Chiara Bertoglio
**Reforming Music**

# Chiara Bertoglio
# Reforming Music

Music and the Religious Reformations
of the Sixteenth Century

DE GRUYTER

ISBN 978-3-11-063681-9
e-ISBN (PDF) 978-3-11-052081-1
e-ISBN (EPUB) 978-3-11-051933-4

**Library of Congress Cataloging-in-Publication Data**
A CIP catalog record for this book has been applied for at the Library of Congress.

**Bibliographic information published by the Deutsche Nationalbibliothek**
The Deutsche Nationalbibliothek lists this publication in the Deutsche Nationalbibliografie; detailed bibliographic data are available on the Internet at http://dnb.dnb.de.

© 2018 Walter de Gruyter GmbH, Berlin/Boston
This volume is text- and page-identical with the hardback published in 2017.
Cover image: Hans Holbein d.J.: The Ambassadors / Die Gesandten, Jean de Dinteville und Georges de Selve, © bpk / Lutz Braun
Printing and binding: CPI books GmbH, Leck

♾ Printed on acid-free paper
Printed in Germany

www.degruyter.com

# Prefaces

## Professor Jeremy S. Begbie

I write this as we approach 2017, the year dedicated to marking the 500th anniversary of the European Reformations. Amidst the massive literature that will doubtless pour forth during those twelve months – in addition to colloquia, conferences and lectures – it will be fascinating to see how much scholarly energy will be given to music, perhaps the most elusive and beguiling of all the arts. Understandably, huge attention has been paid to the battles over visual art that raged so fiercely in the sixteenth century. The re-evaluation of the role of images and our sense of sight during this period has proved to be fertile ground for scholarship. But historians and theologians have been inclined to spend rather less energy considering the ways in which music – in practice and theory – became a heated focus of interest and debate, bound up as it was with the seismic philosophical, scientific and political shifts of the time. In fact, this was an age when music's immense affective and persuasive powers were developed as never before, and this in turn generated entirely new and pressing questions about its proper use. Those who tried to curb and control its place in worship did not, as is often thought, have a low view of music. Just the opposite. They were acutely aware of its potency – indeed, its *theological* potency.

When I first started investigating the place of music in the reform movements of the sixteenth century, I searched in vain for an informed introduction to the field, and one that was sensitive to the complex theological issues at stake. Chiara Bertoglio has provided just this. And despite its substantial length and depth, she still insists that it is only "a stepping-stone for further studies". Yet if it is an introduction, it is one with at least three highly unusual features. To begin with, it is written by an astonishingly able pianist and performer. This gives the text a practice-rooted authenticity, and makes Bertoglio especially alert to the tensions between musical practice and theory which run through her chosen era. Second, although a devout Roman Catholic, Bertoglio's instincts are ecumenical through and through. She is quite properly keen to show that music written within a particular theological or church tradition has the capacity to speak far beyond the boundaries of that tradition. More interested in continuities than discontinuities, she adopts an approach to historical study that refuses to allow *conflict* to be the leading conceptual category. Although fully aware that music can be a highly divisive force, she rightly points out that "it has often been the only means of unity, traversing boundaries and building bridges made of melodies, words and people who crossed the religious divides and weaved an invisible communion". The relevance of this in our own day could hardly be exaggerated. Third, she devotes a whole chapter to women's voices, something which should need no special pleading, but which brings a perspective that has often been woefully under-represented in studies of this sort.

Any reader of this book cannot fail to be immeasurably enriched and pressed to re-think in quite radical ways why music matters, why it is vital that we see it flourish today – and perhaps most especially in the Church. As Bertoglio notes, this is "not the study of a dead object, which can be dissected at leisure and whose relevance for the life of contemporary people is cultural at best. It is instead a field which even today is full of resonances, some of which are among the most important and cherished in the lives of millions of believers". Quite so.

Jeremy Begbie<br>
Duke University

# Sir James MacMillan

Chiara Bertoglio writes "Music allows us to practise an ecumenical approach in a spontaneous and natural fashion: most works of Christian sacred music transcend confessional belonging; and even in those whose confessional identity is more marked, music seems to blur the edges of separation, and to present diversity only as a different perspective, another nuance or a shade of colour which will likely enrich our understanding of faith".

Coming from Scotland where confessional identities have been at their most marked for centuries and where the edges of separation can still tear the heart, I find this a bold and visionary perspective on the role of sacred music in our growing understanding of each other, of denominational culture and of the nature of God Himself. It was only a few years ago that I realised just how blurred the situation was in my own country in this matter – a land where the Reformation is widely regarded as being particularly fierce.

A range of common and conflicting perceptions about Scotland's Reformation period have arisen over the centuries and through the generations. Even though I have lived here most of my life I have always had a niggling doubt that we have never had explained to us the full story of this momentous time. Even although I studied history in a Scottish school I was aware of large gaps and holes in my understanding of the great cultural revolutionary period which shaped this nation's character and soul. Even although I was a music student at one of Scotland's great Universities, I managed to bypass many of the composers and musical narratives which had underpinned the Scottish Reformation process.

A few years ago I attended an exhibition in the University of Edinburgh of the part books of Thomas Wode which challenged some of my perceptions and filled in the considerable gaps in my understanding, explaining the vital continuities, as well as the sharp changes, experienced by Wode himself and his contemporaries in the late 16th century.

It became clear that music and singing were vitally important components in the life of the nation at this time. The eight Wode partbooks formed the centrepiece of the exhibition that also displayed a variety of contemporary objects, including books and manuscripts, musical instruments, paintings and maps. The partbooks, gathered together for the first time from across the world, constitute a unique treasure within Scotland's history, containing the only surviving record for most music found in Scotland during this period. Thomas Wode was responsible for producing the four singing parts for the metrical Psalter, so intrinsically vital for the new reformed liturgy of the day. But he added much more music from before 1560 and from various parts of Europe. These partbooks are illustrated by him and contain fascinating annotations. Wode's life is an encapsulation of the dilemmas and conflicts of the age. He began his ecclesiastical career as a Benedictine monk at Lindores Abbey at Newburgh, Fife and ended it as a Protestant clergyman. Nevertheless, the psalms provided a constant thread through his life and that of the lives of all Christians of the day, regardless of how tossed and turned they were by political and ideological power manoeuvres. The material in the exhibition showed the full extent of music's centrality in the cultural life of Scotland in the late 16th century. I was beguiled by Wode's own illustrations which indicated how ordinary men and women of the time engaged with word and song in the praise of God.

These books preserve one of the most important contributions ever made to Scottish music. As well as his commissioning of new psalm settings in simplified and more homophonic styles suitable for the impending Calvinist age, Wode also included a lot of other music from the time, and crucially from before the great conflagration, and from Scots, English and continental composers. Therefore we are given a glimpse into the musical life of this country at one of its most dangerous hours. The list of composers is astonishing. As well as the Scots, David Peebles, Andro Blackhall, Robert Johnson and Jhone Angus, we find the Englishman Thomas Tallis, who took his own tortured route through the Reformation down south, and continentals like Clemens non Papa, Lassus, Arcadelt and Palestrina.

These composers especially are not immediately associated in the public imagination with the reformed Scottish Church, which took its worship models from Geneva and emphasized the simplest form of unaccompanied psalm singing. However, as Noel O'Regan writes,

> the tide did not turn right away and there were experienced singers and musicians in the Chapel Royal and elsewhere who would have welcomed harmonized psalms and canticles [...] He proceeded to use the remaining pages (of his part books) to build up an anthology of polyphonic music from a variety of sources. As he says in one of his annotations, he was afraid that "musicke sall pereishe in this land alutterlye" (music shall perish and in this land, utterly) and so he set out to preserve as much as he could of it, whether it was pre-Reformation Latin motets by Scottish, English and continental composers, popular religious songs, anthems setting English texts or instrumental dance music.

If only ecclesial, theological and spiritual matters could be left to the leadership and guidance of musicians!

The exhibition of Thomas Wode's partbooks opened up a new vista of understanding of the Scotland of the late 16th and early 17th centuries. It shone a light on the music that musically-literate Scots of the time loved, and loved performing. These collections are evidence of a flourishing musical culture in Scotland as it began its new phase of retreat and isolation. But music respects neither imposed ideology nor geographical and religious boundaries. Wode's work shows that Scotland, in spite of everything, was connected to a wider world, and absorbent of the most important European music of the day.

The power and significance of one of his annotations on these books resounds through the centuries to Scots today. He wrote that singing in four or five parts was "meit and apt for musitians to recreat their spirittis when as thay shall be over cum with hevines or any kynd of sadness, not only musitians, but evin to the ignorant, of a gentle nature, hearing shal be conforted and mirry with uss". (Singing in four or five parts was meet and apt for musicians to recreate their spirits when as they shall be overcome by heavy-heartedness or any kind of sadness, not only musicians but even to the ignorant, of a gentle nature, hearing shall be comforted and merry with us).

These words by a musician at a time of great trial and trouble can be a manifesto even for future generations as to the power of music – especially so when faced with the depredations of iconoclasm and enforced forgetting. If Scotland has to face more cultural revolutions in the future, I hope there will be new Thomas Wodes around to cultivate in the darkness and to preserve all that is good in the human spirit.

Even though my experience of these massive historical, cultural and theological convulsions are limited to the local dimension, I feel that the Scottish story of this important time has, in microcosm, huge universal significance – a significance which is explored and revealed with great authority, insight and optimism through Chiara Bertoglio's meticulous researches.

Sir James MacMillan<br>September 2016

# Acknowledgements

A work of such a scale and scope could be accomplished only with the cooperation and help of many people, to whom I wish to express my heartfelt gratitude.

First of all, my thankfulness goes to my parents, Grazia and Ottavio, to my brother Giovanni and his wife Simona, who endlessly supported me in this long task, encouraging me when forces, enthusiasm and patience were low, bearing with me during my moments of discomfort or fatigue, and celebrating with me the stages of work which were progressively reached. I will never be able to thank you all for your unconditional and generous love, but at least I hope these words will publicly express my indebtedness to your infinite kindness.

Another person whose sincere friendship and Job-like patience were severely tried (but never failed the test) during these years is Ian Chadwick, who read through all Chapters several times, and provided me with a fundamental help both as regards linguistic issues and content. His professional ability and friendly concern, to say nothing of his good-hearted irony and humour were crucial for allowing me to complete this work.

Professor Francis Yapp has unwearyingly read and carefully commented on a draft of this book: his thought-provoking observations, sympathetic evaluations and friendly advice, together with his encouragement, have been a great gift of his generosity and kindness.

Fr. Marco Salvioli OP is another friend I cannot hope to thank enough, not only for his precious advice on theological matters, but also for his brotherly and unwavering support. Professor Nicola Sfredda gave me valuable advice as regards Evangelical theology, particularly in relationship with music, and sustained my efforts by demonstrating his appreciation of my research and of my ecumenical perspective.

Whenever I have doubts or difficulties with the German language (as was often the case when I was writing this book, with old spelling rules and local variants) I know that my friend Antonia Weber is always available for advice, research and a warm-hearted help. I wish to thank her for her consideration and for her precious suggestions.

Another person I wish to thank particularly is Professor Nils Holger Petersen, who supported the publication of this book, and gave me extremely valuable pieces of advice with an exquisite kindness. His words of appreciation for my work gave me some of the happiest moments in my recent past.

A sincere word of gratitude to Professor Ruth Tatlow, another great author, scholar and kind-hearted friend, who found the right words for encouraging me both professionally and personally. I wish also to thank Shanti Vattakunnel, whose unceasing support has frequently sustained my efforts.

My sincere thanks go to Professor Jeremy S. Begbie and Sir James MacMillan for having accepted to preface this book. I am deeply touched and extremely grateful for their words, for their kindness, and for the enrichment their Prefaces bring to my work and to my ecumenical perspective.

Several other people, either friends or colleagues (or both) helped me with my research, by sharing their articles or books, or by checking data for me: my heartfelt thanks goes to Eufemia Giuliana Budicin, Paolo Cavallo, Daniele V. Filippi, don Federico Gallo, Anna Łach, Matthew Laube, Licia Mari, Noel O'Regan, Agata Maria Pinkosz, Thomas Radecke, Marc Smith, Micheline White and Stefano Zuffi.

Along with these scholars and friends who actively helped me, I am deeply indebted to many researchers and authors whose efforts made this book of synthesis possible. As Timothy Snyder beautifully put it, "the tremendous debt to colleagues and earlier generations of historians will be evident in [the following] pages and the notes"[1]. I have constantly tried to reference their work in the proper fashion throughout this book, not only for academic fairness, but also for providing my readers with opportunities to expand their own studies through further readings. In spite of this, the amount of sources consulted for this book may have led me to a paradoxical situation, splendidly summarised by Charles Rosen: since it is not always possible to distinguish between what has been taken from other scholars "and what I thought up on my own", and since "any plagiarism has been inadvertent", the only apology I can offer for unreferenced quotes is that "plagiarism is the sincerest form of flattery"[2].

Thus, many of the merits of this book (if there are any) are not my own; but, needless to say, the responsibility for all errors, imprecisions and flaws is mine and nobody else's.

My last, but certainly not least, expression of gratitude is to God, for his innumerable gifts: I hope that this book will respond, in its own fashion, to the Pauline call to "sing and make melody to the Lord in your hearts, giving thanks to God the Father at all times and for everything in the name of our Lord Jesus Christ"[3].

---

[1] Snyder 2010, p. xvii.
[2] Rosen 1998, p. xii.
[3] Ephesians 5:19–20.

# Contents

**Introduction —— XXV**

**Abbreviations and reference works —— XXXIII**

**Chapter 1 – Framing a century —— 1**
1.1. Introduction —— 1
1.2. Theology: the issues at stake —— 3
    1.2.1. How are we saved? —— 4
    1.2.2. Justified by grace —— 5
    1.2.3. Substantial differences —— 7
1.3. Culture, art and thought in the sixteenth century —— 10
    1.3.1. Thinking the sixteenth century —— 10
    1.3.2. Applied humanism —— 11
    1.3.3. Philosophy and theology —— 12
    1.3.4. Science and literature —— 14
    1.3.5. Visual arts —— 15
1.4. Music —— 17
    1.4.1. Setting a text —— 17
    1.4.2. Travelling music, travelling musicians —— 18
    1.4.3. Genres in vocal music —— 20
    1.4.4. A protagonist: the madrigal —— 21
    1.4.5. A nursery for opera —— 24
1.5. Society and politics —— 25
1.6. Church matters —— 28
    1.6.1. At the roots of the Reformations —— 29
    1.6.2. 1500–1525: Enter Luther —— 31
    1.6.3. 1526–1550: Spreading the word —— 35
    1.6.4. 1551–1575: Consolidating confessions —— 40
    1.6.5. 1576–1600: Finding a *modus vivendi* —— 46

**Chapter 2 – Music, society and culture —— 49**
2.1. Introduction —— 49
2.2. Music and faith: an overview —— 52
    2.2.1. A resounding landscape —— 52
    2.2.2. A time of religious renewal —— 55
2.3. Humanism and music —— 56
    2.3.1. Sounding Greek —— 58

- 2.3.2. Dialoguing with Plato (and Aristotle) —— 60
- 2.3.3. Fashioning antiquity —— 63
- 2.3.4. At the sources of Christian music —— 66
- 2.3.5. "Should God be praised with song?" —— 69
- 2.3.6. Magisterial music —— 72
- 2.3.7. Words, words, words —— 74
  - 2.3.7.1. Moving music —— 75
  - 2.3.7.2. Plain text —— 77
- 2.3.8. Symbol and fascination —— 79
- 2.3.9. "Ornamental neighings": Erasmus on music —— 82
- 2.4. As you like it: aesthetic trends —— 84
  - 2.4.1. Style matters —— 85
  - 2.4.2. A cappella or accompanied? —— 86
  - 2.4.3. Enjoying polyphony —— 89
  - 2.4.4. Seducing or sanctifying? —— 92
  - 2.4.5. Rhetorical questions —— 94
  - 2.4.6. The effects of affects —— 96
  - 2.4.7. Sensing music —— 98

## Chapter 3 – Criticising sacred music —— 101

- 3.1. Introduction —— 101
- 3.2. "Sacred" music? —— 103
  - 3.2.1. Plainchant: the daily bread —— 105
  - 3.2.2. Latin-texted polyphony: resounding feast —— 107
    - 3.2.2.1. Making music for Mass —— 108
    - 3.2.2.2. Mostly motets —— 109
  - 3.2.3. Praying in music —— 110
- 3.3. Crisis, critics and criticalities —— 114
  - 3.3.1. Serving the Word? —— 115
    - 3.3.1.1. Enrapturing melismas —— 115
    - 3.3.1.2. A free rein for Sequences —— 117
    - 3.3.1.3. Hearing the unsaid —— 118
    - 3.3.1.4. "*Intelligo ut credam*": the importance of understanding —— 119
  - 3.3.2. The morals of music —— 123
    - 3.3.2.1. Lady Music —— 123
    - 3.3.2.2. Soft and lascivious —— 126
    - 3.3.2.3. "Moch musick marreth mens maners" —— 128
    - 3.3.2.4. Practical problems —— 132
    - 3.3.2.5. Controlling the choir —— 134

|  |  | 3.3.2.6. | A waste of time and money —— 136 |
|---|---|---|---|

        3.3.2.6. A waste of time and money —— 136
        3.3.2.7. Sounding immoral —— 137
        3.3.2.8. The volume of "wild vociferations" —— 140
        3.3.2.9. Cats, goats, bulls and donkeys —— 142
        3.3.2.10. Virtuous and virtuosos —— 146
        3.3.2.11. Laughable gestures and laudable behaviours —— 149
        3.3.2.12. The force of gravity —— 151
    3.3.3. A letter by Bernardino Cirillo —— 155
        3.3.3.1. The letter's letter —— 156
        3.3.3.2. The letter's spirit —— 161

## Chapter 4 – The reformers' concept of music —— 164

4.1. Introduction —— 164
4.2. Where the Reformers saw eye to eye —— 165
    4.2.1. From word to Word —— 166
    4.2.2. Sources as resources —— 168
    4.2.3. Reforming Church music —— 171
        4.2.3.1. "*A cantantibus intellectus*": words for whom? —— 172
        4.2.3.2. "Not so excellent a thing": the risks of music —— 174
        4.2.3.3. Creation and creativity —— 178
    4.2.4. What's the use of music? —— 180
        4.2.4.1. A gift of God —— 181
        4.2.4.2. "Praise him with lute and harp" —— 183
        4.2.4.3. Chords of concord —— 185
        4.2.4.4. Fostering fervour —— 186
        4.2.4.5. "Faith comes from hearing" —— 187
        4.2.4.6. A "medicine for passions" —— 190
        4.2.4.7. "*Zu Frewde*": the joy of music —— 191
        4.2.4.8. Dispelling devils —— 193
        4.2.4.9. Voicing the Gospel —— 194
        4.2.4.10. Shall or may? Music as *adiaphoron* —— 195
        4.2.4.11. Music for the end of the world —— 197
    4.2.5. Orchestrating praise: the role of instruments —— 199
4.3. Various views: Music for the Reformers —— 202
    4.3.1. Luther: "*Musicam semper amavi*" —— 202
        4.3.1.1. Origins and originality —— 204
        4.3.1.2. The principal principles —— 206
        4.3.1.3. Tuning the tenets —— 210
    4.3.2. Zwingli: nailing the organs —— 212
    4.3.3. "Radical" Reforms —— 216

4.3.4. Bucer: Sacred Music only —— 218
  4.3.5. Calvin: cautions and chanting —— 219
    4.3.5.1. An increasing interest... —— 219
    4.3.5.2. ...And persisting perplexities —— 222
  4.3.6. Anglican antinomies —— 225
  4.3.7. Catholic continuity —— 229
    4.3.7.1. Hearing Mass —— 230
    4.3.7.2. Worship for whom? —— 233

**Chapter 5 – Music in the Evangelical Churches: Luther —— 236**
5.1. Introduction —— 236
5.2. A music-loving Reformer —— 238
5.3. The forms of Reform —— 240
  5.3.1. Latin roots, Evangelical fruits —— 241
    5.3.1.1. Reordering the Ordinary —— 241
    5.3.1.2. Hours of worship —— 245
  5.3.2. Venturing the vernacular —— 246
    5.3.2.1. Translating tradition —— 248
    5.3.2.2. Singing Scripture —— 251
    5.3.2.3. "Christian improvements" —— 253
    5.3.2.4. Starting from scratch —— 256
    5.3.2.5. Forging a repertoire —— 259
    5.3.2.6. Led by the *Lieder* —— 261
  5.3.3. Collecting chorales —— 264
    5.3.3.1. Objects of piety: The Lutheran hymnbooks —— 267
  5.3.4. The daily sound —— 269
    5.3.4.1. A singing Church —— 269
    5.3.4.2. Our daily hymn —— 273
    5.3.4.3. *Lehre:* Learning from the *Lieder* —— 274
    5.3.4.4. *Trost:* Comforted by the Chorales —— 279
    5.3.4.5. Creating communities —— 281
    5.3.4.6. Disseminating doctrines in music —— 282
  5.3.5. A range of genres —— 285
  5.3.6. Music at the borders of Lutheranism —— 288
5.4. Singing in Strasbourg —— 290
  5.4.1. The Strasbourg style —— 292
5.5. The Bohemian Brethren —— 295

**Chapter 6 – Music in the Evangelical Churches: Calvin —— 298**
6.1. Introduction —— 298
6.2. The power of psalmody —— 299
    6.2.1. Metrical psalmody before Calvin —— 300
    6.2.2. Marot: Psalter and verse —— 302
    6.2.3. Preparing for the Psalter —— 304
6.3. The Genevan Psalter —— 306
    6.3.1. Two Reformers, two attitudes —— 308
    6.3.2. Metres and melodies —— 310
    6.3.3. The Genevan Psalter outside Geneva —— 312
    6.3.4. Our daily Psalm —— 315
    6.3.5. Musical flags —— 318
    6.3.6. Psalms in polyphony —— 321
    6.3.7. Instruments and house devotion —— 325
6.4. Constance and Basel —— 328
6.5. The *Souterliedekens* —— 330

**Chapter 7 – Music in the Church of England —— 333**
7.1. Introduction —— 333
7.2. Reforming rites —— 336
    7.2.1. Under Henry VIII —— 336
    7.2.2. Under Edward VI —— 338
    7.2.3. The *Book of Common Prayer* —— 339
    7.2.4. Under Elizabeth I —— 344
7.3. Psalms, psalters and Reformations —— 346
    7.3.1. Coverdale: Continental influences —— 346
    7.3.2. Sternhold: Psalms at Court —— 349
    7.3.3. "The Lord's Songs in a foreign land" —— 351
    7.3.4. Elizabethan Psalmody: the "Sternhold and Hopkins" —— 354
    7.3.5. Singing the Scottish Reformation —— 358
    7.3.6. Psalms, poetry and polyphony —— 360
    7.3.7. Psalms, piety and politics —— 363
7.4. The "Godly Ballads" —— 364
7.5. Our daily music —— 367
    7.5.1. Educating in music —— 367
    7.5.2. Private piety —— 368
7.6. Between Court and parish church —— 371
    7.6.1. Shaping an "Anglican" style —— 374
    7.6.2. Setting the Service —— 377
    7.6.3. Byrd: A Catholic at Court —— 379

## Chapter 8 – Music and the Council of Trent —— 382
8.1. Introduction —— 382
8.2. Trent and tradition —— 384
    8.2.1. Theological themes —— 386
    8.2.2. Self- or Counter-Reformation? —— 387
    8.2.3. Drafts, Debates, Decrees —— 390
    8.2.4. Uses and abuses —— 391
    8.2.5. Fighting "lasciviousness" —— 393
    8.2.6. Singing for the Pope —— 395
8.3. Who was who —— 397
    8.3.1. Ercole Gonzaga: President and patron —— 398
    8.3.2. Giovanni Morone: Monody first —— 399
    8.3.3. Otto Truchsess: Talents and treasures —— 400
    8.3.4. Gabriele Paleotti: Respect and rigour —— 402
    8.3.5. Carlo Borromeo: Influential and idiosyncratic —— 405
    8.3.6. Kerle's *Preces:* The Council's soundtrack —— 405
8.4. The Council on music —— 407
    8.4.1. Setting the stage —— 409
    8.4.2. Enumerating errors —— 410
    8.4.3. A "house of prayer" —— 413
    8.4.4. Rescuing polyphony? —— 416
    8.4.5. Music in the convents —— 418
    8.4.6. Concluding the Council —— 419
8.5. What did not happen at the Council —— 421
    8.5.1. Palestrina: polyphony's saviour? —— 422
    8.5.2. Prescriptions or proscriptions? —— 425
    8.5.3. Open issues —— 427

## Chapter 9 – Music after Trent —— 429
9.1. Introduction —— 429
9.2. Music after Trent —— 431
    9.2.1. Hardly a revolution —— 431
    9.2.2. Purifying worship —— 434
    9.2.3. A new clerical class —— 436
    9.2.4. From global to local —— 438
9.3. Music and liturgy after Trent —— 441
    9.3.1. Reaffirming rituality —— 443
    9.3.2. Revising rites —— 445
    9.3.3. New needs —— 447
    9.3.4. Freeing plainchant from "ineptitude" and "malice" —— 448

9.3.5. Polyphony after Trent —— 452
    9.3.5.1. Exploring post-Tridentine aesthetics —— 454
    9.3.5.2. Polychorality: a new option —— 456
9.3.6. The Cardinals' Commission —— 459
    9.3.6.1. Observing (and by-passing) the "Council's requirements" —— 461
9.3.7. Celebrating with instruments —— 466

9.4. Religious music in post-Tridentine Catholicism —— 467
  9.4.1. Emotional motets —— 468
  9.4.2. Local languages —— 468
  9.4.3. Piety and poetry —— 470
  9.4.4. Devotional music outside Italy —— 473
  9.4.5. Processions and pilgrimages —— 474
  9.4.6. In the sphere of spirituality —— 478

9.5. Reforming Catholicism —— 480
  9.5.1. The theological framework —— 481
  9.5.2. The Jesuits and music: forbidden, admitted, promoted —— 482
    9.5.2.1. The first Jesuits and the unsung Office —— 482
    9.5.2.2. A sensible preaching —— 484
    9.5.2.3. College education —— 486
    9.5.2.4. Performing holiness —— 488
    9.5.2.5. The mission of music —— 489
  9.5.3. Filippo Neri: Laity and *Laude* —— 490
    9.5.3.1. From Florence to Rome —— 492
  9.5.4. Brethren in Christ: The Confraternities —— 495

9.6. Catholic music locally —— 498
  9.6.1. Chapels and patrons —— 498
  9.6.2. Milan: Reforming from the roots —— 500
  9.6.3. Rome: Splendour and spirituality —— 503
  9.6.4. Venice: Enjoying magnificence —— 507
  9.6.5. Mantua: a workshop of the Catholic Reformation —— 508
  9.6.6. Spain: Penitence and pomp —— 511
  9.6.7. Bavaria: the outpost of Catholicism —— 514

**Chapter 10 – Music and confessionalisation —— 519**
10.1. Introduction —— 519
10.2. Building confessional boundaries —— 521
10.3. The confessionalisation of music —— 523
  10.3.1. Faith first —— 523
  10.3.2. Preaching in music —— 525

10.3.3. "As long as I live": music and martyrdom —— 525
  10.3.3.1. "The Story of Brother Henry": sung epics of martyrdom —— 526
  10.3.3.2. "We have become a spectacle": Byrd and the English martyrs —— 528
10.3.4. "Let God rise up": battle hymns —— 530
10.3.5. Pamphlets, broadsheets and polemics —— 530
10.3.6. Enchanting chant —— 532
10.3.7. Conquering space through sound —— 533
  10.3.7.1. Walking singers —— 534
  10.3.7.2. Seizing the Service —— 536
  10.3.7.3. Sung sarcasm —— 538
  10.3.7.4. Paraphrase and parody —— 540
  10.3.7.5. The time of the Antichrist —— 542
  10.3.7.6. Changes in music are changes in doctrine —— 543
10.4. Psalms for all —— 545
10.5. Confessional Contrafacture —— 548
  10.5.1. Songs of scorn —— 550
10.6. The contexts of confessionalisation —— 553
  10.6.1. "Oh Benno, you holy man…" —— 553
  10.6.2. Countering the *Interim* —— 554
  10.6.3. Contesting the calendar —— 556
  10.6.4. Courtly intrigues —— 557
10.7. "Save me, o God": echoes of persecution —— 559
  10.7.1. Silencing songs —— 559
  10.7.2. Martyred musicians —— 562
  10.7.3. Concealing and revealing —— 564

## Chapter 11 – Music beyond confessionalisation —— 567
11.1. Introduction —— 567
11.2. Seeking harmony —— 568
  11.2.1. Tuning the differences —— 568
  11.2.2. Flutes, lutes and Luther —— 569
  11.2.3. Creating communion through prayer —— 572
  11.2.4. Joining theology with praise —— 573
11.3. Finding harmony —— 573
  11.3.1. Consonant doctrines —— 574
  11.3.2. Crossing the confines —— 576
  11.3.3. Sung pleas for unity —— 577
  11.3.4. Bridging social layers —— 577

11.4. Like prayer, like song —— 578
    11.4.1. The thread of psalmody —— 579
    11.4.2. The thread of piety —— 581
    11.4.3. The thread of mysticism —— 582
        11.4.3.1. Defeating the devil —— 585
        11.4.3.2. Consoling and comforting —— 586
    11.4.4. The thread of education —— 587
        11.4.4.1. "The brim around the cup": singing the Catechism —— 590
        11.4.4.2. "By way of pleasant song": enjoying Sunday school —— 593
        11.4.4.3. "Sing like the angels in heaven": publishing Catechism songs —— 596
        11.4.4.4. "Night and day": the forms of sung doctrine —— 597
    11.4.5. The thread of musicianship —— 599
    11.4.6. The thread of solicitude —— 600
    11.4.7. Inspiring hymnbooks —— 602
        11.4.7.1. Vehe: A Catholic pioneer —— 603
        11.4.7.2. Leisentrit: An example of Counter-Reformation —— 605
        11.4.7.3. Sharing songs —— 606
        11.4.7.4. Responses to Calvinist psalmody —— 609
11.5. Music across boundaries —— 611
    11.5.1. Adopting and adapting —— 612
    11.5.2. The challenge of beauty —— 614
    11.5.3. Asserting the sacredness of creation —— 616
    11.5.4. Holy and spiritual songs —— 618
11.6. Musicians beyond boundaries —— 619
    11.6.1. Ecumenism in music —— 621
    11.6.2. Finding the language of musical dialogue —— 623

**Chapter 12 – Music and women —— 625**
12.1. Introduction —— 625
12.2. Truths, myths and stereotypes —— 627
    12.2.1. *Frau Musika* or women's music? —— 628
    12.2.2. Mary Magdalene as a musician —— 629
    12.2.3. Scanty sources —— 631
    12.2.4. Social status —— 632
    12.2.5. Patronesses and prioresses —— 633
    12.2.6. The impact of the Reformations —— 636

12.3. Voices of Evangelical women —— 637
    12.3.1. In the Lutheran Church —— 637
        12.3.1.1. The "virtuous matrons" and their daughters —— 638
        12.3.1.2. Girls "prophesy": announcing the Kingdom's advent —— 640
        12.3.1.3. Cruciger: from the very beginning —— 641
        12.3.1.4. Schütz-Zell: a resourceful Reformer —— 643
    12.3.2. In the Calvinist Church —— 644
    12.3.3. Living (and loving) psalmody —— 646
        12.3.3.1. Creative resonances —— 648
    12.3.4. Among Anabaptists —— 650
12.4. Voices of Catholic women —— 652
    12.4.1. Voices from the Convents —— 653
        12.4.1.1. Voicing resistance —— 653
        12.4.1.2. Convents as cultural centres —— 654
        12.4.1.3. "Only voice and no sight" —— 656
        12.4.1.4. Music for hearers? —— 658
        12.4.1.5. Teaching music to the nuns —— 660
        12.4.1.6. A rich repertoire —— 661
        12.4.1.7. Music for money —— 663
        12.4.1.8. Songs for sanctity —— 665
    12.4.2. (Un)veiled voices —— 666
        12.4.2.1. Aleotti: how many of them? —— 667
        12.4.2.2. Community concerts —— 668
        12.4.2.3. Sessa: better than Monteverdi? —— 670
        12.4.2.4. Bovia, Strozzi, Baptista and their sisters —— 671
        12.4.2.5. The convent scribes: transmitting tastes —— 673
    12.4.3. Reforms, rules and religious women —— 674
        12.4.3.1. Paleotti: muting music —— 675
        12.4.3.2. The Borromeos: between rigour and reform —— 676
    12.4.4. Voices from the laity —— 677
        12.4.4.1. Composing spiritual madrigals —— 678
        12.4.4.2. Voices from Northern Europe —— 679
12.5. Voices from a Christian polyphony —— 681

**Conclusions** —— 685

**Glossary** —— 690

**Bibliography** —— **703**
    Primary —— **703**
    Secondary —— **739**

**Index of Names** —— **795**

**Index of Subjects** —— **817**

# Introduction

> "Three fingers do it", they say of writers;
> but a man's whole body and soul work at it[1].
>
> [Martin Luther]

It is usually said that an Introduction is the part which one finds first in a book, which the author writes last, and the reader never reads. Thus, I have made the unusual decision to start my book by writing the Introduction first, so that it will have a chance to be read, after all. So, in front of me, I have my laptop with a new file open, a pile of books, and two gigantic posters with enormous tables, whose rows represent the hundred years between 1500 and 1599, while lists of facts, people and musical works fill in the many cells.

The plan of my book is already written in detail; hundreds of pages of notes have been taken, digested and ordered; and I feel the usual mixture of thrill and worry that always accompanies the first stages of writing a book.

Why did I choose to explore the role of music in the sixteenth-century European reformations? This is not only a question sometimes I ask myself – especially when the pile of books on my desk sways menacingly or the file of carefully taken notes unexpectedly crashes – but also a question I need to answer for my readers.

I must confess that the first stimulus for this task came from a couple of dear friends of mine, who asked me to prepare a short introduction on a subject of my choice regarding music in the sixteenth century, as part of a cultural project they were creating in my home land of Piedmont. After some reflection, I concluded that what most fascinated me about that epoch was the religious turmoil that shook the foundations of European Christendom, society and thought.

I also realised that there might be the need for a book like the one you are reading now: despite the fact that there is a plethora of excellent studies on individual aspects of sixteenth-century sacred music, perhaps a relatively agile but reasonably comprehensive introduction to the topic – especially with a focus on the religious reformations – ought to be written.

Obviously, this book should be taken only as a guide to research or as an introduction to the music of the European Reformations. The immensity of the sixteenth-century "sacred" repertoire (and the very difficulty in defining what "sacred music" was for sixteenth-century Christians), the quantity of aspects in-

---

[1] *LW* 46, p. 249; *WA* 30$^{II}$, p. 574.

volved (religious, theological, sociological, historical, philosophical, cultural, political, economic...) and the quantity of studies focusing on one or more of these aspects should have discouraged me from undertaking such a task. However, hopefully, this work will encourage further research in a field that has still much to reveal to musicologists, musicians, historians and theologians alike.

Indeed, most of the literature already published focuses on music of a single Protestant confession (e. g. Lutheran, Calvinist, Anglican...), or on the Council of Trent, or on Protestant music, or on the opposition of Reformation and so-called Counter-Reformation, or on individual composers of great renown.

My own viewpoint in this book will be (or will attempt to be) decidedly different from any of the above. First of all, I would like to avoid contrasting one Christian confession against another. This is, for me, more of a necessity than of a choice: in my own religious experience, music has always crossed the confessional boundaries, and I have been constantly enriched in my spiritual insight by the diversity of the confessional perspectives on music. Music allows us to practise an ecumenical approach in a spontaneous and natural fashion: most works of Christian sacred music transcend confessional belonging; and even in those whose confessional identity is more marked, music seems to blur the edges of separation, and to present diversity only as a different perspective, another nuance or a shade of colour which will likely enrich our understanding of faith.

I would like to avoid a confessional approach in this book for yet another reason: in the sixteenth century, even the theological approaches in the different Churches were much less clearly defined than they would later become. Even more so, both the liturgical and non-liturgical repertoire practised by Christians in worship, in church, at home, in schools and in the streets was permeable to external influences, and in many cases different denominations (or what would later be indicated by different denominations...) shared a common ground of praise, repentance and prayer.

One of the hardest tasks for us inhabitants of the post-modern era is to abandon our categorisations when approaching a time when they were, at best, only starting to be constructed: this applies to confessional identities, to aspects of music theory and practice, as well as to considerations of history, politics and relationships between men and women. Obviously, I cannot claim to have succeeded in this respect: however, it is crucial that both writer and reader are constantly aware of how our cultural bias may influence our interpretation of the past.

Moreover, as this book will show, from the musical viewpoint many reformers shared similar concerns and wishes, which were in turn the product of a cultural atmosphere encompassing the religious divides. We will constantly observe, for instance, how the humanist perspective conditioned the insight of several reformers on sacred music in a similar fashion.

Furthermore, the musical aspects of the Christian Reformations in the sixteenth century should also be conceived as part of a broader movement of renewal from the religious, philosophical, artistic and sociological points of view. From this perspective, although the Reformations and their socio-political consequences had a dramatic impact on European history, they were also part of a difficult evolution, of a painful crisis (and yet of a fascinating development) which characterised the "Old World" in the Early Modern era.

I am fully aware that the complexity of such an all-encompassing viewpoint can hardly be sustained in a consistent fashion through a book of this length; once more, therefore, I wish to invite my readers to share this effort with me, and to take into constant account this bird's-eye view even when the necessities of an orderly exposition will force us to accept categories, periodisations and confessional segmentations which should better be avoided.

In the past, music historiography on the sixteenth century has been heavily conditioned by confessional belongings. Memory of the persecutions and of the violence practised by one confession against the other has not always led to humility and reconciliation, but rather to the not-too-hidden effort to demonstrate the (musical) superiority of one tradition over another. Within such a "competitive" approach, what distinguished a confession from another became a kind of "supporting evidence", something that strengthened the alleged supremacy, or at least something that helped to define the historic and social identity of a confessional group.

Therefore, music historiography tended to point out the innovative elements (even when their novelty was only seeming), to focus on diversity and musical revolutions, without caring too much for the perspective on continuity and commonality, which I hold to be at least as important as the former.

While claiming that the confessionalized approach is ideologically conditioned, I am aware that my attempt at an ecumenical perspective is no less "ideological". I would even argue that a neutral approach to matters pertaining to religious conflicts and divisions is possible only if one observes Christianity from the outside: however, in this case, I think that what would be gained in neutrality would be lost in involvement, passion and personal experience. If one's approach must be conditioned by one's belief, convictions and spirituality, I personally favour a perspective tending towards the unity for which Jesus himself prayed (cf. John 17:23) rather than one fomenting division.

I will therefore constantly underline the elements of continuity and similarity among the sacred music of the various Christian churches, believing – as I do

– that music, similar to prayer and worship, can bridge the religious divides and boundaries created by humankind.

Thus, as my research progressed, I decided to abandon (at least in most cases) the term of "Counter-Reformation" to indicate the experience of Roman Catholicism in the sixteenth-century. Whenever possible, I will speak of Catholic Reformation instead: first, since this avoids describing Early Modern Catholicism merely in terms of a reaction to Protestantism; secondly, since it allows us to take into account a process which started well before Luther and continued well after Trent; thirdly, since it de-emphasises the opposition between Catholics and Protestants which I am trying to eschew.

From the temporal viewpoint, however, I have decided to adopt a very clear limitation, and to consider almost exclusively the sixteenth century. This choice was not only determined by safety reasons (my desktop is already groaning under the pile of books as it is), but also by the need to keep the length of this book reasonable without sacrificing a certain quantity of details. Musically speaking, between the sixteenth- and seventeenth centuries several aspects of compositional technique and musical forms or practices evolved, even though the idea of a "Baroque revolution" is now considered to be an artificial construct. Even a summary exposition of the stylistic, musical, theoretical, practical and aesthetic perspectives of the seventeenth century would have required a much longer book.

Within the framework of the hundred years I will discuss in the following pages, and of the hundred cells of the gigantic posters hung in front of me now, one cannot but observe the hardships, sufferings and lacerations striking entire populations, shaking the whole European territory, and affecting the lives of innumerable men and women, the elderly and children, clergy and laity, popes and kings. One wonders, sometimes, whether the sense most lacking among the rulers and religious leaders of the sixteenth century was common sense or the sense of hearing. As a practising musician, I think that music teaches us how really to listen to each other: listening is a process, it is a lifelong learning itinerary, in which the other (with his or her music, personality and words) is accepted and progressively understood, within the framework of a relationship which should be based first and foremost on mutual respect and loving kindness. This kind of listening is conspicuous by its absence in most of the leaders and rulers we will meet in the following pages: few seem to have stopped to consider the consequences of their actions, to try and understand the other, to discern whether the other might have been inspired by God, by sincere love for the Church, or by selfish interest. Very often, all-too-human reasons and considerations have provoked divisions which in turn determined endless sufferings, countless deaths, violence and war.

Although we will see that music has often been an instrument of propaganda, polemics and derision, satire and scorn, if not an outright invitation to violence, it has also accomplished another fundamental – and much more laudable – task: it has often been the only means of unity, traversing boundaries and building bridges made of melodies, words and people who crossed the religious divides and weaved an invisible communion.

If the sixteenth-century concept of art had seemingly lost much of the symbolic value it had possessed in the Middle Ages, it remained however a powerful *symbolon*, something that could "hold together" what the theological discourse was no longer able to do. Theology had moved from the kneeling stool – i.e. from the attempt of talking about God as a consequence of talking with Him – to the academic chair; and its symbolic dimension had got lost in the relocation.

Music continued to inhabit the places of worship – be it in church or at home – and thus maintained a liaison with transcendence which mysteriously "kept together" what humankind was dividing. Music is neither irrational nor asemantic or insignificant, but its symbolic power makes it inherently "polyphonic", contrapuntal, multi-voiced.

Thus, as I wrote at the beginning, in my own experience as a Catholic musician, the music of Lutherans, Calvinists, Orthodox and Anglicans has always been a further gift of beauty, of spirituality and of amazement, helping me to get a little nearer to God, to understand better and more deeply his Word, and to experience his love and truth.

Therefore, I think, studying the music of a time when Western Christianity became separated might help the path of reconciliation that today's Churches are treading with difficulty but also with determination. Even though theological differences cannot be ignored (if the service of truth concerns us all), they might become a little less crucial if our perspective takes into account other elements as well: music may be one of them, being like a thread of beauty unifying the worship of innumerable Christians through centuries and through divisions.

I hope, thus, that this work will be my own humble and simple attempt at contributing to reconciliation, and to the retrieval of a lost *harmony*. The five-hundredth anniversary of Luther's Reformation, which will be commemorated soon, may offer us a chance for reflecting on these issues: in coincidence with the stylistic evolution of music which culminated in tonal harmony, the European *corpus christianum* was splitting itself apart, and losing its capacity for resounding as a polyphony, in which diversity is enriching and not disrupting.

A certain polyphony is found also in the layout of my work, since this book consists of three parts: the first, comprising three Chapters, will try and offer an overview of music theory and of the practice of sacred music at the beginning of the sixteenth century, with a very short historical contextualisation, and a survey of the cultural atmosphere of the time and of the problems of contemporaneous sacred music.

In the second part, with its six Chapters, I will examine first the reformers' perspectives on music, on sacred music and on its functions in the lives of the faithful; then – bowing to the very confessionalisation I have tried to avoid! – I will discuss at some length the theory and practice of music in the different Christian churches; finally, I will explore the role of music at the Council of Trent, showing its impact on subsequent Catholic music.

Part Three will concern cross-confessional perspectives: I will consider first the role of music as an instrument of propaganda and confessionalisation; then how it overcame the confessional walls; and finally I will dedicate a Chapter to women's music within the context of the European Reformations. Hopefully, this "*dodecacorde*" of Chapters will provide a stimulating starting point for more in-depth scholarship.

Unavoidably, my choice of considering the cultural, spiritual and musical processes and evolutions in sixteenth-century music from a variety of viewpoints will provoke several overlapping discussions, and the inescapable repetition of concepts, facts and ideas. Although I understand that this may test the reader's forbearance, I thought that presenting the same facts from different angles might help to grasp the complexity and fascination of the times under consideration.

I must also apologise in advance for my decision to dedicate ample space to the confessions which would eventually develop into the numerically major components of Western Christianity. The obvious omission of Eastern Christianity is due by no means to a lack of consideration, but simply to the necessity of limiting a field of study which is already overwhelming. On a different plane, I had to renounce a thorough and detailed discussion of the concept of sacred music for reformers who, in the long run, did not gather around them as many followers, or did not exert as strong an influence, as the most famous ones, although at that time they may have had a comparable importance.

From the musicological viewpoint, I favoured the history of genres and forms over that of composers of genius. Although the history of music is adorned by immortal masterpieces, whose authorship often belongs to comparatively few individuals, it intertwines with the history of humankind (and of its spirituality) especially in the daily experience of musicianship, which is often made of humbler – but not less meaningful – artistic productions.

Once more, finally, I must stress that this book may have many goals, several of which are surely too ambitious for me, but it certainly does not aim at thoroughness or completeness. It has been conceived and is now offered to the reader simply as an introduction, hoping to serve as a stepping-stone for further studies and as a springboard for original research.

Being more than conscious of these limits, I can simply say that my work has been inspired by three words, three very short words written by Luther with no theological refinement, confessional polemics or pedagogical aim. It was simply the man Martin Luther who wrote: "I love music"; and the very same love still inspires countless believers and non-believers to seek transcendence in the world of sounds.

# Abbreviations and reference works

All Bible quotes are taken from the New Revised Standard Version (NRSV), where not otherwise indicated. Psalms are indicated with the double system stemming from the Hebrew and Greek numbering. All web links were last accessed on August 25th, 2016; some links have been shortened to facilitate reading and typing of web addresses.

The Glossary at the end of the book provides definitions for some musicological and theological terms.

Some of the paintings referenced in the book's text have been uploaded and can be viewed online at http://bit.ly/2cvP8cI.

AEM   *Acta Ecclesiæ Mediolanensis [...]* (Milan: various publishers, 1582–1897); available online at http://bit.ly/2bzgqcs.
BC   Robert Kolb and Timothy J. Wengert (eds.), *The Book of Concord: The Confessions of the Evangelical Lutheran Church*, English translation by Charles Arand, Eric Gritsch, Robert Kolb, William Russel, James Schaaf, Jane Strohl, and Timothy J. Wengert (Minneapolis MN: Augsburg Fortress, 2000).
BDS   Martin Bucer, *Martin Bucers Deutsche Schriften*, edited by Robet Stupperich et al. (Gütersloh: Gütersloher Verlagshaus, 1960ff.).
BSLK   Irene Dingel (ed.), *Die Bekenntnisschriften der Evangelisch-Lutherischen Kirche*, new revised edition (Göttingen: Vandenhoeck & Ruprecht, 2014).
CG   Johann Friedrich Schannat, Joseph Hartzheim (eds.), *Concilia Germaniæ*, 10 volumes (Cologne: J. W. Krakamp, 1759–1775) (Aalen: Scientia, 1970–1996).
Chron.   Juan Alfonso de Polanco, *Vita Ignatii Loiolæ et rerum Societatis Jesu historia*, 6 volumes in *MHSI* (Madrid: various publishers, 1894–1898); available online at http://www.sjweb.info/arsi/Monumenta.cfm.
CIC   *Corpus Iuris Canonici Gregorii XIII [...] in duos tomos divisum [...]*, 2 volumes (Halle an der Saale: Orphanotropheus, 1747).
CŒD   G. Alberigo, G. A. Dossetti, P. P. Joannou, C. Leonardi and P. Prodi (eds.), *Conciliorum Œcumenicorum Decreta* (Bologna: Istituto per le Scienze Religiose, 1973).
Conf.   St Augustine of Hippo, *Confessions*; English translation by J. G. Pilkington, in *Nicene and Post-Nicene Fathers, First Series*, vol. 1. Edited by Philip Schaff (Buffalo NY: Christian Literature Publishing Co., 1887); revised by Kevin Knight, available online at http://www.newadvent.org/fathers/1101.htm; English translation by Albert C. Outler (1955), LoC CCN 55–5021, available online at http://bit.ly/2bLoMmy.
CoR   Aimé Herminjard (ed.), *Correspondance des réformateurs dans les pays de langue française, recueillie et publiée avec d'autres lettres relatives à la réforme et des notes historiques et biographiques, par A. L. Herminjard*, 9 volumes (Geneva: H. Georg etc., 1866-).
CT   *Concilium Tridentinum: Diariorum, actorum, epistularum, tractatuum, nova collectio, edidit Societas Goerresiana*, 13 volumes (Freiburg im Breisgau: Herder, 1901–2001).
DKL   Konrad Ameln, Markus Jenny and Walther Lipphardt (eds.), *Das deutsche Kirchenlied: Kritische Gesamtausgabe der Melodien*; vol. I: *Verzeichnis der Drucke* [RISM B: VIII/1–2], 2 volumes (Kassel: Bärenreiter, 1975/1980).

| | |
|---|---|
| EM | *Early Music* |
| EMH | *Early Music History* |
| fl. | Flourished/floruit |
| fn. | Footnote |
| fol. | Folio |
| Fr. | Father |
| J-AMS | *Journal of the American Musicological Society* |
| J-RMA | *Journal of the Royal Musical Association* |
| JLH | *Jahrbuch für Liturgik und Hymnologie* |
| L-J | *Luther-Jahrbuch* |
| Labbé | Philippe Labbé and Gabriel Cossart (eds.), *Sacrosancta Concilia ad Regiam Editionem Exacta*, 15 tomes, 17 volumes (Paris: Societatis Typographicæ Librorum Ecclesiasticorum, 1671–1672); later edition by Étienne Baluze and Jean Hardouin, 21 tomes, 23 volumes (Venice: Sebastiano Coleti and Battista Albrizzi, 1728–1733); available online at http://patristica.net/labbe. |
| LM | *Lainii Monumenta*, 8 volumes in *MHSI* (Madrid: Gabriel López del Horno, 1912–1917) available online at http://www.sjweb.info/arsi/Monumenta.cfm. |
| LQ | *Litterae Quadrimestres*, 7 volumes in *MHSI* (Madrid and Rome: various publishers, 1894–1932); available online at http://www.sjweb.info/arsi/Monumenta.cfm. |
| LW | *Luther's Works: American Edition*, 55 volumes (St Louis MO: Concordia; Philadelphia PA: Fortress, 1955–1986). |
| Mansi | Giovanni Domenico Mansi et al. (eds.), *Sacrorum conciliorum nova, et amplissima collectio [...] Editio novissima*, 53 volumes (Paris: Welter, 1901–1927); available online at http://www.fscire.it/it/mansi/concili/; reprint (Graz: Akademische Druck und Verlagsanstalt, 1960–1961). |
| MGG | Friedrich Blume (ed.), *Die Musik in Geschichte und Gegenwart. Allgemeine Enzyklopädie der Musik*, 17 volumes (Kassel: Bärenreiter-Verlag, 1962). |
| MHSI | *Monumenta Historica Societatis Iesu*, 157 volumes (1897-), partially available online at http://www.sjweb.info/arsi/Monumenta.cfm. |
| ML | *Music and Letters* |
| MQ | *The Musical Quarterly* |
| MT | *The Musical Times* |
| Nadal | *Epistolae P. Hieronymi Nadal Societatis Jesu ab anno 1546 ad 1577 [...]*, 4 volumes in *MHSI* (Madrid: various publishers, 1898–1905) available online at http://www.sjweb.info/arsi/Monumenta.cfm. |
| NASM | *Note d'archivio per la storia musicale* |
| NRSV | *The Bible. New Revised Standard Version* (1989), available online at http://bit.ly/2bJjbKB. |
| OC | Jean Calvin, *Joannis Calvini opera quæ supersunt omnia*, edited by Edouard Cunitz, Johann-Wilhelm Baum, Eduard Wilhelm Eugen Reuss (Brunswick: C. A. Schwetschke, 1863–1900), 58 volumes in 59 tomes (volumes 29–87 of the *Corpus Reformatorum*, indicated here as *OC* I [=vol. 27]-LVIII [vol. 87]); available online at http://bit.ly/2b3xSrr. |
| OS | Jean Calvin, *Joannis Calvini Opera Selecta*, edited by Petrus Barth et al. (Munich: Christian Kaiser, 1926–1952), 5 volumes. |
| P-KDG | Giovanni Pierluigi da Palestrina, *Erste kritisch durchgesehene Gesamtausgabe*, edited by Franz Xaver Haberl, 33 vols. (Leipzig: Breitkopf und Härtel, 1862–1907). |

| | |
|---|---|
| PG | Jacques Paul Migne (ed.), *Patrologia cursus completus. Series græca*, 161 volumes (Paris: Imprimérie Catholique, 1857 ff.); available online at http://patristica.net/graeca/. |
| PL | Jacques Paul Migne (ed.), *Patrologia cursus completus. Series latina*, 221 volumes (Paris: Imprimérie Catholique, 1844 ff.); available online at http://patristica.net/latina/. |
| RISM | Répertoire international des sources musicales; available online at http://www.rism.info. |
| SCJ | *The Sixteenth Century Journal* |
| SCT | *Sacrosanctum Concilium Tridentinum. Cum citationibus ex utroque Testamento, Juris Pontificii Constitutionibus, aliisque S. Rom. Eccl. Conciliis* (Padua: Ex Typographia Seminarii, 1722); available online at http://bit.ly/2bD8Lff. |
| Sr. | Sister |
| ST | Thomas Aquinas, *Summa Theologiæ*; Latin version available online at http://www.corpusthomisticum.org/iopera.html, English translation at http://www.newadvent.org/summa/. |
| USTC | Universal Short Title Catalogue; available online at http://www.ustc.ac.uk. |
| WA | *Luthers Werke. Kritische Gesamtausgabe*, 65 volumes (Weimar: Böhlau, 1883–1993); available online at http://bit.ly/1LvtcKt. |
| WA BR | *Luthers Werke: Kritische Gesamtausgabe. Briefwechsel*, 18 volumes (Weimar: Böhlau, 1930–1985); available online at http://bit.ly/1LvtcKt. |
| WA DB | *Luthers Werke: Kritische Gesamtausgabe. Deutsche Bibel*, 15 volumes (Weimar: Böhlau, 1906–1961); available online at http://bit.ly/1LvtcKt. |
| WA TR | *Luthers Werke: Kritische Gesamtausgabe. Tischreden*, 6 volumes (Weimar: Böhlau, 1912–1921); available online at http://bit.ly/1LvtcKt. |
| WB | Philipp Wackernagel, *Bibliographie zur Geschichte des deutsches Kirchenliedes im XVI. Jahrhundert* (Frankfurt am Main: Heyder & Zimmer, 1855); available online at http://bit.ly/2bbnOkm; (Hildesheim: Georg Olms Verlag, 1987). |
| WGA | *Johann Walter Sämtliche Werke*, edited by Otto Schroeder (Kassel: Bärenreiter, 1953–1970). |
| Z | Huldreich Zwingli, *Huldreich Zwinglis Sämtliche Werke. Unter Mitwirkung des Zwinglivereins in Zürich*, edited by Emil Egli, Georg Finsler, Walther Köhler, Oskar Farner, Fritz Blanke, Leonhard von Muralt, Edwin Künzli, Rudolf Pfister (Berlin, Leipzig and Zurich: various publishers, 1905–1990), 13 volumes (volumes 88–101 of the *Corpus Reformatorum*, indicated here as *Z* I [=vol. 88]-XIII [vol. 101]); text partially available online at http://bit.ly/2beWHz0. |
| ZVHG | *Zeitschrift des Vereins für Hamburgische Geschichte* |

# Chapter 1 – Framing a century

> It ought to be remembered that there is nothing more difficult to take in hand, more perilous to conduct, or more uncertain in its success, than to take the lead in the introduction of a new order of things[1].
>
> [Niccolò Machiavelli]

## 1.1. Introduction

This Chapter will provide the reader with a brief overview of the main events in the history of the European Reformations of the sixteenth century, and frame them within the larger narrative of the historical, social, economic, philosophical, artistic and religious processes characterising the Early Modern era.

Given the intended readership of this book, I confidently assume that most of what I will discuss in this Chapter will be familiar to my readers, and that probably some of them will be more knowledgeable than I am on several of the topics I will briefly touch upon. Indeed, when one morning I woke up with a "vision" of Chapter One, rising fully fledged as Athena from Zeus' mind, and showing me what a historical introduction to the Reformation era should look like, I also felt that a satisfactory result would be nearly impossible to achieve.

In order to frame the hundred years 1500–1599, a variety of viewpoints should be taken into account: the history of culture and thought, that of economy and explorations; the innumerable artistic achievements of a century which will probably remain unparalleled; the complex alchemies of international and national politics, with wars, alliances, treasons, marriages and commerce; the literary, philosophical and scientific output of the era; a summary of the theological questions which caused the main religious controversies; and, of course, an overview of secular music, which I will mention only cursorily in the remainder of this book.

To provide even a very sketchy narrative of these aspects would require enormous space and a knowledge I will not claim to possess. Instead of a sketch, then, I will merely limit myself to a frame – and to a not very elaborate one.

---

[1] Machiavelli 2010, p. 21.

DOI 10.1515/9783110520811-001

Its main purpose will simply be to give momentum to the following discussion, and to help the reader's view to focus on the canvas it encompasses.

The very terms used for describing the temporal framework I arbitrarily adopted for this book depend largely on the writer's cultural, religious, geographical and historical perspective. Having been schooled in Italy, I grew up with a mind-set which equated the *Cinquecento* with a part of the Renaissance, whereas in other countries it will be known as the Reformation era, or the first post-Columbian age, to remain only within a Western perspective.

Especially as concerns the historical figures of the religious Reformers and their theological issues, I will return to many of the topics summarily sketched here within other sections of this book, especially when a deeper discussion will be necessary in order to comprehend their theology and/or practice of music.

In sum, for those unacquainted with it, this Chapter will neither be nor aim to be a thorough introduction to the sixteenth century; for the educated readers who will honour me by reading the following Chapters, these pages will probably be superfluous; possibly, however, this Chapter will serve as an aide-memoire for recalling what is well known and for paving the way to a more specialised discussion.

Indeed, history should always be construed, understood and interpreted as a process – and as an ongoing one, in which we, as interpreters of the past, are deeply immersed in turn; individual events are seldom isolated watersheds, but more frequently demand to be understood within a complex framework of causes and effects, which normally intertwine with each other and can rarely be extricated from their context.

Of course, such a narrative, as regards the sixteenth century and its religious Reformations, would require a much larger space than that of a historical introduction: the reader interested in a more detailed and less simplistic perspective will find possibilities of further reading in the bibliography listed at the end of the book.

Whilst space limitations will constrain my historical summary within the boundaries of a very concise exposition, I will try and provide the reader with a slightly more faceted overview of the theological issues at stake. The significance of some of the points of contention among theologians of the sixteenth-century is neither patent nor self-evident; however, the reward for delving in some depth into such problems will be immediate.

Firstly, indeed, theological subjects which may seem of minor importance in the eyes of contemporary readers were matters of (literally) life or death for believers of the sixteenth century. Secondly, it will be frequently apparent that matters of "mere" words had impressive repercussions on the complex of faith, and therefore on the daily lives of thousands of people which might know little of theology, but certainly placed faith high within their scale of values. Finally, though some of the theological points raised by the Reformers have little or no relevance to musical topics, many others have important consequences either for the concept of music's role in the lives of the believers, in liturgy and in worship, or for the actual practice of Christian communities.

## 1.2. Theology: the issues at stake

"Teacher, [...] what must I do to inherit eternal life?". This question, asked by an expert in the Jewish law to Jesus (Luke 10:25) is, in a nutshell, not only the basic question to which sixteenth-century theologians strove to find an answer, but, more importantly, the crucial question on the destiny of every man and woman who believes in life after death.

And yet, the very wording of the question reveals a paradoxical truth: "what must I do", from the one side, and "to inherit" from the other. One has to do nothing to inherit, the only conditions being the heir's life and the testator's death. Or, possibly, one could be denied an inheritance if he or she has deeply outraged the testator, who is thus led to modify the will. So, there is something to do, after all: if you wish to inherit, be kind to those who write their will.

Who gives eternal life? For Christians, this is a gift, the supreme gift of God, who created humankind – or rather every man and woman – in His image, and thus wants to share with them, who are by definition finite creatures, His own eternal life.

The Fall of Adam and Eve established a condition of fallenness known as "original sin", which is believed to be normally shared by all human beings[2]. Thus, the second Person of the Trinity, the Son (who is of the same eternal and divine nature as the Father and the Spirit), took human flesh in what is known as "incarnation" and was born to the Virgin Mary. He suffered, was crucified and is risen on the third day; through this sacrifice, Christians believe, he saved humankind: "There is salvation in no one else, for there is no other name under heaven given among mortals by which we must be saved" (Acts 4:12).

This is the core message of the Christian faith, and one which remains both shared and crucial for Christians of all denominations.

---

[2] The exceptions are, of course, Jesus and (for Catholics and many other denominations) his mother Mary.

### 1.2.1. How are we saved?

Problems arise, however, when one asks the question of how actually God saves us, and particularly whether this or that actual person will be saved. Of course, Christ's sacrifice is believed to be more than sufficient for saving every human being in history; but does this mean everyone will be saved, regardless of his or her beliefs or actions? Are there actions which are indispensable for being saved (such as, for example, to be baptised and to believe in Christ)? Or is salvation something which ultimately depends on one's personal choices and behaviours?

The matter is further complicated by some passages of Scripture which are open to various interpretations. From the one side, the Old Testament prophets, Christ himself and his first followers unwaveringly condemned a purely ritualistic observance of precepts, which ultimately leads people to conceive their relationship to God and to others in a utilitarian way: I did this, so you owe me that (prosperity, salvation etc.: cf., for example Proverbs 21:3.27; Hosea 6:6; Matthew 15:1–9; Mark 12:33; Romans 3:28 etc.). Moreover, there is Scriptural evidence showing that people can be saved by a single act of faith and repentance and in spite of an entire life of sin (Luke 23:43). From the other side, the innumerable teachings about right and wrong behaviour in the Bible, from the Commandments to Christ's law of love, bear witness to the relevance of righteousness, charity and holiness (cf. also James 2:17.26).

Before the Reformations, and in spite of some plurality of theological viewpoints, the belief of the Catholic Church could be summarised as: God has saved us in Christ (so the ultimate initiative is that of God's Grace, which is a free gift bestowed to humans); but humans are required to respond freely to this Grace, and this response is embodied and seen in their profession of faith and their loving behaviour to God and to other human beings.

This idea seemed uncontroversial for believers, inasmuch as there appeared to be a clear distinction between the "works of the law" (condemned as an unnecessary ritualism which ultimately destroys one's capacity to love), and the "good deeds" which accompany and show one's faith.

Love and charity, to be sure, are non-measurable quantities. And the Gospel makes it clear (Matthew 20:12; Luke 15:29) that a lifelong righteousness is no worthier, in God's eyes, than a last-minute heartfelt repentance.

In spite of this, the belief gradually emerged that the saints' good deeds are somehow stored in a kind of spiritual treasure, which may be used to help those sinners who would not qualify for salvation. Instead of a Father who "desires everyone to be saved" (1 Timothy 2:4), God was increasingly seen as an impartial judge, in front of whom one needed good advocates.

Moreover, whereas in the first centuries of the Christian era it was believed that either one was saved (and then went to heaven) or damned (and then went to hell), later the Church proposed a third option, which is known as purgatory, and is the state of souls who are ultimately saved, but need to be purified after death and before entering paradise.

It was also believed that one could help his or her dear deceased ones and shorten their stay in purgatory by praying for them and offering good deeds to the Lord on their behalf; the best "deed" of all to be offered was the Holy Mass, which was considered as the re-presentation of Christ's saving sacrifice – thence the practice of offering masses for the dead.

Since humans are frequently prone to want value for money[3], however, many wondered: if two masses are better than one, "how much" better are two than one? How much time in purgatory will be remitted from my dear deceased one in exchange for this mass?

Thus a commercial mentality progressively took hold of such sacred concepts as salvation, mercy and forgiveness, up to the point that "indulgences" (i.e. time-off purgatory) could be actually sold. They even became an easy-money resource for Church authorities whose financial perspectives were not rosy – for example, when Popes spent too much on building the magnificent Basilica of St Peter in Rome, or when an archbishop became indebted to bankers for purchasing a title.

### 1.2.2. Justified by grace

This was the spark which ignited the Reform of Martin Luther (1483–1546): he was outraged at what he perceived to be the Simonic exchange of grace for gold. From Luther's rethinking of the "economy of salvation" (how we are saved, technical name *soteriology*), prompted by his contestation of indulgences, he went on to elaborate his theory of "justification" (i.e. the process by which sinners are "made just" by God and thus saved), which is summarised by the Latin keywords of *sola fide*, *sola gratia* and *sola scriptura*.

By *sola fide* ("faith only"), Luther meant that faith in Christ is the only thing which is actually and necessarily required of men and women to be saved, in opposition to the idea that good works or deeds were equally necessary.

---

[3] Interestingly, in pre-Reformation Strasbourg, there was a saying ("Copper money, copper Requiem") whose meaning corresponds to today's "you get what you pay for". Cf. Trocmé Latter 2015, p. 103.

By *sola gratia* ("grace only") it is implied that God's grace is an entirely free gift by virtue of which we are saved, and is not something one could earn or achieve.

By *sola scriptura* ("Scripture only") a new emphasis is placed on the Word of God as contained and communicated in the Bible, while the importance of transmitted (traditional, from the Latin *traditio*) interpretation of the Bible is downplayed. In fact, for Catholics, the chain of official Church pronouncements (*magisterium*), which are based in turn on what is believed to be a divinely inspired interpretation of the Bible, are as important as the Bible itself for the establishment of dogma. For Luther, all believers have the right to interpret the Scripture in a (relative) freedom, as the Spirit suggests it to them. I added the adjective "relative" to this interpretive freedom, because Luther did not reject in full the one and a half millennium of Church tradition, and he held in high consideration the pronouncements of the so-called Church Fathers (i.e. the holy theologians of the first centuries). It was rather towards the recent magisterial pronouncements that he became more and more critical.

From these basic concepts and points of dissent between Luther and the Catholic Church, a few other crucial problems arise. The first of them is that of free will and predestination, a point on which both Desiderius Erasmus of Rotterdam (c.1469–1536) and John Calvin (Jehan Cauvin, 1509–1564) had much to say. To put it simply: if we are saved by grace only (*sola gratia*), and if our deeds are not decisive for salvation, then we are basically saved or condemned from the very onset of our life. In other words, we are *destined* for heaven or hell *before* we do anything (from the Latin *prædestinatio*, "*præ-*" meaning before and "*destinatio*" destination: cf. Romans 8:29–30). In consequence of this, we are not really free to accept or refuse salvation, to say yes or no to God's love (this freedom is known as "free will"). Radically put (and few Reformers were this radical), our doom has been predetermined for us and there is nothing we can do to change it.

While the idea that we are not the only agents of and responsible for our salvation could be a liberating and heartening one, especially for people who were prone to scruples and spiritual anguish, predestination was ultimately not entirely consoling in turn, as it raised the question, "Have I been destined for the right group?" instead of the previous "Am I doing all I can in order to be saved?"[4].

A second point deriving from the three "*sola*" principles is what is known as the priesthood of all believers. If we are saved by grace only, then those deeds and actions which were deemed to be necessary or very helpful for achieving sal-

---

4 Cf. the summary of such criticism provided in Pettegree 2005, p. 48.

vation cease to be indispensable: the first among them was the Mass intended as the real re-presentation, by a priest who operates *in figura Christi* (in the image of Christ) by virtue of his ministerial ordination, of the sacrifice of the Cross.

Based on Bible quotes (Exodus 19:6, Revelation 1:6 and 5:10), Luther maintained that all believers are "priests": by virtue of the Baptism, all Christians are made one with Christ, and thus share in His divine priesthood. While this point is maintained also by the Catholic Church[5], Luther went on to argue for the irrelevance of ordained priesthood and the equality of all baptised in front of God. (Of course, equality and sameness are two distinct concepts: one may assert, as Catholics do, that one is not "worthier" than another for being an ordained priest, but that there is a diversity of callings and functions in the Church for the good of God's people). Closely related to the changed status of the clergy in relation to the laity was the issue of priest marriage: if the case for clerical celibacy could be made arguing that Christ had not married (and is considered to be the Church's mystical bridegroom), when the *"in figura Christi"* aspect of priesthood was downplayed, there was apparently no reason for prohibiting pastors to marry.

### 1.2.3. Substantial differences

Another aspect on which Luther disagreed with the received dogmas was that of transubstantiation. This nearly unpronounceable Latin-derived word is strictly connected with the topic of Mass as sacrifice (which Luther contested in turn, maintaining that the only sacrifice was that of Christ on the cross, which could not be repeated[6]) and with that of ordained priesthood. The conceptual framework for this dogmatic assertion came from the Christian appropriation of Aristotle's philosophy. For Aristotle, things have a form (an outward appearance) and a substance (their ontological essence). A thing can change shape but maintain its substance (*trans-formation*, change of form): children will grow up, then grow old, their features will change unrecognisably, but still they will maintain their personal identity. A caterpillar will turn into a butterfly, but its DNA will not change.

Conversely, a thing may maintain its outward appearance but change its essence (*trans-substantiation*, change of substance). During the consecration

---

5 Cf. also the Second Vatican Council's Constitution *Lumen Gentium*, Chapter IV, §34; available online at http://bit.ly/1kMW4gy.
6 The Catholic view actually does not intend the Mass as a "repetition" of Christ's Passion, but rather as a re-presentation of the unique sacrifice of the Cross.

(which is one of the core moments of the Catholic Mass), and through the ritual words and acts pronounced and performed by the priest, bread and wine are believed to become the Body and Blood of Christ. Their appearance and their taste (i.e., their *form*) will remain those of bread and wine, but their essence, their substance will be radically changed. This is at the heart of the debate about the "real presence", i.e. whether Christ is truly present in the consecrated bread and wine with his "body, blood, soul and divinity" (following the Catholic formulation of this belief) or they are a mere symbol for His presence, or something like an aide-memoire through which one's prayer is intensified and thus (but indirectly) Christ enters the heart of the believer. On this topic, the Evangelical Reformers held a variety of different opinions.

The belief in the real presence also implied the exaltation, for Catholics, of the moment of the "elevation" (i.e. when the just-consecrated host is raised by the priest and offered for the contemplation of the congregation); sometimes, gazing to the holy host could become almost as important as receiving communion.

Moreover, another related topic was that of the communion "under both kinds", i.e. whether the laity could or should receive both the consecrated bread and wine during communion, or bread was enough. Since – biologically – one's blood is part of one's body, the theological case was made for the "bread-only" communion for the laity – which could be argued for also from a number of practical viewpoints. For Protestants, however, the fact that priests did communicate "under both kinds" while laypeople received only the consecrated bread was a further element of unjust discrimination between clergy and laity.

As an appendage to the transubstantiation doctrine, those who denied the real presence found it even easier to deny any spiritual value to "blessed" (different from consecrated) objects, such as holy water, relics, but also images of saints: if the liturgical consecration did not make of bread and wine the Body and Blood of Christ, even less could a simple blessing confer any particular power to inanimate things. Furthermore, and specifically against the veneration of images, a case could be made on the ground of the Biblical prohibition to worship idols (cf. Exodus 34:17 etc.); however, the destruction of images (iconoclasm), which had been carried out early in the history of the Church (from the eighth century in Byzantium), had also been condemned by an Ecumenical Council (Nicaea 787), which had allowed depiction of holy images. Notwithstanding this, iconoclasm was undertaken again by several Reformers (and mobs) in the sixteenth century, sometimes very violently.

Further within the framework of sacramental theology, there were two more burning issues during the Reformation era. The first regarded how sacraments work: for the Catholic Church, sacraments (such as Baptism, Eucharist, Confirmation etc.) are valid (and thus convey the corresponding Grace) regardless of the holiness or sinfulness of their minister (the priest, the bishop...) and (partly) of their receiver: this concept is known as *ex opere operato*. The only necessary conditions are the presence of the required matter (e. g. water for Baptism, bread and wine for the Eucharist) and the intentional performance of the corresponding rite by the appointed minister. (This will have important implications, which I will discuss in Chapter Four, as concerns the importance of the laity's active participation in public worships: § 4.3.7.2.). However, to complement this, it is also maintained that a proper spiritual disposition in the receiver is needed in order for the Grace of the sacrament to work effectively and fully (*ex opere operantis*).

The rejection of this double doctrine and its combination with the *sola fide* principle brought yet another problematic issue to the fore: was it correct to baptise infants who could not understand, let alone profess, their faith? Most Protestant Reformers continued to hold, together with Catholics, that it was possible and recommendable to baptise children (especially at a time when high infant mortality made it advisable to perform this saving sacrament as early as possible), while others disagreed. It followed, for the latter, that those who had been baptised at birth were not properly baptised, and thus had to receive that sacrament again: for this reason, these Protestant currents came to be known as "Anabaptists" ("re-baptisers").

Last but not least, the *sola* principles also implied the rejection of the idea of intercession. I have mentioned earlier (§ 1.2.1.) that many felt the need for good advocates in the presence of God's justice. The role of pleading the case for sinners was increasingly entrusted to Christ's Mother, the Virgin Mary, and to the saints (many of whom had, so to speak, a sphere of specialisation: childbirth, against particular illnesses, protection of individual trades or crafts etc.). Of course, if one is saved by grace, faith and Scripture only, then the intercession (pleading on behalf of) by Mary and the saints was no longer needed – indeed, seeking such intercession was a practice which had to be discouraged.

I will return to most of these issues in the remainder of this book, especially when their development presents aspects pertaining to musical issues, and I will also try and clarify, when needed, which position was held by the different Reformers on the individual topics. For the moment, this succinct presentation of the major problems should suffice to frame the next Chapters' theological and practical issues.

## 1.3. Culture, art and thought in the sixteenth century

In this section, I will try and briefly summarise the principal cultural issues, achievements and criticalities of the century under consideration.

The first aspect I will discuss here is the relationship between humanism and the so-called "Renaissance": the inverted commas caution against a simplistic historical categorisation which (erroneously) identifies the "Middle Ages" as a period of decay after which the Renaissance represented a welcome rebirth.

### 1.3.1. Thinking the sixteenth century

Humanism was a cultural current which characterised – in various and sometimes conflicting shapes – the perspective of many thinkers in the fifteenth and sixteenth century. Basically, humanism promoted the quest for the sources (*ad fontes*, Latin for "to the sources", was a motto of the time). Humanists encouraged the rediscovery and study of classical antiquity (Greek and Roman): ancient sculptures were taken as models and rules by visual artists, classical Latin as the touchstone of literary elegance, Greek philosophy (Plato, Aristotle, but also Stoicism, Scepticism and Epicureanism) as a source of wisdom and a model of reasoning.

Paradoxically enough, the humanist interest in the past implied rejection of the past and faith in the present and future. In other words, making a Golden Age of classical antiquity brought humanists to downplay what had occurred in between (not only the Middle Ages, but also the very concept of tradition) and to believe that a new era was dawning, one in which a brighter future could be built by joining past wisdom with new brains.

Study of the sources also implied an extraordinary development of philology, linguistics and textual criticism: thus, a crucial attention to the "word". In the following Chapter, I will develop this concept in a thematic fashion: I will discuss a number of issues relating humanism and music, via the "word", under philosophical and theological rubrics grouped by thematic clusters. There, my goal will be to sacrifice historic (chronological) and geographical perspectives (both of which were highly relevant, but also very fluid and subject to external influences) in favour of showing, through examples and quotes, the widely-felt presence of similar (and yet subtly differentiated) concerns. Here I will briefly suggest, instead, a few conceptual and historic points, which will help us to frame the cultural issues at stake.

Frequently, it is maintained that the characteristic features of southern humanism were secular (in spite of the deeply religious convictions of many of its representatives), while northern humanism was "Christian". Though this separation is simplistic, it is true that, for example, in Italy the main focus was on "pagan" antiquity (Greece and Rome), while to the north the "*ad-fontes*" motto meant a return to the sources of Christian belief (the Bible and the Church Fathers, essentially).

## 1.3.2. Applied humanism

From the word, thus, the spotlight shifted to the Word, i.e. the presence of God's *Logos* in the holy texts; from a focus on civic education, culture and politics to one on Christian spirituality and morality. The leading figures of the Christian humanist movement were the Frenchman Jacques Lefèvre d'Étaples (c.1455-c.1536) and the Netherlander Desiderius Erasmus. Both of them realised masterful translations from the Bible, including the erudite *Quintuplex Psalterium* (a Psalter in five languages) and the first French translation of the entire Bible. Erasmus, in turn, made use of his impressive knowledge of classical culture, Biblical studies and the Patristic tradition to promote a movement of spiritual reform, in which individual devotion encouraged and fostered institutional renewal in the Church.

Both of them, in spite of the challenges posed by some of their studies and some of their positions regarding the Catholic Church, did not break with it. Indeed, even though Erasmus' writings had a demonstrable and strong influence on the religious Reformers' thought, he later contended publicly and rather harshly with Luther on the issue of free will.

Actually, although the link between humanism and the Reformations is undoubtedly very strong, it is nevertheless crucial to point out that they cannot be considered as identical or completely consistent with one another: for instance, the humanists' and the Evangelical reformers' overall outlook on humankind was radically different, as the debate on free will between Luther and Erasmus clearly demonstrates. On the one hand, a rather pessimistic consideration of the fallenness of humankind characterised the perspective of many Reformers; on the other, humanist philosophy substantially expressed trust in the possibilities inscribed within human beings.

To these two distinct and yet complementary aspects of humanism (classicist and Christian), a third should be added, which is known as "esoteric humanism". Indebted to the mystical and magical aspects of ancient wisdom, many (particularly among the Neo-Platonists) developed branches of study which could range from astronomy to astrology and occultism. Among the leading figures of this current were Marsilio Ficino (1433–1499) and Heinrich Cornelius Agrippa von Nettesheim (1486–1535), both of whom wrote extensively about music and its influence on human health and behaviour. (While Ficino belongs unequivocally in the humanist field, there is debate as to Nettesheim's stance in this regard).

To the other extreme of human knowledge, humanism also prompted a renewed interest in juridical thought, with extensive studies on Justinian's *Corpus Iuris civilis* (AD529–535).

Humanism led also to the study of classical sources regarding music, in the form of theoretical and philosophical speculation about music. As we will see in the thematic survey in Chapter Two, the principal topics on which this debate focused were the ethos of the ancient modes and their influence on human behaviour, well-being and spirituality, and the importance of words in the relationship text/music. Polyphonic composition was under attack from both fronts, since it limited modal choices (even though there were crucial differences between the Greek modes and those used in the sixteenth century) and it prevented intelligibility. As we will see throughout this book, from the union of humanist speculation with issues of Church reform and purely musical questions significant stimuli for five distinct stylistic features were born: the reduction of imitative complexity in favour of homorhythmic and chordal writing; the application to music of the metres of classical poetry and of their quantitative values; the success of the polychoral idiom as a solution for preserving textual intelligibility without renouncing variety and splendour; techniques of word-painting, aiming at representing analogically the content of individual words or textual fragments; the concept of (accompanied or unaccompanied) monody as the most effective mode for amplifying, through music, the "natural" intonation and rhetoric delivery of speech.

### 1.3.3. Philosophy and theology

In spite of the humanist interest in antiquity, the Greek philosopher Aristotle received an ambivalent treatment in this century. On the one hand, being one of the greatest thinkers of the classical world, he was duly studied and revered; from the other, however, he paid for the humanist reaction against Scholasticism. The Dominican theologian Thomas Aquinas (1225–1274) had in fact structured a great part of his thought upon the conceptual framework of Aristotelian philosophy. Though Aquinas' *Summa* was and remains one of the cultural and religious pillars of the late Middle Ages (and the perspective informed by it is known as *scholastics*), some of Aquinas' later disciples emphasised its purely academic aspect into *Scholasticism*, a kind of speculation against which many humanists rebelled.

Some, including Michel de Montaigne (1533–1592), were led by their reaction to this fixed framework and seemingly closed theological system to doubt the achievability of any absolute truth by the human mind; however, this did not imply, for them, that truth did not exist, but rather that it was not reachable by reason alone.

Montaigne had also embraced, for some time, a philosophical perspective close to that of the French Neo-Stoicism: indeed, a revival and reinterpretation of Stoicism, which had presented virtue as the response to suffering, characterised several thinkers of the era, particularly when political and social turbulences put resilience to the test.

On the other hand, a contrasting solution was proposed by the Florentine Niccolò Machiavelli (1469–1527), whose famous treatise *The Prince* (written in 1513[7]) embodies an idiosyncratic political theory. The controversial ethical stance epitomised by this work suggests that rulers should be ready to undertake morally objectionable acts for the sake of the State and of their own political ends.

In contrast with Machiavelli's argument, another current of sixteenth-century political thought elaborated on the view that power is given to rulers by the consent of their people, under a kind of reciprocal agreement, covenant or contract; thus, if rulers appear to disregard the good of their subjects, the latter have the right to disobey. This idea would acquire immediate relevance to contemporaneous society during several confessional conflicts of the century. Some contemporaneous thinkers justified the use of armed resistance against unfair rulers: among them, François Hotman (1524–1590), whose treatise *Franco-Gallia* was considered to be both debatable and thought-provoking, and a Scottish humanist, George Buchanan (1506–1582), whom we will meet again in Chapters Six and Seven while discussing a very different topic[8].

Ultimately, both theories dealt with the concept of sovereignty, which was further developed in the sixteenth century by the French jurist Jean Bodin (1530–1596).

As concerns philosophy in general, we may add that from the very Dominican order to which Aquinas had belonged came two of the most important and controversial thinkers of the era, i.e. Giordano Bruno (1548–1600) and Tommaso Campanella (1568–1639), both of whom elaborated theories which were to be influential and to give rise to important developments in the following century.

---

[7] Machiavelli 1532, Machiavelli 2010.
[8] See § 6.3.3. and 7.3.5. Cf. Nauert 2006, p. 120.

### 1.3.4. Science and literature

The authority of the ancients was still very influential also in the field of the natural sciences, though the increasing focus on direct observation, on inductive thought and on experience was paving the way for the scientific method of Galileo Galilei (1564–1642).

For physics, the sixteenth century was a momentous epoch: Nicolaus Copernicus (1473–1543) published *De Revolutionibus Orbium Cœlestium* (1543), whose studies in heliocentrism were to revolutionise astronomic thought, also through the research of Tycho Brahe (1546–1601) and Johannes Kepler (1571–1630). Though Copernicus' studies were far from universally accepted by the end of the century, they represented however a challenge to both authority and beliefs in which religious tenets seemed to conflict with scientific observations.

Medicine, also, progressed through the careful and repeated observations of Andreas Vesalius (1514–1564), who furthered (and eventually challenged) the body of knowledge transmitted by Galen's works which had been recently made available in a Greek edition; another anatomist to whom important discoveries are attributed was Michael Servetus (c.1509–1553), who is mentioned here essentially because we will meet him again at a later stage of this Chapter (§ 1.6.4.). Another field in which the sixteenth century brought considerable enhancement of scientific knowledge was that of botany, especially as concerns the use of plants for pharmacopoeia.

As concerns literature, the century was dominated, in Italy, by the work of Lodovico Ariosto (1474–1533), who created the term "humanism", and Torquato Tasso (1544–1595); both excelled in heroic and epic poetry, and many of their unforgettable characters and verses were to become favourite sources for musicians.

The other great current of Italian literature (and another important inspiration for many musicians) was the so-called "Petrarchism" (from Francesco Petrarca, 1304–1374), i.e. a revival of Petrarchan subjects and literary style, which also underwent the influence of the popularisation of Plato's philosophy of love. The initiator of this movement was the humanist Pietro Bembo (1470–1547), who maintained that vernacular literature was not inferior to that written in Latin, and whose views on music and on music education we will discuss in the following Chapters; innumerable imitators followed suit, and also many women poets achieved fame with their published works in the century.

In France, many of the greatest poets and literates of the era concerned themselves with yet another area of humanist interests, i.e. the revival (or remoulding) of ancient metres and their adaptation to the characterising features of their own language. We will see in the following Chapters how Antoine de Baïf

(1532–1589) and Clément Marot (1496–1544) entered the history of music and of its relationship with the Reformations, and how it was hoped that Pierre de Ronsard (1524–1585) would put his poetic talents in the service of the Catholic cause[9].

The century was however also the century of François Rabelais (c.1490–1553), whose humanistic refinement did not prevent him from achieving immortal fame with his bawdy *Gargantua*, while Spanish literature bloomed between sixteenth and seventeenth century with Miguel de Cervantes (1547–1616) and Lope de Vega (1562–1635); and, of course, many of the greatest plays by William Shakespeare (1564–1616) are thought to have been written in the sixteenth century.

### 1.3.5. Visual arts

It was possibly in the arts, however, that the sixteenth century left its most unforgettable traces in human history. In the visual arts, the *Cinquecento* represents probably the unsurpassed height of the Italian *Rinascimento*, and one of the moments in history when artists were most acclaimed and admired. The concept of the imitation of nature, which was one of the battle-cries of humanism, gave way to the idealisation of beauty and to the "improvement" of reality: such concepts were ultimately to lead to the aesthetic perspectives known as Mannerism and Baroque.

The century opened gloriously with Leonardo da Vinci (1452–1519), the precision of whose mathematical studies and technical drawings is counterbalanced by the poetry of his "*sfumato*" (shadowy) painting technique. Raffaello Sanzio (1483–1520) followed suit: his harmonious and elegant style would become a paradigm of earthly (or unearthly) beauty. Raphael's grace was responded by the expressive power and robust creations of Michelangelo Buonarroti (1475–1564), whose Sistine Chapel will be discussed in Chapter Three (§ 3.3.3.1.), and who was intensely involved in matters of Church Reform and spirituality.

The proud Republic of Venice was at one of her moments of greatest splendour in the sixteenth century, and thus could promote artists of the standing of Giorgione (c.1477–1510), Titian (Tiziano Vecellio, c.1490–1576), Tintoretto (Jacopo Robusti, 1518–1594) and Paolo Veronese (1528–1588): we will meet again (§ 9.6.4.) some of them in a painting paying homage to the religious value of

---

9 See in particular § 6.2.2., 6.3.6., 10.3.6.

art while using a poignant musical symbolism. All of them explored new and unforgettable avenues in the realm of colour: from Giorgione's mysterious shadows to Titian's glorious hues, from Tintoretto's dynamic games of light to Veronese's positive assertions of colour; and indeed many of the most epoch-making artists of the era were similar to explorers in their attempts to push to the limits one or more parameters of artistic creation.

The same was true of architects, who experimented with amazing and unprecedented solutions, some of which were extremely daring for their time; in the study of proportions and rhythms, several authors of architectural treatises sought balance and elegance in numerical proportions drawn from music theory.

In the meantime, Italian humanism had crossed the Alps, and among the artists who admired its achievements but were able to find a totally original style was Albrecht Dürer (1471–1528), whose superb drawings and splendid paintings were accompanied by impressive mastery in the technique of woodcut, and whose tormented ("melancholic") spirit bears witness to his deep spiritual itinerary, which was highly problematized by the Reformation. Another artist who experienced those events from the very outset was Lucas Cranach the Elder (c.1472–1553), who portrayed Luther and was one of his close friends, and who contributed to the propagation of Reformation ideas with his woodcuts.

Faith becomes mysticism and vision in the dramatic contrasts of shadow and light and in the "expressionist" painting of Matthias Grünewald (c.1470–1528), while composure and refined psychology characterise the portraits of Hans Holbein the Younger (c.1497–1543), who immortalised the features of many protagonists of the Reformations: one of his paintings will be discussed in Chapter Eleven (§ 11.2.2.). It is, as will be argued, a meaningful blending of symbols, some of which reveal hope for religious peace and harmony, while others betray consternation in the face of the dissolution of unity. The same perplexity and trouble, expressed in a sanguine and yet sarcastic fashion, are discernible in *The Blind leading the Blind* (1568) by the Netherlander Pieter Bruegel the Elder (c.1525–1569), depicting the Gospel parable at a time when warfare and death were arising from religious conflicts.

As the century wore to its end, two other extraordinary artists expressed, each in his own way, a deep religious quest and interior torments, namely the Italian Michelangelo Merisi da Caravaggio (1571–1610) and El Greco (Doménikos Theotokópoulos, 1541–1614). Though their respective styles are as different from each other as can be, both focused intensely on the quest for light as a symbol of faith, and expressed through their art both the anguish and the hope of those times of uncertainty.

The art of neither, however, would have qualified as mirroring the aesthetic principles of the Counter-Reformation: The Catholic prelates who outlined what post-Tridentine art should look like emphasised qualities such as immediacy and simplicity, piety and strict adherence to the Scriptural sources. Symbols, multi-layered interpretations and complex metaphors were certainly not the favourite media for an art which aimed, first and foremost, at instructing.

## 1.4. Music

Different arts have different languages, and simplistic comparisons should be avoided. In spite of this, many of the aesthetic and theological issues discussed in the previous sections were as crucial in the musical field as they were in that of the visual arts.

In this section, I will summarise very sketchily a few crucial aspects of sixteenth-century music, in particular with reference to secular music, with the simple aim of providing an elemental framework to the following discussion of liturgical, sacred and spiritual music[10].

### 1.4.1. Setting a text

One of the pivots around which music aesthetics, theory and practice revolved, in the period under consideration, was the eternal problem of the relationship between words and music in vocal works. Though the topic was not new, nor would it be exhausted in 1600, the remarkable aspect of sixteenth-century music was the variety of responses it gave to the problem.

At the level of improvised music, both "popular" and "cultivated", as well as in some written forms of secular music, the main correspondence between lyrics and music was found in the influence of the rhythm and metre of the text on those of the music. This correspondence could be looser or stricter, frequently depending on the artistic ambitions of the composers/performers; sometimes, texts could be little more than pretexts for virtuoso singing, while on other occasions they could scarcely be defined as "texts" proper, being little more than strings of onomatopoeias.

Metrical structures, which of course depended largely on the language of the text and on the fixed forms of its poetry, could influence more directly the musical structure: thus, even though strophic forms could express only blandly the

---

[10] For further reading, see – for example – Reese 1959; Fenlon 1981; Pirrotta 1984; Fenlon and Haar 1988; Fenlon 1989; Lowinsky 1989; Finscher 1990; Freedman 2013, etc.

meaning of the text, they contributed to building national idioms of musical phrasing and intonation.

In non-strophic forms, "word-painting" techniques implied the illustration, by means of musical gestures and effects, of individual or few words; the unity of composition was thus frequently sacrificed in favour of the direct correlation between textual and musical fragments.

Concern for text/music relationships could also lead composers (and their patrons) to prefer compositional techniques which favoured, instead of hindering, intelligibility: in particular, densely imitative and highly melismatic polyphony could be replaced by chordal writing and homorhythmic structures, at least in alternation with the former technique.

Finally, music could become a rhetorical medium for amplifying the expressive features of speech, by imitating its rhythm, intonation and modulations, and by acquiring a theatrical emphasis. This was particularly true of accompanied monody, which allowed more rhythmical freedom to the singers and where the perfect correspondence between the individual singer and the character favoured subjective identification and emotional responses.

Several of these viewpoints could be adopted by a single composer (sometimes within an individual work or during the same years, but more frequently in succession); others were antithetical, and to choose one instead of another implied a clear aesthetic, and sometimes philosophical, stance.

### 1.4.2. Travelling music, travelling musicians

If a fundamental element for the dissemination of words, and for the prompting and spreading of humanist thinking on verbal issues was printing, this technological innovation had an enormous influence on music too.

With the development of music-printing techniques and strategies by Ottaviano Petrucci (1466–1539), Andrea Antico (c.1480–1538), Pierre Attaingnant (c.1494-c.1552), Antonio Gardano (1509–1569) and the Scotto dynasty[11], to name but the most important, music printing quickly developed into a cultivated/expensive line and also a cheaper and more popular one. At one extreme of the continuum were extraordinarily elegant and refined products, which frequently combined high price with an elite repertoire (often Latin-texted masterpieces of sacred music); at the other extreme, as will be discussed in the following Chapters, were penny-ballads sold by peddlers. While the former

---

11 See Bernstein 1998.

publications represented, for composers, a source of fame and prestige rather than of income, the latter aimed at reaching as large an audience as possible, and frequently made use of music for disseminating ideas (such as religious or political polemics).

Market policies also influenced the trends and orientation of aesthetic taste; printed music widened the audience and readership of musical genres whose origins lay within elite aristocratic circles.

While both languages, i. e. verbal and musical, of Latin-texted Church music were international at the beginning of the century, and frequently bore few traces of national idioms, the influence of vernacular music and the effects of the Reformations diminished the role of Latin-texted polyphony as the supranational paradigm of art-music.

At the beginning of the century, the undisputed protagonist of sacred music was Josquin Desprez (c.1450–1521), whose international fame and widespread appreciation continued posthumously and made him a symbol of artistic perfection. In particular, his ability in combining structural elegance with touching expressivity was admired by the general public (including Martin Luther).

With Heinrich Isaac (c.1450–1517), a focus on the local liturgical traditions in church music was combined with one on the German-texted heritage of vernacular tunes, which were arranged into polyphonic settings. A similar intertwining of the traditional techniques of Latin-texted polyphony with national shades (in the use of the vernacular and in its musical interpretation) characterised the music of Jean Mouton (c.1459–1522). Among the protagonists of the century, stemming from the Franco-Flemish tradition, were other composers such as Nicolas Gombert (c.1495-c.1560), an undisputed master of imitative techniques, Jacobus Clemens non Papa (c.1510-c.1555), whose *souterliedekens* will be discussed in Chapter Six (§ 6.3.3. and 6.5.), Loyset Compère (c.1445–1518), blending Italian influences with northern traditions, Pierre de la Rue (c.1452–1518), who experimented in chromatic and timbral effects, Thomas Crecquillon (c.1505–1557), who favoured tight imitation, and many others whose achievements will be mentioned or discussed in the following pages[12].

Although generalisations frequently risk being naïve, the overall itinerary of sixteenth-century sacred music does present a discernible direction, as suggested by Taruskin:

> The *ars perfecta* came about because musicians had something timeless, universal, and consummate to express: God's perfection as embodied and represented by God's own true church, the institution that employed them. [...] The standards to which musicians

---

[12] See, for example, Wangermée 1968.

serving such an institution aspired transcended the relativity of taste, just as the doctrines of religion are held by believers to represent an absolute truth. [...] By century's end the *ars perfecta* was only one style among many [...]. In a way its fate mirrored the larger fate of the Roman Catholic Church, which was left at the end of the sixteenth century a transformed institution[13].

### 1.4.3. Genres in vocal music

Among secular forms, a typical example of how musical trends and aesthetics dovetailed with market strategies prompted by musical printing is the case of the *frottola*, an Italian form in the vernacular, with simple part-writing and strophic structure.

Though written and printed sources of this genre are typical of the sixteenth century, its origins can be traced back to the earlier unwritten tradition: improvised solo singing was a common practice in fifteenth-century Italy, and much of this experience, as well as (probably) some orally transmitted tunes, were eventually received into the frottola repertoire. The connection between improvised monody with instrumental accompaniment and sixteenth-century frottola is revealed by the frequent presence of homorhythmic and chordal style in its musical settings. The merit for transforming this experience into a cultivated form is traditionally ascribed to Isabella Gonzaga, née Este (1474–1539) and to the musicians at her Mantua court, especially Marchetto Cara (c.1470–1525) and Bartolomeo Tromboncino (c.1470-c.1535).

While the repetition of the same setting on the various stanzas does not allow for deep psychology or for detailed word-painting, the historic importance of the frottola lies in the model it represented for later combinations of Italian verse with music.

Moreover, with time the literary quality of frottola texts gradually increased, and eventually came to include poetry by Petrarch and his sixteenth-century admirers and imitators, the Petrarchists. Though this created a disproportion in artistic value between text and music, it also paved the way for the emergence of the madrigal culture.

The trend leading to the adoption of increasingly refined texts for vocal settings in the vernacular was common to other European countries: for example, poetry by all leading French authors, such as Marot and members of the *Pléiade* (e.g. Ronsard and Baïf), was extensively set to music, and not just by French composers.

---

[13] Taruskin 2010, vol. I, pp. 629–630.

During the century, indeed, the glorious tradition of the French *chanson* subtly differentiated itself into two currents. The first of them is that of the Parisian *chanson*, which frequently adopted rhythmical structures coming from the dance tradition. This did not prevent *chansons* from mirroring very faithfully the poetic metre, since it was frequently built on alternations of stressed and unstressed syllables in regular patterns.

Two of the most important composers of this genre were Claudin de Sermisy (c.1490–1562) and Clément Janequin (c.1485–1558), who is remembered for his vivid and onomatopoeic depictions of "soundscapes" (birdsong, battle sounds, a hunting field etc.).

In the *chansons* by Jean Richafort (c.1480-c.1547), Gombert and Clemens, instead, a more florid and complex polyphony is found; the subjects of some of their *chansons* are more solemn, deep and intense, and these qualities are mirrored in the musical settings.

Influenced by humanist and Neo-Platonic theories, French *chansons* from the mid-century aimed at reviving that (mythical) union of poetry and music whose effects on the soul were transmitted and witnessed to by the writings of the classics. Thus, after the *"vers mesurés à la lyre"* (a classicising denomination for rhyming poetry) by the *Pléiade* poets, Baïf suggested a further evolution by creating French verses in which the rhythm of accents was amplified by and coincided with quantitative metric.

German songs were composed in the form of *Tenorlied*, i.e. polyphonic settings of a tune (either taken from the popular tradition or newly composed in a folk-like style): in the hands of Ludwig Sennfl (or Senfl[14], c.1486-c.1543), and later of Caspar Othmayr (1515–1553), this genre underwent influences from the *chanson* tradition. As we will see in Chapter Five (§ 5.3.2.6.), the *Tenorlied* style and technique suited well the emerging repertoire of Lutheran hymns.

### 1.4.4. A protagonist: the madrigal

In Italy, the *Cinquecento* saw also the success of the *madrigale*, a non-strophic vocal form which drew from the techniques of northern polyphony its refined musical language and from the repertoire of cultivated literature its texts[15]. There was, indeed, a fascinating convergence between the poetical vogue of Pet-

---

14 The composer's spelling of his family name was "Sennfl", as revealed by an acrostic in his *Lust hab ich ghabt zur Musica* (c.1534).
15 See Fenlon and Haar 1988.

rarchism and the emergence of this vocal genre, and while in the period c.1530 – 50 the music of many masterpieces was composed by Franco-Flemish masters such as Philippe Verdelot (c.1480-c.1532), Adrian Willaert (c.1490 – 1562), Jacob Arcadelt (c.1507 – 1568) and Cipriano de Rore (c.1515 – 1565), after the mid-century Italian composers took the lead, while the Flemish-born Orlando di Lasso (c.1532 – 1594) contributed to the success of the genre beyond the Alps.

That the madrigal belonged to the higher spheres of art music was apparent in its appropriation of diverse and varied compositional techniques, which were often blended and employed fluently and flexibly within a single work. The voices could be divided into smaller groups for timbral purposes; homorhythmic sections could be framed by imitations; the musical form depended on that of the chosen poem, and a full palette of rhetorical artifices could be employed both in the text and in its musical setting.

Madrigals became also a favourite genre for word-painting, though sometimes an exaggerated attention to the individual words diminished the overall effectiveness of the piece by fragmenting the musical discourse into minuscule units of meaning.

With increasing frequency, the lyrics incorporated stereotypical interjections (such as *ahimé, deh, oh* etc.), which further contributed to the dissolution of meaningful structures by depriving the verbal text (beside the musical discourse) of its fluency.

Among the disciples of Willaert, whose output of madrigals was widely appreciated and highly influential, Nicola Vicentino (1511-c.1576) undertook fascinating and daring experimentations in the musical language, which he aimed at renovating by reviving the ancient Greek *genera* (see § 2.3.2.). Rore, instead, favoured a more holistic approach to the text, in which naturalness in the musical flow was favoured over detailed depiction. Rore's cycle of madrigals on the last poems from Petrarch's *Canzoniere* (§ 9.4.3.), which are dedicated to the Virgin Mary, represent a beautiful example of the subgenre of the *madrigale spirituale*. Whilst the compositional and stylistic differences between madrigal and motet became less and less apparent, frequently the only observable distinction between spiritual madrigal and motet was in the lyrics' language (vernacular or Latin respectively, though even this rule of thumb had its exceptions). Philippe de Monte (1521 – 1603) was one of the most important composers who achieved substantial stylistic similarity among works of different genres.

Along with Petrarch and the Petrarchists, other privileged sources for madrigal texts were excerpts from Tasso and Ariosto's poems, as well as from the bucolic settings of *Il pastor fido* (1590) by Giovanni Battista Guarini (1538 – 1612).

In the second half of the century, moreover, composers tended to lend unity to their madrigal collections by selecting a single topic or poetry by a single author; the lyrics' mood often determined the music's compositional technique: syllabic settings were considered to be better suited for narrative or dramatic episodes, while melismatic passages for descriptions and introspection. Virtuoso singing was also practised, especially when exceptional soloists or ensembles were available (such as in the famous *Concerto delle donne* in Ferrara, 1580 – 1597).

The road to more fluent settings with a more restrained use of word-painting, which had been opened by Rore, was further explored by Luca Marenzio (c.1553 – 1599) and Carlo Gesualdo da Venosa (1566 – 1613). While Marenzio was a professional musician who gleaned generously from a variety of compositional techniques inherited from earlier traditions, the patrician Gesualdo felt possibly freer to experiment with unusual, unexpected and non-canonical passages and sonorities, frequently using poetry as little more than a pretext for his daring solutions.

Orlando di Lasso impressed his seal on the form of madrigal too, along with so many others; in particular, we will discuss in Chapter Nine (§ 9.6.7.) his cycle of spiritual madrigals on the *Lagrime di san Pietro* (1595). With Lasso, paradigmatically, what lent internationalism to his musical style was no longer the presence of a shared and trans-national idiom of art-music, but rather the composer's personality and his own individual creative power. Though Lasso subtly differentiated among the works he wrote on texts in the various languages, and mirrored the traditional musical idioms typical of the individual vernacular traditions, nonetheless the unifying power of his personality is much more apparent than the differences.

Italian madrigals – and, later, their local counterparts – enjoyed wide success in England too, where the publication of a collection of *Musica Transalpina* (1588) brought the Italian genre to the fore. Madrigals found so fertile a ground in England that they soon started to be written by native composers; indeed, the English interest in madrigals was to remain alive far longer than in Italy.

The national form in Spain was the *villancico*, in which the presence of various musical subjects provided works with variety and a certain degree of complexity. In the Iberian Peninsula, publications from the third quarter of the century bear written witness to the tradition of improvised accompanied monody, which was extensively practised there too.

Returning to Italy, and alongside "high" forms setting "high" poetry, a variety of so-called minor genres flourished in the sixteenth century, especially based on texts in dialect (or mocking dialects and foreign accents) and with abundant use of onomatopoeias and comically fragmented discourse. Orazio Vecchi (1550 – 1605) and Adriano Banchieri (1568 – 1634), both churchmen, were among the most successful composers in these genres; they are known also for their *madrigali rappresentativi*, i.e. madrigals whose texts represent a dialogue though each character is normally represented by more than one voice; Giovanni Giacomo Gastoldi (c.1554–1609), instead, is best known for his *balletti*, i.e. songs whose very name reveals the closeness of their style to that of dance. We will encounter one of Gastoldi's *balletti* in a rather different context, in Chapter Five (§ 5.3.2.3.).

### 1.4.5. A nursery for opera

The interest in representation and dramatic forms, which appears – albeit in a peculiar fashion – in the *madrigale rappresentativo*, is one sign of a widespread concern which was to produce several musical forms throughout Europe, and to pave the way for opera in the seventeenth century. As is known, the history of opera is normally assumed to begin with the experiments of the Florentine *camerate*, whose ideological foundation was at least as important as their artistic value. By ideology, we mean the conceptual framework of studies on music of ancient Greece: the humanist Girolamo Mei (1519–1594) had studied in depth the available sources and written down the results of his research between 1568 and 1573. Since the majority of sources were descriptive and theoretical, abstract knowledge did not hinder the creativity of artists who claimed to revive Greek music, but who were actually responding, with their own artistic imagination, to a set of principles for which little or no musical models were known to them.

Mei's studies were received with particular interest by Vincenzo Galilei (c.1520–1591), father of the natural scientist Galileo, who drew the conclusion that music's force of persuasion was demeaned by polyphony and that only accompanied monody was effective on the human psyche by virtue of its proximity to the "nature" it should imitate. Though accompanied monody was hardly a novelty, for Galilei it should not remain just one of the many options in the composers' palette; moreover, he argued that the union of music and words should not submit musical rhythm to that of verses, but rather to the natural flow of speech. Galilei's theories were to receive musical shape in his own compositions, but most of all in the first operas around the turn of the century. The birth of opera is also connected with the Florentine embodiment of the Northern-Italian tradition of *intermedi* composition: those for the 1589 Medici wedding included works by several of the greatest musicians of the era and distinctly showed the coexistence of the polyphonic madrigal tradition with that of accompanied monody.

It is with Claudio Monteverdi (1567–1643), however, that opera reached the first artistic highpoint in its history, while in his output the dialogue between polyphony and accompanied monody became most fruitful; in Monteverdi's works, the quality of "subjectivity" which is normally associated with the "Baroque" style becomes a crucial aspect of composition.

To conclude this sketchy summary, I will dedicate a few words to instrumental music in the art-music tradition of the century. The connection between vocal and instrumental repertoire was still a very strong one, with vocal music providing themes and structural models to instrumental arrangements (though instrumental dance-music, in turn, influenced some forms of vocal music). Keyboard music acquired increasing importance, with the forms of *ricercare*, which evolved from an improvisatory style to one reminiscent of motet-writing, starting with the works by Marco Antonio Cavazzoni (c.1485–1569), and of the *canzona*, indebted to the Franco-Flemish *chansons* and frequently combining virtuoso sections with multi-voiced chordal sequences. In Venice, *canzone* were to find a fertile ground as a genre for wind instruments, especially when inspired by *chansons* such as Janequin's *La guerre* (1529), which in turn had imitated military sounds with vocal onomatopoeias.

Textures from sung polyphony were frequently adapted for singing as accompanied monody (to the lute, *vihuela* etc.), and numerous treatises explained how extemporaneous arrangements could be realised and embellished.

From all the above, it can clearly be seen that the seventeenth century was not a watershed for music as has been previously maintained in musical historiography, but rather that it reinterpreted and gave written form to practices already in use in the sixteenth century (and in certain cases even earlier). Notwithstanding this, the period of music history commonly known as "Baroque" did have traits of its own, such as the widespread use of continuo accompaniment, the focus on subjective expression and the increasing attention to timbral choices, particularly with the success of the *concertato* style.

## 1.5. Society and politics

In spite of the impressive artistic achievements of the sixteenth century and of the refinement of many courts throughout Europe, living in the sixteenth century was no child's play. Wars were very frequent, and became more and more cruel and disruptive as weapon technology increased its devastating power. Famine and plague struck with deadly regularity. Even religious practice could fail to give hope and answers, as the fractionalisation of the Church appeared to threaten the absolute values of faith.

However, hope was also at hand, and it showed itself very concretely through an impressive demographic boom, by means of which the European population increased by over 25% over the course of the century.

palpably: prices of food (and particularly of cereals) rose with considerable speed, while wages did not rise comparably. Thus, in general, people were poorer at the end of the century than at the beginning, and those living in misery were more and more numerous.

Though civic and church authorities attempted to alleviate the most desperate conditions, initiatives against poverty frequently took the shape of repressive acts, such as the banishing of vagrants; moreover, when and where the religious Reformations undertook the destruction of monasteries, a fundamental source of relief for the poor was demolished in turn.

Cities became more crowded, with significant economic consequences; the urban context came increasingly to the fore as the cradle of capitalism. The emergence of this perspective, moreover, tended to weaken the concept of society as an organism of co-responsibility, and to foster individualistic attitudes.

In the countryside, the seeds of socially disruptive rebellions reaped the frequent harvest of discontent among the peasantry, whose revolts punctuated the century in various zones of Europe, from Naples to the Netherlands and from Hungary to France.

While peasants claimed fairer treatment and property rights, the wealthy were facing the impact of intensive mining and of the introduction of large quantities of silver on the market, especially in Germany. Of course, this produced prosperity both for those who had been shrewd enough to invest in mining (among these, the Augsburg family of the Fuggers) and for some social realities linked with mining (such as, for example, the town of Joachimsthal, whose musical practices will be discussed in Chapter Five: § 5.3.4.4.). On the other hand, the resulting inflation damaged those depending on feudal economic models, among whom many local aristocrats and noblemen (which will be a concurring cause of the Knights' Revolt in 1522).

It should be pointed out, however, that even the greatest European powers, first of all the Valois and the Habsburgs, suffered noteworthy financial troubles, with bankruptcy and failures to repay their debts to bankers[16].

On the positive side, the sixteenth century saw an observable increase in overall literacy, although there was a considerable disproportion between urban and rural contexts (up to six educated burghers for every one literate peasant).

---

16 Cf. Scott 2006.

As we will frequently see in the following Chapters, among the concurring causes for this growing literacy were the humanist ideals of pedagogy and education, as well as religious convictions about the importance of cultural formation. A third element was obviously at least as crucial, and this was the impact of the printing press.

This technological novelty brought revolutionary consequences, whose effects were clearly observable in the religious context. Luther's works were in continuing demand, representing an inexhaustible and safe source of income for German printers.

Obviously, if Luther's writings were so successful and popular, it was because people were interested in them: thus, the correlation between Protestant Reformations and the availability of printing must not be underestimated. The press also favoured the creation and dissemination of literary works in the vernaculars, which became increasingly common throughout Europe.

At the same time, to read – and particularly to read a book on faith or spirituality – could be either a public activity, performed by a literate person for an audience, or a very private occupation: this favoured an increasingly personal relationship to the written texts, and contributed to the emerging individualism.

Nevertheless, networks of kin, trade, interest and faith still represented a series of concentric circles favouring the maintenance of strong social bonds within a community.

This was particularly important when facing troublesome situations such as wars or sieges, which, as mentioned earlier, augmented both in incidence and in deadliness. This was also due to other technological discoveries, leading to the creation of increasingly effective cannons, and to the numerical expansion of armies, many of which were made up of mercenaries such as the Swiss lansquenets.

The hot fronts were numerous, and the breeding grounds for conflicts lay primarily in the large-scale conflict among the main European powers, first and foremost between the Habsburgs and the Valois. (As rightfully suggested by Greengrass[17], however, the great hereditary monarchies were just one of the several forms of government to be found in sixteenth-century Europe).

Beside the wars prompted by confessional opposition, where conflicting religious views frequently dovetailed with political interests, the major menace to Europe came from the attacks from and wars with the Ottoman Turks. In the first half of the century, the most important battles were won by the Turks, culminat-

---

17 Greengrass 2006, p. 60.

ing with the Christians' defeat at Mohács (1526), while in the second half two important victories came to the Christian allies, in Malta (1565) and Lepanto (1571).

The increasing production of vernacular literature, along with the emergence of religious confessions which often were strictly linked to both linguistic boundaries and political issues were factors which contributed to the gradual affirmation of national feelings, particularly in France and Spain. However, these feelings had still far to go before finding manifestation in the idea of nation-states with which we are now familiar.

Weaponry and strategy were also crucial for the success of the European enterprises of conquest outside the Continent: the newly discovered America represented, for both political powers and individual conquerors, a resource to exploit regardless of what its original inhabitants may have thought of the idea. Also to the east, in Asia, the armed ships with which the Spanish and Portuguese sailed the Oceans cannily resembled floating fortresses, and intercontinental empires were soon established by both Iberian monarchies.

Attached to these colonial enterprises, the Catholic Church (and particularly some religious orders such as the Dominicans, Franciscans and Jesuits) engaged in missionary activities, which often also took the form of human and economic development in opposition to the exploitation of native populations by the *conquistadores*. Of course, this was sadly not always the case, and on other occasions the Church was an accomplice to predatory enterprises. When Christian preaching was successful, such as in today's Mexico, Catholic missionaries frequently considered the number of new Christians to be almost a compensation for the loss to the Church of the Protestant lands.

## 1.6. Church matters

But how did the great division between Catholics and Protestants actually happen? And why? We have seen earlier in this Chapter the theological points of contention (§ 1.2.), but the social, spiritual and cultural turmoil of the Reformations involved many more people than those who would have cared for (or have understood) complex theological finesses. In the remainder of this Chapter, I will briefly summarise the most important historical stages of the Reformations; here I will point out some concurring reasons which ignited these religious revolutions.

## 1.6.1. At the roots of the Reformations

Taking a step back in history, we should pause a moment to consider the importance of the Western Schism and of the conciliarist movement on what would eventually happen in the sixteenth century. Between the fourteenth and fifteenth centuries, the Catholic Church had suffered a major trauma, with the coexistence of two (at one point even three) rival claimants to the Papacy, each of whom appeared to have been regularly elected by the Cardinals. The consequent power struggles and the diminution in Papal authority provoked uncertainty and perplexity, particularly among those religious people who cared most for the Church; eventually, the schism was mended by a Council, and it was agreed that this assembly of prelates and theologians would be regularly convened in the future.

Unfortunately, this did not happen, also because several Popes feared that their authority would be undermined by that of the Councils: this fear became palpable when Pope Pius II (1405–1464) issued a Bull (1460) affirming that Council authority was subordinated to the Pope's.

This will justify, at least partially, why Reformers like Luther frequently invoked a Council (to be held preferably in Germany), and the otherwise inexplicable reluctance of sixteenth-century Popes to summon one.

Another concurring factor was a widely-felt anticlericalism, which encompassed a variety of stances, ranging from the criticism of those who were concerned with clerical immorality and wished to reform deeply the Church's spiritual life, to the abusing ditties and songs which expressed the discontent of laypeople against the power and wealth of the clergy.

A particular form of anticlericalism was made of attacks against the Papacy: indeed, this institution, designed for providing pastoral care to Catholics, had gradually degenerated into a princely court, which differed little (in wealth, pride and sometimes immorality) from many secular courts of the era.

Actually, many of the intellectuals and philosophers who criticised the Church prior to the Reformations (and indeed some Reformers as well) did so with the aim of purifying an institution they ultimately believed in and cherished. However, progressively a rift was created between the faith of the "simple people"[18] and that of the educated. The faith experience of the former, while no less intense and sincere than that of the latter, was however based on practices and rituals which could seem to be an end in themselves and to be sometimes little more than magic and superstition. The cultivated, instead, put in-

---

[18] Cf. Scribner 1981, Scribner 1994.

creasing emphasis on the necessity of understanding and meditating on the rituals, and downplayed practice in favour of personal involvement. "Purification by ritual [...] was replaced by forgiveness through understanding"[19], as summarised by Cameron.

Movements which interpreted spiritual renewal as the necessary precondition for all effective Church reform took life in several European countries: the most famous of them is probably that of the *Brethren of Common Life*, a religious order whose principles were those of the *Devotio moderna* proposed by the Dutch theologian Geert Groote (1340–1384). Many of the protagonists of the Reformations, both Catholic and Protestants, had been linked with this approach to spirituality, and some had studied in the schools run by the Brethren (among them, Luther and Erasmus, but also Pope Adrian VI, 1459–1523). One of the most widely read devotional books of all ages, the *Imitation of Christ*, was probably written by Thomas à Kempis (c.1380–1471), who was also influenced by this movement.

Attempts to reform the Catholic Church from the inside took a variety of shapes: from currents whose spirituality was emphatically mystical (as in the case of the Spanish *alumbrados*), to those promoting the spiritual formation of the uneducated (e.g. through extensive preaching in the vernacular), to those focusing on the cultural improvement of the clergy (creation of universities, colleges and centres for theological and exegetical studies).

The centuries before the Reformations had also witnessed the emergence of spiritual movements which ended up with a separation – sometimes to be later mended – from the Catholic Church. The most important of these "heretical" movements were those of the "Lollards", the followers of John Wycliffe (c.1331–1384), and of the Hussites, from the name of their founder, Jan Hus (c.1369–1415), in Bohemia. Eventually, Hus' movement resulted in two distinct branches: a *Utraquist* Bohemian Church, to whom the Catholic Church accorded privileges such as vernacular liturgy and communion under both kinds (thence the name: *communio sub utraque specie*, under the two kinds), and the Bohemian Brethren, to whom the name Hussites is normally applied.

A further relevant figure is Girolamo Savonarola (1452–1498), a Dominican friar who promoted intense spiritual (and also political) renewal in Florence, but who was eventually burnt at the stake as a heretic. Many of his followers, while remaining in the Catholic Church, kept Savonarola's spiritual heritage alive, and managed to maintain a precarious balance between fidelity to his teachings and dogmatic orthodoxy.

---

[19] Cameron 2006, p. 15.

Both the Hussites and the followers of Savonarola, known as the *piagnoni*, made abundant use of vernacular singing as an integral component of their spiritual exercises; as we will see, the Florentine tradition would eventually be resumed by St Filippo Neri (1515–1595; cf. § 9.5.3.) and the repertoire of the Bohemian Brethren will prove influential on that of the burgeoning Lutheran Church (cf. § 5.3.2.3.).

While these movements promoted lay piety, in forms which frequently appealed to both the cultivated and to the uneducated, other attitudes by Christian humanists such as Erasmus had a somewhat ambiguous stance, which I will return to in the next Chapter (§ 2.3.9.). To promote a spirituality based on heartfelt piety and deep understanding was undoubtedly positive; however, this could be linked to a supercilious contempt for the practices expressing the simple faith of simple people. This was not an error Luther was willing to commit, as we will now proceed to discuss.

### 1.6.2. 1500–1525: Enter Luther

It is obviously impossible to summarise the principal historical facts of the sixteenth century in the space of a few pages; as said before, I will simply try and provide a brief panorama, or rather a framework to contextualise the following Chapters.

From the viewpoint of Church life, the first important event of the century was the Fifth Lateran Council, which took place in Rome (1512–1517) and whose main deliberations asserted the primacy of Papal power over that of Councils and cautioned against the emergence of national Churches. Notwithstanding this, in 1516 special privileges were accorded by the Pope to the French ("Gallican") Church. By virtue of this accord, King Francis I of Valois (1494–1547) had obtained for his national Church, with comparative ease, a degree of independence which neither Germany nor England would attain while remaining united with Rome.

A few months after the Council's conclusion, on October 31$^{st}$, 1517, an Augustinian monk by the name of Martin Luther threw a theological stone into the pond of German Catholicism, by sending to his bishop Albrecht of Brandenburg (1490–1545) and by giving publicity (in German) to ninety-five "theses". While their formulation as theological questions in the tradition of university debates was typical of academic discussion, their dissemination among the laity caused considerable turmoil.

Luther, who was a sworn doctor in Biblical studies, was intensely troubled and outraged by the market of indulgences flourishing around the city of Wittenberg, in Saxony, and which had been ultimately fostered by his very own bishop, who needed cash for paying off his debts to the Fugger bankers.

Indeed, beneath the calm surface of the Wittenberg pond, powerful streams were running, which would give an international dimension to Luther's move. Local princes were establishing alliances and testing balances of power in view of the imperial election due to take place in the next few years (1519); Pope Leo X (1475–1521) was absorbed by the task of (and the expenses for) finishing the colossal Basilica of St Peter; the Duke of Electoral Saxony (i.e. Wittenberg's region), Frederick III "The Wise" (1463–1525), stood against the sale of indulgences (but mostly because they competed with his own collection of relics) and was navigating the complex alliances and power struggles of German politics.

For Luther, however, the scandal of selling indulgences was just the most appalling symptom of a crisis of values in the Church, and of a theological construct which he believed in no more: as seen earlier in this Chapter (§ 1.2.2.), his discovery that God saves sinners by grace only had been a crucial turning point for his own spiritual life.

Luther was asked to defend his position in 1518, in Augsburg, in the presence of the Pope's envoy Cardinal Thomas Cajetan (1469–1534), a Thomist to end all Thomists, and in 1519, in Leipzig, against his former friend Johann Maier von Eck (1486–1543). Following the negative outcome of these debates, in 1520 the Pope excommunicated Luther with a Bull, *Exsurge Domine*, which was publicly burnt by Luther.

A further possibility for being heard was given to Luther by the newly elected Emperor, Charles V (1500–1558), under pressure from Duke Frederick, who in the meantime had taken on protecting Luther from physical harassment. At the Diet of Worms (1521) Luther boldly stated his convictions and refused to recant. While his courage and his arguments duly impressed many hearers, ultimately he was condemned for heresy; fearing for Luther's safety, Frederick practically had him abducted by his men, and hosted him in the Wartburg fortress for one year.

Luther did not remain idle, and spent that time working on his translation of the Bible. However, the seeds of Reformation he had planted kept growing, and, in particular, the popular interest in the topics he had raised requested religious leaders to take a stance. Two pastors came to the fore: the methodical and diplomatic, but still very young, Philip Melanchthon (1497–1560), and the older scholar Andreas Bodenstein von Karlstadt (1486–1541). While Melanchthon toiled with theology, writing the *Loci Communes* in which Luther's theories were somewhat systematised, Karlstadt wished to implement in practice the theological principles expounded by Luther, regardless of the congregations' feelings. Considerable turmoil followed, particularly when Karlstadt enforced (or abolished) rituals which were particularly cherished by the laity. Riots accompanied the distribution of communion under both kinds, liturgies without holy vestments, and especially acts of iconoclasm.

News about the Wittenberg facts were circulating, in the meanwhile: in that same year 1521, King Henry VIII of England (1491–1547) had his theologians ghost-write for him an *Assertion of the Seven Sacraments*, countering Luther's opinions and raising enthusiasm in Rome, which led the Pope to proclaim him *defensor fidei*.

At the beginning of Lent 1522, Luther exited from the Wartburg and tried to mend the social disruptions provoked by Karlstadt's initiatives. In particular, Luther maintained that nothing should be forcibly imposed – particularly matters of no immediate urgency – and that respect should be accorded and shown to the uneducated and to those who were not yet ready for major changes. Luther had to face some *faits accomplis*, the most evident of which were the marriages into which some members of the clergy had entered. At the same time, Luther reasserted the validity of infant baptism, the legitimacy of sacred visual art and the real presence of Christ in the Eucharist (in spite of his denial of the transubstantiation). He also undertook important initiatives for the relief of the poor, as well as a liturgical reform: in both tasks, he was ably assisted by Johannes Bugenhagen (1485–1558).

Luther had thus effectively and practically responded to a major problem of all reformers and revolutionaries – i.e. at what speed reforms should be implemented, and what degree of compulsoriness they should have. The same questions were pondered, in that same year 1522, by a Swiss priest, Huldrych Zwingli (1484–1531), who had been in charge of Grossmünster in Zurich since 1518, and had reached "Evangelical" positions even earlier, before Luther came to the fore. What Duke Frederick was for Luther, i.e. both employer and patron, the city council was for Zwingli: thus, Zurich implemented the Zwinglian Reformation in 1522, and from thence the Evangelical[20] ideas spread quickly in German-speaking Switzerland and southern Germany. In 1523, however, Zwingli held a public disputation, in the vernacular and in front of the citizens, where the role of sacraments and images was discussed: while Mass was replaced by the Lord's Supper (symbolic instead of sacrificial perspective) and images were forbidden, Zwingli also maintained infant baptism against Anabaptist positions. Years later (1527), Zwingli and the city of Zurich were going to condemn to

---

[20] I am using the word "Evangelical" as it was intended by most Reformers of the sixteenth-century, i.e. as indicating beliefs and people who contested the Catholic tradition.

death some Anabaptists, whose "heretical" stance was seen as socially disruptive and, thus, potentially compromising the other achievements of the Reformation.

The year 1523 saw other momentous events: it was the second year of the "Knights' Revolt", in Germany, where the intermingling of social discontent with religious matters became apparent, but also the year of the martyrdom in Antwerp of two young Augustinian monks who had converted to Lutheranism (see § 5.3.2.4. and 10.3.3.1.) and of the beginnings of Evangelical preaching in the free imperial city of Strasbourg, initiated by Mathias Zell (1477–1548).

The year after the Knights' Revolt (1524), a major upheaval, known as the "Peasants' War", took hold of southern Germany and later spread northwards. Here too, and perhaps even more clearly than in the Knights' case, the blend of faith with economic and social issues was explosive. This was particularly the case with the Thuringian rebels, who were led by a charismatic guide, Thomas Müntzer (c.1489–1525), whose Evangelical perspective was much more radical than Luther's, and was veined by a mystical spiritualism with apocalyptical overtones. In Lindberg's poignant words, Müntzer "was not looking for a better day" of social justice, "but rather for the end of all days"[21].

The rebel peasants (who actually were not just and not primarily peasants, but rather members of the lower classes) at first did not meet the full strength of the Emperor's armies, since these were presently engaged in the eternal wars between Habsburg and Valois in Italy. In February 1525, eventually, King Francis I was captured by the Emperor after being defeated at the Battle of Pavia; the Habsburg's professional armies thus were free to concentrate against the peasants and scatter them. Slaughter and destruction followed; and after pleading for reasonableness with both rebels and rulers (*An Admonition to Peace*[22]), Luther published a second tract[23] in which he openly advocated the extermination of the murderous peasants. The Peasants' War resulted in the death of about 100,000 people, among them Müntzer himself.

Notwithstanding these facts, which must have troubled Luther deeply, he undertook a fundamental step which his friends had been urging him to make for the last few years, and he got married to a former nun, Katharina von Bora (1499–1552). The reason for such insistence was, of course, highly symbolic: clerical marriage represented one of the most evident and provocative demonstrations of the Evangelical Reform, and it seemed fundamental that its leader

---

**21** Lindberg 2010, p. 149.
**22** *WA* 18, pp. 291–334.
**23** *Against the robbing and murdering hordes of peasants*: *WA* 18, pp. 357–361.

gave the right example. In spite of such propagandistic aims, there is evidence that the Luthers were a happy and loving couple, and that family life provided Luther with many important theological and pastoral insights, both on the plane of his concept of marriage and sexuality and on that of entirely spiritual concepts.

### 1.6.3. 1526–1550: Spreading the word

The year 1526 saw major events in international politics: from the invasion of Hungary by the Turkish army (Battle of Mohács) to the alliance between Francis I (who in the meanwhile had freed himself from imprisonment) and Pope Clement VII (1478–1534) against the Emperor, to the Diet of Speyer, where an essential principle started to appear. This concept is known in its Latin formulation, "*cuius regio, eius religio*" ("Whose realm, his religion"), and it means that the ruler's confessional allegiance determines that of his or her subjects. The official adoption of this principle would have to wait for a few years, but from this Diet the relative weight of the rulers on religious matters substantially increased. Many felt the need for a Council, but most wanted it to be a "German" Council, where religious matters could be settled within an Imperial framework. It will come as no wonder that the Pope was not thrilled about the idea.

Indeed, the Pope had his own problems to care about, since the year 1527 is best remembered for the "Sack of Rome", where Charles V's mercenary soldiers, the payment of whose wages had been delayed, decided to plunder the city at their leisure. That event represented a psychological shock not only for the Pope but also for the entire city and a great part of Italy, and had major repercussions on the fate of many leading artists of the era.

Far to the north, the Reformation had reached Sweden, under King Gustav I Vasa (1496–1560), while Luther, with the help of Bugenhagen, was involved in establishing detailed Church Orders for many cities of today's Germany and for Denmark, and establishing official Visitations on a large scale. This experience demonstrated the low level of religious education of the laity, especially in the country, and thus probably prompted the creation of the Lutheran Catechism by the Wittenberg Reformer. Published in two distinct versions (the "Small-" and the "Large Catechism"), destined respectively for the laity and the pastors, it would become the pillar of Lutheran religious instruction.

Another Diet was summoned, again in Speyer, in 1529, where many allowances which had been made for Evangelical worship and beliefs were suspended. Against such decisions, a coalition of Lutheran princes and free cities gathered under the banner of Landgrave Philipp of Hesse (1504–1567), and presented a joint *Protestatio* (thence the name "protestants") pleading for the maintenance of the previous accords and for an Ecumenical Council.

Frantic attempts were made during the following three years to reach compromises and peace, among which the 1529 Marburg Colloquy (where an entente was sought between Luther and Zwingli, whose positions were by now difficult to reconcile) and the Augsburg Diet in 1530.

The situation had reached such a point that Emperor Charles could no longer avoid a direct intervention, and thus he took part in the Diet: he was then at freedom to go to Germany, since both the Pope (after the sack of Rome) and Francis I were kept at bay, while the Turks had retired from Vienna (which they had besieged the previous year).

On Charles' request, the "Protestants" prepared (or rather asked Melanchthon to prepare) a summary of their theological positions. Melanchthon's masterpiece of theological finesse and diplomacy, the *Confessio Augustana*, was meant to be an Evangelical statement which should have been acceptable for Catholics.

It became apparent that, in spite of Melanchthon's efforts, the Emperor's intention was not to seek an agreement but rather to suppress Protestantism; indeed, a few months were given to Evangelicals to recant, and it became compelling, for them, to create a military alliance in view of an impending war. The League was founded in the following year, 1531, and came to be known as the Schmalkaldic League; its theological foundation was to be the *Confessio Augustana*.

In that same year, Zwingli found his premature death at the battle of Kappel between Catholic and Evangelical Swiss cantons. Zwingli's Reformation was to be taken up by Heinrich Bullinger (1504–1575), who maintained his predecessor's overall orientation but also sought to reconcile Zurich with the other Evangelical realities.

In the meantime (1533), two important cities adhered to the Reformations, namely Geneva and Münster. Both were to play fundamental roles in the history of the Reformations: the former would become the cradle of Calvinism, while the latter, where many Anabaptists had taken refuge (and from which many Catholics and Evangelicals were correspondingly fleeing), would become the theatre of a terrible siege and massacre in 1535.

Things were moving also in England, where Thomas More (1478–1535) had been replaced as High Chancellor by Thomas Cranmer (1489–1556) in 1533, in correspondence with the intricate conjugal issues of King Henry VIII. As is well known, the King had needed a Papal dispensation for marrying Catherine of Aragon (1485–1536), his brother's widow. Since their only surviving child was a daughter, Mary Tudor (1516–1558), the King asked the Pope to retract the dispensation, and thus annul their wedding. On the Pope's denial (which had political along with theological reasons), Henry issued an Act of Supremacy (1534), making him the supreme head of the Church of England, which thus broke with Rome. It should be emphasised that the most evident consequence of that Act at that moment was not the introduction of an Evangelical Reformation in England, but rather the wedding of Henry to Anne Boleyn (c.1501–1536). The first major anti-Catholic undertaking, thus, was the dissolution of monasteries (until 1541), and not a Reformation in the sense of spiritual renewal as elsewhere in Europe.

However, within another European court the Evangelical movement was, quite literally, at the doors. The French court had been rather welcoming to Evangelical ideas, particularly by virtue of Marguerite de Navarre (1492–1549), King Francis' sister, who was deeply interested in spiritual issues and gathered a circle of intellectuals, artists, literates and thinkers, several of whom would later embrace Protestantism.

The King's tolerant and open-minded approach to religious issues was to change following the "*Affaire des Placards*" (1534), when Evangelical posters against the Mass were allegedly pinned on the door of the King's room. The ensuing bitterness against Evangelicals, which increased over the years, led about five thousand of them to leave France – among them Jean Calvin, who fled to Basel. There, he started writing the *Christianæ religionis institutio*, i.e. the first stage of the *Institutes* which were to constitute the dogmatic identity of the Reformed Church.

When, two years later (1536), Calvin was forced by external circumstances to stay in Geneva on his way to Strasbourg, his friend Guillaume Farel (1489–1565), who was seeking with rather unsatisfactory results to implement the Reformation in Geneva, urged Calvin to remain and help him in the task.

In England, these years saw the definitive suppression of monasteries (which were not revived under the Catholic Mary's rule), some new instalments in the romantic affairs of the King (Catherine's natural death, the execution of Anne Boleyn and the wedding to Jane Seymour (c.1508–1537), who was to bear the long-awaited male heir to the King), and, more relevantly, the publication of an English translation of the New Testament (to be followed by the entire Bible) by William Tyndale (c.1494–1536).

In Rome, the new Pope (since 1534) was Paul III (1468–1549), under whose rule (the longest in a century of eighteen Popes) sympathisers to the Evangelical movement and Catholic Reformers interested in mending the rupture with Protestants achieved positions of responsibility in the Church. A circle of Italian Evangelicals gathered around the Spanish theologian Juan Valdés (c.1500–1541) in Naples: among them Bernardino Ochino (1487–1564), the Vicar General of the newly created rigorist branch of the Franciscans, the Capuchins, and Pietro Martire Vermigli (also known as Peter Martyr, 1499–1562), an Augustinian. More loosely connected with Valdés were the Venetian patrician Gasparo Contarini (1483–1542), who had elaborated a theology of justification quite independently of Luther, and Reginald Pole (1500–1558), who was related to the Tudors and would become one of the protagonists of both the Catholic Reformation and of the relationships between Rome and London.

Pope Paul III also requested a commission of prelates to prepare a memorandum for the reformation of the Church, in view of the Council which he had at first announced to take place in Mantua in year 1537. The results of the commission's work had no great immediate impact on the Catholic Reformation, but the abuses listed therein provided Protestant polemicists with a much-welcome and ready-made resource.

In Geneva, Calvin and Farel's joint efforts to reform the city seemed no more successful than those of Farel alone; indeed, in 1538 they were both expelled, and Calvin eventually decided to continue his journey to Strasbourg which had been interrupted two years earlier.

In Strasbourg he was appointed the pastor to the French-speaking congregation, but first and foremost he got to know, from the inside, the secrets of a thriving Evangelical Reformation. Here, under the guidance of Martin Bucer (1491–1551), of Zell and others, Protestantism flourished: one aspect which is particularly relevant for us is the abundant use and presence of vernacular songs in worship, which deeply impressed Calvin and many other visitors.

Bucer's theological stance was marked by his attempts to reconcile the apparently opposing views of Luther and Zwingli: indeed, Strasbourg had adhered to both the Lutheran *Confessio Augustana* and to the *Confessio Tetrapolitana*, of a Zwinglian inspiration.

These years saw also a rapprochement between the Church of England and Lutheranism: Henry VIII had been excommunicated and was considering the idea of joining the Schmalkaldic League. Notwithstanding this, in 1539 the English Church asserted the *Six Articles*, which basically reaffirmed Catholic theology while threatening dissenters with penalties.

Evangelical movements were spreading in the Netherlands too: in particular, the city of Emden (East Friesland) became a centre for Reformed thought (and press), also owing to the presence of the Polish Reformer Jan Łaski (Johannes à Lasco, 1499–1560).

A new attempt at religious pacification was made in 1541, when some of the leading theologians of the era met in Regensburg. After encouraging beginnings, the initiative failed; the atmosphere thus became hotter in Italy for Evangelicals, and both Ochino and Vermigli left the Peninsula (for Geneva and Strasbourg respectively).

In Geneva, Ochino encountered Calvin, who had been recalled there by the citizenry. Calvin had learnt several important lessons from Strasbourg, both as concerns music and in terms of Church organisation. Besides structuring the Church's ministries on the model of Strasbourg, Calvin created the Consistory, a disciplinary assembly in charge of public morality and godliness, and with the power of excommunicating those failing to comply.

After exhausting delays, in 1545 the Ecumenical Council eventually began in the city of Trent, at the borders between Italian- and German-speaking territories. Among the protagonists of its first stage were Cardinal Pole and Cristoforo Madruzzo (1512–1578), who played the host being the bishop of Trent.

The Council's agenda was ambitious, and encompassed theological, pastoral and moral issues. Theologically, among other aspects, it reasserted the dogmatic value of tradition, the Seven Sacraments (whose number had been drastically reduced by the Protestants) and the doctrine of free will enabling human beings to respond to God's saving Grace with the good works necessary for salvation. The Council also stressed the importance of clerical morality (including spiritual renewal and chastity) and education (with the creation of seminaries for the cultural formation of prospective priests).

Evidently, there was nothing conciliatory in the Council, even though several problematic issues denounced by Protestants were positively received at Trent (for example, the criticism of clerical immorality). Thus, unavoidably, at the Council's conclusion (1563) the Church was more "Roman" and less "Catholic" (i. e. "universal") than it was at its beginning.

A fundamental actor of both the "Catholic Reformation" (meaning by this the Catholic Church's self-regeneration) and the "Counter-Reformation" (the attempts and actions undertaken for re-Catholicising Protestant zones) was the Society of Jesus, an order of regular priests (commonly known as Jesuits), founded by the former soldier Ignatius of Loyola (1491–1556). Some of the characterising features of Jesuit activity were the promotion of spiritual renewal, through preaching and the use of "multi-media" experiences (theatre, music, visual arts); the education of the young, through catechism and the foundation of colleges; missionary activity in the farthest regions of the known world, with figures such as St Francis Xavier (1506–1552) in India and Japan, and Matteo Ricci (1552–1610) in China.

The year 1546 saw Luther's death; divisions within the movement arose rather soon, in particular between the "Philippists", who followed Melanchthon's line, and the "Gnesio-Lutherans", who advocated the return of the Lutheran Church to what they deemed to be its original view. Melanchthon, in particular, was accused by some to be too close to Calvinism; thus, the "Gnesio-Lutherans" sometimes threw to their opponents the accusation of "Crypto-Calvinism" (i. e. to be "Calvinists in disguise"), and there could be, in some instances, more tension between Lutherans and Calvinists than between Catholics and Protestants.

The war between the Protestant Princes and the Emperor, which the former had been preparing for since 1530, eventually exploded in 1546. The Schmalkaldic League had already been weakened by the Emperor's shrewd political moves, and was eventually defeated in the battle of Mühlberg (1547), near Wittenberg. The aftermath of the Schmalkaldic Wars could have offered yet another possibility for religious pacification, but neither the Emperor nor the Pope (who moved the Council to Bologna, farther from Germany and closer to Rome) exploited this opportunity effectively. Several Protestants sought refuge in England, where some of the greatest Evangelical theologians of the era were appointed important chairs at English universities (among them, in the following years, Vermigli, Bucer, Ochino and Łaski).

The English situation became indeed more favourable to Evangelicals on the accession to the throne of King Henry VIII's son, the ten-year-old Edward VI (1537–1553). During his brief reign, the *Six Articles* were abrogated, the Lutheran overtones of English Protestantism faded in favour of a more Reformed approach, and Cranmer issued two versions (1549 and 1552) of the *Book of Common Prayer*, the official text of Anglican worship, with increasingly Calvinist features.

Following his victory over Protestants, Charles V proclaimed, in 1548, the so-called Augsburg *Interim:* a provisional settlement, destined to remain in vigour until the Council's conclusion, and in which some liberties were accorded to Protestants (e.g. communion under both kinds and clerical marriage) but many more traditional practices were enforced.

The *Interim* deeply divided Protestants: from the one side, it practically equated Protestantism with Lutheranism, to the deep discontent of the Reformed; from the other, and within Lutheranism, some accepted the Emperor's proposal whereas some rejected it unequivocally.

Those who opposed the *Interim* signed the Magdeburg Confession (1550): politically, this move provoked an imperial ban on and a siege of the city, while theologically it weighed on the elaboration of theories of resistance to unjust power and coercion.

### 1.6.4. 1551–1575: Consolidating confessions

In the 1550s, the Genevan Church increasingly augmented its theological importance (while several dogmatic stances were defined and clarified) and its international prestige: Geneva's firmness in condemning (and executing) the theologian and anatomist Servetus gained for the city the sympathies of many Protestants and several Catholics too.

In England, the Reformation which had started blossoming during Edward VI's rule was suddenly halted by the accession to the throne (1553) of the Catholic Mary Tudor, who quickly defeated her Protestant rival, Jane Grey (c.1536–1554). Many Protestants left England; Emden and Geneva were among the favourite destinations. Living in cities whose Reformed perspective was much more marked than that of their motherland drove many Marian exiles to Calvinist positions. Among those who experienced the Genevan worship and eventually exported it to the British Isles was John Knox (c.1513–1572), the Reformer of the Scottish Kirk.

Under Queen Mary, the Church of England was reunited with Rome (1554); cardinal Pole was sent by the Pope to England to implement the Catholic Reformation, and undertook initiatives which foreshadowed the Council's eventual deliberations; moreover, following the Queen's marriage to Philip (1527–1598), heir to the Spanish throne and son to Emperor Charles V, many of the leading Spanish Catholic theologians were invited to England. Several of these initiatives (and particularly the royal wedding) were ultimately noxious to the Catholic cause: sympathy for Spain and for the Habsburg was far from widespread, foreign domination represented an unwelcome perspective, and Catholicism began to be seen as a Continental threat.

The menace became even more concrete in the following year (1555), when Emperor Charles V began abdicating his powers and ceded the Netherlands to Philip, who left England for the Continent where yet another Valois-Habsburg war was being fought. The loss of Calais, following the unsuccessful participation in the war of Mary's troops as allies of her husband's, did not help to increase her popularity.

The major event of 1555, however, was the Peace of Augsburg. Charles V's brother and heir to the Imperial throne, Ferdinand (1503–1564), arbitrated a settlement with the German powers, in which the principle of "*cuius regio eius religio*" was adopted. The status quo of confessional division was thus acknowledged; a binary opposition of Catholics and Lutherans replaced the shaded situation of the previous decades; and while the principle might seem little more than a re-statement of what had been established at Speyer (1526), the surrounding framework was drastically different, since a third party – Calvinism – had emerged in the meanwhile and was not taken into account at Augsburg.

Thus, the *Confessio Augustana* became officially legal in the Empire along with Roman Catholicism; Catholics were granted the right to worship in the Lutheran territories, whereas Lutherans in Catholic zones were only accorded the possibility of relocating.

The division of Charles V's empire between his son, King Philip II of Spain, and his brother, the Holy Roman Emperor Ferdinand I, which took place in stages in these years, caused the division of what had been a gigantic conglomeration of territories and peoples, and contributed to an increasing popular discontent in the Netherlands, where Philip was seen as a foreign dominator to whom little loyalty was owed.

After one of the shortest pontificates in history, that of Marcellus II (1501–1555), Gian Pietro Carafa (1476–1559) was elected as Paul IV. In spite of his earlier cooperation with open-minded Catholic Reformers such as Contarini and Pole, and possibly also in consequence of his old age, Paul IV adopted a hard line against Protestantism and its sympathisers. The first *Index of the Forbidden Books* was created, and leading Catholic Reformers such as Pole and Giovanni Morone (1509–1580) underwent Inquisition. Paul IV also declared war on Philip II of Spain, regardless of his Catholic faith and of that of his wife, Queen Mary, who was probably the European ruler who most actively engaged in Counter-Reformation activities.

Such activities, however, were doomed to an abrupt end when Mary died (1558) and her half-sister, the Protestant Elizabeth I (1533–1603) accessed the English throne. The Acts of Supremacy and Uniformity were reinstated; the new Queen, however, was able to find a delicate balance between Catholicism (of which the Anglican Church retained many rituals) and Protestantism (whose theological perspective was adopted, while moderating the Calvinist orientation). While her position, expressed in the religious settlement of 1559, undoubtedly succeeded in granting relative peace to England, whose wealth and culture blossomed during her reign, it was also displeasing to many returning Marian exiles who wished the Church of England to resemble more closely the Calvinist models they had observed in the Continent. To the north of England, Scotland was actually implementing its own Protestant Reformation, whose theological and liturgical stance was much closer to Calvinism than Elizabeth's.

Mary Tudor's death permitted her widower, Philip II, to focus entirely on his Spanish kingdom: thus, both Spain and England were entering decades-long rules of fundamental importance for their internal and foreign politics.

On mainland Europe, France and Spain had eventually reached an accord and signed the peace of Cateau-Cambrésis (1559). In that same year, however, the French King Henry II (who had succeeded Francis I in 1547) died unexpectedly, leaving the sceptre in the hands of his widow, the regent Caterina de' Medici (1519–1589).

Her rule, at first, was inspired by comparative moderation to and toleration of Protestantism: Evangelicals were even permitted to worship at court. In spite of this, the power struggles among the parties of the French aristocracy intensified and became tightly connected with confessional issues. The two main factions were respectively headed by the Catholic family of the Guise and by the Bourbons, several of whom were Evangelical.

The Guises, in particular, were exercising remarkable influence on young King Francis II (1544–1560), and – of course – this far from pleased the Huguenots (a name by which Calvinists were often referred to, particularly in France). The Reformed aristocrats thus plotted to extricate the teen-aged King from the Guise orbit (Conspiracy of Amboise, 1560), but failed, and several noblemen were condemned to death.

The young King died in that same year, leaving his widow, the Catholic Mary Stuart, Queen of Scots (1542–1587), to deal with the Scottish Reformation. An Act of the Scottish Parliament, in fact, established the Kirk in 1560: here too, a theological and pastoral structure indebted to the Genevan model intertwined with political power struggles involving international actors such as the Queen Regent of Scotland, Mary, who was a member of the French family of the Guises, and Elizabeth I.

Further riots would arise in Scotland in 1567, where the murder of Mary's husband, Lord Darnley (Henry Stuart, 1545–1567) and the widow's hurried marriage to James Hepburn, Earl of Bothwell (c.1534–1578), whom many believed to be among the instigators of the crime, caused considerable upheaval. Other causes of discontent against the Queen of Scots were her persistence in the Catholic faith which the Scottish Parliament had abolished, especially because the liturgies celebrated for her attracted many Catholics and allegedly hindered the Reformation. Rebellion coalesced around a group of Scottish Lords, who raised an army against the Queen at Carberry Hill; she eventually surrendered without bloodshed, was imprisoned at Loch Leven Castle, and abdicated in favour of her infant son James VI (1566–1625), who was later to inherit the English crown as well (as James I). Disorders followed, both as high-level plots and conspiracies and as a Civil War, which continued until 1573.

The Regent of France Caterina, in the meanwhile, tried to reconcile opposing political and religious factions at the Colloquy of Poissy, 1561. The attempt failed when Calvin's delegate, the great theologian Théodore de Bèze (also known as Beza, 1519–1605), touched the topic of the Eucharist, which was one of the most divisive themes. Nevertheless, Poissy represented a milestone for the official recognition of Protestantism and paved the way for the following year's Edict of Toleration.

The sight of some liberties being accorded to Huguenots outraged both the internal Catholic opposition (the Guises) and Spain; since the Queen Regent was unwilling to embark on yet another Franco-Spanish conflict, she gradually shifted her stance toward Catholicism in the hope of conciliating her powerful neighbour.

Nevertheless, days were numbered for peace in France. When Francis, Duke of Guise, allegedly slaughtered a clandestine Huguenot congregation, the era of the Wars of Religion began in France: it was to last, with interruptions, and with changing fortunes, until 1598.

Among the weapons available to the Huguenot armies, the less violent (but one of the most efficacious) was psalmody: as I will discuss in Chapters Six and Ten (§ 6.3. and 10.3.4.), the publication, in that same year 1562, of the Genevan Psalter, was to represent a unique feat for Reformed spirituality, identity, culture and confessional spread.

Another female ruler was experiencing troubles in those years: Margaret of Parma (1522–1586), Governor of the Netherlands, faced a wave of rebellion and iconoclasm in 1566, which the Dutch Protestants would later remember as the "wonder year". Many Evangelicals who had sought refuge in England or in Emden returned to the Netherlands; the Spanish King Philip, in whose hands authority ultimately lay, reacted by sending a powerful army, commanded by the Duke of Alva (Fernando Álvarez de Toledo y Pimentel, 1507–1582). Margaret resigned her power to Alva, whose "Council of Troubles" was eloquently nicknamed the "Council of Blood".

The resistance of Dutch Protestants coalesced around William of Orange (1533–1584), under whose leadership the rebels obtained several important victories in a confessional war which would last for eighty years. Though it was not a field victory, one of Orange's most important feats was to create a feeling of national identity among the rebels, whose revolt against foreign occupation began to be of a piece with their confessional allegiance. In spite of boundaries which were to be disputed for years, a geographical division between Protestant (to the north) and Catholic provinces was emerging.

Within the space of fifty years, thus, the religious and political face of Europe had dramatically changed. The first generation of Reformers had died (Calvin in 1564); Protestantism had grown, had spread throughout Europe, but was also already deeply fragmented, with a major rift dividing Lutherans from Calvinists. Other currents had progressively flowed into either of the mainstream Protestant confessions, while yet others had established themselves as numerically limited, frequently isolated, but proudly independent.

The more recently-founded Protestant Churches were increasingly likely to be absorbed within the orbit of Calvinism, which acquired a genuinely international dimension. While the Peace of Augsburg and its principle ("*cuius regio eius religio*") had originally concerned German territories, in the age of "confessionalisation" the entire map of Europe bore traces of a similar approach. In parallel with the official or unofficial establishment of geographical boundaries to confessional allegiances, theological statements, "confessions" and catechisms defined the dogmatic identity of the Churches.

After the Council of Trent (concluded in 1563), the Catholic Church undertook energetic initiatives both *ad intra* (internal reform) and *ad extra* (Counter-Reformation and missionary activities). The authority to implement the Council's decision was entrusted to local bishops, who were asked to reside in their dioceses instead of gravitating around Rome as before. To the fragmentation of the Evangelical movement and its increasing tendency to assume national identities, Catholicism responded with ritual uniformity, as embodied in the new liturgical books issued in the post-Tridentine era (cf. § 9.3.2.–4.).

In spite of the emerging divisions, Christians were compelled to unite due to the renewed Ottoman menace, with the attack on Cyprus (1570). Venice, whose naval and economic power was threatened by the Turks, started recruiting allies under the aegis of the Pope, and a Holy League took form. The Turks were eventually defeated at the Battle of Lepanto (1571), which was seen – particularly in the Catholic world – as a sign of God's favour.

In 1570, however, Pope Pius V (1504–1572) had entered the field of English politics by publicly condemning Queen Elizabeth as a heretic: her Catholic subjects were therefore under no obligation of loyalty to her. Many Catholics were not really willing to betray their Queen, and managed to be faithful to both their religious beliefs and to the sovereign. However, as could be expected, the Queen was not flattered by the Pope's initiative, and the subsequent limitation she imposed on Catholics made it more difficult, for them, to maintain this double allegiance.

Protestant faith, in the meanwhile, was taking hold of the Scandinavian countries (Denmark-Norway and Sweden), while the French Protestants, together with the leaders of the Dutch rebellion, met in La Rochelle (1571). Once more, reasons of internal and foreign policy intertwined: a war with Spain was on the Protestants' agenda, but local power struggles were equally compelling, since the Huguenot house of Bourbon was to inherit the French throne if the Valois had no male heir.

Regent Caterina was anxious to pacify the conflicting factions, and – as was common at the time – thought that a convenient marriage could serve the purpose. Thus, a splendid wedding was organised for her daughter Margaret of Valois (1553–1615) to the Protestant Henry of Navarre (1553–1610), a Bourbon.

While Paris was crowded for the wedding, the order was given to the militia to slaughter all Protestants, in what is known as the massacre of St Bartholomew (1572). Whether the order really came from the royal family or somebody claimed to be reporting official commands which had not been issued, remains today an open question. The victims, both in Paris and throughout France, where the carnage spread in the following days, were counted in their thousands. The effects on the surviving Huguenots and on the overall relationships between Catholics and Protestants are easy to imagine.

Thus, the situation found by Henry III (1551–1589), Caterina's fourth son, when he was summoned from Poland by the death of his brother Charles IX (1550–1574) to inherit the French throne, two years after the massacre, was extremely difficult to manage. Consequently, he turned his attention to the party of the *politiques*, i.e. those who believed that national unity should come first, regardless of confessional allegiances. An alliance was established between *politiques* and Huguenots; the Catholic party, however, was united by the goal of preventing the Calvinist Henry of Navarre from accessing the throne after Henry III.

When, in 1584, the Valois line was extinguished with the death of Henry III's younger brother, Francis, and Henry Bourbon, King of Navarre, became heir to the French crown, the Catholic League, with the support of Spain, initiated a harsh and active opposition against the prospect of a Protestant King ascending to the throne.

### 1.6.5. 1576–1600: Finding a *modus vivendi*

In the meanwhile, however, an important theological event had happened in 1580, when the *Formula of Concord*, along with other foundational texts of the Lutheran faith, had been issued. Following in Melanchthon's steps, Lutheranism had downplayed the focus on predestination which was increasingly to be observed in other Churches.

A further occasion for religious upheavals came in 1582, when Pope Gregory XIII (1502–1585) promulgated a calendar reform with the aim of correcting the imprecisions of the Julian calculations on the basis of astronomic observations. Many Protestants were unwilling to submit to Papal authority even on such a practical issue.

Two years later (1584), in the Netherlands, William of Orange was murdered: he left the Netherlands divided by politics and faith, with a continuous stream of southern Protestant refugees migrating to the northern provinces, which had officially declared their independence from Spanish rule in 1581. There, the grounds for the famously tolerant Dutch approach to confessional matters were established, with a climate of comparatively pacific cohabitation.

The struggle between Henry of Navarre and his opponents of the Catholic League continued for five years, from 1584 to 1589. The Catholics argued that he, as a Protestant, had no right to the French crown. To make his position unequivocal on this point, Pope Sixtus V (1521–1590) excommunicated Henry of Navarre (1585); the conflict was fought with armed combats, conspiracies and the murder of the political leaders. At the death of the last Valois King of France, Henry III (1589), Henry of Navarre eventually succeeded him as Henry IV, the first Bourbon King.

Elsewhere, other major events were taking place: Mary Stuart had been executed, by order of Queen Elizabeth, in 1587, after many years of imprisonment; in 1588, the proud Spanish *Armada* had been defeated by the English fleet, in a victory which – analogously to what had happened in Lepanto – represented far more than a mere military success, and symbolised a special divine favour on the Queen, her country and the confession they adhered to.

In the Netherlands, the Dutch United Provinces had become a confederacy, assigned sovereignty to their States General and thus established themselves as a Republic.

Power struggles continued in France, with the siege of Paris, the creation of a rival rule in opposition to Henry IV, and the intervention of foreign powers; eventually, in 1593, King Henry thought it better to embrace Catholicism and entered Paris as the legitimate ruler the following year. Although one of his early Acts, as a King, was to grant freedom of worship to Calvinists, his own "conversion" convinced the new Pope, Clement VIII (1536–1605), to acknowledge him as King of France.

In 1598, furthermore, Henry was to promulgate the Edict of Nantes, which established religious rights and liberties for the Protestant minority in France, and which finally appeased the thirty-year long warfare between Catholics and Huguenots in his country.

While in France this long-awaited religious pacification closed the century of confessional division on a note of hope, as is known the seventeenth century was going to bring the intertwining of religion with politics to the fore once more, with the Thirty Years' War in Germany and the English Civil War, as well as with the continuation, well into the new century, of the Dutch Revolt, to name but the bloodiest.

In the zones where a single confession was professed by a large majority, or where some degree of pacific cohabitation was established, the final decades of the sixteenth century and part of the following strengthened the identity of the Churches, both new and old, further defined their belief and consolidated their practices. However, from the division of the Churches and – especially – from the bloodsheds which accompanied them, new attitudes to faith began to emerge, and the seeds for scepticism and the opposition between faith and reason started to germinate.

Thus, the heritage of the Reformations went well beyond the boundaries of creed and dogma, and created diverse (and sometimes opposing) mind-sets, ways of life, forms of artistic expression (both sacred and secular), economic perspectives, cultural views and approaches to culture – basically, different societies. Their plurality would ultimately enrich the Western panorama, but their conflict continued to devastate it well beyond the boundaries of the sixteenth century.

In this Chapter, I have tried to offer a brief summary of the most important historical events and a sketch of the main features of the sixteenth century. It was a century of nearly unpredictable changes, when many fundamental consequences for the future of society, religion and politics grew out of comparatively minor initiatives, from events of life on which little or no control could be exerted, and from willing or unwilling misunderstandings among religious and political leaders. It was also a century of exceptional artistic splendour, during which, from the one side, artists suffered from the tragedies of the century and sometimes expressed them in their art, but, from the other, art represented an insuppressible manifestation and a repository of beauty, hope and faith, and a form of peaceful resistance to violence and war. It is therefore to art, and particularly to music, that we will turn in the following Chapters.

# Chapter 2 – Music, society and culture

> The true Greek harmony (neither Phrygian
> nor Ionian nor Lydian) is to be found when
> there is complete harmony in a virtuous man
> between his life and language[1].
>
> [Desiderius Erasmus]

## 2.1. Introduction

We live, as many claim, in the "post-modern" era. Regardless of how well this label defines today's world, it can however help us to feel the distance between the contemporary mentality, religious experience, soundscape and society, and those of the period which is commonly referred to as "early modern".

There is a substantial continuity, of course, and the roots of what happens at the dawn of the third millennium delve deep into the middle of the second; however, the two extremes of modernity are also extremely far from each other, and anyone studying sixteenth-century music and religion must be aware of the impossibility of understanding these topics fully.

This Chapter, therefore, aims at providing the reader with a broad overview of how music was thought of, practised and lived in the early sixteenth century, with particular attention to the connection between music and the experience of the sacred.

The cultural panorama of the early sixteenth century was heavily conditioned by the humanistic influence, and this Chapter will discuss in detail many facets of the dialogue between humanistic thought and musical practice. At the same time, not all of the cultural, musical and religious phenomena of the time were directly determined by humanism. For example, printing and music-printing had a dramatic impact on musicianship; new musical instruments saw the light, and new forms of patronage emerged; Renaissance, with its own distinguishing features, was still flourishing in many countries and shaping many social and cultural phenomena.

No less important, and particularly relevant to our forthcoming discussion, was the profound aspiration to spiritual renewal, to be achieved also through the re-establishment of the allegedly lost purity of the original Christian worship.

---

[1] Erasmus, *Adages*, II.v.93, in *Collected Works of Erasmus*, vol. 33, p. 282.

In this Chapter, I will try to sketch an overview of this complex panorama, whose details will progressively emerge in the following Chapters. We will approach the "soundscape" of sixteenth-century life, and the music which constituted its soundtrack; we will also see how the ideal forces driving life, culture and society intertwined with religion and faith.

For example, humanist thought impacted on the theory and practice of music, by encouraging the re-discovery of both classical and Christian sources on music, and by shaping the early-modern reflection on the relationship between word and music. (In particular, as we will see, the humanistic effort to find a "modern" relevance for the ethical theory of the modes will be extremely important for sixteenth-century theorists of religious music). Especially in northern Europe, moreover, the humanists' re-discovery of the past was not limited to the Greek and Latin world: this shaped a common ground of Biblical, Patristic and traditional culture which was shared by most religious reformers, even though their concepts of religious renewal were bound to diverge progressively.

We will see that the typically humanist focus on thought in its verbal expression was sometimes detrimental to a more shaded (and richer) understanding of the meaningfulness of music, particularly as concerns its symbolic value; we will also discuss how these principles dovetailed with the traditional theology of music as expressed in the Magisterial pronouncements of the Catholic Church and in the writings of the Church Fathers. A brief section will also discuss the stance on music maintained by Erasmus, who was one of the most influential and brilliant thinkers of his time.

The last section of this Chapter will deal with the principal aesthetic trends of sixteenth-century music, particularly as concerns works destined for worship: problems such as the presence of instrumental accompaniment to singing, the status of polyphony, the rhetorical power of music and the role of affects and senses in the religious experience will be briefly discussed.

In all this, I will constantly attempt to avoid the risk of "partiality", in both meanings of the term: partial views limit the historian's perspective and prevent a broader understanding of the issues at stake. As concerns sixteenth-century music, for example, "partial" music historiography tends to privilege "art music" (i.e. music composed by musical elites and often destined for social elites; such is the case of many polyphonic works of the time we are discussing) or "progressive" music, which inserts elements of originality and novelty within the existing style and repertoire (e.g. musical aspects which anticipated or broke the ground for the harmonic/tonal perspective). Other forms of music, perhaps less "refined" but certainly no less fascinating and cherished have received minor attention, even though many evident problems in source transmission have their share of responsibility for this.

From their side, historians of the theological thought or of Church studies tended to emphasise the presence, within the Reformers' perspective on music, of concepts and practices which would eventually gain common acceptance, both in the Catholic and in the Evangelic fields (such as, for example, congregational singing as a symbol for the universal priesthood of all baptised), whereas other aspects, of no lesser importance at the Reformers' time, were correspondingly played down. Thus, all aesthetic, historical and theological evaluations must always consider the plurality of possible viewpoints, as well as the context within which music was made and how it was suited to that particular situation: obviously, music aiming at conveying a pedagogical message would have features unlike those of music designed for personal and sometimes mystic piety; music for communal worship required an aesthetic approach radically different from that underlying music for spiritual recreation, and so on.

Nor is it sufficient to discuss the individual attempts and achievements of religious leaders within their local context: broader philosophical, cultural, aesthetic and theological systems were interacting (and sometimes clashing) with each other.

Within this framework, music was rapidly evolving, both theoretically and practically, and was finding new ways while walking on a watershed between past and future. Its theoretical concept was shifting from a scientific perspective to a practical one, while the language of polyphony had to negotiate its way between the extraordinary levels of sophistication and complexity it had achieved and the lingering risk of hyper-rationalism.

Although we will survey each of these aspects in turn, it must be stressed that knowledge of these issues is not enough for achieving a satisfactory understanding of the musical world of the sixteenth-century. Besides theoretical writings on music (which were sometimes authored, ironically, by those least acquainted with practical music) and besides the admirable architectures of masterly polyphony, the daily experience of music and sound was made up of other innumerable elements. It varied depending on geography, urbanisation, social status (from kings to milkmaids, from popes to noblemen, from nuns to merchants, from choristers to drunkards in taverns...), gender, age and ethnicity; it also changed over time, both chronologically and seasonally. It was made of official occasions (from a king's crowning to a city festival, from the patron saint's day to events such as Christmas and Easter) and of spontaneous music-making; of complex cathedral polyphony as well as of improvised lullabies or bell sounds.

I will thus try and provide a brief overview of the cultural and musical experience in the pre-Reformation era: once more, a comprehensive and thorough exposition of any single of the aspects mentioned above would require a very lengthy exposition of its own. My aim here is simply to summarise the most crucial elements in order to provide a framework for the following discussion of Reformation music.

## 2.2. Music and faith: an overview

Time-travellers reaching the sixteenth century from the present-day would be impressed by the soundscape they would find. Perhaps, the most startling difference would be the presence, at night, of true silence, which most of us have nearly never experienced. In contrast to this, daily life was characterised by a multiplicity of sounds, which were probably less noisy but more varied than those of contemporary urban soundscapes.

### 2.2.1. A resounding landscape

Was music more or less present in the lives of sixteenth-century men and women than it is nowadays? This is impossible to say. What is very likely, however, is that people used to make music much more than they do today. To start with, as Pettegree writes, "singing was such a ubiquitous part of pre-industrial society"[2]. Those parts of sixteenth-century music that have been preserved and transmitted in writing are only the tip of the iceberg of the coeval musical practice[3], although that kind of music was heard (at least on particular occasions) by a large section of the overall population. Plainchant was sung in virtually all churches (although in some instances it could be almost inaudible[4]), and religious songs in the vernacular were accessible to all; moreover, even the more solemn and refined of aristocratic music would occasionally be experienced by the humbler social classes, for instance during official celebrations or feasts, and the most beautiful examples of Cathedral music could be heard by virtually any member of the (urban) congregation[5]. Conversely, the most popular folk tunes could reach the ears of the upper classes, for example in the arrangements by celebrated composers[6].

---

[2] Pettegree 2005, p. 41.
[3] O'Regan 2013a, pp. 337–338.
[4] Pettegree 2005, p. 42.
[5] Wagner Oettinger 2001, p. 19.
[6] Wagner Oettinger 2001, p. 20.

## 2.2. Music and faith: an overview — 53

People used to walk long distances, and singing provided some relief during those fatiguing journeys[7]; spiritual songs were particularly popular during pilgrimages, and the litanies sung by pilgrims during their itinerary were absorbed by the musical worship performed at the shrine on their arrival[8].

Similar to songs and beside them, dances were equally widespread in virtually all social layers, and even among the clergy: "Dancing was held to be both a right, differentiated according to social rank, and a duty; consequently both admonitions and prohibitions with regard to dancing were issued"[9]. In some instances, dancing was deemed to be sinful or socially disruptive, while mystical dances found their place within a spiritual framework[10].

Singing together was one of the most popular festive pastimes, and, during workdays, it helped to keep the rhythm of repetitive handwork; furthermore, as Wagner Oettinger points out, "songs were the mass media of the oral culture"[11], since news, stories and gossip were disseminated through singing.

Moreover, oral transmission allowed and favoured personal appropriation of popular songs, whose texts and (perhaps less frequently) tunes might be adapted to the singers' mood, to their musical ability, or to the socio-political situation[12].

Both music and culture were extremely international at the beginning of the sixteenth century: this internationalism was a feature of both people and their music, travelling all across Europe. The high level of professionalism and specialisation of musicians belonging to certain traditions (such as the polyphonic heritage of the Flemish or the instrumental proficiency of certain Italians) made their aristocratic, civic and religious patrons eager to employ the best musicians of the time; thus, compositional styles travelled with those practising them, establishing both a trans-European creative network and a common aesthetical and musical culture[13].

This international exchange was in turn promoted by the increasing success and spread of printing and, particularly, of music printing. During this century, as Collinson states, there was a shift "from a culture of orality and image to one of print culture: from one mental and imaginative 'set' to another"[14]. Of course, literacy and the press impacted dramatically on the process of religious reforma-

---

7 Pettegree 2005, p. 41.
8 Leaver 2006, p. 373.
9 Salmen 2001, p. 162.
10 Salmen 2001, p. 163.
11 Wagner Oettinger 2001, p. 21.
12 Wagner Oettinger 2001, p. 30.
13 Cf. Freedman 2006, p. 165.
14 Collinson 1988, p. 99.

tion and on its very possibility; but in our field too, printed music conveyed ideas which could later be spread by word of mouth or in manuscript copies.

On the other hand, the wide circulation of music and culture permitted the differentiation of music printing depending on market demands, which often did not coincide with the actual location of the printing press. Such was the case in Lyon, where Istrian-born publisher Jacques Moderne (c.1500–1560) produced polyphonic books which were not in high demand in the main cathedral of the town, but which nonetheless enjoyed an important international success[15].

Such phenomena influenced musical style in turn: as argued by Bryant and Quaranta, the need for composers to propose interesting musical "products" to this international market encouraged the spread of the equal-voice style at the expenses of tailor-made solo works conceived for the particular voices of particular singers[16].

Consequently, Haar has defined the combination of greater musical literacy, printing possibilities and commercial success of music as a qualifying element in the transition from Renaissance culture to the new paradigms of early modernity[17].

During this century, thus, music enjoyed some international freedom: and while the increasing importance (both in politics and in culture) of national identity, language and (later) religious confession contributed to dividing the European civilisation, music maintained for a longer period its capacity to permeate boundaries[18].

Nevertheless, cultural currents such as so-called "esoteric humanism" tended to promote the appreciation of local culture and language, sometimes attempting to "canonise" forms of artistry in the vernacular (such as the combination of verse and music) through the application of classicising metres and forms to national poetry[19].

Besides purely religious issues, indeed, political, economic and cultural forces were starting to push towards the emergence of local Churches: Koenigsberger[20] offers a fascinating (although somehow limited) model for explaining the power of the processes at stake.

---

15 Freedman 2006, p. 164.
16 Bryant and Quaranta 2007, p. 118.
17 Haar 2006, p. 24.
18 Cf. Prodi 2014, p. 47.
19 Kim 2005, pp. 103–104. Kim identifies Glarean as an iconic figure of "esoteric" humanism, and Erasmus as the key character of the "exoteric" current.
20 Cf. Koenigsberger 1986, pp. 169 ff.

It is true that, at the end of the sixteenth century, national schools were starting to appear in music too; the presence of new confessional boundaries (sometimes marked by situations of political warfare and instability) did not foster international careers for musicians anymore; moreover, the connection between some confessional identities and church singing in the vernacular favoured a new attention to the musical potentialities of national languages.

Nevertheless, although the unity of the Catholic Church was going to be deeply shaken and broken apart during the sixteenth century, the surviving phenomena of shared musical repertoire and trans-confessional music (cf. § 11.5.–6.) were sometimes one of the few elements of unity within a split Church.

Thus, while a substantial part of this Chapter will focus on theoretical statements on sacred music and on the cultural atmosphere of the time, the rich variety and the pervasiveness of sixteenth-century musicianship should always constitute the experiential frame onto which theoretical disquisitions were superimposed.

### 2.2.2. A time of religious renewal

The religious experience of European Christians at the dawn of the sixteenth century was undoubtedly varied, composite and rich. Christian thought and culture were practised at universities, where theological disputes sometimes suffered from extreme academicism, but might also produce profound spiritual achievements; Christian worship, with its significant musical components, was celebrated in the solemn liturgies of the cathedrals and major abbeys, as well as in the rural parishes and in the minor churches; spiritual musicianship was experienced as a daily part of the religious lives of monks, nuns and friars; lay piety expressed itself in pilgrimages (which, as said before, were highly musical in turn: § 2.2.1.), gilds and confraternities (with their elaborate processions accompanied by singing), as well as in more spontaneous forms.

At the same time, as stated, the yearning for a religious renewal was often felt: although the Catholic Church at the beginning of the sixteenth-century was by no means as universally corrupt as traditional historiography has sometimes asserted, there were nevertheless some highly critical issues, at the moral level, in theology and in spirituality.

Music partook of this aspiration to novelty[21]; for instance, the spirituality of lay movements such as the Florentine *laudesi* was so deeply permeated by music

---

21 Haar 2006, p. 23.

that it would lose its very identity if considered in isolation from its musical experience. It has even been suggested, in consideration of the geographical connection between such spiritual companies and the centres of humanistic thought, that the *laudesi* musical piety might represent the practical actualisation of the humanistic belief in the rhetoric power of the union of music with eloquence (see § 2.4.5.[22]).

Besides the vitality of such devotional experiences, and besides the magnificent artistic results of contemporaneous church music, the actual reality of liturgical practice presented severe critical aspects. Among the issues at stake, a revision of liturgical books was strongly needed, as well as a more thorough spiritual, liturgical and moral education of church musicians. Moreover, the laity's desire for a more active participation in the spiritual life had been sensed by those promoting gilds, confraternities and lay movements, but had yet to be understood within the framework of official worship. Several attempts were made in these directions, although in most cases they did not achieve significant success in the long term[23].

Nevertheless, the desired renewal of both spirituality and church music was not conceived in a revolutionary sense: religious and liturgical reforms had initially the aim of improving and renovating the existing reality, rather than of splitting brusquely from it[24]. At the same time, most of the religious reform movements, both Catholic and Evangelical, concerned themselves with musical issues, and they often "spurred musical activity that was certainly thought of at the time as renewal and rebirth"[25].

Such renewal and rebirth can be understood, however, in a rather humanist perspective (although they should not be simplistically identified with it): we will now move on to consider the most important features of humanism in music, precisely in order to identify those aspects that will be later adopted by religious reformers, as well as those which will remain substantially extraneous to the musical experience of the confessional Churches.

## 2.3. Humanism and music

One of the fundamental features of the movement today known as Humanism is represented by its rediscovery of the classical thought in its Greek and Latin

---

22 Tomlinson 2006, p. 15.
23 Rainoldi 2000, p. 331.
24 Kim 2005, p. 181.
25 Haar 2006, p. 23.

## 2.3. Humanism and music — 57

sources. The humanist enthusiasm for the past, however, did not embody just a nostalgic and antiquarian cult of classicism, nor was it simply a theoretical, speculative and cultural movement concerned exclusively with history. It was instead an approach which had strong implications on the plane of politics and ethics, and the academic study of the classics as practised in the European universities had a profound educational and pedagogic value. Knowledge of the past was a means for improving the present and building a better future.

As regards music, the most direct influence of humanism is found in secular music, mirroring the prevailing secular orientation and interests of the Italian humanists[26]. However, albeit more indirectly, the role played by humanistic thought in providing the academic principles for the Reformations, particularly in Northern Europe, had fundamental importance for the development of sacred music. In Tomlinson's words, "the many sixteenth-century voices advocating the reform of sacred and liturgical music, from whatever doctrinal orientation, may be seen to participate in this Christian humanism"[27].

In turn, humanist thought and practices were highly influential in circles surrounding several Popes of the late fifteenth and early sixteenth century, and expressed themselves also through the cult for the purity of Latin language and its restoration to Ciceronian magnificence even within the context of daily cultural life[28].

As seen in the preceding Chapter (§ 1.3.), between the veneration for past splendour and the optimistic faith in a perhaps even more splendid future, humanism proposed a somewhat critical evaluation of the "Middle Ages" (whose very definition stems from humanistic thought[29]): in music, this implied a shift from the focus on the mathematical aspect of musical art as proposed by Scholastic philosophy, to a new concept of music's powerfully rhetorical value[30]. Moreover, the classical reflection on music actually embodied the coexistence of two complementary concepts: from the one side, music was believed to be a mirror of superhuman harmony, and from the other it was thought to imitate and elicit the human affects. The former view, which had been espoused by medieval Christendom, gradually gave way to the latter, which will characterise the humanist perspective on music[31]. This approach influenced in turn the music of the Renaissance, when the relationship between text and music involved signifi-

---

26 See Palisca 1985.
27 Tomlinson 2006, p. 15.
28 Cf. Batiffol 1912, p. 177.
29 Lindberg 2010, p. 5.
30 Kim 2005, p. 23. See also Caldecott 2009.
31 Berger 2006, p. 313.

cant changes on both the microscopic and macroscopic levels: music underwent the rhythmic and melodic influence of speech, and aimed at both imitating and arousing affects and feelings[32].

Indeed, the attention for the word/music relationship produced three distinct embodiments, which only occasionally overlapped. One of them was the concern for *intelligibility*, which we will see at work in the creation and establishment of chordal writing and homophony. The second was the word-painting or *mimesis* of the text, whereby music illustrated the verbal imagery of the poetry it was set to. The third was the increasing focus on *accompanied monody* as the only credible and convincing way to represent subjectivity and as a rhetoric amplification of the "natural" intonation and rhythm of speech.

Furthermore, as Pettegree points out, "the Renaissance flowering of polyphonic composition inspired both an imitative bourgeois tradition and considerable interest in musical theory", fostering in turn the theoretical speculations on the music of classical antiquity[33].

### 2.3.1. Sounding Greek

As Tomlinson suggests[34], a commonly shared view was that the "physical motions" of music had the power to affect the human soul: although esoteric concepts influenced this outlook, it was also strongly connected with speculations on language as related to both universal and psychic phenomena.

Moreover, the humanist stress on human individuality and potentialities provoked in turn a new attention to concepts such as authorship; creativity became a passport for fame and immortality, and musical works started to be "reified" and to acquire some kind of autonomous personality[35].

Although sixteenth-century knowledge of the actual theory and practice of music in classical Greece and Rome was very imprecise and based on scanty sources, the humanist appreciation for antiquity led to speculation on what was actually known of ancient music: thus, humanist theorists of music focused their attention on issues of tuning, scales and modes (often conflating the Greek *tonoi* with the modes of the medieval Church, but with particular attention to the different powers that Greek theory attributed to the individual modes), as well as

---

[32] This section is indebted to Haar 2006, pp. 23–27.
[33] Pettegree 2005, p. 43.
[34] Tomlinson 2006, p. 19.
[35] Cf. Haar 2006, p. 23 and Wegman 2005, pp. 167–168.

on the importance of monodic singing for the clear perception and for a declamatory delivery of the verbal text[36].

Such topics are faithfully mirrored both by the writings of those who adhered more closely and clearly to humanist aesthetics and by those who were simply influenced by it. For instance, the often-quoted letter (1549[37]) by Bernardino Cirillo, which I will discuss at length in Chapter Three (§ 3.3.3.), clearly relates the "research" of "ancient art" with a confident trust in "the greatness of today's minds", whose ability and knowledge will overcome all obstacles[38]. The cult of antiquity thus became the mark of true progressiveness; on the other hand, the most modern-sounding and experimental of the contemporaneous theories and practices were often justified by their connection with alleged past usage. Such is the case of Nicola Vicentino, whose treatise *L'antica musica ridotta alla moderna prattica* (1555) puts into musical practice most features of the humanist approach to culture: through the supposed recovery of Greek theory, whose modes would lend new affective power to modern music, Vicentino vindicated some of his most startling and innovative attempts in modal theory and practice. So did other musical humanists, among whom Franchinus Gaffurius (also known as Franchino Gafori, 1451–1522), Heinrich Glareanus or Glarean (1488–1563) and Vincenzo Galilei, all of whom frequently referred to ancient wisdom and knowledge to support their own theories and practices, which however differed drastically from one another[39].

Glarean's *Dodecachordon* (1547) explicitly denounces the risk for "modern" theorists to see their systems mistaken for innovations, whereas they were actually led by the desire to revive and reinstate ancient theory[40]. Indeed, in Glarean's case, the appeal to tradition had a strong confessional and religious characterisation besides its musical value[41]: as suggested by Miller[42], whereas Galilei's experimental practices were inspired by the attempt to revive ancient Greek music, Glarean was influenced rather by the Church tradition of monodic plainchant (we will later[43] see other confessional implications of Glarean's *Dodecachordon*).

---

36 Haar 2006, p. 25.
37 *Lettere volgari* 1564, fols. 114ʳ-118ᵛ.
38 *Lettere volgari* 1564, fol. 166ᵛ.
39 Haar 2006, p. 27.
40 Groote and Vendrix 2012, p. 185.
41 Lütteken 2013, p. 45.
42 Cf. in Glareanus 1965, vol. 1, p. 16.
43 See § 2.3.3. and 8.3.3.

A similar viewpoint is proposed by Gioseffo Zarlino (1517–1590), in whose *Institutioni harmoniche* (1558) ancient music is presented as a summit and an artistic highpoint, in opposition to which the Middle Ages stood as the abysmal anti-climax; the process of rebirth of modern music was seen, once more, as one of restoration rather than of renovation or revolution[44]. However, Zarlino's optimistic view of contemporaneous music was such that he did not suggest a supine revival of the Greek modes, since – for him – no further progress and amelioration could improve the quality of "modern" art[45].

In turn, the alleged perfection of ancient art, which the modern could not only imitate but even exceed, was seen (by Christian thinkers indebted to humanism) as mirroring the even greater perfection of heavenly music: such was the view of Federigo Borromeo (1564–1631), whose treatise *De linguis, nominibus, et numero angelorum* (*On the Angels*[46], 1628) asserts that both celestial and human music are of the same kind, and that such experiments as Vicentino's "chromatic" harmony were echoes of and mirrored the unheard-of heavenly music[47].

### 2.3.2. Dialoguing with Plato (and Aristotle)

The principal authorities in the classical discourse on music were also those philosophers who had most deeply influenced the history of Western thought, during the Middle Ages and well beyond them, i.e. Plato and Aristotle.

Although their overall philosophical outlooks were significantly different, on some of the music-related issues their perspective was similar, and thus it became all the more influential on later Christian theology and on the humanist philosophy of music. Indeed, their authority had been referred to well before the humanist appreciation of antiquity, and their theories had been transmitted, commented upon, and integrated within Christian theology (often even providing it with the conceptual tools for shaping its own dogmas) for centuries.

At the same time, a wave of Neo-Platonism characterised the Florentine Renaissance, whence it took some hold of contemporaneous culture, often in contrast with Aristotelian Scholasticism. In turn, many theories and theologies of

---

44 Lockwood 1975, p. 14, fn. 7.
45 Cf. Zarlino 1558, Part II, Chapter 4, p. 62; cf. Berger 2006, pp. 308–310.
46 Borromeo 1628.
47 Quoted in Bizzarini 2012, p. 35.

music proposed by several religious Reformers, both in the Protestant and in the Catholic field, were substantially indebted to Plato's view[48].

Some of the most influential of Plato's passages on music are found in his celebrated *Republic*, where, in particular, a detailed exposition of the moral and affective value of the musical modes is found[49]. The emotional power of music, acknowledged by virtually all human societies, was therefore given a rational understanding through the systematic listing of its effects on feelings and morality. Thus music acquired a highly ethical value, which obviously appealed strongly to the humanist educational perspective and virtuous improvement of society.

Moreover, in Plato's moral evaluation of the modes (as well as in Aristotle's speculations on the same subject, and in the account of classical thought provided by Severinus Boethius, c.480 – 524) the association of individual modes with particular masculine/virile and feminine/effeminate qualities is found: as will be discussed below (§ 3.3.2.1.–3.), this proved very influential on later thought – even when, as should be always pointed out, the original Greek modes had long since disappeared, together with their alleged effects on human behaviour. For Plato, such was the impact of modal music on human beings that certain modes (such as the Ionian and the Lydian) had to be outright banned from a moral society; on the other hand, Dorian and Phrygian music could be useful for disciplining human affects, and – consequently – in ameliorating social life. This drastic distinction between positive and negative music will impart a dualistic feature to most speculations on music written in the sixteenth century[50].

Furthermore, in Plato's *Republic* (398d), the priority of the verbal text over the musical needs dictated by rhythmic and harmonic considerations had been stated. That often-quoted passage is found in a pedagogical treatise (*De liberis recte instituendis*, 1533) by Jacopo Sadoleto (1477–1547), a Catholic churchman who would eventually participate in the discussions at the Council of Trent, and – much later – in Giulio Cesare Monteverdi's ghost-writing for his brother Claudio. For his part, Zarlino, though convinced of music's ethical import and of the significance of its association with words, was by no means disposed to renounce aesthetic evaluations and judgements on music in favour of the exclusive primacy of words.

---

[48] Garside 1979, p. 29.
[49] Plato, *Republic*, Book III, 398b-405a (Plato 1969, pp. 245–269); available online at http://bit.ly/2c1DjeQ.
[50] Koenigsberger 1986, p. 187.

Thus, this Platonic fragment, excerpted from *The Republic* III, acted as the classical authority in support of humanist, religious and early Baroque movements aiming at the simplification of contrapuntal structures and/or at the reformation of sacred music[51].

Finally, Plato's *Republic* provided later theorists of music with another topic, whose importance within the humanist framework of thought should not be underestimated, i.e. a discussion of the educational and pedagogic value of music (cf. *Republic*, 401d[52]). The same subject was developed by Aristotle in his *Politics* (Book VIII[53]), where the usefulness of musical practice for a morally sound education of the young is argued for within the context of the ethical value of the modes.

Thus, humanist and Renaissance theorists were fascinated by both the mysterious and esoteric power of the ancient modes (which could however be rationally understood and systematised) and by their usefulness to moral and educational ends. There was a different shade in the reception of Plato and Aristotle's perspective on music, however: Neo-Platonists were more inclined to see a mystical (and sometimes magical) dimension in music and in reality as a whole, whereas Aristotelians had a more rationalistic approach. Many humanists, nevertheless, did not take sides clearly in choosing between the two Greek philosophers, but rather referred to both of them as to the undisputed authorities of classical thought.

Obviously, a detailed discussion of Platonic influence on sixteenth-century music theorists would largely exceed the limits of this cursory summary; nevertheless, I will briefly mention how two of the leading writers reacted to it.

Vicentino drew from Plato the conviction that music has the primary objective of moving human passions and affects, again within an ethical perspective. The affects conveyed by the words' meaning should be expressed by musical harmony, thus somehow giving primacy to the passions over harmony for its own sake. In consequence, and similar to poets, composers should practise the imitation of affects: in Berger's words, "A chain of imitation starts with the passions and leads through the words of the poet, the music of the composer, and the sounds of the singer, to the listener in whom the imitated passions are to be aroused"[54].

In Vicentino's case, however, it should be said that his own personal and direct knowledge of Greek theory was rather limited. He was particularly interested

---

51 Cf. Berger 2006, pp. 315–316 and Gibson 2009, p. 57.
52 Plato 1969; available online at http://bit.ly/2bXQoQq.
53 Aristotle 1885, p. 250; available online at http://bit.ly/2bWJfVn.
54 Berger 2006, p. 308.

in the *genera* of ancient music, perhaps attributing the apparent decrease of contemporaneous music's visible effects on listeners to its almost exclusive use of the diatonic genus. Thus he promoted the revived use of the chromatic genus (employing semitones) and even of the enharmonic genus (quarter-tones). That he was not alone in such experiments is shown, for example, by a coeval (1558, published 1570) *chanson spirituelle* by Guillaume Costeley (c.1530–1606), *Seigneur Dieu, ta pitié*, employing a nineteen-fold subdivision of the octave (using thirds of a tone) instead of the commonly used twelve semitones[55].

### 2.3.3. Fashioning antiquity

Different from Vicentino, Vincenzo Galilei's knowledge of ancient music benefited from his friendship with philologist and historian Girolamo Mei and from their years-long cooperation. When Galilei returned to Florence in 1572, after his studies with Zarlino (with whom he would enter into a harsh polemic), he tried to revive Greek theory, both by rediscovering and analysing the sources and original texts, and by experimenting on the physical nature of sound. Mei's studies on the sources convinced him that the ecclesiastical modes could not be assimilated to those of ancient Greece: in consequence of this, he developed a critical stance against contemporaneous polyphonic practice[56].

These studies were given public discussion and practical experimentation within the famous *Camerata*, a group of intellectuals surrounding Count Giovanni de' Bardi (1534–1612), and aiming at a revival of the ancient concept of music and performance.

A similar connection between theory and practice shaped the musical beliefs of several composers and theorists of the era. In the fifteenth century, the ethical value of music within a Christian perspective on virtuous life had been argued for by Johannes Tinctoris (c.1435–1511, in his *Complexus effectuum musices*, c.1475[57]); in similar words, and under Quintilian's influence, Gaffurius maintained the moral import of "moderate and virile" music for the achievement of virtue, not only on the theoretical side but in a very practical fashion[58].

The power of music to affect (either positively or negatively) human behaviour was analogously asserted, in a very humanistic style, little less than a century after Tinctoris (1570), by Charles IX, King of France, who drew causal con-

---

55 See also Carpenter 1960.
56 Tomlinson 1998, p. 282.
57 Tinctoris 1963; cf. Kim 2005, p. 134.
58 Gaffurius 1968, p. 15. Cf. Kim 2005, p. 235.

nections between the inherent order of a society's music and its own moral order[59].

Many others were convinced that the choice of modes was fundamental for determining a piece's affective mood, in consequence of the text's emotional features: such was, for instance, the argument maintained by Giovanni del Lago (c.1490–1544), in his *Breve introduttione di musica misurata* (1540), and by Bernardino Cirillo (1500–1575) in the letter we will discuss at length in Chapter Three[60] (§ 3.3.3.). Once more, the "affect" was intended as both descriptive and prescriptive: in other words, both music and lyrics conveyed ("imitated") a particular affect with the aim of arousing a corresponding reaction among listeners and performers alike.

Although such outstanding figures as Francisco Guerrero (1528–1599), in the Preface to his *Vespers* of 1584[61], asserted their adhesion to the Platonic concept of modal ethos, there was not necessarily agreement on which affect was to be connected with a particular mode: as Palisca's assessment[62] points out, even a cursory comparison between modes and affects as seen in the *De harmonia musicorum instrumentorum opus* (1518) by Gaffurius and in Glarean's *Dodecachordon* (1547) shows striking and meaningful differences.

As briefly mentioned before (§ 2.3.1.), Glarean (who was primarily a humanist thinker, with no professional activity as a musician) saw his theoretical effort as transcending the boundaries of musical theory: for him, to understand the musical world by means of modal order and consistency was a form of resistance to the religious chaos experienced by his contemporaries and himself. His idiosyncratic perspective results from the combination of reasoning with a deep spiritual insight and with a humanist framework, aiming at demonstrating that Catholic beliefs and practices could be harmoniously integrated with the wisdom of the ancient[63].

Similar "political" views of the modal ethos were relatively widespread at the time, although obviously the consequences of analogous presuppositions varied depending on the writer's confessional allegiance or philosophical outlook: for many, however, speculation on modal ethos was intrinsically relevant to the daily experience of contemporaneous society. Traces of this attitude may be found, for example, in Giovanni Pierluigi da Palestrina (c.1525–1594)

---

[59] Koenigsberger 1986, p. 183.
[60] *Lettere volgari* 1564, fols. 114$^r$-118$^v$.
[61] Guerrero 1584.
[62] Palisca 1990.
[63] Cf. Fuller 1996, pp. 195–196; Groote and Vendrix 2012, p. 184; Lütteken 2013, pp. 38–39 and 45.

and Claude Le Jeune (c.1528–1600), but also in more popular musical works such as polyphonic *laude*, both in the Catholic and in the Protestant field[64].

Moreover, contrapuntal composition posed insurmountable problems to a consistently modal treatment, since the limitations of vocal range make it impossible to adopt one and the same mode (albeit in octave transposition) for all parts[65]. Furthermore, modal alteration within a single work was admitted among others by Zarlino and by Pietro Ponzio[66] (also known as Pontio, 1532–1596), and modal characterisation was not the unique factor to determine a work's mood, since tempo and rhythmic issues as well as intervallic choices were at least equally fundamental[67]. For Gilles Carlier (c.1405-c.1470), this implied, in turn, that music devoid of the necessary gravity (as was polyphony, in Carlier's view) could not achieve moral results but rather was likely to corrupt the ethical values[68].

As is often the case when too many concurrent explanations are offered for a given phenomenon, none was completely satisfactory: the humanist world felt frustrated by its incapacity to justify the difference between the wonderful effects of ancient music in its modal characterisation and the actual results they could observe in the daily musical experience. For example, Galilei[69] argued for the superiority of vocal to instrumental music on the grounds that human beings had been given the capability to make music in their own body by nature, with the aim not only to entertain, but also to benefit society. Thus, Plato's discussion of the modes and of their affective value started to be understood in relation to his assertion of the primacy of words over harmony; and the power of music to move was gradually attributed to its adherence to the rhetoric delivery of the text, rather than to its intrinsically musical modal features[70]. This concept intertwined with another of the humanists' main concerns, i.e. their focus on persuasion through speech and on the efficaciousness of rhetoric: here, the authority of Quintilian was often invoked, as was his appreciation of heroic music in opposition to theatrical lasciviousness and effeminacy[71].

---

[64] Cf. Powers 1982, p. 84; see also Freedman 2003, p. 308; Haar 2006, p. 32; Fenlon 2009, p. 212, fn. 33.
[65] Berger 2006, p. 319. The distinction between authentic and plagal modes should also be taken into account here.
[66] Zarlino 1558, Part 4, Chapter 32; Ponzio 1595, p. 58.
[67] Cf. Meier 1990, p. 186.
[68] Carlerius/Carlier 2001, p. 53 (§125–127); as translated in Wegman 2005, pp. 50–51.
[69] Galilei 1581, p. 86.
[70] Koenigsberger 1986, pp. 182–183.
[71] Quintilian, *Institutio oratoria*, I.10.31 (available at http://bit.ly/2buxALt); cf. Kim 2005, p. 126.

## 2.3.4. At the sources of Christian music

Although humanist concerns with antiquity focused primarily on the classical Greek and Latin culture, their focus on the rediscovery of the past and of original sources, as well as their interest in linguistic issues, led to new approaches to Biblical studies.

New translations of the Bible were undertaken, both in the Church's languages and in the vernacular, and the pedagogical attitude of the humanists to culture led several of them to advocate a personal relationship of the faithful to the sacred text, either through direct access to Bible-reading or through narrative renditions for the illiterate. This atmosphere of renewed interest encouraged literary versions and appropriations of the most "poetic" among the Biblical books, i.e. the Psalter: this phenomenon would have fundamental consequences within the religious context of Reformed music and worship.

Such linguistic and philological exploration of the Bible was not found exclusively among sympathisers of Luther's Reformation: besides Erasmus, for instance, one of the Catholic protagonists of the Council of Trent, Gabriele Paleotti (1522–1597: cf. § 8.3.4.) similarly advocated the establishment of Biblical studies at the University of Bologna – although his plans were not enthusiastically greeted in Rome[72].

Study of the Bible in the original languages also led to musical results, such as scholarly interest in the Jewish cantillation of the Torah: it was transcribed from oral sources into musical notation by Johannes Böschenstein (1472–1540), an expert in Biblical Hebrew who cooperated with Luther but taught several of his Catholic counterparts as well[73]. (Incidentally, Böschenstein also authored some pre-Reformation sacred songs in German[74]).

Besides the Bible (whose references to vocal and instrumental music will be constantly quoted by virtually all Reformers in support of their view of sacred music), humanism promoted theological interest in the writings of the Church Fathers. Their authority had always been highly considered in theological disputes, since arguments were often maintained by frequent reference to the tradition of the Church; however, the increased spread of linguistic proficiency in Greek encouraged renewed attention to their writings. Moreover, the closeness of the Patristic era and thought to the Apostolic time was seen by religious reformers as guaranteeing a high degree of purity in both belief and Church life:

---

72 Prodi 2014, p. 251.
73 Kim 2005, pp. 281–282.
74 Cf. Classen 2002, p. 12.

since (in spirituality as in music) recovery of the past was seen as the true path for renewal, the Church Fathers might provide religious reformers with the key for genuine regeneration[75].

Within the framework of sixteenth-century debates on (sacred) music, several Patristic authorities were frequently quoted: among them, St Athanasius (c.295–373), St Basil of Caesarea (c.329–379), St John Chrysostom (c.349–407), St Augustine (354–430), St Jerome (347–420) and – naturally – Severinus Boethius.

Boethius' *De Institutione Musica* (c.500–507AD) had probably been the most influential treatise on music of Christian antiquity, and it had played a crucial role in transmitting the classical thought on music (also as concerns its ethical value) to Christian theology. Boethius' importance for Christian theology of music is attested by widespread references to his writings, among others by Aquinas.

Some of Basil's points are also worth recalling, since they will be frequently echoed by sixteenth-century writers. Commenting upon the first Psalm, Basil argued that the delight of psalmody had been devised by the Holy Spirit in order to draw the "human race" toward virtue. "These harmonious melodies of the Psalms", for Basil, were particularly useful for those "who [are] of boyish age, or wholly youthful in their character": these, while seemingly just singing, "may in reality be educating their souls". While the spoken words are easily forgotten, even the inattentive "sing [Psalms] both at home and disseminate [them] in the marketplace. And if somewhere one who rages like a wild beast from excessive anger falls under the spell of the Psalms, he straightway departs, with the fierceness of his soul calmed by the melody".

Moreover, for Basil,

> A Psalm forms friendships, unites the divided, mediates between enemies. For who can still consider him an enemy with whom he has sent forth one voice to God? So that the singing of Psalms brings love, the greatest of good things, contriving harmony like some bond of union and uniting the people in the symphony of a single choir.

I will now outline the main points of Basil's argument, since they are of capital importance for what will follow: Psalms are the delightful means by which people are led to virtue; they are particularly efficacious for the young; when sung, they are easily retained by memory and can be disseminated by singing; they calm and comfort; they create communion and love in a community. By way of conclusion, Basil lists several other functions of psalmody, among which its

---

75 Haar 2006, p. 31.

power against evil forces ("a Psalm drives away demons"), its capacity to restore, its suitability for people of both sexes and all ages, its educational value (particularly in matters of faith), and its power to move by stirring good emotions ("It gladdens feast days; it creates the grief which is in accord with God's will, for a Psalm brings a tear even from a heart of stone"[76]).

Another Church Father whose authority on music would later be quoted by Aquinas was St Jerome: his advocacy of "gravity" in Church music and his criticism of instrumental music (probably determined by its association with pagan worship at his time) contributed to the establishment of long-lasting aesthetic evaluations, such as the connection of musical instruments with lust, impurity and lasciviousness and the refusal of "light" and lively music in worship[77].

Similar to St Jerome, St John Chrysostom was very wary of instrumental music, since he feared that rhythms encouraging bodily motions might blur the distinction between sacred and secular music[78]: such Patristic statements would strongly influence Erasmus' position (and that of several other humanists[79]) on instrumental music and were in turn grounded on Neo-Pythagorean and Neo-Platonist beliefs about the ethics of music[80]. On the other hand, Chrysostom fostered the spread of Psalm-singing, although with some theoretical fluctuations on whether understanding the text was relevant or not to spiritual praise[81].

Although all Fathers listed above were constantly referred to as theological authorities in the musical field, undeniably the major Patristic influence on Christian humanist thought on music was that of St Augustine. Besides his treatise on music, he had extensively written on the subject in other works (such as, for instance, his commentaries on the Psalter), although one of the most quoted among his statements on music is found in his *Confessions* (X.33.49). Here, Augustine acknowledged that music had been instrumental in his mystical experience of God, although his approval of music was not unconditional. Indeed, if music can lead a soul to God (and this is particularly true, as Augustine seems to imply, of people whose imperfect love for God needs to be fostered

---

[76] Basil of Caesarea, *Homily on the First Psalm*, in *PG* 29, cols. 209–213, as translated by William and Oliver Strunk, revised by James McKinnon, in Strunk 1998, pp. 121–122.
[77] Cf. Federigo Borromeo, quoted in Bizzarini 2012, pp. 157–158; cf. also Eco 1988, p. 135.
[78] Chrysostom, *Contra ludos et theatra* 2 (*PG* 56, col. 266); *De Dav. et Saule* 3 (*PG* 54, col. 696); cf. Leyerle 2001, p. 33.
[79] Cf. Koenigsberger 1986, p. 187.
[80] Cf. Kim 2005, pp. 134 and 137.
[81] Cf. Chrysostom, *Exposition of Psalm XLI* (*PG* 55, cols. 155–159), and Willis 2010, p. 43. Cf. however Kim 2005, p. 146.

by sensory experiences), it can also lead astray; its seductive power can attract the faithful to God's beauty, but also distract them from intellectual concentration on the sacred words. Although Augustine had theorised wordless singing (the *jubilatio* or *jubilus*) as the highpoint of mystical exultation in God[82], obviously his cautionary remarks on the importance of verbal understanding were better suited to humanist reception[83].

On the other hand, Augustine's statements on the usefulness of music for the spiritual initiation of "weaker" (or younger) Christians encouraged many religious reformers of the sixteenth century in their use of music for pedagogic and catechetic purposes (a point which Basil had already made[84], as previously discussed: § 2.3.4.).

Augustine's influence on early modern theology of music was enormous, for several reasons: to start with, his status as one of the greatest thinkers of Christianity had rarely been questioned; second, the connection between some features of his thought and Platonic concepts was an added value within a culture undergoing strong Neo-Platonic influences; third, Martin Luther's years as an Augustinian monk certainly contributed to shaping his reception of Augustine's principles.

### 2.3.5. "Should God be praised with song?"

Whereas we will find references to Augustine's statements on music throughout the writings of religious reformers of virtually any denomination, the reaction to the thought of another great theologian of the Catholic Church, St Thomas Aquinas, was not equally favourable. This was partially due to some exaggerations in the later reception of his thought by Scholasticism; however, although explicit quotations of his *Summa Theologiæ* (1265–1274) are scanty in the writings on music of non-Catholic reformers, his discussion of liturgical chant requires some attention here. Indeed, *Quæstio* 91 (article 2) from his *Secunda secundæ* has often been overlooked by those discussing the theological and moral objections to liturgical abuses and the efforts by both Catholic and Protestant Reformers aiming at the purification of rituals. It is however highly relevant, both for those who accepted Aquinas' conclusions and for those who adopted a different theological stance. Of course, all Protestant reformers had once belonged to the

---

**82** Cf. *Enarrationes in Psalmos* 33 [32], II, 8 (v. 3) (*PL* 36, col. 283).
**83** Cf., for instance, Federigo Borromeo (in Bizzarini 2012, pp. 157–158), and the quotation of this passage in ecclesiastical directions for nuns' music (Masetti Zannini 1993, p. 132).
**84** Wagner Oettinger 2001, p. 39.

Catholic Church, and Catholic thought after Aquinas could not overlook the depth of his influence. The extent of his impact on the individual reformers' perspectives cannot be discussed here; however, the history of the reception of Aquinas' *Summa* substantially shaped the theological outlook of the fifteenth and sixteenth centuries, although it faced competition from the nominalist view[85].

I would like here to discuss Aquinas' view in greater detail, because it has hitherto received a proportionally scantier attention by scholars of Reformation music, although – in my opinion – it deserves to be considered as a fundamental source for sixteenth-century theologies of music.

The topic discussed by Aquinas in this *Quæstio* is "whether God should be praised with song". As usual, Aquinas starts by listing some objections (five, in this case) to the subject under consideration. The first objection employs a Pauline quote (Colossians 3:16) which will recur in the writings on music of several religious reformers: since St Paul mentions "spiritual" canticles, and since nothing should be used in worship that is not commanded by Scripture, this seems to imply that "physical" or corporeal singing is contrary to God's commands. We will see that some reformers could have subscribed to this view almost verbatim. Objection 2 quotes St Jerome's criticism of "theatrical" music and strategies used by church musicians to sweeten their singing: once more, critical references to a "theatrical" performance style in sacred music will be frequently found in the forthcoming pages, forming a chain of quotes which links Quintilian to St Jerome and to Aquinas. Moreover, Aquinas' citation of Jerome's criticism of "agile throats" might have been interpreted by Aquinas' contemporaries and by those after him as a reference to virtuoso practices of diminution and melismatic singing.

Quoting the Book of Revelation (19:5) and the Magisterial tradition, Aquinas' third objection contrasts two different viewpoints: from the one side, both "the little" and "the great" should praise God; from the other, however, the Church had advised "the great" not to sing. Here we should observe this distinction between the celebrating priests ("the great") and the laypeople or the clerical singers ("the little"), since this difference will be very relevant to our further discussion.

Objection four makes reference to another Scriptural source (Psalm 33 [32]:2–3), which again will be often found in the reformers' writings. Aquinas' argument is interesting (although we must keep in mind that he is listing here some objections which he is intending to dismantle later): The Psalm describes

---

[85] On Luther's knowledge and reception of Aquinas, cf. Zur Mühlen 2002, p. 81.

Jewish worship as including instrumental music, but the Church should not imitate forms of worship pertaining to another religion. As we will see below (§ 4.2.5.), Calvin made this same point: instrumental music in church mirrored the "economy of law" which is superseded by the Gospel's "economy of Grace"[86].

Finally, objection five maintains that true praise comes from hearts rather than from lips, and singers might be distracted from the words by their very act of singing; moreover, chanting hinders textual intelligibility. Here too, we will find countless mentions of the importance of heart worship in contrast to aesthetic beauty, and considerations about intelligibility will be of the highest relevance to sixteenth-century theology of music. As Viladesau suggests, there is a crucial difference between the expression of an inner and wordless jubilation of the heart (as encouraged by Augustine) and Aquinas' caution against the primacy of sensuous enjoyment over intellectual meditation[87].

Having dutifully listed all possible objections to church singing, Aquinas proceeds – as usual – to argue for the contrary viewpoints. He starts by referring to the Patristic tradition, mentioning the establishment of church singing in Milan by St Ambrose (c.339–397), as reported by St Augustine.

For Aquinas, music (i.e. sung prayer) is useful for moving the soul to devotion, as maintained by Aristotle in his *Politics* (VIII, 5[88]) and by Boethius; he refers in passing to modal ethos, asserting the different effects on the human soul by different melodies; with a further reference to St Augustine, he maintains the importance of music for the "weak" among the faithful, with an argument echoing St Paul's statements on idolothites, i.e. food sacrificed to the idols (1 Corinthians 8:1 and 10:23, although the quotation is implicit here). Again, a similar reasoning will be often used in the Lutheran/Calvinist discussion on *adiaphora* (cf. § 4.2.4.10.), and it is noteworthy that another Dominican, Girolamo Savonarola, would take Aquinas' perspective to the extreme, claiming that public worship (including music) was useful almost only as a "medicine for ill souls"[89].

Against the first objection, Aquinas argues that physical singing does not exclude spiritual devotion; against the second, he echoes St Jerome in warning against vanity and flaunting, but does not see these as an unavoidable appendage to singing. Objection three is not really countered, since Aquinas reaffirms the priority of preaching over singing, even when both move to devotion. Strik-

---

[86] Cf. Calvin's *Commentary on Genesis* 4.20; *OC* XXIII, cols. 99–100; English translation available online at http://bit.ly/2bw1vVd; cf. Clive 1957, p. 93, n. 4.
[87] Viladesau 2000, p. 24.
[88] Aristotle 1885, p. 250; available online at http://bit.ly/2bWJfVn.
[89] Savonarola 1976, vol. 1, pp. 176–185. See Macey 1983.

ingly, Aquinas seems to consider church singing only as a means for encouraging piety, somehow disregarding the (higher?) value of worship in comparison to preaching. The same focus on teaching is found in Aquinas' reply to the fourth objection: he quotes once more from Aristotle's *Politics* (VIII, 6), maintaining that doctrine should not be conveyed with instrumental accompaniment, which is likely to produce mere enjoyment and which is not suited to "spiritual" people. Worship with music instruments, Aquinas argues, is the "figure" of a higher reality: thus he applies some kind of typological reading to music, asserting that Old Testament worship has been replaced by the New.

As suggested by Umberto Eco[90], Aquinas' cautionary remarks against the aural pleasure given by music do not imply his insensitivity to music or his rejection of beauty, but simply a limitation to sensuous enjoyment. Eco further adds that Aquinas' appreciation of music is grounded on his aesthetic theory: the contemplation of proportion and beauty can foster spiritual order and harmony.

Finally, Aquinas responds to the fifth objection by pointing out that music can lead pious singers to be more rather than less attentive to the text they are delivering; and that even though the sung text may not be understood by all hearers, it suffices that they understand why that singing is performed.

As Eco points out, Aquinas' concept of music as an instrument for arousing devotion cannot be reduced to a purely utilitarian view: it has to be understood within the context of the Greek tradition, which was aware of the potentially Dionysian power of music (and particularly of dance-rhythms), and which consistently highlighted the importance of numeric proportions for the musical "science": "Even without reference to Aquinas' sources, it is clear that he conceives of the psychagogic efficacy of music as a relationship between sensible proportion and a psychological state. Thus, the application of this theory to sacred music is in harmony with a traditional theory and is grounded on considerations of form"[91].

### 2.3.6. Magisterial music

Sixteenth-century debates on church music were undoubtedly conditioned by all the above: humanist thought, its classical sources, aesthetic developments and traditional theology of music. Indeed, official pronouncements should always be

---

**90** Eco 1988, pp. 9–10.
**91** Eco 1988, pp. 132–134.

taken with a grain of salt, since they did not always mirror actual practice, nor did they influence it consistently; nevertheless, they constituted a major source for the theology and practice of the Catholic Church, as well as a stable reference and a starting point for further official deliberations.

The most important of these is the Decretal *Docta Sanctorum Patrum*[92] (1324–5), a Constitution by Pope John XXII (c.1244–1334) concerning sacred music. John XXII writes of music in a highly competent fashion, showing his awareness of contemporaneous avant-garde experiments. He criticises the "new school", with its use of mensural patterns and the impression of liveliness it conveys in comparison with the gravity of simple plainchant. Moreover, John XXII carefully lists a number of compositional techniques he finds disturbing in church music, i.e. the practice of hocket, discant and the use of secular music within contrapuntal textures. Furthermore, he complains about the liberties taken by composers with modal theory, the seduction of voice-leading, "intoxicating rather than soothing the ear", and bodily gestures or unnecessary movements by the singers.

Thus, he argues, church music distracts the faithful rather than fostering their devotion: consequently, he condemns the above-mentioned compositional and performance styles, while allowing "the occasional use of some consonance" (i.e. polyphony), since a correct use of counterpoint "would, more than any other music is able to do, both soothe the hearer and inspire his devotion, without destroying religious feeling in the minds of the singers"[93].

Pope John's statements deserve the highest attention, although they were written almost two centuries before Luther's Reformation and thus concerned musical practices which either had been abandoned or had undergone substantial modifications in between. Notwithstanding this, actually, virtually all aspects criticised or prohibited by John XXII will constitute as many topics of discussion for the debates on sacred music in the sixteenth century: among them, the concept of "gravity" as an appropriate quality for church music, the issues with secular music leaking into worship, the problematic relationship with modal theory, the warnings against music's intoxicating power and against unsuitable gesticulations, as well as the appreciation of music as a means for encouraging devotion.

Pope John's Constitution was referred to during the discussions at Trent, thus establishing an explicit connection between the Catholic Church's continu-

---

[92] *CIC* 2, cols. 1149–1150; available online at http://bit.ly/2cnWhuj.
[93] As translated in Weiss and Taruskin 2008, pp. 60–61; cf. Raynor 1972, pp. 36–37; Romita 1936, pp. 47–48.

ing efforts aiming at the reformation of its music[94]. It should be pointed out that John XXII was by no means banning polyphony from church outright, as is often misstated in musicological debates quoting his Decretal[95]; rather, precisely because he appreciated its potentialities and was aware of its technical aspects, he wished to intervene as if pruning it of its deviations.

Similar to what would happen after Trent, also in Pope John's case there were efforts by contemporaneous composers to show their compliance with the requirements of the Church authorities[96]; and later writers referring to this Decretal are thought-provoking not only in what they see in it, but also in what they fail to see or deliberately omit. For example, as Blackburn points out[97], citations of this Constitution by sixteenth-century theologian Martín de Azpilcueta (1491–1586) from the one side mitigate John's criticism of polyphony, and from the other interpret it as a concern for textual intelligibility which was probably not implied in the Pope's statements.

A century after Pope John's Decretal, the Council of Basel (1431–1449) had voiced similar complaints against abuses in church music and encouraged ameliorations, especially as concerned the divine Office. In its twenty-first session (June 9th, 1435), it had condemned the omission or shortening of such important items of the Mass as the Creed, the Preface or the Lord's Prayer, as well as the intermingling of secular songs during sacred services[98]. Thus, even at the official level, there is a substantial continuity in the Catholic Church's concerns for sacred music and in its individuation of problematic issues.

### 2.3.7. Words, words, words

Although our discussion of Christian sources has momentarily distanced us from the main topic of the humanist influence on the debates on sacred music, we will now return to this issue, with particular focus on the humanist concern for textual matters.

Words were crucial for humanist culture: they were philologically studied in the ancient sources, they constituted a formidable tool for human communication and therefore for the progress and improvement of humankind, and they

---

94 Monson 2002, p. 9.
95 Cf. the anthology in Hucke 1984, p. 119.
96 Cf. Strohm 1993, p. 35.
97 Blackburn 2007, pp. 91–92.
98 Session XXI, Chapter VIII, in *Mansi* 29, col. 107 (available online at http://bit.ly/2bgMd3P). Cf. Rainoldi 2000, p. 329.

formed the elements on which rhetoric and oratory were based: for Gray, there is almost a reciprocal identification between Renaissance humanism and eloquence[99]. Words also had accents, measure and length: the rediscovery of ancient poetry fostered a new appreciation of metrical issues and the quest for a correct pronunciation of ancient languages. Last but by no means least, for Christian humanists, words referred to the Word, who ultimately was one of the Trinity's divine persons, and who had revealed the Godhead to humankind also by means of written texts.

We will see that all and each of the above-mentioned items have some musical relevance, and that several impacted onto the perception of sacred music as well. As mentioned in the previous Chapter, the following discussion will therefore be organised by thematic clusters rather than in a chronological order: thus, I will also employ quotations from a period slightly later than that of the Reformations, when they illustrate the consequences of the humanist approach of church music and contribute to our understanding of the perspective of the era.

### 2.3.7.1. Moving music

One key concept of classical and humanist rhetoric is represented by *pronuntiatio*, which may correspond to our "delivery" of a text: it was understood as the combination of *vox* (voice, sound) and *motus* (motion, or the power to move[100]). Thus, the union of word and music was deemed to be the most powerful tool for actively intervening on human souls, since the intellectual content was conveyed by words while music empowered mnemonic faculties and emotional reaction. Language and music together had a dramatic persuasive force, but also were a key for the understanding of the world, through their shared symbolic nature[101]. Thus, both the Renaissance and humanism sought new perspectives for the interaction between text and music, and created a repository of rhetoric devices to enhance the persuasive power of song[102]. On the other hand, the above-mentioned belief in what the ancients said about the effects of modes on human behaviour led some thinkers to posit the (lost) supremacy of that music over oratory and rhetoric: as we will later see (§ 3.3.3.), Bernardino Cirillo was one of them.

Music, and particularly sacred music, had thus the function to "move" human affects and to excite the believers' devotion. As seen before (§ 2.3.5.),

---

99 Cf. Gray 1968, pp. 200–204 and Haar 2006, p. 23.
100 Kim 2005, p. 18.
101 Austern 1988, p. 5.
102 Haar 2006, p. 27.

this was already true much earlier for Aquinas, who claimed that vocal praise was necessary for arousing devotion; in his wake, Cirillo argued that sacred music and painting should "move to religion and piety"[103]; Azpilcueta maintained that in proper sacred music "one hears and understands the words and is moved by them"[104]. Federigo Borromeo, on the other hand, asserted that the true power of music was in its performance rather than in its composition, since "the same thing, said in a certain fashion, will move exceedingly, whereas in another will make no impression at all"[105]: this claim, moulded on humanist beliefs about the power of *pronuntiatio*, is even more startling as regards music.

Similarly, Pontus de Tyard (c.1521–1605) argued that music has the aim to find "such a melody to the text, that all hearing it will feel themselves moved, and let themselves be drawn to the affection of the poet"[106], and we have already seen that Zarlino, though slightly sceptical about attempts to revive ancient music, was nonetheless convinced of music's power to arouse affects and passions[107]. Indeed, connections between music and rhetoric had been drawn already by one of humanism's undisputed models, Quintilian himself, who had highly praised music and its persuasive faculties, though defining it as an auxiliary discipline of rhetoric (a subordinate concept which humanists will often adopt[108]).

The effect of words on the recipients of a rhetorician's speech thus depends not only on the speech's content, not only on the chosen words, but also on acoustic issues such as his or her tone of voice, clear articulation and proper accentuation. Here, those concerned with sacred music faced a problematic and contradictory situation: the received accentuation of liturgical chant in Latin, the position of its melismas and the temporal proportions among syllables did not correspond to those prescribed by classical prosody. It was by no means a purely aesthetic matter: in the humanists' view, this prevented the power of the combination of sacred text with liturgical music to act fully on the believers' souls[109].

Humanist attempts at a reform of plainchant led by rhetoric principles thus represented an effort predating some of the most important musical outputs of the Protestant reformations, i.e. metrical psalmody, as well as a distinct project

---

[103] *Lettere volgari* 1564, fol. 117ʳ.
[104] Blackburn 2007, p. 91 and footnote.
[105] Bizzarini 2012, pp. 38–39.
[106] In Walker 1941, p. 289, fn. 123.
[107] Cf. Berger 2006, pp. 308–310.
[108] Cf. *Institutio Oratoria*, I.10.9 ff.; available online at http://bit.ly/2bLHavx.
[109] Kim 2005, p. 244.

of post-Tridentine Catholic Church[110]. Among such early attempts, Kim mentions the 1521 *Gradual* issued in Cordova (Spain), as well as *De tonis sive tenoribus* (1505) by Paris de Grassis (c.1470–1528), the *Libellus de rudimentis musices* (1529) by Biagio Rossetto (or Rossetti, c.1470-c.1547) and the *Scintille di musica* (1533) by Giovanni Maria Lanfranco (c.1490–1545)[111].

The humanist focus on words thus affected the micro-structure of musical metre and rhythm, but also the larger structures of a rhetorically-inspired musical discourse. This was partially due to the influence of thought developed within the context of universities in northern Europe, but also corresponded to the undecided collocation of music among the entire framework of contemporaneous culture. In fact, on the one hand music had been understood as a scientific subject, whose rational proportions had justified its insertion among mathematics (*quadrivium*); on the other, its affective powers seemed to require its inclusion among the arts of speech, such as poetry, oratory and rhetoric[112].

It should be pointed out that contemporaneous thought on this topic was by no means always consistent, straightforward and unequivocal: if the very nature and understanding of music was still undecided (between *scientia* and *ars*, between mathematics and rhetoric, between theory and practice), so was the identification of the reasons for its power to move: was it a product of modal characterisation (and thus of a purely musical issue)? Did it depend on its connection with the word? In the latter case, when polyphonic beauty diminished intelligibility, did it prevent the action of music's moving power?

For those sharing the latter viewpoint, when the complexity of contrapuntal texture did conceal the words' pronunciation, the powerful union of music with text was undermined, and music had the unwanted effect of diminishing, rather than enhancing, the persuasive power of speech[113]. We will see in the forthcoming discussion that Erasmus of Rotterdam adhered to this view and criticised the incorrect pronunciation of sacred texts in music[114].

### 2.3.7.2. Plain text

For this reason, and particularly in the very last expression of humanism at the end of the sixteenth century, some thinkers maintained that polyphonic music did not merely hide the text, but actually impeached its faculty to move the lis-

---

110 Kim 2005, p. 23 and pp. 148–159 and 170.
111 Kim 2005, pp. 239, 242, 247 and 271.
112 Cf. Tomlinson 2006, pp. 8–9.
113 Kim 2005, p. 113.
114 Cf. Kim 2005, p. 158.

teners' affects. This was the view of Federigo Borromeo, who believed that four- or five-part music "does not move affects", since their interweaving is confusing and impedes perception of metre, "which was the reason of *pathos*" for the old. He also maintained that the moving power of ancient music lay in its combination of "voice, gesture, affect, rhythm, habit, words, occasions, and all voices in unison". He further asserted, following St Augustine's teaching, that ideal church music should be "very similar" to reading and to the clear delivery of a text[115].

This ideal corresponded also to the wishes of Erasmus, who traced back to the first Christian worships a way of singing "closer to modulated recitation than to song"[116]; on the other hand, in his *De natura cantus* (1496), Matthaeus Herbenus of Maastricht (1451–1538) did not reject polyphonic renditions of the text, but underpinned the importance of rational understanding of the words for a full appreciation of music and of its powers[117]. Echoing Pope John XXII's criticism of too strict an interweaving of parts, he claimed that "vernacular songs with simple counterpoint" were highly moving "because their notes, being uttered in syllabic fashion, could be easily made out by all"[118].

Closer to Erasmus' model, Gregory Martin (c.1542–1582), an English Catholic scholar, in 1581 praised the Sistine Chapel Choir with these words: "They deliver every word and every syllable so distinctly, so cleanly, so commodiously, so fully, that the hearers may perceive al that is sung. [...] A bass voice very leisurely, rather sayth than singeth [...]. Every syllable may be heard in thy ears like a Preacher's voice"[119].

A decade earlier, Vincenzo Ruffo (c.1508–1587) prefaced his *Missæ quatuor concinnatæ* (1570) by pointing out his compositional effort aiming at a style in which "the numbers of the syllables" (an expression suggesting prosodic concerns) "and the voices and tones together should be clearly and distinctly understood and perceived by the pious listeners"[120].

Analogous considerations were expressed in the Provincial Council of Sens (Burgundy, 1528), establishing that church songs must be "*distincti ac discreti*" (both words imply clarity in articulation[121]).

---

115 In Bizzarini 2012, p. 40 and pp. 157–158.
116 In Kim 2005, p. 139.
117 Wegman 2005, p. 175.
118 Herbenus 1957, pp. 58–59; in Wegman 2005, pp. 175–176.
119 In Sherr 1994, p. 607, with spelling alterations.
120 As translated in Lockwood 1970, p. 99.
121 *Mansi* 32, col. 1190 (http://bit.ly/2bzaAYG), my translation; cf. Veit 1986, p. 13.

The concern for intelligibility was also of primary import in the Protestant reformers' perspective, as will be discussed at length later (§ 4.2.3.1. etc.), and was one of the foremost concurring factors in the critical stance characterising some of their attitudes to polyphony[122].

Besides their ability to move, words could also instruct and educate: another of the highpoints of humanist thought was its interest in pedagogy and in the improvement of knowledge, literacy and culture. So strong was this characterisation that Kim, in Kristeller's wake, was able to integrate the sometimes conflicting perspectives of humanism and Protestant reformation by qualifying both of them (also) as educational and cultural movements[123].

This process involved increased and more widespread schooling (and the use of music within educational institutions), as well as the transmission of a frame of ethical values to the entire society (and here too music could be highly useful).

As an appendage to this, vernacular culture was also "classicised" in turn, e.g. through the application of quantitative metric principles to local languages[124]: within this framework, the Protestant adoption of vernacular metric psalmody as a qualifying feature of their educational programme combined a cultural aspect with worship and with the transmission of virtue[125].

### 2.3.8. Symbol and fascination

Words can be spoken, sung, heard, written, read and understood. For Christians, however, the Word became flesh (cf. John 1:14) and could be seen and touched (cf. 1 John 1:1). This seeming contradiction is much more than a poetic synaesthesia: it is the principle enabling Christian artistry and a symbolic understanding of beauty. *Symbolon* is what holds together: words, paintings and music may or may not have an immediate meaning, but they have the power to bridge the division of transcendence and immanence by referring to higher realities.

The concept simplistically summarised here had inspired Christian art for centuries, and remained crucial for the Eastern theology of beauty and of the icons. In Western Europe, however, the boundary between Middle Ages and modernity partially damaged this union, and the separation of reasoning from

---

[122] Wegman 2005, p. 175.
[123] Kristeller 1961, p. 10 and Kim 2005, p. 109.
[124] Kim 2005, pp. 103–104.
[125] Joby 2005, pp. 67–68; cf. Kim 2005, p. 176.

intuition, of understanding from contemplation, of meditation from mysticism started to emerge.

Of course, this era was deeply interested in esotericism; however, in my opinion, the very quasi-schizophrenic coexistence of magic beliefs and highly intellectual reasoning is a symptom of the broken unity of symbolic perception.

In worship, awe and amazement started to be superseded by understanding and confessing; the dimension of an almost-ecstatic contemplation was progressively downplayed. While medieval belief was deeply rooted in visual experiences (such as the observation of images) and was strengthened by using the sense of touch (for example in the contact with relics), early modern religiosity started increasingly to focus on hearing and understanding[126].

Listening to sacred music works had originally pertained to the former kind of experience rather than the latter: polyphony had at first been conceived of as a symbol for heavenly jubilation, and as a quasi-ecstatic medium for mystical contemplation. It was a sign of exultation, of praise, of joyful celebration, and a powerful symbol for unity-in-plurality. Although individual words might be not heard or understood, this did not really matter: what did matter was the believers' encounter with transcendence through beauty. As Dean states, at the beginning of the sixteenth century "the performers and their appreciative listeners must have valued sacred polyphony for more generally spiritual reasons and for distinctly musical ones; their attitude might best be described as 'spiritual recreation'"[127].

No less important, moreover, was another concept which gradually started to fade precisely in coincidence with modernity, i.e. that a work of art (not only musical), conceived for worship and made for God's greater glory, would accomplish its function and had a significance even when nobody would see or hear it, or appreciate its beauty.

As said before, these approaches (the symbolic and the cultural ones) were gradually denied in early modernity. In visual art, Jan Molanus (1533–1585) asserted in his treatises on sacred images (1580) that depictions of holy episodes should be firmly rooted in their Biblical accounts, rejecting the medieval symbolic approach[128]. In his wake, Catholic reformer Gabriele Paleotti addressed visual artists in his *Discorso intorno alle immagini sacre e profane* (1582), recommending them to avoid abstraction, symbolism and metaphor, and to limit themselves to a faithful and "natural" depiction of reality[129]. A similar concern for "natural" ren-

---

126 McKee 2003, p. 8.
127 Dean 1997, p. 628.
128 Molanus 1570 and Molanus 1594; cf. Prodi 2014, p. 79.
129 Paleotti 1582; cf. Prodi 2014, p. 121.

dition will be observed in the contemporaneous efforts to reform Latin liturgical plainchant according to the regular rhythm of speech (cf. § 9.3.4.).

In the Protestant area, and even in those Churches which still admitted visual art, the focus was going to be similarly shifted from visual and aural contemplation to rational hearing, from amazement to preaching. This implied an enhanced congregational participation and the conscious effort, on the believers' part, to grasp the meaning of what was preached and to actively apply it to their lives[130]. The primacy of hearing over seeing was obviously favourable to music, although here too the symbolic dimension of music made way for its functional use at the service of the word. Significantly, thus, Glarean[131] questions whether complex polyphonic works are truly *understood* or simply enjoyed: although here his reference to understanding might allude to musical comprehension rather than to textual intelligibility, it is however meaningful that he disavows the legitimacy of a purely aesthetic enjoyment.

As Taruskin admirably summarises, in continental Europe the sixteenth century saw music's struggle to "reflect both the shape and the meaning of the texts to which it was set", while in England the older belief in music's transcendent power was maintained. "The English melismas continued to hide the text, so to speak, from aural view, and thus pre-empt it", continues Taruskin, while mainstream "art-music" in the Continent was more rationalised – and therefore more humane, possibly less divine[132].

On the other hand, another view of music was frequently found, competing with its function as a rhetorical enhancement of the word: music could be relegated to an accessory role, and become a mere "adornment" of speech or liturgy[133]. This or similar words are often read in reference to sacred music, and imply a decorative concept of its value[134].

When the symbolic union of beauty with truth and goodness which had been posited by the medieval theologians and recently reasserted by Ficino[135] started to be felt more feebly than before, aesthetic contemplation could actually become a competitor of spirituality: indeed, Koenigsberger proposes a highly fascinating interpretation of the history of Western music in parallel with secular-

---

130 McKee 2003, pp. 9–10.
131 Glareanus 1965, vol. I, p. 206.
132 Cf. Taruskin 2010, vol. I, pp. 613–614.
133 Rees 2006, p. 342.
134 Compare Ruffo 1570 with the statements by Lodovico Cresollio (1629) and Lelio Guidiccioni (1637) quoted in Lockwood 1975, pp. 30–32. Cf. also § 9.3.6.1.
135 Cf. Aquinas, *De Veritate* (Aquinas 1952, q. 1, a. 1) and *ST* 1, q. 39, a. 8 (with Eco's commentary, in Eco 1988, pp. 44–47 etc.); Ficino 1975, pp. 78, 110, 238.

isation¹³⁶. This encouraged in turn a deep distrust of the seductive power of music: while Augustine's wariness of music's potential to attract listeners without bringing them to divine contemplation had adumbrated such issues, several sixteenth-century reformers will express similar concerns and sometimes even straightforwardly ban musical expression (cf. § 4.3.2.–3.).

### 2.3.9. "Ornamental neighings": Erasmus on music

It is impossible to discuss the topic of humanism and sacred music without dedicating at least a cursory mention to Erasmus' thought. Although his true import on the religious reformations of the sixteenth century has yet to be assessed, and although some of his writings should be taken with a grain of salt, his viewpoint on church music can often be considered to be representative of the humanist movement, and it certainly influenced later discussions of the topic in both the Catholic and the Evangelical field¹³⁷. Moreover, his international stance allows us to regard him as one of the leading figures of so-called exoteric humanism¹³⁸. On the other hand, his treatment of musical topics is not always consistent or straightforward; and it has been suggested that his viewpoint was conditioned by his knowledge of ancient culture rather than by his own personal involvement and interest in music¹³⁹.

Undoubtedly, his insight on music was genuinely humanist inasmuch as he stressed the primacy of word over music, in a variety of fields and situations.

First, there was the issue of intelligibility: for Erasmus, due to polyphonic complexity, as well as for linguistic/cultural reasons (Latin was understood only by few among the faithful, and even many singers did not comprehend what they were singing), and also due to acoustic problems (Erasmus criticised contemporaneous architecture), the text was often not perceived by the congregation, let alone understood. His vexation is mirrored by his famous complaint: "In college or monastery it is still the same: music, nothing but music..."¹⁴⁰.

Second, the choristers' ignorance of prosodic rules led to incorrect accentuation in church singing¹⁴¹: here too Erasmus saw the history of the Church as a history of decay from the original purity of plainchant, part of which had been

---

136 Cf. Koenigsberger 1986, pp. 179–180.
137 Kim 2005, p. 112.
138 Kim 2005, pp. 103–104.
139 Koenigsberger 1986, p. 187.
140 Cit. in Le Huray 2008, p. 11.
141 Cf. Kim 2005, p. 158.

created within a historical context where both Latin and ancient Greek were living languages.

Third, as mentioned earlier, Erasmus would have favoured a soberer style of musical recitation over the contemporaneous elaborated music, also due to historical considerations on the practices of the early Church[142]. These three issues all concurred in undermining the rhetoric power of the association between words and music: inspired by the writings of Lorenzo Valla (c.1405–1457), Erasmus considered rhetoric to be crucial for the outworking of a Christian approach to eloquence as well as a fundamental element of theology. No less important therefore was the possibility of joining a properly designed speech with the persuasive power of music[143].

Fourth, there was a very practical issue: music performance took too long a time during worship. Sometimes, singing was superimposed onto reading and thus covered the liturgical words; in other cases, liturgy was shortened in order to make way for music[144]. Erasmus lists other liturgical abuses such as the insertion of "unlearned" sequences (which sometimes were so long that the Creed had to be curtailed...) and of songs to the Virgin Mary or to the saints during the elevation[145].

Fifth, Erasmus' criticism focuses on inappropriate performance styles: in particular, he disapproves of excessive loudness in singing and of exteriority in the practices of discant and faburden[146]. Interestingly, on this occasion, Erasmus' reference to ancient practices is not veined by nostalgia for an allegedly lost perfection: rather, he maintains that the vocal participation of early Christian congregations in worship produced "thunderous noise and ridiculous confusion", in "a spectacle unworthy of divine worship". A better solution, in his view, is that only those proficient in music should actually sing, while the others should join in the praise "in their hearts"[147]. A similarly condemnable result is obtained, in Erasmus' view, when improvised polyphony is practised; he analogously criticises (perhaps following St Jerome) the "ornamental neighings and agile throats" of English singers. In faburden, he maintains, "the whims of the foolish are indulged and their baser appetites are satisfied"[148]: once more, his

---

[142] Erasmus et al. 1642, col. 2064B.
[143] Cf. Kim 2005, p. 113.
[144] Cf. in Miller 1966, p. 336; cf. Russell 2002, p. 78.
[145] In Miller 1966, p. 337.
[146] Kim 2005, p. 150. Cf. also § 3.2.2. and fn. 17.
[147] In Miller 1966, p. 334.
[148] In Miller 1966, p. 339.

aesthetic (and moral) evaluations of church music are intermingled with a rather elitist and patronising attitude towards lower social classes.

Sixth, Erasmus follows the Church Fathers in their rejection of instrumental music in worship: with particularly harsh words[149], he connects the clamour of musical instruments with dance (echoing Chrysostom). Here a particular feature of Erasmus' thought on music (which will be frequently found in the forthcoming pages) becomes clear: most of his disapproval is based on moral (rather than on musical) grounds, and he is mainly worried about the association of church music with secular practices, and about habits unsuitable for the nobility and elevation which seemingly characterise his ideal of worship[150].

Last but not least, in fact, Erasmus enlists the use of secular melodies in church compositions as another serious abuse in liturgical matters[151].

It should be added, however, that Erasmus did believe (following Quintilian) both in the high dignity and in the social utility of music[152]; and that, although he might be wary of the peasants' rowdy singing in church, he desired that spiritual songs based on Scripture become common in their everyday life: "Would that, as a result, the farmer sing some portion of them at the plow, the weaver hum some parts of them to the movement of his shuttle, the traveller lighten the weariness of the journey with stories of this kind!"[153]. Thus, Erasmus' concern for proper church music intertwined with his scholarly and spiritual interest in the Bible and in making it accessible to all the faithful[154].

## 2.4. As you like it: aesthetic trends

In the preceding pages I tried to offer a cursory picture of the cultural and philosophical trends at the dawn of the sixteenth century and of their relationship to sacred music. Now I will briefly summarise the stylistic orientations of musicianship during the sixteenth century: although some of the aesthetic phenomena were indeed influenced, if not caused, by religious reforms, ideologies and culture, others developed quite independently and on purely musical grounds. All, however, entertained mutual relationships with the cultural atmosphere of the era and with the socio-political changes determined by the Reformations.

---

**149** In Reeve and Screech 1990, p. 151.
**150** Cf. Russell 2002, p. 78.
**151** Koenigsberger 1986, p. 184.
**152** Kim 2005, p. 137.
**153** In Kim 2005, p. 63.
**154** Cf. Tomlinson 2006, p. 14, and Kim 2005, pp. 131–132.

It is fundamental to maintain a margin of independency for musical phenomena when studying their stylistic evolution: all too often, indeed, music historiography has established causal relationships between external factors (such as, for example, the Tridentine decrees on church music) and aesthetic changes (such as the success of accompanied monody, homorhytmic writing or polychoral idiom). Some influence of these external factors is unquestionable, and to deny that many religious reformers and many composers shared analogous concerns (for instance, as regards textual intelligibility) would be unreasonable; however, it is also impossible to determine the extent of a factor's direct influence on a given effect, and sometimes they may both be the by-products of the cultural atmosphere of the era.

Thus, common explanations for observable phenomena may well be the a-posteriori justifications given by later historians for evolutions they wished to canonise.

### 2.4.1. Style matters

From the stylistic viewpoint, part of the history of sixteenth century music can be read as the growing medium for the elaboration of the style of the seventeenth century. Music was evolving in the direction of increasingly national stylistic features, and the success of madrigals paved the way for the first operatic accomplishments. Purely instrumental music also established itself more and more as an independent genre; sacred music saw the survival of traditional musical forms (such as Masses and motets), side by side with blossoming new genres, several of which were directly connected with movements of religious reform.

Another important theoretical issue was the conceptual shift, mentioned above, from a scientific to a practical vision of music: as will be seen later (cf. § 4.2.2. and 4.3.1.1.), the Lutheran pedagogic system and insight influenced this process[155], which paralleled in turn what was happening in the field of visual arts[156].

Finally, this century also saw the gradually increasing success of two particular modes (that would later become the modern major and minor modes) over the variety of the preceding modal system, and the consistent concentration on issues of word/tone relationship[157].

---

[155] Brown 2008, p. 229.
[156] Prodi 2014, p. 44.
[157] Cf. Higman 2000, p. 491.

As Carter correctly points out, however, current musicology tends to conceive of the transition between "Renaissance" and "Baroque" as a process rather than (as traditionally) a rupture. All "Baroque" features listed above (i.e. new aesthetic views, chordal concept, solo singing with continuo accompaniment and the affirmation of tonal perspectives) were germinating latently in the previous era. In Carter's words, "what changes as we move from the Renaissance to the Baroque may be not so much musical or performing styles themselves as the fact that these styles are recorded through notation in different ways"[158]. Styles such as the *recitar cantando* blossomed from well-established pre-extant practices, in what now seems to be a differentiation rather than a revolution, an enrichment rather than a rupture[159]; in Taruskin's words, the so-called musical revolutions of the seventeenth century (opera, continuo, tonality to name but the principal ones) were "only the emergence into print of musical practices that had been in the process of formation over the whole preceding century"[160].

Also the practice of organ or instrumental obbligato accompaniment (in sacred works for solo or a few singers), which was popularised through the publication in 1602 of the *Cento Concerti ecclesiastici* by Lodovico da Viadana (c.1560–1627), was likely to have been almost customary during the preceding century. The *concertato* style found printed evidence in publications from the 1580s (by Andrea Gabrieli [c.1532–1585] and Ascanio Trombetti [1544–1590]), but possibly had been already used in coexistence with the traditional a-cappella performance: "the sound of the music in performance [was] determined less by compositional style than by liturgical and ceremonial context"[161].

### 2.4.2. A cappella or accompanied?

This brief mention of Viadana's *Concerti* and of the questions surrounding the practice of instrumental accompaniment to solo singing lead us to consider this problem, which is still unsolved by today's musicology.

Noel O'Regan has gathered extensive evidence for the likely use of organ accompaniment to singing at the Jesuit *Collegio Germanico* in Rome from 1583[162]; similar practices by Dominican nuns are attested in Treviso (1575), and the

---

158 Carter 2006, pp. 47–48.
159 Cf. Tomlinson 1998, p. 286.
160 Taruskin 2010, vol. I, p. 809.
161 Bryant and Quaranta 2007, p. 118.
162 Cf. O'Regan 2000.

habit of writing down the text only in correspondence to the upper parts of polyphonic works might support the inference that this practice was indeed rather more common than is usually thought[163].

However, the frequent discovery of new documents seems to suggest that the organ was by no means the only instrument played during liturgies. The best proof for such practices, as argued by Korrick, comes from literature complaining against them[164]: indeed, some of the witnesses she gathered implies that instrumental music was played in church side-by-side with dramatic performance and even dancing[165].

Among others, Azpilcueta (1578) listed a number of instruments he would gladly have banned from churches, but which (evidently) were commonly played[166]. Analogously, Protestant reformers or sympathisers of the Reformation counted instrumental music in church among the reasons for their criticism of Catholic practice: to name but one, Andreas Bodenstein von Karlstadt (1486–1541) enumerated organ, flutes and trumpets among the instruments he would have pruned from worship[167].

As could be expected, the greatest support to those advocating the ban of instruments from church came from the writings of the Church Fathers. This was the source of Erasmus' harsh opposition to instrumental music in worship[168], and had been partially determined, in turn, by the association of instruments with pagan worship[169]. It is thus rather striking to find, in Aquinas' discussion of music[170] discussed above (§ 2.3.5.), that instrumental music was unsuitable for Christian worship due to its link with *Jewish* practices: however, as we will see in the forthcoming Chapters, this argument will be found in several other religious writers.

Organ music was deemed by many to be "lascivious": a treatise instructing confessors maintained that the toleration of the wanton and dishonest sound of organs in worship constituted a grave sin on the part of the prelates allowing it[171]. It was not only the organ's timbre, which seemingly excited lustful thoughts, but (more dangerously) the secular pieces that were played on it[172]; both Karl-

---

163 Bryant and Quaranta 2007, pp. 111–115.
164 Cf. Korrick 1990.
165 Cf. Korrick 1990.
166 Blackburn 2007, p. 94.
167 Bodenstein 1905, p. 492; cf. Korrick 1990, pp. 359–360.
168 Cf. Kim 2005, pp. 137, 144, 148.
169 Cf. Rainoldi 2000, pp. 89–94.
170 *ST* 2a2æ, q. 91, a. 2.
171 Lopes 1590, p. 82.
172 Herl 2004, p. 25.

stadt in the pamphlet quoted above and Ludovico Beccadelli (1501–1572) complained against performance of unsuitable music during consecration and elevation[173], i.e. moments of the Mass when particular concentration and attention were required.

"A certain dance" was played by an organ accompanying a solo singer during a public worship witnessed by Cardinal Marcello Cervini, who would later become Pope as Marcellus II, and by Cardinal Guglielmo Sirleto (1514–1585): they reportedly commented that "the weak souls" (perhaps a reference to the often-quoted passage from Augustine's *Confessions*) would receive little help for their contrition from listening to such music[174].

Besides these obvious abuses, there was also some concern about the propriety and morality of instrumental music *per se:* thus, the humanist philosopher and theologian Felice Figliucci (c.1525-c.1590) advised against allowing the young to practise instrumental music[175], since the martial sound of trumpets might excite rage, fury and other similar feelings. Vincenzo Galilei (in a passage briefly referred to earlier[176]) further suggested that instruments, being subhuman objects, could only aim at producing aesthetic enjoyment; whereas humans, to whom Nature had given "sense, movement, intellect, word, speech, reason and soul" should benefit their fellow humans rather than simply entertain them[177].

It may be interesting to note that Galilei might have indirectly alluded here to the Biblical descriptions of inanimate idols (cf. Psalms 115 [114]:5–7 and 135 [134]:16–18), in which case a further parallel might be established between the "cult" of instrumental music and pagan worship. In any case, Galilei's position mirrors the typically humanist belief in the superiority of human beings over the created world, and in their responsibility to maintain their supremacy.

Thus, reasons for taking a stance against instrumental music in worship could be theological (cf. Aquinas), historical (reference to the Church Fathers), moral ("lasciviousness" of either sound or performed works), educational (unsuitability of instruments for the young), spiritual (distraction during the Mass' climax) and philosophical (as maintained by Galilei). Nevertheless, instrumental music in several Christian Churches was going to be practised more and more in the following centuries, and the allegedly wanton sound of organs would eventually become an easily identifiable symbol of church music.

---

[173] Bodenstein 1905; cf. Beccadelli 1804, vol. II, p. 258.
[174] In Jedin 1973 ff., vol. IV, p. 324.
[175] Figliucci 1583, p. 256.
[176] Galilei 1581, p. 86.
[177] Galilei 1581, p. 86.

### 2.4.3. Enjoying polyphony

The evolution of taste, as stated earlier (§ 2.3.7.2.), was increasingly privileging compositional styles which allowed a clearer perception of the text; moreover, the rhetoric interaction between words and music was more easily obtained and had more efficacious results in monodic works or when only few melodic parts were interacting. On the other hand, polyphonic complexity seemed less flexible in conveying affective responses to the text and could even contradict a faithful musical expression of the words when compositional requirements seemed to demand it (e. g. for the sake of variety[178]: cf. Federigo Borromeo's scepticism on the power of multi-voiced music to "move"[179]). This point was clearly made by Mei in a letter to Vincenzo Galilei:

> If in their music the ancients had sung several airs mixed together in one and the same song, as our musicians do with their bass, tenor, contralto, and soprano, or with more or fewer parts than these at one and the same time, it would undoubtedly have been impossible for it ever to move vigorously the affections that it wished to move in the hearer, as may be read that it did at every turn in the accounts and testimonials of the great and noble writers[180].

Was polyphony therefore a dying art? And why did this evolution take place?

Of course, the appearance of new stylistic vogues did by no means imply the rejection of a glorious polyphonic tradition which was neither decaying nor agonising in the sixteenth century. Moreover, I have already pointed out a few reasons for the widespread interest in musical forms which more closely mirrored the humanist belief in the rhetoric of music; on the other hand, a thorough discussion of the aesthetic reasons for this evolution would require a much more extensive treatment than is possible here.

However, resuming the preceding discussion on the crisis of symbolic aesthetics, I will briefly suggest here a possible insight into the concept of polyphony in the sixteenth century.

As mentioned earlier (§ 2.3.8.), from its very beginnings polyphony had been associated with jubilation, exultation, feast and triumph.

For example, in his listing of documental evidence about polyphonic practices in thirteenth- and fourteenth-century Italy, Ciabattoni[181] quotes from medi-

---

[178] Berger 2006, p. 325.
[179] In Bizzarini 2012, p. 40; cf. § 2.3.7.2.
[180] Mei in Palisca 1989; quoted in Strunk 1998, p. 487; cf. *ibid.*, p. 489.
[181] Ciabattoni 2010, p. 21.

eval hagiography regarding Angela of Foligno (1248–1309) and Chiara of Assisi (c.1194–1253). Both of these saints lived mystical and ecstatic moments in which their transcendent experience of God was symbolised also through polyphonic singing[182]. I would argue, therefore, that music (and particularly polyphonic music) was seen as a symbol – if not a medium – of mystical love and joyful union with God.

So close was this association that polyphony was limited during penitential seasons, or in particular liturgical instances where serious concentration was needed (such as, for example, the *Et incarnatus* in the Creed, "out of reverence and because of the gravity of these words", as written by Pietro Ponzio[183]), or within exceptionally ascetic socio-religious contexts (such as, for instance, female claustral monasteries – cf. § 8.4.5. and 12.4.3.). Here, in particular, several interventions of church authorities on the nuns' lives aimed at restricting activities or practices deemed to be excessively pleasurable.

Why were church authorities and religious writers so wary of aesthetic enjoyment? This is another topic whose exhaustive treatment would require a much longer space than what is available here, but I will try and offer a possible explanation.

Within an Augustinian perspective, all that exists is good, since to be is to participate in God's being[184]. Thus, to sin is to choose a lesser good instead of a greater (with God being obviously the greatest good, or rather the Good *par excellence*). The infinite yearning of human souls for the Good can be twisted and deviated: sensuous pleasure can momentarily satisfy a desire which, by its very nature, can be really fulfilled only by the infinite Good. Therefore, to indulge in sensuous delight may divert the human soul from the contemplation of God, which is its ultimate vocation: instead of fostering the soul's yearning for God, musical enjoyment may quell it.

Music can be a God-given instrument for comforting and consoling humans in distress; however, they may content themselves with this temporary consolation and cease their quest for the definitive source of all consolations.

On the other hand, it should be pointed out that joy, pleasure and delight do not necessarily lead human souls astray from sanctity. True, the fallenness of human beings after the original sin tends to turn even good and beautiful things into potential occasions for acting evilly; however, humankind redeemed by the crucified and risen Christ may be free from such bias. The painful condition de-

---

[182] Cf. also the examples listed by Di Fonzo 1998 (pp. 9–10), who mentions other mystics such as Mathelda of Hackerborn (c.1240–1298), the Venerable Bede (c.673–735) and St Fursa (d.650).
[183] Ponzio 1595; English translation by Gary Tomlinson in Strunk 1998, p. 474.
[184] Cf. *Conf.* VII.12.18 (1955, p. 89).

scribed by St Paul (Romans 7:15 ff.), in which one cannot act according to one's good desires, refers rather to unredeemed humankind than to those experiencing the "freedom of the glory of the children of God" (Romans 8:21). Thus, as we will later see (§ 11.4.3. and following), the above-mentioned mystical experiences of God prompted by (polyphonic) music were by no means unheard-of in the sixteenth century: rather, they constituted one of the common features of spirituality across confessional boundaries.

Moreover, the spiritual joy that music can give to both performers and listeners can be considered as a foretaste of heavenly bliss; here too, depending on individual receptivity and disposition, it may encourage one's desire for heaven, or lull the soul into spiritual apathy.

Thus, within the perspective summarised here, we may start to understand the choir of warnings by religious men and women against the risks of excessive musical enjoyment.

We have already seen that St Augustine acknowledged his delight in music; that he was aware that this had somehow attracted him to God; but that he also had the feeling of having sinned when he paid more attention to musical beauty than to its spiritual meaning[185]. Similarly, as mentioned above (§ 2.3.5.), Aquinas (echoing St Jerome) condemns "those who sing theatrically in church not in order to arouse devotion, but in order to show off, or to provoke pleasure"[186]. Commenting upon this passage from Aquinas' *Summa*, Tommaso de Vio ("Cajetan") recommended not to sing for the singer's own delight or to please others; on the same grounds, he asserted that the use of organs in church became illicit when it caused pleasure[187].

The risk represented for spiritual life by aural pleasure was also mentioned during the debates at the Council of Trent, both in a memorandum dated August 8th, 1562 ("It must also be considered whether the kind of music that has now become established in polyphony, which refreshes the ear more than the mind [...] should be abolished from the Masses"[188]) and in a "summary of the abuses" from the same year (recommending to avoid music for the "inane delectation of the ear"[189]).

---

[185] Cf. *Conf.* X.33.49–50 (1955, p. 145).
[186] *ST* 2a2æ, q. 91, a. 2, ad 2.
[187] De Vio 1570, p. 229; cf. Blackburn 2007, p. 95.
[188] *CT* 8, p. 918.
[189] "*Compendium Abusuum*" in Paleotti 1842, p. 266 (10.9.1562); cf. Rainoldi 2000, p. 83; Monson 2002, pp. 9–10; Boyce 2006, p. 140; Weber 2008, p. 164.

### 2.4.4. Seducing or sanctifying?

As demonstrated earlier (§ 2.4.3.), moderation in the enjoyment of music could be argued for on theological grounds; however (as often happens in such cases), the exercise of sobriety in limiting one's pleasurable experiences could also be fostered on purely moralistic grounds.

In fact, I would argue that another fundamental issue in the conception of holiness was at stake here. One possible approach to sanctity considers good behaviour as an almost necessary consequence of one's deep and loving relationship to God, producing in turn a particularly fecund reception of God's grace. The role of music, within this perspective, is to encourage the soul's relationship with and love for God, and thus the influence of music on behaviour is rather indirect (albeit this does not imply to downplay its importance). Morality, instead, results from one's decision to behave properly or ethically, in consequence of a rational process, which may be fostered by rhetorical persuasion (and here music, as we have stated before, may play a more direct role). It was within a moralistic perspective, thus, that both Galilei and Mei cautioned against the sensuous enjoyment one might draw from music, in their correspondence mentioned above (§ 2.4.3.)[190]. Significantly, Mei (in a letter dated May 8$^{th}$, 1572) contrasted words as "sense of hearing", "delicacy" and "delight" with "the complete and efficacious expression of everything [the author] wanted to make understood"[191]. The goal of ancient music (and of a modern music aiming at reviving its splendour) was thus to be *understood*, and not to delight.

It may be suggested, given the humanist and rationalistic framework surrounding this latter debate, that Galilei and Mei were somehow voicing not only a criticism of polyphony, but also some wariness about a kind of spiritual experience verging on the mystical and thus less understandable (and governable?) in purely rational terms. Even more tentatively, I would propose that a connection might have been felt between ecstatic/mystical experiences and femininity. I will discuss this topic more lengthily in the following Chapters: suffice it to say, for the moment, that the respective roles of womanhood and of music within spiritual life may be treated in a similar fashion. While Dante (c.1265–1321), to name but one, viewed both femininity and polyphony as icons of divine Grace

---

[190] Cf. Mei 1960, pp. 115–116; for Galilei, cf. Mace 1964, p. 256.
[191] In Berger 2006, p. 311.

and bliss, and as mediums for holiness[192], the competing position saw both of them as a potential source of temptation[193].

The connection between polyphonic music and a joyful experience of Grace and bliss was significantly posited also by those who were most critical towards it. For example, the Council held in Constance in 1567 asserted that church music should convey a prayerful mood rather than a joyful exultation[194]. On the other side, in the fifteenth century, Gilles Carlier had drawn the connection between joy and polyphony clearly, while admitting both kinds of liturgical performance:

> In many churches [...] Gregorian chant [...] is neglected, and the sweet jubilation and harmonious consonance of voices resound in the divine office – which ritual practice is not observed by well-instituted religious orders that appropriately serve God with doleful and subdued voice – even though both [practices] are good [...]. Both plainchant and musical jubilation [...] draw the soul to divine contemplation, according to the diversity of social positions, personalities, times and places[195].

I would argue, thus, that such quotations may support my point: polyphonic music was often associated with the festive mood; therefore, it was considered as inappropriate for penitential seasons or lifestyles/vocations; moreover, many cautioned against its ravishing power, either because it might lead to mystical experiences of which rational humanists were wary, or because it might seduce without leading to God.

Indeed, the limitations which were imposed on nuns' polyphony (cf. § 8.4.5. and 12.4.3.) cannot be satisfactorily explained, in my opinion, if only the intelligibility issue of polyphonic music is taken into consideration, as I believe that this was not particularly at stake within the context of convent musicianship. It makes more sense, I think, to conceive of such limitations as an element of the asceticism that should have characterised monastic life, in the Catholic reformers' intentions.

As we will see in the forthcoming Chapters, the attitudes of Catholic and Protestant reformers to polyphonic music in worship were extremely varied. What I would suggest here (and develop more thoroughly later: § 4.2.3.3. and 4.2.4.1.) is that polyphony was more welcome among those religious currents whose theology of the created world was more positive; in other words, that re-

---

**192** This view would be shared, in later centuries, among others by Charles Butler (1560–1647), who in 1636 stated that music can help humans to love God, even in ecstatic terms. Cf. Butler 1636, p. 109; Austern 1993, p. 348.
**193** This position is argued for, although in different terms, also in Leach 2006, p. 3.
**194** *CG* 7, p. 488.
**195** Carlerius/Carlier 2001, p. 31.

formers whose position was furthest from Manichaean or gnostic concepts of creation were also better disposed to trust the power of polyphonic music to lift the believers' hearts to God[196].

### 2.4.5. Rhetorical questions

After this digression on the evolution of the concept of polyphony within the theological, philosophical and aesthetic framework of sixteenth-century culture, I will now consider the stylistic issues involved in the text/music relationship.

Rhetoric treatment of music comprehended, as said before (§ 2.3.7.1.), questions concerning metre and rhythm, modal features, as well as the imitation of affects with the aim of arousing these in the listener. As stated by Marsilio Ficino,

> Music is a most powerful imitator of all things. It imitates the intentions and passions of the soul as well as words; it represents also people's physical gestures, motions, and actions as well as their characters and imitates all these and acts them out so forcibly that it immediately provokes both the singer and the audience to imitate and act out the same things[197].

Imitation, in turn, could intervene both at a macroscopic and at a microscopic level; in the latter case, it could concern either speech (when musical features were modelled upon the "natural" intonation and inflection of the spoken word) or single words, including phenomena of word-painting.

Suffice it to mention here the indications by Juan Bermudo (c.1510-c.1565), a Spanish theorist who in 1555 codified musical imitation by means of examples taken from the Gospel. Interestingly, for Bermudo, there is a correspondence between pitch and volume: for instance, words such as *"voce magna"* ("with a loud voice": John 11:43) should be underpinned by ascending melodies, whereas *"silentio"* ("quietly": cf. John 11:28) can be represented by low notes. More predictably, he suggests the use of a rising melody for *"ascendit ad celum"* ("ascended into heaven", a slightly imprecise quote from the Nicene Creed) and of altered notes in correspondence of "sad words". He eventually adds that "he who is a grammatician, poet, and rhetorician will understand best what I mean"[198],

---

[196] Cf. Haar 2006, p. 32 on the use of polyphony within various Evangelical and Catholic contexts.
[197] Ficino 1989, p. 359.
[198] Bermudo 1555, fol. cxxv$^r$; as translated in Borgerding and Stein 2006, p. 436.

thus explicitly establishing a relationship between word-painting composition and the arts of speech.

Another possibility for exploiting the rhetoric resources of verbal language was the use of homophony, which enjoyed considerable popularity in a wide variety of genres and styles practised in the century. Homophonic settings were used at almost all levels of complexity in vocal writing, including works destined for the most solemn liturgies of the Church as well as secular compositions.

The homorhythmic style (as will be discussed in greater detail later) was particularly well suited for giving some degree of complexity to melodies which had been designed with the explicit purpose of being accessible to all: this was the case of religious songs in the vernacular, including Lutheran *Lieder,* Huguenot Psalms and many other spiritual songs. While the "horizontal" conception of genuinely polyphonic settings did present problematic issues as regards textual intelligibility, the "vertical" style of homophony enhanced the words' perceptibility. For this reason and for the sober impression it conveyed, Ponzio recommended it for Lamentation settings and for the *Et incarnatus* in the Creed[199].

We will often see in the following Chapters that "*nota contra notam*" composition, whose tradition can be traced back to the first parallel *organa*, would become very popular among religious reformers; moreover, the principle of one syllable for one note was almost a motto gathering consensus among a wide-ranging spectrum of confessional allegiances. Thus, the Lutheran composer Joachim a Burck (a Burgk, Moller, 1546–1610) chose for his Passion setting a homophonic syllabic style which would have permitted a clear perception of the words[200], and was echoed by Catholics such as Vincenzo Giustiniani (1564–1637), according to whom the "good masters" of the day should apply one note to each syllable[201].

This style was typical for the humanist ode: the origins of this genre can be traced back to humanist Italy, where attempts to revive the metrical forms of ancient poetry had been given musical shape in the late fifteenth century. The joint influence of these and of the *frottole* (cf. § 1.4.3.), whose publication by Petrucci had fostered their international spread[202], encouraged similar creations in early sixteenth-century Germany (cf. the musical settings of Horace's *Odes* by Petrus Tritonius, or Treybenreif, 1465-c.1525[203]). The metrical principles of classical pro-

---

[199] Ponzio 1595, p. 158; English translation by Gary Tomlinson in Strunk 1998, p. 476.
[200] A Burck 1568; cf. Radecke 1996, p. 6. I am very grateful to Dr Radecke for sharing his research with me and providing me with valuable information about Joachim a Burck.
[201] Bizzarini 2012, p. 39.
[202] Blume 1975, p. 79.
[203] Tritonius 1507. Cf. Weber 2008, p. 214.

sody were applied to new poetry both in Latin and in the vernacular languages, for which musical settings were composed[204].

A new impulse for the creation of so-called *"mesuré à l'antique"* music came with the foundation in 1570 of the *Académie de Poésie et de Musique* in Paris, under the leadership of Jean-Antoine de Baïf (cf. § 1.3.4.). Its experiments concerned both language (e. g. replacing the combination of long and short syllables of ancient languages with the stressed and unstressed syllables of French) and rhetoric, in the combination of poetry and music[205]. Musical rhythm was determined by the cadence of the verse, in a highly sophisticated integration of philological knowledge, poetic artistry, musical rhetoric and national awareness. As we will see in Chapter Six (§ 6.2.2. etc.), such attempts will fascinatingly interact with Calvinist aesthetics and theology in the elaboration of vernacular psalmody.

Homophony started to be employed frequently in polychoral writing as well. This style was first practised in Italy around the 1550s, with fascinating results, by such composers as Jacquet de Mantua (Jacques Colebault, 1483–1559) and Adrian Willaert, who applied the *cori spezzati* technique to Vesper settings. Its success was definitively established slightly later (particularly in the seventeenth century), when this particular style seemed to correspond perfectly to the liturgical needs of the post-Tridentine Church. Indeed, it offered exciting possibilities for varying the compositional texture and for increasing the volume of sound without renouncing intelligibility: variety was ensured by the spatial and timbral alternation of the multiple choral ensembles, while the individual choirs often sang in a clear homophonic fashion. Moreover, this particular style was highly appreciated for its suitability for solemn celebrations: in later decades, the number of choirs tended to augment until the whole space of huge cathedrals and basilicas was filled by the sound of competing ensembles.

### 2.4.6. The effects of affects

In considering the word/tone relationships, we have already seen that the humanist view believed in music's power to touch the listener on the basis of modal theory and of its adherence to rhetoric: music could enhance the power of speech to move, in combination with principles of affective imitation. Thus, Bernardino Cirillo, attributing affective power to the modes, could complain: "I cannot hear or see in [music] any part of the above-mentioned ancient

---

**204** Haar 2006, p. 27.
**205** Cf. Higman 2000, p. 502; Weber 2008, p. 19; Lejeune 2010, p. 13.

modes. This is proved by the movements of affects it causes [...]; there is no theory in today's music, but only application of practice"[206]. On the other hand, Thomas More described thus the Utopians' musical style:

> All their music, both vocal and instrumental, renders and expresses natural feelings, and perfectly matches the sound to the subject. Whether the words of the prayer are supplicatory, cheerful, serene, troubled, mournful or angry, the music represents the meaning through the contour of the melody so admirably that it stirs up, penetrates and inflames the minds of the hearers[207].

For Federigo Borromeo, instead, as mentioned above (§ 2.3.7.2.), *pathos* was determined by metre and imitation[208]; around a century earlier, Paolo Cortesi (1465–1510) had written:

> Since the melodious modes of music appear to imitate all the habits of morals and all the motions of passions, there is no doubt that to be entertained by a temperate combination of modes would also mean to get in the habit of passing judgment on the rational basis of morals. This can also be proved, inasmuch as it is evident that all the habits and motions of the soul are found in the nature of the modes, in which nature the similarity to fortitude, or temperance, or anger, or mildness is exhibited, and it can easily be observed and judged that the minds of men are usually brought to those motions just as they are excited by the action of the modes[209].

For Cirillo, thus, affects were represented and conveyed by modes; for More, by the "contour of the melody"; for Borromeo, by prosody; for Cortesi, by modes through imitation.

Indeed, this era also saw an increasing focus on the feeling, emotions and rational evaluations of the individual: we are not too far from the *cogito ergo sum* by René Descartes (1596–1650), a view which will impart an unprecedented stress both on human reason and on the individual; the preceding era, instead, saw both passions and affects as universal (or rather as universally human). This new attitude will be most clearly mirrored in music by the so-called *stile moderno* or *seconda prattica*; nevertheless, also works such as Lasso's *Lagrime di san Pietro* (published in 1595) represent the musical rendition of a soul's personal itinerary to God, in a highly dramatic and individual fashion[210].

---

[206] *Lettere volgari* 1564, fol. 115ʳ, my translation.
[207] More 1995, pp. 238–239.
[208] Cf. in Bizzarini 2012, pp. 38–40.
[209] Cortesi 1510, fols. 72ᵛ-74ᵛ; English translation in Pirrotta 1966; Strunk 1998, pp. 317–318.
[210] Blume 1975, p. 169.

Obviously, affective renditions of the words in sacred music were more likely to apply to devotional texts (such as motets and spiritual madrigals[211]) than to liturgical texts such as the Ordinary of the Mass: indeed, the very concept of liturgy should conceive of personal involvement and piety as necessary and desirable by-products of a communal, ecclesial and universal worship.

Instead, personal piety became increasingly the focus of spiritual life, with aesthetic consequences both in visual and in musical art: for Prodi, there is a deep similarity between the individual enjoyment of music and that of visual art prompted by the establishment of museums and galleries. Both focus on feelings relating to personal experiences, and both are linked to spirituality through the keyword of "piety"[212]. Significantly, however, some church authorities became wary of such increasing musical individualism and of the use of compositional devices aiming at enhancing the expressive pathos. Thus, in the Netherlands, the stylistic limitations on composers fostered, perhaps unwillingly, the elaboration of hidden symbolic languages: music notation became double-layered, and while the first level complied with traditional modal theory, the meaning of the second could be grasped only by the musically competent[213].

Piety in turn fostered the flowering of genres such as the *chanson spirituelle*, in which the stylistic evolution of musical language (which increasingly valued simplicity, intelligibility and adherence to speech) faithfully mirrored the religious needs of sixteenth-century devotion[214].

### 2.4.7. Sensing music

The same principles used in the above discussion of wariness towards polyphony's fascination (§ 2.4.4.) can be thus applied to the use of senses to foster devotion. New forms of spirituality were born in the sixteenth century, several of which attempted to orientate human sensitivity towards contemplation and devotion: The Jesuit theory of the "spiritual senses" is paramount here. Spiritual senses could sometimes be moved by the corresponding bodily senses, in particular sight and hearing; thus, the magnificent architectures and frescoes of new Jesuit churches, which drew the faithful to amazement and awe, were paralleled by an increasingly expressive musical language and by the first Jesuit dramas: these were much more than a spiritual entertainment, since they reportedly

---

211 Atlas 2006, p. 105.
212 Prodi 2014, p. 51.
213 Koenigsberger 1986, p. 186.
214 O'Regan 2009, p. 217.

moved the audience to tears and sometimes accomplished impressive results in the hearers' spiritual lives[215].

Here too, a fluctuation can be observed: music's potential to charm and to move could either be profitably exploited by religious leaders or become dangerous. As Austern convincingly argues, "music was a force of incomparable power, paradox and mystery" within "a culture for whom the mundane and transcendent, or literal and metaphorical, were not entirely separable"[216]; the sense of hearing was perhaps the less "carnal", but it could achieve impressive results on both the physical and spiritual reality of human beings.

Interestingly, therefore, Cristóbal de Morales (1500–1553) prefaced his collection of Masses (*Missarum Liber Primus*, 1544) with a dedication, in which he claimed to have rejected the sensuous appeal of music in favour of expressive sobriety[217]. Francisco Guerrero was in complete agreement with Morales, when he stated that "the abuse of lascivious and effeminate singing the only purpose of which is to caress the ears" was abhorrent to God, as it "cater[ed] [...] to the baser affections and the more vulgar emotions"[218].

In a more ambiguous (or flexible, depending on viewpoints) fashion, Pierre Colin (d. after 1561) presented his 1554 publication of a Mass collection[219] as a blend of musical charm and fascination with rational understanding of the words' meaning[220]. Similarly, Ruffo (1570) was not afraid of claiming his use of "the powerful and sweet sound of the voices" in order to "soothe and caress the ears of the listeners in a pious, religious and holy way"[221], whereas Sadoleto (1533) warned that sensuous music could "turn soul into body and weaken self-control"[222].

On the other hand, Aquilino Coppini (d.1629) and Federigo Borromeo both seemed to agree with one another that music did possess a sensuous power, but that it could be used for spiritual purposes. Coppini stated that "harmony penetrates the souls, and by caressing them with a smooth delight, excites

---

**215** Cf. the reported effects of a play (*Christus Judex*, by the Jesuit Stefano Tuccio, 1540–1597), whose performance in Messina in 1569 was instrumental to the spiritual conversion of many in the audience (Gassner and Quinn 2002, p. 42); similar effects are recorded after the performance of *Cenodoxus* by Jakob Bidermann (1578–1639) in Munich in 1609 (Fisher 2014, p. 225, fn. 127).
**216** Austern 2011, p. 85.
**217** Cf. de Morales 1984, pp. 48–49.
**218** Guerrero 1584, *Preface*; English translation in Stevenson 1961, p. 183.
**219** Cf. Colin 1554.
**220** Cf. Freedman 2006, pp. 165–166.
**221** Latin text in Rainoldi 2000, p. 347; English translation in Weiss and Taruskin 2008, p. 116.
**222** Sadoleto 1533, p. 121; English translation in Palisca 1997, pp. 283–284.

[their] yearning for the excellent things"[223]. Borromeo's assertions parallel Coppini's: people who are "rather carnal than spiritual" can be led to goodness "by the suavity" of music if not by the sung words[224].

This mixed attitude of enthusiasm and wariness, excitement and fear, enjoyment and caution (sometimes present in a single individual or Church at the same time) would characterise many debates on the nature, role and function of church music: Chapter Three, in particular, will point out some of these contradictory and coexisting attitudes, which will foster, in turn, the emergence of highly differentiated musical habits among the various Christian confessions.

In this Chapter, I have attempted to delineate the cultural and musical framework necessary for understanding the intermingling processes of religious and artistic evolution I will discuss later. Humanism, with its interest in antiquity and its efforts to revive earlier theory and practice, was one of the major forces of the intellectual panorama; along with it, a renewed attention to the sources of Christian thought and to the deeply-felt need for a religious regeneration fostered the development of aesthetic considerations as regards the value of music. I have tried and suggested some possible theological and spiritual reasons for the musical evolution in compositional style and taste, particularly as concerns the decreasing awareness of music's symbolic nature and power.

I succinctly sketched the most important stylistic innovations of the century, and how they dovetailed with preceding practices, new theoretical insights and the emergence of the seventeenth-century style.

With this background in mind, we will move, in the next Chapter, to a deeper analysis of the problematic issues in contemporaneous church music.

---

**223** Letter from Aquilino Coppini to Federigo Borromeo, September 5th, 1607; Latin text in Bizzarini 2012, pp. 91–92, my translation.
**224** Bizzarini 2012, pp. 157–158.

# Chapter 3 – Criticising sacred music

> Let them make their motets, *chansons*,
> madrigals and ballads as they please;
> only, let our Church with its deeds
> move to religion and piety.
>
> [Bernardino Cirillo, 1549[1]]

## 3.1. Introduction

Of the three words I used as this Chapter's heading, one is highly problematic. In fact, although the concept of "sacred" music might seem at first self-explanatory, it is equivocal even today, and surely it was conceived very differently (if conceived at all) in the early sixteenth century. Indeed, the emergence of a separation between sacred and secular is one of the characterising features of early modernity; and yet other concepts with which we are commonly acquainted (such as liturgical and extra-liturgical music) need to be questioned and qualified with respect to the early sixteenth century.

Moreover, although the great majority of the European population in the pre-Reformation era was part of the Catholic Church, this should not imply liturgical homogeneity or identical practices. Even within the context of codified liturgies such as the Mass or the monastic Office, there were a great variety of practices (locally determined or varying from one religious order to another, and even within a single order or a single diocese).

I will try to give an overview of this complexity (albeit, once more, a very synthetic one), by considering in turn the musical forms of what we now call "liturgical" and "non-liturgical" music. I will briefly consider the status of plainchant and polyphony (both written and improvised) at the dawn of the sixteenth century, as well as the musical expressions of faith outside liturgy: in particular, given the relevance of this topic to the Reformation in music, I will discuss the vernacular forms of musical piety before Luther.

I will then move on to a survey of contemporaneous criticism of church music. Indeed, music was certainly not the most urgent of the Catholic Church's problems in the early sixteenth century: side by side with luminous examples of

---

1 *Lettere volgari* 1564, fol. 117$^r$, my translation.

charity and sanctity, there were corruption, scandals, and the widespread feeling that changes were required.

Indeed, this challenge was the starting point of both Protestants and Catholic reformers, and – as the following Chapters will show – for most of them music will have a pivotal role as an element of spiritual renewal. However, if we wish to grasp the crucial function of music for the religious Reformations, it is imperative to contextualise this perspective within the framework of the limits and problematic aspects which were pointed out in the church music of the time. I will discuss, in this Chapter, the criticism of Catholic church music as it was expressed *before* the confessional reforms: i.e., in the zones which would later adhere to Protestantism in the time preceding the Reformation, and in the zones which would remain Catholic before the end of the Council of Trent[2].

Thus, I will focus in turn on criticism regarding the text/music relationship, taking into account the humanistic concerns discussed in Chapter Two; later, I will examine the moralistic issues involved in church music, as regards both theory and practice.

I will argue that the meaning and significance of a great percentage of criticism of church music in the Early Modern era will remain elusive to our understanding, since – in my opinion – numerous statements focused on issues of performance practice rather than of composition. Obviously, without any aural witness we cannot imagine what exactly sixteenth-century writers intended to criticise.

I will conclude this Chapter by discussing a famous (and, in my opinion, frequently misunderstood) letter written by a sixteenth-century Italian clergyman, Bernardino Cirillo, in which issues regarding the ethics of church music dovetail with aesthetic considerations on visual art and morality of his time.

Arguably, both Cirillo and his contemporaries criticised contemporaneous church music on moral terms rather than on theological grounds: the concern for a "beautiful" worship which should honour God and give a transcendent experience of amazement to musicians and listeners alike is rarely found in sixteenth-century literature on sacred music, whereas ethical concerns are very frequently voiced throughout European culture.

---

[2] In a very limited number of cases I have quoted witnesses from a later age, but only to reinforce a point that had already been made.

## 3.2. "Sacred" music?

As mentioned in the Introduction to this Chapter, such concepts as "sacred" and "liturgical" music are highly problematic when discussing sixteenth-century church music, and need – at least – to be qualified. Indeed, the very idea that sacred and secular constitute two different and distinct spheres, sometimes in opposition to another, is relatively new: one could even argue that a truly Christian vision would conceive of no separation between sacred and secular, and that what pertains to the daily lives of human beings participates in the sacredness of creation.

In this Chapter, we will often read statements which seemingly testify to a clearly-felt distinction between sacred and secular music (for instance, when complaints were voiced against the presence of secular elements in worship); the point, however, is that great difficulties arise when we try and define what exactly was intended when such concerns were being expressed.

Different definitions of the sacred, as well as different definitions of sacred and liturgical music can lead to dramatically different perspectives[3]. In particular, as Fenlon rightfully points out, our view of the sixteenth-century concept of sacred music is largely shaped by the anathemas of churchmen against liturgical abuses (and this Chapter will discuss many of them). However, Fenlon cautions against taking them too easily at face-value: they should be contextualised as to their socio-religious belonging (in particular, whether they stemmed from a monastic or conciliar tradition[4]); some frequently-recurring words and expressions (such as the famous "lasciviousness") do testify to their writers' concern against wantonness, but do not clarify what was actually intended in musical terms.

Moreover, all complaints and speculations discussed below come from religious *men*, and none emanates from either women or people coming from lower social classes (i.e. people who were neither clergy nor educated laity). What if the "secular" and "lascivious" elements or tunes were actually the expression of the genuine piety of women and uneducated laypeople? Actually, a statement by Erasmus could support such an inference: in a writing of 1532, he explicitly rejects the "alluring songs which the whims of naive women or simple men have added to religious services"[5]; Federigo Borromeo, in turn, claims that "songs and motets" in the Italian vernacular were retained in liturgy out of con-

---

3 Prodi 2014, p. 271.
4 Fenlon 2009, p. 204.
5 In Miller 1966, p. 340: in the original Latin, he speaks of *"muliercularum aut simplicium hominum"*. Cf. Erasmus 1532, p. 247.

cern for the "rough and uneducated" people[6]. Could several of the complaints we will discuss actually mirror rejection or disdain towards alternative (or "lower") forms of devotion? Such questions are probably deemed to receive no answer (nor is it my intention to propose a classist or feminist interpretation of piety). I simply wish to offer a background against which to attempt an interpretation of the statements discussed below; and I hope that – by questioning both the possible attitudes behind them, and the definitions of the concepts adopted – a more complex and nuanced reading will become possible.

As concerns definitions, we face almost insurmountable problems. Is sacred music that performed in churches? This definition wrongfully excludes – for instance – music for pilgrimages and processions, as well as music for private devotion. Within this book, I have adopted the broadest possible definition of sacred music, meaning – perhaps simplistically – music on a religious text. Even here, however, difficulties arise: can polemical songs directed against competing confessions be considered as sacred music? Instinctively, one would answer no; however, they were in turn part of a religious culture and of the expression of religious feelings (which had a much more political and public aspect than they have nowadays).

And is liturgical music that performed during worships? Even here, the concept is not as straightforward as it might appear. For example, what is the status of motets within this definition? Motet texts do not normally belong either to the Ordinary or Proper of the Mass – although they could well be pastiches of Bible excerpts or adaptations of liturgical prayers. Herl offers a concise and somewhat surprising definition of the concept of liturgy before the modern age: official recognition of an element's status within liturgy was almost automatic, since "what was [liturgically] pure was what the cantors, under the supervision of the bishops, wrote in their liturgical books"[7]. Moreover, countering Janota's definition of vernacular singing in church as "extra-liturgical", Herl employs a convincing argument. Since – he maintains – the recitation of Mass texts by the priest (often in a low voice) and his offering of the Eucharist were the only necessary conditions for the validity of worship, then all other elements (including the choir's performance of Ordinary settings) were more or less "superfluous"[8]. Thus, it clearly appears that an attempt to give a definition of early-modern liturgy modelled on our own concept of worship is sadly doomed to failure.

---

[6] In Bizzarini 2012, pp. 157–158, my translation.
[7] Herl 2004, p. 31.
[8] Herl 2004, p. 32.

On the other hand, elements which we would define as clearly non-liturgical, and perhaps even secular, could find their place within the context of worship: as I will discuss at a greater length later (see § 3.2.3.), vernacular songs stemming from popular traditions, and even religious *contrafacta* of secular songs were common practice in many European churches, particularly at certain times of the liturgical year (such as Christmas[9]).

Indeed, attendance at the Mass qualified a "good Christian"; however, devotional forms that today's Catholicism considers advisable but non-compulsory (such as pilgrimages, litanies, processions etc.) were perhaps the most deeply-felt loci of early-modern devotion and faith.

Another important aspect to consider is that Catholic liturgy before Trent was by no means a monolithic set of homogeneous practices. Of course, the Roman Rite was the common heritage of the Western Church, and the basic elements of both Mass and Office were stable; moreover, many devotional practices were widespread throughout Europe. However, there was space for local traditions regarding other elements: sermons, songs, local plainchant variants and musical performance styles (e. g. presence of polyphony or instrumental accompaniment) could vary significantly from one place to another[10]; moreover, sequence and motet texts depended largely on local habits and requirements. There were also long-established regional traditions and rites, some of which – as we will see – were allowed to survive even after the Council of Trent.

### 3.2.1. Plainchant: the daily bread

Although we tend to identify sixteenth-century church music with the magnificent masterpieces of the polyphonic tradition and – albeit less frequently – with the success of the vernacular songs of the Reformation, the presence of plainchant in European churches was quantitatively overwhelming. Moreover, whereas rich polyphony could be satisfactorily performed only by the most accomplished choirs of the greatest ecclesiastical establishments, performance of plainchant was common to small parish churches and to imposing abbeys, to large cathedrals and to remote monasteries. Adalbert Roth has rightfully defined plainchant singing as the "daily bread"[11] of the Papal chapel; the same can be

---

**9** Wagner Oettinger 2001, p. 21.
**10** Herl 2004, p. 24.
**11** Roth 1998, p. 137.

said of practically all other religious institutions (including, incidentally, the Augustinian monastery where Luther lived his years as a monk).

Of course, the plainchant practised in the early sixteenth century was extremely different from that of the "Gregorian" era proper[12]. Indeed, as Baroffio points out, the creative flourishing of the first centuries of the second millennium was followed by a certain decay, as regards both transmission and performance practice. As he suggests, this was probably both the effect and the cause of a flattening process in plainchant practice[13]. Moreover, the use of plainchant as *cantus firmus* for polyphonic compositions had probably had some effect on the reception and practice of monodic plainchant as well (for example, as concerns rhythm and metre).

The contemporaneous Church was highly concerned with these observable problems, and the proper execution of plainchant is often recommended by churchmen of the time. The Council of Trent, as we will see later (§ 9.3.4. etc.), prompted a process of plainchant reform which would eventually produce the Medicean edition in the early seventeenth century. Just after the Council's conclusion, in 1564, Cardinal Federico Gonzaga of Mantua (1540–1565) observed that plainchant had to be perfectly known and performed in order not to become boring or ridiculous[14]; for Azpilcueta, a proper textual and musical performance of plainchant could counterbalance the presence of polyphony (which he did not think of too highly[15]).

Humanist concerns for the proper accentuation, syllabic quantities and pronunciation of Latin were also at stake (although many liturgical texts in Latin had been created in the Middle Ages and not during the allegedly golden age of Latin literature); moreover, notational issues and the force of habit had somehow crystallised the flexibility of earlier practices, their expressive variety and rhythmical fluidity.

The post-Tridentine Catholic Church would thus attempt to restore plainchant to its past splendour (although obviously this process would be led by contemporaneous taste and insufficient knowledge of earlier practices); in the following centuries, plainchant would gradually be assimilated to modern accompanied monody: thus, the feeling for its modal features would gradually become lost in favour of a homologation to the new tonal concept[16].

---

12 Sherr 1998, p. xi.
13 Baroffio 1995, p. 10.
14 Besutti 1993, p. 117.
15 Blackburn 2007, p. 87.
16 Lovato 1995, p. 61.

### 3.2.2. Latin-texted polyphony: resounding feast

Also in the case of polyphony, what we actually know and appreciate of sixteenth-century practice is little more than the famous tip of the iceberg. Through notation, part of the composed repertoire has been transmitted; however, it is the sound of improvised polyphony which is irrecoverably lost. Singing performance practices were more locally characterised than composed polyphony, as they were grounded on the habits and stereotypes upon which the singers of a particular tradition could draw for their performances.

Improvised polyphony, and particularly the English faburden tradition, was harshly criticised by Erasmus, who maintained that it "neither gives forth the pre-existing melody nor observes the harmonies of the art"[17]. Azpilcueta had a completely different opinion: for him, indeed, improvised counterpoint was actually a much better solution than composed polyphony, as it permitted a clearer perception of both the plainchant's original melodic line and of the words[18].

Among composed polyphonic sacred works, modern musicological historiography has given the place of honour to Masses, although perhaps the contemporaneous view was – paradoxically – rather different: as Sherr points out, "the masses and motets over which we enthuse were precisely the pieces that were considered expendable, constantly to be replaced"[19], as the analysis of the Papal choir's repertoire shows.

While fifteenth-century Mass composition had been almost dominated by the Franco-Flemish school, the situation was going to change and evolve in the following years. Within the first two decades of the sixteenth century, such composers as Jacob Obrecht (c.1457–1505), Heinrich Isaac, Pierre de la Rue and Josquin had passed away. Although the mark impressed by their generation on the polyphonic style of the era would continue exerting its influence throughout the sixteenth century, national schools started to show their distinguishing features, and the presence of new confessional boundaries fostered the emergence of local differences. Thus, Atlas identifies "a mainstream tradition", indebted to the fifteenth-century style of the Flanders, and "a group of parallel traditions that ran alongside it"[20].

---

[17] In Miller 1966, p. 339. Whether Erasmus was referring here to the Continental *fauxbourdon* or to the English faburden is open to debate: cf. Wegman 2005, pp. 109–110.
[18] Blackburn 2007, pp. 90–91.
[19] Sherr 1998, p. xi.
[20] Atlas 2006, p. 105. This section is indebted to Atlas' excellent synthesis of the evolution of Mass composition.

### 3.2.2.1. Making music for Mass

Between fifteenth- and sixteenth century, polyphonic Masses could draw upon a series of structural models and compositional techniques. The best-known practice (although by no means the only one) established some degree of unity among the different movements of the Mass Ordinary through the adoption of a recurring compositional element. Depending on which element was chosen and on how it was treated, three types of settings have been identified.

The first and oldest genre is the so-called "*cantus-firmus* Mass", where the composer's contrapuntal elaboration is grounded on a given melody, which could come from liturgical plainchant, secular tunes or could be an original creation by the composer; customarily, the *cantus firmus* was sung by the tenor in long notes.

What we now identify as "paraphrase Mass" employed the given melody in a rather different fashion: instead of being confined to the tenor, it was interwoven within the contrapuntal texture, sung by all voices in turn, and often decorated with more or less rich ornamentation.

The third type is the "parody Mass" (for which, as Ongaro suggests[21], the term "imitation Mass" would be better-suited), for which an entire pre-existing polyphonic composition (motet, madrigal, chanson...) provided the compositional material. This type of composition would enjoy the greatest success in the sixteenth century: in 1588, the theorist Pietro Ponzio discussed the technique of Mass composition in such terms as to show clearly that imitation Masses were by then the compositional style *par excellence*[22].

As Atlas rightfully points out, the value of unity given to Mass settings by the use of a recurring melodic or contrapuntal element was not the only reason for contemporaneous appreciation of this style. Indeed, as stated by German publisher Hans Ott (fl. 1530–1546), a criterion for the evaluation of a composer's work was the degree of variety he could insert within the polyphonic texture. The above-mentioned compositional techniques, therefore, allowed musicians to combine stylistic wholeness with the no less fundamental qualities of fantasy and novelty[23].

As we will see later in this Chapter (§ 3.3.3.), however, Bernardino Cirillo would express perplexity about such compositional techniques, since the use of a single element to create unity among Mass movements conditioned modal

---

21 Ongaro 2006, p. 71.
22 Ponzio 1588 (1959); cf. Ongaro 2006, p. 71.
23 Atlas 2006, pp. 101–102.

choices[24]: thus, the affective variety of the individual pieces could not be satisfactorily paralleled by the adoption of suitable modes.

### 3.2.2.2. Mostly motets

The other great genre of Latin-texted sacred music was the motet. According to the most commonly accepted definition of what was intended by this word in the sixteenth century, we may identify it as a Latin-texted polyphonic work, whose status as a liturgical or devotional composition is open to debate (and constitutes a paramount example of the limits in our understanding of sixteenth-century "liturgy").

Motet texts were actually neither properly liturgical nor non-liturgical: indeed, they were often excerpted from the Proper elements of Catholic worship. However, the actual musical performance of a motet was seemingly unconnected to the original placement of the liturgical element that had inspired the compilation of its text.

Motets could be sung both during the Mass and on other occasions (for example during the Offices, during devotional practices, but also in rather secular contexts). As shown by Crook in a recent article[25], the choice and performance of motets often represented a purposeful appropriation of and an exegetical commentary on Scriptural readings; though motets could be written for a particular liturgical moment (and this could be explicitly stated in the source), this did not prevent their use in other, and unspecified, circumstances. This was far from implying, however, that motets could be chosen carelessly: there is evidence showing that church musicians selected works with spiritual or exegetical connections to the liturgical readings. Printed motet collections from the beginning of the sixteenth century were frequently organised by broad religious subjects, thus resembling devotional books; after mid-century, their structure mirrored the liturgical cycle of the Church year.

The greater freedom of motet-writing in comparison with the fixed texts for Mass Ordinaries was paralleled by a more intensely expressive style: whereas Masses often showed emotional restraint and sobriety, motets were more indebted to humanist theories on word/tone relationships. For example, intelligibility issues were less important in Mass settings than in motets, since the immutability of the Ordinary and its constant repetition allowed listeners to guess those words they could not really understand in the intertwining of voices and imita-

---

**24** Cf. *Lettere volgari* 1564, fol. 116ᵛ.
**25** Crook 2015.

tions. Moreover, motet texts often received a more expressive treatment, due both to their frequently intense affective content, and to the (relative) novelty and freshness of inspiration they could offer to composers in comparison with the innumerable versions of the Ordinary[26].

The use of plainchant in motet composition paralleled that in Mass settings, although differences in the stylistic treatment are observable here too. Cummings suggests an analogy between the use of Gregorian models in motets and the Renaissance idea of *inventio,* inasmuch as a more direct and causal relationship with the plainchant original is found in Masses, whereas in motets the Gregorian melody inspires more flexible "resonances"[27].

Latin-texted polyphony also included Psalms and Canticles for the Office (with particular focus on Vesper settings, where the prescribed Gospel canticle was the *Magnificat*), as well as the antiphons to the Virgin Mary with which the liturgical day was normally concluded. Among these, the *Salve Regina* was also included in special services which were habitually performed on Saturday evenings.

Moreover, the fascinating liturgy of the Holy Week required musical settings of the Scriptural *Lamentations* for the *Tenebræ*[28]. The striking expressive power of these Bible texts and the deeply impressive context for their performance were likely to foster touching musical renditions.

### 3.2.3. Praying in music

Devotion in music took a variety of forms, from those of domestic and individual piety to the spectacular processions which could involve entire cities, or to the rites of confraternities, which often accomplished both a genuinely spiritual and a social role. *Lauda* singing was very popular in Italy as an expression of deep religious feelings, especially in connection with spiritual movements like those encouraged and promoted by Franciscan and Dominican friars.

Indeed, several currents of religious reformation and lay spirituality before the sixteenth century had in common both a critical attitude towards elaborate polyphonic music and the fostering of vernacular singing of spiritual texts: among the leaders of such movements we may recall the already-mentioned Dominican friar Girolamo Savonarola, who balanced his harsh criticism of poly-

---

26 Cf. Atlas 2006, p. 105.
27 Cummings 2006, p. 140.
28 Cf. O'Regan 2009, p. 217, to which this summary is indebted.

phony with his approval of both Latin plainchant and *lauda* singing[29] (which would become a characterising feature of his followers, the *piagnoni*); similarly, the disciples of Jan Hus, while rejecting polyphony, did however create a rich heritage of vernacular songs, several of which were later collected within the first Lutheran hymnals.

Within the field of devotional practices, moreover, public performances of *sacre rappresentazioni* were highly musical in turn, and their settings were likely to exploit the entire emotional palette of the era.

The musical expression of private devotion was represented by spiritual madrigals, *laude* and *canzonette* in Italy, by carols in England, and by spiritual songs in virtually all European languages. As Erasmus reports, the Flemish Beguines used to sing vernacular Psalms and hymns already in the 1480s[30]. The success of such devotional works, particularly within the Italian context, influenced the elaboration and experimentation of new compositional styles and aesthetics. Indeed, as we have seen in Chapter Two (§ 2.3.7. etc.), a combination of several cultural reasons was contributing to the development of vocal music characterised by simplicity and efficacy in the delivery of the text. These features appeared clearly in devotional works such as those listed above, and would condition in turn the elaboration of a vernacular repertory for the Evangelical Churches[31].

It should be said, however, that this vernacular and popular repertoire was not always doctrinally sound and theologically acceptable. Bartolomeo Fernandes (1514–1590), the Catholic Archbishop of Braga, in Portugal, was stunned when members of his flock, in a remote rural region, sang these words to greet him: "Blessed be the Holy Trinity, the sister of Our Lady"[32]. Though the clergyman decided to start an intensive doctrinal education in the area, at first he was careful not to display his shock, out of consideration for the good faith of the peasants.

Latin hymns were part of the Office, from where they could easily migrate to private devotion (also in vernacular translations). Some of these translations

---

**29** Cf. Macey 1998, pp. 91–98.
**30** Reported in Forney 2010, p. 99.
**31** Cf. Rees 2006, p. 341.
**32** Cacegas and Sousa 1619, p. 119, my translation. Cf. Kreuzer 1973, pp. 126–127. There may be a cultural reason for this unorthodox position. As is known, the Iberian Peninsula was deeply influenced by the Muslim culture; and it seems that certain statements in the Qur'ān support the idea that the Christian Trinity is made of Father, Son and the Virgin Mary. Possibly, this distorted view of the Christian teachings came to the early Muslims from their knowledge of a minor heretical sect in Arabia, the Collyridians, who worshipped Mary as a goddess. Cf. Qur'ān, Surah 5, Ayat 116 (available online at https://quran.com/5:116); Hulmes 2004; Cameron 2004.

were fostered by humanist currents: an early example of such attempts is *Der Sequentz Verbum bonum* (c.1496) by Sebastian Brant[33] (c.1458–1521). However, not all of these translations mirrored the metric scheme of the Latin original[34], and consequently it was impossible to sing them on the original tune and without adaptations: thus, as Leaver points out[35], they were more likely to be read from primers within the context of home devotion, whereas in public ceremonies they could be sung (either in Latin or in adapted vernacular versions), alongside carols. In particular, the mixture of Latin with German vernacular appears to be a distinguishing feature of several Christmas songs originating in the pre-Reformation German-speaking world: such carols would enjoy an enduring success among Lutherans and Catholics alike, regardless of confessional belongings.

A similar combination of Latin with German characterised a particular musical realisation for another of the major feasts of the liturgical year: at Easter, within a tradition dating from several centuries already, the entire congregation seemingly participated in a communal singing of *Christ ist erstanden*. This German hymn, inspired by the Latin sequence *Victimæ paschali*, was sung in combination with the Latin original, and the same practice was applied to the Pentecost sequence *Veni Sancte Spiritus*[36].

The tradition of devotional singing in German is attested since the twelfth century: *Leisen* were sung during processions and pilgrimages, and there was a rich heritage of religious songs in the vernacular, which included the penitential *Geisslerlieder* as well as the spiritual output of the Master Singers or the Crusaders[37], together with sacred *contrafacta* of secular songs[38].

On the basis of the extant sources, the debate as to how, when and how much the congregation joined in singing vernacular songs in pre-Reformation Germany is still wide open. It should be said that, in some instances at least, it is only too clear that some historians' viewpoint leads them to choose selectively among the available sources depending on the confessional thesis they wish to demonstrate. In particular, those who would like to see Lutheran singing as a revolution in the history of music will downplay the role of German vernacular singing in the pre-Reformation Church, either denying its performance during worship or challenging lay participation in singing. As will be discussed in Chapter Four (§ 4.3.1.2.–3.), these two features (i.e. the congregation's involve-

---

[33] Kim 2005, p. 183.
[34] White 2011, p. 21.
[35] Leaver 1991, pp. 55–57.
[36] Herl 2004, p. 28.
[37] Cf. Blume 1975, p. 19.
[38] Wagner Oettinger 2001, p. 92.

ment and the very presence of vernacular songs in liturgical contexts) will certainly become distinguishing features of Lutheran singing, but this does not necessarily imply that they were not practised, at least locally, before the Reformation. On the other side, those wishing to demonstrate that Luther did not bring any substantial novelty to liturgical vernacular and congregational singing adduce evidence testifying to the presence of these elements in Catholic worship.

Indeed, it is possible to question, at least in some instances, not only the congregational participation, but the very presence of vernacular singing in church, notwithstanding the numerous written and printed sources of pre-Reformation German hymns[39]: moreover, doubts arise as to the actual spread of these songs[40]. As Brown argues, the wording of some witnesses from the early Reformation era seems to suggest that the introduction of Lutheran congregational singing in the vernacular was considered to be an innovation as radical as some of the most spectacular Lutheran reforms[41].

On the other hand, it is possible to maintain – on the basis of visitation reports – that, in Bavaria, vernacular psalmody and songs were by no means exceptional[42]. Indeed, hymn-singing was integral to the *Kanzeldienst* ("pulpit service"), a form of worship in the vernacular which took place on Sunday morning in between the two main services[43]; singing of German hymns during worship was encouraged in some Catholic dioceses[44]. There are also interesting witnesses of vernacular singing in German monasteries[45], and congregational participation can be argued for (even claiming, with Herl, that "German songs occupied a key role in the liturgy"[46]). Moreover, the *Apology* of the Augsburg Confession, written in 1531 by Justus Jonas (1493–1555) and Philipp Melanchthon, clearly states that congregational singing in the vernacular "has always been held in esteem in the churches. For although in some places more and in some places fewer German songs are sung, still in all churches the people have sung in German; and so it isn't all that new"[47].

Indeed, the complexity of the situation as regards congregational singing of German hymns in the vernacular cannot be accounted for here and should not

---

[39] Cf. Herl 2004, p. 27.
[40] Wagner Oettinger 2001, p. 90.
[41] Brown 2008, p. 227.
[42] Fisher 2014, p. 16.
[43] Herl 2004, p. 27.
[44] Herl 2004, p. 31.
[45] Cf. Brown 2008, p. 227.
[46] Herl 2004, pp. 31–32.
[47] Quoted in and translated by Herl 2004, p. 33. Cf. Brown 2008, p. 226. Cf. *Apology* 24.3–5 (*BSLK*, p. 616; *BC*, p. 258).

be simplistically reduced to a homogeneity it did not have. Nevertheless, we may probably endorse Herl's summary: whereas the merit of introducing vernacular singing in church cannot be ascribed to Luther[48], he did modify its role radically, by making it an essential component of worship "rather than an extra item of little importance"[49].

## 3.3. Crisis, critics and criticalities

In the second part of this Chapter, after the short overview of the principal forms of sacred music in the early sixteenth century, I will focus on the problematic issues pointed out by writers of the era. Such issues will be discussed by dividing them into two broad areas, i.e. those relating to the relationship between text and music and those referring to performance practice and morality.

Unavoidably, some degree of overlapping in the discussion of these aspects will occur, both as concerns source quotation and the similarity of subjects (and I apologise with the reader for this); however, I decided to risk redundancy in order to hopefully achieve greater clarity. Indeed, in my opinion, several common misunderstandings of sixteenth-century thought on religious music have occurred due to either superficial reading or to the projection onto the sources of prejudices or *a-posteriori* interpretations. Although I cannot claim my own interpretations to be free from such stains, I hope that the detailed discussion of all aspects involved may help readers to formulate their own judgements, by taking into account the complexity of a situation which cannot be simplistically reduced to one-word slogans.

I wish also to add that some of the statements I will quote postdate the Protestant Reformations, and a few of them the Council of Trent too. However, since my goal here is to attempt a reconstruction and interpretation of the *mentality* of the era, of what was implied by some particular terms, and of what was felt as problematic or in need of reform, I think that a perfect chronological coincidence is not indispensable, and can be renounced in favour of what slightly-later witnesses can teach us.

---

**48** Wagner Oettinger 2001, p. 90.
**49** Herl 2004, p. 30.

## 3.3.1. Serving the Word?

As I argued in Chapter Two (§ 2.3.7. etc.), concerns with textual issues were typical of humanist culture and would greatly influence the musical thought of the sixteenth century. Summarising briefly some of the aspects I discussed there, humanist study of classical sources fostered questions on where music's power to move came from. For several theorists, it was caused by the rhetoric combination of a properly written text and of its efficacious delivery through music[50]. This view was clearly maintained by Azpilcueta, who condemned those singers who do not "explain" the text and believe that sounds have in themselves the capacity to move. As Blackburn correctly points out, the greatest difference between Azpilcueta and John XXII's Decretal lay precisely in the importance given to the delivery of the text[51]. Thus, words had primacy over purely musical issues; rhythmic and melodic shapes should parallel and enhance those of the speech[52]; in Pierre Colin's view, the very heart of the sentence should be transmitted by music to the spirit of the listeners[53].

For instance, such views found their musical realisation in Adrian Willaert's works written after 1530 and issued as *Musica nova* in 1559: here, virtually all compositional elements were defined on the basis of the requirements of the text[54].

### 3.3.1.1. Enrapturing melismas

As concerns plainchant performance, two main issues were at stake: from the one side, accentuation; from the other, problems posed by melismatic singing.

I have already mentioned, in passing, that humanist concerns for proper metric interpretation of the Latin language and for correct pronunciation and delivery were applied to plainchant, with the support of such theorists as Zarlino. Erasmus had heavily censored the style of plainchant performance that was customary at his time: in order to sing together and to avoid what was perceived as a disordered performance, singers disregarded any difference between long and short vowels. Although this style was appreciated by the uncultivated, it was – in his view – "not saying but baying"[55].

---

50 Cf. Koenigsberger 1986, pp. 182–183 and 187; Mischiati 1995, p. 20; Tomlinson 2006, p. 15.
51 Cf. Blackburn 2007, pp. 90–92.
52 Haar 2006, p. 27.
53 Cf. quotation in Rainoldi 2000, p. 335.
54 Haar 2006, p. 30.
55 Cf. in Kim 2005, respectively pp. 157–158 and p. 269.

The medieval features of plainchant (or, rather, what had been transmitted of Medieval plainchant into the Early Modern era) started to be perceived as barbaric, since they seemingly neglected prosodic rules: thus, the anachronistic application of classical quantitative prosody to contemporaneous plainchant fostered the reform we will analyse in Chapter Nine[56] (§ 9.3.4.).

As concerns melismatic chant, from the one side its vocalisations might represent an instance of the *jubilus* recommended by St Augustine as an almost-ecstatic way of exulting in God (cf. Chapter Two: § 2.3.4.). From the other, it was seen as problematic both ethically and as regards the text. Zarlino claimed that plainchant had to be pruned from melismas in order to enhance its prosodic delivery:

> It would be so praiseworthy and so easy to correct [the barbarisms of plainchant]: through minimal changes, the melody could be adjusted, without losing its original form, since it only consists of the connection of many notes, put under short syllables. With no purpose, they [the notes] make them [the syllables] long, when a single note would suffice[57].

As mentioned in Chapter Two (§ 2.3.7.2.), moreover, the ideal of one-note-one-syllable was gathering a high appreciation throughout Europe, at least among humanist-inspired theorists and composers, both in monody and in homophonic part-writing. For them, melismatic passages prevented proper rhythmic relations between long and short syllables, and could insert so many notes between two consecutive syllables that the meaning of the sentence was hardly retained. Besides this, in my opinion, there was also a moral issue, similar in focus to what I proposed in Chapter Two as regards the symbolic value of polyphony (§ 2.4.3.). Melismas and *jubilus* were powerful symbols of joy and exultation; thus, to indulge in this quasi-ecstatic enjoyment of beauty (which might or might not foster a properly religious praise) could be seen as a moral danger: words of warning in this sense had been voiced already by John of Salisbury (c.1120–1180), who pointed out the risks of music's power over those "feminine types who revel in great melody"[58]. It is in this sense that I suggest a possible interpretation of the words on plainchant of Pope Gregory XIII (see § 9.3.4.), where he spoke of "superfluities" in the performance of plainchant, resulting from "the ineptitude, the negligence, even the malice of composers, scribes and printers alike"[59]. The

---

56 Cf. Lovato 1995, pp. 57–58; Haar 2006, p. 27
57 Zarlino 1558, Part IV, p. 340 – my translation.
58 John of Salisbury 1993, pp. 48–49. In Leach 2009, p. 30.
59 Latin text in Molitor 1901, vol. I, pp. 297–298; English translation in Weiss and Taruskin 2008, p. 117.

Pope's tirade against ineptitude and negligence might simply refer to incorrect accentuation (although his mention of the "superfluities" would remain odd here); "malice", however, makes no sense unless he was condemning the proliferation of melismas as a form of musical intoxication that had not to be indulged in.

In support of my interpretation comes another quote, taken from a 1636 treatise by Charles Butler: "In a Psalm or other pious Canticle [...] the notes [must] answer the number of the syllables [since] this moveth sobriety, prudence, modesty and godliness"[60]. Obviously the musical context of the two statements was radically different, but what I would like to point out is that both seemingly associated syllabic setting with moral restraint.

### 3.3.1.2. A free rein for Sequences
Among the problematic issues of the text/music relationship, one did not concern the delivery of the text, but rather its very nature: sequence texts were among the most controversial aspects in the liturgy of the era.

Since their origin as extensions of the Alleluia, sequences had been both an exegesis of and a prayerful framework for the Gospel; characterised since the eleventh/twelfth century by their poetic structure, they offered an almost boundless creative space to poets and musicians alike. As one might expect, what had initially been conceived as a musical contemplation of the Word soon indulged to purely aesthetic criteria; moreover, for a kind of a legislative void in liturgical matters, tropes and sequences did not undergo the same supervision performed by Church authorities over other elements of the Catholic liturgy.

Thus, as Baroffio suggests, sequences were often selected (and copied) with virtually no control of the text, sometimes multiplying transmission errors until the original text became unrecognisable or incomprehensible, and sometimes selecting the texts only on the basis of their musicality[61].

Sequences proliferated both in number and in length, up to the gigantic figure of several thousands, and sometimes took so long a time for their performance that other fundamental sections of the worship had to be accordingly shortened (cf. § 2.3.9. for Erasmus' criticism of this abuse). In this case, therefore, complaints about church music focused on the role of items performed during worship and on the selection of their texts, which often seemed to be determined by musical – rather than by liturgical – reasons.

---

60 Butler 1636, p. 96.
61 Baroffio 1995, p. 10.

### 3.3.1.3. Hearing the unsaid

A related issue concerns the *alternatim* practice and the use of organs. The habit of presenting longer textual sections of the Mass or the Office antiphonally (i.e. in alternation among two choirs) was extremely old, offering – as it did – both a greater sonic variety to worship, and a possibility for singers to share the strain of long performances. Organ *alternatim* refers to the widespread practice of substituting organ playing for one of the two choirs – with the obvious side-effect that half the text would not be actually sung. At first, however, organs seemingly played the same melodies that should have been performed by the corresponding choir: thus, music could help listeners to remember and imagine the omitted words. Then, some improvisatory elements and embellishment were added, until – eventually – either the original melody was unrecognisable, or it was simply replaced with a totally unrelated work. In some instances, as the sources seemingly attest, secular or even dance music could be played in alternation with the liturgical versicles. In other cases, only the *incipit* of a liturgical item was actually sung, and the organ played most of the remainder; as said before, moreover, motets or vernacular songs could also be performed instead of the prescribed element[62].

Not only (as Cardinals Cervini and Sirleto observed, in the anecdote reported in § 2.4.2.), dance music would do little to enhance the congregation's concentration: the respite granted to singers by *alternatim* practice could easily become an occasion for relaxing manners together with vocal cords. Azpilcueta (possibly referring to choirboys) inveighed against singers who leave their places and speak, joke and laugh together during organ playing[63] and so did Erasmus[64], who also censored a related practice. In Erasmus' words,

> In many churches, a responsory is sung instead of the Introit of the Mass. The Psalm which is usually sung in its entirety is abbreviated. Before the Gospel unlearned prosas are sometimes sung and the Creed is moved forward. An extended Preface is sung before the Canon of the Mass, and the *Sanctus* is sung during the consecration. At the elevation a song imploring the help of the Blessed Virgin or Saint Roch is heard, and the Lord's Prayer is suppressed[65].

Erasmus, thus, condemned the improper shortening of liturgical items, their relocation in inappropriate moments and the distraction caused by less important devotions competing with the highpoints of the Eucharist. (Incidentally: al-

---

62 Herl 2004, pp. 24–25.
63 De Azpilcueta 1578, p. 251. See also Blackburn 2007, p. 90.
64 Kim 2005, p. 150.
65 In Miller 1966, p. 337.

though it is difficult not to share Erasmus' point here, his criticism is once more directed, at least in part, against particularly cherished devotions of the uneducated people. Whereas other reformers will direct their darts against clerical abuses, his references to the "unlearned prosas" and to St Roch, who was popularly invoked against the plague, are rather meaningful).

As mentioned in § 2.3.6., shortenings and truncations of liturgical items had officially been stigmatised by the Council of Basel, but, seemingly, with no revolutionary results: such practices would offer great scope for the Protestant Reformers' critique of Catholic worship[66].

Whilst in one church too many words were omitted, in another there was the contrary problem: the requirements of polyphonic composition and imitation, as well of aesthetic taste and style, fostered the creation of Ordinary settings where the liturgical words were constantly reiterated. When the value of musical and polyphonic beauty as a symbol for transcendence began to be less clearly felt (cf. § 2.4.3.), the seemingly endless repetition of words which could have been pronounced just once (or even omitted) was condemned as redundant. Thus, from the one side the Synod of Constance (1567) forbade the use of organ *alternatim* and complex polyphony for the delivery of the Creed; from the other, it recommended that the words should be clearly understood but not repeated[67].

### 3.3.1.4. "*Intelligo ut credam*": the importance of understanding

This brings us to the issue of intelligibility, which has become a keyword in the musicological debates on the religious Reformations of the sixteenth century, particularly as concerns the Catholic Church and the Council of Trent. Indeed, in consideration of what we have observed about the humanist concern with delivery, and on the basis of abundant verbal and musical evidence, intelligibility was indeed a much-debated topic and a crucial aesthetic matter in the sixteenth century. However, as I hope to show in the remainder of this book, the theological, aesthetic, moral, cultural and stylistic issues at stake were so numerous and complex that the concept of intelligibility cannot be held accountable for all of them.

As we have seen in this very section, for example and paradoxically, no intelligibility issue could exist when the text was not even sung or pronounced. Moreover, the idea that the laity should clearly hear the liturgical words in order to participate actively and consciously in worship was (at best) limited

---

66 Blume 1975, p. 107.
67 *CG* 7, p. 487.

to some progressive churchmen or situations. The presence of a congregation was not indispensable for a Eucharistic worship to be valid; nor was it important for the lay members of the congregation to hear what was said at the altar, as long as they were physically present in church (although this very presence was expendable during considerable portions of the official cult). Furthermore, as mentioned earlier (§ 3.2.2.2.), the fixed parts of the Mass (such as the Ordinary) were so commonly performed and heard, that they constituted no novelty for the listeners; and, perhaps most important of all, since the vast majority of church-goers did not understand Latin, the problem of actually hearing it was of minor importance.

Notwithstanding these provisos, there were indeed numerous grievances against unintelligibility, in particular as regards the most complex polyphonic architectures. Erasmus used no euphemisms: "Modern church music is so constructed", he wrote, "that the congregation cannot hear one distinct word"[68]. Savonarola had the same opinion: "nothing can be understood of what is *said*. Leave alone *figured songs* and sing the plainchant commanded by the Church"[69] (note the use of the verb "to say" in contrast with polyphony).

Stephen Gardiner (1497–1555) reported of a *Magnificat* performance, sung by schoolboys with organ accompaniment, during which, in his words, "I doubt not but God understood them [...] and we could much less mark their words, other than [when they] began the verse and ended it"[70]. Intelligibility problems in this case might or might not be caused by polyphony (Gardiner's boys might simply have sung badly an accompanied plainchant setting). Instead, Palestrina used precise technical terms when writing to Duke Guglielmo Gonzaga (1538–1587): "Since the imitations cause the parts to move in this way, it seems to me that because of the dense interweaving of the imitations, the words are somewhat obscured to the listeners, who do not enjoy them as in ordinary music"[71]. Although the context of Palestrina's statements should be taken into account (he was criticising a composition by his patron), he clearly attributed the responsibility for the text's limited intelligibility to imitations.

---

[68] Cit. in Le Huray 2008, p. 11.
[69] Savonarola 1971, vol. 1, p. 222 (sermon of 5.3.1496), my translation and my emphasis.
[70] Gardiner 1933, p. 488.
[71] Letter of March 3rd, 1570: Mantova, Archivio di Stato, Autografi (Anni 1439–1876), busta 6, cc. 403–404; Mantova Capitale Europea dello Spettacolo, sig. C-2979; translated in Lockwood 1975, p. 25. See also Jeppesen 1953; Besutti 1991.

It is likely that Herbenus too was referring to exaggerated imitations (although his *refractio* has been understood by Wegman[72] as meaning "division", thus perhaps "diminution"), when he wrote:

> So what are your voice refractions to me, when you warble in such a way that I can recognize neither a word nor even one syllable, nor the value of composition? [...] For how will you think your eyes have been gratified if someone who is going to show you some beautiful picture dazzles you all of a sudden, before you can fix your gaze on it, with many multicoloured paintings? I should think that you would be annoyed rather than delighted, because you could render no certain judgment about it. Now, what I say here about the sense of vision I could say about all others as well[73].

Of course, however, proper delivery (and therefore a better intelligibility) of a text can become even more difficult when speakers themselves do not understand what they are reading. Humanistic concerns on pedagogy and education brought out the cultural problem afflicting several members of the clergy. Sometimes even the presiding priest (especially in rural parishes[74]) seemed not to understand the Latin words of liturgy; still more frequently, choristers and singers seemed completely unaware of the meaning of the text.

In another fragment from the excerpt cited before, Stephen Gardiner claimed: "Of the number that sang I dare say a great many understood not what they sang"[75]; similarly, the preface to Loersfeld's Erfurt *Enchiridion* of 1524 asserts that many choristers, not understanding what they sing, damage both themselves and the congregation[76].

Once more, Erasmus had his own opinion on the subject: "They chant nowadays in our churches in what is an unknown tongue and nothing else. [...] The choristers themselves do not understand what they are singing, yet according to priests and monks it constitutes the whole of religion. Why will they not listen to St Paul?"[77]. Indeed, St Paul discussed at length on linguistic issues (referring to the pros and cons of publicly displaying the gift of tongues) in his First Letter to the Corinthians (1 Corinthians 12–14), and in particular he stated: "For if I pray in a tongue, my spirit prays, but my mind is unproductive" (1 Corinthians

---

72 Wegman 2005, p. 176.
73 Herbenus 1957, pp. 58–59; translation quoted (with modifications) from Wegman 2005, pp. 175–176.
74 Besutti 1993, p. 118.
75 Gardiner 1933, p. 488.
76 Loersfeld 1524; cf. Herl 2004, p. 95.
77 Cit. in Le Huray 2008, p. 11.

14:14). As we will see in the following Chapters, those advocating vernacular worship would often base their arguments on such Scriptural quotes.

As regards the laity, the problem was still more complex, since the very first issue was (as mentioned above: cf. § 2.3.5. etc.) whether they *should* understand or not what is said. I will discuss this aspect in greater detail in Chapter Four (§ 4.2.3.1.), since it raises important theological questions. For now, suffice it to say that several churchmen (many of whom were Catholics) advocated vernacular liturgies. For example, in 1513 (i.e. during the Lateran Council), a memorandum called *Libellus ad Leonem* was sent to Pope Leo X by two Camaldolese monks coming from the Venetian elite, namely Tommaso (Paolo) Giustinian (1476–1528) and Vincenzo (Pietro) Quirini (also known as Querini, 1478–1514). In this work, references to the history and tradition of the early Church were used in support of the adoption of vernacular worships understandable by laypeople[78].

We may also recall that, although he did not support the adoption of vernacular for the entire worship, Federigo Borromeo did admit it for "songs and motets" in church, asserting that they benefited the uneducated laity[79].

If the issue at stake here was the language of worship, for others the problem was how music prevented the perception of words, in whatever language they might be sung: among them were Heinrich Cornelius Agrippa von Nettesheim[80], Gregory Martin (who, as seen in § 2.3.7.2., praised the Papal choir's neat pronunciation[81]), Pierre Colin (who proudly claimed that the sobriety of his style permitted to hear not only the words, but the full sentences[82]), and no less an authority than Pope Marcellus, in an incident I will discuss in Chapter Eight[83] (§ 8.2.6.).

Summarising, intelligibility problems could be determined by compositional features (abundant imitations or too numerous voices), by linguistic and cultural problems, and by faulty performance; some of them, as I will discuss now, were seen as inherently ethical in the moral thought of the era.

---

**78** Rainoldi 2000, p. 331; Pecklers and Ostdiek 2011, pp. 48–49.
**79** Bizzarini 2012, pp. 157–158.
**80** Kim 2005, p. 153.
**81** In Sherr 1994, p. 607.
**82** Freedman 2006, pp. 165–166.
**83** Cf. Lockwood 1975, p. 18.

## 3.3.2. The morals of music

The concept of music in terms of moral theology rather than of aesthetic spirituality was indeed deeply rooted in the history of Christian thought. Ferguson[84] maintains that this approach characterised the writings on music of the Church Fathers: given the indebtedness of several sixteenth-century religious thinkers to Patristic tradition, this viewpoint was likely to be adopted by many of them. Moreover, the very fact that we often turn to Azpilcueta's treatises on confession for the discussion of musical issues testifies to a moral concern with music which was intensely felt at the time[85].

Although moral issues are practical by their very nature, I will divide them into theory and practice on musical grounds, meaning by this distinction that I will first discuss moral issues concerning the theory of music, and later those about its practice.

### 3.3.2.1. Lady Music

The first theoretical issue will be mentioned here only in passing, since I have discussed it already in Chapter Two: it regards the impact of modal choices on morality (§ 2.3.3.). For instance, Cirillo stated that the lack of moral/affective results effected by contemporaneous music clearly demonstrated their composers' disregard for modal theory.

In contrast with the succinct summary of this first issue, I will dedicate more attention to the second one, which will recur in a modified fashion among the practical aspects as well, and which has already been briefly referred to in Chapter Two (§ 2.4.4.). How did music relate to sexuality? How did it mirror the relationships between men and women, and the concept they had of each other in the sixteenth century and before?

Once more, I wish to clarify that I do not personally adhere to interpretations of history as an opposition and competition between femininity and masculinity (in my opinion, the best results in the history of humankind are obtained within societies where their complementary qualities concur to establishing a respectful alliance).

However, the overwhelming presence of this topic in the contemporaneous debate requires a detailed treatment. Here I will discuss the connection between

---

[84] Ferguson 1993, p. 275.
[85] Cf. Blackburn 2007, p. 86.

speculation on music and the risk of lasciviousness, whereas later (§ 3.3.2.2.–3.) I will consider how the practice of music could become morally dangerous.

It might be argued that the word "lascivious" is one of the most frequently associated to criticism of music or limitations to its use in the period under discussion[86]. For men, it represented a double risk: from the one side, being "lascivious" meant indulging in sexual pleasure, carnal imagination and licentious fantasies; from the other, it might imply a degradation of their virility into effeminacy. As Gibson convincingly summarises,

> Effeminacy was not only a state associated with women; it was also commonly understood as the natural state of children. It was a condition that boys had to overcome to achieve the social status of adult manhood, but it was also a state to which men were always in constant danger of reverting without rigid self-control and the application of reason[87].

Adult men were deemed superior to women (cf. the Aristotelian view of women as "incomplete men"[88], which had influenced the medieval concept of womanhood[89]), especially by virtue of an allegedly higher rational power[90]: the action of music on feelings and emotions (i.e. on supposedly irrational passions) obviously represented a menace to this status.

As Dean maintains, to over-indulge in music and to be moved to tears by it could be seen as a sign of "a weak moral fibre", and an excessive appreciation of music "was a species of *luxuria*, or lasciviousness"[91].

Thus, for men, lasciviousness proper implied two seemingly contradictory risks: either to indulge too much in the appreciation of women, or to lose male qualities and become too similar to them[92]. On the other hand, within this perspective, for women lasciviousness coincided with the danger of behaving unchastely.

Starting with women, then, we can make a passing reference to a statement by Pietro Aretino (1492–1556), who wrote in 1537: "the knowledge of playing instruments, of singing, and of writing poetry, on the part of women, is the very

---

[86] Leach rightfully points out that *lasciva* might also be mean simply "merry" and "playful", but that it was mostly used in its sexual implications by music theorists: Leach 2006, p. 6.
[87] Gibson 2009, p. 42.
[88] Cf. Aristotle, *On the generation of animals*, 767b 7–9 (Aristotle 1943, pp. 400–403); 737a 26–31 ("the female is, as it were, a deformed male": pp. 174–175) etc.
[89] Cf. Leach 2006, p. 2.
[90] Leach 2009, p. 22.
[91] Dean 1997, p. 623.
[92] Cf. Leach 2006, p. 5.

key which opens the doors to their modesty"[93]. It is likely that Aretino was here under the influence of the Church Fathers: for instance, St Jerome had maintained that properly educated Christian girls should ignore what musical instruments are[94]. It should be pointed out, however, that statements such as that by Aretino were counterbalanced in that same period by those of other thinkers who believed in the educational and moral value of music (see in particular § 11.4.4.).

The reader will not be surprised to find that Erasmus had something to say on this point as well:

> It is customary now among some nations to compose every year new songs which young girls study assiduously. The subject matter of the songs is usually the following: a husband deceived by his wife, or a daughter guarded in vain by her parents; or a clandestine affair of lovers. These things are presented as if they were wholesome deeds, and a successful act of profligacy is applauded[95].

In this case, it will be noted, it is not music *in se* which is dangerous for the girls' chastity, but rather the immoral teaching it conveys through its licentious words.

On the other hand, Cardinal Pietro Bembo wrote about his daughter in these terms in a letter of 1541:

> Since Elena asked me licence to learn to play the clavichord, tell her on my behalf, that I do not think that wishing to learn an instrument is suitable for an honourable woman of noble spirit, and that I do not like at all that she wastes her time in this, just as I did not like that my sister Antonia could play. [...] Indeed, no woman who does not devote herself entirely to practice will play well. To play without being able to do that well is little pleasing and even less praiseworthy. To play well and disregard other more laudable exercises is even more execrable. If she will spend that time in literary studies, she will be praised much more, and her proficiency in the letters will be appreciated much more than that in playing[96].

In this case, Bembo is not against women's cultural achievements in other fields, but considers music as a time-consuming and futile activity: as I will argue later (§ 3.3.2.6.), this opinion sometimes applied to men's music as well.

In Chapter Two (§ 2.4.4.), I have tentatively suggested that a certain analogy can be observed in the respective roles of women and of polyphonic music as regards men's experience of sanctity and Grace. Both, I proposed, could either be seen as vehicles of God's love or potentially sinful distractions from the

---

[93] In Forney 2010, p. 85.
[94] *PL* 22, col. 874. Cf. Viladesau 2000, pp. 15–16.
[95] Forney 2010, p. 104.
[96] In Carrer 1845, pp. 369–370, my translation.

path of holiness: although I personally favour the former view, here we will discuss the latter, with the support of a wide selection of sources.

The connection between womanhood and music is not as far-fetched as it might seem at first: Gibson[97] points out that most allegoric depictions of music (both visual and literary) represented it as a female figure: we will soon encounter Luther's poem on *Frau Musika*, which seems a case in point. Of course, as Austern reminds us, the very word *musica* was feminine in Latin and in several modern European languages: an interesting example of this association in visual art (among the many possible) is the *Allegory of Music* (c.1529) by Hans Baldung "Grien" (c.1484–1545). Moreover, music indicated the art of the Muses, who were female goddesses; however, this connection might also suggest that both women and music could move the affects and passions of men. The Neo-Platonist philosopher Marsilio Ficino, discussing the influence of planets and stars on human behaviour, maintained that songs which are "voluptuous with wantonness and softness" are linked with the erotic power of the planet Venus[98].

### 3.3.2.2. Soft and lascivious

"Lascivious" music, particularly within the sacred sphere, could thus take several forms. First, there was the *musica mollis:* music of too soft and tender a style, but also a music that could in turn soften and mollify the heart of the listeners (remember the bidirectional action of "imitation": from nature to art and from art to nature). Both term and concept of *musica mollis* dated back to Boethius, who (after Plato) theorised the difference between a better kind of music (*durus*), qualified as being "*modesta, simplex, mascula*" (modest, simple, virile) and a lower style (*mollis*), which was "*effeminata, fera, varia*" (effeminate, fierce and changing[99]). In his wake, Isidore of Seville (c.560–636) would propose a rather doubtful etymological explanation, connecting the word *mulier* (woman) to *mollities* (her softness[100]); the connection between chromatic alterations (the note B-flat, indicated as *mollis*) and feminine qualities also became widespread in the Middle Ages[101].

---

[97] Gibson 2009, p. 59.
[98] Ficino 1989; as quoted and translated in Strunk 1998, p. 388. Cf. Austern 1993, p. 347; Tomlinson 1998, p. 285.
[99] Boethius 1867, p. 181, and Boethius 1989, p. 3. Cf. Leach 2009, p. 23.
[100] In John of Salisbury 1993, p. 86.
[101] Cf. Leach 2006, p. 2 etc.; Gibson 2009, p. 58.

## 3.3. Crisis, critics and criticalities — 127

Thus, the numerous warnings found in the sixteenth century against *musica mollis* acquire a rather clear meaning in moral and anthropological terms. Significantly, when Cardinals Giovanni Morone and Bernardo Navagero (1507–1565) had drafted a memorandum for the discussion of music at the Council of Trent (1563), they had suggested to ban "music too soft" from worship[102]. Although their proposal was eventually rejected by the official decrees, similar words were used by another bishop, Gerolamo Ragazzoni (also known as Hieronymus Ragasanus, 1537–1592), during the closing sermon of the Council (on 5.12. 1563), advising the Church to avoid *"molliores cantus et symphonias"*[103]. St Carlo Borromeo (1538–1584) required singers to avoid *"molles flexiones"*[104] and very similar words were used by the provincial Council of his diocese, Milan, in 1565[105].

It is interesting, therefore, to observe what contemporaneous composers thought of the matter. Morales[106] claimed that when music was reproached for its power to weaken exceedingly the souls (*"animos nimis molles efficere"*) or to effeminate (*"effœminare"*) them, the fault was not music's, but rather men's. Indeed, they want music to act in "enticement of their cupidity", to "stimulate and excite their libido" rather than to "restrain the manners of the soul" and its "covetous" appetites "in the service of reason". One of the words used by Morales (*"lenocinium/lenocinans"*, i.e. panderer) is significantly found also in Guerrero[107], in an excerpt I quoted in Chapter Two (§ 2.4.7.). A decade earlier, Sadoleto had voiced a concept similar to Morales', stating that modern music was composed as if it "were designed not to soothe and control the spirit, but merely to afford a base pleasure to the ears"[108].

An exceedingly delicate (*"delicata"*) kind of church music, coming – in Federigo Borromeo's opinion – from "the ancient heathen", could provoke lasciviousness and had been therefore banned by "our fathers"[109]; another bishop, Giovanni Matteo Giberti/Ghiberti of Verona (1495–1543), established that "common and lascivious cantilenas" had not to be performed in church[110].

---

102 Cf. *CT* 9, p. 755, fn. 1. That this was intended as a reference to polyphony is made clear by the "defence of polyphony" written by Ferdinand I in response to this draft. See § 8.4.4.
103 *SCT*, p. 342.
104 In Rainoldi 2000, p. 727.
105 *AEM* 1, p. 27.
106 De Morales 1984, p. 48. All translations are mine.
107 Guerrero 1584, *Preface*. Cf. Stevenson 1961, p. 183.
108 Palisca 1997, pp. 283–284.
109 Bizzarini 2012, pp. 157–158.
110 Lockwood 1966, pp. 44–45. "*Publicæ cantilenæ*" may also mean vulgar and possibly sinful.

Music (at least of a certain kind) could be deemed responsible for encouraging unchaste behaviours: the treatise on confession by Luis Lopes (or López, 1520–1596) censures the "dishonest songs" alongside lascivious organ music[111] (as mentioned in § 2.4.2.); nor should church songs recall "immodest love", as the Council of Toledo (1565–66) established[112].

Moreover, the "mollifying" and effeminising quality of music, in the opinions of some writers, could somehow degrade manhood to womanhood, and humanity to bestiality: in the Aristotelian hierarchic view of the sexes, men were superior to women, and both, in a Christian concept, were superior to soulless beings. These superiorities could be threatened by excessive indulgence to music practice or enjoyment, especially in the absence of rational vigilance and wilful self-control[113].

### 3.3.2.3. "Moch musick marreth mens maners"

Therefore, I will concisely discuss here a few different but complementary ideas of the era: 1) that music *per se* could effeminise men; 2) that music was unsuitable for the education of the young (particularly of boys); 3) that music was inappropriate for churchmen; 4) that music could bestialise humans.

The first idea is perfectly summarised by Gaffurius, who (following Quintilian) condemned "theatrical and effeminate music, which corrupts rather than moulds public morals"[114]. Gaspare, the conservative character in the famous *Cortegiano* by Baldassarre (Baldesar) Castiglione (1478–1529), condenses the point: "I think that music – he said – together with several other vain things, is suitable for women, and perhaps even to some who have the appearance of men, but not to those who truly are men: these must not effeminise their souls with pleasures [Italian: *delicie*] which thus induce them to fear death"[115].

Although in Castiglione's book Gaspare's viewpoint is harshly contested, in my opinion the connection he establishes between the "reduction" of men to womanhood through music and the fear of death is highly significant from a spiritual viewpoint. Of course, we will see (e.g. in § 10.3.3.) abundant examples of men and women who received from religious music the force to face death with great courage; nevertheless, the association is rather uncommon and thus fascinating.

---

111 Lopes 1590, p. 82.
112 *Mansi* 34, col. 562 (http://bit.ly/2bWAKsw); cf. Rainoldi 2000, p. 348.
113 Leach 2009, p. 24.
114 Gaffurius 1968, p. 15.
115 Castiglione 1965, p. 78, my translation.

Although he did not establish the same connection, the English pedagogue Roger Ascham (1515–1568) had a viewpoint similar to the fictional character of Castiglione's Gaspare, and which introduces the second of the points listed above, i.e. that music can be harmful for the young. Ascham maintained that music could "quickly of men [make] women, and thus luting and singing take away a manly stomacke, which should enter and pierce deep and hard study"[116]. In a pedagogical treatise written two decades later, he also stated (following Galen), that "moch Musick marreth mens maners"[117] and thus should be avoided in the upbringing of children. Comparing the first statement with those by Bembo quoted above (§ 3.3.2.1.), it is interesting to point out that here music is in competition with education and culture not in terms of time (as in Bembo), but rather of discipline: music weakens the spirit (or "the stomacke") and diminishes the disposition to serious studies in the young. Similarly, in Agrippa's words,

> In very deed what is more unprofitable, more to be despised, and more to be eschewed, than these Pipers, Singers, and other sorts of Musicians? [...] Which with so many, and diverse voices of songs, surpassing the chirping of all Birds, with a certain venomous sweetness, like to the Mermaids, with voices, gestures and lascivious sounds, do deceive and corrupt men's minds[118].

The symbol of the sirens (which is, incidentally, a recurring one in this kind of literature) holds together the concepts of femininity, music, and a ruinous fate for men.

In a polemic fashion superior to Ascham's (although without his charming alliterations), another English writer, Philip Stubbes (c.1555-c.1610) wrote a tirade worth quoting in full:

> [Music] hath a certain kind of smooth sweetness in it, alluring ye auditory to effeminacy [...] [which] at first delighteth the ears, but afterwards corrupteth and depraveth the mind, making it queasy and inclined to all licentiousness of life whatsoever [...]. If you would have your son soft, womanish, unclean, smothe mouthed, affected to bawdry, scurrility, filthy Rimes & unseemly talking: briefly, if you would have him, as it were transnatured into a Woman, or worse [...] set him [...] to learn Musicke, and then you shall not fail your purpose[119].

---

**116** Ascham 1571, fol. 7ᵛ.
**117** Ascham 1863, p. 15. In this case, I have purposefully maintained the ancient spelling.
**118** Agrippa 1530, pp. 33–34; English translation in Strunk 1998, p. 307 (with slight modifications).
**119** Stubbes 1836, p. 203, with slight adaptations to modern spelling.

Here the links between immorality, femininity and the educational dangers of music could not be clearer. (It should be added, however, that Stubbes' treatise, analogously to Castiglione's *Cortegiano*, is in the form of a dialogue: this negative stance is counterbalanced by that of one of the interlocutors, who maintains that music is "a good gift of God, and [...] delighteth both man and beast, reviveth the spirits, comforteth the heart, and maketh it readier to serve God"[120]).

Cautions against an incorrect use of music were advanced also by Giovanni Francesco Lottini (1512–1572), who wrote that children "should be accustomed to songs written to such words that these could, in their manhood, encourage them to magnificence, to fortitude, and to moral virtues, leaving the delicate and soft [Italian: *molli*] types of music to women, and to those men who live effeminately". Moreover, "those who attend to music with too much study, will become languid"[121].

If this is the concept of music for at least some pedagogues and thinkers of the era, it will come as no surprise that music might be considered as unbecoming for churchmen. William Prynne (1600–1669) expressed the Puritan viewpoint by stating that "The ministers of God ought to abstain from all things which pertain to the enticements of the ears or eyes, from whence the vigour of the mind may be thought to be effeminated"; his condemnation of music regarded mainly the "effeminate, delicate, lust-provoking Musicke" of love-songs, whereas the recommendable psalmody had different musical qualities as well[122].

My last point, therefore, concerns the lowest degree of abjection that humans could be drawn to by music, i.e. their de-humanisation and debasement to a beastly condition. I will discuss this topic also among the "practical morality" of music, since – as we will see – certain performance styles, which were perceived to be similar to animal verses, suggested to hearers that those practising them were degrading themselves to a sub-human level. Here we will treat the topic from the theoretical viewpoint, i.e. how music was deemed responsible in general terms for the de-humanisation of men and women.

The principle according to which music diminished the human status of performers and listeners alike is the same as those operating in addictions, particularly as concerns the immoderate use of alcohol[123]. Similar to wine, music was both pleasurable and exhilarating; however, its consumption might lead to behaviour unworthy of humans (often with sexual overtones) and to a loss of rationality: as Paolo Cortesi pointed out, reporting contemporaneous opinions of

---

120 Stubbes 1836, p. 201.
121 In Guicciardini, Lottini and Sansovini 1588, p. 95 and p. 99 respectively, my translation.
122 Prynne 1632, p. 279; cf. Austern 1993, p. 349.
123 Cf. Leach 2006, p. 7.

music-haters (with which he was in disagreement), "[music's] merriment usually arouses the evil of lust"[124].

For Plato (who inspired both Calvin and Bucer[125]), ears were the funnel through which music was poured into human hearts; this position had been echoed, in 1159, by John of Salisbury: "the ears are almost completely divested of their critical power, and the intellect, which pleasurableness of so much sweetness has caressed insensate, is impotent to judge the merits of the things heard"[126], and Pope John XXII's Decretal spoke of music as "intoxicating rather than soothing the ear"[127].

Our discussion of the power of music to make beasts of men can start by turning again to Sadoleto, who, in the continuation of the fragment quoted before (§ 3.3.2.2.), condemned sensuous music which aims at a mere aural delight, "mimicking the cries of birds and beasts, which we should be sorry to resemble"[128]. It is within this context that he – as stated earlier – cautioned against music's power to de-spiritualise the soul: the powerful concept of Renaissance and humanist *imitatio* implied appropriation and assimilation.

We may also recall an Erasmian quote cited above (§ 3.3.1.1.), where he defined the improper delivery of a Latin sacred text in plainchant as "baying"[129]; Loersfeld's Erfurt *Enchiridion* preface compares the unintelligible singing of church choirs to the "howling" of the Biblical priests of Baal (cf. 1 Kings 18:28) and to a "braying" of asses[130].

This leads us to an important point to stress: singing (or the capacity of producing sounds with the body) is an element that both humans and animals have in common; the distinctive feature of human singing is its union of words with music. In turn, words are not mere sounds, but have a (rational) meaning: if words are made unintelligible, or are not even understood by those singing them, the risk of reverting to a purely "animal" sound production is at hand. And, as discussed earlier in this Chapter (§ 3.3.1.4.), it was not uncommon for church songs in Latin to be made incomprehensible to hearers or not to be understood by the singers themselves.

---

124 Cortesi 1510, fols. 72ᵛ-74ᵛ; English translation in Pirrotta 1966; Strunk 1998, p. 317.
125 Cf. Garside 1979, p. 23, fn. 132. For Plato: *Republic* III, 411 (Plato 1969; available online at http://bit.ly/2bugUqs); for Calvin: *OC* VI, pp. 169–170; *OS* 2, p. 17; for Bucer: *Vorrede* (*BDS* 7, p. 579).
126 In Weiss and Taruskin 2008, p. 53; cf. Dalglish 1978, p. 7.
127 In Weiss and Taruskin 2008, pp. 60–61; cf. Raynor 1972, pp. 36–37.
128 Sadoleto 1533, p. 123; translation in Palisca 1997, pp. 283–284.
129 Cf. in Kim 2005, p. 269.
130 Loersfeld 1524; cf. Herl 2004, p. 95.

The Anglican homily *Of Common Prayer and Sacraments* (published in 1571), quoting from St Augustine's Commentaries on the Psalms[131], stated this difference unequivocally: "We may sing with reason of man, and not with chattering of birds. For ousels, popinjays, ravens, pies, and other such like birds, are taught by men to prate they know not what: but to sing with understanding is given by God's holy will to the nature of man"[132].

### 3.3.2.4. Practical problems

We will now turn to musical practice and on how it was seen to have a moral dimension.

A first ethical issue regards what was felt as a "betrayal" of the plainchant heritage. We have already seen that plainchant performance presented several criticalities in the sixteenth century, as regards clarity of pronunciation, quantitative aspects, the presence of melismas, and other musical aspects I will discuss later in this section. Gregorian chant was part of the Church's heritage: if its dogmatic teaching made reference to Tradition as to an authority comparable to the Bible, its musical tradition could not be treated lightly in turn.

Therefore, to change and modify either the received melodies or their performance was considered to be morally reproachable: John XXII recommended that, in polyphonic elaborations of plainchant, "the integrity of the chant remain intact and that nothing in the prescribed music be changed"[133]: as we will see in the following Chapters, even several Protestant reformers did not reject this musical tradition.

A second point is the use of secular music as the *cantus firmus* of sacred works or as the starting point for paraphrase- or imitation Masses. Incidentally, although this was indeed a serious moral issue, I hope to have shown in the preceding section that the problem of "lascivious" music has many more implications than those connected with this particular compositional technique. Thus, the often-found idea that the Council of Trent banned secular *cantus firmus* from sacred polyphony is fundamentally erroneous.

Bernardino Cirillo was one of those criticising the use of secular *cantus firmus*. He wrote:

> Sometimes they say: "What a beautiful Mass was sung in Chapel". "And which one, indeed?". They reply: *The armed man*, or *Hercules Dux Ferrariæ*, or *La Filomena*. What the

---

**131** *PL* 36, col. 157; English translation in Augustine 1960, vol. I, p. 182.
**132** In *The Second Tome of Homilees* 1571, n. 9; *Sermons* 1839, p. 392. Cf. Kim 2005, p. 189.
**133** In Weiss and Taruskin 2008, pp. 60–61; cf. Raynor 1972, pp. 36–37.

devil has the Mass to do with the armed man, or with Filomena[134], or with the Duke of Ferrara? See that no harvest can be made here of numbers, harmony, motion of affects, of devotion or piety; nor any conformity of subject [can be taken] from the armed man or the Duke of Ferrara[135].

Here Cirillo condemns *cantus firmus* taken from secular chansons (*L'homme armé*), from a *soggetto cavato*, and from a motet which was actually sacred in content (its lyrics had been frequently attributed to St Bonaventure!). However, in my opinion, he does not consider as morally execrable the fact that secular tunes are intertwined within church works; rather, he questions the consistency of the resulting composition. In other words, Cirillo doubts that works whose very compositional structure is determined by a secular piece can be inherently "sacred". The "sacredness" of a work should come (in my interpretation of Cirillo's words) from the inner order and proportions of the piece (the "numbers" and "harmony", obviously on a variety of compositional levels), mirroring the divine *ratio* of the created world: thus (and only in this case) could it bring a "harvest" of "piety and devotion". Instead, when the work was determined by the musical requirements of something that had not been purposefully composed to suit the words of a Mass Ordinary, the result could not be achieved.

A different viewpoint is that taken by Giovanni Battista Doni (1595–1647), who stated, in much clearer terms (but note the later date, which implies a retrospective insight into the great polyphonic tradition!): "What madness impelled those elder and rather celebrated composers of Masses, Jodocus [Josquin], Mutonius [Mouton], Hadrianus [Willaert], and the others of that class to draw the melodies for that sacrosanct and reverend sacrifice not merely from profane subject matter but often from lascivious and contemptible themes?"[136].

In the *cantus firmus* compositions, in consideration both of the long note-values and of the placement of the *cantus firmus* in the tenor part, it would have required both a great attention and an uncommon musical ear to discern and follow the melodic line: to imagine that the average parishioners could do so is probably to overestimate their musical proficiency[137]. According to Dean, acoustical issues would also have complicated the task for listeners[138]; besides

---

[134] Although the known Masses *Philomena [prævia]* are based on Richafort's motet of the same name, Cirillo seems to think of "Philomena" as of a woman's name (instead of a nightingale, as in Richafort's motet).
[135] *Lettere volgari* 1564, fol. 115ᵛ, my translation.
[136] Doni 1647, p. 137; English translation (modified) in Fellerer 1953, p. 581, fn. 18.
[137] O'Regan 2009, pp. 216–217.
[138] Dean 1997, p. 612.

this, most members of the congregation busied themselves with what we would today describe as private devotions while the Mass was performed.

The recognition of the secular model could have been easier in the paraphrase and imitation settings[139]: even in these cases, however, the identification could be made more difficult by embellishments, imitations, and by references to polyphonic models which were likely to be unknown to the majority of the listeners.

### 3.3.2.5. Controlling the choir

If, then, there was a real issue with secular models and *cantus firmus* in sacred works, it regarded, in my opinion, the singers rather than the listeners. Indeed, Dean argues that polyphony was composed and performed primarily for the glory of God, and secondarily to be listened to (almost only) by those very people who sang it. In many cases, the "audience" either was not appreciative of polyphony or simply could not hear it (for acoustic reasons or because there was nobody else besides the choir[140]). Moral concerns about secular *cantus firmus* are more sensible here: a musical proficiency higher than the average could be normally expected of singers of polyphony; and, besides this, singers had obviously to concentrate on their melodic line, and thus they were much more likely to recognise quotations, references and allusions. Therefore, since the morality of church singers was often controlled by Church authorities (cf. § 8.4.3. etc.), I suggest that in many cases they were the true subjects of ethical concerns when the use of secular music within sacred compositions was at stake.

Clearly, there were cases in which this problem did not regard singers only, but rather the entire congregation: for example, when secular works (or adaptations which did not prevent their recognisability) were played on the organ or (in some cases) sung. In an extreme incident, in Forlì (1442), two soldiers reputedly began to sing scurrilous songs during Mass[141]; in more common instances, secular songs were performed by those officially charged with church music. Against such abuses, as mentioned earlier (§ 2.3.6.), there was a pronouncement of the Council of Basel[142]: Azpilcueta referred to this when censoring this practice in his manual for confession. For him, "Secular & bad music with voices & with organs & with other instruments [when it is] intermingled in the divine wor-

---

139 Fellerer 1953, p. 581.
140 Dean 1997.
141 Quoted in Gallo 2011, p. 267.
142 Session XXI, June 9th, 1435, Chapter VIII, in *Mansi* 29, col. 107 (available online at http://bit.ly/2bgMd3P).

ship, is insulting to God & to the Church. Secular music in church is illicit". This constituted a grave sin if "dishonest, vain and secular songs" were sung "during the divine office" by "those who are aware that they are illicit"[143].

Similarly, Agrippa von Nettesheim deplored that "Today music has such great license in churches that even along with the canon of the mass certain obscene little ditties sometimes have equal share"[144].

The subject of singers' morality brings us to another important ethical problem connected with music, i.e. the professionalisation of church music. In correspondence with the spread of polyphonic music, the complex requirements it posed to performers gradually favoured the separation of choir and clergy[145]: moreover, particularly in urban environments where music was provided by professionals, there was practically no need for the congregation to produce its own music[146].

Thus a three-fold separation was established, dividing the priests at the altar from the singing choir and from the attending congregation. We will see the theological implications of this division in Chapter Four (§ 4.3.7.1.), and consider here only its moral aspects.

The professionalisation of church music led indeed to some important social consequences: as Wegman summarises, "Art polyphony had been taken away from its listeners, [...] monopolized and made esoteric by the professionals". These, in turn, were starting to think of themselves as an artistic elite, almost a sect: "They were now the self-appointed custodians of a 'divine' art, a God-given institution with its own rituals and hierarchies, even with its own sinners and heretics (that is, abusers and music haters)"[147].

The separation between choir and clergy caused moral problems to both. During performances of polyphonic music, the priests could find themselves waiting for the music to finish: since not many of them really enjoyed listening to music, the mind was left wandering and found it difficult to concentrate properly on worship when the singing was over.

This happened, for example, in Modena, where Bishop Giovanni Morone had banned "figured music from the Cathedral church" in favour of plainchant, "because the priests were idle and buzzed while the singers sang"[148], as reported by a chronicler in 1538.

---

[143] De Azpilcueta 1569, p. 126.
[144] Agrippa 1530, pp. 35–36; translation in Fellerer 1953, p. 585, fn. 41.
[145] Cf. Reid 1971, p. 42; Mischiati 1993, p. viii.
[146] Cf. Herl 2004, p. 39; Pettegree 2005, p. 42.
[147] Wegman 2005, pp. 168 and 174 respectively.
[148] Quoted in Lockwood 1966, p. 44, my translation.

Even according to Savonarola, "good churchmen, when in choir, praise God and feel a most great delight, so much that sometimes they go beside themselves; but those who do not love God stay there and chatter"[149].

### 3.3.2.6. A waste of time and money

On the other hand, many – especially among the pauperists or those sympathising with them – considered professionalised church music to be a waste of money; others, more generally, thought of music itself as of a waste of time which could be employed for more useful activities.

It was surely from a pauperist viewpoint that Savonarola criticised elaborate polyphony: from the one side, the musicians' salaries could better be used for the relief of the poor; from the other, in Zanovello's opinion, he probably noticed that the lower social classes could not express their faith musically during solemn worships, which mirrored instead the socio-religious experience and needs of the wealthy aristocracy[150].

Following the death of Pope Leo X (in 1521), who had been a great lover and patron of music, satirical poems were penned: one of them invited musicians to mourn and to deeply regret the loss of such a munificent benefactor (as well as the money which would be spent more worthily in the future[151]).

Here and elsewhere, a common complaint was one connecting the topics "waste of money" and "waste of time": since music was seen as a vain pastime for idle people, musicians were almost on a par with beggars; thus, giving them a salary for an activity which was not really a job was to throw money away on people who did not want to work properly.

In consequence, we will find that two of our customary sources of references entertained a very similar opinion: for Agrippa von Nettesheim, "even the divine offices themselves and the sacred prayers and petitions are performed by lascivious musicians hired at great price"[152]; for Azpilcueta, money should not be spent on singers "who know no Latin" and are "frivolous, dissolute and foolish"[153].

---

149 Sermon of 11.2.1497 in Savonarola 1955, vol. 1, p. 161.
150 Cf. Zanovello 2009, pp. 130 and 133.
151 In Dean 1997, p. 623. Dean does not give details of the "*pasquinade*" he quotes; I surmise it can be *O musici con vostre barzellette* (in Ferroni 1978, p. 363), but here no mention is made of the better use that could be made of the money spent on musicians.
152 Agrippa 1530, p. 35; translation in Fellerer 1953, p. 585.
153 De Azpilcueta 1545, Chapter 16, §20. English translation in Blackburn 2007, p. 92.

Similarly, Thomas Becon (c.1511–1567) criticised the rulers' patronage of "drunken musicians" who sing "filthy and trifling songs"[154], and music was intensely felt as an idle occupation by many Jewish-born Spanish Christians[155]. As we will see in Chapter Nine (§ 9.5.2. and following), moreover, St Ignatius of Loyola would adopt a very restrictive view of liturgical music for his fellow Jesuits, precisely on the ground that their time should be better spent than on music; and it was with deep regret that John Merbecke (c.1510-c.1585) stated: "in the study of Music and playing on Organs [...] I consumed vainly the greatest part of my life"[156]. Similarly, the preface to Johannes Loersfeld's *Enchiridion* criticises the singers spending their entire days in choir[157].

### 3.3.2.7. Sounding immoral

Although in the preceding pages we have attempted to bring together and coalesce different opinions as to what made music and music practice moral or immoral, a fundamental aspect still eludes us (and will forever): how did "immoral" music actually sound? What was felt as morally or spiritually reproachable in the aural reality of church music?

Of course, if the soldiers began singing obscene songs during worship, as in the Forlì incident cited above (§ 3.3.2.5.), this was scandalous – and would be just as scandalous today, incidentally. But the complaints about defective aspects of church music were much more nuanced and widespread than such extreme occurrences would justify.

I discussed at some length the topic of "lascivious" music in the preceding pages because, as I wrote earlier (§ 3.3.2.4.), the common idea that it simply meant "secular *cantus firmus* in sacred works" needs to be emendated. The point, however, is that we can identify rather easily a secular *cantus firmus* in a written source, whereas the sound of what sixteenth-century Christians heard in church is lost forever. Nevertheless, by "listening" to the sources, we can get an "aural glimpse" of that lost practice, and perhaps be surprised by what they can reveal.

Before starting our examination of these sources, however, I wish to clarify a fundamental point: many of the witnesses we will hear in the following pages need to be taken with a grain of salt, precisely because we have no aural evidence to compare them with. Sometimes, the needs of polemics, or the wish

---

154 Becon 1844, p. 429.
155 Ramos López 2008, p. 3.
156 Merbecke 1550, fol. a.ij'.
157 Herl 2004, p. 95.

to make one's point clear, would lead our writers to exaggerations or – at least – to employ standard and commonplace expressions, which will tell us very little about the actual reality.

What I think is most interesting in the collection of testimonies gathered here, is how they help us to realise *what mattered* for sixteenth-century listeners of sacred music. We cannot match reality and critique, nor can we compare caricature with portrait in these depictions; however, by observing *which features* are caricatured by the polemicists, we may deduce their aesthetic criteria: a cartoon exaggerating the dimensions of one's nose does not say much about how big the nose actually was, but it does tell us that contemporaneous society prized small noses, and so on.

As a last important proviso, I must add that in many cases even the exact meaning of the words they used escapes us. What is worse, is that very often the same terms have been in continuous and constant use until now, but have adapted their technical meaning in time: therefore, we may not even be aware of our misinterpretations, and simply assume that we know what they meant. This last aspect may slightly be limited by further research and careful comparison of the sources; nevertheless, this is another instance where face-value readings are extremely dangerous.

A clear example of this is a pronouncement of the Church of England (1552), banning from worship "*vibratam illam & operosam Musicam, quæ figurata dicitur*" ("the vibrato and elaborate music, which is called *figurata*"[158]).

What could they exactly mean by this? For twenty-first-century readers, *vibrato* refers to performance practice, while "figured music" refers to compositional technique. Were the Masses by John Taverner (1490 – 1545) normally sung in a vocal style that is reminiscent, in our ears, of Wagner's Valkyries, and were both composition and performance styles to be avoided? Obviously this is a purposefully paradoxical, extreme and anachronistic example, but the fact is that no plausible surmise can be attempted as to the true meaning of this expression.

Another striking example is found in a letter by Giovanni Camillo Maffei (c.1510-a.1573), where those who "praise sweet and smooth singing"[159] are contrasted with those who value "church singing": this seemingly implies that church singing was neither sweet nor smooth.

---

[158] *Reformatio legum ecclesiasticarum* 1571, "De divinis officiis", Caput V, p. 86; English translation in Leaver 2006, p. 398.
[159] Maffei 1562, p. 195.

Thus Phillips could summarise, although slightly bitterly: "We can [...] guess at the type of sound produced by 16th-century choirs, and the evidence suggests that imitation of them would be highly undesirable"[160].

What contemporaneous aesthetics *did* value was a set of qualities listed, ironically, by a writer (Felice Figliucci) who wished to discourage such practices: "They should not try and outdo the others in loudness of voice, high pitch, agility [literally: volubility] of the tongue, or dexterity of the throat. [...] Today's musicians only care for a loud and high voice, and a quick tongue, and an agile [*volubile*] throat, and the like – which are harmful for the body and of scarce utility"[161].

Biagio Rossetto recommended to avoid "vulgar" performance of sacred music, and not to "break" the voice[162]: a recurring advice, since the times of David of Augsburg[163] (c.1200 – 1272), but here again we can only surmise what they meant to deplore.

Another recurring term whose meaning for performance practice is very elusive is *modulatio*, especially when it is associated with its seeming synonym *inflexio*. This happens, for example, in the debate at Trent regarding nuns' polyphonic music, whose words are strikingly similar to the Anglican text quoted above: "[The nuns] should abstain both in choir and elsewhere from modulation [Latin: *modulatione*] and inflection [*inflexione*] of the voices, as well as from the other singing artifice called *figuratum* or *organicum*"[164]. I have purposefully used English words which are closest to the Latin original in my translation, although they are patently unhelpful in conveying the technical details at stake.

The provincial Council of Milan (1565) similarly prohibited the use of "weak inflections" [*molles flexiones*] "and other lascivious singing styles"[165]. We have here still another seeming synonym (*flexio*), whose pairing with the keywords "lascivious" and *mollis* makes it all the more interesting, but gives no clue as to its real sound.

Without a time-capsule, thus, performance practice issues can be discussed only from a speculative viewpoint; however, what we do know is that they mattered for contemporaneous listeners. Federigo Borromeo clearly stated that the perfection of music was not in composition, but in the style of performance[166];

---

160 Phillips 1978, p. 195.
161 Figliucci 1583, p. 256, my translation.
162 Rossetto 1529, III.1, in Rainoldi 2000, p. 721.
163 In Leach 2009, p. 34.
164 Debate of 20.11.1563: *CT* 9, p. 1043.
165 *AEM* 1, p. 27.
166 Bizzarini 2012, pp. 38 – 39.

and a Superior General of the Jesuits banned from their colleges any musical work prompting a performance style[167] (*cantandi modus*) which could be perceived as "indecent". Thus, the possibility – mentioned above – that certain works or compositional styles were indeed associated with particular performance types (and that their combination incurred censorship by religious authorities) may become more likely.

Moreover, the Latin words often used to indicate performance practice (*modus, ratio*) have normally a much stronger and broader meaning than their translations in modern languages. *Modus* and *ratio* are not mere "fashions" superimposed on essence like a varnish: they concur in the essence itself and (particularly in the case of *ratio*) are fundamental conveyors of meaning and order.

We will now discuss performance practice under a few important rubrics, some of which recall topics whose theoretical significance has been presented above. We will consider in turn volume, the impression of effeminacy or bestiality, the presence of national performance styles, virtuoso singing, gestures, tempo and rhythm.

### 3.3.2.8. The volume of "wild vociferations"

As concerns sound volume, the first obvious remark to be made is that volume is not only an objective absolute quantity that can be measured in decibels, but also a relative and subjective impression, in which acoustical and psychological issues are fundamental. Therefore, all problematic topics regarding the occasions for church singing, the kind of music performed, the location and the audience come to the fore again[168], and – at least – we should be constantly aware of their complexity.

In this case, we have a helpful quote from Zarlino's treatise: "one is the way of singing in Churches and public Chapels, and another in private chambers; for there one sings with a full voice (albeit with discretion) [...], whereas in chambers one sings in a softer and sweeter voice, without any clamour"[169]. His words are echoed by Lodovico Zacconi (1555–1627), who spoke of "Churches, or other places when one needs to shout loudly"[170]. It should be noted, however, that both writers were Venetian, and that a rather unrestrained performance style seems likely to correspond to the solemn and sparkling aesthetics of the *Serenissima*.

---

167 Crook 2009, p. 12.
168 Cf. Phillips 1978 and Dean 1997.
169 Zarlino 1558, Part III, p. 204, my translation.
170 Zacconi 1975, fol. 78$^v$, quoted in Wistreich 2007, p. 142, fn. 39.

Zarlino, however, wrote the sentences quoted above immediately after other meaningful statements: "When singing, a singer must not send out his voice with impetus and furore, similar to a beast; but he must sing with a moderate voice, proportioning it to that of the other singers, so that it does not overcome the others' voices, nor prevents hearing them"[171]. The importance of commensurating one's volume to those of the others was also present in Gaffurius' *Practica musicæ*[172], although – as Gardiner reports – this was more observed in theory than in practice: "the boys in the choir sang *Magnificat* in Latin, as loud as they could cry, each one uttering his own breast to the loudest, without regard to how he agreed with his fellows"[173].

Savonarola equates an aristocratic chapel with a "tumult"[174] and Guerrero warns against "vociferations"[175]. The same word ("wild vociferations") is employed by Hermann Finck (1527–1558), who sarcastically wrote: "the singers [suffer] from the delusion that shouting is the same thing as singing. The basses make a rumbling noise like a hornet trapped in a boot, or else expel their breath like a solar eruption"[176]. A similarly colourful description is found in a 1522 Wittenberg pamphlet: "then followeth a sound of a full voice, as it were the sound of a drone or of a leaden pipe"[177].

For the Council of Ravenna (1568), correct church singing should be neither too loud nor too light[178]; and Erasmus voices his disdain for improvised polyphonic practices by defining them a "tremendous tonal clamour"[179], and expressing once more his concern for proper textual delivery: "in many churches and monasteries, by thundering forth in a raucous bellowing, they so fill up the church that all sounds are obscured and nothing can be understood"[180].

Notwithstanding this quotation and those preceding it, Sherr convincingly argues that (in the late sixteenth century) a huge volume of sound was aesthetically more prized in a church or chapel choir than a clear delivery (which was

---

171 Zarlino 1558, Part III, p. 204, my translation.
172 Gaffurius 1496, Liber III, Caput XV (fol. cciiij$^v$); see Kim 2005, pp. 131–132.
173 Gardiner 1933, p. 488.
174 Savonarola 1971, vol. 1, p. 222 (Sermon of 5.3.1496).
175 Guerrero 1584, *Preface*.
176 Finck 1556 (1969); translation in Kirby 1961, p. 213.
177 *De veteri* 1522, fol. Fii$^v$; coeval English translation by William Turner (1534). Quoted in Leaver 2006, p. 376.
178 *Mansi* 35, col. 632 (http://bit.ly/2bMXjzc). The Latin wording is ambiguous, and might refer to pitch instead of volume; the context, however, suggests that loudness is being discussed there. Cf. Weber 2008, p. 143.
179 In Kim 2005, p. 165.
180 In Miller 1966, p. 340.

appreciated in chamber music). Sherr adds that the word "sonorous" seems to be a special favourite in official descriptions of the papal chapels[181]. This was apparently an ideal not only of performance, but of composition as well: thus, in Ruffo's preface to his Mass collection, he wrote of "the powerful and sweet sound of the voices"[182], thus implying that both adjectives could coexist with each other.

At least in some instances (such as solemn celebrations, major feast days and public occasions), therefore, it is conceivable that the huge acoustical space of the cathedrals inherited from the past and of those (sometimes no less gigantic, as St Peter's in Rome) that were being built at the time, might require to be "filled" with sound. When instruments were played during worship, they might also have contributed to creating for worshippers an aural experience of awe and splendour similar in kind to the visual feeling of greatness and majesty inspired by the great cathedrals of the time.

Thus, although we should be aware that our mental depiction of large choirs performing polyphony within huge churches, and being listened to carefully by the audience, is in most cases purely fictional, there is also evidence suggesting that in some cases polyphonic music was indeed offered to an "audience" – although, apparently, the audience was not always thrilled by the treat.

### 3.3.2.9. Cats, goats, bulls and donkeys

We will now review a collection of metaphors used by sixteenth-century writers to describe contemporaneous church music. Ironically, although their sarcasm is patent, no doubt is possible as to whether the music they are referring to is plainchant or polyphony: their descriptions may be exaggerated and merciless, but they certainly do depict bad performances of polyphony. For example, a Wittenberg pamphleteer wrote: "Within a little while after they do let their voice fall so low that thou wouldest ween that they did weep. One man singeth on his part, another singeth on another part, and by and by afterward they wax dumb"[183]. Such a description can apply – in my opinion – only to cacophonic polyphony.

Sixteenth-century writers frequently used analogies taken from the animal world to caricaturise polyphony. The very same pamphleteer quoted above, continues thus: "Anon after one beginneth to crow as it were a hen, which would lay

---

181 Sherr 1994, p. 608.
182 Ruffo 1570, *Preface*; English translation in Weiss and Taruskin 2008, p. 116.
183 *De veteri* 1522, fol. Fii$^v$; coeval English translation by William Turner (1534). Quoted in Leaver 2006, p. 376.

eggs [...]; they do howl so piteously, much like the howling of [March] cats"[184]. Probably the mating season of Italian cats started earlier than in Germany, since the same metaphor is used by Bernardino Cirillo, writing of "certain howlings, bellowings and bleatings that they sometimes seem a January of cats and a May of bulls – not to mention other unflattering associations"[185]. Actually, January was to cats what May was to *donkeys:* thus Cirillo's use of "bulls" is really a euphemism for "asses".

Agrippa describes a similar polyphonic concert, when the choir sings "not with human voices but with the cries of beasts: boys whinny the discant, some bellow the tenor, others bark the counterpoint, others moo the alto, others gnash the bass"[186].

For Karlstadt, during the elevation, music was sung "like the voices of sheep and wolves"[187], and Zarlino (as seen earlier: § 3.3.2.8.) recommended that singers moderate their volume "not to resemble Beasts"[188]. As mentioned above (§ 3.3.2.3.), the moral implications of this kind of singing were pointed out by Sadoleto: humans singing with animal verses put themselves on a par with beasts, and (both similarly and consequently) de-spiritualise their very soul[189].

Yet another animal, the goat, is often mentioned in the musical bestiary, but – probably – at least as much for its behaviour as for its verse. Indeed, the very word *caprizare* (i.e. to move as a goat, "*capra*" in Italian) is at the root of later musical terms such as *capriccio*[190]. Thus Herbenus contrasted the "wondrous simplicity" of some songs with other, more artful songs, that "leapt about like goats [*caprizantes*]"[191]. However, this term is often used not only as an insult, but it sometimes acquires – at least in certain sources – a rather technical quality: the following witnesses, indeed, will lead us to our next subject, i.e. the identification of national performance schools or styles.

In 1492, Gaffurius wrote: "The English sing together jubilantly [Lat.: *concinendo iubilant*]; the French [*Gallici*] sing; the Spaniards display crying, the Ger-

---

**184** *De veteri* 1522, fol. Fii$^v$; coeval English translation by William Turner (1534). Quoted in Leaver 2006, p. 376. In the seventeenth century, several visual artists depicted cats making music (and often it is unmistakably vocal polyphony): cf. Cornelis Saftleven (1607–1681), *A Concert of Cats, Owls, a Magpie and a Monkey in a Barn*; David Teniers the Younger (1610–1690), *The Cat Concert*; Ferdinand van Kessel (c.1648-c.1696), *A Musical Gathering of Cats*.
**185** *Lettere volgari* 1564, fol. 116$^v$, my translation.
**186** Agrippa 1530, pp. 35–36; English translation in Kim 2005, p. 153, with modifications.
**187** Kirkman 2010, p. 144.
**188** Zarlino 1558, Part III, Chapter 45, p. 204.
**189** Sadoleto 1533, p. 123; translation in Palisca 1997, pp. 283–284.
**190** Cf. Campione 2011, p. 242.
**191** Herbenus 1957, pp. 58–59; in Wegman 2005, pp. 175–176.

mans howling; of the Italians none but the Genovese and those who live by their sea do *caprizare*"[192]. This concept is repeated almost verbatim by other writers[193]. Andreas Ornitoparchus (c.1490-a.1520) acknowledges his debt to Gaffurius but adds some picturesque touches: "Hence the English *iubilant*, the French [*Galli*] sing; the Spaniards display crying; as for Italy, those who inhabit the Genovese shores are said to *caprisare*, the others bark; as for the Germans, although it shames to say so, they really howl like wolves"[194]. For Finck, "The Germans bellow, the Italians bleat, the Spaniards wail, the French sing"[195]. Pietro Aaron (c.1480-a.1545) repeats the list, with some personal remarks:

> Since several languages and people exist, consequently there are different kinds of music and pronunciation: just as our own, [there are] those of the French, of the Spaniards, of the English, of the Germans and of other nations. [...] Therefore some of them attributed some titles and names [to the different nationalities]: the French [in Italian: *Franciosi*] sing, the English sing joyfully [*giubilare*], the Spaniards cry, the Germans shout, and the Italians *caprezzare*; but I cannot believe this to come from anything else than envy and malignity[196].

Finally, for Tinctoris, "the English, who are popularly said to shout while the French sing [...] repeat always the very same composition, which is a very poor sign of genius"[197].

I reported all descriptions not for the sake of repetition, but because – besides the amusement these quotes provide – they reveal something of a lost aural reality. Obviously, since the writers employ almost the same words (though differences are meaningful), the verbs are at least stereotypical, and probably plagiarised or quoted. However, national features did exist, and were likely rather marked too. The Papal choir, for example, was clearly made of singers coming from three main traditions, i.e. the Franco-Flemish, the Italian, and the Spanish[198].

As for the French, it may seem at first that they were the only one whose singing was not caricaturised in the descriptions above: whereas all others bellow, howl or shriek, the French simply "sing". However, I have purposefully reported the Latin words used by the authors quoted, since in a number of cases

---
[192] Gaffurius 1492, fol. K5, my translation.
[193] This delightful collection is found in Blackburn 1992, p. 14; the translations are mine. Cf. also Wegman 2003, esp. pp. 181–186 on Tinctoris.
[194] Ornitoparchus 1519, fol. M<sup>r</sup>.
[195] Finck 1556, fol. Ssi<sup>v</sup>.
[196] Aaron 1545, vol. 4, Chapter 1, my translation.
[197] Tinctoris 1975, p. 27. Cf. Wegman 2003, pp. 181–186.
[198] Sherr 1992, p. 601.

the French are indicated as *galli* – a word indicating cocks as well as Gauls. Thus, I would infer that the "*galli cantant*" is not as flattering as it would seem at first; and (tentatively) it might be a shorthand formula for indicating a singing style perceived as characterised by high pitches and shrill voices.

Similarly, I would suggest a similar wordplay as concerns the English. A very ancient tradition, linked to an incident that allegedly occurred to Pope Gregory I (c.540 – 604), and reported by the Venerable Bede, played on the assonance between *Angli* (the English) and *angeli* (the angels[199]). Thus, in my opinion, "*angli jubilant*" was not only a musical-technical description, but also an allusion to angelic jubilations[200].

Nevertheless, the word *jubilare* did seem to imply some technical aspect, and – once more – it may be easier to identify it in caricatured descriptions rather than in appraising compliments. An Erasmian fragment already quoted in Chapter Two (§ 2.3.9.) is a case in point, as here the English are said to sing with "ornamental neighings and agile throats"[201]. As Blackburn points out, our best inference about the English performance style and the meaning of this *jubilare* comes from an analysis of the Eton Choirbook, where complex and long melismas are found, as well as a wide vocal range particularly in the high voices[202]. On the other hand, Seay suggests that the difference found in Tinctoris between *jubilare* (the English) and *cantare* (the French) refers rather to "improvise melodically" and "compose"[203]: although I personally favour a more literal reading, it is indeed true that improvised polyphonic practices were typical of English music.

As concerns the Germans, on the other hand, I think that the recurring verb "*ululant*" is simply an offensive word, perhaps not unconnected with the feeling of superiority that (within a humanistic context) the "heirs of the Romans" could have in comparison with a "barbaric" culture: for example, Livy had written of the barbarians' "*ululatus*" (howling), and of their rough singing[204]. The term will also be used in a very abusing fashion by those deriding vernacular church singing in German[205].

---

**199** Cf. Bede 1853, vol. I, Part II, p. 356.
**200** Cf. also the witness by Marino Sanudo (or Sanuto: 1466 – 1536) as regards the English Royal Chapel in the early sixteenth century: Sanudo 1969, vol. 20, col. 266.
**201** In Kim 2005, p. 165.
**202** Blackburn 1992, p. 16.
**203** Seay in Tinctoris 1957, p. 27.
**204** "*Mox* ululatus cantusque dissonos, *vagantibus circa mœnia turmatim* barbaris, *audiebant*", emphasis added. Titus Livius, *Titi Livii Patavini Historiarum* (*History of Rome*), Book V, XXXIX (Livius 1829, p. 120).
**205** In Groote and Vendrix 2012, p. 180. Cf. Chapter Ten: § 10.3.7.5.

In the Spaniards' case, instead, I suppose that we find another instance of combination of and integration between composition and performance practice. We have already seen such instances: for example, when discussing the *"vibratam illam & operosam Musicam"*[206], or as regards English styles of composition and execution. Obviously, the distinction and separation between composer and performer is a relatively recent phenomenon, although – obviously again – not all those who participated in singing a work had contributed to its composition. Probably, however, at a conceptual level certain compositional styles were inseparable from their own performance style, and both could be nationally characterised.

The "Spanish style" was thus deemed to be particularly suitable for sad or lugubrious occasions: Cortesi mentions a musical style "in which the souls are induced to weeping and compassion by a mode inflected toward sorrows", such as that used for the exequies of popes and cardinals, and adds: "Of this lugubrious manner of singing did the nation of the Spaniards always make use"[207]. The *Lamentations* were performed in a "Spanish manner" during a ceremony with the Pope in 1493, and a contemporaneous witness stated that the Spaniards' voices were particularly suitable for the occasion[208]. Later, Paris de Grassis reported that the 1518 Holy Week *Lamentations* were performed by the Papal choir separately: the first lesson was performed by the Spaniards "*lamentabiliter*" ("dolefully"), the second by the French "*docte*" ("learnedly", whatever this might mean), and the third by the Italians "*dulciter*" ("sweetly"[209]).

Indeed, Italian "sweetness" was not always seen as a positive quality: sometimes, it could represent yet another instance of the risk of effeminacy discussed above (§ 3.3.2.1.–3.).

### 3.3.2.10. Virtuous and virtuosos

But what did Italian "effeminacy" consist of? Interestingly, although singers' efforts to reach high pitches were sometimes condemned, the reproach of such attempts regarded vanity and exhibitionism rather than effeminacy proper. As Leach points out, a historic evolution is observable in the descriptions of feminised singing: whereas in twelfth century an "effeminate" singer was indeed one singing in a female voice's range, in the age of polyphony effeminacy was iden-

---

**206** *Reformatio legum ecclesiasticarum* 1571, "De divinis officiis"; Caput V, p. 86; English translation in Leaver 2006, p. 398.
**207** Cortesi 1510, fols. 72$^v$-74$^v$; English translation in Pirrotta 1966; Strunk 1998, p. 319.
**208** Sherr 1992, pp. 602–603.
**209** De Grassis 1884, p. 66, fol. 805$^r$; cf. Sherr 1997, p. 398.

tified with excessive display of virtuosity, "rapid notes and rests"[210] (possibly associated with the alleged inconstancy and unpredictability of feminine behaviour), and in the "unmanly" revelling in the aural pleasure of polyphony.

We have already observed a long tradition condemning showy singing in church and the display of virtuosity for its own sake. The moral reproach here was not only directed against vanity and pride (two sins harshly condemned by the Church) but also against idolatry and divisions in the community. Indeed, when the all-important function of worship (i.e. to praise God) was turned to human self-glorification, this represented an occurrence of idolatry (since the sinner worshipped himself/herself instead of God). As we will see later, moreover, *prima donna* attitudes were likely to provoke rivalry and envy, thus destroying the community's union.

Last but not least, this point has important theological implications precisely as regards one of the core issues of Luther's Reformation, i.e. the *sola gratia* principle: we will see in Chapter Four how this subject was felt and treated by the most important Reformers.

Following a long Biblical tradition (cf. Isaiah 29:13; Matthew 15:8; Mark 7:6 and many others), the Jewish-Christian heritage condemned a worship made with lips only (especially when its purpose was to obtain praise from other believers) and not with the heart: indeed, Crook argues that one of the meanings of the famous adjective "lascivious", when applied to church music, was precisely an excess of self-referential virtuosity[211].

Thus, Carlier condemned musicians who sing "for the praise of men rather than [the glory] of God"[212]; and Savonarola in turn denounced the outward aspect of singing[213]. For Federigo Borromeo, musicians should practise "the exercise of prayer [that] makes the soul pious and the mind devout", and thus their singing would "move the others to devotion, and music would be made with merit and not with vanity"[214].

Wegman discusses the details and implications of an incident happened in 1486 in Görlitz, where a parish priest forcefully defended polyphonic singing against the complaints of his congregation, which equated it with "*hofereyen*", i.e. vain songs similar to those performed in alehouses[215].

---

210 In Leach 2009, p. 33.
211 Unpublished paper quoted by O'Regan 2013a, p. 340. Cf. John of Salisbury in Leach 2009, p. 30.
212 In Wegman 2005, pp. 50–51.
213 Savonarola 1976, vol. 1, pp. 176–185.
214 In Bizzarini 2012, pp. 38–39.
215 Wegman 2005, pp. 1–3.

Giovanni Battista Possevino (c.1552-c.1622) wrote that "either both mouth and heart sing Psalms and Hymns to God in concord, or else if the heart does not pray, the tongue works and toils in vain; and such prayers count for nothing, or rather they make the blessed Lord angry against us"[216].

Similarly, God required of nuns "not suavity of voice, but purity of heart", as was recommended to Roman religious women in their singing[217]; and Becon (quoting St Jerome explicitly) gave the same advice to young church musicians:

> Let young men hear these things, yea, let them hear whose office it is to sing in the church, that they must sing to God, not in the voice but in the heart, neither must their throat and chaws be anointed after the manner of game-players with sweet ointments, that in the church singing more fit for game-places should be heard, but in fear, in work, in knowledge of the scriptures ought they to sing unto the Lord[218].

On the other hand, the virtues of humility and devotion were recommended to church musicians (among others by Azpilcueta[219] and Rossetto[220]), especially within a context which increasingly praised virtuosity both in composition and in performance[221].

Moreover, as mentioned above, the excessive display of virtuosity by individual singers was likely to encourage rivalry, jealousy, ambition and competitiveness; these, in turn, were often deadly enemies of the communion and concord which should characterise a community of believers. This was particularly serious in the case of church musicians, both because they were somehow part of the official establishment of the Church (and thus should have set a "good example" to the others) and because the very act of singing together should have been an icon of union.

Possevino synthesised this ideal beautifully:

> The act of singing together in a choir must be done in concord and with consonant voices, and in the same tempo; not one *forte* and one *piano*; not one interrupting and another omitting [the words]; not one furiously and another feigning sleep. Rather, be the outer voices' unison and concord the sign of the inner concord, unity and charity, which are particularly sought-after in those dedicated to the angelic office of praising God[222].

---

216 Possevino 1594, p. 29.
217 Cf. Seneca 1604, cc. 78ᵛ-82ʳ; as quoted in Masetti Zannini 1993, p. 132.
218 Becon 1844, pp. 133–134; cf. Kim 2005, p. 190.
219 Blackburn 2007, p. 91 and footnote.
220 Rossetto 1529, in Rainoldi 2000, p. 721.
221 Cf. Garside 1966, p. 41; Haar 2006, p. 23.
222 Possevino 1594, p. 29.

This ideal was not often found in practice: virtuosic polyphony was seen as a symbol of disunion and discord rather than concord both in the Wittenberg pamphlet[223] and by the Hussites[224]; we have already quoted the opinions of Zarlino[225] and Gardiner[226] on singers caring only for their own show and not proportioning their volume to the others.

For religious men and women, musical rivalry could lead to personal enmity and to highly problematic situations within community life. A Bolognese priest who was the confessor to several nuns' convents knowingly wrote in 1593: "As a confessor at many convents, I know for certain that there is so much contention and such warfare among them because of their musical rivalries that sometimes they would claw each other's flesh if they could"[227]. Similarly, excessive displays of solo virtuosity by the organ players were seen as individualistic and could be reproached on the same grounds[228].

### 3.3.2.11. Laughable gestures and laudable behaviours

Another characterising feature of vanity consisted in the singers' gestures. This is an aspect which has not hitherto received widespread attention: we are now accustomed to very reduced bodily motions in singers of polyphony, but – as we will presently observe – this seems to be very different from sixteenth-century practice. The use of exaggerated gestures can also be connected to the topic of virtuoso and soloistic singing discussed above (§ 3.3.2.10.), particularly if (as Bryant and Quaranta suggest) polyphonic music was performed as solo singing with accompaniment[229].

We may start by recalling once more the long line of condemnations of "theatrical" music, particularly in worship (Quintilian, St Jerome, Aquinas, Gaffurius…; cf. § 2.3.3.–6. etc.): "theatrical" could mean exaggerated, showy, and also singing with (excessive) gestures.

Already in Pope John XXII's Decretal the singers' attempt to "convey the emotion of the music by their gestures"[230] had been reprimanded. Carlier (in Boethius' wake) identified "theatrical" music rather by its compositional fea-

---

[223] *De veteri* 1522, fol. Fii^v; 1534 English translation in Leaver 2006, p. 376.
[224] Bossy 1985, pp. 164–165.
[225] Zarlino 1558, Part III, Chapter 45, p. 204.
[226] Gardiner 1933, p. 488.
[227] In Monson 2012, p. 1. Cf. Beggiao 1978, p. 94; see also Monson 1993b.
[228] Blume 1975, p. 107.
[229] Cf. Bryant and Quaranta 2007.
[230] In Weiss and Taruskin 2008, pp. 60–61; cf. Raynor 1972, pp. 36–37.

tures than by its performance: "*musica fracta* rather induces levity, especially that which is excessively rhythmicized in the manner of theatrical ditties [*carminum theatralium*] (which according to the Blessed Jerome are not suitable in church)"[231].

Thus, the church was seen as a space where some of the performed activities could be similar to those of secular plays: notwithstanding this, the very nature of the place required a bodily and vocal approach that should not suggest profane associations[232]. In Vicentino's words, "it is as if God's temple has become a place where lascivious and ridiculous things are performed, as if it were a scene where any kind of buffoons' music can be played"[233].

Zarlino was of the same advice:

> Thus I say, for example, that we occasionally heard somebody shrieking (I can't say 'singing') a song with very rough voices, and with acts, and manners so counterfeited, that they really seemed to be apes. [...] [The singers] must pay attention [...] not to sing with bodily movements, or with such acts and gestures that they will move to laugh those seeing and listening to them[234].

This applies as well, adds Zarlino, to instrumentalists, "who seem to dance" while playing: this concept is found also in the decrees of the Synod of Constance[235], which – alongside with that of Toledo – requested singers to avoid "theatrical gestures"[236].

"Seeing and hearing" are joined also in Bernardino Cirillo's letter[237]; Azpilcueta rebukes singers who make gestures while performing[238], and Gaffurius adds: "exaggerated and unbecoming movements of the head and hands proclaim a foolish singer, for the head and hands do not form a pleasing sound, but a well-modulated voice. Through their imprudent manner many singers are displeasing to those whom they thought they would please"[239].

Finck is – once more – rather picturesque in his description: "fine compositions were monstrously distorted and deformed, with mouths twisted and wide open, heads thrown back and shaking"[240]. It is interesting to note that here

---

**231** In Wegman 2005, pp. 50–51.
**232** Cf. also Don Ercole Tinelli's words (1593) in Monson 2012, p. 1.
**233** Vicentino 1555, Book IV, Chapter XXVI, my translation.
**234** Zarlino 1558, Part III, Chapter 45, p. 204.
**235** *CG* 7, p. 488.
**236** *Mansi* 34, col. 562 (http://bit.ly/2bWAKsw); cf. Rainoldi 2000, p. 348.
**237** *Lettere volgari* 1564, fol. 115ʳ.
**238** Blackburn 2007, p. 90.
**239** Gaffurius 1496, Part III, Chapter XV (fol. cciiijᵛ); English translation in Gaffurius 1968, p. 149.
**240** Finck 1556 (1969); translation in Kirby 1961, p. 213.

both the singers' physical appearance and the performed work are "distorted and deformed": the degradation brought by vanity in human beings applies to their works of art as well.

It should be pointed out, however, that gestures as such were by no means condemned: rather, only their exaggeration was blamed (inasmuch as it could provoke hilarity and that it suggested secular associations). Indeed, Federigo Borromeo attributed to the proper use of gestures part of the expressive force of "ancient music"[241], and Vincenzo Giustiniani wrote that good musicians "show in their faces and gestures the meaning of the concept which is sung, but with moderation and no exaggeration"[242]. Likewise, Thomas Elyot (c.1490– 1546) recommended that music teaching be imparted to children "without diminution of honour, that is to say without wanton countenance and dissolute gesture"[243].

### 3.3.2.12. The force of gravity

We have already seen that one of the several aspects which could concur in the broad semantic field of "lascivious" music was represented by speed and velocity, and that in some cases these were also allegedly "effeminising" factors[244]. In particular, we need now to focus on a further term, "gravity", whose antonym we have already met (i.e. "levity"), and which is another of the keywords of "proper" church music. Thus, for Rossetto, sacred music should be "honest, grave and uniform"[245]; for Federigo Borromeo, in St Jerome's wake, it must be "grave"[246]; Guerrero employs a number of derivatives from the Latin word *gravitas* ("nothing else than a grave and temperate genre of music [...]; music more serious and grave for the divine offices" etc.[247]). Juan Luis Vives (1492– 1540) recommends to Christian women to sing "sweetly, and honest, grave and decent songs"[248]; these qualities are found together in Cirillo's letter, as concerns the ancient Dorian mode's power to move to "gravity and modesty"[249].

In turn, Ponzio writes at length on the suitability of gravity to church music:

---

[241] In Bizzarini 2012, p. 40.
[242] In Bizzarini 2012, p. 39, my translation.
[243] Elyot 1962, pp. 20–22.
[244] Leach 2009, p. 33.
[245] In Rainoldi 2000, p. 721, my translation.
[246] Bizzarini 2012, pp. 157–158.
[247] Guerrero 1584, *Preface*.
[248] Vives 1524; quoted in Forney 2010, p. 121, endnote 2.
[249] *Lettere volgari* 1564, fol. 116ʳ.

> The manner or style (as we wish to call it) for making a motet is grave and tranquil. The parts, especially the bass, move with gravity, and the composer should maintain such ordering of the parts from beginning to end. Likewise, the individual subjects should be grave, even if nowadays some composers make motets and other sacred works in which this is not true. In these sometimes they put the parts together with quick, even very quick motion, using syncopated minims instead of syncopated semibreves and even semiminim and quaver rests, all of which are not suitable to the gravity of motets, so that their works almost seem madrigals or canzoni[250].

It may be pointed out that (both in Latin and in several Romanic languages) words with the root /grav/ indicate low-pitched sounds as well (and thus, incidentally, qualities that are associated with low voice ranges, such as masculinity, old age etc.). The connection between these two musical meanings of *"grave"* (i.e. low and slow) is made by Zarlino also on the basis of cosmographical considerations[251], while Becon affirmed that "music is a more vain and trifling science than it becometh a man, born and appointed to matters of gravity, to spend much time about it"[252].

Music of a serious quality should possess gravity (meaning here that it should abstain from quickness): Butler states this clearly, by writing that "Plain and slow Musik is fit for grave and sad matter, quik Notes or Triple time, for mirth and rejoicing"[253]. For Thomas Morley (c.1557–1602), "grave and sober" music should eschew quick notes which "denote a kind of wantonness"[254].

A similar view was promoted by the Provincial Council of Sens, in 1528: "let the priests and clergymen take care that singing be so instituted, that the ears of the hearers be delighted with a modest and honest gravity in psalmody, with placid and pleasant modulation"[255].

We have already seen that excessive vocal agility was seen as vain, effeminate and unsuitable to church music by Becon[256], Carlier (for whom *"musica morata"* was made of long notes whereas *"musica fracta"* induced levity[257]), Erasmus[258], Herbenus[259], as, in the preceding centuries, by John of Salisbury[260]

---

250 Ponzio 1595; English translation by Gary Tomlinson in Strunk 1998, p. 472.
251 Cf. Zarlino 1558, Part IV, Chapter 15 etc.
252 Becon 1844, p. 429.
253 Butler 1636, p. 96; in Austern 2011, p. 97.
254 Morley 1597, p. 179.
255 *Mansi* 32, col. 1190 (http://bit.ly/2bzaAYG), my translation; cf. Veit 1986, p. 13.
256 Becon 1844, pp. 133–134; cf. Kim 2005, p. 190.
257 Wegman 2005, pp. 50–51.
258 In Kim 2005, p. 165.
259 Herbenus 1957, pp. 58–59; in Wegman 2005, pp. 175–176.

and Pope John XXII (for whom "the music of the Divine Office is disturbed [by] these notes of quick duration"[261]).

Those theorists who had a greater practical experience of music pointed out clearly that the use of short note-values could transform the character of music, regardless of modal choices and even of the verbal text. Zarlino wrote at length on this[262], and Ponzio stated: "The practiced composer can make his music sad or happy as he wishes in any mode, using slow or quick rhythms"[263]. In the seventeenth century, the musical aspect of the Catholic reformation of the preceding century will be interpreted as a reduction of "delicate diminutions" and "vain adornments" by both Lodovico Cresollio (also known as Louis de Cressolles SJ, 1568–1634) and Lelio Guidiccioni[264] (1582–1643).

We will see in the forthcoming Chapters that the concept of gravity as a fundamental and distinguishing feature of sacred music will recur often in the discourses on church singing by Reformers both in the Catholic and in the Protestant field[265].

If the issue of gravity/levity regarded tempo matters (i.e. both the beat and its division), the question of rhythm was no less important. In particular, a rhythmic structure which might suggest associations with dance-rhythms was to be avoided in sacred music. The deliberations of both the Synod of Constance (1567[266]) and of the Synod of Trent[267] (1593) established that music "suitable for dancing" was to be banned from worship; Cardinals Cervini and Sirleto were scandalised by the playing of a dance (or something sounding like a dance) on the organ in church[268]; and Cirillo pointed out the ontological difference between dance- and church music, stating that the former should be as dance-like as possible, but should not pollute the purity of church music[269]. It is also possible that references to dance-rhythm were meant by Lopes (in his treatise on confession, stigmatising "dishonest song and beats [*battute*] in music"[270]), although here the meaning of the Italian original is unclear.

---

**260** In Weiss and Taruskin 2008, p. 53; cf. Dalglish 1978, p. 7.
**261** In Weiss and Taruskin 2008, pp. 60–61 with modifications; cf. Raynor 1972, pp. 36–37.
**262** Cf. Zarlino 1558, Part IV, Chapter 32.
**263** Ponzio 1595; English translation by Gary Tomlinson in Strunk 1998, p. 476.
**264** Cresollio 1629, Liber III, Chapter XXVII, p. 627; Guidiccioni in Suarez 1655, p. 285. Both quoted in and translated by Lockwood (Lockwood 1975, pp. 30 ff.).
**265** Cf. Weber 2008, p. 91.
**266** *CG* 7, p. 488.
**267** *CG* 8, p. 412; cf. Weber 2008, p. 144.
**268** Lockwood 1966, pp. 44–45.
**269** *Lettere volgari* 1564, fol. 116ʳ.
**270** Lopes 1590, p. 82.

To conclude this long section on morality and music, two more aspects will be briefly mentioned, reserving a fuller discussion of each of them for Chapters Twelve (the first) and Eight/Nine (second) respectively[271].

The first aspect concerns the possibility offered by music making for men and women to interact – which could potentially lead to unwanted promiscuity and immorality. This was a source of deep concern regarding female monasteries, which could employ male musicians as music teachers or instrumentalists, thus favouring a physical and artistic proximity that could become dangerous. Moreover, nuns' performance of elaborate music invited male audience to attend their services for the sake of musical beauty: if this was already a problematic aspect *in se* (cf. St Augustine[272]), even greater moral dangers could arise when the voices of particularly gifted nuns were heard from through the enclosure grates.

Music-making brought together not only religious women with male musicians or audience, but also monks with laypeople: thus, the Visitation records for an English Cistercian Abbey in 1526 explicitly commanded, "under penalty of excommunication [...], that lay singers [...] both men and boys are to be excluded from the choir during divine offices. [...] We also condemn that laypeople enter the choir of the friars, sit and speak with them and bring dissolution"[273].

Secondly, music should also not distract the religious people from worship: according to Cajetan, this could become a grave sin[274]; on the other hand, the post-Tridentine Catholic Church will repeatedly stress the importance for both clergy and consecrated people to attend personally to their religious duties, whereas absence from the Office in choir was all too common in the period before Trent (see § 8.4.4.).

---

[271] See § 12.4.1.5., 8.4.2., 9.2.2.–3., 9.3.4. etc.
[272] Cf. *Conf.* X.33.49–50 (1955, p. 145).
[273] In Perry 1888, pp. 712–713, my translation. On this topic, cf. the extremely interesting treatise cited in bibliography as "*Ynconvenientes* s.d." and summarised in Stevenson 1961, p. 333. I did not quote from this because it was probably written in the seventeenth century; however, most of the ideas it expresses were rather common in the preceding century as well.
[274] De Vio 1897, p. 297 (IV).

### 3.3.3. A letter by Bernardino Cirillo

In several instances already, I have alluded to a letter[275] by Bernardino Cirillo. It is an often-quoted document, whose importance for the history of sixteenth-century debates on sacred music has increasingly been recognised, but which (in my opinion) has also been frequently misunderstood.

The very name of the writer has been wrongly quoted in the Spanish translation of his letter and in many of the following documents citing this: Cirillo is sometimes and erroneously referred to as "bishop Cirillo"; several writers assume "Cirillo" to be his first name (the letter is signed simply "Cirillo" in Manuzio's edition, and "Cirillo" can be a first name in Italian), and his family name Franco or Franchi. Indeed, one Cirillo Franco or Franchi (d.1585), a Servite friar, obtained a Master's Degree in Theology on 23.9.1563 in Bologna[276]; he later became Professor of theology, mathematics and music in Bologna, and wrote a treatise on the phenomenon of echo[277]. When John IV, King of Portugal, wrote a reply to Cirillo's letter, almost a century after the original, it is possible that Franco's association with music led the king to mistake him for Bernardino Cirillo.

Bernardino Cirillo was an erudite scholar, a humanist and a churchman; at the time of the letter (1549), he had been from 1535 the archpriest of the Santa Casa di Loreto. The letter's recipient (whose name has in turn been often misspelt as "Guastanezzo" or "Guastenazzo") was Ugolino Gualteruzzi (c.1524-a.1571), even though Cirillo hoped that Ugolino would eventually pass the missive to his father Carlo Gualteruzzi (1500–1577) and to Ludovico Beccadelli, another important prelate. The choice of Beccadelli as the true intended recipient of Cirillo's letter is a particularly clever one, since – more than a decade later – this same Beccadelli would be chairing the committee on the abuses in the Mass at the Council of Trent[278] (cf. § 8.4.2.) and he had been since 1545 the secretary of the Council[279]. The letter mentions several other members of the Roman curia and aristocracy, whom Cirillo hoped to interest in the concerns raised by his writ-

---

[275] It had been published first in *Lettere volgari* 1564, vol. 3, fols. 114ʳ-118ᵛ and later reprinted; it was translated into Spanish and countered by King John IV of Portugal (1604–1656; João IV 1649); translated back into Italian (João IV 1666). A manuscript copy with variants is found in Cirillo's correspondence (Biblioteca Lancisiana, Rome, MS n. 338, vol. II, fols. 7ᵛ-10ʳ). Modern editions in De Angelis 1950, pp. 39–44; English translations in Lockwood 1975, pp. 10–16; Strunk 1998, pp. 368–372; Bertoglio 2017.
[276] Bianchi 1590, p. 112.
[277] Franchi 1575.
[278] Cf. Monson 2002 p. 491.
[279] Palisca 1997, p. 286.

ing, among them Cardinals Alessandro (1520–1589) and Ranuccio Farnese[280] (1530–1565).

### 3.3.3.1. The letter's letter

The letter (dated February 15$^{th}$ or 16$^{th}$, 1549, depending on the sources) has often been simplistically understood as an attack on polyphonic music in church. However, it is worthy of more careful attention, since it takes into account several important elements, many of which have been discussed at length in this Chapter. It is therefore almost a summary of the criticism of sixteenth-century church music – as a Catholic writer saw it: thus, for its objective importance, for the frequent misunderstandings in its interpretation, and for its possibility to recapitulate most of the issues at stake, I will review here its main points[281].

Cirillo claims to have dedicated some thought to the topic of church music for two decades at the time the letter was written, and declares that music can move the affects more efficaciously than either rhetoric or oratory: this is a rather important claim coming, as it does, from someone imbued with humanistic tradition.

It was instead usual for sixteenth-century writers on music to start (as Cirillo did) their exposition by referring to classical culture; accordingly, he lists the (ancient) modes and their effects on the human soul. Interestingly, he mentions only the four modes cited in Aristotle's *Politics*[282] (Phrygian, Lydian, Dorian and Mixolydian), and thus he is clearly not speaking of the church modes[283]. However, Cirillo notes, although modern music "has reached today the refinement and perfection that it never had before, nor could have"[284], it has no vestiges of the ancient modes: and this is proved by the different effects it causes. Cirillo's reasoning is original here: he does not start by considering that modern music has abandoned the Greek modes and *thus* it cannot produce the same effects; rather, he *observes* that the famous effects are not achieved by contemporaneous music, and *thus* deduces that the ancient modes have been abandoned. As Palisca correctly notes, "Cirillo judged the current polyphonic church music by standards he acquired reading ancient authors rather than by the criteria of a trained mu-

---

[280] The best reconstruction of the complex relationships (both political and of friendship) among the members of this circle of cultivated and influential people is in Palisca 1997.
[281] The interested reader is referred to a new annotated translation which will be published in 2017 (Bertoglio 2017, forthcoming).
[282] Cf. Palisca 1997, p. 288.
[283] Palisca 1997, p. 288.
[284] *Lettere volgari* 1564, fol. 115$^r$, my translation.

sician"²⁸⁵. Indeed, here and later Cirillo himself admits his non-specialist expertise in the field, although he writes as a knowledgeable amateur. He also deplores the fact that modern music is only made of practice, with no theoretical speculation: this point might mirror music's difficult transition from *scientia* to *ars*, taking place precisely between the Middle Ages and modernity.

Cirillo then moves to consider church music proper, quoting the liturgical supplication of the *Kyrie eleison:* the function of music should be to move the listeners to an affect of compunction (the Patristic eco from St Basil's homily on the Psalms is very clear here: cf. § 2.3.4.). While we have no evidence that Cirillo knew of the Sens Provincial Council's deliberations (1528), there is a fascinating echo of their words in his statements: church songs, for the Sens Council, should "move to devotion and compunction"; sacred music should "arouse and excite" these feelings, instead of lasciviousness[286].

It is also interesting to note here the rhetorical (and rather utilitarian) function of music for Cirillo: since in a *Kyrie* the believers invoke God's mercy, music could also be thought of as a reinforcement of their prayer, something that should convey the strength of the community's feeling of repentance unto God. For Cirillo, instead, music should convince and persuade listeners to repent, and *then* their sincere supplication would reach God's ears.

The ancients, Cirillo continues, would have used the Mixolydian mode for this purpose, and would have moved all listeners to tears, "and differentiated a *Kyrie* from an *Agnus Dei*, a *Gloria* from a *Credo*, a *Sanctus* from a *Pleni*, and a *Psalm* from a *Motet*"[287]. Here too, an observation should be made: both the liturgical *Kyrie* and *Agnus Dei* are implorations of mercy (although in the former, Christ is invoked as the Lord, "*Kyrios*", and in the latter as God's Lamb); both the *Sanctus* and its sub-section *Pleni* are celebrations of God's glory and majesty; and between Psalm and motet there is a difference in genre (to say nothing of the Psalm-motets!), not (generally speaking) in affect: a Psalm and a motet on the same subject may be affectively closer to one another than settings of a triumphal and a mournful Psalm.

Cirillo then questions the very essence of compositional techniques such as the *cantus firmus* Mass (on secular chanson and on *soggetto cavato*) and the parody Mass, claiming that there can be no "motion of affects, of devotion or piety, nor any conformity of subject" between such *cantus firmus* as "the armed man"

---

**285** Palisca 1997, p. 287.
**286** *Mansi* 32, col. 1190 (http://bit.ly/2bzaAYG), my translation; cf. Veit 1986, p. 13.
**287** *Lettere volgari* 1564, fol. 115ʳ, my translation.

(*L'homme armé*) or *Hercules Dux Ferrariæ* and the subject of the different movements of the Mass Ordinary[288].

Whereas church music, according to Cirillo, fails to move the listeners' affects, this cannot be said of contemporaneous secular music: by observing the effects of dances such as the Pavane or Gaillard on the "good women" of his time, Cirillo notes that these dances achieve results similar to those of the ancient dithyrambs or of the Phrygian mode.

How then could contemporaneous musicians hope to achieve in their sacred works effects as impressive as those they obtained with secular dances? Before replying, Cirillo inserts a very interesting digression, and discusses the *Last Judgment* frescoes painted by Michelangelo in the Sistine Chapel[289] (1508–12). They are beautiful, but they are not well-suited for a church, in Cirillo's opinion, since there are too many male nudes as the artist wanted to display his virtuosity. Michelangelo was a good friend of Beccadelli, and therefore Cirillo's reference is very significant; moreover, the Sistine frescoes did provoke some uproar at the time, and – as is well known – the most scandalous nudities were eventually over-painted and provided with "pants" by Daniele da Volterra (c.1509-c.1566) in 1564.

Cirillo strengthens his point with another example: a knight's attire is splendid when worn by a jousting knight, but it may be "abominable" for others[290]. The term "abominable" used by Cirillo is a rather strong one: I will later discuss a possible interpretation of this stance (§ 3.3.3.2.). The simple moral, however, is that not all fascinating things are suitable for all occasions.

Thus, Cirillo advocates both a sacred and a secular music capable of moving their listeners to their respective affects: devotion and piety in the former case, and a dancing frenzy in the latter. Visual artists and poets of Cirillo's time had researched classical models, and thus recovered and saved their respective arts from the supposedly barbaric condition they had suffered in the Middle Ages; the same should be done by musicians in their field.

Interestingly, three years after the publication in Venice of Cirillo's letter, the Florentine scholar Cosimo Bartoli (1503–1572), who lived in Venice then, maintained that "in his day Ockeghem was, as it were, the first to rediscover music, then as good as dead, just as Donatello discovered sculpture". It is likely that Bartoli knew Cirillo's letter, since there are other similarities between their writings. Bartoli in fact states: "Ockeghem's disciple Josquin was, so to say, a miracle

---

**288** *Lettere volgari* 1564, fol. 115ᵛ, my translation. Cf. Palisca 1997, p. 289.
**289** On this topic and on its link with the subject of the *caprizare*, cf. Campione 2011, p. 242.
**290** *Lettere volgari* 1564, fol. 115ᵛ.

of nature in music, as our Michelangelo Buonarroti was in architecture, painting and sculpture"[291], while Cirillo, when discussing the Sistina frescoes, wrote: "I deem Michelangelo Buonarroti to be a miracle of nature in painting and sculpture", and later: "[I also wish] that today's musicians would try to do in their own profession what the Sculptors, Painters and Architects of our time have done, by recovering art in antiquity"[292].

In spite of this, Cirillo did not aspire to an antiquarian restoration and reconstruction of ancient practices: for example, he maintained that the Greek genera should not be recovered, as – in his opinion – they had been dismissed by the ancients themselves. Rather, study of the modes should suffice for the task, and church music should achieve both "delectation and difference"[293].

The very principles of polyphonic composition, instead, are such that sentences with contrasting verbal meanings are pronounced together: Cirillo's example, however, is sarcastic since it is very hard to find *Sanctus* settings in which "one says *Sanctus*, another *Sabaoth*, still another *Gloria tua*"[294] at the very same moment[295]. Here Cirillo's satire becomes still more pronounced, as he contributes to the musical bestiary discussed earlier in this Chapter (§ 3.3.2.9.) and equates polyphony to "a January of cats and a May of bulls"[296] (or rather asses).

Cirillo then expresses the wish that his ideas will be promoted and disseminated by his correspondent within the Papal circle; moreover, he hopes that Ugolino will find intelligent and honest musicians who could try and put into practice the writer's thoughts.

Cirillo is also convinced that the structural requirements of plainchant should not determine the work: he deplores the (alleged) standardisation of polyphonic writing and favours a compositional style tailored on the affect and meaning of the sacred words. Moreover, he encourages the recipient to speak of the matter with Beccadelli, who will able to work for the amelioration of church music. As Palisca points out,

> Cirillo implies that he does not recognize the artistic value of unifying a Mass. [...]. Quite the contrary, the movements of the Mass should each be as distinct as possible, if they are to express the individual texts and sentiments. He can only see disadvantages in a procedure

---

291 Bartoli 1567, Libro Terzo, pp. 35–36, my translation. Cf. Haar 1988.
292 *Lettere volgari* 1564, fols. 115$^v$-116$^r$, my translation.
293 *Lettere volgari* 1564, fol. 116$^r$, my translation.
294 *Lettere volgari* 1564, fol. 116$^v$, my translation.
295 I am grateful to Professor Noel O'Regan for having drawn my attention to this exaggeration in a private conversation (via email, 2014).
296 *Lettere volgari* 1564, fol. 116$^v$, my translation.

that obliges the composer to repeat the same material almost arbitrarily irrespective of the text[297].

When the main arguments of Cirillo's thesis have been expressed, he turns to Plato almost as an afterthought, quoting at length (and in Latin, in Marsilio Ficino's translation[298]) from the third book of the *Laws:* here Plato distinguishes among the various musical styles and their respective functions, before advocating the control of knowledgeable authorities on the (moral and artistic) value of music[299]. Given the ethical importance of music, it is not the audience's pleasure which should determine its success, but rather this judgement should be made (and put into practice) by those responsible for public morality.

Eventually, Cirillo mentions "a little Madrigal" by Arcadelt, whose "numbers and touching cadences" had made "the unspeaking words speak"; he wishes that sacred music could achieve such (if not higher) expressive results[300]. As Palisca states, "What Cirillo wanted was not simply to comprehend but to be moved, and [...] [liturgical] music stopped well short of arousing the passions. It could not compare in this respect to the madrigal Cirillo praised. [...] Cirillo wanted to be moved by motets and masses as he was by certain madrigals"[301].

Thus, the main concepts expressed by Cirillo can be summarised as: 1) music should move the souls; 2) church music should move to devotion and piety; 3) it presently does not; 4) but the ancient modes did move the listeners; 5) the movements of Mass Ordinary have markedly different affective content; 6) thus it should be impossible to adopt the same mode, the same *cantus firmus* or the same model for an entire setting; 7) for the sake of imitation and of compositional virtuosity, different words (corresponding to different affects) are pronounced at the same time. Several of these points are rather typical of the humanist debate on music discussed in this Chapter and in the preceding: this is unsurprising, in consideration of the humanist education of most members of the intellectual elite Cirillo was addressing his letter to (Palisca points out the connections between the Farnese circle and Girolamo Mei, for instance[302]).

---

297 Palisca 1997, p. 289.
298 Cf. Palisca 1997, p. 288.
299 *Laws* III, 700a-e; Plato 1967, available online at http://bit.ly/2cr9mmQ.
300 *Lettere volgari* 1564, fol. 118ʳ, my translation.
301 Palisca 1997, pp. 291–292.
302 Palisca 1997, p. 287.

### 3.3.3.2. The letter's spirit

Cirillo's letter, therefore, cannot be read primarily as an attack on polyphonic music; rather, its main focus is on the ethos of the ancient modes and on the possibility of recovering their effects on the human psyche and behaviour. He criticises polyphony only inasmuch techniques such as the parody or the *cantus firmus* Mass would prevent composers from assigning a suitable mode to the text, both in its macro- and microstructures[303].

A subtler reading, however, is also possible; and although I propose it tentatively, I think it may help our discussion of some complex aspects.

In several instances throughout the text, Cirillo invites Ugolino to "read between the lines", and to understand what is implicit in his writing[304]. Moreover, there are a few fragments which have hitherto received insufficient attention: 1) "What I am saying of church singing, I say of all other subjects"[305]; 2) the knight's attire is "abominable [...] on the back of that friend of ours"[306] (just after the discussion of Michelangelo's nudes); 3) "I see how the world applies itself to do what is done rather than what it should do; and I believe that Musicians go that way too"[307]; 4) "let them make their motets, *chansons*, madrigals and ballads as they please; only, let our Church with its deeds move to religion and piety"[308]; 5) the quote from Plato's *Laws*[309].

Point 1), together with the reiterated invitations to interpret Cirillo's omissions, seems to suggest that Cirillo is not concerned only with church music, but with other (probably broader and perhaps even more important) topics. I wish to clarify immediately that I do believe that Cirillo's letter is about church music, and it has always been interpreted as such; however, I also think that it is not *only* about church music.

Point 2) raises the question about the identity of "that friend of ours", for whom (as far as I know) no identification has been hitherto proposed. The expression seems to imply that the "friend" was not a friend in the common sense of the term (for example, when Cirillo mentions his real friends in the concluding greetings[310], he lists them by name, with sympathy and reverence): here,

---

303 Cf. Rees 2006, p. 349.
304 *Lettere volgari* 1564, fols. 114$^r$, 115$^v$.
305 *Lettere volgari* 1564, fol. 115$^v$.
306 *Lettere volgari* 1564, fol. 115$^v$.
307 *Lettere volgari* 1564, fol. 117$^r$, my translation.
308 *Lettere volgari* 1564, fol. 117$^r$, my translation.
309 *Lettere volgari* 1564, fols. 117$^v$-118$^r$.
310 *Lettere volgari* 1564, fol. 118$^v$.

Cirillo's use of the words "our friend" seems rather to adumbrate a famous or powerful person whom his reader(s) could easily identify but whose name he preferred not to put in writing. Moreover, Cirillo mentions a warrior's attire, but also a piece of clothing that was not fashionable anymore at his time[311]. On the basis of these elements (warrior's attire typical of the past, easily identifiable person) I would tentatively suggest to recognise in the mysterious friend Pope Julius II (1443–1513), who became known as the "Warrior Pope" by virtue of his military campaigns, during which he personally led his armies. On Palm Sunday, 1507, he was the protagonist of a spectacular triumph, in which he presented himself as both the new Julius Caesar and (even) the Christ entering triumphantly Jerusalem on that very day. However, in the satirical dialogue *Julius Exclusis*[312] (attributed to Erasmus of Rotterdam, although doubts have recently been raised), St Peter banned Julius II from heaven[313], condemning precisely the pope's habit of wearing a "bloody armour" beneath the "priest's cassock". It should be said, notwithstanding this, that Julius II was also a great patron of the arts: he commissioned Michelangelo's *Last Judgment* in the Sistine Chapel – i.e. the very same fresco discussed and criticised here by Cirillo.

The remaining points, in my opinion, fit with this interpretation. The quote from the *Laws* is a clear appeal to the authorities to act as "pastors": if music affects morals, and if the rulers are responsible for public morality, then the evaluation of music's (moral) value should concern them crucially. The wording of points 3) and 4) is no less important: "let *our Church with its deeds* move to religion and piety"[314] (my emphasis), since the world does "what is done" rather than what "it should do".

A last element to consider is that Beccadelli was in the forefront of the Catholic response to the Lutheran Reformation, among those who worked in order to attempt a reconciliation with the Protestants[315]. Moreover, the two Farnese cardinals would be among the protagonists at the conclave which was to take place in

---

**311** Cf. Pietro Aretino, Letter of November 30th, 1537: "Anyone seeing today a knight in *giornea* [...] would think he is either in disguise, or crazy" (Aretino 1864, p. 184); cf. also Castiglione 1560, pp. 144–145.
**312** Cf. Durant 1957, pp. 279–282.
**313** Cf. Stinger 1998, p. 11 etc.
**314** *Lettere volgari* 1564, fol. 117[r], my translation.
**315** I do not include among this evidence Cirillo's use of the same "cats" metaphor that had been employed by the author of the Wittenberg pamphlet (*De veteri* 1522, fol. Fii[v]), because I cannot prove that he had direct knowledge of that source; however, if he did, this might suggest that he was an attentive reader of "subversive" literature regarding the religious revolutions of the era.

that very same year, 1549: although obviously Cirillo could not foresee this, the reigning Pope (Paul III, a Farnese himself and the grandfather of both Alessandro and Ranuccio) was already older than eighty, and many in the Catholic Church were making plans for the future.

Within this framework, I think that Cirillo's letter might acquire an even greater significance than what it deserves for its value for the history of music[316].

Similar to Julius II, the Catholic Church concerned itself with things that had little to do with spirituality and faith. Similar to Michelangelo, who (in Cirillo's opinion) cared more for his fame as a virtuoso artist than for the suitability of his paintings for worship, the Church was often more attentive to outward splendour than to what mattered in spiritual terms. Similar to contemporaneous music (again in Cirillo's opinion), the Church could not move the hearts of the believers, because it was too subject to routine (cf. the musicians' standardised compositional practices, or the excessive power of the requirements of traditional plainchant over the devotional needs of the hearers). However, similar to music, the Church should and could recover the wisdom of the old, and thus hopefully reach new heights in its own art of sanctity.

In this Chapter, we have given a survey of the main features and of the main criticalities of Catholic church music during the sixteenth century. One of its main problems, perhaps, was paradoxically constituted precisely by its excessive focus on moral issues: as we will see in the next Chapters, several religious reformers (Protestant and Catholics alike) will try and recover different stances on church music. Instead of concentrating only on what was wrong or faulty in church music, the *sola gratia* perspective helped to rediscover the dimension of the gift; instead of conceiving music as nothing more than a tool for moving the souls' affects in the desired direction, the attempt was made to revive the mystical dimension of music as a fundamental part of worship. In other words, as several reformers will write, music could come as a gift from heaven, and go back there as the expression of worshipping communities.

---

316 Once more, let me stress that, though I consider my interpretation to be grounded on textual evidence, I do not pretend to be reading Cirillo's mind and cannot argue that mine is "the" correct interpretation.

# Chapter 4 – The reformers' concept of music

> Next to the Word of God, the noble art of
> music is the greatest treasure in the world[1].
>
> [Martin Luther]

## 4.1. Introduction

In the preceding Chapters, I analysed the concept of music – and especially that of "sacred" music – as it was thought of at the beginning of the sixteenth century. We will now focus on the attitude towards music among the religious reformers, thus shifting our attention from a viewpoint more distinctly characterised by musicality to one principally interested in spirituality. Although several of the issues at stake will be consistent with those already observed, the context is fundamentally different: what was (in most cases) a theoretical speculation, or at best a pious desire in the writings analysed until now, will presently become the ground for actual reforms, for concrete actions which will bring substantial changes in the daily musical experience of millions of men and women.

In the first part of this Chapter, I will focus on the common features of both the Protestant and Catholic reformers' viewpoints on music. I will first discuss the relationship between the humanist attention to the word and the reformers' focus on the Word: we will observe how the reformers' statements often echo and are grounded on the very same quotations – from the Bible, from classic philosophy, and from Church tradition.

We will then observe how their criticism of contemporaneous church music mirrored the issues presented in Chapter Three, thus demonstrating that most religious reformers were intrinsically inspired by the philosophical and cultural atmosphere of their time.

Furthermore, we will draw parallelisms among the reformers' ideas about the functions of music, and particularly of religious music: in worship, in pedagogy, in propaganda, in devotion and in exhortation, with some fascinating insights into a mystical perspective.

In the second section, I will examine in turn the most important reformers' theologies of music. I will start with Luther's concept of music, and I will dedi-

---

1 From the *Encomion musices:* in Leaver 2007, p. 322; cf. WA 50, pp. 370–371.

cate a proportionally more extensive treatment to his theology and practice of music than to those of the other reformers. This choice is due both to the chronological primacy of Luther with respect to the other reformers, but also to the undoubtedly stronger emphasis he placed on music in comparison with Calvin or Bucer – to say nothing of Zwingli.

Indeed, it will be on the Zurich reformer that we will progress immediately after, and we will observe the dramatic difference between their respective viewpoints, as well as some unexpected common elements. I will dedicate a brief discussion to the concept of music by so-called "radical reformers" (such as Karlstadt or Müntzer), and then present the theologies of music by Bucer in Strasbourg and by Calvin, highlighting the former's influence on the latter.

A short examination of the Bohemian Brethren's perspective will be followed by a presentation of the most important thinkers on music in the Church of England: here, the lack of a charismatic figure such as those of Calvin or Luther will determine the brevity of this theoretical survey, whereas the history and practice of music in England will be discussed in greater detail later.

Finally, I will summarise the most important differences between the Catholic concept of music and liturgy and those in the Evangelical area: even if the Protestant world does not present (as this Chapter will abundantly show) a homogeneous picture as concerns the treatment of music in worship and in theory, we will observe that some important differences between Evangelicals and Catholics started to emerge from the very beginning of the Reformation.

## 4.2. Where the Reformers saw eye to eye

Although the Reformers' perspectives on music cannot be simplistically equated with the humanist viewpoint, they do share many common elements, particularly as concerns the focus on verbal issues (the word or the Word, and the rhetoric aspect of music), on the ethics of music (in particular within a Platonic perspective), and on the importance of education and pedagogy (both as regards general educational matters and the religious instruction of young and adults alike). The humanistic inspiration of the Reformers and the Platonist influence on their views will be observed in a particularly clear fashion in Switzerland and in its immediate surroundings[2], but also – for example – in the Roman circles of the papal curia.

---

[2] Cf. Kim 2005, pp. 120–123 and 174; Weber 2008, p. 35; Loewe 2013, p. 576.

### 4.2.1. From word to Word

As we have seen in the preceding Chapters, humanism was characterised by its focus on the word[3]: the word with its sound and stress (study of ancient metric and prosody, and focus on *pronuntiatio*[4]); the word with its meaning (philology); the word with its history (study and recovery of ancient sources); the word and its cultural value (cultural exchanges among scholars, both at local and international level); the word, both written and read (educational reforms aiming at enhancing the spread of literacy); the word as what many thoughts are made of (great attention to verbal rationality and speculative reasoning); the word with an almost magical power to move (studies in rhetoric and oratory); finally, the word as a means to interpret the world and what goes beyond it (focus on the theological articulation of belief).

This multifaceted perspective dovetailed with the Christian concept of the Word: the Word as a person of the Trinity; the Word made flesh in Christ (with these two first elements both contributing to a Christocentric perspective); the Word expressed in human words in the Bible (spread of Biblical knowledge, both as academic research on the sources and as enhanced knowledge of Scripture by the laity); the Word in worship (meaning both that the Church prays *through* the person of Christ, who is God's Word, and that the Church prays using words); the Word and belief (and here again, both the Word as the divine Person in whom the believers profess their faith, and the way of expressing that faith); the Word and the spread of faith (catechesis and missionary activity; rhetoric and sermons[5]; hymnology as an evangelising tool; the Evangelical focus on faith); and finally the Word and tradition (here too, meaning both that Christ is the guarantor of the Church's tradition, and that the use of the same words and the same quotes through the ages establishes a chain of interpretations, exegesis and belief).

It is easy to see how the concerns for the word intertwined with those for the Word; and how both could have important results concerning the concept and the practice of music. In worship, the word needed to be clearly pronounced, distinctly heard, and understood, so that it could instruct and educate the congregation (Kim points out that "the four attributes of *pronuntiatio* – accuracy, clarity, elegance, and compatibility" had to be applied "to the art of musical composition and performance"[6] for sacred works); through words the commun-

---

3 Cf. Brauner 1994, p. 337.
4 Cf. Kim 2005, p. 16.
5 Cf. Kim 2005, p. 19.
6 Kim 2005, p. 324.

ity's belief was expressed and its cultual acts were performed; music was seen as a fundamental component of a Christian education of youths[7]; finally, the Biblical words could be spread in music and sung in prayer; and the Bible itself could and should provide the reasons and the justifications for musical practices in the Church.

Although all of these elements could (and did) foster distinctive musical practices, and sometimes contributed to creating an immensely rich heritage of sacred music, in many cases – as we have seen in the preceding Chapters – this could also imply a very partial view of music. Its own symbolic value was often denied, and music could be reduced to a function of the word; its mystical aspects and its *own* power to move (not only as a rhetorical accessory of discourse) were frequently ignored[8].

As we will see, the religious Reformers' positions on these matters can be seen as constituting a continuum ranging from the strictest opinions of those considering music as a disruption of and distraction from the purest concentration on the word/Word, to the openness of those who knew and felt that music had a symbolic and spiritual value of its own, and who admitted to the presence of a mystical dimension of musical beauty[9].

Moreover, if the primacy of the word/Word was accepted by most religious reformers, how this had to be understood with respect to the Bible was not as straightforward a matter as it might appear at first: did the Bible have a transcendent meaning which could be conveyed also in other words (meaning by this another continuum spanning translation to paraphrase to subjective rewriting)? Or did the original words matter[10]? Besides their theological import, these questions had also crucial musical consequences. Could Biblical words be interpreted and adapted to Church worship[11]? Should worship make use only of what is prescribed by the Bible, and of the very words it contains? Could the translations of Biblical words be paraphrased in order to become more "musical", i.e. more suitable for musical renditions and communal singing? Should the Biblical words, when sung, be distinctly perceptible, or could their expressive value be conveyed almost mystically through the beauty of sounds? Here too, we will see in the forthcoming pages that answers to these and to similar questions were extremely different within the various Churches in the sixteenth century.

---

[7] Kim 2005, pp. 119–120.
[8] Cf. the view of fine arts as "similar to oratory" in the perspective of Catholic reformer Gabriele Paleotti: Prodi 2014, p. 95, and Chapter Eight: § 8.3.4.
[9] Cf. Viladesau 2000, pp. 25–26.
[10] Cf. Ferguson 2011, p. 140; Zim 2011, p. 1.
[11] Cf. Leaver 2006, p. 378.

### 4.2.2. Sources as resources

We have seen in Chapter Two (§ 2.3. and following) that the concern for sources was crucial within a humanist perspective: the ancient sources had to be studied in their original language, were quoted at length in any speculative debate and often constituted the ultimate authority for scientific study (before Galileo) and even for the evaluation of contemporary artistic creations (literary, visual...). We have also seen how this applied to music, where "ancient" sources were rather fragmentary and difficult to interpret as to practice (whereas visual art was judged on the basis of classical canons, music could not be compared with the actual sound of Greek music), but they were extensively quoted and deeply appreciated in theory (writings on music by philosophers such as Plato or Aristotle, theory and physics of music and acoustics, legends on music in ancient literature, influence of ancient rhetoric, oratory and prosodic principles on the concept and practice of music). Within a Christian perspective, this study of the sources became also a principle encouraging the study of and debate about the Christian sources on music: first and foremost, the Bible (which actually could provide arguments in support of practically whatever viewpoint on music), then the Patristic tradition and the pronouncements of the Church in the past.

For example, the Platonic component of Calvin's thought on music was very clear (especially as regards the moral and affective power of music: from this viewpoint his perspective was very close to Bucer's[12]), and equally clear were the Christian sources on which he relied to ground it: in Erasmus' wake, the principles of history, Scripture and Patristic tradition were declined – in Calvin's theology of music – as references to Church practice, to St Paul's authority, and to St Augustine[13].

In most cases, the philosophical tradition (largely "pagan") and the Christian heritage were considered to be two complementary and non-conflicting components and sources of the Reformers' reflection on music, although – when a conflict did arise, at least in how some radical reformers interpreted them – preference was normally accorded to the Christian tradition. Such an opposition is clearly observed, for example, in Becon's view: in his opinion, "all Scholemasters & teachers of youth" should have taught their pupils "these verses of David [...] in stede of Virgile, Ovide, Horas, Catullus, Tibullus, Propertius,

---

[12] Garside 1979, p. 29.
[13] Kim 2005, pp. 117–118.

&c."[14]. In this case, the Bible was not seen only as a religious book, but as having also an aesthetic and cultural value – so high a value, actually, that it could satisfactorily replace humanist learning.

The Bible was held by almost all Reformers (with the only exception of the most extreme "spirituals" who claimed to be directly inspired by the Holy Ghost) to be the ultimate reference when doctrinal or pastoral difficulties arose.

In the Bible, the Reformers could find stories relating the powerful effects of music on human behaviour (even if it was conditioned by superhuman forces: cf. David quietening Saul by the sound of his music, 1 Samuel 16:23), on the inanimate world (such as the fall of Jericho's walls: Joshua 6:20) and on the spiritual life (such as the influence of music on prophecy: cf. 2 Kings 3:15[15]); there were testimonies on the (Jewish, apostolic and early Christian) use of sung and instrumental music in both official and private worship, which were sometimes interpreted with radically different results (in support or against music and instruments); there were instructions and commands as to the (Jewish and Christian) use of music in worship, which in turn led to sometimes highly conflicting conclusions.

The Biblical attestations of the powerful effects worked by music on humans are quoted in Luther's *Encomion Musices*[16] (1538a), and his reliance on the Biblical model for hymn-writing is shown in his letters (1524[17]), thus shaping a circular itinerary from Word to music and to words again: the Word bears witness to the value of music, which in turn binds itself to the Word and puts its expressive resources at the service of words. This attitude should also be understood in connection with the contemporaneous shift in the concept of music from *scientia* to *ars*, and from the mathematics to the humanities[18]. On the other hand, Zwingli deduced from his readings of the Old Testament the reasons for banning instrumental music from churches[19] whereas the Italian Reformer Peter Martyr Vermigli analysed the musical episodes in Exodus 15 in support of the adoption of music by the Church[20].

Excerpting from Pauline fragments, however, the Reformers could find arguments both in favour of and against music: for example, discussing the very

---

[14] Becon 1542, sig. A6ᵛ-A7ʳ; in Zim 2011, p. 4.
[15] Cf. St Ambrose's *In psalmum David CXVIII expositio* 7.26, *PL* 15, cols. 1289–1290 (Vulgate IV *Regum* IIII:14); cf. Zarlino 1558, Part I, Chapter Two.
[16] See in Leaver 2007, p. 322; Sfredda 2010, p. 26; cf. *WA* 50, pp. 364–374.
[17] *LW* 49, p. 68.
[18] Cf. Blume 1975, p. 13; Leaver 2007, p. 35; Sfredda 2010, p. 26.
[19] Marcus 2001, p. 729.
[20] Leaver 2006, p. 386.

same Chapter from the First Letter to the Corinthians (1 Corinthians 14), Erasmus found support for advocating "speech-like singing", whereas Luther noticed St Paul's acknowledgement of music's communicative power[21]. For Zwingli, however, St Paul's stress on the "prayer of the heart" (cf. Ephesians 5:19 and Colossians 3:16) did not imply merely that prayer must be heartfelt, but also that is must *remain* in the heart (thus virtually denying legitimacy to vocal expressions of the heart's prayerful feelings[22]). While agreeing with Zwingli on the topic of instrumental music, on the grounds of 1 Corinthians 14:13[23], Calvin excerpted from St Paul[24] and from the tradition of the early Church[25] in order to justify his choice of allowing only unaccompanied unison psalmody in the worships of the Genevan Church[26]. References to the apostolic tradition were also made at the Council of Trent, but in this case they were in support of the retention of "ceremonies, vestments, and outward things"[27] (including music) in Catholic worship.

Among Patristic sources, the place of honour in the Reformers' theology of music undoubtedly goes to St Augustine (even though St Jerome is discussed very often too). The reader will recall from our brief discussion of Augustine's theology of music in Chapter Two (§ 2.3.4.) and of how it was interpreted in the sixteenth century, that, in the *Confessions*, Augustine's position on music was not that of unconditional approval. He admitted to music's power to lead the soul to God (as had happened in his own experience), but deemed it to be a help for the weak (and thus not indispensable for all believers) and even considered an excessive aural delight to be a grave sin.

Of this complex, nuanced and slightly controversial stance, the former Augustinian monk Luther took only the most positive aspects. Certainly, Luther's theology of music is not just indebted to Augustine's, but imbued with his teaching and shaped by his spiritual perspective[28]; so strong was this link, that the Catholic historian of Church music Rainoldi has defined Luther as the greatest writer on music in the Western Church since Augustine himself[29].

---

[21] Kim 2005, pp. 121–122.
[22] Garside 1966, p. 53.
[23] Korrick 1990, p. 362.
[24] *OC* X¹, p. 12; *OS* 1, p. 375.
[25] Garside 1951, p. 568; Garside 1979, pp. 10 and 28.
[26] Cf. Blankenburg 1975, p. 517; Noll 2007, pp. 16–17; Lindberg 2010, p. 373; Sfredda 2010, pp. 82–83.
[27] *CT* 13, p. 714.
[28] Portnoy 1949, p. 238.
[29] Rainoldi 2000, p. 706.

However, the distance between Augustine's wavering statements and Luther's enthusiasm cannot be summarised more clearly than by Luther's own words:

> While the Passion was being sung, he observed with the utmost attention, saying: "Music is an excellent gift of God. It rather frequently urged and stimulated me to preach with joy. St Augustine had such a conscience that he imagined to be sinning as he enjoyed music. He was a fine man. Were he living in our century, he would feel the same as we do"[30].

On the other hand, Augustine's position – with both its pros and its cons – was shared by Calvin: interestingly, Buszin points out that Augustinian theologies of music were likely to emerge where and when church music was problematized in the history of Western spirituality[31]. Thus, Calvin followed the Patristic tradition in advocating "gravity" in church music and in fearing the excessive fascination of aural pleasure[32].

### 4.2.3. Reforming Church music

In this section, we will review the Reformers' thought on what needed to be modified in the musical tradition they had inherited from the Catholic Church. Clearly, most of the issues we will be discussing in the following pages have been already treated in Chapter Three: however, while the preceding Chapter aimed at framing the situation of sacred music and of its problematic aspects within the context of contemporaneous culture, we will now see how the most important Reformers reacted to these same problems.

Among the problems we will discuss, some are more theological than properly musical: for example, the very nature of worship was questioned by many Protestant reformers, since the *sola gratia* principle could be interpreted as depriving of meaning the entire function of rituality (and so thought some of the most radical Reformers). Moreover, the *sola scriptura* principle could in turn be interpreted as denying validity to all traditional forms of prayer and cult unless they had been prescribed specifically by the Bible; and the focus on the universal priesthood of all believers had profound musical implications as well. As efficaciously summarised by McKee, "Generally, worship became less mechani-

---

30 *WA TR* IV, p. 313, no. 4441, my translation. Cf. Kim 2005, pp. 121–122; Sooy 2006, p. 49.
31 Buszin 1958, p. 11.
32 Cf. Calvin 1960, p. 895; *OC* II, p. 659; *OS* 4, p. 342; *OC* VI, pp. 169–170; *OS* 2, p. 15; see also Garside 1979, p. 20; Herl 2004, pp. 108–109.

cal and individualistic for Protestants and more demanding; it required understanding, active attention, and some specific acts of participation in a common service. Visual arts with their many layers of meaning for individual appropriation give way to verbal art, the corporate focus of a gathered people"[33].

#### 4.2.3.1. *"A cantantibus intellectus"*: words for whom?

One of the most frequently discussed interventions of the Reformations on church music regards the matter of intelligibility. We have seen in Chapter Three (§ 3.3.1.4.) that this topic was felt in a very nuanced fashion in the Catholic Church, regarding (as it did) the debate on whether the sung words had to be discernible (in polyphony, in melismatic singing...), whether the laity and/or the singers should be able to understand them, and whether the liturgy had to be performed aloud, in the vernacular, and/or include vocal participation by the congregation.

In consequence, the effort to enhance the intelligibility of what was sung took a variety of shapes in the Protestant and in the Catholic reformations. It could take the form of unaccompanied and syllabic monody (whose particularly simple musical style had also the obvious purpose of allowing all members of the congregation to sing it), or of homophonic and syllabic harmonisations (with or without instrumental accompaniment); or else, it could simply favour less elaborate imitative writing and a simpler musical style in a genuinely polyphonic musical composition.

Moreover, this concern for intelligibility (not only as regards music, but also Scripture's reading and explanation in services) could also foster architectural considerations, both as regards the criticism of existing buildings (whose huge dimensions did not favour the clear delivery of speech and song) and the concept of new edifices[34].

The syllabic style (in monody or in homophonic harmonisations, depending on the confession and on the performance context) was widely adopted in the Protestant Churches[35], and had been influenced by the creation and spread of humanist odes[36]. Lutheran Chorales were in principle syllabic[37] (though more complex elaborations were possible); this same concern for clarity in textual delivery was seen in multi-voiced settings of Lutheran *Lieder*, such as those found

---

[33] McKee 2003, pp. 9–10. Cf. Hendrickson 2003, p. 54.
[34] Cf. *WA TR* III, p. 611, no. 3781; English translation in Leaver 2006, p. 374.
[35] Weber 2008, p. 214.
[36] Kim 2005, pp. 119–120.
[37] Haar 2006, p. 32.

in the 1524 collection by Johann Walther[38] (1496–1570). However, as soon as confessionalisation started to appear and the Lutherans and Calvinists strove to distinguish themselves from each other, the Lutherans began to maintain that intelligibility was still important, but not indispensable[39].

On the other hand, a clearly humanist concern for delivery and *pronuntiatio* is observable both in Luther's *Deudsche Messe* (1526) and in the *Book of Common Prayer Noted* (1550) of the Church of England: as Kim comments, "they illustrate characteristic insights of the humanist reform of plainchant of the day"[40]. Indeed, as Shaw points out, the often-quoted statements by Cranmer on the importance of syllabic style are rooted in a pre-existing practice[41]; however, undeniably the concern for the proper delivery and understanding of the text was of primary import for the Church of England, as pronouncements issued during the reigns of Edward VI (1552[42]) and Elizabeth (1559[43]) clearly confirm.

Of course, for the text to be understood it needed to be – at least – pronounced: thus, the *alternatim* practice was often criticised, not only for its omission of the corresponding text, but also for the attention it drew on the solo organist; this primacy of an instrumental soloist was seen by many as detrimental to the unity and communion of the congregation[44].

If the condemnation of textual omissions was the basic requirement for a proper liturgy, the debate as to the language of worship followed suit: as seen in Chapter Three (§ 3.3.1.4.), in fact, this topic was freely discussed in the Catholic Church as well. Indeed, in both the Catholic and Lutheran Churches, a certain flexibility was always maintained: vernacular elements were occasionally admitted in the Catholic worship (which however remained basically in Latin[45]), and (as we will see in a greater detail later: § 5.3.1. and following) the Lutherans did not ban Latin music and prayers from their own liturgy. Actually, for the Lutherans, it was the singers who had the duty and the right to understand what they were singing (the principle was known as "*cantus a cantantibus intellectus*"[46]): this applied both to congregational singing in the vernacular and to polyphonic singing in Latin by the choir. Indeed, according to the Lutheran theologian Eras-

---

[38] Walther 1524. Cf. Leaver 2006, p. 379.
[39] Cf. the debate between Andreae and Bèze in Irwin 1983, p. 161.
[40] Kim 2005, p. 15 and p. 255.
[41] Shaw 1975, p. 697.
[42] Leaver 2006, p. 398.
[43] *Injunctions* 1559; *Injunctions* 1914, p. 435; cf. Le Huray 2008, p. 33; Bray 2004, p. 344.
[44] Blume 1975, p. 107.
[45] Rainoldi 2000, p. 352.
[46] Brown 2008, pp. 230–231.

mus Alber (c.1500–1553), those who condemned Latin worship as a papist practice were inspired by the devil[47]. The permission for upholding Latin rites alongside those in the vernacular was frequently deduced from 1 Corinthians 14, where the possibility of praying in (unknown) tongues is admitted. On the basis of the same Scriptural quote, the Catholic Robert Bellarmine (1542–1621) maintained that understanding was preferable but not indispensable for worship[48] (see § 4.3.7.2.[49]), while some explanation and instruction for the laity in the vernacular was encouraged also in the Roman Church[50].

The Calvinist Church adopted a much more uncompromising stance, abolishing the use of Latin in worship[51], criticising the unintelligibility of Latin psalmody[52] and the fact it had been taken away from the multitude of the laypeople: for the Calvinists, thus, "singing with understanding" (cf. 1 Corinthians 14:15) became a crucial criterion for a proper Christian worship[53].

All of these themes will be discussed more deeply later in this Chapter and in the following ones; this short survey aimed merely at pointing out how the principal Reformers stood in relation to issues of intelligibility and delivery, and whence did their convictions originate.

### 4.2.3.2. "Not so excellent a thing": the risks of music

A similar brief review will be now proposed as regards moral issues, which will closely mirror those discussed in Chapter Three.

The risks posed by excessive aural enjoyment to a proper concentration on heartfelt prayer and on the Word of God were particularly clear in the Calvinist field: Théodore de Bèze criticised "popish" music for the pleasure it endeavoured to cause[54], while Pierre Viret (c.1511–1571) defined it as "lascivious", aiming only at "giving delight to the ears, and detaining them, and in the meanwhile distracting the hearts from feeling and understanding the sung words, which must be understood by all". The Reformed Church did not admit "in God's temple any lascivious and dishonest music", nor any which "could prevent the understanding of what is sung, without which it would be better to sing nothing". Therefore,

---

47 Alber 1556, fol. Y2ʳ. Cf. Herl 2004, p. 108.
48 Bellarmino 1599, Book II, Chapter 16 (pp. 187–188).
49 Cf. Kolb and Nestingen 2001, pp. 127–128.
50 Weber 2008, p. 84, p. 90, p. 168.
51 Blankenburg 1975, p. 517.
52 Reid 1971, p. 38.
53 Garside 1979, p. 27.
54 Cf. Irwin 1983, p. 161.

Viret continues, "we explain to the people what is sung, and we sing only in an intelligible tongue, using a plain and very modest music, and giving to each syllable one note only, as the ancients did"[55].

A similar view was fostered by Catholic authorities as well: at the Provincial Council of Sens (1528), while advocating a kind of church music which "delights the ears of the hearers", the Fathers also prohibited music which "arouses and excites to [...] lasciviousness, titillating heart or soul"[56].

Notwithstanding this, one of the clearest condemnations of the usual themes of lascivious, effeminate and dance music in worship was that written by Zwingli, in his commentary to Amos 5:23:

> What would the farmer-prophet [Amos] do in our times, if he saw so many different kinds of music in the temples, and heard so many different rhythms of *basses danses, tourdions, saltarelli*, and other proportions, while the effeminate canons went to the altar in their silk surplices? Truly, he would cry out so that the whole world could not endure his word[57].

Thomas Becon was almost as strict as Zwingli in his criticism of music:

> All other outward melody is vain and transitory, and passeth away and cometh to nought. Vain and transitory it is indeed; notwithstanding, music may be used, so it be not abused. If it be soberly exercised and reputed as a handmaid unto virtue, it is tolerable; otherwise it is execrable and to be abhorred of all good men. So ye perceive that music is not so excellent a thing, that a Christian ought earnestly to rejoice in it[58].

Another criticality we have already discussed in Chapter Three (§ 3.3.2.5.) and will further analyse in its theological implications toward the end of this Chapter (§ 4.3.7.1.) is that concerning the professionalisation of church music. Many in the Evangelical field pointed out that the act of worship, which should involve the whole congregation as the symbolic image of the entire Church, had become the prerogative of the clergy from the one side, and of professional singers from the other. We will see that, though this situation was seen as problematic by many Catholics as well as by the most important Evangelical reformers, the theological principles on which this criticism was grounded were different, and so would be the attempted solutions[59].

---

55 Viret 1556, pp. 71–72.
56 *Mansi* 32, col. 1190, available online at http://bit.ly/2bzaAYG, my translation.
57 *Z* II, pp. 352–353; available online at http://bit.ly/2bOSm9I.
58 Becon 1844, p. 430.
59 Cf. Rainoldi 2000, p. 352; McKee 2003, p. 10; Witvliet 2003, p. 211; White 2005, pp. 63–66 and 72; Wetzel and Heitmeyer 2013, pp. vii-viii.; etc.

Certainly, however, the question of professional singers contributed to the extreme aversion felt by many Reformers against church music, which was considered by some (as discussed in § 3.3.2.6.) to be a waste of time and money, as well as the pharisaic practice of a purely outward worship. Among those surrounding Luther, Andreas Karlstadt (*De Cantu Gregoriano Disputatio*, 1521–2[60]) was one of the harshest in his criticism: he believed that the intrinsic difficulty of Catholic church music required from singers so high a concentration on music that their own prayer would become almost negligible[61].

Closest to Karlstadt's position was Zwingli, who considered the very act of singing as a distraction and a form of vanity, disrupting the soul's concentration and promoting a proud display of one's musical abilities[62].

A strong focus on interiority, and on the purity of a silent and heartfelt devotion characterised also Calvin's attitude to worship and to music, especially in his first statements on the subject. For him, indeed, the individual's intentions, and the sincerity of the soul's prayer were primary concerns: the focus on the spiritual (as opposed to carnal) reality of God fostered a spiritualised concept of prayer and worship[63].

It should be pointed out, however, that such concerns were by no means an exclusive preoccupation of the Evangelicals. We will see in greater detail in Chapters Eight and Nine how these topics were felt in the Catholic Church[64]; suffice it to mention now the interest in a heartfelt devotion expressed by both Biagio Rossetto[65] (who worked alongside the Catholic reformer Ghiberti) and Federigo Borromeo[66], among many others.

In Chapter Three (§ 3.3.2.12.) we have also seen that "gravity" (as opposed to levity and frivolity) was considered by many to be a necessary feature of a proper church music, and that there was a long Patristic and magisterial tradition supporting this view. Whereas some of the declarations by the Council of Trent substantially agreed on this view[67], it was Calvin who developed more fully this topic. He advocated a style of singing which was not "light and fickle, but rather had weight and majesty, as said by St Augustine. And also, that there is great

---

[60] In Barge 1905, vol. I, pp. 491–493.
[61] Cf. Blankenburg 1975, p. 510; Herl 2004, p. 108.
[62] Cf. Garside 1966, pp. 49 and 53; Blankenburg 1975, p. 510; Koenigsberger 1986, p. 191. For a summary of Zwingli's concept of music, see § 4.3.2.
[63] Cf. Whale 1936, p. 162; Garside 1979, pp. 8–9.
[64] Cf. § 8.2.2., 8.2.4., 8.4.3., 9.2.2.–3. etc.
[65] Rossetto 1529, quoted in Rainoldi 2000, pp. 720 ff.
[66] Cf. the letter A115 in Bizzarini 2012, p. 132.
[67] Cf. *SCT* p. 156.

difference between the music made for rejoicing at table and at home, and the Psalms sung at Church, in the presence of God and of his angels"[68]. The qualities of "weight and majesty" clearly stem from a humanistic context, similar to that inspiring Pontus de Tyard[69], and revealed the Patristic influence of St Jerome and Chrysostom[70]; of course, St Augustine had had once more a key role in shaping the Reformer's viewpoint[71]. For Blankenburg, *"poids et majesté"* mirror rather melodic/rhythmic simplicity than tempo issues: indeed, in our discussion of the *gravitas* in Chapter Three (§ 3.3.2.12.) we have seen that those advocating it in church music were also complaining against excessive diminutions (thus the condemned quickness was rather in the beat's division than in the beat proper); however, Blankenburg himself hastens to add that "an inappropriate fast [tempo] was out of the question"[72]. In my opinion, as mentioned in Chapter Three, *gravitas* concerned both the beat and its division, as the beat's speed might suggest dance-like associations, whereas a rich ornamentation could foster a joyful and too-pleasing delight in the beauty of melody.

Moreover, Calvin's stress on the ontological difference between a kind of music made for delighting the human beings and one made to please God mirrors the concerns expressed by Bernardino Cirillo: "The praises of the Lord God [should be] sung differently from the secular things"[73]. Vicentino was of the same advice:

> Compositions for four voices that are settings of Masses and other Latin texts must be serious and not greatly agitated. Since Masses and Psalms are church compositions, it is essential that their movement be different from that of French chansons and of madrigals and *villotte*. Some composers set these works in a way that upsets the entire subject of the Mass, which requires a means of movement that is grave and more filled with devotion than with worldly pleasure. [...] One should certainly strive to make a great difference between a composition that is to be sung in church and one that is to be sung in the chamber, and the composer should carefully sharpen his judgement and set his compositions according to the subject and purpose of the words[74].

A topic that can be only touched on in passing here, but which would be worthy of more attention, is that of the attitude towards dance by the religious reform-

---

[68] Calvin 1542, "Epistre au lecteur", my translation; *OC* VI, pp. 169–170; *OS* 2, p. 15. Cf. Sfredda 2010, pp. 81–82; Garside 1951, p. 568.
[69] Cf. De Tyard 1555.
[70] Cf. Hunter 1999, pp. 279–280.
[71] Cf. Garside 1979, p. 28; Kim 2005, pp. 119–120.
[72] Blankenburg 1975, p. 531.
[73] *Lettere volgari* 1564, fol. 117ʳ, my translation.
[74] Vicentino 1555, Book VI, Chapter XXVI, p. 84ᵛ; English translation in Lockwood 1975, p. 17.

ers. We have already considered Zwingli's criticism against music reminiscent of dance-rhythms in church, as well as how scandalised were Cardinals Cervini and Sirleto when they heard similar tunes played by the organ; we have also considered how gestures suggesting dance-like associations were considered as unsuitable for church music. Not only in church, however, but also outside it, some Reformers strictly limited the practice of dance (although, as we will see later, some Lutherans actually encouraged it with spiritual aims: § 12.3.1.1.). For example, the Geneva Consistory often condemned "dancing and unseemly singing"[75] almost as criminal offences: "Anyone who sings indecent, dissolute, or outrageous songs or dances the fling or some other similar dance shall be imprisoned for three days and shall then be sent before the Consistory"[76]. As we will discuss in the forthcoming pages, the different theological concepts entertained by the Reformers about such crucial dogmatic aspects as creation and incarnation were largely responsible for their attitude towards music (and the enjoyment of music), dance and the arts.

### 4.2.3.3. Creation and creativity

Indeed, the Reformers' approach to visual art was also conditioned by two other issues which were deeply rooted in the characterising features of their theology. As seen in Chapter One (§ 1.2.2.), the *sola gratia* principle, by denying any decisive value to human merits for achieving salvation, also deprived the cult of the saints of its validity: in medieval theology, the good works of the saints contributed to constituting a treasure of Grace from which sinners could draw to obtain mercy; the saints were also seen as mediators (intercessors) between Christians and God. If, on the contrary, God's mercy was purely gratuitous, then devotion to the saints became unnecessary at best and harmful at worst, and there was no need to foster it through visual depictions in churches and at homes[77].

Secondly, the *sola scriptura* principle brought to light that the Old Testament had forbidden visual representations (particularly with reference to carved images: cf. Leviticus 26:1; Exodus 20:4–5). Although (as seen in § 1.2.3.) the Church had already dealt with this topic during the iconoclasm controversies in the eighth century, those Reformers who rejected more strongly the authority of tradition in favour of Scripture were forced to consider images as idolatrous[78]. Interestingly, however, the Catholic Bishop Vittore Soranzo (1500–1558), while or-

---

75 Lindberg 2010, p. 249.
76 In Hughes 1966, p. 58; cf. *OC* X$^2$, No. 111, p. 192.
77 Leaver 2006, p. 374.
78 Cf. Irwin 1993, p. 18.

dering the abolition of allegedly unseemly images, stated that the most beautiful church was one entirely white[79].

The destruction of images from former Catholic churches could take very violent forms during the crucial years of the Reformations, and resemble more closely riotous devastation than religious purification, at least in certain cases. Churches were spoiled of statues (first and foremost), walls were whitewashed, pictures were destroyed or vandalised, and in some cases organs were nailed or dismantled.

Indeed, at first (1522) Luther himself had been rather close to iconoclastic positions: "See, that is the proper worship, for which a person needs no bells, no churches, no vessels or ornaments, no lights or candles, no organs or singing, no paintings or images, no panels or altars [...]. For these are all human inventions and ornaments, which God does not heed, and which obscure the correct worship, with their glitter"[80].

He was however to change his attitude rather soon, as shown in the *Invocavit* sermons against Karlstadt (who maintained a rigidly iconoclastic stance[81]): Luther would eventually foster a concept of visual art as a catechetic tool in the service of evangelisation[82].

Against Zwingli at the Marburg colloquy (1529), Luther would express his viewpoint more clearly, in connection with other fundamental theological points, in particular as concerns the nature of the Eucharist. The path from this to visual (and sometimes to musical) art is not obvious, so it may need to be briefly summarised. Reformers such as Karlstadt and Zwingli asserted that Christ could not be present in the consecrated bread and wine since – after his Ascension to heaven – he is "at the right hand of God"[83]. Against them, Luther based his concept of the Eucharist on the principle of the *communicatio idiomatum:* Christ is both a Person of the Trinity (i.e. has a divine nature) and a human being by virtue of his incarnation, and these two natures communicate with each other[84]. Thus, the fact that his glorified human body is "at the right hand of God" does not limit his possibility to be present in the Eucharist. This implies that the "finite", created and bodily nature of a human being, but also

---

[79] Prodi 2014, p. 24.
[80] *WA* 10$^{I/1}$, p. 39 (translation of this passage by Carl Christensen: Christensen 1979, p. 43).
[81] Eire 1989, pp. 67–68.
[82] Leaver 2006, p. 374.
[83] Cf. Acts, 2:33 etc., as well as the Nicene Creed.
[84] On the connection between Luther's theology of the Incarnation and music, cf. Hendrickson 2003, pp. 251 ff.

of bread and wine, is "capable of the infinite (*finitum capax infiniti est*)"[85]. This stance mirrors a substantially positive view of the created world, of the body, of the physical component of the universe. Thus, the human senses are created good in turn[86]; they need not be denied in favour of a purely spiritual worship, nor do they inescapably lead to an opposition of carnal and spiritual. So, finally, the appreciation of music which pleases the ear is not evil or sinful; and therefore the celebration of the beauty of the created world in visual art is both legitimate and commendable. In Lindberg's words, "To Zwingli, who like Karlstadt had the sound pastoral intuition that the externalization of religion put God at human disposal", the principle that the finite is capable of the infinite "suggested idolatry. But to Luther this meant not only that ordinary bread and wine may communicate the presence and promise of God, but that all creation may serve the creator. This is the theological foundation for Luther's profound appreciation of nature and art as vehicles for communicating the gospel"[87].

Similarly, Christophorus of Padua (1500–1569), who was, incidentally, the Father General of the *Augustinian* Order, stated at the Council of Trent that "Outward signs arouse the people to devotion, just as song and sound incite to devotion in church"[88], and we will soon discuss the stance of Gabriele Paleotti, a Catholic reformer, as concerns the theological justification of secular visual art[89].

Calvin's position is, again, more nuanced and complex. He did not forbid visual art as such (indeed, he maintained that it could be inspired by the Holy Ghost[90]), but he did not admit it in church buildings (as we will discuss later, this position was remarkably similar to his view of instrumental music: § 4.2.5.); since music was based on invisible sounds, which might seem closer to the spiritual (non-bodily) nature of God, it was seen as more appropriate for worship than visual depictions of a spiritual reality[91].

### 4.2.4. What's the use of music?

In this section, we will briefly consider the common features as well as the differences in the principal Reformers' views of music and of its function in the believ-

---

[85] Cf. Lindberg 2010, p. 181.
[86] Cf. Auksi 1995, p. 217.
[87] Lindberg 2010, pp. 184–185.
[88] *CT* 13, p. 714.
[89] Prodi 2014, p. 94 and fn. 121.
[90] Cf. Calvin 1960, II, ii, 16.
[91] Cf. Spelman 1948, p. 249; Joby 2005, p. 1 and p. 71.

ers' lives. The functions we will take into account are: 1) music as a gift of God in the created world; 2) as a means for praising Him in worship; 3) for creating communion; 4) for fostering piety and devotion; 5) for instructing and conveying the Word; 6) for moving and promoting ethical behaviours; 7) for comforting; 8) music as a mystical force, also against the evil; 9) music as a means for propaganda; 10) music within the principle of *adiaphora*. It will be noted that several of these functions mirror very closely those listed by St Basil in his praise of psalmody quoted in Chapter Two (§ 2.3.4.).

### 4.2.4.1. A gift of God

The very first aspect we will consider is almost a continuation of the preceding paragraphs, since music was seen by most Reformers as a gift of God: this perspective, in turn, refers to a theological understanding of the created world.

We have briefly mentioned above (§ 4.2.3.3.) that a Chalcedonian (i.e. dogmatically orthodox) concept of Christ's divine and human nature is at the root of the Christian appreciation for the physical world, and particularly for the physical aspect of human life. Since God, who is a purely spiritual being, took a human flesh and lived a human life in Christ's incarnation, then human beings (with their physicality, their sexuality, their bodily experiences, their voice, sight, hearing, their creativity, their feelings, their rationality...) are intrinsically good. Besides the theology of Incarnation, the other fundamental theological theme that enters into this discussion is that of creation. The Biblical narration of Genesis emphasises that all creatures are pronounced "good" by their Creator, and thus affirms unequivocally the goodness of the created world.

Notwithstanding this, a recurrent heterodox current in the history of the Christian thought tends to deny the double nature of Christ, and thus to describe Him either as a God who presents Himself in human form (but without really being a man), or as a particularly holy man (who is not divine): the transcendent nature of God is seen as ontologically incompatible with the finite reality of the human being. The corollary of such a position is – rather obviously – a somehow contemptuous view of the physical reality, and an emphasis on the spiritual world *in opposition* to it. (Incidentally, one of the historical manifestations of this heresy is called Manichaeism, and St Augustine's spiritual experience had been deeply marked by his own former belonging to and then rejection of Manichaeism. This element should be taken into account, remembering Luther's education as an Augustinian monk).

Both for Luther's Augustinian perspective and (undoubtedly) for his own personal and strong attachment to music, his theology of music tends to see it in the best possible light. He defined it as "the greatest treasure on earth after

God's word", and the creature that should be praised most[92]. Moreover, for him music is a "gift of God, to which I assign the place next to theology"[93]. As Leaver rightfully points out, this concept stresses the difference between a view of music as a human invention (i.e. merely a product of human creativity) and the idea that it is a God-given reality, which – similar to other creatures – is trusted to humans for their good by God's providence. Significantly, Luther's repeated definitions of music as a "gift of God" mostly coalesce at the very same time of his Genesis lectures, in which, obviously, his theology of the created world was being developed, discussed and preached[94]. The beauty of music thus becomes a symbol of and mirrors the beauty of its Creator[95]. Inspired by the Wittenberg Reformer, later Lutherans further developed this viewpoint: for example, Johannes Mathesius (1504–1565) defined music as a "divine and heavenly thing", as well as a "glorious gift of God"[96].

Calvin did use the very same expression as Luther, defining music (alongside with the visual arts) as "a gift of God", whose aim is to foster the human quest for a spiritual joy. Notwithstanding the seeming similarity, it should be pointed out that here Calvin (differently from Luther) inserts immediately an "aim": music is seen as a God-given tool (provided with a manual of instructions) rather than as a gift proper[97].

In fact, whereas Luther's definitions of music are found in his *Encomion musices* (the "praise of music"), the context of Calvin's statements is rather different. Actually, Calvin's discourse mirrors more closely the reasoning discussed in Chapter Two as regards the risks and perils of musical enjoyment (§ 2.4.3.): although the true spiritual joy of human beings is in God, Calvin writes, they sinfully attach themselves to lesser and vain kinds of joy. Thus, God created music (as well as similar gifts) as a "means in order to occupy us in that spiritual joy which He recommends to us so much"[98]. Calvin's view of music in the created world is therefore substantially positive, but not as unconditional and enthusiastic as Luther's.

---

[92] From the *Encomion musices:* in Leaver 2007, p. 322. German text: "*In summa die edle Music ist nach Gottes wordt / der höchste Schatz auff Erden*"; Latin: "*Hoc unum possumus nunc afferre, quod experientia testis est. Musicam esse unam quæ post verbum Dei merito celebrari debeat*". Cf. *WA* 50, pp. 370–371.
[93] *WA TR* I, p. 490, no. 968: "*Die Musica ist eine schöne Gabe Gottes, und nahe der Theologie*".
[94] Leaver 2007, pp. 70 and 89.
[95] Irwin 1983, p. 158.
[96] Brown 2005, p. 50.
[97] Garside 1979, p. 22.
[98] *OC* VI, pp. 169–170; *OS* 2, p. 16.

Also in Calvin's case, his statements will be echoed by his followers: for example, the Calvinist publisher Tielman Susato (c.1510-a.1570) prefaced his first *Musyck boexken* (1551) with these words: "music is an exceptional heavenly gift, created by God and given to humankind"[99].

It should be said, however, that expressions echoing those by both Luther and Calvin (I would even say that they are closer to Calvin than to Luther!) were written by the supposed champion of Catholic church music, Palestrina: "the utility and pleasure afforded by the art of music is a gift of heaven greater than all human teachings"[100].

It may be interesting to note, moreover, that there is a significant consistency between the Reformers' viewpoints on creation, on sexuality, and on music: Calvin's more restrictive and rigorist perspective on all these aspects in comparison with Luther's, as well as a certain tendency of the Genevan Reformer to moralism, are faithfully mirrored by his reduction of acceptable church music to one particular and sober musical style; on the other hand, both the Lutheran and the Catholic Church will admit in their worships a variety of musical forms, somehow mirroring their more inclusive concept of the goodness of creation.

### 4.2.4.2. "Praise him with lute and harp"

Indeed, the second feature of music we will discuss, after its role within creation as a gift of God, is precisely its function in worship and for praising God. Although this function of music is probably one of the most ancient in "sacred" music, it was not accepted without problems by the Reformers: indeed, this point was one of the most complex for them to solve, as it involved the entire concept of worship, liturgy and of the Eucharist.

Briefly summarising what has been discussed in Chapter One (§ 1.2.2.), we may recall that many problems were bound to a very simple question: why should humans praise God? The traditional answer was that by praising God they could acquire merits which could eventually lead to their salvation, and that this satisfied a "debt of praise which was owed to God"[101]. Moreover, for Catholics, Christ had commanded to perform the sacrifice of Mass as a re-presentation of his own sacrifice on the Cross, by virtue of which humanity had been redeemed. Thus, it was not by their merits alone that humans could be justified, since God's Grace had been earned for them by the crucified and risen Christ;

---

[99] *Het ierst* 1551; English translation by Eugeen Schreurs in *Het ierst* 1989, p. 6, with adaptations.
[100] Palestrina 1567, *Dedication*; English translation in Lockwood 1975, pp. 22–23.
[101] Brown 2005, pp. 23–24.

however, good works were still crucial, and the performance of the Eucharistic sacrifice was the good work *par excellence.*

Most Evangelical Reformers, however, denied validity to this approach: both by rejecting the value of works for justification (the *sola gratia* doctrine) and by refuting the sacrificial aspect of the Mass. As one of the consequences of this approach, all things that had traditionally been conceived as embellishing the sacrificial performance (such as rituals, music, vestments etc.) lost their value (i.e. to make the offer more beautiful in God's eyes) and became mere frills.

Those who did maintain something of the traditional worship, conceived it in a new and different manner: in McKee's words, "from something done to please God and earn divine favour, to worship as a response to God's gift and obedience to God's word"[102], as well as a means for the edification of the congregation through the proclamation of the Gospel[103], following the model of the early Church[104].

From a theological viewpoint, this solution was not without its own problematic issues, mirroring the criticalities of the Lutheran concept of freedom. From the one side, if God saves humans regardless of their merits, worship becomes almost superfluous; from the other, since it is commanded by the Bible (i.e. by God's Word) and has a high pastoral function, it cannot be abolished[105].

Still other important conceptual differences were observable among the Evangelical churches: as Brown summarises, "Whereas Lutherans regarded their hymns as a form of preaching or proclamation, for Calvin the sung Psalms were categorized as congregational prayer"[106].

For Luther, however, there was a mystical dimension of music which should not be overlooked, and which fostered the maintenance and enhancement of liturgical beauty[107]: a Christian congregation singing God's praise was united through music to the heavenly choir of the angels and of the saints. In Loewe's words, "Whenever human beings used their voice to sing God's praises, *musica humana* and *musica cælestis* were conjoined"[108].

It may be interesting to mention that this view was widespread among Catholics as well. For Zarlino,

---

102 McKee 2003, p. 10.
103 Cf. Brown 2008, pp. 221–222.
104 Sfredda 2010, p. 32.
105 Irwin 1983, pp. 159–160.
106 Brown 2005, p. 24.
107 Cf. Leaver 2007, p. 224.
108 Loewe 2013, pp. 591–592.

It is enough to say in supreme praise of music that the Bible, without mentioning other sciences, places music in Paradise, where it is most nobly practiced. And just as happens in the heavenly court, called the Church Triumphant, so in our earthly one, the Church Militant, the Creator is praised and thanked with nothing so much as with music[109].

We have already quoted (§ 4.2.3.2.), in our discussion of the qualities of "weight and majesty" that church music should possess, that Calvin similarly considered the Church's praise as performed "in the presence of God and of his angels"[110]. However, in his 1541 Church Orders (significantly, in the section dedicated to marriage) he advocated the introduction of "church song to encourage the people to pray and praise God"; in his 1542–3 *Form of Prayers* he mentioned singing as one of the two possible forms of public prayer (the other, naturally, was in words alone[111]). Music thus was "an incentive for us, and as it were, an organ for praising God and lifting up our hearts to Him"[112]. This exhortative function of music (i.e. to foster both public congregational prayer and personal devotion) was a typical feature of Calvin's theology of music[113], which also stressed the role of the Holy Spirit in inspiring forms of art worthy of being part of worship[114], as had happened to the Biblical David when he composed the Psalms[115].

A fascinating concept of praise is that expressed by Peter Martyr Vermigli, who (significantly commenting upon Augustine's *Confessions*) included sacred dancing among the commendable possibilities for praising God: "As it is lawful to sing, and we use singing to give thanks unto God, and to celebrate the praise, so also by a moderate dancing, we may testify the joy and mirth of the mind"[116].

### 4.2.4.3. Chords of concord
The third function of sacred music as seen by the religious reformers, though distinct from the preceding, can also be considered as its consequence, i.e. the power of music to create communion, unity and a feeling of belonging within the community of believers. When a group of worshippers expresses its faith and praise in singing, this very act contributes to establishing a concord of

---

**109** Zarlino 1558, Part I, Chapter 2. English translation in Strunk 1998, p. 296.
**110** Calvin 1542, "Epistre au lecteur", my translation; *OC* VI, pp. 169–170; *OS* 2, p. 15. Cf. Sfredda 2010, pp. 81–82.
**111** *OC* VI, pp. 169–170. Cf. Calvin 1541 and 1542; in Sfredda 2010, pp. 80–81, my translation.
**112** *OC* VI, pp. 169–170; *OS* 2, pp. 15–16; English translation in Garside 1979, p. 21.
**113** Cf. *CoR* 4, p. 155; and Reid 1971, p. 38 (translation). Cf. also McKee 2003, pp. 19–20.
**114** Joby 2005, p. 69.
**115** Cf. Calvin 1543, "Epistre au lecteur", *OC* VI, p. 171.
**116** Vermigli 1994, p. 133; quoted in Leaver 2006, p. 386.

which the communal singing is both a symbol and a concurring factor, as already St Basil had maintained in the homily quoted in Chapter Two (§ 2.3.4.). Thus, Herbenus had defined heavenly music as "full of unity and perfection where all voices resound together, sung by all, most melodiously without any mistake at all"[117], likely suggesting the musical symbol of unisonance as a paradigm of communion. Although he presented his own viewpoint from a negative perspective, Karlstadt substantially agreed with him when he rejected polyphony because it represented a plurality which he saw as conflicting with the ideal of absolute unity[118].

Against Karlstadt's view, Luther saw no contradiction between plurality and unity, considering polyphony to be an efficacious metaphor for the very possibility of their coexistence. He described his view of polyphony thus: "While one and the same voice continues in its course, several voices play, exult, and adorn it with the most delightful gestures all round it in wondrous ways, and so to speak lead a kind of divine dance"[119]. Therefore, although different Reformers had different ideas on which kind of music was best suited to express unity and communion, most of them agreed on the power of music to unify the congregation and build its harmony – and this not just on the human level, but also in a transcendent and spiritual perspective.

### 4.2.4.4. Fostering fervour

When a congregation is unified in singing, it is likely that a fourth function of music can emerge, i.e. its possibility both to mirror and foster piety, devotion and a religious feeling. We may recall here that music was often seen in the humanist context as a rhetorical means for enhancing the moving power of words. Through music, then, the sacred or pious words could penetrate more deeply into the souls of both listeners and singers, strengthen their religious feelings, and encourage devout and proper behaviour in daily life (again, a point made by Basil in his homily). Thus, the expression of theology in music was seen as fundamental for the spiritual edification of Lutheran congregations[120], and Calvin repeatedly discussed the power of music to inspire devotion[121]: music can "move and inflame the hearts of men to invoke and praise God with a more ve-

---

[117] Herbenus 1496, p. 33; English translation in Loewe 2013, p. 602.
[118] Cf. Alber 1556, fol. Y2ᵛ, and Herl 2004, p. 108.
[119] Luther 1538a, 5.2; WA 50, p. 373; English translation in Loewe 2013, p. 602; cf. Leaver 2007, p. 318.
[120] Leaver 2007, p. 224.
[121] Spelman 1948, p. 249.

hement and ardent zeal"[122]. Théodore de Bèze agreed with Calvin in acknowledging the power of music to move the affects and foster devotion[123], and Vermigli similarly maintained that "Music has power to arouse the affections of the faithful to piety"[124].

The same view was shared by the Lutherans: in his *Apology* (1531), Melanchthon wrote that German hymns could "arouse [the people's] faith and fear"[125]; we may also recall that the same idea was expressed by Christophorus of Padua at Trent[126].

Music is, by its nature, a relational activity; and while it is of course possible to make and enjoy music for one's own pleasure in solitude, the privileged social dimension of music is evident. Thus, outside church, the function of music as a help for devotion was commonly acknowledged, but frequently took the form of a non-individual practice. And this aspect was particularly valued within religious societies which, as demonstrated by Longfellow[127], could nourish suspicions about solitary devotion.

### 4.2.4.5. "Faith comes from hearing"

The fifth function of music for the Reformers consists in its being at the service of the Word as a means for instruction, catechesis, teaching and evangelisation: singing was perfectly suited for conveying belief and spiritual edification to congregations (as maintained, once more, by Basil[128]). As we have seen before, both due to the humanist interest in verbality and education, and to the Evangelical focus on the *sola scriptura* principle, this was a core concern for the Protestant Churches. Obviously, this function implies the submission of music to words and, consequently, a reduced interest in the aesthetic and symbolic value of music *per se*, as well as (almost unavoidably) the subordination of instrumental to vocal music.

We have seen that one aspect that characterises the emergence of many Evangelical Churches with respect to the Roman Catholics is the increasing focus on *congregational hearing* versus the *individual (visual) contemplation* typ-

---

[122] *OC* VI, pp. 169–170; *OS* 2, p. 15; English translation in Strunk 1998, p. 365.
[123] Cf. Irwin 1983, p. 161.
[124] Vermigli 1994, p. 133; quoted in Leaver 2006, p. 386.
[125] In *BC*, p. 69.
[126] *CT* 13, p. 714.
[127] Cf. Longfellow 2012.
[128] Willis 2010, p. 201.

ical of medieval piety[129]. Indeed, Luther often quoted a Pauline fragment (Romans 10:17) stating that "Faith comes from hearing"[130], and he maintained that "miracles for the eyes are by far inferior to those for the ears"[131]. This led to an unprecedented focus on sermons, on their rhetorical strategies, on the hearers' expectations about their form and content, and on the overall aural experience of the congregation, of which music was, of course, an integral component[132].

In fact, his concept of music as closest to theology from the one side stresses Luther's belief in the semantic and rational value of music, and from the other suggests an alliance between music and theology, both of which are at the service of the Word. Moreover, he also stated that music has a crucial pedagogical value, since it may help in giving (religious and human) education to the young in a pleasurable fashion: *"und also das Güte mit Lust"*[133] ("and so the good with pleasure", in a literal translation[134]).

In his focus on the value of music both as a rhetorical support to the Word (whose meaning was conveyed more effectively by musical rhythm and melody than by a simple prose[135]) and as an emotional force with the power to move, Luther was rather close to Herbenus[136]; however, the practical results of this perspective were radically innovative. Lutheran worship, while maintaining many features of the Catholic liturgy (as we will see in § 5.3.1. and following), changed profoundly the significance of cult itself: worship acquired the dimension of teaching, instruction and education, and became the ideal context for the proclamation of the Gospel[137]. As Luther stated, "Everything is to be done for the sake of God's Word, so that it may have free course and ever restore and give life to souls, that they may not become weary"[138]. For him, singing was a "*sonora prædicatio*"[139], a preaching in sounds, and thus had almost a ministerial quality

---

[129] Cf. McKee 2003, pp. 9–10.
[130] Quoted in Lindberg 2010, p. 34; *NRSV* "Faith comes from what is heard".
[131] "*Ocularia miracula longe minora sunt quam auricularia*" (*WA* 44, p. 352). Cf. Guicharrousse 1995, p. 180.
[132] Cf. Pitkin 2015, p. 18
[133] Luther in Walther 1524; the translation in Strunk 1998, p. 361, renounces a literal rendition of this fragment.
[134] Cf. Sfredda 2010, pp. 25, 28 etc.
[135] Portnoy 1949, p. 238.
[136] Loewe 2013, p. 581.
[137] Brown 2008, pp. 220–221.
[138] *Von der Ordnung des Gottesdienstes in der Gemeinde* (1523), *WA* 12, p. 36, *LW* 53, p. 13, transl. altered. In Brown 2008, p. 221.
[139] Cf. *WA* 50, pp. 371–372; *LW* 53, p. 323.

and certainly an indispensable function for the spiritual growth of a community. Conversely, as will be discussed in greater detail in the following Chapters, catechism (especially when it was sung) was transformed into prayer (and thus a part of worship) in turn[140]. Congregational singing thus became, in Leaver's words, "a rich experience in which theology was expressed in musical forms, undergirded by pedagogical and catechetical concerns"[141].

Luther's perspective was eagerly adopted by his followers. Prefacing the 1553 *Psalmodia* by Lucas Lossius (1508–1582), Melanchthon explicitly wrote: "The principal cause of music is so that divine doctrine may be comprehended by song and propagated more widely and conserved for longer. Our ears are drawn to song, and delightful harmonies penetrate deeper into our minds and cling more tenaciously in our memory"[142].

Already in 1530, however, the Augsburg Confession had stressed the importance of "ceremonies [...] in order to teach those who are ignorant"; in his *Apology* to this very Confession (1531), Melanchthon added that "German hymns" were used in the Lutheran Church "in order that the [common] people might have something to learn"[143]. Similarly, the theologian Johannes Brenz (1499–1570) clearly included music among the means for the proclamation of the Word: "When we speak of the preaching of the Word of God, we do not understand only that preaching which takes place publicly in the pulpit, but also what takes place in the public songs of the church"[144], and music gradually started to be considered to be the *viva vox evangelii*, the true voice of the Gospel[145]. In still later Lutheran documents, such as the 1579 Church Orders of Nördlingen, pastors were encouraged to foster congregational singing for catechetic (rather than liturgical) purposes[146].

Notwithstanding this, an important observation by Bernard Kreuzer should be mentioned here: indeed, music was seen as a form of theology by the Lutherans; however, the artistic nature of music could sometimes conflict with the strictest requirements of dogmatic precision and theological refinement: thus,

---

140 Brown 2008, p. 238.
141 Leaver 2007, p. 224.
142 Melanchthon, in Lossius 1553, fol. ij'; English translation by Grantley McDonald in Groote and Vendrix 2012, p. 186.
143 Both this quote and the preceding are in *BC*, p. 69; cf. Grindal 2011, pp. 2–3.
144 Johann Brenz, quoted in Blankenburg 1961, pp. 567–568. See Hartmann 1862, p. 155.
145 Leaver 2007, p. 277.
146 Herl 2004, p. 67.

"When the hymnody does not mirror faithfully the dogmatic theology of a Church, then we find that it mirrors the practical theology of the people"[147].

In the Calvinist Church, the educational and instructional value of music was felt rather differently: as we will see, the focus on music as an efficacious means for teaching the young was common to practically all Christian confessions in the sixteenth century, but Calvinist worship did not aim at instilling particular concepts and beliefs through music as the Lutheran did.

On the other hand, the beginnings of Protestantism in England were marked by similar uses of music. John Jewel (1522–1571), the Bishop of Salisbury, reported in 1560 to Vermigli what was happening in London at the time, when large crowds gathered (*after* the service) for singing hymns together: "This sadly annoys the mass-priests, and the devil. For they perceive that by these means the sacred discourses sink more deeply into the minds of men, and that their kingdom is weakened and shaken at almost every note"[148].

Thus, music's combined power to move and to convey instruction was largely used both for the spread of Reformation ideas and for affirming and confirming particular confessional beliefs. As we will see, particularly in Chapter Ten, both the propagandistic aspect and the dogmatic function were crucial at a time when different confessions were just starting to establish and promote their own beliefs, and needed to present them clearly and efficaciously both to their own members and in the face of competing confessions.

### 4.2.4.6. A "medicine for passions"

As discussed in the preceding lines, the power of music to move could be seen as a component of its instructional and educational purpose; however, we may also mention it briefly as a distinct function (the sixth in our list), by considering its affective and moralising potential. In other words, music can *instil* both doctrine and moral values through its words (function five); it can *move the affects* to devotion and piety (function four), but it can also build a soul's or a community's moral values by virtue of its inner order and harmony which stimulate in turn an analogous moral order and harmony (function six). As Luther wrote, music could "break the proud, [...] soothe the haters – and who shall count all those masters of the human heart, the affections and impulses or spirits that drive all virtues or vices?"[149]. Furthermore, music was a "noble, salutary and happy

---

147 Kreuzer 1973, pp. 126–127.
148 Jewel, Letter of March 5$^{th}$, 1560, in Robinson 1842, p. 71.
149 Luther 1538a, 3.6–7; *WA* 50, p. 371; English translation in Loewe 2013, p. 600; cf. Leaver 2007, pp. 316–317.

creature", which could become "on occasion medicine for your passions against shameful lusts and evil company"[150]. Loewe rightfully comments that Luther seems to attribute to music the power of creating a "habit of goodness" in those practising it, which would help them in their battle against vice and evil[151].

We have already seen that even Becon, whose praise of music was much more restrained than Luther's (the most encomiastic adjective he employs for describing it is "tolerable"), still believed that music could act as a "handmaid unto virtue"[152]; and Calvin expressed in turn a similar conviction. Calvinist Psalm singing could therefore become a tool for the self-education of Christians, also from the ethical viewpoint[153]: doubtless, this view was strongly influenced by Calvin's Platonic approach to music[154]. Freedman efficaciously synthesises Calvin's position by stating that, for him "music was a maker of moral fibre rather than principally a manifestation of worldly civility"[155].

### 4.2.4.7. "*Zu Frewde*": the joy of music

Notwithstanding this, for Calvin himself music had yet another function, i.e. that of providing Christians with a source of joy and consolation for their souls (and also for this function St Basil's writings had provided the Reformers with an authoritative model). As discussed earlier (§ 4.2.4.1.), Calvin believed that music could replace worldly pleasures with a spiritual bliss which would in turn lead the souls to God, the true source of all happiness[156]. Interestingly, on this very topic of spiritual enjoyment, the difference between Luther's unconditioned love for music and Calvin's caution becomes clearest. Calvin does believe in music's power to give joy, and sees in this very possibility one of its most important spiritual functions; however, he feels it necessary to justify the value of music *notwithstanding* this seemingly minor and non-fundamental role. Though music is more pleasurable than properly useful, "it ought not on that account to be judged of no value; still less should it be condemned"[157], since God "render[ed] many things attractive to us, apart from their necessary use"[158].

---

150 Luther 1538a, 6.2; *WA* 50, p. 373; English translation in Loewe 2013, p. 604; cf. Leaver 2007, p. 318.
151 Cf. Loewe 2013, pp. 581, 591, 598.
152 Becon 1844, p. 430.
153 Cf. Joby 2005, pp. 67–68.
154 Kim 2005, pp. 117–120.
155 Freedman 2006, pp. 169–170. Cf. Garside 1951, pp. 568–569.
156 *OC* VI, pp. 169–170; *OS* 2, p. 16.
157 Quoted in Calvin 1960, vol. 2, p. 721, n. 4.
158 Calvin 1960, vol. III, x, p. 721. Cf. Koenigsberger 1986, p. 184.

On the contrary, Luther seemingly never felt the need to justify the joy of music. There is a plethora of declarations by the Wittenberg Reformer which testify to three points: a) that music gives joy; b) that good Christians are joyful; c) consequently, that the joy of music helps in the making of good Christians.

We have already seen how he discarded Augustine's controversial feelings about music, by labelling his perplexities as "scruples" and by adopting only his most positive declarations[159]; his union of "good" and "joy" in the 1524 preface can be similarly recalled here[160]. Similar concepts are found again in his *Preface* to the 1545 collection[161], where joy is the characterising feature of both the Christians and of their singing, and will be further developed by Mathesius (music is given to humankind "for enjoyment", "*zu Frewde*"[162]); however, music did not merely express the spiritual "happiness" of a serene soul. On the contrary, this "*Frewde*" was closely linked to another key-concept, that of "*Trost*", comfort or consolation. Music did not simply convey a soul's joy; it could also restore that joy when external (such as persecution, illness, suffering…) or internal causes (such as one's own sin) had troubled it. Mathesius stated this clearly: "let him who needs joy, comfort, and life hold fast to the text and learn it well, and sing it to a good Gregorian melody"[163].

Similarly, in the *Encomion musices*, Luther had affirmed that music could "cheer the miserable" and "encourage the despairing"[164]; among Calvinists, this viewpoint was maintained by Susato, who wrote that music could "eschew melancholy, […] dispel trouble, […] alleviate heavy minds, and […] gladden worried hearts"[165]. Fascinatingly, the Puritan William Fulke (1538–1589) asserted that the voice of God is for humans like "a most pleasant harmony, as it were of harpers singing with their harps", through which the "minds of men are subdued and brought under to the obedience of God, and filled with the pleasant sweetness of his amiable Grace"[166]. The Anglican divine Richard Hooker (1554–1600) held a similar viewpoint, by maintaining that music "carrieth as it were into ecstasies, filling the mind with an heavenly joy and for the time in a manner severing it from the body"[167].

---

159 WA TR IV, p. 313, no. 4441. Cf. Kim 2005, pp. 121–122; Sooy 2006, p. 49.
160 Luther in Walther 1524; translation in Strunk 1998, p. 361.
161 Luther 1545.
162 Cf. in Brown 2005, p. 50.
163 Mathesius 1586, vol. 3, fol. 25ʳ. Translation in Brown 2005, p. 91.
164 Luther 1538a, 3.6; WA 50, p. 371; English translation in Loewe 2013, p. 600; cf. Leaver 2007, p. 316.
165 Het ierst 1551; English translation by Eugeen Schreurs in *Het ierst* 1989, p. 6.
166 Fulke 1573, fol. 91ʳ.
167 Hooker 1876, book V, Chapter 38, p. 160.

### 4.2.4.8. Dispelling devils

If music could both express joy and restore it in the middle of life's ordeals, it could also serve to fight against the father of evil, Satan; on the other hand, it had mystical powers (eighth function in our analysis: it will come as no surprise that this role was listed by Basil too). There were Biblical witnesses to music's force against the evil, particularly in the oft-recounted positive effects of David's music on King Saul, who was affected by an "evil spirit from God" (cf. 1 Samuel 16:14 ff.) tormenting him.

Luther developed this theme, in a very Basil-sounding statement, arguing that "Even the Holy Ghost honours [music] as the instrument of his own function, bearing witness in Holy Scripture [...] that she drives out Satan, that is the instigator of all vices"[168].

Furthermore, he stated that "The devil, the creator of saddening cares and disquieting worries, takes flight at the sound of music almost as he takes flight at the word of theology"[169]; music is also a "great enemy of Satan, and an instrument to drive away temptations and evil thoughts"[170]. As Loewe rightfully notes, this function of music made it strikingly similar to the actions attributed to divine Grace by traditional theology[171].

A mystical perspective is also found in Luther's description of the very essence of music:

> Nothing is without sound, or sounding number, so that the very air, which on itself is invisible and impalpable, and imperceptible to all the senses, and least musical of all things, but utterly mute and of no account, yet in motion sounds and can be heard and even touched; in this the Spirit signifies marvellous mysteries of which this is not the place to speak[172].

Echoing Luther, the presence of the Holy Spirit's power in music was also mentioned by Paul Eber[173] (1511–1569).

It is highly significant that later Lutherans such as Jakob Andreae (1528–1590) based their arguments in favour of purely instrumental music (and against Calvinists) precisely on their belief in this thaumaturgic and mystical power of

---

**168** Luther 1538a, 3.8; *WA* 50, p. 371; English translation in Loewe 2013, p. 600; cf. Leaver 2007, p. 317.
**169** *LW* 49, pp. 427–428; *WA BR* 5, p. 639.
**170** *WA TR* I, p. 490, no. 968.
**171** Loewe 2013, p. 598.
**172** Luther 1538a, 3.7; *WA* 50, p. 371; English translation in Loewe 2013, p. 600; cf. Leaver 2007, p. 314.
**173** Paul Eber, in Herman 1560 (*WB* 788, pref. 67, p. 609); as translated in Brown 2008, p. 217.

music: since music was inhabited by the mysterious force of God's Holy Spirit, the blessings it conveyed did not come from its association with words, but rather from its very supernatural essence[174].

### 4.2.4.9. Voicing the Gospel

Last but not least, the ninth function of music we can find in the writings of religious reformers is one which will be discussed at length in Chapter Ten (§ 10.3.5. etc.), i.e. its role as an instrument of propaganda (and here too Basil provided a model for the Reformers, when discussing the role of Psalm-singing in the marketplace). Suffice it to say, for the moment, that hymn- or Psalm-singing became an extremely powerful means for stating and defending the identity of a religious group, for spreading their belief, and for proclaiming their faith in the presence of opposing or persecuting groups.

A summary of the functions listed above is found in a statement (1568) by the Lutheran Cyriacus Spangenberg (1528–1604): for him, through the communal singing of sacred hymns,

> God is praised [...], the human creature is spurred to true devotion; all the chief articles of divine doctrine (especially the promise of the gospel) are called to mind; the singer is strengthened; the neighbour is taught, encouraged and exhorted, and the hearts of both are comforted; the soul is rejoiced, the conscience stilled, hope increased, the cross lightened, fear and sadness are diminished; the angels are delighted, the devil put to flight and brought to shame[175].

In a similar fashion, Myles Coverdale (1488–1569) described the multiple benefits of Psalm-singing: "to comfort a man's heart in God, to make him thankful, & to exercise him in his word, to [en]courage him in the way of godliness, and to provoke other men unto the same"[176].

However, as Blume points out[177], all these functions did not always coexist peacefully with one another, and sometimes the needs of one could conflict with those of another: in particular, worship and instruction, mystics and theology, homiletics and praise became sometimes difficult to harmonise together.

---

[174] Irwin 1983, p. 161.
[175] Spangenberg 1568 (*WB* 896, pref. 77, p. 632); as translated in Brown 2008, pp. 217–218.
[176] Coverdale 1535a, quoted in Zim 2011, p. 34 (with minor spelling alterations).
[177] Blume 1975, p. 5. This concept is found also in Baroffio 1995, p. 12.

### 4.2.4.10. Shall or may? Music as *adiaphoron*

It will come as no surprise to the reader that the overall view of music in the Lutheran Church was and would continue to remain extremely positive in the subsequent centuries: incidentally, Western music is highly indebted to Luther's love for music, since it fostered a musical culture to which we owe an extraordinary heritage.

However, in agreement as a musician can be with Luther's perspective, it does elicit a rather important theological problem, which is summarised with the word *adiaphora:* here too we must insert a brief digression in order to explain this concept and its roots.

Martin Luther discussed at length the topic of Christian liberty, against what he perceived as the obligations and impositions of the Catholic Church. In his own personal spiritual itinerary, he had experienced excruciating suffering in realising his own inability to live up to the expectations and precepts of the Church; thus it had come as a liberation, for him, to realise that humankind is saved by Grace alone (*sola gratia*). Therefore, with the exception of what the Scripture commands on God's behalf, many other things, which were traditionally part of a Christian life, suddenly became non-compulsory. Though Luther's stance may seem (and actually was) rather revolutionary, it was by no means as extreme as those of other Reformers (such as Karlstadt), who tried and uprooted numerous practices of the Catholic Church, some of which were highly cherished by the laity. On the contrary, Luther followed St Paul's invitation to moderation in 1 Corinthians 8: while affirming that eating food sacrificed to the idols was indifferent to one's salvation (cf. § 2.3.5.), Paul was concerned for the faith of the "weak", who – having not yet reached the perfection of Christian liberty – could be scandalised by seeing a Christian doing what they deemed to be sinful. Therefore, out of concern for their sensitivity, Paul claimed: "If food is a cause of their [i.e. my brethren's] falling, I will never eat meat, so that I may not cause one of them to fall" (1 Corinthians 8:13).

Following Paul's example, Luther – differently from some of his colleagues – was not prepared to forbid certain practices, but – as long as they were not harmful in his eyes – he allowed their continuation. Such matters, which were "indifferent" to salvation, but which might be maintained unless they became superstitious, were called *adiaphora*[178].

Music in worship, being a component of ceremonies, was officially considered as *adiaphoron* by the Lutheran Church. However, in 1586 and 1597 delega-

---

[178] This subject constitutes the topic of Irwin 1983, in which it is discussed in great detail and to which this section is indebted.

tions of Lutherans and Calvinists met to discuss, among other subjects, the question of *adiaphora*, and it became clear that the Lutheran view had progressively shifted from an (officially) neutral or adiaphoric consideration of music, to an (almost) explicit affirmation of its being an integral and non-renounceable part of worship[179]. This brought to light also a crucial difference in the understanding of the *sola scriptura* principle by the Lutherans and the Calvinists (who, in this subject, were theoretically closer to Zwingli, although their respective practical conclusions were markedly different). For the Lutherans, what was not forbidden by Scripture could be done; for the Calvinists, what was not commanded by the Bible should not be done[180]. Therefore, the Lutherans affirmed straightforwardly the goodness of music (including instrumental music and vocal music in languages other than the vernacular), perhaps on grounds more aesthetical and experiential than rigorously theological: the justification for their position was grounded on the concept of music as a divine gift and not as a human invention. On the other hand, the Calvinists were adamant in defending a strictly adiaphoric quality of music.

Paradoxically, therefore, the Calvinists' position was more flexible than the Lutherans', who – in turn – probably started to affirm unequivocally their convictions on the indispensability of music precisely in polemics with the Reformed party[181].

Among other Reformers, the adiaphoric view was more common, as in these statements by Vermigli (1587):

> I affirm that faithful and religious singing may be retained in church; but I do not confess that any precept exists on this matter in the New Testament. Wherefore if there be a church which does not use it, for just cause, it may not rightly be condemned, provided that it does not defend this matter illicitly by its nature or by the precept of God nor stigmatize other churches where singing and music are used or exclude them from the fellowship of Christ[182].

Interestingly, Cajetan, in his commentary on Aquinas' *Summa,* adopted an almost-adiaphoric view of (secular) organ music in church, basing his argument on the fact that purely instrumental performance abstracted music from the meaning of the (omitted) words[183].

---

[179] Cf. Hendrickson 2003, p. 55.
[180] Leaver 2006, pp. 389 and 392.
[181] Irwin 1983, p. 160.
[182] Vermigli 1587, Classis Tertiæ, Chapter 13, p. 677; English translation in Irwin 1983, p. 168.
[183] Mischiati 1995, p. 19.

Though they are not properly "functions" of music, but rather qualities attached to it in the thought of several Reformers, I will include here two further elements in order to complete our overview of their concept of music, i.e. the experiential-practical trait of their perspective, and the connection between music and apocalyptic views.

As concerns the first feature, indeed, we constantly need to take into account the personal imprint given by several Reformers to the Churches which would eventually name themselves after their founder. Therefore, while sometimes particular Popes were rather influential on stylistic features in either visual art or music, often the personal attitude of Evangelical Reformers toward music is more dramatically discernible in the overall orientation their Churches would have in this respect. The Reformers' attitude could be determined by their own musical talent, disposition and skills; by their practical experiences as regards music and faith (uses or abuses; positive or negative effects of Catholic or Evangelical music practice; the congregation's response to music etc.); by personal meetings and encounters, or by personal contrasts (for an example of the former, cf. Calvin and Bucer; of the latter, cf. Luther and Karlstadt); or, finally, by confessional influences or oppositions (sometimes a group's identity, also as regards music, was built and delimited by the attitudes of the competing groups).

For example, Luther backed his opinion that music deserved "the highest praise" just "next to the Word of God" by stating that "experience confirms" this fact[184]; similarly, Calvin claimed that he "[knew] by experience that singing has great force and vigour to move and inflame the hearts of men"[185].

### 4.2.4.11. Music for the end of the world

The other characterising feature in a substantial part of contemporaneous literature on sacred music is its "apocalyptic" aspect. First of all, I need to clarify that modern Biblical criticism often questions an interpretation of the Book of Revelation as describing catastrophes to come: a more spiritual (and probably more correct) view tends to read it as a contemplation of the redemption of the world realised through Christ's sacrifice and resurrection, as well as of the battle between the victorious Redeemer and the forces opposing Him[186]. However, though such contemporary exegeses are grounded on early Christian interpretations of the Book of Revelation, by the time of the Reformations it had been

---

[184] *LW* 53, pp. 323–324.
[185] Calvin 1542; *OC* VI, p. 170; translation in Garside 1951, pp. 568–569.
[186] Cf. Corsini 1980.

read since long as a vision of the future. Furthermore, the daily experience of men and women in several European countries of the time was so tragically affected by events such as famine, plague, wars and invasions that the catastrophes described in the Book of Revelation were terribly easy to apply to their own times. Thus, from the one side many religious people of the sixteenth century had a rather strong impression that they were living in the last times of the world; from the other, this consciousness (combined with the renewed attention to Scripture) led them to interpret the Book of Revelation as closely mirroring their own reality. Whereas some images in that Book clearly demanded to be interpreted in a symbolic fashion, others could (or seemed in turn to demand to) be seen as indicating actual people: this was particularly the case with the Antichrist. In the transmitted interpretation of some of the Bible books attributed to St John (such as the Letters and the Book of Revelation), the Antichrist and/or the false prophet came to represent a false Messiah, a highly charismatic person who could deceive and lead to perdition many former Christian faithful, and whose appearance would indicate the last days of the world. Therefore, the task of unmasking the Antichrist was seen as both an announcement of the imminent second coming of the true Christ, and a mark of the true Church, which has remained faithful to Him and has not been misled by the Antichrist. Unavoidably, those opposing a particular Christian confession were easily labelled as Antichrist: many Evangelical Churches tended to agree in identifying the Pope (whomever he was) as the Antichrist, but some Evangelical Reformers could be in turn identified as such by both Catholics and other Protestants.

Within this framework, music accomplished some very different functions. Firstly, through polemical hymns the idea that the end of the world was close and that somebody was the Antichrist could be easily spread (cf. § 10.3.7.5.). Secondly, non-polemical hymns might have an apocalyptical vein which expressed itself either as a consolation for the suffering/oppressed Christians (i.e. fostering their resilience and patience in the belief that their distress would end soon) or as an urgency to convert since the world was nearing its end: several examples of such approaches are found in English popular ballads[187]. Thirdly, among the many horrible facts which were allegedly announcing the last times, there were also positive and comforting signs: as the prophet Joel (2:28), quoted in the Acts of the Apostles (2:17) had revealed, in the last days "your sons and daughters will prophesy". Many, especially in the Lutheran context, understood this announcement as applying to their own children: within the framework of lay piety and of the Lutheran education of the young (both of which made abundant use of

---

[187] Willis 2009, p. 307.

music), the words of the Bible and of the Gospel were indeed proclaimed in singing by boys and girls, thus fulfilling the Scriptural prophecy[188] (see also § 12.3.1.2.).

### 4.2.5. Orchestrating praise: the role of instruments

The last musical issue regarding which a comparison of the Reformers' viewpoints will be made concerns their view of musical instruments. This topic includes several different subjects, namely: a) organ as an accompanying instrument for congregational or choral singing; b) organ in the *alternatim* practice; c) other instruments as an accompaniment to singing; d) purely instrumental music in church; e) secular instrumental music in church; f) instrumental music and/or accompaniment outside worship (e. g. at homes or for private devotion).

As stated before (§ 2.4.2.), the Biblical references to instrumental music seemingly provided evidence in support of almost all positions; therefore, there was a great variety of attitudes – often determined by personal taste as much as by theological convictions – on this topic.

As can easily be imagined, Luther's position was the most inclusive and enthusiastic of all. He had stated it by these words:

> The stringed instruments of the [...] Psalms are to help in the singing of this new song: and Wolff Heinz and all pious Christian musicians should let their singing and playing to the praise of the Father of all grace sound forth with joy from their organs, symphonias, virginals, regals, and whatever other beloved instruments there are (recently invented and given by God), of which neither David nor Solomon, neither Persia, Greece, nor Rome, knew anything[189].

As Leaver rightfully comments, while praising the human ingeniousness in creating new and marvellous instruments, Luther stresses that they are in turn gifts of God: a similar discourse, as will be recalled, characterised Luther's vision of music in general as well, and obviously implies that a God-given reality is trusted to humans so that they may use it to praise Him[190].

The Lutheran view of instrumental music and accompaniment became progressively more detailed and refined in correspondence to polemical confronta-

---

**188** Cf. Brown 2008, p. 257.
**189** Plass 1959, No. 3100.
**190** Leaver 2007, p. 91.

tions with other confessions or Reformers. We may recall that Karlstadt had a particularly strict stance against instruments such as trumpets, flutes and organs in church[191], and that his approach to organ music was considered by Alber as a sign that Karlstadt was "diabolically" inspired[192].

Another Reformer characterised by a particularly critical stance against instrumental music was Zwingli, who attacked the use of instruments in Catholic worship very harshly[193]; once more, however, the Calvinist approach was more nuanced. The moment when the Lutheran and Calvinist attitudes on the topic were most clearly enunciated and compared with one another was in 1586, in the encounter we mentioned earlier as concerns the *adiaphora* (§ 4.2.4.10.). The Lutheran Andreae advocated the use of instruments (and even of purely instrumental music) in worship by quoting the therapeutic and thaumaturgic efficacy of David's lyre on Saul's spiritual illness: this demonstrated, in his eyes, that music *in se* had the power to move, regardless of its being combined with words; what really mattered to Lutherans was that purely instrumental music had a clearly distinguishable "sacred" character[194]. To this, the Calvinist Bèze replied that music's beneficial power to draw the soul to God depended on the understanding of its words by the listeners: and this could apply neither to polyphony nor to purely instrumental music[195].

The Calvinist stance was grounded on their founder's: while acknowledging the positive mention of instruments in the Old Testament, Calvin maintained that their suitability for worship was bound to the old Law, which had been superseded by the new. His position was probably inspired by St Jerome's rejection of instrumental music for worship[196]. Calvin consequently labelled instruments as "*puerilia elementa*", "childish elements"[197], in reference to 1 Corinthians 13:11, where Paul states: "When I was a child, I spoke like a child, I thought like a child, I reasoned like a child; when I became an adult, I put an end to childish ways". Within the Calvinist understanding of God's Grace, the actions and prayers practised by Jews and Catholics in order to (simplistically put) earn God's favour were considered as part of the "economy of the (old) law". This view was more radically negative than it may appear at first, since Paul had expressed his condemnation of those who did not trust Grace alone and tried to justify

---

191 Cf. Bodenstein 1905; Korrick 1990, p. 360.
192 Alber 1556, fol. Y2ᵛ, and Herl 2004, p. 108.
193 Marcus 2001, p. 729.
194 Irwin 1983, p. 164.
195 Herl 2004, p. 109.
196 See Rainoldi 2000, p. 323.
197 Cf. Blankenburg 1975, p. 517; Koenigsberger 1986, p. 185; Sfredda 2010, pp. 82–83.

themselves through the old practices of the Law: cf. for instance Galatians 2:21 ("I do not nullify the grace of God, for if justification comes through the law, then Christ died for nothing") and 5:4 ("You who want to be justified by the law have cut yourselves off from Christ; you have fallen away from grace"). Incidentally, the difference between Calvin's view of instrumental music as belonging to the "old" worship and Luther's mention of the stringed instruments in support of the "new" song (cf. above) is worth noting.

Consequently, for Calvin, to make use of "childish" elements which did not belong to grown-up Christians was similar to falling again into the belief that the actions of human beings could justify them. Alongside with this argumentation, Calvin himself repeatedly stressed the essentiality of words to church music[198], and attacked organ music as "a very ridiculous and inept imitation of papal worship"[199]. Instrumental music could distract both players and listeners from concentration and focus on the Word; it contravened Paul's command to pray "with understanding" and in "known tongues" (cf. 1 Corinthians 14:13); when used in accompaniment to singing, it could hinder intelligibility of the sung words; furthermore, it suggested secular associations which were unsuited to church music[200]. Summarising, then, Calvin did neither forbid nor reject instrumental music, but it had no place in Calvinist worship: it may be interesting to note (as briefly mentioned earlier: § 4.2.3.3.) that his stance about visual art closely resembles that on instrumental music[201].

Playing of purely instrumental music at the consecration was seen as simply idolatrous by Pierre Viret[202], whereas Vermigli maintained seemingly contradictory viewpoints on this topic: in 1545 he had allowed instrumental accompaniment to singing[203], whereas elsewhere he denounced the organs' "rumbling" which prevented understanding of the sacred words, and approved of the Papal Chapel (although he did not identify himself as a Catholic any more) inasmuch as it made exclusive use of unaccompanied singing[204].

Biagio Rossetto, in his 1529 *Libellus de rudimentis musices*[205], deemed wind instruments (such as flutes, trumpets, trombones and horns) inappropriate to church music since they were too reminiscent of martial (or possibly hunting)

---

**198** Cf. Viladesau 2000, pp. 26–27.
**199** Quoted in Hunter 1999, p. 280. Cf. Spelman 1948, p. 250.
**200** Cf. Korrick 1990, pp. 359–362.
**201** Cf. Joby 2005, p. 1.
**202** Cf. Viret 1584, p. 197.
**203** Vermigli 1994, p. 133.
**204** Cf. Vermigli 1587 and Irwin 1983, p. 168.
**205** Rossetto 1529; quoted in Rainoldi 2000, p. 724.

sounds. It is interesting to observe that the mention of music "*della caccia*" or "*della battaglia*" in the Council's discussions on music (cf. § 8.4.2.) may have regarded also this presence of instruments whose sound was associated with hunting or battling.

Henry Peacham the Younger (1578-c.1644) justified the practice of instrumental music in the English Royal Chapel by referencing to the Bible and to its descriptions of Jewish worship[206]: thus it becomes evident that the same excerpts could be interpreted as fostering instrumental music in church *since* the Jews used to play for the glory of God, or as countering it *since* it belonged to a surpassed tradition.

## 4.3. Various views: Music for the Reformers

In the first half of this Chapter, we have obliquely considered the Reformers' theologies of music in order to see which subjects were at stake and how they were treated. In this second half, we will briefly discuss the individual theologies of music of the most important Reformers, both Evangelical and Catholic. Unavoidably, this will imply that subjects treated above will have to be shortly recalled; however, before considering (in the next Chapters) how the characterising features of confessional theologies of music were put into practice, it is expedient to succinctly summarise their principal points.

### 4.3.1. Luther: *"Musicam semper amavi"*

Already in the first half of this Chapter, it will not have escaped the reader's notice that Luther's opinions were referred to very often. In this second half, the space devoted to the Wittenberg Reformer will be considerably lengthier than that dedicated to others, for several reasons. First of all, there is a chronological aspect: Luther's Reformation was among the first important facts for the religious history of the sixteenth century and most subsequent Reformers had to take into account his positions on various aspects of Church reform, including music.

Moreover, among the Reformers Luther was probably the most passionate about music, though perhaps he was not the most musically accomplished; in consequence of this (as well as of other concurring factors), music had a place

---

[206] Peacham 1906, p. 97; cf. Strunk 1998, p. 347.

of prominence in the Lutheran Church, both at Luther's time and in the following centuries.

Furthermore, the theology of music found in Luther's writings and practised in the hymns he wrote or promoted is almost unparalleled in the history of the Western Churches, as concerns the quantity of writings, the quality of music's role in his view, and the continuity of his thought on music throughout the decades. In Luther's theology, music has a fundamental role at all levels and ages of a Christian's life.

Finally, in several instances (though by no means in all) Luther's thought on certain musical topics was subsequently adopted by other Reformers: by discussing it here, we will often need simply to recall the key-concepts at a later stage of our discussion. As Rainoldi points out[207], actually, several of Luther's intuitions on music and liturgy were adopted by the Catholic Church as well: a few of them already in the sixteenth century, whereas others had to wait until the Second Vatican Council (1962–5) to find a positive acceptance among the Roman Catholics.

As is well known, indeed, the man Martin Luther's deep love for music accompanied him throughout his life. His knowledge of music theory dates back from his study years in Erfurt (1501–5); he was an accomplished amateur player of both flute and lute (which he often played with his friends after dinner), and knew enough of composition to be able to write contrapuntal works, besides elaborations and creations of hymn tunes. He had even planned to devote an entire treatise on music (besides the occasional writings we will refer to in the forthcoming pages), but this plan was never accomplished; nevertheless, some notes have survived, and they start – significantly – with a declaration of love: "Music I have always loved"[208]. (Notwithstanding this, Leaver rightfully points out that not all of Luther's references to music are simplistically enthusiastic, and that in some instances he could express rather critical stances about certain aspects of music[209]).

Among Luther's principal writings on music there are several prefaces to hymn and motet collections[210], the most important of which are probably the two 1538 works, i.e. the Latin *Encomion Musices* (1538a) prefacing the *Symphoniæ iucundæ* collected by Georg Rhau (1488–1548) and the German poem known as *Frau Musika*[211] (1538b); moreover, there are scattered but frequent ref-

---

207 Rainoldi 2000, p. 706.
208 *WA TR* V, p. 557, no. 6248; cf. Plass 1959, no. 3092; *WA* 30$^{II}$, p. 696.
209 Leaver 2007, p. 6.
210 Luther 1529 (lost), 1538a-b, 1542, 1545; Luther in Walther 1524.
211 Cf. Leaver 2007, p. 11; Sfredda 2010, pp. 24–25; Loewe 2013, p. 576.

erences to music in the *Tischreden*, the "table talks" reported by his friends and students.

### 4.3.1.1. Origins and originality
Among the fundamental traits of Luther's theology of music are its Biblical sources (in particular his understanding of the created world in his interpretation of Genesis), its Patristic influences and – paradoxically – the polemics with Karlstadt, which forced him to elaborate and defend his concept of music and of its role in worship[212].

As we have repeatedly seen, however, Luther's theology of music was undoubtedly influenced by St Augustine's, although Luther's stance does not show any trace of Augustine's doubts and perplexities[213]. However, Luther was neither a music theorist nor a professional musician, but rather a gifted amateur whose primary concerns were pastoral; notwithstanding this, when treating musical topics, he sometimes let his intuition and/or his practical (personal and congregational) experience of music lead him at least as much as theological considerations. In other words, Luther was primarily a theologian and a pastor (and not a musician), but he sometimes let the musician prevail over the theologian's rigour[214].

We have seen earlier in this Chapter (§ 4.2.4.5.) that Luther's *Encomion musices* reveals the influence of Herbenus on two of its core-concepts (music at the Word's service and the affective power of music), as well as a mystical view of music as a means for crossing the distance between immanent and transcendent[215]: this mystical perspective, which included a deeply symbolic concept of polyphony, is both one of the most fascinating features of Luther's thought on music, and one of those that a rationalistic and academic view of musicology and theology has often tended to neglect. As Viladesau states, music "was to be valued not only as a vehicle for sacred texts, but also as being in itself a mirror of God's beauty and thus a means for reaching the soul directly with a message about God that is inexpressible in words"[216]. This symbolic view was doubtlessly influenced by the medieval thought on music (a feature which is apparent also in his categorisation of music[217]), but it conveys – in my opinion – a much

---

212 Cf. Horne 1985, p. 27; Sooy 2006, p. 15; Brown 2008, p. 208.
213 Cf. Portnoy 1949, p. 238; Rainoldi 2000, p. 706.
214 Cf. Blume 1975, p. 8.
215 Cf. Loewe 2013, pp. 581 and 591–592.
216 Viladesau 2000, pp. 25–26.
217 Loewe 2013, p. 595.

deeper understanding of music than those expressed by theorists and theologians who merely focused on combinations of words and music.

The liminal position of Luther's concept of music between Middle Ages and modernity is evident also in the uncertainty of its theoretical collocation. Indeed, Luther repeatedly asserted that music belonged to the sciences of the *quadrivium*, and that it was the first of them: writing to Ludwig Sennfl in 1530, Luther established the primacy of music among the other mathematics ("the prophets [Psalmists] did not make use of any [quadrivial] art other than music, attaching their theology neither to geometry, nor arithmetic, nor astronomy, but to music"[218]); in asserting that "music is the best of the arts" he also stated its supremacy over all seven of the liberal arts[219].

On the other hand, Luther demonstrated a clearly modern outlook in pointing out the artistic-practical significance of music (from *scientia* to *ars*: cf. § 2.3.7.1.) as well as its rhetoric, emotional and poetic value (music among the humanities[220]).

In Luther's concept of music as "next to theology"[221], Oberman points out a possible indirect influence of Aquinas' thought, inasmuch as both theology and music are "subalternated sciences" taking their principles from higher sciences (revelation and arithmetic respectively[222]). However, the connection between theology and music is not a loose one or just a matter of principle: for Luther, they are strictly linked to one another by the very object of them both, i.e. God himself and his Word. For Luther, the prophets "held theology and music most tightly connected, and proclaimed truth through Psalms and songs"[223]. Luther's view of music as capable of "proclaiming truth" should not be overlooked, since it is an uncommonly clear statement of the songs' value as an artistic form of preaching.

The kinship of music and theology is also shown by the similarity of their effects (such as, for example, the possibility of repelling the devil[224], or the joy they both can arouse[225]); moreover, the very first collection of "Lutheran"

---

[218] Luther to Sennfl, October 1530, in *WA BR* 5, p. 639. Quoted in Loewe 2013, p. 595.
[219] Loewe 2013, p. 596.
[220] Cf. Blume 1975, p. 13; Sfredda 2010, p. 26.
[221] *WA TR* I, p. 490, n. 968.
[222] Oberman 2000, p. 202.
[223] "Prophetæ [...] in musicam digesserunt, ut theologiam et musicam haberent coniunctissimas, veritatem psalmis et canticis dicentes". *LW* 49, pp. 427–428; *WA BR* 5, p. 639. In Leaver 2007, p. 94. Cf. also *LW* 53, pp. 323–324, and *WA TR* I, p. 490, no. 968.
[224] Cf. *LW* 49, pp. 427–428; *WA BR* 5, p. 639 (quoted above: § 4.2.4.8.), and Leaver 2007, p. 93.
[225] Sooy 2006, p. 30.

hymns (the *Achtliederbuch*[226]) stressed their correspondence to the "pure Word of God" taken from Scripture, thus establishing the proximity between singing and evangelisation. Leaver succinctly summarises the fundamental role of music for Luther: "These early Lutheran hymns were [...] clearly and self-consciously the Word of God in song that would allow the people to learn and experience fundamental theology as they sang"[227].

Music, thus, acquires the role (similar to theology) of a "lifeline" bridging the abyss of human sin: after the Fall, both remain as signs of the original order and beauty in the created world, as well as instruments by which humans can interpret and give meaning to reality[228].

As a conclusion to this section, we may briefly summarise the many functions of music within Luther's theological and pastoral perspective (following a scheme suggested by Rainoldi[229] with integrations). Music has a "cathartic and psychological" function (including its thaumaturgic properties and its power against the forces of evil, temptations and the devil, as well as its capability to give joy and move the affects); it has a pedagogical function (creating the "habit of goodness" mentioned by Loewe[230]); it is akin to theology and catechesis in the proclamation of God's Word (*kerygma*); it unifies a community of believers; it conveys the gifts of the Holy Spirit and is a gift of God itself; it has a mystical function in crossing the separation between immanent and transcendent; and it is fundamental in worship and liturgy.

### 4.3.1.2. The principal principles

In the preceding pages, we have seen how music was thought of by Luther and what were its fundamental functions and actions. I will now proceed to illustrate how music relates to the principal pillars of Lutheran theology, i.e. the three principles of *sola fide*, *sola gratia* and *sola scriptura*, as well as the universal priesthood of all believers[231].

Recalling the theological overview of Chapter One (§ 1.2.1.), the *sola fide* principle implied – as Leaver suggests – that the content of faith (i.e. the "confession") was not only known and understood, but also believed and lived. Music

---

226 Luther 1524.
227 Leaver 2007, p. 108.
228 Horne 1985, p. 27.
229 Rainoldi 2000, pp. 313–315.
230 Loewe 2013, p. 591.
231 Leaver 2006, p. 377 and Leaver 2007, p. 299 (to which this section is indebted); see also Weber 2008, p. 27.

helped to spread the theological dogmas, to retain the catechism in one's mind more easily, and to recall it during daily life. To this I would add that the saving *fides* implied not only to "believe" something, but also to trust someone: the beautiful and comforting experience of church music, appealing to the believers' favourable disposition to and taste for beauty, could foster their willingness to trust God and to confidently abandon themselves to His will.

The *sola gratia* principle is linked to the doctrine of justification: as seen earlier (§ 4.2.4.2.), this implied a radically new comprehension of Mass and liturgy, as well as of all human actions. Luther countered the Catholic concept of the Eucharist as a sacrifice (since, for him, the only sacrifice had been that of Christ on the Cross), and as a merit or good work (since nothing done or acted by humans could justify them in the eyes of God); Luther's idea of the Lord's Supper as a *beneficium*, *testamentum* and *donum* stressed that it was a gift and a promise going from the Godhead to humankind rather than vice-versa. Human rites, therefore, served to praise God, to announce the Gospel and strengthen the congregation's faith (and *fides*) in God by nourishing their trust in Him[232]. Within this perspective, music could express the community's faith and praise, help them to understand and retain the Gospel, and convey their hope and trust.

According to the Catholic viewpoint, the re-presentation of Christ's sacrifice in the Mass had such a great power to save that the very performance of ritual acts had a crucial import for salvation (and therefore the congregation's understanding of what was happening at the altar had a relative importance). Within the Lutheran framework, instead, if worship had an inherent and inalienable catechetic dimension, understanding acquired a much greater value (although it never reached the compulsoriness found in other confessions: as we will see in Chapter Five[233], Luther allowed the maintenance of the Latin language in worship). This perspective obviously had consequences as regards the musical matters of intelligibility and congregational participation in communal singing.

Besides this, Luther's focus on Grace helped to develop similarities and parallelisms between the action of Grace as well as its nature from the one side, and those of music from the other. Both music and justification primarily came from God to humans as freely given gifts, and were not a product of human works or accomplishments[234]; music was inhabited by the divine Grace, and – similar to it – acted on the souls promoting and fostering sanctity and godliness. Notwithstanding this, obviously, music remained in a state of subordination to Grace,

---

[232] Cf. Leaver 2007, p. 303; Brown 2008, pp. 220–221.
[233] See § 5.3.1. and following.
[234] Leaver 2007, p. 89.

being itself an effect and a gift of Grace, which was the only way of salvation and justification[235].

The implications of the *sola scriptura* principle for music have been already mentioned on several occasions, and we will shortly summarise them here. For Luther, "The notes bring the words to life"[236], and therefore they were crucial for announcing, preaching, memorising and recalling God's Word, as well as for praying with the very words of Scripture[237]. He wanted Scripture-inspired songs in the vernacular, "so that the Word of God may be among the people also in the form of music"[238], as a "*sonora prædicatio*"[239] which would allow all the faithful to have a direct experience of and contact with the Word[240]: through spiritual songs Luther hoped that "the holy Gospel which now by the grace of God has risen anew may be set forth and given free course"[241]. As Blume puts it, "That is precisely the decisive basic idea of the Protestant *Lied*: it is the biblical word itself, not its substitute; it is an essential part of the liturgy, not its appendage"[242]; music, along with the preacher's sermon, became an interpretation of and a commentary on Scripture[243]. Notwithstanding this, however, Luther did not reject polyphonic singing, being convinced that musical beauty was no less necessary than intelligibility[244].

As Lucas Osiander (1534–1604) wrote in 1569, "it is and remains God's Word, whether it is read or sung"[245]: consequently, so fundamental was the importance of Lutheran hymns that they could be cited as theologically authoritative sources[246] in such important confessional statements as the Augsburg Confession (1530), the *Formula of Concord* (1577) and the *Book of Concord* (1580).

The primacy of the Word in worship was shown by its centrality in Luther's *Deudsche Messe*, where it had to be proclaimed in singing without shortening the Biblical lessons[247]; the Scripture was sung on precisely indicated melodic formulae. These were inspired by the Passion tones – which had been in use only dur-

---

235 Loewe 2013, pp. 597–598.
236 *WA TR* II, p. 518, no. 2545b.
237 Cf. Rainoldi 2000, p. 706.
238 *LW* 49, p. 68.
239 Cf. *WA* 50, pp. 371–372; *LW* 53, p. 323. Brown 2008, p. 219.
240 Brown 2005, p. 14.
241 *WA* 35, p. 474; *LW* 53, p. 316; translation altered in Brown 2008, pp. 214–215.
242 Blume 1975, p. 43.
243 Mischiati 1995, p. 25.
244 Sfredda 2010, p. 25.
245 Hemmel 1569 (*WB* 907, pref. 81, p. 639); cf. Brown 2008, p. 235.
246 Brown 2005, p. 15.
247 Leaver 2006, p. 378.

ing the Holy Week – therefore establishing a connection between the core mystery of Christ's death and resurrection and the congregational worship performed each Sunday[248].

Luther's new understanding of the Eucharist's value and significance had profound implications as concerned the role and nature of priesthood, which shifted from being ministerial and ordained to a general involvement of the entire congregation.

This implied that the congregation acquired a radically new role in worship and in the very concept of the Church, since it ought to understand what happened in liturgy in order to be able to follow it and join in heartfelt prayer and singing; moreover, preaching became another responsibility and right of the laity, which could and should announce the Word of God in deeds, words, and in singing (we will see numerous examples of how this was realised in practice in Chapter Five). Hymn-singing thus became the musical and aural expression of the congregation's unity in receiving, accepting, spreading and praising the Word of God[249].

Luther maintained this stance also by referring to the practice of the early Church, wondering: "Who doubts that originally all the people sang these which now only the choir sings?"[250]. (Incidentally, this question points out the difference between Luther and Erasmus: we may recall that Erasmus considered positively the fact that the unavoidable disorder engendered by congregational singing had been reduced in later epochs[251]).

As Brown rightly suggests, however, the Lutheran attitude underpinned the *possibility* for laypersons to participate in congregational singing in a language they could speak and understand: this was not a compulsory matter, as Karlstadt would have liked it to become[252] (and, indeed, one of the distinguishing marks of Luther's approach to liturgy was precisely the radical reduction of compulsoriness in a wide variety of situations). Therefore, as we will see in the next Chapter (§ 5.3.3.1. etc.), the actual degree of congregational participation in Lutheran worship was by no means homogeneous among different communities[253].

---

[248] Leaver 2007, p. 298.
[249] Cf. Brown 2005, p. 14; Leaver 2007, pp. 300–302; Sfredda 2010, p. 32.
[250] *LW* 53, p. 36.
[251] Cf. in Miller 1966, p. 334. See § 2.3.9.
[252] Brown 2008, p. 223.
[253] Herl 2004, p. 178.

### 4.3.1.3. Tuning the tenets

Music also related to Luther's understanding of the principal dogmas of the Christian faith, i.e. the Trinitarian nature of the Godhead, God as Creator (of the world and of humankind), the fallenness of humans and their redemption through the incarnation of Christ, his death and resurrection, and the gift of eternal life.

As concerns the Trinitarian dogma, Luther considers God the Father as the creator of music (in a very singular fashion, incidentally: "Music was impressed on or created with every single creature, one and all"[254]); God the Son as the Father's Word, through whom all revelation is made (including the capacity of music to "proclaim the truth"[255]); God the Holy Spirit as "honouring" music and making use of it to convey spiritual gifts to humans[256].

We have argued above (§ 4.2.4.1.) that Luther's favourable and positive understanding of the created world and of its physical aspect was undoubtedly influential on his vision of music. His concept that the physical and created reality is "capable of the infinite" gave both to music and to humanity the possibility to be united with God by his Grace; the concept of music as a creature itself fostered a responsible and grateful acceptance of this gift, which was not primarily a self-assertive expression of humans, but rather their thankful use of a God-given reality[257]. The good use humans could make of God's gift was to sing His praise and to employ music in the service of the Word. The rootedness of Luther's view of music in God's act of creation is significant and rather unusual, and it allows him to understand music in its deep relationship with the mystery of God's Word and of Revelation[258].

In response to the disorder introduced in the created world by human sin, music remained as a trace and a witness of the original order, harmony and beauty (cf. § 4.2.4.1.), as well as a means through which (by God's Grace) this order could be experienced again; on the other hand, within the importance of liberty for Luther's theological framework, music was seen as a powerful symbol of the joyful freedom of the redeemed and saved Christians[259].

---

[254] Luther 1538a, 1.6; *WA* 50, p. 369; English translation in Loewe 2013, p. 600; cf. Leaver 2007, p. 314.
[255] *LW* 49, pp. 427–428; *WA BR* 5, p. 639. Cf. Leaver 2007, p. 94. Cf. also *LW* 53, pp. 323–324, and *WA TR* I, p. 490, no. 968.
[256] Luther 1538a, 3.8; *WA* 50, p. 371; English translation in Loewe 2013, p. 600; cf. Leaver 2007, p. 317.
[257] See Anttila 2013, pp. 84–96.
[258] Sooy 2006, pp. 2 and 56.
[259] Cf. Hoelty-Nickel 1960, p. 156.

Indeed, as Østrem has fascinatingly demonstrated, music was a poignant metaphor of – or rather a symbol for – Luther's view of the freedom given by the Gospel in comparison with the unachievable demands of the Law. In Luther's words, "What is Law, is not done voluntarily; what is Gospel is done voluntarily. In this way God has preached the Gospel also in music, as can be seen in Josquin, from whom all composition flows gladly, willingly, mildly, not compelled and forced by rules, as *des fincken Gesang*"[260].

The dogma of Christ's incarnation was linked, once more, to the theme of finite's capability for the infinite; moreover, as Auksi writes, "Luther's positive valuation of art rests on the lesson of the Incarnation"[261]. On the other hand, Christ's incarnation is intrinsically connected with the redemption of humankind he realised on the Cross: Sooy argues that music, representing a primeval order, is closely associated with redemption, i.e. to Christ's restoration of the lost order[262].

Through Christ's death and resurrection, eternal life is promised to redeemed humankind. For Luther, music fostered the faithful's belief and hope in resurrection: as he had criticised the Catholic teaching on Purgatory, he also disapproved of the texts used in the Catholic liturgy of the dead. He wrote in 1542: "We have collected the fine music and songs which under the papacy were used at vigils, masses for the dead, and burials. […] But we have adapted other texts to the music so that they may adorn our article of resurrection, instead of purgatory with its torment and satisfaction which lets their dead neither sleep nor rest"[263].

Luther's theology of music can therefore be analysed from a plurality of viewpoints, including its relation with the Augustinian background of the Reformer's thought and with the medieval reflection on music, the implications of Luther's concept of music as a gift of God, the role of music within the framework of liturgy and praise, the consideration of the affective value of music and of its potential for fostering a lasting Christian joy in the hearts of the believers: all of these aspects are discussed at length by Anttila[264], who carefully analyses the many facets of Luther's idea of music.

Almost all of these themes were further developed by the later generations of Lutheran theologians, and several of them were also accomplished (or even professional) musicians: among them we may cite Nikolaus Selnecker (1530–1592),

---

[260] *WA TR* II, pp. 11–12, no. 1258, as translated in Østrem 2003, p. 51. See also Anttila 2013, pp. 178–183.
[261] Auksi 1995, p. 205.
[262] Sooy 2006, p. 20.
[263] *LW* 53, pp. 327–328; *WA* 35, pp. 479–480. Cf. Sfredda 2010, p. 27.
[264] Anttila 2013.

who contributed to the elaboration of the *Formula of Concord* and who was an organist and composer of church hymns, and Lucas Osiander, a fine composer and eminent churchman[265]. Indeed, in consideration of the role attributed by Lutherans to music and to those appointed to its performance in Church, it was not unusual for Cantors to continue their education until pastorate[266]. Thus, several other Lutheran theologians accepted and elaborated on their founder's view of music: for Johann Walther (1496–1570), there was an alliance without competition between music and theology, which were "heavenly sisters"[267]; and, if for Luther the notes gave life to words[268], for Mathesius "the text [was] the soul of a melody"[269]. The impressive quantitative and qualitative growth of Lutheran hymnody thus revealed, from the one side, the Lutherans' profound understanding of the connection between music and the Word of God, i.e. the "sole"[270] channel of the Spirit's soteriological action; from the other, a truly artistic and mystical appreciation of the beauty of music.

### 4.3.2. Zwingli: nailing the organs

Chronologically close to Luther's, the Reformation enacted by Zwingli in Zurich offers a radically different viewpoint as concerns the role of music in theology and worship[271]. Actually, whereas Luther was a gifted amateur of music, Zwingli was a highly talented musician (he is defined as "the most gifted of the three great Reformers" by Blankenburg[272]). His studies in music and the humanities had been thorough, and he was an excellent performer on a variety of instruments, as reported by his contemporary Bernhard Wyss (1463–1531):

> I never heard of anyone who in the art of *musica*, that is, in singing and all instruments – lutes, harps, large and small fiddles (*gigen, rabögli*), pipes, *schwegeln* (as proficient as any Swiss), the *tromba marina*, the dulcimer, the cornett, the horn, and anything else that would be invented, – when he saw it would soon know how to handle it and who, in addition, was so erudite as he[273].

---

[265] Leaver 2007, pp. 278–279.
[266] Herl 2004, p. 43.
[267] Koenigsberger 1986, p. 191.
[268] Cf. *WA TR* II, p. 518, no. 2545b.
[269] Mathesius, in Herman 1562, fol. A6ᵛ (*WB* 841, p. 614); in Brown 2005, p. 52.
[270] Cf. Brown 2008, p. 219.
[271] This section is indebted to Garside 1966.
[272] Blankenburg 1975, p. 509.
[273] Wyss 1901, p. 5; English translation in Blankenburg 1975, p. 509.

Furthermore, Zwingli was also a good composer, having written the music for the first known modern performance of an ancient Greek comedy (i.e. Aristophanes' *Plutos*) in the original language, as well as text and music for *Hilf Gott, das Wasser geht mir bis an d'Seel* (a paraphrase of Psalm 69 [68], 1525); *Hilff Herr Gott, hilff in diser not*, also known as the *Pestlied* (because it had been composed during a plague), and the so-called *Kappeler Lied*. This song (*Herr nun heb den wagen selb*) was written in 1529 after the peace treaty of Kappel, stipulated between Catholics and Protestants cantons: its lyrics display the influence of the *Meistersinger* tradition, and its melody is adapted from a love-song[274] (*Ich weiß mir ein Maidlein hübsch und fein*).

Notwithstanding this, Zwingli's attitude to church music was among the strictest in the Reformation era, possibly due to the influence on his thought of Erasmus' criticism (cf. § 2.3.9.): Zwingli's approach to prayer was characterised by an intense yearning for internal purification and personal conversion, in the belief that the external forms of worship should add nothing to the transcendent essence of faith. Consequently, ideally prayer should be individual, heartfelt, pure and spiritual: for him, Catholic church music was merely an outward clamour and an ostentation made for earning the appreciation of other humans rather than a religious act pleasing to God[275]. As Garside comments, "With that sentence, Zwingli reveals the extremity of his reach. What he seeks is nothing less than an irreducible purity of worship – in other words, an absolutely private prayer: the individual withdrawn from the world and from his fellow men, absolutely alone in communion with his heavenly Father"[276].

Therefore, whilst Luther's experience of music encouraged him to promote its use in worship, Zwingli realised the power of music to move but found it distracting from the purity of contemplation. Blankenburg interestingly argues that possibly their different stance was due to the different kinds of musical experiences they had had in their personal lives: Luther was more deeply involved in "the realm of the folk song, the *musica naturalis*", and thus could foresee its usefulness in the daily lives of the faithful; whereas Zwingli's more professional attitude conditioned his view of music and brought him to consider elaborate music ("*musica artificialis*") as less suited to worship[277].

---

**274** Cf. Jenny 1962, pp. 32 and 52; Koenigsberger 1986, p. 191; Viladesau 2000, pp. 26–27; Marcus 2001, p. 732; Wagner Oettinger 2001, p. 207; McKee 2003, p. 12; Leaver 2006, p. 394; Sfredda 2010, p. 79.
**275** Blankenburg 1975, p. 510.
**276** Garside 1966, pp. 42–43.
**277** Blankenburg 1975, p. 510.

Nevertheless, Zwingli was aware of the necessity for communal worship, especially for the purpose of instructing the laity (as Hustad wrote, "Zwinglian liturgy tended to be more didactic than devotional"[278]). At first he had proposed the congregational singing of a few liturgical items such as the *Gloria* and *Credo*, as well as of Psalms and hymns, by two alternating choirs of men and women in antiphonal fashion: when this suggestion was rejected he opted for congregational declamation and a Scripture-centred worship[279]. Indeed, in 1525 he had asserted that singing and "other ceremonies" could be maintained as they could "make everyone bow to the Lord and [...] attract many people"[280]. As Koenigsberger suggests, therefore, it is possible that Zwingli regarded the absence of music from worship merely as a provisional and temporary measure, which his untimely death prevented him to update and modify[281]; and Marcus points out that Zwingli's attacks on church music were not aimed at an Evangelical style of congregational hymnody (as it was practised, for example, in Basel), but rather at Catholic polyphony and instrumental music. The traditional view of Zwingli as the arch-enemy of church music may therefore be more a consequence of his successor's (i.e. Heinrich Bullinger) stance than of his own convictions[282].

However, the different approaches maintained respectively by Zwingli and by the Basel reformer Johannes Oecolampadius (also known as Huschin, Heussgen etc., 1482–1531) were extremely clear to their contemporaries, one of whom (Johannes Buchstab, 1499–1529) wrote in 1528: "Huschin [Oecolampadius] upholds the singing of Psalms, but Zwingli [...] cannot tolerate Psalms"[283].

Though Zwingli's ultimate intentions concerning church music cannot be definitely and finally established, in consequence of his death at a young age, what does remain as a historical fact is that in Zurich both the celebration of Mass and church music were suspended in 1525. The first motivation for his decision was his conviction, quoted above, that outward ceremonies disrupted concentration on prayer: incidentally, Buchstab's assertion needs to be qualified since Zwingli actually fostered the prayer of Psalms, so long as they were privately recited and not sung in church. Even so, in a sermon of 1528 he argued that psalmody was typical of Jewish religiosity and therefore had no role in a Chris-

---

[278] Hustad 1952, p. 114.
[279] Sfredda 2010, p. 79; Viladesau 2000, pp. 26–27.
[280] Cf. Z IV, p. 14; available online at http://bit.ly/2bOhVXm.
[281] Koenigsberger 1986, p. 192.
[282] Marcus 2001, p. 729.
[283] In Stähelin 1927, vol. 2, pp. 173–177; quoted in Marcus 2001, p. 730.

tian worship[284]. Zwingli understood St Paul's recommendation to "sing and make melody to the Lord in your hearts" (Ephesians 5:19) as implying that God's praise had to be sung *only* in the hearts, and not actually in audible music: this conviction had already clearly emerged in his *Schlußreden* (or *Sixty-Seven Articles:* 1523[285]). For Zwingli, "the words of Paul in Ephesians 5 [:19] and Colossians 3 [:16] concerning psaltery and singing in the heart give no help to those who protect their swan songs by them. For in the heart, he says, not with the voice"[286].

The second reason for Zwingli's choice was his rejection of the pomp and hypocrisy he associated with choral singing, polyphony and organ music[287]. Organs were nailed, destroyed or sold in Zurich and Berne; church singing was to be reinstated in Zurich only in 1598[288]. As Leaver points out, however, there were not only theological reasons for Zwingli's choice: indeed, politics had some weight in determining this orientation. In fact, the authorities in Zurich aimed at establishing a theocracy with distinctive and characterising features: the creation of a form of worship radically different from the Catholic Mass was functional to stress the diversity of this new society with respect to the medieval concept of Church and State[289].

This novelty results clearly from Zwingli's service order, which came into use in April 1525: though it was inspired by the *Manuale Curatorum*[290] of Johann Ulrich Surgant (c.1450–1503), it also represented a drastic innovation[291] (vernacular language, congregational participation, speech only).

Though the reasons listed above (pastoral, theological and political) were sufficient in order to justify Zwingli's choices, it is interesting to mention the difference between his view of the created world and Luther's, which mirrors their contrasting positions as regards church music. Zwingli maintained that "Body and soul [are] two most widely different things. What differs more widely from the clearness and light of the mind and intelligence than the dull inactivity of the earth and the body?"[292]. If we recall how crucial for his theology of music Luther's understanding of finite's capacity for infinity was, we can easily see

---

**284** Marcus 2001, p. 729.
**285** In Z II, n. 20 (14.7.1523), pp. 348–354; available online at http://bit.ly/2bYxKsL.
**286** Z II, p. 621 (*De canone missæ libelli apologia*; text available online at http://bit.ly/2cjOT1l). Translation in Garside 1966, p. 53.
**287** Cf. Marcus 2000, pp. 167–170; Marcus 2001, p. 728.
**288** Koenigsberger 1986, p. 192; Rees 2006, p. 345.
**289** Leaver 2006, p. 393.
**290** Surgant 1506.
**291** Cf. Blankenburg 1975, p. 509.
**292** Zwingli 1983, p. 160.

that Zwingli's different stance on both music and the physical reality consistently reflects their dissimilar perspectives[293].

### 4.3.3. "Radical" Reforms

The label of "Radical" Reformers has been applied to a variety of religious leaders of the sixteenth century, more or less appropriately (in several instances, it mirrors the political views and projections of contemporary historians and sociologists rather than the actual outlook of the people under discussion). We may adopt it here for the sake of simplicity, in order to indicate those Reformers who promoted an understanding of "Reformation" as a complete break with the past, sometimes involving the imposition of their concept of Church on those who were not in agreement with them. This grouping is also useful for a discussion of church music, since several of the "Radical" Reformers shared a very critical opinion of church music and often proposed its outright abolition.

Many traits of Andreas Bodenstein von Karlstadt's perspective on music have already been mentioned, since they were paradoxically important for shaping Luther's view in opposition to it. Their different opinions on the matter became particularly evident when (in March 1522) Luther left the Wartburg Castle in order to limit the novelties Karlstadt had been imposing on the Wittenberg congregations. Indeed, one of the principal divergences among them lay precisely in Karlstadt's tendency to force ritual and moral changes on the community, whereas Luther favoured both a greater gradualness and more respect for the "weak" among the faithful.

As quoted earlier (§ 4.2.3.2.), Karlstadt had expressed his views on church music in his *De Cantu Gregoriano Disputatio* (1521–2), criticising the use of instruments and elaborate polyphony, whose performance required the singers to concentrate on music rather than on the sung words of prayer, and whose multiplicity of voices seemed to contradict the unisonance of communal praise. Even plainchant was not enthusiastically endorsed by Karlstadt who, similar to Zwingli, favoured personal and intimate contemplation over the outward expression of music[294].

Whereas Thomas Müntzer was no less radical than Karlstadt in many aspects, his view of music was more positive and shaded. Prior to the manifestation of his criticism of the Catholic Church, indeed, Müntzer had interestingly

---

[293] Sooy 2006, p. 43.
[294] Cf. Korrick 1990, p. 360; Herl 2004, p. 108; Groote and Vendrix 2012, p. 180.

composed the music for the Office of St Cyriacus. At that time (1515–6), Müntzer had acted as the chaplain to a female monastery in Frose, whose church was dedicated to that saint; possibly, this early compositional effort represented for him a test-bed for his later attempts to create an Evangelical liturgy[295].

In 1524, Müntzer published one of the first German Masses with music after that by Kaspar Kantz (c.1483–1544), which had been issued two years earlier. Müntzer's *Deutsch Evangelisch Messze*[296] for the city of Allstedt was little more than an adaptation of the German translations of liturgical texts to the corresponding Gregorian music (unaccompanied monody) taken from the Catholic worship. The question whether this project was considered by Müntzer to be a definitive accomplishment or rather as a transitory experiment remains unanswered, since he died only one year after its publication[297]. The conflict between the conservative musical aspect of Müntzer's *Deutzsch Kirchenampt* (1523) and the radicalness of his theological approach is shown by the mere mention of its title: "Instituted for the purpose of lifting the perfidious cover that hid from the world the light now shining again in these hymns of praise and divine Psalms, for the edification of a growing Christendom, conforming to God's immutable will for the annihilation of the ostentatious deportment of the godless"[298].

The common points between Müntzer's *Messze* and Luther's German Mass (cf. § 5.3.1.1.) are in their use of the vernacular, in their new understanding of priesthood (which reduced the role of the ordained ministers in favour of the congregation), in the adaptation of Mass texts to the Evangelical theology and in the insertion (or, rather, promotion) of congregational vernacular hymnody.

However, there were also important differences (particularly from the musical viewpoint) in their respective outlooks. Blume interestingly compares the German versions realised by both Müntzer (*O Herr Erlöser alles Volks*) and Luther (*Nun komm, der Heiden Heiland; Erhalt uns, Herr, bei deinem Wort; Verleih uns Frieden gnädiglich*) of the Latin hymn *Veni redemptor gentium*. Müntzer's chant corresponds strictly to the Gregorian model, whose text is translated and adapted to suit the melodic shape of the original song[299]: as Blume notes, the result was not ideal for easy memorisation or to be sung by entire congregations, as it was rather unidiomatic and lacked the rhythmic and melodic clarity and immediacy

---

**295** Cf. Bubenheimer 1989, pp. 92–94; Lindberg 2010, p. 138.
**296** Müntzer 1524.
**297** Leaver 2006, p. 381.
**298** Müntzer 1523; Müntzer 1968, p. 25; English translation in Gritsch 1989, p. 48.
**299** Brown 2005, p. 37.

of Luther's hymns[300]. Songs such as Müntzer's *Es wart gesant Gabriel* or *Lasst uns von Herzen* are rich in melismas but devoid of the attractiveness found in Luther's hymns. In Blume's words, this "German Gregorian chant" (not very different from those used by the Bohemian Brethren) could be useful, at most, "for the group singing of a small, rigidly organized sect"[301].

A further important point of disagreement between Luther and Müntzer lay in the focus of their hymnody: the former reproached the latter for neglecting a properly Christological concentration on the mystery of redemption realised by Jesus in favour of the presentation of His life as merely a model for those of the faithful[302].

### 4.3.4. Bucer: Sacred Music only

Martin Bucer's view of church music and of music in general was perhaps one of the most strictly indebted to the humanist and to Erasmus' viewpoints. Clearly humanist is Bucer's belief in the importance of music for the education of children and the young: its introduction closely paralleled the religious reforms he introduced in Strasbourg[303]. Furthermore, the influence of Plato's view of musical ethics is clear in Bucer's *Foreword* to the 1541 Strasbourg hymnal[304], and his attitude to music (more prudent and less wholehearted than Luther's) reveals the humanist concept of music as functional to the word (or, in this case, the Word) and the worry that its emotional power might overcome this purpose[305]. Bucer was close to Erasmus also in fostering a moderate approach to the reformation of church music[306].

Notwithstanding his moderation, Bucer was harsh in classifying secular love-songs as "*teufflische*", "devilish"[307], and was perhaps one of the most radical of all reformers in advocating the total elimination of secular music from a Christian society, in favour of sacred songs. In his 1541 *Foreword*, he stated: "Thus music, all singing and playing (which above all things are capable of mixing our spirits powerfully and ardently), should be used in no other way except

---

300 Pettegree 2005, p. 44.
301 Blume 1975, p. 37.
302 Buszin 1963, p. 45; cf. Janson 1995, p. 25.
303 Garside 1979, p. 25; Weber 2008, p. 35.
304 *BDS* 7, p. 579. Cf. Garside 1979, p. 29.
305 Sfredda 2010, pp. 82–83.
306 Kim 2005, pp. 117–118.
307 *BDS* 7, p. 579; cf. Rainoldi 2000, p. 331, Trocmé Latter 2015, p. 40 and Weber 2008, p. 91.

for sacred praise, prayer, teaching, and admonition [...] so that absolutely no song and no instrumentalizing may be sung or used except by and for Christian spiritual activities"[308].

On the other hand, and different from other Reformers, Bucer admitted in worship (and, of course, in private devotion and as a recreational activity) not just the Psalms, but also hymns and songs[309]. Consequently, the importance that music came to have in the spiritual life of the Strasbourg community is clearly shown in the following question and answer taken from the Latin 1544 Catechism of the Alsatian city: "Q. What is the third general church practice? A. Songs and psalmody. [...] Q. Should all sing in church? A. Surely: indeed Paul wrote that exhortation to all Christians equally"[310].

### 4.3.5. Calvin: cautions and chanting

In Calvin's case, as in Luther's, his opinions on music and on church music have already been quoted frequently in the first half of this Chapter: however, I will summarise them here in a more organic fashion in order to provide the reader with a comprehensive overview of his perspective.

The principal sources for studying Calvin's position about music are a passage from his *Institutes* (1536, p. 184), the *Articles* of 1537 and the "Letter to the Reader" (or Epistle, or Preface) from the 1542 *Forme des prières*, with the 1543 addition.

#### 4.3.5.1. An increasing interest…

As presented in Chapter One (§ 1.6.3.), Calvin's personal itinerary underwent some important influences and experiences which progressively shaped his theology and his pastoral concept; these are particularly evident as concerns his musical perspective. There is an observable evolution and a progressive refinement in his position[311], and it can be argued that his theoretical and theological viewpoint did not only determine, but was also partly determined in turn by his practical experiences and the encounters he had with other Reformers (particularly during his stay in Basel, 1535, and with Bucer in Strasbourg, 1538).

---

308 *BDS* 7, pp. 578–579. English translation in Garside 1979, p. 25. Cf. Trocmé Latter 2015, p. 40.
309 Garside 1979, p. 26.
310 *Catechismus* 1544, fols. 49ᵛ-50ʳ, my translation.
311 Cf. however Vanderwilt 1995, p. 68, and Joby 2005, pp. 68–69, fn. 18.

His starting point about music was his solid humanistic education (including particularly strong influences from Plato's and Erasmus' philosophies of music) and his constant reference to the Bible, which was – throughout his life – the ultimate authority when theological matters were at stake. As Garside efficaciously synthesises, although four dimensions are discernible in Calvin's theology of music (i.e. "pastoral, historical, Augustinian and humanistic"), they are "ultimately [...] fused [...] and made indissolubly one in Scripture"[312].

The first important references to music in Calvin's writings are found in his *Institutes* (1536): music does not appear to be particularly important within his theological outlook, though he admits Psalm- and congregational singing for giving praise to God at the end of liturgy. Whereas in the first edition his rather cautious approach is shown by the words "Yet we do not here condemn speaking and singing provided they are associated with the heart's affection and serve it", a first evolution in his thought is shown in a later edition, where he added "but rather strongly commend them"[313].

The year after, in 1537, Calvin wrote the *Articles*, fostering singing of Psalms in the vernacular for the Geneva community and claiming for psalmody a constitutive role in liturgy: in Garside's words, "from a position essentially indifferent to its value, Calvin has moved to one of very nearly unqualified acceptance"[314]. This stance was grounded on the usual Scriptural references, but also on the practice of the early Church (a point stressed also by Bucer).

In 1538, Calvin arrived in Strasbourg, where he had the opportunity of discussing with Bucer and meeting with his congregation. As said, Calvin had already developed his personal positive stance on congregational psalmody in the vernacular, but there he had the possibility of seeing in practice how a congregation could be shaped and spiritually nourished by the constant habit of singing together. He noticed how eagerly the Strasbourg community chanted sacred songs (strikingly different from the "coldness" he had observed in Geneva[315]), and this was probably the triggering factor behind his first Psalm collection (1539), as well as the propelling force for his Genevan Psalter (1542).

Though Calvin underwent Bucer's influence as concerns the utility of congregational singing and the desire to provide his community with sacred songs to replace secular music, he did not agree with the Strasbourg Reformer on which kinds of music could be admitted in worship: whereas both Luther

---

312 Garside 1979, p. 29. This section is indebted to this article by Garside.
313 Cf. Garside 1979, pp. 15 and 27.
314 Garside 1979, p. 9.
315 Cf. *OC* X$^1$, p. 12; *OS* 1, p. 375.

and Bucer made use of hymns alongside with Biblical texts, Calvin would always admit almost exclusively Scriptural texts, and particularly Psalms[316].

In the 1543 addition to the Psalter Preface, another element is given particular evidence, i.e. the quality of "moderation", which points out manifestly both his discernment in the choice of suitable music and musical styles, and his belief in music's power to become "an encouragement to believers, fostering their heartfelt desire for and praise to God"[317].

Calvin's approach to music is thus starting to delineate itself more clearly: though the music of metrical Psalms would eventually become no less important for Calvinists than hymnody for Lutherans, Calvin's choice of admitting only psalmody in worship mirrored their very different attitudes. Calvin's option represented a much clearer rupture with the traditional practice inherited from the Catholic Church in comparison with Luther's; furthermore, whereas Luther tended to embrace music inclusively, Calvin preferred to shield his congregation from the risks of music by limiting its use and allowing only a particular musical form. For Luther, most kinds of music could be profitably put at the service of God's Word; for Calvin, most of them should be avoided and prohibited[318].

We have already seen, however, several positive assessments of music in Calvin's words: these concentrate mainly on music being a gift of God for the spiritual rejoicing of humans[319]; on its power to move (which should be properly channelled); on the Scriptural and traditional arguments in favour of music; on the positive pastoral experiences provided to congregations from the practice of singing Psalms together.

Furthermore, Calvin endorsed music on humanistically-inspired grounds, seeing music as close to poetry (whereas it was close to theology for Luther) and concentrating on the possibilities offered by their alliance[320]; moreover, he considered music as a crucial educational element, especially when it possessed the qualities of moderation, majesty, gravity and temperateness which were particularly appreciated by humanists[321] (though here Augustine's influence is also extremely clear). Calvin stated: "Touching the melody, it has seemed best that it be moderated in the manner we have adopted to carry the weight and majesty appropriate to the subject"[322].

---

316 Cf. Garside 1951, pp. 571–572; Garside 1979, pp. 25–28; Herl 2004, p. 99; Sfredda 2010, p. 80.
317 Cf. *OC* VI, pp. 169–170; *OS* 2, pp. 15–16.
318 Cf. Garside 1979, p. 19; Auksi 1995, p. 216; Sooy 2006, pp. 58–59.
319 *OC* VI, pp. 169–170; *OS* 2, p. 16.
320 Spelman 1948, p. 249.
321 *OC* VI, pp. 169–170; *OS* 2, pp. 15–16; cf. Kim 2005, pp. 119–120.
322 *OC* VI, pp. 171–172; *OS* 2, p. 18.

Calvin also acknowledged the emotional and moralising force of music, making an explicit reference to Plato: "there is scarcely anything in the world which is more capable of turning or moving this way and that the morals of men, as Plato prudently considered it [music]. And in fact we experience that it has a secret and almost incredible power to arouse hearts in one way or another"[323]; as quoted above (§ 4.2.4.4.), music can "move and inflame"[324] human hearts to religious zeal and to the praise of God.

Calvin's appreciation of church music is also due to his understanding of its value as a gift of the Holy Spirit (a point on which his perspective is very close to Luther's): the Holy Spirit is involved in the creation of works of visual art as well as music, as He inspired King David to compose the Psalms and leads the faithful to praise the Lord in music[325].

### 4.3.5.2. ...And persisting perplexities

We have repeatedly seen that this positive evaluation of music, together with the many reasons Calvin adduced to foster it, was counterbalanced by several cautions and perplexities as concerns the risks and dangers which could be attached to music making. As Sternfeld put it, "faith in the elevating powers of music must perforce have its corollary in the fear of a corruptive influence which vulgar and cheap music would exercise"[326].

Light and frivolous music had to be eschewed; church music had to be characterised by peculiar and distinguishing features, different from those of secular songs or dances[327]. Whereas Luther could adapt the very music used "at table" and "in [...] homes" to religious hymns, this contamination was absolutely unconceivable for Calvinist psalmody; on the other hand, while sharing Zwingli's fear of the alluring power of music[328], Calvin sought to channel this capacity to the service of devotion and piety.

To achieve this end, music should be neither too attractive nor too complex[329]: simple and sober music would not distract from the sung words but rather give them a favourable support. The responsibility for directing the power of

---

[323] *OC* VI, pp. 169–170; *OS* 2, p. 16. Cf. Freedman 2006, pp. 169–170.
[324] *OC* VI, pp. 169–170; *OS* 2, p. 15.
[325] *OC* VI, pp. 171–172 and 169–170 respectively; *OS* 2, p. 17.
[326] Sternfeld 1948, p. 103; cf. Garside 1979, p. 23; Sfredda 2010, pp. 81–82.
[327] Cf. *OC* VI, pp. 169–170; *OS* 2, p. 15.
[328] McKee 2003, pp. 19–20. Cf. Garside 1979, p. 19, where is stated that Calvin sought a musical style "generally fitting the sacred service".
[329] Calvin 1960, p. 895, *OC* II, p. 659; *OS* 4, p. 342. Cf. Sfredda 2010, pp. 82–83.

music and making it useful for moving the hearts to prayer was trusted by Calvin to words: the sacred words of the Biblical Psalms acted as an antidote to the rebellious and uncontrollable affective and emotional force of music[330].

Indeed, Calvin neatly separated this seemingly sub-rational power from the textual component of songs: "in speaking now of music, I understand two parts: namely the letter, or subject and matter; secondly, the song, or the melody"[331]. Actually, evil texts and words had in turn a great capacity for degrading human beings; when they were accompanied by seductive music, this debasing influence was correspondingly increased[332]. Music *per se* (and consequently instrumental music, which could not be controlled by words) could also intoxicate with pleasure and immoderate joy, and thus become a threat to the spiritual life of the faithful. Thus, Calvin pointed out that the invention of the harp could be traced back to the descent of Cain (cf. Genesis 14:21):

> Although the invention of the harp, and of similar instruments of music, may minister to our pleasure, rather than to our necessity, still it is not to be thought altogether superfluous; much less does it deserve, in itself, to be condemned. Pleasure is indeed to be condemned, unless it be combined with the fear of God, and with the common benefit of human society. But such is the nature of music, that it can be adapted to the offices of religion, and made profitable to men; if only it be free from vicious attractions, and from that foolish delight, by which it seduces men from better employments, and occupies them in vanity[333].

Instrumental music, as seen above (§ 4.2.5.), was to be rejected for its lack of verbal content, for its connection with Jewish worship (the *"puerilia elementa"*[334]) as well as because it allegedly contravened the Pauline command to pray "in a known tongue":

> To sing the praises of God upon the harp and psaltery unquestionably formed a part of the training of the law, and of the service of God under that dispensation of shadows and figures; but they are not now to be used in public thanksgiving. We are not, indeed, forbidden to use, in private, musical instruments, but they are banished out of the churches by the plain command of the Holy Spirit, when Paul, in 1 Corinthians 14:13, lays it down as an invariable rule, that we must praise God, and pray to him only in a known tongue[335].

---

[330] Freedman 2006, pp. 169–170.
[331] *OC* VI, pp. 169–170; *OS* 2, pp. 16–17.
[332] *OC* VI, pp. 169–170; *OS* 2, p. 17.
[333] Calvin 1999a, Chapter Four (*OC* XXIII, pp. 99–100).
[334] Cf. Blankenburg 1975, p. 517; Koenigsberger 1986, p. 185; Sfredda 2010, pp. 82–83.
[335] *OC* XXXI, p. 662, as translated in Calvin 1999b (Commentary to Psalm 71 [70]:20–24).

It is clear, therefore, that Calvin's theology of music lacks the symbolic dimension discussed in Chapter Two (§ 2.3.8.), and that the epistemological richness of music is for him a danger rather than a value[336].

We have seen, thus, that Calvin had a positive concept of music in general, although he saw it in a subordinate function with respect to words and had doubts as regards the potentially corruptive power of its emotional content. We will now consider in greater detail the only form of church music he did allow in worship, and with which he would eventually have liked to replace all other kinds of music even in the secular sphere, namely psalmody.

In the *Preface* to the 1542 Genevan Psalter, Calvin underpinned most of the notions discussed until now, i.e. the dangers of music, its force in combination with words, the necessity for understanding the words (implying they had to be sung in the vernacular and without instrumental accompaniment or polyphony), and the importance of wisely choosing a text: the divinely inspired Psalms, when sung in unaccompanied monody and in the vernacular, seemed to correspond to all requirements of church music with none of the risks that might be associated with it[337]. Though the Biblical Psalter could not (for chronological reasons) mention Christ explicitly, it was for Calvin the quintessentially true form of Christian prayer, since it prophetically anticipated Christ's coming and several facts of his life, death and resurrection (this interpretation of the Old Testament is called "typological reading"). Calvin stressed that psalmody had been used by the Church from its very beginnings, stating: "We wish [the Psalms] to be sung in the church as we have it from the example of the ancient church and also the testimony of Saint Paul, who says that it is good to sing in the congregation with mouth and heart"[338]. Calvin wished therefore to re-establish an Apostolic practice, and to educate the laity to pray with divinely inspired words[339], sung in their own language. For Calvin, thus, psalmody should eventually become the musical accompaniment for the entire lives of the faithful, replacing secular music and being sung in all daily situations: in private devotion, harmonisations of the Psalm tunes were admitted alongside monodic singing. In this way, Psalms would interweave the congregation's time, at work, at home and in church, and "no longer could Sunday worship be separated from that of the rest of the week; all of time was offered to God in the same biblical prayers. [...] The scope might be nar-

---

336 Cf. Butin 1994, p. 430.
337 Higman 2000, p. 499. Cf. Garside 1979, p. 24.
338 *OC* X¹, p. 12; *OS* 1, p. 375.
339 Cf. *OC* VI, pp. 171–172; *OS* 2, p. 17. Cf. Sfredda 2010, p. 80.

row, but the appreciation for beauty was channelled rather than cut off"[340], as McKee summarises.

What mattered most, however, for Calvin as for Zwingli, was the purity of worship and of the individual's prayer[341]. Cultual acts should mirror the intimate and sincere devotion of the soul: otherwise, rituality and ceremonies would become mere hypocrisy and ostentation. As he wrote, "unless voice and song [*cantum*], if interposed in prayer, spring from deep feeling of heart, neither has any value or profit in the least with God"[342].

Within the Evangelical understanding of Christian liberty, moreover, the compulsoriness of liturgical acts gave way to the faithful's initiative, and their participation in public actions of worship had a meaning only if such acts were the expression of the congregation's piety[343]. Stressing the spiritual nature of God, Calvin (similar to Zwingli) fostered the heart's contemplation of transcendence: as Joby suggests, Calvin's consideration of God's invisible and impalpable nature might have encouraged his adoption of music (an invisible and impalpable form of art) as an appropriate accessory to prayer[344].

### 4.3.6. Anglican antinomies

The different origins of the English Reformation in comparison with those on the Continent, the presence within it of several important spiritual leaders instead of a single charismatic figure, and the fact that the practical implementation of theological theories often depended on the reigning sovereigns (who did have religious authority but seldom could be considered as theological guides) make it difficult to present an "Anglican theology of music" (at least in its early period) as I have tried to do for those by Luther, Bucer and Calvin in the preceding pages.

Thus, statements from individual theologians active in England during the sixteenth century are of little help here, since several (and sometimes sharply contrasting) theories of sacred music coexisted with another, particularly under the influences of Continental Reformers: undoubtedly, they all contributed to the theological debate about music and to the growth of a cultural conscience

---

340 McKee 2003, pp. 28–29.
341 Garside 1979, p. 8.
342 Calvin 1975, p. 100; *OC* I, p. 88; *OS* 1, p. 103.
343 Whale 1936, p. 162.
344 Joby 2005, p. 71.

about it, though – practically – both the confessional orientations and their musical style largely depended on the musical and religious taste of the powerful.

The most reliable statements concerning an overall theological perspective on music in the Church of England come therefore from collegial works, expressing the Church's official position and mirroring the sensitivity of its leaders on the subject.

In c.1540, an episcopal commission composed a *Rationale* (i.e. a ceremonial book), where assertions on the functions and value of music are found. Music is considered to be a tool for delivering God's Word to the faithful, so that the congregation may penetrate into its spiritual depth; singing could foster the believers' piety and encourage their spiritual life; and it could act as a reminder of God's promise and as a bridge between the Church living on earth and that already in heaven. Moreover, worshippers should be granted the possibility of understanding properly and clearly the words, which were of the utmost importance for their spiritual growth[345].

A similar stress on the clarity of pronunciation and on the intelligibility of the words is found in the *Reformatio legum ecclesiasticarum* of 1552, recommending that "words [be pronounced] methodically and distinctly" and chant be "clear and connected so that all things may attain to the feeling and understanding of the hearers"[346]. We have already seen, on the other hand, that Cranmer (who actually could rightfully be considered as both a deeply spiritual and a powerful religious leader) had attempted to find an Evangelically-inspired style of sacred music led by syllabic principles of declamation which could suit the peculiarities of the English language[347].

Even among those who, in the Church of England, were closer to the Calvinist positions, music was rarely denied its symbolic dimension and its capacity to move; there was awareness, however, that – precisely by virtue of this power – music could be either very useful or potentially very dangerous. The "godly" (i.e. those who fostered a Calvinist orientation in the Anglican Church, frequently in consequence of their experience of Reformed worship during the Marian exile) could sometimes oppose even the chanting of liturgy, let alone the complex polyphony or instrumental music in church, while, of course, metrical psalmody was not only admitted but actively encouraged.

Debate often focused on the keyword of "edification", since one of the main goals of several Reformers was to "build", quite literally, the new Church: it was

---

[345] Kim 2005, p. 189.
[346] *Reformatio legum ecclesiasticarum* 1571, fols. 43$^{r\text{-}v}$; English translation in Leaver 2006, p. 398.
[347] Cf. Shaw 1975, p. 697; Le Huray 2008, p. 7.

crucial, therefore, to evaluate whether music was a "constructive" activity or rather a distraction. Occasionally, the love for music by the religious leaders (bishops, theologians or sovereigns) might simply overcome all theological arguments; there were also, however, earnest efforts to establish whether music had an edifying power, and, if so, which music was recommendable and why.

Thus, for Richard Hooker, church music "doth much edify if not the understanding because it teacheth not, yet surely the affection, because therin it worketh much. They must have hearts very dry and tough, from whom the melody of Psalms doth not sometime draw that wherein a mind religiously affected delighteth"[348]. Here, references to the touching power of sacred music (explicitly quoting St Basil, cf. § 2.3.4.) support the "edifying" value of music though limiting it to the affective sphere.

Frequently, judgements of value about music were not grounded on its objective qualities, but depended on its subjective reception by the hearers, the faithful (and sometimes the musicians themselves).

A Zwinglian influence on the English perspective came from Heinrich Bullinger, Zwingli's successor in Zurich, who dedicated several sermons from his *Decades* to King Edward VI. While discussing the forms of prayer, in the fifth Decade (dedicated to Lord Henry Grey, 1517–1554: Latin version from c.1549–51), Bullinger maintained:

> If ye list to sing, sing Psalms and spiritual songs. Whereunto this also may be added; that even in those kinds of songs, [the apostle] requireth rather the song of the heart than the warbling of the voice; so far off is it that he at any time alloweth uncomely shriekings, either public or private. [...] No man can or ought to disallow moderate and godly singing of Psalms, whether it be publicly-used in holy assemblies, or at home in private houses. [...] Ye shall also find this, that by certain decrees of councils it was ordained, that no other thing should either be read or sung in holy assemblies but only the canonical scripture[349].

Bullinger continues by endorsing Erasmus' stance, that "the singing used in the ancient churches was no other than a distinct and measured pronunciation, such as at this day in some places is used in pronouncing of the Psalms, the Gospel, and the Lord's prayer"; he also stresses that "singing, howsoever it be an ancient institution, nevertheless was never universal, and of necessity thrust upon the churches; but it was free".

Bullinger continues his discussion by resorting to some of the arguments previously discussed: the non-Scriptural origin of many sung texts, their being

---

[348] Hooker 1876, book V, Chapter 38, pp. 161–162.
[349] Bullinger 1852, p. 192.

in an unknown tongue, the professionalisation of music, the consequent rivalries among musicians. Bullinger concludes by stating that "it is a hard thing so to limit or restrain singing, which otherwise is tolerable, lest at some time it exceed and go beyond the appointed bounds"[350]. For Bullinger, thus, singing was not commanded but practised; not forbidden but discouraged.

Indeed, the official pronouncements of the Church of England after Elizabeth's accession (1559 *Injunctions*) echoed several of Bullinger's views, which were for that matter far from uncommon among the Reformers. In spite of this, complex music and artistic polyphony remained in use both in the Chapel Royal and in several important institutions throughout the Kingdom, as will be discussed in Chapter Seven (§ 7.6. etc.).

Later in the century, two important writings defending music were printed in England, namely *The Praise of Musicke* (1586) and the *Apologia musices* (1588): the latter was authored by John Case (c.1539–1600), while the former used to be attributed to him (though scholarly debate is open). The *Apologia* frankly endorses the Lutheran musical practices and the quality of their performances, while quoting from Andreae's arguments against Bèze which have been discussed earlier in this Chapter (§ 4.2.4.8.).

The *Praise of Musicke* derives from the Patristic tradition and early Christian practices a first argument in favour of music; it also maintains the inherent goodness of music, which cannot be despised without despising, at the same time, the creative work of God, since He is the first and foremost author of harmony. Echoing many other religious writers on music, the author of the *Praise* argues that music is a gift of God, and that singing represents its highest and purest form, while some "kind of intemperance and wantonness" could be found in contemporaneous instrumental music. Here too, however, the fault is not in music *per se*, but rather in how it is practised and used. A list of the beneficial powers of music follows, including the discussion of its ability to move, with references to the ancient modes; therefore, the importance of music for education is maintained.

Between Bullinger and the *Praise of Musicke* a huge space was left open for discussions, interpretations, theologising and practising music: we will discuss in Chapter Seven how the theological and philosophical debate on church music which had found practical application in the Evangelical Continental Churches was peculiarly understood and applied in practice by the Church of England.

---

[350] Bullinger 1852, pp. 192–197; cf. also Willis 2013, to which this section is indebted.

### 4.3.7. Catholic continuity

Also in the case of the Catholic Church, it is problematic to synthesise a "Catholic" theology of music: since the Reformation of the Catholic Church did not constitute a new confessional entity (with the possibility of experimenting new solutions, as well as with the need of differentiating itself from other confessions) and since some important decisions, initiatives and statements were the product of an assembly (at the Council of Trent) rather than of a single individual, it is difficult to summarise *one* and a *new* theology of music for the Catholic Church: there were indeed many Catholic theologies of music, and they were often deeply rooted in the centuries-old tradition of Catholicism.

Therefore, thoroughness could only be reached by writing a *history* of the Catholic theology of music, whereas here I am trying to offer a picture of the situation in the sixteenth century: an easier path, in order to achieve this objective, is to point out how the Catholic position differed from those of the Evangelical Churches discussed above.

Paradoxically, the absence of a single influential leader comparable to the Evangelical Reformers (as seen in § 1.6.3., eighteen Popes ruled from Peter's Chair during the sixteenth century) and the lack of an official reflection on sacred music within this period are noteworthy – although obviously the Catholic Church had more pressing and difficult matters to deal with at the time[351]. However, this very situation helped to preserve a truly "Catholic" (i.e. "universal") approach to church music: together with the Lutheran Church, Catholics maintained and made use of a large variety of musical styles, both in worship and outside it[352]. Though there were a number of particular orientations, of individual theologies, of musical styles typical for certain places, religious orders, liturgical traditions and ritual contexts, the Council of Trent would eventually avoid sectarianism in its official pronouncements, and preserve the Church's "universality" in the variety of its charismas.

Whereas several Evangelical Reformations were closely linked to a particular geographical or linguistic context, the Catholic Church chose to favour its international vocation over localism, by maintaining the use of the Latin language in the liturgy. To be sure, there were excellent reasons for advocating the use of the vernacular (which the Catholic Church would eventually promote in the twentieth century, after the Second Vatican Council); however, vernacular elements were not only permitted but actually encouraged in private or public devotional

---

[351] Mischiati 1995, p. 25.
[352] Cf. § 8.2.4., 8.4.2., 8.5.3., 9.3. and following.

activities, while liturgy had to express the atemporality (and thus the link to eternality) and the universality of the worshipping Church.

### 4.3.7.1. Hearing Mass

Several theological topics concerning liturgical and stylistic choices fostered by the Catholic Church before and after Trent will be discussed in Chapters Eight and Nine; here we will concentrate on a single (albeit fundamental) topic which deeply involved the relationships between Catholic and Evangelic theologies of music, i.e. the role of laity in worship and the different understanding of priesthood.

Once more, there were good Scriptural grounds for defending either position. As discussed in Chapter One (§ 1.2.2.) and earlier in this Chapter (§ 4.2.3. and 4.3.1.2.), the Evangelicals could maintain that all faithful were made "priests" by virtue of their Baptism; on the other hand, for Catholics, Jesus had conferred particular ministries to the Apostles, and their functions had been transmitted to their successors (although certain traits of Western Catholic priesthood, such as the compulsory celibacy, emerged at a later historical stage).

Indeed, the contemporary Catholic view of the laity's participation in liturgy and worship is very close (and probably indebted) to that of the Evangelical Churches, and, nowadays, the priesthood of all baptised is not seen in competition with the peculiarities of the ordained ministry or in alternative to it; however, in the sixteenth century the situation was very different.

Though Catholic piety was by no means restricted to the celebration of the Eucharist, and there were several other liturgical or devotional activities (in church, outside it or in private contexts) where the Catholic laity could be deeply involved both spiritually and creatively, undoubtedly the Mass was considered to be the most important liturgical act by the Catholic Church, and it envisaged very little interaction between the celebrating priests and the congregation.

Of course, ideally those attending Mass should have joined in prayer (albeit often with particular devotions which were not directly related to what happened at the altar) and thus mystically contributed to the sacrifice performed by the priest; however, devotion largely depended on the individual's good disposition and willingness to concentrate, and was probably not fostered by the liturgical shape of the rite. When music was performed audibly, it could have sustained the piety of churchgoers by virtue of its beauty, though it is likely that this was not the case with the majority of listeners.

The "low Mass", thus, was read by the priest, to whom the altar servers responded: the liturgical texts were delivered in Latin and probably were not even audible, let alone understandable, by most participants. The laity could – especially in some contexts and places – sing vernacular songs, but (as discussed in the preceding Chapters) the extent of this practice as well as the actual participation of the congregation cannot be established with any likeliness. Furthermore, when several Masses were simultaneously celebrated at the different altars present in most churches, the laity could not properly be involved in any one rite, and would probably try and follow the sequence of elevations at the many altars[353]. As previously mentioned (§ 1.2.3.), at several points in the history of the Catholic Church, even a frequent communion was discouraged, and it was replaced by the visual contemplation of the consecrated host at elevation. In order for the rite to be valid, however, the priest and his liturgical acts, together with the matter of the bread and wine, were the only indispensable elements: the presence of the laity was accessory, as – obviously – was their understanding and their prayerful participation. Though this may seem (and from a certain viewpoint actually was) inappropriate and erroneous, the fundamental presupposition of Catholic liturgy should not be overlooked: as Herl rightly points out, congregational participation or understanding "mattered little, for the liturgy was sung for its own sake and for God's, not for theirs"[354].

On the other hand, several Evangelical Churches shifted the meaning of worship from sacrifice to instruction or education: the priest was replaced by the preacher, and if Calvinist Psalm-singing aimed at letting the God-inspired words be sung by the laity, the Lutheran hymns joined theology with praise.

This process, though different from those happening in the Catholic Church, had (similar to them) its pros and its cons. We have seen that two of the main purposes of Lutheran hymn-singing were *Lehre* and *Trost*, i.e. to provide instruction and to comfort. Though these were excellent ideals, in practice and historically this could (and sometimes did) lead to a dualistic divarication between individualistic fideism and liturgical rationalism[355]. On the other hand, the maintenance of Latin worship in the Catholic Church fostered – in the long run – an output of liturgical music aiming at "entertaining" the laity "while" the Mass was celebrated (all the more since even choral singing was not indispensable for the validity of a Eucharistic rite[356], and was only an appendage to enhance solemnity[357]), alongside with the creation of a devotional repertoire whose disjunction from liturgy unavoidably verged on the theatrical style in

---

353 Cf. Herl 2004, p. 35; Weber 2008, p. 134.
354 Herl 2004, p. 175.
355 I am grateful to my friend Prof. Marco Salvioli OP for clarifying this point to me.
356 Herl 2004, p. 32.
357 Rainoldi 2000, p. 352.

turn[358]. Devotion became increasingly private, and "spirituality" replaced the "official corporate life of the Church as the ordinary vehicle for the faith-life of the believer"[359].

Though the post-Tridentine Catholic Church did indeed promote the laity's education and piety, the separation between clergy and congregation did persist, and was particularly clear precisely during Eucharistic liturgies. The reader may recall that such a view was already found in Aquinas' discussion of sung praises of the Lord[360], where the supremacy of preaching over singing was maintained. This concept was held in 1562 by Francisco de Cordova (also known as Franciscus Cordubensis, fl. 1562–1586), a Franciscan Friar, who stated: "Singing is the meanest office; indeed it is not even the property of ministers of the church but of all Christians"[361]. Though this assertion does foster the laity's participation in singing (as it is the "property [...] of all Christians") it also stresses the radical difference between ordained ministry and lay involvement.

On the other hand, Gabriele Paleotti drew an interesting parallelism between secular visual art and the "order" established in the Church by the presence of ordained ministers and lay faithful: for Paleotti, just as there existed both lay and consecrated Christians, so it was possible that secular art coexisted alongside with sacred images. Therefore, secular paintings or sculptures participated in religion itself by virtue of their position in the order of the created world[362]. This concept of "order", which is inherent to the very idea of the clerical state for Catholics (as the expression "sacred orders" testifies) helps to understand why a congregation-centred worship was hardly imaginable in the Catholic Church, as (in White's words) it would have "dissolved divinely ordained hierarchical relations between the clergy and the laity, between men and women, and between the sacred and the profane"[363].

Indeed, in that same *Quæstio* (see § 2.3.5.), Aquinas had also underpinned that the congregation ought only to understand *why* the rite was performed, and not necessarily *what* it consisted of.

---

**358** Prodi 2014, p. 264.
**359** Rasmussen 1988, p. 281.
**360** *ST* 2a2æ, q. 91, a. 2; cf. § 2.3.5.
**361** *CT* 13, pp. 619–620, cit. in Monson 2002, pp. 31–32.
**362** Prodi 2014, p. 94 and fn. 121.
**363** White 2005, p. 67.

#### 4.3.7.2. Worship for whom?
Therefore, a proper understanding of the focus and of the motivations of worship (different for Catholics and Evangelicals, as well as among different Evangelical confessions) is fundamental in order to comprehend the function of liturgy and of rituality (including music).

For the Catholic Church, as stated in Chapter One (§ 1.2.3.), the Mass was valid regardless of the congregation's understanding and participation; similarly, it maintained that the sacraments had a spiritual force of their own ("*ex opere operato*") which did not depend on the holiness of those ministering them. The beauty pursued by the Catholic Church in the visual appearance of its buildings (paintings, sculptures, architecture, mosaics...) and in the aural appearance of its rites (polyphony, instrumental music etc.) stressed the fact that worship was an act directed primarily towards God (and therefore all efforts to adorn the liturgy were made, at least theoretically, in order to please Him).

Here our discussion of the symbolic value of music comes again to the fore: though obviously on a different plane as the sacraments, music as a *symbolon* could be a vehicle of Grace from God to humans and of praise from humans to God. Through its beauty, music could bear witness to the beauty of God and (at the same time) please Him; and, as long as it was conceived as an act for the glory of God, it accomplished its function. Similar to the *ex opere operato* of the sacraments, it was both pleasing to God and beneficial to humans for the very fact that it had been performed.

The Calvinist and Zwinglian focus on the purity of the faithful's intentions and of their internal disposition, as well as the Lutheran attention to the pedagogical dimension of worship stress a different concept: since God saves the human beings by His Grace only – and not by virtue of what they do in response to it – then the quest for beauty as a way to make the human participation to liturgy more pleasing to God loses (at least partially) its significance. Where liturgical beauty continued to be pursued (such as, for example, in the Lutheran Church) it was conceived rather as a means for attracting the congregation and for lifting their hearts to the contemplation of eternal realities than as something which God Himself could enjoy.

Though both dimensions of worship (i.e. praise "to God" and edification "for humans") should ideally be kept together, the Catholic Church of the sixteenth century chose to privilege the former. The Catholic stance was synthesised by St Robert Bellarmine, whose statements are worth quoting since they represent a different interpretation of the Pauline discussion on "praying with understanding" and on the prayer in known tongues:

> The chief end of those canticles [of the ancient Church] was the instruction and consolation of the people, for these were done in conferences in place of exhortation, and therefore it was right for them to be understood by many, and unless it was done in a known language, or unless an interpretation soon followed, the chief fruit of these conferences would have been lost. But the chief end of the divine offices is not the instruction or consolation of the people, but the worship of God, and what the people need to know from the divine offices is explained by pastors. [...] The prayer of the Church is not made to the people but to God for the people. So there is no need for the people to understand so as to be profited, but it is enough if God understands. In the same way, if someone were to pray in Latin before a king on behalf of some rustic, the rustic would certainly be able to perceive the fruit of it, even if he did not understand the prayer of his advocate[364].

Already in 1530, the *Confutatio Pontificia* written by Catholic theologians in response to the Augsburg Confession had made use of Aquinas' argument: the laity's understanding of the liturgical words was unnecessary so long as they comprehended their aim[365]. In Besutti's thought-provoking analysis,

> Polyphonic singing raises the sacred words to heights of ineffable beauty, and this is one of the highest acts of glorification of God realised by man. However, sacred words are symbols as well. They are loaded with transcendent meanings, which cannot be simplistically reduced to their semantic meaning. In this sense, perceptibility is not a primary value any more[366].

As we will often see in Chapters Eight and Nine, efforts were actually made in the Catholic Church in order to enhance both the intelligibility of sung texts and the participation of the laity in worship: we have also already considered the fact that the constant repetition of liturgical texts such as the Mass Ordinary implied and brought familiarity with their words[367], and that explanations of the liturgy and of the Bible in the vernacular were fostered by the Council of Trent[368]; however, even when similar initiatives were enacted by Evangelicals and Catholics alike, they often had slightly (or highly) different meanings and reasons.

For example, as we will see, vernacular singing inspired by Luther's hymns was encouraged by several Catholic Reformers too; however, the dimensions of *Lehre* and *Trost* were at least downplayed, if not outright absent, in the Catholic

---

**364** Bellarmino 1599, Book II, Chapter 16, pp. 187–188; English translation in Bellarmino 2013, pp. 129–130.
**365** Cf. Kolb and Nestingen 2001, pp. 127–128.
**366** Besutti 1993, p. 121, my translation.
**367** Mischiati 1995, p. 20.
**368** *SCT*, p. 159; cf. Weber 2008, p. 168.

promotion of hymn singing[369]: as Bellarmine said, "instruction and consolation" were of secondary importance.

Summarising, then, the concept, function and importance of lay participation in the Eucharistic sacrifice is determined by the Catholic understanding of the Mass: although it is musically correct to compare the distinctive worship forms practised by the Christian confessions in the sixteenth century, it is theologically inappropriate inasmuch as the focus, purpose, object and primary receiver of a Catholic Eucharist, of a Calvinist prayer or of a Lutheran worship were different.

This Chapter has surveyed the positions on sacred music in the Christian Churches of the sixteenth century both thematically and from the confessional viewpoint. Though considerations about the criticalities and the abuses in worship were often similar among most – if not all – religious Reformers, their respective stances as regards the functions and modes of church music were often different, and sometimes outright irreconcilable with one another. Starting from the same (or almost the same) Scriptural sources, being imbibed with the same cultural atmosphere we have pictured in the preceding Chapters, and facing the same or very similar pastoral problems, the theological and practical results achieved by the various Reformers establish a continuum ranging from the rejection of all church music to the acceptance of almost all musical forms in worship. In the next Chapters, we will move from theology to practice, and consider in turn how music was made, experienced, enjoyed and utilised in the Christian Churches of the sixteenth century.

---

**369** Cf. Brown 2005, pp. 23–24, and Wetzel and Heitmeyer 2013, pp. vii-viii.

# Chapter 5 – Music in the Evangelical Churches: Luther

> Music remains always with God; [...]
> In heaven, after the Last Day [...]
> All people will be singers,
> They will use this art only[1].
>
> [Johann Walther]

## 5.1. Introduction

We have seen how the viewpoints on music within the framework of the religious Reformations in Early Modern Europe had some common elements as well as some dramatic differences. Now we will move on to the consideration of the individual Churches' approach to music in the actual reality of their worship and of their experience of the sacred.

A few provisos should however be kept in mind: first, that the conventional use of confessional labels was by no means a rigid, static and fixed frame, particularly at the beginnings of the Reformations; second, that even when boundaries were starting to be established, musical practice proved itself to be much more permeable and fluid than confessional limits.

Furthermore, we will see that the composite world of the non-Roman Churches could make use of very different forms of church music, so that there might be a greater similarity between the music of a particular Evangelical confession and that of the Catholic Church than between two different Protestant Churches: as Blume correctly points out, a "Protestant" musical style is not identifiable, since individual Churches did possess idiomatic musical features, but none was universally accepted (and typical only of the non-Catholic Churches[2]). From the theological discussion of the preceding Chapter, moreover, the typical repertoires of the principal Evangelical Churches have started to emerge, alongside with the maintenance of a number of Catholic practices by some Protestant confessions[3].

---

1 Walther 1970, vol. 6, p. 156, lines 145–151.
2 Cf. Blume 1975, pp. xii and 3.
3 Cf. Sooy 2006, p. 10; Groote and Vendrix 2012, p. 179.

## 5.1. Introduction

One common feature of the music-making of most Evangelical confessions can however be identified, i.e. their focus on congregational singing in the vernacular. This in turn produced a more widespread musical literacy and fostered the use of music for private piety, promoting the composition of devotional works in a variety of styles and languages[4].

This Chapter will focus therefore on Luther and on Lutheranism. Even though we have already discussed Luther's outlook on music, here I will briefly examine his own experience of music, as a composer, as a performer, as a perceptive listener, and as a person whose spiritual insight was profoundly connected with his love for music.

I will then present Luther's interventions (and his "non-interventions") in the liturgical tradition of the Catholic Church, both as regards the Mass – in Latin and in German – and the Office. As is well known, however, Luther's main contribution to the history of Western music is his focus on vernacular singing: I will discuss the multiple origins of the songs adopted or created by Luther and his circle, and consider songs stemming from the Latin tradition of the Catholic Church, as well as those coming from pre-existing vernacular traditions (both sacred and secular), together with Luther's original works. Other composers and poets cooperated with him both in the early years of the Reformation and later, and innumerable musicians adopted Lutheran songs, with their artistic and symbolic value, as sources of inspiration for more complex contrapuntal and instrumental renditions. Although this process continues – albeit in a variety of different forms – until the present day, I will limit my discussion to the sixteenth century: it is important, however, to be constantly aware of the fecundity of the Lutheran tradition and of its flexibility, which will take in later centuries a Protean-like variety of forms and prove itself to be an almost inexhaustible source of musical inspiration.

I will then focus on how the vernacular singing promoted by Luther affected his followers' daily lives: I will discuss the role and value of hymn-books both within domestic worship and in the congregational experience, as well as the function of Lutheran *Lieder* within liturgy. Besides this, vernacular singing was deeply inscribed into the laity's everyday practice: as a form of catechetic instruction, within the context of education and pedagogy, as a source of comfort and consolation, as a sacred alternative to secular songs, as a means for creating a feeling of confessional identity, and as a crucial demonstration and application of Luther's theology of the universal priesthood of the believers.

---

4 Higman 2000, pp. 502–503.

Another function of Lutheran songs should also be pointed out, i.e. their fundamental role in spreading Luther's message and ideas among wide layers of the contemporaneous society. We will see the reasons for the exceptional importance of *Lied*-singing as a propagandistic tool, and discuss the advantages it offered in comparison with other forms of verbal and non-verbal communication.

The Lutheran tradition prided itself on having several other musical forms, among which I will succinctly present the Lutheran Passion and litany, as well as the Latin-texted musical works which will demonstrate Luther's effort to preserve and to renovate the existing musical and liturgical traditions side by side with his undeniable and creative innovations.

This Chapter will also include the discussion of Lutheran traditions outside the boundaries of present-day Germany (particularly in Northern Europe and Scandinavia), as well as of musical experiences which are definitely not ascribable to Luther, but whose interaction with Lutheranism justifies their presentation here. In particular, I will speak briefly about the Bohemian Brethren's tradition, as well as about the musical aspect of Bucer's reformation in Strasbourg: this will also help us to introduce the subject of Chapter Six, since Calvin's concept of and attitude towards music cannot be understood in isolation from his own experience in the Alsatian Church.

## 5.2. A music-loving Reformer

We have already seen in Chapter Four (§ 4.3.1.) that Luther was an accomplished amateur musician, who particularly enjoyed music-making with friends; moreover, he was a perceptive listener and a sensitive critic of music, who prized Josquin's works highly. Luther's musical criticism may have been slightly amateurish and inconsistent, as Blume points out, but some of his remarks reveal a careful listening habit and a lively interest in contemporaneous music[5].

His Reform is set against a richly musical background, due not only to his own sensitivity and love for music, but also to the flourishing artistic life in the city of Wittenberg. Since Duke Frederick the Wise (whose political stature was inferior only to the Emperor's) aimed at establishing a musical chapel similar in splendour to the Emperor's, during the time of Luther's ministry in Wittenberg its activity was impressively fostered and promoted[6].

---

5 See Blume 1975, pp. 7–8 and Østrem 2003.
6 Leaver 2006, p. 391.

Luther could therefore have direct experiences of high-quality polyphonic music, which probably encouraged him to compose his own contrapuntal works: A Psalm-motet titled *Non moriar sed vivam* (Psalm 118 [117]:17), written in four parts and attributed to Luther, has survived within a humanistic play (*Lazarus*, 1545) by Joachim Greff (1510–1552).

The Psalm fragment after which Luther's motet is named had a great importance in Luther's spiritual life: he wanted it written (together with the attached melody) on his room's walls, and adopted it as his motto[7]. Indeed, it represents perfectly the key discovery of Luther's spirituality, as well as that which would have prompted his Reformation: indeed, Luther had developed his view of justification and salvation precisely by overcoming his anguish about God's wrath and discovering His mercy and Grace instead. The realisation that he "would not die" ("*Non moriar*", in Latin) for his sins, but rather receive life ("*sed vivam*") by God's mercy so that he may tell ("*et narrabo*") his brothers and sisters the good news (the "Gospel": "*opera Domini*") of salvation was the fundamental event in his personal life as well as the foundation of the Evangelical theology.

The importance of music for Luther's own religiousness is shown also by another episode. During a moment of particularly harsh spiritual distress (October 1530), Luther wrote to the Catholic musician Ludwig Sennfl, who was one of the best composers of that time in the German-speaking world, with the following request:

> I ask if you would have copied and sent to me, if you have it, a copy of that song: *In pace in idipsum* [cf. Psalm 4:8]. For this Tenor melody has delighted me from youth on, and does so even more now that I understand the words. I have never seen this antiphon arranged for more voices. I do not wish, however, to impose on you the work of arranging [i.e. setting polyphonically the melody]; rather I assume that you have available an arrangement from some other source. Indeed, I hope that the end of my life is at hand; the world hates me and cannot bear me, and I, in turn, loathe and detest the world; therefore, may the best and [most] faithful shepherd take my soul to him. And so I have already started to sing this antiphon and am eager to hear it arranged. In case you should not have or know it, I am enclosing it here with the notes; if you wish you can arrange it – perhaps after my death[8].

In fact, Luther was not as close to death as he imagined, and he did survive for more than fifteen years after penning this request to Sennfl; however, liturgical music linked to the Office of Compline continued to constitute a red thread in his

---

7 Leaver 2007, p. 52.
8 *LW* 49, pp. 427–429; *WA BR* 5, p. 639.

spirituality, particularly in connection with the idea of death[9]. While the antiphon *In pace in idipsum* was sung at the end of the day in Lent, a Responsory for the same liturgical Hour (*In manus tuas Domine*) constitutes the Latin text for the tenor part of a motet by Caspar Othmayr (*Verba Lutheri ultima*[10]), whereas the other parts sing, in German, Luther's last words, thus framing his earthly life with a musical homage.

## 5.3. The forms of Reform

As we have seen in the preceding Chapter (§ 4.3.1.2. etc.), the Lutheran Church, alongside with the Catholic, made use of the most varied musical repertoire, from both the textual and the musical viewpoint. The musical roots of the Lutheran Church came, on the one hand, from the Catholic liturgical tradition; on the other, from the vernacular heritage of sacred and sometimes secular songs.

Songs excerpted and modified from the popular secular and sacred tradition, as well as new ones composed in the same style, could be the expression of deep spiritual feelings, or convey a dogmatic teaching, or indulge in satire and polemics, or else spread news in the form of ballads[11]; properly religious songs were elaborated from translations of the pre-existing Latin-texted plainchant or pious songs in Latin and German *Leisen*; the creation of art songs in German was fostered and eventually became the favourite form of the urban burghers; the continuation of the Catholic polyphonic repertoire stemming from the Franco-Flemish tradition provided an artistic expression for the most cultivated and musically accomplished members of the Lutheran society[12], and organ music was encouraged. Within this framework, however, there was a high degree of fluidity and permeability between popular and cultivated art forms[13]; and though all musical forms were admitted within the omnivorous musical culture of Lutheranism, undoubtedly the most important and widespread form was that of the vernacular song, characterised by rhythmic and melodic simplicity, syllabic or quasi-syllabic style, and the use of regular repetitions favouring memorisation

---

[9] For an account of the Protestant view of night-time and slumber as symbols of death, cf. Ryrie 2012 (esp. p. 75).
[10] Lejeune 2010, p. 7.
[11] Wagner Oettinger 2001, pp. 32–33.
[12] Blume 1975, p. 3.
[13] Sfredda 2010, p. 18.

and singing by all members of the congregation: through this style, in Pettegree's words, "the pure word of Scripture was made manifest in the new music"[14].

We will now consider in turn the principal musical forms of the Lutheran Reformation, while reminding the reader of the difficulty that can be sometimes encountered when trying to label univocally a fluid and creative repertoire.

### 5.3.1. Latin roots, Evangelical fruits

We have seen in the preceding Chapter (§ 4.3.1.2.) that Luther's theological understanding of the Lord's Supper was profoundly different from that of the Catholic Church, but it remained closer to the Catholic view than to that of Zwingli. Whereas the theological meaning changed substantially, however, the liturgical schemes of the Lutheran Mass continued to mirror rather closely those of the Catholic Mass. The most important differences lay in the possibility of choosing the language of worship and/or to combine Latin and the vernacular, as well as in the encouragement given to congregational singing and participation (for example by the elimination of concomitant rites and thanks to the new focus on Bible reading and on the sermon[15]).

#### 5.3.1.1. Reordering the Ordinary

Luther's writings on liturgical topics are found principally in three works, two dating from 1523 (*Von der Ordnung des Gottesdienstes in der Gemeinde* and the *Formula Missæ et Communionis*[16]) as well as the *Deudsche Messe*[17] (the "German Mass") of 1526[18]. The *Formula Missæ* was a liturgical form close to the Catholic Mass and in Latin, whereas the German Mass was intended to benefit the uneducated laity through the use of vernacular texts: in Luther's description of the *Deudsche Messe*, the musical novelties he had inserted with respect to the traditional formula were made explicit and thoroughly described[19]. Alongside with

---

14 Pettegree 2005, pp. 42–43.
15 Pettegree 2005, p. 40.
16 *WA* 12, pp. 205–220 and *LW* 53, pp. 19–40.
17 *WA* 19, pp. 72–113 and *LW* 53, pp. 61–90.
18 A useful table comparing the Roman Mass with the *Formula Missæ* and the *Deudsche Messe* is found in Herl 2004, p. 29; it can also be matched with a table found in Leaver 2007, pp. 217–218, where Luther's liturgical orders are related to Johann Spangenberg's *Cantiones ecclesiasticæ* (1545). See also Wessler 2011.
19 Leaver 2006, p. 382.

these two forms (which were in turn rather fluid and should not be considered as rigidly prescriptive schemes), particular attention was given to domestic piety, which came to constitute a true pillar of Lutheran devotion[20]. In the coexistence of these forms, Pelikan has rightly seen a combination of "Catholic substance and Protestant principle"[21]: the emphasis on the Word and on its comprehension and proclamation by the laity was fostered principally through the vernacular hymns, which could be combined with or could replace almost any liturgical item of both the Latin and the German worship[22]. Blume synthesises efficaciously the various possibilities that Luther's liturgies left open to choice as regards language and structure: the Mass could be performed integrally in Latin or in German; vernacular *Lieder* could replace almost any prose item in either version, or supplement them; and they could also be added *ad libitum* at certain specific moments of the worship[23]. In particular, the hymns which were inserted between the Epistle and the Gospel (and which came to be indicated as *Graduallieder*) shifted the focus from the choir which had traditionally sung the Gradual or Sequence to the congregation, representing the faithful's prayerful and communal response to the first Biblical reading and their introduction to the proclamation of the Gospel[24].

Whereas we have already seen that many practices similar to these had already been used (sometimes rather extensively) on a local basis by the Catholic Church, undoubtedly Luther gave to the vernacular *Lied* both an unheard-of impulse and an incredible spread.

The flexibility of the Lutheran liturgy was from the one side an extraordinary quality of the new worship, but from the other it had in itself the seeds of a liturgical decline which would be observable in the following centuries. Luther's rejection of fixed and rigid formulations opened the door to a pulverisation of liturgy, where few common traits were discernible among a number of different local rites[25]. On the other hand, the diversity of Lutheran liturgies may also mirror a pre-existing local variety which dated back to the Catholic tradition in those areas[26].

Luther's *Formula Missæ* of 1523, therefore, represented no liturgical revolution with respect to the Catholic Mass. It was performed in Latin, though German

---

20 Sfredda 2010, p. 22.
21 Pelikan 1964.
22 Brown 2008, p. 224.
23 Blume 1975, p. 63.
24 Leaver 2007, pp. 300–302.
25 Cf. Blume 1975, pp. 4 and 52.
26 Herl 2004, p. 24.

songs could be sung after the *Gradual*, the *Sanctus* and the *Agnus Dei* and might be inserted at other moments: indeed, in several instances Luther expressed his favourable view of Latin worship, which possessed for him a more solemn and celebratory character with respect to that in the vernacular. The conservative approach shown in the *Formula Missæ* becomes particularly clear when one notices that a few among the rites and practices it maintained were to be abolished by the Catholic Church itself after the Council of Trent. It can be argued, therefore, that the greatest novelty in this worship order lay in its theological meaning (where the sacrificial aspect was denied) rather than in its outward shape[27].

Though Luther's German Mass was undoubtedly more different from the traditional Catholic Mass than the *Formula Missæ*, it was by no means a religious revolution in turn. First of all, as discussed earlier (§ 3.2.3.), there are good grounds for maintaining that the use of German songs and liturgical paraphrases was practised, at least locally, before Luther's Reformation[28]. Secondly, the *Deudsche Messe* of 1526 is predated by several other vernacular orders by other religious reformers, as has been briefly mentioned in Chapter Four (§ 4.3.3.). There is evidence for vernacular Masses performed in Basel by Wolfgang Wissenburger (or Wissenburg, c.1494–1575), in Pforzheim by Johann Schwebel[29] (1490–1540), in 1522 in Nördlingen by Kaspar Kantz, alongside with Strasbourg and Nuremberg, and, especially, by Müntzer in Allstedt (1524). From the musical and liturgical viewpoint, Müntzer's vernacular Mass is the closest to Luther's and is likely to have influenced him (though Luther was very critical of Müntzer): the similarities regard form, musical style, theological approach and pastoral concerns[30].

On the other hand, the possibility of omitting the *Gloria* which is found in several vernacular liturgies (many of which are unrelated to each other) fosters the surmise that this practice predated the Reformation (not only during the penitential seasons, but also for extra-theological reasons such as the need of shortening winter services in cold churches[31]). In general, however, Lutheran liturgies maintained the traditional five items of the Ordinary, though they could be replaced with their vernacular paraphrases: Luther's hymn on the Creed, *Wir glauben all an einen Gott* was based on a pre-existing vernacular translation of the

---

[27] Cf. Blume 1975, pp. 58–59; Herl 2004, p. 28; Kim 2005, p. 184; Pettegree 2005, p. 44; Brown 2008, p. 220; Sfredda 2010, p. 20.
[28] Herl 2004, p. 29.
[29] Kim 2005, p. 183.
[30] Cf. Blume 1975, p. 59, and Leaver 2006, p. 381.
[31] Herl 2004, pp. 28–29.

symbol of faith, though it is impossible to establish how and when it may have been used before the Reformation[32].

As concerns the Proper elements, first of all their variety was drastically reduced in consequence of the Lutheran curtailing of the cult of the saints: besides the feasts celebrating Christ's deeds, only a few solemnities of the Virgin Mary and of the Apostles and Evangelists were maintained. Most elements of the Proper could be replaced with vernacular hymns, which were chosen in accord with the liturgical time of the year and the Gospel of the day, for which they represented a spiritual resonance and a congregational response[33].

Notwithstanding this, the most interesting connections between theology and (musical) practice in Luther's *Deudsche Messe* are found concerning the role of Scripture and the meaning of the entire worship.

As a consequence of the *sola scriptura* principle, the New Testament and later the Bible were made available to all those who could read them or have them read by a literate person. This focus on the Word is mirrored by its role in Luther's Mass, where both the Epistle and the Gospel had to be delivered neatly, accurately and understandably in chant. Furthermore, the "words of institution" by which Jesus had established and commanded the Eucharistic celebration had been amplified by the Catholic Church into the so-called Canon (which was composed of both Biblical fragments and ecclesiastical prayers and was normally pronounced in a low voice by the priest). Luther advocated the elimination of non-Biblical words from this highpoint of the Mass, and the retention of the *Verba testamenti* only (i.e. the Gospel words of institution). Both the Biblical readings and the *Verba testamenti* had to be chanted, in order to be more audible and more solemn; moreover, Luther decided to attract the congregation's attention to Christ's words by having them sung in the traditional Passion tones, originally used during Holy Week: thus, a meaningful connection was established between the mystery of Christ's passion, death and resurrection and the Church's prayerful gathering. Thus, in Leaver's words, "the *Deutsche Messe* was essentially a musical service of worship, a combination of chant and hymnody, with the sermon and the paraphrase of the Lord's Prayer being the only spoken elements of the liturgical form"[34].

The melodic formulae, inspired and indebted to those traditionally adopted in the Catholic liturgy, and with particular attention to modal choices[35], had

---

32 Cf. Herl 2004, p. 58; Leaver 2006, p. 328.
33 Cf. Blume 1975, p. 52; Brown 2005, p. 10; Bergquist 2006, pp. 335–336.
34 Leaver 2007, pp. 292–293. Cf. also pp. 188, 192 and 298 to which the last paragraph is indebted.
35 Cf. Hendrickson 2003, p. 26.

been adapted to the linguistic peculiarities of the German vernacular and simplified from melismas in order to enhance their intelligibility: moreover, in some cases, Luther had also gleaned some melodies from popular non-liturgical tunes, thus demonstrating his attention for the uncultured laity[36]. (Incidentally, we may note how different Luther's constant concern for the needs of the uneducated was in comparison with Erasmus' contempt towards them and their music: cf. § 2.3.9.). As Kim interestingly points out, Luther's choice to create a vernacular plainchant in syllabic style and with references to the Latin Gregorian tradition predates and resembles the process which will eventually lead to the elaboration of an Anglican form of plainchant as shown in the *Book of Common Prayer Noted*[37] (cf. § 7.2.3.).

In general, thus, Luther's liturgical reform can be characterised as considerate, wise and balanced, and surely not (as sometimes it has been portrayed) as a hasty improvisation or a rash revolution[38].

Notwithstanding this, it should be observed that in actual practice the situation could be rather different from that ideally envisaged by the Reformers: congregational attendance at the Sunday service was not always satisfactory, and the considerable length that a typical worship could reach (with hymns, sung sections, and a very long sermon) fostered the habit of attending just the sermon, which normally occupied the second of the three hours constituting a complete service[39].

### 5.3.1.2. Hours of worship

The other traditional pillar of Catholic liturgy alongside with the Mass was the Liturgy of the Hours (or Office). It was intended as an expansion of the Eucharist, which could encompass the entire day of the faithful, and consisted of several moments of prayer scattered throughout the day (and sometimes also during the night), whose structure was largely made of Psalms and Biblical canticles, along with hymns and readings. The complete liturgy of the Hours was typically a prerogative of the clergy and of religious men and women, since the quantity of variable elements rendered it necessary to read the sung or recited words, which could practically not be memorised in their entirety. Thus, the illiterate laity could not actively participate in this worship, whilst the quantity and length of the prayers rendered the performance of this liturgy almost unconceivable

---

36  Cf. Leaver 1989, p. 271.
37  Kim 2005, pp. 15 and 255.
38  Leaver 2007, p. 188.
39  Cf. Herl 2004, pp. 30, 49, 53.

for those active in secular life. (We will see in Chapter Nine the idiosyncratic attitude of a Catholic Reformer as concerned the sung Office: cf. § 9.5.2.1.). Despite this, shortened and simplified devotional forms modelled on the structure of the Office had been realised (some of which were in the vernacular) for religious men and women who did not belong to monastic orders as well as for the laity. (Incidentally, the popular Catholic devotion of the Rosary had been conceived as a substitute for psalmody, with the one-hundred-and-fifty *Ave Maria* representing the corresponding number of Psalms of the Psalter[40]).

In Luther's *Ordnung des Gottesdienstes* (1523), the only Hours which were preserved were Matins and Vespers: their structure (and therefore their musical items) mirrored closely those of Catholic worship, though locally the number of Psalms sung at each Hour was often reduced from five to three.

Luther's own piety was deeply marked by his familiarity with the Psalter: during his years as a monk, his days had been interspersed with the Liturgy of the Hours, and his Biblical expertise obviously contributed to his knowledge of and love for psalmody (though it never acquired for Lutherans the character of exclusiveness it would assume for the Calvinist Church). For him, the Psalms (similar to hymns) had a double function: from the one side, to give consolation by affirming God's promise; from the other, to express both praise and supplication.

Lutheran Vespers were well attended by the laity particularly on Saturdays and Sundays: on Saturdays and vigils, a sermon was added, with the usual appendage of hymn-singing, and those wishing to communicate on the following feast day were given the possibility to confess. Sunday Vespers were characterised by a greater solemnity, and could include polyphony as well as a catechism hymn relating to what had been taught during the day[41].

### 5.3.2. Venturing the vernacular

In this section, we will discuss both the importance of Lutheran songs in the devotional lives of the faithful, and their different forms and origins. Indeed, from Luther's theses of 1517 until 1523, the community of his first followers who would eventually become the so-called Lutheran Church did not possess a musical repertoire of its own: insomuch as these years have come to be known as the "song-

---

40 Brown 2008, pp. 237–248.
41 Cf. Blume 1975, p. 51; Herl 2004, pp. 35, 63–64; Brown 2008, pp. 237–248.

less period"[42]. (Obviously, given Luther's love for music, it is hard to believe that early Lutheran piety was truly "songless": rather, it had not yet a specific repertoire).

In 1523, the year of Luther's *Formula Missæ*, this need for Evangelical *Lieder* started to be felt very clearly. Luther himself wrote to several poets asking them to compose Psalm paraphrases in the vernacular. He stated: "Poets are wanting among us, or not yet known, who could compose evangelical and spiritual songs, as Paul calls them (Colossians 3:16), worthy to be used in the Church of God (after the *Gradual* and also after the *Sanctus* and *Agnus Dei* etc.)"[43].

Luther's own first known *Lied* (which we will discuss later: § 5.3.2.4.) dates from the same year, and in 1524 a small collection of eight songs comprising his own creations or adaptations, as well as some by Paul Speratus (1484–1551) was published: it has become known as the *Achtliederbuch*[44]. These first hymns feature already the multiplicity of sources used by Luther and his followers in the creation of the Lutheran repertoire, which will be discussed in the following pages: they were elaborated from popular religious songs (the *Leisen*), from translations of Latin liturgical items, and some were newly created. The extensive use of the *contrafactum* technique (see § 5.3.2.3.) was typical for Luther's inclusive approach to church music, and is a feature which clearly distinguishes him from the mainstream humanist attitude: the neat separation between secular and sacred advocated by the culture of the time was absorbed, in Luther's view and practice, by a sacralisation of the entire created world. In many cases, pre-existing songs were simply "improved in a Christian manner", in the words which would be printed on many later hymnal title-pages. Even before the *Achtliederbuch*, the spread of Lutheran hymns was guaranteed by their being printed as loose sheets[45] (broadsides).

The first Lutheran vernacular hymns were indicated in a variety of ways: the use of terms such as *Kirchenlied* or *Kirchengesang* stressed their belonging to public worship (*Kirche* meaning Church), but failed to point out their function for private and home devotion; they might also be called *Psalm*, thus establishing a correspondence between the Biblical songs and those written by contemporaneous poets and musicians. The word "Chorale" which eventually became the most common is not frequently found before a 1586 collection by Lucas

---

[42] Bergquist 2006, p. 333.
[43] *WA* 12, p. 218; *LW* 53, p. 35.
[44] Luther 1524. See Ameln 1956.
[45] Cf. Leaver 1998, p. 283.

Osiander[46] (§ 5.3.2.6.). It would indicate a melody which could be sung in unaccompanied unison by the congregation and/or by the choir, and which could also be harmonised in polyphony.

### 5.3.2.1. Translating tradition

A first source for the Lutheran vernacular hymns comes from the Catholic plainchant heritage of canticles and hymns in Latin. Luther's knowledge of the Latin repertoire dated back to his studies as a boy at the Latin schools in Mansfeld (from 1491) and Magdeburg (from 1496), and, of course, had been fostered by his training as an Augustinian monk. In several instances, Luther and his collaborators translated the original Latin text into German, adapting both translation and melody to suit the idiosyncrasies of the German language and the necessities of congregational singing. For this task, he enlisted the help of two musicians: Conrad Rupsch (c.1475-c.1530), who was Duke Frederick's *Kapellmeister*, and the young bass Johann Walther.

One of the first of such translated hymns (1523) was the German version of *Veni Redemptor gentium*, which Müntzer would translate in turn as a German song in that very same year. Luther's version would become the enormously popular *Nun komm, der Heiden Heiland*.

Five of the 1524 *Lieder* were similarly inspired by Latin models: *Christum wir sollen loben schon* from *A solis ortus*; *Jesus Christus, unser Heiland*, from *Jesus Christus nostra salus*; *Mitten wir im Leben sind* from *Media vita*; *Komm Gott Schöpfer, Heiliger Geist* from *Veni Creator Spiritus*, and *Komm, Heiliger Geist, Herre Gott* from *Veni Sancte Spiritus* (this last one being the Pentecost Sequence in the Roman Church). Several other Chorales, among which are many of Luther's most popular ones, would later be derived from Latin models.

While discussing this process, Brown correctly points out that it exposes one of the many myths surrounding Luther's songs, i.e. that they are taken from secular melodies. Though this sometimes was the case, the inverse path was much more frequent: several of Luther's hymns originated within the ecclesiastical (and cultivated) tradition of the Church, and from this they were adopted by the laity and brought to secular contexts, whereas Lutheran *contrafacta* of properly secular songs rarely reached the status of church music[47].

---

[46] Cf. Blume 1975, pp. 14 and 29; Leaver 1998, p. 283; Sfredda 2010, pp. 29 and 32; Cameron 2012, p. 259.
[47] Brown 2008, p. 211. Cf. Leaver 2007, pp. 24–25 and 209–210; Sfredda 2010, p. 28.

## 5.3. The forms of Reform — 249

Other Chorales were translated, by Luther or by others, from movements of the Mass Ordinary: among them *Allein Gott in der Höh sei Ehr* (c.1522 by Nikolaus Decius [c.1485-a.1546]), whose text was a paraphrased translation of the Latin *Gloria* and whose melody was adapted from the Easter *Gloria*; Luther's Creed paraphrase *Wir glauben all an einen Gott* (1524, from pre-existing models), the German *Sanctus* translated as *Jesaja dem Propheten* (which connected the Latin liturgical text with its Biblical context: 1526 text and 1545 music), and the *Agnus Dei* paraphrases *Christe, du Lamm Gottes* (by Luther, c.1528) or *O Lamm Gottes unschulding* (by Decius, c.1522, published 1531).

The Mass Proper was by its nature variable. Its components varied according to the time of the year (e.g. Advent, Christmas, Lent, Easter...), with individual feasts (celebrating Christ, the Virgin Mary, the Saints etc.), and depending on the Biblical readings of the day. Moreover, the very nature of the variable elements was varied in turn: though historically the Proper elements of the Mass were limited in number and clearly defined, a looser concept of Proper may include several other components. Some of them were poetic elements (such as hymns, sequences etc.), other in prose (such as the Collects), short semi-poetic forms, often with internal repetitions (such as Responsories, Introits or Antiphons etc.); moreover, musically (though not liturgically), Proper items included motets as well.

The Catholic form of the Sequence proved itself to be fundamental for the Lutheran Church, both as concerns performance of Latin or translated/adapted Sequences within the Lutheran worship, and as regards the model provided by Sequences for new Lutheran compositions. Indeed, of the three musical elements which, in the traditional liturgy, were inserted between Epistle and Gospel reading in the Mass (i.e. *Gradual*, *Alleluia* and Sequence), it was perhaps the Sequence which was the most interesting for Luther and his first followers, and it represents a fascinating example of how an ancient tradition was maintained and reshaped by the Lutheran Church[48].

In the Sequence, the key message of Biblical readings of the day was poetically interpreted, given voice in singing and made prayer for the congregation. Moreover, the Sequence model was adopted for the vernacular versions of such liturgical items as the *Gloria* and the *Sanctus*.

Indeed, well before Luther's Reformation there existed vernacular songs inspired by or modelled on Latin Sequences. They were known as *Leisen* (where "*Leise*" was the abbreviated form of the liturgical invocation *Kyrie, eleison*), and – as seen earlier: § 3.2.3. – were often performed in a particular *alternatim*

---

[48] Cf. Herl 2004; Leaver 2007, pp. 236 and 241.

form with the Latin original interposed with the German paraphrase. This practice was common especially with the Easter, Pentecost and Christmas Sequences, which originated respectively *Christ ist erstanden* (twelfth century), *Nun bitten wir den Heiligen Geist* (thirteenth century) and *Gelobet seist du, Jesu Christ* (fourteenth century), all of which were reworked and adopted by Luther. Indeed, visitation records in Wittenberg describe this antiphonal performance very precisely: "At Easter and until the Sunday after Ascension one shall sing after the Alleluia *Victimæ paschali* together with *Christ lag in Todesbanden*, verse by verse, until both alike are completed; at Pentecost the sequence *Veni Sancte Spiritus* with the hymn *Nun bitten wir den Heiligen Geist* [are sung], as arranged above"[49].

Apparently, the Latin originals which were most consistently adapted and elaborated by the Lutherans were those already popular; moreover, particular attention was given to Latin Sequences which had been created in the German-speaking world. Here too, therefore, the main novelty of Luther's approach is found in the integration of older traditions and practices within a new liturgical concept, and in the importance they were given as an expression of congregational piety[50].

At a later stage of the Lutheran Church, moreover, the Sequence model would also inspire the creation of two idiosyncratic expressions of Lutheran devotion, i.e. the verse-motet (*Spruchmotette*) and the Cantata[51].

Similar to Sequences, Responsories were adapted and adopted by Lutherans too, in a typical combination of tradition with innovation. A fascinating element of the Catholic Responsories – which obviously appealed strongly to the Scripture-inspired Lutheran piety – was their Biblical origin, as well as the melodic beauty of the plainchant originals. A particular case was that of the funeral Responsories of the Catholic Church, whose text was considered to be unsuitable for the Lutheran approach to the mystery of death, but whose tunes were judged as too beautiful to be forgotten (cf. § 4.3.1.3.). Thus, both the form and the melodies of the ancient Responsories were preserved, while new texts stressing the Christian doctrine of resurrection were excerpted from the Bible[52].

Another important source for Lutheran translation/paraphrases was represented by Latin hymns in poetic form, several of which came from the Ambrosian tradition. It is possible that Luther's paraphrases were paradoxically encour-

---

**49** Visitations: Wittenberg 1528 and 1533; in Pallas 1906, vol. II, Part 1, pp. 1 ff. See Boës 1958, p. 7; English translation in Leaver 2007, p. 228.
**50** Cf. Blume 1975, p. 17; Herl 2004, p. 58; Leaver 2007, p. 241.
**51** Leaver 2007, p. 237.
**52** Cf. Leaver 2007, pp. 235–241, to which this section is indebted.

aged and prompted by those which Müntzer was realising at the same time, and against which Luther probably wanted to provide an alternative (both from the doctrinal and from the musical viewpoint). Luther's own versions, in fact, are characterised by an attractive rhythm and metre, and a close interaction between speech accentuation and melodic lines, which favours memorisation and the rhetoric combination of words and music. Luther's example would be followed by many members of his Church both at his time and later: for example, Nikolaus Herman (c.1500–1561) combined a Christmas Latin plainchant antiphon melody with a strophic structure typical of folk dances, thus demonstrating once more the tendency of Lutheranism to cross the boundary between secular and sacred music[53].

Even the Latin Collects, which were prayers usually recited by the presiding priest, linked to the day's theological focus and normally in prose, were translated into German and appended to prayer- and hymnbooks for the laity in the Lutheran Church; sometimes, they could provide textual material for the creation of devotional musical compositions such as motets or spiritual madrigals[54].

### 5.3.2.2. Singing Scripture

Whereas all the preceding translations and adaptations from Latin originals were elaborations of parts of the Catholic rites, Lutheran songs on Biblical Psalms and canticles were grounded on an even older tradition, which could date back to Jewish worship well before Christ's birth.

We have already observed Luther's familiarity with the Psalter, and the presence of Psalm-singing in the Lutheran Office of the Hours. Beside this, however, the Biblical Psalms were also the source for innumerable adaptations which would greatly enrich the Lutheran hymnody. Indeed, Luther's 1523 appeal to poets such as Georg Spalatin (or Burkhardt, 1484–1545) asked them precisely to write Psalm paraphrases in the vernacular:

> Following the example of the prophets and Fathers of the Church, I intend to make vernacular Psalms for the people, that is, spiritual songs so that the Word of God, even by means of song, may live among the people. Everywhere we are looking for poets. Now since you are so skilful and eloquent in German, I would ask you to work with us in this and to turn a Psalm into a hymn as in the enclosed example of my work (Psalm 130: *Aus tiefer Not schrei ich zu dir*). But I would like you to avoid new-fangled, fancied words, and to use expressions simple and common enough for the people to understand, yet pure and fitting. The

---

53 Cf. Blume 1975, pp. 16 and 37; Brown 2005, p. 84.
54 Cf. Brown 2005, pp. 243–244.

meaning should also be clear and as close as possible to the Psalm. Irrespective of the exact wording, one must freely render the sense by suitable words[55].

A few elements should be pointed out among Luther's words, i.e.: a) his reference to the Biblical and Patristic tradition; b) his goal that "the Word of God, even by means of song, may live among the people"; c) the task of "turning a Psalm into a hymn"; d) the precise stylistic directions he gives to Spalatin ("simple", "common", "pure", "fitting" etc.); e) the character of paraphrase and not of faithful translation he envisaged.

Thus, Luther combined a noteworthy liberty in the treatment of the Biblical text with a corresponding love and concern for Scripture: in his opinion, precisely by avoiding exaggerated philological scruples one could be actually more faithful to the Word. If the rendition of a Biblical text intended for prayer and singing could not be easily understood, sung and memorised by all, its literal fidelity would not be mirrored by fidelity to the spirit, which required that the Word "may live among the people". Rightfully, then, Grindal observes that Luther's version of Psalm 46 [45] (the enormously popular *Ein feste Burg ist unser Gott*, 1528–9) "is not a paraphrase of Psalm 46, but a sermon on the Psalm, with its images updated from ancient Palestine to medieval Saxony"[56]. (It should be noted, however, that Luther's Psalm-*Lieder* eschewed too direct a reference to contemporary events in politics or religion, whereas other coeval versions, such as those by Justus Jonas, were more explicit and could easily become the starting point for polemical *contrafacta*. On the other hand, the Calvinist attitude to Psalm-singing favoured quasi-literal translations with no substantial paraphrase or updating, though sometimes they could be no less inflammatory: paradoxically, their claim to be the faithful rendition of the original Biblical text fostered their adoption as battle-hymns in certain situations. See § 6.2., 6.3.5., 10.3.4. etc.).

Lutheran congregations would not have been drawn to piety and godliness by painstaking exegetical efforts or refined humanistic renditions (though Luther himself was concerned with both): they needed to feel the proximity of the Psalms to their daily lives, joys, worries, prayers and praises. Thus, Luther selected among the Biblical Psalms those which could express most immediately the spiritual needs of the faithful, and even indicated the Psalms which were best suited to particular situations in a person's life.

---

55 *LW* 53, p. 221; English translation in Targoff 2001, p. 68.
56 Grindal 2011, p. 4.

Beside the Psalm paraphrase mentioned by Luther himself in his letter to Spalatin quoted above (Psalm 130 [129]: cf. § 5.3.2.2.), he wrote at least four other Psalm-hymns between 1523 and 1524 (on Psalms 12 [11], 14 [13], 67 [66] and 124 [123]), followed by Psalms 128 [127] and 46 [45], mentioned above, in the following years; the Biblical model was divided into stanzas whose rhythm and tune favoured their immediate spread and success[57].

### 5.3.2.3. "Christian improvements"

Beside paraphrased translations and melodic adaptations of Catholic and Biblical originals, the second great source of inspiration for Lutheran hymnody came from pre-existing vernacular songs, most of which (though not all) had a religious content from their very origin (or at least had already been widely known in their sacred version if this was based on a secular model). In this case, however, a "sacred" origin did not necessarily mean that the pre-existing songs came from the Catholic heritage: in many cases, other confessional provenances are found.

Catholic songs in the German vernacular predating the Lutheran Reformation had a variety of origins in turn. As seen before (§ 3.2.3.), they could be translated paraphrases of Latin Sequences: in this case, the transition from the Latin model to the Lutheran hymn was not a direct one, but it had been mediated by the Catholic paraphrase, on which normally the Lutheran hymnographers intervened in order to "Christianly improve" them.

Other Catholic songs were the expression of medieval piety, particularly within specific devotional contexts: as discussed in Chapter Two (§ 3.2.3.), for example, the Crusaders had their own musical repertoire, alongside those of the penitent confraternities (the *Geisslerlieder*), those used for pilgrimages or processions and those coming from the cultivated tradition of the *Meistersinger*, as well as anonymous expressions of popular piety, especially for Christmas.

Together with traditional Catholic vernacular songs, the other great source of inspiration and of songs for the Lutheran repertoire came from the Hussite tradition of the Bohemian Brethren. Singing had been a fundamental component in the spiritual life of the followers of Jan Hus, and they had gathered an impressive collection of vernacular songs in Czech. Their first printed hymnal appeared in Prague (1501) and was the first example of this kind in Europe; in 1531, Michael

---

57 Cf. Fisher 2001, pp. 624–625; Pettegree 2005, p. 50; Brown 2008, p. 240.

Weisse (c.1488–1534) published a collection[58] of German translations of Hussite songs[59].

Contrary to myth, then, only a minority of Luther's songs did actually come from secular models. Indeed, as mentioned before (§ 3.2.3.), there were Catholic precedents for this practice too: many religious songs had originally been secular, though it is impossible to establish whether the sacred piece had the aim to replace its secular model or simply to exploit its popularity in order to convey religious feelings.

Similarly, several Lutheran *contrafacta* of secular songs were not immediately adopted within public worship: they were firstly intended for domestic use, and only the most successful of them eventually made their way into church[60]. Indeed, as Brown points out, "Lutheran polemicists identified church music based on worldly melodies as a distinctly Roman Catholic abuse"[61].

Among the chorales authored by Luther himself, indeed, only one was originally a secular song, and its complex story probably betrays a certain dissatisfaction with the result. Luther's *Vom Himmel hoch da komm ich her* was a *contrafactum* of the secular song *Aus fremden Landen komm ich her* (which seemingly was in turn an elaboration of the dance-song *Mit Lust tret ich an diesen Tanz*). First of all, however, it should be pointed out that Luther had imagined it as a Christmas carol to accompany a manger play (and thus not properly for a standard liturgical context). Moreover, after the song had been included in two prints from the 1530s with Luther's text and the secular tune, in 1539 a new tune was given for Luther's lyrics (and in later editions still other combinations were envisaged[62]).

Among Luther's followers, however, *contrafacta* of secular songs were more extensively practised. A hymnbook printed in 1571[63] specifically states in its titlepage that secular songs of various origins had been "Christianised" with the explicit purpose of replacing the originals with their religious versions. Speratus transformed *Ich armes maidlein klag mich sehr* into *Ich armer Sünder klag mein Leid*; Lazarus Spengler (1479–1534) adapted the tune of a song on the battle of Pavia to the words *Durch Adams Fall ist ganz verderbt* (1529): though eventu-

---

58 Weisse 1531.
59 Cf. Blume 1975, p. 19; Blankenburg 1975, p. 594; Settari 1994; Sfredda 2010, p. 31. More on Hus and the Bohemian Brethren's music later in this Chapter (§ 5.5.).
60 Cf. Wagner Oettinger 2001, p. 92; Leaver 2007, pp. 12–13; Brown 2008, p. 211.
61 Brown 2008, pp. 213–214. Cf. Selnecker 1569.
62 Cf. Blume 1975, pp. 30–31; Koenigsberger 1986, p. 190; Leaver 2007, p. 17.
63 Knaust 1571. Cf. Sfredda 2010, p. 70.

ally his text was given several other melodies, the lansquenets' strain transmigrated even into Catholic hymnals where it remained in use for centuries[64].

Other *contrafacta* were even more striking, such as for example those based on the tune known as *Madre non mi far monaca* (or *La Monica*), of unknown origin, which was transformed into the German religious songs *Von Gott will ich nicht lassen* (1563; 1572[65]), *Helft mir Gotts Güte preisen* (1571; 1575[66]) and several others. A secular song by Hans Leo Hassler (1564–1612), *Mein Gmüth ist mir verwirret*, was given religious words as *Herzlich thut mich verlangen* (1599) or the Passion Chorale *O Haupt voll Blut und Wunden* (1656), which would later be immortalised in Johann Sebastian Bach's *Matthäus-Passion*, as well as several others. In turn, a delightful Italian *balletto* by Giovanni Giacomo Gastoldi, *A lieta vita*, became the very popular *In Dir ist Freude*[67] (1594).

If Calvinists would be opposed in principle to such practices, these were by no means universally accepted in the Lutheran world[68]; however, the lasting success of some of such *contrafacta* (several of which are still in use to the present day, and have gained acceptance also among other Christian confessions) confirms that contrafacture could be immensely useful for spreading a religious message.

Among the most important composers of *contrafacta*, Hans Sachs (1494–1576) deserves a special mention. It is not certain whether this Nuremberg shoemaker, whose modern fame has been ensured by Richard Wagner in his opera *Die Meistersinger von Nürnberg* (1867), did actually adhere to Lutheranism, though several of his *contrafacta* do express a very critical stance against the Catholic Church, and sometimes go further than Luther himself in his "tuning" of traditional songs to the needs of the new confession[69]. Moreover, an evolution has been observed in Sachs' output, which gradually abandoned religious themes typical for the Catholic confession (such as invocations to the Virgin Mary or the saints) in favour of a Christocentric view; furthermore, he contributed with several Psalm translations to the repertoire for the German Mass, and he Evangelically "corrected" pre-existing songs with the *contrafactum* technique between 1524 and 1525. He was more daring than Luther also in his use of secular songs for religious purposes, and – in his case – it is rather clear that he wished

---

64 Cf. Blume 1975, p. 31.
65 See in Magdeburg 1572.
66 See in Figulus 1575. Cf. Wendland 1976, pp. 191 and 192.
67 Curiously, it came back to Italy as a religious song which is sung up to the present day as *Gioia del cuore* in the Catholic Church. Cf. Mischiati 1995, p. 19; Rainoldi 2000, pp. 318–319.
68 Cf. Brown 2005, p. 52.
69 Otten 1993, p. 231.

his *contrafacta* to supersede their secular or Catholic models in the mouths and hearts of the faithful[70].

It should be said, however, that Sachs' *contrafacta* (similar to those of the tradition closest to Luther himself) eschewed violent polemics against or derision of their Catholic models: their composers tried instead to purify them from what they perceived to be erroneous or incompatible with the Evangelical belief while preserving the common traits which still united the two confessions. This was not always the case: an impressive output of satirical, polemical or propagandistic *contrafacta* was created in the sixteenth century by members of most confessions. We will discuss this unpleasant page of music history and of the Reformations in Chapter Ten (§ 10.3.7. and following).

### 5.3.2.4. Starting from scratch

We have seen until now that Luther and his followers translated and paraphrased traditional liturgical, religious and secular songs in order to enrich the repertoire of their new Church. Incidentally, we should remember that the concept of authorship, which was starting to emerge in this period (cf. § 2.3.1.) was by no means like that which we are acquainted with nowadays. Suffice it to recall that the theological debate (as well as those in several other disciplines, not only in the humanities) was principally made of commentaries upon pre-existing writings, and/or collations of various authoritative sources. In music, too, the *contrafactum* technique was just one among the many which made use of musical elements by other composers (from the *cantus firmus* compositions to the parody and paraphrase techniques, etc.). This is to say that whilst we tend to consider as "Luther's hymns" only those which are original by today's parameters, at his time the common perception might have been rather different.

On the other hand, the aura of piousness and greatness which started to surround Luther already during his earthly life, but even more impressively after his death, is also mirrored by the disproportionate quantity of hymns which began to be attributed to him: in a hymnbook (1594[71]) compiled by Seth Calvisius (or Kalwitz, 1556–1615) no less than one hundred and thirty-seven songs are attributed (in both text and music) to the Wittenberg Reformer.

Of course, the actual figures are decidedly lower. Contemporary scholarship substantially agrees in ascribing thirty-seven chorale texts to Luther, which are

---

[70] Cf. Wagner Oettinger 2001, pp. 92 and 104; Russell 2002, p. 167; Leaver 2007, p. 15; Brown 2008, p. 211.
[71] Calvisius 1594.

found in combination with different melodies (sixty in total), plus liturgical adaptations for the Mass or the Hours. Several of the melodies for Luther's chorale texts can be attributed with good likeliness to his pen: about fourteen are probably original by him, thirteen are his own adaptations of pre-existing tunes and ten were adopted in their bequeathed form[72].

Luther's chorales avoid the responsorial form, since his concept of communal worship and of the universal priesthood of all believers would have been at odds with the presence of a soloist alternating with the whole of the congregation[73].

From the textual viewpoint, Luther's hymns have some remarkable features. A first noteworthy aspect is that Luther himself adhered very strictly to the principles he had set for the "German poets" in his letter to Spalatin quoted above (§ 5.3.2.2.): simplicity first. It has been observed that, writing in a language famous for the length of its words, Luther's chorale texts are mostly constituted by monosyllables or very short words, which is a rather ascetic exercise[74]. This choice emphasises the rhythmic strength of his verses (frequently adopting iambic or trochaic metres), which sometimes reaches a cadenced beat not unlike that of dance-rhythms: whereas elsewhere critics of church music expressly forbade the "contamination" of sacred music by dance elements, here Luther seems to deliberately choose the opposite strategy, with the purpose of enhancing the emotional and quasi-physical involvement fostered by his religious songs.

In order to facilitate memorisation, Luther also made use of refined rhetorical devices, such as assonances, alliterations and rhymes, though these literary finesses are always functional to his religious aims and never effected for the sake of poetic polish. In some instances, the formal structure has also a symbolic value with theological and catechetical significance, and in most cases Luther's verbal choices are imaginative and memorable, and they adopt a very immediate style, often directly addressing the faithful in an engaging fashion[75]. Indeed, parallel to shifting the pastoral focus from the visual paradigms of medieval piety to the aural dimension of modernity, Luther took care not to indulge in rationalism, and somehow replaced the figurative depictions of the preceding era with the appealing imagery of his chorales.

Stanzas are inspired by a secular poetic structure (the *Barform*) practised in the German tradition of the Master singers, with two *Stollen* and an *Abgesang* re-

---

[72] Cf. Blume 1975, p. 45; Bergquist 2006, p. 333.
[73] Cf. Rainoldi 2000, p. 313.
[74] Cf. Marcus 2001, p. 727; Sfredda 2010, p. 29, to which this section is indebted.
[75] Cf. Sfredda 2010, pp. 29 and 37.

sulting in an AAB form: both at the formal level and as regards content, Luther's choice would be extremely influential on subsequent chorale literature[76].

The various literary and religious sources of Luther's chorales have been discussed in the preceding pages; here we can briefly add that all of his hymns show a clear vision of their pastoral purpose and a correspondingly apt use of the available rhetoric and poetic strategies, specifically suited to the object and matter of the song. Thus, he adopted a rather epic tone when describing the martyrdom of his first followers (*Ein newes Lied*, see below); a heroic style to reinforce the feeling of belonging and identity (e.g. *Ein feste Burg ist unser Gott*, or *Erhalt uns, Herr, bei deinem Wort*); in other instances, he used chorales to counter effectively (though normally not belligerently) other confessional teachings he wanted to contest. This was the case with *Nun freut euch, lieben Christen g'mein* (1523), where the Catholic doctrine on justification is opposed through the efficacious and immediately fascinating proposal of an alternative view. Similarly (as observed in § 4.3.3.), Luther's rejection of Müntzer's theology as expressed in his hymns is manifested in the composition of chorale texts conveying his own perspective[77].

The very first known hymn written by Luther, *Ein newes Lied wir heben an* (1523[78]) shows also some features which will not be very common in his subsequent chorale output. It is not primarily a prayer or a praise (though both of these dimensions are clearly present), but rather a "news song", inspired by the tradition of the so-called *Bänkelsänger* (or ballad-mongers). It recounts (and was prompted by) the persecution and death at the stake of two Augustinian monks who were martyred in Brussels (July 1523) for having refused to recant their Lutheran opinions. Incidentally, Coats justly points out that Luther's celebration of these martyrs in singing and the consequent propaganda which such news could gain for the Lutheran cause drew upon that very veneration of the saints that the Reformation aimed at reducing[79]. Paving the way for numerous subsequent chorales, this hymn was first printed as a broadsheet (probably after having been spread by word of mouth) and then found its way into the first Lutheran hymnals. Two years later (1525), Luther would return to this particular genre to commemorate another Evangelical martyr, Heinrich von Zütphen (c.1488–1524) in the *Geschicht von Brüder Hainrich inn Diethmar verprent*[80].

---

[76] Cf. Blume 1975, p. 41; Leaver 2007, p. 13; Sfredda 2010, p. 29.
[77] Cf. Buszin 1963, p. 45; Janson 1995, p. 25; Wagner Oettinger 2001, p. 45; Brown 2008, p. 209.
[78] *LW* 53, pp. 211–216; cf. Wagner Oettinger 2001, pp. 61–69, 87, 260–263.
[79] Coats 1994, pp. 20 and 27.
[80] Cf. Pettegree 2005, p. 50; Lindberg 2010, pp. 266 and 283.

From the musical viewpoint, Luther demonstrated a masterly knowledge and an indisputable talent for composing unforgettable tunes. As seen before (§ 4.2.3.1. and 5.3.), he favoured the simple syllabic style, but achieved variety and expressiveness through a thorough exploitation of the limited melodic ranges he could employ; moreover, his melodies often follow and amplify the normal intonation of speech, thus reinforcing expressively the text's inherent features.

He also frequently used thematic "building blocks", choosing a formulaic compositional style based on fragments found in the pre-existing musical literature: this helped to establish meaningful connections, both within the Lutheran repertoire (among different chorales, but also within a single work) and outside it. This also conferred unity to the works and to the repertoire they were establishing, and undoubtedly favoured congregational memorisation, while connecting the new songs with the traditional plainchant heritage. For example, as Blume points out, the *incipit* of *Aus tiefer Not* employs a rather common melodic formula which is found in several sacred and secular works of the era, among which a *Miserere* by Luther's favourite composer, Josquin[81].

Luther's melodies demonstrate in several instances a modern sensitivity for the major and minor modes which would eventually become the keystones of modern tonality, although the tunes are clearly rooted within the ancient tradition of both ecclesiastical song and the secular melodies of the *Meistersinger*[82].

### 5.3.2.5. Forging a repertoire

Luther's example would be followed by numerous poets, musicians and lyricist-composers in the Lutheran tradition, often establishing fruitful artistic alliances and cooperations: among them Ludwig Helmbold of Mühlhausen (1532–1598) who wrote poetry for music in the humanistic fashion but in a direct and engaging style. Helmbold collaborated with the musicians Johannes Eccard (1553–1611) and Joachim a Burck, who underlined the syllabic style and intelligibility of his own musical settings, as well as the inspiration he had drawn from the Italian form of the *villanella*[83].

Among Luther's closest collaborators, however, Walther played probably the most fundamental role, together with Rupsch. They were the first musicians enlisted by the Reformer for the task of revising and adapting the melodies for the germinal cells of the Lutheran repertoire; Walther was among the first to set pol-

---

[81] Blume 1975, p. 41.
[82] Cf. Leaver 2007, pp. 59, 61 and 208; Sfredda 2010, pp. 30 and 37.
[83] A Burck 1572; cf. Blume 1975, p. 144 and Weber 2008, p. 228.

yphonically the new tunes. A further fundamental contribution by Walther to the Protestant musical heritage is constituted by his Passion settings, where the plainchant renditions of the Gospel narrative are interspersed with the multivoiced interventions of the people.

In the 1551 edition of Walther's *Gesangk Buchleyn*, the hymn collection comprised seventy-four German chorales along with forty-seven Latin *Cantiones*; some were in four-part homophonic settings, whereas others revealed more ambitious polyphonic goals and were intended for domestic use.

Walther was a fine polyphonist, who employed the new chorale melodies also within the composition of complex multivoiced works; some of his settings are inspired by the Franco-Flemish tradition of *cantus firmus* composition. However, whereas the tenor had traditionally been constituted by a Latin plainchant melody in augmentation, Walther's compositions make use of the German chorales in their regular rhythmic values, while the other parts are set in imitative counterpoint. Walther was undoubtedly inspired by the polyphonic *Lied* repertoire, as well as by the Italian genre of the *frottola*; however, an evolution in his style has been observed, with a prevalence of imitative *cantus firmus* settings in the earlier years and a later tendency towards quasi-homophonic compositions, in some of which the chorale melody was assigned to the highest voice[84].

Walther's *cantus firmus* interpretations of chorale melodies are an homage to stylistic features typical of the late Middle Ages, in the style of the *Tenorlied*; the tenor represents the compositional fulcrum around which the other voices revolve, without having great possibilities of expressing the rational meaning of the text in other than a symbolic fashion. The tendency towards homophony and syllabic settings reveals instead the influence of contemporaneous humanistically-inspired trends as well as the effort to find an efficacious, expressive and affectively poignant union of text and music[85]. (An interesting discussion of Walther's theological aesthetics is found in Hendrickson's research[86]).

Thus, in the early Reformation period, chorale melodies could be harmonised (often in four parts), or be employed within polyphonic works of greater musical complexity; later, other forms of composition on chorales would include instrumental works such as organ Chorale preludes, variations, fugues etc., as well as works in the *concertato* style.

Taruskin delineates the aesthetic boundaries within which the early Lutheran polyphonic music flourished, by stating that "even at its fanciest, Lutheran

---

[84] Cf. Blume 1975, pp. 18, 60, 78 and 80; Higman 2000, p. 495; Rainoldi 2000, p. 313; Bergquist 2006, pp. 335–336; Leaver 2006, p. 391; Lejeune 2010, pp. 7 and 8; Sfredda 2010, pp. 28–29.
[85] Cf. Blume 1975, pp. 78–80. See also Weber 1989.
[86] Hendrickson 2003, pp. 21–29.

church music was a town music, not a court music [...]. Its aesthetics ignored the rare and the recondite, seeking beauty in the commonplace. It did not reject the *ars perfecta* but placed limits on its exercise. Within those limits [...] masterpieces could be created"[87].

As Blume correctly points out, however, the particular status accorded to music (and consequently to the principal musical expression of Luther's Reformation, the chorale) gave to chorales an almost "consecrated" quality, since they represented the Word of God which Luther would disseminate among the laity through music. Whether the chorale was employed for compositions echoing the German polyphonic *Lied* style or that of the Franco-Flemish motet, it always maintained its individuality and its characteristic features, which composers did not feel entitled to modify according to their own taste[88].

### 5.3.2.6. Led by the *Lieder*

Harmonisations of chorale melodies (which were normally given to the tenor at first, as *Tenorlied*, and only later to the soprano) were originally intended for private devotion and spiritual recreation rather than for congregational singing. The use of placing the chorale at the highest voice was fostered and spread by the appearance in Germany of the translations of the Calvinist Psalter by Ambrosius Lobwasser (1515–1585: cf. § 6.3.3.); however, in most cases of the Lutheran Church's early period, the likely actual performance practice in congregational contexts did not consist of spontaneous four-part singing by the church-goers. Rather, both men and women would normally sing the chorale melody in octaves, while it is possible that at least in some instances the remaining parts were played on instruments. This practice, of course, was consistent with contemporaneous musical trends towards accompanied monody.

Gradually, four-part singing became more common, and with this process a terminological change happened as well: the term "chorale" had been adopted to indicate Luther's songs inasmuch as they represented the Evangelical equivalent of traditional plainchant (i.e. monody), whereas later it started to indicate its four-part performance by extension[89]. If the chorale melody was at the soprano, this style began to be called *Cantional*.

This particular fashion for presenting the chorale melody offered an undeniable advantage, as it permitted to reconcile two opposing wishes which were in-

---

[87] Taruskin 2010, p. 769.
[88] Blume 1975, pp. 104–105; cf. Sfredda 2010, p. 106.
[89] Cf. Blume 1975, pp. 134–135; Herl 2004, p. 166; Bergquist 2006, p. 346; Rees 2006, p. 343; Sfredda 2010, p. 25.

herent to the Lutheran theology of music. From the one side, indeed, the principle of congregational participation in the liturgy seemed to require simple monodic melodies which were immediately learnable and could be sung by all members of the community; from the other, the appreciation for music's beauty *in se* and Luther's own passionate commitment to music could not exclude polyphony from Lutheran churches. A first compromise was found when polyphonic stanzas sung by the choir were presented in alternation with monodic singing by the community. In 1586, however, Lucas Osiander could proudly show the advantages of the new style which would become known as *Cantional:* in complex polyphony "an amateur can certainly not sing along but only listen since he is not acquainted with Figural music [...]. Therefore I have placed the chorale in the discant so that it is truly recognisable and every amateur can sing along"[90].

The influence of Osiander's hymnal on those following it was so inescapable that it has been defined by Siegele as a "musical *Formula of Concord*"[91].

In this style, all parts sing in the same rhythm, which faithfully mirrors that of the original melody: its simplicity and plainness, and the solution it offered for the tensions between congregation and choir, were obviously a brilliant achievement, but not one without negative side-effects. As Blume slightly severely summarises, Osiander's work "represents that point of development at which the practical needs of the church and artistic values separated decisively for the first time"[92].

Whereas Osiander's proposal was explicitly aimed at offering a response to the devotional and musical needs of worshipping congregations, chorale melodies were also employed in the creation of pious works for private use, either at home or within the context of Latin schools or universities; being often conceived for the spiritual recreation of amateur musicians and/or for pedagogical purposes, they frequently took the form of *bicinia* or *tricinia*, i.e. simple polyphonic arrangements for two or three voices.

Vernacular translations and paraphrases of Psalms made by Lutheran poets and writers were also employed in the creation of German Psalm-motets. One of the most important early composers who left a significant in this genre (inspired by earlier works in Latin) is the Catholic Thomas Stoltzer (c.1480 – 1526), who, towards the end of his life (1525 – 6), wrote a Psalm-motet on Luther's version of Psalm 37 [36] (*Erzürne dich nicht*), followed shortly after by three more, all of which were included in Protestant collections only: his example was not fol-

---

[90] Osiander 1586, *Preface*. English translation in Herl 2004, pp. 113 – 114; cf. *ibid.*, p. 129, and Marcus 2001, p. 738.
[91] Siegele 1989, col. 429.
[92] Blume 1975, p. 136.

lowed by other Catholic composers. This might be in part due to the relatively scanty occasions on which such works could be performed during public services (the most likely context for their liturgical performance being before or after the Gospel and during Communion): later collections explicitly mention that they had been conceived for use at schools and in the educational context. Such works may also have been a particular initiative by the composers, who (as Stoltzer stated himself) could be inspired by "a special pleasure in the very beautiful words"[93].

This subjective inspiration is mirrored by the individuality and expressive quality of many motets on Psalm texts and/or melodies, or on chorales, written – among others – by Balthasar Resinarius (c.1485–c.1544), Wolff Heinz (c.1490–c.1552), Benedictus Ducis (c.1492–1544) and Sixt Dietrich[94] (c.1494–1548).

In such works, the composers' approach to the sacred text is different from that encountered and discussed above. Comparing the 1597 *Lieder auf den Choral*[95] by Johannes Eccard with *Lied* motets by the same composer, Blume points out that in the former the composer is at the service of the text, which is made available to all, whereas in the latter he interprets the text and creates more ambitious works for the cultivated amateurs and the musical elite (schools, choirs, accomplished music lovers[96]). In such elaborate compositions, the words were emphasised through expressive renditions, with affective contents similar to those observed at about the same time in the Catholic area: both fields would take a fundamental inspiration for motet settings from Orlando di Lasso and his school, whose influence would be crucial and long-lasting[97].

The interesting fact that, in Stoltzer's version of Psalm 37 [36], the lower parts could be played on crumhorns instead of being sung[98] leads us to the topic of instrumental music in Lutheran chorales, and particularly of whether, how and when the organ participated in chorale performances.

Once more, it should be stressed that no certainty can be drawn from the available sources, and there is no universal consensus among scholars: furthermore, generalisations are always dangerous, since many choices depended on

---

93 Quoted and translated in Blume 1975, p. 101. On this topic, cf. *ibid.*, pp. 100 and 152, to which this section is indebted.
94 Cf. Leaver 2006, p. 392.
95 Eccard 1597.
96 Blume 1975, p. 152.
97 Cf. Bergquist 2006, pp. 346–347.
98 Lejeune 2010, p. 8.

those in charge of liturgical music, on the available resources, and on the orientations of the congregations and/or of the civil authorities.

What does seem most likely, is that early Lutheran practices followed fairly closely the Catholic model, and that *alternatim* performance was possible between organ and choir, or organ, choir and congregation. Purely instrumental preludes could also be played, and sometimes motet tablatures (i.e. organ transcriptions from vocal works) could be performed. Organ accompaniment for congregational singing was not practised in the early years of the Reformation, and would become common only at a later historical stage. It is possible that other instruments could (at least locally) accompany part-singing, particularly in the most solemn festivities: this practice would contribute to the establishment of *concertato* performances in the following century.

In Wittenberg (1536), *alternatim* performances with organ playing are documented for the *Kyrie* and *Gloria*[99], as well as organ pieces before the sermon; the importance of organs for Lutheran church music would gradually be increased, and distinctive instrumental forms on chorales would appear and flourish in the centuries to come[100].

### 5.3.3. Collecting chorales

If the chorale is the musical symbol of Luther's Reformation, the hymnbook is its visible and tangible incarnation; just as chorales took on pre-existing traditions and practices, but gave them new spread and new significance, so hymnals drew upon pre-Reformation models but also revolutionised their function and circulation; finally, both chorales and the books collecting them became a formidable tool for shaping a distinctive Lutheran piety and for radiating the Word of God and its Lutheran interpretation.

Lutheran songbooks were modelled upon medieval prayerbooks (which had been relatively widespread among the wealthy and educated laity, but which were normally not provided with music) and *hymnaria* (which did have music, but were not intended for lay use; moreover, they obviously were in Latin).

A few figures may help in grasping the dimensions of this phenomenon. Estimates based on the two main catalogues available for German hymns include around two thousand hymn editions in the sixteenth century[101], with Lutheran

---

[99] See the diary of Wolfgang Musculus, as quoted in Kolde 1883, p. 216.
[100] Cf. Herl 2004, pp. 48, 130, 151; Leaver 2006, p. 392; Rees 2006, p. 343; Sfredda 2010, p. 116.
[101] Brown 2005, p. 5.

publications virtually monopolising the market. After the Reformation, the maximum vitality of non-Lutheran hymnal publishing reached no more than about thirty percent of the total, with Catholic hymn-printing representing between ten and fifteen percent of the total in the most favourable situations[102].

The impressive production of German hymnals with music is also shown by the nearly three hundred songbooks published in less than fifty years (1524 – 1570), more than two-thirds of which were intended for Lutherans[103].

It should be said, however, that hymnals were often the product of private entrepreneurship rather than of official Church initiatives: thus, repertoire choices largely mirrored the demands of the potential customers and the list of the most cherished pieces in the burgeoning Lutheran musical repository.

Beside hymnals, Lutheran hymn-printing included a huge quantity of broadsheets, as well as hymns with music transmitted in forms different from hymnals proper[104]. Study of the number, assortment and spread of hymnbooks does not automatically and reliably mirror the actual practice of Lutheran hymn-singing, as we will soon discuss; however, the two phenomena are strictly connected, and without the possibilities offered by the pinting press, the Lutheran Reformation would have missed a formidable pastoral, spiritual and propagandistic possibility[105].

The very first Lutheran hymn collections were issued in 1524: in the *Achtliederbuch* we find eight chorale texts with four tunes. However, already in the *Enchiridion oder handbuechlein*, published in Erfurt in the same year, there are twenty-six texts with fifteen melodies. Here, the compiler's eclecticism in choosing the sources for his selection of hymns is clear: besides paraphrased translations and adaptations from Latin and German hymns, there are also popular religious songs coming from the unofficial tradition. In Garside's words, "The *Enchiridion* [...] neglects virtually none of the textual and musical expressions of mediaeval piety"[106].

Since the very beginning of Lutheran hymnal-printing, the importance of lay initiative is apparent, both as concerns the publishing process and the composition and selection of hymns: these were written not only by spiritual leaders such as Luther himself, but also by lay men and women (sometimes people

---

102 Brown 2005, p. 7.
103 Herl 2004, p. 88.
104 Cf. Brown 2005, p. 14; Brown 2008, p. 237.
105 Blume 1975, p. 46.
106 Garside 1967, p. 164. Cf. Konrad Ameln in Loersfeld 1983.

who had formerly been in religious life) and published by clever printers throughout Germany[107].

Indeed, among others, the 1524 *Enchiridion* includes a song by a woman hymnographer, Elisabeth Cruciger (c.1500–1535), and her hymn was going to be reprinted in many subsequent collections (on Cruciger see also § 12.3.1.3.).

In that same year 1524, another collection was issued, i.e. the already mentioned *Geystliche Gesangk Buchleyn*[108] by Walther, which originally comprised thirty-eight polyphonic songs along with five Latin *Cantiones*, and whose immense popularity is testified by its numerous editions: this publication, however, was not primarily intended for the common parishioner, but rather for the musically educated.

Among polyphonic collections, the most important after Walther's *Gesangk Buchleyn* is probably that by Georg Rhau[109], issued in 1544 as *Newe Deudsche Geistliche Gesenge*, and comprising 123 pieces, ordered according to the liturgical year. It is an "ecumenical" assortment, since several Catholic composers are found among the high-level musicians contributing to the collection, and since many works could be used for both Catholic and Evangelical liturgies. The most prominent composers featured in Rhau's collection are Martin Agricola (1486–1556), Arnold von Bruck (c.1500–1554), Lupus Hellinck (c.1493–1541), Stephan Mahu (a.1480-a.1541), Lucas Osiander, Balthasar Resinarius (who is represented by as many as thirty works), Ludwig Sennfl and Thomas Stoltzer. The broad-mindedness of the compiler is shown by the inclusion of a Latin *Pater Noster – Ave Maria* motet by Arnold von Bruck; indeed, however, most similar collections of the era and from the German area cannot be ascribed univocally to a particular confession. This confessional ambiguity is particularly clear in the cases of Latin motet collections, published in Augsburg and Nuremberg in the first half of the sixteenth century, where the choice criteria seem to be inspired by musical rather than by confessional reasons[110].

The fluidity of musical boundaries is shown also by another interesting collection by Johann Spangenberg (1484–1550), whose very title (*Cantiones ecclesiasticæ / Kirchengesenge Deudsche*[111]) reveals its bilingual structure. In this case, the book's confessional belonging is clearly Lutheran, inasmuch as it mirrors rather faithfully the Latin and German Mass Orders issued by Luther in 1523 and 1526 respectively. The Latin section, intended (as Spangenberg explains in

---

107 Cf. Brown 2005, p. 7.
108 Walther 1524.
109 *Newe deudsche* 1544.
110 Cf. Rasmussen 1995, p. 115; Bergquist 2006, pp. 335–336; Lejeune 2010, p. 6; Ropchock 2015.
111 Spangenberg 1545.

the *Preface* to the German part) "for schoolboys and learned" (and therefore for ecclesiastical establishments in urban contexts where Latin schools or universities were present), offers the liturgical material for all Sundays and the principal solemnities of the year; the German part, conceived "for lay-people and the uneducated" (and thus for countryside and rural parishes), includes in turn German plainchant and hymns organised according to the liturgical year[112].

### 5.3.3.1. Objects of piety: The Lutheran hymnbooks

In the preceding paragraphs, we have taken into consideration some examples of the variety in music publishing for the Lutheran Church in the sixteenth century, including monodic chorale collections, books with harmonised versions of chorales, collections intended for church musicians, clergy or educated amateurs etc. However, it is the songbook proper which is the most common and most symbolic representative of Lutheran piety. Used as we are today to find in Lutheran churches (as well as in most Catholic churches in the German-speaking area) a huge number of songbooks available for use by church-goers, as well as more-or-less technological boards for indicating the hymn numbers, we tend to assume that Lutheran songbooks belong to the church, at least inasmuch as the church is the privileged location for their use, even when they are owned by the faithful who bring them to worship.

In the sixteenth century, the situation might have been very different, though this is another topic on which much debate is still underway.

For example, Brown pithily states that "The Lutheran hymnal of the sixteenth century was foremost and most typically not a church book but a household book"[113]. And indeed, seemingly the principal use of hymnals was for home devotion. Hymn singing was encouraged in families, where parents (with the most educated members of the household, who might be their children) were deemed responsible for teaching the hymns, explaining their doctrinal and spiritual content, and singing them together with the entire family and their servants[114].

However, many hymnals were (at least at first) too expensive for most families, and many among the faithful did not possess a sufficient literacy (let alone the ability to read music) for using them properly[115]. Moreover, there is evidence of the practice of choir music in the Wittenberg liturgies, whereas no such evi-

---

112 Leaver 2007, p. 216.
113 Brown 2005, p. 12.
114 Cf. Paul Eber in Herman 1560 (*WB* 788, pref. 67, p. 609); in Brown 2008, p. 236. See § 5.3.4.4.
115 Cf. Blume 1975, p. 65; Hsia 1992, p. 109.

dence has survived as regards the congregation's participation in singing or their use of hymnbooks; on the contrary, Luther complained in 1529 that the community was reluctant to learn new songs. Seven years later, Wolfgang Musculus (1497–1563) described the absence of lay participation in the Wittenberg worship[116], and in 1540 the reports on the magnificent choral performances in Luther's city support the inference that early Lutheran congregations did not sing very often or very willingly in church. As a consequence, their use of hymnbooks seems even less likely[117]; moreover, if and when the congregation sang, they probably did so by memory, while singing from hymnbooks was probably more typical for clergy and church musicians, who could thus teach (by their very singing) new hymns to the bystanders[118].

For those who could read and afford to buy songbooks, thus, these were primarily a tool for domestic piety and instruction; they could be taken by their owners to church services, but this was not as widespread a practice as contemporary reality may suggest[119]. Moreover, a comparison between surviving prints of hymns and the songs whose use was prescribed in liturgical books for the city of Nuremberg shows that only a small number of them were present in both sources, thus suggesting that printed hymns were not primarily intended for use in church[120].

Indeed, what we do know is that only at a local level was the use in church of hymnbooks for singing common, and this happened (interestingly) in areas near the borders of the German-speaking zones such as Strasbourg, Riga and Rostock[121]. However, the title-pages of the first Lutheran hymnbooks mention some instances of congregational singing, by stating that song collections had been created not only "to sing in the church, as is already the practice to some extent in Wittenberg"[122], but also "for every Christian to have on hand for constant exercise and meditation on spiritual songs and Psalms"[123], thus stressing the double destination for church and home of these early collections; on the other hand, several hymnals dating from the second half of the sixteenth century were explicitly designed for use at home[124].

---

116 See the diary of Wolfgang Musculus, as quoted in Kolde 1883, p. 216.
117 Cf. Herl 2004, p. 101, to which this section is indebted.
118 Herl 2004, p. 152.
119 Brown 2008, p. 206.
120 Cf. Herl 2004, pp. 90, 94–95.
121 Herl 2004, p. 106.
122 Luther 1524, title-page; English translation in Brown 2008, p. 211.
123 Loersfeld 1524, title-page and preface; English translation in Brown 2008, p. 211.
124 Brown 2008, p. 235.

Eventually, however, the spread of hymnals and of their use in church was one of the concurring factors which prompted and fostered congregational singing in Lutheran worship, together with the increasing success of the *cantional* style, the Pietist focus on lay involvement and the establishment of organ accompaniment to communal singing[125].

It should be said, however, that Lutheran hymnbooks very soon started to be identified as a musical and visible symbol of the Reformation. In the famous painting known as *The Ambassadors* (1533) by Hans Holbein the Younger, one of the numerous symbols used by the painter to convey information about the sitters as well as messages about his own political and religious view is precisely a Lutheran song collection[126] (a 1525 edition printed in Worms of Walther's *Geystliche Gesangk Buchleyn:* see § 11.2.2.).

### 5.3.4. The daily sound

In several instances we have already briefly touched upon the role and importance of chorales for Lutherans in the sixteenth century, on a great number of occasions and in various contexts. In this section, we will discuss this topic in a more thorough and systematic fashion, by considering in turn the role of chorales within and outside Lutheranism, i.e. internally (in church, for liturgy; at home and outside church, in daily life) and externally (as a tool for spreading the Lutheran message).

#### 5.3.4.1. A singing Church

Within early Lutheran worship, music was varied as concerns both genres and performers. Luther's concept of the universal priesthood of all believers brought him to advocate congregational singing also in vernacular plainchant and not only for the strophic chorales; however, as has been briefly mentioned in our discussion of hymnbooks above (§ 5.3.3.), even the easier and more immediate strophic forms did not immediately and everywhere encounter the success hoped for by the Reformers[127].

Theoretically, congregational singing was the perfect expression of a worshipping community, where praise and prayer were expressed in music, teaching

---

[125] Herl 2004, p. 130.
[126] Leaver 2006, p. 396.
[127] This section on congregational hymnody is indebted to Herl 2004; here p. 162.

was conveyed in and could be retained through singing, and the Word of God could be proclaimed, prayed and lived in the chorales. Indeed, in some cases, this actually happened: for example, Church orders issued in 1579 for Nördlingen instructed pastors to foster lay appropriation of the hymns, in consideration of the spiritual power of the sung Word[128]. However, in many other cases, this ideal – which was clearly present in Luther's view – was mistakenly assumed to be the actual and generalised reality of early Lutheran worship especially when, in the nineteenth century, the need started to be felt for a renovation of liturgy in the Lutheran Church. As commonly happens in a religious context, the possibility for renewal was sought in the recovery of ancient practices, deemed to be more "original" and authentic than later accretions. By trusting Luther's writings with a descriptive quality they did not have, and by carrying out a selection among the available sources of witness, nineteenth-century historians contributed to creating what Herl maintains to be the myth of early Lutheran congregational singing[129].

As Herl convincingly demonstrates, this myth did mirror actual reality only locally, and (often and notably) not in properly Lutheran contexts: for example, in Bucer's Strasbourg or in the Calvinist areas. Indeed, when hymnals started to be actually used in church, they became fundamental for encouraging the congregation to sing[130].

An interesting piece of evidence which Herl (building on Ameln's research[131]) brings in support of his assertions is a negative proof: early hymnals faithfully transmitted the original rhythmic values of the chorales, whereas in the following century this precision started to disappear. Since congregational singing normally lacks rhythmic precision and tends towards value homogeneity, the appearance of errors in rhythmic notation and in the transmission of note durations in seventeenth-century hymnals supports the inference that the flattening effect of congregational singing was not felt until then[132].

Moreover, we have already seen (both in this Chapter and in the preceding) that Luther was by no means adverse to professional or trained choirs, and that congregational singing was not meant to replace entirely the performance of polyphony. Listening to the Word when it was proclaimed in singing by a choir was

---

128  Herl 2004, p. 67.
129  Herl 2004, p. 176.
130  Herl 2004, p. 177.
131  Ameln 1980 and 1986.
132  Herl 2004, p. 171.

no less important than delivering or praying it in music through congregational singing[133].

Terminology may be slightly confusing here, and so a short clarification is needed. We have already seen that the very word "chorale" was etymologically linked to the Latin expression *choraliter* (i.e. in unaccompanied monody) as opposed to *figuraliter* (i.e. in polyphony); however, by Luther's time, the "choir" (i.e. an ensemble of trained singers) could sing (and often did sing) in polyphony, whereas unaccompanied monody tended to be sung either by those proclaiming a text in music (e.g. a Gospel reading, or the Words of Institution etc.) or by the congregation[134] ("congregational singing"). Obviously, the choir might support the congregation when it sang, and might sing unaccompanied monody in turn when this was needed (for example, if the congregation stood silent when it was supposed to sing).

Notwithstanding this, the primary task for choirs (if sufficiently accomplished) was precisely to sing polyphonically; and, rather unavoidably, they tended to invade an increasing part of the worship's music, to the detriment of congregational singing[135].

For instance, in the second half of the sixteenth century, visitation records increasingly report dissatisfaction over the predominance of choir over congregational singing; Luther's hymns could be almost forgotten locally, since the congregations did not sing them frequently enough[136]; abuses similar to those described as regards pre-Reformation Catholic practice started to appear, with organ music and polyphony replacing liturgical items which should not have been considered as expendable. (Seemingly, the only element which was stubbornly preserved for the congregation to sing was the Creed[137]). This phenomenon was particularly evident within urban contexts, whereas the limited financial and cultural resources of the countryside prevented the expansion of choir singing: in some instances, the precise directive is found that congregations should sing when there was no available choir[138].

This caused two contrasting and seemingly contradictory results: from the one side, those wishing to involve the congregation more effectively tended to suppress Latin singing in favour of the vernacular; from the other, those wishing to preserve high-level music tended to relegate the lower social classes and the

---

133 Leaver 2007, p. 224.
134 Leaver 2007, pp. 209–210.
135 Bergquist 2006, pp. 335–336.
136 Herl 2004, p. 107.
137 Cf. Herl 2004, pp. 54–56, 58 and 68.
138 Herl 2004, pp. 164, 56 and 67.

uneducated to a secondary role, and to privilege the needs and capabilities of the upper and cultivated citizenry[139].

As we have seen, a good compromise and a satisfactory balance was found in the alternation of choir and congregation in strophic *Lieder:* the choir might interpret polyphonically the chorale melody, for example in a chorale motet (while the listening congregation could follow the tune and mentally rehearse it), and then the entire assembly could join in singing[140]. (Beside the *alternatim* practice, we may recall that the cantional style was one of the options available to Lutherans for reconciling the musical exigencies of both choir and congregation[141]).

Later, when the organ started to be commonly used for playing along during singing, it provided a much-welcome support to the congregation, and encouraged them to sing more boldly; of course, the other side of the coin was that the choir's role was correspondingly reduced and – eventually – minimised or suppressed altogether[142].

It is time, then, to focus our attention precisely on the choir or *schola*, since we have seen it competing for space with the congregation. It was an institution closely linked to the presence of educational possibilities: since Luther had maintained the intelligibility criterion that singing had to be understood by the singers (and not necessarily by the listeners), in order to obtain a theologically consistent performance of Latin-texted polyphony, it was necessary that enough Latin-speaking singers were available[143]. We will shortly discuss the role of music within Lutheran pedagogy: suffice it to say for now that most polyphonic choirs were directly connected with the presence of Latin schools or universities, and that many singers were recruited among the schoolboys and students.

It should be added, however, that in many instances there was more than one choir: the *chorus choralis* limited itself to monody and mainly supported the congregation, whereas the *chorus figuralis* or *chorus musicus*, constituted by the musical elite of the most accomplished singers, was in charge of polyphony[144].

The role of the *chorus choralis*, therefore, was a strongly didactic one: schoolboys and children were taught the Lutheran hymns as part of their religious and

---

139 Blume 1975, p. 122.
140 Cf. Herl 2004, p. 129, and Leaver 2007, p. 205.
141 Cf. Herl 2004, pp. 113–114 and 129.
142 Herl 2004, p. 151.
143 Leaver 2007, p. 224.
144 Cf. Herl 2004, p. 44; Sfredda 2010, p. 33.

cultural education, so that they could sing the chorales for the gathered congregation until it had learnt them in turn, and support it in its efforts to join in singing. (Indeed, students attending Latin schools had to speak Latin only: the use of German was allowed exclusively when the pupils had to sustain the congregation in vernacular singing[145]). Members of this monodic choir could even be directed to stand in the church's nave in order that their support to the congregations might be more effective[146].

On the other hand, the *chorus figuralis* could also alternate its polyphonic performances with those singing in monody[147]: in several instances, as we have seen, this alternation produced bilingual performances where Latin polyphony (normally on liturgical texts) was interspersed with monody in German[148] (translated plainchant or hymns inspired by liturgical texts).

It should be added, however, that the unbalance sometimes observed between Latin polyphony and vernacular congregational singing was partly a consequence of the confessionalisation process: since Calvinists were in principle against the presence of polyphonic music in Latin during worship, Lutherans reacted by according to this kind of music an increasingly larger scope within their liturgies[149].

### 5.3.4.2. Our daily hymn

Beside their use in churches, however, on which (as discussed in the preceding paragraphs) several doubts remain, Lutheran hymns were ubiquitous in the lives of the faithful. As Brown concisely summarises, "Though each sphere of musical activity – the church, the school, and the home – developed to some extent its own repertoire, one notable feature of the Lutheran hymns was their use in both public and private, learned and lay contexts"[150].

Brown himself painstakingly analysed sixteenth-century testimonies regarding daily life in the Lutheran city of Joachimsthal, drawing a fascinating picture of lively musical and spiritual experiences. Doubtless, the situation was not the same everywhere, and, probably, much depended on the presence of such an inspiring figure as that of Johannes Mathesius, who was the religious leader of Joa-

---

145 Brown 2005, p. 10.
146 Cf. Herl 2004, pp. 113 and 162.
147 Leaver 2007, p. 295.
148 Brown 2005, p. 81.
149 Cf. Herl 2004, pp. 110–111.
150 Brown 2005, p. 8.

chimsthal and to whose deep spirituality, enlightened human approach and love for music the Joachimsthalers were unquestionably indebted[151].

In Joachimsthal, the interaction and reciprocal support that music and spirituality gave to each other, as well as the contribution that both brought to the human, cultural and educational development of the city, were extraordinary and almost idyllic. Musical practice involved people from all social layers, conditions and ages, and ranged from complex Latin polyphony sung by the educated citizens and by the Latin school students to the vernacular religious songs cherished by all. Lutheran music also succeeded in establishing favourable social cooperation, bridging (through its spiritual content and its communal practice) class differences as well as the separation between clergy and laity, and fostering a responsible involvement of all the faithful in their own spiritual growth as well as their undertaking of a "pastoral" role with respect to their neighbours[152]. By means of the hymns, catechetic teaching and instruction were transmitted to all social levels, and lay spirituality was promoted: though some dogmatic finesses might be lost in transmission, hymns generally proved themselves to be an excellent tool for communication and communion[153].

Though obviously music was not a creation of the Lutheran Reformation, Brown points out the acuteness of Lutheran pastors and preachers in exploiting its value for religious purposes and in promoting its spread in a virtuous circle[154]. Through the clergy's action, Lutheran hymns became part of the Joachimsthalers' daily lives, both in official occasions (worship, festivities, schooling) and in private contexts[155] (family life, children's games and personal prayer).

When Luther's vision succeeded in being put into practice, the result was remarkable: at the beginning of the seventeenth century, a Spanish Carmelite friar, Thomas à Jesu (1564–1627), was impressed by how Lutheran hymns had become an essential component of the laity's daily experience, being sung at home, at work, in the markets, as well as in urban and rural contexts alike[156].

### 5.3.4.3. *Lehre:* Learning from the *Lieder*

We will now see how the Lutheran theoretical affirmation of the hymns' value in providing both *Lehre* and *Trost* was realised in practice.

---

151 Brown 2005.
152 Brown 2005, p. 30.
153 Brown 2005, p. 76.
154 Brown 2005, p. 43.
155 Brown 2005, p. 27.
156 A Jesu 1613, p. 514; Robinson-Hammerstein 1989, p. 161.

## 5.3. The forms of Reform — 275

The capacity of hymns for transmitting religious instruction was widely acknowledged – and sometimes even feared: Luther himself warned against the risk represented by deceptive hymns which could convey erroneous messages[157]. Within the "apocalyptic" perspective mentioned in Chapter Four (§ 4.2.4.11.), Luther was obviously referring to the rise of the false prophets which would appear near the end of the world to deceive the faithful (cf. Matthew 24:4 – 14 etc.); however, his implicit equating of hymn-writers with prophets is significant (and not isolated).

The dimension of teaching and instruction was – of course – particularly important for the young, although we must remember two fundamental aspects: 1) that life expectancy was rather low in the sixteenth century (about 28 – 30 years, though the data are misleading due to the high rate of infant mortality[158]) and thus the population was – on average – rather young; 2) consequently, that religious education of young people was not just one of the many differentiated pastoral concerns, but rather one of the most important: as Bireley effectively summarises, the religious reformations of the sixteenth century (Catholic and Evangelical alike) were "youth movements"[159].

Luther himself was convinced of the importance of music for education, from both the human and the spiritual viewpoints. The Reformer had explicitly stated: "Necessity demands that music be kept in the schools. A schoolmaster must know how to sing; otherwise I do not look at him. And before a youth is ordained into the ministry, he should practise music in school"[160]. As a consequence of such statements and of the pastoral actions inspired by this view, theological and musical teaching were integrated in the education of both clergy and musicians alike[161]. A similar view inspired primary schooling as well: if education was a crucial concern for Lutheran Reformers (both for humanistic reasons and for the sake of the new confession's survival, which depended on the younger generations), music was not to be neglected at any stage of the educational curriculum[162]. Though this vision was probably originally Luther's, it was shared by most of his fellow Reformers, such as Melanchthon, Johannes Bugenhagen and Justus Jonas, whose interest in music is testified by their prefaces to

---

[157] Cf. Luther 1545.
[158] Cf. Konnert 2008, p. 22.
[159] Bireley 1999, pp. 118 – 119.
[160] *WA TR* V, p. 557, no. 6248; English translation in Leaver 2007, p. 278.
[161] Leaver 2007, p. 278.
[162] Leaver 2007, p. 277; cf. Wagner Oettinger 2001, p. 191.

musical collections and by the role they assigned to music in the Church orders they designed[163].

If – as said above – the education of the young nearly approximated the education of the entire population, it must be said that the very concept of "Reformation" implied that the Church in general, and its members in particular, should constantly consider themselves as pilgrims on the path of life[164] (or, with a more modern and less spiritual expression, as people in continuing education).

In particular, one of the key concerns of Luther himself was for the illiterate and uneducated people who had attended the Catholic Mass without being able to understand it, and without receiving religious instruction in terms they could comprehend. Though pre-Reformation piety could be very deep and involving, and its symbolic dimension could be very strong, it was often combined with superstitious or syncretic practices, which a theologian educated within a humanist framework could not accept. For the uneducated people, who could not read and who could probably not even understand, follow and memorise a lengthy sermon, music became an extremely efficacious tool, conveying "pure" doctrine in an easy fashion and joining it with both prayer and enjoyment[165].

There was, thus, a circular interaction, prompted by music, between faith and doctrine: doctrine was transmitted through music and formed the object of faith, but faith was expressed and strengthened in turn when the believers prayed with music on doctrinally sound texts[166]. Moreover, the union of teaching and prayer helped Lutheran theologians to re-establish a fundamental balance that late Scholasticism had sometimes lost: whereas pure theology could become arid and sterile, and be reduced to a merely academic subject, hymns (which could be cited as authoritative sources in theological debates) helped to maintain spiritual theology within a prayerful relationship to its "object", i.e. the Word of God[167].

This view was strongly supported by Melanchthon, who believed in the power of music to communicate doctrine and – at the same time – was a convinced supporter of education within a humanist perspective[168].

It should be noted, however, that though one of the pillars of humanism was its educational concern, the presence of (religious) music within this framework

---

163 Leaver 2007, p. 42.
164 Kim 2005, p. 110.
165 Wagner Oettinger 2001, pp. 43–44 and 60–61.
166 Leaver 2007, p. 170.
167 Cf. Brown 2005, p. 18; Leaver 2007, p. 170.
168 Cf. Kim 2005, p. 110; Melanchthon, "Preface" to Lossius 1553.

was by no means obvious: for example, both Erasmus and his disciples did not attribute too crucial a role to music in their educational projects[169].

In Lutheran Latin schools, on the other hand, music was almost omnipresent, both inasmuch as students "received" it as a part of their education, and as they offered it in turn to the congregation. As concerns the former case, the schoolboys' days were framed by hymn-singing and interspersed with music teaching (both theoretical and practical); as regards the latter, we have already seen that the interaction between and intersection of groups constituted by Latin school students and members of the church choirs was extremely close[170].

Here too we can observe a circular process. Adult teachers "gave" music to schoolchildren in the form of both musical teaching and compulsory practice. Schoolboys, in turn, "gave" music to adults both in the form of choir singing in church and on religious festivities, and in the form of instruction and teaching proper.

In fact, we have already seen that church choirs – often made up of Latin school students – were fundamental for the uneducated laity's rote learning of hymn texts and melodies; moreover, the pupils could transmit part of what they were taught at school (such as, for example, explanations of the hymns' theological content) to their parents and elders, who often had not received an education at the same level as their children's[171].

The instructional aspect of Lutheran religious education was particularly evident in the case of the catechism, which was the official context for the transmission of the contents of faith. Catechism was taught mainly on Sundays, though even here instruction was not only made of spoken words, but also included music. Through hymns, the substance of what was taught and explained became easier to memorise; moreover, the contribution of music to the establishment of a prayerful mood prevented religious instruction from becoming just a set of propositions to memorise, and helped it to enter into dialogue with both spiritual contemplation and daily life.

For this purpose, Luther devised the so-called *Katechismuslieder*, corresponding to the six sections into which catechism teaching was divided. They were sung in combination with what had just been learned, but they might also be used at homes, either with direct educational purposes or – indirectly – for spiritual entertainment which would have helped to refresh the knowledge and experience of catechism teaching.

---

**169** Brown 2005, p. 59.
**170** Cf. Brown 2005, pp. 10, 57 and 59.
**171** Cf. Wagner Oettinger 2001, p. 47; Leaver 2007, p. 295.

Moreover, when (in the sixteenth-century, but even more in the seventeenth) composers combined the melodies of the six catechism hymns to create so-called *Quodlibets*, this musical process became a powerful and fascinating symbol for the unity and integration of all teachings of the Church[172].

Interestingly, on the one hand, Luther revised and modified the medieval concept of prayerbooks, which ceased to be repositories of prayers and became closer to catechisms, showing a conspicuous presence of Biblical teachings; on the other, catechism (in music) became in turn a form of prayer[173].

Within this perspective, a curious by-product of Lutheran catechetic and musical pedagogy may be mentioned here: Mattheus Le Maistre (c.1505–1577) published in 1559 a song collection destined for schoolchildren, where the Lutheran catechism (interestingly translated into Latin!) was set to music in a blend of the purest humanistic fashion (homophonic and closely mirroring speech) and of imitational techniques[174] (such as the canon).

If hymns were integral to catechetic instruction of the young, their spiritual and dogmatic value was recognised at all levels (and indeed up to the highest) of homiletics and theology. For example, Cyriacus Spangenberg issued a four-volume anthology of sermons on Luther's hymns[175], and the practice was not uncommon: Mathesius made use of hymn quotations in support of specific theological points in his sermons, and sometimes hymns became the very focus of his preaching. (It should be added that such *Liedpredigten* were also found among the Bohemian Brethren[176]). Brown interestingly points out that Mathesius' sermon on Psalm 46 [45], being grounded on Luther's *Ein feste Burg*, enacts a multi-layered exegesis: "Luther's hymn serves as a gloss on the Psalm, and the two together serve as the basis for the evangelical proclamation of the text. The hymn is treated with a respect only a little less than that accorded to the Psalm itself"[177]. Similarly, Spengler's famous chorale *Durch Adams Fall* was used as a doctrinal authority in the redaction of the *Formula of Concord*[178].

We have thus briefly seen how the function of *Lehre* assigned by Luther to hymns was put into practice and exploited (in catechism, pedagogy, education

---

172 Cf. Brown 2005, pp. 52 and 67; Leaver 2006, p. 379; Leaver 2007, pp. 113 and 299; Brown 2008, p. 216.
173 Brown 2008, p. 238.
174 Le Maistre 1559; cf. Blume 1975, p. 104.
175 Spangenberg 1571; cf. Brown 2005, p. 11 and 278.
176 Pollmann 2006, p. 309.
177 Brown 2005, p. 101.
178 Leaver 2007, p. 170.

of adults and homiletics); now we will consider how the function of *Trost* was conceived and experienced by sixteenth-century Lutherans.

### 5.3.4.4. *Trost:* Comforted by the Chorales

Indeed, when these two dimensions are considered in isolation from each other, the risk of misunderstanding the pastoral efforts of the early Lutheran clergy is at hand. Of course, all generalisations (both positive and negative) are always simplistic and fail to take into account the actual and individual experiences lived by real people and not by the "average" person: thus, we must always remember that the modes and contents of early Lutheran preaching depended not only on Luther's ideas or even on his writings or directives, but also on each pastor's spirituality, personality, congregation, culture and inclinations.

This proviso is particularly important when discussing the topic of *Trost* or consolation/comfort, since opposing views have been expressed on this subject – and, probably, though they seemingly contradict each other, in practice they did coexist with one another. For example, the capacity of pastors to effectively communicate the theological and spiritual peculiarity of the Reformation to the uneducated laity could locally be rather limited; and it has also been questioned whether the message of Luther's Reform, as it was perceived by the laity, was really as "comforting" as it was supposed to be (cf. § 1.2.2.).

On the other hand, whilst homiletics might sometimes have given ground for such critical concerns, the view of justification and salvation transmitted by Lutheran hymns was much more heartening, both inasmuch as the chorales' poetic form required and implied literary imagery and beauty which were in themselves "comforting", and as the joy transmitted by music's own beauty and by the positive feeling of communal singing was a source of consolation in turn[179].

Moreover, hymns could also be used by the faithful in distress to reassure and appease themselves outside official worship: Mathesius recommended meditation and singing of chorales to anyone in need of consolation, "so that he may have and be his own choir"[180].

We have repeatedly seen, indeed, how closely the theory and practice of communal singing mirrored Luther's theology of the universal priesthood of all believers; and, actually, hymns did not just render each Christian "his own choir", but also his own (and his neighbours') pastor.

Indeed, Eber expressed this conviction very clearly and rather strikingly:

---

[179] Cf. Hsia 1992, p. 109; Brown 2005, pp. 15, 24, 30, 53, 241.
[180] Mathesius 1586, vol. 3, fol. 25ʳ. Translation in Brown 2005, p. 91; cf. *ibid.*, pp. 24 and 53.

> Christian fathers and mothers who hold God's Word dear will be able to manifest their diligence in accustoming their children and servants to the hymns, and singing along with them themselves, and sometimes explaining and expounding one stanza after another. And such household sermons without doubt yield great benefit, so that many simple, unlearned people are able to comfort and encourage themselves more amid distress and temptation with one of these hymns than from a lengthy and carefully arranged sermon[181].

Here a theological revolution can be seen at work: lay (and married) men (and women) can proclaim the Gospel through hymns with spiritual results which may exceed those of a "lengthy and carefully arranged sermon". Incidentally, the theology of conjugality modelled on Christ's relationship with the Church is one contribution of Luther and his Church to modern theology which the other Christian Churches have greatly benefited from. Luther fostered family devotion (the *Hausandacht*), within which the melodic simplicity of chorales could accompany prayer and instruction: chorales were ideally suited to all members of virtually all households, due to their rhyming structure, easy vocabulary and limited melodic range[182]. Nevertheless, literate households could find their music among more complex forms of religious songs – such as, for instance, those represented in a collection (1582) by Leonhard Lechner[183] (c.1553–1606).

Luther believed that household piety could become the sanctuary where holiness was preserved and transmitted, in the face of a hostile and debauched world: "the world shall become so thoroughly Epicurean that there will be no more public preaching in the whole world, and nothing but Epicurean abomination shall be spoken of in public, and the gospel will be preserved only in homes by fathers"[184].

Preaching – in the broadest meaning of the term – thus was not just a prerogative of the clergy, but also not only of the male head of the family: we have already seen (§ 4.2.4.11.) that both "sons and daughters" were expected to prophesy as the end of the world came closer (cf. Joel 2:28), and in fact women and children were entitled to announce the Gospel (outside official worship, of course).

Brown reports a few delightful anecdotes recounted by Mathesius, such as the comfort and spiritual (as well as physical) strength given to a woman in difficult labour by a passing schoolboy's hymn singing, or the consolation he had

---

**181** Paul Eber in Herman 1560 (*WB* 788, pref. 67, p. 609); in Brown 2008, p. 236.
**182** Marcus 2001, p. 725.
**183** Lechner 1582. Cf. Hsia 1992, p. 109.
**184** *WA DB* 11$^{II}$, p. 123. Cf. Brown 2008, p. 257.

received himself during a period of distress when he heard a chorale sung by schoolchildren[185].

The attachment of the laity to hymn-singing (at least in such idyllic contexts as Mathesius' Joachimsthal) was indeed impressive. By popular request, an extra hour of hymn-singing was added to Sunday services in Joachimsthal[186]; ensemble musicianship was also practised for hours in the *convivium musicum*, where laypeople and clergy could gather for music-making from 1558[187]; when Mathesius referred in his sermons to some particularly cherished hymns, he stressed their belonging to the congregation by such expressions as "your German hymn" or "your *feste Burg*"[188]. Even though lay participation in official worship could sometimes fall short of clerical expectations, the laity's fondness for Lutheran hymns was shown on a number of occasions. This was particularly evident when relatively young Lutheran communities were exposed to confrontation with rival confessions or subject to forced conversions or persecutions: in such cases, hymns really became a spiritually indispensable force for strengthening and unifying the community[189].

### 5.3.4.5. Creating communities

Indeed, though chorales could be spiritually beneficial for the individual, one of their primary functions was to build that feeling of union and belonging.

When a congregation sang a chorale in unison, the very act of singing became a powerful symbol of identity and communion; the official adoption of vernacular singing, even when it had already been privately or unofficially practised in the pre-Reformation Church, helped the faithful (even the most humble and uneducated) to perceive their own belonging to the congregation and the congregation's belonging to their own culture[190]. Moreover, the performance style and the peculiar compositional features of Lutheran chorales helped the community to define itself not just within its own boundaries, but also in comparison with other Christian confessions. The reciprocal identification between hymn-singing and Lutheranism was in certain instances so strong that Wagner Oettinger could express this feeling in a concise and efficacious fashion: "If Luther saved music

---

[185] Brown 2005, pp. 72–73.
[186] Brown 2005, p. 82.
[187] Brown 2005, p. 46.
[188] Brown 2005, pp. 102–103.
[189] Brown 2005, p. 25.
[190] Leaver 2007, pp. 300–302.

for the Evangelical Church, then it is also true that music saved the Evangelical Church for Luther"[191].

Hymn-singing did not accomplish only spiritual functions – or, rather, not only directly. It also responded to musical needs, offering occasions to experience music and practise musicianship, both individually and communally. Thus, we have already seen that in several instances the explicit or implicit purpose of sacred *contrafacta* of secular songs was to supersede the "frivolous" or "unchaste" texts of the originals through religious and moral messages. A similar replacement, however, was also the purpose of newly composed chorales with no connections to pre-existing secular music, inasmuch a successful religious hymn might offer a spiritual alternative to secular songs.

On other occasions, the Lutheran clergy allowed the continuation of pre-Reformation practices which were seemingly rather typical of Catholic devotion (such as Christmas manger plays or singing around bonfires at St John's feast). The pastors' wisdom in recognising the overall innocence of such cherished activities and in understanding the sincere piety they were expressing – albeit perhaps naively – was matched by their shrewdness in using hymns and chorales as an antidote to superstition. By adeptly choosing the accompanying songs for such devotional rites, they could give a new, and solidly "Lutheran" meaning, to practices which other Evangelical confessions would have rejected altogether[192]. (Incidentally, such broad-mindedness will frequently disappear from later Lutheranism[193]).

Hymn-singing represented a unifying tool for the entire society in its different social, cultural and economic characterisations: though civil authorities actively fostered the most complex musical activities of the Church, considering an excellent polyphonic choir to be a source of pride and a musical flag for the entire community, simple chorales were the ground on which all citizens could meet and express their faith[194].

### 5.3.4.6. Disseminating doctrines in music

We have seen how crucial was hymn singing for fostering Lutheran spirituality in church and outside it, as well as for creating the congregation's identity. We will

---

[191] Wagner Oettinger 2001, p. 209. Cf. *ibid.*, p. 45; Hsia 1992, pp. 107–108; Pettegree 2005, p. 46; Fisher 2014, p. 172.
[192] Brown 2005, pp. 79–80.
[193] Cf. Pettegree 2005, p. 75.
[194] Cf. Blume 1975, p. 3; Wagner Oettinger 2001, p. 1; Brown 2005, pp. 79–80; Brown 2008, p. 232.

now see how chorales were useful for asserting this identity towards (or against) the others, and for spreading the Lutheran message (though more on this topic will be found in Chapter Ten: § 10.3. and following).

The power of Lutheran hymns as a means for propaganda and for spiritual conversion was acknowledged by Lutherans and by their opponents alike. The Jesuit Adam Contzen (1571–1635), who was the confessor to Elector Maximilian I of Bavaria (1573–1651), stated that "the songs of Luther and Bèze have killed more souls than their writings and sayings"[195].

On the other hand, Tilemann Heshusius (1527–1588) had written:

> I do not doubt that by this one song of Luther's, *Nun freut euch, lieben Christen g'mein*, many hundreds of Christians have been brought to faith who would otherwise have been unable to hear Luther's name; but the noble, precious words of Luther have won their hearts, and compelled them to acknowledge the truth, so that, in my judgment, the hymns have been no small help in spreading the Gospel[196].

The hymn quoted by Heshusius had been one of the very first among those written by Luther (1523), and was the poetic and musical counterpart of his theological writings against the doctrine of free will. Whereas Luther's dispute with Erasmus on this topic and his exposition of the same in the Heidelberg Disputation[197] could arouse the interest of a limited number of learned and theologians, his chorale gave to the "abstract theological propositions" a "subjective and affective reference"[198], together with an impressive and immediate spread[199].

Similarly, another key concept of Lutheran thought, i.e. that of the "*fröhliche Wechsel*" (i.e. the "joyful exchange" between Christ's divine wealth of Grace and the sins of his Bride, the Church[200]) is given musical form and a simple expression (suitable even for children at Christmas) in a song by Nikolaus Herman (c.1560), *Lobt Gott ihr Christen alle gleich*[201].

It should be stressed that the success, popularity and efficaciousness of Lutheran hymns are not due merely to the overall idea of spreading the Evangelical teaching through music, but also to the specific value of their literary and musi-

---

[195] Contzen 1621, Liber Secundus, p. 100. Cf. Brown 2005, p. 1; Fisher 2014, p. 33.
[196] Tilemann Heshusius, "Preface" to Magdeburg 1565; English translation in Brown 2005, p. 16.
[197] Luther's "Heidelberg Disputation" (1518): *LW* 31, p. 40. For the polemics between Luther and Erasmus, cf. Rupp and Watson 2006.
[198] Brown 2005, p. 17; cf. *ibid.*, p. 16 and pp. 215–216.
[199] Cf. Wagner Oettinger 2001, p. 36.
[200] Cf. *WA* 26, pp. 4–10 etc.
[201] Brown 2005, p. 85.

cal features, which conferred unto them, in Blume's opinion, a "high aesthetic rank, far above so many songs of the period which were fitted together more or less mechanically"[202].

Sung words could obviously reach those who could not read by themselves (or would not have read theological treatises), and this clearly was an advantage of hymns over books; however, another non-negligible pro they possessed lay in the very intangible nature of music. Cornelius Becker (1561–1604) saw this clearly:

> That God's Word so rapidly spread forth from Saxony to other places in Germany, unhindered by the awful tyranny of the papacy, and succeeded so well, was promoted above all by Luther's Psalms and other hymns since these could not be so easily interdicted as his other books and writings, as the hymns were spread in letters and in the minds and memory of pious Christians, and communicated to people in foreign places[203].

We have already seen that Luther's very first hymn, *Ein newes Lied*, was strictly connected with the oral tradition of news songs[204], on whose stable popularity Luther's Reformation consistently built[205]; and many (if not most) of his chorales had at first been conceived primarily for extraliturgical use and for propagandistic purposes. This is witnessed by their first publication in the form of broadsheets, which could be sold at markets (or clandestinely, as might be the case), easily hidden, and read/sung aloud for those who could not read[206]; other written means of diffusion included letters and manuscripts[207]. The spread of a song was virtually uncontrollable by hostile authorities; it could reach people of all social classes and all levels of education, and travel – sometimes impressively – across political and geographical boundaries[208], influencing in a short time a large number of people[209], especially if the tune was fitting, easy and attractive[210] (or perhaps already popular with another text). Indeed, it is possible that the triggering factor prompting Luther to compose his hymns was precisely a ban on the written and printed word: in 1522, his translation of the New Testament into German had been prohibited in Ducal Saxony, and perhaps his

---

202 Blume 1975, p. 36. Cf. Wagner Oettinger 2001, pp. 1, 24 and 209; Herl 2004, p. 156.
203 Becker 1602 (*WB* 1060, pref. 100, p. 680); English translation in Brown 2008, p. 210.
204 Cf. Pettegree 2005, p. 50; Lindberg 2010, p. 283.
205 Wagner Oettinger 2001, p. 17.
206 Mager 1986, pp. 25–26; Brown 2008, p. 209.
207 Brown 2005, p. 9.
208 Wagner Oettinger 2001, p. 206.
209 Wagner Oettinger 2001, p. 34.
210 Wagner Oettinger 2001, p. 25.

output of hymns represented also an alternative strategy for spreading his thought[211].

Lutheran hymns penetrated into the fortresses of his opponents, who sometimes did (or could do) nothing to prevent their spread: for instance, they were sung in the chapel of Wolfenbüttel's Catholic Duke, and clerical attempts to forbid them were met with strong opposition[212].

Sometimes, Lutheran songs could contain and convey a specific message countering a particular Catholic doctrine: we have already discussed the role of *Nun freut euch* and *Durch Adams Fall*, but this trend was by no means limited to these two songs. In other instances, instead, music maintained elements typical for Catholic worship even after the Reformation had reduced their importance: thus, several Lutheran polyphonic works were grounded on Latin hymns celebrating the Virgin Mary[213] (we must remember that Luther did not wish to abolish the Marian cult among his followers).

However (with a brief allusion to the subject of Chapter Ten, especially § 10.3.), the songs' potentiality to reach a wide audience and to convey a message was also exploited (by Lutherans as by members of other Christian confessions) for polemical purposes, particularly through the process of contrafacture. Polemical *contrafacta* of pre-existing songs granted several benefits: they built upon the already-established success of the tune (and sometimes of its text, especially when the *contrafactum* changed only a few words of the original); they offered the possibility for inter-textual references to their model; they allowed multiple interpretive layers which could sometimes elude censorship[214].

### 5.3.5. A range of genres

We have seen so far a rather extensive sample of Lutheran religious music in the sixteenth century and how it was used within the Lutheran society. I will now briefly consider other musical forms which represent further aspects of the Lutheran repertoire.

Early Lutheran musical settings of the Gospel narrative of Christ's Passion took several forms during the sixteenth century, the principal of which were the so-called "responsorial Passion" and the polyphonic version.

---

211 Brown 2008, pp. 209–210.
212 Brown 2005, p. 10.
213 Blume 1975, p. 28.
214 Cf. Wagner Oettinger 2001, pp. 10, 90, 101 and 102; Pettegree 2005, p. 69.

The text used for musical settings of the Passion was in most cases an adaptation of the *Passionsharmonie*, issued in 1526 by Johann Bugenhagen[215], in which the four versions of the last hours of Christ as narrated by the Evangelists were fused into a single exposition; later in the century, the four Passions would be differentiated (probably by Johann Walther).

Credit for the creation of the Lutheran "responsorial" Passion is given to Walther himself: this musical form is essentially monodic (the parts of the Evangelist and of Christ) with simple multi-voiced sections representing the crowd. The melodies for recitation were inspired by the traditional Passion tone, which was however adapted by Walther so as to be suited to the peculiarities of the German language[216].

A completely different possibility had been made available to composers in the last decades of the sixteenth century. Usually indicated as "through-composed Passion", it is entirely polyphonic in a style reminiscent of motets, although the characters (Evangelist, Christ, and crowd) are identified by different compositional textures. Among the most interesting examples of this genre are the *Deutsche Passion nach Johannes* by Joachim a Burck (1568[217]); the fascinating Passion according to St John composed by Leonhard Lechner in 1593[218] and printed the following year (in this version, the Seven Last Words of Christ are incorporated within the text); and the highly dramatic and emotionally rich interpretation offered by Christoph Demantius (1567–1643) in 1631[219]. With the St John Passion (1561[220]), written by the Italian-born composer Antonio Scandello (1517–1580), the influence of the northern Italian style of Vincenzo Ruffo and Cipriano de Rore started to be felt in Germany, where it would affect – among others – the Passions by Orlando di Lasso[221].

Another Lutheran vernacular interpretation of a traditional devotional form of the Catholic Church is the Litany. Luther wrote his German version of the Litanies in 1529, adopting the characteristically antiphonal style which often distinguished Lutheran church music: a first choir of schoolboys would propose the first line, whereas the second choir with the entire congregation would respond. Here again, the physical collocation of the boys' choir would mirror

---

215 Cf. Bugenhagen 1985.
216 Blume 1975, p. 179; cf. Lejeune 2010, p. 8; Sfredda 2010, pp. 28–29 and 123.
217 A Burck 1568.
218 Lechner 1960.
219 Demantius 1631.
220 Manuscript at the Sächsische Landesbibliothek – Staats- und Universitätsbibliothek Dresden, Mus.Gri.11, RISM ID 211003879.
221 Cf. Blume 1975, pp. 180–183, to which this section is indebted; Lejeune 2010, p. 8.

their integration within the praying community: the Wittenberg Church Orders prescribe in fact that they should stand "in the middle of the church" and sing "with the congregation"[222]. Luther's version of the litanies is a case in point for demonstrating how he "reformed" church music: the traditional genre was maintained, but its content was modified (e. g. suppressing the typical focus on the intercession of the saints) and its form was also reinterpreted from a basically responsorial structure (which assigned to the congregation a secondary role) to an antiphonal shape[223]. When the German Litany was resorted to in moments of hardship or difficulty, in the role that had been of processions and votive worships in the Catholic Church, it was often performed in association with hymns such as *Wenn wir in höchsten Nöten sein* by Paul Eber[224].

It will come as no surprise to the reader who has followed me up to now that musical forms seemingly typical for the Catholic worship were maintained and actively practised in the early Lutheran liturgy, which is contrary to the commonly-held perception. This was the case, for example, of Latin monodic singing (i. e. what is imprecisely but concisely indicated as Gregorian chant).

Erasmus Alber explicitly stated the importance of aesthetic (or rather spiritual and symbolic) reasons for defending the use of Latin plainchant: "In churches where there are schoolboys and educated citizens, it is excellent to sing Latin chants alongside German hymns. It is not now possible to create such beautiful melodies that these Latin chants have. [...] And the Latin text sounds much better under the same notes than the German"[225].

An impressive example of such attention to the ancient liturgical heritage is represented by the *Psalmodia* (1553) by Lucas Lossius[226], where traditional plainchant melodies were adapted for Lutheran worship. The book, which resembles more closely Catholic Gregorian collections than Lutheran hymnbooks, exposes a liturgical paradox: both in repertoire choices and in their performance, certain members or local realities of the Lutheran Church were more conservative than their Catholic counterparts. As we will see in Chapters Eight and Nine[227], indeed, Catholics would undertake a heavy revision and modernisation of plainchant, whereas it would be preserved in a more faithful fashion by the Lutherans. Undoubtedly, however, collections such as Lossius' demonstrate once more that stereotypes regarding liturgical repertoire, musical practice in worship, congre-

---

**222** In Sehling 1955, vol. 1, p. 701 (Wittenberg 1533).
**223** Cf. Fisher 2015, p. 51.
**224** Cf. Leaver 2007, p. 196; Brown 2008, p. 244.
**225** Alber 1556, fol. Y2$^v$; English translation (from a later edition) in Leaver 2007, p. 212.
**226** Lossius 1553.
**227** See § 8.2.4., 8.4.2., 9.3.2.–4. etc.

gational participation and language of the liturgy need – at least – to be constantly qualified.

In Joachimsthal, for example, use of the Latin heritage of the Catholic Church was common in association with the educational context of the Latin school, where it permitted to establish meaningful theological connections with the ancient tradition of the Church[228] (especially when the plainchant hymns which were retained were those attributed to such Fathers of the Church as St Ambrose).

Curiously, moreover, the very "new" chorales by Luther started to be translated into Latin for use at school (for example, *Ein feste Burg ist unser Gott* became *Arx firma noster est Deus*); their Latin text could also be used for polyphonic compositions which often did not employ the melody associated with the German version as a *cantus firmus*.

Latin polyphonic music frequently did not show a clear confessional mark of belonging, and thus works originally conceived for worship in a particular Church (or by a composer belonging to it) could easily find their way into the liturgies of another confession; collections such as the *Officia paschalia de Resurrectione et Ascensione Domini*[229] and the *Vesperarum precum officia*[230], published in 1539 and 1540 respectively by Rhau, are the impressive testimonies of the vitality and importance of the Latin-texted polyphonic repertoire[231]. This was particularly true in some zones of Germany (e. g. north/east), were the influence of a humanist educational concept was more strongly felt, whereas in the centre vernacular singing had a clearer primacy[232].

## 5.3.6. Music at the borders of Lutheranism

Early Lutheranism was rather closely connected with German-speaking territories or minorities, whereas Calvinism would show from its beginnings a more international (or multilingual) vocation. Notwithstanding this, the influence of Lutheran practices extended well beyond confessional boundaries, and fostered – for example – reflections on music and worship among members of other con-

---

[228] Brown 2005, p. 60; cf. Rainoldi 2000, p. 318; Groote and Vendrix 2012, p. 181; Wetzel and Heitmeyer 2013, pp. 24–25.
[229] *Officia Paschalia* 1539.
[230] *Vesperarum precum* 1540.
[231] Cf. Blume 1975, pp. 104 and 113; Rees 2006, pp. 342–343; Brown 2008, p. 230; Sfredda 2010, p. 105.
[232] Kremer 2001, p. 126.

fessions or of groups which did not yet have a confessional identity and were simply trying and experiencing Evangelical forms of thought, prayer and worship[233].

Moreover, early Lutheranism did not present itself as an iron-cast set of beliefs and practices, and thus local variants could be significantly idiosyncratic: this happened, in particular, when the local pastor was a Reformer in his own right, or when the geographical distance from the centres of the Reformation prevented a very close contact with the Wittenberg tradition, or else when the use of languages or dialects different from Luther's German required substantial adaptations or translations.

For example, the hymn collections in Low German edited by Joachim Slüter (c.1490–1532) in Rostock[234] date back from the earliest years of the Reformation: though they are indebted to Luther's Wittenberg tradition, they possess a distinctive and individual quality as well, which would exert its influence on the northern countries of Denmark and Sweden as well as (via Coverdale) on the Anglican tradition to come[235]. Slüter, however, had a markedly different approach from Luther's, inasmuch as he advocated the outright abolition of Latin singing: it was eventually maintained, but only with the aim of benefitting the Latin school students[236].

The stance of Peder Palladius (1503–1560), the first Evangelical bishop of Zealand and a fundamental figure for the Danish Reformation, was very different. In 1537, together with Bugenhagen (and with the approval of both Luther and Melanchthon), he created a Danish and Norwegian Church Order, in which vernacular liturgies were indicated for the rural zones, whereas a combination of Latin and Danish was advocated for the urban churches. This coexistence of Latin and vernacular would characterise Danish worship: in 1569 Hans Thomissøn (1532–1573) issued *Den danske Psalmebog*[237], a hymnbook which is also the first example of music printing with movable type in Denmark, and which collects several Lutheran chorales translated into Danish and adapted to this language, together with Danish traditional folk songs. Four years later (1573), Niels Jesperssøn (1518–1587) edited a *Gradual* (*En Almindelig Sangbog*[238]), with the aim of preserving part of the traditional repertoire of the Catholic

---

[233] See Leaver 1991, p. 102. For an excursus of Lutheran hymnody in Masuria, see Narocka-Wysocka 2009.
[234] Slüter 1525 and 1531.
[235] Cf. Pettegree 2005, p. 47; White 2011, p. 22.
[236] Cf. Kremer 2001, p. 126.
[237] Thomissøn 1569.
[238] Jesperssøn 1573.

Church, though within the context of a renewed Evangelical worship. Jesperssøn thus continued in the wake of Palladius, fostering Latin liturgy but admitting vernacular hymns for the sake of the uneducated.

The importance of Latin worship for the Danish Church is indirectly shown by the fact that Lossius dedicated his *Psalmodia* (1553) to the King of Denmark; and the high consideration in which the liturgical books by Thomissøn and Jesperssøn were held is testified by their compulsoriness for all Danish churches (where they had to be chained to prevent stealing or vandalism). Danish worship was in turn very influential on the liturgical concept of Coverdale, who explicitly mentioned his indebtedness to what he had observed and heard there during his travels in northern Germany and Scandinavia[239] (cf. § 7.3.1.).

The tendency to favour the Latin plainchant tradition over chorales in the vernacular was present also in Sweden and Finland, where – in spite of a creative output of vernacular hymnody as well as translations from German originals – vernacular hymns were slow in gaining recognition and success. On the other hand, congregations seemingly joined in singing Gregorian melodies, some of which had been translated into Swedish or Finnish. However, even when hymns in Swedish did replace Latin Introits, Graduals and Communion antiphons, it is possible that the chorales were not sung by the entire congregation. The influence of Gregorian culture on these Scandinavian countries is also shown by the practice of alternating stanzas sung by men and by women in hymn singing[240].

## 5.4. Singing in Strasbourg

The Reformation in Strasbourg cannot be seen as a mere local variant of Luther's Wittenberg, since it definitely possessed qualities and features of its own, both from the liturgical and from the theological viewpoints. Indeed, the Strasbourg Church was not among those signing the Augsburg Confession in 1530 due to its stance on the Eucharist which the Lutherans saw as closer to Calvin's than to their own. Notwithstanding this, the Strasbourg Reformation actually had points in common and contacts with both the Lutheran and the Calvinist Church, and acted as a bridge between the two, especially as concerns the treatment and the role of church music[241]. It also showed features clearly different (and some-

---

239 Cf. Schousboe 1975, pp. 612–615, and Leaver 1991, p. 107.
240 Schousboe 1975, pp. 617–620; Hendrickson 2003, pp. 44–51.
241 Cf. Herl 2004, p. 97.

times outright opposed) to Zwingli's, though on some aspects of spirituality several common points can actually be found between Bucer and Zwingli. Thus, though the Strasbourg Reformation cannot be considered as an appendage of Luther's, I have decided to discuss it here so that it could constitute – here too – a bridge between Lutheranism and Calvinism.

Martin Bucer's view of music has already been discussed in Chapter Four (§ 4.3.4.), and so only a few of its most important features will be briefly recalled here. His perspective was rather unique, inasmuch as it had common elements with almost all other major Reformers, though he did not adhere totally to any of their positions.

Similar to Luther, Bucer was a convinced supporter of music, and believed very strongly in its value for spirituality and for the cohesion of a community. We have already seen (§ 4.3.4.) that he considered music to be one of the pillars of the Church's life, and in his Catechism (1543 version[242]) he explicitly stated that music was almost as crucial as communal worship for Christian life.

Similar to both Luther and Calvin, Bucer supported musical education for children: since their age is naturally inclined for music and singing, this good disposition can (and should) be exploited for conveying educational and religious messages to children. Bucer also deemed parents responsible for teaching sacred hymns and songs to their offspring[243], while choirs of schoolchildren were in charge of presenting the new songs to the congregation in turn[244].

Similar to Calvin, however, Bucer repeatedly stressed the importance of heartfelt participation, without which singing would become a sterile practice: he even stated that "it is a disgrace to God not to pray or sing with the heart"[245].

Moreover, Bucer countered Zwingli's opinions on music by pointing out the positive references to worship music in the Bible, as well as the practice of the ancient Church, affirming that "those who decry the use of song in the congregation of God know little either about the content of Scripture or about the practice of the first and apostolic churches and congregations, which always praised God with song"[246].

Notwithstanding this, Bucer's stance was one of the strictest among the early Reformers in envisaging the complete abolition of all secular music and its total replacement with religious music[247].

---

[242] *BDS* 6/3.
[243] Bucer 1541; cf. Honegger 1982, pp. 9–10.
[244] Cf. Trocmé Latter 2015, p. 154.
[245] *BDS* 1, p. 275; English translation in Garside 1979, p. 12.
[246] *BDS* 1, p. 276; English translation in Garside 1979, p. 12.
[247] *BDS* 7, pp. 578–579; cf. Garside 1979, pp. 11 and 25; Rainoldi 2000, p. 331.

Though this perspective may seem exceptionally severe to modern eyes, undeniably Bucer succeeded in fostering a high-quality church music and in conveying popular enthusiasm for singing in the field of religious music. The printing of secular songs in Strasbourg effectively diminished considerably in parallel with the publication of the first Strasbourg hymnbooks[248]. Several reports of the time attest to the beauty of Strasbourg liturgies and to the extent of congregational participation in singing; Strasbourg was also one of the few places where hymnals were certainly used by the laity in church. A *Cantor* was in charge of coordinating musical performances: here too Bucer insisted that he should be a man of faith and irreproachable morality, and not merely a good musician[249]. (Notwithstanding this, two of the most important Strasbourg musicians who actively cooperated with the Reformers underwent some troubles for improper moral conducts[250]).

### 5.4.1. The Strasbourg style

The Strasbourg community developed a distinctive liturgy and a particular musical style, which was to become very influential on subsequent attempts by later Reformers. The modifications to worship instituted by the Strasbourg Church were much more radical than those found in Luther's Wittenberg, inasmuch as from 1524 Latin was almost entirely replaced by the vernacular, in a liturgy increasingly focused on the Bible, and within which congregational singing was fostered. Bucer wrote in that same year: "We use in the congregation no hymn or prayer that is not drawn from Holy Scripture"[251]. From the very outset of the Strasbourg Reformation, hymns by Luther were included in virtually all forms of worship[252].

The process of translation and adaptation of the traditional Gregorian melodies to the Alsatian language created a unique style of German plainchant; Bucer aimed at establishing a new kind of communal singing grounded on Scripture. As a corollary of such liturgical reforms, complex polyphony was abolished and the need for an Evangelical style of church music was increasingly felt.

Whereas the 1524 liturgy still followed the schemes of traditional Catholic worship (albeit translated into the vernacular), after Bucer took the lead of the

---

248 Cf. Trocmé Latter 2015, p. 158.
249 Cf. Garside 1979, p. 13; Honegger 1982, p. 7; Herl 2004, pp. 99, 106 and 164.
250 Cf. Trocmé Latter 2015, pp. 31–32.
251 In Leaver 1991, p. 38.
252 Cf. Trocmé Latter 2015, pp. 36–37.

Evangelical Church in Strasbourg (1525) a new structure was devised, which was inspired by the Catholic Mass but which abandoned many non-Biblical elements found in the Catholic rite. As pointed out by Trocmé Latter, surviving evidence suggests that those in charge of implementing the Reformation in Strasbourg were less interested than Luther in creating a vernacular counterpart of the Latin Mass with the same solemn qualities: "The priority for Strasbourg in 1524 was to enable laypeople to understand the liturgy and participate in it through song"[253].

As stated by Bucer himself, no prayer or singing was admitted except those based on Biblical texts; all should be sung or spoken in the vernacular because the aim of liturgy was to improve the worshippers, who could not adhere properly to what was said unless they were able to understand it[254]. Different from Luther's model, the early liturgical forms in post-Reformation Strasbourg did not include the participation of choirs to sustain congregational singing[255].

The lively interest in liturgical matters and the concern they provoked in Strasbourg is mirrored by the quantity of publications on the topic (forty-four in less than forty years, from 1524 on).

The focus on the Word of God in Strasbourg worships was paralleled by a corresponding attention to the single individual's response to it, and to the resulting unity of the congregation in showing its adherence to the Word. Thus, the frequently reported beauty of Strasbourg worships was in fact the result of the deep spiritual involvement of a community which was striving to purify itself and to achieve a heartfelt communal prayer.

On the other hand, alongside plainchant and hymns, some space was reserved for spoken prayers, readings and sermons, in a higher percentage than in Lutheran worship: as Honegger suggests, this attention to the spoken word may be due to the stronger humanist influence on the Strasbourg Reformation in comparison with that of Wittenberg[256].

Hymnbooks with musical notation started to appear in Strasbourg very early, and showed from the very beginning the characteristic features and the typical appearance of Evangelical hymnals. They were intended for use both at home and in church, both privately and congregationally[257]. Particular mention is deserved for the zeal and entrepreneurship showed by Strasbourg printers, to

---

**253** Trocmé Latter 2015, p. 47.
**254** Bucer 1524, sig. I ii$^v$ in *BDS* 1; see Honegger 1982, p. 7.
**255** Cf. Trocmé Latter 2015, p. 43.
**256** Garside 1979, p. 11; Herl 2004, p. 97; Pettegree 2005, p. 47; Leaver 2006, p. 385; Sfredda 2010, p. 79.
**257** Cf. Trocmé Latter 2015, p. 127.

whose personal initiative the publication of the first service books and hymnals is at least partly due[258].

Along with new, original and local songs, these early Strasbourg hymnals included several Lutheran hymns, though with new melodies by Strasbourg composers – especially Matthias Greiter (c.1494–1550), who was *Cantor* at the Cathedral of St Thomas, and Wolfgang Dachstein (c.1487–1553), organist at the same church; eventually, in 1541, a hymnal prefaced by Bucer was issued[259].

Organ music was actually not enthusiastically supported in Strasbourg, at least in the early Reformation years; however, the very first known organ chorales were composed by a Strasbourg organist, Hans Kotter (c.1480–1541), who was active in Freiburg (Switzerland). Only in 1598 was organ music definitively admitted in Strasbourg, on the condition that it did not prevent the orderly performance of worship[260]. Indeed, the Strasbourg religious leaders managed, in time, to find a balanced middle-way between excessive austerity and purely outward splendour: rejecting the signs of what was deemed to be medieval "extravagance", they sought a soberer worship style "which involved spiritual values, and everyone's participation in the singing of hymns"[261]. At the same time, outward liturgical elements were curtailed (such as complex polyphonic and instrumental music) and control was exercised on forms of musicality and bodily expression which could potentially undermine the values of a Christian society.

A peculiarity of the early Strasbourg hymnals is the increasing quantity of metrical Psalms, and, actually, in his 1524 treatise[262], Bucer had established the primacy of psalmody over other forms of prayer and worship, advocating the use of vernacular metrical Psalms – a stance which would be extremely influential on Calvin's own liturgical concept. Bucer's wishes were soon realised when Jakob Dachser (d.1567) published in Strasbourg a complete Psalter with melodies in 1538[263].

Notwithstanding this, the repertoire of the Strasbourg hymnals was by no means limited to psalmody, and songs on lyrics of non-liturgical and non-Scriptural provenance were commonly found in the hymnbooks. For Trocmé Latter, the primary purpose of this inclusion was not rote learning, but "to encourage

---

258 Cf. Marcus 2001, pp. 731–732; Herl 2004, p. 97; Trocmé Latter 2015, p. 57.
259 Cf. Herl 2004, p. 98; Leaver 2006, p. 388; Sfredda 2010, p. 79.
260 Cf. Honegger 1982, pp. 7–8.
261 Trocmé Latter 2015, p. 251.
262 Bucer 1524.
263 Blume 1975, p. 133.

people to sing them, to absorb them, and to reflect on their relationship with their neighbours and with God"[264].

We will discuss in Chapter Six (and have already seen in Chapter Four[265]) the importance of Strasbourg's example for Calvin; it should be said, however, that the Strasbourg Reformers (Bucer, but also Peter Martyr Vermigli) were also fundamental for the English Reformation, to which they brought both their particular style of worship and an Evangelical theology inspired by Luther's views though not coincident with them[266]. Influences from Strasbourg hymnals are also found in the northern zones of Germany, in Scandinavia, and – later – in such important cities as Leipzig, Augsburg, Bonn and Magdeburg. As Trocmé Latter interestingly observes, while Wittenberg was primarily a university city, Strasbourg owed its international influence to its role as a haven for the refugees: thus, Wittenberg's influence on Evangelical musical practices throughout Europe was frequently mediated "by other centres of Protestantism that had adopted similar musical practices and were exposing them to religious refugees and other visitors. [...] One of the clearest demonstrations of this process was in Strasbourg's reach across Europe"[267].

## 5.5. The Bohemian Brethren

The history, theological views and worship style of the Bohemian Brethren are very special, and would deserve a more complete and detailed treatment than what is possible here: this brief presentation of their main features has been collocated at this point in consideration of the musical influence they had exerted on Luther's view and on the development of the Lutheran musical repertoire.

The *Unitas fratrum* ("Unity of Brethren"), as the Bohemian Brethren called themselves, was a component of the Hussite movement (i.e. those adhering to the theology of Jan Hus) which had settled since the second half of the fifteenth century in a wooded region in Bohemia.

After the death of their founder, the Brethren established congregational singing in the vernacular, fostering the composition of new Czech songs and attaching great importance to communal singing, which could also include polemical or belligerent features. The impressive force of their hymn-singing in hostile situations (such as the Hussite Revolution, 1419-c.1434) became both an example

---

264 Trocmé Latter 2015, p. 243.
265 See § 4.3.4., 4.3.5., 6.2.3., 6.3.1. etc.
266 Kim 2005, p. 74.
267 Trocmé Latter 2015, p. 239.

and a model for the Lutheran and (especially) for the Calvinist approach to communal singing[268].

Their hymns were strictly unaccompanied, monodic and in the vernacular[269] (and these qualities will be found in the Calvinist worship discussed in the next Chapter[270]); they regarded polyphonic music as a "frivolous assault on the ears [and] an empty pastime"[271]. On the other hand, Luther was indebted to the Hussite musical viewpoint as concerns their inclusion of secular tunes in their worship. In a later edition of their hymnbook (1575), this choice was explained and justified, by stating that "our singers took up [secular melodies] intentionally, in order that the people be attracted to a grasp of the truth more easily through the familiar sounds"[272].

Though the first Hussite songbooks were manuscript, from the very first years of the sixteenth century they published printed hymnals; however, since many of these were not under the direct control of their religious guides, in 1555 an official songbook was prepared by a commission (though the musical responsibility is probably to be ascribed mainly to a single individual, Jan Blahoslav, 1523–1571). This beautifully crafted hymnbook is indebted in turn to the Calvinist Psalter, though it includes an impressive number of hymns alongside the Psalms admitted by Calvin, reaching little less than 750 songs. This number is matched by the musical practice of the Brethren, who sang as many as thirty songs each day as part of their worship[273].

Striking as the Czech hymnals could be, however, the most important influence exerted by the Hussites over the music of other Reformation movements came from the publication of a German version of their hymns, translated, edited or newly written by Michael Weisse in 1531 as *Ein New Geseng Buchlen*[274], as well as of a later publication[275] by Johann Horn[276] (Jan Roh, c.1490–1547).

Weisse's hymnbook, with its more than 150 songs (though not all possess a melody of their own), is the most complete German songbook of the era, and is carefully organised according to the liturgical year: it was conceived essentially for use by the members of his community, although several songs from this rep-

---

268 Pettegree 2005, p. 53.
269 Blankenburg 1975, p. 599.
270 See § 6.3. and following.
271 In Abraham 1974, p. 32.
272 *Gesangbuch* 1575. English translation in Wagner Oettinger 2001, p. 5.
273 Cf. Blankenburg 1975, pp. 593–594 and 600; Settari 1994.
274 Weisse 1531.
275 Horn 1544.
276 Cf. Blume 1975, p. 19; Blankenburg 1975, p. 594.

ertoire later migrated to those of other confessions; however, it also shows influences from Walther's *Gesangk Buchleyn*. It includes many songs regarding Christ's Passion, as well as several hymns dedicated to various moments of daily life (in consideration of the omnipresence of hymn-singing in the Brethren's days). Moreover, the very familiarity of the Brethren with communal hymn-singing allowed Weisse to include more complex and less immediate songs than those chosen by Luther: whereas both Luther and Weisse had taken inspiration from the medieval repertoire (though, in Weisse's case, the choice of songs had been mediated by the Czech repertoire of the Brethren), Luther favoured strophic models, whereas Weisse included pieces derived from difficult plainchant originals[277].

When adopting pre-existing melodies, Weisse conformed to the Brethren tradition of not modifying them for textual reasons, whereas – as we have seen earlier in this Chapter: e.g. § 5.3.2.3. – Luther rarely left a melody untouched[278].

Though Luther was careful not to be associated too directly with the Hussite movement, his favourable statements regarding Hus and his spirituality are matched by his interest in the Hussite repertoire as well as in the principles behind their hymn singing as a means for enlivening the spiritual life of a community, as well as for transmitting teaching and building a sense of identity and belonging[279].

In this Chapter, we have considered in turn the various forms of Lutheran liturgical and extraliturgical music, in its origins, in the principles behind it, in the practice (from the ideal in the Reformers' vision until its criticalities and problematic aspects), and in the daily experience of those belonging to the Lutheran Church. Though reality might sometimes differ from the utopian descriptions of later historians or from the hopes of the leaders, generally speaking the Lutheran Church was among the richest in musical beauty, and among those which benefited most from musical practice. In turn, the history of music must acknowledge its indebtedness to Luther's vision, and to the splendid musical heritage his Church has produced in the sixteenth century and in more recent times.

---

277 Blankenburg 1975, p. 595.
278 Blankenburg 1975, p. 597; Gangwere 2004, pp. 292–293.
279 Cf. Marcus 2001, p. 730; Pettegree 2005, p. 54.

# Chapter 6 – Music in the Evangelical Churches: Calvin

> Among the other things which are proper
> for recreating man and giving him pleasure,
> Music is either the first, or one of the principal;
> and it is necessary for us to think that it is a gift
> of God deputed for that use[1].
>
> [Jean Calvin]

## 6.1. Introduction

The role of music within the worship of Bucer's Strasbourg, discussed in the preceding Chapter, was of enormous importance for the birth of the Calvinist tradition in Geneva and (later) on a global scale. This Chapter will focus on the role of metrical psalmody for the Reformed world: I will present the central figures who contributed (either with text or music) to the creation and affirmation of metrical psalmody in the vernacular, starting with Marot's first versifications, discussing the contributions of the Strasbourg musicians and theologians to the development of Calvinist psalmody, and I will also introduce the so-called Genevan Psalter in its textual and musical features, in its performance and in its tangible reality as represented by Calvinist songbooks.

The unprecedented success of the Genevan Psalter led to its early translations into several languages, although many of these versions were not conceived primarily or exclusively for use in the Reformed churches: in particular, I will examine Lobwasser's translation into German, and those appearing in the Netherlands, with a brief mention of the rather surprising translations into Latin of the Reformed Psalter. Discussion of English and Scottish metrical psalmody will be found in the next Chapter.

Similar to what happened in the Lutheran context, where (as seen in Chapter Five) vernacular songs gradually took hold of virtually all occasions of social musicianship, the Reformed psalmody's presence in the believers' lives went well beyond the official congregational worship: it was practised at home, at school and within the education of the young, and quickly became a mark of confes-

---

[1] Calvin 1543, "Epistre au lecteur", *OC* VI, pp. 169–170; English translation in Garside 1951, p. 570.

sional identity, both in times of peace and of war, during persecution and exile, but also as a means of evangelisation when the Reformed Church expanded its presence, even outside Europe.

Similar to Lutheran songs, moreover, the Genevan psalmody was seen as the starting point and the inspiration for polyphonic renditions by many composers such as Claude Goudimel (c.1514–1572), Paschal de L'Estocart (c.1538-a.1587), Le Jeune and several others; moreover, although psalmody in worship was strictly monodic and unaccompanied, there is a remarkable tradition of instrumental versions of Reformed Psalms for devotional use.

Calvinist psalmody also influenced, more or less directly, the composition of spiritual songs in the vernacular, which often surpassed confessional boundaries – though in some cases their text had to be modified to suit diverse theological and spiritual outlooks.

Finally, I will discuss the musical traditions of other Evangelical Churches, some of which were influenced by Calvin, whereas in other cases clearly stood in polemics with him: however, in several instances, their musical output had some relationship with the Reformed Psalter (in the form of cause, effect or influence), and thus can be presented here: in particular, we will examine the musical experience of the Church in Basel and the original Dutch psalmody of the so-called *Souterliedekens*.

## 6.2. The power of psalmody

At the very core of Calvinist spirituality and worship, Psalm-singing represented a mark of identity for Calvin's followers, as well as their only form of official communal musicianship, their privileged form of prayer, both in public and in private, a form of religious entertainment and consolation, a repository of spiritual strength for individuals on all occasions (both joyful and sad) of their lives, and the very shape of their relationship with God and with His Word, since – as Calvin stated, quoting St Augustine[2] – when a Christian prays with a Psalm, God is praised in His very words[3].

---

2 Cf. *Enarrationes in Psalmos* 144, I (*PL* 37, col. 1869).
3 *OC* VI, pp. 171–172; *OS* 2, p. 17. Cf. Ryden 1959, p. 109; McKee 2003, pp. 19–20 and 28–29; Sooy 2006, p. 8; Sfredda 2010, p. 8; Zim 2011, p. 150.

### 6.2.1. Metrical psalmody before Calvin

Before discussing the origins, features and uses of Calvin's Psalter, I should briefly outline some traits of metrical psalmody in the sixteenth century, as well as give a synthetic history of Clément Marot's contribution to this genre.

The Psalter had always been a form of prayer for the Church, and the Liturgy of the Hours (cf. § 5.3.1.2.) was mostly composed of Psalms. However, these were sung in Latin, and constituted one of the distinguishing marks of religious and monastic life. The number of Psalms contained in the eponymous book in the Bible (one-hundred-and-fifty), and the considerable length of some of them made it practically impossible for the illiterate to pray with the Psalter. Only a few Psalms (among which the penitential Psalms, such as the *Miserere*, Psalm 51 [50], or the *De profundis*, Psalm 130 [129]) were widely known and commonly used by lay persons: normally, a selection of the most famous Psalms was included in the Books of Hours for the literate laity.

The Latin version used was, normally, St Jerome's *Vulgate*, which often mirrored the literary beauty of the Psalms' poetry, but which obviously favoured literal fidelity over aesthetical considerations.

Within the framework of humanist thought, however, poems such as the Psalms seemed to require more literary polish; Christian humanists wished that the masterpieces of Biblical poetry would be put in a condition to compete with the refinement of classical metrics and prosody.

Obviously, moreover, a rhyming (or at least a rhythmically cadenced) poetry is easier to retain, and this was a benefit not just for the illiterate: a memorised repository of Biblical prayers for virtually all occasions of one's daily experience could sustain and comfort the faithful, and give a (spiritual) meaning to even the most distressing occasions of life.

There was, however, another side of the coin: as any translator of poetry knows well, the balance of fidelity and beauty is a delicate one. Or rather: what one gains in fidelity to the original text's literary beauty, one loses in fidelity to the original's meaning.

The more aesthetic and rhetoric devices and limitations translators apply to their poetic translation (such as, for instance, rhyme, metric, alliterations, onomatopoeias, allusions to the sounds of the original text etc.), the more difficult it will be to use the words which most faithfully mirror those of the original in the language of destination. Naturally, moreover, even without any particular literary aim, there is never a perfect correspondence of meaning between a word in one language and the "corresponding" word in another. It is, of course, a particular instance of the eternal problem of fidelity to the letter or to the spirit.

In the case of metrical psalmody, however, the problem becomes even thornier. Translations of the Bible have always been treated with the greatest care, because – for believers – the Bible is in itself the translation of God's Revelation to humankind in a human language. There is, therefore, a slight contradiction – or rather a problematic issue – at stake in the very choice of preparing (and of using in worship) a metrical Psalter: though, for instance, Calvin admitted only Psalms in his Church's worship precisely because they were the very Word of God, a "poetic" translation of the Psalter was likely to be considerably less faithful than a non-metrical one.

This was not just a theoretical problem: when undertaking a metrical translation of the Psalter, a poet was allowing himself or herself a greater degree of liberty towards the original than they would have had in a literal translation. Thus, they felt entitled to use this liberty even when a greater fidelity would actually have been possible, and to choose – among the available verbal possibilities – those which they liked the most, or mirrored their own viewpoint, or that of their confessional allegiance. While Luther's interpretations of the Psalms in his hymns did not conceal the process of "updating" and adaptation that the originals had undergone, Calvinists could be convinced that the Psalm they had memorised and sung so frequently were an exact transposition of the Word of God into music: and since sometimes the poet's hand is rather clearly discernible, the translator's influence on the Calvinist Biblical reception could be both strong and unnoticed at the same time.

In order to demonstrate this point, I will briefly compare here a "translation" with a metrical interpretation of the same Psalm fragment (Psalm 2:1–2). The translation of King James' Bible reads: "Why do the heathen rage, and the people imagine a vain thing? The kings of the earth set themselves, and the rulers take counsel together, against the Lord, and against his anointed".

The "Sternhold and Hopkins"[4] metrical translation (see § 7.3.2.–4.) reads: "Why did the Gentiles tumults raise? / What rage was in their brain? / Why did the Jewish people muse / seeing all is but vain? / The kings and rulers of the earth / conspire, and are all bent / Against the Lord, and Christ his Son, / whom he among us sent". The former version makes use of thirty-two words; the latter of forty-seven. The poetic version is much more emotional and polemical than the former (especially when read within a context of confessional opposition: note also the reference to the "Jewish people"); moreover, the "Sternhold and Hopkins" interprets in a Christian sense ("Christ his Son") the reference of the former to "his anointed".

---

4 Sternhold and Hopkins 1562, pp. 27–28.

As we will see, the Calvinist metrical translations were more literal than the "Sternhold and Hopkins", and in particular eschewed the anachronistic (though theologically sanctified by the typological reading which was traditional for the Church) substitution of such words as "anointed" or "son" with "Christ". Indeed, the Catholic polemicist Artus Désiré (c.1510–1579) found in Marot's Psalms just two passages which were, from his viewpoint, doctrinally objectionable; and, as Higman suggests[5], the Calvinist Psalms were generally acceptable by Christians of all denominations. It was rather within the "arguments" (i.e. the short summaries of the individual Psalms added to the Calvinist psalters) that less shareable opinions could be found. In particular, the typological readings identifying the "heathen" with the Catholic persecutors, while rarely stated in an explicit fashion, were nonetheless commonly acknowledged and clearly constituted a problem for readers of other allegiances. And, of course, the delicate balance of fidelity and literary beauty in Psalm paraphrases should constantly be considered, especially when dealing with Psalms having a highly polemical or belligerent content.

Even when the poets/translators were seriously concerned with literal fidelity, moreover, they rarely translated directly from the originals, and often used, as their primary source: 1) an existing translation into their own language; 2) the Latin *Vulgate*; 3) or the Greek translation of the Septuagint (we will discuss, for example, Coverdale's curious choice in the next Chapter[6]: see § 7.3.1.).

### 6.2.2. Marot: Psalter and verse

Though the Psalm versifications by Clément Marot would eventually play a crucial role in the birth and the success of both the Calvinist psalmody and of the Calvinist Church in general, they had not been conceived – as had, for example, Luther's hymns – for the needs of a particular Church or with pastoral purposes, but rather as a spiritual and artistic interpretation of the Bible within the context of the French Royal Court.

Marot's first Psalms, thus, were rather a literary effort prompted by religious feelings than a Bible translation proper; they originated within the literary culture of humanist France, and were the expression of an artistic and social elite with spiritual concerns. Marot was actually one of the most refined poets in France, and particularly well-established at the court of King Francis I, as

---

5 Higman 2004, esp. pp. 39–44.
6 Cf. Ferguson 2011, p. 139.

well as a *valet de chambre* to the King's sister, Marguerite of Navarre, Duchess of Alençon and Berry, who was an extremely cultivated, clever and also deeply spiritual woman.

Marot started to interpret the Biblical Psalms in French verses in 1532–3: though he had become interested in Evangelical ideas a few years earlier (1526), similar to many other contemporaneous literates and humanists, he was not yet explicitly committed to the Reformation at the time.

Marot's Psalms obtained an immediate and impressive success at court and amid the leading European nobility; among those who favourably received his verses (at that time or later) were the King himself, his sister, Emperor Charles V, Caterina de' Medici, the King's son who would access the throne as Henry II, and even Henry's mistress Diane de Poitiers (c.1499–1566). Diane, in particular, is said to have particularly appreciated Marot's setting of the penitential Psalm 130 [129]; and – reportedly – in 1542 Henry composed the music for Marot's Psalm 128 [127] during a period of infirmity[7]. Marot's verses could also be sung at court to pre-existing French tunes, though it is not known which melodies were used in that context. It is likely, however, that refined *chansons*, rather than folk songs, might have provided the melodies, given the links between the humanist atmosphere within which Marot was operating and the French *chanson* of that time.

In the meanwhile, Marot had been involved in activities associated with Reformation movements, and had been suspected of having had a hand in the "*Affaire des Placards*" (1534) during which Reformation ideas had penetrated to the very heart of the Catholic French monarchy (cf. § 1.6.3.). Marot thus left France for Italy, where he took refuge at the court of Ferrara, whose Duchess Renée (1510–1574), a great patroness of the arts in turn, was said to nourish Protestant ideas. Indeed, many members of the European Reform-minded elite had passed from her court, and several were there at that moment (possibly Calvin as well, though this is not certain: cf. § 10.6.4.).

What we do know is that Calvin appreciated Marot's Psalms, and selected some of them for his first (1539) anthology of Psalms and Canticles, published in Strasbourg (see § 6.2.3.). The next year (1540), Marot allegedly[8] sent thirty of his Psalms in manuscript to the Emperor: clearly, until then Marot's Psalms might have had an Evangelical flavour, but were not directly associated with the Reformations, nor were they banned or condemned as "heretical" works. In 1541, however, forty-nine of the Psalms in Marot's version were published

---

7 Cf. Quitslund 2008, p. 11.
8 On this topic, see Wursten 2008.

in Antwerp and in Paris, prefaced by Calvin himself, and in the following year (1542) Marot joined the Reformer in Geneva. Before his death in 1544, Marot was able to put into French verses only roughly a third of the Psalter (forty-nine Psalms, plus other Scriptural poems), and Calvin would have to find other poets for the remaining hundred Psalm paraphrases[9].

### 6.2.3. Preparing for the Psalter

As seen in Chapter One (§ 1.6.3.), after the publication in 1536 of the *Institutes of the Christian Religion*, Calvin was invited by Guillaume Farel to contribute to the Reformation in Geneva. In the *Institutes*, Calvin expressed his ideas about church music for the first time, and his cautions regarding music were such that the role which Calvinist psalmody with music would eventually assume for the Church in Geneva could not be foreseen at that time.

Calvin's early approach probably appealed to Farel, since the liturgy he had established in Geneva was as songless as Zwingli's in Zurich. However, the practical result of Farel's musical asceticism was seemingly not the "heartfelt" devotion which the abolition of music should have favoured; rather, Calvin's later mention of the "cold"[10] Genevan worship was likely to mirror the impression he received from this unmusical cult.

On the contrary, Calvin had witnessed a different situation in Basel, and had received reports (such as those by Gérard Roussel, c.1500-a.1550) about the ardour and zeal of the Strasbourg community, where, as we have seen in Chapter Five (§ 5.4.), music was an integral and important component of worship[11].

In 1537, Calvin proposed to the Council of Geneva his *Articles* for the reorganisation of the Church: in the thirteenth article, he envisaged a role for music (and particularly for Psalm-singing, though he did not specify either on which tunes they had to be sung, nor which texts had to be used) within the framework of a spiritual rejuvenation and a deep reform of Christian life. Although he was building upon the pre-existing rites established by Farel in Neuchâtel a few years before, Calvin's insertion of congregational psalmody in public worship represented an interesting novelty, especially within a situation marked by several liturgical and religious criticalities. (Interestingly, in Neuchâtel, Farel had coop-

---

[9] Cf. Reid 1971, pp. 40–41; Blankenburg 1975, pp. 518 and 531; Blume 1975, p. 133; Garside 1979, p. 15; Prescott 1991; Marcus 2001, p. 735; Pettegree 2005, pp. 55–56; Brooks 2006, pp. 176–177; Lindberg 2010, pp. 268–269; Groote and Vendrix 2012, p. 168.
[10] Cf. *OC* X$^1$, p. 12; *OS* 1, p. 375.
[11] Cf. *CoR* 1, No. 167, pp. 406–407; Garside 1979, pp. 6–7 and 13–14; cf. Higman 2000, p. 497.

erated with Matthieu Malingre [d.1572] and others who wrote poetry for music, though not intended for worship and to be sung on secular melodies. Such *chansons*, which were either spiritual or polemic, would later be gathered in an expanded collection which would become known as the *Chansonnier Huguenot*[12]).

Calvin regarded psalmody not as an expendable element of worship, but as a priority; however, the political and religious situation in Geneva prevented him from seeing his proposals fully enacted, and he had to leave the city. Another opportunity, however, was waiting for him: on Bucer's invitation, he arrived in Strasbourg where he was put in charge of the small congregation of the French exiles. In Strasbourg, he could observe directly the effects of nearly fifteen years of communal singing in the German-speaking congregation: it took him virtually no time (merely four months) to start working on a French psalmody for his own community. At this stage, the availability of ready-made French Psalms written by the best French poet of the era must have seemed providential to Calvin, and he turned to Marot's versions as the germinal nucleus of what would become the Genevan Psalter.

In 1539, the first fruits of Calvin's efforts would see the light of day: a short collection (*Aulcuns Pseaulmes et Cantiques mys en chant*) was published in Strasbourg, including a selection of Marot's metrical Psalms, together with six more Psalms Calvin had personally translated, as well as the Canticle of Simeon (excerpted from the Gospel of Luke, 2:29–32, and which the Catholic Church had usually sung at Compline), the Decalogue and the Creed.

It has been noted that at this stage Calvin was not restricting singing to Psalms[13]: the Decalogue is excerpted from the Pentateuch, Simeon's Canticle from the New Testament, and the Creed is not found in the Bible[14]. From this I would infer that the *Aulcuns Pseaulmes* were intended not only for worship, but rather as a reference book with the "essentials" for Christians, in Calvin's view. In the Psalms, a faithful could find a prayer for all occasions; the Ten Commandments summarised Christian ethics and morality and the Creed epitomised the main dogmas of the Christian faith (i.e. its doctrine). As for Simeon's Canticle, which may seem an odd choice among such "essentials" (the Lord's Prayer or the *Magnificat* would have been more obvious) I would suggest that Calvin was providing a prayer for dying people. Simeon's canticle is attributed in the Gospel to an old man who prays to God that he may "go in peace"; and the reader may remember that Luther's last words were interwoven in the *Verba Lutheri*

---

**12** Cf. Spelman 1948, p. 249; Garside 1979, pp. 7–8, 14–16; Higman 2000, p. 497.
**13** Joby 2005, pp. 93–94. Cf. also Pollmann 2006, p. 309.
**14** Cf. Garside 1979, p. 14; Honegger 1982, pp. 8–9; Higman 2000, p. 497; Sfredda 2010, p. 80.

*ultima* with a Latin Responsory which was usually sung by the Catholic Church at Compline, immediately before this very canticle. Compline, the last canonical Hour of the day, at the very border of night, was commonly seen as a symbol of (and the preparation for) a person's death: thus – in my opinion – Calvin's inclusion of the Canticle of Simeon among the *Aulcuns Pseaulmes* aimed at providing a prayer taken from the Gospel (and speaking of God's promise, symbolised by Christ's light) for the last moments of a faithful's earthly life[15].

Calvin took the tunes to which his own Psalm translations were set from those composed or arranged by Greiter and Dachstein for the German Strasbourg liturgy: in turn, some of them could originally have been popular (or even secular) melodies, though obviously the sources were not mentioned. If Calvin was aware of their secular origin, he clearly regarded this solution as provisional and not ideal: he intended to associate Psalm-singing with a particular musical style, characterised by sobriety, majesty and by a close interaction and reciprocal support between text and music. As regards Marot's Psalms, instead, they were accompanied by melodies whose origin is uncertain, though it is likely that the Strasbourg composers had at least contributed to arranging them – if not composed them from scratch[16].

## 6.3. The Genevan Psalter

After Calvin had been summoned back to Geneva, in 1541 he issued the first edition of the Genevan Church Orders; the following year (1542) his treatise entitled *La Forme des Prières et Chantz Ecclesiastiques* was published: its complete heading included a significant reference to the practice of the old Church. The book comprised an order of service as well as a second section consecrated to singing, which was clearly considered to be a form of prayer; here, a selection of thirty-five metrical Psalms with melodies was included. The importance of music within Calvin's thought was now signified by its insertion among the improvements in the education of children, both for their own sake and for the goal of teaching the new songs to the entire community[17].

At that moment, Marot was in Geneva: thus Calvin took advantage of his presence and in 1543 a new edition of the Psalter was issued, including forty-

---

15 See Chapter Five (§ 5.2.) for another instance exemplifying the connection between slumber and death, as well as their symbolic understanding within the framework of Compline.
16 Cf. Reid 1971, pp. 41–42; Blankenburg 1975, pp. 517, 519 and 522; Garside 1979, p. 15; Wagner Oettinger 2001, p. 207; Rees 2006, pp. 345–346; Weber 2008, p. 37.
17 Cf. Joby 2005, pp. 66–67; Sfredda 2010, pp. 80–81.

nine metrical Psalms (all of which were in Marot's verses) and Simeon's Canticle. Moreover, also the Psalms which had already been published in Calvin's previous collections were revised and retouched in order to mirror more effectively the theological and spiritual viewpoint of the Reformer. The 1543 edition also comprised a rewritten and substantially enlarged Preface by Calvin, which represents his most extensive writing on music: the importance of the Strasbourg experience on his approach to music is seen in his strong promotion of Psalm-singing, though the continuing presence of cautions and limitations is also noteworthy.

Briefly summarising what we have already seen in Chapter Four (§ 4.3.5. and following), we may recall the principal points of Calvin's 1543 Preface: a) a humanistically inspired belief in the joined power of text and music, and – as a corollary – the importance of vernacular worship; b) music should support and not hinder the text's intelligibility: thus, no polyphony or instruments are allowed in worship; c) the power of music must be controlled, lest it seduces and debauches humans; d) psalmody should satisfy the need for music and replace secular songs; e) it is also the most perfect form of prayer since it is divinely inspired[18].

Since the city of Geneva had become a favourite harbour for Evangelical refugees suffering persecution in their own countries, a fairly-large Italian-speaking community could be found there, under the spiritual leadership of Massimiliano Celso Martinengo (1515–1557). In 1554, a collection of twenty rhyming Psalms in Italian, including also Simeon's Canticle and the Commandments, all with their tunes, was printed for the exile community[19]. Further editions were issued in the following years, expanding the number of Psalms (sixty in the 1560 edition[20]) and religious songs (the Creed, the Lord's Prayer and a Gospel fragment were added), while Philibert Jambe-de-Fer (c.1515-c.1566) published, in the same year 1560, a collection of fifty polyphonic settings of these Italian Psalms.

At Marot's untimely death, Calvin turned to Théodore de Bèze for the remaining circa one hundred Psalm versifications – a task Bèze began in 1551 and completed by 1562. Once more, we must remember that these literary interpretations are "the result of the poet's imaginative engagement with the texts we find in Scripture"[21] and not a mere translation.

The literary style, however, fittingly represents what would later become known as "Calvinist aesthetics", marked by a simple and immediate vocabulary,

---

**18** Cf. Garside 1979, pp. 6–7; Higman 2000, pp. 497–499; Joby 2005, pp. 66–67; Sfredda 2010, p. 80.
**19** See Schreich-Stuppan 2009.
**20** *Sessanta Salmi* 1560.
**21** Joby 2005, p. 73.

avoidance of verbal excesses and formal sobriety – features which, though originating within this context, would later inspire texts for both Reformed polyphonic works for private use and Catholic versifications of the Psalms[22].

Parallel to the increase in number of the Psalms included in the successive editions, fitting melodies for each Psalm were provided. Debate is open as to the composers of these tunes, though among them were almost certainly the *chantres* Pierre Davantès (c.1525–1561), Guillaume Franc (c.1505-c.1571) and Loys Bourgeois (c.1510-c.1561), who was chapel master at St Peter's in Geneva and is the only named among the collaborating musicians. Though Calvin was not directly involved either as author of the texts or as composer of the tunes, his supervision of the entire project is indubitable.

Some Strasbourg tunes were maintained, though others migrated from one Psalm to another: for example, Greiter's melody which had originally been linked to Psalm 119 [118] and to Psalm 36 [35], was later combined to Bèze's versification of Psalm 68 [67], in an association which would eventually become one of the most successful in the entire Psalter. (Incidentally, this tune would also be adopted by the Lutheran Church, and immortalised by Johann Sebastian Bach [1685–1750] in the concluding Choir of Part I in his Matthew-Passion, *O Mensch, bewein dein Sünde groß*[23]).

The complete Psalter, including all 150 Psalms (plus two canticles), was eventually published in 1562; the figures involved in the Genevan Psalter project are immense and unprecedented. The edition resulted from the cooperation of thirty printers; some 27,000 copies were produced in Geneva, and within the first year as many as 35,000 copies had appeared in print[24].

### 6.3.1. Two Reformers, two attitudes

Though superficially there are common elements between the strategies adopted by Luther for the early hymnody of his Church and those found in the process originating the Genevan Psalter from the musical viewpoint, the differences are striking. True, some of the melodies associated with the Genevan Psalms were not composed *ex nihilo*: among their sources, there are common melodic formulae of the time, echoes of the medieval and Gregorian heritage, even sec-

---

22 Higman 2000, p. 500.
23 Honegger 1982, pp. 12–14.
24 Cf. Monter 1967, p. 181; Reid 1971, pp. 41–42; Hunter 1999, p. 278; Higman 2000, pp. 497–500; Joby 2005, pp. 66–67; Pettegree 2005, pp. 55–56; Brooks 2006, pp. 176–177; Lejeune 2010, p. 11; Lindberg 2010, pp. 268–269.

ular or popular tunes which had undergone a long process of purification via the Strasbourg sacred hymnody. We may recall that the musical sources of several of Luther's hymns were similar to these; moreover, if the Genevan tunes (when taken from pre-existing material) were reworked and adapted to suit the text's needs, it is also true that Luther rarely took a prior tune without retouching it for his chorales.

Notwithstanding this similarity, the overall approach of the two Reformers was radically different. In the case of several Lutheran chorales (particularly when contrafacture technique was applied), it is likely that the pre-existing melody, and sometimes even the text associated with it in the original model, provided the inspiration for the Lutheran chorale. In other words, although the theological view behind most of Lutheran chorales is clear and consistent, in many cases of contrafacture the existing song gave the input for the creation of the new one, as regards rhythmical structure, melody and overall form. In most cases of the Genevan Psalter, on the contrary, the creative priority is attributed to the verses, to which – sometimes – a pre-existing tune might be adapted.

Tunes coming from preceding traditions, thus, were used merely as the raw material for building the distinctive traits of the Genevan psalmody. As concerns the Gregorian inspiration, for example, the Latin Easter Sequence *Victimæ paschali laudes* is found in the *incipit* of Psalm 80 [79] (*O Pasteur d'Israel escoute*); we may recall that Luther's and Walther's adaptation of the same plainchant melody (*Christ lag in Todesbanden*) had been worked out from the German *Leise* for Easter *Christ ist erstanden*[25]. Among the many other melodic similarities, the *incipit* of *Puer natus est nobis* resembles those of the German *Freut euch, ihr lieben Christen all* as well as of Psalm 19 [18] from the Genevan Psalter (*Les cieulx en chascun lieu*); the beginning of Psalm 84 [83] (*O Dieu des armées combien*) mirrors a Latin trope (*Deus Pater Filium suum hodie misit in mundum*[26]).

The use of tunes coming from the medieval heritage of religious songs is also consistent with Calvin's repeated stress that his Church Orders were connected to the "ancient practice" of the Church; and the possible use of folk songs is congruous with the rather common habit among early Evangelical movements of singing Psalms on famous melodies known by all[27].

Notwithstanding this, Calvin and his co-operators clearly strove for a unique and distinctive musical style, which might have made use of pre-existing material, but which had digested and appropriated it so that the resulting unity in the

---

25 Cf. Blankenburg 1975, p. 522; Leaver 1991, pp. 48–49; Rees 2006, p. 344; Forney 2010, p. 107.
26 Cf. van Rensburg and Spies 2011, pp. 16 ff.
27 Cf. Pidoux 1962, vol. I, pp. 10 ff., and Pidoux 1955; Blankenburg 1975, p. 521.

collection's musical conception was much more evident than the provenance of its original sources.

The aesthetical principles governing its music mirrored closely (and were the consequence of) those behind its literary shape: simplicity and sobriety; humanistically-inspired and classicising metrical structures, based on two note-lengths only; strict adherence of both the melody and its rhythm to those of the classical prosody; and proper delivery of the text, which was set in a syllabic style.

In a simplistic though perhaps efficacious fashion, it can be said that Luther took what "the people" liked (either as pre-existing songs or as a stylistic model) and made use of it for religious purposes; whereas the underlying principle behind the Genevan Psalter seems the goal of shaping a *forma mentis*, of educating (in the broadest possible meaning of the term) those who would be constantly making use of it. Though the definitive shape of both Lutheran chorales and Genevan Psalms was given to them by educated and cultivated people, the creative interaction between the musical output of upper and lower social classes is more bidirectional in Lutheran hymnody, and quasi-unidirectional in Calvinist psalmody. In Luther's case, the vivacity and spontaneous expressivity of popular music were exploited for spiritual and educational aims, and sometimes even melodies coming from "cultivated" traditions (such as those of the plainchant heritage) were given a rhythmic and structural form mirroring that of folk music; in Calvin's case, a musical style was created which would be easy to learn, to appreciate and to cherish by people from all levels of society and education, but which had been basically designed "from above".

### 6.3.2. Metres and melodies

Even though the substantial revisions realised on the melodies of the Genevan Psalter or their new composition finally resulted in a peculiar, distinctive and unique melodic style, the most striking musical quality of the Psalter lay in its rhythmic shape. The relationship between text and music was actually played on the rhythmical level rather than on word-painting or the expression of single words. The verses' rhythm shaped that of music; however, as long as music adhered to the metrical scheme and did not contradict the intonation patterns of speech with its melodic shape, the tune could enjoy a certain degree of liberty and creative freedom.

Calvin's poets made use of an impressive variety of prosodic schemes (one-hundred-and-ten in total), all based on the juxtapositions of long and short syllables, and this multiplicity of verse patterns is faithfully mirrored by their musical settings.

Obviously, this variety represented a challenge for composers and the faithful alike: the former could use a single melody for different Psalms only in a very few cases (melodies and Psalms are in a relation of roughly four to five), and – consequently – the latter were exposed to a very high number of different songs, whose diversity could have prevented most congregations from learning them effectively.

The challenge was largely won, however, and Calvin's pedagogical insight played a fundamental role in this victory. Similar to Luther, he had the Psalms extensively taught to children, who in turn drew the entire congregation in communal singing.

The variety of tunes had two other fundamental consequences. From the one side, most of the later editions of the Genevan Psalter were going to include musical notation of the tunes, since it was impossible to memorise them unless one had already had a long familiarity with Calvinist worship. (Music was often printed in movable type, with characters made of a single note with its portion of stave). From the other, when this familiarity was reached and the Psalms memorised, texts and tunes became inseparable from each other. This strong identity of melody and Psalm increased dramatically the power of the music (even when it was wordless) to evoke a particular text, and would prove itself fundamental both when Psalms had to be used as a confessional flag (e.g. during persecution, or for propaganda) and in the spiritual life of the believers[28].

During public worship, the congregation was led by the *chantre* and sustained by the schoolchildren; moreover (as we have repeatedly seen), no other musical form except unaccompanied singing in unison was admitted: no instruments, no polyphony, no harmonisations. This performance style was seen by Calvin as symbolising the congregation's unity and the absence of any intermediation between their prayer or praise and the Lord who had inspired it. Of course, however, no prohibition was issued as to the use of instruments, polyphony and harmonisations in private contexts, for spiritual recreation and for artistic enjoyment: we will soon present some such realisations by Calvinist composers. So astonishing and widespread was the success of these harmonisations that in Paris, the Catholic Sorbonne demanded the Parliament to forbid their performance[29].

---

**28** Cf. Blankenburg 1975, pp. 522–523, pp. 529–531; Blume 1975, p. 133; Garside 1979, p. 28; Marcus 2001, p. 736; Pettegree 2005, pp. 58 and 61; Rees 2006, pp. 345–346.
**29** Cf. Spelman 1948, p. 250; Garside 1967, p. 162; Hunter 1999, p. 279; McKee 2003, pp. 19–20; Sooy 2006, p. 52; Lejeune 2010, p. 11; Sfredda 2010, pp. 80–83.

### 6.3.3. The Genevan Psalter outside Geneva

Actually, the success of the Genevan Psalter quickly reached an international and multilingual dimension, which was fundamental for the spread of Calvinism in general. That is, metrical psalmody (which at first had been all but a strictly Evangelical vogue) gradually started to be identified more and more strictly with the Reformed confession, and to act as a formidable means for its dissemination in the Netherlands, England, Scotland, Hungary, Poland, Bohemia, Italy, Germany, Switzerland etc.

We will now discuss only the most important among the early translations of the Genevan Psalter (which obviously were metrical in turn, and in the majority of cases made use of the Genevan tunes, though sometimes with indispensable alterations[30]).

I have mentioned, in passing (§ 5.3.2.6.), the German version by Lobwasser, which however was not the first German Psalter with music to appear: it had been predated by a collection including all Psalms by Burkhard Waldis (c.1490–1556), published in 1553[31] and harmonised by Johann Heugel (c.1510-c.1585). In 1569 another polyphonic Psalter[32], edited by Balthasar Bidenbach (1533–1578) and Osiander after the work of Sigmund Hemmel (c.1520–1565) was published in Tübingen: this so-called *Hemmel Psalter* has been defined by Leaver as "a Lutheran equivalent of the Genevan Psalter"[33].

There was seemingly no immediate need for yet another translation; however, during a journey in France, the Lutheran humanist and jurist Ambrosius Lobwasser came across the Genevan Psalter harmonised by Goudimel in the Jaqui edition (Goudimel 1556: see § 6.3.4. and 6.3.6.), and was fascinated by the literary results achieved by Marot and Bèze. It is therefore likely that his initiative to translate the Psalter into German so that it could be sung to the Genevan tunes was prompted at least partially by aesthetic and cultural reasons (both literary and musical), beside theological and spiritual motivations. His enterprise was ultimately very successful: the Lobwasser Psalter contributed to the spread of the Calvinist confession in Germany but was widely adopted also by members of and congregations belonging to other Churches, and would play a crucial role in the establishment of the *cantional* style for Lutheran chorales[34] (cf. § 5.3.2.6.).

---

30 Cf. Reid 1971, p. 42; Blankenburg 1975, p. 546; Rainoldi 2000, p. 324.
31 Waldis 1553.
32 Hemmel 1569.
33 Leaver 2004c, p. 151.
34 Cf. Blankenburg 1975, pp. 549–550; Blume 1975, pp. 48–50 and 134; Rainoldi 2000, p. 324; Marcus 2001, p. 736; Weber 2008, p. 186.

In the Netherlands, too, the presence of Reformed worship dealt a strong blow to the polyphonic tradition of which the Low Countries prided themselves. At first, Evangelical ideas had spread among the cultivated citizens, and several musicians had adhered to the Protestant confessions; as entire towns embraced the Reformed creed, however, the visual and aural symbols of Catholicism were eliminated from many churches. Though organ accompaniment to Psalm-singing was obviously out of the question within a Calvinist-inspired worship (as established by the 1574 Synod of Dordrecht), not all congregations were happy to suppress organ music: thus, in a few cities (among which Amsterdam), organ music was granted a space by the civil authorities, within public concerts framing the unaccompanied sung service. Thus, some of the greatest organists of the time, such as Peter Swybbertszoon (or Swibberts, c.1535–1573), his son Jan Pieterszoon Sweelinck (1562–1621) and Cornelis Schuyt (1557–1616) were granted the possibility of expressing their talent, albeit outside the official worship[35].

Vernacular psalmody in the Netherlands had not been introduced with Calvinism: in 1540 the first Dutch Psalter, called *Souter Liedekens* (or *souterliedekens*, i.e. Psalter songs), had been published[36], with metrical rhyming Psalms on pre-existing tunes (see § 6.5.); these songs, with the several polyphonic versions realised in the following years, started to be perceived as "Calvinist" only at a later stage, when the Reformation was gaining ground in the Netherlands. In the meanwhile, selections from the Psalter in Dutch translations suitable for singing at Calvinist services had been published in England for the Dutch exiles since 1551; in 1566, Jan Utenhove (c.1516–1566) completed the Dutch Psalter which would take his name, and in which tunes from the *souterliedekens* (some of which had a decidedly secular origin) appeared alongside those from Calvinist Geneva[37]. Though the Utenhove Psalter, well before its completion, was already in use by the Dutch exiles in England (and in Emden, during Queen Mary's rule in England), the Reformed Church in the Netherlands would eventually adopt the Genevan Psalter officially, as a replacement of the *souterliedekens*, only in 1568 (ratified in 1578) in a translation by Petrus Datheen (or Dathenus, c.1531–1588[38]). Datheen had sought to avoid the contaminations with the secular repertoire which could be found in Utenhove's Psalter, and to follow strictly the metrical pattern of the Genevan Psalter in his Dutch translation: the possibility of using the same melodies for Psalm-singing in French or in

---

35 Cf. Joby 2005, p. 96; Forney 2006, pp. 246, 263, 270; Lejeune 2010, p. 19; Sfredda 2010, p. 19.
36 *Souter Liedekens* 1540.
37 Utenhove 1566.
38 Datheen 1566.

Dutch was undoubtedly a great advantage of his version within a multilingual context such as that of the Low Countries.

Polyphonic sacred music for use outside worship continued to be practised and cherished in the Netherlands. Sweelinck himself was the appreciated composer of Latin-texted works as well as of polyphony on the tunes of the Genevan Psalter; Jean Louys (or Louis, c.1530–1563) had published in Antwerp (1554–5) five-part settings of *Pseaulmes de David* in French[39], based on both texts and melodies of the Genevan Psalter and with a polyphonic style much more complex than that of the *souterliedekens* settings. Among other polyphonic works on spiritual texts in Dutch for domestic use, we may mention a 1568 collection of songs by Noé Faignient (b.1540-b.1600) as well as another with works by various composers, including Jan Belle (fl. 1545–1566), Jacobus Clemens non Papa, Ludovicus Episcopius (c.1520–1595), and Gerardus van Turnhout (c.1520–1580), issued in 1572 by Phalèse[40].

Though this survey of translations and adaptations of the Genevan Psalter (or sometimes of the concept behind it) for use by Reformed Churches in Europe has been perforce cursory and summary (and has purposefully omitted discussion of Scottish psalmody, which will be treated in Chapter Seven: § 7.3.5. etc.), a short mention is due to the Latin versions of the Genevan Psalter. We have already mentioned that metrical versions of the Psalter were by no means confined to those necessary for the Calvinist worship, and that Psalm versifications might be the expression of the poets' personal devotion as well as of their literary ambitions. Within the humanist revival of poetry in Latin, unavoidably the turn for metrical versions of the Psalter in Latin would eventually come: one of the most interesting examples of such attempts is found in Buchanan's output. His *Paraphrasis Psalmorum poetica* (1566[41]) adopted Horatian verses and after its publication was set to music by Statius Olthof (1555–1629). This version would be consistently used, particularly in Lutheran Latin schools, but also – occasionally – in Lutheran worship, with a few of Buchanan and Olthof's Psalms making their way into Lutheran hymnbooks.

However, it is even more striking to consider that a Latin metrical version suitable for singing on the Genevan tunes and in four-part harmonisations was prepared by Andreas Spethe in 1596: though it was obviously intended

---

**39** Louis 1555.
**40** Faignient 1568 and *Een dvytsch* 1572. Cf. Reid 1971, pp. 47–48; Blankenburg 1975, pp. 565–566; Pettegree 2005, pp. 62–63; Forney 2006, pp. 253–254, 264, 266; Lejeune 2010, p. 19; Sfredda 2010, p. 97.
**41** Buchanan 1566.

for educational purposes, the itinerary leading to Latin poetry of tunes specifically conceived for vernacular singing is impressive[42].

Thus, alongside the support provided by Calvinist psalmody to the spread of the Reformation, and to the fundamental role it played in the spiritual lives of an enormous number of Reformed believers from Calvin's time to our own, the Genevan Psalter also had a great impact on artistic and literary creations in the sixteenth century and later. Many poets (not just among Calvinists) undertook their own Psalm versifications as a way of expressing their spirituality; the musical and literary style of the Genevan Psalter imposed itself as a valid alternative to the competing French models of the time; and its significance for the Lutheran *cantional* style (which would in turn become extremely influential on later composers of all confessions) is one of the key events in the development of sixteenth-century music[43].

### 6.3.4. Our daily Psalm

Though their musical and textual origins had been very different, both Lutheran hymns and Calvinist Psalms were quickly adopted outside official worship, soon becoming a way to praise and pray to God during work, leisure, suffering, travel, entertainment etc.; a mark of identity; a source of inspiration for composers; a medium for propagating faith and for strengthening a community in the face of adversities.

Of course, the primary context for Psalm singing was within official worship; and though it might seem that Calvinist psalmody was soberer and potentially less engaging than other kinds of worship, its results could be extremely touching and emotionally involving. We will see in Chapter Twelve (§ 12.3.3.) that the human and spiritual impression made by congregational Psalm-singing on those participating in it (in Strasbourg, but it is likely that this happened in Geneva as well) was so strong that the faithful could be moved to tears[44].

Indeed, in Reid's words, Calvinist psalmody "soon became woven into the fabric of sixteenth century Calvinist thought and life – one might even say it became part of the Calvinist mystique"[45]. As Calvin had advocated, Psalm-singing soon began to replace secular music also within the private contexts of music-making. (The substitution was not as complete as Calvin would have wished,

---

42 Cf. Blume 1975, pp. 145–146; Weber 2008, pp. 56–57; Porter 2009, p. 229.
43 Cf. Blume 1975, p. 135; Higman 2000, p. 500; Joby 2005, p. 83.
44 Cf. Erichson 1886, pp. 21–22.
45 Reid 1971, pp. 53–54.

rather obviously, and several reprimands of the Geneva Consistory attest to the fact that secular music and even dancing were alive and well even within the fortress of Calvinist morality[46]).

On the other hand, music could be employed in turn for the purpose of instilling the moral principles of the Reformed Church into the hearts of the faithful: a collection such as the *Chrestienne instruction touchant la pompe et excez des hommes desbordez et femmes dissolues* (1551) included – slightly ironically – a song on "the damnable and detestable vice of dancing"[47].

Through psalmody and through Calvin's catechism, Reformed theology entered into the very core of the faithful's lives, and was able to shape their idea of God, their way of relating with Him and their daily lives in a much more effective way than what printed books or sermons could have hoped to achieve[48]. Psalmody thus had a strong pedagogical and moralising function, and it was seen as a way to Christianly educate children, to transmit faith to them, and to mould the ethics of a Christian (i.e. Calvinist) society[49].

On the one hand, thus, parents were responsible for fostering Psalm-singing at home; on the other, children were the first beneficiaries of Psalm teaching, and were entrusted with the task of teaching to the entire congregation the tunes they had learnt. The importance of music teaching (though music was seen primarily as an educational instrument and not for its own sake) is shown by its weighty presence in the college students' timetable: four hours of music-learning weekly, plus singing as a part of daily prayers and public worship on Wednesdays and Sundays[50].

Outside liturgy, those possessing a sufficient degree of literacy and musicianship could venture into the numerous arrangements of Calvinist Psalms which started to appear. Composers responded favourably to Calvin's wish to create a repertoire of sacred music for private use, and an ever-increasing number of possibilities became quickly available. These included simple homorhythmic settings for more than one voice (from the *bicinia* and *tricinia* to four- and even five-part harmonisations), as well as more complex polyphonic forms, and even instrumental arrangements and possibilities to sing the Psalm tunes with instrumental accompaniment.

Undoubtedly, homorhythmic settings were among the favourite shapes of private Psalm-singing, since they did not require an extremely high level of mu-

---

46 Cf. Hughes 1966, p. 58; cf. *OC* X$^2$, No. 111, p. 192. See also § 4.2.3.2. etc.
47 *Chrestienne Instruction* 1551; see Pollmann 2006, p. 309; cf. also Louison Lassablière 2003.
48 Reid 1971, p. 37.
49 Rainoldi 2000, p. 323.
50 Hunter 1999, p. 279.

sical proficiency but were challenging enough to permit musical enjoyment at homes and with friends. Of course, both homorhythmic and polyphonic settings could be seen by some as exceeding the strict limits of unaccompanied monody; thus Goudimel felt the need for justifying his decision by stating: "We have added three parts to the Psalm tunes in this little book, not to be sung in church, but for rejoicing in God in the home. This should not be considered wrong, since the tune as it is used in the church remains intact, as if it appeared by itself"[51]. It is interesting to note that Goudimel hastened to say that he had left the church melody "intact": apparently, both the Psalm texts and their official melodies were seen as partaking of the status of divine Word, which could not be tampered with.

This form of musical and spiritual entertainment gained success in a short time: Frederick III (1515–1576), the Calvinist Elector Palatine of the Rhine, is reported to have sung Psalms with his spouse before and after meals; during official dinners, Psalms were played for his guests by his chapel of wind instruments[52]; in fact, arrangements of the Genevan tunes were also available for instruments (in particular the lute and similar) and were widely used by amateurs throughout Europe.

However, also at the other extreme of the social ladder comparable practices were common, as is witnessed by Catholic observers of the time. Claude Haton (c.1534-c.1605) stated that Huguenots sang Psalms "to move their hearts", and Michel de Castelnau (c.1520–1592) acknowledged the power of the "harmonious and delectable" Psalm-singing for encouraging and fostering the faithful to endure persecution[53]. In the seventeenth century, Antoine Godeau (1605–1672), the Bishop of Grasse, wrote:

> Those whose separation from the Church we deplore have rendered famous the version [of the Psalms] they use thanks to the agreeable melodies that learned musicians gave to them when they were composed. To know [the Psalms] by heart is, among them, like a mark of their communion, and – to our great shame – in the cities where they are most numerous, one can hear Psalms from the mouth of artisans, and, in the country, from those of labourers, whereas Catholic are either dumb or sing dishonest songs[54].

Godeau was right in acknowledging the power of Psalm-singing to create communion, a sense of identity, and a seal of unity within the congregation. Calvinist culture distinguished itself through Psalm-singing; identity and unity were

---

51 Goudimel 1565, "Preface"; English translation in Parrish 1986, p. 127.
52 Blankenburg 1975, p. 551.
53 Cf. Haton 1857, vol. I, p. 49; de Castelnau 1823, XXXIII, p. 55; Reid 1971, p. 44.
54 Godeau 1676, "Preface", my translation.

strictly dependent upon one another, and Calvinists felt entitled to claim the Psalms as their own particular spiritual property: as Reid states, "The Psalms were *their* songs which they sang as the elect people of God in a covenant relationship with Him"[55]. Psalm-singing accompanied particular moments in the lives of Calvinist communities: for example, they sang while building a new temple, which was both the physical locus of communal prayer (where psalmody would have resounded frequently) and the outward appearance of their identity, of their being a "Church"[56]. As a contemporaneous observer stated (1567),

> They worked so cheerfully that many a heart would have rejoiced and many would have been moved to pious tears, if only the doctrine had been sound. On working days they used, moreover, to teach one another the Psalms in the evening, which fostered a truly godly exhilaration, the more so because each understood the fine words of the holy Scriptures which he sang[57].

### 6.3.5. Musical flags

If this was the function of Psalm-singing during times of (relative) peace and serenity, their role in times of war, persecution, exile or martyrdom was perhaps even more essential. During conflicts, for example (as in the case of the French Wars of Religion, between 1562 and 1598), metrical Psalms became true battle-hymns for Huguenot armies[58]: in Reid's opinion, the pugnacious use of psalmody by Calvinists was not motivated by internal reasons (such as an inherently warlike content of the sung texts or of their music), but rather by the fact that their confession had to endure the longest, hardest and most prolonged situation of belligerency, during which they obviously turned to their musical flags as a mark of identity and a source of strength[59]. In fact, in 1558, King Henry II of France (who had appreciated Marot's metrical psalmody in his youth) had banned Psalm-singing precisely due to its confessional connotation – which might encourage riots and violence. He was accused by Calvinists, however, of having prohibited the holy songs of the Psalter while vacuous and lewd secular songs were permitted[60].

---

[55] Reid 1971, pp. 43–44.
[56] Van Orden 2000, p. 276. Cf. Garside 1979, p. 5; Pettegree 2005, p. 61; Lindberg 2010, pp. 268–269 and 283.
[57] Van Vaernewijck 1873, p. 109. English translation in http://bit.ly/2bvhPEA.
[58] Higman 2000, p. 499.
[59] Reid 1971, p. 36; cf. Lindberg 2010, pp. 260 and 283.
[60] Brooks 2006, p. 177.

The atmosphere of persecution surrounding the Calvinist faith, particularly after the execrable massacre of St Bartholomew (1572), discouraged some printers from continuing their otherwise successful publications of musical works based on the Genevan tunes[61]. However, this did not dissuade Calvinists from singing them, and in several cases the Calvinist martyrs reportedly went to the gallows with their Psalms on their lips (see § 10.3.3.[62]).

Another interesting instance in which metrical psalmody acted as a source of spiritual comfort, a flag of identity and a tool for spreading the Gospel was within missionary or extra-European contexts. Calvinists could find themselves in foreign lands for a number of reasons: during geographical explorations, commercial travels, missionary actions proper (in a later epoch) or when they had been expelled from a country and sought not only refuge, but rather the possibility of building a new life in a distant land[63].

In 1564, a colony of French Huguenots, led by René Goulaine de Laudonnière (c.1529–1574), fled to Florida for both religious and political reasons and established a settlement there (Fort Caroline, today Jacksonville). They were accompanied, of course, by their Psalters, and used them to thank God for their safe arrival in America, as Laudonnière reports:

> On the morrow about break of day, I commanded a trumpet to be sounded, that being assembled we might give God thanks for our favourable and happy arrival. There we sang a Psalm of thanksgiving unto God, beseeching him that it would please him of his grace to continue his accustomed goodness toward us his poor servants, and aide us in all our enterprises, that all might turn to his glory and the advancement of our King[64].

Native Americans were intrigued by the Europeans and by their ubiquitous Psalm-singing, and were happy to learn some Psalms by rote.

It did not take long, however, for Europeans to bring their religious and political conflicts into the New World, and soon the Huguenots came into battle with Spanish colonists, who eventually defeated them. When Jean Ribaut (1520–1565), one of the military leaders of the French, was captured and condemned to decapitation by the Spanish, he reportedly went to death singing "*Domine, memento mei*". Recounting this episode, Warner[65] notes that no Psalm begins with these words, and that perhaps Ribaut adapted the beginning of Psalm 132 [131] to his particular situation. However, what I personally find

---

61 Blankenburg 1975, p. 541.
62 Cf. Diefendorf 1991, p. 138; Pettegree 2005, pp. 62–63.
63 See, for example, Stevenson 1966; Stevenson 1973; Ogaspian 2004.
64 Quoted and translated into English in Hart 1898, vol. I, p. 114 (spelling modernised).
65 Warner 1984, p. 81.

more interesting, in this witness, is that either Ribaut sang in Latin, or the Spanish soldier telling the story was familiar enough with the Genevan Psalter to recognise which Psalm was sung and to report it in the form a Catholic would have normally used.

One of the Huguenots who managed to escape the massacre, Nicolas Le Challeux (d. after 1565), reported some other interesting facts regarding Psalm-singing in the New World. The natives who had enjoyed listening to Huguenot psalmody had retained their favourite tunes (in particular the penitential Psalm 130 [129], *Du fonds de ma pensee*, which was the French version of the *De profundis*, and Psalm 128 [127], *Bienheureux est quiconques sert à Dieu volontiers*), and they used to sing them as a way to recognise whether the Europeans they met were amicable French or hostile Spaniards[66].

Hundreds of miles to the north of Florida, in North Carolina, the natives were no less eager to hear Psalms: Thomas Harriot (1560–1621) reports that

> The Wiroans with whom we dwelt called Wingina [a Roanoke chieftain] and many of his people would be glad many times to be with us at prayers, and many times call upon us both in his own town, as also in others wither he sometimes accompanied us, to pray and sing Psalms; hoping thereby to be partaker of the same effects which we by that means also expected[67].

At the opposite coast of today's United States of America, Sir Francis Drake (c.1540–1596) landed with his companions in California in 1579. His chaplain, Francis Fletcher (c.1555-c.1619), reports on their arrival:

> Our general with his company in the presence of those strangers fell to prayers. [...] In the time of which prayers, singing of Psalms, and reading of certain chapters in the Bible, they sate very attentively; and observing the end of every pause, with one voice still cried, oh, greatly rejoicing in our exercises. Yea, they took such pleasure in our singing of Psalms, that whensoever they resorted to us, their first request was commonly this *Gnaah*, by which they intended that we should sing[68].

The meaning of this "*gnaah*" has been often discussed among scholars; at first (1942), Heizer had suggested that it might be a transcription of *koyah*, the natives' word for "singing". In a later study (1974), though, he recanted his identification as unlikely. However, since Kelsey demonstrates that some words which had originally been considered a part of native American languages were actually de-

---

66 Le Challeux 1579, p. 96; cf. Stevenson 1975, pp. 639–642; Warner 1984, p. 81.
67 Hariot 1590, p. 27; spelling modernised.
68 Vaux 1854, p. 124; spelling modernised.

formations of Spanish words, I would suggest that "*gnaah*" could be an Englishman's transcription of the natives' pronunciation of *cantar*, Spanish for singing[69].

After some pure Psalm-singing, however, Drake and his companions reportedly shifted to a less ascetic type of music: according to Francisco Gomez Rengifo (d. after 1580), their communal prayer was followed by singing to the accompaniment of viols[70].

Obviously, those reported here are merely examples chosen from many other possibilities; however, they help us to get a picture of how deeply psalmody was interwoven within the lives of those practising it (whether Huguenots or members of other Christian confessions particularly attached to Psalm-singing).

### 6.3.6. Psalms in polyphony

As we have repeatedly seen, Calvin's prescription to use exclusively unaccompanied monody in public worship did not prevent the Genevan tunes from becoming favourite sources of inspiration for composers, who exploited their fascinating melodies as well as their solid rhythmical structure. A particular feature of the Genevan tunes was that their use within musical works was not exclusive: on the one hand, it did not represent as clear a mark of confessional allegiance as was their monodic singing; on the other, it did not prevent composers from dedicating themselves to other types of music, either religious pieces for other confessions or secular works.

So (as we will discuss again in Chapter Eleven: § 11.6. and following, etc.), Catholics such as Clément Janequin, Jacob Arcadelt, Pierre Certon (a.1510–1572), Andreas Pevernage (c.1542–1591) and Lasso composed polyphonic works on the Genevan tunes; in the Protestant field, they inspired Richard Crassot (c.1530-a.1580), Philibert Jambe-de-Fer, who edited the first complete Huguenot Psalter (Lyon 1555) and others (some of whom will be briefly presented below). Several of them were very active in the production of spiritual and religious music for use by French Evangelicals in private contexts, both on Psalm texts and on devotional literature (and sometimes on religious *contrafacta* of secular songs). Obviously, the degree of complexity of this religious literature varied

---

[69] Cf. Heizer 1974, pp. 53–78 (for the 1942 study) and 23–24; Kelsey 1990, p. 459.
[70] Warner 1984, p. 89.

enormously: the more complex the polyphonic settings were, the less evident the confessional inspiration becomes[71].

Loys Bourgeois had been one of the musicians most directly involved in the creation of the Genevan Psalter, for which he had written several melodies, including some of those which would become very popular. In 1547 he issued in Lyon a collection of four-part homorhythmic harmonisations of fifty Psalms[72] (not all of which were among the 1542 Genevan tunes). The title under which he published his work is very meaningful, as it specifies the musical style (*contrepoint égal*) and the theological concept behind it (*consonnante au verbe*). His versions "resound with" the Word: their homorhythmic setting allows the Word to shine in its purity, unhindered by rich polyphony, and both music and the Word are "harmoniously" (i.e. "consonantly") merged with one another. Obviously, this approach was clearly humanistic, and paralleled the efforts of other French composers who created *chansons* in the strophic, syllabic and homorhythmic style called *vaudeville* or *voix-de-ville*, in contrast to the non-strophic and polyphonic *chanson*. Bourgeois' influence on later settings would be great: though obviously this style would become just one of the many possibilities for composers, undoubtedly it remained one of the favourites.

It is clear that, for him, if unaccompanied monody was not sufficient for satisfying all musical needs of his contemporaries, then (privately) they could sing in parts, but preferably in a style allowing the Word to be clearly perceived; his goal (consistent with Calvin's) was thus to provide a valid alternative to secular music. He stated his position very clearly in 1550, when he lamented the lascivious style of contemporaneous songs, against which he proposed "holy and divine things". He wrote: "Concerning texts, I mean those of a Psalm or Spiritual canticle, since it is not the duty of a Christian to sing other things. Music is given by God with no other goal than for rejoicing in Him"[73].

In 1565, Jean Servin (c.1529–1609) was the first to write three-part settings of the entire Psalter, dedicated them to a former Catholic Cardinal who had converted to Protestantism[74], and just before issuing his settings of Buchanan's Latin Psalms he published two volumes of collected spiritual *chansons*.

---

[71] Cf. Reid 1971, pp. 41–42; Blankenburg 1975, pp. 531–532 and 541; Higman 2000, pp. 499–500; Brooks 2006, pp. 177–178; Freedman 2006, pp. 169–170; Rees 2006, pp. 345–346; Porter 2009, p. 245; Lejeune 2010, p. 12.
[72] Bourgeois 1547.
[73] Bourgeois 1550, sig. D2, my translation. Cf. Reid 1971, pp. 41–42; Blankenburg 1975, pp. 532–533; Hunter 1999, p. 278; Brooks 2006, pp. 176–177; Freedman 2006, p. 169–170; Sfredda 2010, p. 95.
[74] Cf. Servin 1565, Servin 1579.

His Latin settings closely resemble Franco-Flemish motets, but with a clear emphasis on the meaning of the words: among the expressive resources he employs for this goal are homorhythmic passages and word-painting, such as – for example – in the musical depiction of instruments in Psalm 30 [29][75].

Another composer we have already seen at work was Claude Goudimel, who wrote Psalm settings at different stages of his career. In the 1550s, he had written complex polyphonic settings in a motet-like style on individual (though numerous) Psalms; in the following decade, he wrote two entire Psalter collections, the first of which (1564) is in a very simple homorhythmic fashion, with the Genevan Psalter tune either at the *superius* or at the *tenor*; the 1568 setting is less simple and indulges in some ornamentation[76].

The Psalm compositions by Paschal de l'Estocart (who was born in the same city as Calvin) similarly fluctuate between sobriety and daring polyphony: his complete versions of the Psalter were published in 1583 and dedicated to King Henry IV[77].

Though also Claude Le Jeune wrote two complete settings of the Psalter, respectively in three and four/five parts, which were posthumously published and would eventually be very successful in the following centuries, his most interesting contribution to the heritage of Psalm settings is the so-called *Dodecacorde*. Le Jeune was even more closely associated than his predecessors with a Christian humanist elite, by virtue of his cooperation with Antoine de Baïf (who, incidentally, wrote a Psalter in French rhymes in turn) and his *Académie de poésie et de musique*[78]. Baïf and Le Jeune experimented with the *vers mesurés à l'antique* (cf. § 2.4.5.), where musical rhythm is strictly determined by the metrical structure of quantitative prosody, and some of Le Jeune's Psalm settings will be numbered among the most daring musical experiments in the combination of verse and music[79].

The title of his fascinating collection of twelve Psalms, *Dodecacorde* (1598), immediately suggest references to Glarean's treatise; however, the true theoretical model for Le Jeune's work is Zarlino, since the modal ordering of the twelve Psalms follows Zarlino's plan and his definition of the modes. Le Jeune adopted both texts and melodies of the Genevan Psalter as the basis for his work (and this choice, coming from one who was Henry IV's court composer at the time of the Edict of Nantes, was highly meaningful): notwithstanding this, Le Jeune

---

75 Servin 1579, fol. K ij$^v$.
76 Spelman 1948, p. 250; Higman 2000, p. 499; Brooks 2006, pp. 177–178; Lejeune 2010, p. 12.
77 De L'Estocart 1583; cf. Higman 2000, pp. 499–500; Lejeune 2010, p. 13.
78 Cf. Blankenburg 1975, pp. 541–542; Higman 2000, p. 499.
79 Cf. Brooks 2006, p. 179; Rees 2006, pp. 345–346; Lejeune 2010, p. 13.

combines the strict self-imposed formal limitations with a great creative freedom in underpinning both meaning and affects of the text. His polyphonic and rhythmical textures are complex and demanding, and demonstrate that aesthetical refinement is not incompatible with Calvinist principles.

As we have seen was the case with other composers in Chapter Two (§ 2.3.2. etc.), Le Jeune's avant-garde experiments were always connected with a rediscovery of the past: for example, he employed the Lydian mode writing in F but omitting the B-flat, thus justifying a compositional experimental innovation with a reference to antiquity. If this was a typical procedure for humanistically-inspired composers, within the framework of the Evangelical Reformation it acquired a new meaning: as Freedman points out, Le Jeune's structural use of the twelve modes mirrors the Protestant attempts to give new meanings to tradition, and to "reform" the Church by going back to its Biblical and Patristic sources[80]. In the words of Catherine Randall, "The Calvinist ideology was to redetermine space by occupying it"[81].

Le Jeune's selection of the twelve Psalms which would constitute his *Dodecacorde* is refined and pondered: he deliberately chose texts whose "mood" or affect could be effectively mirrored by the affective value of the corresponding mode. For example, Zarlino's fifth mode was deemed to express a plaintive and doleful mood; and among the Genevan tunes written in this mode, Le Jeune selected the only one Psalm which was characterised by this same emotional value. Notwithstanding this, as Freedman demonstrates, "Le Jeune's treatment of Psalm 102 [...] is not simply a musical realisation of affective states already present in the original text and tune. It can also be seen as an attempt to assimilate the Genevan Psalter to a theoretical ideal"[82]. This ideal consisted in the aim of establishing a strong connection between the still young Calvinist tradition and the august modal system of antiquity as it was presented by a prominent Catholic theorist. It also reconciles classical (and pagan) traditions with Christian poetry, through music; and it represents a musical parallel to an interior path of self-discovery and introspection led by Biblical meditation[83].

In the seventeenth century, almost twenty years after Le Jeune's death, and within a complex political and religious situation, his *Dodecacorde* was re-issued by Pierre Ballard (c.1580–1639) in a twofold version: from the one side, the original setting; from the other, a *contrafactum* where the original Psalm

---

[80] Freedman 2003, p. 297.
[81] Randall 1999, p. 31.
[82] Freedman 2003, p. 302. This section is indebted to Freedman 2003 and to His 1999.
[83] Cf. His 1999, pp. 191 and 205; Freedman 2003, pp. 297–308; Brooks 2006, p. 179; Rees 2006, pp. 345–346.

texts were replaced with devotional lyrics. Paradoxically, the Psalter's words (sacred for all Christians) were deemed to be non-recommendable by the publisher, whose "devotional" version was aimed at attracting Catholic customers who would have feared too close an association with the Calvinist Psalter. (Obviously, the Psalm tunes, which were integral to Le Jeune's compositional structure, could not be erased in the same way as the compromising texts).

The result, as could be expected, was not really convincing from the artistic viewpoint (one wonders what Le Jeune would have thought of it, in consideration of his attention to the text/music relationship); instead, a broader and multi-confessional audience continued to enjoy for a long time another collection by Le Jeune[84], based on the devotional poetry of the *Octonaires de la vanité du monde* (set to music also by L'Estocart[85]). Though these pious lyrics were no less Calvinist than the Genevan Psalter, they were less identifiable as such, and could appeal to Christians of all confessions for their spiritual exercises in music; moreover, since the music they were set to had been conceived purposefully on their words, the result was obviously more convincing and successful[86]. As Freedman summarises, in the *Octonaires* "modality [...] is not a means to 'express' an emotional condition, but is instead a constellation of ideal forms against which a process of spiritual reflection is staged"[87].

### 6.3.7. Instruments and house devotion

We have already seen that Calvin's opposition to instrumental music and accompaniment in church did not apply to music outside worship: thus, Reformed organists could perform in church concerts in the Netherlands, and Psalm arrangements for instruments were performed by musically educated burghers and by the court chapels of important rulers[88].

More unusual and unexpected (and clearly pointing towards practices which would establish themselves in the seventeenth century) is a report about what happened in Gdańsk, where the Calvinist faction gained momentum around the last decade of the century, with the usual accompaniment of liturgical reforms (iconoclasm, abolition of outward signs, ceremonies and polyphony). However, evidently unaccompanied monody was too harsh an imposition for

---

[84] Le Jeune 1606.
[85] De L'Estocart 1582.
[86] Cf. His 1999, pp. 191, 104, 206–207.
[87] Freedman 2003, p. 306.
[88] Cf. Blankenburg 1975, pp. 537 and 551; Warner 1984, p. 89; Rees 2006, pp. 345–346.

the congregation: they obtained to have the Psalter sung "in four parts in the choir, and the organ was played with them"[89], in what is the earliest known example of organ accompaniment to Reformed singing.

In Geneva, however, the organs had been frequently destroyed and their pipes melted; moreover, as Latour demonstrates, private instrumental music could be the object of official censorship whenever its association with dancing was possible. The performance of Psalm transcriptions, particularly for plucked-string keyboard instruments, was instead considered as a licit activity[90].

We have already seen that the religious repertoire for private use flourished – perhaps precisely as a consequence of the limitations imposed on polyphony and instrumental music in church. Psalm settings in a variety of forms could be composed, and several of them differed only in the origin of their texts from the *chansons spirituelles*. As we have seen in the case of the *Octonaires*, and rather ironically, lyrics written by contemporaneous poets belonging to a particular confession were more easily adopted as recreational pieces by members of other Churches than were the Biblical words of the Psalter.

Spiritual songs could be sometimes very close in language and style to secular *chansons*; their lyrics could be adapted and translated from Latin hymns, or be the original artwork of religious poets such as the Catholic Guy du Faur de Pibrac (1529–1584) or the Calvinists Eustorg de Beaulieu (c.1495–1552) and Antoine de la Roche Chandieu (1534–1591). If such texts, by Catholic and Evangelical poets, were set to music by Catholic and Evangelical composers alike, similarly motet compositions could migrate to the private sphere and be sung and appreciated by educated burghers as well as by the nobility.

A text by the Huguenot Guillaume Guéroult (c.1507–1569), *Susanne ung jour*, appears to have been particularly favoured by composers of all confessional allegiances, among whom was Orlando di Lasso (1560); frequently, the *tenor* of such settings is quoted from the first known version of this spiritual song, which was published in 1548 by the composer Didier Lupi (c.1520-a.1559). On several occasions, collections of spiritual songs could be assembled by publishers, including works on religious texts by several composers, often regardless of their confessional allegiance: one such example is the *Jardin musical*, a series of four volumes including a total of nearly a hundred works by some of the leading composers of the time, published in Antwerp by Hans de Laet (1556[91]).

---

89 Cf. Hartknoch 1686, p. 760; quoted and translated into English in Herl 2004, p. 132.
90 Cf. Latour 2015, pp. 24 ff.
91 *Jardin musical* 1556; cf. Brooks 2006, p. 178; Forney 2006, pp. 252–254; Porter 2009, p. 233.

In other cases, spiritual *chansons* did not simply share vocabulary and style with secular songs, but actually were religious *contrafacta* of existing works: for example, the Reformed theologians and editors Simon Goulart (1543–1628) and Jean Pasquier (fl. 1570s) systematically revised the contemporaneous repertoire of secular songs transforming several of them into devotional works. Goulart's work was not merely an artistic accomplishment, but had the religious and social aim of building a frame for Protestant piety within the context of a mostly Catholic society. As in the case of Le Jeune's *Dodecacorde* (cf. § 6.3.6.), a parallel can be drawn between the aesthetic and spiritual endorsement of closed and contained spaces emphasised by the Reformed architecture, the devotional works using architectural similes, and the focus on devotional music for private worship[92].

In 1597, Goulart issued a collection of fifty French Psalms modelled on five-part polyphonic works by Lasso[93], plus twenty other polyphonic Psalms adapted from contemporaneous European composers. The arranger's skill is shown by his ability to convincingly transform vocal works originally written on texts in French, German, Italian or Latin into French psalmody; indeed, as shown by Freedman, the language of Psalms seems to have become so familiar to Reformed lyricists that several of their most daring (and artistically best) *contrafacta* acquire an unexpected fluency and naturalness[94].

Alongside paraphrases of and "Christian corrections" on works by Orlando di Lasso, other *contrafacta* were realised on compositions by Antoine de Bertrand (c.1530-c.1581), Guillaume Boni (c.1530-c.1594) and many others. Among such collections are the *Recueil du mélange d'Orlande*[95], the *Mellange d'Orlande de Lassus*, on lyrics by Jean Pasquier[96] and the *Thrésor de musique d'Orlande*[97]. In several instances, contrafacture was easily done, for example replacing the word "*amour*" with "*Dieu*" or "*Seigneur*" (as happened, for example, with the famous song *Tant que vivray* by Claudin de Sermisy[98]).

The phenomenon of "spiritualisation", or religious contrafacture, could also apply to songs on traditional and popular tunes: a collection such as the *Veel-*

---

[92] Cf. Freedman 2000.
[93] Lasso 1597.
[94] Cf. Freedman 2011, p. 37.
[95] Lasso 1570.
[96] Lasso 1575.
[97] Lasso 1576.
[98] Cf. Blankenburg 1975, p. 544; Brooks 2006, p. 178; Freedman 2006, pp. 169–170; van Orden 2006, p. 210.

*derhande Liedekens* (1558[99]) could coexist – for private devotion – with the Genevan Psalms and be used and appreciated by the Dutch Reformed though it would not be employed in official worship[100].

As we can easily note, therefore, spiritual contrafacture of secular models could be admitted or not in worship, but certainly was practised at least within the private sphere by poets and musicians alike from practically all confessional backgrounds.

## 6.4. Constance and Basel

Towards the end of this Chapter, and analogously to what has been done in Chapter Five with Strasbourg (§ 5.4.), a few words will be dedicated to the musical situation of German Switzerland and Constance. Geographically, this region was at the very heart of the Reformation movements, undergoing influences from Strasbourg and Geneva, and nourishing at its core such different realities as Zwingli's Zurich or Oecolampadius' Basel.

When congregational singing was allowed in church, its repertoire was not local or national, but rather drew upon those of the surrounding German-speaking territories. In Bern, church singing was admitted in 1558 (though it was only in 1574 that the Church officials explicitly authorised it); Zurich was the last city to reintroduce church singing, on the eve of the seventeenth century.

One of the most interesting situations is found in Constance, whose Reformer Johannes Zwick (c.1496–1542), though theologically indebted to Zwingli, adopted however a very different stance from the Zurich reformer as regards church music. In fact, Zwick advocated congregational singing in church, giving primacy to Psalm-singing but permitting also other musical possibilities. His Preface to what would become known as the "Constance hymnbook" counters Zwingli's positions with sound theological and pastoral arguments, which would be quoted by those advocating church singing against Zwingli's prohibitions in northern Switzerland and eventually promoted the reintroduction of music in Zurich[101].

The publication of Swiss Evangelical hymnals in German was initiated with a songbook issued in Sankt Gallen in 1533 (under the supervision of Dominik Zili [1494–1571]), and immediately afterwards came the first "Constance" hymnbook

---

[99] *Veelderhande liedekens* 1558.
[100] Pollmann 2006, p. 306.
[101] Cf. Gérold 1954, p. 438; Blankenburg 1975, pp. 513–515.

(1533–4), which actually was commissioned by the city of Constance but published (ironically) in Zurich by Christoph Froschauer (c.1490–1564), and edited by Zwick himself in cooperation with Ambrosius Blarer (1492–1564); the influence of Bucer's Strasbourg is clearly discernible in the theological approach behind it. Its success was immediate: a second edition was issued by 1537, and the 1540 edition (*Nüw gsangbuechle von vil schönen Psalmen und geistlichen Liedern*[102]) would become known as "the" Constance songbook.

Similar to the hymnal published in Strasbourg the following year (1541[103]), the Constance songbook (with texts in the local dialect) drew from many sources and confessional provenances (only the Bohemian Brethren tradition was excluded), and included, among others, songs by the Strasbourg composers Greiter and Dachstein[104].

In Switzerland, as in many other German-speaking regions, a widespread tradition of religious ensemble music within private contexts (the *Geistliche Abendmusiken*) flourished and fostered a rich experience of musicianship and spirituality[105].

The case of Basel was rather unique. The Evangelical Reformation was officially brought to the city in 1529 by Johannes Oecolampadius under the influence of the Wittenberg Reformers and of Erasmus. Nevertheless, congregational singing in the vernacular had been in use there for three years already, fostered by Oecolampadius, who was adverse to Catholic ceremonies but favourable to congregational singing since his contacts with Wittenberg had persuaded him of its importance, and notwithstanding the Zwinglian orientation of his theology. In fact, Basel can be considered to be the first Swiss Reformed city to admit congregational singing within worship, and to foresee its importance as a means to convey both religious principles and piety, particularly to the illiterate. Oecolampadius' stance corresponded to those of the Wittenberg and Strasbourg Reformers also as regards the importance of musical education for children.

We have already seen (§ 4.3.2.) that even contemporaneous observers were aware of Basel's deviation from pure Zwinglian doctrine as regards Psalm-singing; moreover, this was practised within the framework of a worship resembling the Catholic Mass (to which, of course, Zwingli was unfavourable).

The Basel congregation made use at first of the Strasbourg hymnal, and later of the "Constance" songbook, which in its 1559 edition comprised more than two hundred tunes (including all Psalms and nearly a hundred other songs, most of

---

[102] Zwick 1540. See Ameln 1955.
[103] Bucer 1541.
[104] Cf. Marcus 2001, pp. 731–732; Gangwere 2004, p. 291; Sfredda 2010, p. 79.
[105] Cf. Koenigsberger 1986, p. 195.

which had their own tunes), and was one of the most comprehensive hymnals of the era.

Two facts, however, were soon to modify religious and musical life in Basel (its "second Reformation"): Basel's new preacher from 1552, Simon Sulzer (1508–1585), was on friendly terms with some of the major Lutheran theologians of the time, and it was under his leadership that organ music (which had been abolished by the Reformation, though the organ had not been destroyed) was reinstated into use as early as 1561; even more strikingly, the appointed organist was the Catholic Gregor Meyer (c.1510–1576) from Solothurn, a friend of Glarean.

The city also harboured many Huguenot fugitives after the massacre of St Bartholomew, thus making the need for a Reformed Psalter more pressing: Basel eventually adopted that by Lobwasser. Goudimel's settings were later adapted to Lobwasser's lyrics by Samuel Mareschall (1554–1640), a musician from Tournai, who also expanded the Basel repertoire to include hymns (harmonised by himself) from a variety of confessional provenances[106]. His harmonisations are in the cantional style, which he introduced into Switzerland, and were likely intended for the Cathedral choir, with the congregation supplementing it in singing the chorale melody[107].

## 6.5. The *Souterliedekens*

As mentioned earlier, I have decided to insert here a short discussion of the *souterliedekens* tradition in consideration of their connections with sung psalmody and of the interaction between this repertoire and some Reformed Churches outside Geneva, though it must be emphasised that the *souterliedekens* ("Psalter songs") were not translations of the Genevan Psalter.

Published in 1540 by Symon Cock[108] (c.1505-a.1548), and possibly edited by the Utrecht nobleman Willem van Nyewelt (or Nijevelt, d.1543), the hymnal enjoyed a widespread and immediate popularity, with more than thirty editions before 1613, nine of which were printed by Cock; beside the complete Psalter with melodies, it included hymns such as the *Te Deum* and canticles, making a total of 159 texts. The tunes, as seen above (§ 6.3.3.), were often taken from the secular repertoire, comprising folk songs alongside dance tunes and *chansons*, possibly in connection with the efforts of Christian humanism to replace secular with spi-

---

[106] Cf. Mareschall 1606.
[107] Cf. Blankenburg 1975, p. 516; Blume 1975, p. 146; Weber 2008, p. 39; and particularly Marcus 2001, to which this section is indebted.
[108] *Souter liedekens* 1540.

ritual music. Thus, this hymnbook was not conceived exclusively for Evangelicals, since religious vernacular singing was customary in the Flanders from the fifteenth century (also thanks to the pious practices of the Beguines). It is noteworthy, moreover, that the *souterliedekens* were never condemned by the Catholic Church, and had been published with the imperial *imprimatur*; furthermore, their texts were translated from the Vulgate and not from the Hebraic original.

The strophic settings are often based on contrafacture, with a very unprejudiced source selection: for example, Psalm 74 [73] (*Waer om wilt ghi ons verlaten?*) was set to a secular tune, *Den lustelijcken Mey*, whose content can be inferred from the inclusion of its score in a painting with rather secular overtones by Maarten van Heemskerck (1498–1574), depicting the Muses with Apollo (c.1555). Similarly, a tune whose traditional text tells the story of three poor musicians in winter (*Het ghinghen drie ghespeelkens*) was associated with some of a Christian's basic prayers.

Harmonisation and polyphony on the tunes of the *souterliedekens* were realised by several composers, some of whom were among the leading musicians of the time: in 1556–7 Jacobus Clemens non Papa issued an arrangement of one-hundred-and-forty pieces from the *souterliedekens* in three parts, in syllabic style with imitative passages. The last of his arrangement collections, published by Susato in 1557[109], includes compositions on texts which are not found in the Biblical Psalter, such as the Creed, the Lord's Prayer or the *Ave Maria*. Clemens' example was followed by his disciple Gerardus Mes (fl. around 1561, the year when his arrangements were issued by Susato[110]) and Cornelis Boskoop from Delft (c.1525–1573), who published fifty four-part Psalm arrangements in Düsseldorf (1568[111]). The simple style of these works seems apparently more suited for domestic devotion.

Though the *souterliedekens* had not been linked to the Reformation from the outset, their adoption by Reformed Netherlanders (both in their homeland and abroad) gradually established this association, and made it increasingly inadvisable for Catholics to sing them. Eventually, as we have seen before (§ 6.3.3.), Dutch refugees in England first, and Evangelicals in the homeland later,

---

**109** Clemens 1557.
**110** Mes 1561.
**111** Boskoop 1568.

would favour translations from the Genevan Psalter (Utenhove and Datheen) for their communal worship[112].

In this Chapter, we have observed the genesis, development and spread of Calvinist psalmody and of the spirituality it promoted and conveyed. Though the musical repertoire and its performance practice, as fostered by Calvin, were limited in comparison with the forms admitted in Lutheran and Catholic worship, it became fundamental not only for the Reformed Church, but also for the overall development of musical language in Europe. The close association between the rhythms of verse and music favoured the exportation of a humanistically-inspired style from the upper social classes to popular culture; the Reformed contribution to the spread of the cantional style would prove itself extremely influential on the later evolution of harmonic thought; and the close identification between the Genevan tunes and the Reformed Church was one of the most striking examples of musical appropriation on the part of a social or religious group in the sixteenth century.

---

[112] Reid 1971, pp. 47–48; Reese 1959, p. 355; Blankenburg 1975, pp. 565–566; Blume 1975, p. 133; Atlas 1998, p. 525; Gangwere 2004, p. 293; Forney 2006, pp. 253–254 and 264; Rees 2006, p. 344; Forney 2010, pp. 94–99 and 107.

# Chapter 7 – Music in the Church of England

> If it were not the Queens' majesty did favour that excellent Science [of music], singing men and choristers might go a-begging[1].
>
> [John Bossewell, 1572]

## 7.1. Introduction

The uniqueness of the English Reformation, whose theological, social and historical features are neatly distinguished from most Continental patterns, is mirrored by its musical tradition, which is unique from the one side, but conflates many influences from Lutheran, Calvinist, Strasbourger and Catholic backgrounds from the other.

The musical heritage of the English Reformation builds upon a pre-existing tradition of Cathedral singing, of idiosyncratic liturgies, of monastic practice and of rural musicianship: although several of these elements were deeply undermined and scattered by the religious and political instability of the first half of the sixteenth century, many of them were later incorporated, albeit in a modified form, within the great variety of the Anglican liturgical and spiritual practice.

Indeed, the most peculiar aspect of the English Reformation (in comparison with those confessional identities which have survived into modern times and were not absorbed by other mainstream Churches) is represented by the weight of the English rulers' influence on confessional allegiances; moreover, the personal attitude of the English Kings and Queens to music often proved to be crucial for the destiny of English music.

As concerns its musical output, the path of the English Reformation can be observed in the succession of liturgical changes and modifications, as well as in the publication of hymn-books and of the *Book of Common Prayer*. Moreover, the English metrical psalmody developed under both Lutheran and Reformed influences, as is mirrored by the successive publications by Coverdale, Robert Crowley (c.1517–1588) and others, up to the enormously successful "Sternhold and Hopkins". This Chapter will also discuss the musical output and practice of the Scottish Kirk: as happened in the preceding Chapters with other experiences,

---

[1] Bossewell 1572, fol. 14$^r$.

the discussion of different Churches within a single Chapter does neither imply to downplay their distinct nature and peculiar features, nor – of course – to merge them into a single reality.

Other peculiar forms of English music were the so-called "Godly Ballads", and here too the presence of sacred and religious music in the daily experience of the laity regularly exceeded the temporal frame of official worship; on the other hand, within the Anglican context we will observe the long-standing survival of two rather distinct forms of musical practice, i.e. the solemnity of worship at Court or in the major cathedrals and the simpler forms of parish music.

Among the distinguishing features of Anglican music, I will shortly present the typical "verse" composition, spanning from verse anthems to verse services; some attention will be given to the use of instruments in the worship of the Church of England, and to the leading figures of English sacred music in the sixteenth century (although several of the major composers of early Anglican music were in fact Catholics).

I have stated that the first observable feature of Anglican liturgy and music is its dependence on the religious orientation of the English sovereigns. Though in some cases they were deeply concerned with spiritual issues and personally interested in a life of piety, their religious and confessional choices were normally determined more by their upbringing and by matters of internal and foreign politics than by theological considerations proper. As a consequence, the field we are considering more specifically in this book – i.e. sacred and liturgical music – was not only subject to the confessional directions impressed by the English rulers on the Church of England, but also by their own musical tastes and by diplomatic and economic questions.

On the other hand, since theological considerations were not the primary motor of the English Reformation, this allowed the cohabitation of various theological and liturgical trends: though this coexistence was not always pacific, and in some instances became particularly difficult, the musical traits of the English Reformation sprang from a blend of practically all other principal Western traditions. It should be stressed, moreover, that the labels used for describing the confessional situation in England (such as "Anglicans", "Catholics", "Puritans", "Calvinists"...) are conditioned by interpretations *ex post*, and mirror separations and divisions which were not always clear in the sixteenth century[2].

The musical tradition in England before the Reformation was a rich and artistically fruitful one, with Catholic rites peculiar to the British islands, with a noteworthy though brief season of polyphonic Mass composition, and with the

---

[2] Cf. Leaver 2004a, pp. 152–153; Owens 2006, p. 359.

particular singing styles transmitted both by the surviving musical sources and by the written descriptions by contemporaneous listeners, as well as with a flourishing background of non-liturgical music (be it on sacred or on secular texts). Indeed, liturgical works influenced and inspired the composition of music which was not destined for worship: for example, "part-songs" employed (in miniature) a style of counterpoint similar to cultual music, with imitations at the beginning of the verses and prolonged vocalises towards their endings[3].

In Chapter Two (§ 2.3.9.) we have already mentioned, however, that the peculiar qualities of English church music were criticised with particular vehemence by Erasmus, both in their aural features and as concerned the financial and human resources they demanded[4]. Indeed, whereas one of the distinguishing marks of Luther's Reformation lay in his fostering of professional musicianship alongside with musical education of all layers of the population, the early English Reformation tended in the opposite direction, particularly on ethical grounds[5].

On the other hand, the importance of the Crown for the English Reformation is mirrored by an attention to the outward appearance of liturgy (for example for diplomatic purposes) which is not only unique in the panorama of the early Reformation era, but is also in marked contrast to some of the viewpoints maintained by the religious reformers on the Continent. Thus, the unique blend of royal solemnity with Evangelical sobriety, of pomp with simplicity and of splendour with pastoral concerns will mark the peculiar features of Anglican Church music, and place it very close to the Catholic experiments of the same period.

Therefore, in comparison with the Continent, the official status and the political relevance of the Crown and of Parliament's interventions on religious matters led to a reduced radicalness and to a greater conservativeness in the overall approach to liturgy and to theology, as well as to a shift in the power balance of Church and Crown in favour of the latter; on the other hand, these same factors allowed the English Reformation to be marked by a greater liturgical uniformity in comparison with – for example – the variety of Lutheranism[6].

In consequence of the relevance of the King or Queen's religious orientation for the overall shape of English spirituality and liturgy, it was a fortunate circumstance for English music that some of the most important rulers were personally favourable to music and sometimes passionate about it. Under Henry VIII, court music flourished impressively; an amazing quantity of instruments was available

---

3 Bray 2006, p. 495.
4 Kim 2005, pp. 160–161; Atlas 2006, p. 112.
5 Kim 2005, p. 173.
6 Cf. Shaw 1975, p. 694; Kim 2005, p. 172; Owens 2006, p. 360; Le Huray 2008, p. 1.

to his court musicians; and – according to Erasmus – the King was also a good composer of music himself; later, Elizabeth's appreciation of music would prove itself to be crucial for the survival and expansion of Anglican music[7].

## 7.2. Reforming rites

Due to the dependence of English liturgy on the rulers' orientation, I deemed it advisable to adopt a chronological approach to describe the most important stages of evolution in early Anglican worship. We will therefore observe in parallel the presence of official acts – which sometimes resemble real swerves in comparison with the preceding King's or Queen's approach – and the attempts of churchmen and musicians to keep pace with the innovations, and sometimes even to anticipate them with their experiments and their publications.

Between the Act of Supremacy of 1534 and the Edict of 1689, church music in England had to undergo an impressive sequence of modifications, both in its overall orientations and in its practical shape. In general, however, in the sixteenth century the tendency was to move from a Lutheran-inspired approach to one closer to Calvinism, which provoked in turn a reduced need for complex church music and a diminution in the liturgical output of composers such as John Taverner and Christopher Tye (c.1505–b.1573). Indeed, as Taruskin points out, Taverner's compositional style maintained a symbolic dimension which much Continental polyphony had lost: he "remained true to an older attitude, according to which the music contributed something essentially other than what human language could encompass". Music by the English composers, "aspiring to raise the listener's mind up above the terrestrial, provided a sensory overload"[8].

### 7.2.1. Under Henry VIII

Since their appearance, the first Continental Lutheran hymnbooks had made their way into England, where they enjoyed limited dissemination among the Evangelical sympathisers, especially in the cultivated classes. A primer published in 1530 by George Joye[9] (c.1495–1553) included hymns derived from Lutheran

---

7 Cf. Erasmus 1519, pp. 332–333; Bossewell 1572, fol. 14ʳ; Peacham 1906, p. 97 (cf. Strunk 1998, p. 348); Shaw 1975, p. 698; Lejeune 2010, p. 15.
8 Taruskin 2010, vol. I, pp. 613–614; cf. Rainoldi 2000, p. 326; Leaver 2006, pp. 395–396.
9 Joye 1530.

models: however, they were intended not as musical works, but rather as devotional poetry for meditation[10].

As seen in Chapter One (§ 1.6.3.), in 1534 Henry VIII promulgated the Act of Supremacy, which had – for the field we are studying – two main consequences: the first was to establish a direct correlation between the rulers' creed and that of the country; the second was to attribute to the Royal Chapel an incontestable primacy as the model for worship and for liturgical music.

Notwithstanding this, however, in the following years King Henry VIII would take other steps affecting dramatically the musical life of England. The 1536–41 seizure of monastic properties by the Crown caused the dissolution of several important musical realities; frequently, written sources of polyphonic music were destroyed in turn; fortunately, however, the English choral tradition was maintained in the thirteen major collegiate Cathedrals, as well as in the Royal establishments (e.g. Windsor Castle) and in the colleges at Cambridge, Eton, Oxford and Winchester, which allowed the maintenance of Latin offices and the preservation of a particular and distinctive practice[11].

As discussed in the historical overview of Chapter One (§ 1.6.3.), in fact, at that time the overall orientation of the English Reformation was still very uncertain. In 1539, the Parliament approved an Act (*For Abolishing Diversity in Opinions*), which would also become known as the "Six Articles" or – more graphically – as the "bloody whip with six strings", which substantially endorsed the reinforcement of distinctly Catholic practices[12]. It could be said, thus, that the separation from Rome apart, the general style of the Church of England under Henry VIII was very close to that of Catholicism[13].

Notwithstanding this, experiments were made in the field of vernacular sacred music, which started to be written in English by the leading composers of the time from the 1540s (such as Tye, Thomas Tallis [c.1505–1585], John Sheppard [or Shepherd, 1515–1558] and William Mundy [1529–1591]), thus establishing a solid background of knowledge and expertise in the setting to music of sacred words in the English language. This experience would prove to be very useful and profitable at a later stage of the English Reformation, when the need for new music in the vernacular for worship would be felt[14].

The only substantial concession made by Henry VIII to the requests of the English Reformers was the elaboration of an English Litany (or "procession")

---

10 White 2011, p. 22.
11 Cf. Shaw 1975, pp. 694–695; Le Huray 2008, p. 2.
12 Cf. Leaver 1991, p. 108.
13 Cf. Owens 2006, pp. 359–360.
14 Cf. Bray 2006, p. 501 and Le Huray 2008, p. 172.

in 1544, published in two editions with music[15] (at least one of which was printed by Grafton in London). It is clearly influenced by Luther's version of the Litanies (in Latin), and it results from the combination of several pre-existing forms of Litany: though other English versions already existed, this was the first to be provided with its own tunes. The process initiated with this publication was then continued by the Archbishop of Canterbury, Thomas Cranmer, on the King's behalf; other processional forms from the Latin tradition were gradually translated into English and provided with original music[16].

On the other hand, some steps were taken towards an English liturgy (though for now within a basically private dimension and without any congregational participation) with the so-called "King's Primer" (*Primer* 1545), whose hymns and offices could be sung in semi-public contexts such as collegiate or choral institutions; however, the songs included in the Primer were only translations of hymnody coming from the Latin Breviary, with no new or original creations. The non-metrical nature of hymns included in Primers preceding the 1545 official book made it impossible to sing their poetry to existing songs, and only declamatory plainchant models could be employed[17].

In the meanwhile, however, Evangelical influences from the Continent continued to be felt and actually increased in England, particularly as a consequence of the presence in leading theological posts of English universities (Oxford and Cambridge) of Strasbourg reformers such as Vermigli and Bucer.

### 7.2.2. Under Edward VI

In 1547, the situation was going to change abruptly, with the accession to the throne of Edward VI (who was only ten years old at the time) and a decided shift in the direction of Evangelically-inspired reforms. From the one side, several of the surviving institutions which were still practising high-level church music were abolished or dismantled; from the other, more substantial efforts were made to create vernacular liturgies and forms of worship. Soon after the King's coronation, a Visitation was ordered with the aim of verifying the discontinuance of Catholic rituality (with the prohibition of sequence singing in Winchester, for example), and in the very same year a vernacular liturgy was performed at Westminster. In April (on Easter Monday), Compline was sung in

---

15 *An exhortacion* 1544.
16 Cf. Leaver 1985, p. 112; Le Huray 2008, pp. 4–5.
17 Cf. Leaver 1991, p. 115; Bray 2006, p. 497; Quitslund 2008, p. 13; White 2011, p. 26.

English in the King's Chapel; a few months later (November 1547), in the Mass celebrating the Parliament's opening session, three items from the Mass Ordinary (namely the *Gloria*, *Credo* and *Agnus Dei*) were performed in English.

Both at Lincoln Cathedral (1548) and at York Minster (1552) a syllabic singing style was fostered, with the Lincoln Injunctions establishing that the choir "shall from henceforth sing or say no anthems of our Lady or other Saints, but only of our Lord, and them not in Latin; but choosing out the best and most sounding to Christian religion they shall turn the same into English, setting thereunto a plain and distinct note for every syllable one: they shall sing them and none other"[18].

In York, similarly, the Dean and Chapter of the Minster received instructions that "there be none other note sung or used in the said church at any service there to be had, saving square note plain, so that every syllable may be plainly and distinctly pronounced, and without any reports or repeatings which may induce any obscureness to the hearers"[19]. In this case, the concomitant presence of syllabic style and avoidance of repetitions is worth noting.

Unavoidably, this quick succession of contrasting ordinances and rules caused uncertainty, confusion and perplexity both among the congregations and among church musicians: these sometimes risked losing their jobs, and even when the danger was not so impending, they were never sure which direction church music was going to take in the future.

In 1548, the *Order of the Communion* was published[20] and its use was prescribed starting with Easter of that year. Vernacular liturgy thus became more common in the principal churches of London, where "both matins masses and evensong"[21] were performed in English. The nature of the *Order of the Communion*'s interventions on liturgy was more additive than detractive, with several liturgical items being inserted before the *Agnus Dei*[22].

### 7.2.3. The *Book of Common Prayer*

The following year (1549) was a momentous time for the history of English liturgy, with the appearance of Cranmer's *Book of Common Prayer*. Following a Parliamentary *Act of Uniformity* promulgated in January of that same year, the use of

---

**18** In Le Huray 2008, p. 9 (cf. *ibid.*, p. 8). Cf. Leaver 1991, p. 104; Kim 2005, p. 229; Owens 2006, p. 360; Rees 2006, p. 347.
**19** In Le Huray 2008, p. 25.
**20** *Order* 1548.
**21** In Arnold and Wyatt 1940, p. 7.
**22** Cf. Kim 2005, p. 229; Leaver 2006, pp. 382–383.

a new liturgical book, *The Boke of the Common Prayer and Administracion of the Sacramentes, and other Rites and Ceremonies of the Churches after the Use of the Churches of England*[23] was approved and mandated for worship in England, replacing all the Latin liturgies.

Whereas the first liturgical reforms in England had added new elements to the pre-existing Catholic rituals, these new orders tended to go in the opposite direction, and reduced – both in number and in complexity – the demanding rites of the Catholic Church. The many Hours of the monastic office were compressed into Matins and Evensong, and the Mass was replaced with the Communion service. Notwithstanding this, the basic structure of the Mass Ordinary was maintained, and thus (when the literary and musical configuration permitted it), earlier Latin-texted polyphonic settings could be adapted to English translations of the liturgical texts: choral foundations, at that time, survived in around forty ecclesiastical institutions.

Among such adaptations there are *contrafacta* of John Taverner's Latin-texted works, as for example those in the "Wanley" Partbooks: this impressive manuscript collection (recently edited and published by James Wrightson[24]), comprising ninety works from the Edwardian period, is a fundamental witness of the major composers' response to the challenges of the liturgical reforms of the era. Though the contributing musicians include composers from various confessional backgrounds (e. g. Christopher Tye, Robert Okeland [fl. b.1548] and William Whitbroke [c.1501–1569]), this collection demonstrates a considerable unity in its liturgical style and purpose, and an intense adherence to the principles of sobriety and restraint fostered in the Edwardian years. Moreover, notwithstanding their common adoption of the syllabic style, this by no means implies a uniformity or dullness in the artistic results: several of the works included in these partbooks employ imitative processes typical of advanced polyphonic composition, though reconciling them with the needs for a clear articulation, delivery and intelligibility.

Notwithstanding these efforts, it should be emphasised that the 1549 liturgical organisation was still provisional, and was going to be reworked in the following editions of the *Book of Common Prayer* (especially in the more decidedly Evangelical version of 1552[25]); however, even though the Latin titles survived for the offices, the process of translating the liturgy into English was already completed.

---

23 *Common Prayer* 1549.
24 Wrightson 1995; see also Wrightson 1989.
25 *Common Prayer* 1552.

The 1549 *Book of Common Prayer* was a compendium of the preceding attempts at vernacular liturgy, inasmuch as the 1545 *Primer* provided the basic material for Matins and Evensong (and through it the 1544 Litany gained access to the 1549 publication), and the 1548 *Order of the Communion* was reworked in the Lord's Supper[26].

The greatest part of merit for the compilation of the 1549 *Book of Common Prayer* must be attributed to Cranmer, though he was not the only author of this accomplishment. However, he left a personal mark on the collection's texts, which convey some of the idiosyncratic features of his literary style. In particular, as Bray demonstrated, Cranmer's inclination for verses starting with "for" or "and" – which are apt to be set to music as upbeats – influenced the peculiar style of English musical compositions in the decades to come, and provided a sharp contrast to the Latin texts which church composers were acquainted to setting to music before the Reformation[27].

Surely, however, at first the publication of the *Book of Common Prayer* must have troubled church musicians, who lacked directions as to the possibility of maintaining polyphony on feast days. The answer to some of their musings came the following year (1550) with the publication of the *Book of Common Prayer Noted*[28] (i.e. with music). Here, along with his own original compositions of *Gloria* and *Credo* settings, John Merbecke, the organist of St George's Chapel at Windsor Castle, reworked the traditional plainchant repertoire in order to adapt it to both the English translation and the syllabic principles.

Indeed, the extent of Merbecke's reworking of the traditional tunes is such that Leaver proposes to indicate it as "musical setting" rather than as "plainsong", with reference to the similar approach adopted by Luther in his creation/elaboration of the *Deudsche Messe*[29]: both testify to the effort to rethink the stylistic and melodic heritage of monody in accordance with humanistic and Evangelical principles and linguistic requirements proper to the vernaculars. Merbecke sought a rhythmical style of intoned declamation which could faithfully mirror the patterns typical of the English language, and adopted a mensural notation which mirrored and emphasised his aesthetical choice.

Though these principles are in accord with Cranmer's pursuit of the syllabic style, they cannot be reduced to a consequence of his statements; rather, as

---

26 Cf. Harper 1991; Bray 1995; Leaver 1991, p. 131; Leaver 2006, p. 383; Rees 2006, p. 347; Le Huray 2008, pp. 13, 18 and 28; Lejeune 2010, p. 16; Sfredda 2010, p. 124.
27 Bray 2006, p. 501; cf. Kim 2005, p. 229.
28 *Common Prayer* 1550.
29 Leaver 1989, pp. 273–274.

Kim[30] emphasises, they should be understood against the background of similar trends operating throughout Europe and among all confessional Churches, in partial consequence of experiments such as the humanistic ode and of the influence of personalities such as Erasmus.

As mentioned before (§ 4.2.3.1. and 4.3.6.), Cranmer had supported the adoption of a syllabic style for liturgical music since 1533, when he had written to Henry VIII with regard to the Litany translation, stating:

> As concerns the *Salve festa dies*, the Latin note, as I think, is sober and distinct enough; wherefore I have travailed to make the verses in English and have put the Latin note unto the same. Nevertheless, they that be cunning in singing can make a much more solemn note thereto. I made them only for a proof, to see how English would do in song. [...] The song that should be made thereunto would not be full of notes, but, as near as may be, for every syllable a note, so that it may be sung distinctly and devoutly[31].

Cranmer's endorsement of the syllabic style would prove itself to be undoubtedly important for the development of Anglican church music, and several later injunctions show the continuing permanence of this concern in the early period of the English Reformation. Besides the already-quoted injunctions for Lincoln Cathedral and York Minster, in 1571 Winchester Cathedral was ordered "that in the choir no more shall be used in song that shall drown any word or syllable, or draw out in length or shorten any word or syllable, otherwise than by the nature of the word it is pronounced in common speech, whereby the sentence cannot be well perceived by the hearers"[32]. In this case, the adherence of church music to the prosodic and rhythmical patterns of speech is even more important than a properly syllabic style[33].

Though Merbecke's efforts were consonant with the aesthetic ideals of his time and with the liturgical principles of the Church of England, his *Book of Common Prayer Noted* did not gain an immediate widespread success and recognition, for two main reasons: the first was the accession to the throne of Mary I in 1553 (see below), and the second was the publication of the second edition of the *Book of Common Prayer* in 1552.

From the liturgical viewpoint, though the 1552 edition conveyed important theological differences with respect to that of 1549, it can be said that the overall

---

30 Kim 2005, p. 255. See also Weber 1989.
31 In Cox 1846, p. 412.
32 In Le Huray 2008, p. 38.
33 Cf. Shaw 1975, pp. 698–699; Leaver 1991, pp. 132–133; Higman 2000, p. 501; Kim 2005, pp. 12–15, 163, 255 (etc.: this section is indebted to Kim 2005 in general); Rees 2006, p. 344; Le Huray 2008, p. 22; Weber 2008, p. 52.

influence of the 1549 edition was to shape the structure, principles and forms of Anglican liturgy for the following centuries. As concerns music, however, the impact of the 1552 revisions was more deeply felt, and certainly contributed to limiting the effect of Merbecke's setting in those hectic years.

The 1552 edition reveals the strong mark of the Evangelical movements active on the Continent, insomuch as it marked "the furthest Zwinglian influence to be officially approved by Parliament", in Shaw's words[34]. Indeed, the very concept of the Eucharist was quickly changing in the direction of a Zwinglian or Calvinist approach, and this obviously implied a reduction in the presence and importance of "art music": "Music, possibly the most mystical of all liturgical ornaments, was severely pruned"[35], as Le Huray states.

As in the 1549 edition, also the 1552 book did not include music notation, and church musicians had to devise their own strategies in the absence of specific directions. Some of the changes brought by the new edition on the preceding liturgical structure had important consequences concerning the musical shape of worship: for example, the addition of tropes to the *Kyrie*, the introduction of penitential prayers on the Decalogue, the displacement of the *Gloria* and the elimination of the *Agnus Dei*. What had been composed or adapted after the appearance of the 1549 book had now to be radically modified or replaced: in two of the most important musical sources of the time (the Wanley and Lumley partbooks) there are testimonies of such efforts. Notwithstanding this, the focus of Anglican music was starting to be found in Matins and Evensong (with their repertoire of anthems and canticles), with a decreasing importance accorded to music for the Communion service[36].

With the publication, in 1553, of Cranmer's *Forty-Two Articles*, it was clear that the Church of England was evolving in the direction of an increasingly Calvinist approach. One of the greatest historians of Anglican church music, Le Huray, states this clearly: "By the summer of 1553, the future of the English choral tradition was certainly in question. Is it too fanciful to see, in the accession of a Catholic monarch, its ultimate salvation?"[37].

With Mary's coronation (1553), the official orientation of the Church in England reverted to Catholicism, and so did liturgy and all musical practices linked to worship. Catholic liturgical books were reprinted, and even the most complex forms of polyphony preceding the Reformation were allowed again. Just as psalmody represented, for both Henry VIII and Edward VI, an allusion to the priestly

---

34 Shaw 1975, p. 696.
35 Le Huray 2008, p. 28.
36 Cf. Kim 2005, p. 2; Leaver 2006, p. 384; Le Huray 2008, p. 19.
37 Le Huray 2008, pp. 28–29. Cf. Owens 2006, p. 360.

role of kingship, as will be seen later in this Chapter (§ 7.3.1.–2.), for Queen Mary elaborate polyphony was a way to self-represent herself in her role as the modern equivalent of the Biblical Queen Judith[38].

While in England the Marian years arrested the process of limitation in the role of music which had marked the Edwardian period, they also forced many Evangelicals to leave their country and to seek refuge on the Continent, where they were welcomed by Protestant communities and could experience the Psalmodic worship which was practised especially in the Reformed zones[39].

### 7.2.4. Under Elizabeth I

In 1558, Elizabeth became Queen, and restored Protestantism after the Catholic period under Queen Mary. However, the theological and liturgical orientations which the Church of England would take under Elizabeth were different from those marking the final years of Edward's short rule; nor can it be said that the point from which Elizabeth started was the same reached at Edward's death.

Even within a Protestant theological framework, in fact, many elements which were normally associated with Catholicism were reinstated in worship; Elizabeth's stance about music was, in most cases, a middle-way between those of the "godly" returning from exile (with their psalters, of course) and of the Catholics. As quoted in the epigraph to this Chapter, in 1572 John Bossewell (d.1580) could state that "If it were not the Queens' majesty did favour that excellent Science [music], singing men and choristers might go a-begging"[40].

Indeed, the Queen's role in mitigating the initiatives of the clergy who would have favoured a more clearly Protestant stance is evident in what happened at the Convocation of the Province of Canterbury in 1563. In that year, the former exile Alexander Nowell (c.1507–1602) led a group of more than thirty like-minded Evangelicals to request that liturgical changes be implemented. Along with vestments and ritual gestures, they requested the abolition of "all curious singing and playing of the organs". The Queen's opposition to such initiatives was probably the main reason why this Protestant line was not adopted[41].

The Prayer Book issued in 1559[42] mirrored the Queen's attitude: though it was basically a reprint of the 1552 *Book of Common Prayer*, it moderated its

---

38 Cf. Page 1996.
39 Cf. Leaver 2004a, pp. 155–156; Pettegree 2005, p. 65; Owens 2006, pp. 361 and 365.
40 Bossewell 1572, fol. 14ʳ.
41 Cf. Fincham and Tyacke 2007, pp. 41–42.
42 *Common Prayer* 1559.

most extreme positions as regards liturgy and reintroduced some Catholic practices which had been endorsed in the 1549 version but proscribed in the second edition[43].

That edition would become a reference model for subsequent revisions, and its version dating from after the English Civil War (1662) represented the milestone for Anglican Liturgy in the following centuries.

The Elizabethan *Injunctions* of 1559[44] synthesised the Queen's attitude to worship music, permitting the singing of hymns or canticles, avoiding any pronouncement about metrical psalmody, fostering aesthetical principles consonant with ideals of sobriety and clear declamation, but also leaving a space open for complex music.

The relevant text reads:

> Because [in] divers collegiate and some parish churches heretofore, there hath been livings appointed for the maintenance of men and children, to use singing in the church, by means whereof the laudable science of music hath been had in estimation and preserved in knowledge, the Queen's Majesty neither meaning in any wise the decay of anything that might conveniently tend to the use and continuance of the said science, neither to have the same in any part so abused in the church, that the common prayer should be the worse understanded of the hearers, willeth and commandeth that first, no alteration be made of such alignments of living, as heretofore hat been appointed to the use of singing or music in the church, but the same to remain. And that there be a modest and distinct song so used, in all parts of the common prayers in the church, that the same may be as plainly understanded as if it were read without singing. And yet nevertheless, for the comforting of such as delight in music, it may be permitted that in the beginning or in the end of common prayers, either at morning or evening, there may be sung an hymn or suchlike song, to the praise of Almighty God, in the best sort of melody and music that may be conveniently devised, having respect that the sentence of the hymn may be understanded and perceived[45].

While the *Injunctions* provided official protection to the choral foundations, they also fostered intelligible and sober singing, without renouncing the beauty of complex music, though always respecting aesthetic criteria inspired by Evangelical principles. The "hymn or suchlike song" which these *Injunctions* permitted cannot be simply equated with (metrical) psalmody; the purposefully vague term may virtually include all kinds of sacred-texted music. The careful formulation of these *Injunctions*, combined with another particular feature of the English Reformation, i.e. the survival of episcopal authority and of the corresponding ec-

---

43 Cf. Shaw 1975, p. 696; Le Huray 2008, p. 32.
44 *Injunctions* 1559.
45 *Injunctions* 1559; *Injunctions* 1914, p. 435; Bray 2004, p. 344.

clesiastical institutions, contributed to the unique development of Elizabethan music[46].

Evaluations about the overall orientation of liturgical music in the early period of the English Reformation are complex, and, in particular, resist generalisations. It would be unfair to assert, as was sometimes done, that the Anglican Church was adverse to music: of course, much depends on whether by Anglican Church one indicates the King or Queen who was its Supreme Head or Governor, or the clergymen who were in charge of designing the liturgies, or those who had to implement them.

We will now turn our attention to another string of publications which paralleled the orders of liturgy and *Books of Common Prayer* (and which represents at least as efficaciously the identity of the Church of England), i.e. metrical psalmody, which will be discussed in comparison with the Scottish experience.

## 7.3. Psalms, psalters and Reformations

Though, by the end of the century, both in England and (even more) in Scotland, sung metrical psalmody would become a typical feature of the post-Reformation worship, the beginnings of Psalm-paraphrases in both countries are found within the framework of private devotion (whereby "private" means "unofficial", but not perforce "individual"); as frequently seen so far, Psalm-singing was seen to be a spiritually profitable alternative to secular singing. Indeed, as Quitslund remarks, "Without either the liturgical function of metrical Psalms in Continental Protestant Churches or a strong tradition of lay devotional song in English Catholic practice, the most obvious context for metrical psalmody was indeed amusement"[47].

### 7.3.1. Coverdale: Continental influences

We have already encountered on several occasions in the preceding Chapters the name of Myles Coverdale. This English theologian, who was a member of the Augustinian order as Luther had been, spent several years in Continental Europe, where he experienced the Evangelical movements which were spreading there and the liturgies, psalters, hymnals and Bible translations they employed.

---

46 Cf. Willis 2013, pp. 134–135.
47 Quitslund 2012, p. 239; cf. *ibid.*, pp. 237–238.

Encouraged by the Continental Reformers and their example, Coverdale prepared an English translation of the Bible (based on Latin, English and German sources), which he dedicated to the King in 1535[48], and which of course included a complete translation of the Book of Psalms. Indeed, Coverdale's translation of the Psalter is based neither on the original Hebraic text nor on the Vulgate (or the Septuagint), but on a Latin paraphrase published in 1532[49] by John van Campen (Johannes Campensis, c.1491–1538). (Incidentally, another early translator of the Psalter into English, George Joye, based in turn his Psalm versions of 1530 and 1534 on the Latin Psalters authored, respectively, by Bucer and by Zwingli). Coverdale's continuing interest in the Psalter is demonstrated by his later translations of the Psalms (in 1535, 1539 and 1540).

Parallel with his Bible translation, Coverdale worked on a hymnal, the *Goostly Psalmes and Spirituall Songes*[50], which reveals influences from German and Scandinavian Lutheranism, but also from the Strasbourg Reformation, five of whose tunes are included in the collection. Indeed, one of the most inspirational sources for Coverdale's collection were the *Geistliche Lieder* published in Wittenberg between 1529 and 1533[51], but probably via Slüter's *Geystlyke leder*[52] (cf. § 5.3.6.), and possibly with Danish influences as well. A Lutheran flavour is found not only in its textual and musical components, but even in the style and content of the preface and in the very title of the collection.

We have seen in Chapter Four (§ 4.2.4.9.) that Coverdale listed the functions of Psalm-singing in a way which is clearly reminiscent of Luther's principles, to which he added: "By this thou mayest perceive, what spiritual edifying cometh of godly Psalms and songs of God's word; and what inconvenience followeth the corrupt ballads of this vain world"[53].

Coverdale's aim was clearly to foster the introduction of a Lutheran-inspired liturgy into England: at that time, indeed, Henry VIII was looking with favour to alliances with the Lutheran princes. Moreover, the King – who was a keen music lover, as previously mentioned (§ 7.1.) – was also interested in psalmody: in particular, he liked to fancy himself in the image of David, the king-prophet (as well as poet and musician) to whom the Psalms are ascribed[54].

---

48 Coverdale 1535b.
49 Van Campen 1532. Cf. Ferguson 2011, pp. 138–139.
50 Coverdale 1535a.
51 Luther 1529, Luther 1533.
52 Slüter 1531.
53 Coverdale 1535a (p. 5: http://bit.ly/2cODhXT); spelling modernised following Pearson 1844, p. 539.
54 Cf. Tudor-Craig 1989.

Coverdale's writings bear witness to his particular interest in a syllabic form of chant. According to his ideal, worship should be introduced by

> two good sober singing men, which (commonly a quarter of an hour afore the sermon) begin a Psalm; and all the people, both old and young, with one voice do sing with them, after such a fashion that every note answereth to a syllable, and every syllable to one note commonly, and no more, so that a man may well understand what they sing[55].

These statements are a precedent for Cranmer's famous endorsement of the syllabic style discussed earlier in this Chapter (§ 7.2.3.).

Coverdale's collection is one of the most interesting and influential editorial projects of the early English movements following Evangelical principles. It comprises forty-one texts (only four of which have no German model; fifteen are Psalm settings); they make extensive use of the strophic form, but there are references to the local traditions (for example using the Sarum rite tune for the *Christe qui lux es* plainchant).

Coverdale's influence would actually prove to be fundamental for the subsequent developments of English psalmody and rituals: some of his melodies would later be elaborated in the "Sternhold and Hopkins", thus establishing some continuity and connections between the early attempts at vernacular psalmody in England, and the practice of Psalm-singing which would acquire a constantly increasing importance during Edward VI's rule[56].

It should be pointed out, however, that the first translations of the Psalter into Anglo-Saxon had appeared in the eleventh century and that, before vernacular Bibles started to be associated with Lollardy and the Books of Hours replaced psalmody for lay piety, there had already been a certain spread of vernacular Psalters in England[57].

If the King's momentary sympathy for the Lutheran princes and principles had possibly fostered Coverdale's efforts, Henry VIII's subsequent harsh reaction against the Evangelical movements caused, among other things, the burning of "heretical" books such as Coverdale's collection; Cranmer's attempts to revise the Breviary (1538, 1543–46) could not be issued in printing[58].

A repertoire similar in style and scope to Coverdale's, and similarly revealing Lutheran influences, was circulating in Scotland in manuscript and/or broad-

---

55 Coverdale in Pearson 1844, p. 469.
56 Cf. Leaver 1991, pp. 79, 103–104, 107 and 131; Pettegree 2005, p. 65; Rees 2006, p. 344; Le Huray 2008, pp. 370–371; Quitslund 2008, p. 17; White 2011, pp. 22–25; Zim 2011, p. 34.
57 Cf. Quitslund 2008, pp. 11–12.
58 Cf. Le Huray 2008, p. 4 and White 2011, p. 26.

sheet form from 1546 (*Gude and Godlie Ballatis*), though the first printed copies of the collection date from two decades later (1565[59]). It is also known as the "Wedderburn Psalter", since it is frequently attributed to one of the Wedderburn brothers from Dundee (but doubts have recently been advanced on their role as compilers). This collection includes versifications, partly adapted from Coverdale's hymns, and partly translated directly from Continental models[60]. As we will see in the forthcoming pages, however, this was never an official book of the Scottish Kirk, though its contents were well known in the country and possibly familiar to the Reformer John Knox; its primary destination was domestic devotion[61].

In the meanwhile, Henry VIII's death and Edward's accession to the throne had left the door open for substantial implementations of Protestantism in England, as repeatedly seen in the preceding pages. During Edward's reign, for example, many Continental Evangelicals fleeing persecution found refuge in London, where they gathered in congregations on the basis of their language and provenance. Thus, by the presence of these refugees in London, the experience of sung congregational psalmody was brought to England, where it was heard and, probably, appreciated, by many people who could not travel onto mainland Europe[62].

### 7.3.2. Sternhold: Psalms at Court

Another milestone for the history of early English Protestantism was the publication of the first Psalm collection by Thomas Sternhold (1500–1549), who was a court gentleman under Henry VIII and Edward VI. As the reader will remember from Chapter Six (§ 6.2.2.), this context was not dissimilar from that of Clément Marot's first Psalm versifications, which had been composed primarily for use at the French court, and had been probably sung on contemporaneous secular tunes. Moreover, Marot was held in high esteem among the English cultural elite (particularly Thomas Wyatt [1503–1542], and other court poets), thus paving the way for a positive acceptance of his metrical psalmody and stimulating analogous attempts to translate the Psalter into English verse. Thus, similarly to French metrical psalmody, also in England this form of spiritual poetry originated from within the secular context of the court, from which it gradually mi-

---

59 *Ane Compendious* 1565.
60 Cf. Duguid 2014, to which this section is indebted.
61 Cf. Reid 1971, p. 51; Higman 2000, p. 501; White 2011, p. 30; Dawson 2012, p. 50.
62 Cf. Leaver 2004a, p. 161.

grated to the church. Sternhold dedicated his first collection to the young King, affirming that "as your grace taketh pleasure to hear them sung sometimes of me, so ye will also delight not only to see and read them yourself, but also to command them to be sung to you of others"[63].

Isolated metrical psalmody in English had been already written by several authors; the most interesting efforts in this sense are those by John Croke (1489–1554), who composed some Psalms in English metre during King Henry VIII's reign, though their destination for singing is doubtful. There is, instead, evidence that metrical Psalms written by Wyatt, and inspired by the Penitential Psalm paraphrases by the Italian Pietro Aretino, were sung at the English court[64]. Other early versified translations of Psalter selections include those by Henry Howard, Earl of Surrey (c.1515–1547) and Thomas Becon, whose views on music and pedagogy we encountered in Chapters Three and Four[65].

In 1549, during Edward VI's rule, Robert Crowley issued the first complete metrical Psalter in English with music (*Psalter of David*[66]); its tunes were inspired by those of the Sarum rite, and their melodic settings are syllabic, in consonance with Cranmer's aesthetical principles. Crowley's collection also included translations of the Gospel canticles and of two Latin hymns; this suggests that the compiler may have envisaged a liturgical use for his work[67]. Notwithstanding this, the very wording of the collection's title reveals its primary intended use to be spiritual entertainment: "The Psalter of David newly translated into English metre in such sort that it may the more decently, and with more delight of the mind, be read and sung of all men"[68].

Though also the Psalm versifications by Sternhold dated back to Henry VIII's last years, their success was established during Edward VI's reign; actually, as maintained by Quitslund, the Psalm selection written by Sternhold was inherent to the educational programme designed to shape the young King's feeling of his own religious/political predestination. During Edward's reign, metrical Psalms could also be sung in parishes, though no official endorsement for this practice had been issued[69].

---

63 Sternhold 1549, fol. Aiii<sup>r</sup>.
64 Cf. Quitslund 2008, pp. 14–15.
65 See § 3.3.2.6., 3.3.2.10., 3.3.2.12., 4.2.2., 4.2.3.2., etc.
66 Crowley 1549.
67 Cf. Leaver 1991, pp. 138–139; Le Huray 2008, p. 371; Sfredda 2010, p. 125.
68 Crowley 1549, as quoted in Quitslund 2012, p. 240.
69 Quitslund 2008, p. 9 etc.; cf. Pettegree 2005, p. 65; Sfredda 2010, p. 97; Le Huray 2008, p. 172.

Sternhold's metrical Psalms were issued first as a collection of nineteen paraphrases (*Certayne Psalmes*, c.1549[70], published by Withchurche), while a further collection, comprising thirty-seven Psalms versified by Sternhold with seven additional paraphrases by John Hopkins (c.1520–1570) was issued after Sternhold's death[71]. These forty-four Psalms represented the kernel of the "Sternhold and Hopkins", the future complete Psalter whose importance for the spirituality of English-speaking Evangelicals was immense.

As we have already seen, Mary Tudor's accession to the throne forced many Evangelicals to leave England (in particular, foreign Protestants were banished), while many others decided to remain in England, to worship clandestinely and to hide their confessional allegiance. As will be discussed in Chapter Ten (§ 10.3.3. etc.), many Evangelicals were led by the experience of persecution, martyrdom and exile to identify themselves with Biblical examples of exiled people, and to integrate these Scriptural models within their forms of prayer.

### 7.3.3. "The Lord's Songs in a foreign land"

The forty-four metrical Psalms of the first, partial "Sternhold and Hopkins" were among the items brought by numerous exiles to the Continent; indeed, it was precisely by their connection with that period of martyrdom and persecution that these Psalms conquered the unique place they maintained for so long at the very heart of English Protestantism.

The English refugees found asylum in several cities of the Continent, many of which were in today's Germany and Switzerland. In some places, the exiles were accorded permission to worship independently, whereas elsewhere their forms of worship were influenced more closely by the local communities. In the former case (e.g. in Emden and Frankfurt), adaptations from the liturgical orders of the Edwardian era (in particular the 1552 *Book of Common Prayer*) were employed, and metrical Psalms were considered, for the first time, to be an integral component of worship. In the latter case (e.g. Strasbourg and Zurich), the exiles gained first-hand experience of the Continental Evangelical traditions. Strasbourg, indeed, was the haven where many of the spiritual leaders of Edwardian Protestantism sought refuge, while Emden became a hotbed for the publication of English Evangelical books.

---

70 Sternhold 1549.
71 Sternhold and Hopkins 1549.

In Frankfurt, a profitable interaction between the English exile community and that of the French refugees was established: The French practice of singing Marot's metrical version of the Decalogue before the Lord's Supper was imitated by the English, for whom a paraphrase was created, on Marot's model, by William Whittingham (c.1524–1579). Some of Whittingham's versifications were included a collection published in Wesel (c.1555–6, *Psalmes of David in metre*[72]) by Hugh Singleton (d. c.1593), including also several canticles: the "Wesel Psalter" was to influence numerous later publications.

It was from the exiles' community in Geneva, however, that the most significant contributions to the history of English metrical psalmody were to come: the English congregation in Geneva was the only one not to use the 1552 *Book of Common Prayer* for its official worships[73]. In 1556, the *Forme of Prayers and Ministration of the Sacraments*[74] was issued there, comprising the refugees' liturgy (modelled on the hybridisation of Genevan practices with the forms adopted by the French-speaking exile community in Frankfurt[75]), a selection of fifty-one metrical Psalms, and the Decalogue. This collection drew upon the first incomplete "Sternhold and Hopkins", but with substantial revisions. The melodies are by unknown musicians; in spite of their similarities with Genevan and German models, they are by no means dependent on them. The same applies to the theological concept behind the metrical versions, since the spirituality of the Marian refugees was profoundly marked by their condition as exiles, which they interpreted as a mark of their election as the people of the alliance, on the model of the persecuted and exiled Israel. As Quitslund writes, "led by William Whittingham, they both rewrote the Edwardian Psalms of Sternhold and (to a lesser extent) Hopkins to reflect their own theological, psychological, and literary concerns, and added ever-larger numbers of new paraphrases that expressed the particular situation and ideology of their community"[76].

The 1556 *Forme of Prayers* was the first to officially include metrical psalmody within the framework of an English worship inspired by Evangelical principles.

Moreover, under the influence of Calvinism, Whittingham revised the extant Psalm versifications in order to prune them from too free a paraphrasing and excessive poetic liberties. Indeed, the title-page's claim that the 1556 version had been checked with the original Hebraic text was an overstatement; however,

---

72 *Wesel* 1556.
73 Cf. Leaver 2004a, p. 157.
74 *Forme of prayers* 1556.
75 Cf. Leaver 2004a, p. 158.
76 Quitslund 2008, p. 6.

the connection between this publication and the centre of Calvinism bestowed on it a halo of authoritativeness: its musical features suited and expressed perfectly the leading principles of the Calvinist aesthetics (unaccompanied monody in the syllabic style and with limited note-values[77]). This 1556 edition of the *Forme of Prayers* would also provide the model for the later liturgy of the Scottish Kirk.

The main problem with the 1556 edition was that it included just one-third of the Psalter's texts; thus, this publication was considered to be provisional and did not stop the Anglo-Scottish exiles in Geneva from continuing their task.

In the 1558 edition[78], in fact, the versified Psalms were already sixty-two; however, in this version there was no more a perfect identity between texts and tunes, and a single melody could be used for several paraphrases. However, lyrics and tunes were not paired haphazardly: shared melodies worked as exegetical tools, by pointing out common features among the different Psalms they were sung to.

Notwithstanding this, it should be emphasised that even the proximity to the very core of Calvinist spirituality did not prevent the English exiles from developing their own specific and individual theological insights. Undoubtedly, upon their return to England, the Marian exiles would bring what was felt as a distinctly Calvinist mark to the spirituality of their motherland: for example, while in exile they had replaced the Anglican clerical hierarchy (which resembles that of Catholicism, with bishops, priests and deacons) with one of Presbyterian inspiration. A major influence on the English exiles' adoption of this model came from the communities of Continental Evangelicals who had worshipped in London during the Edwardian era, under the supervision of Jan Łaski. His Church Orders (the *Forma ac Ratio*[79]) were thus exported by these London-based Continental Evangelicals when they had in turn to flee during Mary's reign: being in exile strengthened the bonds between English-born and foreign Evangelicals who had to leave England, and favoured their common adoption of similar liturgical practices. It is thus to Łaski's ultimate influence that Leaver attributes a major role for encouraging the use of metrical psalmody in worship[80]. This may be one reason why Whittingham's publications also show some remarkable traits of independence from the Genevan Calvinist model[81].

---

[77] Cf. Duguid 2014, p. 25.
[78] *Forme of prayers* 1558.
[79] Łaski 1554.
[80] Leaver 2004a, especially pp. 158–160.
[81] Cf. Blankenburg 1975, pp. 565–566; Shaw 1975, p. 700; Pettegree 2005, p. 65; Le Huray 2008, pp. 372–373; Quitslund 2008, pp. 156–157, 169 and 217.

A third, enlarged version of the *Forme of Prayers* was issued in Geneva in 1560–1[82], by then comprising nearly ninety Psalms, paraphrases from the Lord's Prayer, the Decalogue and the *Nunc Dimittis* (cf. § 6.2.3., about the similar choices in Calvin's 1539 *Aulcuns Pseaulmes*), to be sung on more than sixty tunes, nearly a third of which came from the French Genevan Psalter. In the meanwhile, as seen earlier in this Chapter (§ 7.2.4.), the major event for the refugees had been Elizabeth's accession to the throne, which allowed them to return to their homeland.

As Duguid points out[83], the reception of the Genevan 1560–1 *Forme of Prayers* in Britain was varied: those who followed Cranmer's liturgical models favoured the earlier Genevan versions (and this was particularly common among the English), whereas those who remained faithful to the liturgical practices established in exile tended to prefer the new publication (and this attitude was frequently found among the Scots).

### 7.3.4. Elizabethan Psalmody: the "Sternhold and Hopkins"

If the refugees had worked on metrical psalters from Geneva, as soon as the Elizabethan Settlement was issued the English publishers in the motherland did not remain idle. At first, of course, there was no certainty about the kind of music which would be allowed or prescribed in worship; those building on the Anglo-Genevan Psalter for the creation of a repertoire of English metrical psalmody were doing so in the hope that it would find a role in the English worship, but without having any guarantee in this sense. In 1559, the Queen did establish that a "hymn or such like song" could be performed at Matins or Evensong, but no specific mention of the Psalms was made[84].

This vague disposition was enough, however, to encourage the initiative of the London-based printer John Day (or Daye, c.1522–1584), who prepared a metrical psalter based on the 1558 edition of the Genevan *Forme of Prayers* and with Psalm paraphrases by Sternhold, Hopkins (to whom fifty-eight Psalm paraphrases are attributed) and Thomas Norton (1532–1584), who adopted both Sternhold's perspective and his metrical structures. The complete Psalter, including upwards of sixty tunes, plus canticles, hymns and prayers, was ready by 1562, and was published as *The Whole Booke of Psalmes, collected into English*

---

82 *Forme of prayers* 1560.
83 Cf. Duguid 2014, p. 48.
84 Cf. Shaw 1975, p. 698; Russell 1996, p. 280; Pettegree 2005, p. 65.

*Metre*, though it is now better known as "the Sternhold and Hopkins"[85]. Since the proportion between tunes and texts was roughly of one to three, the grounds for the independence of the English tradition from its Genevan models were established.

The origins of this enormously successful Psalter, which have painstakingly been traced and collected by Beth Quitslund[86], reveal the superimposition of several theological, literary and spiritual layers, bearing trace of the turbulent historical milieu, of the composite social and cultural sources concurring in its creation and of the multiple forces active in its elaboration. It is easy to see, for example, how different was the role of psalmody among the courtly context of Sternhold's first versifications for young King Edward and those in the exiles' communities in Geneva (who obviously were still in contact with their motherland and thus did not experience a total isolation from what was happening there), or upon their return to England. For example, several tunes which had been used in Geneva for Psalm-singing were replaced by new ones for the 1562 publication, "in the stead of those sung in Calvin's city"[87], thus marking a clear separation between the Genevan tradition and the Elizabethan context, although within an overall and undeniable continuity.

Moreover, Quitslund demonstrates the bidirectional influence between metrical psalmody and the Reformation process in England: from the one side, the history of English metrical psalmody mirrors the theological and political history of those complex years; from the other, it also influenced the evolution of the very concept of the "Church of England" and its retrieval of a specific identity, unifying under the same prayerful and musical flag believers who could have very different viewpoints as to the theological perspectives of English Protestantism.

The complete title of this collection points out the multifaceted concept lying behind it: fidelity to the Scripture ("conferred with the Hebrew") and to the official indications of the English Church ("according to the order appointed in the Queen's majesty's injunctions", in spite of the fact that Queen Elizabeth had not officially endorsed congregational Psalm-singing[88]); suitability for domestic devotion ("very mete to be used of all sorts of people privately for their solace & comfort"); aiming at the replacement of secular music with psalmody ("laying apart all ungodly Songs and Ballads which tend only to the nourishing of vice and corrupting of youth").

---

**85** Sternhold and Hopkins 1562.
**86** Cf. Quitslund 2008.
**87** Cf. Quitslund 2008, pp. 5–6 and 211.
**88** Cf. Quitslund 2012, p. 242.

As concerns the melodic material of the 1562 "Sternhold and Hopkins", it is interesting to note that scholars have been hitherto unable to trace secular origins for most of its tunes. There are, however, melodic influences and borrowings from both the Genevan Psalter and Lutheran sources.

As concerns the performance practice of English metrical psalmody, debate is open in contemporary scholarship. The nickname of "Geneva jigs" by which Psalms were contemptuously referred to by contemporaneous critics is read by some as witnessing an early actual performance style, characterised by lively tempo, whereas others argue that the nickname purposefully mocked a singing style which was grave and solemn from the outset. Actually, we have already observed (cf. § 5.3.4.1.) that congregational singing tended to modify the musical features of religious songs, for example by standardising note-values and slowing down the tempo. While no scholarly agreement has been reached so far as to the quick or slow beat of early Psalm singing, it seems safe to assert that, by the end of the century, congregations were singing Psalms rather calmly, and apparently enjoyed this performance style. Seemingly, moreover, the Psalms' various moods were not mirrored by corresponding tempo choices[89].

The impressive dissemination of the "Sternhold and Hopkins" (some hundred-and-fifty editions, for an estimate printing of more than two hundred thousand copies by 1603) made it an extremely influential interpretive filter through which the Biblical Word was transmitted to the faithful.

From the textual viewpoint, thus, the "Sternhold and Hopkins" versifications quickly became "the" metrical psalmody of the Church of England; however, the same stability was not observed in the tune repertoire associated to them. The remarkable musical variants of the following years were partly due to the printers' initiatives (or to their carelessness), partly to the lack of official supervision on the repertoire, and partly to the trend of later editions to mirror (instead of prescribing) the singing practice. In fact, in the last decades of the century, the repertory of tunes was modernised and simplified, with the emergence of the popular-sounding "Common Tunes" by which the congregations sought to replace the chaotic associations of texts and tunes contradictorily suggested in the frenzy of new publications.

Most crucially, the Church of England did not issue official orders concerning sung psalmody, which therefore developed with a considerable degree of spontaneity and freedom[90]. Notwithstanding this, however, Psalm-singing was actively encouraged: from the time of its publication, the "Sternhold and Hop-

---

**89** Cf. Temperley 1979, vol. I, p. 64; Watt 1991, p. 64; Marsh 2013, pp. 430–431.
**90** Cf. Duguid 2014, p. 201 etc.

kins" provided valuable material for congregational worship, since metrical psalmody did not yet represent a mark of confessional allegiance to the Puritan current. As Quitslund points out, although the theological approach conveyed by the 1562 Psalter was more radical and closer to Continental Protestantism than Elizabeth would have liked, "The ecclesiastical authorities nevertheless ensured its success by enthusiastically supporting the practice of public Psalm-singing before and after sermons and at common prayer. For most of the remainder of the century, singing Psalms and hymns from *The Whole Booke of Psalmes* was a normal, nearly universal experience in English Churches"[91].

Thus, the "Sternhold and Hopkins" quickly became "a standalone, multimedia guide to devotional practice"[92], and individual Psalms were suggested for private use on particular occasions of one's life, with special focus on the climate of persecution which had characterised the exiles' spirituality[93].

In later epochs, the literary quality of the "Sternhold and Hopkins" versifications started to be criticised (sometimes rather harshly), until it became almost an icon of low-quality poetry. This criticism, however, was not felt until the last decade of the sixteenth century, when the 1562 Psalter began to be seen "by many as a national embarrassment"[94], as White argues, and Quitslund[95] offers a rather entertaining sample of such statements. However, as Hamlin points out, equating the popularity of the "artless verse"[96] of the "Sternhold and Hopkins" with its appeal to the uneducated is to mistake the nature of its success, which encompassed all social classes. Moreover, using these metrical Psalms as a form of spiritual entertainment bridged the gap between sacred and secular, while their musical settings encompassed the whole spectrum of their composers' confessional allegiances, from Catholics to Puritans[97].

---

**91** Quitslund 2008, p. 6.
**92** Willis 2010, p. 191.
**93** Cf. Shaw 1975, p. 800; Bray 2006, p. 502; Milsom 2007, pp. 29–30; Le Huray 2008, p. 377; Quitslund 2008, p. 265 (etc.: this section is indebted to Quitslund 2008 in general); Sfredda 2010, p. 97; Willis 2010, p. 191.
**94** White 2005, p. 73.
**95** Quitslund 2008, pp. 1–2.
**96** Lewis 1954, p. 247.
**97** Cf. Hamlin 2000, pp. 37–39 and 51.

### 7.3.5. Singing the Scottish Reformation

The history of the Scottish Psalter presents a rather different narrative from that of the "Sternhold and Hopkins", although the beginnings of both traditions had been similar. In Scotland, as will be recalled, in 1560 the Parliament implemented the Reformation. The ground for it had been prepared by John Knox's missionary activity (1555–6) and by popular upheavals following his definitive return to Scotland (1559).

The Scottish Kirk thus abolished the celebration of the Catholic Mass, adhered to the Calvinist confession and introduced a Geneva-inspired worship, which obviously demanded the availability of metrical psalmody; however, as shown by Duguid[98], while the 1562 *Whole Booke* was built on the Genevan *Forme of Prayers* of 1558, the Scottish compiler of the Kirk's metrical Psalter, Robert Lepreuik (or Lekpreuik, fl. 1561–1581), based his work on the latest *Forme of Prayers* (1560–1). Lepreuik's *Forme of Prayers* made no use of the pre-Reformation Scottish repertoire of the *Gude and Godlie Ballatis*, probably (as argued by Duguid[99]) since their texts were deemed to be closer to Lutheran Psalm-paraphrases than to Reformed metrical versifications. The Scottish *Forme of Prayers* was translated into Gaelic in 1567 (*Foirm na n-Urrnuidheadh*[100]), becoming the first printed book ever in that language.

The different sources for the two British psalter traditions explain their divergence in concept and details. Moreover, by officially mandating the purchase and use of Lepreuik's 1564 *Forme of Prayers*[101] (the "Psalm buik") to all ecclesiastical institutions, and later (1579) to all wealthy households, the General Assembly of the Scottish Kirk bestowed upon this publication its full liturgical authority. Indeed, this authority was already inherent in some of the metrical Psalms, which had been written in Calvin's Geneva and sanctioned by being used by the persecuted (and therefore elected) community of the exiles. While much depended, in England, on the initiative of printers, in Scotland the ultimate supervision and responsibility on the metrical psalter was in the hands of the Kirk.

Therefore, the connection between tunes and texts, and the consistency with which later editions of the Scottish Psalter maintained the original associations mirror the different status of metrical psalmody in England and in Scotland.

---

**98** Cf. Duguid 2014, pp. 82 ff.
**99** Cf. Duguid 2014, p. 86.
**100** *Foirm* 1567.
**101** *Forme of prayers* 1564.

## 7.3. Psalms, psalters and Reformations — 359

Consistency in the association of tunes and texts implied that Scottish congregations had to learn a higher number of tunes by heart, especially where literacy (and musical literacy) were uncommon. Memorising Psalms and singing them was crucial for the new Reformed Kirk, since there were few authorised preachers: thus, metrical psalmody became a form of catechesis, of exegesis and of prayer at the same time. As pointed out by Dawson, the prevalence of oral culture in sixteenth century Scotland made repetition, particularly in song, the preferred form for the rote learning of the basics of faith[102].

Help, both in singing the Psalms and in learning them, was given to the congregations by the pupils of the *"sang schwylls"*, the "song schools". At first, these pre-Reformation institutions seemed to suffer a blow from the Reformed style of the Evangelical worship: as there was no more need for either trained choirs or organ music, the existing establishments for the musical education of the young were closed. Of course, sacred polyphony still continued to be practised (in the schools as well), and also autonomously produced in Scotland by composers such as Andro Blackhall (c.1535–1609) and David Peebles (fl. 1530–1576, d. c.1579), but it was not admitted in public services; Blackhall's Psalm settings were intended for solemn public festivities, such as patrician weddings or royal events[103]. Interestingly, Latin psalmody was composed and performed in Scotland for non-liturgical purposes: Peebles composed a four-part setting in Latin of Psalm 3, and (as seen in § 6.3.3.), the humanist poet George Buchanan wrote metrical versions of the Psalms in classical Latin, which he dedicated to Mary Queen of Scots. As seen in §6.3.3., Buchanan's Latin Psalms received a polyphonic setting in Germany by Statius Olthof, but it was in the musical version by Jean Servin that these Psalm paraphrases were presented in 1579 to Buchanan's pupil James VI King of Scotland[104]. By offering his work to the young King, Servin hoped that his compositions would be successful as a form of courtly spiritual entertainment, in a context which was obviously unavailable in Geneva where he lived at the time. Servin was thus trying to reconcile humanist with Evangelical trends by underpinning their common interest in the primacy of the word/Word[105].

Possibly as a consequence of Servin's initiative, indeed, within a few weeks, the Scottish Parliament realised that the "art of music & singing [...] is almost decayed and shall shortly decay without timely remedy be provided". This "time-

---

[102] Cf. Dawson 2012, pp. 44–46.
[103] Cf. Dawson 2012, p. 50.
[104] Servin 1579.
[105] Cf. Porter 2009, pp. 229–233, 245–251.

ly remedy" was fortunately enacted, and music schools were fostered again in Scotland[106].

Both in England and in Scotland, as elsewhere in Continental Europe, the practice of Psalm-singing as a devotional activity outside worship was fostered, and, of course, it underwent fewer restrictions than those applied to liturgical use. Indeed, and significantly for a Calvinist-inspired Church, music students reportedly sang four-part harmonisations of the Scottish Psalms, possibly even during the Kirk's worship, as specified in the music teacher's duties (Ayr, 1583): "shall sing in ye Kirk ye fo[u]r parts of music"[107]. Probably, however, the most common form of harmonisation of Psalm tunes in church, both in England and in Scotland, was through improvised discant[108].

### 7.3.6. Psalms, poetry and polyphony

While the actual practice of part-singing in the Kirk is difficult to ascertain, undoubtedly the musically literate could sing Psalms in polyphony in their homes. Harmonisations of Sternhold's Psalms are attested in England from the Edwardian era. In 1553, among others, Francis Seager (or Segar, Seagar, fl. 1549–1563) published nineteen metrical Psalms[109], with motet-like music in four parts. The metre adopted here is regular and stanzaic, allowing the use of repeated musical structures and the setting of several texts to a single musical tune. Great importance was given to the power of music to give depth and beauty to schematic versifications: as John Case stated about music, "flat verse it resyth sublime"[110]. Moreover, parallel to the publication of the *Whole Booke of Psalmes*, John Day prepared a four-part setting of its complete tune repertoire (1563, "Parsons' Psalter"[111]), favouring tenor-based harmonisations.

Two years later, he issued a further collection (*Certaine notes*[112]) including settings of hymns and canticles. Some of the best-known works of contemporaneous English church music were included in this collection (among them Tallis' *If ye love me*): together with Sheppard's *I give you a new commandment* it shows

---

**106** Cf. Weber 2008, pp. 56–57; Porter 2009, pp. 229, 238, 250; Munro 2010, pp. 65–70, p. 78.
**107** Pagan 1897, p. 75, as quoted in Duguid 2014, p. 223.
**108** Cf. Duguid 2014, p. 226.
**109** Seagar 1553.
**110** Case 1586, p. 66. Cf. White 2011, p. 26, and Zim 2011, p. 149.
**111** *Whole psalmes* 1563.
**112** *Certaine notes* 1565. As regards the dating of this collection, cf. Duguid 2014, p. 193; see also Aplin 1981.

a tendency to adopt a strictly syllabic style for the first section of a piece, and to allow the presence of some imitations in the concluding part[113].

In the meanwhile, a new English metrical Psalter was authored by Matthew Parker (1504–1575), who was the Archbishop of Canterbury at the time of its publication (c.1567). The nine tunes associated with Parker's Psalms were offered in a four-part harmonisation by Thomas Tallis; the underlying perspective on singing practice is shown in the prefatory instruction: "The Tenor of these parts be for the people when they will sing alone, the other parts, put for greater queers, or to such as will sing or play them privately"[114].

Among the most important of the early English harmonised metrical Psalters, we should briefly mention the three collections composed by William Daman (c.1540–1591), and published in 1579 and in 1591 (two settings[115]), the second of which is singular inasmuch as it features the Psalm tune in the upper part. Daman's printer, Thomas East (or Este, c.1540–1609), published in 1592 another Psalter[116] with four-part harmonisations by young composers of such standing as George Kirbye (c.1565–1634), John Dowland (1563–1626) and Giles Farnaby (c.1563–1640). East's collection is unique in that it comprises the entire text of the Psalter and the four parts are all printed side-by-side and not in partbooks[117]. These early harmonisations display a wide variety of musical styles, ranging from simple homorhythmic counterpoint to more imitative polyphony.

In 1585, the printer John Wolfe (c.1548–1601) issued a collection (*Musike of Six, and Fiue Parts*[118]) including sixty harmonised Psalms by John Cosyn (d.1609), whereby a new tune for Psalm 67 [66] (the "London" tune) was inserted in the melodic repertoire along with harmonisations of the traditional tunes[119]. The century closed on a further collection by Richard Alison (c.1560-b.1610), *The Psalmes of Dauid in Meter* (1599[120]), which, similarly to the preceding, had not been conceived for public performance in churches during worship, but rather for private spiritual enjoyment.

The so-called "Penitential Psalms" were also the object of particular interest: Catholic recusants under Protestant rule saw them as embodying their plea for

---

113 Cf. Bray 2006, p. 498; Quitslund 2008, pp. 203, 211 and 264.
114 Parker and Tallis 1567; cf. Ellinwood 1948 and Stevens 1979.
115 Daman 1579; Daman 1591.
116 *Whole booke* 1592.
117 Cf. Shaw 1975, p. 700; Strunk 1998, p. 376.
118 Cosyn 1585.
119 Cf. Duguid 2014, p. 120.
120 Alison 1599.

God's mercy, but they were no less popular among non-Catholics. From a purely artistic viewpoint, their sorrowful lyrics offered many interesting stimuli to the composer's creativity, which, in "art-music", could employ many rhetoric strategies taken from plaintive secular models. Among the English composers of Penitential Psalm settings for devotional use were William Byrd (c.1539–1623), John Mundy (1555–1630), Thomas Campion (1567–1620) and John Dowland.

In Scotland, another fascinating project survives in manuscript partbooks. The half-brother of Mary Queen of Scots, Lord James Stewart (c.1531–1570), Earl of Moray, had asked Thomas Wode (fl. 1560–1592) to collect and copy the Psalter harmonisations which Moray had commissioned to several composers, among whom David Peebles. Once more, political reasons were at work, since the Earl (who would become Regent to King James VI at Mary's abdication) considered these psalter harmonisations to be a foundational element of the Protestant Kirk and of its legitimacy.

As stated above, among the musicians involved was David Peebles, who was requested to compose in a "plaine and dulce" style, without complex polyphony and in a fashion reminiscent of the Genevan harmonisations (with the tune in the tenor part). Other contributors were John Angus (fl. 1543–1595), the arranger of most canticles and prayers, and Andro Kemp (fl. 1560–1570), while John Buchan (fl. 1562–1608) contributed two Psalm-settings. Since the Wode project predated the publication of the Kirk's *Forme of Prayers*, it is interesting that it was not interrupted when the official Psalter was published; this is particularly fascinating in consideration of the fact that the first Scottish *Forme of Prayers* did not include the canticles and hymns found in the Wode partbooks. The Wode partbooks represent today one of the most important sources for Scottish music from the early Reformation era, and a valuable witness of the fluid boundaries between private devotion and public worship[121].

Although it is impossible here to list thoroughly the metrical psalters and the editions of metrical psalmody in the English and Scottish languages, I will only mention, in passing, the English psalters issued in the 1590s by Richard Schilders (c.1538–1634) in the city of Middelburg, in Zeeland[122]: in Schilders' psalters, for the first time, prose translations of the Psalms were juxtaposed to their metrical versions. The Schilders prints, which were illegal in England since they violated the Royal patents for psalter printing, had possibly a political significance: as maintained by Duguid, they represented an attempt to join the two British tra-

---

[121] Cf. Dawson 2012, p. 50; see also the exhibition booklet for the exposition *"Singing the Reformation. Celebrating Thomas Wode and his Partbooks. 1562–1592"*, Main Library, University of Edinburgh (The Wode Psalter Project Team), 2011; available online at http://bit.ly/2cgtfJW.
[122] *Psalmes of David* 1594 (and subsequent editions).

ditions, possibly in view of the accession of the Scots' King James VI to the English throne following Queen Elizabeth's death (1603).

### 7.3.7. Psalms, piety and politics

Indeed, political aspects were frequently intertwined with religious matters in England and Scotland: as we know, sung psalmody in worship had started to be systematically practised by the Marian exiles, and it represented their heritage and the witness of their suffering. Thus, when the religious stance of Queen Elizabeth, of her successors or of the spiritual leaders appeared to be too close to Catholicism in the eyes of the returning exiles or of their descendants (the "godly"), psalmody became a form of protestation, and represented the religious and spiritual identity of the Evangelicals who would later be known as "Puritans".

Several scholars whose research focuses on English metrical psalmody have also pointed out the fundamental role of Psalm-singing in attaching popular culture to the values of the Reformation. Within a few decades, Psalm-singing had won a unique place in the lives and hearts of the English Protestants. Several reasons have been advanced for this phenomenon, and they are probably all concurring, rather than competing, factors.

One such reason was probably the powerful feeling of belonging, and the aesthetical pleasure drawn by the congregation from the very act of singing together, particularly with loud voices[123]. Psalm tunes became more and more cherished in parallel with the emergence and success of the Common Tunes, which not only were simple, easy and immediate, but also created a net of internal references by way of recurring motifs; this in turn increased the parishioners' feeling of familiarity and "aural homeliness", if I may say so. Indeed, in Leaver's opinion, the "popular attachment" to metrical psalmody constitutes a valid indicator of the impact of Protestantism on the English society[124].

English parishioners, by the end of the century, could thus maintain that they "have had more pleasure, and their minds more lifted up to devotion, [than] with all the solemn music of organs and voices: whether it were the matter, or the meter, or the maker, or the music, or all together that so ravished them"[125], as reported by John Harington (1561–1612).

---

[123] Cf. Craig 2010, p. 108; Marsh 2013, pp. 391–392.
[124] Cf. Leaver 2004a, p. 153.
[125] Harington 1804, vol. I, p. 190.

The occasions for singing Psalms within services progressively augmented in number and gained official acceptance. Typically, Psalm-singing framed the sermon at both ends; psalmody accompanied communion and burial rites, as well as sacred actions taking place outside the church. The penetration of metrical psalmody within the high spheres of society and religion is also shown by the use and careful choice of appropriate Psalms on official dynastic occasions during Elizabeth's reign[126].

The tunes of the "Sternhold and Hopkins" started to be used also independently of their original Psalm-texts: for example, they were employed in a 1583 publication by Thomas Roberts, providing the musical accompaniment to a metrical catechism for the doctrinal instruction of children and the young[127], while John Rhodes (fl. 1588–1606) used Psalm-tunes (such as those for the XV, XXV or "any ordinary Psalm") for the devotional and recreational poetry contained in *The Countrie Mans Comfort* (1588[128]). The lyrics included in this collection already show a clear mark of Evangelical sensitivity, inasmuch as their focus is constantly and unmistakably on the Christ – even when they celebrated the saints' feast-days[129].

## 7.4. The "Godly Ballads"

The brief mention of the *Countrie Mans Comfort* with which the preceding section ended brings us to the subject of religious music not intended for singing in church[130].

The phenomena of religious ballad printing, selling, transmission and singing have often been seen in opposition to the culture of psalmody; however, recent studies suggest that they should rather be seen side-by-side, and contribute together to the interpretation and understanding of musicianship and piety in the sixteenth century.

Similar to what happened in Germany, where religious broadsheets were used as a means for conveying news, to entertain, instruct, provide ethical models and foster devotion, also in England the impressive spread of "penny-bal-

---

126 Cf. Temperley 1979, vol. I, p. 48; Marsh 2013, p. 409.
127 Roberts 1583; cf. Willis 2010, p. 173.
128 Rhodes 1637.
129 Cf. Watt 1991, p. 65; Willis 2010, p. 199.
130 On the topic of ballads and cheap print, cf. Watt 1991, to which this section is indebted. Cf. also Würzbach 1981 (1990) and Fumerton 2012.

lads" co-involved several social layers and gradually extended itself well beyond the limits of the urbanised population.

Ballads on religious subjects served both Catholics and Protestants for the propagation of confessional teachings from the very first years of the English Reformation; however, many ballads (especially in the first years of the Elizabethan era) had a more spiritual purpose and were aimed at fostering piety rather than at challenging or spreading beliefs.

Together with the phenomenon of contrafacture, which was often associated with such forms of "popular" culture, the dissemination of cheap-print religious songs was part of a Europe-wide movement, in which the accessibility of economic broadsheets favoured the propagation of tunes and texts alike (often in combination with visual imagery).

The output of ballads written by early English Reformers does not try and convey detailed dogmatic teachings or to oppose the Catholic doctrine: instead, it attempts an appropriation of the subjects and forms of Catholic popular culture within the new perspective fostered by the Evangelicals. (The reader may recall that one of the features of Calvinism, in Randall's opinion, was to redefine spatial or cultural realities through occupancy[131]; cf. § 6.3.6.).

The potentially educational function of religious music, whose primary and intended recipients were the uncultivated people (although, as said, they were by no means the only consumers of cheap ballads), was clear for some of the first English Reformers. For example, John Ponet (or Poynet, c.1514–1556) endorsed this view in writing: "Ballads, rhymes and short toys that be not dear and will easily be born away, do much good at home among the rude people"[132].

The culture of penny-ballads was undoubtedly primarily a culture of entertainment; however, as argued by Ponet (and similarly to what happened on the Continent, especially in the Lutheran areas), the practical advantages of cheap prints (such as their inexpensiveness and easiness to carry and conceal) could be profitably used by preachers and religious reformers.

Thus, in the early Elizabethan era, "the writers of metrical Psalms and 'moralized' ballads borrowed the tunes of secular song as their route to the people's hearts"[133].

The main themes found in religious ballads are often those which all people cared for most: from the fight against evil and sin to death, salvation and damnation, with a strong focus on ethics and morality: Watt classifies her repertoire

---

[131] Randall 1999, p. 31.
[132] In Collinson 1988, p. 103.
[133] Watt 1991, p. 40.

of ballads by dividing them as "religio-political", "social morality", "death and salvation" and "stories". Similar to what happened in the Lutheran areas, moreover, "apocalyptic" themes are often found in this popular repertoire (cf. § 5.3.4.3. and 4.2.4.11.); roughly a quarter of the total, instead, focused on devotional subjects regarding introspection, discernment and conscience.

The doctrinal viewpoint on afterlife is often not straightforwardly "Catholic" or "Protestant", but frequently represents the people's "practical theology", which was often more nuanced and flexible than that of dogmatic Churches[134]: in Watt's words, "the resulting patchwork of beliefs may be described as distinctively post-Reformation but not thoroughly Protestant"[135].

Notwithstanding this, and regardless of the sometimes imprecise doctrinal teachings transmitted by the godly ballads, they concur to portray "a coherent layman's theology"[136]. It should be emphasised that one of the goals of cheap ballads was to profit their sellers (and therefore too complex doctrinal messages would have been counter-productive); and as to their religious content and value, their aim was to contribute to shaping a society's ethics, fostering piety and transmitting simple instruction. A secondary goal of godly ballads, at least for a certain period, was to contribute to the self-definition of an Evangelically-inspired identity, often in opposition to that of Catholicism.

Generally speaking, then, in England as in Germany and in several other European countries, the combination of text, music (and sometimes woodcuts) which characterised the popular culture of ballads and similar songs was a liminal object between literacy and illiteracy, orality and printing, musicianship and instruction. It also represents a fascinating insight into what really mattered for the faithful, and into what was perceived and received among the population of what was discussed by theologians. Although it cannot be assumed that religious ballads were the *product* of the less cultivated social layers (since in most cases the texts originated at a much higher level of literacy than that of their primary users), they certainly mirror what the "people" was interested in, and what they were willing to own, to sing and to transmit in turn[137].

---

[134] Kreuzer 1973, pp. 126–127.
[135] Watt 1991, p. 327; see also *ibid.*, pp. 86–127.
[136] Pettegree 2005, p. 73.
[137] Cf. Watt 1991, pp. 40–41; 86–127; 325–237 etc.; Pettegree 2005, pp. 72–73; Willis 2009, pp. 305–307; Willis 2010, pp. 184, 189 and 307.

## 7.5. Our daily music

Whereas we have already observed several important differences in the worship styles and practices of the various Churches, the forms taken by religious musicianship in private contexts were more similar to one another in most European countries: in the domestic sphere, dissimilarities could be more pronounced among social classes than among countries or confessional allegiances (with obvious exceptions).

A still different situation concerns the role of music in education, since here there was a public dimension which could not be always assimilated to those in worship, but which also could depend more closely on the official orientation of the confessional Churches.

In England, as elsewhere, music – in all forms it took – was a fundamental component of the education to faith and religion. Sung metrical psalmody, particularly in the early years of the Reformation, was thought to have an educational value, to foster a habit of devotion and responsiveness to God, to channel in a spiritual direction the spontaneous emotions of the believers, and also to be a form of spiritual entertainment; after the Marian experience, however, this recreational function was downplayed in favour of the others[138].

### 7.5.1. Educating in music

If we consider first the educational function, we may adopt the categorisations proposed by Willis, who however stresses that the actual situation was much more fluid than groupings may suggest[139]. Music's "educational" functions can be therefore schematically classified in three categories: 1) musical works with a specifically pedagogical function; 2) spread of one confession (to the detriment of others); 3) "Protestantisation" (i.e. the fostering of an Evangelical frame of mind and behaviour through music).

As concerns the musical education of children and the use of music for their religious instruction, contemporary scholarship suggests that music was less ubiquitous and more expendable in English schools than it was in the Lutheran areas of Germany: in many cases, it was left to personal/institutional initiative and was not officially mandated by the Church.

---

**138** Cf. Quitslund 2012, pp. 240–241.
**139** Willis 2010, p. 163.

On the other hand, English children were undoubtedly familiar with religious music, especially with Psalms, which were sung and performed in a variety of private and public contexts; moreover, canticles, hymns and religious songs (up to carols or ballads) were an essential component of the Elizabethan soundscape and certainly contributed to shaping the religious framework of the young. We have already seen how this familiarity with psalmody was exploited by Thomas Roberts, who structured his metrical catechism so that it could be sung on Psalm-tunes: I will touch on this subject again in Chapter Eleven (§ 11.4.7.4.).

I will dedicate some space to the propagandistic use of music in the Christian Churches in Chapter Ten (e.g. § 10.3.5.); suffice it to recall, for now, the importance of Psalm-singing to "annoy the mass-priests, and the devil" mentioned in John Jewel's letter to Peter Martyr Vermigli quoted in Chapter Four[140] (§ 4.2.4.5.). Notwithstanding this, the belligerent dimension of much Psalm-singing in Continental Europe was less pronounced in England, where the Psalms' main functions were prevailingly to foster education, piety and to comfort. As Willis points out, though music did not receive the same official support and encouragement from English Reformers as it did in Lutheran Germany, undeniably it played a fundamental role in the spread and consolidation of Evangelical ideas and behaviours in England[141].

### 7.5.2. Private piety

To this end, naturally, what exceeded the limits of officially promoted or compulsory activities was at least as important as what happened within them. The first (musical) rudiments of a child's religious instruction were provided at home, though the issue of general and musical literacy is always crucially at stake from this viewpoint: how widespread was the capability of reading a line of music (let alone a polyphonic piece)? And what about that of learning, singing and spreading the text of a Psalm or of a religious song?

It is possible that such skills were more common that we normally infer: many more people than those who could write were probably able to read a text, and musical notation could serve merely as an aide-memoire for tunes which had actually been learned by rote. We have already seen that the private use of the "Sternhold and Hopkins" as well as of Archbishop Parker's Psalter was explicitly envisaged by their authors, who purposefully imagined flexible

---

[140] Jewel, Letter of March 5th, 1560, in Robinson 1842, vol. I, p. 71.
[141] Willis 2009, p. 309. Cf. Willis 2010, pp. 163, 172–173.

performance possibilities (from monody to harmonisations and/or with instrumental accompaniment) to suit the musical needs and capabilities of a wide variety of users.

Private Psalm-singing was encouraged and fostered, particularly among the "godly", but not always successfully, as testified by Nicholas Bownde (d.1613): "The Psalms are sung in many places, after a plain, distinct, and profitable manner, and may be everywhere if men will, yet men content themselves with that, and are not mindful to sing at home by themselves alone, or with the rest of their household"[142].

Minister James Melville (1556–1614) efficaciously summarised the goal of Christian life for his parishioners (in Anstruther, Scotland), as being "homely with God": this habit to a godly life was interwoven with prayer, especially in the form of sung Psalms interspersing the daily activities of the laity[143]. In Scotland, indeed, the Kirk endorsed from its outset (*First Book of Discipline*, 1560) the practice of Psalm-singing at home, not only with immediate devotional purposes, but also for improving the quality of sung psalmody in the church: "Moreover men, women, children, would be exhorted to exercise themselves in the Psalms, that when the Kirk convenes and does sing, they may be the more able together with common hearts and voices to praise God"[144].

The same concept is found in an earlier (1553) collection by Christopher Tye, where music represents an accessory to the metrical version of the Bible, but the focus is on the spiritual value of the text: "The acts of the apostles [...] with notes to each chapter, to sing and also to play upon the Lute, very necessary for students after their study, [...] and also for all Christians that cannot sing, to read the good and Godly stories of the lives of Christ [and of] his apostles"[145].

Metrical psalters, in turn, obeyed the same principles outlined here by Tye, i.e. to encourage knowledge of God's Word and a Christian behaviour fostered by familiarity with the Bible, and doing so through the pleasant medium of music. As Thomas Morley stated, music should "draw the hearer, as it were, in chains of gold by the ears to the consideration of holy things"[146]. Even more clearly, this was stated in the Psalm collection (1599) by Richard Alison[147]: "because the whole Book of God to idle scholars may seem too tedious, we have the Psalms of David more compendiously teaching doctrine fit for us". We will see in Chapter

---

[142] Bownde 1595, p. 241, as quoted in Marsh 2013, p. 439.
[143] Melville 1598, "Epistle Dedicatorie", fol. 2$^r$, as quoted in Dawson 2012, p. 34.
[144] Cf. http://www.swrb.com/newslett/actualNLs/bod_ch03.htm.
[145] Tye 1553, title-page.
[146] Morley 1597, Part III; in MacClintock 1982, p. 97.
[147] Alison 1599, sig. A2$^r$.

Eleven (§ 11.4.4.1.) how close was Thomas Roberts' stance to Alison's; here I would like to point out two significant aspects in Alison's viewpoint. Firstly, music is seen (echoing once more St Augustine's statements) as a help for the weak and the young; secondly, the Psalter is regarded as a summary of the entire Bible.

There was also a noteworthy fluidity between the secular and the religious repertoire destined for private music-making, both as concerns the instrumental/vocal destination of the works (whose instrumentation was normally flexible) and the migration from the sacred to the secular sphere and vice-versa. Contrafacture was practised in both directions: for example, the secular song by Sheppard *O happy dames* was transformed into an anthem (*I will give thanks unto the Lord*), while a sacred work by Tallis (*Purge me o Lord*) became secular as *Fond youth is a bubble*, though the moralising text of the secular version closely mirrors the process undergone by Calvinist Psalms when they were given more neutral and simply devotional texts (cf. § 6.3.6.).

Whereas – as we have stated before (§ 7.3.4.) – there was little or no contamination between secular music and the "Sternhold and Hopkins" Psalm tunes, the polyphonic repertoire destined for church choirs was more open to secular infiltrations. Possibly, this was due to the greater audibility and evidence of a secular tune in monody conceived for singing by all members of the congregation; the secular origins of polyphonic *contrafacta* were probably less recognisable by the average church-goer.

A fascinating article by John Milsom[148] analyses the background of works which had traditionally been attributed (even in a printed collection by John Day: *Mornyng and Evenyng Prayer and Communion*, 1565[149]) to Thomas Caustun (c.1520–1569), but which actually were just *contrafacta* of works by Sebastiano Festa (c.1490–1524), Nicolas Gombert, Rogier Pathie (c.1510-a.1564) and Philippe van Wilder (c.1500–1554). According to Milsom, Caustun's *contrafacta* may have been intended for publication from the outset, at a time when there was insufficient availability of syllabic works in English for singing in the major ecclesiastical institutions. The urgent need for such a repertoire to be ready and available for use encouraged the production of *contrafacta* such as those by Caustun, and the acceptance of pre-existing polyphonic works regardless of their origin (as concerns geographical and linguistic provenance as well as the content of their original texts[150]).

---

**148** Milsom 2007.
**149** Caustun 1565.
**150** Cf. Milsom 2007, pp. 26, 29–31; cf. also Aplin 1978, 1979, 1980 and Leaver 1991, p. 116.

Contrafacture also applied to Latin-texted works, as mentioned earlier (§ 7.2.3.), with the purpose of giving a new, "Evangelical" meaning and significance to pieces conceived for and belonging to the traditional repertoire. Such was the fate of *Gaude, gloriosa Dei Mater*, an antiphon by Tallis whose text is typical of the Catholic veneration of the Virgin Mary[151]: under the Reformation, it was transformed into a Protestant piece through the use of Psalm texts.

Sacred polyphony and religious works similar to French *chansons spirituelles* or Italian spiritual madrigals were also popular among the musically literate (we will see some examples of this repertoire later in this Chapter: § 7.6.3.), and contributed to unifying through the medium of music – though in different ways – the religious experience of many believers in Elizabethan society[152].

Prefacing his *Songs of Sundrie Natures* (1589), William Byrd clearly suggested the various contexts for the practice of devotional music: his music, he claimed, was conceived "to serve for all companies and voices: whereof some are easy and plain to sing, other more hard and difficult, but all, such as any young practitioner in singing, with a little foresight, may easily perform"[153]. The most refined musical works on Scriptural or devotional texts were principally destined for members of the upper and educated classes, and were particularly appreciated by patrician women, as the diary of Lady Margaret Hoby (1571–1633) demonstrates[154].

## 7.6. Between Court and parish church

The very outset of the English Reformation had been deeply marked by the confiscation of ecclesiastical properties and dissolution of monasteries, which had brought about in turn the impoverishment of England's choral tradition (including the destruction of written sources of the early English polyphonic repertoire). However, as we have seen before (§ 7.2.1.), at no point of the English Reformation in the sixteenth-century was this tradition actually destroyed, although in several instances its future was very uncertain.

The major ecclesiastical institutions (such as great Cathedrals, the Royal Chapel and some colleges belonging to the most important educational establishments) preserved and maintained a living choral practice, though the actual

---

151 Corpus Christi College MS 566; cf. Milsom 1982, pp. 429–431.
152 Cf. Bray 2006, pp. 496–497; Lejeune 2010, pp. 17–18; Willis 2010, p. 189.
153 Cf. Byrd 1589a, "To the courteous reader".
154 Cf. Hamlin 2012, p. 229.

modes of its enactment and the kind of music performed were subject to change according to the official orientation of the Church.

Recent studies have pointed out the variety of situations which could be found in the different social, economic and geographical contexts. Some parish churches were able to maintain their choirs, while these were virtually annihilated in London; on the other hand, three of the principal choral institutions of the country were found in the City (the Chapel Royal, St Paul's and Westminster). It is true, however, that while the 1559 *Injunctions* explicitly fostered the survival of choral institutions which were existent, they provided no funding for this purpose and no detailed indications about their musical style and repertoire; by promoting congregational singing, they potentially supported the feeling that professional church music was superfluous. Indeed, by the end of the century parish choirs were virtually extinct.

In spite of this, there are numerous documents witnessing to the willingness of many parish churches to invest in music-related improvements (perhaps of less an expensive nature than maintaining a choir); and while it is true that many existing organs were not restored and organ-building was in crisis, research has shown that the fundamental reasons for these phenomena were contingent, and not inherent, to religious issues (e.g. financial problems, unavailability of know-how etc.). No official prohibitions were issued concerning the use of organs in church, although isolated attempts to limit their use were undertaken by local authorities. In spite of a general crisis in organ maintenance and construction, the instruments owned by several parishes were in use at the end of the century. Moreover, there was a fascinating tradition of lay choral singing which managed to survive in spite of the limitations imposed on ecclesiastical choral institutions[155].

Thus, there was a significant degree of variability concerning the types of pieces to be sung (e.g. Masses, anthems, canticles, Psalms etc.), the compositional styles (syllabic, imitative, polyphonic...) and the settings (monody, harmonisation, presence of instruments, polyphony etc.).

As seen in our discussion of many other religious contexts, while the simplest forms of church music could enter into the worship of the most important institutions, the reverse migration was very unlikely: so, there soon emerged two distinct musical traditions of different complexity, the simplest of which characterised parish churches, and the most complex one pertaining almost exclusively to major establishments.

---

[155] Cf. Fincham and Tyacke 2007, pp. 64–66 and 104; Craig 2010, pp. 105–108; Marsh 2013, pp. 397–403; McCullough 2013, pp. 109–110; Willis 2013, p. 131.

## 7.6. Between Court and parish church — 373

Of course, the existence of a similar differentiation was typical of all contexts in which polyphony was maintained (as in the Lutheran and Catholic Church). It could be seen as mirroring the distinction between daily plainchant and festive polyphony which has been discussed in Chapter Two[156] (§ 2.4.3.), and also (of course) the different availability of financial and human resources for church music in cathedrals from the one side or parish churches from the other.

Within the former context, a rather conservative form of worship and liturgy remained in use, with the continuing and regular performance of Offices and the active practice of polyphony: the repertoire sung there included anthems on Biblical texts performed in polyphony, and was enriched by such composers as Tallis, Byrd, Thomas Morley and Thomas Tomkins (1572–1656), among others. It should be emphasised, however, that this tradition was perceived and conceived as an elite product (both as concerns the artistic elite composing and performing it and the social layers involved), and suffered moments of economic, political and numerical uncertainty. On the other hand, worship in parish churches was centred on metrical psalmody[157]: this had been fostered – as mentioned earlier – by the returning exiles, who would have wished this practice to entirely replace all other competing forms of church music. Apart from the great choral institutions, for that matter, this actually became a reality in the majority of parishes throughout the country: conversely, the most common context for public psalmody in the last decades of the sixteenth century was during worship[158].

Thus, metrical psalmody and its harmonisations, though they may constitute an artistically less fascinating field than that of high vocal polyphony, were quantitatively prevailing and – therefore – sociologically and religiously more significant.

Whilst this double tradition was neither numerically balanced nor equally fostered and promoted, it persisted rather pacifically for years; however, it was doomed to become a true opposition at the later epoch of the Civil War (1642–51), when metrical psalmody came to be associated with Puritanism and the cathedral choral tradition with Anglicanism.

---

[156] Cf. also the instructions issued by Bishop John Grandisson (1292–1369) for Exeter in 1337 (so-called *Ordinale Exoniense*); cf. Le Huray 2008, pp. 29 and 139.
[157] Cf. Sfredda 2010, p. 125.
[158] Cf. Quitslund 2012, p. 237.

### 7.6.1. Shaping an "Anglican" style

Cathedral music started to represent a harbour against and an alternative or response to the Genevan influence, as well as the musical flag of the independence and individuality of the Church of England. Music became a symbol for the Anglican Church's self-identification as the "true continuation of all that was best in the European Catholic tradition"[159], in Le Huray's words.

This process involved (if not caused, as it was previously maintained in scholarship) the creation of a rather idiosyncratic musical language, typical of the English musical style. The tendencies at work between the sixteenth- and seventeenth centuries were gradually building this peculiar musical language; the Evangelical and humanist attention to the word/Word and its perceptibility encouraged the use of syllabic settings, fostering a clear "presentation" of the text. This, in turn, provided the background for the trends toward "re-presentation" and an increasingly expressive, almost pictorial concept of the text/music relationship. Notwithstanding this, however, Church music eluded a theatrical and over-emphasised rendition of the text, favouring instead moderation, gravity and solemnity; though sacred music was not immune from the contemporaneous aesthetical trends, it maintained some restraint and privileged a comparatively sober, plain and conservative style[160].

As Le Huray argues, these trends were certainly in dialogue with the processes of religious reformation, and probably were furthered by them, though confessional reasons cannot be deemed to be the only forces responsible for such an evolution[161]. Among the concurring causes, a major role was played by the influence of Italian madrigals on the English musical panorama, as well as by the change in the technique of composition, in the direction of vertical simultaneity instead of successive and horizontal writing.

A typical feature of English church music, which dated back to the pre-Reformation era but was maintained both in the physical distribution of space and as an expressive musical resource was the partition of the choir in two halves, called *decani* and *cantores*, which favoured antiphonal practices (particularly for musical versions of the canticles) and gave birth to other types of alternation (e.g. solo vocal passages with instruments vs. choral sections, or various choral groupings[162]).

---

159 Le Huray 2008, p. 46.
160 Cf. Le Huray 2008, p. 146 and 154–155.
161 Le Huray 2008, p. 135.
162 Cf. Bray 2006, p. 498; Rees 2006, p. 348.

## 7.6. Between Court and parish church — 375

Moreover, as Le Huray points out, Elizabeth's political skills allowed her to perceive the value of a Catholic-like approach to liturgy for diplomatic purposes and as a means to offer a particular view of the Church of England to international visitors[163].

Duke Frederick I of Württemberg (1557–1608), who travelled to England with his secretary Jacob Rathgeb (1578–1614), who later (1602) published his memories, was vividly impressed by the worship he attended on August 20$^{th}$, 1592 at Windsor Castle:

> The music, especially the organ, was exquisitely played; for at times you could hear the sound of cornet[t]s, flutes, then fifes and other instruments; and there was likewise a little boy who sang so sweetly amongst it all, *ornamenting the music in such a way* with his little tongue that it was really wonderful to listen to him. In short, their ceremonies were very similar to the Papists, as above mentioned, with singing and all the rest[164].

The similarity between the Chapel Royal performance and those of the "papists" was thus clear and impressive even to contemporaries, though its music was subtly fascinating for listeners. Significantly, this amazement was caused by the use of instruments (of which a striking variety is listed) as well as by the melismatic singing of the treble.

The quality of the Chapel Royal's music was a constant concern for the Crown, also in consideration of Elizabeth's love for music and of her conviction about its usefulness for diplomacy; the Chapel could number around thirty-two Gentlemen and a dozen boys, together with instrumentalists of whose expertise the Duke of Württemberg could bear witness.

Towards the last decades of the sixteenth century, substantial economic investments were made in order to restore or rebuild organs in the English territories, thus showing the increasing interest in musical practices which were labelled as "popish" by those identifying themselves more closely with the Reformed approach. At the same time, a numerical increase in the quantity of choral works composed by musicians employed in church establishments could be observed[165].

Also as concerns the use of musical instruments, a pronounced difference can be found between the most prestigious ecclesiastical institutions and the daily reality of parish life. Whereas here the task of realising music for services

---

163 Le Huray 2008, p. 34.
164 As quoted and translated in Rye 1865, pp. 15–16; translation modified for the section in italics (German original: "*und colorirt dermassen mit seinem Zünglein*").
165 Cf. Temperley 1979; Leaver 2006, pp. 399–400; Owens 2006, pp. 361, 363 and 366; Rees 2006, p. 346; Le Huray 2008, p. 45; Quitslund 2008.

was entirely dependent upon the human resources of the parish itself, and the increasing presence of metrical psalmody virtually annihilated polyphony and (often) the use of musical instruments in church, in Cathedrals and similar institutions the situation was markedly different, and the organ was not the only instrument in use. (As Marsh has fascinatingly studied, however, a particular kind of musical instruments did not suffer the fate of parish organs: church bells maintained their social, ritual and spiritual role, frequently remaining virtually untouched by the Reformation, with just a few adjustments to the principles of the new confession[166]).

It is possible that cornetts and sackbuts had been employed at the Cathedral of Canterbury since before the Reformation (around 1532) and it has been argued that a specific space was assigned to wind instrument players within the Cathedral of Carlisle less than a decade later (1541).

On August 31$^{st}$, 1566, the day of her arrival at Oxford, Queen Elizabeth was greeted with a worship service at the Cathedral, when the *Te Deum* was performed ("sung to cornet[t]s"[167]); however, such practices were probably rather exceptional until the last quarter of the sixteenth century, when the use of cornetts and sackbuts in church is reported with ever-increasing frequency. In detail, cornetts usually doubled the high-pitched parts, whereas sackbuts played with the lower voices.

The increasing fondness for organ playing, on the other hand, and the increasing difficulty of the organ parts provoked a significant change in the very process of recruitment of organ players: before the Reformation, the members of a major institution's Chapel who could play the organ with sufficient proficiency were entitled to the task; later, some of the best English organists of the time were elected to a Chapel precisely by virtue of their organ playing[168].

The higher requirements placed on organists after the Reformation were partially a consequence of the increasing spread of a particular form of composition which was typical of English music, i.e. the so-called *verse-composition*.

Though the practice of alternating solo and ensemble groupings was by no means a novelty, the form it took in England was original; the other qualifying feature of verse-composition (i.e. instrumental accompaniment) had a clear direct forerunner in some performance practices for metrical Psalms. Together with religious songs, Psalms were often sung as accompanied solo monodies, with lute or similar (often plucked-stringed) instruments. The combination of al-

---

**166** Cf. Marsh 2013, pp. 454–470.
**167** Nichols 1823, vol. I, p. 209.
**168** Cf. Owens 2006, p. 362; Le Huray 2008, pp. 65–66 and 125–127.

ternation with *obbligato* accompaniment produced the most typical traits of post-Reformation verse-composition, which (in opposition to that practised earlier, in Catholic England) requires the use of instruments as a necessary condition.

This strategy, however, presented both artistic and practical benefits: the solo parts (which were obviously both more demanding and more evident) could be entrusted to the best musicians, whose number was rather limited (especially in provinces) in relation to the higher quantity of average performers; moreover, the timbral difference between vocal soloists and instruments increased the emotional power of the singing voices in comparison to the more homogeneous blend (and more neutral timbre) of purely vocal polyphony[169].

### 7.6.2. Setting the Service

This particular compositional style was applied both to individual anthems and to entire services, which could however be set also in traditional polyphony. A complete musical "service" was made up of the sum of the three services of Matins, Evensong and Communion, corresponding to the shape taken by English post-Reformation liturgy during the Edwardian era. Matins and Evensong comprised musical settings of the canticles (*Venite, Te Deum* or *Benedicite, Benedictus* or *Jubilate* for Morning Prayer, and *Magnificat* or *Cantate Domino, Nunc Dimittis* or *Deus Misereatur* for Evening Prayer), whereas music for the Lord's Supper resembled the Catholic *Ordinarium Missæ* with the exception of the *Agnus Dei* and with a different order of the liturgical items. Musical settings of complete services could be unified through the use of a recurring *incipit*, similarly to what happened to Catholic Mass settings in the pre-Reformation era. Among the most ancient and significant examples of service settings, a special mention should be made of Thomas Tallis' *Complete Service* in the Dorian mode, which is one of the most beautiful and remarkable of the early musical fruits of the English Reformation; on the other hand, Byrd's *Second Service* is one of the first to employ the verse-composition style for service settings[170].

After the Collect, both at Matins and Evensong, an anthem could be sung: this form is another peculiarity of English church music which would originate a series of masterpieces both in the century under analysis and in those to come.

Though choral anthems in English (normally indicated as "full anthems", in homorhythmic and syllabic style) show similarities with *concertato* motets, to-

---

[169] Cf. Le Huray 2008, pp. 217 and 225.
[170] Cf. Shaw 1975, p. 701; Bray 2006, p. 506; Rees 2006, pp. 347–348.

wards the end of the century "verse anthems" (with alternations between accompanied monody and choral passages) started to be composed. Anthems were normally set to texts excerpted or paraphrased from the Bible, similar to the "antiphons" (*antiennes*) from which their name derives; both as regards anthems and motets, at first English composers seemed to favour texts chosen from a single Scriptural source, and it was an Italian musician working at Elizabeth's court, Alfonso Ferrabosco the Elder (1543–1588) who successfully established the practice of combining several textual sources together in his motets. On the other hand, some of the most beautiful anthems written in the second half of the sixteenth century were the work of such composers as Tallis, Tye and Richard Farrant (c.1525–1580), whereas William Byrd attempted the creation of musical works suitable for both church and domestic performance, as verse anthems or consort music. His 1588–9 published works (see § 7.6.3.) demonstrate a truly flexible approach to the actual sound of performance, having been probably created for solo voice with accompaniment by viols, but whose performance by voices alone is equally possible[171].

Among the greatest composers of the time, the career and output of Thomas Tallis exemplify an artist's creative response to the political and religious changes of sixteenth-century England. The beginnings of his musical activity date back to the pre-Reformation era, when he was employed as an organist in abbeys and cathedrals such as Canterbury, Dover and Waltham. In 1542 he became a member of the Chapel Royal, and obviously had to follow with his compositions the different confessional and artistic requirements of the successive sovereigns who determined the country's confessional and liturgical orientation (from Henry VIII to Elizabeth, including the years of Edward and Mary's rule). Some of his works mirror the confusing alternation of opposing liturgical indications, and their text was changed from Latin to English (or vice-versa) in consequence of the King or Queen's confessional allegiance. (As concerns Tallis' own choices, modern scholarship tends to agree on his continuing adhesion to Catholicism, though such matters are extremely difficult to establish for someone so closely associated with the Crown). Not only the works' texts were subject to change with time, but also the favoured compositional style: as mentioned earlier (§ 7.3.6.), Tallis' *If ye love me* is one of the most splendid examples of how homophonic settings which succeed in delivering a text in a perfectly understandable fashion could also reach artistic heights whose simplicity implies by no means a downplaying of beauty. On the other hand, Tallis' extraordinary ac-

---

[171] Cf. Shaw 1975, pp. 702–703; Higman 2000, p. 501; Rainoldi 2000, p. 327; Bray 2006, p. 506; Rees 2006, p. 348; Le Huray 2008, p. 142; Weber 2008, pp. 56–57; Sfredda 2010, p. 125.

complishment as a polyphonic composer is abundantly shown by his justly famous *Spem in alium*, whose forty-part texture rivals the most complex achievements of the Flemish polyphonists[172].

### 7.6.3. Byrd: A Catholic at Court

Whereas no certain statements can be pronounced about Tallis' confessional allegiance, William Byrd (who probably studied with him) was definitely a Catholic throughout his life, and became an important representative of the Catholic resistance during the harshest times of persecution and martyrdom (see § 10.3.3.2.).

Notwithstanding this, Byrd was a faithful and esteemed musician in Elizabeth's Chapel, and his loyalty to the Queen was shown ample appreciation: in fact, Elizabeth conceded to both Tallis and Byrd an exclusive right to publish music for more than two decades. In homage to the Queen, the two composers published in 1575 a joint collection (*Cantiones quæ ab argumento sacræ vocantur*[173]), to which each contributed seventeen pieces, and in which musical symbolism referring to Elizabeth is frequently found.

Byrd's musical output reveals the difficulty of his situation, in which sincere fidelity to his faith struggled with his equally sincere loyalty to the Queen. Some of his major achievements are found in the field of Latin-texted music, whose artistic quality is reached by practically only his "Great" Service among his English-texted works.

His Latin-texted sacred output includes, among others, three Mass Ordinary settings (c.1595, set for three, four and five parts respectively) and a large number of *Gradualia*, collected in two volumes (1605 and 1607[174]), with Proper settings, including those for such clearly Catholic feasts as those in honour of the Virgin Mary, of All Saints, and of the Corpus Christi. Both the *Gradualia*'s texts and the explicit declaration of allegiance found on their title-page did not conceal the composer's confessional belonging and its courageous vindication. Since the possession of this collection was mentioned among the elements relevant to the conviction of a Frenchman in Britain[175], obviously Byrd's *Gradualia* were not conceived for public worship, and could be performed only within private

---

[172] Cf. Higman 2000, p. 501; Owens 2006, pp. 364–365; Lejeune 2010, p. 17; Sfredda 2010, p. 125.
[173] Byrd and Tallis 1575.
[174] Byrd 1605 and Byrd 1607.
[175] Cf. Brett 2007, p. 196.

liturgies or for domestic devotion[176]. As argued by Milsom, however, the survival of several collections of Latin-texted religious music (composed both in the time preceding and in that following the Reformation) among the libraries of private collectors such as John Baldwin (c.1560–1615), Robert Dow (1553–1588) and John Sadler (1513–1596) and the continuing vitality of the composition of new Latin-texted sacred repertoire by such composers as Byrd testifies to a widespread interest in a kind of music which could not be publicly performed[177].

Whereas Byrd's earlier collections of Latin motets often rely on texts excerpted from liturgical sources, his 1589 and 1591 volumes of *Cantiones Sacræ*[178] reveal his increasing concern for texts selected personally by the composer (often in agreement with his spiritual leaders), combining and adapting words from various sacred provenances. As argued by Bray[179], the presence of penitential motets within these collections can be interpreted within the framework of Byrd's increasing determination to be officially identified as a Catholic recusant. Byrd's choices reveal a self-aware and discerning initiative: the composer wished to set to music words which mirrored and expressed the religious feelings, concerns and needs of the Catholic community and of himself[180] (cf. also § 10.3.3.2.).

Notwithstanding this, in 1588–9, Byrd published collections of English-texted religious works (Psalms and songs), several of which had been written some time before, titled respectively *Psalmes, Sonets, & songs of sadnes and pietie* (1588) and *Songs of Sundrie Natures*[181] (1589). They were to be followed, in 1611, by another collection of *Psalmes, Songs and Sonnets*[182]. As the title itself shows, Byrd set to music metrical Psalms in English; as Bray maintains, it is likely that the intended recipients of these versions were Catholic recusants – though, of course, devotional works were less denominationally bound than liturgical music – and they certainly show the closeness of Byrd's spiritual horizon to that of psalmody[183]. Almost all pieces included in this collection can be performed in a variety of mixed settings for voices and viols, either doubling or replacing the ones with the others (it is likely that the favourite performance style envisioned by the composer was solo voice with instrumental accompaniment).

---

[176] See McCarthy 2007.
[177] Cf. Shaw 1975, p. 794; Brett 1989; Milsom 1995; Monson 1997, p. 363; Higman 2000, p. 501; Atlas 2006, p. 116; Owens 2006, pp. 365–366; Lejeune 2010, p. 17; Sfredda 2010, p. 125. On Byrd's *Gradualia*, cf. especially McCarthy 2007.
[178] Byrd 1589b and Byrd 1591.
[179] Bray 2011, p. 63.
[180] Cf. Le Huray 2008, p. 142.
[181] Byrd 1588 and Byrd 1589a.
[182] Byrd 1611.
[183] Cf. Bray 2011, pp. 69–74.

Notwithstanding the variety of Byrd's compositional techniques and of his works' intended users, his style is constantly recognisable thanks to the elegance and expressiveness of his melodic writing, which often indulges in word-painting and frequently struggles for a perfect cohesion between text and music[184].

As this essential and sketchy overview aimed at showing, English religious music expressed itself in a variety of forms which could easily compete with the other major musical traditions of Continental Europe, creating new and totally idiomatic musical genres and compositional styles.

In comparison with other European countries which were affected by the social, religious and political changes of the Protestant Reformations, England represents a unique case under many aspects. As discussed in this Chapter, the peculiar features of the history of its Reformation had clear repercussions on its liturgical and non-liturgical religious repertoire, on the origins, musical/literary style and organisation of its worship, and on the particular traits of its major composers' lives, religious experiences and insight into life and spirituality.

From the one side, the Elizabethan era was a "golden age" for music as it was for so many other fields of culture and creativity, and the Queen's love for and appreciation of music allowed several Catholic composers to employ and cultivate their artistic gifts in relative creative freedom and within a situation of economic certainty and a stimulating musical environment. Notwithstanding this, many tensions were felt at all levels of English society, and not only between the contemporaneously competing religious confessions: as we have repeatedly seen in this Chapter, the opposition between Cathedral and parish music not only mirrored a similar division within the Church of England, but paralleled and pre-cognized a confessional conflict which was going to explode in the following century.

---

**184** Cf. Shaw 1975, p. 702; Higman 2000, p. 501; Bray 2006, pp. 503 and 506; Le Huray 2008, p. 386; Lejeune 2010, p. 18; Zim 2011, p. 150.

# Chapter 8 – Music and the Council of Trent

> The whole plan of singing in musical modes should be constituted not to give empty pleasure to the ear, but in such a way that the words may be clearly understood by all, and so that the listeners' hearts may be enraptured to the desire of the heavenly harmonies and to contemplation of the joys of the blessed[1].
>
> [Draft for a Decree at the Council of Trent]

## 8.1. Introduction

The collocation of this Chapter within the discussion of the European Reformations aims at considering the effects of the Council of Trent on music from the viewpoint of reform and renewal rather than of opposition and reaction. Even though many of the Tridentine deliberations (both theologically and liturgically) were conditioned by what had happened and was happening throughout Europe, it would be profoundly incorrect to evaluate Trent (and especially the itinerary of sixteenth-century Catholic Church) in relation only to Evangelical reforms or as a response to them.

Moreover, as we will see, the true priorities of the Council of Trent were much more focused on issues which were crucial and central to the Church's life, rather than on the relatively minor issues of musical style and practice. On the other hand, this downplaying of music's role might have (at least partially and locally) affected the overall success of the attempted re-catholicization of Europe. In other words, Catholic churchmen sometimes lacked the insight into the power of musicianship for devotion, identity and worship that characterised so many of the Evangelical reformers.

Actually, instead of concerning themselves primarily with genuine musical matters, the relatively scanty rulings of the Council on music involve principally liturgical and moral issues, which only secondarily impacted onto actual musical practice.

Indeed, well before the Council, there had been attempts at a religious reform of sacred music; we will briefly examine the role played by the Papal chap-

---

[1] "Compendium Abusuum" in Paleotti 1842, p. 266 (10.9.1562), my translation. Cf. Rainoldi 2000, p. 38; Monson 2002, pp. 9–10; Boyce 2006, p. 140; Weber 2008, p. 164.

els in the establishment of what would later become known as the so-called "Tridentine aesthetics". The discussion of what was appreciated within the Chapels' music and what was considered to be problematic can give us an idea about the overall aesthetic perspective of the Catholic Church at the time; among others, I will present a well-known episode showing Pope Marcellus' concern for a correct style of church music.

As elsewhere in Europe, broad aesthetic, religious and social movements dovetailed with the initiatives and outlooks of individual people (mostly men, indeed): in the Catholic Church, such leading characters were – among others – those of Cardinals and bishops such as Carlo Borromeo, Gonzaga, Morone, Paleotti, Vitellozzo Vitelli (1531–1568) and Otto von Waldburg (1514–1573). Other key figures concerned with the role of music at the Council of Trent were those of Jacobus de Kerle (c.1531–1591), who composed the *Preces speciales* for the Council itself, and Emperor Ferdinand of Habsburg, who actively intervened in musical matters. On the other hand, we will see that the role played by Palestrina and his *Missa Papæ Marcelli* as concerns the Tridentine discussion of sacred music was probably less important than musicological mythology has frequently asserted in the past.

Among the discussions relating to liturgical issues at the Council, I will briefly mention those regarding the use of vernacular languages in the liturgy: it is a controversial aspect which points out how similar matters were seen on either side of the confessional boundaries.

Eventually, I will consider the actual decrees of the Council concerning music, in particular the famous ban on "lascivious" music and the limitations on polyphony in female monasteries. Of primary import for the subsequent history of Catholic Church music, however, was the Council's attribution of authority in implementing its decrees to local bishops. As we will see, the few lines of the Council's official statements on music should both be read in the context of and abstracted from the preceding discussions: from the one side, their formulation mirrors the long debates antedating their publication, both at the Council and before it; from the other, the deliberate omission of certain sentences, terms or entire topics from the official decrees' wording has a great significance in itself.

Finally, I will briefly compare the Council's decrees on visual art with those on music, pointing out both the similarities among the Fathers' concept of various kinds of artistic creation and the differences between them.

## 8.2. Trent and tradition

Although the debates at Trent and the Council's rulings cannot be reduced to a mere response to the Evangelical Reformations, it is undeniable that several of the most important points under discussion were precisely those on which Luther and the other Reformers had broken with the Catholic Church's tradition. Thus, the theological agenda of the Council was determined by what needed to be clarified, in the Fathers' eyes, rather than by a wish to reshape, redefine or simply restate the entire theology of the Catholic Church.

The Council did not aim at creating a systematic corpus of pronouncements: instead, as concerns the theological aspects, it limited its interventions to the issues on which controversies had arisen with the Protestants, deriving its statements in most cases from preceding magisterial and theological declarations (though on certain topics the Council actually had to structure the Catholic perspective in the absence of previous official assertions) and taking its subjects from the "errors" it aimed at confuting.

Though the main theological themes were the same as those discussed in the preceding Chapters as regards the Evangelical viewpoints, therefore, the implications of Trent's discussions for music were not as immediately discernible as in the case of some Evangelical Reformers. For example, we have seen in Chapter Five that Luther's statements on the principles of *sola fide, sola gratia, sola scriptura* and on the universal priesthood of all believers found an almost immediate application in the practical treatment of music within the Lutheran Church. This was due to a double cause: first, Luther was an individual who had a considerable (though at first geographically limited) power to enact his liturgical, moral and theological reforms within the boundaries of his flock; second, though he was careful not to reject all Catholic beliefs and practices (and we have seen how many of them were adopted by the Lutheran Church), nevertheless he was not bound by those ties of tradition, collegiality and theological consequentiality which Catholics had to consider constantly. We have seen, for example, that there is a substantial consistency between Luther's theological stance on dogmatic issues and his treatment of music, but also that, on some occasions, he favoured his own personal convictions and his taste for music over what a strict theological reasoning would have implied (as in the matter of *adiaphora*, for example).

The Catholic theologians at Trent were in a very different situation. Indeed, they did accept Luther's challenge and discussed at length the subjects of disagreement between the Catholic position and his. However, whereas both the pastoral needs and the necessity of defining the shape of a new Church organisation compelled Luther to design the practical consequences of his theology (at the liturgical, pastoral and moral level), this was not the case with the Catholic Fathers. The Catholic Church already had at its disposal centuries-old traditions of practices and of how to deal with their evolution, and so did not need to deduce them afresh from the Council's doctrinal clarifications (which in turn were often no more than the elucidation and restatement of what had already been affirmed and believed).

Thus, for example, the need for the Catholic Church to reflect on the nature of the Mass, Eucharist and priesthood did not imply a speculation on how these dogmatic issues dovetailed with the very concept of liturgy, with the role of music within it (or of lay participation) or on how to make practice more consonant with the theological principles at stake.

Indeed, both the theological teachings and the actual liturgical and devotional practices of the Catholic Church were the result of the progressive stratification, superimposition and clarification over centuries, in dialogue with social, cultural and artistic challenges posed by the successive contemporaneities. In many cases, practice and theory corresponded remarkably well (and this is rather surprising, if one considers how complex their respective origins had been); in others, however (and especially on relatively minor issues such as the actual shape taken by music in worship), the evolution in musical taste (i.e. a properly and exquisitely musical/aesthetical topic) was at least as important as the theological principles it had to answer to.

This introduction has aimed at establishing the framework for understanding how and why music was discussed at Trent, and the context for that debate. If the Fathers had been gathered for a conference aiming at discussing the role of music in the Catholic Church's theology and practice, they could well have found implications for music in virtually all of the topics under analysis. Obviously, however, this was neither their aim, nor their priority.

Moreover, though the Council of Trent did have a crucial importance for both theology and practice of the Catholic Church in the following centuries, it was by no means as neat a dividing line for the Catholic Church as the establishment of the Lutheran Church had been for those adhering to it. Thus, whereas the Lutheran or Calvinist theologians of music needed perforce to refer to Luther or Calvin's writings on music in order to draw the essential traits of their confession's perspective, Trent was just a stage (albeit an important one) within the history of the Catholic Church. It was a crucial moment of reflection, an important occasion for discussing and clarifying major theological issues; but it was by no means a radical revolution (especially as concerns music).

### 8.2.1. Theological themes

The most important theological challenges posed by the Evangelical theologies concerned Revelation (cf. the *sola scriptura* principle), the topics of sin, free will and justification (the *sola fide* and *sola gratia* principles), the Sacraments (*ex opere operato*), particularly the Eucharist (what role for transubstantiation? Mass as sacrifice?) and priesthood (universal? ministerial?). Moreover, the Evangelical movements had significantly challenged the Catholic Church on other issues, which were more closely associated to practice and ethics, among which the residency of bishops within their diocese, the clergy's education and morality as well as the role of the laity/congregation within worship.

The Council reaffirmed that Revelation was not expressed entirely in the words of Scripture, but needed the Church's authoritative interpretation which had been uninterruptedly handed down within the Apostolic tradition: thus, several of the consequences for music drawn by the Evangelical Reformers from the *sola scriptura* principle did not apply to the Catholic Church (such as, for example, the focus on psalmody).

Against the Anabaptists (but together with most of the major Reformers), the Catholic Church restated the value of infant baptism which delivered children from original sin: the redeemed believers are justified by God's Grace (as Luther believed) but (differently from Luther's view) they are given free will and asked to cooperate with Grace in order to accomplish the gift of salvation bestowed on them by God. (Incidentally, it must be pointed out that several oppositions between the Evangelical views and that of the Catholic Church were based on reciprocal misunderstandings and on the radicalisation of certain positions: the joint document on justification which has recently been issued by theologians from both sides[2] overcomes one of the major dogmatic obstacles to the communion of the Western Churches).

As we have seen in Chapters One and Four[3], however, the *sola fide* and *sola gratia* principles and the Evangelical view on justification had important consequences on the concept of the Sacraments, on the value of works (the greatest and most perfect of which was considered by Catholics to be the Eucharist) and on the perspective on priesthood. The affirmation of the *ex opere operato* principle in the Catholic view, thus, implied a reduced focus on the active participation of the laity in the Mass (and thus, as concerns the subjects discussed here, on intelligibility issues, on the use of vernacular and on the insertion of

---

2 Cf. http://bit.ly/1nX7RYW.
3 See § 1.2.1.–2., 4.3.1. and following.

hymns which all could sing in public worships). The continuing presence of the doctrine of the works (as the believer's necessary response to God's Grace) implied, for music, that those kinds of music which were not directly functional to immediate benefits for the congregation (e.g. memorisation of doctrines or of Biblical excerpts) could still be employed as "adornments" of liturgy, i.e. as a means of making worship more beautiful for God's sake.

Among the moral issues, those destined to have the utmost importance for music were those concerning the behaviour of the clergy, as we will see in detail later in this Chapter (§ 8.4.3.–5.): it was precisely within this context that music was actually discussed at Trent, and this collocation is highly significant. Although, as we have just seen, Luther, Calvin and other Reformers had drawn important musical consequences from their view of the theological issues listed above, the Catholic Church did not deem it necessary to rethink theologically the significance of music in worship and devotion, but rather treated it as a matter pertaining simply to the moral sphere.

### 8.2.2. Self- or Counter-Reformation?

It is thus very important to constantly keep in mind the existence of two realities in the Catholic thought and practice during the second half of the sixteenth century. From the one side, the Roman Church underwent a process of reflection, purification, renewal and clarification which was prompted by the Evangelical Reformations, but which was also the consequence and continuation of its centuries-old tradition, both as concerns its dogmatic speculation and its constantly-needed sanctification and atonement. From the other, starting before Trent and especially after it, the Roman Church also actively strove to regain the formerly Catholic territories and their population, and to avoid the loss of yet more countries to the Evangelical faith. In the former case, we should speak of "Catholic Reformation"; in the latter, the term "Counter-Reformation" may be acceptable.

In Jedin's view, thus, "Catholic Reformation" implies the Church's renewal within its own boundaries; "Counter-Reformation" is its "self-affirmation" in its struggle against the spread of Protestant ideas[4]. For Catholics, the former comprises the explicit reflection on music at Trent and such issues as the liturgical and moral abuses, intelligibility and incorrect delivery of the Latin texts; the latter implies the use of music in order to contrast its effective employment

---

4 Jedin 1957, p. 43.

for propaganda by the Evangelicals (cf. also Chapter Ten on this topic, e.g. § 10.3.7.). At Trent, however, the "Counter-Reformation" use of music did not represent an official subject for discussion, although several members of the Catholic Church (particularly those who came from territories where Evangelical confessions were successful) were aware of the propagandistic value of music, and in some instances were in favour of adopting it in turn. The faithful's need for a musical expression of their belief and piety had been shrewdly and intelligently seized by several Evangelical Reformers; and whereas the Catholic Church was slow on the uptake and did not immediately understand the role which music could play as a means to fascinate and conquer the laity, the increasing creation of devotional works for domestic use united Catholic with Evangelical practices on a common ground[5].

Generally speaking, however, music was seen mostly within the framework of the Church's self-renewal (or better, of its renewal in Christ); thus, the official line taken by Trent on music and the attitudes to music of some among the major Catholic Reformers were similar in both style and content to those of the moderate Evangelicals[6].

It can be said, therefore, that Trent did not aim at reforming Catholic music, but rather at comprehending it within the Church's own Reformation; its official pronouncements concerned general approaches and basic principles rather than stylistic, aesthetical or practical details[7]. Where discontinuities can actually be discerned on the compositional-technical level between the pre- and post-Tridentine sacred output of Catholic musicians, they can rarely be attributed directly, exclusively and unmistakeably to the Council's action: in most cases, Trent's directives at least dovetailed with (if were not caused in turn by) the tendencies of contemporaneous musicianship in dialogue with the cultural and religious ferments of the era.

Catholic Reformers were undoubtedly aware of the several problems found in their time's liturgical music (which have been discussed in Chapter Three, § 3.3. and following): polyphony, as will be recalled, presented criticalities including the use of secular models or *cantus firmus*, the difficulty of achieving affective differentiation within the homogeneity given to Mass movements by modal or compositional needs and choices, as well as performance styles and practices which were deemed to be inappropriate for worship. Trent, as will be discussed in the remainder of this Chapter, encouraged a reform of plainchant

---

5 Cf. O'Regan 2013a, pp. 344–345.
6 Cf. Kendrick 1996, p. 6; Monson 2002, pp. 1 and 4; Weber 2008, pp. 10–11; Fenlon 2009, p. 199.
7 Cf. Weinmann 1919; Fellerer 1953, p. 576; Lockwood 1966, p. 41.

repertoire and performance styles: however, the increasingly common practice of accompanying monody with instruments qualified this focus on the "Gregorian" repertoire not merely as a conservative initiative, but also as intensely forward-looking.

Similarly, Catholic composers increasingly adopted homorhythmic writing (and, obviously, were not the only ones to do so, as the previous Chapters have abundantly shown). This was in consonance with the Council's concern for intelligibility (which was by no means the only focus of its deliberation on music, as musicological myths have it, but was however a not negligible preoccupation), while it cannot be maintained that there was a direct and exclusive cause/effect relationship between the two. Rather, the frequent references found in post-Tridentine Catholic works to a musical style "conforming to the Council's indications" resemble more often an *ex-post* claim of orthodoxy rather than a deliberate effort to adapt one's compositional style to the alleged directives of the Council. The post-Tridentine atmosphere, in other words, seemed to legitimise composers in invoking the Council's authority as the warrantor for stylistic choices which were – in most case – their own, and corresponded more to the musical and cultural aesthetics of their time than to purported demands on the part of the Catholic authorities.

This inversion of the received causal order between the Catholic Reformation and artistic trends was noted already by Hubert Jedin in 1957, though within a different context[8]. The centrality of beauty in all of its manifestations which had characterised the Renaissance was, in Jedin's view, something against which the Catholic Reformation wished to intervene. The post-Tridentine artistic, religious and moral ideals were at first oriented towards sobriety instead of opulence, simplicity instead of splendour, interior life instead of outward appearance, and towards asceticism and austerity instead of magnificence. Though each and all of the latter qualities were soon going to take hold of Baroque religious art and music, the artistic principles of the seventeenth century and their germinal presence in the sixteenth were exploited rather than created by the religious climate of the Catholic Reformation.

Within the perspective of the Catholic Reformation, therefore, the reflection on music at Trent was practical rather than theological, moral rather than Scriptural: although there were ample grounds for discussing the theology of music and its relationship with the Bible (as the preceding Chapters have shown), these aspects did not receive a thorough discussion. Music was examined *within liturgy* (thus omitting a discussion on its overall significance, value, meaning and

---

[8] Jedin 1957, p. 51.

theological shape) and as concerned liturgical *abuses* (so without analysing what positive contribution music could give to worship, or how it theologically related with it).

These omissions should not be interpreted as weaknesses on the Council's part. As stated above (§ 8.2.), the Council could not aim at developing each and every aspect of Catholic theology – and, as much as one loves music, it is difficult to deny that it was not the most urgent matter for the Catholic Church to discuss.

### 8.2.3. Drafts, Debates, Decrees

The framework of Trent's discussion of music, thus, was rather limited in scope: what had to be done on the plane of "behaviours" in order to suppress the negative aspects of music in worship. Most of the themes which were discussed at Trent have already been presented at some length in this book (particularly in Chapters Three and Four): given the particular viewpoint on music adopted at Trent, i.e. the debate on liturgical abuses, many of these malpractices had already been pointed out by people interested in religious reforms for a long time, both among those who would leave the Catholic Church and by those who would remain inside it.

It must be emphasised that by "discussions at Trent" I mean both those happening formally (e.g. the preparatory meetings of the theologians and the official discussions by the commissions and by the entire assembly) and those which did not have the mark of officialdom but were in fact no less important.

The Council offered those interested in the fate of the Church the possibility of meeting, of sharing ideas and perspectives and of discussing the different features of one's experience of Church and of belief within the diverse geographical, social and confessional realities coexisting in Europe (and not only there) in the sixteenth century. Moreover, the Council's final documents underwent – especially in some cases – an incredible amount of drafts, corrections, discussions and revisions; the debate, in some measure, and especially by means of letters, was also open to those who were not physically present at Trent, or were not entitled to speak officially. Cirillo's letter to Gualteruzzi discussed in Chapter Three[9] (see § 3.3.3.) is one such example: Cirillo had written it in the hope that Gualteruzzi would pass it to Beccadelli – who was going to assume a leading stance in the Council's discussion of liturgy and of music's role within it.

---

9 *Lettere volgari* 1564, fols. 114$^r$-118$^v$.

Moreover, the Fathers could count on a rich and abundant amount of material for their debate on these topics. Most of them could report on their own experiences – what they had seen and heard, or what had been recounted by those in contact with them. This did not concern only the negative side (abuses) but also the positive, since there had been attempts to reform church music on several occasions and in some particular contexts (see, for example, the constructive cooperation between Bishop Ghiberti and the famous musician Biagio Rossetto in Verona[10]). Elsewhere (as in some German dioceses) reforms had been advocated and sometimes undertaken as concerns the integration of clerical morality/sanctity, proper liturgy and the possibility – for the laity – to participate more actively in worship[11]. No less important were the stimuli in the direction of the so-called *Devotio moderna*, whose influence dated back to the preceding centuries, with its increasing focus on spirituality and interior improvement of the individual and on lay piety[12]. The typical post-Tridentine "innovation" of the establishment of seminaries had been actually invented and implemented by Cardinal Pole in England. Attempts at a Catholically "reformed" church music had also been enacted by composers, such as – to name but one – Pierre Colin in his 1554 *Liturgicon musicarum*, which explicitly mentions such efforts on the part of the composer himself[13].

### 8.2.4. Uses and abuses

On the subject of liturgical abuses, the Fathers at Trent could also count on an extensive literature, both official (e.g. the Council of Basel in the fifteenth century[14]) and unofficial (cf. the *Libellus ad Leonem*, 1513, at the time of the Fifth Lateran Council, but also the sometimes harsh criticism voiced by Protestant polemicists against what were perceived as "popish" abuses in church music). Furthermore, there were spontaneous submissions, such as that sent to Beccadelli's Committee by Stanislaus Hosius (or Stanisław Hozjusz, 1504–1579), who had been appointed Prince Bishop of Warmia (Ermland) in order to fight Protestantism there. Hosius listed the following abuses:

---

10 Cf. Rainoldi 2000, p. 332.
11 Cf. Rainoldi 2000, p. 331.
12 Cf. Rees 2006, p. 349.
13 Cf. Colin 1554.
14 Cf. *Mansi* 29, cols. 105–108 (http://bit.ly/2c83JqU). Of course, the Council of Basel was a controversial topic in the sixteenth century.

> Around the moment of the elevation of the most holy Sacrament, when, as it were, a lofty silence ought to be observed by everyone, and a focused commemoration of the Lord's death, organs make a great noise and musicians sing, and some other things intrude which, apart from the fact that they are untimely, also frequently appear to recall something licentious and to distract souls from spiritual inclination. In the singing at the time of the sacrament, there has begun to be much licentiousness, against the custom of the ancient church. For prophetic and apostolic words in the Epistles are sometimes omitted and mutilated. The Creed is not recited complete, nor the Preface, which is the act of thanksgiving [Eucharist], and the Lord's Prayer, too, is suppressed, for the sake of music made together by singers, musicians, and instruments[15].

Hosius' list does not only represent a specimen of the inventories of abuses which were reported to and debated by the Council Fathers, but also a summary of the most important issues discussed in the preceding Chapters. It will not escape the reader's notice that there is often very little difference between a list such as that quoted here (written by a Catholic Bishop who was well-known for his successes against Protestantism) and those created by Evangelical polemicists or by humanists.

Hosius complains against untimely music, but also against its power to "recall something licentious" (he uses the Latin word *lascivum*, which we have already discussed at length in Chapter Three and which will return later in this Chapter[16]): this was often the case, as it was felt at the time, with organ music (with dance-like overtones, excessive duration or virtuosity[17]). Another interesting point made by Hosius is his appeal to the "custom of the ancient Church": though it is not historically circumstantiated, it does however represent a significant reference to the Church's tradition to legitimate his stance. This point is a delicate one: from the one side, as seen above (§ 8.2.), the Catholic Church conceived Tradition as an uninterrupted chain unifying the Scripture's interpretation of Scripture itself (e.g. the presence of internal quotations between different books of the Old Testament), the Apostles' interpretation of the Old Testament (as transmitted, for example, in their Epistles) and the Church's interpretation of the Bible and of Revelation in its entirety. From the other, though the Protestants contested some aspects of the latter (especially in its most recent expressions), they did in turn refer their claims on church music to both the Old and the New Testament, but also to several Patristic sources (cf. § 4.2.4. and following). Finally, Hosius joins in the choir of complaints against the omission of

---

**15** Morandi 1804, vol. 2, p. 258; English translation in Monson 2002, pp. 6–7 (with modifications).
**16** See § 3.3.2.2. and 8.4.3.
**17** Cf. Fellerer 1953, pp. 578–579.

some of the crucial texts of the Mass: the Creed, which expresses the Church's communal belief; the Lord's Prayer, which even Luther (in his *Deudsche Messe*) did not wish to be sung but rather spoken[18], and the Preface (which Luther had replaced with the *Verba Testamenti*).

In order to recall the variety and the types of "abuses" discussed in Chapter Three (§ 3.3. and following) and which would constitute the background of the Fathers' debates on music, I will employ (in a modified form) a very useful list drawn up by Felice Rainoldi (2000) in his treatment of music at Trent. The criticalities of church music can be grouped as: 1) use of melodies or models with secular origins and texts within sacred compositions; 2) unsuitability of the affective qualities of particular pieces of music for the moment of worship when they were performed; 3) polytextuality, i.e. the concomitant delivery in polyphony of one or more different texts while the liturgical words were being sung; 4) *alternatim* with the organ (implying omission of the liturgical text); 5) replacement of indispensable texts (such as those of the *Ordinarium*) with music on other (optional) words; 6) troping; 7) unintelligibility (which might be due to unending repetitions or excessive imitations/melismas[19]).

Moreover, as we have seen in Chapter Three (§ 3.3.2.2.), the subject of "lascivious" music could not be reduced solely to the presence of secular *cantus firmus* or models in sacred pieces (as it comprehended a much larger semantic field which included performance practice as well as anthropological concepts).

### 8.2.5. Fighting "lasciviousness"

Considering that both the discussion of music at Trent and the decrees resulting from it took place within the framework of liturgical abuses and clerical behaviour (including ethics and morality together with liturgical practices), then our discussion of "lasciviousness" in Chapter Three (§ 3.3.2.3.) may be usefully recalled here in some of its main and most pertinent aspects.

First: by some, music as such was seen as dangerous for morality (cf. Aretino, Bembo, Stubbes etc., quoted in § 3.3.2.1.–3.). Second: Dean[20] argues that the primary – if not the only – listeners of sacred polyphony were the singers themselves. (Therefore: the presence of secular tunes in polyphonic music, which would have probably gone unnoticed by a merely listening "audience", was cer-

---

[18] Leaver 2007, pp. 292–293.
[19] Rainoldi 2000, p. 333; cf. *ibid*, pp. 329 and 331; cf. Damilano 1977.
[20] Dean 1997, p. 628.

tainly an issue for those singing it). Third: at least in some of the major ecclesiastical institutions, church singers were (preferably) clerics or unmarried men. (For instance, as seen in § 3.3.2.12.: already in 1526 lay singers were forbidden to enter the monastic choir and interact with the monks in England[21]; as is well known inasmuch it affected Palestrina's career, in 1555 Paul IV dismissed the married singers from the Papal Chapel[22], and, in other instances, Papal singers were evaluated more on their moral behaviour than on their musical capabilities[23]. Moreover the 1565 Council of Milan convened by Carlo Borromeo established the moralisation of church singers as one of its goals[24] and Agrippa von Nettesheim was not the only one who complained against "lascivious" *musicians* rather than lascivious *music*[25]). Fourth: the presence of boys within church choirs had educational implications beside and together with moral considerations. Fifth: if there were "listeners" to the singers' polyphony, at least some of these listeners were in all likelihood priests (for example, those performing the Mass). This implied: a) that priests would have to wait for polyphony to finish (cf. the "buzzing" of the priests in Modena, 1538[26], quoted in § 3.3.2.5.); b) that they could be distracted or provoked to "lascivious" thoughts by the kind of music performed. All this was in turn due to the professionalisation of music performance caused by complex polyphony[27]: if church singers should ideally belong to the clerical class (though obviously not all of them were actually priests), this did not imply in the least the reverse, i.e. that all priests could sing polyphony passably. (It may also be recalled that, for Aquinas, the celebrating priests ought better not to sing: cf. § 2.3.5.).

Attempting to sum up all of the above, I think that a rather clearer picture emerges of how the Council's pronouncements on music should be understood. The performance of "lascivious" music (in all meanings of this term) by singers who belonged to the clerical status or were educated for this purpose or (at least) were perceived to be "close" to the clergy was – first and foremost – a moral danger for them. It could also represent a distraction (if not an outright temptation) for the priests performing the liturgy; and, only thirdly, this applied to the laity participating in the worship.

---

21 In Perry 1888, pp. 712–713.
22 Brauner 1994, p. 337.
23 Cf. Sherr 1994.
24 *AEM* 1, p. 27; cf. Fenlon 2009, pp. 201–202.
25 Agrippa 1530, p. 35; translation in Fellerer 1953, p. 585.
26 Cf. Lockwood 1966, p. 44.
27 Mischiati 1993, p. viii.

One of the main issues of the Catholic Reformation was the moralisation of the clergy, as it was believed that godly pastors could set a good example to their flocks and that, vice versa, their scandalous behaviour was deeply disrupting for the Church (and a formidable weapon in the hands of Protestant propaganda). I would therefore argue that the proper context for interpreting the Council's rulings on music is precisely that of the clergy's moralisation: this will be particularly clear as concerns the *Decretum de reformatione* in the XXIV Session, but in general constitutes the interpretive framework for the entire discussion which will follow later in this Chapter.

### 8.2.6. Singing for the Pope

Even though the Papal Chapels epitomised under many aspects exceptional situations, which neither could nor should be considered as representative of a widespread condition, they nevertheless deserve a succinct discussion here. Indeed, they could be seen as a model by other Catholic realities; moreover, they were so closely associated with the centre of Roman Catholicism as to become a window through which Popes and Cardinals saw church music. Conversely, they also represented the window through which church musicians understood their relationship with the Roman Curia and with the Church it hierarchically represented. Indeed, Pope Gregory XIII, in his Bull *De Communi Omnium* (1578[28]) explicitly stated that the other chapels in the world should take inspiration from the Cappella Giulia both as concerned the "offices, divine rites and ceremonies" and on the plane of devotion: the Chapel had to set a "great example" to encourage others in the accomplishment of "acts of piety"[29].

I mentioned the Papal Chapels in the plural, since the *Cappella Giulia*, founded by Pope Julius II in 1513, represented the "Vatican" aspect of church music (it performed at St Peter's during public, semi-public or official liturgies) whereas the *Cappella Sistina* (the Sistine or Pontifical Chapel, named after Sixtus IV [1414–1484] who reorganised it in 1471) represented the "Pope's" music, to whose service it was entirely dedicated.

Some Popes were actively interested in the musical and liturgical level of their Chapels, and occasionally undertook reforms in order to improve their quality (both in singing and morality); notwithstanding this, Papal music was not always reputed to be an audible manifestation of Rome's importance and

---

**28** *Collectio Bullarum* 1752, vol. 3, pp. 113–117.
**29** *Collectio Bullarum* 1752, vol. 3, p. 113, my translation; cf. Rostirolla 1993, p. 47.

centrality for Catholicism. In the second half of the sixteenth century, however, an increasing concern for the beauty of Papal music was shown not only by the Popes but also by the Cardinals surrounding them. The results of such interest were observable in the increasingly laudatory impressions received and transmitted by visitors and listeners participating in its sung liturgies[30].

In the sixteenth century, several Popes concerned themselves with the Chapels' music, each in his own particular fashion and idiosyncratic style, starting with Pope Julius II who – as stated above – established the Cappella Giulia. Around 1518, his successor, Leo X, chose Elzéar Genet (better known as "Carpentras", c.1470–1548) as choirmaster with several aims: to turn the musician's talent away from secular composition, and to realise in practice the Pope's idea of sacred music while providing the Chapel with a high-level repertoire for daily use. As Sherr[31] points out, although Leo appreciated elaborate Mass settings and motets, he encouraged his *maestro di cappella* to compose polyphony for the Liturgy of the Hours, thus revealing a deep and profound concern for the artistic quality of ferial worship music. Pope Paul III included the reform of church music among those aspects in need of specific attention: for him, "reform" did not simply mean the redefinition of theological issues, but also their practical enactment and their relationship with the experience of faith, of which music was an integral component. In the troubled years following the Sack of Rome (1527), the presence of extraordinary musicians such as Jacob Arcadelt, Costanzo Festa (c.1485–1545) and Cristóbal de Morales within the Papal Choir was part of the Pope's programme for reforming the Church also by means of culture, beauty and artistic magnificence.

His successor, Julius III (1487–1555), who had been the Bishop of Palestrina, is remembered as Giovanni Pierluigi da Palestrina's patron: thanks to the Pope's benevolence, the composer became *magister cantorum* of the Cappella Giulia in 1551[32] (chapel master in 1553) and was admitted to the Sistine Chapel without an examination in 1555[33]. During both Paul III's and Julius III's rules, the Sistine Chapel sang a repertoire analogous to what was fashionable in Italy at that time: along with works by Arcadelt, Festa and Morales, those by contemporaneous masters such as Jacquet of Mantua and by "classics" such as Josquin or Mouton.

On Julius' death, in 1555, Marcellus II succeeded him: notwithstanding one of the shortest reigns in the history of papacy (merely three weeks), he left his

---

30 Cf. Rostirolla 1993, p. 41; Dean 1997, p. 626.
31 Sherr 1997, p. 396.
32 See Rostirolla 1977.
33 Cf. Rostirolla 1993, p. 41; Brauner 1994, pp. 333–335.

own mark on the history of Roman music. As reported by the Council's secretary, Angelo Massarelli (1510–1566), on Good Friday (April 12th, 1555), the day when Christ's death was memorialised, the Pope was displeased by the joyful style of the music sung by the Sistine Choir. Thus, he summoned the singers and reprehended them, recommending that what was sung on the days of Christ's Passion should be delivered in an "effective" fashion and so that "what was delivered could be heard and perceived"[34].

Indeed, in the Papal Chapels, polyphony was abundantly performed, both in alternation with plainchant (the Holy Week *Lamentations* being precisely one of those instances) or in entirely polyphonic settings (for example in Mass Ordinaries or in *Magnificats*[35]). As Sherr maintains[36], however, it is likely that the Sistine Chapel could often have sung with only a single singer to a part; and – in spite of their frequent performance of polyphonic works – the quantitative majority of the music sung by the Papal Chapels was plainchant, which was considered to be much less expendable than the polyphonic masterpieces on which musicological studies have focused their attention[37].

Before and during the last grouping of the Council's sessions (1561–3), the Sistine Chapel's repertoire mirrored the uncertainty in which church musicians (and particularly those who were closer to the papacy) were operating as regards the musical styles appropriate for worship. Thus, as shown by Brauner[38], the conservative repertoire performed in the early 1560s tended to favour the "safe" option provided by composers such as Josquin, Pierre Moulu (c.1484-c.1550), Mouton and Richafort.

After the conclusion of the Council, and particularly during Palestrina's second appointment as master of the Cappella Giulia (1571–94), both Chapels experienced a time of renewal and rejuvenation, both as regards their artistic level and their practical organisation[39].

## 8.3. Who was who

The tone and results of debates on music at Trent depended greatly on their protagonists. Some of them can easily be identified as being not only the principal

---

**34** *CT* 2, p. 256, my translation; see Rainoldi 2000, p. 336, fn. 16. Cf. Lockwood 1975, p. 18.
**35** Cf. Brauner 1998, pp. 168–170.
**36** Cf. Sherr 1994, p. 618.
**37** Cf. Sherr 1998 (*Introduction*).
**38** Brauner 1994, p. 338.
**39** Cf. Brauner 1994, pp. 336–339; Rostirolla 1993, p. 42.

agents of the Council's deliberations on music, but also as the leading figures of the assembly general. I will shortly present the views on music of some of the most important of such figures, i.e. Ercole Gonzaga (1505–1563), Giovanni Morone, Otto Truchsess von Waldburg, Gabriele Paleotti, Vitellozzo Vitelli and Carlo Borromeo. Later, I will briefly discuss the role played by other personalities who, though they were not among the ecclesiastical standard-bearers at the Council, did however exert a notable influence on its decisions on music.

### 8.3.1. Ercole Gonzaga: President and patron

Ercole Gonzaga, who descended from one of the most important families in the nobility of the Italian peninsula, was a man of great ability as a ruler, both in the religious and in the civil field. He was highly concerned about the reform of the Catholic Church, though he joined his attention for a spiritual renewal with a considerable practical sense and juridical talent. In his view, a properly ordered and intensely spiritual Church could and should lead the entire society to a corresponding order and peace. In his library, alongside Patristic writings, there was space for Evangelical writers such as Melanchthon, Zwingli and Luther, and he was well informed on the religious and cultural ferments of the era. Though he was often a favourite candidate for papacy, he was never elected as Pope; however, he was entrusted with the presidency of the Council until his death. He was highly appreciative of the polyphonic schools of Northern Europe, whose grandiose Latin-texted settings represented for him a repository of moving artistry. His patronage of music was evident from the 1530s, when he established a musical chapel, and it became even clearer with his support of Jacquet of Mantua. Jacquet not only was chosen as the master of Ercole's Chapel, but also enjoyed a friendly relationship with Cardinal Gonzaga, who – in turn – subsidised the publication of several of Jacquet's works. It is probably not too far-fetched to suppose that the friendship between the Cardinal and his composer, as well as Ercole's appreciation of music, were not without influence on the eventual results of the Council's debates on music. We will see, moreover (§ 10.6.4.) that Cardinal Ercole Gonzaga was lucidly aware of the possibilities offered by music as an instrument of persuasion and as a means of combating the spread of Protestantism: whereas in other cases such strategies were conceived for the illiterate, as a replacement for pamphlets and treatises, in his case the use of music for propaganda was meant for members of the upper classes[40].

---

[40] Cf. Besutti 1993, pp. 111–112; Nugent 1990, pp. 270–271 and 280; Nugent 1997, p. 246.

## 8.3.2. Giovanni Morone: Monody first

Though he was in turn not indifferent to music in the least, Giovanni Morone, Bishop of Modena, adopted a very different stance from Gonzaga's. As discussed in Chapter Three (§ 3.3.2.5.), between 1537 and 1538, Morone had attempted to abolish polyphony from the Cathedral Church of his diocese, replacing it with simple plainchant. His radical experiment seems to have been unique in sixteenth-century Italy; even though it was short-lived, it represents a clear indication of Morone's position towards polyphony. As we have also seen, however, it must be noted that Morone's initiative was judged very positively by many in Modena: as the contemporaneous writer Thomasino Lancillotto (c.1503–1554) reports, the reintroduction of polyphony was ill-accepted by "many citizens", since when plainchant was sung "everybody could understand and sing in their hearts with the priests"[41].

At Trent, Morone would promote a rigorist attitude to polyphonic music; it is significant, however, that between the Modena experiment and Trent, Morone would be the object of a hard persecution by the Inquisition (on Pope Paul IV's orders), including a long imprisonment from 1557 to the Pope's death in 1559, on the charge of alleged Lutheran sympathies. Although Morone was eventually not only freed but fully rehabilitated and became one of the leading figures at Trent, the suspicion of heterodoxy which fell on him could have been fostered by some of his reforming initiatives (such as the ban on polyphony) which were perceived as too abrupt and hasty. Moreover, the chronicler Lancillotto pointed out that the "citizens" (i.e., probably, the laity) could "sing in their hearts" when plainchant was performed. Though this form of lay involvement was decidedly inferior to the Evangelicals' congregational singing, nevertheless there is an interesting proximity between this "heart-singing" and that desired by Calvin (who, in turn, did not admit polyphony in worship) or Zwingli.

At Trent, Morone's most important initiative as regards music was his drafting of forty-two proposals for discussion at the XXIV session, in 1563, together with another Papal legate, Bernardo Navagero[42]. The third point in their list suggested that the Council forbid the "*musica troppo molle*" (the reader will remember our discussion of *mollis* and its implications in § 3.3.2.2.). The suggestion was eventually omitted from all official decrees (though Hieronymus Ragasanus quoted its wording in the Council's concluding sermon[43]), but Morone and Nav-

---

41 Quoted in Lockwood 1966, p. 44, my translation.
42 Cf. *CT* 9, p. 755, fn. 1.
43 *SCT*, p. 342.

agero's draft had been sent, in the meantime, to Emperor Ferdinand I of Habsburg, who would react with vehemence against this perspective[44] (see § 8.4.4.).

### 8.3.3. Otto Truchsess: Talents and treasures

If Morone was favourable to the limitation of polyphony in Catholic worship, another of the principal actors at Trent actively sought to spread its appreciation among the Fathers who had gathered there. Cardinal Otto Truchsess von Waldburg, Prince-Bishop of Augsburg (and thus responsible for a diocese which was on the very borders of Protestantism) and Protector of Germany, was famous for his fostering of the arts, and particularly of music, both in Bavaria and in Rome, where he had resided since at least 1568. Here, he became acquainted with Palestrina, and it is likely that the attribution to Waldburg of the title of Bishop of Palestrina (1570) constituted a further connection between the composer and the prelate.

However, Waldburg's appreciation for Palestrina dated back several years earlier, and is clearly shown by a singular but fundamental initiative taken by Waldburg in the early 1560s. Starting in 1561, works by Orlando di Lasso were sent to Rome, and compositions by Italian musicians were dispatched in turn to the Bavarian Court of Munich, the city where Lasso had settled at the time (though he was not yet the *maestro di cappella* there).

Upon receipt of Lasso's works, Waldburg wrote back from Rome to Munich expressing not only his own enthusiasm, but also that of other Cardinals: "[the musical works have] pleased not only [Cardinal] Vitelli in particular, and everyone here, but especially Cardinal Borromeo, who has had them copied and wishes to have them performed in the Papal Chapel"[45]. As Lockwood rightfully points out, "This exchange reflects a vivid interest on the part of Vitelli and Borromeo in polyphonic works written outside the Roman musical circles accessible to them"[46]. We will see in the next Chapter that these particular prelates were going to play an important role in the musical reception of Trent (§ 9.3.6. and 9.6.2.).

In turn, a Mass by Palestrina (*Benedicta es*) was sent to Munich: interestingly, Lasso would later make use of the same model as Palestrina's Mass (i. e. Josquin's *Benedicta es cælorum Regina*) for one of his *Magnificats*, thus implicitly

---

[44] Cf. Lockwood 1957, pp. 78–79; Lockwood 1966, pp. 42–44; Palisca 1997, p. 285 and fn. 13; Monson 2002, pp. 12–13.
[45] Quoted and translated in O'Regan 1999a, p. 139.
[46] Lockwood 1966, p. 46.

acknowledging the importance of this exchange for his own compositional research. Together with Palestrina's, another Mass setting was forwarded to Munich: it is the Mass *Ultimi miei sospiri*, previously attributed to François Roussel (c.1510-a.1577) but now assigned to Giovanni Maria de Rossi[47] (c.1522–1590). De Rossi, who was later to become the Maestro di Cappella at the Cathedral of Mantua (the post that had been Jacquet's), had been in charge of accommodating Ercole Gonzaga's household during their stay in Trent for the Council. It is noteworthy that de Rossi's Mass is based on a secular madrigal, in consideration of the fact that this musical exchange was promoted by some of the most influential among the Cardinals active at Trent and in the Catholic Reformation[48].

It should be emphasised, however, that this correspondence seems not to have been aimed primarily at matters of Church or sacred music reform: nowhere in Waldburg's surviving correspondence does he specify particular stylistic qualities which the works should possess, or what features they should have. The exchange regarded "good music", without any specific demands on what purposes it should achieve or how it had to be composed[49].

In the meantime, Waldburg had had still other opportunities to demonstrate his interest in music, first and foremost his establishment, in Augsburg's Cathedral, of a musical Chapel (1561): this initiative would later become the aural symbol of the renewal of Catholicism in the southern German-speaking territories.

In that very same year 1561, Waldburg had met with Jacobus de Kerle, who had been since 1555 the organist and Chapel master at the Cathedral church in Orvieto, and who would become in 1562 the master of Waldburg's own private Chapel. The acquaintance between Kerle and Waldburg promoted the composition of Kerle's *Preces speciales*[50], which were to play a crucial role in the Council's consideration of and reflection on music (see § 8.6.3.).

Another leading figure of contemporaneous music with whom Waldburg had a fruitful relationship was Glarean, who dedicated his *Dodecachordon* to the Cardinal. Glarean's choice is not only an homage to a powerful clergyman, but also represents a commitment of trust and responsibility from the theorist to the Cardinal, who could actively shape the concept of music within the self-reforming Catholic Church. Indeed, as will be recalled (cf. § 2.3.1.), Glarean maintained that the future of music should germinate from the rediscovery (*restitutio*) of the past, in a creative but not revolutionary fashion. Given the deep spiritual meaning attributed by Glarean to music theory, it is not unlikely that his dedica-

---

[47] Cf. Bente 1989, p. 170.
[48] Cf. Leichtentritt 1944, p. 325; Haberl 1966, p. 32; Leitmeir 2002, pp. 163–164.
[49] Cf. Lockwood 1966, pp. 47–48; O'Regan 1999a, p. 138.
[50] De Kerle 1562.

tion represented something in the line of Cirillo's letter discussed in Chapter Three[51] (§ 3.3.3.): music could become a symbol for the path that the Catholic Church should undertake – for Glarean, this led to the rediscovery and rethinking of Tradition[52].

### 8.3.4. Gabriele Paleotti: Respect and rigour

If Morone's stance was adverse to polyphony (as shown by his experiments in his own diocese), and Waldburg's was decidedly positive (to the point that his evaluations on music seemed to be made on purely aesthetical grounds), that of Gabriele Paleotti, Archbishop of Bologna, can be qualified as intermediate between the two.

Similar to Morone (whose diocese was geographically very close to his own), indeed, Paleotti placed actual and restrictive limitations on the practice of polyphony, albeit in a particular context as that of the female monasteries. After the Council's conclusion, in 1580, Paleotti forbade polyphonic singing to nuns in Bologna with the only exception of Mass and Vespers on the convent's patron saint feast (once a year). Paleotti's injunctions were left substantially unmodified by his successors Alfonso Paleotti (1531–1610) and Ludovico Ludovisi[53] (1595–1632) – on this topic, see § 12.4.3. and the following sections.

Gabriele Paleotti's rigour is particularly surprising in consideration of his very moderate position on several other issues, to say nothing of his own love for music. He had been taught music by Domenico Maria Ferrabosco (1513–1574), who was a famous composer of the time, and with whom Paleotti remained continuously in contact afterwards. From 1562 to 1566, the two men were in correspondence, and Paleotti was active in helping his former teacher and his family. It seems, however, that the advantage of this friendship was reciprocal: in 1562, Paleotti requested Ferrabosco to send him information about the main exponents of the French clergy, and particularly on Charles de Guise, the powerful Cardinal of Lorraine (1524–1574), who was expected in Trent for the Council.

The connection between music and intelligence seems to have been a permanent feature for the Ferrabosco family: Domenico's son, Alfonso the Elder, whose godfather at his baptism was Gabriele Paleotti's brother Camillo (1520–

---

51 *Lettere volgari* 1564, fols. 114$^r$-118$^v$.
52 Cf. Leichtentritt 1944, p. 320; Leitmeir 2002, pp. 121–122; Groote and Vendrix 2012, p. 185; Lütteken 2013, p. 45.
53 Cf. Monson 1993a, pp. 144–146; Monson 2012, p. 4.

1594), was prosecuted by the Inquisition in 1579 under suspicion of espionage, and Gabriele Paleotti played a crucial role in mitigating his condemnation.

Besides the musicians' political and religious intrigues, Paleotti's continuing interest in music is shown also by his own practice of music: according to his brother, who was his first biographer, Gabriele enjoyed playing the lute and singing in his free time during his entire life[54].

Paleotti's attention for the arts was not limited to music: as seen in Chapter Two (§ 2.3.8.), he is also remembered for his *Discorso intorno alle immagini sacre e profane* (1582[55]), which mirrors his concern for the establishment of a fruitful dialogue between the Church and the arts. The stance taken in his *Discorso* is very balanced, and inspired by Christian-humanistic principles; the bishop's writings on art convey that same poise which characterised his spiritual and pastoral attitude.

For Paleotti, visual arts should express the intense spirituality of the best post-Tridentine era under the inspiration of nature and realism; his rejection of the symbolic and allegoric representations, as well as of theological abstractions in visual art is typical of his time but very significant for us. Although here Paleotti was not expressing his views on music, I think that his position is (at the very least) a piece of evidence that can be added to our discussion of music's symbolic value (see § 2.3.8.). It may be recalled that a parallelism was made there between polyphony as an expression of mystical beauty and joy, and femininity: both could be seen as moral dangers or as (potentially sanctifying) anticipations of the eternal bliss. I would argue, therefore, that the seeming contradiction between Paleotti's love for music and support of musicians from the one side, and his limitations on *female polyphony* and on symbolic art from the other are not a mere oddity, but rather mirror a mentality which was widespread at his time.

Moreover, the ideal of "naturalism", which Paleotti proposed to visual artists, was also present in the musical field (for example, as concerned the "natural" delivery, accentuation and pronunciation of the liturgical texts in music). Here, too, those who focused more strictly on the adherence of music's melodic shape and rhythmic patterns to those of speech were also those who feared the unclear delivery (but much greater artistic beauty and fascination) of a richly melismatic or polyphonic compositional style.

As years went by, however, Paleotti would adopt an increasingly rigorist viewpoint on art: instead of the serene dialogue he offered to artists in his *Dis-*

---

[54] Cf. Monson 2002, p. 13; Monson 2003, p. 6 etc.
[55] Paleotti 1582.

*corso*, in the 1590s Paleotti considered the possibility of creating an Index of the forbidden images (on the model of that of the forbidden books). The post-Tridentine years had not brought the results hoped for by the Catholic Reformers: at the dawn of the seventeenth century, Paleotti could only observe that – in the field of the visual arts – the abuses which had been denounced by the Catholic Reformers had not decreased, and the first manifestations of the Baroque style were pointing in a direction which was diametrically opposite to his wishes[56].

Although this discussion of Paleotti's viewpoint on art was indispensable in order to frame his stance and his contributions at Trent, it has taken us chronologically too far, and we need to return to the years of the Council and to those immediately after it.

At the Council, Paleotti was one of the leading actors, and his influence was such that Paolo Prodi (the major expert on Paleotti in our times) stated that "the reform decrees from the last two sessions were almost entirely the work of Paleotti"[57]. We will see, later in this Chapter (and in Chapter Twelve[58]), that the Council occupied itself with the issue of music in female monasteries, and that Paleotti's idiosyncratic reception of the Council's decrees applied also to the problem of intelligibility. While it is true that, contrary to the commonly held opinion, the Council of Trent's decrees on music did not regard primarily this topic, it is also true that several leading churchmen interpreted them as going in this direction, and thus contributed to the misinterpretation of Trent by music historians which has gained such widespread acceptance in the following centuries. In his narrative on the Council, Paleotti focuses clearly on the subject of intelligibility, and points out the very topics which would become predominant in the successive reception of Trent:

> As concerns music in divine service, even though some would have rather condemned it, the others (and especially the Spaniards) thought that it should by all means be retained. [This was maintained] on the ground of the ancient custom of the Catholic Church, [and] in order to arouse the faithful's affect to God, provided that [music] should be devoid of lasciviousness and wantonness, and provided that, so far as possible, the words of the singers should be comprehensible to the hearers[59].

I quoted the entire passage on music from Paleotti's memories since it presents several points of interest. Once more, the "ancient custom" of the Church is in-

---

56 Cf. Prodi 2014, pp. 11, 29, 94 (and fn. 121), 107 and 121.
57 Prodi 1959, vol. 1, p. 183; English translation in Monson 2002, p. 13.
58 See § 8.4.5. and 12.4.3. (and following).
59 Paleotti 1842, p. 270; English translation in Monson 2006, p. 404 (with integrations and modifications of my own).

voked in defence of musical practice, and we find again the idea that music has the power to move the faithful's hearts to God. Yet again, we find the keyword "*lascivia*" (in the original Latin), as well as the concern for intelligibility which seems to be fundamental in Paleotti's view[60].

### 8.3.5. Carlo Borromeo: Influential and idiosyncratic

Along with Paleotti, another authoritative interpreter (as well as a protagonist in his own right) of the Council, to whom the traditional reception of Trent's decrees on music is highly indebted, was Cardinal Carlo Borromeo. Though his activity in the field of music was particularly pronounced in the aftermath of Trent (and therefore will be discussed at length in Chapter Nine: § 9.6.2.), we can now briefly mention his cooperation with several musicians such as Vincenzo Ruffo, Costanzo Porta (c.1528–1601), Giovanni Matteo Asola (1524–1609) and Biagio Pesciolini (c.1535–1611), in the effort to find a musical style conforming to the Council's requirements (or to what Borromeo felt them to be). Besides his interaction with musicians, as will be seen in the next Chapter (§ 9.3.6.), Borromeo worked also with other churchmen with the same goal: it can be said, therefore, that his influence was crucial for the creation of a musical style characterising a considerable portion of the Catholic output after Trent[61].

### 8.3.6. Kerle's *Preces:* The Council's soundtrack

Whereas the music by composers such as the Northern Italians mentioned above (§ 8.3.5.) was actually and discernibly influenced by the Council (or by how Borromeo interpreted it), and though Kerle was by no means less involved than them in the matter of music at Trent, the fact that Kerle's ecclesiastical representative was Waldburg instead of Borromeo or Paleotti posed less specific requirements on his style.

Kerle's compositional activity comprised an extensive output of sacred music (Masses, *Magnificats*, hymns, Psalms and motets). The composer's wide-ranging journeys throughout Europe and his prolonged stays in different countries had provided him with first-hand knowledge of the major compositional styles of his time. Kerle had recently met Waldburg when the Cardinal commis-

---

60 Cf. Sherr 1978, p. 94; Monson 2006, p. 404; Fenlon 2009, p. 203; O'Regan 2009, p. 215.
61 Cf. Leichtentritt 1944, p. 324; Haberl 1966, p. 32.

sioned from him the *Preces speciales pro salubri generalis Concilii successu et conclusione* (i.e. "special prayers" for the Council's positive outcome).

Kerle's *Preces* (published in 1562 in Venice by Gardano[62], together with his *Sex Missæ*) are ten four-part responsories, dedicated to the five Cardinals who were Council legates (Ercole Gonzaga was among them). The *Preces* are set to Latin texts by Petrus (Pedro) de Soto (1493–1563), a Spanish Dominican friar who had been Professor of Theology in the Bavarian Academy of Dillingen since its foundation by Waldburg, and who was involved in Counter-Reformation activities (among which, sadly, the events leading to Cranmer's execution under Queen Mary, in 1556).

The text had been partially written by Soto already in 1551 (and possibly prompted by Waldburg in turn) and had circulated extensively in Germany in the meantime. It had even been published in 1558 in Dillingen by Sebald Mayer (the university's printer), though the wording had been partially modified to adapt it for the German Church, under the heading of *Preces speciales pro Salute Populi Christiani*[63].

As Soto lived at Waldburg's residence from the summer of 1561, he could participate in the Cardinal's daily worship which was accompanied by Kerle's music. Though Kerle's encounter with Soto could probably have fostered their co-operation, it is certain that the main stimulus for Kerle's composition of the *Preces* and for their use and dissemination (both at Trent and in printing) came from Cardinal Waldburg.

The ten responsories can be grouped under four headings: the first three are *"pro Concilio"*, the fourth and fifth *"pro populi Christiani unione"* (for the union of the Christian people); the sixth *"pro remissione peccatorum"* (for the forgiveness of sins), and the seventh to tenth are *"contra Ecclesiæ hostium furorem"* (against the fury of the Church's enemies). In Kerle's settings, each responsory is similar to a string of motets.

Taking inspiration from ancient practices, Kerle followed the modes' order in setting the texts to music: in so doing, he faced the problem of how to eschew the affective quality of the seventh mode (which was allegedly cheerful or even "lascivious", and thus inappropriate for serious occasions). This "frivolous" mode was given an earnest quality by transposing it a fifth lower: this seemingly minor issue becomes interesting when one considers that Glarean's treatise on modal theory was dedicated to Kerle's patron, Waldburg.

---

[62] De Kerle 1562.
[63] De Soto 1558.

The four-part texture was not always maintained by Kerle, who set the concluding doxology (the *Gloria Patri*) to three parts, possibly as an homage to the Trinity who is praised with those words, and adopted other flexible arrangements for the versicles and for the last responsory.

Kerle's compositional style is particularly interesting for the skilful and clever balance he achieved between backward-looking traditionalism (shown, for example, in the avoidance of word-painting and in the occasional use of chromatic harmonies) and the modern orientation to homophony and polyphonic simplification.

Though Kerle did not renounce a refined polyphonic style, the words are distinctly pronounced and the rhythmic and melodic patterns mirror closely those of speech; the overall sobriety in the responsories' compositional style corresponds both to their penitential mood and to the aesthetic ideals which were most appreciated by the Fathers. In Kerle's *Preces*, the evolution from the Franco-Flemish to the expressive but restrained Roman style is clearly observable, and the composer constantly refrained from employing too complex, rich or convoluted techniques.

In the year of their publication, Kerle's settings of the *Preces* were often sung at Trent during solemn worships (probably at the opening of each session), though – if one wishes to use contemporary definitions – they belong to the devotional rather than to the properly liturgical repertoire. Undoubtedly, however, the very context of their performance (within the Council itself) gave them an extraordinary exposure, and it is very likely that their repeated execution represented a kind of demonstration of what sacred music should be and become, countering the worries of those Fathers who complained against musical abuses of the past[64].

## 8.4. The Council on music

In the first section of this Chapter we have briefly introduced the framework for the Council's discussions and rulings on music, as concerns the overall context (objectives and limits of the debate as well as its subordination to matters of more urgent importance) and the main protagonists of its negotiations on music.

---

[64] Cf. Leichtentritt 1944, pp. 320–322 and 326; Fellerer 1951; Fellerer 1953, p. 588; Haberl 1966, pp. 33–36; Meier 1990, pp. 185–186; Rainoldi 2000, pp. 336–337; Leitmeir 2002, pp. 118–122; Forney 2006, p. 263.

We will now move on to the Council proper, though it is very important to keep constantly in mind its way of proceeding and the relative importance of the various items discussed below. First: music *per se* was not debated at the Council, and it was examined only within the framework of other topics (abuses in the Mass, institution of the seminaries, discipline in the female monasteries). Second: once a topic had been defined, those charged with the task would proceed to compile a draft, gathering all relevant information (theological arguments, practical experiences, pastoral needs, complaints, suggestions etc.). Third: such drafts often underwent more or less formal discussions, which could include epistolary exchanges with people who were interested in the topic (for a variety of reasons) and/or who were deemed to be able to profitably contribute to the subject. As a consequence, several drafts could be prepared and, in some cases, written witnesses of this preparatory work can be studied. Fourth: the commission's draft was submitted officially to the Council Fathers, who might discuss (and possibly approve) it as it was, but more often requested further modifications. These could be enacted by the commission (which would then send back the results of its revision to the Council Fathers) or – if only minor corrections were needed – they could be ratified directly by the assembly. Fifth: When an official decree was finally approved[65], it had to be sanctioned by the Pope, and then to be put into practice locally. In some instances, Roman Commissions were instituted with the task of continuing the Council's work and implementing its directives.

From what we have just seen, it appears clear that a huge number of papers were produced by the Council, by those working officially on its behalf and by those interested in its activity. Thus, it is always fundamental to consider: a) who wrote a certain document; b) whom it was intended for; c) which stage of the discussion was it produced at; d) how it was received.

In the discussions on the Council's stance about music, as Monson (2002) has very justly pointed out, provisional drafts have often been considered on the same plane as the official decrees. On the other hand, the opposite risk should also be avoided: whereas only the canonically approved decrees had formal value, the non-definitive discussions have in turn a significant importance, though a relative one. In fact, they mirror the concerns, ideas, attitudes and evaluations on a certain topic by the leading churchmen of the era; and they influenced the eventual reception of the official decrees. Those who had followed the writing of a decree, through all stages of its complex drafting, were likely to re-

---

[65] For the decrees' texts: *CT* 8, pp. 918, 922, 927, 963; Romita 1947, pp. 59–64. See also *CT* 2, pp. 256–257; *CT* 12, p. 714.

tain, as their interpretive framework, even those aspects which would later be dropped from the decree's wording (for the sake of synthesis, or because there was no consensus about them). Since in several instances those who participated in such preparatory discussions were also those who would be responsible for the decrees' enactment in their dioceses, this point is of the utmost importance and has sometimes been insufficiently considered.

Summarising: it is incorrect to treat the unapproved texts in the same way as the official decrees; but it is also wrong to abstract the decrees from their background, which influenced their reception by the bishops after the Council.

Moreover, in our specific field, doubts are permitted as to how many musicians actually read the official texts of the Council. In several cases, I deem it arguable that only word-of-mouth knowledge was passed to practical musicians: as we will see in the next Chapter (§ 9.3.6.), statements such as "conforming to the Council's decrees" started to be used (sometimes rather inappropriately) with a vague meaning which has perhaps been taken too seriously by modern musicology.

### 8.4.1. Setting the stage

When topics with musical implications started to be taken into consideration at Trent, the Council had already been working for fifteen years, though – obviously – in much shorter time-slots: from 1545 to 1547 (sessions I to XI, Trent and Bologna), from 1551 to 1552 (sessions XII to XVI, Trent) and from 1562 to 1563 (sessions XVII to XXV, Trent). Only in this latter gathering was music considered.

Notwithstanding this, expectations about the Council's discussions on music had been nourished for a long time: even Cirillo's letter[66] (§ 3.3.3.) can be considered an anticipated contribution to the Council, as it had been written between sessions XI and XII (1549).

Even before the Council started, in 1543, the Bishop of Vienna, Friedrich Grau ("Nausea") von Waischenfeld (also known as "Blancicampianus", 1496–1552, who died in Trent during the Council) had written for Pope Paul III a summary of issues needing consideration, some of which regarded music: though Grau did not live to contribute actively to the Council's discussions on music, his draft provided the basic scheme for many of them. His intervention[67] focused on some fundamental issues (ordered here according to their topic and not to the

---

66 *Lettere volgari* 1564, fols. 114$^r$-118$^v$.
67 Grau 1865, pp. 585–586. See Schaefer 1994.

original). As concerns texts, he denounced: a) errors, imprecisions and inadequacies in missals, breviaries etc.; b) texts which are not based on Scripture; c) texts in the vernacular; d) text not focused on the Eucharist or on Christ's Passion. As regards text/music relationships, Grau complained about the subordination of liturgical texts to musical needs (e.g. repetitions or shortenings). As regards compositional issues, he stigmatised music encouraging wantonness and maintained that church songs should possess the necessary gravity and seriousness. As concerns the musicians' behaviour, he blamed the (musical) incompetence of some and their inappropriate performance styles; he also instructed that optional, non-liturgical prayers should be distinct and separated from the Mass[68].

As mentioned earlier, it was not before 1562 that music entered officially among the topics under debate at Trent. In June, Emperor Ferdinand had sent a Reform *libellus* to the Council, advocating the introduction of vernacular psalmody and hymns in worship. Very few of the suggestions included in his writing were going to be accepted, since many of them seemed too close to the Evangelical positions in the Catholic clergy's eyes[69].

### 8.4.2. Enumerating errors

Soon, however, in July 1562 (in view of the XXII session), a Commission chaired by Ludovico Beccadelli (the Archbishop of Ragusa whom Cirillo hoped his letter would eventually reach) was officially charged to work on the "abuses" committed in the celebration of the Mass. While the Commission was working, the Jesuit Peter Canisius (or Pieter Kanijs, 1521–1597, later to be proclaimed a saint by the Roman Catholic Church) sent to Bishop Hosius a list of abuses, which however arrived to its recipient on August 8th, too late to be incorporated in the first draft[70].

On that very same day, in fact, the Commission presented the results of its meetings to Cardinal Ercole Gonzaga, who was the President of the Council. The draft denounced, among other things, the use of unauthorised texts (stating that no new Introits or prayers should arbitrarily be introduced); of inappropriate tropes (such as those in honour of the Virgin Mary within the *Gloria*); and some problematic issues of polyphony in general.

---

68 Cf. Rainoldi 2000, pp. 333–334; Monson 2006, p. 28.
69 Cf. Lockwood 1966, p. 43; Rainoldi 2000, p. 337; Monson 2002, pp. 15–17.
70 Cf. Monson 2002, p. 7. On Canisius' attitude to music, cf. *Chron.* 4, p. 262.

The drafts dating from August 1562 have significant links with the Decretal by John XXII analysed in Chapter Two of this book (§ 2.3.6.). The Pope had complained against music which "intoxicated rather than soothed the ear"; however, in his opinion, (polyphonic) music "would, more than any other music is able to do, both soothe the hearer and inspire his devotion, without destroying religious feeling in the minds of the singers"[71]: these words are quoted almost verbatim in the draft of August 8th.

In fact, Beccadelli's committee asked the Council Fathers "Whether the kind of music that has now become established in polyphony, which refreshes the ear more than the mind and which seems to incite lasciviousness rather than religion, should be abolished from the Masses, in which things are often sung, such as *della caccia* and *la battaglia*"[72].

It will not escape the reader's notice that this question faithfully mirrors the concerns voiced by Cirillo in his often-quoted letter[73], which Beccadelli probably knew. Moreover, we have briefly mentioned in Chapter Four (§ 4.2.5.) that Biagio Rossetto's criticism (1529[74]) of wind instruments in church may have referred precisely to their association with venery and jousting.

It should be stressed that musical settings exemplified by those mentioned here were being condemned not on the basis of elements such as secular *cantus firmus* or models, but on a much more audible ground: here, the secular component is the vocal imitation of *sounds* such as those of battling or hunting. It can be recalled that already John XXII had expressed his aversion to similar aural effects (such as hockets), which were distracting and potentially ridiculous; and also Friedrich Grau, in his intervention, repeatedly advocated the elimination of comical elements from sacred music. Moreover, as seen in Chapter Three (§ 3.3.2.9.), the fear of aural effects with too explicit and "unholy" connotations (such as beasts' cries) was intensely felt. Furthermore, as Monson is once again right in pointing out, the proponents of the quoted text were simply inviting the Fathers to express their opinion on the matter: if analogous starting points on matters of systematic theology were to be considered as dogmatic pronouncements, the Catholic Church's belief would be very different from what it is[75].

Since musical matters were only a minimal part of the numerous liturgical abuses listed in the document dated August 8th, a little more than ten days later the text was sent back to the Commission to be considerably shortened.

---

71 In Weiss and Taruskin 2008, pp. 60–61; cf. Raynor 1972, pp. 36–37; Romita 1936, pp. 47–48.
72 *CT* 8, p. 918, English translation in Monson 2002, p. 8.
73 *Lettere volgari* 1564, fols. 114r-118v.
74 Rossetto 1529; quoted in Rainoldi 2000, p. 724.
75 Cf. Lockwood 1966, p. 41; Monson 2002, p. 8; Lejeune 2010, p. 12.

In another draft datable approximately to August 25th, it was proposed that the kinds of music used in worship should be reduced to those prescribed by John XXII in his 1324 Decretal (cf. § 2.3.6.). Rainoldi[76] interprets this as meaning that the only non-monodic form of music the proponents of this option would admit was the "*organum*": it will be recalled, however, that Pope John's discussion was much broader than this, and that the Council's Commission's reference to the Decretal could simply have been aimed at establishing a theological and historical connection with a previous magisterial pronouncement[77].

On September 10th, 1562, a *Compendium Abusuum* was issued afresh by the Commission: it was structured in nine Canons, the eighth of which dealt with musical issues. Here, the matter of intelligibility became central: liturgical texts had to be delivered clearly, so that they may "placidly descend" into the ears and hearts of the listeners; it was also suggested that the holy lessons should be read first with a "simple and clear voice", so that nothing escaped the listeners. When music was employed, the Canon continued, it should not be composed for the "inane delectation of the ears", but so that "everybody could perceive the words". However (and this is an interesting point), the function of music was not merely to submit itself to verbal delivery and possibly increase its rhetorical function: the Fathers demonstrated that they were conscious of music's symbolic and mystical power ("so that the listeners' hearts may be enraptured to the desire of the heavenly harmonies and to contemplation of the joys of the blessed"[78]).

Music is seen here as a true anticipation of heavenly bliss, as it enables the listeners to be drawn to contemplation of the divine beauty: though such statements were not an absolute novelty, they were also not typical of the aesthetical perspective of the time, and opened up a fascinating space for considering music as an agent of divine Grace and an instrument used by God in order to encourage humans in their path to sanctity.

Though this draft from September 10th is undoubtedly interesting and has been quoted (perhaps even too often) in musicological debates on Trent, it was still not the definitive version. Some, among whom the Spanish Bishops of Coimbra, Granada and Segovia, proposed that the nine Canons should be shortened still further. It is probably at this point that the Spaniards' defence of music, quoted by Paleotti and mentioned above (§ 8.3.4.), took place; in Pale-

---

[76] Rainoldi 2000, p. 338.
[77] Cf. Monson 2002, p. 9.
[78] "*Compendium Abusuum*" in Paleotti 1842, p. 266 (September 10th, 1562); Latin text also in Rainoldi 2000, p. 38; my translation. Cf. Monson 2002, pp. 9–10; Boyce 2006, p. 140; Weber 2008, p. 164.

otti's papers, moreover, a reference to the ancient customs of the Church was made – and they were actually invoked by Christophorus of Padua (the Father General of the Augustinians who was one of the major theologians active at the Council), who quoted from Patristic sources in support of the maintenance of church music, ceremonies and vestments[79].

### 8.4.3. A "house of prayer"

The numerous efforts to summarise the initially bulky list of abuses reached eventually their goal when a still further draft, submitted on September 14th, was approved three days later (September 17th, 1562, *Decretum de observandis et vitandis in celebratione missarum*[80]). Here, the section regarding music is extremely succinct and concise, and was included within a decree "concerning the things to be observed and avoided in the celebration of the Mass". In Monson's translation, it reads: "Let them keep away from the churches compositions in which there is an intermingling of the lascivious or impure, whether by instrument or voice"[81]; other forbidden things were "secular actions" and "chattering, walking, uproars, clamours", in order that "the house of God may be truly seen and said to be a house of prayer" (cf. Isaiah 56:7, Matthew 21:13, Mark 11:17, Luke 19:46; cf. John 2:13 ff.).

Since this synthetic statement was the only one officially approved as regards music, it is worthy of some attention in spite of its objectively vague wording. First observation: though there is no better translation into English than "compositions", the original Latin *musicas* may indicate "kinds of music", potentially including performance practices beside composed works. Second observation: there is no mention, here, of the "secular": David Crook has rightfully pointed out that the previous wording (which included the word *profanum*) was replaced here by *impurum*, which has a similar but not identical meaning. In detail, the "purity" which church music should possess obviously includes the absence of unchaste overtones, but also implies, in my opinion, a kind of "suitability to the sacred", a ritual godliness. We may recall here our discussion of the "purity of heart" which is necessary for praising God in a way pleasing to Him (§ 3.3.2.10.). Rainoldi efficaciously points out this element: for him, the

---

[79] *CT* 13, p. 714; cf. Monson 2002, p. 10 and fn. 24.
[80] In *Mansi* 33, cols. 132–133 (http://bit.ly/2bxVlSK).
[81] "*Ab ecclesiis vero musicas eas, ubi sive organo sive cantu lascivum aut impurum aliquid miscetur*" (*CT* 8, p. 963); *Canones* 1564, p. 112. Translation in Monson 2002, p. 11.

Council wished to insert a discontinuity between "common social practices" and the holy mysteries, both as concerns behaviour and repertoires[82].

My third observation regards the context for the prescriptions about music: the mention of "chattering, walking, uproars, clamours" (cf. Azpilcueta[83]), and – especially – the reference to the Bible have not hitherto received sufficient attention. In an episode narrated in all four Gospels, Jesus was horrified to see the merchants and money-changers selling animals for the ritual sacrifices or exchanging coins in the proximity of the holy halls of the Temple in Jerusalem. Thus, an outraged Jesus overturned the tables of the money-changers and drove the sellers out from the Temple, while proclaiming that God's house should be a "house of prayer" and not a "market" or a "robbers' den". In John's version, a significant remark is added (John 2:17): "His disciples remembered that it was written: 'Zeal for your house will consume me' (Psalm 69 [68]:9)".

I deemed this Scriptural digression necessary, because it may add several significant and meaningful layers to the interpretation of the Council's decree. As is well known, the spark which had triggered Luther's Reformation had been his outrage at the selling of indulgences (an abuse which can be seen as representing all too well the market of holy things condemned by Jesus himself). Though under many aspects the Council aimed at opposing several of the theological stances maintained by the Evangelical theologians, it also substantially agreed with several of the criticisms they had voiced concerning the corruption found in certain institutions of the Catholic Church. If, as I suggested as regards both Cirillo's letter[84] – cf. § 3.3.3. – and Glarean above in this Chapter (§ 8.3.3.), several among the most serious discussions on sacred music in the sixteenth century may be interpreted as mirroring even greater concerns for the spiritual life of the Church, then I would argue that here too the purification of church music is seen within the framework of a much greater and important process of atonement.

My fourth observation, which is a consequence of the preceding, concerns the "lascivious and impure". Our lengthy discussion of the word "lascivious" in its several layers of meaning (cf. § 3.3.2.2.) finds here its justification. It will be clear, by now, that the common interpretation of the Council's decrees on music as "banning secular *cantus firmus* from polyphony" is grossly inadequate and – at best – extremely limited. No mention is made here of polyphony, or of

---

[82] Rainoldi 2000, p. 339.
[83] De Azpilcueta 1578, p. 251. See also Blackburn 2007, p. 90.
[84] *Lettere volgari* 1564, fols. 114$^r$-118$^v$.

*cantus firmus*, or of the secular. The process by which this decree was elaborated did mention more specific aspects of musical composition (but also there, as said before, it censored explicit aural references to secular activities such as hunting and battling rather than *cantus firmus* or parody composition: § 8.4.2.), but the actual decree omitted such detailed references.

What the decree does say, in my opinion, is something much more profound and spiritually important. In the Temple of Jerusalem, where the Gospel episode of the merchants took place, there was a complex spatial organisation, culminating in the *sanctum sanctorum:* the more sacred (and inner) a space was, the less numerous were the categories of people admitted within it. (Incidentally, the Gospel merchants were not actually operating within the Temple itself, where such trade would have been forbidden; however, Jesus showed by his action that he wished all "intermingling of the lascivious or impure" to be removed from the house of God). Interestingly, in the lines immediately preceding Paleotti's recollection of the debates leading to this decree in his memories, he reports that some clergymen suggested expelling female public sinners from the churches after the Gospel during Masses. The proposal was not accepted for fear of even greater scandals, but – in my opinion – it is yet another proof of the climate surrounding the discussions on musical matters (music, femininity, lasciviousness, temptation).

Summarising, then, I think that the Council's Decree of September 1562 on music should be interpreted: a) as a symbol of (or at least a parallel to) the purification needed by the Catholic Church and fostered by the Council; b) as inviting sobriety (in opposition to wantonness and vanity) and rigour (as opposed to "vain pleasure" of the ears); c) as fostering the purification of things (or people) which were close to the sacred.

The holy vessel, which would contain the Eucharistic species, needed to be constantly purified; the priests and clergy, who were in contact with the holy mysteries, were forcefully invited by the Council to purify their morality; music, which was an integral part of the Eucharistic celebration, needed to drop what was superfluous, wanton or vain, and to recover its "heavenly" vocation (as described in the August draft).

It will be noted, moreover, that no words are employed in the Decree on the issue of intelligibility, contrary to musicological legends. Once more, it is undeniable that concern on this matter was common among the Catholic clergy (as it was in other Christian confessions), and that the topic had been mentioned in most drafts and discussions leading to the eventually published Decree; yet, in the officially approved text, it had disappeared. As we will see, notwithstanding this, it will still continue to play a major role in the post-Tridentine debates on music and on the reception of the Council, even by those who had participated in almost all stages of the Decree's elaboration[85].

### 8.4.4. Rescuing polyphony?

Another deliberation issued in September 1562 was also going to have some bearing on musical aspects: by affirming the importance of teaching the contents of faith to the laity, in the form of catechetical instruction, the Council was paving the way for a systematic, nearly-official and widespread use of vernacular songs in the Catholic Church, within the framework of religious instruction of children (and adults[86]: cf. § 11.4.4. and following).

Though the extensive debates on the liturgical abuses had led to the highly significant, but comparatively succinct and undetailed Decree of September 1562, the subject of music was to be discussed again less than a year later.

In May 1563, Giovanni Morone and Bernardo Navagero, recently chosen as Papal legates, initiated a new wave of reforms, by writing a list of forty-two articles for discussion in the XXIV session of the Council. As we saw above (§ 8.3.2.), they proposed the elimination of *molliores musicorum cantus* (or *"musica troppo molle"*) from worship[87]. Once again, I would like to recall to the readers' attention the semantic multiplicity of *mollis* as discussed in Chapter Three (§ 3.3.2.2.). Morone and Navagero's draft was sent to Emperor Ferdinand, who replied (on August 23$^{rd}$, 1563) in worried tones to what he perceived to be a menace to polyphony.

Indeed, the Emperor's interpretation of *molliores modulationes* as *cantus figuratus* was just this – an interpretation, as he states himself:

> If it be a matter of eliminating straightforwardly figural singing from all churches of the world, We do not approve of this. We think, in fact, that the divine gift of music (which not infrequently arouses to greater devotion the human souls, especially those of the expert and studious of the arts) must by no means be expelled from the church[88].

---

**85** Cf. Monson 2002, pp. 10–11, 19–22 (Monson's article is the reference study on the Council and music, and represented a turning-point for the musicological reception of Trent); cf. also Koenigsberger 1986, p. 186; Mischiati 1995, p. 19; O'Regan 2013a, p. 340; Prodi 2014, p. 262.
**86** Cf. Scheitler 2010, pp. 163, 184–185.
**87** Cf. *CT* 9, p. 755, fn. 1.
**88** In Pastor 1950, p. 630, fn. 66; my translation.

(Incidentally, the difference between Ferdinand's "expert and studious" and the idea that music was a help for the "weaker souls" is noteworthy).

How influent was Ferdinand's letter on the Council's discussion? Music historians have debated this topic for centuries, with opinions ranging from those which define the Emperor as the "saviour of church music" to those which discard the former interpretation as a myth or a legend. The only fact that can be established is that the Fathers actually suspended their debates on this issue until they received the Emperor's reply to the draft (thus demonstrating that his opinion was undoubtedly taken into consideration); on the other hand, his interpretation of the draft may have been too extreme, and – besides this – polyphony was not without its advocates at Trent[89].

In the meantime, however, another topic which would eventually have important musical consequences had been discussed and approved on July 15$^{th}$, 1563 (session XXIII, c. XVIII[90]): it established that clerics should learn singing "and other good arts" as a part of their education. Though the type of singing alluded to here was primarily plainchant, polyphonic singing was going to be actively taught and practised in most seminaries instituted after Trent[91].

Upon arrival of the Emperor's letter, a new draft was prepared, submitted (on September 5$^{th}$) and discussed later in that month. This new version, which was to be officially approved with comparatively minor corrections on November 11$^{th}$ (*Decretum de Reformatione*, session XXIV, Canon XII[92]) refrained from giving precise indications on musical matters: its most important directive (and that which would prove most influential on the future of church music) entrusted the ruling on ceremonial aspects such as music and its enactment to local authorities (bishop, synods, local councils etc.).

The Decree is translated by Monson as:

> Let them all be required to attend divine services and not by substitutes; and to assist and serve the bishop when celebrating or carrying out other pontifical functions, and to praise the name of God reverently, clearly and devoutly in hymns and canticles in the choir established for psalmody. [...] With regard to the proper direction of the divine offices, concerning the proper manner of singing or playing therein, the precise regulation for assembling and remaining in choir, together with everything necessary for the ministers of the church, and suchlike: the provincial synod shall prescribe an established form for the benefit of, and in accordance with the customs of, each province[93].

---

**89** Cf. Lockwood 1966, p. 42; Rainoldi 2000, p. 341; Monson 2002, pp. 16–17.
**90** *CŒD*, p. 751.
**91** Cf. Rainoldi 2000, p. 341.
**92** *CŒD*, p. 767.
**93** *CT* 9, pp. 983–984. Translation by and in Monson 2002, p. 18. Cf. Weber 2008, pp. 97–98.

In this case, matters concerning the proper delivery of a text are actually mentioned, but it is extremely interesting that the topic under discussion is *not* intelligibility (i.e. what the *hearers* can perceive or understand) but rather delivery (i.e. how the sacred words are *pronounced*).

This change of perspective is, in my opinion, not to be overlooked. In the Evangelical world, the primary focus of concern was what the *congregation* could hear and comprehend (thus fostering their participation in worship, through the passive act of listening on the occasions when they could not join in more actively). Here the focus, instead, is on *God*, to whom praise is addressed: the act of adoration, conveyed by means of the sacred words, had to be enacted in the best possible fashion, as was appropriate to the divine majesty.

### 8.4.5. Music in the convents

The third occasion on which music was debated at Trent was during the very last session (XXV), immediately after the approval of the preceding decree, and when the reform of female religious orders was treated. As Monson cleverly puts it, musicology has often overlooked the only documentable instance when polyphony really ran the risk of being banned. On November 20th, 1563, the Council Fathers were invited to discuss a Canon whose text read:

> Chapter 7. [...] Let the divine services be accomplished by [the nuns] with voices raised, and not by professionals hired for that purpose; and in the sacrifice of the Mass let them make the responses that the choir usually makes; but let them not usurp the role of the deacon and subdeacon of reciting the Lessons, Epistles, and Gospels. Let them abstain both in choir and elsewhere from modulation and inflection of the voices, as well as from the other singing artifice called *figuratum* or *organicum*[94].

We may observe a few important elements in this draft (though, once more, it was not approved in the form quoted above). First, there is an element in common with the (approved) Decree of November 11th, i.e. the stress that religious men and women should personally undertake the prayerful duties to which they were committed by their state, and not leave them to substitutes. Second, we can note that the liturgical role of nuns is driven back to what tradition had established, and that the office of publicly proclaiming the Scripture is re-

---

[94] *CT* 9, p. 1043; English translation partially taken from Monson 2002, pp. 20–21, quoted here with my own modifications: I take *organicum* to be a synonym of *figuratum* and not a reference to organs as instruments.

served for the clergy. Third (what matters most for us here), the Commission proposed to abolish "figured" music outright in female convents, together with *"vocis modulatione atque inflexione"*.

Once more, we can harvest here the results of our previous discussions (§ 3.3.2.1.), as regards the connections between the dangerous charms of polyphony and those of femininity; moreover, I think that the draft's mention of "modulation" and "inflection of the voice" represents yet another instance of an expression whose exact meaning eludes us. I believe that they can be safely assumed to indicate performance practice styles, probably similar to those discussed in Chapter Three (§ 3.3.2.7.): in particular, I deem the association between this description and the word *artificium* to be significant. Though our surmises on how sixteenth-century music actually sounded are purely speculative, I think that what was at stake here, beside the possibility to sing polyphonically, was also an artificial way of singing (of ornamenting?), which was felt as vainglorious, ostentatious and conceited. If the nuns' music was perceived as "natural", it could be practised; if it betrayed an artificiality similar to those of the women's "seductive" arts, it should be banned.

Fortunately, however, a more moderate stance was eventually adopted by the Council, and the Decrees approved on December 4th, 1563, did not include prohibitions on nuns' music, though – obviously – the religious superiors still had the power to enact almost whatever limitations they deemed necessary. We will discuss at a greater length, in Chapter Twelve (§ 12.4.1.–2.), the extraordinary musical life, repertoire and experiences which characterised many Catholic female monasteries, as well as the skilful and sometimes very shrewd strategies they enacted to defend their musicianship when it was at risk of being limited[95].

### 8.4.6. Concluding the Council

The XXV session was also the very last of the Council, which was rather hastily brought to its conclusion after so many years of debates and such long interruptions in between the official sessions. As mentioned above (§ 3.3.2.2. and 8.3.2.), the final sermon by Ragasanus touched in passing on the topic of *molliores cantus*, though this did not have actual implications for church musicians. Instead, a last decision which did have some weight on music was the resolution to entrust

---

[95] Cf. Beggiao 1978, p. 94; Masetti Zannini 1993, pp. 125 and 128; Kendrick 1996, p. 11; Monson 2002, pp. 19–22; Monson 2006, p. 403; Weber 2008, p. 99.

the Holy See with the task of preparing (along with the *Index* of forbidden books and with the Catechism) a revised Breviary and Missal (it will be recalled that this necessity had been expressed well before the Council's opening by Friedrich Grau, the Bishop of Vienna[96]).

As mentioned earlier (§ 8.4.4.), therefore, the Council's decision which would practically have the greatest importance for music and musicians was its choice to entrust local authorities with the power to interpret, implement and enact its reticent decrees[97].

Though in some instances this choice could partially be imputed to external factors (such as the haste to conclude the Council which seized the Fathers toward its ending), it was also, in my opinion, a precise and wise strategy. It recognised, albeit implicitly, that musicianship took diverse forms in diverse contexts (social, geographical...) and answered to different needs for different people and groupings (praise, propaganda, instruction...).

What the Council did define (corresponding to a precise need of the Catholic Church) was the overall orientation to sobriety, simplicity and sincerity in music for worship. One shivers at the thought of what an *Index* of the forbidden music would have done to Catholic music. While the official responsibility for the forms which Catholic music would take in the following centuries was entrusted to bishops and synods, I think it arguable that the unofficial responsibility was given by the Council to musicians themselves[98]. Of course, the local ecclesiastical authorities had the power of placing certain limitations on music, and did often make use of this power; nevertheless, the only ones who normally possessed the necessary knowledge for discussing music's technical aspects were the professional musicians (and churchmen only when they were musicians in turn). Clearly, this led in some instances to musical anarchy and to abuses sometimes greater than those censored by the Council; however, on other occasions, it encouraged musicians to reflect creatively on how to put their music at the service of liturgy.

On a more indirect level, as Weber points out, the Council fostered the establishment of new relationships between liturgy and piety[99]: we will see in the next Chapter the forms this connection was going to take in the first post-Tridentine era.

Among the other decisions of the Council which had some relevance to musical issues, it is worth mentioning the debates on the use of the vernacular. We

---

96  Cf. Rainoldi 2000, pp. 333–334; Monson 2006, p. 28.
97  Cf. Monson 2002, pp. 3 and 19.
98  Cf. Fenlon 2009, p. 200; Prodi 2014, p. 17.
99  Weber 2008, p. 161.

have seen in the preceding Chapters that congregational singing in the vernacular had a crucial role not only for the spiritual life of Evangelical believers, but also within their official worship (up to the complete replacement of Latin liturgies, in certain cases). We have also seen that Luther's use of vernacular singing was undoubtedly innovative, creative and fascinating, but that it built upon existing practices of the Catholic Church, at least at the local level.

The topic was discussed at the Council of Trent (it had also been brought to the Fathers' attention during the preceding Lateran Council, in 1513, thanks to the *Libellus ad Leonem* by Quirini and Giustinian, cf. § 3.3.1.4.). In 1562, a large majority (four out of five) of the Bishops discussing a draft on liturgy expressed a favourable opinion on the use of vernacular in worship; however, in September of the same year, a more cautious line prevailed (probably in reaction to the Evangelicals' use of vernacular worship as a confessional flag). Vernacular worships were in general not permitted (with a few exceptions), though preaching in the local languages was allowed and encouraged, as well as explanations of the Latin liturgy for the sake of the illiterate. Vernacular hymnody could find its way within official cults, and this happened with a certain frequency especially in "borderline" contexts, such as territories close to Protestantism or in culturally distant missionary milieus[100] (for example in China).

## 8.5. What did not happen at the Council

The concluding section of this Chapter bears a provocative title: after our previous analysis of what the Council did state on music, of how it arrived at those statements, and of the people and theological ideas behind them, I will now briefly discuss what was *not* said or written or established at the Council.

Obviously, as we have seen in the introductory section of this Chapter, very numerous issues pertaining to music and to its role within the Catholic worship were not touched on at the Council, for a number of reasons already discussed. It is not my goal here to restate what has already been said there: instead, my aim is to point out a few topics which have been the object of musicological mythology for years and are still transmitted in some histories of music, notwithstanding the valuable efforts of musicologists who have carefully dismantled such legends.

---

[100] Cf. Herl 2004, p. 34, to which this section is indebted; cf. Rainoldi 2000, p. 331, fn. 6; Brown 2005, p. 9; Weber 2008, pp. 168 and 170; Fisher 2014, p. 16.

Indeed, two such myths have already been – hopefully – discarded in the preceding discussion, i.e. that the Council banned secular *cantus firmus* or models from sacred polyphony, and that polyphony itself was at risk of prohibition in Catholic worship.

### 8.5.1. Palestrina: polyphony's saviour?

This latter legend is strictly connected with the most famous of all fables surrounding the Council of Trent and music, i.e. that concerning Palestrina's *Missa Papæ Marcelli*. I have deliberately avoided discussing it until now, because only after all that has come before will the reader be able to judge autonomously on the contents of this story. Of course, like all myths, it can reveal to us something about the background originating it, and it is based (albeit very loosely) on actual facts which we have already discussed in the previous pages.

In a few words, the legend has it that the Council intended to forbid polyphony in Catholic worship, on the grounds that it prevented a proper understanding of the sacred words; fortunately, however, a performance of Palestrina's *Missa Papæ Marcelli* persuaded the Fathers that polyphony and intelligibility were not incompatible; thus Palestrina could be considered to be the saviour of polyphony. (Ironically, Palestrina is already the second saviour of polyphony we have met in this Chapter, in the august company of Emperor Ferdinand).

This myth originated in the early seventeenth century (in a treatise by Agostino Agazzari[101]), and gained widespread acceptance in the early nineteenth century (thanks to Palestrina's biographer Baini[102]), until it was given immortality in a "musical legend" by Hans Pfitzner (1869 – 1949), *Palestrina* (1915 – 7).

The origins, history and reasons for rejecting the Palestrina myth are exhaustively summarised in Lockwood and Jeppesen's essays attached to the former's critical edition of the *Missa Papæ Marcelli*[103], to which I refer the reader who wishes to get more information about this work and the issues connected with it.

The date of composition of this Mass, published in 1567 within the *Second Book* of Palestrina's Masses[104], has been disputed by many during the last two centuries, as has the title under which it is known. We have already seen that, during his extremely short pontificate, Pope Marcellus demonstrated considerable interest in matters of church music, encouraging his singers to choose (and

---

101 Agazzari 1607.
102 Baini 1828 (cf. pp. 34 ff.).
103 Lockwood 1975.
104 Palestrina 1567.

## 8.5. What did not happen at the Council — 423

perhaps to compose) sacred music works in a style and affect suitable to the liturgical occasion, in order that the text could be clearly pronounced and heard.

Furthermore, another letter by Cirillo has been preserved on the subject of church music[105], inferentially dated to the summer of 1574 by Palisca and addressed to an unknown recipient, who is indicated only as "Messer Annibal".

In his discussion of this letter, Palisca suggests some possibilities for the identification of this Annibal (or Annibale), the most likely of which is Annibale Rucellai (d.1601). Notwithstanding this, I would propose here an alternative, i.e. Annibale Zoilo (c.1537–1592). The closest connecting link between Zoilo and Cirillo is represented by the former's brother, Giovanni Domenico (or Giandomenico[106], 1531–1576), who was *maggiordomo* of the Ospedale di Santo Spirito in Sassia in 1573[107] (Cirillo was there as the administrator from 1555–6 to his death in 1575). Giovanni Domenico commissioned all adornments, with the only exception of the altarpiece, in the third chapel on the right in Santo Spirito in Sassia[108]; within the same church, Cirillo is portrayed as the commissioner of a painting by Livio Agresti (1505–1579), depicting Jesus' healing of the paralytic: close to this painting, a commemorative stone in honour of Giovanni Domenico is found, dedicated to him by Annibale[109].

It is therefore very easy to surmise that Cirillo was acquainted with Annibale Zoilo, and it is suggestive to mention that Annibale Zoilo died in Loreto, where he had been *Maestro di Cappella* since 1584 at the Santa Casa where Cirillo had been Archpriest from 1535 to 1553 (though at the time of Zoilo's appointment in Loreto, Cirillo was already dead. After Cirillo, the pastoral care duties at the shrine of Loreto were entrusted to the Jesuits).

If my supposition is correct, it would demonstrate that Cirillo was particularly able at hand-picking the recipients of his letters on church music: Beccadelli, to whom Cirillo intended his 1549 letter to be delivered, would become, in 1562, Chair of the Commission charged to discuss liturgical abuses at the Council of Trent; Zoilo, in turn, was going to be entrusted, in 1577, by Pope Gregory XIII (and in the company of Palestrina) with the task of revising the Catholic Church's plainchant (cf. § 9.3.4.).

In this 1574 letter, Cirillo stated that, shortly after his writing of the famous 1549 letter, he "happened to come upon Cardinal Marcello Cervini, later Pope

---

**105** It is quoted and translated in Lockwood 1975, pp. 26–27; Palisca 1997 (pp. 291 ff.) discussed it at some length.
**106** Cf. Casimiri 1932 and 1940.
**107** Cf. a manuscript bill of sale (Roma, Ospedale S. Spirito, Pergamene, sig. 70/607).
**108** Cf. Vanti 1936, p. 135 and n. 11.
**109** Cf. Pietrangeli 1994, vol. 14, Part III, p. 85.

Marcellus", and to have "a long discussion with him about the content of the letter". When he got back to Rome, Cervini sent Cirillo "a Mass that conformed very closely to what [Cirillo] was seeking", and which gave him "great consolation and pleasure", since it showed that his "thought and purpose had been taken up and in some measure put into execution"[110].

It has therefore been supposed that this Mass, sent by Cervini to Cirillo, may have been Palestrina's *Missa Papæ Marcelli*, though this theory presents several (and severe) chronological criticalities – partly due to our insufficient knowledge of certain important facts, such as when this meeting of Cervini and Cirillo took place, and when Palestrina's Mass was composed.

It is true that, in comparison with other contemporaneous Masses (and with other works by Palestrina himself) the *Missa Papæ Marcelli* does adopt a style which, in several instances, favours intelligibility more than the others do; the composer himself defined his own compositional style as a "new manner" in the preface to the printed edition of 1567[111]. (Interestingly, Taruskin sees Palestrina and Ruffo's "intelligible" style as "coerced" and "official", though one in which "beautiful and moving" results could be achieved[112]). Notwithstanding this, there are sections, in this Mass, where the dense polyphonic texture and imitative processes cannot be taken as an example of musical settings allowing perfect intelligibility.

There are, indeed, in the entire *Second Book* of Palestrina's Masses, numerous sections where the compositional style is close to homorhythmic, and – granting one of Cirillo's wishes – the simultaneous delivery of different textual segments by the vocal parts happens more rarely than in the composer's preceding output and in the works by composers of the previous generation. As Palisca correctly maintains, however, granted that this Mass actually was that sent by Cervini to Cirillo (which is highly debatable), it would have corresponded exactly to just that one (i.e. intelligibility) among the numerous issues and wishes discussed by Cirillo; not, for instance, to his aspiration to a touching and "moving" music in the style of Arcadelt's madrigal[113].

Notwithstanding this, the absence of an identifiable pre-existing model for Palestrina's Mass constitutes another element which would have satisfied Cirillo, since – as we observed in § 3.3.3. – he complained that the adoption of a recurring *cantus firmus* or model prevented composers from differentiating among the various movements of Mass Ordinaries on the modal and affective plane.

---

110 Cf. De Angelis 1950, pp. 44–46; English translation in Lockwood 1975, pp. 26–27.
111 Palestrina 1567.
112 Taruskin 2010, vol. I, p. 653.
113 Palisca 1997, p. 291.

It must be stressed, however, that scholars such as Jeppesen[114] suggested 1562–3 as the possible date of composition for the *Missa Papæ Marcelli:* though this surmise is debatable, it would make it impossible for Cervini to have known it (he died in 1555), and would instead increase the likelihood of a connection between this Mass and the Council of Trent. However, the numerous chronological uncertainties about the dating of Palestrina's *Second Book* of Masses make it very difficult to surmise whether these works were composed before the last sessions of the Council, and – if so – whether they were performed there, and whether they could influence the Fathers' deliberations on sacred music. (It is for this reason that I dedicated more attention to Kerle's *Preces* than to Palestrina's *Missa Papæ Marcelli* when discussing the Council, since in the former case we are certain that Kerle's works were performed at Trent, whereas no indisputable data are available as concerns Palestrina).

Moreover, as we have seen, it can hardly be said – on the grounds of the documents available to us – that the Council's majority was in favour of a ban on polyphony. As Leitmeir correctly points out, what the *Papæ Marcelli* legend does tell us is only that, at the beginning of the seventeenth century, the idea that polyphony had been under threat of elimination could be believed. The origins of this story from a Jesuitical background suggest, in Leitmeir's opinion, that the legend may have had the function of a veiled threat: when polyphony was no longer at any risk of being suppressed (provided that it had been under such a threat at any time of its history), church authorities could have had some interest in warning composers "not to leave the orthodox line", under fear that "otherwise the ban might still be enacted"[115].

If the *Missa Papæ Marcelli* story was a classical instance of what *did not* happen at the Council (or at least what we have no historical certainty about), it is perhaps more interesting for us to point out a few more issues of what the Council did not affirm or did not take a stance on.

### 8.5.2. Prescriptions or proscriptions?

We may start this concluding survey by briefly comparing music with the visual arts. As Prodi succinctly and efficaciously summarises, also in their case the Council only gave negative indications as to what should be avoided in churches.

---

[114] In Lockwood 1975, p. 130.
[115] Leitmeir 2002, p. 132 (cf. *ibid.*, p. 131). Cf. Jeppesen 1975, pp. 110–111, 114 and 124; Atlas 2006, p. 114; Bergin 2009.

This included "secular and lascivious" images (once more!) and those unsuitable to the place's holiness; for visual arts too, moreover, the local bishops were held responsible for the enactment of the Council's decrees. Prodi rightfully comments that these indications are seemingly oriented against "the artistic splendours of Renaissance and Mannerism" rather than against the iconoclastic stances of some Evangelical confessions[116]. This thought-provoking observation encourages similar considerations about music.

Though we have seen that some awareness about the mystical and symbolic value of music did emerge at the Council, most of the drafts and of the approved decrees quoted earlier in this Chapter seem to tolerate rather than to foster music, especially as concerns that with a higher artistic complexity and value. It is true that the Council's eventual decrees did not substantially change the existing situation of Catholic church music (the best that can be said is that they fostered a sober, simple and intelligible style as opposed to a "lascivious and impure" one), whereas Evangelical Reformers such as Calvin (to say nothing of Zwingli) started from similar considerations but did actually enact a ban on polyphony. However, what does strike the observer is that attitudes to music close to those of the strictest Evangelical Reformers were not uncommon among Catholic Reformers at Trent, whereas enthusiastic stances such as those revealed in Luther's writings and in those of his followers are remarkably less frequent.

Moreover (and again following a cue given by Prodi [2014] in his discussion of visual art after Trent), the post-Tridentine concept of painting and sculpture tended to emphasise some specific functions: a) visual art should be strictly adherent to Scriptural narratives (and therefore avoid allegory and symbolism); b) it should accomplish a catechetic function (i.e. instruct those contemplating it); c) it should move the observers to devotion; d) it should encourage moral behaviours.

Transposing these indications onto the musical plane, we can find interesting parallelisms. The rejection of allegory and symbolism in figurative art mirrors the cautious attitude toward polyphony and the rejection of polyphonic forms preventing intelligibility (notwithstanding the fact that their greater power of fascination could be mystically more efficacious than that of simpler musical forms). Both functions a) and b) mirror an attention to the word/Word which we have already observed among the characterising features of both humanism and Evangelical Reforms. In turn, all of them parallel the increasing importance assumed by the "content" of faith (*what* was to be believed, especially in con-

---

[116] Prodi 2014, p. 17.

trast with what the other confessions maintained) to the detriment of an all-encompassing and integrated experience of faith.

As concerns the visual arts' role in fostering devotion, we have already observed how a similar task was entrusted to music, by those appreciating it within most Christian confessions (including, of course, the Catholics, though this topic was not mentioned in Trent's decrees); in some instances, as we have seen, the power to move was attributed to a proper use of the modal theory.

Finally, as regards morality, it is unnecessary to restate here how moral concerns were relevant to the concept of music by the Catholic Reformers of the sixteenth century, both in the negative (the worries about "lascivious" music…) and in the positive (ethical power of music, sometimes depending on its modal/affective qualities). Thus, the Council's decrees on music, as those on figurative art, tended to privilege negative indications over positive recommendations.

### 8.5.3. Open issues

I will now draw the reader's attention to some issues which the Council left open, and on which liberty was left to musicians and/or to local ecclesiastical authorities, or on which later pronouncements were to be expected.

One topic which was not treated was that of non-liturgical music (which was obviously a major one): this corresponded however to a choice which can be observed also in other fields (such as those of the visual arts or of the devotional practices), where the lead was going to be assumed by individual realities (such as new religious orders or spiritual guides).

Generally speaking, moreover, the Council tended to indicate aesthetical/spiritual models to the arts, rather than detailing its prescriptions: from the one side, this fostered creative interpretations and enactments by both churchmen and artists; from the other, this led to considerable differences between one diocese and the other, one bishop and his successor etc.

As we have seen, furthermore, though the issue of textual intelligibility was constantly referred to by several Catholic Reformers, it did not receive official mention within the Council's pronouncements. Ironically, however, most composers who were going to allude to the "Council's decrees" in the post-Tridentine era, would do so precisely as concerned matters of textual intelligibility. However, we have already seen from the very beginning of our discussion of music (in § 2.3.7. and following), that the tendencies toward musical styles allowing a clearer perception of the words (such as homorhythmic writing or accompanied monody) were already at work: though the concerns for the word/Word may have actively contributed to this process, it was already in the making when the Council took place, thus rendering the decrees' influence difficult to estimate.

Among the technical issues the Council decrees did not mention was the use of instruments in church, on which (as will be recalled) several Evangelical Reformers placed strict limitations or at least debated at length; similarly, and though broad aesthetic guidelines can be found in the decrees, no particular form of polyphony or of music in general is explicitly forbidden or discouraged[117].

In the next Chapter we will see how these guidelines were received, interpreted, enacted and perceived; to which spiritual movements they appealed most; which forms of piety corresponded most closely to their requirements; in short, how the Catholic Reformation (and the Counter-Reformation) were experienced and built in musical forms.

By providing an overview of the strategies and processes governing the Council of Trent, of its priorities and limitations and of its protagonists (prelates and laypeople, clergymen and musicians), this Chapter has framed the succinct decrees on music approved by the Council within the framework of the Catholic Reformation. Though the few words of the decrees did not provide precise indications or concrete prohibitions, this did not prevent their brief wording from being frequently misunderstood by later scholarship. However, by analysing the process leading to their formulation, their cultural, religious, aesthetical (and human) background has been provided. This will prove to be fundamental for attempting an interpretation of the Council's reception among spiritual leaders and musicians of the post-Tridentine Catholicism.

---

[117] Cf. Monson 2002, pp. 1–2, 12 and 22; Monson 2006, p. 406; Morucci 2012, p. 264; Prodi 2014, p. 263.

# Chapter 9 – Music after Trent

> I have considered it my task, in accordance with the views of most serious and most religious-minded men, to bend all my knowledge, effort, and industry towards that which is the holiest and most divine of all things in the Christian religion – that is, to adorn the holy sacrifice of the Mass in a new manner[1].
>
> [Giovanni Pierluigi da Palestrina]

## 9.1. Introduction

Given the preceding discussion on what the Council's deliberations regarding music actually were and on how they originated from within the framework of sixteenth-century Catholic culture, we may now consider whether the Council was really a watershed for Catholic church music or not. As we will see, one of the major influences of the Council on sacred music came from a decree which seemingly had very little to do with music, i.e. that leading to the creation of seminaries for the education of prospective priests. Moreover, since the Council had delegated the power to implement its decrees to local authorities, I will briefly point out how local synods reacted to the Council's view on sacred music.

Indeed, whereas the transmitted view of the Council tended to attribute a substantial uniformity to the post-Tridentine Catholic liturgy, it will be suggested that a noteworthy variety of liturgical practices did in fact survive well after Trent. Differences could be found depending on geographical localisation, temporal chronology, as well as among various religious orders and confraternities.

Nevertheless, after the Council a certain unity was actually promoted, especially through the publication of liturgical books such as the Roman Missal and Breviary; at the musical level, a reform of plainchant was attempted, and initially entrusted by the Pope to Palestrina and Zoilo: it would eventually lead to the publication of the controversial so-called *Editio Medicæa*.

We will also see that the common belief about the impact of the Council on the repertory of sequences needs to be qualified, as is that regarding the Council's effects on polyphony. The issues relating to textual intelligibility were cer-

---

[1] Quoted in and translated into English by Lockwood 1975, pp. 22–23.

tainly at stake, but they should not be understood in isolation from the overall aesthetic frame, from the contemporaneous stylistic evolution, and from the moral aspects discussed earlier in this book. We will observe, however, why and how a commission of Cardinals was instituted for the evaluation of polyphony, and what were the results of their experiments.

The musical world, in turn, was not impermeable to the Council's decrees, and (more importantly) to how they had been received and interpreted by local authorities: several composers reacted – sometimes in a highly personal fashion – to the evolving taste and to what they deemed to be the Council's requests.

Outside liturgy proper, music played a major role in the lives of the Catholics, both as regards the lay and clerical nobility and for the lower social classes. Catholic devotional music thus included motets, vernacular works (some of which even found their way within liturgy), spiritual madrigals both in Italy and abroad, as well as pilgrimage songs, litanies, and several other forms. Actually, music was involved in the mystical experiences of many religious men and women, and in the daily devotional practices of laypeople, within the framework of the keyword of post-Tridentine spirituality, *pietas*. Although neither devotion nor non-liturgical music were regulated by the Council's decrees, nevertheless (on an indirect but not less effective level) both were probably the best expressions of post-Tridentine piety.

Moreover, music was not unrelated to the architectural innovations characterising the Catholic Church after the Council, and this will be seen in a particularly clear fashion as concerns the Jesuits' promotion of a multi-sensorial approach to faith.

This will bring us to the discussion of two of the newly-established Catholic Orders, which made an idiosyncratic use of music both in their liturgical and extra-liturgical worship and in their catechetic efforts.

The Jesuits, founded by St Ignatius of Loyola, placed severe limitations on their own use of music in the Office, but employed it abundantly both as a means of involving all senses in the contemplation of the divine mysteries, and as a tool for spreading the Catholic doctrine and spirituality, particularly within the context of their newly-established colleges and as a component of the Jesuit dramatic output.

Music was no less important for St Filippo Neri and for his congregation of the Oratory, which would in turn deeply influence Federigo Borromeo and his later ruling of the Milanese diocese. Thus, through music, a certain degree of continuity was established between the spiritual movement promoted earlier in Florence by Savonarola and some among the leading figures of the Catholic reformation.

The rich variety of forms taken by post-Tridentine Catholic spirituality included the blossoming of many confraternities, which often had an impressive musical life, and of local musical chapels, sometimes depending on lay aristocratic patronage, and sometimes on ecclesiastical structures. In Rome, the Papal chapels flourished, also due to the presence of such musicians as Palestrina and Tomás Luis de Victoria (1548–1611); in Milan, the leadership of St Carlo Borromeo had multiple (and sometimes contradictory) effects on church music, often depending on his highly personal interpretation of the Council's decrees; at the same time, the independent-minded Republic of Venice played a major role in the creation of a rather unique musical style, in which some respect for the Council's concern for intelligibility was often combined with a happy disregard for its aspiration to sobriety; in Mantua, a lay ruler's ambitious projects for the courtly chapel produced some of the most interesting and ground-breaking results in the entire Italian panorama, whereas other Catholic courts such as those in Bavaria (where Orlando di Lasso was the musical protagonist) and in Spain (with such figures as Guerrero and Morales) were experimenting in their own right and with highly stimulating and artistically splendid results.

It must be emphasised that the geographical spread and local variety of Catholic liturgy and devotion in the sixteenth century will constrain us to limit our discussion to a few paradigmatic examples: the omission of detailed accounts and of even cursory mentions of many more local realities should not be understood as downplaying their importance and specificity, but merely as a necessity imposed by space limits.

## 9.2. Music after Trent

We have seen in the preceding Chapter that a number of myths (or at least of imprecise narratives) surrounded what happened at Trent and what the Council actually decided. Some other untruthful or inaccurate ideas encircle the Council's reception, its influence on music and the broader causes for such processes.

### 9.2.1. Hardly a revolution

Generally speaking, it can be said that the actual, documentable and clear influence of the Council on the music which was written, published and performed in its aftermath was very limited (geographically, chronologically and as concerns the composers and churchmen involved). Attempting some comparisons, it can be said that the Lutheran Reformation fostered a new understanding and appreciation of music, and was inclusive in its adoption of pre-Reformation musical genres and styles along with the new (or newly understood) ones; within the Calvinist approach there is a clear discontinuity between pre- and post-Reformation practices; in the Church of England, pre- and post-Reformation music styles coexisted, though they did not merge as smoothly as they did in Luther's concept; in the Catholic Church, Trent is only a stage within an evolution in the concept and practice of religious music – an evolution in which no ground-breaking discontinuities are discernible.

Moreover, as Boyce correctly points out[2], when the Council did enter into technical aspects of music (though they were not mentioned in its approved decrees), it could do so only on the basis of what already existed in music, and obviously not about what the future was going to create. In other words, the Council could sanction or condemn only works or styles pertaining to the past, and though it might have exerted some influence on the future of church music, it could not anticipate its actual evolution.

Thus, among the incorrect beliefs regarding Trent's impact on music, recent musicology has pointed out that – contrary to common opinion – the post-Tridentine Church neither possessed nor successfully enacted a consistent and centralised policy, and a noteworthy degree of freedom and diversity was observable at the local level.

Moreover, though Trent did constitute a stage of the Catholic Church's thought and pronouncements on music (and inserted itself within the religious and cultural milieu of the era), it did not represent a point of rupture between what was before it and what was to come. In particular, and not only on the musical plane, the Council did not consider the Catholic Church's recent past as a repository of corruption (as regards either music or religion in general), and therefore the Council cannot be identified as the turning-point in which all preceding criticism of church music converged and to which it pointed. Complaints about "abuses" in past musical practice were not universally felt or shared, and they did not form a steadfast chain of tradition, since their provenance can be traced back at least to two different origins (one magisterial, and the other within spiritualist movements).

Thus it is unfair and incorrect to conceive of the Catholic Church's music as of a spiritually increasingly decaying repertoire (forming the object of unanimous condemnation by both its hierarchy and its spiritual leaders), to which the Council forcefully responded, forbidding certain types of music and favour-

---

2 Boyce 2006, p. 143.

ing others, and eventually causing a revolution in the compositional orientations represented by the "Catholically-reformed" style of Palestrina, Ruffo etc.

On the contrary, many negative judgments on the pre-Tridentine Catholic music were determined by the progressively decreasing sensitivity towards the symbolic value of music (and particularly of polyphony). The several forms taken by its criticism (as seen in Chapter Three: § 3.3. and following) should be interpreted within the context of their origin (cultural, geographical, social, spiritual etc.). The Council's impact on the subsequent output was reduced, in consequence of the lack of (musical) focus within its debates, of the non-specificity of its decrees, and of the liberty (up to arbitrariness) it left to local authorities, as well as of the impossibility for the Council to predict the future of church music and foster or condemn its later orientations.

Furthermore, as observed in the conclusions of the preceding Chapter (§ 8.5.3.), the Council did not concern itself with non-liturgical music: neither was pre-Tridentine music in general unspiritual and profane, nor did the Council have any substantial impact on its subsequent repertoire (except, as said, in the indirect but fundamental sense that Trent influenced Catholic spirituality, which expressed itself in a great variety of musical styles). The works by Ruffo and Palestrina which have been seen as mirroring most faithfully the alleged ideals (or prescriptions) of the Council represent only a fraction of the contemporaneous output; moreover, some of their characterising features were probably more influenced by ecclesiastical patrons and authorities, as well as by local spiritual movements, than by the Council as such.

Musicology often took into consideration only (or mostly) certain genres of sacred music, favouring (for obvious reasons) the written over the unwritten, and therefore the "cultivated" over the "folkloric", but also (among the "cultivated" written works) the larger settings which best corresponded to the Romantic idea of "masterpiece" over less complicated, but perhaps more significant and common, forms of monodic or polyphonic music.

Was then the Council merely a negligible quantity within a music history developing quite independently of it? I think not: instead, I deem it important to limit the study of the Council's influence on music to the areas where that influence could actually be perceived and can therefore be analysed. If one considers Trent as a watershed in Catholic church music, its impact will result indeed insignificant, ungraspable and elusive. If, instead, one focuses on what the Council actually said (i.e. on the spiritual and theological background of its decrees, as well as on their origins) and on how it acted on subsequent Catholic spirituality and theology (which in turn were mirrored by contemporaneous music), then its true importance will become observable and analysable.

The Council promoted and encouraged particular styles and orientations in Catholic piety, and built mind-sets, perspectives and goals which were going to be translated into music and musical practices by composers and spiritual leaders alike. With Trent, the Catholic Church accepted the challenge of the emerging modernity, giving to its worries, provocations and weaknesses a response – the first of many to follow. Possibly, the very fact of having assented to this dialogue, of having tried and formulated an answer to such confrontation instead of burying itself in the contemplation of the past represents the greatest contribution of Trent to Church history.

### 9.2.2. Purifying worship

Within the particular field of music, we observed in Chapter Eight that the Council's debates progressively reduced in length and specificity the initial drafts by the Commissions. Though the sake of synthesis may have had its weight on this choice, it probably (and more importantly) mirrored a lack of consent among the prelates on the details of style and repertoire to promote or forbid in church music. In consequence of this, the decrees – as we have seen – are declarations of principle rather than meticulous prescriptions; and precisely in this quality, perhaps, lay their most appreciable and important heritage. What Trent did define, as regards music, was that it required "purity" *inasmuch* as it belonged to the sphere of the sacred. By stating that ritual holiness was requested from music as from all other things or people which were in close contact with the mysteries of faith, the Council implicitly (but forcefully) affirmed the status of music as an integral part of worship.

Sacramentary theology in the Catholic perspective stated that material elements (such as bread, wine or water), in their humble, touchable and created nature, were "capable of the infinite", and that God's unlimited power had chosen such humble matters as irreplaceable vehicles of his Grace. On the other hand, as a sign of respect for God, the material elements which were going to constitute an integral part of the Catholic sacraments had to be the best available and to correspond to certain requirements of purity. (This concept of a continuing dialogue between Creator and creatures, between God's grace and the response given by the material world is a typical trait of Catholic theology).

Though music was undoubtedly no sacrament, it partook of some features of this theological view (cf. § 4.3.7.2.). We can thus say that, for Catholics, God's saving Grace (omnipotent by definition) had chosen to enter into dialogue with human freedom (which was required to act and correspond at its best); God's sanctity, from which every created element took its origin, had decided to "need" the presence of material elements to dispense its holiness in the sacraments. Similar to human freedom and to the material elements of the sacraments, music – which participated in the celebration of the holy mysteries – needed to "purify" itself so as to make itself "worthy" (in the measure possible for created things) to convey human praise to the presence of the Lord.

In practice, the acknowledgement of music as a vehicle of God's Grace and of the Church's praise implied the striving for a liturgical uniformity which could and should mirror the unity of the Church in its worship. Since, as Jesus had stated (cf. Matthew 18:20), his disciples' union in prayer made their prayer his own, then – wherever the Church gathered in praise – Christ himself was praising the Father with them and in them. In consequence of this, if the same liturgical forms were employed by the entire Church (including the same liturgical language, i.e. Latin, and the same liturgical books, such as the Roman Missal and Breviary whose creation was prompted by the Council), this both mirrored and fostered the prayerful unity of Catholicism. This did not prevent differences (sometimes very relevant) from emerging within the Catholic Church: the most striking of them concern the use of music within a Counter-Reformation context (such as that observable in Germany) and within one of Catholic Reformation (as, for instance, in Italy).

On the other hand, the Council's acceptance of the dialogue of Catholicism with modernity was going to encourage the activity of innovative religious orders and congregations, engaging in an intense and dense presence in the laity's daily life. Music was going to represent an indispensable element both for devotional gatherings (e.g. of those following particular forms of spirituality or of the numerous Catholic confraternities), and for the development of the individual soul-searching, devotion and piety which characterised a large portion of post-Tridentine spirituality.

As Prodi[3] rightfully suggests (though in the field of the visual arts), an adequate study of the Council's influence on the arts should take into account three fundamental elements: a) the local regulations and their enactments, mirroring the institutional attitude to artistic issues; b) the interaction between art and the forms taken by liturgy and devotion; c) a study of the reception, in the artistic field (both in treatises and in actual creations) of the Council's decrees and overall attitudes[4].

To complement what is written above, however, another element must be clearly stressed once more (it has been briefly mentioned in the previous Chap-

---

[3] Prodi 2014, p. 72.
[4] Cf. also Schreiber 1951, vol. I, pp. lvi-lix and 381–425.

ter: § 8.3.4.). It is obviously important and fundamental to verify carefully what the Council's decrees actually said, distinguishing this from both their preparatory drafts and their later interpretations, which were often highly personal if not outright faulty (and in many cases were probably based on oral transmission rather than on direct knowledge). Notwithstanding this, the importance of an event such as Trent for the history of music is found also (and perhaps first and foremost) in its reception: though this could include or be based on (partial) misunderstandings, even these become part of the event's historical significance.

Finally, and in anticipation of what we will see in this Chapter, a consistent portion of Catholic "sacred" music was not performed in churches or during worships; and a large percentage of this nonliturgical output was not under the direct control and supervision of the clergy. Of course, the cultural and social framework of the era (with the Inquisition, the *Index* and so on) made spiritual anarchy and "relativism" (to use a contemporary term) practically impossible; however, the looser control on the devotional activities and repertoire permitted the cross-confessional repertoires mentioned in passing in the preceding Chapters and to which Chapter Eleven (§ 11.5. and following) will dedicate greater attention[5].

### 9.2.3. A new clerical class

As we have seen, one of the most influential decisions of the Council as regards music was to entrust its implementation to local authorities, i.e. Bishops (and superiors of the religious orders, whose organisation was partially independent from that of the secular clergy) and local Synods or Councils. Though, broadly speaking, most of what will be discussed in this Chapter relates to how individual bishops, religious authorities or dioceses received, interpreted and enacted the Council, in this section I will analyse only two of such issues, among those more immediately relating to official matters of Church organisation: first, I will briefly introduce the post-Tridentine creation of the seminaries, and second, how some local synods interpreted the Council's decrees about music.

As we have seen, the Council was highly concerned with the moralisation and culture of the clergy, in the conviction that the Reform of the Catholic Church started from reforming its pastors; and that the highest possibilities of

---

[5] Cf. Fellerer 1953, p. 576; Fenlon 1989, p. 58; Baroffio 1995, p. 16; Kendrick 1996, p. 5; Boyce 2006, p. 143; Monson 2006, pp. 402–403; Fenlon 2009, p. 204; Prodi 2014, pp. 72, 77, 270–271 and 275–276.

success came from the education of prospective priests. This education had to comprise both cultural matters (priests had to be able to fully understand the Latin liturgies they were celebrating; they should preach efficaciously and knowledgeably, without delegating the ministries of preaching and confessing to friars) and religious/ethical issues (pastors had to set a good example to their flock, with the prohibition to marry and to have illicit relationships, and with a higher degree of control on economic matters).

For the purpose of creating a priestly class with higher levels of godliness, morality and culture, seminaries were created (albeit at an irregular pace), in which (following a Council decree of the XXIII session, as mentioned in § 8.4.4.) music and singing were considered to be fundamental educational matters.

Though seminaries must not be confused with Jesuit Colleges, the former took many of their structures and inspirations from the latter, and sometimes they shared at least a part of the teaching body. It will be interesting, therefore, to compare the role of music within different educational systems, created or restructured during the sixteenth century by confessional Churches or closely associated with them (from the Latin schools in Lutheran Germany to the education of children in the zones adhering to the Reformed or Anglican confessions, to Jesuit colleges and seminaries): though a detailed comparison would need a discussion whose dimensions would largely exceed those available here, I will try and suggest some ideas on this topic in Chapter Eleven (§ 11.4.4. and following).

Seminaries also provided the clerical class with a number of children and boys who were capable of singing and who received specific musical instruction: their presence was going to offer increasingly interesting musical possibilities to composers and musicians operating in the cathedral chapels of many Catholic dioceses. The level of and the importance in which music education was held at seminaries is witnessed by the appointment of no less a musician than Palestrina as master of music at the Seminario Romano (1566–71).

When and where music-loving bishops were in charge, the stress placed on music education of seminarians could be even higher: for example, by order of Giulio Feltrio della Rovere (1533–1578), boys studying at the seminary of Ravenna had to learn counterpoint along with singing, and even to send essays of their compositional activity to the Cardinal.

In other instances, however, the emphasis on music could be seen as a negative factor: for example, in Vigevano (where a seminary was established in the late 1560s), Cardinal Borromeo's visitation found that musically gifted children enjoyed privileges over those less able to sing, and that musical talent was deemed to be more important than piousness or advancement in their non-musical studies. Though the energetic Milanese Cardinal intervened to limit such discriminations, this was not to the detriment of music: clerics continued to receive instruction in both figural singing and plainchant, and to sing in church at all canonical hours except the very first of the day.

Finally, we may recall the connections between rhetoric and music outlined in Chapter Two (§ 2.4.5.), also as regards a humanist/post-humanist attitude to music (conceived as a tool for amplifying and enhancing the rhetorical effect of words). Since seminarians received a thorough education in rhetoric, which was considered fundamental for effective preaching, it is highly suggestive to regard the focus on rhetoric and the fostering of music as complementary tools for empowering the strength of the word/Word in the post-Tridentine Catholic Church[6]. The effects of this focus on rhetoric, both musical and verbal, are observed in the output of several clergymen whose religious education took place after the Council. As demonstrated by Getz[7], there is indeed a close resemblance between musical works (by Vincenzo Pellegrini, c.1562–1631, and Andrea Cima, 1580–1627, among others) and sermons written within the same cultural and religious milieu (in her case-study, this is represented by the period leading to Carlo Borromeo's canonisation in Milan). Musical and verbal rhetoric were employed in a similar fashion and made use of analogous structures.

### 9.2.4. From global to local

As concerns the role of music in the liturgy of the Catholic Church, initiatives were taken both on a centralised plane and at the local level. One of the major steps enacted in Rome was the creation of a new institution, the *Congregatio pro Sacris Ritibus et Cæremoniis* (Congregation for the Holy Rites and Ceremonies), instituted by Pope Sixtus V in 1588, with the purpose of maintaining a constant surveillance on ritual uniformity and propriety over local initiatives and liturgies[8].

Local synods and councils were convened in most dioceses after Trent, in order to interpret and enact the Council's decrees with regard to the specific religious, geographical, social and cultural reality of the individual bishoprics. It is obviously impossible here to discuss thoroughly the wealth of documents produced by such gatherings in the last decades of the sixteenth century. I will

---

6 Cf. Borgerding 1998, pp. 592–593; Marvin 2002, p. 5; Rees 2006, p. 354; Weber 2008, p. 172; Morucci 2012, pp. 264 and 270; Mari 2013, pp. 160–161.
7 Getz 2015.
8 Rainoldi 2000, p. 356.

therefore limit my discussion to a sample of such statements, which exemplify how Trent was received, interpreted and enacted within some dioceses. This discussion is useful especially inasmuch it reveals which meanings were attributed to the Council's decrees and how they were "translated" into practice by those in charge of its realisation. Moreover, since several of the bishops summoning such diocesan gatherings were among those who had contributed to drafting and revising Trent's decrees, the local synods' interpretations often reveal the principles and ideas behind the Council's rather vague statements.

Generally speaking, the themes most frequently found within the decrees on music by local councils are those regarding "lascivious" music (often with clear references to performance practice) and to intelligibility.

As we have repeatedly seen, though intelligibility and clarity of pronunciation are obviously related to one another, they are by no means synonymous: proper delivery implied that singers and readers had to show their respect for God's Word by putting all their efforts into its proper rendition (meaning that the intended recipient of their diligence was God, to whom liturgy was directed, and only secondarily the listeners), whereas intelligibility showed concern for what the hearers could perceive and understand.

I think that a concern for intelligibility proper can be identified in the decrees of the Council of Cambrai (1565), which specify that the Creed must be performed without polyphony (unless it be very simple), whereas figured music is allowed for other items of the Mass Ordinary[9]. Similar concerns for intelligibility are found in the Synods of Constance (1567) and Toledo (1565–6). In the latter case, the recommendation is found that figural music, when present, should "attract" the listeners to the sung words rather than to surprising, curious or unexpected effects of a purely musical nature[10]. The Council of Ravenna (1566–8), summoned by Giulio Feltrio della Rovere, analogously commanded intelligible music[11]; the Cardinal's continuing concern for this topic is found in the similar ordinances issued by him several years later for Loreto.

The indebtedness of such concerns for the word/Word to humanism is clearly shown by the Synod of Besançon (1571), where a humanistic treatise on music was explicitly quoted[12].

On other occasions, the stress was laid on the affective qualities of church music rather than on its relationship with the text. While admitting polyphony

---

9 *Mansi* 33, col. 1401; available online at http://bit.ly/2bOd1vV.
10 *Mansi* 34, col. 562; available online at http://bit.ly/2bWAKsw.
11 *Mansi* 35, col. 631; available online at http://bit.ly/2bMXjzc.
12 Cf. *CG* 7, col. 487; *CG* 8, col. 203 etc.; Romita 1947, pp. 64 ff.; Fellerer 1953, pp. 590–592; Fabbri 1993, pp. 17–18; Weber 2008, pp. 142–144; Morucci 2012, p. 270.

of a more complex kind for such liturgical items as the *Gloria* and *Sanctus*, the Synod of Constance underpinned that its quality should express a prayerful rather than an exceedingly joyful mood[13]. The provincial synod of Trent (not to be mistaken for the Council of Trent), in 1593, echoed the famous decree of the Council stating that church music should refrain from "lascivious" music with dance-like overtones[14]. Though the similarity with the Council's decree is shown by the recurring use of "lascivious", the Synod was more specific in mentioning dance as one activity which church music should not bring into the listeners' minds; "lascivious" music was also forbidden by the Council of Ravenna (1566–8[15]), as well as by the Synods of Prague (1565[16]), of Besançon (1571[17]) etc.

The provincial Synod of Milan (1565) once more made use of the word *lasciva*, though here it referred to "*canendi ratio*", i.e. a way of singing, which may imply performance styles rather than compositional techniques (which can however be alluded to by the preceding "*prophana cantica sonive*"). This interpretation is supported by its condemnation of the "weak [*molles*] inflections [*flexiones*]", and the "voices oppressed by the throat rather than expressed by the mouth" ("*voces magis gutture oppressæ quam ore expressæ*"[18]), thus establishing an interesting opposition between throat (i.e. melismatic vocal virtuosity) and mouth (articulation and delivery of the words). References to performance practices are also present in the decrees of the Council of Ravenna, where singing with too weak or too loud voices was forbidden[19].

In Toledo (1565–6) the provincial Synod also established that the sounds employed for praising God should avoid a style reminiscent of the theatre, of "unchaste" love, and of battle sounds[20] (the echo of the Tridentine decree's draft is particularly clear here, as are those of the Patristic sources behind it and of Quintilian[21] – cf. § 2.3.3.–4.).

---

[13] *CG* 7, p. 488.
[14] *CG* 8, p. 412.
[15] *Mansi* 35, col. 631; available online at http://bit.ly/2bMXjzc.
[16] *CG* 7, p. 29.
[17] *Mansi* 36bis, col. 76; available online at http://bit.ly/2byq0kU.
[18] *Labbé* 21, col. 57.
[19] *Mansi* 35, col. 632; available online at http://bit.ly/2bMXjzc.
[20] *Mansi* 34, col. 562; available online at http://bit.ly/2bWAKsw.
[21] Cf. *CG* 7, p. 29; *CG* 8, pp. 199 and 412 etc.; Rainoldi 2000, p. 348; Weber 2008, pp. 142–144; Morucci 2012, p. 270. For a collection of decrees from provincial Councils and Synods, cf. Fellerer 1953 and Weber 2008.

## 9.3. Music and liturgy after Trent

The Council of Trent, advocating the creation of liturgical books to be adopted by the entire Catholic Church, with only few exceptions being granted to ancient rites, aimed at uniformity in the cultual practice of Catholicism (which was characterised by a wide variety of liturgies before the Council).

However, study of Catholic liturgical forms after Trent must take into account that practical differences continued to exist, mirroring diversity at the geographical, social, cultural and spiritual levels, as well as the impact of individuals such as bishops or superiors of religious orders on the musical and liturgical practices of those under their guidance. Of course, time played a non-negligible role as well, both inasmuch as changes in the theological and musical perspectives paralleled those affecting society as a whole, and as the chronological alternation of religious guides sometimes implied a noticeable diversity in the liturgical, spiritual and musical orientation of a religious order or a bishopric over time. This could also mean, obviously, that limitations on music which had been first proposed, but later overruled at the Council, could still be enacted by those spiritual leaders who felt inclined to do so.

The need for a reform within the Catholic Church and its music was commonly felt, before, during and after the Council; however, the interpretation of which reforms were needed and of how they had to be pursued varied greatly, and depended in a significant measure on the spiritual streams vivifying religious life in the Catholic areas. Though there were strong centralising tendencies, they did by no means exhaust the spiritual energies unleashed by the Council, or the variety in the musical and spiritual attempts at reformation and regeneration.

It is important to stress, once more, that there was considerable fluidity between liturgical and sacred repertoire, and between the sphere of religious and that of secular music, in parallel to a social situation in which "the sacred" was still largely intertwined with what we would today define as secular. Notwithstanding the religious people's recurring concerns that nothing "secular" should enter into close contact with the "sacred" (cf. the worries about ritual purity in music, clergy etc.), the sacred still maintained a public dimension which is largely lost today, and which impacted strongly on the political, economic and social lives of an urban or (even more so) a rural community.

Though classifications are always rigid and schematic, they cannot be avoided for the sake of clarity; however, I would argue that the distinctions between sacred, secular, liturgical etc. are best understood as a *continuum* ranging from the strictest and purest forms of liturgical music (which I think can be identified with plainchant) to works of an entirely secular character, and comprising, within itself, Mass settings, *Magnificats* and other works for the Liturgy of the Hours or other official liturgies (e. g. Office of the Dead), motets, spiritual songs (in accompanied monody or polyphony, or suitable for both), *lauda*-style songs, litanies, processional songs and so on.

Only a few of the genres listed above (and of the many more which can be included within the *continuum*) were destined exclusively for performance within or outside churches; most could migrate from one situation to another, in some instances after having undergone some textual or musical modifications, but in other cases in a substantially unaltered form.

In order to illustrate this diversity, Monson usefully juxtaposes some of the seemingly most typical examples of Tridentine or post-Tridentine music (such as the *Preces speciales* by Kerle or the *Missa Papæ Marcelli* by Palestrina) with other no less typical works (though dramatically different from one another) such as Byrd's *Gradualia* or *Xicochi xicochi conetzintle*, a Christmas lullaby in Nahuatl (vernacular of the native Nahuas) composed by Gaspar Fernandes[22] (1566–1629).

It is therefore too simplistic, not to say entirely erroneous, to reduce this diversity to an allegedly uniform "Counter-Reformation" style, whose presumed qualities are too easily identified with an archaising musical style and a primary concern for intelligibility[23].

As regards geographical diversity, it is true that the Council aimed at imposing a unified rite to the entire Catholic Church (see § 9.3.2.); however, it is also true that it permitted the continuation of local rites which were at least two centuries old. Later in this Chapter, however[24], we will see that this permission was exploited not only by practically all who could boast such ancient rites, but also by those wishing to obtain approval for much newer ones. Ironically (as we will observe in greater detail in the following pages), some among the protagonists of the Council (i.e. those who had fostered the adoption of unified liturgies) were also among the proudest supporters of the particular liturgy of their own diocese. Such attitudes mirror a strong affection (of laity and clergy alike) for local traditions, rites and liturgical forms, which were felt to be an integral part of a community's spiritual experience, history and life.

Among the myriad of possible examples of this local diversity, we may mention the permanence of texts and musical settings dating from the pre-Tridentine era and featuring regional variants or idiosyncrasies in the Spanish repertoire (for example the Iberian tunes for the *Vexilla regis prodeunt* or the *Pange lingua*,

---

22 Monson 2006, p. 418.
23 Cf. Kendrick 1996, pp. 7 and 13; Monson 2002, p. 27; Herl 2005, p. 23; Monson 2006, p. 406; Fenlon 2009, pp. 200–201; Prodi 2014, p. 69.
24 See § 9.6.2. and 9.6.5.

as well as Guerrero's inclusion of a motet whose text did not conform to the Roman rite in his collection of 1597[25], etc.); or the surprising creation of new sequence cycles by Bernard Klingenstein (c.1545–1614) in Augsburg in 1605 (notwithstanding the post-Tridentine reduction in the sequences' importance and number elsewhere in the Catholic Church), and many more examples we will encounter in the following pages.

On the other hand, when ritual uniformity could not be avoided, it is also interesting to observe the strategies enacted to eschew it: one such example is the replacement of the organ with other instruments in the Holy Week liturgies (when, obviously, the ban's aim was to permit vocal music only, and not to replace a "sacred" instrument such as the organ with "secular" instruments such as lutes and archlutes[26]).

Alongside with geographical diversity, as mentioned above, there was chronological variety: under this heading we can list phenomena such as the changes imposed by new spiritual leaders, the evolution in the reception of the Council's decrees over time, and the responses given by the Church to new aesthetical challenges (which, as mentioned earlier in this Chapter, could not be foreseen by the Council: see § 9.2.1.).

We have seen (cf. § 8.2.6.) how the changes in the leadership of the entire Church (in the Papal succession) and in the Council's stages were paralleled by the fluctuating repertoire of the Papal Chapels, ranging from extreme conservatism to the adoption of modern music such as that composed by Palestrina – notwithstanding the opinion of those, such as Pietro della Valle (1586–1652), who considered even Palestrina's output to be too old-fashioned. Though such fluctuations are particularly clear within a context as close to the centre of Catholicism as the Papal Chapels, such variances are constantly observable in several other cases (some of which will be discussed later in this Chapter: see e.g. § 9.3.5.1.), and especially when a spiritual leader was particularly interested in music, be it on the positive or on the negative side[27].

### 9.3.1. Reaffirming rituality

Even though, as seen, the Council's decrees on music could hardly be considered to be liturgical revolutions, it has also been said that their few words on music

---

[25] Guerrero 1597.
[26] Cf. Fabbri 1993, p. 22; Baroffio 1995, p. 12; Leitmeir 2002, p. 161; Borgerding and Stein 2006, pp. 439 and 445; Monson 2006, p. 405.
[27] Cf. Fellerer 1953, p. 589; Fabbri 1993, pp. 22–23; Brauner 1994, p. 342; Körndle 2006, p. 488.

were entirely spent on that conceived for and employed within liturgy. It is precisely in this field that the more clearly observable and direct consequences of the Council are to be found.

The Council's attention to liturgical music also represents a critical stance against the modifications introduced within the received liturgy by the Evangelical confessions, and the rejection of ceremonies and of the traditional theological understanding of liturgy by some of them. This reaffirmation of liturgy's intrinsic value against its emptying of significance by some Protestants was symbolised particularly through the maintenance of Latin worship and of the received plainchant repertoire (though, as we will see, in a revised form).

The reappraisal of plainchant, even if it expressed itself in the debatable form discussed below (§ 9.3.2.–4.), represented therefore a declaration of principle, as well as the first seed of the plainchant movement which was going to represent a constant feature in the Catholic Church from the seventeenth century onwards.

Among the most direct and clear institutional interventions on the practice of worship are the abolition of Offertory versicles and of many tropes and sequences. However, these alleged novelties, in most cases, were simply acknowledgements of a change in taste which had appeared long before Trent, or the official recognition that certain genres and repertoires were no longer fashionable or cherished.

Similarly, the appearance of the unified and "new" liturgical books confirmed the longstanding liturgical practice of having the Mass recited by the celebrant alone, implying that the (musical) interventions of the singers and (when admitted) by the laity were nothing more than dispensable and ornamental accessories.

It can be said, therefore, that the impact of Trent on liturgy was admittedly strong and long-lasting, but that – in most cases – it influenced the future mainly by its acceptance and sanctioning of the past.

Among the true "novelties", however, the consequences of the Council included the modification of certain liturgical texts and of their position within Catholic worship, the officially ordered revision of plainchant (in itself a historical innovation) and its rhythmical and sometimes mensural reinterpretation, the appearance of institutional prescriptions ruling the presence of music in worship (the *Cæremoniale*) and the publication of unofficial liturgical books (such as the *Directorium Chori*, the *Manuale chorale* etc. – see § 9.3.2.–4.).

Many liturgical books with musical notation (such as Antiphonals, Graduals and Choral Psalters), however, were conservative in appearance, inasmuch as their musical type maintained the existing notational style and approach, transposing into print the forms of the preceding manuscript tradition, and conforming to the standard set in the early sixteenth century by the Giunti press in Venice.

Though the revision of plainchant was entrusted to musicians and did involve melodic changes, it must however be stressed that its focus was on the texts rather than on music – in other words, music had to be modified in order to better accommodate the text, and not for musical requirements. The traditional Latin-texted plainchant repertoire was seen as desperately needing a thorough revision because it no longer corresponded to the humanistically-inspired ideals of metric and accentuation, in consequence of the alleged "barbarisms" introduced by medieval practice[28].

### 9.3.2. Revising rites

The last quarter of the sixteenth century witnessed the appearance of numerous revised liturgical books, testifying to the largely shared interest which musicians and churchmen alike were taking in the creation of a "purified" plainchant and/or liturgy. Among the earliest published attempts in this direction are a *Pontificale* (published in Venice in 1572 by the Giunti press[29]), and a *Graduale*, edited and published in the same city eight years later by Lichtenstein[30]. Again in Venice, in c.1587, Gardano published another *Graduale*[31] whose edition had been realised by musicians of the standing of Ludovico Balbi (c.1545–1604), Andrea Gabrieli and Orazio Vecchi.

Rome responded to the entrepreneurship of the Republic with the 1595 *Pontificale romanum*[32], which had been approved as a reference publication by Pope Clement VIII, and whose musical revision had been realised by such musicians as Giovanni Andrea Dragoni (c.1540–1598), Luca Marenzio and Giovanni Maria Nanino[33] (c.1544–1607).

Several years earlier, however, and immediately after Trent, Rome had taken another fundamental initiative whose responsibility had been entrusted to the

---

**28** Cf. Fellerer 1953, pp. 593–594; Borromeo 1993, p. 232; Baroffio 1995, p. 12; Gozzi 1995, p. 45; Rainoldi 2000, pp. 351 and 356.
**29** *Pontificale Romanum* 1572.
**30** *Graduale* 1580.
**31** Balbi 1587.
**32** *Pontificale Romanum* 1595.
**33** Cf. Baroffio 1995, pp. 12–13; Rainoldi 2000, p. 355.

Holy See by the Council itself, i.e. the publication, under Pius V, of the Roman Breviary (1568[34]) and of the Roman Missal (1570[35]).

These books represented the core of Catholic liturgy, as they contained the texts for – respectively – the Office of the Hours and the Mass. Through this publication, the Catholic Church aimed at obtaining ritual uniformity at a universal level, although obviously this "universality" only regarded Roman Catholics and did not take into account the permanence of ancient rites. Notwithstanding this, such an initiative represented, under many aspects, a great novelty, both at the level of cultual details and at that of its overall significance. As concerns the actual practice, the liturgical revision curtailed the saints' feasts throughout the year, and (as mentioned before: § 9.3.1.) did not include tropes, whereas only few sequences were prescribed. As concerns the broader perspective, Rainoldi[36] has correctly pointed out that this publication replaced the local authority of bishops with that of the Holy See as the warrantor of the sacredness of liturgy. Whereas before 1568–70 it was the bishops' responsibility to supervise on the liturgy performed in their dioceses, afterwards Rome became the only subject entitled to approve or disallow a particular liturgy.

As we have just seen, the revised Missal included only few sequences of the thousands which had been written during the Middle Ages. It must be stressed, however, that the often-heard statement that "the Council forbade sequences" is another of the several myths concerning music at the Council. It is true that several prelates in Trent expressed complaints as to the overabundance of sequences and to the lack of official supervision on their texts; and it is true that the new Missal made use of just four (five since 1727); however, no mention of the sequences is found in the official decrees.

Moreover, it should be said that the sequence repertoire had been drastically limited also as a consequence of the theological imprecisions found in its poetical texts. The quest for dogmatic precision is a typical consequence of the confessional divisions appearing in the sixteenth century; and the requirement that poetry be theologically accurate conflicts with the symbolic value of literature (and therefore parallels the mistrust in music's symbolic power discussed in Chapter Two etc.[37]). Limiting the use of sequences, however, did not limit the texts sung in churches to those officially approved; instead, it ironically prompted the composition of new religious poetry to be set to music for use in church

---

[34] *Breviarium* 1568.
[35] *Missale* 1570.
[36] Rainoldi 2000, p. 350.
[37] See § 2.3.8., 2.4.3. etc. Cf. also Kreuzer 1973, pp. 126–127.

(e.g. for motets), and whose literary value was often decidedly inferior to that of the forgotten sequences[38].

### 9.3.3. New needs

An important consequence of these publications for music was that this newly imposed uniformity implied that a musical setting of Catholic liturgical texts could be performed anywhere in the Catholic world (and sometimes by non-Catholics as well). This represented an amazing opportunity for composers (and printers), whose market could virtually embrace the entire Catholicism. In particular, the new Breviary fostered the composition of many works for the liturgical Hour of the Vespers, including hymns and *Magnificat* settings. Moreover, many pre-Tridentine liturgical settings needed to be revised or entirely rewritten in accordance with the new texts: those years, therefore, saw a hectic and lively activity on the part of composers in order to provide a new repertoire or adapt the old one to the revised books.

As happened elsewhere in non-Catholic Churches, moreover, the appearance of new liturgical books prompted the creation of musical and literary works based on the new texts. Giovanni Battista Possevino, for instance, translated into Italian the hymns of the Roman Breviary (1594[39]): similar to what had happened to Luther's chorales, thus, they became sources of spiritual instruction, meditation and prayer. Though Possevino in several instances translated the same Latin hymns which had inspired Luther's vernacular chorales (for example, the Latin *Veni creator Spiritus* became Luther's *Komm Gott Schöpfer, Heiliger Geist* and Possevino's *Spirto che creasti il mondo, vieni*), the Catholic versions drew upon the tradition of the medieval prayerbooks (cf. § 5.3.3.), which included vernacular hymns destined for reading rather than for singing.

On the other hand, the Breviary and Missal became a source of inspiration for musicians, to whom they provided a wealth of new or revised texts for motet writing; the changes brought by the new books to the Church's calendar implied not only the suppression of feasts already in use, but also the necessity for new Proper settings for the freshly created or modified liturgies which occasionally replaced the older ones[40]. As argued by Peter Ackermann[41], the publication, within the post-Tridentine Catholic repertoire, of motet collections whose organ-

---
**38** Cf. Rainoldi 2000, p. 345, fn. 32 and pp. 362–363; Leitmeir 2002, p. 161.
**39** Possevino 1594.
**40** Cf. Borgerding and Stein 2006, p. 439; Rees 2006, p. 355; O'Regan 2013a, p. 338.
**41** Cf. Ackermann 2002, pp. 31–43.

isation mirrors that of the liturgical year possibly demonstrates a concern aiming at rendering motets (and their performance) an integral part of the liturgy and not mere appendages to it.

### 9.3.4. Freeing plainchant from "ineptitude" and "malice"

Whereas both Breviary and Missal contained the holy texts sung during the Eucharist and the Office, the *Cæremoniale Episcoporum* (1600[42], under Clement VIII) was more of a manual of instructions for the correct performance of Catholic rites. Actually, the *Cæremoniale* regulated the development of ceremonies presided over by bishops (i.e. primarily those ordinarily performed in Cathedral churches, but also those celebrated in less important institutions during the Bishop's visitations); however, obviously, the *Cæremoniale* also represented a model for the less solemn celebrations in parishes, abbeys, shrines etc. It thus became the reference book for church musicians, and particularly organists and choirmasters, who could find therein indications as to which versicles or Ordinary items (e.g. the Creed) could not be replaced with organ *alternatim*. Instruments other than the organ were forbidden; moreover, both organ and polyphony were excluded during such rites as exequies and penitential seasons. However, as we have seen in the previous pages, neither of these prescriptions as regards instrumental music was strictly respected: indeed, the use of instruments other than the organ became increasingly common in the seventeenth century and later. It should be added, however, that along with the Roman *Cæremoniale Episcoporum*, many dioceses created their own ceremonial book, which often modified both prescriptions and limitations found in the Roman model[43].

Whereas both Breviary and Missal were compulsory for almost all Catholic churches, another important initiative from the same years, i.e. the revision of plainchant, did not formally have the same status, though many erroneously considered it as equally compelling, due to both its spread and its official origins.

The need for such a revision had been often expressed in the second half of the sixteenth century (and in agreement with what was attempted in roughly the same years within several Evangelical Churches). The reader will recall our discussion of Zarlino's proposals for a "purification" of plainsong (which would

---

[42] *Cæremoniale* 1600.
[43] Cf. Fabbri 1993, p. 22; Baroffio 1995, p. 12; Gozzi 1995, p. 52; Leitmeir 2002, p. 161; Herl 2004, p. 23; Monson 2006, pp. 403–405; O'Regan 2006, pp. 78–79; Rees 2006, p. 355.

have meant, for him, the drastic reduction of melismas and the adoption of a syllabic style: cf. § 3.3.1.1.[44]); plainchant forms corresponding to the contemporaneous taste (i.e. inspired by early modern and humanistic ideals) had been actually experimented in such unconventional situations as was Mantua's Santa Barbara (see § 9.6.5.); and the Pope had even (though indirectly) received a self-candidacy for this task. In fact, Paolo Animuccia (d. c.1563, not to be mistaken for his more famous brother Giovanni [c.1520–1571]) wrote in 1566 to a Roman acquaintance, offering his services to the newly elected Pope Pius V for that purpose. Animuccia was certain that Pius would undertake a thorough reform of the Papal Chapels and of their repertoire, including both polyphony and plainchant, so that "the words can be understood and be accompanied by the devout music necessary for ecclesiastical functions"[45].

Eventually, neither the initiative was taken by Pius V, nor was it entrusted to Paolo Animuccia. With a Brief dated October 25th, 1577, Pope Gregory XIII (1502–1585) formally requested Palestrina (who was the master of the *Cappella Giulia* at that time) and Annibale Zoilo to undertake a thorough revision of the plainchant repertoire[46].

The Pope's Brief has already been cursorily mentioned in Chapter Three (§ 3.3.1.1.): we have seen there that the Pope's request to Palestrina and Zoilo was to purify plainsong from the "barbarisms, obscurities, inconsistencies and superfluities" which centuries-old accretions had brought. As discussed there, it is interesting to note that Pope Gregory attributed such accumulations to "the ineptitude, the negligence, even the malice of composers, scribes and printers alike"[47], possibly suggesting a link between the sensuous pleasure of melismatic singing and the risks of inebriation "maliciously" pursued.

Palestrina and Zoilo were neither philologists of the language, nor musicologists: their editing criteria were inspired by their own practical experience as church singers, by humanist principles of prosody and accentuation, as well as by the use both of them had made (and were making) of plainchant as the *cantus firmus* for their polyphonic works.

This influence was actually bidirectional: from the one side, Palestrina and Zoilo received a tradition dating back to the late Middle Ages and reaching its peak during Humanism, and which (for both contrapuntal exigencies and humanistic aesthetics) proposed a metrical (or mensural) interpretation of plain-

---

[44] Zarlino 1558, Part IV, p. 340.
[45] Quoted and translated in Sherr 1984, p. 76.
[46] Latin text in Molitor 1901, vol. I, pp. 297–298; English translation in Weiss and Taruskin 2008, p. 117.
[47] Translation in Weiss and Taruskin 2008, p. 117.

chant. From the other side, the effect of Palestrina's engagement with plainchant on his own compositional output is clearly observable in a group of Masses he wrote on *cantus firmus* excerpted from plainchant antiphons and hymns. These compositions seem also to show that the task set to Palestrina and Zoilo by the Pope had deep spiritual overtones for them. Reforming (and "purifying") plainchant from its "barbaric" accretions was a highly symbolic undertaking: it is likely that Palestrina, similar to Cirillo and to Glarean, saw the duty of reforming church music (and therefore the Church's prayer) as a means for achieving the purification of the Church *in se*.

Moreover (cf. § 8.3.4.) metrical prosody was then conceived as an instrument for conferring order unto nature. In other words, correct accentuation meant that the "natural" accents of speech were respected by metrical settings, even though these had a regularity and elegance in their accentuation patterns which largely exceeded those of spontaneous speech. The deep philosophical and aesthetic implications of such an attitude did not escape a humanistically inspired culture: humans could neither overturn the eternal laws of nature (symbolised by the "natural" accentuation of the words), nor could they eschew their God-given vocation of ordering and giving beauty to nature. We have seen in Chapter Eight how this view shaped the post-Tridentine perspective on visual art as well (cf. Paleotti's *Discorso*) and how it mirrored contemporaneous values and concerns.

Alongside mensural and metrical interpretations of plainchant, a tendency could be similarly observed both in Catholic and Lutheran singing, i.e. the increasing homogenisation of rhythmic values. Whereas earlier plainchant singing practices had eschewed rigid rhythmic schemes, and Lutheran Chorales had been characterised by a high variety of rhythmic values (differently from the binary quantities of Calvinist psalmody), this rhythmic plurality was progressively reduced to homogenous quantities. This was due to the influence of complex ensemble compositions (both vocal and instrumental) on the church tunes they were set to, and to the aesthetic principle which saw in the feature of *æqualitas* a symbol for the atemporality of church singing.

While Palestrina and Zoilo were attempting to realise the task set for them by the Pope, another Italian musician, Giovanni Guidetti (c.1532–1592) was working on the *Directorium Chori*, which would eventually be published in 1582[48], earning Pope Gregory XIII's praise, and reprinted until c.1750. This collection, comprising (among others) hymns and antiphons, is based on the ancient Vatican antiphonals, and was conceived for the *hebdomadarius* and the *cantor* (i.e.

---

[48] Guidetti 1582.

those in charge of choral performance in Cathedrals as well as in collegiate churches).

This book is known for its particular notational features: the note forms adopted by Guidetti are created with the purpose of attributing proportional durations to both *accentus* and *concentus*, and their function is explained in the editor's *Preface*. Guidetti's work, thus, went in the same direction as that of Palestrina and Zoilo, in that it sought to apply prosodic schemes to the Catholic plainchant (it is possible, incidentally, that Palestrina supervised on Guidetti's work, or was at least consulted about it). Moreover, the *Directorium* fosters the *recto tono:* lengthy liturgical items in prose (such as prayers and Biblical readings) had to be delivered mostly on a single pitch. Recent scholarship has revealed, however, that Guidetti was not establishing new rules (particularly as concerns the *recto tono* practice), but rather spreading a style which was already in use within the Papal liturgies[49].

Guidetti's work also bears witness to an important overall approach: The Catholic Church was not concerning itself with solemn and festive liturgies only, but also with the propriety and aesthetical beauty (according to the canons of that time) of daily liturgies. In this case, too, as in that of Palestrina and Zoilo, music could be interpreted as a symbol for the overall spiritual orientation of post-Tridentine Catholicism: though its most conspicuous artistic creations (both visual and aural) are characterised by splendour, greatness and magnificence, the true core of post-Tridentine spirituality lay in a scrupulous and careful reformation of daily life, i.e. of the seemingly minor issues of everyday behaviour, liturgy, prayer and singing[50].

We have briefly left the narrative of Palestrina and Zoilo's efforts to concentrate on those originating Guidetti's *Directorium*. Indeed, the enterprise started by Palestrina and Zoilo was eventually not concluded by them: its story is a very complex one, which lasted for decades and whose most important result was the publication, in 1614–5, of the so-called *Editio Medicæa*, a *Graduale* ultimately edited by Felice Anerio (1560–1614) and Francesco Soriano (c.1548–1621), to whom it had been entrusted in 1608 by Pope Paul V[51] (1552–1621).

The *Editio Medicæa* (whose name comes from that of its printing press) was never sanctioned as an official book of the Catholic Church; however, as mentioned earlier, it practically enjoyed this status due to the official initiatives be-

---

[49] Kim 2005, p. 247.
[50] Cf. Rainoldi 2000, p. 355; Kim 2005, pp. 245–247.
[51] *Graduale* 1614 and *Graduale* 1615. Cf. Besutti 1993, p. 119; Brauner 1994, p. 341; Baroffio 1995, p. 13; Gozzi 1995, p. 44; Lovato 1995, pp. 57–61; Rainoldi 2000, p. 353; Kim 2005, pp. 245–246; Atlas 2006, p. 114; Haar 2006, p. 27; Weber 2008, p. 52; Prodi 2014, p. 121.

hind it and to the increasing reverence bestowed on whatever came, even partially, from Palestrina's pen. For these reasons, it became the reference model not only for further interventions on the "Gregorian" repertoire, but also for the overall concept of plainchant in the Catholic Church (classicising prosodic principles, focus on the intelligibility and proper declamation of the sacred words).

Notwithstanding this (or precisely for this reason), the *Editio Medicæa* has been the object of as strong a criticism as its spread and influence have been universal. It is true that it popularised a view of plainchant which was almost totally unhistorical and disrespectful of the musical origins and "authentic" performance of plainsong. (The very fact that it treated *all* Catholic plainchant as a homogeneous repertoire, the so-called "Gregorian chant", belies its steamroller and cavalier attitude). Moreover, not even the value of consistency can be acknowledged to the *Editio Medicæa*, since its complex editorial history, the interventions by multiple revisers, and the variety of the original repertoire (as well as the absence of clearly stated editing criteria) caused a rather patchy final result.

However, it would be unfair to attribute all responsibilities for the "decay" of plainchant singing in the Catholic Church to the *Editio Medicæa*, as would be the simplistic statement that the editors could not distinguish between plainchant used for polyphony and plainchant for monodic performance. It is true that the *Editio Medicæa*'s influence should not be underestimated: for instance, recent studies have shown that older liturgical books were corrected by hand "*ex Soriano*" (i.e. according to Soriano's edition), thus demonstrating the *Medicæa*'s status as a reference text. It is also true, however, that the *Medicæa* was simply a part (though an important one) within a broader and wider process of evolution in taste, which was going to include the increasingly frequent performance of plainchant as an accompanied monody and with tonal features. Moreover, though the editors actively operated on the received tunes, it is also possible that (similarly to what has been established in Guidetti's case) some of the modifications eternalised by the *Medicæa* were already in use, at least partially and in selected contexts, within the Catholic liturgy[52].

### 9.3.5. Polyphony after Trent

In the preceding Chapters we have often seen how polyphony was critically evaluated, both by Catholics and by non-Catholics, how it was discussed at the Council, and how Trent's decrees on music were interpreted as concerns poly-

---

[52] Cf. Baroffio 1995, p. 13; Ruini 1995, p. 33; Rainoldi 2000, p. 354.

phony. We have also seen how later musicological mythology elaborated on the alleged risks undergone by church polyphony in Trent; how the other highly debated topic of intelligibility related with the decrees and their enactment; and how the criticism of polyphonic music mirrored an evolution in the overall aesthetic concept along with spiritual, theological and pastoral concerns. Within the present section, I will briefly present some aspects of post-Tridentine sacred polyphony, without obviously pretending to exhaust such a large topic.

Even when local Councils went into greater detail than Trent had done in describing which kinds of music could be performed in church, in the overwhelming majority of cases polyphony placidly continued to be permitted, performed and enjoyed; at most, as had happened in Toledo (1565–6), Church authorities established that it should aim at "attracting the listeners' souls" to the sung words instead of merely entertaining them[53]. Elsewhere, and within the highly idiosyncratic context of Mantua's Santa Barbara (§ 9.6.5.), the path for a true reform of Catholic Church music was found in the quest for a balanced relation between plainchant and polyphony. Their different symbolic value was exploited, reserving polyphony for the most festive occasions (during which, however, plainchant was also sung) and stressing the importance of plainsong as a perhaps humbler, but sometimes more efficacious form of prayer in music[54].

On the other hand, the passionate debates surrounding church music and the role of polyphony within it are mirrored by such witnesses as a satirical play (*Dialogus musicæ*, Fulda, 1583[55]), originating within a Jesuit context, in which a donkey favours the cuckoos' monody over the nightingales' polyphony, on the grounds that the former sings in a fashion which is closer to the donkey's braying. Curiously, some of the arguments quoted against polyphonic music (and thus conforming with the ass' perspective) are excerpted from the criticism voiced by Cornelius Agrippa von Nettesheim in 1531 (an author we encountered rather often in Chapter Three of this book: § 3.3.2. and following): seemingly, then, criticism of polyphonic music was seen as an outright asinine stance within such a typical example of Counter-Reformation context as a German Jesuit college[56].

---

[53] See Mansi 34, col. 562 (http://bit.ly/2bWAKsw). Cf. Rainoldi 2000, p. 348.
[54] Cf. Fenlon 2002, pp. 196–198; Padoan 2003; Mari 2008, p. 483.
[55] Martinus Thomaeus, *Dialogus musicæ*, (1583): Fulda, Hochschul- und Landesbibliothek, Sammelhandschrift der Societas Jesu in Fulda, MS 4° C 13, fols. 150ʳ-155ʳ.
[56] Cf. Körndle 2006, p. 488.

### 9.3.5.1. Exploring post-Tridentine aesthetics

Though, obviously, official pronouncements (such as those of the Council of Trent or those of the local synods or bishops) had a non-negligible effect on the kind of music performed in church, we have often seen that their influence should be neither over- nor underestimated. Their role and impact intertwined with those of the evolution in musical taste and language with which they entertained a relationship of cause, effect and of parallel development; official statements were the product of a cultural and aesthetic milieu, and partially conditioned it in turn.

The language of music was exploring new paths, in the years after Trent and as the seventeenth century approached; new compositional opportunities could be exploited by musicians (in church as outside it) and old forms could be maintained or reinterpreted according to changing taste. Basically, church musicians had several coexisting styles at their disposal (and this very possibility of choosing was an element of novelty): polychoral settings, also in combination with instruments (and playing with space in an increasingly spectacular fashion); accompanied monody or settings for few vocal parts with continuo; and polyphony in the *stylus antiquus* or *ecclesiasticus*, which drew upon the preceding tradition of imitative writing, but with increasingly solemn and archaising features. The emotional and affective dimension was progressively confined within the two former compositional styles, whose expressive power intensified as the Baroque grew closer; in the meantime, works in the *stile antico* acquired an increasingly clear trait of Olympian purity and transcendence.

All three forms were focused on the word/Word: the polychoral idiom, with its frequent use of homorhythmic structures, allowed a clear perception of the text; monody was a privileged option for clear delivery (and fostered word-painting and affective amplification of the text's meaning); polyphony, in order to correspond to these ideals, had to partially renounce its most fascinating features and became spiritualised, almost disembodied[57].

In several instances, *stile antico* compositions sacrificed the composer's display of technical proficiency in polyphonic writing, in favour of a simpler style which allowed a clearer pronunciation of the words and, in consequence of this, their better intelligibility. In fact, whereas (as we have often seen) this topic was omitted in the Council's official decrees, it was frequently stressed by many prelates who had gathered in Trent and were in charge of the Council's implementation at the local level. In several cases, some bishops actively con-

---

57 Cf. Fellerer 1953, p. 590; Lovato 1995, p. 61; Mischiati 1995, p. 20; Leitmeir 2002, p. 152; Boyce 2006, p. 143; Rees 2006, p. 356; O'Regan 2013a, pp. 342–343.

tributed to the subsequent misunderstanding of Trent's decrees by stating that the Council had commanded church music to favour intelligibility.

For example, Carlo Borromeo, archbishop of Milan, explicitly stated: "I would like you to speak to the master of the chapel there and tell him to reform the singing so that the words may be as intelligible as possible, as you know is ordered by the Council"[58]. It must be stressed that – once more – it is difficult for us to understand what, in Borromeo's statements, referred to compositional issues and what to performance practice. It is certain, however, that Borromeo took an active interest also in musical composition, as is evidenced by his request to Vincenzo Ruffo to write a Mass "as clear as possible"[59].

Similar relationships between composers and ecclesiastical patrons grew increasingly common, up to the point that the "intelligible style" became almost a new trend, an option among the others, or a slogan which could be pinned over new compositions in order to foster their success. Thus, Ruffo himself prefaced his *Missæ quatuor concinnatæ ad ritum Concilii Mediolani* (1570[60]) – the reference to official Church pronouncements could not be clearer – by claiming that his compositional style permitted the "clear and distinct" understanding and perception of the words by the listeners. Similarly, Costanzo Porta, a Franciscan friar who had been a student of Adrian Willaert, wrote to his patron Giulio Feltrio della Rovere and pointed out that his Masses had been composed, in compliance with the latter's requirements, "so that the words could be clearly perceived"[61]. It has been argued, however, that della Rovere's reforming efforts (including his attention to the issue of intelligibility in musical settings) may have been inspired by Borromeo's, whom della Rovere considered as his model[62].

Another instance of correspondence between composers and patrons revealing an interest in intelligibility is that between Palestrina and Guglielmo Gonzaga, Duke of Mantua. In this case, the musical relationship between the two was more shaded and complex than in those mentioned before: firstly, Guglielmo Gonzaga was not a clergyman (though he was very actively interested in church matters, as we will see later in this Chapter: § 9.6.5.); secondly, Palestrina was not the only one to send musical works to the other, since Guglielmo was an amateur composer himself and occasionally had some of his works delivered to Palestrina.

---

[58] In Lockwood 1975, p. 20.
[59] Cf. Lockwood 1970, pp. 88–100; Rees 2006, p. 350.
[60] Ruffo 1570.
[61] In Morucci 2012, pp. 281–282, fn. 54, my translation. Cf. Sherr 1984, p. 77.
[62] Cf. Morucci 2012, pp. 283–284.

Thus, in 1568, Palestrina could offer his own creations to the Duke, proposing the "intelligible style" as one among the many options available ("If in this first attempt I shall not have fulfilled the wishes of your Excellency, I beg you to inform me how you prefer it, whether short, or long, or written so that the words can be understood"[63]). On the other hand (cf. § 3.3.1.4.), when Palestrina had to comment on his patron's compositions, he attributed the occasional lack of intelligibility to the complexity in the imitational texture[64].

In still other instances, it is apparent that mentioning the "Council's decrees" on the title-pages or within the dedicatory letters of published Masses was little more than a homage paid to the ecclesiastical authorities, and that it was much more common for composers to refer to these alleged decrees on intelligibility than to modify their compositional style for the sake of the listeners[65].

In some cases, instead, there was some observable improvement, both as concerned compositional techniques and performance practices: we have already mentioned the enthusiastic report by the Englishman Gregory Martin on the clear perceptibility of the Sistine Chapel choir's delivery (*Roma Sancta*, 1581[66]), but we should not forget the recent studies according to which "it is evident from other sources that loudness or full sonority, not good diction, was the sound ideal of a church or chapel choir in the late 16$^{th}$ century"[67].

### 9.3.5.2. Polychorality: a new option

An interesting stylistic possibility which could unite both aspects – i.e. solemnity with clarity – was that of polychorality. Interestingly, the first attempts in the polychoral idiom had been created in a context both historically and geographically close to the Council, i.e. northern Italy in the middle of the sixteenth century (though polychoral experiments can be traced back even earlier and their remote origin is inspired by antiphonal singing and recitation). Among the

---

63 Letter of February 2$^{nd}$, 1568: Mantova, Archivio di Stato, Autografi (Anni 1439–1876), busta 6, cc. 397–398; Mantova Capitale Europea dello Spettacolo, sig. C-2976; cf. Rees 2006, p. 351; translated in Lockwood 1975, p. 24.
64 Letter of March 3$^{rd}$, 1570: Mantova, Archivio di Stato, Autografi (Anni 1439–1876), busta 6, cc. 403–404; Mantova Capitale Europea dello Spettacolo, sig. C-2979; translated in Lockwood 1975, p. 25.
65 Cf. Lockwood 1970, p. 134.
66 Martin 1581, Martin 1969.
67 Sherr 1994, pp. 607–608; cf. Monson 2006, pp. 404 and 408. Cf. also Fellerer 1953, pp. 581 and 592; Rainoldi 2000, pp. 342 and 347; Atlas 2006, p. 114; O'Regan 2006, p. 77; Weber 2008, p. 103; Fenlon 2009, p. 203; O'Regan 2013a, p. 341.

first important accomplishments of this style are Psalms for *cori spezzati*, written for the liturgy of the Vespers by Adrian Willaert and Jacquet of Mantua.

The vocal ensemble, sometimes (and increasingly often) with instrumental accompaniment, was split in two or more groupings, which could be (and actually were, with growing frequency) spatially separated. Even in its simplest form (two groupings facing each other), this situation fostered a much higher involvement of the listeners in the performed music: the aural result was more varied (since the different provenance of the sounds created a fascinating and Protean musical milieu), and the audience was surrounded by sound. The musical impression was not dissimilar from the visual effects realised in several late Renaissance and early Baroque churches, where the ceiling seems to have been broken and the observers can have a glimpse into heaven itself: one such example is found in the Cathedral Church in Parma, whose splendid frescoed dome was painted c.1530 by Antonio Allegri, "Il Correggio" (1489–1534).

On the other hand, the variety provided to this style by the juxtaposition of several groupings allowed composers to employ a relatively static technique as the homorhythmic style without risking dullness; the advantage brought by the use of homorhythmic settings was, in turn, that of allowing a very clear declamation and perception of the words. It is interesting, however, to point out a singular aspect: though it is true that polychorality seemed optimally suited for post-Tridentine church music (thanks to its balance of intelligibility with variety), it is also true that its success underpins yet another instance of misinterpretation of Trent. As we have seen, what Trent officially stated was not that church music should be intelligible; rather, it set down some aesthetic principles which seemingly pointed to sobriety rather than to grandiosity, to interiority rather than to outward splendour. Though the polychoral style did foster a clear comprehensibility of the text (what the Council had *not* requested), it quickly became an enormously luxurious – not to say ostentatious – style, which actually did *not* correspond to the Tridentine principles of spiritual reformation.

Whereas the first Tridentine guidelines, in Taruskin's opinion, were aimed in the direction of challenging the Evangelical aesthetics "on its own ground", by adopting similar principles of "modesty", later "the Catholic reaction to the Reformation [...] took on a mystical, enthusiastic and antirationalist character", whose aesthetic embodiment was represented by the promotion of "pomp and spectacle"[68].

While one of the means by which this purpose could be achieved was the adoption, in the sacred sphere, of word-painting techniques developed in the

---

[68] Taruskin 2010, p. 771.

secular domain, the other strategy was to pursue a continuing inflation of the size and volume of church music. And no style could be more suited than the polychoral idiom for this goal. From northern Italy – and particularly from Venice, where it flourished magnificently – this style migrated and was quickly espoused by Roman composers and audiences alike. Noel O'Regan has fascinatingly described the role played by the dissemination of Lasso's works in Rome for the adoption of the polychoral idiom by Roman composers, though the influence of Kerle and of his *Preces speciales* should not be overlooked in turn[69]. In Rome, a compositional style close to the *cori spezzati*, though not exactly identifiable with it, was adopted already in the Second Book of *laudi* published in 1570 by Giovanni Animuccia[70]: the composer's choice, as will be discussed later in this Chapter (§ 9.4.3.), was interestingly connected with the social provenance of the participants in St Filippo Neri's prayers at the *Oratorio*[71].

Polychorality was practised also by Palestrina (though this aspect of his output is lesser known than others), by some of his followers, and was exported to Spain where it entered the repertoire of the *villancico*. The first works by Palestrina in which a clear distinction between two choirs dialoguing in consecutive Psalm-verses is found are those published in 1575[72], while Victoria integrated the new style in some of his compositions of the following year[73]; other Roman composers followed suit[74]. As time went on, polychorality showed a tendency to magniloquence: the number of the groupings employed by the composers grew steadily, and it became more and more common to combine them with instruments (in particular with winds, whose sound was obviously likely to empower the grandiosity of the aural result). In Venice, as in some Spanish cathedrals (such as Seville and Toledo), wind players were employed from the second half of the sixteenth century.

Polychorality is also frequently found in the works by Jacobus Gallus (also known as Handl or Carniolus, 1550–1591), whose monumental *Opus musicum* (1587[75]) represents not only a repository of sacred works for virtually all liturgical needs (with more than 350 motets), but also a catalogue of compositional idioms, with occasional presence of *cantus firmus* elaborations alongside imitative

---

69 Cf. O'Regan 1984; O'Regan 1999a, pp. 144–147.
70 Animuccia 1570.
71 Cf. O'Regan 2006, p. 80.
72 Palestrina 1575.
73 For Victoria's polychoral works, see the recent research by Noel O'Regan (2012 and 2013b).
74 Cf. O'Regan 1999a, pp. 150–151.
75 Handl 1959.

works, word-painting and other compositions with dense expressivity and typical post-Tridentine sobriety.

At the turn of the century, the increasing imposingness of church architecture was aesthetically matched and aurally filled by polychoral works. As Rainoldi efficaciously put it, "polychorality dilated spaces even more than it did with time"[76]. It is interesting to observe that this phenomenon was more common within contexts (such as the Papal Rome or the Republic of Venice) which wished to emphasise and show their splendour and magnificence and to impress visitors with the aural symbol of their grandeur. The summit of polychorality (at least in quantitative terms) would be reached in the second half of the seventeenth century, when as many as ten or twelve groupings sang at solemn festivities in Rome; it must be added, however, that this style spread well beyond the boundaries of southern Europe and became popular also in Germany and elsewhere in the seventeenth century[77].

### 9.3.6. The Cardinals' Commission

In the case of the polychoral idiom, as we have seen just, its success represented (and was caused by) the intersection between the Council's reception, with its lights and shadows, the evolution in musical language, and the aesthetics of the time. It is therefore difficult, if not outright impossible, to ascertain how each of these elements impacted on the final result.

There are, instead, historical facts which probably had a comparatively minor effect on the history of music, but whose narrative is easier to establish and to recount.

Such is the episode of the Cardinals' Commission of 1565[78], which was another by-product of the Council and had a certain responsibility in the later understanding and reception of Trent.

As the reader will remember, the Council had discussed topics of musical relevance between 1562 and 1563. Already in the following year, and precisely in August 1564, Pope Pius IV (1499–1565) established a Roman Commission charged to enact some of Trent's decrees for the reform of Roman institutions. It must be stressed, however, that the difference between this Commission and the Council's discussions and decrees was huge, notwithstanding the impor-

---

[76] Rainoldi 2000, p. 357, my translation.
[77] Cf. Morelli 1993, p. 187; Carter 2006, p. 41; Rees 2006, pp. 353–354.
[78] See Maniates 1979, pp. 492ff.

tance of the people involved on this Commission (from the Pope who instituted it to those participating in its discussions) and the role played by some of them at the Council. The Council was responsible for major issues regarding the entire spectrum of Roman Catholicism; the extent of the Commission's influence was – at least officially – much more local and limited.

Cardinals Carlo Borromeo and Vitellozzo Vitelli, both members of this Commission, were entrusted with the duty of reforming the Papal music Chapels. It will be recalled (cf. § 8.3.3.) that Borromeo and Vitelli had already been involved in musically-related issues: when, in 1561–2, Cardinal Waldburg had fostered the exchange of musical works between Rome and Munich, he had done so partially in response to Vitelli's specific demand and interest. Moreover, both Vitelli and Borromeo are mentioned by Waldburg as having been among the listeners of the works received and as having appreciated the works heard. It must be stressed, however, that neither Vitelli nor Waldburg had requested on that occasion any particular kind of music to be sent, nor had there been any emphasis on qualities such as intelligibility (or sobriety, or length...).

In the first months of 1565, instead, Borromeo's correspondence reveals an increasing concern and interest in church music and in its intelligibility. We have already encountered, in this Chapter, some excerpts from Borromeo's letters, and we will discuss them in greater detail toward the conclusion of this Chapter[79]; suffice it to say, for now, that Borromeo actively sought and commissioned polyphonic works whose text could be clearly understood.

It is also likely that Borromeo's request to his newly appointed choirmaster Vincenzo Ruffo prompted his composition of the Masses later collected as *Missæ Quatuor* (1570): whatever judgement is given to their artistic quality, the intelligibility of their texts cannot be denied.

When sufficient material had been gathered, the Cardinals organised an experimental audition at Vitelli's palace (April 27th or 28th, 1565), where some such works were performed and listened to, with the specific purpose of evaluating "whether the words could be understood" (*"si verba intelligerentur"*[80]).

It is noteworthy, incidentally, that *Masses* (i.e. Mass Ordinaries) were performed on that occasion. We have seen, in fact (cf. § 3.2.2.2.) that the constant repetition of the *Ordinarium* items in the Mass made intelligibility problems much less urgent in their case than in others. Those who regularly took part in Eucharistic services were likely to know by heart the Latin text of the Mass

---

79 See § 9.3.5.1., 9.3.6., 9.6.2.
80 Rees 2006, p. 350.

Ordinary, and thus were able to follow the words – if they felt inclined to do so – even if and when imitations or dense polyphonic texture hid them partially.

In the case of the Cardinals' Commission, as in several others seen until now, therefore, we can observe how the actual decrees of the Council underwent an interesting process: from the one side (and this was obviously both foreseen and desired by the Council), what had been left vague or general in the decrees was detailed and declined into practice by local authorities. From the other side, however, this process of actualisation implied also the reduction of a broader aesthetic and theological view to an array of instructions and to set phrases.

These could reach heights of unwilling irony, as was the case with composer Giovanni Animuccia. In 1566, he was paid by the Cappella Giulia for five Masses "*secundum formam concilii*" (i. e. "according with the Council's requirements"). When he had them published (1567[81]), the composer's preface stated that he had sought to write them so that "the music may disturb the hearing of the text as little as possible"[82]. It is easy to observe how long had been the itinerary of the Council's decrees within the short space of five years, from the reticent Tridentine statements to the notion that the ideal of church music was to disturb as little as possible.

Given how widespread was this concept by that time, however, and considering that the Council's pronouncements on music had progressively been understood as prescribing textual intelligibility, the Cardinals' effort in 1565 is appreciable. Though their knowledge of music was that of refined amateurs (but, of course, not that of professionals), they had wanted to experiment in person on the comprehensibility of the Mass settings offered to their hearing. (Here too, however, there is an irony: probably, highly cultivated churchmen who wrote in Latin as in their first language and who had assisted to or celebrated innumerable Masses, could grasp the words of sung Mass Ordinaries much better than most illiterate church-goers).

### 9.3.6.1. Observing (and by-passing) the "Council's requirements"

When (September 1565) Borromeo left Rome for his diocese of Milan, the work started by Vitelli and himself came to an end; however, the topic of intelligibility would continue to play a crucial role for Catholic church music (and particularly for the concept Borromeo had of it).

---

[81] Animuccia 1567.
[82] Quoted in and translated into English by Monson 2002, p. 24.

Notwithstanding this, it is also important to note that works decidedly different from the aesthetic criteria appreciated by those prelates in the post-Tridentine years continued to be performed and composed, even within the closest circles of the Papal sphere. The Cappella Giulia continued to sing Masses on secular *cantus firmus* in 1568 – including one by Matthaeus Pipelare (c.1450-c.1515) on that very *L'homme armé* which had been so often criticised. Years later, other *L'homme armé* settings were included by Palestrina in his 1570 and 1582 published Mass collections[83]; in others of his settings, secular *cantus firmus* were avoided only in the title, but not in practice (thus a Mass on *Io mi son giovinetta* was called *Missa primi toni*, and one on *Je suis déshéritée* was modestly indicated as *Missa sine nomine*).

A musician who, similar to Palestrina, has come to be closely associated with post-Tridentine reformations of music, namely Francesco Soriano (one of the *Medicæa* editors), was however no less nonchalant in his practice, calling *Missa sine titulo* his paraphrase settings of madrigals. Cipriano de Rore was even more creative, and gave a polish of "sacredness" to his works on secular models by simply translating their title (e.g. *Quando lieta sperai*) into Latin[84] (*Quando læta sperabam*).

Generally speaking, even though Roman composers made some efforts to satisfy the stylistic preferences of their post-Tridentine ecclesiastical patrons, the effects of the Council's reception on musical composition are more clearly discernible in other areas of the Italian peninsula (and particularly in the zones under Borromeo's supervision or influence). Even where the title-page homage to the "Council's requirements" did correspond to actual compositional efforts, a true novelty could be observed in the composer/work/patron relationship: musicians were assuming new responsibilities in the choice of stylistic elements and in evaluating their suitability to aesthetic/theological demands.

It was sometimes no easy task: composers were probably more sensitive than average prelates to the symbolic and artistic value of music, and though they could rationally adhere to the post-Tridentine aesthetic ideals (or simply pay homage to them without any personal conviction), they could undergo the strong fascination of a less intelligible (but probably more enrapturing) kind of music. One such example of an attempted reconciliation between austere sobriety and glorious beauty is found in Francisco Guerrero's *Preface* to his *Liber vesperarum* (1584[85]), where both aspects are stressed – and Guerrero's tone

---

[83] Palestrina 1570; Palestrina 1582.
[84] Cf. Fellerer 1953, pp. 586–587; Lockwood 1966, pp. 41, 46–48, 54; Sherr 1978, p. 94; Rorke 1984, p. 172; Rainoldi 2000, pp. 345 and 357; Atlas 2006, pp. 112–113; Monson 2006, p. 404.
[85] Guerrero 1584.

seems to testify to the composer's sincere quest for a compositional style corresponding to both artistic and ecclesiastical exigencies.

Once more, it is necessary to underline that references to the "Council's demands" rarely implied direct knowledge of the decrees on the part of the composer; rather, we should imagine a cultural climate in which the ecclesiastical patrons of church musicians were giving instructions (either in person or through local synods), musicians were discussing with one another on what they had heard about the Council, and printers were eager to boast the compliance of their newly-published collections with the "Council's decrees".

A brief overview of some such statements may help to clarify the point. The preface to Palestrina's *Second Book of Masses* (1567) invites us to consider a few important aspects of its wording: "I [...] have considered it my task, in accordance with the views of most serious and most religious-minded men, to bend all my knowledge, effort, and industry towards that which is the holiest and most divine of all things in the Christian religion – that is, to adorn the holy sacrifice of the Mass in a new manner"[86].

Palestrina's sentence should be compared with Giovanni Animuccia's preface to his *First Book of Masses* of the same year (a fragment of which has been quoted earlier: § 9.3.6.):

> Being led to this by the judgment of these men, I have sought to adorn these divine prayers and praises of God in such a way that the music may disturb the hearing of the text as little as possible, but nevertheless in such a way that it may not be entirely devoid of artifice and may contribute in some degree to the listener's pleasure[87].

It is interesting to observe that both composers explicitly mention the external influences they underwent: Palestrina mentions the "views of most serious and most religious-minded men", and Animuccia claims to have been "led [...] by the judgment of these men". Both, moreover, speak of their compositional activity as of the task of "adorning" the Mass (cf. § 2.3.8.): music is seemingly seen as an embellishment which should not distract hearers from the text's meaning.

These words can be contrasted with those by Lodovico Cresollio quoted in Chapter Three (§ 3.3.2.12.), where he maintained that sacred music, at Palestrina's time, consisted merely of "delicate diminutions and vain adornments to the words, from which no benefit of piety came forth to the listeners"[88].

---

[86] Palestrina 1567, "Preface". English translation as found in Lockwood 1975, pp. 22–23.
[87] Animuccia 1567, "Preface". English translation as found in Lockwood 1975, p. 23.
[88] Cresollio 1629, Liber III, Chapter XXVII, p. 627; English translation as found in Lockwood 1975, p. 30.

Interestingly, however, Palestrina's words specify that he sought to "adorn the holy sacrifice of the Mass": a sentence which not only underpins the concept of Mass as sacrifice (against which Luther had actively fought) but also suggests the idea that music embellished the liturgical words *for God* (which, as previously discussed, was a typical trait of Catholic church music: see § 4.3.7.2.). Similarly, and though Animuccia mentions "the listener's pleasure", he also points out that his task was to "adorn these divine prayers and praises of God". Both composers, finally, mention stylistic aspects: Palestrina speaks of a "new manner" of writing church music, and Animuccia describes the strategies he employed for his own "new manner". Indeed, the Masses collected by both composers comprise homophonic sections in *Gloria* and *Credo* settings, whereas the other items of the Ordinary sometimes display a richer imitative style.

The statements discussed here can be further compared with an excerpt from Ruffo's own preface to his *Missæ Quatuor* (1570):

> I was to compose some Masses (as they are called) which should avoid everything of a profane and idle manner in worship, and so that the powerful and sweet sound of the voices should soothe and caress the ears of the listeners in a pious, religious and holy way. [...] Guided by your help, I composed one Mass in this way: so that the numbers of the syllables and the voices and tones together should be clearly and distinctly understood and perceived by the pious listeners[89].

Some of Ruffo's expressions are especially noteworthy, among which the sound ideal favoured by the composer ("the powerful and sweet sound"), the "soothing and caressing" of the listeners' ears (cf. Animuccia, but also Pope John XXII's Decretal), the external guidance (as in Palestrina's and Animuccia's prefaces) and the concern for intelligibility. It is interesting, however, that here the key concern seems to be for the listener, and the mystical dimension suggested by Palestrina and Animuccia is intriguingly downplayed here. Ruffo's reference to the "numbers of the syllables" is also worth mentioning as an example of humanistic influence on the concept of sacred music.

An analogous reference to patronage and aesthetic ideals is found in Costanzo Porta's words addressed to Giulio Feltrio della Rovere, claiming that the composer, following "an order given by Your Lordship", had set to music some Masses characterised by textual intelligibility, easiness, limited length, but not devoid of artistic qualities[90]. Here too we find references to factors other than musical

---

[89] Ruffo 1570; as translated into English by Weiss and Taruskin 2008, p. 116, with modifications.
[90] In Morucci 2012, pp. 281–282, fn. 54. Cf. Sherr 1984, p. 77.

## 9.3. Music and liturgy after Trent — 465

inspiration as the driving force of the compositional activity, and the stress on the possibility of clearly understanding the text[91].

As mentioned above, the composer/patron/work balance was changing, as a consequence of social, cultural, religious and economic variations. In parallel with the evolution of music from the medieval *scientia* to the modern *ars* and with the reification of the musical work as a means for the composer to achieve artistic immortality (cf. § 2.3.1.), composers were invested with an increasing responsibility and (as I argued in Chapter Eight: § 8.4.6.) were the ultimate subject in charge of interpreting, understanding and enacting the Council's perspective on music.

An implicit recognition of this status can be found, in my opinion, in the fact that no *Index* of prohibited music was ever created by the Catholic Church. It is true that this lack of centralised and official indications exposed music to the risk of arbitrary decisions by church leaders and of anarchy on the part of musicians. Since Borromeo's active engagement in and supervision of church music was more the exception than the rule, it can be said that often the need was felt for a deep reflection on how to put into practice the general guidelines of the Council on music.

Much was left to personal initiative; and whereas no *Index* of forbidden musical works is found, sometimes musical collections could be included in catalogues of prohibited books. For example, the *Catalogus hæreticorum* constantly kept up-to-date by the Munich Jesuits includes Lutheran chorale settings and psalmody on tunes coming from the Bohemian Brethren tradition. It would be interesting to know, however, whether the prohibition was determined by the lyrics' content or by the music, or by the dissemination which music had guaranteed to the words[92]. Notwithstanding this, other Jesuits operating in Counter-Reformation Germany fostered the publication of a sacred music collection including several parodies of secular works[93]. Such seeming contradictions not only demonstrate that – in the absence of a clear leadership in musical matters – much was left to the decisions of local authorities; but also that music normally enjoyed a considerable degree of freedom, in which actual bans and prohibitions were much less frequent than in other fields of human creativity and culture.

---

**91** Cf. Leichtentritt 1944, p. 324; Fellerer 1953, pp. 586–587; Lockwood 1975, pp. 24–25; Sherr 1984, p. 75; Monson 2002, p. 26; O'Regan 2006, p. 78; Rees 2006, pp. 351–352; Morucci 2012, pp. 283–284.
**92** Cf. Crook 2009, p. 5 and pp. 51–52.
**93** Leitmeir 2002, p. 153.

### 9.3.7. Celebrating with instruments

Similar differences in practice, as well as the progressive overcoming of scruples and strictures on church music, can be observed concerning the use of instruments in Catholic worship.

The use of the organ was normally accepted, though the Papal Chapel sang *a cappella*, and restrictions were sometimes placed on the use of organs in monasteries: though organ music was generally welcome, the feeling was that the "purest" kind of church music was unaccompanied singing. Notwithstanding this, in several convents not just one organ, but two were commonly in use; and Gregory Martin's report (1581) on Roman church music explicitly mentions organs, but also "cornett or sagbut or such like"[94].

Nonetheless – as mentioned above (§ 9.3.4.) – the *Cæremoniale Episcoporum* forbade the use of organs on penitential occasions. We have also already seen that this recommendation was not always obeyed, and that in some cases the organs might keep silent, but other instruments took their place.

Beside that particular case of plucked-string instruments replacing the forbidden organ music during Holy Week, in the late sixteenth century and early seventeenth century the presence of instruments other than the organ in Catholic worship increased noticeably, though study of this matter is elusive (due to terminological imprecision in several sources and to the lack of fundamental data). It can be said, however, that the participation of wind instruments in church music grew increasingly common, and was particularly associated with festive occasions[95].

It is interesting to contrast the words on organ music in worship found in Paris de Grassis' ceremonial book (1516) with the practice witnessed in Venice roughly fifty years later. The Papal master of ceremonies prescribed that the organist must "not stop playing until the Cardinal Bishop has finished [his] prayer", and that he had to "shorten or lengthen his accompaniment so that the Cardinal be not compelled to haste more than usual or to wait"[96]. This is consistent with observations by Haberl about the unusual length of some of Palestrina's *Magnificat* settings, whose duration was determined by the rites taking place during their performance[97]. On the other hand, the order of priorities in Venice

---

[94] In Sherr 1994, p. 607.
[95] Cf. Fellerer 1953, pp. 578–579; Monson 1993a, p. 151; Sherr 1994, p. 607; Gozzi 1995, p. 52; Herl 2004, p. 25; Monson 2006, p. 405; Rees 2006, p. 354; Mari 2008, pp. 478–479 and 497–498; Groote and Vendrix 2012, pp. 180–181.
[96] De Grassis 1580, p. 18 (Chapter XVII), my translation; cf. Gozzi 1995, p. 53.
[97] In *P-KDG*, vol. 17, p. i.

seemed to be rather different: here, musical needs seemingly came first. On November 28th, 1564, when the organists at San Marco were musicians of the standing of Claudio Merulo (1533–1604) and Andrea Gabrieli, the orders were as follows: "The Procurators order that none among the Canons, Sub-Canons, or any other priest dare interrupt the organs' sounds while they are played, but they must keep quiet and patient until the organists will have finished their sounds; and [only] when each of these organists will have finished his sounds, will the priests continue their orders and habits"[98].

We will see later in this Chapter (§ 9.6.4.) that Venice was undoubtedly an untypical example of the purest post-Tridentine Catholicism, and it cannot be said that there is a straight line of evolution connecting de Grassis' organists who adapted their playing to liturgical necessities with the Venetian priests who had to wait patiently for their organists' inspiration to fade; however, what can be observed is that instrumental music in church was left practically unscathed by the Council, and indeed became increasingly common in the years following it.

## 9.4. Religious music in post-Tridentine Catholicism

While discussing the auditions organised by Borromeo and Vitelli in 1565, we observed that the Cardinals tested the intelligibility of polyphonic Mass settings, though their text was particularly well-known to devout Catholics. Indeed, the most important of Trent's debates on music had taken place within the discussion on abuses in the celebration of the Mass: though nothing too definite came regarding music from the Council, the other genres of sacred music (performed either in church or elsewhere) received even less official attention from the Council.

Thus, post-Tridentine religious music could find its space in church and during worships, whilst flourishing within a creative interaction with the non-liturgical (and even secular) world. The provenance of the religious texts set to music was very heterogeneous; the stylistic variety of their musical settings was partly due to the substantial freedom enjoyed by Catholic sacred music (if this was true of Mass Ordinaries, it was truer of other religious compositions), and partly to the fluidity of the boundaries between church music, spiritual works and secular music.

---

**98** Quoted in Dalla Libera 1961, p. 54, my translation.

### 9.4.1. Emotional motets

Motets often became the favourite *locus* in which the persuasive and affective power of music could be exploited to "move" listeners to devotion. Whereas *stile antico* Mass settings were more restrained in their emotional palette, motets not only could, but rather should make use of compositional artifices aiming at a thorough spiritual involvement of their listeners. Borgerding[99] has fascinatingly drawn parallels between the development of post-Tridentine rhetoric in homilies, sermons and devotional literature from the one side, and motet composition from the other. Both motets and sermons were normally based on Scriptural excerpts, which they interpreted and whose meaning was transmitted in a colourful fashion to the audience. Thus, both music and speech were allowed to reflect and meditate on the Word, and to re-present it to the listeners in order to arouse their devotion.

Motet composition also raises interesting points of a more technical nature, concerning the language and stylistic choices available to composers. Indeed, analysis of the compositional models adopted in post-Tridentine motet-writing has shown the quest for a delicate balance between retrospective trends and attempts at exploration of new aesthetic fields[100]. Since the occasions for performance of motets within post-Tridentine liturgical ceremonies were limited, several published motet collections of the late sixteenth century were conceived for private devotion at least as much as for official worship.

### 9.4.2. Local languages

Along with Latin motets, vernacular singing continued to be occasionally practised in Catholic churches, although in some instances the strong identification of vernacular singing with the Evangelical confessions rendered problematic a practice which dated back to the pre-Reformation era.

In the Catholic German-speaking zones, however, vernacular hymns could be sung after sermons or catechism, and during activities such as processions, Eucharistic or Marian devotions etc.[101].

In Bavaria, the practice of Catholic vernacular singing gained momentum after Trent instead of being discouraged due to its association with Protestan-

---

[99] Borgerding 1998, pp. 592–593.
[100] Cf. Fromson 1992, pp. 244–245; Monson 2006, p. 402.
[101] Cf. Scheitler 2010.

tism. Vernacular hymns were permitted also in Wroclaw (Breslau, Poland), in 1592, by the local Synod, decreeing that it was an ancient practice, "useful for the devotion of the people" and therefore "laudable"; however, the only allowed vernacular songs were those found in an official Catholic booklet, while Protestant collections had to be removed[102].

Elsewhere, the acceptance of vernacular singing was even more cautious and conditional. For instance, in France, the Council of Avignon (1594) permitted French carols at Christmas but only when the bishop's consent had been previously obtained[103].

On the other hand, very inclusive attitudes could be found within extreme situations such as Catholic missions: for example, in 1615 the Jesuit missionaries working in China were permitted to celebrate both Mass and the Office in Mandarin Chinese, upon a request made to Pope Paul V by St Robert Bellarmine. This fact is particularly striking if one compares this initiative by Bellarmine with his statements on the expendability of linguistic comprehension in worship[104] (see § 4.3.7.2.).

Outside the liturgical framework (but by no means outside the religious sphere), sacred-texted music for devotion flourished in post-Tridentine Catholicism. As Prodi has pointed out, the keyword for connecting the artistic world with that of history, at the time we are considering presently, is "piety"[105]. The most genuine and significant expressions of post-Tridentine Catholicism are perhaps to be found within this intersection of devotion, contemplation, introspection and creativity; moreover, a fascinating aspect that should not be neglected is the closeness of the world of Catholic piety to those of many Evangelical confessions. Of course, the objects to whom piety was addressed could vary, sometimes very substantially, between one confession and one another (for example, Marian devotion was typical for the Catholic areas); however, the forms taken by this piety– in music but not only there – could be very similar, if not identical or even coincident, among the different Christian Churches of the era.

Notwithstanding this, whereas in some Evangelical confessions (such as, for example, Lutheranism and partly Calvinism) the separation between the musical repertoires of worship and piety could be minimal, and in certain cases non-existent, within the Catholic field only certain fractions of the religious repertoire

---

**102** *Acta* 1595, p. 79ᵛ-80ʳ. I wish to thank my friends Agata Maria Pinkosz and Anna Łach for helping me to consult this source.
**103** *Mansi* 34, p. 1351, available online at http://bit.ly/2by8pI3.
**104** Cf. Bellarmino 1599, Book II, Chapter 16, pp. 187–188. Cf. Weber 2008, p. 185; Monson 2006, p. 410; Pecklers and Ostdiek 2011, pp. 48–49.
**105** Prodi 2014, p. 13.

were common to worship and devotion, while others were exclusive for either of them.

However, one of the most remarkable fruits of the Council (even from the musical viewpoint, as we have previously seen) was that it started a spiritual renewal involving all social layers and their artistic expressions. While it is true that the Council did not regulate piety and devotion, nor did it set guidelines on forms of prayer outside liturgy proper, it is also true that the religious climate fostered by the Council produced innumerable forms and works of art, all expressing the commonly-felt desire for a deeper and more intense spirituality. Though the secular repertoire has been studied more often and more deeply than non-liturgical sacred music, this was not considered a minor genre at the time, and that repertoire was highly relevant to the lives and spiritual experiences of those composing and practising it.

Among the genres which were common to both worship and devotion are motets, which were often sung during the Mass, but which were normally performed as a form of spiritual entertainment. On rarer occasions, Mass settings and *Magnificats* could also be sung outside service (and such was the case, for example, of the Cardinals' Commission audition); however, the core of the Catholic devotional repertoire was constituted by religious poetry set to music, as in the case of spiritual madrigals, *laude* and similar forms.

### 9.4.3. Piety and poetry

*Laude* were simple strophic compositions, which were particularly well suited for congregational non-liturgical singing. This practice was highly appreciated and common in Florence and central Italy, where the long-term effects of Savonarola's preaching were still observable; the musicianship and sociability of children and young people had been channelled to the religious sphere, where *laude* were sung both in the impressive processions and public rites involving thousands of people, and in the more intimate contexts of confraternities and religious groups.

It is perhaps no coincidence that the first blossoming of *lauda* printing in Italy coincided with the conclusion of the Council, in that very year 1563. Serafino Razzi (1531–1613), a Dominican friar from Florence, edited a volume of pre-existing religious poetry set to music, the *Laudi spirituali*[106]: here, spiritual contrafacture was practised at its most, with secular and carnival songs such as *Tre*

---

[106] Razzi 1563.

*ciechi siamo*, by Giovanni Domenico da Nola (c.1510–1592), becoming a praise of the theological virtues (*Tre virtù siamo*).

Again in 1563, Giovanni Animuccia, who lived in Rome but was Florence-born, published his *Primo libro delle laudi*[107], as the result of his participation in the devotional activities of St Filippo Neri's Oratory. Northern Italy replied to these publications originating from the centre of the peninsula with yet another collection, edited by Giovanni del Bene (1513–1559), the archpriest of St Stefano in Verona, and titled *Musica spirituale*[108], issued "for the Christian people's enjoyment". This publication included poems from a wide range of provenances (comprising religious poetry by Petrarch), and the musical settings were signed by such composers as Willaert, Giovanni Nasco (c.1510–1561), Ruffo, Maistre Jhan (c.1485–1538) etc.

Petrarch remained a favourite source of inspiration for musicians in the spiritual sphere as he was in that same period in the secular context: the long poem *Vergine bella, che di sol vestita* which concludes the *Canzoniere* was often divided into separate sections, which were set to music in cycles of spiritual madrigals (among others by Cipriano de Rore, published in 1548; by Asola in 1571, and by Palestrina, in 1581[109]).

We may observe here a substantial formal difference between *laude* and *madrigali spirituali:* the former are characterised by strophic lyrics, while the latter (which may or may not adopt strophic forms) are closer in style to secular madrigals, of which they often are textual *contrafacta*. Spiritual canzonets are characterised by a style simpler than madrigals, being often set for three voices, and with frequent use of homorhythmic writing.

In the last four decades of the sixteenth century, collections of spiritual music in Italian were constantly issued, witnessing to the interest of the public for this repertoire. The spiritual madrigals, whose musical and verbal language was directed to the cultivated layers of society, were appreciated and performed both by the laity and by religious men and women (including cloistered nuns), and within the cultural/religious gatherings of academies and oratories. Spiritual madrigals could also be included within mostly-secular collections, continuing a pre-Tridentine habit (whereas publications entirely dedicated to spiritual madrigals were an exquisitely post-Tridentine creation).

The connection between post-Tridentine piety and devotional compositions is clearly shown by the active interest taken by Carlo Borromeo in the creation

---

[107] Animuccia 1563.
[108] Del Bene 1563.
[109] De Rore 1548; Asola 1571; Palestrina 1581.

of collections of spiritual madrigals: we will see later in this Chapter (§ 9.6.2.) that he fostered such initiatives within the framework of devotion and interior renewal.

Occasionally, spiritual *contrafacta* did not merely modify the secular madrigals' text, but intervened even on their language, thus creating motet-like forms (an operation which in itself testifies to the fluidity of boundaries between musical genres of the era). Such was the case of the *contrafacta* realised by Aquilino Coppini on some of Monteverdi's secular madrigals (see § 9.6.2.).

Among the authors of spiritual poetry for madrigals were such diverse figures as Luigi Tansillo (1510–1568), who had been known for a licentious youthful work banned by the *Index*, but who later expressed his repentance in the *Lagrime di san Pietro* (text published in 1585[110]), Gabriele Fiamma (1533–1585), the bishop of Chioggia near Venice, and the Benedictine monk Angelo Grillo (c.1557–1629). Both Fiamma and Grillo adopted new stylistic features in their religious poetry, which progressively distanced itself from the Petrarchan model and showed the first traces of Baroque subjectivism and a taste for verbal effects, artifices and emotionally powerful choices. Spiritual madrigals fostered the identification and empathy with the feelings and emotions of the Biblical characters they often portrayed, and the rhetorical, persuasive and affective power of music was increasingly exploited to arouse devotion and spiritual sentiments.

In some instances, the use of contrafacture regarded works whose secular origin was betrayed not only by the text (which was accordingly modified), but also by their music. Such was the case of a highly sensuous secular motet by Orlando di Lasso, *Anna mihi dilecta*, which was transformed into a religious-texted piece as *Christe, Dei soboles* without losing any of its musically voluptuous features.

The evolution in the madrigals' lyrics encouraged composers to adopt corresponding musical artifices in their settings, and fostered – especially in northern Italy – a growing interest in spiritual madrigals, while *laude* and canzonets received comparatively minor attention[111].

---

[110] Tansillo 1585.
[111] Cf. Lockwood 1970, p. 94; Rorke 1984, pp. 173–175; Kendrick 1996, p. 14; Haar 2006, pp. 235–237; Kendrick 2006, pp. 340–341; Monson 2006, pp. 409–410; O'Regan 2006, p. 87; Rees 2006, p. 353; Weber 2008, p. 161; Crook 2009, pp. 17 and 27; Bizzarini 2012, pp. 18–21; O'Regan 2013a, p. 346; Prodi 2014, p. 13.

### 9.4.4. Devotional music outside Italy

Outside Italy, the output of devotional music featured significantly different traits in the zones where Catholic and Evangelical communities shared the same language, and in those whose population was in the majority Catholic.

As we will see in Chapter Eleven (§ 11.5. and following), in fact, confessional boundaries could be crossed rather easily by spiritual music intended for private prayer (due in part to the adroit strategies of publishers, who wished their products to appeal to as many believers as possible, regardless of their confessional allegiance). The French-speaking world was a typical case in point: we have already seen (cf. § 6.3.6.) that spiritual settings by composers such as Le Jeune and L'Estocart were purchased, sung and appreciated by Huguenots and Catholics alike, with occasional modifications to the lyrics when they were too clearly characterised as belonging to Calvinism.

In France as in Italy, the verbal and musical language of the *airs spirituelles* or of the *chansons spirituelles* was very close to those of their secular analogues, and contrafacture was similarly practised. Lyrics for spiritual songs were also frequently excerpted or adapted from translations (more or less faithful) of Latin hymns, but could also be original creations. Among such spiritual poetry for music, great popularity was achieved by the *Quatrains* written by Guy du Faur, sire de Pibrac: his lyrics were set to music by Guillaume Boni, Jean Planson (c.1545-a.1612), Lasso and L'Estocart.

The case of Antoine de Bertrand is particularly interesting, since the composer's own experience followed that of his works. At first, in fact, it was Bertrand's secular output (originally setting to music lyrics from Pierre Ronsard's *Les Amours*) which was given a sacred text by Simon Goulart. Two years after the publication of Goulart's collection, Bertrand himself issued a book of *Airs spirituels* (1582[112]), which were the result of the composer's spiritual itinerary, leading him from the secular world of love poetry to a Jesuit-inspired Catholic perspective.

In France too, moreover, Latin motets were frequently performed in extra-liturgical contexts, and Lasso's published collections testify to their composer's success not only among ecclesiastical choral establishments, but also in the private sphere[113].

Similar forms of spiritual music were practised also in the Spanish-speaking zones, and could receive the attention of such composers as Guerrero, whose

---

112 De Bertrand 1582.
113 Cf. Brooks 2006, p. 178; van Orden 2006, p. 210.

*Canciones y villanescas espirituales* (1589[114]) show stylistic features very different from those used by the same composer for his Latin-texted output.

In Spain and in its extra-European dominions, however, the musical form of the *villancico* was the most typical and successful among all genres of spiritual music. The genre, as a whole, progressively migrated from the secular to the sacred sphere, to which – after Trent – it remained closely associated. Its success was such that it increasingly overshadowed motets; and though it was a non-liturgical form, it often found its way within official worships. For example, *villancicos* were sung instead of the prescribed Responsories at Matins on Christmas Day, and were created on texts conceived for such important feasts as Epiphany, Corpus Christi (especially in Seville), feasts of Our Lady and public rites such as processions and pilgrimages.

Instrumental accompaniment was typical for *villancicos*, as were their triple-time rhythms with dance-like overtones and homorhythmic settings; another feature which had characterised sixteenth-century *villancicos*, i.e. their refrain structure, became expendable in the following centuries, when the term *villancico* started to merely indicate religious songs in the vernacular, which increasingly made use of polychoral settings. *Villancicos* were even set to native languages of the Latin American Spanish colonies, and a flourishing repertoire of sacred music in the vernacular was composed and performed throughout the zones under Spanish domination[115].

### 9.4.5. Processions and pilgrimages

Among the practices which were common to virtually all Catholic communities, both in Europe and outside it, the rites of pilgrimages and public processions were (and still are, at least in some areas) among the most cherished and beloved by the faithful.

These were normally highly musical events, where musical forms specifically dedicated to individual saints, shrines or feasts intertwined with other forms with a more general profile. A genre which could be sung within the churches, but was particularly well suited to accompany the progress of walking groups was the litany.

We have already seen (cf. § 5.3.5. and 7.2.3.) that litanies were by no means an exclusively Catholic practice, and that new litanies in the vernacular had been

---

114 Guerrero 1589.
115 Cf. Borgerding and Stein 2006, pp. 426, 446–447; Rees 2006, p. 353; O'Regan 2013a, p. 347.

among the first creations of both the Lutheran and the Anglican Reformers. However, within the Catholic field, the reaffirmation of some particular litanies and the downplaying of others represented a clear stance against what the Evangelicals promoted and discouraged in turn: in Alexander Fisher's words, "the litany was perhaps the most insistently 'confessional' form of sounding prayer and music"[116].

So, for example, the Litanies of the Virgin Mary commonly known as *Litaniæ Lauretanæ* (from the shrine of Loreto) became a great favourite in the centuries to come, along with the Litanies of the Saints: both types underpinned the belief in the intercession of the saints and of the Virgin Mary held by the Catholic Church, against the denial of that possibility by Evangelicals. On the other hand, the Marian Litanies *Ex Sacra Scriptura*, whose text was excerpted from the Bible, were less fostered[117]. We will see in Chapter Ten (§ 10.3.7.1.) that occasionally the public open-air dimension of litanies was exploited within the context of confessional opposition and that it could serve as an instrument for the definition of confessional spaces[118].

Even when the public display of sung litanies in processions was not directed against other confessions, it still represented an opportunity for those participating in it to offer a public demonstration of devotion: as we will see later in this Chapter (§ 9.5.4.), this feature was particularly important for confraternities, where a genuine emphasis on spirituality was often linked with a non-negligible social aspect.

Musically, litanies could take several forms: they could be simply recited, or delivered in heightened recitation; they could be chanted or performed in *falsobordone* (chordal heightened recitation), and there were polyphonic settings as well. The first published example of these is represented by the *Litaniæ deiparæ Virginis Mariæ ex Sacra Scriptura depromptæ* written by Costanzo Porta in 1575[119], scored for double choir and conceived for use at the shrine of Loreto; among others, the Loreto litanies were set in polyphony by Orlando di Lasso[120]. Practically all of these forms could be combined with one another, exploiting the call-and-response structure of litanies and contrasting two or more groupings (or the solo/ensemble alternation), often through the use of different compositional strategies and not only of spatial juxtaposition.

---

**116** Fisher 2015, p. 46.
**117** Cf. Fisher 2015, p. 49.
**118** Cf. Fisher 2015, p. 50.
**119** Porta 1575.
**120** Fisher 2015, pp. 71–73.

Since in most cases the simplest forms among those listed above could be sung by the entire congregation, this alternation became a powerful aural and social symbol of communion and inclusiveness. The sound of sung praise literally embraced those participating in the rite, and they could join in singing to express their faith and prayer[121].

Though litanies were by no means the only sung prayers performed during processions and pilgrimages, they were an almost universal feature of these open-air devotions, which could include also Psalms, hymns, *laude*, and even polyphonic motets (which were obviously performed by professional singers), often with a focus on Eucharistic devotional texts, especially in the case of Corpus Christi processions. This point, as Fisher[122] correctly underpins, should not be overlooked: though processions and pilgrimages involved all social layers and were particularly cherished by the poor or illiterate, who could join in singing the simple chants performed, the sung repertoire was often created by the clergy and by a cultivated elite, and thus cannot be considered as an expression of the "common people".

Pilgrimage and processional songs often resulted from contrafacture processes, whereby pre-existing songs, whose tunes were well-known by the faithful, were adapted to suit a particular occasion or to celebrate an individual saint, his or her shrine, and miracles which had happened there. Such texts often show a stress on the communal dimension of prayer and plea, whereas the repertoire of spiritual songs for private devotion discussed above (§ 9.4.3.–4.) focuses on the individual soul's relationship to the sacred.

From the formal viewpoint, many pilgrimage songs are set in responsorial structures, in which the variable part of the text (e.g. that narrating the saint's deeds or the prodigies at the shrine of destination) was sung by a soloist, and the pilgrims joined in singing a formula with invariable text.

In the case of pilgrimages outside town, the itinerary covered by the pilgrims could be long and wearisome: music, then, had the goal of alleviating their burden, as was explicitly recognised by many. For example, in his *Guide for Crusaders, Pilgrims and Procession-makers* (1584), the Tyrolean parish priest Melchior de Fabris affirmed that "When the journey brings to [pilgrims] any difficulty or fatigue, they may comfort themselves with Psalms, canticles, and sacred songs, so that their devotion will be strengthened, and their weariness re-

---

**121** Cf. Kendrick 2009, pp. 21–22 and 46; O'Regan 2009, p. 220; O'Regan 2013a, p. 347; Fisher 2014, pp. 44–45.
**122** Fisher 2014, p. 287.

lieved"[123]. (The reader will recall that a similar function was acknowledged to music by many Evangelical Reformers as well: cf. § 4.2.4.7.).

Processions, in contrast with pilgrimages, were normally less lengthy and demanding, but more solemn; their frequent urban setting permitted to alternate the procession's movement with static moments (e.g. in front of churches), where the participants in the procession could be greeted by music. This was obviously an opportunity for the different ecclesiastical institutions (parishes, abbeys, confraternities) to display and show their specificity in music; thus, on such occasions, professional musicians were hired with the purpose of offering to the incoming faithful an essay of their accomplishment, which thus symbolised aurally the importance of the institution they were representing.

The proportions of such displays of faith could be impressive: a contemporaneous witness reports on a procession in Cremona (1596), in which "Forty-six schools and companies of the Christian Doctrine led the procession, with a great number of boys and girls, who sung the Litanies of the Virgin with great devotion"[124].

On still other occasions, such as Holy Week processions, professional singers could participate in the procession's itinerary; therefore, it was imperative that the type of music which was sung allowed a peripatetic performance. Such was the case of some Passion settings, which could be performed during the rite of the Stations of the Cross: for example, in a version by Gasparo de Albertis (c.1480-c.1560), the multivoiced interventions of the *turba* feature homorhythmic settings which could even be sung from memory[125].

Similarly to what happened during processions, also on a church's feast day, and/or on special solemnities, even those institutions which did not normally have a permanent choir or vocal ensemble turned to hired professionals to celebrate with splendour their holiday.

Such public events represented a beautiful opportunity for people of all social classes and education to listen to music, sometimes of the highest level: analogously to the visual artworks displayed in the churches for the benefit of all faithful, these musical performances were offered both to God and to all believers regardless of their provenance, wealth or culture.

A favourite occasion for music of a particularly solemn style was the celebration of Vespers, particularly in the post-Tridentine era, when Psalms and *Magni-*

---

[123] De Fabris 1584, fols. 60$^v$-61$^r$ (see http://bit.ly/2bdc9P8); translated into English in Fisher 2014, p. 316.
[124] Quoted in Kendrick 2009, p. 45, my translation.
[125] Cf. Ongaro 2006, p. 68; O'Regan 2009, p. 220; O'Regan 2013a, p. 351; Fisher 2014, pp. 18, 277, 287 and 296.

*ficat* canticles started to be set to increasingly complex music, often in polychoral settings, whereas the opening hymns were characterised by a normally soberer style, and by allusions to their plainsong model.

### 9.4.6. In the sphere of spirituality

Though the Catholic Church was perhaps slower and less enthusiastic than several Evangelical confessions in employing music as a means for conveying religious instruction and arousing devotion in the laity, it acknowledged the importance of communal singing for these purposes. Religious music was a fundamental part of the spiritual and musical experience of nearly all faithful, who could listen to public ceremonies such as those already discussed, participate in sung rites such as processions, confraternity rites and public devotions, and sing or perform religious music both at home and in educational establishments.

For this latter purpose, collections of *bicinia* and *tricinia* were published with increasing frequency: they often included musical forms reminiscent of those which could be performed within liturgy (such as motets), but the inclusion of spiritual songs and madrigals within their content testifies to the educational and private destination of these books[126].

Properly liturgical settings, such as Mass Ordinaries, could be transcribed for instrumental performance: the process of appropriation of worship music for domestic use is efficaciously described by Coelho and Polk as an itinerary from the liturgical to the secular (by the omission of the sung text), from the fixed-form to an adapted structure (by the transcription of isolated portions of larger settings), and from the idiom of vocal polyphony to that of instrumental music (by the addition of passages typical for the technical characteristics of the instruments in use[127]).

What has been said above, however, needs a few qualifications by way of conclusion of this section of Chapter Nine. The splendour of and high participation in public ceremonies such as processions and pilgrimages must not overshadow the overall tendency to the "privatisation" of piety and devotion which characterised modernity from its early years until the postmodernity we are living in; the undeniable importance of music in the congregational life of

---

[126] Cf. Rorke 1984, p. 174; O'Regan 2006, pp. 83 and 90; Forney 2010, p. 101; O'Regan 2013a, pp. 338, 344–345 and 352.
[127] Coelho and Polk 2006, p. 540.

Catholics must not eclipse the patent difference between the meaning of communal singing for several Evangelical confessions and the less frequent and less common occasions on which Catholics could express their faith in music. Moreover, the diverse approaches to worship by the different Churches should be once more pointed out: Luther maintained some liturgical structures of the Catholic tradition but reinterpreted the role of the congregation so that it could express its belief in music and interact with the pastors; Calvin reshaped worship and gave pre-eminence to congregational psalmody; in the Catholic Church, the most frequent opportunities for the laity to sing their faith remained outside the liturgy of the Mass (though congregational hymns could be admitted within Eucharistic worship, as seen before: § 4.3.7.1.).

Similarly, and though religious singing at home was a common feature in the spirituality of most Western Churches, it must be stressed that forms of domestic worship such as the Lutheran *Hausandacht* were not correspondingly fostered by the Catholics; hymn-collections similar to those issued by the Lutherans, when edited by Catholics, were conceived for use in public rather than for home devotion. (Ironically, while congregational singing from hymnbooks has become a symbol for Lutheran worship, in the sixteenth century it was more likely for Catholic rather than Evangelical songbooks to be used primarily in church than at home).

On the other hand, as Prodi has correctly observed, the success of publications such as collections of spiritual madrigals for private devotion underpins some important religious and social trends of the era. The increasingly subjective and intimate settings of spiritual music for private devotion pointed out a transition of individual piety from the communal to the domestic, and from the pervasive presence of religious music on all occasions of daily life to the allocation of specific times and places for personal devotion[128].

As Rasmussen suggests, early modern religiosity is characterised by "a definite abandonment of the official corporate life of the Church as the ordinary vehicle for the faith-life of the believer. What replaced it is called 'spirituality'"[129]. Though this could be in several instances more genuine, heartfelt and sincere than some communal expressions of faith which characterised the religious experience of the preceding generations, it also represented an impoverishment of the social dimension of faith and of its mystical aspect of communion.

---

[128] Cf. Prodi 2014, pp. 260 and 278; cf. Masetti Zannini 1993, p. 123; Brown 2005, pp. 22 and 160.
[129] Rasmussen 1988, p. 281.

## 9.5. Reforming Catholicism

We have seen so far, in this Chapter, the official initiatives undertaken by the Catholic establishment for the implementation of the Council, and the principal forms taken by Catholic music within liturgy and outside it.

In this second section of the Chapter, I will discuss how music related to the driving forces of Catholic reformation: we will see its connections with post-Tridentine theology and practice, and we will consider how music was seen and exploited by some of the most important Catholic Reformers and by the institutions they created and/or were responsible for.

In the last paragraphs of the preceding section, the uneasy balance between the public and the private sphere of piety, and the cautious and precarious attitude of Catholic leaders towards (musical) forms of devotion characterising the Evangelical Churches have been pointed out. Similar contradictions were by no means the exception. From the one side, we will observe, therefore, a splendid flowering of lay piety in confraternities, oratories, schools and other forms of religious sociability, and the adroit exploitation of the rhetoric and affective power of music both in the grandiose forms taken by Catholic church music between the sixteenth and seventeenth century, and in the persuasive and touching forms of private piety. From the other, a certain prudence about (if not outright distrust of) the emotional power of music remained observable within some areas of the Catholic world. The enthusiastic and pervasive adoption of music by the Lutherans as a means of propaganda, prayer, instruction and consolation was not matched by the Catholic Church as a whole.

Notwithstanding this, and especially at the level of so-called "art music", the recognition of music's capacity to fascinate, move and portray the glorious heavenly Church fostered the composition and performance of an extraordinary repertoire of Catholic sacred music in the post-Tridentine era. An increasing tendency to "theatrical" forms of affective involvement likened music to preaching, and some of the cleverest among the Catholic Reformers were no less enthusiastic than Luther in employing music for their devotional activities. Thus, it is only from the overall consideration of the Catholic perspective that its relative caution in comparison with other realities can be observed[130].

---

[130] Cf. Borgerding 1998, p. 595; Rainoldi 2000, pp. 347 and 353; Wagner Oettinger 2001, pp. 70, 86 and 87; O'Regan 2006, p. 90; Lindberg 2010, p. 344; O'Regan 2013a, p. 353.

### 9.5.1. The theological framework

As concerns the role of music in Catholic worship, its post-Tridentine conception derived from the main theological statements of the Council, such as its underpinning of the *ex opere operato* value of the sacraments and of their objective reality. As Prodi[131] points out, the multiple ways in which rituality was used and empowered after Trent are – at the same time – complementary and contradictory. They included an increasingly formalistic approach: since the validity of liturgies and sacraments depended only on their proper performance, it became crucial to codify precisely what was necessary for their correct execution. Moreover, the role of the clergy was stressed: it was on their proper actions that the sacramental life of the Church depended, and in parallel with the attempts to reform the education, behaviour and sanctity of Catholic priests, their social role was emphasised. A secondary consequence of this attitude, for Church music, was that the outward and apparent substance of rituality gained momentum (and was symbolised precisely by this attention to the ritual details and to the role of priests). Thus (and in parallel with the blossoming Baroque aesthetics, with its taste for splendour and its attention to the affective/sensuous dimension of spirituality) music increasingly acquired the role of an embellishment and a rhetoric empowerment of worship.

The theological perspective of the Council had important effects also on Catholic architecture, at least locally and within particular contexts, and some of them impacted in turn on music. The attention of Catholic theology toward the Eucharist (with the restatement of beliefs such as those in the transubstantiation and in the real presence) fostered a new focus on the altar, as the locus in which the sacrifice of Mass was performed. Thus, in several Catholic churches where a religious community was present, the choir stalls were moved from before the altar to behind it. The organ followed this replacement of the choir and was relocated in turn in a lateral zone of the presbytery; both choir and organ could be doubled symmetrically by a second instrumental and vocal grouping on the other side of the presbytery. As Mischiati correctly observes[132], this rearrangement of the church space had consequences on music: first of all, it emphasised the distinction between the plainchant-singing clergy and the professional singers performing more elaborate settings; secondly, the large choirbooks which used to be positioned in between the two halves of the choir were definitively replaced by partbooks.

---

[131] Rainoldi 2000, p. 361.
[132] Cf. Mischiati 1993, pp. ix-x; Mischiati 1995, pp. 21–22. Cf. Leaver 2006, p. 373.

Several of the new Catholic churches, moreover, were large buildings with highly resonant acoustics, which, from the one side, increased the aural effect of the performed music, and, from the other, influenced the kind and style of the musical works and performances, favouring (both acoustically and aesthetically) the qualities of grandiosity, splendour and brilliancy over restraint and moderation.

Here too, however, generalisations are helpful but also dangerous, as they cannot faithfully mirror the variety of the spiritual experiences and approaches, of the manifold realities and of the geographical and social diversity in the post-Tridentine Church. In order to attempt at least to give the feeling of this multiplicity, I will now introduce some of the most significant spiritual experiences of Catholic Reformation, and discuss how music was considered and made use of within their framework.

### 9.5.2. The Jesuits and music: forbidden, admitted, promoted

Though the most extensive, thorough and influential use of music for religious purpose by a Catholic order was probably that of the Congregation of the Oratory (which will be discussed later: § 9.5.3. and following), it was the Order of the Jesuits which came to be most closely identified with the Catholic Reformation and the Counter-Reformation. And, indeed, within the relationship to music of the Society of Jesus one can observe, as if in miniature form, the same contradictions and complexity we have noted within Catholicism as a whole.

Both in the attitude of its founders and in its overall policy, the Society of Jesus displayed a twofold approach to music: caution and limitations from the one side, enthusiasm and creativity from the other. These two aspects were partially separated from one another chronologically, since the alliance between Jesuits and music grew increasingly as the history of the Order progressed; however, they were also distinct as to the subjects involved, since the restrictions on music concerned its use by the members of the Society themselves, whereas the exploitation of the affective, pastoral and propagandistic role of music was directed mostly to the laity to whom the Order addressed its efforts.

#### 9.5.2.1. The first Jesuits and the unsung Office

Interestingly, however, the initial cautions and limitations against music were not motivated by a mistrust of music by the founders, or by a lack of musicianship and appreciation of its beauty: indeed, St Ignatius reportedly enjoyed music deeply, and resorted to it in moments of particular suffering as a means of consolation and comfort. The Society's Founder frequently asked a fellow priest, Fr. André Frusius (also known as des Freux, c.1515–1556), to come and play for him the clavichord; and a lay brother sometimes came and sang "devout hymns" for him[133].

It may come as a surprise, therefore, to know that St Ignatius imposed heavy restrictions on the practice of music in the Constitutions regulating the lives of the Order's members. Jesuits not only were exempted from the obligation of singing the office – a duty which was a common feature for religious men and women – but were actually forbidden to do so. This revolutionary and unexpected indication was not without its reasons, since the singing of the Office was felt by many to be an exhausting imposition. Indeed, from a theological viewpoint, there are a variety of vocations within the Church, and the time and energies spent by monks and nuns in prayer are not required by lay people or by religious men and women whose peculiar call is preaching, or caring for the ill, the elderly etc. This does not mean (nor did it mean for Ignatius, whose *Spiritual Exercises* are a summit of Catholic spirituality) to downplay the importance of prayer for all Christians: it was just a matter of how it was celebrated and which features it should possess.

For St Ignatius, music was not indispensable for praying well; and, as he wanted his followers to be entirely dedicated to preaching and to the care of souls, he believed that a good preacher must pray well, but that praying well does not perforce mean praying with music.

Indeed, celebrating the complete Liturgy of the Hours could be trying, especially for those outside monastic life. On occasions, it could even be a counterproductive activity, since its length could become an obstacle to concentration: within the early sources of the Society, the anecdote is recounted of a Cardinal telling Fr. Gerolamo Ottello (1520–1581) that he found the choral celebration of the Hours very distracting, and that "Matins especially, even when not sung, left them so exhausted that they could not apply themselves to anything else"[134].

The prohibition on members of the Society to sing communally the Office was not appreciated by many. Some Jesuits would have liked to perform sung liturgies, and occasionally attempted to establish that practice at their Houses – though both St Ignatius and his successors were strict against local superiors who had allowed this. Sometimes, it was the local population which deemed

---

**133** Cf. *Fontes narrativi* I, p. 636; Culley and McNaspy 1971, p. 216 (this section is indebted to this article); Monson 2006, p. 415.
**134** *LM* 3, p. 600.

it improper, if not outright scandalous, that the Jesuits did not sing: the Rector of the Jesuit College in Prague, Fr. Ursmar de Goisson (1524–1578) wrote in 1556 that "This Bohemian people is very attached to church ceremonies, especially singing, towards which their devotion and affection are such that they think we are a new race and unworthy of the priesthood or of the Christian religion – because we do not sing Vespers and Mass"[135].

Moreover, the ascetic liturgy of the early Jesuits did not appeal to listeners: without any musical splendour, people were not attracted to their services and worships[136]. The greatest problems, however, arose when Pope Paul IV decided to impose the regular celebration of sung Offices on the Jesuits. The contrasting views of the Pontiff and of St Ignatius are perfectly summarised by Culley and McNaspy: "For the founder of the Society, having choir meant being monks, which he was determined that Jesuits not be. For Paul IV, being religious meant having choir"[137].

The encounter between the Pope and the early Jesuits was rather tempestuous, as the protagonists reported soon afterwards:

> With much great commotion [the Pope] reprehend[ed] us first [...] saying that we had been rebellious toward him by not accepting choir; further, that we were helping heretics by this, that he was afraid that some day a devil would appear among us, and that saying the office in choir is an essential matter of religious life and of divine law[138].

Before the Pope could actively intervene and compel the Jesuits to perform something as far from their outlook as polyphony, the followers of St Ignatius decided to forestall the menace and to submit to the lesser evil; the founder himself decided that *falsobordone* singing could represent a passable and acceptable compromise[139].

### 9.5.2.2. A sensible preaching

Though – as we have seen – St Ignatius' view of music for his followers was among the strictest and most restrictive in the entire spectrum of Catholicism, the use of music for spreading the Gospel was perfectly admissible and actively encouraged.

---

135 *LQ* 4, p. 410. English translation by Culley and McNaspy 1971, p. 224.
136 Cf. *Epistolæ Mixtæ* 1900, p. 479. Cf. Culley and McNaspy 1971, p. 219.
137 Culley and McNaspy 1971, p. 225.
138 *LM* 8, p. 673; English translation by Culley and McNaspy 1971, p. 225.
139 Cf. Culley and McNaspy 1971, pp. 217, 223–224; Crook 2009, p. 9.

St Ignatius had fostered the view that the faithful should experience the beauty and goodness of God with their spiritual senses, whose perceptiveness could be both stimulated and channelled by a proper use of the physical senses and of imagination. Thus, in their architecture, in their dramas and in their music, the Jesuits sought to involve the people facing them within a multisensory and fascinating experience of sacred beauty. The use of music for this purpose paralleled, once more, the cultivation of rhetoric: as mentioned earlier in this Chapter (§ 9.5.), a distinctive feature of post-Tridentine Catholic preaching was its tendency to a theatrical approach, which was mirrored by the kind of music and drama associated with it by the Jesuits.

Whereas elsewhere in the Catholic Church an effect of Trent was to foster sobriety and moderation in sacred music, here amazement, fascination and spiritual seduction were actively sought, thus paving the way for the ecstatic and enrapturing spirituality of the Baroque era. These feelings could be aroused either by moving and touching words and music (for example through meditations on Christ's Passion, or through the use of nuptial similes for the relationship between the soul and God) or by the glorious assertion of the triumph of Catholicism over its enemies, which was celebrated with splendid buildings and with equally magnificent musical and theatrical creations.

Here too, however, and even within the Jesuit field, perplexities as to the advisability of such strategies were occasionally voiced. For example, Jeremias Drexel (1581–1638) censored the use of music with too complex and rich features, and Johann Georg Wittweiler (c.1556–1633) condemned a "frivolous" kind of music, "for many will never stop with their pipes and trombones"[140].

Notwithstanding this, the overall orientation of the Society was favourable to music as an instrument for spreading the Gospel: and this applied to their apostolic work at all social and cultural levels. As Filippi puts it, the Jesuits were "eager to handle and experiment with a most diverse range of cultural artefacts", ranging from "the simplest catechetical songs" for the young or uneducated, up to the most refined artworks combining high poetry and complex musical settings[141]. In France, for example, they fostered the publication of spiritual songs in the vernacular: one of the first fruits of this concern is the *Paraphrase des hymnes et cantiques spirituels* (1592[142]), by the French Jesuit Michel Coyssard (1547–1623), whose catechism included (from its second edition on) songs for fa-

---

[140] Both quoted in and translated into English by Fisher 2014, p. 50. Cf. also Hanlon 1961, p. 437; Schmidt 1993, p. 248; Auksi 1995, p. 217; Borgerding 1998, pp. 592–593; Rees 2006, p. 353; Sooy 2006, p. 39; Crook 2009, p. 28; Fisher 2014, pp. 43 and 54.
[141] Filippi 2016a, p. 78.
[142] Coyssard 1592.

cilitating its memorisation and for interiorising its content. As Filippi has recently demonstrated, moreover, the international network of the Society of Jesus started very early to work as a cultural system through which, for example, interesting collections of spiritual lyrics, suitable for setting as madrigals, could be spread and disseminated among Catholic composers[143].

Similar strategies were adopted by Jesuits within diverse geographical areas, and the use of easy forms, analogous to the *laude,* for teaching the holy doctrine was rather common in their colleges and educational institutions: we will see in Chapter Eleven (§ 11.4.4.) numerous examples of these activities in Italy, in Germany and elsewhere, and the very context of that Chapter will suggest interesting parallels between Catholic and Evangelical educational perspectives[144]. Indeed, a remarkable trait of Jesuit activities was their capability to maintain distinctive features, which were common to virtually all of their branches, but – at the same time – to develop a noteworthy ability to adapt the forms taken by their message to the cultural and social reality they were encountering.

### 9.5.2.3. College education

Jesuits soon became famous for the quality of the education they offered to their students in colleges, seminaries and universities: the musical experience within their educational establishments became one of the most fascinating, complex and rich within the Catholic Church, and comprised the sung liturgies (Mass and Hours), religious music as part of the educational and cultural activities, music for catechetic instruction and musical components within the dramatic output of Jesuit colleges[145]. Along with these, music was also practised within the framework of activities such as academic gatherings and public debates, as well as during the encounters of the lay Marian Congregations fostered by the Jesuits. Moreover, music was promoted as a profitable and constructive pastime: for instance, Bellarmine reportedly enjoyed playing music, wrote spiritual poetry suited for musical settings and practised devotional contrafacture[146]. Leitmeir[147] has convincingly demonstrated that the Jesuits of Dillingen actively fostered the creation and publication of a collection of easy and enjoyable three-part compositions. They had observed the spread of this musical form among

---

143 Filippi 2016a, p. 69.
144 Cf. Duhr 1907, pp. 459–460; Strauss 1978, p. 234; Wagner Oettinger 2001, p. 50; Crook 2009, pp. 8 and 10; O'Regan 2009, p. 225.
145 Cf. Leitmeir 2002, pp. 124–125; Körndle 2006, p. 479.
146 Filippi 2016a, p. 74.
147 Leitmeir 2002, pp. 124, 130–132, 138, 145, 149 and 152–153.

the young, and – with a strategy highly reminiscent of those by Luther and other Evangelical Reformers – decided to counter the success of secular and "lascivious" *tricinia* with a repertoire having similar musical features but a sacred content.

Jesuits were careful not only to provide their students with healthy religious music for their spiritual entertainment, but also to avoid unhealthy contaminations. On occasions, it was not sufficient to give their pupils a valid and pleasurable alternative to secular singing, and the presence of "lascivious" music had to be actively countered.

Already in 1575, the Superior General of the Jesuits, Everard Lardinois (also known as Mercurian, 1514–1580) had set down rules for the choice of music to be allowed in Jesuit Colleges, fostering the performance of sacred and liturgical works and prohibiting vacuous music. "Good" music was represented first and foremost by Masses, motets, spiritual songs and hymns – as long as they had not been written by "heretics" and had officially obtained ecclesiastical approval. "Bad" music was that with lewd texts, but also that whose aural features were "vain" or "obscene". Crook[148] has fascinatingly demonstrated how Mercurian's rules were received and enacted, fifteen years later, by the Superiors of the Jesuit College of Munich. Crook's examination of the "prohibited" works (i.e. of the pieces which were deemed to be "obscene" or "vain" by the Jesuit pedagogues) is not only interesting *in se*, but is also fundamental for our understanding of sixteenth-century evaluation of music and of its morality.

In fact, when the objectionable aspect of a musical work is in its text, the reasons for the Jesuits' censorship are obvious even to present-day eyes (for example, erotic madrigals on explicit lyrics). Sometimes, contrafacture permitted pieces originally set to unseemly texts to be "purified" and therefore allowed by the superiors; in other instances, however, the "vanity" and lasciviousness were found in the music itself. This was the case, for example, of works where liturgical plainchant tunes were satirically quoted, or of a motet by Lasso where a Psalm text was irreverently fragmented. The actual listing of the permitted and of the forbidden works is extremely helpful (as is its careful interpretation by Crook) because it sheds some light on the complex debate on "lascivious" music which we have discussed on many occasions so far.

Curiously, however, some of the works whose texts in praise of wine had earned them a place among the forbidden pieces in the Munich catalogue were included and performed within Jesuit plays. Indeed, it is probably within the framework of theatrical activities that music was practised during the first

---

[148] Crook 2009, to which this section is indebted.

(and musically strictest) years of the Society, since – as Pastina wrote – music "was present in the Jesuit theatre from the beginning"[149].

### 9.5.2.4. Performing holiness

Jesuit plays could reach impressive dimensions both as regards the quantity of people involved (up to a thousand actors) and the quality of the contributing artists (among whom Orlando di Lasso[150]).

This attention to quality was by no means exceptional. Indeed, the focus on music which characterised several Jesuit Colleges in the latter decades of the sixteenth century is also shown by the level of some of their music masters: suffice it to say that the first *moderator musicæ* at the Germanic College in Rome was a musician of Victoria's standing, and that some of his successors were chosen from among the leading musical figures in Rome. Indeed, one of the merits of this fruitful interaction between education and music was that it fostered the experimentation of new polychoral solutions, since the appointment of important composers at the College provided students with excellent musical teaching, but also their *moderators* with a high number of trained young singers, with whom elaborate settings could be performed and experimented[151].

Obviously, the quantitative and qualitative dimensions of some Jesuit plays aimed at creating a strong impression on the audience; and if this was conceived as a means of arousing the piety of devout Catholics, it could be even more useful within the framework of confessional opposition.

Indeed, music was seen by the Jesuits not only as a means to help the memorisation of prayers or religious knowledge, but also as an instrument for spreading the Catholic faith and for opposing the competing confessions (which were in turn using music for the same purpose). In Filippi's thought-provoking words, "Vernacular vocal music loomed [...] as a sonic space to be Christianized and Catholicized"[152]. This clearly results from an examination of the Jesuits' musical output within the areas where confessional boundaries were closest or still fluid and contested. We will see in the next Chapter some examples of such musical wars of religion (§ 10.3.7. and following), which are saddening for the separation

---

[149] Pastina 1958, col. 1160.
[150] Cf. Körndle 2006, pp. 479, 482, 486 and 490 (and the entire paper, to which this section is indebted); see also Culley and McNaspy 1971, p. 214.
[151] Cf. O'Regan 2013a, pp. 345–346.
[152] Filippi 2016b, p. 76.

they bear witness to, but also slightly comforting in comparison with other – much bloodier – forms of hostility[153].

### 9.5.2.5. The mission of music

Moreover, music was actively used by the Jesuits within missionary contexts: it could even be said that the geographical and cultural distance in which some of them were working fostered a freer and more creative approach to music. It seems, in other words, that outside Europe the risks of "lascivious" music were less strongly felt, and that music was seen only in its most positive features. Indeed, as Culley and McNaspy rightly point out, the constant attention of Jesuit missionaries for music is singular if one considers the trying (and sometimes extreme) conditions of their daily life[154].

In Japan (1596), for example,

> On the day of Our Lord's Ascension, [...] in order that the feast could be celebrated more solemnly, the Father Rector of the College sent some Brothers to sing Mass with musical instruments. [...] Many came from the villages with music, according with their habit, congratulating each other. During the same feast we gave something to eat to more than five hundred poor people[155].

In Macao, the feast of the Assumption (1595) was celebrated with the performance of a play, depicting "how faith defeated the Japanese oppression", and with "music and vocal accompaniment": as the chronicler reports, "everybody is greatly content"[156].

Sung psalms and catechism sustained the faith of the Japanese Christians not only on festive occasions, but also when facing martyrdom. A touching account of the death of St Paul Miki (c.1556–1597) and his fellows narrates that Anthony, a nine-year old boy who had been crucified, "looked toward heaven and called upon the holy names – 'Jesus, Mary!'. He began to sing a psalm: 'Praise the Lord, you children!' (He learned it in catechism class in Nagasaki. They take care there to teach the children some psalms to help them learn their catechism)"[157].

---

153 Cf. Guillot 1991, p. 75; Hsia 1992, pp. 100 and 101; Leitmeir 2002, p. 127; Carter 2006, p. 45; Monson 2006, p. 416; Weber 2008, pp. 205–206; O'Regan 2013a, p. 345; Fisher 2014, p. 179.
154 Culley and McNaspy 1971, p. 244.
155 Fróis 1599, p. 72, my translation.
156 As quoted and translated in Tang 2016, p. 232 (chronicle dated January 16th, 1596).
157 Bolland and Henschen 1658, vol. I, p. 761. English translation in Wright 1993, p. 35.

In less sad circumstances, in Goa, Indian children had sung polyphonic litanies when the victorious Portuguese had conquered Daman[158] (Damaõ, 1559); a few years later (1565) another missionary reported that the "new Christians greeted us with their drums and cornetts, and though their music was not so good, we liked their goodwill very much. [...] On the day of the Immaculate Conception of Our Lady [...] we invited the Viceroy [...] who came with many nobles of his Court, and Vespers were celebrated with music of his wonderful instruments"[159].

Analogous practices were reported from the Americas: in Brazil (1550s), some of the most important and basic Christian prayers and doctrines had been translated into a native language and set to music with melodies similar to those sung by the natives, and a school of music was inaugurated already in 1553. The year before (1552), a Jesuit missionary wrote from Brazil stating: "Since [the natives] are so fond of all things musical, if we played and sang among them we would win them over"[160]. Works among the most sophisticated of the European polyphonic repertoire coexisted and were performed along with new compositions, where the traditional idioms of polyphony acquired new nuances thanks to the influence of native music[161].

Such practices were applied not only by Jesuits, however: for example, the Franciscan missionary Bernardino de Rivera de Sahagún (1499–1590) composed an impressive *Psalmodia* (1583[162]), whose songs establish meaningful relationships between the basics of the Christian faith and the traditional Aztec culture of Mexico, where he had been sent.

An example of such cross-cultural references is his likening the Christian angels to the image of birds, traditionally employed by the Aztecs to symbolise a shape taken by dead heroes when appearing to mortals[163].

### 9.5.3. Filippo Neri: Laity and *Laude*

If Jesuit and Franciscan missionaries showed remarkable skill and ability in adapting the musical forms of preaching and prayer to local indigenous realities outside Europe, in the very heart of Catholicism the need for a similar approach

---

[158] Kendrick 2009, p. 19.
[159] *Diversi avisi* 1565, p. 292.
[160] In Leite 1956, p. 383, as quoted and translated in Filippi 2016b, p. 364.
[161] Cf. Monson 2006, pp. 417–418.
[162] Sahagún 1583.
[163] Pollmann 2006, pp. 310–311.

was equally felt. In fact, the mission of St Filippo Neri was within the walls of Rome, where both the poor and the most cultivated citizens flocked to the meetings of his Oratory. The variety in the social provenance and in the level of education of those participating in the Oratory's prayers was paralleled by the diversity in the musical repertoire which was practised there: from the simplest monodic *lauda* forms to polyphony.

Though the official Papal approbation for Neri's Congregation came only in 1575, meetings had been taking place for roughly a quarter of a century already. The Oratory – as Prodi[164] points out – represented the symbol for two fundamental realities: it was both the *space* and the *time* of prayer. Spatially, it marked a place which was adjacent to but not identical with the church: it represented sacredness and spirituality, but it was not the *locus* of liturgy. As we have seen, the Council had focused its interventions regarding the form and meaning of prayer exclusively on liturgy, and though the energies bursting out from Trent had promoted and fostered a new attention on piety, it had not been codified or even discussed at the Council. The Oratory, thus, represented a *consequence* of the Catholic Reformation focus on spirituality and piety; however, it was also an *alternative* to Trent's exclusive attention to liturgy, and to the latent risks of dualism inherent within the Council's perspective. In fact, the communal aspect of prayer was identified with liturgical moments – during which, however, the limited participation of the laity did not encourage their perception of the assembly's communion; on the other hand, the spiritual experience of the individual tended to subjectivity and intimacy, and the ecclesial dimension of faith risked being dangerously downplayed.

By providing his followers with a context in which the life of faith could be experienced with other believers but outside the fixed forms of liturgy, Neri created a *locus* which represented a connecting point between the sacred world of liturgy and the secular world of daily life. If – as we have seen in Chapter Eight: § 8.4.3. – one of the tendencies observable in Trent's debates and decrees was to emphasise the sacredness of the sacred, i.e. to restate the importance of ritual purity and clerical sanctity, Neri acted within a different (but complementary) perspective. Of course, he was as concerned as anyone with personal sanctity and the value of liturgy; however, he foresaw the risk of a drastic divarication between an unreachable (and clerical) purity and the daily life of the majority of the believers. Thus, he tried and provided an intersection between the two, in which a genuine and life-changing experience of prayer could be accessible

---

**164** Prodi 2014, p. 48.

to all, and enliven their normal activity (in their jobs, families, spare time) through a profound spirituality.

### 9.5.3.1. From Florence to Rome

Music was an essential component of the Oratory's activities, and it became a powerful tool for enhancing the emotional impact of the Biblical narratives; music acted as the interpreter through which the episodes and the characters of Scripture were presented and re-presented for the pious participants in Neri's meetings. Cardinal Cesare Baronio (or Baronius, 1538–1607) witnessed the "marvellous utility and consolation" brought to listeners by the conjunction of preaching with *lauda* singing at the Oratory, stating that "it seemed that, as much as the present times allow, the ancient apostolic manner had been renewed"[165]. Once more, the path for the true reformation of the Church was found in the recovery of the spirit (if not of the letter) of the apostolic era.

The reasons for Neri's attention to the musical aspect of spirituality were determined not only by his own love for music, but also – at least as importantly – by the influence of the Florentine tradition of *lauda* singing on his own spirituality. Neri had personally participated in *lauda* singing in Florence, in the 1520s, at the Dominican convent of San Marco where Savonarola had fostered this activity and revived the tradition of religious singing; and even in Rome, where Neri's Oratory started its mission, the Florentine community played a crucial role in the establishment and success of his spiritual exercises with music.

Spiritual songs had been a typical feature of the companies of *laudesi* already in the Middle Ages, but that tradition had been rejuvenated, and then particularly cherished and thoroughly practised by Savonarola and his followers. The groups of *piagnoni* (as Savonarola's disciples had come to be known), however, sang only monodic songs: the reader will recall Savonarola's harsh criticism of polyphony discussed in Chapters Two and Three[166]. For the Dominican friar, complex polyphony was distracting, vain and outward; and his endorsement of simple monodic *laude* was perfectly balanced by his severe criticism of polyphony.

Notwithstanding his ascetic and rigorous approach, however, neither Savonarola nor his followers condemned the contrafacture of secular melodies to suit religious texts – and this feature was to be adopted in sixteenth-century Oratorian *lauda*-singing. Indeed, the somewhat hybrid quality of the Oratory – between

---

**165** In Rinaldi 1656, Part I, p. 254.
**166** See § 2.3.5. and 3.3.1.4., 3.3.2.5.–6., 3.3.2.8., 3.3.2.10. etc.

church proper and lay home – fostered the use of secular borrowings and *contrafacta*, within a musical atmosphere which grew freer and freer as time went by.

It should be pointed out, however, that (similar to many Evangelical Reformers) one of the objectives of spiritual *contrafacta* realised by Neri's followers was to supplant their secular models. One of Neri's closest musical collaborators was the Blessed Giovanni Giovenale Ancina (1545–1604), who actively fought against "licentious" music and – allegedly – destroyed a collection of madrigals by Jean de Macque (c.1548–1614) before the composer's eyes.

As reported by Baronius, in the 1570s the fundamental structure of Neri's spiritual exercises at the Oratory had been already established, with readings, homilies and music, though their actual shape varied according to the hour of the day and the period of the liturgical year.

Oratorian *lauda* singing quickly obtained an immense dissemination and success, prompting the publication of *lauda* collections both in Rome and within relatively distant Italian cities such as Turin, Venice and Naples. Among the editors and composers of such collections were Giovanni Animuccia (who issued three volumes within roughly fifteen years, from 1563 on), Francisco Soto de Langa (c.1534–1619), who oversaw the publication of other five volumes, and Giovanni Arascione (1546-a.1589).

The Oratory's *laude* could be monodic and on simple tunes, in the wake of the medieval and Savonarolan tradition, but also in three or four parts, and were set to pre-existing or new pious texts.

Smither helpfully classified the lyrics of early Oratorian *laude* within four main categories: "dramatic dialogues, narrative-dramatic dialogues, narrative-monologues, and narratives"[167]. Notwithstanding this, elements such as supplication and spiritual advice could be common to all categories; in most cases, dramatic elements such as dialogues or – at least – monologues were found, and only rarely was the direct speech of one or more characters entirely replaced by third-person narrative[168].

Some of Animuccia's *laude* borrow from the compositional style of the *canzonetta*, and their three-part settings often contrast two high-pitched voices with a lower one: his compositional strategies are particularly interesting inasmuch as they pave the way for the *concertato* motets. The complexity in the vocal settings which Animuccia's *laude* could reach is witnessed by the rich eight-part

---

[167] Smither 1969, pp. 189–190.
[168] Cf. Koenigsberger 1986, p. 194; Monson 2006, pp. 413–414; O'Regan 2006, p. 87; Rees 2006, p. 354; Fenlon 2009, pp. 208–209 and 213; O'Regan 2009, p. 226; Bizzarini 2012, pp. 18–19; O'Regan 2013a, p. 345; Prodi 2014, pp. 31 and 48.

texture employed in his second *lauda* collection (Animuccia 1570), though the clear perception of the text was always actively sought by the composer. This publication, furthermore, included Latin motets alongside vernacular works, and their openness to compositional experimentation is testified by the presence of polychoral attempts. As I briefly mentioned earlier in this Chapter (§ 9.4.3.), Animuccia – whose Florentine origins probably were one further element of proximity between Neri and himself – was consciously trying new compositional styles for the benefit of the participants in the Oratory's spiritual exercises. The composer also emphasised his quest for a refined and innovative musical idiom, which would satisfy the musical tastes of the educated without becoming incomprehensible or unattractive for the average listener. His attempts, however, were principally due to the need for a kind of music which would appeal to the noble and cultivated audience which had begun to flock to Oratory devotions. Animuccia summed up his efforts by stating:

> The said oratory having been expanded [...] with a concourse of prelates and of the most important gentlemen, it seemed to me appropriate in this second book to increase the harmony and the number of voices in concert, varying the music in diverse ways, now with Latin words and now with vernacular; now with more voices, now with fewer; sometimes with one type of verse, other times with another; interfering as little as possible by means of imitation or inventions, so as not to obscure the meaning of the words in order that their effectiveness, with the aid of the harmony, might penetrate more sweetly the hearts of those who listened. And many wise and devout people told me that they were highly moved to devotion when these *laudi* are sung[169].

Soto de Langa's third collection of three- and four-part *Laudi spirituali* (1588[170]) was significantly dedicated to Federigo Borromeo: in this and in similar cases, both text and music are deliberately simple, with a constant use of homorhythmic textures paralleled by the choice of regularly strophic poetic forms[171].

We can observe here, thus, as in several of the religious and musical experiences recounted before, that many Catholic Reformation movements were associated with the exploration of new musical languages by the union of a creative approach to spirituality with the active quest for new (or renewed) ways in which it could be both expressed and fostered. The closeness between such experiments and those characterising several contemporaneous Evangelical confes-

---

[169] Animuccia 1570; English translation by and in O'Regan 2006, p. 80, with integrations by myself.
[170] Soto 1588.
[171] Cf. Haar 2006, pp. 235–237; Weber 2008, p. 202; O'Regan 2009, pp. 226–228; Bizzarrini 2012, p. 9.

sions is striking, and seems to demonstrate how spiritual reform intertwined with musical creativity.

### 9.5.4. Brethren in Christ: The Confraternities

After the religious and musical efforts of both Jesuits and Oratorians, another distinctive trait for post-Tridentine Catholicism must be briefly mentioned, i.e. that of confraternities. A common feature associating these three realities was that they fostered the dynamic participation of the laity in their activities; though their spiritual leaders were normally members of the clergy, lay involvement was actively sought and promoted, and was mirrored by the kind of music performed.

Indeed, participation in the Sunday Mass was a distinguishing feature of any "good" Catholic, and – though beautiful music could be one of the elements appealing to the faithful and leading them to one church instead of another – it was not the determining factor for their going to church.

Participation in a confraternity's activity, or in a Jesuit or Oratorian gathering, instead, was a free choice. Thus, while the overall concept of liturgical music was primarily oriented to the embellishment of worship "for God", the music performed within optional religious meetings was conceived primarily "for the audience", and had an active role in attracting them to the encounters. (This function, with a special focus and concern for the young, is pointed out by an early biographer of Carlo Borromeo, who wrote of "songs [...] used during the service to arouse devotion and to attract the people, especially the young"[172]). This is one reason why Catholic music not intended for liturgy is closer (in both shape and concept) than liturgical works to the music of several Evangelical confessions: the common focus of Evangelical music and of Catholic non-liturgical music on the laity favoured the appearance of structural similarities between the two.

One specificity of confraternities in comparison with the spiritual experiences of lay followers of Jesuit and Oratorian spirituality was their public and outward dimension. Participation in the spiritual life of a confraternity did not only bring spiritual benefits to its members both in the present life and posthumously, but it also represented a mark of belonging and a source of corporative pride.

This feature was mirrored by the musical aspect of confraternity life, in which the three dimensions of sacred music (for God, for participants and for listeners) were very closely interrelated.

---

[172] In Bascapè 1592, Book I, Chapter X, p. 36 (sig. E2ʳ); as translated in Filippi 2015a.

Confraternities had a complex system of rites, some of which aimed primarily at fostering the holiness of their members (both individually and corporately), whereas others were firstly conceived as a public display (for example processions).

Processions were a core element within the life of a confraternity, and were held on a variety of occasions, such as – for example – the patron saint's feast-days, Lent, Holy Week or Corpus Christi ceremonies, visitations by ecclesiastical authorities, but also for events more immediately connected with social life (such as the greeting of pilgrims or the participation in pilgrimages). On many such occasions, the participation of professional musicians was almost compulsory for guaranteeing a proper representation of the confraternity's importance for observers.

The processional repertoire of confraternities varied – obviously – from one to another, and depended on the economic and human resources of the group, as well as on its purposes. The quality of the music which hired professionals could provide was clearly different, normally, from that offered by the confreres. Generally speaking, however, the genres listed in our previous discussion of procession music (cf. § 9.4.5.) were also those typical for confraternity processions, ranging from the simplest *lauda*-like forms to polyphonic motets in Latin.

Members of some confraternities were required by their statutes to sing some particular forms of devotional music besides participating in the official liturgies. For example, in Como, the spiritual/musical programme of a Confraternity is summarised in a distich: "Let the tongue sing praises, hymns, songs of jubilation and love / and let the heart answer to these"[173].

Indeed, as O'Regan justly points out, the undeniable public dimension of confraternity life should not overshadow the equally important and genuine component of piety: actually, the goal of setting up a magnificent feast in God's honour was not considered as being in latent contradiction with the purpose of demonstrating the confraternity's own magnificence[174].

If singing at the feasts organised by the confraternities was an important source of income for musicians, many of them were in turn members of one or more of such organisations: actually, there were even confraternities of musicians, such as the *Compagnia dei Musici*, officially approved in 1585. Some members of that pious gathering joined their creative forces to compose a Mass for three choirs, the *Missa Cantantibus organis Cæcilia*, which was most likely intended to be a musical homage to the patron saint of musicians.

---

[173] Quoted in Rainoldi 2000, p. 360, my translation.
[174] O'Regan 2013a, p. 352.

This joint initiative is a meaningful symbol of the power of confraternities to create a bond, a feeling of alliance and brotherhood among their members, motivated by their common devotion and by their sharing of the same profession: once more, it was an important and successful attempt to bridge the distance between liturgy and daily life, which was to become one of the key challenges for Catholicism in the modern era[175].

Spiritual gatherings with music within the framework of confraternities had also a clear confessional connotation, and sometimes represented an explicit response to Evangelical practices, doctrines or trends. A particular form of confraternity devotion was the adoration of the Blessed Sacrament which took place during forty consecutive hours (the *Quarant'Ore*). While the origins of this practice have been traced back to Milan, its great flowering took place in Rome (mainly thanks to the Jesuits and Oratorians) but it was popularly encouraged in many other Catholic contexts: its forceful reaffirmation of the doctrine of transubstantiation and of the real presence represented an unambiguous challenge to the Protestant denial of one or more of these beliefs.

The *Quarant'Ore* devotion was also fostered in Florence, and Nils Holger Petersen has fascinatingly studied its role within the spirituality of the *Compagnia dell'Arcangelo Raffaello*, a *laudesi* confraternity (with ties to the Dominicans) of young boys. The *Compagnia* used to provide a splendid setting for its *Quarant'Ore* devotion, investing considerable economic resources for the creation of a magnificent visual display and of an involving and immersive musical experience. From the viewpoint of music history, such initiatives are particularly interesting since they created the cultural background for the first operatic experiments; from the viewpoint of Church history, they underpin the close interrelation between dogmatic/confessional issues (the Catholic view of the Eucharist), pastoral/educational concerns (focus on the spirituality of the young), and a clever use of multisensorial experiences for the promotion of devotion and piety[176].

---

**175** Cf. O'Regan 1994, p. 556; Rainoldi 2000, p. 359; Forney 2006, p. 255; O'Regan 2006, p. 81; O'Regan 2009, p. 220; O'Regan 2013a, pp. 350–351; Fisher 2014, p. 17.
**176** See Østrem and Petersen 2008 and Petersen 2012. Cf. also Eisenbichler 1998, on the importance of this confraternity for the social and religious life of the city, and for the role played by its devotional practices for the development of the musical language and forms (for instance, Jacopo Peri [1561–1633], Giulio Caccini [c.1550–1618] and several members of the Florentine academies had close links with the *Compagnia*).

## 9.6. Catholic music locally

After having discussed the overall aesthetic and theological trends of the post-Tridentine Catholic music in the first part of this Chapter, and the use and experience of music within some particular religious realities in its second section, we will now move on to a brief survey of how post-Tridentine Catholic music was experienced locally.

Once more, I wish to stress that no comprehensiveness should be expected from such a survey: my only aim is to provide the reader with some significant examples of the rich geographical and musical variety found in the Catholic Church of the late sixteenth century.

This survey will start from Italy, where many elements of interest can be observed: from the very presence of the papacy to the great diversity prompted by different forms of ruling and competing ecclesiastical and civil authorities, not forgetting the presence of one of the liveliest milieus of artistic creativity, patronage, cultural speculation and international relationships.

### 9.6.1. Chapels and patrons

Throughout the Italian peninsula, the sixteenth century saw the birth and flourishing of numerous musical Chapels, sponsored by individual collegiate churches, cathedrals and even minor ecclesiastical realities. This phenomenon is connected by Piperno[177] with the increasing divarication in the respective interests of church and civil authorities during the sixteenth century, bringing out the necessity for the Church to affirm itself, on the local plane, and sometimes in competition with lay rulers, as an active subject in the cultural life.

On the other hand, it is rather at the level of less important churches, as well as of the institutes of religious life, that the creation of musical Chapels had a more spiritual quality and a less pronounced political dimension.

When a Chapel was connected to a canonical Chapter, it frequently had a more pronounced clerical mark, whose distinguishing traits are identified by Mischiati[178] as including the clerical provenance of the singers, the connection with an educational establishment, and the physical collocation of the singing body within the choir stalls proper.

---

[177] Piperno 2008, p. 205; cf. also p. 204.
[178] Mischiati 1993, p. vii.

In the case of Chapels sponsored by churches entrusted to the secular (i.e. non-regular) clergy, it was much more common, instead, for the musicians to be lay professionals, who were permanently employed by the ecclesiastical establishment.

Musical ensembles whose main (or even exclusive) focus was on sacred music could also be employed by lay rulers. Their Chapels were normally not provided with schools for children (and consequently had to employ adult male singers also for the high-pitched parts); on the other hand, their connection with civil social life and its requirements implied their close interaction with instrumentalists. Such Chapels had thus a twofold role: from the one side, to represent aurally (and often visually too) the power, importance, wealth and diplomatic weight of their employer; from the other, to symbolise the ruler's commitment to the spiritual welfare and religious life of his or her subjects[179].

Of course, patronage was not limited to civil potentates, and was often practised, with regard to music, by ecclesiastical establishments (as seen before), but also by individual authorities. One such leader was Cardinal Giulio Feltrio della Rovere, whose deep interest in and strong support of music has been carefully traced and narrated by Morucci[180].

Coming from one of the most powerful Italian aristocratic families, whose rule and/or influence reached to such important centres as Urbino, Ravenna and Loreto, Cardinal Giulio was actively engaged in the spiritual climate following Trent (though it is uncertain whether he actually took part in the Council or its discussions). As the Protector of the Holy House of Loreto (a shrine to which Bernardino Cirillo had been closely linked), he issued a manual regarding liturgy and its music (*Constitutiones almæ Domus*, 1576), which has been counted among the most representative examples of post-Tridentine aesthetics and spirituality[181]. In his role as the Archbishop of Ravenna, he endorsed a thorough reform of liturgical music, including virtually all of the main points of the post-Tridentine view on sacred music: prohibitions on "lascivious" music and instrumental accompaniments, fostering of intelligibility and creation of seminaries where, as we have seen, young clerics received a careful musical instruction, whose results Giulio Feltrio wanted to ascertain personally.

That Giulio Feltrio was not inclined to delegating musical matters to his subordinates is also shown by his interaction with Costanzo Porta, which has already been mentioned in passing above (§ 9.3.5.1.). Porta asserted that his Masses

---

**179** Mischiati 1993, pp. vii-ix; Piperno 2008, p. 203.
**180** Morucci 2012, to which this section is indebted.
**181** Cf. Verstegen 2007, p. 90.

had been composed, on Giulio's requirements, in an intelligible fashion, being "easy, [...] short and [...] melodious"[182].

### 9.6.2. Milan: Reforming from the roots

In terms of active cooperation between ecclesiastical leaders/patrons and musicians, of the connection between spiritual renewal and pastoral actions involving music, and of the preference shown for a sober and almost ascetical aesthetic perspective, della Rovere was both close and indebted to the viewpoint of Carlo Borromeo, the Cardinal Archbishop of Milan.

We have already frequently met with this protagonist of the Catholic Reformation on a variety of occasions (including his membership of the Cardinals' Commission): I will now recall his main contributions to post-Tridentine music, discussing his own experience and that of his archdiocese, as well as his influence on many other ecclesiastical contexts of the era, and on the artistic output of musicians such as Matteo Asola, Biagio Pesciolini, Vincenzo Ruffo as well as that same Costanzo Porta who worked closely with della Rovere.

One of the major Italian cities, and the heir of an august (and somehow idiosyncratic) tradition dating back to St Ambrose' times, Milan was a cultural centre in which music played a crucial social role in the sixteenth century[183].

Carlo Borromeo, who was an amateur musician himself, intervened energetically in the musical field – as indeed in most others: as listed by a seventeenth-century biographer, he improved the quality of church music by augmenting the quantity of performers (and their salaries), he interfered on the style of polyphonic music favouring "devotion" over "delectation", censored the presence of instruments other than the organ in church music, and connected the topics of church music and clerical morality by requesting of singers both an exemplary life and to belong to the clergy. He also promoted the use of music as a tool for drawing the laity to worship and devotional activities, with the double purpose of promoting the spiritual life in his diocese and diminishing the appeal of secular entertainments[184].

Indeed, the devotional experience of the Cardinal himself was nourished by music[185]: it is reported that motets (among others, by Lasso) were sung during the hour Borromeo dedicated daily to prayer. When, on one such occasion, the

---

[182] Florence, Archivio di Stato; Archivio di Urbino, filza 88, fol. 187ʳ. Cf. in Sherr 1984, p. 77.
[183] Cf. in particular Kendrick 2002 and Getz 2005.
[184] Giussano 1855, pp. 126–127 (Book II, Chapter IX).
[185] See Filippi 2013 for a thorough exposition on this topic.

Cardinal was the object of an attempted murder, he asked the singers to continue their performance, so that the sung prayers could be concluded regularly[186]. As Filippi remarks, this is evidence of Borromeo's inclusion of motets within his concept of "spiritual entertainment"[187].

Between January and March 1565 – the very year the Cardinals' Commission was established – Borromeo frequently wrote to his vicar, Nicolò Ormaneto (c.1515–1577), on topics regarding the reform of church music: seemingly, his main concerns at the time were about the intelligibility of polyphonic works. As mentioned earlier (§ 9.3.6.), Borromeo urged Ruffo to send him a sample of "clear" liturgical music, first a motet and then Masses; the "post-Tridentine" output of the composer eventually resulted in the publication of such Mass collections as that of 1570. The aesthetic approach encouraged by Borromeo and put into practice by his Chapel Master is marked by the sacrifice of imitations and diminutions in favour of a homorhythmic and syllabic style, which drew on the experience of earlier composers but acquired, within this context, the status of a musical manifesto[188].

Borromeo, however, did not enlist the cooperation of Ruffo only: he also prompted Nicola Vicentino ("don Nicola of the Chromatic music", as the Cardinal defined him) to compose a Mass in his own style, so that the comparison of the two might give grind to the mill of the Cardinals' judgment.

At the same time, Borromeo demonstrated his interest in devotional music as well: in a fashion strikingly similar to Luther's invitation to the German poets (cf. § 5.3.2.2.), Borromeo appealed to the lyricists of his time, hoping they would write "words on spiritual and devout subjects", thus creating a "collection of decent madrigals such that every good man can sing them"[189].

Borromeo's success in encouraging a true spiritual reform within his diocese and outside its boundaries, also by means of music, cannot be denied: however, and rather ironically, most of his initiatives (both in music and as concerns the whole of religious life) achieved their greatest accomplishments precisely when they embodied only the spirit of the Council while sacrificing fidelity to the letter of its pronouncements. The strength of Borromeo's personality and of his rather

---

**186** *Relatione* 1570, fol. A3ᵛ; see also Anfosso 1913, p. 241, as translated in Filippi 2015a.
**187** Filippi 2015a. I am grateful to Daniele V. Filippi for sharing this paper with me.
**188** Cf. Lockwood 1970, p. 131; Lockwood 1975, p. 20; Rorke 1984, p. 172; Mischiati 1995, pp. 20 – 21; Rainoldi 2000, pp. 346 – 347; Rees 2006, p. 351; Lejeune 2010, p. 23; Campione 2011, p. 244; Bizzarini 2012, p. 8.
**189** Letter to Ormaneto, March 31ˢᵗ, 1565; as quoted in and translated by Lockwood 1970, p. 94. Cf. also Leichtentritt 1944, p. 324; Lockwood 1966, pp. 48, 50, 53; Lockwood 1975, p. 20; Rorke 1984, p. 173; Ghiglione 1986, pp. 1014 – 1015; Rainoldi 2000, p. 346, fn. 36; Weber 2008, p. 203.

idiosyncratic interpretation of the Council, in other words, obtained the greatest results for the post-Tridentine Church especially when they did not correspond too closely to the Council's decrees. Thus, for example, the later identification of Trent's influence on music with the issue of intelligibility largely depended on the stress laid by Borromeo on this subject[190].

As we have just observed, the other topic on which Borromeo's efforts focused in relation to music was the morality of the clergy. Since he strongly advocated clerical status for church singers, his attempts to prune unbecoming elements from sacred musical works should be interpreted, once more, within the framework of the overall moralisation of the clergy which characterised the interventions of many Catholic reformers after Trent[191].

Of course, the moralisation of pastors was merely intended as the first step towards the improvement in morals and holiness of the entire society. As concerns the laity, for example, people were attracted to evening services at Santa Maria presso san Celso by the sacred works of an appreciated madrigalist such as Simon Boyleau (fl. 1544–1586). At first, the same strategy was applied by Borromeo (different from other prelates) as concerned the Milanese nuns: their music was seen as a powerful means for captivating the hearers and for encouraging their attendance at sacred services. Later, however, Borromeo's attitude became increasingly strict, and resulted in some heavy limitations on musical activities in the female monasteries, especially when these involved interaction with the outside world[192] (see § 12.4.3.2.).

It is true that Cardinal Federigo Borromeo's perspective on many issues was indebted to that of Carlo, his cousin and predecessor as Archbishop of Milan; however, in several aspects – among which precisely that of the nuns' musicality – he adopted a different and somewhat gentler stance than Carlo's.

Indeed, Federigo's approach to reforming the Catholic Church was conditioned by Filippo Neri's style at least as much as it was by Carlo Borromeo's. During the 1580s, in fact, Federigo took part in the spiritual activities of the Oratory in Rome, and even chose Neri as his father confessor. At the *Oratorio della Vallicella*, Federigo could not fail to become familiar with *lauda* singing (Francisco Soto even dedicated to him his third collection of *laude*, published in 1588); he also experienced the usefulness of pious contrafacture exploring the whole expressive and sentimental array of secular music for spiritual purposes.

---

[190] Cf. Haar 2006, p. 32; Monson 2006, p. 404; Fenlon 2009, p. 202; O'Regan 2009, p. 215; Prodi 2014, p. 73.
[191] Cf. Lockwood 1966, p. 53; Koenigsberger 1986, p. 187; Getz 2001, pp. 155 and 168; O'Regan 2006, p. 77; Fenlon 2009, pp. 201–202.
[192] Cf. Kendrick 1996, pp. 17, 57, 60–62, 67–68; Getz 2001, p. 152; Macy 2011, p. 350.

The effectiveness of this strategy was employed, in the first decade of the seventeenth century, by Aquilino Coppini, who – on Federigo's request[193], and as briefly mentioned in § 9.4.3. – collected madrigals and secular works by Claudio Monteverdi and other famous composers of the era, and "spiritualised" them, not only adapting their lyrics to sacred subjects, but rather intervening on their features so that their emotional power could be channelled in the service of spirituality. As Coppini himself put it, "There is [in Monteverdi's madrigals] a wonderful power to move the passions exceedingly"[194]; the goal of this undertaking was – again in Coppini's words – to "clothe music with spiritual words, so that God and his Saints be praised in churches and private houses"[195].

Between "churches and private houses", however, Coppini failed to mention another crucial context where spiritual madrigals were employed upon active encouragement by Federigo Borromeo, i.e. that of female convents. Convinced as he was of the power of music to move and of its mystical potentialities, he positively encouraged the nuns' musicianship: whereas this was seen as a potentially disruptive and sinful activity by other prelates, Federigo understood it as a means for fostering the religious women's holiness, in a process where they played an active and conscious role. Indeed, Federigo himself recounted to a nun his first-hand experience of how touching the music by composers such as Luzzasco Luzzaschi (c.1545–1607) could be; this direct knowledge may have paved the way for his understanding of music within the framework of mystical contemplation[196].

### 9.6.3. Rome: Splendour and spirituality

While the Milanese scene was dominated by such figures as those of the Borromeos, in Rome the situation was slightly different. Paradoxically, and notwithstanding the presence of the Pope, the religious musical panorama in Rome was more shaded and less unified by the controlling figure of the spiritual leader. In fact, besides the Pope, Rome housed many other powerful authorities (such as the Cardinals of the Curia, or many leaders of religious orders),

---

**193** Cf. Banchieri 1628, p. 120; see also Sartori 1952, p. 405.
**194** Coppini, letter of July 1609 to Hendrik van der Putten (also known as Erycius Puteanus, 1574–1646); as quoted in Fabbri 1985, pp. 152–153.
**195** Coppini 1608; quoted in Vogel 1887, p. 428. Cf. Rorke 1984, pp. 170 and 174; Kendrick 1996, p. 73; Kendrick 2006, pp. 342 and 345; Rainoldi 2000, p. 340; Bizzarini 2012, pp. 8–9.
**196** Cf. Kendrick 2006, pp. 339, 343–344; Macy 2011, p. 350; Bizzarini 2012, pp. 35–36; Monson 2012, pp. 4, 15, 20–21, 28.

whose spheres of influence might collide, and whose concept and promotion of music could noticeably differ.

Ecclesiastical patronage flourished thanks to members of the Curia who often were relatives of the Popes; musical Chapels multiplied, also due to the high number of confraternities active in the city; new religious orders such as the Jesuits, the Oratorians and the Theatines made ample use of music for their services and spiritual exercises; popular religiosity often expressed itself in music, in the form of *sacre rappresentazioni* and processions (which increased exponentially in correspondence with the Jubilee of 1575); and, of course, the Papal Chapels continued to attract some of the best musicians of the era and to offer some of the most refined music one could hear in Europe[197].

Under the direction of Palestrina and Animuccia, the Cappella Giulia knew a perhaps unprecedented splendour, thus somehow realising the wishes of Pope Gregory XIII, who intended it to become an example and a model for all other (Catholic) churches "in the entire world" [198].

It is therefore all the more significant that both Papal Chapels maintained in their repertoire several sacred works on secular *cantus firmus* or polyphonic models, well after the Council and its ban on "lascivious" music: works such as Masses on *La Castagnia* or *Ultimi miei sospiri*, as well as *En doleur en tristesse* by Noel Bauldeweyn (c.1480–1529), *Je suis déshéritée* by Nicolas de Marle (fl. around 1550), and possibly the *Missa Le villain jaloux* by Antoine de Févin (c.1470–c.1511) were copied and performed by the Papal singers until the late 1570s. Once more, this suggests that there was no crusade against such compositional practices, and that their later abandonment was not only or not just a consequence of an alleged prohibition by the Council, but rather – or at least partly – a result of an evolving taste.

The situation changed substantially in the second half of the 1580s, when the retrospective and pre-Tridentine repertoire of the Papal musicians was absorbed by new and "post-Tridentine" trends, with the figure and works of Palestrina taking progressively hold of the Roman scene[199].

Since the aim of this book is not to provide a "history of music" in the traditional sense, and even less to discuss thoroughly (or even satisfactorily) the great composers of the era, I will not attempt a survey of Palestrina's output, which cannot be done in a few lines or pages, and for which so many excellent studies

---

[197] Cf. Morelli 1993, pp. 175 and 178; O'Regan 2006, pp. 76–77 and 81; O'Regan 2009, pp. 216 and 228; O'Regan 2013a, p. 351.
[198] *Collectio Bullarum* 1752, vol. 3, pp. 113–117. Cf. Rostirolla 1993, p. 42 and p. 47.
[199] Cf. Sherr 1978, pp. 93–94; Borromeo 1993, p. 236; Brauner 1994, pp. 340–341; Rainoldi 2000, p. 357; Monson 2006, p. 409.

already exist. I will therefore mention just a handful of elements relating to the topic under discussion, and refer the reader to the available specialised monographs, some of which are listed in bibliography. (The same applies to all major composers of the era, and particularly to Lasso whom I will discuss shortly[200]).

Indeed, the figure of Palestrina came to be associated with the Catholic Reformation, with post-Tridentine church music and even (though less pertinently) with "Counter-Reformation" at a very early stage of music historiography, and was seen as the musical representative of the Council's musical ideals even by many of his contemporaries. In Taruskin's words, "Palestrina was the quasi-official musical spokesman of Catholic power, Byrd its clandestine servant in adversity"[201].

Of course, the vastness and diversity of his compositional output make it difficult to point out clearly what such ideals actually did consist of; indeed, and with the usual provisos regarding Carlo Borromeo's personal interpretation of the Council's deliberations, it is easier to see Borromeo's aesthetical principles embodied in Ruffo's Masses than to handpick the "post-Tridentine" features of Palestrina's music.

It is true, however, that Palestrina was as close as possible to the spiritual and ruling centres of the Catholic Reformation; indeed, he had been Chapel Master at a Roman Basilica (Santa Maria Maggiore) where that same Carlo Borromeo was archpriest, and later he fulfilled important roles at such institutions as the *Seminario Romano* and the Papal Chapel. Undeniably, Palestrina shows by his career choices and his works that he willingly assumed the role of musical symbol of the Catholic Reformation, and that he probably considered it as a spiritual mission[202] (beside the obvious practical aspects involved). It should be stressed that his identification as "the" composer of the Roman Catholic Reformation was beneficial not only to him, but also to the Church authorities, who appraised his accomplishments also within the framework of the Church's self-representation and diplomatic relationships with Catholic secular rulers.

As seen before, not only did Palestrina cooperate with the Catholic Reformers by supervising the actual performance of liturgical music (as choir master) and by writing an impressive collection of sacred works, but he also undertook some seemingly less exciting activities such as the revision of plainchant; in

---

**200** See, for example, Jeppesen 1946 (1970); Jeppesen 1953; Schaefer 1994; Marvin 2002 for Palestrina; for Lasso, Bergquist 1999; O'Regan 1984 etc.
**201** Taruskin 2010, vol. I, p. 630.
**202** See also Schaefer 1994.

turn, this undertaking influenced his own aesthetic concept, and prompted his compositions on Gregorian melodies.

Palestrina was also clearly concerned with matters of textual delivery and intelligibility, as shown by such examples as his *Second Book of Masses* (Palestrina 1567) with their use of homorhythmic writing in the verbally lengthiest parts of the Ordinary and the avoidance of imitative devices which could hinder textual comprehension.

While Palestrina observably strove for a clearer declamation of the text, he normally avoided too direct an illustration of the individual terms by means of word-painting: the close association of this technique with the world of (secular) madrigals possibly was one concurring factor in discouraging its adoption by a composer aiming at the purification of sacred music.

On the other hand, Palestrina knowledgeably made use of what means both tradition and liturgical directives had sanctioned: as shown by Powers[203], his Offertories for the winter season (beside other collections such as those of hymns, *Lamentations* and *Magnificat*) represent a true repository of such techniques, employed in the service of the post-Tridentine principles.

While the ideal commitment of Palestrina to the principles of the Catholic Reformation is shown by his aesthetical choices, his connection to the institutions where these were enacted is clearly demonstrated by his professional engagements. The same can be said of Tomás Luis de Victoria, who – during his Roman years – was employed as *moderator musicæ* at such a core centre of the Counter-Reformation as the *Collegio Germanico*, committed to the education of Catholic missionaries preparing themselves for being sent to the regions of Germany which had adhered to Lutheranism.

In Victoria's case, the degree of personal involvement in the spiritual renewal of the Catholic Church is particularly clear[204]: his compositional output seems to have been entirely focused on liturgical and sacred works, and even the polyphonic models he adopted for his parody Masses were almost exclusively taken from religious pieces. A recurring trait of his creative perspective is the mystical vein which seems to pervade his artistic inspiration: the typically post-Tridentine attention to the purity of lines and sobriety of style is frequently combined with a personal touch which seems to embody the *pietas* which characterises the Catholic Reformation. It may come as a surprise, therefore, to see how such a prototypical post-Tridentine composer seemed to challenge the Catholic Reformation

---

**203** Cf. Powers 1982, p. 84; Nugent 1997, p. 249; Atlas 2006, p. 114; Boyce 2006, p. 142; Cummings 2006, p. 156; Haar 2006, p. 35; Leaver 2006, p. 400; Fenlon 2009, pp. 203 and 212; O'Regan 2013a, p. 339.
**204** See also Hruza 2002.

aesthetics with one of his works, the *Missa pro Victoria* (published 1600[205]). As the reader will recall (cf. § 8.4.2.), during the Council's discussions on church music, the *battaglia*-style pieces were among the few actual examples of erroneous practices mentioned by the Council Fathers. Nevertheless, Victoria's Mass is modelled on the 1529 chanson by Janequin known as *La guerre*[206] (or *La Bataille de Marignan*).

### 9.6.4. Venice: Enjoying magnificence

Whereas, as seen in the case of Palestrina, political and diplomatic considerations of his patrons were by no means incompatible with artistry and with a deep spiritual inspiration, the Republic of Venice made little or no attempts at concealing such apparent mixtures of sacred and secular.

Indeed, at the end of the sixteenth century, Venice was flowering at its best, both as concerns economic prosperity and political importance. The Chapel of San Marco, the Venetian Basilica, was the musical incarnation of such power and wealth: indeed, formally it was the Doge's private Chapel (and this is highly suggestive of how interconnected political and religious matters were in the city), and actually it represented the aural image of the *Serenissima*'s splendour in front of visitors, diplomats, international merchants and of the citizens themselves[207].

This intertwining of politics, art, religion and economy is observable on a number of planes, though it should be stressed that it did not necessary imply corruption at the spiritual level or a disregard for faith proper. It was instead rather unique and somewhat typical of Venice to succeed in the seemingly impossible task of being a wealthy merchant, a conquering warrior and a sincere believer (though perhaps not a very contrite one) at the same time, while fashioning itself as an international power rivalling the great European courts but proudly maintaining its Republican rule.

Thus, the innumerable diplomatic and commercial connections enjoyed by the Republic were exploited also for the task of recruiting excellent musicians for the Chapel, whatever their provenance; the local liturgies, practices and sacred music repertoire were passionately defended by both civil and religious authorities alike, in the face of the attempts at uniformity of post-Tridentine Cathol-

---

[205] De Victoria 1600.
[206] Leichtentritt 1944, p. 326; Higman 2000, pp. 493–494; Atlas 2006, p. 115 and fn. 13.
[207] See Ongaro 1986.

icism; the city's splendour was symbolised by the totally non-ascetic style of its religious music, with multiple choirs and wind instruments whose rich sound was likely to convey an efficacious image of power and beauty. Musicians such as Willaert or Andrea Gabrieli and his nephew Giovanni (c.1554–1612) succeeded in creating the unique features of Venetian sacred music and in establishing the proper environment for the development of polychorality and of the interaction between instruments and voices in religious music.

The connection between religious and political ritual practices is apparent in the collection of Andrea Gabrieli's sacred works, published posthumously, where one of the most splendid works is a sixteen-part Mass, composed for the visit to Venice of a group of Japanese patricians. Andrea Gabrieli is also considered to be a pioneer of the purposefully creative blending of voices and instruments, which is commonly known as the *concertato* style.

As said before, however, all this did not imply that the sphere of the sacred was simply swallowed up by that of the secular. As in the justly famous painting *The Wedding at Cana* (1563) by Paolo Veronese, the theatrical scenery and splendid setting did not prevent art from being – quite literally – at the feet of the Christ: in this oil on canvas, actually, the greatest Venetian painters of the era are depicted as musicians, sitting below Jesus, and thus contributing by their art to the beauty of the feast He consecrated by his presence[208].

### 9.6.5. Mantua: a workshop of the Catholic Reformation

Though the actual forms taken by this interaction were palpably different, Church and State were by no means two totally independent entities in yet another city of northern Italy, Mantua. A duchy ruled by the Gonzaga family, whose links with the reformation of the Church and its music we have already seen in the previous discussion of Cardinal Ercole Gonzaga's efforts (in § 8.3.1.), the city entertained important dynastic and political relationships with the dukes Este of Ferrara.

Both duchies were first-rank cultural centres, promoting art and music and attracting thinkers and religious leaders from throughout Europe. In 1556–7, Guglielmo Gonzaga officially took charge of the duchy of Mantua. The young ruler soon became one of the protagonists of the Italian Catholic reformation, in a very

---

[208] Cf. Egan 1961, p. 192; Rosand 1977, pp. 514–515, fn. 8; Koenigsberger 1986, p. 193; Bryant 1993, pp. 68–71; Rowland-Jones 1998, pp. 416–422; O'Regan 2006, p. 76; Bryant and Quaranta 2007, p. 107.

personal and idiosyncratic fashion. He was a highly cultivated person, and had undergone the influence of his uncle Ercole, in whose rich and wide-ranging library he could find the seeds for a deep and open-minded spiritual vision.

As we have already seen, Cardinal Ercole had been the patron of Jacquet of Mantua and was such a protagonist of the Catholic Reformation that he presided over the Council sessions in Trent. Church matters were no less important for Duke Guglielmo, notwithstanding his status as a secular ruler; indeed, here as in Venice (though in a completely different style), the attempt was made to realise a harmonisation of political power, religious reform and liturgical music.

Guglielmo was moved by a personal interest in both spirituality and music at least as much as by outward reasons of political prestige. As we have seen, he was an accomplished composer in his own right, who corresponded with Palestrina and sent him the results of his creative efforts – some of which were even published; moreover, he was successful in securing for his musical Chapel the services of another great musician of the era, the Flemish composer Giaches de Wert[209] (1535–1596).

Just as having a famous transalpine Chapel master meant ideally to connect the liturgy performed in Mantua to those of the most important European Cathedrals, so what should merely have been a prince's private church was fashioned by Guglielmo into a splendid, large and impressive basilica, dedicated to St Barbara.

Built in two stages (1562–7 and 1569–72), the basilica was granted numerous and rather unheard-of privileges, in consequence of the Duke's tireless efforts and negotiations with the Roman authorities. By building the basilica and obtaining for it a liturgy of its own, Guglielmo claimed for himself a role which exceeded that of a civil ruler: while this was seen by many as an undue interference in the religious field, it is likely that for him this meant simply to realise fully his God-given vocation as a "pastor" of his subjects.

Thus, the new basilica requested (and eventually obtained) to be allowed a Missal, a breviary, a rite and a plainchant repertoire of its own, which were shaped after those used in Rome, but still differed significantly from all existing models.

The plainchant in use at Santa Barbara was thoroughly revised: Duke Guglielmo took an active interest in the task, but also enlisted the cooperation and advice of many of the leading church musicians of the era, including Palestrina. Thus, Mantua's revision of plainchant somehow predated the Roman undertaking of Palestrina and Zoilo, as well as the resulting *Editio Medicæa*.

---

**209** Cf. Besutti 1993; Nugent 1997; Ongaro 2006; O'Regan 2006.

The principles behind the Mantua amendments were by and large those corresponding to post-Tridentine ideals: clear delivery, consistent use of the modes, curtailing of melismas, correspondence between verbal and musical accents etc. Alongside the revised chants, new pieces were purposefully added and constitute a repertoire unique to Santa Barbara.

All this was fascinating and certainly testified to Duke Guglielmo's spiritual interests. There was only one minor problem, however: as the reader will recall, the Council of Trent had just prohibited the use of liturgies which were not sanctioned by a two-century long usage.

One can easily imagine that the task of obtaining approval for a brand-new liturgy was almost certainly doomed to failure. It is highly amusing, for today's readers, to browse the long and unceasing correspondence between Mantua and Rome on such matters. For example, in 1572 the following argument was proposed: it is well that no liturgy be approved that has not been in use for two hundred years; however, since Mantua's rite would be sanctioned in two centuries from now, an immediate approval would just be a "moderation of [the Papal bull's] fixed time, not a derogation in [its] principles"[210].

After many years of mediation, Santa Barbara's liturgy was eventually ratified in 1583 by Pope Gregory XIII, and thus became a pioneering example of post-Tridentine Catholic reformation. It is worth noting, here as in the case of Cardinal Carlo Borromeo, that several of the leading characters of the Church's spiritual renewal, who seemingly embodied the very spirit of Trent, were also among the least willing to accept the liturgical uniformity the Council had tried to impose.

Guglielmo Gonzaga also intervened concerning polyphonic sacred works, commissioning new pieces both in Mantua and outside the boundaries of his duchy. While it is no wonder to find his endorsement of the use of liturgical plainchant as the compositional basis for contrapuntal works, it is perhaps more surprising to discover his liking for complex imitative works, whereas many other reformers were favouring homorhythmic settings. Duke Guglielmo thus seems to be among the few who understood and appreciated the symbolic value of polyphonic beauty, to which intelligibility may justifiably be sacrificed, at least occasionally.

Indeed, though his efforts for Santa Barbara's idiosyncratic liturgy may seem disproportionate and certainly implied (even from the economic viewpoint) a

---

[210] Archivio di Stato di Mantova, Archivio Gonzaga, busta 907 (49), January 29th, 1572, letter by Aurelio Zibramonti (d.1589) in Rome to Guglielmo Gonzaga in Mantua, as quoted in Besutti 1993, p. 119, my translation.

considerable burden, apparently Duke Guglielmo achieved what he hoped for. Contemporaneous witnesses testify to the citizenry's involvement in and participation to the rites in Santa Barbara, often connecting such results with the beauty and appeal of its music: when organist Francesco Rovigo (c.1540 – 1597) played on the extraordinary instrument by Graziadio Antegnati (1525 – 1590) in the basilica, such was the crowd attending that "it looked as if there was constantly a jubilee in the church"[211].

Thus, Guglielmo Gonzaga can truly be considered to be a religious reformer in his own right, who remained faithful to the Catholic Church, but at the same time strove to modify what he deemed to be ameliorable – starting from the reality nearest to him, but also giving an example for other reforms in the entire Church[212].

Whilst the examples of Milan, Rome, Venice and Mantua are certainly significant and emblematic, depicting a few iconic cases of how music and spirituality intertwined in post-Tridentine Italy, they are obviously not representative of the complexity and variety in the liturgical practices, pastoral attitudes and local traditions in sixteenth-century Italy. Rather, by discussing in some detail their diversity, I hope to have given the readers at least an impression of how drastically different the actual realisations of a broadly similar spiritual framework inspired by the Council's ideals could be.

### 9.6.6. Spain: Penitence and pomp

I will now proceed to describe briefly two other fundamental Catholic realities outside Italy, i.e. Bavaria and the Spanish court. It is self-evident that in this case too my choice has been to favour two very different contexts, but using them (as those preceding them) just as pretexts symbolising a complexity and diversity which no single Chapter might hope to exhaust. Thus, the omission of other no less important European milieus (such as those in France, in the Catholic Low Countries, in Eastern Europe, in Austria, in Portugal etc.) is neither a negligent omission nor a disdainful downplaying of their importance. It is just a means – albeit perhaps a debatable one – for keeping this Chapter within rea-

---

**211** Letter by Girolamo Cavazzoni (c.1525-a.1577) to the Duke of Mantua, July 3$^{rd}$, 1565; quoted in Mari 2008, p. 479.
**212** Cf. Besutti 1991; Besutti 1993, pp. 118 – 121; Ruini 1995, p. 35; Fenlon 2002, pp. 196 – 198; Fenlon 2009, pp. 202 – 203; Mari 2008; Mari 2013. I am grateful to Professor Licia Mari for sharing her research with me.

sonable limits of length. The reader will find opportunities for enlarging the geographical extent of this discussion within the bibliographical suggestions[213].

While in both the Iberian and the Italian peninsulas the actual presence of non-Catholic communities was neither as overwhelming as in the Protestant countries nor as strong as in the disputed zones, the political situation and the ways in which politics interacted with religious matters were significantly different. The power balance between local authorities and great sovereigns on the secular plane, and that between local bishops and the Pope had distinctive features proper to the two peninsulas; moreover, on the spiritual level, the strategies enacted in the territories of today's Italy, Spain and Portugal by different religious orders and diocesan authorities to bring about the spiritual renewal prompted by the Council were rather idiosyncratic.

Officially, the Synod of Toledo (1565–6) included discussions on church music which largely reasserted the main themes examined in Trent. It may be recalled that, in the debates on music preceding Trent's deliberations, the Spanish delegation had had a crucial role. When local synods such as that of Toledo had to realise in practice what Trent had established, the usual topics emerged afresh: permission to use polyphony, but only in the service of the sung words; "purification" of the aural shape given to God's praises from suggestive references to theatrical gestures, unchaste love, and battle sounds.

Though such expressions will be very familiar to our readers by now, it is perhaps worth mentioning that Toledo stressed a concern for the hearers which was not as common, in the Catholic field, as these trite sentences may suggest. The Council of Toledo, in fact, required that the "minds of the hearers" be "urged to devotion" by the sung words, so that they may pay more attention to "what is delivered" than to the "curious" melodies[214]. By reading carefully these expressions, we may notice that the "curiosities" mentioned here are likely to refer to the use of madrigalisms rather than to imitational devices proper, and that music is seen as a rhetorical empowering of the word, to which – however – the hearers should be attracted not just by intellectual understanding, but rather by emotional and spiritual affects.

Analogously to official pronouncements, which mirrored those of the centralised Church, but also featured distinctive traits, both the liturgical and non-liturgical music of Catholic Spain had qualities of its own. For example, musical settings for the Office collected by the Spanish composers normally adhered

---

**213** See, for example, for Spain, Stevenson 1964, Robledo Estaire 1984, Knighton 1996, Dumanoir 2003, Carreras and García 2005, Wagstaff 2007; for Portugal, Rees 1991; for Hungary, Király 2014; for Poland, Smialek 1989 and Morawska 2002, etc.
**214** *Mansi* 34, col. 562 (http://bit.ly/2bWAKsw).

## 9.6. Catholic music locally — 513

to the aesthetical and ritual principles of post-Tridentine Catholicism, but did not renounce the local tradition, represented by melodies typical for the Hispanic liturgy (cf. § 9.3.). Other idiosyncratic traditions such as the sacred dances performed in the Cathedral of Seville were not abolished after the Council, and continued to express in a unique fashion the beauty and specificity of the Spanish tradition.

Even more impressively, and as seen earlier in this Chapter (§ 9.4.4.), after Trent the previously rather secular form of the *villancico* became increasingly associated with devotional texts, and represented a striking instance of vernacular singing performed within the framework of official liturgy. Thus, *villancicos* could truly represent an efficacious and attractive form for involving the laity in devotional practices which "sounded" familiar to their ears. Notwithstanding this (or precisely for this reason), not many examples of devotional songs in the vernacular dating from the sixteenth century have survived, perhaps testifying to the minor social and artistic recognition which could be expected of a composer specialising in this repertoire in comparison with the more august compositional forms in Latin.

Thus, it is rather to the ambitious collections of motets published by composers such as Guerrero and Morales that we should turn to realise how the artistic demands of compositional technique, the respect for a proud and august local liturgical tradition and the requirements of the post-Tridentine Church were reconciled with one another[215].

A significant example of such an attitude is found in the last collection of motets by Guerrero (1597[216]), where the composer decided to include a work composed nearly three decades earlier, and whose text did not correspond any more to those admitted in the post-Tridentine liturgies: here, possibly, considerations of both an artistic and a traditional order overcame the composer's fidelity to the requirements of the new unified rites.

In turn, Morales was particularly careful about and showed an admirable respect for the plainchant formulae on which his *Magnificat* settings are built: artifices such as direct quotation, paraphrase, excerpting fragments for motivic allusions within imitative writing and respect for the modal features of the plainchant model were all signs of the homage paid by the composer to the liturgical tradition of the Church[217].

---

[215] Cf. Borgerding and Stein 2006, pp. 437–449 (to which this section is indebted); cf. also Salmen 2001, p. 166; Weber 2008, p. 103; O'Regan 2013a, p. 347.
[216] Guerrero 1597.
[217] Cf. Borgerding and Stein 2006, pp. 439 and 444.

A similar attitude of reverent veneration for the plainchant heritage is found in the liturgical practices admitted within the monastery of *El Escorial*, which was considered by Philip II to be the prayerful stronghold (*"alcázar y templo"*, "fortress and temple") of post-Tridentine Catholicism. Here, complex polyphony was forbidden, and only the simplest forms of part-singing on *cantus firmus* were admitted; the liturgical focus was on plainchant, whose tradition Philip II strenuously defended, even in the face of the Roman attempts to revise this heritage which would result in the *Editio Medicæa*.

On the other hand, a very different situation was found in another royal monastery, that of the *Descalzas Reales* in Madrid. Here, a musician of Victoria's standing was employed, in the service of a convent where two female members of the ruling family had retired. At the *Descalzas*, Victoria had at his disposal a high-quality team of professional musicians, and the status of Royal Chapel granted to the monastery church implied generous funding from and frequent attendance by crowned listeners.

Some ambivalence could thus be observed in the case of Philip's attitude to polyphony and to liturgical music as a whole: from the one side, virtually no polyphony was performed at the Escorial (except, of course, when his own musical Chapel visited the monastery); from the other, the choice of a musician of Victoria's prestige for another royal monastery such as that of the *Descalzas* testifies to Philip's strong interest in high-level polyphony and his understanding of its role within liturgy[218].

### 9.6.7. Bavaria: the outpost of Catholicism

If the *Escorial* was a fortress of Catholicism, it represented the spiritual stronghold of the Roman Church which resisted Protestantism by virtue of asceticism, repentance, prayer and moralisation. The situation was very different within a geographical context closer to the Evangelical Reforms, and which constantly had to face the opposing confessional groups. As an example among the many possible of this situation, I will succinctly present the case of Bavaria, in what is today's Southern Germany. One reason for this choice is the liberality of the Bavarian Dukes' investments in art, which was conceived as an appealing means to attract believers through visual and aural beauty, but also as a way of asserting the duchy's power and wealth in the face of other rulers (especially

---

[218] Cf. Nugent 1997, p. 251; Noone 1998, p. 24 and fn. 29; Borgerding and Stein 2006, pp. 429–431; O'Regan 2006, pp. 75–76; Rees 2006, pp. 351–352; Ramos López 2008, pp. 6–7.

those who had adhered to Lutheranism or Calvinism) and of the superior authorities.

The Dukes' ambitions are shown by the splendour and pomp which characterise many of the artistic realisations they promoted: from the polychoral style, which embodied the sumptuous aspect of post-Tridentine music, to the building of churches (and of the corresponding musical repertoire) which represented Bavaria and its Dukes as the non-receding citadel of German Catholicism. Beside the Dukes' personal undertakings, moreover, much was due to the presence of the Jesuits in Bavaria and to the influence of such a leading figure of the Catholic Reformation as Cardinal Waldburg[219].

No less important, obviously, was the role played by Orlando di Lasso and by the excellent choir he had at his disposal in Munich. Though Lasso should be considered as embodying the spiritual climate of post-Tridentine Catholicism no less than a Palestrina (or a Victoria, to say nothing of a Ruffo), his interpretation of how this milieu should find a musical incarnation was highly personal and very different from those of the musicians just mentioned.

His musical style was a unique blend of various influences and musical experiences: from the chromaticism which characterised many experiments of the Italian madrigalists, to the humanist attempts at *vers mesurés* practised in France, to the popular song culture of the German countries, to the polyphonic heritage of the Flemish school, and to the burgeoning polychorality which was enjoying success in Venice. And, of course, all of these styles were not simply mixed or merged by Lasso, but rather reinterpreted and fashioned according to his unique artistic and spiritual personality, as mentioned in Chapter One (§ 1.4.4.). In Taruskin's words,

> Whereas the earlier cosmopolitan ideal – the ideal of the *ars perfecta*, brought to its peak by Palestrina – had been ecumenical (that is, reflective of religious universalism and hence nation-transcending), Lassus was brought up in the age of music printing and was an eager and ambitious child of the burgeoning age of worldly music commerce. Thus his brand of cosmopolitanism was not ecumenical but polyglot[220].

In particular, Lasso's attention to the emotional and affective value of the text, and his tendency to pictorially portray its images and details (especially in his late motets) not only contrasted with the soberest styles of declamation of some post-Tridentine composers, but also represented an element which greatly fascinated the German composers of the Lutheran zones. Indeed, Lasso's influ-

---

**219** Cf. Bryant 1993, pp. 70–71; Schmidt 1993, p. 248; Bergquist 2006, p. 341.
**220** Taruskin 2010, vol. I, p. 713.

ence on the "art-music" of the first generations of Lutheran composers (among whom Joachim a Burck and Johannes Eccard) is not to be underestimated.

Not only was Lasso's influence determined by the stylistic choices of his compositions; he also represented a pivotal figure between musical Catholicism and Protestantism by virtue of works which might appeal to devout music lovers of both confessions, and which often set the model for musical forms which would later characterise one or the other of the competing fields.

Actually, Lasso composed circa a hundred works on German-texted lyrics, many of which had a religious content. Indeed, he also wrote a Psalm collection (*Teutsche Psalmen: Geistliche Psalmen*, 1588[221]), on fifty German Psalm translations written by Catholic convert Kaspar Ulenberg (1549–1617) with the aim of offering a Catholic alternative to the spread of Lutheran German psalmody. Though here the "Counter-Reformation" attitude is clearly observable, this did not prevent Lasso's setting from offering an admired stylistic model for composers of both confessions.

Another aspect of what the Catholic Reform demanded of musicians was the adaptation of the existing liturgical repertoire to the needs of the post-Tridentine Church. For Lasso, this meant the creation of numerous liturgical works during the two last decades of the century, when the Freising rite which had been in use needed to be replaced by the centralised Roman liturgy. This liturgical repertoire included hymns, responsories and *Lamentations* for use by the Catholic musicians throughout the Church year.

The hymn-cycles composed by Lasso in the years 1580–1 represent his creative response to the liturgical needs of post-Tridentine Catholicism in Bavaria, but also a means by which his employer, Duke Wilhelm V (1548–1626), sought to affirm Munich's stance at the very heart of the Catholic Reformation. By adopting the "Roman" Breviary and strongly affirming Bavaria's union and identification with Rome, liturgical choices became an explicit commitment to the values of "Roman" Catholicism and of its post-Tridentine renewal[222].

Beside "Counter-Reformation" undertakings such as the German Psalms, and responses to Catholic Reform requirements such as the composition of new liturgical items, Lasso represents the spiritual climate of the time also through his devotional works, which symbolise the post-Tridentine attention for piety.

---

[221] Lasso 1588.
[222] Cf. Zager 1999.

The best known of his efforts in this field is undoubtedly the justly famous cycle of the *Lagrime di San Pietro*[223] (1595), composed by Lasso shortly before his death (1594) on lyrics published one decade earlier by the Italian poet Luigi Tansillo. As seen before (§ 9.4.3.), Tansillo had evolved from licentious to devotional poetry; and indeed for Lasso too this undertaking had a deep spiritual meaning and represented his own prayerful request for God's mercy as his days were nearing their end. The heartfelt devotion and the composer's humble penitence are touchingly shown by this masterpiece, where all stratagems and techniques of madrigal settings are put at the service of an intense and remorseful supplication.

On the other hand, sincere as Lasso's religiosity was, this did not prevent him from maintaining his own very personal and idiosyncratic style throughout his compositional career: neither did he renounce writing parody Masses in obsequy to what were perceived to be the Council's deliberation, nor could his style be classified and understood in the same terms as those of the typical post-Tridentine composers. It was precisely by constantly being himself, with the unique traits of his artistic personality, that Lasso could pledge the sincerity of his spirituality. And this permanence of constant stylistic features, in spite of the variety of artistic influences undergone by Lasso and of the internationalism of his inspiration, was what permitted many of his secular works to be given sacred or devotional lyrics by his admirers (both Catholic and Lutheran): of course, in certain cases (such as the contrafacture of *Anna mihi dilecta* mentioned earlier in this Chapter: § 9.4.3.) the results might remain at best inferior to Lasso's own spiritual works, but certainly they mirrored the concept of Lasso's music as being both highly spiritual and deeply touching and emotional at the same time[224].

The figure of Lasso with whom I have concluded this Chapter represents an ideal summary of what has been said in the whole of it: we have examined the aesthetic and spiritual principles behind the musical efforts of the post-Tridentine Church; how they were locally interpreted and enacted; how they prompted official and centralised initiatives such as the reforms of the liturgical books, as well as the forms taken by devotional poetry and music. We have also seen how music was thought of and employed by religious movements and orders which symbolise the very efforts at self-reform characterising the best part of six-

---

[223] For the role of this work within the framework of the Bavarian Counter-Reformation, see Fisher 2007.
[224] Cf. Leichtentritt 1944, p. 326; Blume 1975, p. 169; Higman 2000, p. 493; Bergquist 2006, p. 346; Forney 2006, p. 266; Crook 2009, pp. 24–27; Porter 2009, pp. 250–251; Fisher 2014, pp. 108–110.

teenth-century Catholicism, as well as a few examples of how this reality was experienced at the local level.

The position of Lasso on the boundaries between Catholicism and Protestantism will thus bring us to the next Chapter and the last section of this book, focusing on interconfessional topics and how they were embodied in musical practice.

# Chapter 10 – Music and confessionalisation

> The hymns by Luther and Bèze have killed
> more souls than their writings and arguments[1].
>
> [Adam Contzen]

## 10.1. Introduction

The power of music to move, to excite, to unite and to strengthen a community of believers, which, as seen in the previous Chapters, was widely acknowledged in the sixteenth century, was often used by religious reformers throughout Europe. This was seen both in the first age of the Reformations, when individual viewpoints had to be asserted – sometimes in opposition to other competing outlooks – and in the later age of "confessionalisation".

In both cases, even though efforts were made to recompose and reconcile theological differences, personal divergences and confessional oppositions, other forces were pushing in the contrary direction, and aiming at the creation of new confessional profiles, clearly distinguished from all the others.

Confessional identities thus were defined both in relation to the competing structures of belief, and within their own dogmatic boundaries. Both approaches led to an unprecedented stress on the catechetic and theological profile of the individual communities, and music was often conceived as a tool for spreading and affirming the particular creed of a congregation; on the other hand, music became a powerful way of uniting the believers, sometimes in open opposition to other confessional views.

It should be said, moreover, that the process of confessionalisation sometimes had important effects on the later musical historiography: in other words, our reception of the entire history of music in the Reformation era has often been conditioned by the confessional allegiances of the music- and Church historians who studied and transmitted it.

When Christian confessions started to separate, music played a major role, both in a pacific and in a more belligerent fashion. Music was essential to worship for most confessional Churches; it helped in creating a feeling of belonging to a community, and sometimes the identification of a particular confession with its specific musicianship was so clear as to become a one-to-one relationship,

---

[1] Contzen 1621, Liber Secundus, p. 100.

constituting a confessional flag. This was particularly the case with Lutheran vernacular songs and Huguenot Psalms; moreover, if the Lutheran hymn texts could have intertextual or implicit references which might be understood in polemics with other beliefs, even Psalm translations were not as neutral as they may seem (both in consequence of the undeniable presence of bellicose elements in the Psalms themselves, and sometimes of their potentially idiosyncratic translations; even more frequently, of the "argument" summaries which favoured particular typological interpretations[2]).

As mentioned before, music was also a very useful propaganda weapon: singing arose sometimes spontaneously, conveying a confessional message; occasionally, it assumed the value of a public manifestation, which could have the goal of disrupting other confessional worships. The power of music was especially striking when it was the medium used by martyrs and persecuted Christians to convey their belief in times of suffering and death. On the other hand, the musical flag was often lifted by pugnacious confessions in times of warfare.

Confessional hymns were a tool for promoting a particular belief, but also needed to be disseminated in turn: this could be done first and foremost by singing them, but also through manuscript and printed copies, both bound (such as hymn-books) and unbound (such as broadsheets).

However, musical propaganda was not limited to the positive public display of one's confessional allegiance: it also presented itself as an active opposition to other beliefs, from the milder forms (such as attracting proselytes through the beauty of one's worship) to the less pleasing (such as the occupation of the other's acoustic spaces, the ridicule of another's beliefs, the identification of the other as the Antichrist or the opposition to particularly cherished elements of the other's faith).

A particularly fecund source for the study of propagandistic songs in the religious hostilities of the sixteenth century comes from *contrafacta*, i.e. pre-existing songs whose text was adapted to suit the specific needs of an individual, a community or a situation. In some cases, pious *contrafacta* aimed simply at offering a devotional alternative to their secular lyrics, whose connection with highly popular tunes had determined their widespread adoption; in other cases, confessions aimed at adapting the text of other Churches' hymns or liturgical songs to their own belief; obviously, however, *contrafacta* were also highly useful as polemic songs, for derision, or as a mass-medium for spreading news or doctrines.

---

2 Cf. Higman 2004.

All forms of propaganda music were most likely to be found in those territories whose confessional allegiance was fluid – either because of the co-existence of different beliefs or as a consequence of the confessional fluctuations of their rulers; moreover, specific events (such as the Augsburg *Interim*, the so-called *Kalenderstreit* or the controversial canonisation of St Benno) were likely to prompt a huge quantity of new songs or adaptations.

If music might be useful to the aggressive parties, it was however of primary importance also for those persecuted, and sometimes it underwent forms of repression itself; musicians – who had experienced internationalisation for a long time already – often found themselves forced to deny or renounce their particular beliefs in order to survive or to be able to work; institutions which had used to employ musicians were frequently dismantled, and some musical compositions are eloquent witnesses of the human and spiritual distress endured by their composers in those difficult times.

## 10.2. Building confessional boundaries

The process of confessionalisation impacted heavily on the daily lives of those experiencing it, at all levels of several European societies. Nevertheless, since its origins can be traced (at least partially) to the field of theological debates, it involved a large amount of theoretical reasoning, of dogmatic clarifications and of doctrinal definitions. These, of course, produced palpable effects as regards the shape and meaning of worship and devotion, the presence of religious elements in daily life, and tangibly shaped the political and social experience of a great part of the European population – even when it did not provoke such execrable by-products as wars, persecution, exile and murder.

Music, of course, by its nature is better suited for praying than for debating, for worshipping than for theological discussions, for praising than for instructing in a doctrine. It may seem, therefore, that music was closer to what the different Churches still held in common (such as the expression of faith, of praise, of repentance, of supplication...) than to what was separating them (such as dogma and doctrine); and in fact this is basically true, as the next Chapter will show.

However, there are elements in the confessionalisation process which actually relied abundantly on musical expression, and which we will see in the forthcoming pages[3]. Indeed, both music and the visual arts had to respond to the

---

[3] Cf. Ziegler 1995; Blume 1975, p. 29; Fisher 2014, p. 15.

challenges of confessionalisation, one of which was the transformation of the individual's or the community's religious identity from a set of practices to one of beliefs; and while dogmatic content had always been expressed by art (both musical and visual), the necessity for precision often came to the fore with an unprecedented cogency[4].

While in the first years of the Protestant experience there was considerable fluidity and permeability among what would subsequently become distinct confessions, and sometimes allegiance was a matter of shades, of sympathy or of degrees, later the need was felt (and often promoted by the religious leaders) for clear lines to be traced between Catholics and Protestants, and between one form or another of Protestantism. The creation of a group's identity often implied the demonization of another; to describe the "other", often in a markedly negative light, was a necessary stage in the self-definition of one's own community. Parallel to and concomitant with the delineation of confessional boundaries, which erased (often for political reasons) all middle ways, compromises and (frequently) possibilities of dialogue, the line between the sacred and the secular started to appear with increasing clarity: as we have repeatedly seen, and though the difference was certainly felt in the sixteenth century, these two fields maintained a permeability which was going to decrease in the centuries to come. And, in all of these processes, music was often far from neutral, and it frequently became an essential instrument for the creation of group identity[5].

The extent, influence and importance of political considerations in the process of confessionalisation need always to be taken into account: this intermingling of spirituality with strategy, of prayer with opportunism, of renewal with rebellion also impacted on the aural experience of faith, and on how sounds of a very different nature (spiritual or profane) contributed to shaping the musical habitat of many European citizens. As Wagner Oettinger succinctly puts it, "it is difficult to draw the line between political songs that are religious and religious songs that are also political"[6]. On the other hand, in the words of another scholar in the field, "Religious sentiment coloured politics in such a way that those who cared little about power struggles among nobles did care desperately that France was being polluted with heresies"[7].

---

[4] Cf. Kaplan 2007, p. 30; Crook 2009, p. 52; Prodi 2014, p. 16.
[5] Cf. Hsia 1992, p. 108; Fisher 2001, p. 617; Wagner Oettinger 2001, pp. 9 and 202–204; Haar 2006, p. 241; Crook 2009, p. 53; Willis 2010, p. 184; Groote and Vendrix 2012, p. 163; Fisher 2014, pp. 3, 10 and 298. This Chapter is particularly indebted to the research of Fisher and Wagner Oettinger, to which readers interested in these topics are invited to refer.
[6] Wagner Oettinger 2001, p. 2.
[7] Van Orden 2000, pp. 272–273.

What role had the singing of a Latin, traditional *Te Deum* after the public burning of the Papal bull and of the *Corpus iuris canonici* by the first Lutherans rebelling against the Pope in Wittenberg (December 10$^{th}$, 1520)? Was it protest, prayer, praise or propaganda? Or all of these together?

What was the connection of religious polemical songs with the pre-Reformation heritage and tradition of anticlerical verse-writing?

The power of music to move (the crowds, beside the individual souls) was clear and acknowledged. Public order needs could thus require official actions which may seem farcical in today's eyes, such as prohibiting public singing and sung references to the Bible, as happened in the Low Countries. Here, the confessional opposition had a particularly clear political overtone; thus, in Ghent (1572), *contrafacta* of the Lord's Prayer praising Alva counterbalanced the proud singing of the *Wilhelmus*.

The very story of this song, which is now the Dutch anthem, is iconic of this dovetailing of politics and religion as well as of the capability of music to both transcend and reinforce the confessional boundaries. The melody of the *Wilhelmus* came actually from the Catholic field, where it had been a political song in turn, and it was adopted by believers from a variety of confessions (including the Anabaptists); in association with verses attributed to Filips van Marnix van Sint Aldegonde (1540–1598), it gave voice to the Protestant cause, sometimes supplanting other genuinely religious songs which had previously expressed the Evangelical identity in opposition to Catholics[8].

## 10.3. The confessionalisation of music

Though the preceding pages will have already suggested to readers that it is impossible to define just one and a single function for religious songs within the process of confessionalisation (and it would be rather wrong to attempt such a definition), it is not only possible but also advisable to categorise these functions, even if they are normally found in an inextricable combination.

### 10.3.1. Faith first

Of course, the first and foremost function of religious singing was precisely that of praying and of moving the soul to the love for God. I deem it likely that in the

---

8 Cf. Reid 1971, p. 50; Pettegree 2005, pp. 41, 67–71; Lindberg 2010, p. 83; Fisher 2014, p. 4.

episode of book-burning quoted above (§ 10.2.), the main purpose of the early Lutherans who sang the *Te Deum* was to pray and praise the Lord. Similarly, when – years later – zones which had already belonged to Lutheranism were officially re-Catholicised from the above, the attachment shown by many lay people and families to the Lutheran hymns was often and principally a matter of genuine faith and spirituality[9].

Thus, and even if the Calvinist Psalm-singing frequently had a propagandistic and even belligerent dimension which we will shortly discuss in turn, their psalmody was primarily an act of faith. An anecdote regarding a Huguenot community in Bas-Poitou (Vendée) can shed some light on this connection of prayer and propaganda: after the Catholic priest had finished his worship, which was attended by Huguenot sympathisers, they began their Psalm-singing; those who did not adhere to Evangelical views used to leave the church at that point, and reappeared when the Psalmodic appendage to worship had eventually been completed[10]. Ostentatiously abandoning a service, in the early 1560s, was the means chosen also by one Mrs Bell, of the Holy Cross parish in Canterbury, for showing her disapproval of Psalm-singing; since she also was found owning an unauthorised prayer book, she was probably a religious dissenter[11].

Though, as we have repeatedly seen in the preceding Chapters, religious songs in the vernacular were not created by Luther and even had locally a place within the framework of official worship, their spread and the force of their spiritual and public power were undoubtedly new and unprecedented: the German version of Psalm 130 [129], *Aus tiefer Not*, was sung in Landshut "in the public streets in front of homes [...], in the churches, during the Mass and the sermon"[12]. Luther drew on the pre-existing experience of how communal singing could shape a "culture of belonging"[13], in Fisher's words, and – at the same time – mould the spirituality, devotion and faith of the believers, who soon adopted Luther's hymns as their most cherished sung prayers even in contexts as private as their very homes[14].

---

9 Cf. Brown 2008, p. 257; Lindberg 2010, p. 83.
10 In Reid 1971, p. 45 (see also pp. 36–54); Rainoldi 2000, p. 324; Lindberg 2010, pp. 268–269.
11 Willis 1975, p. 31; cf. Marsh 2013, p. 446.
12 From the Landshut city council to Albrecht V, October 20th, 1555; Munich, Bayerisches Hauptstaatsarchiv, Kurbayern Äußeres Archiv 4263, fols. 208$^r$-211$^v$. Quoted in Fisher 2014, p. 34.
13 Fisher 2014, p. 32.
14 Cf. Brown 2005, p. 9; Groote and Vendrix 2012, p. 187; Fisher 2014, p. 16.

## 10.3.2. Preaching in music

As seen so far in this Chapter, singing religious songs thus meant to pray, to affirm, keep and maintain a group and its identity, but also to spread the content, teachings and meaning of one distinct confession.

It is impossible to deny the genuinely religious content of the first Lutheran songs; however, the context in which they appeared first was not that of churches or chapels, but rather that of marketplaces where they were sold and spread as broadsheets[15]. As Pollmann puts it, "the role of song is most evident at the stages when the battle for the reformation was being waged in inns and market squares, near pyres and gallows. Yet songs were often packed with Scriptural references and often tried to convey quite complex messages"[16].

Singing religious songs like those by Luther therefore meant to disseminate the doctrine they conveyed. Preaching thus became a prerogative of laypeople, who could independently and autonomously take the initiative of singing, even though in some cases they might be prompted to do so by external factors. For example, in Braunschweig (1527), a Lutheran publicly charged a Catholic preacher of lying about the doctrine of works and then reinforced the Evangelical point by intoning a freshly composed Lutheran song (*Ach Gott, vom Himmel sieh darein*[17]).

## 10.3.3. "As long as I live": music and martyrdom

Though the Bas-Poitou Catholics may have found the Huguenot Psalm-singing slightly tiresome, or the Catholic preacher in Braunschweig may have liked the musical interruption of his sermon very little, these were not – sadly – the most troublesome occurrences of confessional contraposition. Religious singing had indeed a pre-eminent role in the situations of martyrdom and persecution, which cruelly struck Christians of virtually all denominations at the hands of other Christians.

Frequently, people condemned to death for their faith started singing their religious songs during the very last moments of their earthly life (we may recall how the Japanese child-martyrs resorted to sung psalmody while they were sharing, literally, the experience of Christ's cross[18]: cf. § 9.5.2.5.). In this case, of

---
15 Cf. Mager 1986, pp. 25–26; Brown 2008, p. 209.
16 Pollmann 2006, p. 309.
17 Herl 2004, pp. 89–90.
18 Bolland and Henschen 1658, vol. I, p. 761. English translation in Wright 1993, p. 35.

course, singing had a variety of functions: once more, I think it safe to assert that the martyrs resorted to singing primarily as a particularly moving way to pray just before (or while) undergoing suffering and death. Of course, however, singing ceased to be a private and intimate prayer and became a public act, in which, sometimes, the most courageous among the assisting crowd joined in singing with the martyr. This happened frequently in the case of Huguenot Psalm-singing (we have already seen, in § 6.3.5., an example of how Psalms were sung by a Huguenot leader just before his death by decapitation in America[19]), but was not unheard-of in the case of Catholics as well: for example, in England, several martyrs went to the gallows with Latin Psalms on their lips, some of which were penitential in character, whereas others were joyful and jubilating and still others invoked God's justice and wrath on the persecutors[20]. On the other hand, as Duguid fascinatingly suggests[21], one reason why the English "Sternhold and Hopkins" Psalms were not supplanted in use by Parker's (which were seemingly preferable for a variety of reasons) was precisely because the "Sternhold and Hopkins" Psalms had a history. They were the Psalms which had consoled both exiles and martyrs; thus, their literary shortcomings were abundantly compensated by the role they had played in building the spirituality and identity of the English Evangelicals. The refugees were also led by their condition of persecuted exiles to meditate on their experience in Biblical terms: this is shown by their creation of penitential songs based on the public confession found in Chapter Nine of the Book of Daniel, but updated to mirror more closely their own context. There is further evidence demonstrating how the exiles' prayer maintained a deep bond with the clandestine congregations of Evangelicals who remained in the motherland, and who frequently suffered persecution and martyrdom in turn[22].

### 10.3.3.1. "The Story of Brother Henry": sung epics of martyrdom

While many martyrs from all confessions asserted their faith in singing, the narratives of their deeds could be spread through singing in turn. Such accounts were by no means limited to the Catholic field, even though the Evangelicals rejected the traditional forms of and beliefs in sanctoral intercession.

---

19 Warner 1984, p. 81.
20 Cf. Reid 1971, p. 36; Warner 1984, p. 81; Monson 1997; Diefendorf 1991, p. 138; Pettegree 2005, pp. 60 and 63; Lindberg 2010, p. 260.
21 Duguid 2014, p. 119.
22 Cf. Leaver 2004a, pp. 164–171.

I have mentioned briefly, in Chapter Five (§ 5.3.2.4.), that the occasion for composing his first hymn was given to Luther precisely by such an occurrence. Three of his fellow Augustinian monks, who sympathised with his views, had been sentenced to death: the first two of them, Heinrich Voes and Johannes Esch, were burnt at the stake in 1523, in Brussels, whereas their companion, Lambert Thorn, died in prison five years later[23]. Luther's hymn honoured the martyrs' steadfast belief, constancy and courage. Different from many of the hymns which would follow it, thus, the ballad *Ein newes Lied wir heben an* (1523[24]) did not contribute to the success of the Lutheran confession by disseminating its original teachings, but rather by eliciting wonder, rebellion, amazement, wrath and even disgust among those who heard of the sad doom of these monks.

As Wagner Oettinger suggests, with this song Luther managed to create a non-traditional space for the veneration of holy people: though no prayers for intercession are addressed to the first Lutheran martyrs, the author inserted himself and his work within the tradition of the songs of deeds, portraying the virtues of holy or heroic people[25].

Two years later, a similar occasion encouraged Luther to pen a similar hymn[26] on the martyrdom of another Augustinian monk, Heinrich von Zütphen, who was killed in northern Germany. These hymns by Luther, though representing a minority of those created by the Reformer (who afterward specialised in paraphrases from Psalms and liturgical items, or in prayers in verse) obtained however a huge success both for the Reformation's cause and for themselves: many later songs on other Evangelical martyrs such as those belonging to the Anabaptist camp were shaped on Luther's early models[27].

Martyr songs not only used to describe how martyrdom took place, but, as Pollmann puts it, "by giving details of interrogations they were also teaching believers how to articulate, defend and provide Biblical evidence for their beliefs. Moreover, they made sense of the suffering, explained how the Lord looked upon His chosen people, reviled those who refused to witness"[28]. This was particularly crucial for minority communities, such as those of Anabaptists or of a branch of these, the Hutterites.

---

[23] The circumstances of Thorn's death are still a topic of debate among historians.
[24] *LW* 53, pp. 211–216.
[25] Wagner Oettinger 2001, p. 62.
[26] *LW* 32, pp. 263–268.
[27] Cf. Coats 1994, pp. 20 and 27; Wagner Oettinger 2001, pp. 61–69, 87, 260–263; Lindberg 2010, pp. 266 and 283.
[28] Pollmann 2006, p. 302.

Hymns on Calvinist martyrs were also composed and sung: for instance, *Antwerpen rijck, o Keyserlicke Stede* commemorated the death at stake of Christoffel Fabritius (d.1564). The lyrics were set to the tune of Psalm 79 [78] as translated by Petrus Datheen to suit the Genevan tunes (*De heid'nen zijn in Uw erfdeel gevallen*). Following the success of this hymn, the associated tune became a favourite choice for new songs during over a century, and was used by members of several Christian denominations, including Catholics and Anabaptists[29].

### 10.3.3.2. "We have become a spectacle": Byrd and the English martyrs

If Protestant hymns celebrated the heroic deaths of Evangelical martyrs on mainland Europe, the persecution against Catholics in England was at times among the fiercest and bloodiest of the century. In particular, the fate of Jesuit missionaries sent with the purpose of re-Catholicising England could be horrible when they were discovered: their brutal executions involved hanging and quartering, and the tales and depictions of such killings were recounted in printed texts, often combined with graphic imagery.

The martyrdom of St Edmund Campion (1540–1581) and of his fellows, notably, provoked considerable – and justifiable – uproar. William Byrd, who (as said in § 7.6.3.) was a Catholic in the service of the Anglican Court, reacted to this violence by means of his artistic gifts: his moving consort song *Why do I use my paper, ink and pen* (on lyrics by Henry Walpole [1558–1595], a Jesuit and a martyr himself) and his motet on *Deus, venerunt gentes* are probably to be connected with these gruesome facts. The latter work is the musical setting of the first verses of Psalm 79 [78], which was often chosen by English martyrs as their last prayer, and which was officially recommended for beseeching the re-Catholicisation of England.

The fourth verse of this Psalm, moreover, reads "*Facti sumus opprobrium*" ("We have become a taunt to our neighbours", Psalm 79 [78]:4), which echoes the words uttered by Campion just before being executed ("*Spectaculum facti sumus*", "We have become a spectacle", 1 Corinthians 4:9[30]).

Abundant inspiration for English Catholic composers wishing to give musical expression to their despondency came also from the book of the *Lamentations* of Jeremiah; however, a touching musical correspondence between Byrd and Philippe de Monte was based on a text taken from yet another Psalm (137

---

**29** Cf. Pettegree 2005, pp. 70–71. The website "Nederlandse Liederenbank" lists 134 songs on the tune of Psalm 79 [78] (http://bit.ly/2bezMDC), including settings of Psalm 44 [43] in Utenhove's version ("*Wy hebben Heer ghehoort*").
**30** Cf. Monson 1997, pp. 356 and 358.

[136]): The Flemish Master of Emperor Rudolf II's musical Chapel sent Byrd the first half of the doleful Psalm set in polyphony, and received from Byrd his own setting of the second part.

Byrd's support of the Catholic cause is also shown by his work on liturgical items proper: his efforts for the replacement of the Sarum rite with the Roman liturgy clearly indicated his commitment to the promotion of post-Tridentine Catholicism, of its unity and its values within his own country.

It is likely that Byrd's steadfast commitment to the Catholic cause resulted, at least partly, from his connection with a Jesuitical milieu: between 1589 and 1591 he issued two collections of sacred works on Latin texts, some of which were excerpted from contemporaneous writings of Jesuit provenance; as mentioned in Chapter Seven (§ 7.3.6.), his *Gradualia* (which claimed compliance with Catholicism from the very title-page) soon came to represent the musical expression of the Catholic community, particularly as concerned its most cultivated and socially high-standing members[31].

A fragment from Psalm 27 [26]:4 ("*Unam petii a Domino*", "One thing I asked of the Lord"), set to music by Byrd within the *Gradualia*, was very loaded, in turn, with religious-political meaning. As argued by Monson[32], it represented a rather overt supplication for obtaining freedom to practise the Catholic faith, and it was so strictly connected with the Jesuits' efforts to re-Catholicise England that the same fragment was used as an epigraph to the quintessentially Ignatian *First booke of the Christian exercise* (1582[33]).

Such works had of course a "political" meaning too, but they also helped in establishing a set of values, of beliefs and of mutual encouragement which was shared and felt by the English Catholics[34].

While the means employed by Byrd to assert his own faith were neither bloody nor violent, in other instances the confessional opposition occasioned not only riots and uprisings, but actual wars – some of which would explode with extreme cruelty and have decades-long duration in the seventeenth century.

---

**31** See McCarthy 2007.
**32** Monson 1997, p. 366.
**33** *First Booke* 1582.
**34** Cf. Monson 1997, pp. 348, 354–355, 363, 370; Atlas 2006, p. 116; Bray 2006, pp. 499–500; Monson 2006, pp. 416–417; Crook 2009, pp. 4–5; O'Regan 2013a, pp. 348–349. Cf. especially Brett 2007, McCarthy 2007 and Bray 2011.

### 10.3.4. "Let God rise up": battle hymns

The use of Psalms as battle hymns was typical of the Huguenot armies: this happened within the context of the Wars of Religion (France, 1562–98), where Protestants showed a marked preference, in such belligerent situations, for Psalm 68 [67]: "Let God rise up, let His enemies be scattered"[35].

Indeed, even a Reformer whose efforts were eventually not crowned by lasting results, such as Müntzer, had led his armies to be slaughtered to the sound of religious hymns[36], but local rebellions and manifestations were also often accompanied by spiritual songs. In Magdeburg (1550–1), Lutherans opposing the Augsburg *Interim* (see § 10.6.2.) defended their city against the attackers while singing "Do as the Maccabees did and strive for God's Word"[37], while Psalm-singing characterised many confrontations between competing groups during the French disorders in 1557[38]. In Aix-en-Provence, in 1562, the consul organised a Catholic mob which systematically practised violence against the Huguenots while singing anti-Protestant songs[39].

Whereas the most obvious way for disseminating a song and its spiritual and dogmatic content was by singing it (and of course a hymn or Psalm sung by a martyr at the stake or a warrior in battle had an emotional power we can hardly imagine), there were other, and not less important, opportunities for spreading the word.

### 10.3.5. Pamphlets, broadsheets and polemics

We have mentioned already (cf. § 5.3.3. and 7.4.) that broadsheet and pamphlet printing were among the most effective media of sixteenth-century communication. Songs might be illustrated by woodcut images, and even the people who were not able to read the lyrics themselves could learn them by rote and spread them in turn.

Seemingly, and as far as it is possible to estimate the printing volumes by the number of surviving copies of polemical pamphlets, the Protestants were much more active in this field than their Catholic counterparts (up to a proportion of

---

35 Reid 1971, p. 36; cf. also pp. 41 and 47.
36 Cf. http://to.pbs.org/2bCdQET.
37 Cf. Jacobs 1871; quoted in Olson 1972, p. 70.
38 Cf. Higman 2000, p. 499; Wagner Oettinger 2001, p. 140; Pettegree 2005, p. 60; Lindberg 2010, pp. 268–269.
39 Cf. Davis 1973, p. 89.

five to one). It cannot be directly inferred from this, however, that this situation resulted from the Catholics' neglect for or underestimation of this possibility. Conceivably, indeed, the printers themselves were disinclined to publish Catholic works (probably by fear they would attract less numerous buyers than their competitors), and the Catholic polemicists often had to resort to self-funded publishing when they wanted their pamphlets to be printed and distributed.

Parallel to polemical pamphlets, belligerent songs were printed in very high figures and at a very reasonable price, making them affordable for most potential buyers. They often expressed resentment and capitalised on all kinds of public discontent; satire was widely employed, and songs circulated in a variety of social contexts and of geographical locations[40].

Alongside cheap print, it was possible to disseminate a polemical or religious song also by means of manuscript copies: in this case, of course, it was also possible for copyists to intervene on the text, and – if necessary – to adapt a song originally conceived for a different city or context to those typical for their situation.

Though the level of inflammatory verses found in many broadsheet songs and pamphlets was hardly found in more official and explicitly spiritual products such as hymnbooks, these were clearly yet another efficacious means for spreading a message, a doctrine, a set of beliefs: indeed, they had the considerable advantage over broadsheets of allowing their editors many more possibilities for shading and refining their message, and for framing it within a much more complete and complex framework of prayers and dogmas.

This cursory summary of how a song with a confessional content could be spread (and thus could contribute to the confession's dissemination) applies, of course, not only to songs whose primary function is propaganda, but also to virtually all other functions of religious songs. Beside spiritual aims proper (such as prayer), social purposes (such as the creation of group identity) and apostolic activities (such as the dissemination of particular beliefs), we will now turn to two other functions, which are somewhat complementary to each other, i.e. the power of songs as a tool for opposing other confessions and for defending the original traits of one's own allegiance. I will articulate the first of these two functions under a variety of rubrics, which will be examined in turn in the following pages.

---

**40** Cf. van Orden 2000, pp. 272–273; Wagner Oettinger 2001, p. 205.

## 10.3.6. Enchanting chant

Possibly, the less violent and aggressive way of opposing a competing confession in music was to attract believers by the beauty of one's music, or to influence their stance on religious matters through the use of seducing and easily memorisable tunes.

We have already seen, especially in Chapters Five and Six, how cunningly, wisely and effectively was music employed by many Protestant Reformers to this end. Indeed, as mentioned previously (§ 5.3.4.6.), both Lutherans and their opponents recognised how fundamental Luther's hymns had been for spreading his doctrine (in the words of Tilemann Heshusius and Adam Contzen respectively). Similarly, the effects of Calvinist Psalms and of Strasbourg's congregational singing on the dissemination of the Protestant views are difficult to establish, but they were certainly of primary importance.

In the climate of confessional opposition, however, it may come as a surprise to learn that the Catholic Church – and especially the Jesuits – soon understood the value of music for re-attracting believers to their churches, and that they purposefully acted to this end.

For example, in 1563, the French Jesuit Edmond Auger (1530 – 1591) advocated the use of music when writing to his superior. He suggested asking Pierre Ronsard, the "first poet of the kingdom", to make Psalm translations which would obviously compete with those by Marot, "for singing at home, in shops and while traveling". Indeed, he maintained, the French are strongly attracted by singing, and "the devil has won over a whole world of them" by exploiting this "weakness". Indeed, continued Auger, "This would be a battle like that in the time of St [John] Chrysostom against the songs of the Arians", and, if people had Catholic "Mass, sermons, catechism and holy Psalms", they would have "no occasion to be led astray by any novelty". The French Jesuit, thus, wanted to fight against the Reformation on a musical ground: theology might become of secondary importance, since – according to Auger – people were conquered by the power of music rather than by fine reasoning, and only later did they undergo the influence of competing doctrines. Notwithstanding this, Auger concludes: "It is not fitting that these [i.e. the Catholic Psalms] be sung in church, or anywhere except in private places"[41]. This, of course, was a clear, undeniable and probably a strategically crucial difference: Psalms, hymns and spiritual songs could be very similar across the confessional divide, but what mattered was their use for congregational singing.

---

41 *LM* 7, p. 475. Translation in Monson 2006, p. 416.

If there the musical war opposed Catholics to Huguenots, in Alsace the contention was between Bucer and his Catholic counterparts. At the dawn of the seventeenth century, indeed, the competition of rivalling Churches was mirrored by a genuinely musical opposition of styles. The city of Strasbourg, proudly Evangelical, was in fact promoting a retrospective appreciation of polyphonic music belonging to the Franco-Flemish tradition; the bishopric and the Jesuits of Molsheim, instead, supported new styles such as the accompanied monody, also by inviting composers of international standards to Alsace.

Music was effectively practised by the Jesuits in Vienna too, where their College prided itself with appreciated musical performances. In 1564, Jerome Nadal (1507–1580), who had been among the first ten members of the Jesuit Society, wrote: "On Saturday evenings they also sing the *Salve* with other hymns and prayers to Our Lady; and on Sundays after Vespers, the litanies – all with the organ [...] This is very suitable against the heretics; they are upset by this, and the Catholics, on the contrary, receive great consolation"[42].

Thus, music (performed, promoted, composed and published) was seen in a variety of perspectives: as an element which would enrich the beauty of worship in the eyes of God and of the congregation, but also as a weapon against the "heretics", both for persuading and for "upsetting" them[43].

### 10.3.7. Conquering space through sound

This weapon could become much sharper when music became an instrument for conquering, through sound, the spaces belonging to other confessions. We have already met with street vendors who sold and sang Luther's hymns in German market squares, and with mobs intoning Huguenot Psalms in Bordeaux, Rouen and other French cities. At a fair in Givry (Burgundy, 1561), for instance, groups of Evangelicals overturned the stands of Catholic peddlers, while singing Psalms. As maintained by Pettegree, "this use of the Psalms for the insolent appropriation of public space undoubtedly played a large part in the rising sense of anger and frustration among the Catholic population – an anger that fuelled the extraordinary passions of the Religious Wars. So too did the violence that accompanied the Psalm singing"[44].

---

[42] *Nadal* 2, p. 496.
[43] Cf. Honegger 1982, p. 17; Rainoldi 2000, p. 353; Wagner Oettinger 2001, p. 50; Leitmeir 2002, p. 127; Brown 2005, p. 1; Monson 2006, p. 416; Crook 2009, pp. 27–28.
[44] Pettegree 2005, p. 60.

Sometimes, the Calvinists' Psalms were fought by other sounds, in a kind of a musical duel where each confession strove to overcome the other in decibels. Thus, in December 1561, the pealing of bells in the Church of St Médard, in the Paris *faubourg* of St Marcel, disrupted a Huguenot meeting when Psalms were sung and sermons were preached[45].

On the other hand, in an episode detailed in Chapter Six (§ 6.3.4.), when the Calvinist in Ghent sang Psalms whilst building their new church, as touchingly recounted by Marcus van Vaernewijck (1518–1569), the physical occupation of space by those constructing a sacred edifice was acoustically mirrored by the seizure of an aural space through Psalm-singing.

This kind of conquest may seem of minor importance today, since the noisy background of today's cities and the proportionally scanty use of aural signals with respect to visual communication have considerably slighted the perception of aural spaces. In the sixteenth century, however, aural spaces did matter and had an almost tangible quality: suffice it to say that, in the rural areas, the extent of a parish church's territory was set by the reach of the pealing of its bells, and that bells at shrines were similar to signposts to help pilgrims in finding their way.

While bells gathered Catholics for public prayers in Counter-Reformation Bavaria, the German practice of having civic musicians playing from the "piper's tower" had a social and religious dimension in turn: in Ingolstadt (1584), an ordinance prescribed that civic musicians "play, in all four directions [of the compass], several motets or other songs, appropriate to the time", but explicitly excluded both "scandalous songs" and "Lutheran Psalms" from the repertoire they were permitted to perform[46].

### 10.3.7.1. Walking singers

Civic musicians playing all around the compass were certainly occupying an ample share of the acoustic space; however, the advantage of being aboveground was counterbalanced by the scarce mobility of piper's towers. Another way of physically appropriating the aural space of other confessions was to exploit the potential of processional singing, which had the benefit of allowing the singing community to gradually advance on an itinerary while spreading its songs all around it.

---

**45** Cf. Davis 1973, p. 73.
**46** Stadtarchiv Ingolstadt, A II 36a, fols. 4$^{r\text{-}v}$, quoted in and translated by Fisher 2014, p. 212 (cf. also pp. 11 and 19); cf. Reid 1971, p. 45; Mager 1986, pp. 25–26; Pettegree 2005, p. 64; Brown 2008, p. 209.

Processions might be made outside the city's walls by pilgrims reaching a shrine: in this case, the wideness of the aural horizon allowed their songs to spread to considerable distance. This was particularly useful for Catholic Counter-Reformers when the pilgrims' itinerary bordered on Protestant territories. In 1583, the master carpenter Jean Pussot (1568–1626) wrote in his journal about the "White Processions", where pilgrims clad in white sang "various songs, prayers, litanies, Psalms and prose verses, like the *Ave Maria*, the prose songs of the Nativity and Assumption of Our Lady, *Deus benigne, Stabat Mater, Christi fideles, Averte faciem* and many other things of great devotion"[47]. Once more, such processions were held in an area (today's Champagne) which was both linguistically and religiously on the boundary between competing confessional allegiances.

Other processions were often taking place within city walls, and, for Catholics, a favourite occasion for such public displays of faith was the Feast of Corpus Christi. Processions on the feast-day honouring the real presence of Christ in the consecrated particles were an opportunity for prayer, of course, but also for asserting the Catholic belief in transubstantiation which had been contested by Protestants.

Seemingly, Corpus Christi processions spared no efforts in musical splendour: in Ingolstadt (1588), an observer reported that they involved music played by "trumpets and military drums, trumpets and trombones, singing and bell-ringing, salvos of joy, the noise and rejoicing of all people"[48].

It should not be imagined, however, that Protestants simply waited for such processions to pass by and finish – not always, at least. Already in 1529, in Göttingen, Lutheran hymns such as *Aus tiefer Not*, sung by Lutheran crowds, disturbed a Corpus Christi procession; the same happened in Dieppe, in 1559, when another such procession promoted by the Archbishop of Rouen was blocked by a gathering of two thousand Calvinists who sang "for hours" Marot's Psalms[49]. Since the planned procession would have been musical in turn, this is yet another instance of a competition for aural spaces[50]. In Lyon (1551), Huguenot processions whose soundtrack was obviously psalmody were organised at the same time as Corpus Christi processions, whereas in Sens (1562) the two parades faced each other producing riots and violence[51].

---

[47] Pussot 1858, pp. 18–19; as quoted in and translated by Crouzet 2006, p. 94.
[48] Scherer 1588, pp. 2–3, as quoted in and translated by Fisher 2014, p. 251.
[49] Cf. Hannay 1998, vol. II, p. 6.
[50] Cf. Reid 1971, p. 46; Eire 1986, p. 192; van Orden 2000, p. 277; Herl 2004, pp. 89–90; Fisher 2014, pp. 30, 251, 298 and 302.
[51] Cf. Davis 1973, pp. 73–74.

In Edinburgh (1558), the city's patron saint's feast-day was celebrated, as always, with a procession in honour of St Giles. During a pause, when the saint's statue was left unguarded, it became the object of violent iconoclasm; however, in the words of a seventeenth-century historian, David Calderwood (1575–1650), "Search was made for the doers, but none could be deprehended; for the brethren assembled themselves in such sort, in companies, singing Psalms, and praising God, that the proudest of enemies were astonished"[52].

### 10.3.7.2. Seizing the Service

If such a clash of opposing musical expressions of faith was striking when it happened in open-air contexts such as those described above (§ 10.3.7.1.), it became even more impressive when it took place within the very buildings which used to symbolise the Church's unity. On various occasions, in fact, musical protest intruded into churches, with more or less disruptive consequences. Indeed, an episode which happened in Milton (Kent) in 1545 constitutes an ideal bridge between our discussion of processions and that of liturgical disagreements: there, a conflict arose among the sexton, the churchwardens, some parishioners and the minister regarding whether the Litanies revised by Archbishop Cranmer could (or should) be performed processionally, outside the church, or within it. Catholic practices thus conflicted with Evangelical innovations, and the aural space became one object of contention[53].

As told by Fisher[54], congregational singing in the German vernacular was often introduced by the laity, rebelling against their Catholic pastors. The flock's initiative might become rather worrying for the celebrating priest: in Ottering, near Regensburg, the curate – under menace of death – reportedly allowed his parishioners to sing *Aus tiefer Not*; in Au, near Munich, the laity sang vernacular Psalms "against [the priest's] will", and "when he begins to sing a Catholic song to them, they remain silent". In Ulm (1527), the Franciscan church was occupied by singing protesters[55]. In Lübeck (1529) and in Lüneburg (1530), sermons were interrupted by the congregation's singing of Luther's hymn *Ach Gott, vom Himmel sieh darein* (though sometimes secular songs might work at least as well for this purpose, as happened in Wittenberg in 1521). On the other hand, in Beelitz (Brandenburg), a Lutheran congregation interpreted the Psalms of the Lutheran Lobwasser as symbols of Calvinism: one particularly outraged pa-

---

52 Calderwood 1843, vol. 1, pp. 346–347, as quoted in Duguid 2014, p. 202.
53 Cf. Mears 2013, pp. 48–49.
54 Fisher 2014, p. 36. See also *ibid*, p. 35.
55 Stadtarchiv Ulm A 3680, fols. 148, 150; *Ratsprotokolle* 8, fol. 40.

rishioner threw a candelabrum at the organist who had started playing a Lobwasser Psalm during worship (eventually, it was not the organist, but his unlucky wife who was hit by the poorly-aimed candelabrum-throw[56]). Spontaneous singing of forbidden or unsanctioned German songs was often seen by Protestants as a purposeful rebellion against the Catholic clergy and the tradition they represented. So dangerous could such incidents become, that in Salzburg (1565) the Catholic Archbishop forbade laypeople from joining in singing until the first line of the song had been intoned in its entirety by the celebrating priest[57].

Whereas in such cases the formerly Catholic congregation showed its new allegiance by means of song, in other instances groups or individuals belonging to a confession would burst into another's places of worship with the purpose of disrupting their services.

In many cases, it should be said, such disturbances seem to have been caused by riotous fringes of the population, and to have mirrored a disposition to violence and aggressiveness at least as much as one to spiritual reformation.

For example, when (in September 1528) a group of young protesters irrupted into St John's cathedral in Toggenburg (near Sankt Gallen, Switzerland) to disturb a Vesper service, they accompanied their profanation of the consecrated particles with reportedly "roguish" songs. A drunkard sang a Calvinist Psalm rather impromptu during a Catholic service (Antwerp, 1565); the demolition of a Passion scenery representing the Mount of Olives was similarly performed while singing, and Catholic Masses were frequently interrupted by such iconic hymns of Lutheranism as *Erhalt uns, Herr, bei deinem Wort*. This happened, for example, in Munich (1558), when, for two consecutive Sundays in June, a small crowd of about twelve people interrupted the celebration at the Augustinian church by singing that highly provocative song[58].

The interruption of a religious service by singing a religious song was however less disturbing than to ridicule another confession's teachings, its members or its songs.

---

**56** Cf. Nischan 1994, p. 153.
**57** Cf. Reid 1971 p. 52; Herl 2004, pp. 89–90; Brown 2008, p. 256; Fisher 2014, pp. 14, 35 and 37.
**58** Cf. Müller 1911, p. 133; Janssen 1966, p. 262; Eire 1986, p. 113; Scribner 1987, pp. 110–112; Bowers 1999, p. 449; Wagner Oettinger 2001, pp. 45–46; Pettegree 2005, p. 63; Owens 2006, p. 36; Fisher 2014, pp. 1–2.

### 10.3.7.3. Sung sarcasm

Lutherans had a noteworthy repertoire of sarcastic songs, especially against the Pope: one of the most famous examples is the "children's song" *Nun treiben wir den Papst hinaus* (1541), which was inspired by the custom of "driving out" winter at the beginning of spring, but which actually suggested "throwing out" the Pope. Of course, papacy as an institution (rather than its embodiment in the person of the actual Pope) was a favourite target for Evangelical polemical songs. Lutheran children were trained, by songs such as *Erhalt uns, Herr*, to identify the Pope with one of the two "archenemies of Christ", and the Scottish *Gude and Godlie Ballatis* did not hesitate in defining him as a "Pagan full of pride"[59]; but collections such as those published by Pierre de Vingle (1495–1536) in the 1530s show that these sentiments were widely shared. It should be said, however, that this approach was not exclusive to the Evangelicals, and that strongly polemical writings and songs against the Pope and papacy had appeared well before Luther's Reformation[60].

Other songs, such as *Hört ihr Pfaffen andere meer* (1525, on the tune of *Resonet in laudibus*) made fun of priests and Masses: anticlerical feelings prompted the creation of a huge number of polemical songs throughout Europe. Among these, an interesting example is the satirical Decalogue *Das sind die Heyligen zehen Gebott* (1531?) by Erasmus Alber, in which the Ten Commandments are replaced by the anti-Commandments which, according to the author, regulated the lives of depraved Franciscans. Calvin had also his share as the victim of polemical songs (cf., for example, *Calvinus du und dein Kind*, 1592[61], contrafacture of *Venus, du und dein Kind* by Jacob Regnart [c.1540–1599]) but Catholics did not refrain from reviling against Luther in turn: "*Ach Luter du vil böser man*" ("Ah, Luther, you very evil man") by Hieronymus Emser (c.1477–1527), fourth stanza of *Ach Benno du vil heilger man* (1524), is a direct attack on the Reformer in the form of a song, and so is *Was han ick dummer Monnich gedaan?*[62], mocking Luther's marriage[63].

Frequently, polemical songs attacked particular aspect of the others' beliefs: rather obviously, this happened frequently with those elements of the old faith against which the Reformers had rebelled.

---

59 *Ane Compendious* 1621, sig. M3.
60 Cf. Wagner Oettinger 2001, pp. 32, 129, 131 and 185; Groote and Vendrix 2012, p. 178; Pettegree 2005, p. 67; Fisher 2014, p. 218.
61 *Fuenff schoene* 1592.
62 *Historia manuscripta Hamburgensis 834*, AD 1542; as quoted in ZVHG 1847, vol. IV, p. 232.
63 Cf. Blume 1975, p. 34; Wagner Oettinger 2001, p. 129.

One such example was the cult of the saints and of the Virgin Mary: since both of them had been particularly cherished by popular devotion and piety, one of the most effective ways for uprooting what was perceived as idolatrous by many Reformers was precisely to ridicule it.

Indeed, the pre-Reformation and Catholic repertoire of devotional songs maintained a strong focus on the Virgin Mary. Nikolaus Herman, whom we met in Chapter Five as the composer of early Lutheran works (§ 5.3.2.1. and 5.3.4.6.), stated that Catholic songs used to be "for the most part intended for the invocation of the highly-praised Virgin Mary and the dear saints". Though he wrote with noteworthy reverence of the Virgin and of the saints, he complained that "no one knew how to sing or speak about the Lord Christ" except as in terms of "a strict judge, from whom no grace could be expected, but only wrath and punishment"[64]. Thus, he continues, religious songs addressing intercessors such as Mary or the saints were particularly treasured by the pre-Reformation laity. In other cases, songs were composed which openly contested this aspect of Catholic spirituality: a polemical song documented in Strasbourg c.1525, *Merckt jr herren myner sag*, for example, is particularly harsh against the veneration of the saints and against pilgrimages[65].

Herman recounts that many, among the elder, still remembered and could sing some pre-Reformation songs in honour of the Virgin Mary. While in some zones these simply tended to be neglected, as the Evangelical Reformations succeeded in downplaying the cult of the saints, other Reformers decided to build on the popularity of these songs but to address them to Christ instead of to his Mother. Thus, contrafacture of the *Salve Regina* could produce hymns such as *Salve Rex Christe*; when these processes were enacted within communities which had not yet officially adhered to Protestantism, however, they could be persecuted by local authorities[66].

On other dogmatic aspects, several polemical songs were penned, challenging the other confessions on their particular beliefs. For example, as we have seen in Chapter Five (§ 5.3.2.4.), Luther's *Nun freut euch* (1523) was certainly not a properly polemical song, but nevertheless it supported and successfully disseminated the Lutheran view of salvation and works, thus implicitly countering the received teaching of the Catholic Church.

Still another *contrafactum* on the *Resonet*, which however was created by a Catholic polemicist, attacked in turn the Lutheran doctrine of the priesthood of

---

[64] Herman 1562, fols. B3$^r$-B3$^v$ (*WB*, p. 616), as quoted in and translated by Brown 2005, p. 31.
[65] Cf. Trocmé Latter 2015, p. 164.
[66] Cf. Wagner Oettinger 2001, pp. 54–55, 70; Fisher 2014, p. 37.

all believers on Scriptural grounds: similar to the Biblical characters of Korah, Dathan and Abiram (cf. Numbers 16), who claimed a right to priesthood without being entitled to it, so Lutherans advanced pretentions to a ministry which was proper to the ordained clergy in the eyes of Catholics[67].

### 10.3.7.4. Paraphrase and parody

Indeed, contrafacture lent itself easily to the possibility of mocking the religious songs of other believers by paraphrasing them. This happened, for example, during a votive procession held in Göttingen in 1529, when the Catholic litanies were at first disrupted by vernacular Psalm-singing, and later they were satirised by changing the traditional response to litanies (i.e. *"ora pro nobis"*, pray for us) into *"Ohr ab, zum Thor aus"* (roughly corresponding to "Shut up and clear out"[68]).

The French Catholic polemicist Artus Désiré, whose literary output is virtually entirely intended as a holy war against the Evangelical Reformations, made use of the same strategy, though in a more organised and consistent fashion. His *Contrepoison des Cinquante-Deux chansons de Clément Marot* (1560[69]) is a systematic parody of the fifty-two Psalms translated by Marot into French. By using the same metric and poetic schemes as Marot, Désiré consciously de-sacralised what was going to become the core devotion of Calvinism. Thus, for example, in his parody of Psalm 13 [12] (fourth stanza), Marot's *Que celuy qui guerre me fait / Ne die point, Je l'ay deffait* is turned by Désiré into a direct attack to Calvin (*Que Calvin qui guerre nous faict...*); in Désiré's same *chanson*, the two most famous Reformers are jointly targeted: "How long will the error last / of Martin Luther false at heart / and of Calvin our adversary?"[70].

Désiré's paraphrase of Marot's version of Psalm 114 [113], *Quand Israël hors d'Egypte sortit*, "When Israel went out from Egypt", was no less explicit in denigrating Calvin. It read: "When Jehan Calvin went out of France / and parted from the God of Jacob / To live in a foreign land / He became the great enemy of God"[71].

However, as the Gospel has it, "all who take the sword will perish by the sword" (Matthew 26:52). When, in 1561, Désiré himself was caught and imprisoned, his Huguenot antagonists were quick to pen a *contrafactum* of the *contra-*

---

67 Wagner Oettinger 2001, p. 134.
68 Lubecus 1967, pp. 15ff., as quoted in and translated by Scribner 1987, p. 61.
69 Désiré 1560.
70 Désiré 1977, p. 21.
71 Désiré 1977, p. 14, my translation.

*factum*, reading: "When Désiré went out of Paris / and departed toward Spain / [...] He was discovered, by God's will / to Whom be praise"[72].

As Pineaux points out[73], this rebound of paraphrases was by no means typical for the Huguenot polemicists, who could and did satirise Catholic religious songs but normally left the psalter untouched.

Indeed, though the only form officially admitted within Calvinist worship was, as we have repeatedly seen, unaccompanied psalmody, there were several printed collections of songs destined for use by the Huguenots, and which – notwithstanding the frequent use of *"chansons spirituelles"* in their title-page – often belong to the polemical repertoire rather than to the devotional proper. Such collections frequently draw liberally on popular tunes from the Catholic heritage and from the secular repertoire, whose lyrics undergo systematic contrafacture. The first song-book of such *contrafacta* had been issued already in 1533 by Matthieu Malingre[74], who had been a Dominican friar; a group of fourteen songs listed by the Inquisition (Toulouse, France, 1540 – 9) were similarly associated with secular melodies; and in the *Recueil de plusieurs chansons spirituelles* (1555[75]), which enjoyed considerable success, we find lyrics of such an unmistakable character as *"La Sorbonne la Bigotte"* or *"La Papauté est contre Christe"* ("the Sorbonne, that bigot", or "Papacy is against Christ"[76]). Within this same collection, however, *contrafacta* of sacred traditional songs could mirror more closely the original: it is the case, for example, with *Grand conditeur de tous les cieux* on the tune of *Conditor alme siderum*, or of *Verbe Divin, verbe eternel* on *Verbum supernum prodiens*. In spite of this, the lyrics of *Dy moy ami ou s'en ira*, set to the Gregorian tune of the *Dies iræ*, challenge directly the original Latin sequence, though their subject is seemingly the same (i.e. death). In this case, the musical reference to the Catholic model is thus exploited for reinforcing the Evangelical views against the doctrine of purgatory.

A curious instance of polemics on polemics is the song *Poures Evangelistes*, which is set to the tune of *Lutheriens retirez-vous meschans* ("O Lutherans, retire, you evil"): though the content of the new song is clearly marked by the climate of confessional opposition, it has no direct reference to the members of other Churches.

---

[72] Désiré 1977, pp. 13–14, my translation.
[73] Jacques Pineaux, "Introduction", in Désiré 1977, p. 14.
[74] Malingre 1533.
[75] *Recueil* 1555.
[76] Cf. Pollmann 2006, p. 306.

Toward the end of the songbook, however, the level of polemics increase, and many songs are found which abuse the papacy, the Mass and many Catholic rites in a rather explicit fashion.

It should be pointed out, in this context, that promoting the use of devotional *contrafacta* was not always a safe option for the religious Reformers: as demonstrated by the trial records of Genevans charged with singing illicit songs, several defendants maintained they were not singing the original licentious text, but rather some pious hymn whose words had possibly escaped their accusers. As Latour suggests, all *contrafacta* had a "palimpsest of meaning"[77], and it was impossible, particularly in the short term, to erase completely the lewd associations of a secular song in favour of its new spiritual lyrics.

### 10.3.7.5. The time of the Antichrist

Other forms of musical polemics involved playing on the very act of singing and how it was perceived by members of other confessions. For example, the Catholic Bonifacius Amerbach (1495–1562) from Basel wrote that "the people howl the Psalms which have been translated into German", whereas the Carthusian monk Georgius Carpentarius (c.1487–1531) mentioned the "rough" style of the laypeople's chanting of vernacular Psalms[78].

The Franciscan theologian Konrad Klinge (c.1483–1556) similarly drew on the pre-existing and traditional imagery (cf. § 3.3.2.9.) which associated German singing with "howling" to develop an elaborated and Scriptural metaphor: "Their songs in the vernacular are merely the howling of wolves against Christ's sheep and their pastors"[79].

The wolf *par excellence* which – according to Scripture again – was going to attack Christ's flock, and particularly as the last times were thought to approach, was of course the Antichrist. We have already seen (cf. § 4.2.4.11.) that an "apocalyptical" vein (meaning by this the announcement of and expectation for disastrous events preparing the end of the world) was often present in the writings of many Reformers of all allegiances, and that labelling one's theological opponents as the Antichrist was a very common practice for many polemicists.

These topics were of course abundantly developed in songs, which actually become poignant indicators of how this view was felt and shared by people of all social and cultural provenances. In Wagner Oettinger's study of propaganda

---

77 Latour 2015, p. 27.
78 Groote and Vendrix 2012, p. 180; cf. Marcus 2000, p. 165.
79 Klinge 1562, p. 209.

songs in the Reformation era, roughly a quarter of the songs under discussion (i.e. 56 over 221) include one or more references to "apocalyptical" themes. Many of them, of course, are quick in identifying the Pope as the Antichrist. This echoes, on the aural plane, what was done, in a very graphical fashion, by Lucas Cranach the Elder in his well-known *Passional Christi und Antichristi* (1521), where Christ's saintly deeds preceding his death on the cross were ruthlessly juxtaposed to the greedy and sinful acts of the Pope, portrayed as the Antichrist.

"Apocalyptical" subjects were particularly frequent in Lutheran songs dating from the 1520s, though they frequently are primarily religious songs; the identification of the Pope as the Antichrist was seen principally as a confirmation that the last times were approaching, that Christ's faithful had to endure persecution and suffering, but that they would soon receive their prize from the Lord's hands[80].

### 10.3.7.6. Changes in music are changes in doctrine

Finally, I will discuss another function of religious and polemical songs within the context of confessionalisation, i.e. that of defending the idiosyncratic teachings of one's confession. Songs, as we have seen, were useful for disseminating ideas and doctrines; moreover, some particular forms of religious songs had soon come to be strictly associated with particular confessions. Thus, as the boundaries between allegiances hardened, as confessional fluidity disappeared, and – especially – as political decisions influenced drastically the religious belonging of the people, to adopt or to refuse a particular song or a form of singing had a great impact on the self-representation of a community and on how it represented itself to others.

Though the episodes I will briefly relate here refer to a period which does not form the object of this book (early seventeenth century), I wished to mention in passing the polemics surrounding the adoption of Calvinist psalmody by Lutherans since they perfectly summarise the issues at stake and why they constituted important matters for the people involved.

The reader will recall from Chapter Six (§ 6.3.3.) that the translation of the Genevan Psalter into German by Ambrosius Lobwasser had met with great success and had played an important role in the development of the *cantional* style in the performance of Lutheran chorales. In Brandenburg, from 1613, the official attempts to replace the Lutheran hymnbooks with Lobwasser's Psalms were felt

---

**80** Cf. Wagner Oettinger 2001, pp. 32, 171, 175, 182, 201 etc.

(as they actually were) to be pointing to the penetration of Calvinism into Lutheran lands.

The Lutherans reacted with vehemence: as one of them wrote, "when the music in the temples is changed, the teaching is changed as well; that is, when people sing in a new and foreign manner in the churches, a transformation of the doctrine generally follows"[81].

Not only, however, the risk was feared that a change in the sung repertoire would eventually lead to a change in the content and practice of faith; the problem, for many Lutherans, was that the Genevan Psalms were merely translations – albeit not literal, in consequence of poetical needs – of the Old Testament book, whereas the Psalm paraphrases sung in the Lutheran tradition made use of typological reading. By stating clearly that – for instance – the Messiah promised in the Psalms was, for Christians, the Lord Jesus, Lutheran hymns were felt by believers to be more comforting, more consoling and ultimately closer to their lives. The Calvinist approach, instead, seemed to them as favouring literal and slightly antiquarian or philological renditions, which failed to appeal to the Lutherans' hearts.

Thus, when authorities tried and imposed the adoption of Lobwasser's psalmody, the Lutherans rebelled: they would remain silent instead of singing, or else they would simply intone the hymns they were used to; in some instances, they even resorted to violence and open rebellion.

When a similar incident happened in Elbing (today's Elbląg in Poland), in 1655, those complaining against the replacement of Lutheran hymns by Lobwasser's Psalms argued that, since the name of Christ was not mentioned in the Calvinist Psalms (because, of course, they were translations from the Old Testament), they could not be considered as "Christian" songs proper. Against this argument, it was maintained that confessional difference did not perforce imply a different musical repertoire, and that Lutherans had not been always fastidious in adopting only songs created within their own field[82] (and this was, of course, a good point).

Such discussions, however, are highly significant and symptomatic of how crucial were songs for the believers; how strongly they identified themselves as members of a community, and their own congregation as belonging to a confession by means of music; and, of course, how biting, irritating and painful

---

[81] Polycarp Leyser (1552–1610), in Becker 1602, as quoted in and translated by Brown 2008, pp. 254–255 (cf. *WB* 1060, pref. 100, pp. 679–684).
[82] Cf. Herl 2004, pp. 157–159; Brown 2008, pp. 254–255.

could sarcasm become, when it attacked songs so dear and so cherished by entire communities.

## 10.4. Psalms for all

The episodes mentioned towards the end of the preceding section of this Chapter lead us to discuss the role of Psalm-singing within the context of confessionalisation. The complexity of this subject should be clear to readers by now. Psalms basically are a form of prayer whose pre-eminent status within the Christian (and the Jewish) tradition is guaranteed by their belonging to the Scripture, by the alleged authorship of King David and (for Christians) by the fact Jesus himself used them for praying and the Church has uninterruptedly maintained this practice. Notwithstanding this, in the sixteenth century they became a matter of division, separation and sometimes of violent opposition.

As discussed in the previous Chapters, the Hebraic Psalms had been frequently used in their Greek translation of the Septuagint, until – in the Western tradition – the monastic practice favoured St Jerome's Vulgate and progressively disseminated the custom of timing the hours of prayer throughout the day with a selection of Psalms.

Vernacular – and sometimes rhymed – translations of the Psalms had appeared very early in the history of European literature; in Italian, for example, a version of the penitential Psalms in tercets had long been attributed to Dante but – whatever its authorship – testifies to the long-dating tradition of Psalm-paraphrases in the vernacular.

Indeed, such a practice had normally been understood as a mark of devotion and piety, and in the early Reformation era it still had this connotation, although in certain contexts the prohibitions issued by Church authorities against vernacular translations of the Bible might be understood as limiting vernacular Psalm-paraphrases as well. In France, for example, in 1526 a ban against complete Bible translations had been issued; at the same time, as we have seen in Chapter Six (§ 6.2.2.), Marot's early Psalms were deeply appreciated by staunch Catholics, and – as Higman points out[83] – as late as 1561 a commission of Catholic theologians gave explicit approval to the Psalm paraphrases by Marot and Bèze (even though Higman suggests that the members of the commission could have been more Evangelically-minded than average).

---

**83** Cf. Higman 2004.

In spite of this, in 1545 Marot's Psalms had been forbidden; in general, as time progressed, Psalm-singing in the vernacular became so closely associated with Calvinists that Christians of other confessions found it increasingly unadvisable to do the same in public. This was particularly true for Lutherans who wished to eschew accusations of "crypto-Calvinism" in the age of confessionalisation[84].

Similarly, in 1619, George Wither (1588–1667) clearly stated that Catholics "have of late years disapproved the translation of these *Psalmes* into the vulgar tongues, and scoffed at the singing of them in the reformed Churches [and] in scorn termed them *Geneva Jigs*, and *Beza's Ballets*"[85]. It is open to debate, therefore, whether the hundreds of Scots singing Psalms under Mary Stuart's window the night of her arrival in Scotland (1561) intended this impromptu performance as a homage or a provocation to their Catholic Queen – or possibly both[86].

As seen before (§ 6.2.1.), moreover, no translation is totally neutral; and even less so when it is realised by strongly motivated believers whose primary aim is not philology, but rather piety (first), literary beauty and – sometimes – the promotion of a confessional view. Luther's Psalm paraphrases were more explicit in adapting the chosen Psalm to a Christian perspective, and often in updating their wording so as to mirror particular situations currently experienced by the contemporaneous Lutherans. The Calvinist Psalms, though seemingly closer to the Scriptural text, could still be read and interpreted in a typological fashion which made them no less pertinent to contemporaneous issues, and sometimes even inflammatory.

To start with, many Biblical Psalms are far from "politically correct" even in their original version: they often speak of warfare, of destroying the enemies of God and of his people, but also of the righteous enduring persecution or exile. In 1560, for example, after the unsuccessful Conspiracy of Amboise, Bèze was accused (by the Genevan Consistory!) of purposefully increasing the instigations to violence contained in Psalm 140 [139] in his translation[87].

Secondly, and precisely through their association with music (and with tunes which, as seen in Chapter Six[88], were in turn very closely bound to a par-

---

[84] Cf. Laube 2014, p. 85.
[85] Cf. Wither 1619, sigs. B4ᵛ-B5.
[86] Cf. MacDonald 1991, p. 107; Duguid 2014, pp. 203–204 and 220.
[87] Kelley 1973, pp. 124–125.
[88] See § 6.3.2.

ticular text), an impressive interplay of cross-references could be built and exploited[89].

Moreover, phenomena of appropriation could update some details of the Psalms' texts to make them mirror even more closely the situation of the believers. For example, when – in April 1562 – the Prince de Condé arrived in Orleans, the crowd greeted him by singing an adaptation of Marot's version of Psalm 124 [123], with the text modified from "Israel" to "Orleans"[90]. The same Psalm was intoned by an imposing crowd gathered in Edinburgh (1582) for celebrating the return of John Durie (1537–1600) from exile:

> At the Netherbow they took up the 124th Psalm, 'Now Israel may say', etc., and sang in such a pleasant tune in four parts, known to the most part of the people, coming up the street all bareheaded till they entered the Kirk, with such a great sound and majesties, that it moved both themselves and all the huge multitude of the beholders[91].

The *Estreines au Cardinal*, written in 1561, similarly adopted the metrical structure of Marot's translation of Psalm 38 [37] (*"Las, en ta fureur aigue / Ne m'argue / De mon faict, Dieu tout puissant"*), adapting it to the contemporaneous political situation (*"Au Cardinal de Lorraine / Porte estreine / Le saige Dieu tout puissant!"*[92]). The connection between the original text and its corresponding tune is made explicit in the 1562 *Cantique et action de Grâce au Seigneur* (*"O bienheureux tous nobles Princes"*), which celebrates the Huguenot victory in Lyon making references to Antichrist imagery[93], set to the melody of Psalm 7 (*"Mon Dieu, j'ay en toy esperance"*). Other such creations were an Ode on the Battle of St Giles (1562), on Psalm 81 [80], or a song celebrating the end of the war (*Echo parlant à la paix*), set to the melody of Psalm 33 [32][94].

An interesting case of psalmody, propaganda and persecution is that involving Jérôme-Hermès Bolsec (d. c.1585), a former Carmelite who actively engaged in public theological polemics and disputes with Calvin in Geneva, and who was therefore imprisoned for more than two months before being banished from the city.

During his incarceration, Bolsec penned an extremely poignant *contrafactum* of Psalm 23 [22] from the Genevan Psalter (the famous "The Lord is my shep-

---

**89** Cf. van Orden 2000, p. 276; Fisher 2001, pp. 651–652; Wagner Oettinger 2001, p. 45; Herl 2004, pp. 89–90; Pettegree 2005, p. 50; Forney 2006, pp. 253–254; Brown 2008, pp. 254–255.
**90** Hannay 1998, vol. II, p. 6; cf. Foxe 1965, vol. VI, p. 700; Gillingham 2008, vol. I.
**91** Cf. Calderwood 1843, vol. 8, p. 226, as quoted in Duguid 2014, p. 205.
**92** Tarbé 1866, p. 41.
**93** Cf. Pettegree 2003, p. 120.
**94** Pettegree 2005, pp. 67–69.

herd"). His version was particularly efficacious for a number of reasons: it exploited the dissemination of a well-known Psalm and of its tune; it suggested that its author be equated with the Biblical King David to whom the Psalm was ascribed; it also hinted to hearers that the author was the object of unjust persecution, thus probably disquieting those who had sought refuge in Geneva to escape persecution in turn; finally, it managed to convey the core of Bolsec's theological disagreement with Calvin, on the complex doctrine of predestination, in a simple and easily memorisable fashion. Indeed, in the times following Bolsec's condemnation, evidence is found that his *contrafactum* was sung by Genevan dissidents, to the irritation of the Calvinist religious authorities[95]. This episode will thus help us to move on to consider the role of *contrafacta* in the field of polemics and propaganda.

## 10.5. Confessional Contrafacture

Indeed, the last paragraphs of the preceding section form an ideal bridge with what will now follow: in the upcoming pages I will analyse the purposes fulfilled by *contrafacta* – not only of Psalms, as in the preceding pages, but of religious and secular songs in general – within the framework of confessionalisation.

Here too, as in the case of using a Genevan tune for *contrafacta* or paraphrases, the intertextual net of references, both musical and verbal, could be exploited – and often was – to convey multiple layers of meaning, both conscious and unconscious.

As Fisher has efficaciously summarised concerning the city of Augsburg, the process of contrafacture often started with a well-known tune which might come from the secular tradition or from a Lutheran song (which might have in turn secular origins); from this a new song was created, often by literate authors, and could be printed and sold; in turn, this *contrafactum* could be copied by hand and progressively modified to mirror the contemporaneous situation[96]. Thus, the resulting *contrafacta* were felt, at the same time, to be radically new (since they often spoke of the news of the day) and as having a history, whose meaning was rooted in the melody's existing tradition and on its preceding *contrafacta*.

On the other hand, and especially in the case of very popular tunes, it is highly unlikely that any new *contrafactum* aimed at replacing the song it was

---

95 Cf. Latour 2015, pp. 31 ff.
96 Fisher 2001, pp. 651–652.

built on; rather, it exploited its popularity and the intertextual potential it expressed. It was not a matter of "improving" (or "Christianly improving") a preceding text, but rather of enriching the meaning of the *contrafactum* by exploiting its history. Thus, such *contrafacta* are an invaluable resource for understanding the religious and social climate experienced by those living the years of confessionalisation and denominational opposition[97].

We have already seen on several occasions that one function of contrafacture, at all levels of musical and literary refinement, was to replace the secular words which had been traditionally associated with a successful tune, so I will not discuss this function here. More significant, within the context of the present Chapter, are those *contrafacta* created with the aim of supplanting a religious song typical of another confession.

Thus, such a symbol of Lutheran polemics against Catholicism as *Erhalt uns, Herr* was transformed – possibly by the Jesuits or by someone close to them – into a variety of Counter-Reformation songs, which exploited its huge success in the service of the opposing view. Luther's attack against the two archenemies of the Lord, i.e. the Pope and the Turks, was turned, in these *contrafacta*, into denunciation of the heretics ("*Den Ketzern wehr*") and of the Turks – who apparently were one of the archenemies for members of all denominations.

Fisher correctly cautions against simplistic assumptions on how successful such *contrafacta* actually were at the level of popular culture: instead, he does maintain that the association of Catholic propaganda with unmistakably Lutheran tunes may have been striking for the hearers[98].

While Counter-Reformation Catholics did not disdain the use of Lutheran tunes for spreading their message, and thus somehow appropriated their opponents' melodic heritage, the confessions' feelings of ownership with regard to songs might be rather contradictory. When Lutherans had transformed pre-existing (and thus Catholic) songs into hymns for their Church, they felt that the resulting song was now their own; however, this did not imply that Catholics disown or stop singing tunes which had been traditionally theirs for centuries. Thus, the association between tunes and confessional identity could become rather complex in some cases, especially when multiple appropriations, paraphrase and *contrafacta* had been created[99]. This is the case, for example, of a German pamphlet (c.1525) where Catholic polemical songs are built on models coming ultimately from the "Gregorian" tradition (such as *Dies est lætitiæ*,

---

97 Cf. Brednich 1974, vol. 1, p. 63; Wagner Oettinger 2001, pp. 112, 115 and 135.
98 Cf. Fisher 2014, pp. 22 and 183.
99 Cf. Wagner Oettinger 2001, p. 46.

*Omnis mundus, Resonet*) but which had already been taken up by the Lutherans for their own songs[100].

On the other hand, precisely because Catholics were reluctant to abandon their melodic heritage when it had been partially appropriated by the Protestants, a situation potentially dangerous arose for those faithful to Rome: Evangelical songs, which often were built on familiar plainchant models, might penetrate easily within the homes – and sometimes the churches and worships – of the Catholics.

The need was felt, therefore, for an orthodox repertoire to be created, both at the level of simple tunes accessible to all, and as concerns more elaborate works: the competition between opposing factions was increasingly played on the grounds of beauty, amazement and splendour, especially in those situations where the Jesuits' creative strategies were coupled with the economic resources of powerful Catholic rulers such as the Bavarian Wittelsbach family[101].

Alongside functions such as replacing texts of a secular content or whose confessional identity was under attack, or as disseminating a confession's beliefs by exploiting a successful melody, *contrafacta* – as we have seen – were also used for polemical purposes. While rather often polemical *contrafacta* seem to be intended primarily for those whose confessional perspective is analogous to the author's, there are others (such as a Catholic *contrafactum* on *O du armer Judas*, titled *O jr vill armen Christen*, c.1525) which seem to be genuine attempts to convince the adversaries, though the tone of their lyrics was sometimes rather unlikely to be favourably listened to by its intended audience[102].

### 10.5.1. Songs of scorn

A subcategory of polemics – and a rather disturbing one, to be honest – is made of songs purposefully designed in order to offend, mock or abuse another confession, its members or its beliefs.

When biting *contrafacta* were created by Protestants on pre-existing Catholic songs, they could have the added bonus – if one wishes to consider it as a positive aspect – of being potentially useful for disrupting those services and celebrations of the Catholics when the original was sung. We have seen such an ex-

---

100 Wagner Oettinger 2001, p. 120.
101 Cf. Fisher 2014, pp. 31, 38, 40.
102 Cf. Wagner Oettinger 2001, p. 120.

ample earlier in this Chapter (§ 10.3.7.4.), when the traditional Latin "*ora pro nobis*" answer was turned into a warm invitation to the Catholics to go packing.

Similarly, a *contrafactum* of the Christmas hymn *Dies est lætitiæ*, which had already originated a German devotional paraphrase, became *Ain Doctor in dem Sachsser land* (c.1525), which in its first stanza manages to abuse cardinals, bishops and the Pope (who is identified, once more, as the Antichrist, and is accused of simony[103]).

In many cases, satirical *contrafacta* of religious songs had no properly spiritual or doctrinal aims and contents: rather, they played on the typical *topoi* of anticlerical literature, by scorning the morals of debauched clergy and joking about the behaviour and dogmas of the Catholic faith. Such practices represented the Early-Modern updating of medieval customs such as the carnivalesque idea of the world-upside-down[104].

Sadly, however, Catholics might use their own plainchant for ridiculing the others in turn: the *Te Deum*, a hymn which normally had praised God for granting victory to his people, was sometimes employed in mock processions when Protestants were arrayed in ritual vestures, mounted on donkeys and offered to public contumely[105].

The *Te Deum* originated numerous insulting paraphrases in turn. We will see in the following pages the role played by another *Te Deum* parody (1532) within the context of the court of Ferrara; at around the same time, another *contrafactum* appeared in Bologna. Starting with the words *Te Lutherum damnamus*, the hymn leaves no doubts as to its content even after reading only its first lines: "We curse you, Luther, / we acknowledge you a heretic. / The whole world / detests you, father of error"[106].

Another *Te Deum* paraphrase abusing Luther (and Hus, for good measure) was included within a mock liturgy of the Hours written by the Scandinavian Carmelite Poul Helgesen (Paulus Heliae, c.1485-c.1535), together with satirical adaptations from the first verses of the Gospel of Matthew ("*Liber generationis Antichristi, filii perditionis*", i.e. "The book of the generation of the Antichrist, the son of perdition" instead of "The book of the generation of Jesus Christ, the son of David"[107]) and of John ("*In principio erat error, et error erat apud Lu-*

---

103 Wagner Oettinger 2001, p. 89.
104 Cf. Bardsley 2007, p. 177.
105 Cf. Davis 1973, p. 84. See also Scribner 1994, p. 164; van Orden 2000, pp. 276–277; Wagner Oettinger 2001, pp. 89–90, 122–123; Pettegree 2005, pp. 67–69.
106 Bologna, Civico Museo Bibliografico Musicale, MS Q27. Quoted, in Lawrence Rosenwald's translation, from Weiss and Taruskin 2008, p. 90.
107 Translated from the Latin and not quoted from *NRSV*.

*therum*", i.e. "In the beginning was the error, and the error was with Luther", instead of "In the beginning was the Word, and the Word was with God"[108]).

Another extremely well-known plainchant song was the Easter Sequence *Victimæ paschali laudes:* we have already seen, in Chapter Five (§ 5.3.2.1.), that Luther himself adopted its tune for *Christ lag in Todesbanden* (via the German *Leise* for Easter *Christ ist erstanden*), and that it was found even in the Genevan Psalter as the beginning of Psalm 80 [79] (*O Pasteur d'Israël escoute*, cf. § 6.3.1.).

Even though such quotations testify to the widespread appreciation for this beautiful Sequence, which united Christians of all Western denominations, some of them felt rather comfortable in parodying it for satirical purposes or for promoting their confessional view. The author of *Invicti Martini laudes intonant Christiani* was certainly candid in his praise of Luther, though it is debatable how consonant with Luther's own views it was to put him, by means of musical reference, on the same level as the risen Christ[109]. The parody asks the "righteous and pious Martin" to deliver the "doctrine of the living Christ" to the faithful; it accuses the "Roman Judea" not to believe in Christ's resurrection and affirms: "We know that Christ is truly risen / through Martin['s teachings]. / Defend us, o victorious Martin, Alleluia". The text is quoted in a short treatise by the Catholic polemicist Peter Sylvius (or Penick, 1470–1547), who affirms to have heard it sung in Nuremberg; he contrasts this laudatory parody of the *Victimæ paschali* with a derogatory version, possibly by his own (*Perfidi Lutheri fraudes exhorrent Christiani*), and upon which he comments at length: the same Sequence, in the same book, is thus borrowed by the two competing fields to advance their theological and polemical positions.

Another *Victimæ paschali* contrafacture, originating from a Carthusian monastery in Basel, is directed against Luther's teachings. The text here begins: "*Pessimas Lutheri fraudes / fugiant Christiani. / Luther dispergit oves / quas Christus congregarat*", translated as: "Let the Christians avoid / the terrible frauds of Luther. / Luther dispersed the sheep / which Christ gathered"[110].

These few, but significant examples, are merely a selection aiming at providing a feeling, an impression and a picture of how virulent polemics could become, of how astutely it exploited the familiar tunes and songs, and of how unashamedly it made use of liturgical songs: indeed, what should be pointed out here is that mocking *contrafacta* were made not only from the opponent's sacred

---

[108] Cf. Steidl 1918, p. 48; Nugent 1990, pp. 233–237.
[109] In Sylvius 1529, fols. A$^v$-Aij$^r$; see also Legg 1891, p. 34.
[110] Cf. Basel, Öffentliche Bibliothek der Universität, MS AN.II.46; cf. Nugent 1990, pp. 233–237 to which this section is indebted.

songs, but also from one's own, as long as they provided a satisfactory and potentially successful starting point for the creation of a polemical work.

## 10.6. The contexts of confessionalisation

In a similar exemplary fashion, and without any pretence to completeness, I will now propose a short survey of particular contexts which – for geographical, religious or historical reasons – were at the frontline of confessional opposition.

We have already seen, for example, that Catholics were much more disposed toward the use of music for confessional purposes in those territories which were closest to the boundaries of Catholicism, or where Catholics and Protestants actually shared a space and competed for primacy: some of the several possible examples include sensitive areas such as the Netherlands, Bavaria and Austria.

Indeed, it has been noted that the highest concentration of Catholic songbooks was found in those German cities which were geographically closest to Protestantism, such as Cologne, Ingolstadt, Mainz, Munich and Speyer; arguably, the vivacity and appeal of Lutheran singing prompted a similar and opposite reaction from the Catholic camp. Similarly, the propagandistic potential of open-air devotions such as processions (as seen in § 10.3.7.1.) was particularly useful in those areas whose confessional allegiance was threatened by the Protestants: this explains the increasing promotion of shrines such as those of Amberg, Bettbrunn, Dettelbach, Neukirchen and Taxa, whose geographical position was very close to Evangelical zones. As Fisher put it, in Bavaria the concepts of confessionalisation and Counter-Reformation can be usefully employed "given the proximity of the religious frontier and the remarkably intense atmosphere of confessional persuasion and propaganda"[111].

### 10.6.1. "Oh Benno, you holy man..."

Indeed, it was precisely in the Bavarian city of Munich that one of the first events to prompt the composition of polemical songs took place. In 1523, the very year in which Luther's song on the martyrs of Brussels was published, a Papal bull canonised St Benno of Meissen. Probably, this eleventh-century holy man little expected his belated proclamation as a Catholic saint to become the occasion

---

[111] Fisher 2014, p. 15. Cf. also *ibid.*, pp. 3, 13, 298; Monson 2006, p. 416; Wagner Oettinger 2001, p. 9.

for harsh polemics: indeed, and though the canonisation had been strongly supported by civil authorities and thus had important political overtones, the timing of the Pope's decision was seen as a direct challenge to Luther's position on the cult of saints.

The Catholic polemicist Hieronymus Emser, who had been involved in Benno's process of canonisation, was therefore harshly attacked by Luther, who called him "the goat of Leipzig" (in spite of an earlier sympathy between them). Possibly, following Luther's turn to songs with *Ein newes Lied*, Emser was encouraged to change the locus of their theological debates from pamphlets and dogmatic essays to songs. This implied, of course, a drastic modification in the intended audience of their arguments, from that of learned readers to that of all who were capable of singing or listening to a song. Emser's song *Ach Benno du vil heilger man* was not only a powerful tool for propaganda and persuasion (and one rarely used by early Catholic polemicists), but also a statement of values: first, it reasserted the importance of the cult of saints, which the laity cherished dearly; secondly, it affirmed the Catholic endorsement of religious vernacular singing, which Luther seemed to have appropriated with *Ein newes Lied*.

After praising St Benno, "you very holy man", in three stanzas exalting his piousness, the song turns to abusing Luther ("you very evil man"), accused of offending St Benno who had done nothing against him (which is, actually, a good point). Emser's song is rather effective, especially in its first section (the encomium of St Benno) in summarising the dogmatic teaching of the Catholic Church on the intercession of saints; notwithstanding this, data regarding the printing figures of Emser's *Ach Benno* seem to suggest that it did not enjoy a success comparable to Luther's songs[112].

### 10.6.2. Countering the *Interim*

Years later, the tense climate of confessional opposition, often fuelled by political and economic reasons at least as much as by theological issues, actually caused (and was going to provoke in the future) several armed conflicts, among which the Schmalkaldic War of 1546–1547. Notwithstanding Emperor Charles V's victory at the Battle of Mühlberg (April 24th, 1547), an attempt at theological conciliation between Catholics and Protestants was deemed indispensable: thus, an imperial decree which came to be known as the *Augsburg Interim*

---

112 Cf. Wagner Oettinger 2001, pp. 52–53, 69, 81–87; Fisher 2014, p. 301.

was issued the following year, after consultations with religious leaders of both sides (cf. § 1.6.3.).

Though the *Interim* had been devised as a compromise which should have satisfied both parties, as often happens it displeased both. The Evangelical pastors frequently refused to abide by it, seeing the *Interim* as a manoeuvre against the Reformation rather than as a quest for religious peace. Thus, the *Interim* also brought division within the Evangelical field, between those who agreed with it and those who firmly rejected its terms.

What interests us here, however, is the impressive flowering of polemical songs and *contrafacta* prompted by the *Interim:* most of them, as Wagner Oettinger points out, were the work of theologians and mirror their authors' Scriptural knowledge and spiritual concerns.

To be authored by theologians did not mean, for a song, to have a content to which the uneducated people could not adhere: the atmosphere of discontent following the *Interim* was very widespread and involved practically all social layers. However, as Wagner Oettinger is careful to state, these songs might well speak the people's mind, but probably not as the people itself would have expressed it[113].

A typical example of such an artistic/polemical creation is a *Beatus vir*, published as a broadside in Magdeburg by Pancratius Kempff in 1548. The lyrics, in Latin and in German, are a parody of Psalm 1: instead of the original text ("Happy are those who do not follow the advice of the wicked"), this *contrafactum* reads: "Happy is the man who trusts in God and does not approve of the *Interim*, for it has the Devil behind it"[114]. The broadside, with its combination of printed music, lyrics (with evident Scriptural references providing intertextuality) and visual imagery, represents a refined work exploring a multimedia communication which was highly symbolic and rich in interpretive possibilities[115].

The most outraged within the Lutheran field (among whom the so-called "Gnesio-Lutherans", who advocated the return to the sources of the Evangelical movement against the position of Melanchthon) sometimes felt the need for updating some of the most inflammatory songs of the first Reformation years, by adding stanzas or changing words in order to mirror more closely the present situation.

---

113 Cf. Wagner Oettinger 2001, pp. 137–143.
114 Quoted in and translated by Scribner 1994, p. 178.
115 Cf. Wagner Oettinger 2001, pp. 145–153.

New versions of older songs such as Luther's *Ach du arger Heinze*[116] were penned, thus connecting the feeling of unfairness and persecution experienced by the Gnesio-Lutherans with the burnings and executions suffered by the first Lutherans of the previous generation; at the same time, some of the most iconic of Luther's hymns (such as *Ein feste Burg*) were prohibited in cities such as Nuremberg during the *Interim* due to their potential for social disorders.

However, as in the case of *Ein feste Burg* – which is primarily a Psalm paraphrase, and only secondarily a polemical song – it should be emphasised that the levels of acrimony and verbal abuse found in the previous pages are normally missing from the *Interim* songs: as Wagner Oettinger points out, most of them are prayerful in mood, invoking God's defence against heresy, and some may even be interpreted as supporting the union among Christians of different confessions[117].

### 10.6.3. Contesting the calendar

Though on a different scale, another event which prompted the composition of several songs expressing confessional opposition was the so-called *Kalenderstreit*, the uproars which arose in several cities when the Gregorian calendar was introduced in 1582. Though the calendar reform had been designed on the basis of astronomic calculations which had little to do with theology, many Protestants resented a change which was felt to be a papist imposition.

In some instances, the only or most effective way of expressing dissent was precisely by means of song: in a village near Würzburg, Bergrheinfeld, the Lutherans continued using the hymns corresponding to the Julian calendar even after the Gregorian reform was implemented. In Augsburg, Protestant songs decrying the calendar reform were brought into the city from the neighbouring Lutheran zones; they were often modified by Augsburg Evangelicals to suit the city's particular situation, and distributed clandestinely in manuscript copies or spread by means of singing. Several records of trials held against the sellers and distributors of such songs preserve important witnesses on the role of music as a valued resource for expressing (and sometimes for fomenting) confessional division[118].

---

116 *LW* 41, p. 255.
117 Wagner Oettinger 2001, p. 167. Cf. *ibid.*, p. 164; cf. Pettegree 2005, p. 50.
118 Cf. Fisher 2001, pp. 616 and 650; Fisher 2004, pp. 27–70 and 280–281; Brown 2008, p. 256.

While in most of the cases described above music was used as a mass-medium for expressing, disseminating and provoking dissent over confessional matters, I will now turn to a very different case, which symbolises in turn another fundamental dimension of music as an element of confessional opposition.

### 10.6.4. Courtly intrigues

Alongside the popular horizon of the Reformations and their appeal to the feelings, culture and beliefs of wide layers of sixteenth-century society, another – and no less important – battle was fought at the high levels of the European aristocracy, in courts, in diplomacy, and in those centres of wealth, power and artistic patronage which contributed in moulding the allegiances, alliances and politico/religious shape of sixteenth-century Europe.

A thought-provoking example of how confessional beliefs, culture and creativity could interact with each other at such a high level is that of the court of Ferrara. The future Duke of the city, Ercole II d'Este (1508–1559), got married in 1528 to Renée, daughter of Louis XII, King of France (1462–1515). While Ercole was able to secure for his court the services of artists and musicians of the highest level (such as Maistre Jhan and Cipriano de Rore), his wife gathered a circle of equal importance, but of a rather different nature. In fact, with Renée, the court of Ferrara (which had already been known for a rather tolerant approach on matters of faith) became a meeting point for "heretics" and religious dissidents who had been expelled from numerous other courts and cities both in today's Italy and outside it.

Indeed, such a protagonist of the French Reformation as Clément Marot took refuge in Ferrara in 1535, where he became the duchess' secretary; the consequences of the same "*Affaire des Placards*" which had made it unadvisable for him to stay in France had encouraged the musician Jeannet de Bouchefort (fl. 1530-a.1572) to seek protection at the same court. It is very likely, moreover, that even Calvin sojourned in Ferrara in 1536, though under the false name of "Charles d'Espeville". It can be surmised that one of Calvin's aims (if, as it seems, he actually resided in Ferrara) was to persuade Renée to convert officially to the Reformed faith: given both her ancestry and her standing as a ruler's wife, her profession of faith would have profited the Reformed cause enormously.

With such a gathering of Reformers and sympathisers, something was bound to happen. And of course it did. On Good Friday (April 14th, 1536), Jeannet publicly refused to submit to the traditional devotional practice of the veneration of the cross and left the church under the astonished eyes of the congregation and of the other musicians. Eventually, Jeannet was interrogated by the Inquisition, discharged and permitted to move back to France.

Notwithstanding the comparatively mild treatment of his singer by the Inquisition, it is very likely that the chapel master at the time, Maistre Jhan, felt rather worried about the climate at court, to which many of his compatriots had contributed by embracing the Reformed principles more and more openly.

Thus Jhan started setting to music a *Te Lutherum damnamus*, whose lyrics had been published by Giambattista Faello (or Faelli, d. c.1557) in 1532, within the framework of a treatise by the Capuchin friar Giovanni da Fano[119] (1469–1539).

It has been argued that the intended reader for both Giovanni da Fano's tract and Jhan's composition was Renée, whose Reformed sympathies had been and were going to be targeted by a series of high-profile Catholic theologians. Though this is of course possible, I am personally not certain that a musical setting of a *Te Lutherum damnamus* could have been (and have been deemed to be) really effective in order to persuade a woman of Renée's culture and fortitude to abandon her convictions.

As we have repeatedly seen even in the case of the unlearned layers of society, most satirical works were written to be sung and enjoyed by those whose ideas were the same as the polemicist's. It seems to me rather unlikely that Ercole could have expected a polemical *contrafactum* to convince his wife to revert to pure Catholic principles.

On the other hand, I agree with Nugent[120] that Jhan would not have dabbled in his employers' religious and private affairs unless instructed to do so by Duke Ercole. It seems to me probable, therefore, that both Jhan and Ercole saw this artistic undertaking as a means of distancing themselves from the positions of Jeannet and of Renée respectively.

While other parodies of the *Te Deum* are textual paraphrases which can be sung on the traditional plainchant tune, in this case Jhan's motet exploits the metrical similarity between the liturgical text and its polemical version, and is purposefully designed to suit both texts.

Though Jhan's *Te Deum / Te Lutherum* is perhaps one of the most striking examples of the intrusion of confessional opposition within the high layers of society and of complex polyphony, two other works originating from the same political and aristocratic sphere and with similar purposes are discussed by Nugent: a four-part motet (*Cantemus Domino*, published 1544) and a polyphonic

---

**119** Da Fano 1532.
**120** Nugent 1990, pp. 249–250.

Mass (*La fede unque debbe esser corrotta*, published 1555), both by Jacquet of Mantua[121]. These works connect the worries about the equivocal confessional stance of the Ferrarese Este court with the leading figures of the Catholic Reformation, among whom Cardinal Ercole Gonzaga (cf. § 8.3.1.) and Cardinal Cristoforo Madruzzo, who was the Prince Bishop of the Council's city, Trent[122]. Such examples fascinatingly show how confessional opposition intertwined with politics and was expressed by music not only in the streets and marketplaces of the German cities, but also within the close circles of the cultivated nobility.

## 10.7. "Save me, o God": echoes of persecution

Though it is licit to wonder how pleased Renée was with the motet her chapel master had written on the *Te Lutherum* lyrics, the game of persuasion, propaganda, politics and preaching staged at the court of Ferrara may have involved some psychological persecution, but was nevertheless played on the highest levels of cultural refinement and symbolic allusions.

Elsewhere, as we have seen abundantly in this Chapter, the game might become much tougher, and music could be played or sung during battles, raids, riots, rebellions and capital executions.

### 10.7.1. Silencing songs

In turn, on multiple occasions, music could be an object of persecution itself, and be limited, prohibited or banned depending on the political and religious circumstances – and this had often, and understandably, some harsh consequences on the actual lives of many musicians throughout Europe.

In Toulouse, for example, in 1542 a list of seventy-six forbidden books and of fourteen songs was issued by the Catholic authorities: the latter included (Huguenot) spiritual *chansons* or *noels*, which, similar to the proscribed books, had to be yielded to the Inquisition under pain of the crime of heresy[123]. Risks for those owning or singing "heretical" songs might be considerable indeed: Jacques Duval, a tailor from Paris, was condemned to the stake where he had to be burnt together with his book of *Chansons spirituelles*; to prevent his exploitation

---

[121] Colebault 1544; Colebault 1555.
[122] Cf. Nugent 1990, to which this section is indebted. Cf. also Reid 1971, p. 40; Fenlon 1980, pp. 76–77; Prizer 1998, p. 296; Freedman 2006, p. 158; Ongaro 2006, pp. 62–63.
[123] Bordier 1870, vol. I, p. xxvii.

of his last moments for propagandistic purposes, he was threatened with having his tongue cut before leaving the prison[124].

Other cases were less tragic but not less meaningful: as seen in Chapter Seven (§ 7.6.3.), to be found in possession of a copy of Byrd's *Gradualia* was a suspicious element, which weighed against Charles de Ligny (d.1624) when he was convicted in 1605 by the British authorities[125].

When Henry II of France forbade public Psalm-singing (1558) for reasons of public order, harsh polemics ensued: indeed, as we have seen in Chapter Six (§ 6.2.2.), at the earlier time when Marot's Psalms were nothing more than a pious exercise by a great French poet, the King himself (as a *dauphin*) had sung them together with many other members of the Court. Moreover, as the Huguenot polemicists were eager to point out, it seemed rather paradoxical to prohibit psalmody while allowing the public singing of licentious love-songs or piquant ditties[126] (cf. § 6.3.5.).

After Henry II's ban, a long series of official interdictions ensued, including a particularly strict prohibition against public singing in Lyon (1564): though the primary target of this ordinance was certainly Huguenot Psalm-singing, it is likely that it did not intend to strike exclusively against the Reformed. As we have seen above, in fact, Catholic songs had to be limited in turn (§ 10.3.7.1.), since they often instigated social disorder and violence.

Reasons of public order, supported by Pope Adrian VI's complaints to Emperor Charles V, led to the prohibition of selling polemic and satirical songs on lyrics abusing the Pope in the city of Nuremberg (1523[127]).

Counter-Reformation authorities might be very wary about public singing, precisely because in many cases it was the only possibility left for dissenters to express their stance. Thus, in Münster, the case is reported of a Lutheran who was prosecuted for and charged with having sung the hymns proper to his confession in his garden[128]. Indeed, though most bans concern congregational and public singing, some were enacted even against private worship at homes or devotional activities involving music.

We have already seen that trial records are one of the historians' sources as concerns the polemical songs on the *Kalenderstreit* in Augsburg[129], and the Lutheran repertoire, though officially forbidden, was pointedly maintained in use

---

124 Bordier 1969, vol. I, p. xxx.
125 Brett 2007, p. 196.
126 Cf. Brooks 2006, p. 177.
127 Cf. Scribner 1981, pp. 73–74.
128 Hsia 1992, p. 107.
129 Fisher 2001, p. 617.

by the Protestants during the Counter-Reformation of the city[130]. Similar bans were enacted against Evangelical congregational singing in cities whose traditions were very different from one other, such as – for example – Salzburg and Basel; in many Bavarian towns Lutheran songs were prohibited, though there were often no significant efforts, on the part of Catholic authorities, to create a valid alternative to the musical void they were thus establishing.

As early as 1528, in Strasbourg, a group of orphans was repeatedly admonished for having publicly sung devotional songs to the Virgin Mary and the saints: it should be emphasised that singing in the roads was a socially acceptable source of income for many students and poor children throughout Europe at the time. Five years later, ordinances were issued concerning the proper kind of songs allowed in the city and their correct performance style: as Trocmé Latter points out, here – as elsewhere – prohibitions regarded both the pre-Reformation sacred repertoire and the secular songs[131].

The situation in Calvin's Geneva in the years 1542–52 has been thoroughly investigated in a recent study by Latour[132], which discusses the cases of illicit singing and music-making brought before the Consistory (more than a hundred in ten years), following its deliberations against forbidden songs and the ensuing penalties for disobeying (up to a three-day imprisonment). The cases analysed in Latour's study range from the relatively hilarious mischief of two women singing scurrilous songs during the catechism lessons to others which were potentially much more disruptive, such as that of Bolsec we have seen earlier in this Chapter (§ 10.4.).

As shown by Latour, the implementation of religious discipline by the Consistory was seen to be central for the maintenance of social order and harmony; to allow behaviours considered to be disruptive or damaging for the social ethics would have meant putting in danger the entire community, by making it the object of God's wrath. On the other hand, by manifesting the community's cohesion in the judgment of illicit behaviours, the Consistory's deliberations (which represented the entire community) were functional for the maintenance of social union and stability.

The great importance given by the Consistory's rulings to the seemingly minor crime of illicit singing was grounded on Calvin's Platonic beliefs on the power of music to move (cf. § 4.3.5.1.), and thus justifies the seriousness with which such issues were treated.

---

130 Fisher 2004, pp. 27–70 and 280–281.
131 Cf. Trocmé Latter 2015, pp. 157–158.
132 Cf. Latour 2015.

If illicit songs were sometimes persecuted, hymnbooks could become in turn the targets of official censorships: though this is not very surprising as regards song collections typical for the worship of a particular denomination (such as a Lutheran songbook or a Genevan psalter), the case is reported of a prohibition, issued in the Low Countries by their Regent, against a French psalter on the ground that it employed the Genevan melodies (and not on the basis of its vernacular lyrics[133]). Given the strict association between the Calvinist tunes and the confession they represented, in certain situations the melody alone was sufficient to convey a precise message of identity and belief[134].

It seems clear, thus, that Catholics were not the only ones to legislate against music or dancing. Indeed, the very disruption or suspension of Catholic Masses in many Protestant territories implied – beside the religious aspect proper – also a forced interruption in the musical practices of the Catholic Church. Similarly, the abolition of certain forms of church music (such as polyphony or instrumental music) from the worship of some Evangelical confessions was equivalent to a prohibition to perform works which had been intended for the Catholic liturgy.

To summarise, and though greater or lesser limits were imposed by virtually all confessions on some particular types of singing, music or dancing, the reasons for doing so could vary significantly: many Protestants banned musical activities on moral grounds, and, indirectly, forbade the continuation of musical practices which had been bound to the traditional worship (though what happened to Byrd's *Gradualia* in England is a case of confessional persecution proper); Catholics enacted limitations against singing in order to block the dissemination of Protestant ideas or for reasons of public order or security.

### 10.7.2. Martyred musicians

I have already mentioned, in passing, that many of the restrictions imposed on music and musicianship for confessional reasons had a strong impact on the lives of musicians. This obviously applied to any member of a particular confession, inasmuch as they were not free to express their faith or prayer in singing. But this was even truer of professional musicians, who often felt harshly the hardships of confessionalisation.

---

133 Forney 2006, pp. 253–254.
134 Cf. Dobbins 1992, pp. 11–12; van Orden 2000, pp. 274–280; Fisher 2001; Brown 2005, p. 23; Lindmayr-Brandl 2005, pp. 90 ff.; Marcus 2000, pp. 169–171; Pettegree 2005, p. 67; Brown 2008, p. 256; Crook 2009, pp. 4–5; Groote and Vendrix 2012, p. 180.

## 10.7. "Save me, o God": echoes of persecution — 563

While, in the era immediately preceding the Reformations, an international career had been proportionally common among musicians of talent, later their viable options were drastically curtailed, either because complex musical forms were practised no more within certain Reformed zones, or because their confessional allegiance would have conflicted with that of their prospective employers, particularly when these were ecclesiastical institutions.

Thus, the case was not infrequent of musicians who had to face the difficult choice between losing some important job opportunities or of renouncing or silencing their beliefs.

For some, the choice might be even more difficult. As seen in the preceding Chapter (§ 9.4.4.), the musician Antoine de Bertrand had abandoned the secular subjects of his preceding output and had become a pioneer of Catholic devotional songs in France. The preface to his *Airs spirituels*, posthumously published in 1582[135], maintains that he had been martyred precisely for composing such spiritual music, "by those who detest these ecclesiastical hymns"[136]. Words in praise of Bertrand were published in the following years: among others, by the Jesuit Michel Coyssard in his *Traicté du profit que toute personne tire de chanter en la Doctrine Chrestienne*[137] (1608).

During the French Wars of Religion, however, many Protestant musicians had to suffer persecution or duress: among them was Claude Le Jeune. Reportedly, when he had to abandon Paris in 1590, his compositions were salvaged from burning by a Catholic colleague of his, the composer Jacques Mauduit[138] (1557–1627).

The fate of Claude Goudimel and Philibert Jambe-de-Fer was even sadder: both were among the victims of the execrable Massacre of St Bartholomew in 1572. That unforgettable date not only brought to an abrupt end the lives of artists of their standing, together with those of thousands of other innocents; it also represented a turning point as concerns the creation and dissemination of Reformed devotional music and the progressive extinction of musical publishing of a recognisable Evangelical identity in centres – such as Paris and Lyon – which used to be at the frontline of such entrepreneurship[139].

Other musical activities which had been practised rather freely suddenly became dangerous: one of the traditional literary and performative contests organised by several cultural societies in the Low Countries, taking place in Ghent in

---

135  De Bertrand 1582.
136  Van Orden 2006, p. 210.
137  Coyssard 1608. See van Orden 2005, p. 164.
138  Brooks 2006, pp. 176–177.
139  Blankenburg 1975, p. 541.

1539, and in which music was frequently performed, was later deemed to be imbued with "heretical" ideas[140]. In this as in other situations, thus, musicians could be forced to become very careful; their right to artistic and religious expression could be considerably downplayed; even their freedom to experiment in the artistic field could be subject to considerations of opportunity and prudence. On the other hand, in those contexts where the coexistence of different confessions had been established for some time and was officially and somehow peacefully regulated, opportunity – rather than faith proper – might dictate to musicians the transition from one denomination to another; sometimes, moreover, such decisions could even be retracted at a later stage[141].

### 10.7.3. Concealing and revealing

In still other cases, the possible conflicts between the musicians' personal beliefs and the professional choices they were more or less compelled to make might surface – on close scrutiny – from their compositions. In the late sixteenth century, the compositional language of so-called "art music" could count already on a full arsenal of symbolic allusions and meaningful associations – sometimes accessible only to the musically initiated – but which could convey a powerful and significant message to those able to decipher it.

For instance, Ludwig Daser (c.1525–1589), whose musical training and career had been bound to the Catholic Court of Munich, expressed his proximity to Evangelical positions while composing the work which best represents the core of the Catholic faith, i.e. the Creed for a Mass Ordinary (*Missa Ave Maria*). Here, by inserting the word "nostrum" within the sentence proclaiming belief in Christ ("*Et in Dominum* nostrum *Jesum Christum*", "And in *our* Lord Jesus Christ") Daser managed to convey a feeling of confessional identity and appropriation, as if, for the composer, the Catholic Church was no more entitled to calling Christ "hers"[142].

In a similar, though even more complex fashion, scholars have traced a possible net of allusions and references connecting three works by English composers, i.e. two Masses by Tallis (*Puer Natus*) and Tye (*Euge bone*), as well as a *Suscipe quæso Domine* by the former. The two works by Tallis are linked by their uncommon scoring (seven-part choir), whereas both Masses emphasise the "*Ben-*

---

140 See Brachin 1975.
141 Cf. Forney 2006, p. 258; Groote and Vendrix 2012, pp. 166–167 and 175.
142 Groote and Vendrix 2012, p. 172.

*edictus qui venit*" in the *Sanctus*. As Bray suggests[143], if the occasion prompting the composition of these three works was the absolution, given by Cardinal Reginald Pole, to England from the sin of heresy (1554), then the greeting "*Benedictus qui venit*" ("Blessed is he who comes in the name of the Lord", cf. Psalm 118 [117]:26, Matthew 23:39) was addressed to the Cardinal, hailed as a "good man" ("*bone*"). Possibly, moreover, the "*puer natus*" (the "born child") was a symbol of England's new birth (an expression often interpreted as a symbol for Baptism: cf. Isaiah 9:6 and John 3:3–8).

We have already seen, earlier in this Chapter (§ 10.3.3.2.), how many of Byrd's works had taken as clear a stance as possible, for one in his situation, as a denouncement of and complaint for the martyrdom of Campion and his fellows (Alexander Briant [1556–1581] and Ralph Sherwin [1550–1581]).

When, some five years after Campion's mission to England, two other Jesuit priests (St Robert Southwell [c.1561–1595] and Henry Garnet [1555–1606]) were sent to England as missionaries, Byrd's greeting to them was once more expressed by means of music. In July 1586, the Jesuit William Weston (1550–1615) mentions Byrd among those who celebrated the arrival of Southwell and Garnet in the house of a Catholic gentleman, by the name of Richard Bold (d.1602). Byrd's *Circumspice Hierusalem* is a magnificent and touching work, which expresses the joy, expectation and hopes nourished by the persecuted recusants when the "sons of Jerusalem" (i.e. the Jesuits missionaries) were to arrive on the English shores.

Exactly as the musically literate could read between the lines – of counterpoint or musical symbolism – to understand a hidden confessional meaning, so the religiously literate could interpret symbolically the several Scriptural and traditional references embodied within the lyrics chosen by Byrd[144].

Indeed, most musicians belonging to persecuted communities throughout Europe adopted strikingly similar symbolic strategies: references to Jerusalem as the promised land (but also as the lost and devastated city, abandoned by God but deeply regretted by his people), to Israel as the chosen people (who had in turn to endure exile, persecution and the seeming forsaking by its God) and to several other typical elements of Scriptural imagery abound in their sacred and devotional works.

Many of such compositions are of an almost shocking beauty and succeed in blending a touching emotionality with an otherworldly serenity. Though these musicians were suffering themselves for the divisions brought by confessionali-

---

**143** Bray 2006, p. 493.
**144** Cf. Monson 1997, pp. 350 and 358.

sation, and were expressing the pain of the members of their community, their music somehow unites them.

It is as if the very fact of suffering for one's faith was actually much more important, crucial and meaningful than which confession they represented and which confession was persecuting them. Suffering for Christ, in short, and expressing this suffering through music was the means by which the persecuted were truly in communion, though probably they did not know it and possibly would not have understood it.

Thus, though this Chapter has dealt with the painful and often shameful topic of confessional opposition, and with the fact that frequently music lent itself in becoming an instrument of persecution, oppression and violence, the message I would like to leave in conclusion is very different, and in some way connects this Chapter with the following. Music might have been a tool in the hands of those who wished to divide the Church and to separate people by means of power, propaganda and politics; but, in its truest and purest nature, music was much more than this.

Even when unnoticed or unacknowledged by those living the confessional turmoil, music was discreetly cooperating to maintain a thread, albeit a fragile one, among those who used to profess the same faith and to pray together to the same God: the next Chapter will develop this topic in greater detail.

This Chapter has surveyed the functions of music within a situation of confessional opposition: it was, of course, an instrument for praying, but also for creating a group identity, for disseminating doctrines and for opposing those of the competing confessions, as well as for vindicating the particular elements of one's own denomination. Sadly, music was also used within contexts of violence, persecution, riot and war, and it was even employed for mocking or ridiculing the teachings of other confessions. Psalms and *contrafacta* were of particular importance, thanks to the possibilities they offered for a multi-layered interpretation. Music was also crucial where and when the confessional opposition was most strongly felt, due to geographical or historical reasons. In turn, music itself could be persecuted, banned and prohibited, and such limitations frequently impacted rather harshly on the lives of professional and amateur musicians alike. On the other hand, occasionally, music could become the only possibility for expressing, showing and maintaining one's beliefs, and for encouraging the persecuted communities in their struggle; in particular, the symbolic value of music and its semantic tradition were exploited, in conjunction with religious exegesis. Thus, even though music could express and sometimes did foment division, it also wove a spiritual unity among those who suffered for their faith.

# Chapter 11 – Music beyond confessionalisation

> Lord God, Father in heaven,
> Do not turn from us with Your grace.
> In their final need, have pity
> On those whom Your Son has redeemed.
> Bestow on them peace and unity,
> Make them ready for Your Service[1].
>
> [*Interim* song, 1555–1558]

## 11.1. Introduction

The previous Chapter focused on the rather painful subject of confessional opposition, with music playing sometimes too active a role between hostile factions. This Chapter, instead, will consider the capacity of music to overcome religious antagonism, and to offer an alternative to contrast and conflict.

Indeed, as I have argued in the very introduction to this book, music is theologically suited to become a symbol of unity, communion and reconciliation; moreover, historically, the need for a reform of church music was common and widespread, and often there was not so great a disagreement between several reformers' viewpoint on music as was to be found on other theological problems. The humanistic influence on the speculation about intelligibility did not depend on confessional allegiance; so-called "art music" enjoyed an international status which facilitated its inter-confessional penetration.

There were indeed several shared elements among the various confessions' worship and music types: psalmody was practised, in one form or another, by virtually all Churches; the need for devotional music was widespread, and piety was fostered even at a mystical level by musical practice. Pedagogy became crucial (also due to humanistic influence) for most Churches and most societies, with music playing a major role both as a subject of instruction and as a catechetic tool; the increased literacy which was so essential for the spread of Protestant hymn-books encouraged similar efforts on the Catholic side as well.

Music itself was crossing boundaries: besides the existence of a common repertoire antedating all Reformations – and which several Churches prided themselves on maintaining – the most beautiful or popular musical works were likely to be adopted (or adapted) by different confessional Churches; more-

---

[1] As quoted by and translated in Wagner Oettinger 2001, p. 277.

over, new Latin-texted works became a common heritage of several Churches which had not entirely abolished Latin worship, and speakers of the same mother tongue could share a vernacular devotional repertoire regardless of their confessional belonging.

Moreover, professional musicians themselves were more likely than most of their contemporaries to travel across confessional and national boundaries, and most of them wrote liturgical or devotional music for Churches or individuals belonging to Christian confessions different from their own. Thus, in an age of religious division, music acted as a reminder of past unity, and perhaps as the hope for a unity to come.

## 11.2. Seeking harmony

Before entering into a historical discussion of the forms taken by music as an element of communion in spite of the confessional divisions during the sixteenth century, I wish to examine briefly the theological reasons for its vocation as an instrument of unity: some of them have been cursorily mentioned in the previous Chapters, but it is perhaps necessary to summarise them here.

### 11.2.1. Tuning the differences

The first reason which can be adduced, in my opinion, for the particular status and call of music to communion lies in its very nature. Indeed, few other human activities can claim to be as permeated by the idea of "plurality-in-unity" as music is. At its very root, for Christians, music's "polyphonic" nature can be seen as mirroring in a particularly close and impressive fashion the nature of the Triune God, who is believed by the Church to be One in Three divine Persons. It is neither a monadic and self-contained God, as in the most radical monotheisms, nor a fragmented vision of the Godhead, as in polytheism: rather, it is a hard to grasp and yet fascinating perspective which sees plurality as a gift, and unity as a necessity.

Most forms taken historically by music can be interpreted as symbols of this tenet of the Christian faith: unison singing, as in the liturgical unaccompanied monody, stresses the communional aspect as seen in the single melody, but mirrors the Church's plurality in the cooperation of multiple human voices to the overall sound. Polyphony is an even clearer and more transparent image of the Trinity: the interweaving parts convey an impression of utmost freedom, and yet of cogent consistency, logic and coordination. The single part's submission to the needs of contrapuntal rules can be seen as a symbol of the loving acceptance of the other which eventually produces an interplay which is enjoyed by all.

Plurality, as seen in the trace left by contrapuntal concepts in the harmonic language, is found also in chordal writing; unity is expressed here either by the (single) melody sustained by the harmonic texture or by the very simultaneity of sound production which is inherent in all chordal structures.

Even in the case of unaccompanied melodies sung or played by a single person, this symbol can be identified (though, to be sure, in a less convincing and clear fashion): it is only from the temporal interaction of pitches and durations that the logical and expressive unity of the melody can arise.

It is therefore not by chance that frequently (and not only within the Christian culture) music has represented "harmony" in its quintessence[2]: this is abundantly seen in the history of literature, of music aesthetics, of philosophy, of theology, of mathematical and astronomical sciences, and even in fields such as the history of art.

### 11.2.2. Flutes, lutes and Luther

It is in fact to a painting that I will briefly turn now, as it represents in a particularly meaningful fashion this role of music during the years of confessional opposition: namely, to the justly famous *The Ambassadors* (1533) by Hans Holbein the Younger, presently at the National Gallery in London (see http://bit.ly/2cvP8cI). The German-born artist had recently settled in London, during the turbulent years of the early Protestantism. In *The Ambassadors*, Holbein portrayed two diplomats from the Continent, i.e. Georges de Selve (c.1508–1541), on the right-hand side of the observer, and Jean de Dinteville (1504–1555), who was the French ambassador in London. De Selve, in particular, in his capacity of Ambassador in Venice, and of priest and Bishop of Lavaur, had been entrusted by Rome with delicate missions aiming at reconciling the opposing confessional views. Holbein's masterwork owes part of its fame to the unusual, fascinating and yet troubling use of the graphical deformation known as anamorphosis, revealing a giant skull to those observing the painting from a particular angle. (Another skull is painted, as a pin, on Dinteville's hat).

While these are certainly symbols for the fugacity of life and possibly for the disquietudes felt by many religious people of the time, as well as for the ephem-

---

[2] Cf. Spitzer 1963.

eral knowledge of human science, it is to the musical symbols in the painting that I will turn now. Between the lute and the flute case (and who knows whether the choice of these particular instruments was in turn an allusion to Luther's family name...), a hymnbook is depicted in great detail. It can therefore be identified precisely as the tenor part of the *Geystliche Gesangk Buchleyn* by Johann Walther (second edition, 1525). The book is open on two recognisable songs: to the left, there is the hymn *Kom heiliger Geyst*, in Walther's elaboration of Luther's adaptation of the Sequence for Pentecost (*Veni Sancte Spiritus*). To the right, we can identify the first lines of *Mensch wiltu leben seliglich*, a song by Luther on the Ten Commandments.

To the various interpretations which have been advanced for Holbein's choice, I would like here to add my own. The Commandments refer clearly to the Law; the Spirit, invoked in the Pentecost Sequence, is the giver of life. Law and the Spirit are juxtaposed and partially (but not entirely) contrasted in Romans 8:2: "For the law of the Spirit of life in Christ Jesus has set you free from the law of sin and of death". The contrast is only seeming, however: St Paul further explores the topic by stating: "[God] condemned sin in the flesh, so that the just requirement of the law might be fulfilled in us, who walk not according to the flesh but according to the Spirit" (Romans 8:3–4. Other relevant Pauline quotes are from Galatians 3:2–5).

What might then Holbein have implied by his musical choices? One interpretation might be that he simply contrasted the Law against the Spirit: in which case the painting would take sides within the harsh debate on the works (of the law) as seen by the most extreme polemicists.

However, I think that a more shaded and theologically complex interpretation can be advanced. By choosing *Luther's song* on the Commandments, Holbein seems to suggest that, even for the Wittenberg Reformer, there was a Law which had to be taught, respected and honoured as a gift of God. Indeed, the Commandments can be seen as the embodiment of Christian love in the practical lives of human beings; and, of course, Christian love is a direct emanation of God's Holy Spirit.

Moreover, the very feast of Pentecost evoked by the *Veni Sancte Spiritus* is full of implications, being, as it is, the source of the Church's unity and of its diversity. The Apostles and Mary, receiving the gift of the Holy Spirit, are made one: the narration of Pentecost in Acts 2 begins precisely by stating that "they were all together in one place"; shortly thereafter, however, "all of them were filled with the Holy Spirit and began to speak in other languages" (Acts 2:1.4).

Further still, it is the Spirit who enables to Church to interpret Scripture, which may be symbolised by the Commandments. Most important, finally, the saving Grace is identified by Christian theology as the Grace of the Holy Spirit.

Thus, Holbein seems to suggest, Law and Grace are not in competition, not in opposition: they are merely two facing pages of the same book, the book of God's love for humankind. Thus, the choice of conveying such a complex theological message by means of a hymnbook acquires its greatest significance: Law and Grace are in *harmony* with one another, a harmony powerfully symbolised by music itself.

The centrality of the concept of harmony (through music) within Holbein's painting is further stated by the symbols of the flutes and of the lute. On the one hand, the lute has a broken F-string (the sixth counting from either side, and F is the sixth note counting from A): the strings still in order, thus, are ten as the Commandments, but the number six has always meant imperfection (since it falls short of seven, the symbol of fullness). These symbols all imply a broken harmony, and the imperfection of human nature (as humans appeared on the *sixth* day of Creation) which is redeemed only by Grace. On the other hand, however, Rasmussen[3] reminds us that lute and flute had been traditionally associated respectively to Venus and Mars, who are the mythological parents of Harmony.

Though the multiple layers of the complex symbolism embodied within Holbein's painting cannot be exhausted here (and certainly are not exclusively focused on musical symbolism), it seems to me that some concepts are clearly stated in *The Ambassadors* and summarise the first theological reason for seeing music as an instrument of unity. First, confessional oppositions had broken a fragile but fundamental harmony: a single broken string makes the lute (an instrument whose harmonic potential is acknowledged) practically unusable. Second: harmony should be found between Law and Grace, between the Commandments (the God-given rules for living "harmoniously" with other humans and with God Himself) and the Spirit who enables humans to live freely and according to the law of love. Third: the only way for preventing unity from degenerating into homologation, and diversity from degenerating into alienation is by seeking harmony. It is the Spirit who, by enabling the Church to speak the diverse languages of humankind (as in the very miracle of Pentecost) allows Christianity to be "harmoniously" united by love while admitting variety and difference of charismas[4].

On the ground of practical musicianship, a comparable complexity of meanings had been offered by Claude Le Jeune with his *Dodecacorde* (cf. § 6.3.6.),

---

[3] Rasmussen 1995, pp. 121–122.
[4] Cf. Rasmussen 1995, p. 115; Leaver 2006, p. 396; Zuffi 2011, pp. 176–177. I am grateful to my friend and colleague, the art historian Stefano Zuffi, for sharing his research on Holbein with me.

where, as seen above, the iconic Calvinist psalmody was put into dialogue with the traditional modal theory as codified by the Catholic Zarlino[5]. This was seen as symbolising a perspective inspired by concord and by the idea, once more stressed, that a variety of modes and moods combined in an orderly fashion produced harmony, plenitude and perfection. The suggestion has been advanced, moreover, that also George Buchanan's metrical version of the Psalter in Latin (which were to be set to music by Statius Olthof and Jean Servin, cf. § 6.3.3.) was intended as an effort aiming at the "restoration of harmony at a political level"[6].

### 11.2.3. Creating communion through prayer

If the inherent capacity of music to reconcile unity with plurality is the first theological reason for its being among the protagonists of an interconfessional dialogue, two other reasons, of no lesser importance, should be briefly discussed in turn.

Indeed, music is an integral element of liturgy and worship for the great majority of the Christian Churches. Music, as we have seen, enhances the beauty of the praises of God; moreover, by "moving" the believers' hearts and feelings (cf. § 2.3.7.1.), it contributes to uniting (once more) the potentials for rationality and for emotionality which constitute the complexity of human experience. Thus, music is not an accessory to prayer, but rather it can be considered to be one of its fundamental components. To be sure, exactly as one can pray without uttering or even thinking any words, similarly prayer without music is absolutely possible. However, and especially within the context of communal prayer, music takes an active and crucial role in giving shape to the praying congregation and in channelling the individual sentiments into a deep and intense communion.

Therefore, as recent ecumenical meetings have clearly shown, it is easier to restore communion among the various Christian Churches by means of communal prayer than of theology. Though the importance of dogmatic clarification is not to be downplayed, in the service of the truth, it is nevertheless evident that Christians belonging to different confessions find it much easier to pray than to discuss together.

---

5 Freedman 2003, p. 305.
6 Porter 2009, p. 253.

Though the fragmentation of the sixteenth-century Church resulted in the separation of worships and in the interruption of the visible communion of liturgy, nevertheless a trace of the lost unity might be seen in the continuing prayer of the Christians, of which music was normally a constituting element. Moreover, as we will see in the following pages, not infrequently Christians shared at least a part of their musical repertoires, if only those performed for private devotion. Music, as linked to prayer, was thus a powerful connection which still united the divided Churches.

### 11.2.4. Joining theology with praise

Thirdly and finally, we have already discussed (cf. § 2.3.8.) the symbolic nature of music, and how it truly embodies the very concept of *symbolon* as something which holds and keeps together the expression of faith, its experience, and the various spiritual, psychological and physical dimensions of the human beings and of their interaction. Though the rational, architectural and analytical side of music is fundamental for understanding it fully and properly (and of course this aspect of music was particularly clear during the Early Modern era), music as a *symbolon* both encompasses and transcends all this. While theological discussions, important as they are, can quickly lose sight of the mysterious reality of God, of the mystical dimension of faith, of the ultimate transcendence of the divine nature, music – with its beauty, fascination and power to inspire awe, amazement and enchantment – may help in "keeping together" contemplation with meditation, dogma with prayer, praise with thought, preaching with jubilation.

Thus, a music which is properly Christian is frequently much more apt to cross confessional boundaries than are written devotional works or even visual artworks. Since music resists to being too narrowly codified and described, it embodies a fullness of meaning which can easily be shared by all those who identify themselves as Christians (and, to be sure, also by many who do not[7]).

## 11.3. Finding harmony

While in the first section of this Chapter I have tried to offer a short survey of three theological reasons justifying the analysis of music as transcending the

---

7 Cf. Prodi 2014, p. 279.

confessional boundaries, I will now consider how these concepts dovetailed with the actual history of sacred music in the sixteenth century.

### 11.3.1. Consonant doctrines

The first point I will make will not need to be extensively demonstrated here, since I think that it will result clearly from all that has come before in this book. It is that music united several confessional denominations since the viewpoints on music maintained by many Reformers (both Catholic and Evangelical) were not as drastically different as those regarding other aspects of dogma, ethics or liturgical practice.

From Chapter Two to Chapter Four we have in fact surveyed the stance of several spiritual leaders both on the problems of contemporaneous sacred music and on the value of music and the functions it could accomplish. Partly in consequence of the cultural perspective shared by many Reformers (who, it should not be forgotten, had been all educated in the Catholic faith and frequently had studied the same books), and of the impact of the humanistic thought on their aesthetical horizon, the criticism they voiced, the criticalities they pointed out and the solutions they suggested shared several points. In other words, if one considers the continuum ranging from the total rejection of music as a sinful or harmful activity to the enthusiastic greeting of music as a gift of God, the Reformers' positions were not uniformly distributed, and many of them tended to concentrate within a relatively narrow spectrum.

Many of their theologies of music had common elements and cultural references; many of the practical criticalities pointed out by one were echoed by another; but also many of the suggestions for what was seen as an improvement of church music were shared by many.

Even at the level of official worship, the forms of liturgical music as practised by Catholics, Lutherans and Anglicans still maintained several common traits; and the devotional works composed for private use, as well as the popular songs with a spiritual content showed many elements of similarity through the confessional panorama.

Musically speaking, Luther's Reform was extremely inclusive and tended to enrich the Catholic tradition rather than to deny it; the Council of Trent can hardly be seen as a rupture with the past; and the music practised in Queen Elizabeth's England shared many traits with those of Lutherans and Catholics.

To be sure, many of these resemblances were due to the stylistic and aesthetical features of sixteenth-century music rather than to the official deliberations of Councils or Consistories. This very reason, however, confirms once more the capacity of music to affirm its own values (many of which are, in my opinion, genuinely spiritual) in the face of confessional division[8].

Many common trends, as seen earlier, can be traced back to the humanist attention to the word, which found a particularly fertile ground in the centrality assigned to God's Word by the Evangelicals. The intertwining of a stylistic evolution of a purely artistic order with the influence of humanist principles on the Reformers could be observed in the shape of Lutheran chorales, in the clear delivery and fidelity to the syllabic style found in the Calvinist psalmody, in the reform of plainchant enacted by the Catholic Church and in the concerns for intelligibility voiced by many of its leaders, as well as in the principles behind the creation of Anglican hymnals and liturgies.

At the level of so-called "art-music", such concerns were expressed by the increasing use of homorhythmic writing and word-painting, by the emergence of polychorality, or by the exploration of metrical combinations of prosody and music, as well as by the attempts to reinforce and to mirror the words' power through modal choices; paradoxically, a further shape taken by these ideas could be the mnemonic meditation of the omitted texts in the instrumental works based on liturgical or sacred songs[9].

Many, both among the musicians and among the theologians reforming the music of their Churches, might have subscribed to the fascinating words of Byrd's famous dedication of the *Gradualia* (though, perhaps, few could have expressed that viewpoint so beautifully):

> The holy words in which are sung the praises of God and the citizens of heaven deserve nothing less than a heavenly harmony, to the extent we can attain it. Moreover, in the [sacred] words themselves (as I have learned from experience) there is such hidden and mysterious power that to a person thinking over divine things, diligently and earnestly turning them over in his mind, the most appropriate measures come, I do not know how, and offer themselves freely to the mind that is neither idle nor inert[10].

There is a mystical dimension in this statement by Byrd which should not be overlooked, and to which we will shortly return, as another of the elements recurring within the musical experiences of members of several Christian Churches.

---

**8** Cf. Monson 2002, p. 4; Bergquist 2006, p. 340; Leaver 2006, pp. 371–372; Leaver 2007, p. 227.
**9** Cf. Blume 1975, pp. 131 and 169; Rees 2006, p. 356.
**10** As translated by McCarthy 2007, p. 11; cf. Kerman 1994, p. 88.

### 11.3.2. Crossing the confines

Along with the common aspirations of spiritual leaders to a "reformed" Church music and with their common belonging in the cultural atmosphere of the era, another element which should be taken into account is the internationalism of musical languages and practices, especially when contrasted with the increasing tendency of confessional Churches to identify with particular linguistic, geographical or political areas.

The trends leading to the codification of vernacular languages and to the establishment of local political identities were among the forces which prompted the birth of individual States and nations, and which partly contributed to the disintegration of the *corpus christianum*. The influence of local authorities and power struggles on the events leading to the religious schisms of the sixteenth century is of course widely acknowledged and needs not to be reaffirmed here.

While, as we have seen in the preceding Chapter (§ 10.7.2.), the increasing confessionalisation of Europe limited the musicians' freedom to build international and Europe-wide careers like those of their predecessors, still music (also by means of printing and of the large circulation of music books) continued to bridge not only the linguistic and national boundaries, but also those of confessional differences. The nature of music as a transnational and supranational form of art allowed it to cross the confessional divides too. In consequence of this, music also contributed to the creation of a trans-confessional language of piety and devotion. Since spiritual works for private devotion (as we have frequently seen in the preceding Chapters) were likely to be used by members of different confessional denominations, elements typical for the composer's (or lyricist's) confessional allegiance could migrate to, and be accepted by, members of other Churches. Moreover, as we will see in greater details later in this Chapter (§ 11.6.1.), but as has been already observed on several occasions previously, there was no direct connection between the destination of a composer's output and his or her confessional allegiance. It was instead rather common for members of a Church to write music destined for other Churches: this contributed from the one side to the maintenance of a language of sacred music which obviously had confessional and national "dialects", but also featured many common elements; and, from the other side, somehow hybridised the music of one confession with traits coming from the "dialect" of another[11].

---

[11] Cf. Prodi 2014, pp. 47 and 279; cf. also Blume 1975, p. 86.

## 11.3.3. Sung pleas for unity

While confessional opposition was starting to provoke local and sometimes large-scale episodes of violence (from riots and executions to systematic massacre and to wars), many were hoping that conciliations could be achieved, and that – at least – the differences which appeared increasingly to be unavoidably irreconcilable could coexist peacefully.

We have already seen that, in Holbein's painting, music can be seen as the symbol of a harmony for which many prayed and many (like the "Ambassadors") worked. A few years before (1530), the Diet of Augsburg, which had been intended as an attempt to find an entente among the opposing factions, had been opened with a performance of Ludwig Sennfl's *Ecce quam bonum*. The work, a Psalm-motet setting in four-part the words of Psalm 133 [132], is a clear appeal to peace and harmony: "How very good and pleasant it is / when kindred live together in unity!"[12].

As seen in Chapter Ten (§ 10.6.2.), moreover, among the *Interim* songs there are some which directly appeal to unity and peace in prayer. For example, *Herr got vater jm himmelreich* (c.1555–8, quoted in the epigraph to this Chapter), though clearly connected with polemical songs prompted by the *Interim*, is however prayerful in mood and shows concern for the unity and peace of Christians: "Lord God, Father in heaven, / do not turn from us with Your grace. / In their final need, have pity / on those whom your son has redeemed. // Bestow on them peace and unity, / make them ready for Your service"[13].

## 11.3.4. Bridging social layers

Another historical aspect of music could also bridge very easily all confessional boundaries. Divided as they might be by dogmatic differences and worship styles, people belonging to the lower economic and cultural layers of society had to face the same kind of problems. Their daily lives were marked by similar worries, struggles, mishaps, but also by similar hopes and joys. These feelings were, of course, both relevant to the religious aspect of life, and expressible by music. Thus, for example, as Wagner Oettinger has shown[14], a whole category of *contrafacta* based on the *Resonet* plainchant tune display remarkable similar-

---

12 Cf. Dunning 1970, pp. 158–165; Nugent 1990, p. 231; Leaver 2007, p. 52.
13 As quoted in and translated by Wagner Oettinger 2001, p. 277.
14 Wagner Oettinger 2001, p. 126.

ities in subjects and style, even though they originate from among both Catholics and Evangelicals. These *contrafacta* deal, very concretely, with themes which mattered to family mothers and fathers, such as the costs of living (and of dying), or social and religious practices. Singing, praying and struggling for life were features common to most people in the European societies of the sixteenth century, and similarly common was the plainchant repertoire to which they turned when in need of a tune with which to express their feelings and worries.

These *contrafacta* feature frequently polemical tones, but their attacks are directed against the higher social classes and their exploitation of the poor rather than against other Christian confessions. The theology they express, when references to God are made, is very simple and very true:

> Pay attention to me with regards to faith: / who doesn't charge interest and sell things? Enough of everything grows as God commanded, / [thus] the merchants make these problems, / you pious people. [...] // With God, one doesn't gain many riches, / [and] we know that love doesn't [make one rich]. / Now they are called "Evangelical". / How is it that they do not know poverty / you pious people[15]?

It is very helpful for today's readers to consider such musical expressions. They show us what many people felt; how social issues dovetailed with the principles of theology and of politics which seemingly drove all confessional changes; how, indeed, the subjects exploiting the poor and weak might change, while the overall perspective remained substantially unmodified.

## 11.4. Like prayer, like song

If in the preceding section we have taken into account some historical reasons behind the continued permanence of common traits in the music of different confessions, in this section I will examine in turn some actual elements shared by the various denominations.

---

[15] *Wir wissen woll den grossen trüg* (c.1525), stanzas 15 and 22, as quoted in and translated by Wagner Oettinger 2001, p. 395.

### 11.4.1. The thread of psalmody

The first topic is, of course, psalmody. In several instances already we have seen that Psalm-singing was a common feature to virtually all Christians: from the Catholic monks praying daily in Latin with the Liturgy of the Hours to the Lutherans who frequently adopted Psalm-paraphrases, and including the distinctive psalmody of the Reformed, the Psalm collections used in England, the *souterliedekens* and innumerable other examples. Psalms were sung or recited by Christians of all denominations during funeral vigils[16].

What has perhaps been neglected in my exposition until now is the use of vernacular psalmody by the Catholics: indeed, all examples of psalmody quoted above are in the vernacular (though of course some confessions maintained the practice of singing Latin Psalms), with the only exception of the Catholic Liturgy of the Hours.

Exactly as, for instance, Lutherans sang Latin Psalms along with German translation and paraphrases, vernacular psalmody was by no means unheard-of among Catholics. Indeed, at the outset of the French Wars of Religion and during the last sessions of the Council (1562), a plea was submitted to Pope Pius IV. It read:

> It remains to speak of the way to serve God. In this regard it has been observed that even as in the early Church the singing of Psalms and public prayer in a language understood by everyone encouraged Christians to fear God and in their devotion frequently to invoke him in fraternal brotherhood, so it likewise provoked their enemies to want to hear what there might be about this religion that made men live better and made them more devout toward God. So we see in our time that those who are separated from us draw into their company all those who hear them singing the Psalms and praying. And seeing that this is a good thing and praiseworthy, and something the church has employed for such a long time, it would be a good thing to accept by the same stratagem into our Church the singing of Psalms in the vernacular with the public prayers; and every bishop could order just this in his diocese[17].

The long quote was, I think, necessary, for pointing out some aspects which are worth discussing. First: the proponents hastened to recall how Psalm-singing was sanctioned by and deeply inherent to the tradition of the (Catholic) Church; moreover, having being practised since the earliest years of the Christian era, it had accomplished a crucial role not only as an excellent form of prayer, but also as an efficacious propagandistic tool. Secondly, it is significant that the propo-

---
16  Fisher 2014, p. 157.
17  *CT* 13, p. 524. As quoted in and translated by Monson 2002, p. 31.

nents refrain from considering the Protestant psalmody merely as a good idea for recruiting music lovers, but rather acknowledge its value and honestly consider it to be a praiseworthy deed. Thirdly, the importance of *vernacular* singing is specifically recognised, and official pronouncements by the Catholic authorities are urgently advocated.

Though the Council remained silent on this issue, the practice of Catholic Psalm-singing in the vernacular is documented by several printed collections of metrical Psalms, and was especially common in the zones closest to Protestantism, such as France, Germany and Poland[18]. In Chapter Ten (§ 10.3.6.) I quoted the statements of the Jesuit Edmond Auger on the appeal of sung psalmody to the music-loving French and how urgent it was for Catholics to create a similar repertoire to combat the influence of Protestantism[19].

This need was widely felt, and some poets promptly responded: Philippe Desportes (1546–1606), for example, toiled on a metrical version of the Psalter which was consciously challenging the success of the Genevan collection. Desportes' Psalms, whose literary quality was malignantly criticised by François de Malherbe (1555–1628), were actually interesting for musicians precisely by virtue of their immediacy and simplicity; moreover, they granted more creative liberty to composers in comparison with the Genevan Psalms, which had become so closely identified with their tunes as to make alternative versions difficult to create and to promote. Finally, and rather obviously, the confessional overtones of the Marot/Bèze Psalms could not be ignored, and it was of course much more advisable for Catholic musicians to turn to a new version coming from their very field.

Curiously enough, however, many of the "Catholic" harmonisations of Desportes' "Catholic" psalter imitated closely the homophonic settings typical for the chordal adaptations of the Genevan tunes. Once more, from an artistic viewpoint, Geneva had succeeded in creating a consistent aesthetical perspective, which quickly became a model and a paradigm.

Another famous poet of the era, the same Jean-Antoine de Baïf, whose *Académie* had pioneered the *vers mesurés à l'antique* (cf. § 2.4.5.), also authored a collection of Psalm-paraphrases[20], which were presented to Pope Gregory XIII (1573), thus establishing a meaningful and significant connection between the classicising experiments of the *Académie* and the artistic interpretations of the Psalter. Differently from Marot and Bèze's Psalms, Baïf's psalter did not adopt

---

18 Cf. Ruff 2005, pp. 25–26.
19 *LM* 7, p. 475. Cf. Pettegree 2005, p. 61; Monson 2006, p. 416.
20 See http://bit.ly/2b5MTtY.

a rhymed structure, but rather exploited the quantitative principles of classic poetry: his attempts, therefore, were judged – and are still considered – to be a unique witness of how humanism, notwithstanding its paganising traits, could become a tool for ennobling through culture the religious efforts of the Counter-Reformation[21].

While the traces of the Calvinist Psalter were clearly observable in the poetical and musical style of its Catholic competitors, the case of the German Psalter created by Kaspar Ulenberg was even more striking. A theologian and a priest who had been educated in the Evangelical faith, Ulenberg wrote an entire rhyming and stanzaic Psalter, supplied with a Catechism and with more than eighty tunes (1582[22]). The curious side of Ulenberg's efforts, which appear as a clear challenge to the spread of Evangelical models, is that they actually mirror many of the Genevan tunes: not only, thus, was the Calvinist aesthetics adopted, but even its melodies were subsumed. Notwithstanding this, Ulenberg's collection was abundantly used by the Jesuits in their Counter-Reformation activities, and a selection of his Psalms was set to music by Lasso himself[23] (cf. § 9.6.7.).

Other Catholic composers who engaged in vernacular psalmody include (but are not limited to) Jacob Arcadelt, Arnold von Bruck, William Byrd, Pierre Certon, Lupus Hellinck, Clément Janequin, Stephan Mahu, Andreas Pevernage, Ludwig Sennfl and Thomas Stolzer[24].

## 11.4.2. The thread of piety

Many of the Catholic Psalms and Psalm-paraphrases had been conceived for the private devotion of the faithful or for the non-liturgical worship of confraternities, gilds and pious gatherings; as we have repeatedly seen, this repertoire was very likely to be adopted by households belonging to a variety of Churches. This applied, as has also been stated previously, to spiritual songs as well, and here too the confessional denomination of lyricist and composer could have little or no impact on the songs' adoption by members of the other groups.

---

**21** Cf. His 1999, p. 194; Higman 2000, pp. 499–502; Rainoldi 2000, pp. 324–325; Brooks 2006, p. 177.
**22** Ulenberg 1582.
**23** Cf. Blankenburg 1975, p. 550; Weber 2008, pp. 186 (and fn. 1) and 205; Fisher 2014, pp. 108–109.
**24** See § 5.3.3., 6.3.6., 7.6.3. Cf. Blankenburg 1975, p. 532; Higman 2000, p. 499; Rainoldi 2000, p. 324; Brooks 2006, p. 177.

This was partially in consequence of how widespread was the focus on interior growth, meditation and piety among practising Protestants and Catholics alike. In Germany (Augsburg), the Jesuit Peter Canisius fostered the performance of traditional *Kirchenlieder* in the vernacular, within the framework of a spiritual revival of piety. Collections such as the *Sacrarum ac aliarum cantionum trium vocum*, by Gerardus van Turnhout (1569[25]) are typical examples of how music dovetailed with religiosity and fervour in the daily lives of musically literate Christians. Hymns suited for blessing the table are found side-by-side with Latin motets which could also be sung within official liturgies; the highly successful spiritual song *Susanne ung jour* was juxtaposed to thanksgiving hymns. For the many religious leaders who cared for the godliness of their flock, it was imperative to foster its spiritual advancement not only during the official and communal worships, but also on all occasions of daily and family life. Since the ordinary experiences and vicissitudes of life were likely to differ more drastically among members of distinct social classes than among members of different denominations who belonged to the same economic or cultural group, then the devotional repertoires suited for the uneducated, for the literate or for the aristocrats could transcend confessional boundaries more easily than social spheres[26].

Spiritual music was often seen as a means for holding together content and experience of faith, dogmatic knowledge and heart-warming feelings, catechesis and prayer. Though, within an integrated religious perspective these elements should actually be strictly joined, I will now turn separately to the former and to the latter members of these pairs, and point out how music was seen, by Reformers of all denominations, within the context of mystical experience and of religious instruction.

### 11.4.3. The thread of mysticism

The mystical dimension of music (as of faith in general, indeed) is always difficult to evaluate and to describe; and yet, in spite of this difficulty, it has always played and still plays a fundamental role in the lives of the believers (and of many so-called non-believers). Shaky as the ground may be, thus, it is necessary to focus briefly on this topic, especially since within this dimension of faith the confessional divergences might become marginal.

---

25 Van Turnhout 1569.
26 Cf. Weber 2008, p. 185; Forney 2010, p. 101. See also § 11.3.4.

The reader will recall our discussion (§ 2.3.7.1.) of how several thinkers and writers about music (and religious music specifically) considered its power to "move" (the passions, the affects, the deeds...) as one of its greatest merits. In Chapter Twelve (§ 12.3.3.) I will discuss the touching experience of communal singing lived by an Antwerp exile in Strasbourg[27].

We have also seen (§ 2.3.8., 2.4.3., 3.3.2.1.) that the common association between music and femininity could be seen as a positive or negative quality, depending on the author's perspective. For men, both music and the love for a woman were seen as potentially sanctifying or depraving forces, which might appeal to the highest or to the basest passions of the soul. Thus, for many – among whom Charles Butler, in his *Principles of Musik in Singing and Setting* (1636) – music could favour an ecstatic experience of God's beauty, which would in turn increase the soul's love for Him. In Butler's words,

> Besides these ordinary special uses of Divine music, we read of certain extraordinary; whereby strange things were brought to pass, both touching the Evil and the Good Spirit. Touching the Evil Spirit, in that it was used for the quieting of Men possessed, and for the expulsing of the foul fiend [...]. And for the Good Spirit, the like Music was used by the Prophets, thereby (as it seemeth) to excite a special Enthusiasm, or divine Rapture for some present Oracle[28].

Though ecstasy and rapture were uncommon experiences (and were seen with suspicion by many spiritual leaders), the heart-warming power of music was acknowledged by such different figures as Calvin (who admitted to the "coldness" of the songless Geneva in comparison with the musically appreciative Strasbourg congregation) and Federigo Borromeo. It was on the latter's encouragement, it will be recalled (cf. § 9.6.2.) that Aquilino Coppini decided to put in the service of piety the highly emotional power of Monteverdi's madrigals[29].

The hypothesis has been advanced that Borromeo made use of these spiritual madrigals while preaching spiritual exercises to the nuns of the Milanese convent of Santa Marta, where mysticism was particularly appreciated and fostered[30].

Mysticism should not be interpreted, though, as implying a diminished rational power and a more or less extravagant behaviour. For most spiritual leaders, it rather meant a profound experience of God, which should have encour-

---

27 Erichson 1886, pp. 21–22.
28 Butler 1636, pp. 114–115, spelling modernised.
29 Coppini, letter of July 1609 to Hendrik van der Putten; as quoted in Fabbri 1985, pp. 152–153.
30 Cf. Rorke 1984, pp. 174–175.

aged, if genuine, a more intense (rather than a vaguer) comprehension of life and of its meaning.

Thus understood, a mystical experience was likely to occur at the highpoints of life, when one's faith was challenged and put at stake. In such situations, what had been sown in the ordinary experience of life should resurface, with both its results (i.e. a deeper knowledge of and love for God) and the instruments and accessories (such as music) that had favoured it.

Thus, Christians whose spiritual life was shaped by the practice of Psalm-singing were likely to request it when facing agony: Psalm 103 [102] was chosen by Scottish Protestants such as Elizabeth Adamsoun (d.1555, i.e. before the Scottish Reformation) and James Lawson[31] (1538–1584) for accompanying their own last moments with religious music. Adamsoun told her relatives that this Psalm had led her to experience and "taste of the mercy of my God"[32]. Similarly, the Anglican bishop John Jewel allegedly wished Psalm 71 [70] to be sung during his agony[33]; perhaps more surprisingly, crew members of a sinking ship, in 1593, sang "with doleful tune and heavy hearts" Psalm 12 [11], just before being drowned by the strife of the elements[34]. The sailors' resorting to sung psalmody, their knowledge of the Psalter and their clinging to this religious practice in a moment of terrible distress all bear witness to how deeply this practice had pervaded the spirituality of the English by the end of the century.

Another experience embodying this same principle was witnessed by the Catholic priest St Filippo Neri, who accompanied the last moments of the earthly life of a musician from Castel Sant'Angelo, by the name of Sebastiano. During his agony, Sebastiano was terrified by demonic visions and by the idea that he would be damned forever. At the arrival of his father confessor, Neri, the demons were quickly dispelled, and Sebastiano gave praise to God, exclaiming: "Long live Christ, long live Filippo, through whom I have been freed from hell". Then – in Neri's biographer's words – Sebastiano became "very happy, and he started to sing the spiritual Lauds which were sung at the Oratory, and particularly that which begins: *Gesù, Gesù, Gesù, ognun chiami Gesù*"[35]. Sebastiano then was comforted by angelic visions and died peacefully in Neri's arms.

Though in this particular case the author attributes to Neri's holy presence the merit for banishing the demons which were tormenting Sebastiano, the power of music to drive away the evil forces was acknowledged by spiritual lead-

---

31 Calderwood 1843, vol. 4, p. 201, as quoted in Duguid 2014, p. 206.
32 As quoted in Ryrie 2006, p. 122.
33 Featley 1609, sig. ¶¶6ʳ; cf. Quitslund 2012, p. 244.
34 In Clarke 1805, p. 46; cf. Marsh 2013, pp. 435–436.
35 Bacci 1622, p. 99, my translation. Cf. Fenlon 2009, pp. 208–209.

ers of all denominations. As seen in Chapter Four (§ 4.2.4.5.), John Jewel reported how Psalm-singing "annoyed the devil"[36], while Luther repeatedly affirmed the power of music to exorcise Satan[37].

### 11.4.3.1. Defeating the devil

For Lutherans, this was not just a theoretical statement or a dogmatic assertion (for Bugenhagen, "when Music is embellished with holy words, it puts the evil spirit to flight"[38]), but was actually observed in practice. In 1559, in the village of Platten near Joachimsthal, a girl named Anna, daughter of the smith, was possessed and tortured by the devil, who started to speak through her. The individual and joint efforts of the local Lutheran pastors could do nothing to free her from the diabolic possession; however, when Anna was brought to a service where prayers were said and hymns were sung for her by the entire congregation, the demon was finally defeated and she was liberated[39].

Among Catholics, demons seemed just as scared by hymn-singing as they were among Lutherans. Another Anna, who was a noblewoman from the lineage of the Bernhausens, and who was lady-in-waiting to Sybille von Fugger, was possessed by the devil in turn, together with another female member of the famous banker's household. In her case, too, ordinary exorcism performed by the clergy (namely Jesuits) had been unsuccessful. In January 1570, the girl – who was only seventeen at the time – was brought to the shrine of Altötting, together with her patrons and with a clerical figure of St Peter Canisius' standing. For two days in a row, litanies were "devoutly performed in figural [polyphony]" for her; on the second day, "when they began to piously pray the litany of Our Lady all together, the demon soon began to quiver"[40]. Though in this case the ultimate deliverance from the diabolic possession was due to St Peter Canisius' prayers, which were uttered and not sung (as the chronicler clearly states), the presence of communal singing and its importance within the ritual of exorcism should not be underplayed.

Though today's most sceptical readers may be perplexed by such accounts, they mirror important truths which are held to be matters of faith by most Chris-

---

**36** Cf. Robinson 1842, p. 71.
**37** Cf. Luther 1538a, 3.8; *WA* 50, p. 371; *LW* 49, pp. 427–428; *WA BR* 5, p. 639; *WA TR* I, p. 490, no. 968.
**38** In Rhau 1955, vol. I, p. xvii, as quoted in and translated by Hendrickson 2003, p. 38.
**39** Cf. Brown 2005, pp. 103–104; Pettegree 2005, p. 49.
**40** Cf. Eisengrein 1581, fols. 125$^v$-147$^r$. Cf. Soergel 1993, pp. 123–124. Translated by Fisher 2014, pp. 307–311. See also Fisher 2015, pp. 68 ff.

tians: that evil forces exist and are adverse to humankind; that they can be defeated by God's Grace; that this liberating Grace can and should be invoked in prayer; and that the communal prayer of the Church (possibly with the help of singing, whose beauty sharply contrasts with wickedness and despair) is more powerful and effective than that of any individual member of the congregation.

Music, thus, expresses, mirrors and creates that concord of hearts which strengthens the communion of a congregation; this communion, in turn, ultimately reflects the belief that, when the Church prays, it does so through and with her mystical bridegroom, the Christ.

### 11.4.3.2. Consoling and comforting

Phenomena of diabolic possession, however, were fortunately uncommon, and precisely for this reason the tales of successful exorcisms have been transmitted in writing. Much more frequently, of course, people fell ill, suffered and hoped to be relieved from their pain.

In Chapter Five (§ 5.3.4.4.) we encountered the case of a woman whose difficult labour was eased and brought to a happy ending when she heard a Lutheran hymn sung by a passing boy[41]; and a brief mention has been made, in Chapter Nine (§ 9.5.2.1.), of St Ignatius of Loyola's reliance on music to be comforted in his darkest hours. As recounted by a witness, "[for] the whole time that I was in Rome, Father Frusius was called from the German College (when Ignatius was in bed, feeling out of sorts) to play the clavichord for him – without singing, since even this helped him; as well as a very simple and virtuous brother, who sang many devout hymns"[42].

Music was also used as a means to recount miracle tales: from the one side, this was in itself a source of comfort for the suffering, who were encouraged to hope and pray for their own healing; from the other, music helped to transform miracle songs from chronicle to prayer, and to give an orthodox meaning to prodigies, while downplaying their superstitious side.

The mystical power of music extended itself well beyond the physical comfort it could convey, and often it was seen as an instrument for the healing of souls: the cases are reported of nearly-prodigious conversions following the per-

---

**41** Cf. Brown 2005, pp. 72–73. On music's thaumaturgic power as seen by sixteenth-century Christians, see also Kendrick 1996, p. 14.
**42** *Fontes narrativi* I, p. 636.

formances of touching spiritual plays, both in Italy (Messina, 1569) and in Munich (1609[43]).

### 11.4.4. The thread of education

While many of the effects of religious music quoted above maintain a mysterious nature, whose acceptance or rejection by today's readers largely depend on one's religious outlook, another of the functions of music on which Reformers of nearly all denominations were remarkably in agreement was its pedagogical value, which is much easier to convey in writing and to evaluate. As argued by Robert Bireley, Western history has seldom witnessed so strong a pedagogical concern as that of the sixteenth-century Reformers: for both Catholics and Evangelicals, the religious growth of children and the young was essential (particularly when competing confessions faced each other), and the locus where it could take place was represented by education and schooling[44].

Once more, the cultural framework within which the European Reformers were operating was fundamental, and their attention to educational principles was highly indebted to the humanists. For spiritual leaders who were as imbibed with humanist principles as, for instance, Philip Melanchthon was, any effective reform of the Church should be integrated with a reform of the entire society by means of a widespread education. This laudable perspective had however a risky side, i.e. the potential marginalisation of those who remained untouched by the educational reform (due to social, intellectual or economic reasons). Actually, such a division between learned and unlearned came to be clearly visible in the very musical practices of the Lutheran Church, where – as seen in § 5.3.4.1. – a competition for musical space in worship soon set the plainest forms of singing practised by the "simple folk" against the complex music performed by professionals or accomplished amateurs.

On the other hand, the stress laid by the Evangelicals on the verbal content of faith as expressed in readings, sermons and, of course, in singing, emphasised the primacy of hearing and thus contributed to enhancing the value and appreciation of music as an educational instrument[45].

In Lutheran Germany, for example, religious education was embodied in and, at the same time, encompassed the teaching of the other subjects; school

---

**43** Cf. Chapter Two (§ 2.4.7.); see also Gassner and Quinn 2002, p. 42; Fisher 2014, p. 225, fn. 127.
**44** Cf. Bireley 1999, pp. 118–121; Crook 2009, p. 8.
**45** Cf. Blume 1975, p. 122; Wagner Oettinger 2001, p. 24; Kim 2005, p. 110.

ordinances of the time bear witness to the importance given to music within the educational curriculum and how music, culture and religion were deeply interrelated[46]. (It should be emphasised, however, that this was by no means an unavoidable by-product of humanist ideals: though all humanists were supportive of educational improvement, not all of them were as enthusiastic about music. This could be observed, for example, in the relative downplaying of religious music by Johannes Sturm [1507–1589] in Strasbourg, whose outlook was influenced by Erasmus' views[47]).

This applied to virtually all levels of education (though, of course, with different qualitative results), ranging from rural parish schools to Latin schools and universities, where singing was a fundamental component of religious services.

Pupils were instructed in music and through music; musical education was important *in se* and as a medium for conveying those teachings which were deemed to be most crucial for the children's lives, i.e. catechetic, moral and spiritual learning.

Moreover, the children's accomplishment in music worked also as a means for spreading both Lutheran music itself and its religious content: as we have seen in Chapter Five (§ 5.3.4.3.), the hymns and songs learned by school students as part of their curricular education were transmitted to the entire community during congregational worships, and to their families during household devotion. This was seen as a keystone for the survival and dissemination of Protestant ideas, Evangelical faith and Lutheran values[48]. Moreover, the presence of advanced students who could master the Latin repertoire (and understand it) was judged by Luther and his followers as an indispensable requirement for ensuring the possibility of maintaining the tradition of Latin-texted polyphony[49]. Though many in the congregation were probably unable to understand what was sung, the singers' proficiency in the Latin language was the only necessary condition for this music to be a legitimate form of prayer; moreover, Luther's educational perspective involved – as seen in § 5.3.4.3. – the commitment to children of the responsibility for explaining such songs to their family[50].

Though Luther was probably the religious Reformer most enthused by music, a similar perspective was by no means unique to him and his Church. As briefly mentioned in Chapter Five (§ 5.4.), Martin Bucer unequivocally supported the musical education of the youngest members of the community.

---

46 Wagner Oettinger 2001, p. 191.
47 Brown 2005, p. 59.
48 Cf. Leaver 2007, pp. 277 and 295; Wagner Oettinger 2001, p. 47.
49 Brown 2008, p. 224.
50 Brown 2008, pp. 230–231.

Music, he affirmed, was a means for "leading [children] to the good by joyful means", especially since children were naturally disposed for music[51].

In Basel, the importance of teaching sung psalmody to children had been acknowledged by Oecolampadius (cf. § 6.4.) and was further fostered by Mareschall, whose adaptation of Goudimel's Psalm settings to Lobwasser's translations in High German mirrored the educational purpose of his endeavour. The four-part harmonisations featured within Mareschall's collection, which included Lutheran songs along with Lobwasser's psalmody, made his book perfectly suitable for the pedagogical aims of religious education with and through music[52].

A similar perspective was inherent to Calvin's vision too: The Reformer shared the humanist belief in the possibility of moral growth, improvement and self-education, and believed in the power of music to effect an overall bettering of the individual's character, and, therefore, of the society's godliness. For him, as for many other Reformers, metrical psalmody was an amazing synthesis of prayer, religious and ethical teaching, literary refinement and spiritual beauty; by rendering it even more pleasing and retainable, music actively cooperated in the establishment of a truly Christian society[53]. A particular case of a pedagogical use of psalmody is the role played by Sternhold's *Certayne Psalmes* within the framework of the religious and moral education of the young King Edward VI in England, in order to instil in the sovereign an increasing awareness of his God-given vocation as a saintly ruler, based on King David's model[54] (cf. § 7.2.3.).

On the other hand, and similar to Luther, Calvin availed himself of the schoolchildren's cooperation for the purpose of familiarising the congregation with the Psalmodic repertoire and its tunes[55].

Music was extensively practised and actively promoted also within the framework of Jesuit colleges, starting from c.1560, and it became a fundamental element of the Jesuit plays, aiming at conveying religious, spiritual and moral teachings in an effective, touching and yet pleasant fashion. At the same time, perplexities still lingered as to the risk, feared by many, that the theatrical quality of such dramatic music might somehow pollute the style and features of church music proper[56]. It can be argued, however, that the Jesuits' educational

---

[51] "*Mit lustlichen mitle zum güten gefürt sein wil*". Bucer 1541 A3ᵛ. Cf. Honegger 1982, pp. 9–10.
[52] Cf. Marcus 2001, pp. 739 and 741.
[53] Joby 2005, pp. 67–68.
[54] Cf. Quitslund 2008, p. 9 etc.
[55] Pettegree 2005, pp. 55–56.
[56] Cf. Körndle 2006, p. 479; Crook 2009, pp. 9–10.

engagement and concerns were among the principal causes prompting their interest in music, since, as we have seen in Chapter Nine (§ 9.5.2.1.), their religious family had not been enthusiastically supportive of musical activities at its outset.

An ordinance issued in Antwerp in 1588 testifies to the ubiquitous role of religious music during the days of schoolchildren: "each morning [the students] should kneel and sing or read the *Veni sancte Spiritus* with a versicle and collect, and each evening as they leave, sing a song in praise of the Virgin (*Laudes Diva virginum* [sic]) or the hymn *Christus qui lux es et dies* [sic] in Latin"[57].

### 11.4.4.1. "The brim around the cup": singing the Catechism

In this case, as – for instance – in the Psalm-singing of the schoolchildren in Calvin's Geneva, Oecolampadius' Basel or Bucer's Strasbourg, the primary function of music was to foster piety, to embellish prayer and to educate the pupils to love the practice of devotion.

In other cases, which again can be seen as a red thread among most confessional Churches, music was placed at the service of religious instruction, of catechesis, and served as a means of helping the children to retain the dogmas of faith and of making the process of their learning more agreeable. At the same time, a side-effect of sung catechism which no Reformer would have reasonably downplayed was that children were likely to sing spontaneously the catechism songs they had learned, thus helping – more or less consciously – the dissemination of the confessional dogmas. Moreover, as suggested by Scheitler, the practice of singing Catechism songs fostered an interactive approach to religious teaching, whose dialogic form was empowered by the musical expression of the attending laity[58].

As Hsia correctly points out, the importance of catechetical songs can only be grasped by considering how closely the processes they triggered resemble the dynamics of storytelling: "Catechistic songs", he argues, "represented musical narratives in verse; storytelling was the central act of religious propagation". Thus, the impact of spoken and sung narrative is hardly measurable by today's standards, but can be imagined when we consider that "storytelling provided one of the main forms of entertainment"[59].

---

[57] 1588 Ordinance of the Guild of St Ambrose. Antwerp, Archief van de Onze Lieve Vrouwekathedraal, Scholastria 25, fol. 25ᵛ. Quoted in Forney 2010, p. 111; translation taken from *ibid.*, p. 101.
[58] Cf. Scheitler 2010, p. 184.
[59] Hsia 1992, p. 102.

The concept that music was a pleasant help for the hard task of learning was, possibly, yet another trace of the humanist culture and influence on the Reformers. In my opinion, in fact, it represents an embodiment of a famous Lucretian simile (*De Rerum Natura*, 4:12): here, Lucretius maintains he chose to expose his doctrine, which "seems / in general somewhat woeful unto those / who've had it not in hand / [...], in song / soft-speaking and Pierian". Thus, just as physicians "touch / the brim around the cup"[60] of a bitter medicine with honey to dupe a child into drinking it, similarly the poet-philosopher seeks to lure his readers into swallowing his difficult teaching by means of sweet song.

Possibly, however, Lucretius' simile had been reinforced through its adoption by a Church Father, St Basil, whose beautiful endorsement of psalmody has been quoted in Chapter Two (§ § 2.3.4.). Indeed, Basil maintained that

> When the Holy Spirit saw that humankind was ill-inclined toward virtue and that we were heedless of the righteous life because of our inclination to pleasure [...], he blended the delight of melody with doctrine in order that through the pleasantness and softness of the sound we might unawares receive what was useful in the words, according to the practice of wise physicians, who, when they give the bitterest draughts to the sick, often sear the rim of the cup with honey[61].

Echoing Lucretius even further, as quoted in Chapter Two (§ 2.3.4.), Basil maintained the particular value of psalmody as an educational instrument for the young or the "wholly youthful in their character".

The influence of this viewpoint, frequently summarised as *"miscere utile dulci"*[62], is clearly discernible in the words of the Anglican Thomas Roberts, who in 1583 authored a metrical catechism suited for singing on the "Sternhold and Hopkins" tunes. He wrote:

> He, that considereth the dull untowardness of our nature in learning of heavenly things, the tediousness that easily creepeth upon us, the scorn that many have to teach, and others to be taught by their Pastors and Masters, the difficulty and infinite travail in teaching, and the small increase of continual labour with them, besides the diligence of the adversaries, in blasting abroad their poison, and how necessarily therefore the people of God are to be foreseasoned and confirmed with the counterpoison of truth against them, shall easily perceive this to be no idle or vain Poetry, but a needful and Christian policy[63].

---

[60] All quotes from William Ellery Leonard's translation (1916). Cf. Lucretius 2004, p. 104.
[61] Basil of Caesarea, *Homily on the First Psalm*, in *PG* 29, cols. 209–213, as translated by William and Oliver Strunk, revised by James McKinnon, in Strunk 1998, p. 121; with adaptations.
[62] Horace, *Ars poetica*, 342–343 (Horace 1836).
[63] Roberts 1583, sigs. A2$^{r\text{-}v}$, spelling modernised.

Roberts also stressed the importance of complementing religious instruction with prayer, by adding: "When you have done singing so much as you will, it were good to add that prayer for the Church of God, in the 28 Psalm 9 verse"[64]. In Chapter Four (§ 4.2.4.5.), we have seen that Melanchthon's words, while prefacing Lossius' *Psalmodia* (1553) were highly consonant with the Lucretian/Patristic approach[65], and Johannes Bugenhagen was in substantial agreement. He wrote:

> I should like hymns for the young to be purer, [...] so that the young might become accustomed by their singing to commit to memory the sacred writings, like the school boys here at Wittenberg, whom we train in a very short and most delightful exercise, when they go twice a day, morning and evening, from school into the church. By this exercise, as though by a game, our young people learn the Holy Bible, so that they return with greater enthusiasm to their scholastic pursuits[66].

Another printed text, chronologically situated midway between Melanchthon's and Roberts', seems to make exactly the same points:

> In particular the reason for singing, especially in places where to sing like this is a novelty, is because thus the pupils learn more easily, and especially those who do not know very well how to speak or how to read, and those of uncouth mind, the peasants, and women; since the memory is reinforced by singing [the material] and the teaching is made more sweet; also in places where rude songs are commonly sung, [it is better] to sing those holy and good songs; we also have the example of the early church which sang in the morning and in the evening the praises of God. For these and other similar reasons, the church today causes sacred things to be sung[67].

These lines were written by a Spanish Jesuit, Jaime (also known as Diego or Giacomo) Ledesma (c.1519–1575), framing his treatise on the proper way to teach Christian doctrine: the publication (1573) of his method in Italy represented the apex of a Jesuit initiative for spreading internationally the catechetical techniques experimented in Spain[68]. Such techniques included the combination of sung formulae with simple verbal contents, metrical patterns which favoured memorisation, and the frequent use of first-person plural pronouns and verbs, stressing the ecclesial dimension of catechism. The musical aspect of religious instruction comprised both songs which were structured with the purpose of

---

[64] Roberts 1583, sig. B4ʳ. Cf. Willis 2013, p. 173.
[65] Cf. Groote and Vendrix 2012, p. 186.
[66] In Rhau 1955, vol. I, p. xvii, as quoted in and translated by Hendrickson 2003, p. 38.
[67] Ledesma 1573, p. 9. Quoted in and translated by O'Regan 2009, p. 225 (with modifications).
[68] Cf. Filippi 2015b, p. 2.

conveying precise dogmatic contents, and others which were more loosely – but not less fundamentally – connected with the process of learning, including – but not limited to – sung prayers[69].

As Filippi remarks, "if the roots of this phenomenon are distinctly Spanish, the contribution of the Jesuits was to be decisive for its international dissemination and its inclusion in a systematic pedagogical strategy"[70]. Indeed, much earlier in the century (c.1527, though the earliest surviving edition is of 1554) a compendium of Christian doctrine in verses to be sung had been written by St John of Ávila (1499–1569), who had also stressed the importance of a warm personal relationship between religious instructors and disciples[71]. The *Doctrina christiana* written by St John of Ávila was transmitted to the Roman headquarters of the Jesuits, and then translated into Italian in 1555, thus providing a fundamental model for the later Italian catechisms.

### 11.4.4.2. "By way of pleasant song": enjoying Sunday school

In Ledesma's homeland, Spain, and namely in Gandía, near Valencia, analogous practices were successfully employed in 1554, as related by Juan Alfonso de Polanco (1517–1576), the Jesuit who was Ignatius' secretary:

> A certain one of our brothers went around parts of the town at fixed times every day with a bell, inviting children to sacred learning. Two boys went along with him, and they taught the doctrine to the rest by way of pleasant song. [...] When the listeners were counted, the number had risen to five hundred, and throughout the town the only thing that was heard sung, by young or old, day or night, was Christian doctrine. Indeed, workers in the city and farmers in the field eased their labour with this singing; and mothers at home who did not know it, unashamedly learned it from their children[72].

Beside the impressive number of those who attended the Jesuit teaching, I would like to point out a few details in Polanco's account: teaching was imparted "by way of pleasant song", as in the examples quoted before; religious singing had reportedly taken the place of secular songs, even outside the contexts appointed for prayer and religious instruction; elders were willing to be taught by their children, as in many other situations observed so far.

---

69 Filippi 2015b, pp. 13–14.
70 Cf. Filippi 2015b, pp. 3–4.
71 De Ávila 1971, vol. VI, pp. 454–480. Cf. Nalle 1992, p. 111; O'Malley 1993, p. 116.
72 *Chron.* 4, pp. 350–351. As translated by Culley and McNaspy 1971, p. 222. Cf. *LQ* 3, p. 89. See also *LQ* 3, pp. 169–172 and p. 434; *LQ* 7, pp. 704–705.

With similar successes to report, it is no wonder that the Jesuits' sung catechism received approval from above and was thus encouraged in many contexts where Ignatius' followers were operating. At the First General Congregation of the Jesuits, in 1558, an official pronouncement had been requested: "Is it appropriate to teach Christian Doctrine in song, for experience shows that children are more easily attracted to it that way and that greater success results?". The very formulation of the question made a negative answer very unlikely to be given; and indeed Diego Laínez (1512–1565), who had been appointed as Loyola's successor, allowed sung catechesis to be imparted when it produced good results[73].

In spite of this, both the potential usefulness, and the problems which the similarity of Catholic and Protestant techniques might pose, were clear in the eyes of the Catholic Reformers; Ledesma himself explained that complex situation as follows: "although, where the heretics sing similar things, and it is forbidden by the superiors to sing them, it is necessary that Catholic singing be done for the edification of Catholics and with the superiors' permission, so that they do not seem to side with the heretics"[74].

In those same years (1560), in Casas Ibañez, near Albacete, the results of musical instructions were described with similarly enthusiastic expressions:

> It melted my hard heart to see the eagerness with which the children came to doctrine, and they went singing it in the streets and fields, so that almost nothing else was heard. Some women were crying with devotion, and when we asked them why they didn't know the Ten Commandments, they said, "Because they didn't teach it to us like now in the streets"[75].

Here too, sung catechism brought abundant harvest both as regards piety (the women who "cried with devotion") and knowledge, and pious songs became the favourite repertoire sung by the children. In the same year, St Peter Canisius (who authored a fundamental Catholic Catechism, in two versions of different length and complexity, similar in concept to Luther's two Catechisms) explicitly fostered the practice of singing metrical versions of the Catechism[76].

Similar results (though with particular focus on the mnemonic function of music) were reported by a Jesuit preaching in Fulda, Germany (1586): "For a whole year I have been labouring with our village boys but could not make them remember even the words of the Lord's Prayer. But now that I have taught

---

73 *Institutum* 1757, vol. 1, p. 481 [CXXXVII]. Cf. O'Malley 1993, p. 122.
74 As quoted and translated in Filippi 2016b, p. 16.
75 *LQ* 6, p. 949. As translated by Nalle 1992, p. 112.
76 In Canisius 1905, vol. 4, p. 331.

them how to sing, they learn the Apostles' Creed and the Ten Commandments in a few hours, and I doubt they will ever forget them"[77].

These basic texts of the Christian faith were taught in singing by missionary Jesuits in such diverse contexts as Indonesia (thanks to the efforts of St Francis Xavier) and in Brasil, in the native Tupi language (1577)[78].

A similar repertoire was included in a book by Franciscus Sonnius (also known as van de Velde, c.1506–1576), the Catholic Bishop of Antwerp who had participated at the Council of Trent and was at one of the front-lines of Counter-Reformation. His compilation, published in 1571, was entitled "A suitable manner for youth to learn sweetly through song": it comprised metrical monodic settings of vernacular versions of the Lord's Prayer, *Ave Maria*, Creed and the Ten Commandments[79]. Seemingly, however, religious instruction with music had been practised for many years in Antwerp, and even within the context of charity educational establishments for poor or orphaned children[80].

Notwithstanding this, sung catechism was not always welcomed by the Catholic authorities in the Low Countries. Jacob Vallick (c.1515-a.1571), the parish priest of Groessen, reports in his *Ouwe Kerckenboek* (c.1568) that the Sunday afternoon meetings he organised for the religious instructions of children were extremely well attended, and that the songs on the Commandments, on the Creed and on the Lord's Prayer were particularly liked by his pupils. Vallick continues by stating:

> And that did a lot of good among the people, and they became very skilled at it, but then I was forbidden to do so by my superiors, by the Dean and the Bailiff, and I was prohibited on pain of death, but the preaching was not prohibited, only the singing. But when I sang no more, people no longer came[81].

The reason for such serious a threat from Vallick's superiors is difficult to guess and seems in contradiction with other examples from the Netherlands. Did perhaps sung vernacular catechism sound suspicious, at least locally? Was Vallick using "heretical" tunes or lyrics? What was behind such a decision will probably remain mysterious, but the causal connection drawn by Vallick between singing and attendance is certainly worth observing.

---

77 Quoted in Duhr 1907, pp. 459–460; translated in Strauss 1978 p. 234. Cf. Wagner Oettinger 2001, p. 50.
78 In van Orden 2015, p. 137.
79 Sonnius 1571; cf. Forney 2010, p. 91.
80 Forney 2010, p. 91.
81 Quoted from van der Heyden 1921, p. 37; translation by Pollmann 2006, pp. 311–312.

### 11.4.4.3. "Sing like the angels in heaven": publishing Catechism songs

In c.1591, an extended version of Sonnius' *Een bequaem* was published, under the title of *Die Christelycke Leeringhe*, by Rutgeert Velpius in Brussels[82]. The additions regarded both the musical settings (which were here in four-part harmonisations) and the textual aspect, which included more religious songs. The preface underpinned the mnemonic function of music as a help for remembering catechetic instructions, and – exactly as in Ledesma's case and in many others we have seen so far – the idea was stressed that religious songs could profitably replace the lewd ones in the impromptu daily singing of the laity[83].

Similar books were written and published throughout Europe by pastors from all denominational provenances. Collections such as those created by the Scotsmen David Peebles and Andro Kemp, with Psalms, hymnody and religious instruction proper ("*The XII Articles of The Christian Fayth*") were in turn commonly used and frequently copied in the Scottish song schools after the Reformation[84].

As Scheitler suggests, many catechism songs can be classified according to four categories: metrical songs on the contents of faith, sung versions of the catechism texts, narrative songs and songs in which the affective dimension of faith was stressed and fostered[85].

When, in 1576, a new Italian edition of Ledesma's successful catechism book (*Dottrina Christiana a modo di dialogo*) was printed in Carlo Borromeo's Milan, an accompanying collection of religious songs was issued in turn, comprising *Lodi e canzoni spirituali per cantar insieme con la Dottrina Christiana*. Here, as in Velpius' *Christelycke Leeringhe*, the musical aspect consisted of simple four-part harmonisations of pleasant and uncomplicated tunes; they could be adapted to several texts, and were certainly created primarily as aide-memoirs[86]. The preface states:

> These *laude*, printed here separately from the *Dottrina*, are to be sung by the pupils at the beginning, in the middle, and at the end in the quantity and the way judged necessary by the teacher of the doctrine. Singing the doctrine and the *lodi spirituali* by two choirs is useful for a number of reasons. First, to make it easier to commit to memory, as experience has already made clear. Second, to make it more attractive for pupils to come to the *Dottrina* at times when they are otherwise invited to play games, as on feast days. Third, those who can only just speak can learn [better] through the medium of song; they do not learn as quickly

---

82 *Christelycke leeringhe* 1591.
83 Cf. Forney 2010, p. 100.
84 Munro 2010, p. 70.
85 Scheitler 2010, p. 168.
86 Cf. Ledesma 1576; O'Regan 2009, p. 225.

without singing. Fourth, to teach with minimum effort: because when everyone sings the *Credo* they all take part, and readily, whereas simply listening to one after the other takes a lot of time and is boring. Fifth, to avoid the scurrilous songs that are generally sung wherever youngsters – and older people – gather when they do not know any other songs. Sixth, so that those who hear and do not come to the *Dottrina* will also learn. Seventh, so that the pupils will learn to sing with as much ease as possible so that they will know and want to sing either the *Dottrina* or [other] praises of God our Lord. Eighth, to imitate the usage of the Roman Catholic Church, which sings the canonical Hours night and day. And finally to sing like the angels in heaven who continually sing: Holy, Holy, Holy to the Lord God[87].

This somewhat lengthy quotation is particularly interesting in its careful enumeration of virtually all the reasons for using music in catechism which were listed individually or partially in the texts and prefaces of other Reformers from all denominations. Similarly, Filippi's survey of Catholic sung catechisms lists a series of functions or objectives which music could help to achieve in religious instruction: among them, the possibility of memorising more easily the dogmatic definitions, the attractiveness of music, its potential for creating a feeling of community and for spreading doctrine outside the church walls, its value for contrasting "lewd" songs and for sacralising the daily life of children and adults alike[88].

This approach was not limited to the Catholic milieu, however: we have already seen (cf. § 4.2.4.5.), that Luther warmly recommended that the union of the commendable with the joyful be constantly practised[89]; and that these principles – so close, indeed, to those of many other religious Reformers – were arguably put into practice within Lutheran schools such as those of Joachimsthal. As correctly suggested by Brown[90], indeed, the multiple functions (cultural, ethical, pedagogical...) accomplished by music at a Lutheran school did not obscure the fact that the principal of them was and remained the religious education of children and young.

### 11.4.4.4. "Night and day": the forms of sung doctrine

Most Churches reserved a special dedicated time for catechetic instruction proper, particularly on Sunday afternoons; there, teaching was framed by prayers and

---

[87] As quoted in and translated by O'Regan 2008, p. 239. Cf. Rostirolla 2001, pp. 318–319; Østrem and Petersen 2008, pp. 57 ff.
[88] Filippi 2015b, p. 42.
[89] Luther in Walther 1524; cf. Strunk 1998, p. 361 and Sfredda 2010, p. 25.
[90] Brown 2005, p. 67.

songs, thus assuming the shape of a religious service, of an act of worship. Among Catholics, the members of the *Arciconfraternita della Dottrina Christiana* in Rome sang *laude* during both their weekly instructional meetings and the catechism competitions held annually on the Sunday after Epiphany[91].

Jesuits made use of music when teaching catechism in a variety of contexts: in the Sicilian city of Messina (1555), around three-hundred-and-fifty children received religious instruction by the Jesuits every Sunday; reportedly, the younger children were taught the catechism songs by the older "with such great enjoyment" that "night and day they sang nothing else in the streets and marketplaces of the town"[92].

During the weekly sung catechism teaching at the Jesuits' church in Vienna, a responsorial musical style was adopted (1569): here the Lord's Prayer was sung first by a boy from an elevated podium, and then repeated by the others; then a girl proposed the Apostles' Creed and was responded by the bystanders. The scheme was repeated until the entire lesson had been delivered[93].

For the Reformed, the sung aspect of Sunday schools was centred on unaccompanied psalmody, as would be expected; among the Anglicans, the situation was similar except when, in the major ecclesiastical establishments, more complex kinds of music were available; Lutherans could profit from the hugest musical repertoire for catechesis, comprising the *Katechismuslieder* (Catechism songs) which Luther had purposefully composed on the six sections in which religious instruction was articulated[94].

Though these were among the best-structured accomplishments of catechism in music, the basics of the Christian faith were sung by members of many Churches: following Luther's *Dies sind die heil'gen zehn Gebot'*, included in the *Erfurter Enchiridion* of 1524 and set to the tune of a crusaders' song (*In Gottes Namen fahren wir*), in the wake of a pre-Reformation tradition, the Ten Commandments had been set to music in Strasbourg by Wolfgang Dachstein (1526), whose song was reworked by Calvin into *Oyons la Loy que de sa voix*. In 1533, Antoine Saunier (d. a.1547) created a successful *contrafactum* of Claudin de Sermisy's *Au boys de deuil* (actually *Au joly boys, en l'ombre d'ung soucy*), on lyrics paraphrasing the Commandments. Marot in turn contributed to Huguenot *chansonniers* with his own version (*Lève le cueur* [sic], *ouvre l'aureille*, 1545[95]).

---

91 Cf. O'Regan 2013a, p. 346. See also Hsia 1992, p. 101; Crook 2009, p. 10.
92 *Chron.* 5, pp. 184–185.
93 Cf. Duhr 1907, pp. 455–456; O'Malley 1993, p. 122; Scheitler 2010, p. 169.
94 Cf. Leaver 2006, p. 379.
95 Cf. Forney 2010, pp. 94–99.

Among Catholics, a song on the Commandments (as on many other basics of Catholicism) is included in Michael Vehe's *Ein New Gesangbuechlin* (1537[96]: see § 11.4.7.1.), as, for example, in Sahagún's *Psalmodia* (cf. § 9.5.2.5.); as we have just seen, before being forbidden to do so, the Dutch curate Jacob Vallick used to have children sing, among others, the Commandments prior to 1568[97].

### 11.4.5. The thread of musicianship

During the previous discussion of how pedagogical and catechetic concerns were common to religious Reformers both Catholic and Evangelical, and of how many of them made use of music for educational purposes, another element which united spiritual leaders of all denominations has surfaced: several Reformers saw in devotional music a resource for offering a sanctioned repertoire to replace the secular or scurrilous songs favoured by the "rude people".

It was imperative, for many pastors, that the natural tendency of most human beings toward singing be channelled into the service of their spiritual growth. This became even more urgent, for Catholics, when they realised the impressive results music had achieved for the dissemination of the competing confessions. On the other hand, as repeatedly seen in the preceding pages, it was easier for the devotional repertoire than for that of official worship to migrate from one confession to another[98].

Many among the shrewdest and most creative Reformers from all fields were quick to exploit the success of secular forms (such as, for example, madrigals) and to either transform them through contrafacture into sacred works, or create new works similar in form to their secular counterparts.

For example, Leitmeir has fascinatingly discussed the causes and history of the collection *Triodia Sacra* prepared by Bernhard Klingenstein, the Augsburg Cathedral *Kapellmeister*, on behalf of the local Jesuits in 1605[99]. The collection astutely relied on the commercial success of *tricinia*, whose perfect balance between excessive simplicity and difficulty made them perfectly suited for the needs of the educated music-lovers, and hurried to offer itself as a devotional alternative, whose primary intended users were the students at the Jesuit university of Dillingen[100] (see also § 9.5.2.3.).

---

**96** Vehe 1537; Vehe 1567, pp. 11–12.
**97** Pollmann 2006, pp. 311–312.
**98** O'Regan 2013a, pp. 344–345.
**99** Klingenstein 1605.
**100** Leitmeir 2002, p. 145.

The aim of replacing profane songs with catechism hymns was reportedly achieved in northern Spain, where the Jesuits succeeded in conveying religious teaching in music so well that, "on those hills" where the remotest villages lay, the only songs which resounded were the Lord's Prayer and the others learnt at catechism. Even in urban contexts such as Syracuse (Sicily) or Murcia (Spain) the catechism songs were spontaneously intoned by the children in the streets[101]: as reported, in 1557, by Giovanni Filippo Casini (1520–1584) to Diego Laínez, "The most distinguished children, the children of barons and gentlemen, attend our schools: they learn the doctrine in Italian verse and go around the city singing it in public, instead of other idle songs"[102].

Warnings from religious leaders against secular music, to which sacred works should be preferred, could transcend the field of vocal music, and instrumental performance of dances was discouraged in favour of transcriptions from sacred works. This happened, in *La Montaigne des pucelles / Den Maeghden-Bergh* (1599) written by the Leiden schoolmistress Magdaleine Valéry, to the fictional character of Emerence, a young Dutch girl, to whom the teacher ("*la maistresse*") recommends to prefer devotional pieces – such as canticles, Psalms or "honest songs" – to dances or "light songs" ("*chansonnettes legeres*") when playing the spinet. Later, the *maistresse* praises music as it helps to "forget many fantasies which would otherwise trouble man"[103].

Here music is seen to be a powerful psychological force, in driving to the good not only the deeds, but rather the thoughts, fantasies and spiritual aspirations of the schoolgirls educated by the *maistresse*.

### 11.4.6. The thread of solicitude

Indeed, among the pedagogical concerns of many Reformers of all denominations we should finally list one more common trait: if music was a valuable tool for conveying religious instruction to the children, it also was a precious means for drawing to the good – and ultimately to God – the souls of those who were weaker in their faith. While young age was commonly associated with instability in one's choices of faith (and, of course, the young were deemed to be more vulnerable to the preaching and fascination of the competing confessions), sometimes this "weakness" depended on causes other than one's age.

---

**101** *Chron.* 4, pp. 432–433; *Chron.* 6, pp. 301–302, 555, 697. Cf. O'Malley 1993, p. 122.
**102** As quoted and translated in Filippi 2015b, pp. 6–7.
**103** Valéry 1599, folios B4ᵛ and C4ʳ. Quoted from Vanhulst 2008, pp. 276 and 278, my translation from the French. Cf. Forney 2010, pp. 104–105.

(The reader will recall that such a belief can be traced back to St Basil, to St Augustine[104] and to Aquinas[105]).

Even some among the Reformers who were least enthusiastically supportive of music could thus understand the reasons for employing music for educational purposes when the "weak" were concerned.

This somewhat patronising attitude extended itself also to another category of vulnerable people, such as those lacking literacy or the intellectual means for grasping the meaning of the contents of faith. As seen in some of the previous quotations, in fact, music was frequently considered to be particularly useful for helping those who could not read to retain the words and definitions which were considered as indispensable for any Christian to know.

A curious agreement can be observed between Cardinal Federigo Borromeo and Queen Elizabeth I. As cursorily mentioned in Chapters Two and Three[106], Federigo Borromeo's opinions on the matter were entirely in the wake of the great theologians Augustine and Aquinas. For Borromeo, in the ancient Church, psalmody was closer to utterance than to singing. "Later, however, for the sake of those men who are carnal rather than spiritual, the Church allowed another way of singing, so that those who were not moved by the words could be persuaded by the suavity [of music]". It is for this reason, Borromeo continues, that vernacular singing of "songs and motets in our language" was preserved: the uneducated were in fact to receive "a greater benefit by this permission"[107].

The very same concepts (i.e. preference for clear delivery and sober singing, concern for the music lovers) are expressed in a strikingly similar fashion in the Elizabethan *Injunctions* of 1559, quoted in Chapter Seven (§ 7.2.4.).

Whereas other writers such as Giovanni Animuccia (*Preface* to the First Book of Masses, 1567: cf. § 9.3.6.1.) and Gabriele Paleotti[108], to quote but two, were in agreement with this perspective on the function of art and beauty for attracting to faith, it is interesting to contrast this view with that of Ignatius of Loyola. The Founder of the Jesuits in fact decreed: "For one who experiences devotion in listening to those chanted services will suffer no lack of places where he can find his satisfaction; and it is expedient that our members should apply their efforts to the pursuits that are more proper to our vocation, for glory to God our Lord"[109].

---

104 Cf. *Conf.* X.33.49–50 (1955, p. 145); see Chapter Two (§ 2.3.4.).
105 *ST* 2a2æ, q. 91, a. 2.
106 § 2.3.1., 2.3.7.2., 3.2. etc.
107 In Bizzarini 2012, pp. 157–158, my translation.
108 Cf. Prodi 2014, p. 95.
109 *Constitutiones* 1970, pp. 261–262. Cf. Culley and McNaspy 1971, p. 217.

For Ignatius, thus, it was perfectly admissible that the music lovers might enjoy listening to beautiful sung services; however, in his opinion, it was not the Jesuits' mission to provide for that need with their sung Offices. Of course, here Loyola was justifying his position on the incompatibility of the times of monastic prayer with the apostolic activities of the Jesuits (and, as we have seen, the Founder himself could be counted among those who loved listening to music). Moreover, his position was limited to how the Office had to be performed, so that the use of music and other artistic disciplines for winning over people and leading them to spirituality was far from forbidden to the Society's members.

I would argue, thus, that Loyola's statement can be seen as the exception confirming the rule: whenever the religious Reformers expressed concern for the faith of the younger, weaker or illiterate among the members of their flocks, music was resorted to as a sweet and yet powerful medium for attracting them to God[110].

### 11.4.7. Inspiring hymnbooks

In the cases discussed above (i.e. the cross-confessional use of psalmody, the fostering of piety and devotion, the mystical and thaumaturgic value of music, its educational role) it is sometimes difficult to establish which confession first established a practice which the others adopted later – and indeed it is very likely that many common practices predated the sixteenth-century Reformations. In another case, instead, i.e. the creation and dissemination of hymnbooks, there is a clear confessional forerunner[111].

It should be very clear by now that the primacy of the Lutheran Church in making the use of printed hymnals widespread is indisputable (though, of course, the model for many Lutheran hymnals came from preceding traditions, such as the Hussites', and from the use of medieval prayerbooks and *hymnaria*[112] – cf. § 5.3.3.).

In spite of this, the input for the creation of Catholic hymnbooks with German religious songs came undeniably from the acknowledgement of how well these books worked for the Evangelical communities and from the wish to exploit this resource in turn.

---

110 See also Wagner Oettinger 2001, pp. 60–61.
111 On the history of German Catholic hymnbooks, cf. Fugger and Scheidgen 2008.
112 Cf. Rainoldi 2000, p. 325; Marcus 2001, pp. 724–725; Brown 2008, p. 228.

The dependence of Catholic hymnals on their Lutheran models is observable at a number of levels, from the very aesthetical appearance of the Catholic hymnbooks, which closely resemble their Evangelical forerunners, to the choice of repertoire. Indeed, and though the Catholic hymnbook compilers could have drawn from the rich supply of medieval religious songs in the vernacular, they preferred to rework and adapt Lutheran songs for Catholic use or to compose new songs.

As seen in Chapter Five (§ 5.3.3.), however, the dissemination of Catholic hymnbooks in the German-speaking territories was not comparable to that of the Lutheran hymnals: vernacular hymn printings between 1520 and 1600 only amount to forty-six Catholic issues over more than seven hundred of their Evangelical counterparts[113]. This disproportion is likely to be due not only to the chronological priority of Lutheran hymnals in the market of religious publications, but probably rather to the different emphasis placed on the use of vernacular songs by Evangelical and Catholic spiritual leaders. While, as seen in Chapter Five (§ 5.3.3.1.), in the early Reformation era the most likely context for the use of Lutheran hymnbooks was for home and private devotion (and thus, theoretically, this non-liturgical frame should have been common to both confessions), it is no wonder that the Catholic clergy hesitated in promoting forms of piety which were too strictly reminiscent of Lutheran practices and over which the ecclesiastical authorities could perform little or no supervision.

Thus, paradoxically, it was more likely for Catholic hymnbooks to be used publicly rather than privately, though in most cases such public use would have been outside liturgy proper. Interestingly, however, a noticeable warming in the Catholic attitude to congregational singing chronologically corresponds to the Lutherans' strongest efforts for the involvement of the laity in church singing[114] (1560s). Notwithstanding this, even when Catholic hymnals imitated most closely an Evangelical model explicitly conceived for household devotion, they made it clear that the proper Catholic use of such collections was during official worships (for example for singing before or after the sermon[115]).

### 11.4.7.1. Vehe: A Catholic pioneer

The first known Catholic hymnal in German is the work of the Dominican friar Michael Vehe (1485–1539), who published his *New Gesangbuechlin* in 1537. His

---

113 Brown 2005, p. 22.
114 Herl 2004, p. 33.
115 Brown 2005, p. 22.

pioneering effort consisted of forty-seven songs, amounting to about two-thirds of the latest Lutheran hymnal. On the one hand, thus, even the bare figures reveal the different approach of Catholics and Evangelicals to hymnbooks and vernacular singing: though Catholics could draw upon an august tradition of sacred songs (while Lutheranism was an extremely recent movement at that time), they did not foresee the potential of communal singing for the spiritual lives of Christian communities, and were generally slower than the Evangelicals to adopt it. To be sure, Vehe explicitly stated that his hymnal was meant to be used by laypeople, both in public non-liturgical worships such as pilgrimages, and within the framework of the Mass, as an optional element before or after the sermon[116]. Though publicly performed, however, these songs were deemed to be not as integral to worship as communal singing was for Luther.

On the other hand, however, Vehe's hymnal – and those taking it as a model – are discussed here instead of Chapters Nine or Ten since they represent, in my opinion, an element in common among different Churches rather than a weapon in a confessional war.

Indeed, in Vehe's collection, no trace is found of polemical songs, references to the Evangelicals or allusions to the emerging confessional divisions. In place of violent attacks, we only find prayers in music; and, indeed, Vehe seemed more than willing to incorporate some of the beautiful musical and spiritual creations of his confessional adversaries within his collection. Occasionally, he interpolated new stanzas amid those of Lutheran songs, with the aim of integrating their confessional perspective or of stressing the Catholic viewpoint on certain theological topics: this happened, for example, as regards the Eucharistic stanzas added by Vehe to the Lutheran version of *Jesus Christus nostra salus*, which had become the enormously successful *Jesus Christus unser Heyland*[117].

As seen earlier in this Chapter, within the discussion about the theological reasons for the unifying power of music (§ 11.2.3.), when song is really intended to be an integral component of prayer and praise, then the confessional divergences fade and may even become negligible, inasmuch as all Christians are united by the wish, the need and the necessity to exalt and invoke the Lord[118].

---

**116** Cf. Vehe 1537, fol. 2b; cf. Herl 2004, p. 33.
**117** Vehe 1567, pp. 109 ff.; cf. Scheitler 2010, p. 166.
**118** Cf. MacCulloch 2003, p. 153; Wetzel and Heitmeyer 2013, pp. 30–31.

### 11.4.7.2. Leisentrit: An example of Counter-Reformation

Thirty years after Vehe's hymnal, Johann Leisentrit (1527–1586), a Catholic priest, tried his hand in turn at the creation of a Catholic hymnbook. The city of Bautzen, in Lusatia, where Leisentrit practised the care of souls was close to the regions of Moravia and Bohemia where Protestantism was at its strongest.

Leisentrit's hymnal had true Counter-Reformation purposes, inasmuch as its aim was to contribute to the conversion of those who had abandoned Catholicism, the "old Apostolic Christian Church which rightly believes the truth", in the very words of his title.

As seen on several occasions, when the Catholic authorities realised the power of Evangelical singing they reacted either by banning it or by imitating it: Leisentrit's choice to fight the Evangelical movements on their own musical ground was neither the easiest nor the most common, and it was misinterpreted by many of his fellow Catholics.

Not only, moreover, the typically Lutheran encouragement of the *Hausandacht*, of the household piety expressed through family sung worships was not paralleled by most Catholic authorities; as Brown correctly (though perhaps slightly too categorically) points out[119], there was also a significant difference as to the overall concept of the functions of music.

While I would not go as far as to state that the dimension of *Trost* (comfort and consolation) was absent from Catholic songs, it is undeniable that the emphasis given by Lutherans to this aspect was unparalleled in the Catholic field. On the other hand, the Catholic preference for songs celebrating the holy deeds of saints and invoking their intercession possibly reduced the feeling of personal attachment and even ownership which characterised the Lutherans' relationship to their repertoire.

Moreover, most of the texts in Leisentrit's collection made use of Luther's translation of the Bible as their source: this created a somewhat awkward feeling of inconsistency, which may have impacted on the ultimate success and dissemination of such songs.

Leisentrit's task thus involved creating translations from traditional Latin hymns, whose linguistic shape was radically different from that of German poetry, and adapting the plainchant tunes to the metrical and prosodic qualities of the vernacular. Of course, Luther himself and his followers had had to tackle similar problems, but for Leisentrit it was also imperative to camouflage the origins of songs coming from the Protestant repertoire, lest his superiors blocked the publication of his hymnal or accused him of heresy.

---

**119** Brown 2005, pp. 23–24.

In Wetzel and Heitmeyer's words, Leisentrit's hymnal "is possibly the most comprehensive collection of interconfessional songs of the sixteenth century"[120], but this does not prevent it from also being the expression of an entirely Catholic mentality veined by Counter-Reformation ideals. In spite of this, and notwithstanding Leisentrit's clear stance, owing to which his hymnal is much more clearly "Catholic" than Vehe's (of course, thirty years of confessional opposition had elapsed between the two), his effort was met with suspicion by the Catholic authorities, and – seemingly – his task was given ultimate approval only due to the Pope's direct intervention.

This impressive and imposing collection comprises nearly two-hundred-and-fifty songs, roughly a third of which are adapted from the Protestant tradition (in some cases, it has been demonstrated that Leisentrit made use of oral tradition rather than of the written texts of Lutheran hymnals); new hymns appear in about the same number, and possibly are Leisentrit's own creations. These figures suggest that the quantity of truly widespread Catholic songs in the vernacular which predated the Reformation was actually rather limited, in spite of an overall large traditional heritage, and Leisentrit himself presented his accomplishment as an effort to endow the repertoire of his Church, which he deemed to be rather poor[121].

The context envisaged by Leisentrit for the use of his hymnal was, of course, that of public non-liturgical devotion, as stated in the title itself: "to be sung in and in front of houses, but at the appointed times [...] and in an orderly manner"[122].

The impact of Vehe's and Leisentrit's work is hard to establish and such attempts were relatively isolated in the Catholic field, especially in comparison with the remarkable efforts of the Protestants in hymn-writing. In spite of this, they represented a fundamental precedent and a model for several contemporaneous and later publications, some of which will be briefly discussed in the following pages.

### 11.4.7.3. Sharing songs

Indeed, one of these Catholic compilers of hymn collections was not only a friend of Leisentrit, but also a contributor to his hymnbook. Kryštof Schweher (also known as Christoph Hecyrus, c.1520–1593), a Bohemian Catholic priest,

---

[120] Wetzel and Heitmeyer 2013, p. viii.
[121] Cf. Marcus 2001, pp. 724–725; Brown 2005, pp. 21–23 and 158; Wetzel and Heitmeyer 2013, to which this section is indebted.
[122] Quoted in and translated by Brown 2005, p. 212.

had actually already published (Nuremberg, 1561[123]) a collection of more than sixty songs in Latin and German for schoolchildren (*Veteres ac piæ Cantiones*), while sharing with his friend Leisentrit part of his collection of German songs; thus, twenty-four of the songs in Leisentrit's hymnal were contributed by Hecyrus and are found in the latter's *Christliche Gebet und Gesang* (Praha, 1581[124]). This collection is considered to be the oldest Bohemian Catholic hymnbook, and comprises more than fifty songs, several of which originated within the tradition of Czech Protestantism[125].

Similarly, Laube[126] has recently studied how musical repertoires were partially shared by Lutheran and Calvinist congregations in Heidelberg, a city whose confessional allegiance – by virtue of the *cuius regio* principle – frequently changed in the age of confessionalisation. The situation there was complex: there were attempts at reconciliation between Calvinists and Lutherans; at the same time, both theologically and practically, there were also concerns that no confessional syncretism might arise. Thus, from the one side, typically Lutheran practices such as Latin songs and organ accompaniment were fostered (by Lutherans) or rejected (by Calvinists) since they were seen by both as marks of confessional identity; from the other, however, study of the hymnbooks reveals the presence of an overlapping repertoire. The 1567 Heidelberg hymnbook[127], inspired by a model from Bonn, is clearly divided into two sections, the first of which is made of Biblical Psalms and Canticles, while the second includes hymns and sacred songs, thus mirroring in its articulation the qualifying types of congregational singing practised by the two confessions. The tunes found in this hymnal are similarly "ecumenical", with roughly two thirds of the melodies coming from Lutheran and one third from Calvinist sources.

Even though the confessional history of Heidelberg was rather uncommon, however, Laube demonstrates that this "ecumenical" trend in hymnals was not unique; the Heidelberg repertoire was similar to those found in other areas characterised by different confessional allegiances, and the need for complete vernacular psalters was felt not only by Calvinists (though, of course, the actual worship practices remained different and distinct). Laube thus cautions against two risks in the study of music and confessionalisation: a) to assume that members of a particular confession uniformly adopted a musical repertoire which was both unique to their confession and shared by all members of that

---

123 Hecyrus 1561.
124 Hecyrus 1581.
125 Cf. Wetzel and Heitmeyer 2013, p. 43.
126 Laube 2014, to which the following paragraphs are indebted.
127 *Psalmen* 1567.

confession regardless of their geographical, linguistic, cultural and social situation; b) to downplay the importance of "local social, theological or political characteristics [which] might have created different results among confessionally unified areas"[128].

The 1569 (reissued 1574) *Gesang Postill*[129] by the Graz parish priest Andreas Gigler (d.1570) is similarly made of a repertoire of songs both Catholic and Lutheran, and can therefore be seen as uncommitted to the confessional opposition of one denomination to another. Though Gigler took evidently as his model Nikolaus Herman's *Sontags-Evangelia* (1560[130]), however, his Catholic inspiration is clearly discernible in the destination of Gigler's hymnal as a book to be used for private devotion during public worships in church.

"Postil", in fact, was the name traditionally attributed to collections of sermons whose internal organisation mirrored that of the church year, and whose texts could be used both as the basis for actual sermons or for private meditation; originating from before the Reformation era, their dissemination and spread gained momentum in the sixteenth century. If Gigler's *Gesang Postill* explicitly drew the connection between such publications and devotional music, Crook suggests[131] that the structure of many motet collections purposefully resembles that of postils and had a similar exegetical aim. While many of such collections originated from Lutheran contexts, the first of them to appear in print was the *Novum et insigne opus musicus* (1565[132]) by a Swiss Catholic composer, Homer Herpol (c.1510-c.1574).

Returning to hymn collections, another anthology inspired by Herman's was that of *Sontags Evangelia* by Johann Posthius (1537–1597), a famous poet and physician of a Calvinist confessional allegiance. In this case, and typically for a Reformed Christian, the destination for private devotion was equally clear, but the context was that of home prayer and worship. Indeed, the stimulus for composing this collection came to Posthius from a forced confinement within the walls of his home due to a prolonged illness: hymn-singing, thus, represented a kind of a contemplative and interior spiritual exercise[133]. It is interesting thus to observe how a Lutheran collection became the model for both a Catholic and a Reformed work.

---

128 Laube 2014, p. 101.
129 Gigler 1569.
130 Herman 1560.
131 Cf. Crook 2015.
132 Herpol 1565.
133 Cf. Brown 2005, p. 160.

Georg Witzel (1501–1573), who had been a Catholic priest before adhering to Luther's Reformation, but who afterwards returned to the Catholic Church, contributed some hymns to Vehe's hymnbook, but also published his own collections of vernacular religious songs. His *Odæ christianæ* (1541) for the laity comprise songs, prayers and poetry, while his *Psaltes Ecclesiasticus* (1550) includes the German translations of liturgical texts (such as Mass and Office), of Psalms, and of liturgical and non-liturgical prayers. His collection, however, has no musical notation[134].

Other collections were issued by Adam Walasser (c.1520–1581) in 1574 and 1581 (*Catholische Teutsche und Lateinische Gesang*), including numerous folksongs; by Johannes Haym von Themar (d.1593) in Augsburg (1584 and 1590); Catholic songs were also collected locally as in the Innsbruck hymnbooks (1587, 1588 and 1589, under Jesuit influence and with Catechism songs[135]) and in the Tyrolean hymnal[136].

Interestingly, however, and notwithstanding the fact that Lutherans did not lack hymnals of their own, a recent study by Thomasz Jeż has demonstrated that a Catholic liturgical order, the *Agenda* (1591[137]) by Hieronim Powodowski (1543–1613), was owned and used by the Protestant community in Wrocław; handwritten corrections show how the Catholic liturgy was adapted to Protestant worship by modifying Marian texts so that they could mirror a more clearly Christocentric theology and by simplifying the order of liturgy[138].

### 11.4.7.4. Responses to Calvinist psalmody

Whereas many of the preceding can be understood to be Catholic responses to the Lutheran tradition of hymnbooks and congregational singing in the vernacular, Kaspar Ulenberg's collection of rhymed Psalms[139] (cf. § 9.6.7. and 11.4.1.) reveals instead its Calvinist models.

Even from the viewpoint of the melodic sources it is always important to keep into account the numerous borrowings and passages of particular tunes from one confession to the other: for example, many famous Lutheran chorales have Genevan origins. Other tunes were shared by Lutherans and Calvinists because both repertoires had undergone the influence of Strasbourg sources, while

---

134 Cf. Wetzel and Heitmeyer 2013, p. 31.
135 Cf. Scheitler 2010, p. 166.
136 Cf. Rupprich 1973, p. 263. See Witzel 1541; Witzel 1550; Walasser 1574; Haym 1590.
137 Powodowski 1591.
138 Cf. Jeż 2007 (particularly pp. 41–42).
139 Ulenberg 1582.

some Genevan tunes found their way into Lutheran hymnals via the Bohemian Brethren repertoire, which in turn gleaned melodies from the Calvinist Psalter. On a more abstract plane, we have already observed (cf. § 5.3.2.6. and 6.3.3.) how the development of the cantional style, which was to become a landmark of Lutheran chorale singing, drew its ultimate origins from Calvinist homophonic settings of the Psalms, via Osiander[140].

If Ulenberg's task was undertaken with the explicit purpose of opposing the success of the Huguenot songs, also the distinguished Orientalist, theologian and poet Guy Le Fèvre de la Bodérie (1541–1598) acknowledged that his poetical efforts were a response to the Reformed psalter. His preface to his *Hymnes Ecclesiastiques* (1578) states:

> Considering that David's Psalms, translated into our vernacular, through the sweetness of music and of melodious singing that has been attached to them, have enticed and misled not only your people but also the congregations and preaching of the so-called Reformed religion, I thought it expedient (as a remedy and antidote) to translate the Church hymns, and other spiritual canticles composed by the Holy Doctors and ancient Fathers, who are the columns and pillars of our unique Religion, with the purpose of trying – by this means – to bring back and regain by the sweetness of verses and of the songs those who – for the pleasure of the ears and of music – would otherwise have strayed from the circle of the Catholic Church[141].

He also compares the attractive songs of the Reformed to those of the sirens who first enrapture and then bring to death those who listen to them.

Le Fèvre quickly understood the potential of the Catholic devotion to the Virgin Mary and to the Saints for counteracting the success of the Reformations, and thus adopted the strategies of the Reformed with an idiosyncratic Catholic focus on Marian devotion. The framework for Le Fèvre's collection, however, is drastically different from those prompting publications such as Vehe's hymnal: though both took from the Evangelicals the cue about creating collections of religious songs, the intended readers of both are completely different. Vehe, it can be assumed, had in mind the bourgeois literate citizens of German towns, whereas Le Fèvre's translations compete with Marot's Psalms within the framework of their original destination, i.e. as refined literary and spiritual achievements for the highly educated within a humanist perspective. Thus, Le Fèvre's choices mirror the compiler's own cultural perspective – which was first of all a philologist's – and have Neo-Platonic overtones which are typical of the kind of society he was addressing. Moreover – and most important for us –, different from

---

140 Cf. Leaver 2004c.
141 Le Fèvre 1578, as quoted in Galand-Hallyn and Hallyn 2001, p. 300 (my translation).

Vehe's, Le Fèvre's collection has no musical notation. The author himself regretted this absence, but deemed it better to test the efficacy of his translations by publishing them first, and then see whether any "good musicians" were willing to undertake the task of setting them to music. (Curiously, Le Fèvre expressed the wish that musicians would give "a soul" to his verses, echoing – probably unawares – a similar statement by Luther[142]). The contents of Le Fèvre's collection, as well as his reference to Chrysostom's use of music in his struggle against the Arian heresy seem a response to Edmond Auger's hopes, as expressed in his 1563 letter to his superiors[143] (cf. § 10.3.6.).

## 11.5. Music across boundaries

It has been frequently observed, throughout this book, that musical works conceived for devotional use were most likely to cross the confessional boundaries, both at a time when these were still indistinct, and also when they took the form of solid walls. However, as the preceding paragraphs have made clear, even works which could find a place within the official worship of a Church (such as, for example, Lutheran chorales) might migrate to another confession; there, they might even be included within publications overtly aiming at confessional propaganda.

This section of Chapter Eleven will therefore discuss a few examples of how music transcended confessional delimitations: hymns or devotional works might be adopted by several confessions (possibly in consequence of their common reliance on a pre-Reformation repertoire); non-polemical *contrafacta* and adaptations could be made of particularly cherished songs; new vernacular or Latin-texted works could address believers of different denominations.

Indeed, as discussed already, often the hardest boundaries for sacred musical works to overcome were those of language and culture, instead of those of confessional allegiance. In certain zones of Europe, a neat identification of the population of a geographical area as being "Evangelical" or "Catholic" would have been difficult to establish, whereas others applied the principle of "*cuius regio, eius religio*"; and, in actual practice, in the lives of the believers, there could be many examples of a comparatively pacific cohabitation among different communities. It was common, for many, to identify themselves as "good Christians" rather than with their particular allegiance when dictating their wills; and a

---

142 Cf. *WA TR* II, p. 518, no. 2545b.
143 On Le Fèvre's hymns, cf. also Céard 2008.

social and religious climate of lessened tension could be observed in several European regions between c.1550 and c.1580. In spite of councils and theologians' meetings, in spite of diets and deliberations, examples of what we would now define as confessional ambiguity could be easily observed, such as married Catholic clergy distributing communion under both kinds, or Catholic hymns including such an "Evangelical" statement as "salvation comes to us from Grace and Goodness, works do not help anymore"[144].

Music, indeed, was among the religious elements which were most likely to permeate the lives of faith of different communities. As Blume stated, "In those areas in which both denominations used the same texts, a common literary tie lasted for centuries, and anyone who would exclude music composed by non-Protestants would arrive at a very incomplete picture of Protestant Church music"[145]. The same applied, of course, to many other confessions as well.

### 11.5.1. Adopting and adapting

Especially between confessions such as Catholicism and Lutheranism, which accepted within their worships music with texts in both vernacular and Latin, and set in a variety of styles from plainchant to polyphony, the shared repertoire could be quantitatively impressive. This did not imply, of course, that the performance style, the congregational participation in, the degree of compulsoriness of and the importance given to a similar repertoire were equal; simply, it meant that some works which could be heard in a Lutheran church on a given Sunday were not unlikely to be sung in the Catholic church next-door too (perhaps with some textual changes, if needed[146]).

Clearly, this sharing of a similar repertoire was favoured when professional musicians could be employed by Churches with different allegiances: either a musician could change his confessional stance and be employed by his new Church, or a Church might wish to employ a musician from a different denomination (for example, when he was particularly famous or gifted[147]).

The process of confessionalisation, moreover, did not always imply a musical revolution, or the rejection of pre-Reformation practices and repertoire. As seen in Chapter Five (§ 5.3.5.), a collection such as the Protestant Lossius' *Psalmodia* (1553) resembles more closely modern Catholic liturgical plainchant

---

144 Quoted by and translated in Hsia 1992, p. 41; cf. *ibid.*, p. 175.
145 Blume 1975, p. xiv.
146 O'Regan 2013a, p. 346.
147 Cf. Leaver 2006, p. 372.

books than typical Evangelical hymnbooks, and – especially after the Catholic plainchant reform of the *Editio Medicæa* – older practices could survive for a longer time among Lutherans than within the Catholic Church[148].

We have also seen, in Chapter Five (§ 5.3.5.), that several of Rhau's collections of sacred music far from represented a break with the past (see the *Officia paschalia* of 1539 or the Vespers of 1540), in terms of repertoire (including works by deceased composers, such as Obrecht or Josquin), of compositional style (polyphony on plainchant models) and of liturgical destination[149]. This did not mean, as we will see later in this Chapter (§ 11.6.1.), that new works by contemporaneous Catholic composers were banished from Lutheran worships[150].

Though the percentage of shared repertoire was probably highest between Lutherans and Catholics, even other confessions whose perspective on music was more restrictive could both lend to and borrow from other repertoires. We have already discussed (cf. § 6.3.1.) that among the sources for the Genevan tunes the heritage of Catholic plainchant is clearly discernible[151]. A famous statement about music teaching in Scotland is open to different interpretations. James Melville maintained that, fourteen years after the Reformation, he had been taught plainchant by Alexander Smith (d. a.1574), a musician "who had been trained up among the monks in [St Andrews] Abbey", and who was imparting knowledge to his pupils on "the gam[ut], plain-song" beside harmonisation of Psalm-tunes. Melville's memory is intriguing, although it is likely, as suggested by Duguid, that Melville was referring to monodic Psalm-singing[152]. Other examples of preservation and/or elaboration of pre-existing models are found in such different contexts as Coverdale's *Goostly Psalmes* in England or the Dutch *Souterliedekens*[153].

Virtually no-one, indeed, could work in isolation from the Catholic plainchant and polyphonic tradition; moreover, many Reformers felt the pressure and the need for a confessional repertoire to be available quickly. The variety of liturgical events in the Church year, or the number of Psalms to be set to music, and – at the same time – the necessity of having songs ready as soon as possible implied the impossibility of starting from scratch. Moreover, this would have also disconcerted the congregation, which was more likely to

---

148 Wetzel and Heitmeyer 2013, pp. 24–25.
149 Rees 2006, pp. 342–343; cf. also Ropchock 2015.
150 Groote and Vendrix 2012, p. 181.
151 Cf. Blankenburg 1975, p. 522; Leaver 1991, pp. 48–49.
152 Duguid 2014, p. 218; see Melville 1842, p. 29; cf. Munro 2010, pp. 69–71.
153 Rees 2006, p. 344.

learn new words to familiar tunes, or even new adaptations of known melodies, than a totally novel repertoire of entirely unknown songs.

### 11.5.2. The challenge of beauty

For many music-loving Reformers, moreover, the beauty of a tune or of a composition could become the necessary and sufficient ground for performing it. This is a very important point, as it affirms the value of music *per se*, but not (or not only) in the sense popularised by nineteenth-century supporters of "absolute music"; instead, music was seen as having a value of its own *as* an element of religious life. In other words, when a sacred work was admitted by a Church in spite of its provenance from a different confession, this was not done with the purpose of transforming a service into a concert; instead, the principle was implicitly affirmed that a beautiful musical work in the service of God could be fundamental and even indispensable for the spiritual growth of a congregation, even when its text or provenance would have otherwise discouraged its adoption.

On this topic, a famous controversy about music among early Lutherans occurred in 1543, when Georg Rhau issued a collection of responsories (*Responsorium numero octoginta*) in Balthasar Resinarius' settings[154]. The publication was preceded by the forewords of two among Luther's closest friends and followers, i.e. Johannes Bugenhagen and Rhau himself; however, the disagreement between the two is palpable. In his capacity as one of the first Lutheran theologians, in fact, Bugenhagen strongly disapproved of the presence, in the Responsories' texts, of statements of dubious Lutheran orthodoxy. To be sure, the Catholic texts had undergone revisions "so as not to cause offense to the devout", though, "through negligence"[155] (on Rhau's part), a few references to Catholic doctrines remained. For Bugenhagen, however, church music of the proper style should not merely be contented with having a passable text, but rather positively mirror the theological and spiritual perspective of the Church.

For Rhau, instead, to publish these Responsories meant to preserve a precious heritage. Moreover, the beauty of a truly "sacred" music had the power of redressing the doctrinal fallacies found in a text: in Hendrickson's words, a "Gospel-inhabited music" would "accomplish what the text failed to do", and

---

**154** See Rhau 1955.
**155** In Rhau 1955, vol. I, p. xvii, as quoted in and translated by Hendrickson 2003, p. 38.

"could correct, develop and refine texts which erred from the Gospel revealed in the Holy Scriptures"[156].

It can be argued, in my opinion, that Rhau's viewpoint was more consonant with Luther's than Bugenhagen's; indeed, Luther himself had set an example for his followers when requesting the Catholic composer Ludwig Sennfl to set to music a Psalm fragment to be used for his funeral (cf. § 5.2.), on the ground that Sennfl was one of the most celebrated of the contemporaneous German composers. Thus, Rhau was simply following in Luther's footsteps when he enlisted the cooperation of musicians such as Arnold von Bruck (who was the Emperor's *Kapellmeister*) for his sacred music collections, and when he included Bruck's *Pater Noster – Ave Maria* motet within one of them (cf. § 5.3.3.[157]).

Almost as if reciprocating, a *Crucifixus* setting by the unequivocally Evangelical composer Johannes Eccard was included in such an unequivocally Counter-Reformation collection as Klingenstein's *Triodia* (see earlier in this Chapter[158]: § 11.4.5.), and similar examples are easily found in similar publications. Such an open-mindedness may seem surprising to today's readers, who would expect a stricter and narrower confessional perspective from compilers of "confessional" collections such as Rhau or Klingenstein. More predictably, composers chose rather freely from the melodic and compositional heritage of other confessions when selecting a model or a source of inspiration for their own works. While Rhau justified his choices theologically, maintaining that the beauty of a musical setting could make the doctrinal errors of its text negligible, for most musicians the only criterion to be applied when choosing a model was inherent in its musical qualities[159].

Even Rhau, however, and – of course – Luther himself to an even higher degree, had frequently felt the need for adapting, adjusting and retouching the text (an operation which might or might not include the tune or musical setting) of the non-Evangelical works they were adopting.

We have already found numerous examples of such non-polemical *contrafacta* in most of the preceding Chapters, and I will now only briefly summarise some cases showing that virtually all confessions paraphrased and made *contrafacta* of other confessions' songs.

---

156 Hendrickson 2003, p. 39; cf. *LW* 53, p. 324.
157 Cf. Blume 1975, p. 86; Rasmussen 1995, p. 115; Bergquist 2006, pp. 335–336; Lejeune 2010, p. 6.
158 Cf. Leitmeir 2002, p. 138; see also Ropchock 2015.
159 Cf. Blume 1975, p. 117; Groote and Vendrix 2012, pp. 193–194.

### 11.5.3. Asserting the sacredness of creation

What I would like to point out here, beside the many examples I could list, is a fundamental concept: by adopting a tune from another confession, the Reformers were not (or at least not only) stealing or plagiarising from a copyrighted repertoire, and not even exploiting the success of a catchy tune. Rather, they were adopting a history and a tradition, since every song has an origin which is often both multiple and composite in turn. Tunes were sung, orally transmitted, imperceptibly changed, sacralised and de-sacralised, used for expressing prayer or secular love or jokes. By integrating formulas whose origins were ultimately unknown and unknowable within their sacred songs, church musicians had operated, for innumerable years, a process of sacralisation, which paralleled and mirrored some of the most fundamental tenets of the Christian faith: that all which exists was created good, and that God has made the human being holy, and even divine, by taking a human body Himself.

Thus, virtually all repertoires – from plainchant to polyphony – bear traces, more or less hidden and identifiable, of motifs and songs which did not originally speak of God; this is however perfectly consonant with the style of the Holy Scriptures, which are in turn interspersed with human narratives, songs, poetry and wisdom.

If this justifies the adoption of "secular" tunes, fragments or formulas within the "sacred" repertoire, the same applies – even more convincingly – to the adoption of a music used by some Christians for praying by other Christians who are no more in full communion with the former.

While today's ecumenical concept, as accepted by many Churches, sees their variety as a sisterhood of confessions, it is true that, in the early Reformation era, many Churches saw themselves as the only "true" Church, faithful to its Saviour and Bridegroom. Nevertheless, and possibly in spite of what the compilers of hymnbooks or composers were aware of, music was somehow weaving, even then, the sisterhood which is starting to bloom today. And this is a powerful experience and a meaningful symbol also for today's Christians, who may suddenly feel "at home" when, attending a service of another confession, they unexpectedly hear a tune they are familiar with.

Thus, the tune of Luther's *Dies sind die heil'gen zehn Gebot'* had a long way behind it before the Wittenberg Reformer adopted it: and a long way it was, quite literally, since it had used to be sung to accompany the marches of crusaders and those of pilgrims (attested from the twelfth century onwards, in *Tristan und Isolt* by Gottfried von Strasbourg [c.1180-c.1215]), until it became widespread, in the Lutheran world, as the song on the Commandments, which are the signposts of Christian life[160]. This tune had been intrinsically bound, in the German-speaking world, to the words of prayer normally associated with it, which appeal to God for his mercy and grace – which are, of course, indispensable for Christians wishing to live according to the Commandments. Moreover, in my opinion, a subtle exegesis was suggested by Luther's choice of this tune, by associating the pilgrimage melody with the circumstance that the Commandments had been given to Israel during its years of wandering in the desert[161].

Though the tune's way had already been long, however, it continued even after its acceptance in the Lutheran hymnbooks: Vehe included it, in a modified form, in his 1537 hymnal (as "*Ein Bittlied zusingen zur zeit der Bittfartten im anfang der Procession*"[162], a "song of prayer to sing at the time of pilgrimages at the beginning of the procession"[163]).

As seen in Chapter Five (§ 5.3.2.3.), a song on the battle of Pavia (*Was wölln wir aber heben*) lent its tune to Spengler's *Durch Adams Fall:* and even though the quintessentially Lutheran lyrics by Spengler made the song unacceptable for Catholics, the melody found its way into Catholic hymnals as *Der grimmig Tod mit seinem Pfeil*[164]. Even more surprisingly, in a later era even the most polemical and anticlerical of Luther's hymns, i.e. *Erhalt uns*, was included (in a textually modified version, of course) within Catholic hymnbooks until the present-day[165].

Analogously, a pre-Reformation *Leise*, based in turn on the Latin Sequence for the Christmas midnight Mass (*Grates nunc omnes*), was reworked by Luther and Walther (1524) into a Christmas song (*Gelobet seist du Jesu Christ*). Significantly, and in spite of Vehe's and Leisentrit's own "Catholic" versions of the song, Luther's hymn enjoyed such a widespread success that it was his version, and not theirs, which would be later included in many Catholic songbooks[166].

An extremely successful song such as Nikolaus Herman's *Wenn mein Stündlein vorhanden ist*, which is a touching and yet very consoling Christian meditation on death, was frequently printed in Lutheran hymnals, but – what is perhaps most surprising – was disseminated even in the Calvinist territories, both

---

160 Leaver 2007, pp. 118–119.
161 Blume 1975, p. 20.
162 See Vehe 1567, p. 85.
163 Fisher 2014, pp. 284–285; my translation.
164 Blume 1975, p. 31.
165 Wagner Oettinger 2001, p. 202. Cf. Honegger 1982, p. 16, as regards the similar fate of *Aus tiefer Not*.
166 Blume 1975, p. 21.

as a pamphlet and in songbooks: as suggested by Brown[167], the rather unexpected adoption of this Lutheran hymn might be due to the extreme challenges posed by the event of death to one's faith, calling for a form of comfort and consolation in music which Calvinists might possibly fail to find within their usual repertoire.

### 11.5.4. Holy and spiritual songs

What happened at the level of chorales and hymnbooks happened also at the level of "art-music", as the previous Chapters have already abundantly shown. We have seen, for example, that the French *chanson spirituelle* was among the musical forms most likely to cross the confessional boundaries. Given the importance of this genre for the French-speaking musical culture of the era, and given the focus which most confessions were putting on personal piety, a large repertoire of devotional songs was created: the features common to all compositions belonging to this genre were much more clearly discernible than the divergences suggested by the confessional allegiances of lyricist, musician and printer. A kind of osmotic exchange could foster reciprocal influences, borrowings, adaptations and fluctuations between the forms of religious poetry practised by devout Christian poets of either Evangelical or Catholic provenance[168].

The input for the great blossoming of the spiritual song came actually from the Reformed world: while unaccompanied monodic psalmody was the only form admitted in church, the effort to eradicate secular music in favour of sacred songs in the home encouraged the success of this genre. As a consequence, a certain "Reformed" flavour hovers around many spiritual songs by Catholic composers such as the priest Clément Janequin[169]. On the other hand, however, a collection such as that of *Sacræ Cantiones* by L'Estocart[170] (whose earlier output suggested strong Calvinist sympathies, if not a Calvinist allegiance) resists being labelled as either Catholic or Reformed: though its dedication and its French *chansons spirituelles* clearly belong in the Huguenot sphere, its Latin-texted works seem to point to the composer's interest in the liturgy and tradition of the Catholic Church[171].

---

[167] Brown 2005, p. 157.
[168] Cf. Pineaux 1971, pp. 449–455.
[169] Blankenburg 1975, p. 543.
[170] De L'Estocart 1582.
[171] Cf. Groote and Vendrix 2012, pp. 171–172.

Among the lyricists whose *chansons spirituelles* were most frequently set to music were Marot and Eustorg de Beaulieu, but one of the most successful songs, *Susanne ung jour*, was written by the Calvinist poet Guéroult. As seen in Chapter Six (§ 6.3.7.), the lyrics appealed to a large number of composers of all allegiances, and this in spite of the propagandistic intentions which had prompted the creation of the poetic work. The lyrics' success among composers was echoed by the dissemination of the musical settings based on it, such as those by Lasso, Le Jeune, de Rore and Eustache du Caurroy[172] (1549–1609).

We have already seen, in Chapter Six (§ 6.3.6.), that, ironically, the *chansons* by Le Jeune which were set to Huguenot moralising poetry found it easier to be appreciated by a multi-confessional public than happened to his own Psalm-settings, even though psalmody was practised by Christians of all denominations[173]. Curiously, however, some of the Huguenot Le Jeune's *Airs* (1608) were used, as late as 1642, within a Jesuit publication (*Cantiquou spirituel*), consisting of Breton religious poetry to be used for catechism instruction[174].

Though these are just a few among the many possible examples, the unforeseen itineraries which sacred music could travel through and among competing confessions are, in my opinion, the best testimony of how the interior needs of beauty-loving Christians unite them and allow them to employ the same or similar works as a help for their spiritual life. Music, as we have seen, was able to claim for itself a space: and this space could become a place of worship, open for Christians of all denominations.

## 11.6. Musicians beyond boundaries

Songs, published hymnbooks, printed or manuscript partbooks, copied or orally transmitted tunes were, in many cases, likely to cross confessional boundaries, as we have seen so far in this Chapter.

As we have also demonstrated, however, the career of many professional musicians was still remarkably international, though, as seen in Chapter Ten (§ 10.7.2.), the process of confessionalisation might partially hinder their possibilities to travel and be employed, or their possibility to profess and practise their faith.

---

[172] Forney 2006, pp. 253–254.
[173] Cf. His 1999.
[174] *Cantiquou* 1642. Cf. Riou 2000, p. 114.

Of course, when Western Europe was Catholic in its majority, and the official language of church music was in most cases Latin, it was much easier for musicians to be employed in a context which might differ radically from that of their formation. When Christianity became fragmented, musicians professing the same allegiance as their employer were more likely be given a place, and those whose first language was the same as that of the vernacular liturgies which were being established had, of course, a greater familiarity with its idiosyncrasies and could set it to music more confidently.

Thus, confessional and linguistic barriers started to weigh much more heavily on the musicians' lives. However, as the preceding pages have abundantly shown, many other elements remained which could be exploited by musicians wishing to write or work in spite of confessional boundaries.

As we have seen, several confessions did not reject the preceding Catholic heritage, and this constituted both a model and a repository of creative ideas which many musicians continued to utilise. Moreover, certain cultural – and therefore stylistic – traits were common to the aesthetic perspectives of several Churches. We have repeatedly seen how the humanistic concerns about the word/Word had influenced both some of the properly theological reflections on the reform of music and some of the actual shapes taken by "reformed" Church music. Though these shapes might sensibly differ from one confession to the other, it is undeniable that some similar concerns had been voiced, and put into practice, by those who were reforming church music throughout Western Europe. Thus, aesthetical principles, musical forms and actual compositions could represent the intersection among the repertoires of the different Churches, and several composers, particularly among the greatest of the age, could be equally appreciated by their fellow coreligionists as well as by members of other Churches.

We have frequently seen, for example, that the works of William Byrd appealed to those valuing music among both Catholics and Anglicans – and this is particularly significant in consideration of his increasing commitment to the Catholic cause; collections such as the *Psalms, Sonets & Songs* (1588) and the *Songs of Sundrie Natures* (1589) were certainly conceived to please and to have something to offer to members of both confessions[175].

A motet collection by Andreas Pevernage, the *Cantiones sacræ* (first published in 1578[176]), represented both in its musical content and in its prefatory statement a clear declaration of Catholic allegiance by the composer, at a time when

---

175  Bray 2006, p. 503; Rees 2006, p. 356.
176  Pevernage 1578.

confessional turmoil was endemic in the Low Countries. Notwithstanding this, a later edition of the same collection (1602[177]) was adjusted so as to appeal to a trans-confessional readership: while the Catholic liturgical subtext remained evident to those sharing the composer's allegiance, the Biblical sources of the motet texts could be used by and appeal to Protestants as well[178].

Lasso, being employed at a Court which was both at the frontline of Counter-Reformation and, at the same time, very close both geographically and linguistically to Protestant zones, was in turn a musician whose admirers were not only among those sharing his confessional views. Moreover, the composer himself saw to it that his works could reach as large a public as possible: not only the lyrics for his vocal settings are in a variety of languages to satisfy virtually any cultivated musician or music lover, but also the textual sources and musical models for his pieces came from many different confessional traditions. Lasso could write on Genevan Psalm tunes, while interpreting in a highly emotional way the verbal nuances of the text; this same aspect (an intense meditation of the Word producing a direct engagement of music and of the individual with Scripture) was of course entirely in accord with Lutheran views, and was embodied in the numerous German-texted devotional works by Lasso. This is probably one of the reasons for his becoming the spiritual father of the main exponents of the early Baroque Protestant style in music[179].

### 11.6.1. Ecumenism in music

Compilers of Protestant sacred music collections often turned to Catholic composers and their works as a valuable resource. It has been argued that some motet- and Psalm-collections such as those issued by Berg & Neuber in Nuremberg (1553–5) are Protestant compilations "living on Catholic composers"[180]; at the beginning of the seventeenth century, a composer such as Michael Praetorius (or Schultheiß, 1571–1621) who was to become a symbol of Lutheranism in music, was willing to insert works by the champions of musical Catholicism (such as Palestrina and Costanzo Porta) within his *Musarum Sioniarum Motectæ et Psalmi*[181].

---

177 Pevernage 1602.
178 Cf. Hoekstra 2013; Crook 2015.
179 Cf. Blankenburg 1975, p. 545; Blume 1975, p. 169; Forney 2006, p. 266.
180 Hans-Joachim Moser, as quoted in Blume 1975, p. 165. Cf. *ibid.*, p. 86.
181 Praetorius 1607.

The motet *Tristitia obsedit me* (published 1612) by Claude Le Jeune is an interesting example of a cross-confessional perspective in music: its *soggetto ostinato* is based on the motet *In te Domine speravi* by the Catholic (though with Evangelical sympathies) Lupus Hellinck; both Le Jeune and Hellinck may have been asked to compose their respective works (and, in Le Jeune's case, to make references to Hellinck's motet) by their Este patrons[182].

The lyrics of Le Jeune's motet are excerpted from two meditations on the Psalms 51 [50] and 31 [30], written by Savonarola during his imprisonment, before being executed and while suffering terribly for the tortures he had endured. Savonarola's two prayers for mercy were widely known, and musicians such as Willaert, de Rore, Vicentino, Lasso and Byrd set to music *Infelix ego*, the companion poem; Le Jeune's choice to set to music *Tristitia obsedit* (to which only Clemens non Papa had turned his attention before) is all the more interesting, as it somehow creates a chain connecting people who were Christians and artists, and who cared for the reformation of the Church: Savonarola was burnt as a heretic though he did not abandon the Catholic Church; Hellinck was close to Evangelical spheres but in turn remained faithful to Catholicism; Le Jeune was one of most representative among the Calvinist musicians, though his works circulated among Catholics and were adapted for their devotional use.

The Catholic Thomas Stoltzer, who was and remained a priest in spite of Evangelical sympathies, was asked by Mary of Hungary (1505–1558) to set to music Psalms 12 [11], 13 [12], 38 [37] and 86 [85] in Luther's translation (1525–6): these settings came to be regarded as the beginning of a typically Lutheran compositional tradition, i.e. the genre of Psalm-motets[183].

We have already seen (cf. § 5.3.3.) that Rhau's collection of *Newe Deudsche Geistliche Gesenge* featured composers both Catholic (such as Bruck, Hellinck, Mahu, Sennfl and Stoltzer) and Evangelical, and that the result is an interconfessional compilation; the same editorial criteria were applied in Rhau's other collections between 1538 and 1545, where works by Catholic and Evangelical composers could suit the liturgical demands of both confessions.

In Augsburg and Nuremberg, up to well after mid-century, Latin motets were collected on the main ground of their musical beauty rather than of their confessional content or the belief of their composers[184].

These few examples have had the sole purpose of illustrating the permeability of confessional borders to music; indeed, the practice of writing sacred music

---

182 Cf. Macey 1999, pp. xv-xvi; Macey 1998, pp. 237 ff.; Lejeune 2010, p. 13.
183 Blume 1975, pp. 85 and 100–101. See also Thompson 1984.
184 Bergquist 2006, pp. 335–336; cf. Blume 1975, pp. 85–86 and 117; Carter 2006, p. 46.

for the rites or devotions of Churches different from the musician's continued both in the sixteenth century and later. Of course, this could be difficult, unadvisable and risky within situations of particularly strong confessional opposition; and it could be unlikely and even unthinkable for composers living in zones where a total historical and geographical homogeneity of confessional allegiance was undisputed.

### 11.6.2. Finding the language of musical dialogue

However, when such positive interactions were observable, they always implied an enrichment in the aesthetical perspective – and, consequently, in the overall theological vision – of the Church.

Exactly as a song, tune or motif extracted from the repertoire of a Church and paraphrased or adapted to suit the needs of another could (and should) never be considered in isolation from its history, so the cultural implications and mind-sets of a composer's confession could hybridise those of the Church he or she was composing for.

Moreover, if the composers in question wished not to disgust, scandalise or outrage their patrons, they had to elaborate a musical language, choose lyrics and negotiate a result which would be acceptable to both the patrons and the composers themselves.

Obviously, in many cases it could and should be argued that the stimulus for such compositions or for being employed by another Church was not (primarily) an ecumenical concern, especially since ecumenical dialogue and wishes for unity are a relatively recent achievement of the Christian Churches as a whole (and even today, this is felt with a different degree of urgency by some Churches than by others).

However, by finding this musical language of dialogue, musicians were doing precisely what the ecumenical movement is striving to do now: not just to find an acceptable compromise, but rather to put into dialogue each Church's tradition, history, thought and practice with those of the others. In both music and ecumenism, the result cannot be convincing, true and satisfactory if only the intersection of traditions, history, thoughts and practices is sought: this would represent an impoverishment for all, who would have to renounce a huge part of their reality. On the contrary, fullness and beauty are reached when a language is sought and found which allows each to communicate its true and deep identity to the other; and, sometimes, the greater and more historically significant one's tradition had come to be, the greater their contribution to the other Church could become. Though my discussion in this book is mainly limited to the sixteenth century, it is impossible to neglect what Bach's Catholic Mass setting has brought to the history of the Catholic Mass, or what the dialogue of Georg Friedrich Händel (1685–1759) with Lutheran, Catholic and Anglican traditions has given to each – to name but two of the greatest.

Possibly, then, just as I have argued (in the introduction) that the sense of hearing is sometimes missing in the narratives of what has led to the separation of the Churches in the Reformation era, similarly music can teach something to all those who have an ear for the unity of the Churches.

In this Chapter, a number of threads which had been scattered throughout the preceding Chapters have been gathered and re-woven, with the purpose of showing the multiple forms taken by interconfessional music in the sixteenth century. The theological reasons for this role of music have been discussed: music can reconcile plurality with unity; its being a fundamental component of prayer makes it a source of communion and its symbolic nature makes it inherently suited for "keeping together" what would otherwise become separated. We have seen the historical reasons for this mission of music: among them, the common aspirations of many to a reform of church music, the influence of humanist concept, culture and perspectives, music's vocation for internationalisation and the similar social problems faced by members of all confessions. We have seen where and how there could be a profitable interexchange among Churches: for example, in their psalmody, in their focus on piety, in mystical experiences, in pedagogy, and in their use of similar strategies for similar ends (e.g. the publication of hymnbooks). Finally, we have seen that both music and musicians could overcome confessional boundaries with comparative ease: this could be due to the maintenance of a pre-Reformation common repertoire, to the choice of sometimes sacrificing textual orthodoxy in favour of musical beauty, to the creation of non-polemical *contrafacta* and of new works (both in Latin and in the local vernaculars) which appealed to members of more than one confession. In conclusion, I have argued that the attempts made by musicians who composed sacred music for members of another confession may become a paradigm and an actual model for the aims and methods of ecumenical dialogue. We will see, in the next and last Chapter, how the specific viewpoint of womanhood can also contribute to this perspective.

# Chapter 12 – Music and women

> In order that you have not to complain, "May we never sing at all? Must we become like wood and stone?", then sing these songs, which so suitably express God's love for us, and admonish us so truly not to miss out on the salvation we have been offered[1].
>
> [Katharina Zell]

## 12.1. Introduction

The last Chapter of this book focuses on women's music, and I feel first the duty to justify my choice, both as regards my decision to dedicate a Chapter to women's music, and its collocation at the end of this work. To devote a Chapter to female musicianship does not mean to segregate it, or to posit its fundamental and intrinsic otherness in comparison to men's music, or to adhere to the "female quota" ideology. On the contrary, I wanted to point out the women's contribution to both musicianship and sanctity, to both artistry and theology in the sixteenth century, in the awareness that their voices (often preserved more scantily than those of their male counterparts) might be suffocated unless they receive specific attention. Moreover, whereas judgements of artistic value based on gender are ridiculous either way, I do believe that there are distinguishing features, proper to the female approach to faith and to music, which can and should be highlighted: while trying not to adhere to stereotypes, my being a woman musician and believer leads me to listen with particular care to the musical experiences of female singers, instrumentalists and composers, who lived as nuns, mothers, wives or unmarried women five centuries before my own life.

An analogous reason justifies my choice of concluding this book with the present Chapter: it does not imply the hasty relegation of female musicianship to the very last pages (as a duty to be accomplished or a forced homage to be paid), or the unfair dedication of one twelfth of my book to a half of humankind, but – obviously – a very different approach. First of all, although this Chapter focuses entirely on female musicianship, this was by no means absent from all the previous pages. Indeed, women's voices have resounded throughout this book, as their music resonated throughout the century under consideration.

---

[1] Katharina Schütz Zell (Zell 1534, *Vorrede*); quoted in McKee 1998, vol. II, p. 60.

Their being mixed with those of men simply implies a worshipping covenant, a rich complementarity which posits sexual diversity as inherently good, as the Book of Genesis states. Second, this Chapter immediately follows that dedicated to music as a means for achieving cross-confessional unity: I see the female contribution to religious music in the sixteenth century as one means of reconciliation, since women's voices were sometimes those of the most oppressed human beings, and thus those with which the Crucified Lord most readily identified Himself.

This Chapter thus will start with some theoretical considerations, during which themes often found in the preceding Chapters will be cast in a new light: the subjects of "lasciviousness" and "effeminacy" (which were often connected in the most common criticism of church music), will be cursorily mentioned here.

Within the Catholic world, the musicianship of nuns is among the most studied in a field which deserves a much greater attention: I will discuss both the musical restrictions that several monasteries had to endure, and their creative efforts to express their artistry and spirituality regardless of such limitations. In some cases, it needs to be stated that music was actively encouraged within claustral walls, both as a licit recreation and as a mystical itinerary.

Evangelical women brought their distinctive contribution to the heritage of Lutheran hymnody, whereas phenomena of creative appropriation of Reformed psalmody by women shed a new light on the spiritual experiences of early modern women.

Throughout the confessional divides, sacred and devotional music was listened to, practised and composed by lay and religious women, in unaccompanied singing, polyphony, instrumental performance and accompanied monody; although the greater part of this artistic world and of this spiritual experience is irrecoverably lost to us, the scanty examples I will provide in this Chapter may help us, at least, to imagine and pay homage to it.

I would like to state, finally, that this Chapter will have even less pretences to thoroughness than those preceding it. From the one side, the state of the art as concerns our knowledge of musical works composed by sixteenth-century women, their biographies, their ideas, as well as data about the musical experience of coeval women leaves still much to be desired. I hope that this Chapter may encourage further research about some of the figures we will be considering.

From the other, I have omitted (for reasons of consistency) discussion about two categories of female musicians. In the first category belong those whose main compositional activity took place in the sixteenth century, but by whom no sacred or religious works survive. In the second category are women musicians who were born in the sixteenth century, but whose sacred compositions were written or published in the seventeenth century: among them the nuns Claudia Sessa (c.1570-c.1619), whose sacred works were published in 1613; Sulpitia Cesis (1577-a.1619), whose *Motetti Spirituali* were issued in 1619; and Caterina Assandra (c.1590-a.1618), who published several sacred works in the seventeenth century and whose op. 1 is lost. No works by the laywoman Adriana Basile (c.1580-c.1640) have been preserved, and the *Son de la Má Teodora*, attributed (?) to the Cuban musician Teodora Ginés (1530–1598) would be definitely out of place within a discussion of religious music.

## 12.2. Truths, myths and stereotypes

When studying the relationship between women and sacred music in the sixteenth century, there are some truths to be avowed, some stereotypes to problematize or qualify, and some myths to dispel. The aim of this Chapter is to provide a starting point for each of these three tasks, while contributing to an assessment of present knowledge in the field. Though these three aims will guide us throughout the Chapter, I will provide some examples of them from the start, since they will help us to frame the entire discourse.

Among the undeniable truths, we must acknowledge an impressive disproportion in the surviving sources as regards the music of women and of men, as well as the presence of objective social and religious factors which have conditioned and caused this situation.

Among the stereotypes to problematize is, for example, the lack of opportunities for professional musicianship for women in the sixteenth century: this is in turn an objective fact, but we should always consider that the possibility of choosing one's occupation freely and depending on one's talents and inclination was a comparative luxury for most human beings then, both women and men.

Among the myths, I would count, for example, the lingering idea that monasteries were oppressive establishments, which young women were forced into entering and where their talents, their femininity and their artistry were mortified. Though, of course, such situations did exist, the picture that emerges from most sources and from many of the best studies in the field is very different, and portrays thriving realities where creativity, beauty and sincere spirituality were given the possibility of flourishing, at least within certain limits.

In this Chapter, we will encounter women who actively engaged in musical activities linked with the sphere of the sacred; they could be professional, amateur, or quasi-professional musicians, aristocratic patronesses, hymnographers, editors, scribes, publishers and collectors of religious songs, girls whose education included music (either institutionally or privately), nuns in urban or extra-urban contexts, as well as women to whom music provided comfort, hope, expression or courage in situations of hardship, persecution or grief.

### 12.2.1. *Frau Musika* or women's music?

The century we have been considering throughout this book is also the century when the first collections of sacred music written by women were printed: it was a momentous beginning, and a symptom of a dawning change[2].

Though, as said, women's music has been encountered rather often in the preceding Chapters, the overwhelming presence of male figures may leave the reader with the impression that the greatest acknowledgement of women's musicality was the identification of *"Frau Musika"* as a woman by Luther (cf. § 3.3.2.1.). And that the association between femininity and music was not always seen in such a favourable light as Luther's is an actual, if disturbing, reality: we have discussed at length the implications of such concepts as the "lascivious" or "effeminising" power of music, the idea that it could debase a man's *virtue* (from the Latin *vir-tus*, with *"vir"* being "man"), and, conversely, the belief held by some that women making music were somehow less modest, less serious and therefore less respectable than those who remained silent.

This belief, as readers will recall, was maintained by influential figures of such standing as Pietro Aretino and Pietro Bembo (cf. § 3.3.2.1.), who actively discouraged musical practice by young girls, seeing it either as a waste of time or as a first step on the slippery slope to immorality; analogous concepts were argued for in many other moral books for women in several European countries[3]. The same idea was also maintained by another Venetian humanist, Giovanni Michele Bruto (1517–1592), who in 1555 cautioned against the potentially corrupting effect of music in the education of young aristocratic girls. The author published his treatise on the education of girls in Antwerp, where he had taken refuge for the "heretical" stances he was accused of maintaining; his statements are worth quoting, since they summarise many of the points we have seen in the preceding Chapters as regards the topic of music, education and femininity. For Bruto,

> It seems to most people that great adornment and grace are given to a dear and gentle girl, who becomes famous and illustrious among the others, by reaching accomplishment and

---

[2] Cf. Bowers 1986, pp. 116–117; Drinker 1995, pp. 251–252; Pendle 2001, pp. 60–61; Koldau 2005a, p. 220.

[3] Cf., for example, and as concerns Spain, Ramos López 2008, p. 3; see also Ramos López 2005.

expertise in singing or in playing various instruments. With strong and powerful reason, not only I cannot recommend this, but I deem that she ought to avoid and flee from it entirely, as from a grave danger. [...] [Music] is a sweet and agreeable bait to grave and important evils. [...] Our girl will be therefore entirely removed from the use of music; and since, under an honest veil of virtue, it opens the door to many vices, all the more it should be avoided, since the hidden peril is the greatest. Be the use of singing, and of a luring harmony allowed to those [men] who need respite and relax, being weary from boring and grave concerns. [...] We will have no doubts that a tender and delicate girl [...], should she learn such a luring art, would languish, become weak [*molle*], lascivious and effeminate. [...] Leaving music to the light-hearted and otiose, let our girl learn not only how to sew and embroider as it is becoming for a gentlewoman, but also how to spin and weave[4].

It is all too easy to wonder at Bruto's apparent inconsistencies: if music "effeminises" a woman, why should it be practised by those (men) who are made weary by grave concerns? And why should typically feminine activities such as sewing and embroidering make a girl more "virile" (*virtus*), whereas an art practised by many men would damage her by making her more feminine?

It is not my aim, however, to engage in a futile argument with the author of these inconsistent lines; rather, I quoted them at length because they are the clearest summary of the many oppositions encountered by music-loving girls and women: music is deemed to be an adornment to women; it opens the road to vice, while seeming a virtue; it may be conceded as an entertainment to those who know how to resist it; it makes people languid, weak, lascivious and effeminate; it is a waste of time which could be more profitably spent in other and more useful activities.

Though Bruto's position was undoubtedly extreme, and close to those of the fiercest opponents of music and of its educational value, we have abundantly seen, in the preceding Chapters, that many of the worries he expressed were shared, perhaps in a lesser degree and with a more shaded perspective, by many other thinkers of the era.

### 12.2.2. Mary Magdalene as a musician

Indeed, if Music was frequently depicted and symbolised as a woman, it could be personified as several mythological, religious and historical figures, from the Muses to St Cecilia; a less common symbol, though a very significant one, is the association between Music and the Gospel figure of St Mary Magdalene.

---

4 Bruto 1555, pp. 34–40, my translation.

As is known, tradition sometimes conflated into and identified with a single woman the portraits of three female characters of the Gospel: Mary the sister of Martha and Lazarus of Bethany; Mary who had been possessed by seven demons; the prostitute who washed Jesus' feet with her tears. Moreover, Mary Magdalene had been the first to see and to talk with the risen Christ, who had asked her to bear witness to his resurrection with the other disciples. Thus, the fascinating figure of the Magdalene could represent femininity as corruption (the prostitute), as an irrational and obscure force (the demonic possession), but also as mystical love (the Mary who listened to Jesus in contemplation) and as Christ's chosen one for announcing the main belief of the Christian faith (the witness of his resurrection).

Though no mention is made of music in connection with any of the Gospel's Marys, traditional iconography has frequently associated the Magdalene (especially as a prostitute) with music; for example, the so-called Master of the Female Half-Lengths (fl. 1525–1550) depicted Magdalene as a lute-player, possibly in consideration of the unchaste symbolic overtones suggested by the round shape of the instrument (the same kind of implications which caused the association of the musical symbol for the b-flat with femininity). As shown by Slim, however, music could figure in such portrayals also as a symbol of the past relinquished by Magdalene the saint, and be represented by a lute-case which conceals the score of a licentious song[5].

Thus, the symbolic associations between music and femininity might range from the exaltation of both (also in connection with the sanctifying power ascribed by some to both) to the harshest condemnation and contempt; in either case, both music and femininity were considered in their abstract, general, symbolic and sometimes stereotypical essence. Valerio Bona (c.1560-c.1620), an early seventeenth-century composer, in his dedication of an Introit collection to Carmelite nuns explicitly likened the integrity of virgin women to the harmony of a polyphonic concord[6]; on the other hand, one of the most frequent symbols for the danger of women's musicianship was that of the sirens, who drive men to perdition with their singing[7].

The actual reality of female musicianship obviously differed from such abstractions, but was, nevertheless, in some degree conditioned by the frames of mind they revealed. From the one side, as we will see, belief in the sanctifying power of music, particularly in association with its feminine characteristics,

---

5 Cf. Slim 1980, p. 465; Slim 1992.
6 Cf. Bona 1611, p. 3, in Kendrick 1996, pp. 11–12.
7 Gibson 2009, p. 63.

might encourage the devotional use of music by religious women (for example in monasteries or within movements of spiritual reformation); from the other, an underlying wariness about the dangerous power of music, of femininity, and of their even more perilous association could prompt several limitations to the musicianship of women.

### 12.2.3. Scanty sources

Though we will see throughout this Chapter many examples of both approaches, the first consequence of restrictive attitudes to the music of women is a depressing paucity of sources.

I have argued, in Chapter Three (§ 3.3.2.7.), that many of our evaluations about sixteenth-century criticism of sacred music are hopelessly flawed by our impossibility of hearing how it actually sounded. In the case of women's music, we lack not only the aural evidence, but even the written sources. In most cases, and sadly, the music of sixteenth-century women has been silenced forever.

Obviously, the rarity of preserved sources implies by no means a musical inferiority. It is not far-fetched to posit that the life of sixteenth-century women was permeated by the ubiquity of music no less than men's: at least quantitatively, it is safe to assume that women made music as much as men did. The same cannot be asserted with the same confidence as regards the quality and achievements of their music: as far as the documents in our possession let us infer, none of the greatest masterpieces of sixteenth-century music were composed by a woman.

There are many reasons for this, and I will try and summarise a few of them. First of all, there is the problem of musical literacy, which often represented a degree of knowledge and culture which was higher, more specialised, and thus rarer to achieve than general literacy. If, for example, in mid-sixteenth-century England just twenty percent of adult men could sign a paper, only five percent of adult women could do the same[8]. It seems safe to assume that those who were musically literate represented a minority among the minority who could write their own names[9]. Rather obviously, therefore, musical literacy was a kind of a privilege, and was often combined with a social status higher than the average; it should be pointed out, however, that religious factors (such as the educational concerns of the Reformers or the opportunities for learning

---

8 Cressy 1993, p. 314.
9 Cf. Mackerness 2010, p. 53.

which many nuns could find in a convent) were a positive cultural element for many women of the sixteenth century.

Clearly, however, the fact that more people could read and write words than music caused a lamentable situation: a comparatively high number of religious hymns and poems by sixteenth-century women have been preserved, while written music which can be safely attributed to women is much rarer. Arguably, many of such lyrics were destined for singing, either on pre-existing tunes (whose title or *incipit* is occasionally specified) or on melodies which could be created by the author of the verses; the surviving traces of such musical works are, however, minimal.

Of course, many accompanied monodies sung by both women and men in the sixteenth century were largely improvised; the subject of their lyrics could also be a religious topic or a spiritual poem. Since this kind of music could be practised in solitude or in very small groups, it is rather probable that this was one of the favourite shapes taken by the musical creativity of women[10].

Nevertheless, and though the scantiness of written sources will recur throughout this Chapter, we will see that proportions change dramatically depending on the social status of the women under consideration.

### 12.2.4. Social status

The social class whose female voice is hardest to perceive today is, of course, that of peasants and of the poor and uneducated urban people. Inferentially, we may assume that singing was an extremely common activity for women belonging to those classes: indeed, as we have seen in Chapter Two (§ 2.2.1.), singing was a much welcome relief which could lessen the fatigue of repetitive tasks. The informal and spontaneous singing of vernacular religious songs could also bring comfort and hope, and give a spiritual meaning to the hardships which underprivileged women frequently had to endure.

Probably, singing was also an important moment of family life: mothers sang lullabies to their babies (and many lullabies have touchingly religious lyrics), and later gave their children the basic religious instruction by teaching them sung prayers or repeating with them the catechism songs.

Though singing is, of course, a form of art itself, we may wonder whether sixteenth-century uneducated women were also "composers": did they create

---

[10] Cf. Koldau 2005a, pp. 231–232.

new songs? Did they practise contrafacture? Did they adapt, modify or combine pre-existing songs?

Arguably yes; but, of course, the problem of authorship and preservation in the repertoire of oral tradition is insurmountable. In most cases, the popular songs we know are the result of collective authorship, in which no single "composer" can be identified, and in which the traces of female creativity are even harder to recognise.

The situation was slightly better for women belonging in the middle-class, especially if there were professional musicians in their family or a particular interest in music-making. The possibility for women of this class to become, at least, amateur musicians depended also rather largely on where they lived, since in certain zones of Europe it was much more common for girls to play or sing at a good level than in others. The religious Reformations certainly contributed to the dissemination of some basic musical knowledge among girls, particularly among the Evangelicals.

Music learning could involve interaction with men, and thus could be seen as a suspicious activity by some; however, musical abilities could also be an extremely profitable knowledge for prospective nuns, whose dowry might be reduced or waived in exchange of their musical proficiency (see § 12.4.1.7.).

Women of this class might also be actively engaged in music publishing, editing and collecting (for example by creating compilations of religious musical works for private use or for publication[11]).

In spite of Bruto's contrariety, many aristocratic women received musical education, and some reached a considerable degree of proficiency: of course, this was a consequence of the less pressing needs posed by daily life for the wealthy, of the role played by music as a refined pastime, and of the availability of professional musicians in the musical Chapels and courts of the nobility.

### 12.2.5. Patronesses and prioresses

It was not infrequent, for noblewomen, to become patronesses of music and musicians, and sometimes to foster the creation of works in genres which were normally neglected by male patrons; in particular, and especially in Italy, noblewomen tended to sponsor secular (rather than religious) music and the

---

[11] Koldau 2005a, p. 232; cf. Brown 2005, p. 8. On women active in the field of Protestant music publishing, such as, for example, Kunegunda Herrgott (also Kunigunde or Kunegund Herrgottin, d.1547), cf. Jackson 1997 and Snyder and Huebert-Hecht 1996, p. 269.

creation of chamber music works for small ensembles. This situation is of course related to social issues: the small size of the performing forces matched the idea that a domestic context was the appropriate framework for women's initiative, and the male preponderance in the field of sacred music corresponded to their prevalence in Church hierarchies[12]. The case of Queen Elizabeth of England, who was the sponsor of an exceptional Chapel performing superb Church music is only the exception which confirms the rule, since she was the Supreme Governor of the Church of England and an extremely powerful civil ruler. She also fostered programmes for the improvement of musical education.

Among the Habsburgs, Margaret of Austria (1480–1530) and her niece Maria of Hungary, in their capacity as governors of the Habsburg Netherlands, were the first female members of their family to become patronesses of music at an international level, establishing an excellent musical Chapel and collecting works of the greatest musicians of the time (such as Lasso, whose sacred works were particularly cherished by Maria[13]).

Among others, we will see how the religious beliefs of Elisabeth von Braunschweig-Lüneburg (1510–1558) prompted her composition of spiritual songs, and how the musical education received by Louise Juliana of Orange Nassau (1576–1644), William of Orange's daughter, encouraged her in her efforts to promote psalmody in Heidelberg, at the court of her husband, Frederick IV, Elector Palatine[14] (1574–1610).

While the acknowledged public role of the aristocrats' wives allowed them a certain degree of independent enterprise, for example in patronage, for many women of the lower classes, including professional singers, marriage could put an end to their public performances, or represent a serious obstacle to their compositional activities. Their possibility to practise music at a high level largely depended on their husbands' decisions and on the time they could spare from housekeeping and caregiving.

Female musicians who entered a convent might have many more possibilities, in this respect, than married women, though, of course, frequently the public appearances of nun musicians were limited (at least visually) and their freedom to perform outside the monastery was minimal (with exceptions I will discuss later: § 12.4.2.2.).

Of course, the post-Tridentine enforcement of enclosure in female monasteries represented a serious limitation for the musical activities of many religious

---

12 Cf. Bowers 1986, p. 132; Pendle 2001, pp. 61–65.
13 Koldau 2005a, p. 223. See also Thompson 1984.
14 Koldau 2005a, p. 225.

communities, as we will see in the next pages; however, and paradoxically, the very fact that the interactions between nuns and male musicians were strictly reduced encouraged the religious communities to provide autonomously for their musical needs. On the other hand, this could imply that it was difficult for a young nun to reach a high level of musical accomplishment unless somebody in her community had already reached the degree of competence necessary for transmitting musical knowledge and expertise[15]. Clearly, moreover, while musical activities were normally an integral component of what it meant to be a nun, most religious women were not at liberty to dedicate many hours to purely musical practices, since the rhythm of their lives was articulated and regulated so as to include several spiritual and domestic duties, potentially conflicting with artistry[16].

Nevertheless, the importance of music in the lives of many Catholic nuns also represented a meaningful symbol which acknowledged the intellectual and spiritual role of women expressed in the bodily reality of their voices or instrumental performances. As we will see later in this Chapter, when crowds gathered in the convent churches where some particularly gifted nuns were singing or performing, this was one of the rare opportunities for sixteenth-century women to be the only active subject in an artistic and religious field. Indeed, as maintained by Kendrick, "of all the arts, music [provides] us with the best guide to the symbolic and mental world of these [enclosed] women"[17].

The musical ensembles of nuns performing in some monasteries which were particularly focused on musical proficiency also represented the context most similar to Chapels in which women could participate. As regards the particular field examined in this book, i.e. religious music in the sixteenth century, this was indeed one of the most serious and hindering limitations for women: since there was no need for female musicians in Chapels, they could not hope for a professional employment in the field of sacred music. This, of course, implied that educating a girl in the skills necessary for a church musician was a waste of time and resources, unless she was to become a nun; moreover, compositional abilities were acquired by male church musicians through practice, by imitation and apprenticeship, and they could test the aural result of their first compositional attempts with their colleagues. Another problem was that the pitch range of an all-male vocal ensemble was normally self-sufficient, whereas

---

15 Bowers 1986, p. 141.
16 Bowers 1986, p. 141.
17 Kendrick 1996, p. 22.

an all-female choir had to employ instruments (when permitted) for the low-pitched parts.

Thus, and in parallel with the fields in which Italian aristocratic patronesses were most active, also in composition the sacred output of female composers was frequently inferior to their secular works, and small-scale or devotional pieces were favoured[18].

### 12.2.6. The impact of the Reformations

We will also see how the history of the religious Reformations intertwined with various aspects of women's music. On the one hand, where congregational singing was encouraged, introduced and implemented, women had a new and sometimes revolutionary possibility of making themselves heard in church. On the other, leadership was and remained mostly male (with the exception of some numerically smaller confessions), or tended to be reabsorbed by men after some concessions to women had been made.

Occasionally, however, spiritual hymns, songs and sung prayers composed by women were appreciated and widely adopted: this was frequently seen as a prophetic or apocalyptic sign, as a particular gift of the Holy Spirit reserved for the last times.

The religious Reformations, both Catholic and Evangelical, actively fostered the musical education of girls. Following Luther's letter *To the Christian Nobility of the German Nation* (1520[19]), which explicitly promoted schooling and education for girls, many Evangelical movements provided children of both sexes with at least some basic knowledge in literacy; music, of course, was never missing from the schoolchildren's days. On the other hand, and following the Jesuits' focus on education and schooling, among Catholics several women consecrated their lives to the cultural and spiritual improvement of girls, and here too music was seen to be a fundamental element of the curriculum[20].

Notwithstanding this, the Evangelical Reformations also implied that many monasteries were destroyed, and former nuns re-entered the world as wives and mothers; though we will see that this phenomenon could be seen in a very positive or very negative light, these women frequently possessed a degree of liter-

---

18 Cf. Bowers 1986, pp. 135 and 138; Harrán 1995, p. 36; Pendle 2001, pp. 61 and 84.
19 *WA* 6, pp. 404–469.
20 Koldau 2005a, p. 230.

acy and musical accomplishment which was rare indeed among contemporaneous housewives.

At the same time, many Reformers had encouraged mothers and wives to undertake a genuinely pastoral role within their household: not only, as could be expected, as the first educators of their children, but also with their servants and – with provisos – with their husbands.

On some occasions, those Reformers with the strictest moral views imposed, as we have seen, some important limitations on the use of secular music in daily life; as demonstrated by Latour[21] (cf. § 10.7.1.), women were no less subject than men to disciplinary rulings and penalties for singing secular songs, though their self-defence frequently stated that the immoral words had been replaced with religious lyrics on the same tune.

At the apex of religious division, women could risk much more than a fine or a short detention for their faith; by examining the repertoire of martyrdom songs, we will find hymns praising the virtues of female martyrs, songs composed by persecuted women and instances in which musical resistance was virtually the only weapon left to dissident women for expressing their belief and their stance.

## 12.3. Voices of Evangelical women

Following the pattern adopted for Chapters Five to Nine, I will now proceed to discuss the role of music in the lives of Evangelical women, and later in those of Catholic women, particularly within the Catholic Reformation and the post-Tridentine spirituality.

### 12.3.1. In the Lutheran Church

If we pause a moment to recall some of the most typical of Luther's teachings (cf. § 4.3.1. and following), we will immediately observe what consequences they could produce for women's music. As just seen, Luther had promoted the cultural education of young girls, especially with the aim of allowing them to read the Bible (*sola scriptura* principle). Moreover, his assertions about the priesthood of all believers implied a divine consecration of all members of the Church, female and male alike. His positive doctrine of creation and of marriage, his theology of music, his concept of hymn-singing as providing Christians with both *Lehre* and

---

[21] Latour 2015.

*Trost*, as well as the focus on congregational singing and on the role of parents as the first pastors of their household form a picture whose shape will be familiar by now. Mothers and fathers were responsible for transmitting faith, and vernacular hymns were an exciting possibility for passing on both the verbal content of faith, which was in turn embroidered with Scriptural quotes and reminiscences, and the values on which a Christian life should be grounded.

Though I would not surmise that the role of women (sisters, wives, mothers, grandmothers) had been passive in the pre-Reformation Church, or that they had not actively participated in the religious education of their children, or that they had not sung religious songs to their family with the double purpose of to educate and entertain, it is certainly true that Luther's focus on and theological reasoning about music was probably unprecedented.

The impulse given by Luther's Reformation to hymn-singing was similarly momentous, and this prompted the composition of a huge number of new vernacular hymns in the sixteenth century.

Whereas in the field of Latin-texted "art music" the problems listed earlier (such as the impossibility of being professionally engaged as a Church musician) constituted a major obstacle for the musical creativity of women, in the field of vernacular songs it is likely that women contributed extensively: they certainly helped to retain, preserve, transmit and disseminate songs, and it is more than likely that they created new hymns, or adapted and practised contrafacture on pre-existing songs. The near-absence of women's names as authors or composers of hymns in the Lutheran hymnbooks is certainly discouraging, but – in a culture where the concept of authorship was sensibly different from today's – it can be safely surmised that many women should be attributed, at least, the co-authorship of several hymns. The very role of mothers as the catechists of their family was likely to stimulate their creativity, to foster their imagination and to encourage them to find new and efficacious ways of transmitting their faith to their children.

### 12.3.1.1. The "virtuous matrons" and their daughters

As Paul Eber, prefacing Herman's *Sontags-Evangelia*, explicitly affirmed, there were "many virtuous matrons here who at their last end were able to comfort themselves very effectively by means of the German hymns [...] and to explain them word by word and employ them with such a rich spirit that it was a cause of great wonder to the pastors and other learned men present"[22].

We will shortly see that the amazement with which male observers wondered at the Scriptural wisdom and theological knowledge of (unlearned) women were seen, by many, as an eschatological sign of the last-times effusion of the Holy Spirit as promised in the Bible (Joel 2:28; Acts 2:17).

Where and when the efforts to make the congregation sing were successful, women were not only entitled, but rather required to sing in church; nevertheless, it seems that in most cases this was their only vocal contribution to public services, and that the official roles of church musicians (such as organists or cantors) were still reserved for men.

In such exceptional and advanced environment as Joachimsthal (cf. § 5.3.4.4. etc.), however, the pupils of the girls' school were the intended recipients of a whole repertoire of vernacular hymns, many of which were authored by Herman. Among such songs, some mirror Herman's efforts to embody the Lutheran doctrines and devotions within the framework of girls' and women's lives: there are hymns which could be danced by the girls and others in the form of lullabies. The girls' choir, led by the schoolmistress, took part in the public worships, often by singing in alternation with that of the boys' Latin school, and probably responding antiphonally to their Latin stanzas with vernacular verses.

This official presence of a girls' choir at Lutheran worships was however rather exceptional, and has been reported only scantily elsewhere (for example in Hof[23]). Nevertheless, as pointed out by Brown, for the Joachimsthalers the church was the *locus* of socially permissible public musicianship. There, to share and show one's talents was not considered to be a vacuous display or, even worse, a potentially immoral seductive luring, but rather as the partaking of a community in the gifts and talents which had been given to singers by God[24].

The pedagogical ideas behind Herman's *Sontags-Evangelia* made a strong impression on a schoolmistress in Cham, Magdalena Heymair (c.1535-a.1586), who later recounted: "When I read this, it made me glad, and I thought, 'O God, would that I had grace from thee to set the Sunday epistles in songs, for thy praise'"[25]. Her wish was granted, and in the following years she gradually completed five collections of rhyming versions of the Epistle lessons, of the

---

[22] Paul Eber, in Herman 1560, p. 5 (*WB* 788, pref. 67, p. 609); as translated by Brown 2005, p. 111.
[23] Cf. Brown 2005, pp. 47 and 58.
[24] Cf. Herl 2004, pp. 163–164; Brown 2005, pp. 47, 85 and 115; Koldau 2005a, pp. 232–233; Koldau 2005b, p. 419.
[25] Heymair 1578, fols. A5$^v$-A6$^r$, as quoted in and translated by Brown 2005, p. 163.

Acts of the Apostles and of three books from the Old Testament (Ecclesiasticus, Tobit and Ruth). For Heymair, songs were the most efficacious means for transmitting and memorising the Scriptural teachings which were the daily bread of Lutheran schoolgirls; her works were published and frequently reprinted, enjoying a considerable dissemination particularly within the female circles of the South-German nobility. Heymair's main talents, however, lay in the fields of pedagogy and poetry: therefore, she did not compose new tunes for her songs, but rather drew on the pre-existing repertoire of sacred and secular songs[26].

### 12.3.1.2. Girls "prophesy": announcing the Kingdom's advent

Another particular context where Lutheran songs have been collected, preserved and transmitted (and therefore arguably sung and possibly composed) is that of the Lutheran *Damenstifte*, i.e. the female communities resulting from the conversion to the Lutheran faith of former Catholic convents. Though many Catholic convents and communities were in fact dismantled and dismembered by the Reformation, and most former nuns re-entered "the world" as wives and mothers, other religious communities chose to adhere to the Evangelical faith but to maintain their form of life as a female congregation. The archives and libraries of such *Damenstifte* provide us with handwritten collections of hymns, which bear witness to the choices and interest by these religious women in vernacular songs[27].

Here, as in the case of lay women, the question about the possible female authorship of song texts and/or melodies is both pressing and unanswered. In discussing cases such as that of Elisabeth Cruciger, which we will shortly consider, it is unavoidable to wonder if hymn-writing was an exceptional activity for Lutheran women, if perhaps they created songs which were transmitted under the name of their male scribes or adapters, or if the culture of prayer, improvisation and creative poetry was common but has not been preserved. What is certain is that after the first revolutionary moments of the Evangelical Reformations, where the thirst for novelty dovetailed with apocalyptical expectations which favoured the "prophetical" role of women, the crystallisation of the Lutheran Church as an institution tended to diminish the role of female creativity[28].

Indeed, if we recall the idea that, for Lutherans, hymns had an authority close to Scripture's, and that sermons and confessions of faith could be structured on hymn-texts or take from them substantial arguments, it becomes appa-

---

26 Cf. Brown 2005, p. 163; Koldau 2005a, p. 230.
27 Cf. Koldau 2005b, pp. 917–918.
28 Cf. Classen 2002, pp. 6 and 13.

rent that the hymn's author was conversely invested with a considerable prestige and influence. Of course, and precisely because hymns were so close to the Word of God, the ultimate authorship of a hymn recognised by the Church as authentically hers was ascribed to the Holy Spirit. As the passage of the Prophet Joel quoted in the Acts of the Apostles states, "In the last days it will be, God declares, that I will pour out my Spirit upon all flesh, and your sons and your daughters shall prophesy" (Acts 2:17).

This was the framework for interpreting statements such as this one by Gregor Strigenitz (1548–1603): at his times, he maintained, one can "find among women and girls many who, through the grace of the Holy Spirit, understand Scripture better and can speak from it more wonderfully than a doctor under the papacy"[29]. Though neither the women's intelligence nor their wisdom or creativity are denied, Strigenitz's perspective is clear: it is a wonder that women are more knowledgeable of Scripture than Catholic doctors, but it is a wonder operated by the Spirit as a sign of the last days.

### 12.3.1.3. Cruciger: from the very beginning

It was within this framework that the contribution of Elisabeth Cruciger to Protestant hymnody should be understood. Née von Meseritz, she had been a nun, and then left the monastery to get married in Wittenberg to Caspar Cruciger (1504–1548) in 1524. In that same year, both the Erfurt *Enchiridion* and Walther's *Gesangk Buchleyn* (cf. § 5.3.3.) were issued; both included an (anonymous) hymn, *Herr Christ, der eynig Gotts Sohn*, which was frequently reprinted within coeval collections; eventually, seven years later (1531), it was attributed to Elisabeth Cruciger in a hymnbook[30] by Andreas Rauscher (d. a.1535).

The attribution, which was reasserted in many other vernacular hymnbooks of the sixteenth century, was later disputed (particularly in Latin publications) in favour of Andreas Knoepken (c.1468–1539), a Reformer from Riga. As argued in Haemig's article, one possible reason for denying the authorship to Cruciger could be that her name had become unwelcome in certain Lutheran circles, since her husband's and her son's theological writings had been used by Melanchthon's opponents during intra-confessional struggles[31].

Another reason could be tied to prejudice, and to the reluctance of some male religious leaders to avow that a woman could write a hymn whose beauty,

---

**29** Strigenitz 1610, p. 97; as quoted in and translated by Haemig 2001, p. 37; cf. Grindal 2011, p. 2.
**30** Rauscher 1531.
**31** Cf. Wengert 1989 and Haemig 2001, p. 32 etc.

depth and significance entitled it to an authority close to Scripture's. This attitude, which conflicts with the idea that the gift of prophesy could be accorded to all Christians, became significantly more and more common as the apocalyptical perspective of the early Reformation era faded, and as the institutionalised aspect of the Church took hold of gender-based roles and identities.

In the sixteenth century, instead, such eschatological ideas were widespread, and it is within such a framework that a Lutheran theologian, Simon Pauli the Elder (1534–1591), dedicated in 1588 a long commentary to Cruciger's hymn[32], explicitly stating it had been composed under the guidance and inspiration of the Holy Spirit.

If, as seems more than likely, the hymn *Herr Christ* was actually written by Cruciger, she demonstrates a deep theological insight and a profound spiritual feeling. One source of inspiration for her text may had been a Christmas hymn by Aurelius Prudentius Clemens (348–413), *Corde natus ex parentis*, with which Cruciger may have been familiar during her years as a nun. Indeed, this hymn acquired a well-earned and lasting fame and was included within a number of hymnals in the following centuries.

As concerns the tune associated with the lyrics of *Herr Christ*, it bears a marked resemblance to a secular song, *Mein Freud möcht sich wohl mehren*, which was included within the "*Lochamer Liederbuch*", an important handwritten collection of German songs (c.1450). It cannot be established with any degree of certainty whether the association between lyrics and tune, as well as the necessary adaptation of the melody, were realised by Cruciger or by another person.

Such was the success of Cruciger's hymn that it appeared, in a rather faithful translation into English, in Coverdale's *Goostly Psalmes* (c.1535: cf. § 7.3.1.); a decade later, it was translated into the Scottish dialect and appeared in the *Compendious buik* attributed to John Wedderburn[33] (c.1505-c.1553).

Spiritual hymns authored by other Lutheran women have been preserved, among which are those by another figure who lived the events of the Reformation on the front line, Duchess Elisabeth of Braunschweig: differently from her letters, which testify to the numerous struggles endured by the Duchess, the mood of her hymns is rather joyful and interwoven with praise and hope. Her daughter Anna Maria (1532–1568) wrote spiritual poetry as well, and sometimes even the corresponding music has been attributed to her pen, though her musical authorship is open to debate[34].

---

32 Cf. Haemig 2001, to which this section is indebted.
33 Cf. Haemig 2001, pp. 22, 23, 35; Koldau 2005b, pp. 420 and 423; Grindal 2011, pp. 6 and 10; White 2011, pp. 21–23 and 30.
34 Cf. Bainton 1971, p. 141; Pendle 2001, p. 75; Koldau 2005b, p. 140.

### 12.3.1.4. Schütz-Zell: a resourceful Reformer

We have already seen (cf. § 5.4.) how important congregational singing was for the Reformers in Strasbourg, and the influence their communal singing would play on Calvin and on his pastoral perspective. One of the Strasbourg pastors, Mathias Zell, had married in 1523 Katharina Schütz (c.1497–1562): their wedding was one of the first which publicly involved a former Catholic clergyman and represented a clear declaration of principles by the couple.

Katharina, who had received a remarkable education in the vernacular and probably knew some Latin as well, was very active as a pamphleteer and writer; she shared with her husband a strong pedagogical concern. While Mathias wrote two catechisms, Katharina issued, among other works, the Strasbourg edition of Michael Weisse's translation of the Bohemian Brethren hymnal (which had been originally published in 1531: cf. § 5.5.). Katharina Zell divided Weisse's hymnal into four separate booklets (1534), prefaced it and added commentaries[35].

Katharina's collection presented itself as a "*Leer: Gebett und danckbuoch*", i.e. a book for learning, praying and giving thanks. It included, therefore, songs destined for particular times or activities of the day or of one's life, and songs for the dead, for the dying and about the saints (in an Evangelically-correct fashion, of course).

The first intended recipients of Katharina's efforts were, in all likelihood, Christian mothers, who could find within her collection a repository of lyrics and songs for most occasions of daily and family life. Through her collection of songs, families could enact, relive and interiorise the teaching and prayer received and practised during weekly worship, and embody the principle that family life was a privileged *locus* for a true Christian experience.

By publishing her work in four pamphlets, Katharina managed to keep the price extremely low (a few pennies), so that even "children and the poor" could afford it; her theological insight is shown in her prefaces, which have numerous original elements worth mentioning. For example, her references to female Biblical figures and to their musical practices are typical for women editors or authors of hymnals (such as Heymair, for example), but are normally missing from prefaces written by men. Her aim is clearly stated:

> When so many filthy songs are on the lips of men and women and even children, I think it well that folk should with lusty zeal and clear voice sing the songs of their salvation. God is glad when the craftsman at his bench, the maid at the sink, the farmer at the plough, the

---

**35** Zell 1534.

dresser at the vines, the mother at the cradle break forth in hymns of prayer, praise, and instruction[36].

These statements will sound familiar to our readers: in fact, they faithfully echo Erasmus' wishes (discussed in § 2.3.9.).

Katharina Zell's prefaces maintain that singing is the best means for praising God, and that spiritual hymns sung while performing the daily family duties – such as doing the washing-up or cooking – please God more than those sung by priests, monks or nuns in their convents.

Occasionally, in her editorial work, Zell suggested more than one tune for the lyrics in her collection: for example, an older melody which would have eased the process of memorisation together with a new tune which was considered to be more beautiful. She also attached commentaries to many of the selected songs, explaining the spiritual framework and theological context of the hymns[37].

### 12.3.2. In the Calvinist Church

It is possible that Calvin's favourable impression of the Strasbourg worship was, in some measure, indebted to the efforts of the Zell couple to involve the congregations in sung hymnody. On the other hand, the very beginnings of what would later become the Genevan Psalter were in turn connected with female creativity, piety and patronage. The reader will recall (cf. § 6.2.2.) that, at the time of his first metrical Psalm translations, Marot was *valet de chambre* to Marguerite of Navarre, sister to King Francis I. Marot's Psalmodic poetry was appreciated by many aristocrats at Court, among whom Marguerite herself.

Though she never formally abandoned Catholicism for the Reformed confession, she wrote a collection of *Chansons spirituelles* (published in 1547 but reprinted until the seventeenth century[38]) in which traits typical of Evangelical spirituality are easily found. For example, she focused intensely on the concept that salvation is given only through and by Christ, while neither works nor the intercession of saints possess by themselves the power to save.

Also in Marguerite's case, however, her contribution to sixteenth-century spiritual art does not include the creation of new music for her lyrics: the mel-

---

[36] In McKee 1998, vol. II, p. 61; as translated by Bainton 1971, p. 72.
[37] Cf. McKee 1998. See also Bainton 1971, pp. 71–72; Pendle 2001, p. 75; Koldau 2005a, pp. 232–233; Koldau 2005b, pp. 454, 459–466; Lindberg 2010, p. 243; Trocmé Latter 2015, pp. 124–126.
[38] See de Navarre 1971. Cf. Cholakian 2006.

odies to which her poems are set are taken from the pre-existing repertoire (not disdaining secular songs[39]).

Other women from her family took an even clearer stance: her daughter Jeanne d'Albret (1528–1572), encouraged by Bèze, became a Calvinist in 1560. One of her literary works (set to music which might have been composed by Jeanne herself) has autobiographical overtones, being a dialogue in which a monk attempts to re-convert Calvinist girls to Catholicism. Catherine de Bourbon (1559–1604), Jeanne's daughter, was in turn both a musician and a fine writer[40].

In the Netherlands, the first female member of the Reformed Church whose works were printed, albeit posthumously, was Cornelia Teellinck (c.1553–1576). She had authored a highly appreciated and widely disseminated commentary on the profession of faith she had pronounced at the moment of her confirmation; her sister Suzanna published it together with some poems by Cornelia. One of these, *A Song Composed on the Death of Her Husband*, is to be sung on the tune of the Lord's Prayer and represents a touching expression of deep feelings, which is however framed by a dense intertextual net of Biblical allusions. Thus, Teellinck's grief is not only and not merely a personal sentiment in the style of an individualistic confession, but – contextualised as it is within an Ecclesial perspective – it acquires the status of a shared and almost universal lamentation[41].

Reformed women could also become active patronesses of both religion and the arts; among them, I have already briefly mentioned Louise Juliana of Orange Nassau, who had received music lessons by such a great musician as Claude Le Jeune; following the composer's death, his sister Cécile dedicated to Louise Juliana his three-part setting of fifty Psalms, thus underlining Louise's role as a religious woman, her personal piety, but also her activity in favour of the arts and of the sciences.

Indeed, both monodic and polyphonic Psalm-settings originating from the Reformed milieu were mostly in the vernacular, which Natalie Zemon Davis has defined as "the language of women and the unlearned"[42]. This very fact reveals something about their intended recipients: though their refined verses and musical settings were beyond the reach of many, they were also simple enough to be enjoyed by literate women with some musical knowledge. Thus, creations like the Psalms by Bourgeois, Goudimel and Le Jeune implicitly affirmed that the privileged locus for self-expression of a woman's religious feelings and artistic

---

39 Pendle 2001, p. 73.
40 Cf. Bainton 1973, pp. 45–46 and 75; Pendle 2001, p. 74.
41 Schenkeveld-van der Dussen 2010, pp. 217–219.
42 Davis 1975, p. 86.

gifts was a domestic ambiance. This corresponded to Calvin's ideals: from the one side, he had wished for psalmody to become an all-encompassing frame for the daily musical experience of his followers; from the other, the only context for female voices to resound in Reformed churches was as part of a Psalm-singing congregation. Though, in comparison with pre-Reformation practices, this could be an improvement, at least locally, undeniably it still represented a rather rigid shell within which the space for female creativity and inspiration was constrained[43].

### 12.3.3. Living (and loving) psalmody

Though psalmody was the distinguishing feature of the Reformed confession, it was also, as we have repeatedly seen before, a common trait of many more Christian Churches. I will therefore consider here how psalmody was lived (and loved) by women across the confessional boundaries.

The practice of sung congregational psalmody represented, indeed, a fundamental factor in the history of female religiosity, both as concerns the public role of women in Psalm-singing and its influence on their own creativity.

As concerns the role of congregational singing, in those areas where it had not been practised during worship prior to the Reformations, its establishment meant that convents would no longer be the only context for women's voices to resound in worship[44]. This relative (or sometimes absolute) novelty was frequently exploited by Reformers such as Coverdale and Jewel as a propagandistic tool, used to counter the alleged marginalisation of laywomen in the Catholic Church. There were even some radical reformers such as John Cotton[45] (1585–1652), who felt the duty of explicitly affirming that women's participation in the congregation's psalmody did not violate the Biblical precept according to which women should keep silent in church (cf. 1 Corinthians 14:34).

Pace the scruples of Cotton and the cutting remarks of polemicists, the true revolution of congregational psalmody was a matter of profound and moving spirituality. Already in 1525, Gérard Roussel, an old friend of Calvin's and later addressee of an important letter by the Reformer, witnessed with amazement

---

43 Cf. Davis 1975, p. 78; Garside 1979, p. 25; Hufton 1996, p. 412; Pendle 2001, pp. 76–77; Schenkeveld-van der Dussen 2010, p. 62.
44 White 2005, pp. 63–64.
45 Cotton 1650, p. 43.

the beauty of the sung liturgies in Strasbourg, stating that the "singing of women together with the men was so wonderful that it was a delight to hear"[46].

Twenty years later, and from the same Alsatian city, a similar – but perhaps even more touching –report was sent by an Antwerp exile, who wrote:

> On Sundays [...] we sing a Psalm of David or some other prayer taken from the New Testament. The Psalm or prayer is sung by everyone together, men as well as women with a beautiful unanimity, which is something beautiful to behold. For you must understand that each one has a music book in his hand; that is why they cannot lose touch with one another. Never did I think that it could be as pleasing and delightful as it is. For five or six days at first, as I looked upon this little company, exiled from countries everywhere for having upheld the honour of God and His Gospel, I would begin to weep, not at all from sadness, but from joy at hearing them sing so heartily, and, as they sang, giving thanks of the Lord that He had led them to a place where His name is honoured and glorified. No one could believe the joy which one experiences when one is singing the praises and wonders of the Lord in the mother tongue as one sings them here[47].

The participation of women's voices, thus, contributed to creating a welcoming atmosphere, in which the exile found refuge and spiritual warmth.

Obviously, for some Catholic observers this same experience was far from praiseworthy. It is impossible to establish whether the harsh condemnation of congregational psalmody by Florimond de Raemond (1540–1601) was due to his objection to women's singing in church or to his disappointment for the success of psalmody and, consequently, of the Reformations it represented. Certainly, however, his judgement cannot be mistaken as laudatory:

> The Minister, thus, after that short prayer, begins a section of a Psalm of David, in French, in a loud voice: the whole people follows, men, women, children and valets, batmen and chambermaids: what a dishonourable thing! [...] Frequently, when a crowd is present, all disorderly rise and lower their music as well as they can; thus, instead of raising the soul to devotion, in this confusion of discording voices, music without music is not just ridicule, but annoying and nearly brutal, without law, without order, without harmony[48].

Raemond then censures the display of virtuosity by the nice-voiced girls in the smaller congregations, and the attention with which the young men listened to the prowess of these "sirens" (thus connecting, once more, femininity with music and seduction).

---

**46** *"Mire assonant mulieres viris, ut jucundum sit audire"*, CoR 1, pp. 406–407, as translated by Garside 1979, p. 13.
**47** Erichson 1886, pp. 21–22, as quoted in and translated by Garside 1979, p. 18.
**48** De Raemond 1610, p. 1010, my translation.

Frequently, to introduce Psalm-singing (either in public or in relatively private contexts) could represent a first step for those with Calvinist sympathies or those wishing to present their own Calvinist belief within a new situation. Among the women who acted to this end were Louise Juliana of Orange, as we have seen earlier in this Chapter (§ 12.2.5.), but also another powerful woman, Inger Ottesdotter Rømer of Austrått (c.1475–1555), who established Lutheran Psalm-singing in her Norwegian household already in 1529[49]. A similarly "godly" household was also that of Elizabeth Campbell of Kinzeancleugh (d.1574), a friend and supporter of John Knox in Ayrshire, Scotland: her proud claim to descend from a longstanding Protestant tradition dating back to Lollardy was actualised in her active fostering of Psalm-singing and prayers among her family and friends[50].

### 12.3.3.1. Creative resonances

As concerns the role of psalmody for female creativity, it offered women of all social classes and cultural levels an extraordinary repository of poetical beauty and imagery, as well as a spiritual mind-set which could shape the horizon of their own devotion and piety.

Attempting a rather daring metaphor, one could almost say that the Book of Psalms came to represent, for many Evangelical poets, what Petrarch's models had been for their Petrarchist imitators.

The musical settings of the Psalter which we have encountered so far could suit women with all degrees of musical ability and general literacy: those unable to read could learn many Psalms and their tunes by rote, while the more educated and refined women could perform vocal and instrumental arrangements of the Psalms as a form of spiritual entertainment. Psalmody almost became the religious and aural context, the sacred and beautiful place where women were entitled to create beauty in turn – be it poetry, performed music, or prayer[51].

As concerns England, metrical psalmody was of course practised even in the remotest rural parishes, but here too, among the cultivated, the French settings were appreciated as a refined devotional activity. This encouraged in turn the creation of literary responses to the Psalter, written by women and men alike.

Among the surviving examples of this creativity are two musical settings, for voice and lute, of paraphrases of the penitential Psalms 51 [50] and 130 [129] by

---

49 Cf. Marshall 1989 and Pendle 2001, p. 75.
50 Cf. Dawson 2012, p. 42.
51 Cf. Witvliet 2003, p. 211; Austern 2011, pp. 77, 114, 211; White 2005, pp. 62, 66, 72.

Mary Sidney Herbert, Countess of Pembroke (1561–1621). In yet another Psalm-paraphrase by Sidney Herbert (on Psalm 68 [67]), a song of victory is daringly intoned by a choir of women, who explicitly identify the space of communal worship and of congregational singing as a "freer sky"[52] allotted to them for their spiritual enjoyment. Thus, what could have represented a further shell which framed the opportunities of women's participation in worship, could actually become a virtually infinite possibility.

The great Scottish Reformed poetess Elizabeth Melville (Lady Culross, c.1578-c.1640) is similarly remembered for her outstanding literary output, among which several sacred *contrafacta* of famous secular songs are found.

Since numerous other Psalm paraphrases written in Britain by sixteenth- and seventeenth-century noblewomen survive, the question about their musical performance is pressing but remains unanswered. Here too, it seems safe to surmise that at least improvised musical settings might have been realised, since there were sound theological reasons (the Scriptural model) and musical traditions for justifying this practice.

The extent to which congregational singing provided a space and a meaningful frame for women's spiritual and creative literature is revealed by other coeval songs, such as a penitential poem written by an anonymous "handmaid" in the Wesel Psalter (cf. § 7.3.3.). Analogously to what happened to Teellinck in the Netherlands, the subjective outpouring of intimate and highly personal feelings (of contrition, in this case) acquires a much higher and communal value, thanks to the Ecclesial dimension provided by the appropriation of the Church's language of prayer[53].

Sternhold's Psalms (with influences from Coverdale's hymns) were also the ultimate inspiration behind the religious songs authored by Lady Elizabeth Tyrwhit[54] (c.1510–1578), who employed formal structures which directly mirror Sternhold's metrical psalmody, but who was spiritually indebted to a variety of confessional traditions. Indeed, in her case as in many other examples of religious poetry written by women, the confessional diversity seems to be conceived in terms of plurality and enrichment, rather than opposition and polemics: Tyrwith's work, in White's words, "peaceably recalls the content of traditional Latin hymns even while it celebrates the capacity of the laity to replace them with new vernacular works that also emphasize the layperson's engagement with the Word"[55].

---

52 As quoted in White 2005, p. 77.
53 Cf. White 2005, pp. 62–63, 68–70, 78; Austern 2011, pp. 83–84, 96–100.
54 See Felch 2008.
55 White 2011, p. 28. Cf. *ibid.*, pp. 21 and 26.

### 12.3.4. Among Anabaptists

The case of the Anabaptist women is worth a separate discussion, for a number of reasons. First, their community was among those enduring the greatest and longest persecutions: this encouraged its members to express their suffering, to ask for strength and mercy, to revive the bonds of solidarity and identity within their Church, all by means of singing. Moreover, within their communities, women had a role which was more active and more affirmative than elsewhere, and this encouraged in turn their creativity and their artistic and spiritual expression. Finally, literacy was more common among Anabaptist women than in many other religious and social groups, since it was deemed to be an indispensable means for entering in a personal dialogue with Scripture, and this favoured the transmission of their thoughts, memories and prayers.

As Joldersma[56] rightfully points out, when a woman was tried for her faith, she had to face male-only authorities, and this put her in a situation of even greater powerlessness and alienation. Indeed, an anonymous martyr song (*Babels Raets Mandamenten*) by a Mennonite author (found in collections of 1562–3) points out precisely this: "They harmed two maidens physically / Those tyrants were hardly aware / That each one of us is borne in pain / Being procreated by women / They haven't learned any reasonability / From this experience through nature / They almost totally neglect this matter / That is why they became tyrants"[57].

The courage shown by many Anabaptist women when facing torture, imprisonment and death is therefore impressive, as is their voice as preserved in their writings, their hymns, and martyrdom narratives by the members of their Church, published in collections or independently.

One such woman was Anna Jans of Rotterdam (also known as Anneke Esaiasdochter or Jansz, c.1509–1539), whose Anabaptist faith had been revealed to her fellow-travellers precisely by her singing while she crossed the North Sea from Britain to the Netherlands. She is remembered for a song which gained considerable dissemination at her time, and was known as the "Trumpet Song", *Ick hoorde de Basuyne blasen*, to the tune of *Na Oostland wil ik varen*. Jans' lyrics are unusually graphical in their content, though interwoven with Scriptural references, particularly from Revelation and the Psalms:

---

[56] Joldersma 2010, p. 176.
[57] In Cramer 1904, vol. II, p. 585; as quoted in and translated by Snyder and Huebert-Hecht 1996, p. 384.

At Borsom and Edom, so the author has read / The Lord is preparing a feast / From the flesh of kings and princes / Come all you birds / I will feed you the flesh of princes / As they have done, so shall be done to them / You servants of the Lord, be of good cheer / Wash your feet in the blood of the godless / This shall be the reward for those who robbed us[58].

Martha Baerts (d.1560), who was a housemaid martyred in Ghent, left a song titled *To My Sister Betken, A Lovely Spiritual Song* (beginning as *O Godt ghy zijt myn Hulper fijn*). This literary composition, set to the *souterliedekens* tune of *Wel hem de Godes vrede staet* (possibly an adaptation of the Lutheran *Wohl dem der in Gottes Furcht steht*) is a confession of faith involving a narrative of Baerts' trial. The author also encourages her brothers and sisters of faith to endure persecution with her same serenity: "I pray all those who hear this song, / Pray, do not be frightened off / From taking on the cross: / God can help us to endure"[59].

One of the most important Anabaptist hymn-writers was Soetjen Gerrits (also known as Soetken Gerrijts, c.1540–1572), who authored a collection of ninety-eight songs, published in 1592 under the title of *Een Nieu Gheestelijck Liedtboecxken*[60]. Gerrits was a blind woman, and therefore was unable to read and write by herself: thus, we should note that her literary achievements had to be dictated to somebody else, and this testifies to the great respect, authority and veneration which surrounded her. Indeed, apparently her advice was held in high consideration, even by the Anabaptist leaders who frequently asked for her opinion. This was due, in all likelihood, to the deep spiritual wisdom of Gerrits, and to her impressive knowledge of the Bible, in spite of the difficulties posed by her disability. Indeed, her songs are full of Scriptural allusions, which are minutely referenced in the collection. Notwithstanding this, her songs are also fully inserted within the actual and living experience of her community, mentioning, for example the martyrs of Delfshaven (1548–50) and Rotterdam (1558). Several of her songs were later incorporated within Anabaptist hymnbooks destined for both private and communal worship[61].

Here, as in many other cases we have met and will meet again soon, the tunes to which Gerrits' songs are to be intoned are taken from the pre-existing repertoire (frequently secular), though the variety of Gerrits' choices is remarka-

---

**58** Joris s.d., fol. 68ʳ. Translation cited from Snyder and Huebert-Hecht 1996, p. 340.
**59** As quoted in and translated by Joldersma 2010, p. 185. Cf. also van der Poel and Joldersma 2010, p. 33; Joldersma 2010, p. 183.
**60** Gerrits 1592.
**61** Cf. Snyder and Huebert-Hecht 1996, pp. 387–388; Schenkeveld-van der Dussen 2010, pp. 61 and 207.

ble (seventy-nine different tunes). I would like to point out, however, that the use of contrafacture by so many of the hymn-writers in the sixteenth century is not to be considered only in the negative (i.e. as a lack of musical originality or creativity); rather, music may have played a considerable role precisely in stimulating the hymnographers' creativity. The frequent presence of similar terms or themes in the original (be it sacred or secular) and in the new lyrics suggests that the idea for the new texts came to the poetess also via a creative engagement with the musical repertoire of the era.

A hymn collection of the same name as Soetken's was published in 1607 by Vrou Gerrits (c.1580–1605), and comprises fifty-one songs, mostly dedicated to other women (in several instances, their names are embodied through acrostics in the text). Vrou Gerrits preferred to use tunes coming from the sacred repertoire as the basis for her *contrafacta*.

Other women hymnographers from Anabaptist circles include Janneken van Aken (or van Houtte, d.1557), and Elisabeth Dirks (also Lijsbeth or Lijsken, d.1549), who sang her pious songs from inside the prison cell where she had been confined; in Germany, Ursula Hellriegel (c.1530-a.1543) and Walpurga Marschalk von Pappenheim (d. a.1571), who wrote a song to the tune of Luther's *Aus tiefer Not*, preserved in a hymnal of the Swiss Brethren[62].

Though the large use of contrafacture by these women hymnographers may seem disappointing for musicologists studying the history of early women composers, it is however extremely significant from the viewpoint of the social and religious history of how music dovetailed with spirituality. We may have little to say about the purely musical features of songs whose tunes were borrowed from the pre-existing repertoire; but we should point out how important music was for these women, and how directly it was correlated with their experience of the sacred, even (or particularly) within the framework of martyrdom and of a heroic witness of their faith.

## 12.4. Voices of Catholic women

Though, sadly, on several occasions Catholics assumed the role of persecutors, equally sadly they also were victims of persecution themselves in other contexts. Thus, Catholic women had also to endure suffering and harassment, and sometimes this found, in turn, some form of musical expression.

---

[62] Cf. Snyder and Huebert-Hecht 1996, pp. 338–340, 390–392 etc. (also as regards the doubts on the attribution of Marschalk's song); Koldau 2005b, pp. 491–494; Pollmann 2006, p. 303.

## 12.4.1. Voices from the Convents

Indeed, where the Evangelical Reformations took charge of a zone, the most common fate for Catholic convents would be the dissolution of the religious community. It is possible and likely that some nuns (particularly those who had not been enthusiastic about religious life from the outset) were only too glad to leave the monastery and get married; however, this was far from being a universally shared reaction. Not only did many religious women take their vows seriously and did not wish to act against what they had promised; they also were reluctant to abandon what had become their world – the community of sisters, an orderly life of prayer and work, and probably also the possibility of intellectual and artistic accomplishments which most busy mothers would have regarded as a dream[63].

Of course, former nuns who had received a good or sufficient musical education could find new ways to employ their gifts as wives and mothers; but the most complex and refined of the nuns' musical achievements were unlikely to be replicated within the framework of family life.

### 12.4.1.1. Voicing resistance

In other cases, the communities of nuns might also enact more or less open and desperate forms of resistance against the dissolution of their monastery. We have seen earlier in this Chapter (§ 12.3.1.2.) that some Catholic communities became Evangelical *Damenstifte*, which in turn practised a rich musical repertoire. Elsewhere, rebellion might take a musical shape and thus closely resemble the examples seen in Chapter Ten.

In Geneva, before Calvin's arrival but after the first seeds of Protestantism had been planted, a congregation of Poor Clares fought against the Reformation by means of their convent bells. These were not just a form of aural/spatial appropriation such as those seen in Chapter Ten (§ 10.3.7. and following), but also a powerful reminder of how the nuns remained faithful to their routine of prayer, since the bell, at intervals, called the sisters to their liturgical duties. The bell's sound, thus, was felt as irritating and provoking by those adhering to the Reformation and for the civil authorities implementing it, and riots ensued between Protestants and Catholics who defended the Poor Clares[64].

---

63 Cf. Pendle 2001, p. 75.
64 Cf. Solfaroli Camillocci 2005, p. 283, quoting from the journal of Sr. Jeanne de Jussie (1503–1561) (de Jussie 1611, pp. 12, 22–23, 154, 163, 172–177, 194, 211–212).

In Germany, the Benedictine nuns of Lüne were in a similar situation and adopted analogous strategies. In this case, the source for reconstructing their experience comes from the letters of their abbess, Mechthild Wilde (r.1504–1535). When Duke Ernst I "The Confessor" (1497–1546), who was one of the strongest supporters of Luther's Reformation, sought to implement Protestantism in Lüne, the nuns successfully carried out a seven-year long rebellion against it.

The abbess' letters demonstrate how closely the identity of the nuns (both as individuals and as members of a community) depended on their continuation of the usual worship, of which singing was an integral part. When the Lutherans intoned "*suos teutonicos Psalmos et leysas*" ("their German Psalms and *Leisen*"), the nuns replied by continuing their own Latin songs unhindered. The Duke tried to wear down the nuns' musical defences, for example by seizing their bells in 1533 (once more, bells represented a powerful sonorous flag). Nevertheless, abbess Mechthild's letters repeatedly point out that nuns continued their sung liturgies "in the usual way", even in the face of increasingly frequent disruptions, since the regularity of worship represented the aural symbol of their faithfulness to their vows. On the other hand, as Koldau correctly points out, the literary form of the abbess' letters is in turn highly revealing of how the practice of Latin plainchant had shaped the very mind-sets and language of the religious women, whose writing was constantly interspersed with Latin fragments taken from liturgy[65].

Indeed, while witnesses about forms of musically armed self-defence like those of the Lüne or Genevan nuns are scanty, the dense interweaving of female monastic life with musical practices was a trait common to monasteries throughout Catholicism.

### 12.4.1.2. Convents as cultural centres

It is important to point out that being a nun was a condition shared by a much higher percentage of sixteenth-century women than it is today, and might involve roughly a third of the Italian girls from patrician families[66]. Many of these aristocratic women were kept up-to-date about social, cultural and political issues by the secular members of their families: thus, news from outside the convent penetrated inside it, reducing the effects of enclosure on the seeming isolation of monastery life. If this provided a door from society to community,

---

65 Cf. Koldau 2005a, p. 241; Koldau 2005b, pp. 456, 681–684.
66 Hufton 1996, p. 370.

other doors were kept open from monastery to society, and one of them was music.

That convent music might become a symbolic violation of enclosure was clearly seen and stated by a Bolognese priest, maintaining that "while [the nuns'] bodies remain within the sacred cloisters, [singing] cause[s] them to wander outside in their hearts, nourishing within them an ambitious desire to please the world with their songs"[67].

Of course, convent music was, primarily, a fundamental component of worship's beauty and of its worthiness as an offering to God (within the Catholic concept of works and merits). It was also an element which, in many cases, was deeply enjoyed, loved and cherished by those inside the convent walls as well as by those outside them. Finally, it was one of the principal ways for nuns to create, maintain and show their identity as a community, and occasionally also as individuals.

The combination of an increasing number of consecrated men and women, of a more widespread musical literacy which allowed them to perform and sing polyphony and instrumental music, as well as of the spiritual renewal prompted by the Catholic Reformation produced a general blossoming of convent music in the years around and after 1570. From the second half of the sixteenth century onwards, the number of written testimonies about the musical activities and expertise of Italian nuns augment exponentially, and they have been intensely studied by the leading scholars in the field[68].

Though the quantity of written documents about the beauty, importance and social relevance of nuns' music bears witness to how fundamental a component it was of sixteenth-century religious musicianship, the written sources from inside the convents are proportionally sparse. The kind of repertoire performed by the nuns was difficult to take outside the convent (although devotional works sung and performed by the laity at home were likely to enter the monastery walls), and therefore its transmission and that of its performance were problematic and difficult. Fundamental questions remain open, such as, for example, those relating to the authorship of music performed in the convents, particularly for devotional purposes and as a form of entertainment, e.g. during the sacred plays which were regularly enacted in several monasteries[69]. On the other hand,

---

[67] In Archivio Generale Arcivescovile, Bologna, Misc. Vecchie 808, fasc. 6, as quoted in and translated by Monson 2010, p. 30.
[68] Cf. Morelli 1993, p. 178; Kendrick 1996, p. 57; Monson 2012, p. 2.
[69] Cf. Monson 1992; Harrán 1995, p. 41; Monson 1995; Kendrick 1996, pp. 22–23; Pendle 2001, pp. 67–68; Koldau 2005a, p. 238. This section is indebted to the studies of Kendrick, Monson and Reardon in particular.

we are indebted to many nuns throughout Europe for copying, collecting and transmitting a heritage of sacred music, both liturgical and devotional: though such manuscript collections have frequently been lost, they represented a way of appropriating the works chosen by the scribe, and of affirming her involvement in their performance and preservation[70].

In several instances, we know that individual nuns did practise composition, but in most cases none of their works has been preserved: a young nun at the Modenese convent of San Geminiano, Faustina Borghi (b. c.1574), was reportedly "exceedingly virtuoso in counterpoint [and] in playing the cornetto and organ"[71], suggesting she was able to compose or at least to improvise polyphonically; at the same convent, another nun musician mentioned earlier in this Chapter (§ 12.1.), Sulpitia Cesis, was appreciated as a composer. Though, as said there, her works were not published before 1619 and thus exceed the time-span of my discussion, the Modenese chronicler informs us that she had authored a motet performed already in 1596, when a religious procession was greeted at the convent's doors with her composition.

Frequently, the impulse for an intense focus on the quantity and quality of a convent's music could come either from the presence of highly gifted nuns or from the particular interest of the abbess or prioress in music. This was the case, for example, of the Augustinian monastery of Inzigkofen (Baden-Württemberg, Germany), where the patrician abbess Amalie von Hohenzollern (1557–1603) was an enthusiastic supporter of music; therefore, under her rule, the nuns practised polyphonic singing, performed instrumental music and studied composition[72]. (We will frequently note that music was a particular focus in many female monasteries following the Augustinian rule: the reader will recall how important St Augustine's writings were about music for the Christian theology of music, and that Luther himself had lived for years as an Augustinian monk).

### 12.4.1.3. "Only voice and no sight"

As we have seen in Chapter Eight (§ 8.4.5.), however, the flourishing musical heritage and practices of nuns were challenged, in the sixteenth century, not only by the suppression of monasteries by the Evangelical Reformations, but also by the Catholic Reformation at the Council of Trent. We will see, in the forthcoming

---

70 Cf. Classen 2002, p. 1.
71 Cf. Spaccini 1911, vol. I (16), p. 34; as quoted in and translated by Bowers 1986, p. 120.
72 Koldau 2005a, pp. 242–243.

pages, that in fact the post-Tridentine atmosphere was not always favourable to convent music: while the most restrictive measures proposed at the Council were eventually not approved, the margin for action accorded to local authorities was such that there was ample room for imposing strict limitations.

The Council had been particularly concerned with the behaviour of nuns, by enforcing and sometimes imposing enclosure to those orders and congregations without a monastic vocation. The very architecture of convent churches was shaped in function of the separation of the nuns from the world, with one section reserved for the religious community and another for those not belonging to it (including the celebrating priest). By secluding the nuns' choir from the sight of the bystanders, its presence was revealed only by the sense of hearing, which, correspondingly, became the principal instrument for entering into communication with the nuns.

This experience was faithfully recorded by Gregory Martin (1581):

> This is the old Rule of Religious women, and this is renewed by that holy Council [...] that thou shalt never see a Nun out of her cloister, and being in the Church thou shalt only hear their voices singing their service most melodiously, and the Father himself, that is, their Ghostly father heareth their confessions through a grate in the wall, where only voice and no sight goeth between [...] And in Bononie [=Bologna] and Rome having been many times at their service in their chapels and hearing their goodly singing, never did I see one of them[73].

Indeed, the sound of nuns' voices was frequently compared to those of angelic choirs, and therefore acquired an extremely positive and sanctifying value. However, and even though the sense of hearing and the voices' beauty were considered to be far less dangerous than sight and visual beauty, there was by no means a unanimous and total approval for nuns' music.

We have seen (§ 3.3.2.7., 8.4.5.) that what really worried the religious authorities was the presence of "artifice" in the nuns' singing. Conversely, the proper way for nuns to perform their religious duties in music was that closest to a "natural" delivery of the words (a highly humanistic concern, as seen earlier in this book). Thus, as Antonio Seneca (1542–1626), a clergyman close to Carlo Borromeo, wrote in 1604, nuns had to "be present day and night in the choir for the Divine Offices and, according to the rite of their order, recite these with devotion, attention, and with the proper distinction of points in an even, clear, and distinct voice, with good words, expressed intelligibly"[74].

---

73 Martin 1969, pp. 141–142.
74 Seneca 1604, as quoted in and translated by Montford 2006, p. 1012.

In the eyes of most Catholic Reformers, a proper, sober and modest way for nuns to sing the Office was that of avoiding pure aesthetical delight (by the nuns themselves and by those hearing them), as well as pride, vanity, interaction with outside musicians and an excessive squandering of time and economic resources.

From the viewpoint of musicians and musicologists, of course, this may seem a restrictive and punitive perspective (and, of course, in the hands of particularly strict Church authorities, it was indeed so); however, theologically, it is undeniable that the first aim of religious life is not artistic perfection. Though such concerns might degenerate into narrow-mindedness and arbitrary, mortifying and limiting prohibitions, the particular finality of monastic life in the Church should always be kept in mind in the following discussion.

On the other hand, the rules about enclosure could be more flexible than may appear, as is testified by the following witness (1596):

> At Monte Cavallo [today's Quirinale, in Rome], in the church of San Silvestro, [...] Monsignor read the low Mass, and gave communion to twelve girls and twelve widows, who, when the Mass was finished, went in procession to their monastery, which is in front of that church. The Reverend singers, while Monsignor said the Mass, sang a Motet after the Creed, another during Elevation and another during Communion. After Mass, Monsignor entered the sacristy, while the girls went in procession to the monastery; while they passed, the singers sang the *Te Deum*[75].

At the very heart of the post-Tridentine Rome, thus, a procession of nuns could be observed, within a worship which included several motets and a *Te Deum*.

Though exceptions (such as this) were certainly possible and the panorama was far from uniform, undeniably Trent indirectly sanctioned many limiting interventions by the local bishops on the nuns' musicality. I will succinctly comment about some of them and their impact on the nuns' lives.

### 12.4.1.4. Music for hearers?

As concerns polyphonic singing, Seneca argued that it should be prohibited in female monasteries, together with *concertato* and solo singing, in favour of unison plainchant singing. He maintained that God did not seek "sweetness of voice", but "purity of heart" in the nuns; that nuns whose aim in singing was their own delight, instead of God's glory, were sinning; and that they should only sing in "plainchant with their organs, where these are available, and with-

---

75 Quoted in Frey 1985, p. 165, my translation.

out other instruments", such as "viols, violins, citterns, lutes etc."[76]. We will see, in some particular instances discussed in the forthcoming pages, that Seneca's principles were actively applied by some local bishops, sometimes with very negative consequences on nuns' music.

Much, however, depended on whether the nuns were singing for an audience or for themselves. Although the positive effects of their music's beauty were numerous and undeniable (such as a higher presence and spiritual enjoyment by the laity), many Catholic Reformers were very concerned about the nuns' showing-off with their voices. Thus, several limitations concerned what could be heard by the laity rather than what was sung by the nuns: for example, *lauda*-singing in the vernacular could be permitted to Florentine nuns provided it happened outside the church, lest laypeople could hear it[77].

Also don Ercole Tinelli, a Bolognese priest who had been the father confessor at several female convents, was highly perplexed about the opportunity of such practices. He wrote in 1593 to Cardinal Alessandro de' Medici (1535–1605, later Pope Leo XI), stating: "You know that men flock much more than is respectable to nuns' churches as if to plays and other frivolous, unholy places"[78].

Indeed, in some contexts, listening to the music of some particularly famous nuns had become something close to a tourist attraction. In a list of twelve not-to-be-missed things to do in Venice, listening to the nuns of San Zaccaria or Le Vergini was put on a par with sights such as the Piazza and Basilica of San Marco which still score top marks in any of today's visitors' guides to Venice[79].

The picture is emerging, then, of two distinct kinds of worries for the ecclesiastical authorities, which caused in turn two kinds of limitations: from the one side, the spiritual risks for the interior life of nuns, whose musical practices might lead them to vainglory and pride; from the other, the moral risks deriving from the interaction of nuns with men (or the nuns' self-display, even if this involved their voices only). Even though the "angelic" aspect of nuns' singing was frequently mentioned by the hearers, and regardless of the careful hiding of the nuns' visible appearance, many Church authorities felt (with some reason) that the very mystery surrounding their concealed persons could be extremely attractive for hearers.

---

[76] Seneca 1604, fols. 78ᵛ-82ʳ; cf. Masetti Zannini 1993, p. 125; Montford 2006, p. 1012. See also Beggiao 1978, p. 94 and Macy 2011, p. 350.
[77] Monson 2006, p. 410.
[78] Archivio Segreto Vaticano, Sacra Congregazione dei Vescovi e Regolari, posiz. 1593, B-C, as quoted in and translated by Monson 2012, p. 1.
[79] Sanudo 1980, p. 62.

Several regulations, thus, were issued with regard to enclosure, and some of them had the result of limiting musical practices: female convents were forbidden to employ male instrumentalists, especially if musicians had to enter the space of enclosure for playing the organ; moreover, nuns could not receive lessons from male musicians, because the close relationship between music teachers and their students could potentially lead to something else.

### 12.4.1.5. Teaching music to the nuns

As summarised earlier (§ 12.2.5.), while the obligation for nuns to provide autonomously for their music could actually encourage their musical proficiency, its combination with the lack of adequate and external teaching produced an unavoidable diminution in musical quality: since girls usually entered convents at an early age, it was likely that their musical training was not yet accomplished.

Limitations were also issued ruling the presence of male musicians in the exterior church of monasteries, though in this case the direct contact between them and the nuns would have been minimal: the symbolic power of antiphonal singing between choirs of men and women was however too charged, and their musical dialogue was deemed to be inadvisable.

Such restrictions, nonetheless, were far from universally adopted: for example, in Siena, in the seventeenth century, the bishops Camillo Borghesi (1552–1612) and Alessandro Petrucci (c.1560–1628) adopted milder stances, and the female monasteries under their jurisdiction were entitled to employ male musicians provided that they asked for and explicitly obtained the bishop's permission.

Even in those dioceses where the official line was stricter – or strictest – there were often several ways for the nuns to bypass the regulations. The simplest, and often most efficacious strategy, was to try and obtain a special episcopal licence allowing them to employ male musicians as performers or teachers. It was normally easier to obtain permissions for players or singers than for teachers, since the former would be needed only occasionally, for example in solemn circumstances such as the patron saint's feast or a novice's profession, while teaching could require prolonged and frequent meetings.

Notwithstanding this, there is documentary evidence that some flexibility could be obtained: in Toledo, in the years 1597–1600, the Augustinian nuns of San Torcuato employed a (male) teacher who gave them lessons in polyphony and counterpoint[80]. In Spain, indeed, Baade's studies[81] demonstrated that the requirement for musician nuns to teach their sisters only appears in the 1650s: this seemingly implies that in the first post-Tridentine era music teaching was supplied by external mentors. The combination of moral concerns with the increasing abilities of musician nuns inside the convent caused a decrease in the demand for external teachers in the late seventeenth century.

We have already seen, however (cf. § 9.6.6.), that in Spain there were notable exceptions in turn, such as the *Descalzas Reales* in Madrid, where male musicians of Victoria's standing were permanently employed to provide the monastery with an exceptionally refined and high-quality music. It may be inferred that the presence of female members of the royal family among the nuns was not totally irrelevant to such an unusual setting[82].

### 12.4.1.6. A rich repertoire

Inside the convent walls, however, and out of male ears' reach, few limitations could be imposed on the nuns' musical activities. In the Bolognese convent of Sant'Agnese, for example, the nun Elena Malvezzi (1526–1563) collected – and probably performed – keyboard transcriptions of secular vocal works.

While transcribed songs might suggest their original lyrics to their performer, secular songs were sometimes intoned in turn. The custom was so widespread, and so objectionable, that more suitable repertoires were promptly collected. Thus, prefacing his collection titled *Libro Primo delle laude spirituali* (Venice, 1563), the Dominican friar Serafino Razzi stated: "I wonder that many, who rule the monasteries and the persons consecrated to divine worship and totally subtracted to the world [...] tolerate that the most lascivious kinds of music are sung there, and even songs which would be less than honest also amid a brigade of secular people"[83].

Drawing from the Dominican tradition (which had never entirely abandoned the Savonarolan practice of *lauda*-singing), Razzi collected ninety-one tunes for 146 texts; the lyrics' authors included women such as Lucrezia Tornabuoni de' Medici (1425–1482). Caterina de' Ricci (1522–1590), to whom the collection was dedicated, was in turn a nun at the monastery of San Vincenzo in Prato

---

[80] Baade 2010, p. 264.
[81] Baade 2010.
[82] Cf. Bowers 1986, p. 142; Masetti Zannini 1993, p. 128; Kendrick 1996, p. 67; Reardon 2002, pp. 24–26; Borgerding and Stein 2006, pp. 429–431; Montford 2006, pp. 1007 and 1013; Baade 2010, pp. 265–267; Macy 2011, p. 350.
[83] Razzi 1563, my translation.

and wrote a *lauda* text, intended to be sung to the tune of a *lauda* by Feo Belcari (1410–1484) found in Razzi's collection, and describing her miraculous healing through the intercession of Dominican saints[84].

It is also worth noting that the Dominican female monasteries which had kept alive the practice of *lauda* singing (Santa Lucia and Santa Caterina in Florence, and San Vincenzo in Prato) were connected on the one hand with Savonarola, who had been a Dominican friar in turn, and on the other with St Augustine, whose monastic rule is followed by the Dominican nuns. As discussed by Macey[85], *lauda*-singing in these monasteries helped to preserve the heritage of the Savonarolan *laude*, at least as far as their original tunes are concerned: some of these are actually included within Razzi's collection in spite of the bans surrounding the lyrics which the Florentine *piagnoni* had sung to them[86].

Apparently, however, the problems about which kind of music was performed, sung and practised by the nuns within their convent walls was not solved as easily as the collectors of *lauda* books would have liked. As Kendrick has fascinatingly narrated, visitation records at the Humiliate monastery of Santa Maria Maddalena al Cerchio in Milan (1575) have preserved a kind of trial undergone by some musician nuns, regarding "licentious" songs which had been found in the cell of one of them. The nun found guilty of the compromising possession of carnival songs stated that her family had sent them to her as a gift, but that she was unaware of the songs' meaning since they were written in the dialect of Bergamo. The interrogation records, however, are interesting especially inasmuch as they offer us a glimpse of the musical practices in the nuns' daily lives. Sr. Prospera Vittoria Cavenaghi, questioned about her musical activities, stated: "In polyphony I sing only sacred pieces; I never sang with Sr. Paola Giustina except in church, and in the refectory or the washing-room, and outside church sometimes with Sr. Laura Bezona, Sr. Prospera Corona, and Sr. Claudia Sulpitia"[87].

Whether the book of *bergamasche* had simply been left unopened in the nun's cell or it had actually been used for singing or playing is open to debate; however, collections of devotional songs in the vernacular were also found in possession of the Milanese nuns, to whom they had been presented in turn. One such collection was the *Thesauro della Sapientia*, better known as *Devotis-*

---

[84] Cf. Razzi 1563, fols. 32ᵛ-33ʳ; de' Ricci 1850, pp. 15ff.
[85] Cf. Macey 1992.
[86] Cf. Monson 1989, p. 113 etc.; Macey 1992, p. 457; Pendle 2001, pp. 70–72.
[87] *Esamina* dated February-March 1575, Archivio Storico Diocesano Milanese XII, vol. 97, fasc. 2, fol. 10ᵛ, as quoted in and translated by Kendrick 1996, p. 55. Cf. *ibid.*, pp. 50–56.

*sime compositioni rhythmice* (Bologna 1525[88]), a compilation of pious poetry authored by a Poor Clare nun from the monastery of the Corpus Domini in Ravenna (possibly Angela Morandi), and destined for the recreation of nuns. Though no music is found in the *Thesauro* and there is no mention of the tunes to which the lyrics should be sung, the stanza/refrain structure of some of the poems confirms the statement of another of the questioned nuns, Sr. Paola Giustina Carpani, who declared that this religious poetry was sung by some of her sisters[89].

The interrogation records also testify to the nuns' frank and rather outspoken style when answering the questions of their inquisitors; indeed, while in some cases the limitations to nuns' music make present-day readers pity them, it seems also abundantly clear that many nuns were all but passive and acquiescent to such rulings.

Actually, some nuns showed a remarkable shrewdness in turning the musical restrictions to their advantage. For example, in the Bolognese convent of Sant'Omobono (1585), Church authorities had required that the organ be dislodged from the external church where both the instrument and its player could be seen. Sr. Giulia Montecalvi, the organist, promptly jumped at the chance of getting a better instrument, and "happily spent some fifty *scudi*" for a new, and much better instrument to be placed in the enclosed church; and since enclosure limited sight but not hearing, the organ, "resounding excellently well, [...] still created delightful harmony for those outside"[90].

Indeed, music was seen to be a fundamental component of convent life in many monasteries of the Catholic world; and, in spite of all limitations, it was frequently encouraged, promoted and fostered by several Church authorities, and cherished, practised and valued by the nuns themselves.

### 12.4.1.7. Music for money

Actually, music had a value, and it could have a monetary value too: many monasteries accepted postulants who could not pay for the requested dowry if the girls were musically gifted and trained. Sometimes, this took the form of a real contract with their parents: girls would be invited to postpone their admission to the convent in order to perfect their musical education (especially within

---

[88] Cf. Graziosi 1996, pp. 307–308; Graziosi 2005, pp. 150–151. See *Thesauro* 1525, *Thesauro* 1568.
[89] *Esamina* dated February-March 1575, Archivio Storico Diocesano Milanese XII, vol. 97, fasc. 2, fol. 10ʳ, as quoted in and translated by Kendrick 1996, p. 56.
[90] Bologna, Archivio di Stato, Demaniale, 31/5845 [Sant'Omobono], as quoted in and translated by Monson 1992, pp. 194 and 205.

those contexts where external music teachers were not available in the convent); the dowry waiver or reduction could also be withdrawn if, for some reason (illness, unsatisfactory proficiency or unwillingness) the nun was later judged to be unable to fulfil her musical duties. Moreover, frequently the ability to play the organ, teach music or sing particularly well could raise the social condition of a nun coming from a poor family: instead of remaining a *conversa* (the normal destination for uneducated sisters who performed the manual duties), she could become a *professa*, i.e. the condition normally reserved for patrician, wealthy or educated nuns.

Juan Luis Vives, a humanist author who did not approve of music-making girls, admitted however that organ lessons could be given to girls destined for religious life. He wrote:

> I do not permit or wish that girls learn music, and even less that they enjoy listening to it anywhere – at home or outside it, at the door, at the window, by day or by night, and I say this with good reason. [...] However I would agree that a Christian virgin, should she wish to learn to play the organ a little in order to become a nun, should be taught a lot from an early age[91].

In 1584, the Archbishop of Florence, Alessandro de' Medici, explicitly stated that the musical necessities of the convent were the only admissible reason for accepting a girl as a prospective nun without a dowry; his line was confirmed one year later (August 1585), when young Bartolommea, an orphaned or abandoned child, was received into the monastery of Le Murate with the only provision of her beautiful voice[92]. Ippolita Calvi, a candidate for convent life at Santa Maria Maddalena al Cerchio in Milan, who asked Carlo Borromeo for a similar dowry waiver in 1578, was however less fortunate, since Borromeo's vicar thought that the convent already had too many musicians[93].

All this was obviously due to the fundamental necessity for liturgical music in convents; but worship, as seen before, did not represent the totality of monastery music (although Seneca's *Prattica* expressly forbids music-making in parlatories and outside worship). Indeed, if the possession and use of illicit songs was dangerous for nuns such as those at Santa Maria Maddalena al Cerchio, in the same city of Milan music was actively encouraged as a form of licit recreation for nuns.

---

**91** My translation from the Spanish edition (1584), p. 111. This section is missing in the Latin edition (Vives 1524). I interpret "*de enhora buena*" (sic) as meaning "from an early age".
**92** Cf. Lowe 2003, p. 275. See also Baade 2005; Monson 2005, p. 4; Baade 2010, pp. 262–263; Monson 2012, p. 3.
**93** Cf. Kendrick 1996, p. 68.

## 12.4.1.8. Songs for sanctity

Cardinal Federigo Borromeo, in particular, believed that the most efficacious reform of convent life was not that imposed on the nuns, but that in which they were actively involved; thus, he consistently made use of music with the purpose of offering something so beautiful, engaging and fulfilling to nuns that other, and more dangerous, kinds of recreations might lose their attractiveness. The repertory he imagined for this aim was substantially made up of spiritual *contrafacta* of secular madrigals, thus explaining his interest in this genre and his fostering of this activity, as discussed in Chapter Nine[94] (§ 9.6.2.).

Similarly, whereas some religious leaders were highly concerned and worried about the power of nuns' music over the external listeners, and by the lingering suspicion that the pleasures of the ear might lead to something else, others saw the positive effects which could come from this admiration and spiritual enjoyment. There could be a theological and mystical reason for this connection of cause and effect: the nuns' voices expressed beauty in an invisible fashion, and thus were the symbol of a presence and an absence at the same time; this mirrored in turn the belief in Christ's invisible presence in His Church and the eschatological dimension of "already but not yet" which characterises any Christian experience.

In Siena, the Archbishop Ascanio I Piccolomini (c.1548–1597) found "great consolation"[95] in the nuns' polyphonic singing accompanied by the organ, when he visited, in 1593, the monastery of Sant'Abbondio; and this in spite of his limitations on the music-making of another convent, that of the *Convertite*, where he had forbidden the use of plucked string instruments. The 1534 rule of the *Convertite* of Rome, of which Carlo Borromeo requested a copy, actually foresaw the good results of the nuns' festive music-making, since it prescribed to sing the Office "so that the laity may be moved to devotion"[96].

Though a certain pride and vanity could certainly have played a part in such displays, it should be always underlined that, in most convents, the first goal of a beautiful worship was precisely to make a beautiful worship, i.e. to adorn liturgy so that it pleased God. This concern is apparent both in some Bishops' ordinances, such as those by Petrucci in Siena, and in the price the nuns themselves were disposed to pay for music. For example, the nuns at the Florentine monastery of the Crocetta spent two thirds of their budget for the titular feast-day (1593)

---

[94] Cf. Montford 2006, p. 1013; Macy 2011, p. 350.
[95] Biblioteca Comunale Siena, MS E.V.19, fols. 109$^v$-110$^r$; as quoted in Reardon 2002, p. 28.
[96] Archivio Storico Diocesano Milanese XII, vol. 50, fols. 19 ff., as quoted in and translated by Kendrick 2006, p. 62.

on music, demonstrating how important this was in their eyes and in those of the bystanders[97].

Music, in convents, had also the role of fostering intense spiritual experiences and mysticism. In the same convent of the Crocetta, a miraculous event took place in which music played a key role: while she was at table with her sisters, the monastery's founder, Sr. Domenica Narducci da Paradiso (1473–1553), "heard resounding in the church an extraordinarily sweet song, so that she immediately left the table and ran to the oratory inside the monastery, and she found that angels were processing around the altar of the church, and celebrating and singing with sweetest harmony, they were blessing God"[98].

Here music was the true sign of God's blessing on the monastic community and on its prioress.

Federigo Borromeo thought that

> The songs and sounds made in God's honour were heavenly joy and delights, and it was possible to call earthly angels those sacred virgins who [...] celebrated the divine praises with harmonious concerts; he even exhorted them to recreate themselves by singing some sacred songs, both for being restored from human fatigue, and for keeping themselves more united with God[99].

Music in female convents, thus, could take a number of shapes and be considered from a plurality of viewpoints: it could be the angelic praise of spiritual beings or an occasion for showing-off; it could be an instrument for "moving" both hearers and nuns to devotion or an encouragement for illicit behaviour; it could be, in sum, a sanctifying or a depraving activity, an opportunity for creative and spiritual agency or something which had very little to do with the vocation of religious women.

### 12.4.2. (Un)veiled voices

As we have seen, the subject of convent music is still largely unexplored, in spite of the fundamental achievements of many scholars in the field; notwithstanding this situation, which prevents this Chapter from aiming at thoroughness, I will present some key figures of musician nuns, with the proviso that they represent merely the famous tip of the iceberg.

---

[97] Cf. Reardon 2002, p. 25; Harness 2006, pp. 224–228.
[98] Del Nente 1743, p. 275; as translated in Harness 2006, pp. 225–228.
[99] As quoted in Bizzarini 2012, pp. 32–33 (my translation); Rivola 1656, p. 758.

### 12.4.2.1. Aleotti: how many of them?

The extent to which research remains to be developed is shown in an exemplary fashion by the case of Raffaella Aleotti. Although she is considered to be the first woman ever to have published a collection of polyphonic sacred music, and one of the two nuns whose music was printed in the sixteenth century, scholars are still debating about such a negligible biographical issue as to whether she was two women or just one.

The irony of the situation comes from a rather puzzling narrative by her/their father[100], the architect Giambattista Aleotti (also known as "L'Argenta" from his birthplace, 1546–1636), who prefaced a madrigal collection by his daughter, and described his household so confusingly, that there is no consensus as to how many daughters he was actually writing about. There is, in fact, a published collection of sacred music by Raffaella Aleotti (c.1570–a.1646), who was a nun (and even the prioress) at the Augustinian monastery of San Vito in Ferrara; and a printed collection of madrigals, *Ghirlanda de Madrigali* (1593[101]) by Vittoria Aleotti (1575–a.1620). The main open question is whether Vittoria changed her name into Raffaella upon entering religious life, or Vittoria and Raffaella were two distinct women.

The odds are presently in favour of Vittoria/Raffaella being the same person; the Baptism registers of the church of Santa Maria in Vado seem to confirm this theory[102]. It appears in fact that Giambattista's first daughter, Beatrice, had at first manifested an inclination to religious life, and therefore had received music instruction. The second daughter, Vittoria, learnt music by listening to her elder sister's lessons; later, she expressed the wish to enter the convent in turn. Seemingly (because Giambattista, toward the preface's ending, speaks of "my other daughters" who are in the convent together with the composer Vittoria), at a certain point there were at least three Aleotti sisters at the monastery. This is consistent with information about the death of a Sr. Valeria Aleotti in 1625, while the fact that Beatrice later married can be explained with a change of mind on her part.

While the need for further research on Raffaella Aleotti and her family may be pressing, in the following lines I will discuss her accomplishments as a musician nun and a composer of sacred music regardless of the attribution to her of Vittoria's secular output.

---

**100** Quoted in and translated by Bowers 1986, pp. 129–130.
**101** Aleotti 1593b.
**102** Scherf 1998, p. 49; quoting from Gialdroni (preface to Aleotti 1986).

Raffaella's *Sacræ Cantiones quinque, septem, octo, et decem vocibus decantandæ* were printed in 1593[103] and are a collection of sixteen motets on texts taken from the Scripture or from liturgy, with a prevailing presence of excerpts from the liturgies of Christmas and of the Virgin Mary, and with a fascinating presence of lyrics from the Song of Solomon. It is very likely that her works were performed by the sister nuns at her monastery: the lower-pitched parts were probably played instrumentally or sung an octave higher by the nuns.

The compositional strategies employed by Raffaella Aleotti are consistent with the style fashionable at her time, with a juxtaposition of chordal and imitative passages, which are however frequently determined by the text's content. For example, in her *Facta est cum angelo* (on the Christmas Gospel of Luke 2:13–14), the concord of the angelic choir's praise is symbolised by homorhythmic writing, whereas imitations are used for describing the context and events. Her mastery of compositional technique is shown by the variety of her creative solutions, and by her adoption of a range of styles including polychorality and fluent counterpoint.

### 12.4.2.2. Community concerts

Raffaella's extraordinary musical gifts are testified not only by her works, but also by a number of written witnesses by those who heard the musical ensemble of the San Vito nuns led by her. The historian and chronicler Marco Antonio Guarini (c.1570-c.1638) defined her as "remarkable over any other and peerless in playing the organ", "extremely knowledgeable in music" and the composer of "several motets and highly appreciated madrigals"[104].

Though one could suspect some paternal pride in Giambattista Aleotti's statement that the "perfection and excellence in music" of the San Vito nuns "surpass[ed] that of all the most famous ensembles of women that have been heard for a long time"[105], it seems that Giambattista was actually understating the case.

Ercole Bottrigari (1531–1612) provides us with a more detailed and enthusiastic description of the nuns' concert. The twenty-three nuns (who were clearly visible by the bystanders) entered in line, bringing their instruments, and sat or stood around a long table; the ensemble conductor led them with a long baton. The concerts, continued Bottrigari, had been going on for decades, and this ex-

---

103 Aleotti 1593a.
104 Guarini 1621, p. 376, my translation.
105 In Gaspari 1961, vol. 3, p. 19; as quoted in and translated by Bowers 1986, p. 129.

plained the quality of their music; in consequence of this, the nuns were also self-sufficient as regards the music teaching needed, and were in high request by the elites of both the musical field and of the nobility[106]. The variety of instruments participating in the concerts was listed by Giovanni Maria Artusi (1540–1613) as comprising *cornetti*, trombones, violins, *viole bastarde*, double harps, lutes, cornamuses, flutes, harpsichords, as well as the singers[107].

The fame of the nuns' musical skills reached the ears of Pope Clement VIII, who was deeply touched by their performance when he heard them playing in 1599. In the words of a contemporaneous chronicler, the nuns

> cultivate all kinds of virtue and good disciplines, and particularly music, in which they highly progressed under the lead of Giulia Fiaschi, a famous organist and expert in music[108]. [...] Many people, who came on purpose, could only praise exceedingly and admire such a noble and skilled concert, whose angelic melody powerfully drew from the eyes of the Pontiff, Clement VIII, many tears of emotion. [...] Among the nuns there were excellent composers, sweet voices and extraordinary players[109].

Interestingly, the ensemble of the San Vito nuns seemed to have been less limited by enclosure than many others: not only could they be seen when playing, but they reportedly were allowed to leave the convent to perform for patricians in Ferrara (for example during a concert at the Este court in 1592). However – or precisely for this reason – a follower of Carlo Borromeo who was appointed Bishop of Ferrara, Giovanni Fontana (1537–1611), in 1599 hastened to adapt the nuns' rules to those of the post-Tridentine Catholic Church. Among others, his decree established that worship had to be sung by the nuns themselves, without hiring lay or clerical musicians, that no external music teaching could be given to nuns, not even by female musicians, and that the only permitted instruments were the organ and harpsichord. Seemingly, after these dispositions, the extraordinary quality and social visibility of the San Vito musicians decreased in the following years[110].

---

**106** Bottrigari 1599, pp. 49–50; English translation in Bottrigari 1962, pp. 58–60.
**107** Artusi 1600, fols. 1ᵛ-2ʳ; translated in Carruthers-Clement 1982, p. 10.
**108** Newcomb (1980, vol. I, pp. 29, 167, 172) suggests that Giulia Fiaschi (a female name) may be a misprint for Giulio Fiesco (c.1519–1586).
**109** Guarini 1621, pp. 375–376, my translation.
**110** Cf. Carruthers-Clement 1982; Bowers 1986, pp. 116–117, 125–126, 142; Pendle 2001, pp. 70, 85–90.

### 12.4.2.3. Sessa: better than Monteverdi?

If aristocrats and patricians eagerly waited for an opportunity to hear the Ferrarese nuns of San Vito, noble listeners could also be found in large numbers at the Church of the Milanese convent of Maria Annunciata.

Here, the star musician was Sr. Claudia Sessa, among whose admirers were Margaret of Austria, Queen of Spain (1584–1611) and the Duke of Savoy; the Archduke Albert VII of Austria (1559–1621) and his spouse, Isabella (1566–1633), during their visits to Milan, allegedly escaped their official duties in order to be free to hear her singing. The nobility of Parma and Mantua heard her too, and seemingly compared her singing with Claudio Monteverdi's (to his detriment, it is said).

Sessa was famous for her splendid voice, for her taste in ornamenting, for her expressiveness and the incisiveness of her musical personality. Such was the beauty of the worship where she sang, that "many were compelled to remain outside [the church], and it seemed as if any ordinary feast became, by her singing, the titular feast of the church", as witnessed by a contemporaneous writer, Girolamo Borsieri (1588–1629). Her interpretations were so inspiring that she conveyed the impression of being, at the same time, "a musician and an actress"; her personality seemed to beautify the works she was singing.

She was moreover a charming person and a nun happy to be what she was; invited by Queen Margaret to follow her to her Spanish court, Sessa politely refused and kept faith to her religious vows.

Sessa was undoubtedly more than what we would describe today as just a performer, inasmuch as her interpretations were more than the simple execution of a score; indeed, Borsieri affirms that she died shortly after having begun to "compose those same musical works which she sang at the feasts", where "composing" seems to indicate the transcriptions of musical works she had already imagined, created and actually performed[111].

The only surviving works by Claudia Sessa are *Occhi io vissi di voi*, an Italian-texted motet whose language and lyrics are given their sacred meaning (a lamentation of the Virgin Mary) only by their context, and *Vattene pur lasciva orechia humana*, both published in 1613[112]. These two works were included in a collection of works by various composers, dedicated to "the sung mourning of the Virgin Mary about the face of the dead Jesus", on lyrics by Angelo Grillo.

The only puzzling aspect of Borsieri's account, which is currently the most detailed source regarding Sessa's musical personality, is that he concludes by af-

---

111 Cf. Borsieri 1619, pp. 51–54; see also Bowers 1986, pp. 126–127 and 131.
112 *Canoro* 1613.

firming that she died young, though – on the basis of the information we possess – she was close to fifty at the moment of her death: an age which few sixteenth-century writers would have regarded as youthful.

### 12.4.2.4. Bovia, Strozzi, Baptista and their sisters

Another Italian musician who started her activity within convent walls was Laura Bovia (c.1565?-1629), who had been educated by the nuns of San Lorenzo in Bologna and had become "as dear as a precious jewel" to the nuns, not least for her beautiful voice. In 1578, the girl was removed from the monastery, provoking considerable uproar among the nuns, who complained about the "great wrongdoing and offense" they had suffered. They had educated her carefully as a musician, and – just when she had reached the height of musical perfection – she had been taken away "because she was pressingly sought-after by other monasteries"[113]. The complaining prioress hinted that Archbishop Paleotti might have had a hand in this wrongdoing, since he wanted the girl "for his monasteries" as they lacked organists. (The reasons why this inference seems unlikely will be seen shortly: § 12.4.3.1.).

Eventually, Laura was returned to San Lorenzo, where Federico Pendaso (or Pendasio, c.1525–1603, a Mantuan theologian) heard her during Holy Week 1581, when huge crowds came to the nuns' worship to hear her playing and singing. Pendaso, together with several other high-level churchmen, was acting as a head-hunter for the Gonzagas, who were interested in Laura's talent with the purpose in mind of making her a lady-in-waiting at their court. Possibly, they were also thinking of establishing a female musical consort similar to the Ferrarese *Concerto delle dame.*

Eventually, having spent ten years at the monastery, Laura left it for the Medici court in Florence (1584), where there was a similar female ensemble; in 1582, her talent had been acknowledged once more by composer Camillo Cortellini (1561–1630), in the dedication of his *Primo Libro de' madrigali a cinque voci.*

Undoubtedly, the outraged prioress complaining about Laura's estrangement had some reason: though the excellent music teaching received by Laura had been prompted (and possibly paid for) by her uncle (or probably father) Giacomo Bovio, the convent of San Lorenzo was a musical centre in the city of Bologna. Indeed, such was the nuns' interest in music, that they were the objects of an

---

[113] Cf. Bologna, Archivio di Stato, Demaniale, 120/1460 (S. Lorenzo), as quoted in Monson 2005, p. 8, my translation.

official inquiry by the Church, with the charge of having resorted to the devil himself in order to be helped to find a missing viola[114].

Though many other musician nuns could be listed (and many more are still to be discovered, especially outside Italy), I will conclude this section with a brief mention of another artist, Lorenza Strozzi (c.1516–1591), a Dominican nun from one of the most important aristocratic families in Florence, who lived at the monastery of San Niccolò in Prato. She authored a collection of Latin poetry (published in 1588[115]) of a clear humanist inspiration, taking as her model the metres of classical odes but also those of famous hymns from the plainchant heritage. Since, in this case, she frequently indicates which hymn of the Office she had taken as her metrical model, it can be inferred that her own hymns may have been sung on the model's tunes. If this was the case, her literary creations should be framed within the Christian humanist movement discussed in the preceding Chapters, and comprising such works as Buchanan's Latin translations of the Genevan Psalter or Baïf's experiments[116] (cf. § 6.3.3. etc.).

I mentioned previously that Raffaella Aleotti was one of the two nuns whose music had appeared in print in the sixteenth century. The other was Gracia Baptista, a nun from the Iberian Peninsula about whom, alas, no biographical information is available. All we have is one of her compositions, an intabulated hymn for keyboard instrument, included within the first (and only) published volume of a planned collection of keyboard anthologies, the *Libro de cifra nueva* (1557[117]). It is the first instrumental composition which can be attributed with certainty to a woman composer.

Gracia Baptista's *Conditor alme siderum* figures among works by the greatest masters of the era, such as Antonio de Cabezón (1510–1566) and Francisco Hernández Palero (c.1533–1597); this prestigious inclusion testifies to the appreciation which presumably surrounded Baptista and her works. Interestingly, the editor's preface suggests that, among the anthology's intended users, there were girls who studied music in order to prepare themselves for religious life.

Baptista's *glosa* on the seventh-century plainchant melody is close in style to the transcription of a keyboard improvisation; nevertheless, in my opinion, it is fascinating to observe the recurrence of the number three in the work (written in the third tone, in three parts and with thirty-three semibreves). This choice might

---

114 Cf. Fenlon 1980, p. 134; Bowers 1986, pp. 120–121; Monson 2005, pp. 7–10; Monson 2010, pp. 31–37, 49 etc.
115 Strozzi 1588.
116 Stevenson 2002, p. 111; Graziosi 2005, pp. 156–157.
117 Venegas de Henestrosa 1557.

be an homage to Christ, to whom the plainchant hymn is dedicated, and whose earthly life was traditionally believed to have lasted thirty-three years.

Other famous musicians among the Iberian nuns of the era include the Poor Clare Blasina de Mendoza (last third of the sixteenth century) and the *professa* Bernardina Clavijo del Castillo, a Dominican nun at the monastery of Santo Domingo el Real in Madrid and an appreciated harpist and organist, whose father Bernardo (1549–1626) was a composer in turn[118].

### 12.4.2.5. The convent scribes: transmitting tastes

We owe to consecrated religious women of the sixteenth century also another valuable realisation: some of them collected devotional songs and poetry (perhaps partially created within the monastery in turn) and thus helped to preserve a precious musical heritage.

One such scribe and editor was Sr. Catherina Tirs (d.1604), who completed in 1588 a collection of nearly eighty spiritual songs in Low German and Latin. She was a Sister of Common Life, i. e. a follower of the reforming movement known as *Devotio moderna*, and lived in a monastery which adopted the Augustinian rule, the Kloster Niesing (or Mariental) in Münster.

The *corpus* of songs collected by Tirs had evidently a high value for the community in which she belonged: it was not just their musical history, but also a living description of the main features of their spirituality and artistry. As Classen rightfully suggests[119], a songbook such as Tirs' epitomises the theological insight and the literary and musical heritage of the community.

Some of the songs she transcribed and helped to preserve reveal, by their dependence on Dutch models, the connection between the German-speaking followers of the *Devotio moderna* and its roots; moreover, there is frequently a deep mystical inspiration, in which music is seen as an instrument of elevation and also a consoling reality, especially in a context of asceticism and identification with Christ's sorrows. The *Devotio moderna* followers had actually created an impressive body of spiritual poetry and songs, whose composition was actively fostered and constituted one of their favourite forms of expression. Since the meditation and contemplation which characterised this spirituality were based on the ability to read, the connection between literacy, literary creativity and devotion is particularly clear, and encouraged the creation of a massive repertoire of religious poetry and songs.

---

[118] Cf. Lorenzo Arribas 2011, to which this section is indebted.
[119] Classen 2002, p. 11.

Other songbooks from the same spiritual milieu testify to this rich tradition, and date back to the last decades of the fifteenth century or the first half of the sixteenth. The relative freedom to interact with the laity which characterised the form of life of many sisterhoods and brotherhoods of the Common Life are shown by the presence of many tunes taken from the secular repertoire, to which spiritual lyrics have been applied. For example, a spiritual song on a secular tune is reported to have been sung first, in a community of the Common Life, by a married woman, by the name of Hillegont Aerontsdochter.

The same interaction between high culture of a humanistic spirit and the direct immediacy of vernacular and popular creativity is found in the poems by Berta Jacobs (also known as Suster Bertken or Christina Hospenthal, c.1426–1514), one of which found its place in the *Utrecht Liederbuch* (c.1500), set to an anonymous tune. Also from the beginning of the sixteenth century is a songbook by Anna of Cologne, which collects devotional poetry with a mystical content, as favoured by many religious women in the pre-Reformation era. The songs represented in Anna's collection have some traits in common with the Italian *laude*, such as the prevalence of vernacular lyrics and the shape in which they have been preserved (mainly with the verbal text alone). Similar traits are found in other analogous anthologies compiled by women, frequently belonging to religious communities (e.g. those by Marigen Remen and Lijsbet Ghoyvaers). Though the attribution of these songs presents the usual problems of anonymity, collective authorship and oral transmission, such collections represent a fascinating insight into the spiritual world and artistic expressivity of religious women in the early modern era[120].

### 12.4.3. Reforms, rules and religious women

In this section focusing on music by Catholic nuns in the sixteenth century, we have encountered both individual figures and situations in which sacred music was practised, taught, written, sung and performed. We have also seen that limitations, inquiries and obstacles were set by some exponents of the Catholic hierarchy for convent music, while others supported the musical practices. Prelates belonging to either category were concerned about spiritual reformation and the renewal of the Catholic Church, beginning from the interior life and outward behaviour of the consecrated people. However, while for some – such as Federigo

---

[120] Cf. Pendle 2001, p. 72; Classen 2002, pp. 10, 154–155; Koldau 2005a, p. 248; van Aelst 2010, p. 99; van der Poel and Joldersma 2010, pp. 27–30; van der Poel 2010, p. 14.

Borromeo – music could be an efficacious instrument for promoting the sanctity of religious women, for others its dangerous aspects were more cogent and compelling.

I will succinctly present, in the following pages, the decrees and initiatives taken with respect to convent music by two of the most important Catholic Reformers, whose importance for the Tridentine and post-Tridentine Church has been discussed in Chapters Eight and Nine (§ 8.3.4.–5., 9.6.2.).

### 12.4.3.1. Paleotti: muting music

The elder of the two is Gabriele Paleotti, the Archbishop of Bologna. Within his diocese, there were significant examples of high-level music within female convents, such as, for example, that of Santa Cristina della Fondazza. According to the surviving descriptions of the nuns' music, we know that they performed complex music, which was highly appreciated and attracted many listeners, and which involved vocal soloists and choir accompanied by instruments (not only the organ, it seems).

In spite of the overall reformist attitude of Paleotti, whose stance about music and the arts was certainly not among the strictest, both during and after the Council, his approach to the music of nuns was decidedly rigorous. In 1580, in his capacity as local authority in charge of the implementation of Trent's decrees, he turned the screw against musical practices in female monasteries, with the *Ordine da servarsi dale suore nel loro cantare e musica*. Indeed, his episcopal decrees seem to be the actualisation of the Council's draft (November 20th, 1563) about nuns' music, instead of its real decree (December 4th: cf. § 8.4.5.).

Paleotti in fact permitted the performance of polyphony within the nuns' worship only once a year, on the monastery's feast day – thus excluding such solemn feasts as Easter, Christmas or Pentecost. On such feasts, only motets were allowed, during Mass or at the end of Vespers, in conformity with the existing festive practice at the monastery of San Guglielmo. The singing nuns had to stay "down below in the chapel where the other nuns stand"; instrumental music was forbidden, except "the viol for the bass part where necessary, with the permission of their superiors, and, in their cells, the harpsichord". No music masters were allowed to teach or to rehearse with the nuns. (Thus, when we consider Paleotti's attitude with respect to convent music, the charge of having removed Laura Bovia from her monastery in order to employ her musical talents in "his monasteries" seems to be rather unfounded). In 1584, Paleotti increased the stringencies even further, by issuing the prohibition about organs in the outer church which Sr. Giulia Montecalvi of Sant'Omobono so successfully turned to her favour in the following year. Though special permissions could always be asked for (though not always granted), and though the nuns' love for music frequently found alternative paths for expressing itself, undeniably the strictures imposed by Paleotti in their performance of complex music were painful to endure and very limiting for the nuns; they also provided a model (probably unwelcome by the nuns) for his successors, who continued in his wake well into the seventeenth century[121].

### 12.4.3.2. The Borromeos: between rigour and reform

Though they were not always of the same mind about how to achieve the Catholic Reformation they both cared for, Gabriele Paleotti and Carlo Borromeo were likeminded about nuns' music. The Milanese Cardinal forbade female monasteries to employ outside musicians as teachers or as performers in the outer church. He instructed that in the external churches of monasteries under regulars' ruling no polyphony be sung, and that no secular music be owned by the nuns. Enclosure was strictly reinforced; the Archbishop consistently went his way also when faced by public opposition, especially by the most influential patrician families.

As Kendrick[122] points out, and though Carlo Borromeo was not isolated in pursuing the moralisation of female convents via limitations on their music, the uniqueness of his conduct lay in its consistency and in the concept of unauthorised music-making by nuns as constituting a grave sin.

Though the direction of Borromeo's episcopal regulations is clear and coherent, it represents however an evolution: as seen earlier in this Chapter (§ 12.4.1.8.), he had been interested in female monastic rules which actually promoted music-making as a means for moving the hearers, and had even shared this perspective at an earlier stage of his life.

However, while the episcopal restrictions on the nuns' music in Ferrara sadly succeeded in curtailing their musical activities in the long term, Carlo Borromeo's initiatives did not. In 1595, roughly ten years after his death, the level of monastic music-making in Milan was excellent and highly admired by the contemporaneous hearers. Indeed, Milan could pride itself on the presence of numerous monasteries whose music was renowned, and which actually competed in musical excellence, since this represented the public manifestation of the institution's importance.

---

[121] Cf. Monson 1992, pp. 191–194; Monson 1993a, pp. 144–150; Pendle 2001, p. 169; Monson 2012, pp. 4 and 41–43.
[122] Kendrick 1996, p. 68.

In that year, the Milanese historian Paolo Morigia (1525–1604) expounded at length on the musical panorama of the city's monasteries, affirming that music (both instrumental and vocal) was widespread in almost all convents; in some of them, he maintained, "there are voices so fine they seem angelic, and like sirens they allure the nobility of Milan to come to hear them". The best musicians, in Morigia's opinion, were those at Santa Maria Maddalena and at the Assunta; so fine was their music that "one hears select voices that are concordant in harmony, and minglings of divine voices with instruments, so that they seem to be angelic choirs that please the ears of the listeners and are praised by connoisseurs"[123]. The parallel between musical proficiency and sanctity was often drawn by other writers as well: describing the mastery of the Cremonese nun Sr. Corona Somenza (c.1530–1609), the artist Antonio Campi (c.1522–1587) clearly associated "the holiness of her life, [...] her many virtues, and [...] her excellence in music of every sort"[124].

Thus, implicitly, the deep connection between sanctity and singing, between godliness and gamut, between beauty and bounty was reaffirmed; and in spite of the attempts by and of the fears of some Church authorities (or perhaps precisely because they did not work as expected), many female monasteries could face the threshold of the seventeenth century with the musical talents they harboured, and cultivate them in a social and religious environment which continued to produce an abundant artistic harvest.

### 12.4.4. Voices from the laity

Under the label of "Catholic lay women", as the reader will easily imagine, an extraordinary variety of social positions, geographical contexts, levels of culture and class, differences of age and family condition are grouped. Girls educated at the Venetian *ospedali* were initiating in the sixteenth century the glorious musical tradition which was going to characterise these institutions in the following centuries (in 1575, at least one such ensemble was giving public concerts along with the usual worship routine). In spite of increasing post-Tridentine limitations on non-monastic forms of lay consecration, women belonging to the tertiary orders were encouraged to sing devotional music in their private gatherings. Processions of girls and boys who attended catechism were seen and heard in the

---

[123] Morigia 1595, pp. 186–187, as quoted in and translated by Bowers 1986, pp. 125–126.
[124] Campo 1585, Libro Terzo, p. I, as quoted in and translated by Bowers 1986, pp. 125–126. Cf. also Kendrick 1994; Kendrick 1996, pp. 17, 60–67, 73; Pendle 2001, pp. 68–69; Reardon 2002, pp. 24–25; Macy 2011, p. 350.

streets of many European cities, singing litanies or more complex musical forms. Aristocratic women wrote religious poetry which was sometimes set to music, on improvised tunes or on melodies from the popular or cultivated tradition[125]. And the listing could continue for long.

Thus, in this case as in many others encountered so far, I will not even attempt a thorough assessment: once more, I will only limit myself to a survey exemplifying some particular situations and conditions.

### 12.4.4.1. Composing spiritual madrigals

Among the scanty surviving sources, a spiritual madrigal (*Quando spiega l'insegn'al sommo Padre*) composed by a sixteenth-century woman, Paola Massarenghi (also spelt as Mazzarenghi or Massarengo, and also known as Madonna Paola da Parma, b.1565) has partially been transmitted. It was included in a collection of madrigals (*Il Primo Libro de madrigali a cinque voci*[126]) published in 1585 by Arcangelo Gherardini, a Servite friar from Siena who had studied with Salvadore Essenga (d.1575) in the company of Orazio Vecchi.

Little is known about Massarenghi: her younger brother, Giovanni Battista (1569-c.1596) a composer in turn, was supported by Ranuccio Farnese in his musical studies – a circumstance which leads us to infer that their parents were possibly wealthy members of the bourgeoisie with important benefactors.

The text for Paola's madrigal is excerpted from a stanza of a spiritual poem by Gabriele Fiamma, Bishop of Chioggia, who had published a collection of *Rime spirituali* in 1570[127] which attracted the attention of several composers of madrigals.

In another case, two entire collections of spiritual madrigals by a woman composer would seem to have vanished, although there may be a simpler and less saddening explanation.

The name of Maddalena Casulana (c.1544-c.1590) is comparatively famous, not only because her four madrigals included in *Il Desiderio* (1566[128]) are the first secular polyphonic works by a woman to have appeared in print, as far as is known, but also for the bold and proto-feminist wording of her preface.

No sacred works by Casulana survive; we have the text for a Latin motet (*Nil magis iucundum*) she wrote in 1568 for the wedding of Wilhelm V of Bavaria to Renée de Lorraine (1544–1602), and which was performed together with *Vos*

---

[125] Cf. Masetti Zannini 1993, p. 123; Berdes 1996; Pendle 2001, pp. 73–74; Kendrick 2009, p. 45.
[126] Gherardini 1585.
[127] Fiamma 1570.
[128] Bonagiunta 1566.

*sacræ adeste tonis* by another woman, Caterina Willaert. The music of both pieces has been lost, but neither text would have qualified for inclusion among sacred music proper.

The mystery surrounding Casulana's two books of "*spirituali*" stems from their inclusion in a catalogue of printed music issued by Vincenti in 1591. Apparently, however, the catalogue's compiler mistook her two books of secular madrigals for spiritual pieces, so – hopefully – the loss is only seeming and Casulana never wrote two books of spiritual madrigals[129].

Female creativity was also at work in the creation of a collection of spiritual madrigals set to music by Philippe de Monte in 1581[130]. As Filippi fascinatingly narrates[131], only two poets are identified by name as the authors of the madrigals' lyrics, and both are women, i.e. Laura Battiferri degli Ammannati (1523–1589) and Vittoria Colonna (1490–1547). It is particularly interesting to observe that de Monte explicitly acknowledged the role of Jesuits in selecting and proposing the madrigal texts to the composer[132]. Indeed, as Filippi points out, "in the central decades of the sixteenth century, the Society [of Jesus] managed to appeal to some of those Italian intellectuals who had inhabited the gray areas of the age of reform and Reformation"[133], and thus to win for the Catholic cause the talents and energies of several members of the *intelligentsia* of the time – among whom a leading figure of the Italian cultural panorama such as Colonna.

### 12.4.4.2. Voices from Northern Europe

In the case of Anna Bijns (1493–1575), as in many others encountered so far, we can infer a musical performance or destination for some or many of her literary works, but no evidence is available about her actual involvement in musical creation. Nevertheless, I will dedicate a few lines to her work, since it is highly relevant to our discussion on the religious Reformations. An unmarried Catholic laywoman from Antwerp, close to the Franciscan Minorite friars, Bijns was an appreciated pedagogue both at school and privately; her poetry, which reveals remarkable mastery of a complex metrical structure such as the *referein*, is highly committed to the cause of the Counter-Reformation, and was fostered by the Catholic hierarchy precisely for this reason; indeed, in her time her writings had

---

[129] Cf. Bowers 1986, pp. 116–119; Fenlon 1989, pp. 243, 251–255; Pendle 2001, pp. 85–86.
[130] De Monte 1581.
[131] Filippi 2016a.
[132] Filippi 2016a, p. 66.
[133] Filippi 2016a, p. 78.

enormous dissemination and success, and her stinging verses proved very useful for the Catholic cause[134].

Similar to Anna Bijns, Brussels-based Katharina Boudewijns (c.1520-a.1603) was a Catholic poetess who felt the confessional instability and conflict of her time deeply. Differently from Bijns, however, Boudewijns wrote lyrics explicitly destined for singing and with precise indications of the tune; moreover, Boudewijns' poetical style is less sharp and more sorrowful, especially when she describes the Calvinist ruling (1581–5) and what it meant for Catholics to experience such a situation.

After her husband's death, in 1587 Boudewijns had her poetry published (*Het prieelken der gheestelycke wellusten*[135]), in a collection comprising twenty-five songs, devotional poetry, Christmas carols, and two dialogued plays (one between the Bride and the Groom of the Song of Solomon, and one between Love and Harmony who deplore the sorrows caused by confessional divisions).

Among her poems, *A Fine Air on the Holy Sacrament* (*Een schoon Liedeke van 't Heilig Sacrament*) is set to the tune of a secular song ('*S winters en 't somers even groen*, on which also the Anabaptist Soetken Gerrits composed a song) and is an appeal to Calvinists to recant their teaching which deviate from Catholic dogma. The rhetorical device of addressing one's confessional opponents has been already found in other examples in Chapter Ten (§ 10.3.7.3.), but in Boudewijns' case, more than in others, the reader's feeling is that she actually intended her song to be a persuasive tool for Calvinists, and not just a stylistic artifice destined for her fellows Catholics[136].

Among others, in Germany, another poetess was actively struggling for Catholicism and against the Evangelical movements, but in this case she was a member of the high aristocracy, i.e. Princess Margaretha von Anhalt (1473–1530). She wrote a *Historie von dem Leiden, Sterben, Auferstehung und Himmelfahrt unsers Herrn und Heilandes Jesu Christi*, published posthumously in 1553, which was conceived as a text to be sung for the devotional practices of her household, and whose structure mirrored that of the monastic Office. Nothing is known, unfortunately, of the tunes on which this poetry would have been sung[137].

These few examples are just representative of what sixteenth-century women created, lived and composed: from the so-called "art music" of professional composers to the devotional expression of nuns or laywomen, aristocrats or

---

134 Cf. Aerke 2010, p. 160; van der Poel and Joldersma 2010, pp. 33–36.
135 Boudewijns 1587.
136 Cf. Schenkeveld-van der Dussen 2010, p. 60; van Gemert 2010, pp. 222–229.
137 Cf. Koldau 2005b, p. 390 and p. 418.

bourgeois, to the polemical songs which flourished in the disputed territories. The variety of these women's achievements sharply conflicts with the paucity of the surviving musical sources; however, by sampling a few of these religious and musical creations, I hope to have given the reader a glimpse of what (and of how much) has been lost.

## 12.5. Voices from a Christian polyphony

Even though I have been compelled, by the requirements of an orderly exposition, to adopt once more a structure based on confessions for this Chapter, I would like to conclude it with an interconfessional section. Though women could take their pens up against the teachings of another confession not unlike their male counterparts, also in their case the connection between music and spirituality could transcend the confessional boundaries.

Arguably, the lesser involvement of women in the theological debates, and their higher concern with mysticism and devotion produced a more shaded and less polarised situation, which resembles more closely a continuum of spiritual practices and attitudes than a neatly divided field.

In this last section, I will present a selection of contexts for women's spiritual music-making, and we will see that the presence of music in the spiritual and religious life of women took similar forms throughout the confessional divisions.

Even though we have repeatedly seen, in the previous Chapters, that the Catholic hierarchy was not particularly supportive of private singing of vernacular devotional songs – favouring its adoption in public circumstances and devotional gatherings – it has also been maintained that many vocal and instrumental works on religious texts, and/or arrangements and elaborations of traditional or confessional tunes were widely disseminated, and could often transcend their users' confessional affiliation.

As concerns the simple vernacular songs on religious lyrics, Lutheran chorales and vernacular hymns, as well as Calvinist Psalms, frequently aimed at becoming the soundtrack of daily life, beside their communal use in public worship. Though it was unlikely that the songs which most clearly represented a particular confession and characterised its identity would be adopted by members of other Churches, the large heritage of songs whose confessional features were neutral could be intoned by housewives doing their daily chores irrespective of their confessional allegiance.

Otherwise, when religious songs did actually become confessional flags, the repertoires would be obviously different, but the practices and the functions of music might be rather similar: to strengthen one's faith (and also that of her listeners, perhaps her family and children), to create a feeling of belonging and identity, to instil a sacred presence within the framework of daily life and to provide relief, respite and comfort amidst the fatigue and pain of the day.

Where middle-class women received musical teaching, it was likely that the performance (instrumental or vocal) of religious music was fostered by parents, guardians and educators more than that of secular music – though possibly the latter was more enjoyable for many.

As we have seen in the preceding Chapter, therefore, music was not only the object of teaching in many schools for girls throughout Europe, but also a teaching medium for conveying the content of faith and a religious frame of mind; religious instruction in music was another occasion on which many girls of virtually all confessional allegiances could sing and listen to music.

The ability to read music and play an instrument was obviously more common in certain social and geographical contexts than in others: from the one side, the illiterate were unlikely to be able to read a musical score; from the other, some societies had a more favourable attitude to music than others, and the approach to women's music was yet another question.

Virtually everywhere, however, at least some establishments in which a musically gifted girl could learn to read music, play and sometimes compose were available: from the Italian and Spanish convents to some song- and music schools in Scotland, from the Lutheran girls' schools to those in the Low Countries, where music was particularly cherished and loved.

The ubiquity of musical practices in a city like Antwerp was widely acknowledged, provoking amazement, admiration and sometimes even perplexity in the observers. There, the most remarkable consequence of the religious Reformations on women's music was the increasing focus on and promotion of the spiritual repertoire, which corresponded to the common concern of all religious reformers for piety and morality.

The Italian historian Lodovico Guicciardini (1521–1589) was a witness of music's omnipresence in the Flanders[138], and he specifically pointed out the women's knowledge of, and participation and ability in music. Polyphonic music (in which devotional works had a significant role) and instrumental transcriptions from the sacred repertoire were published, sold, bought and performed in many occasions of daily life[139].

---

138 Guicciardini 1567, p. 70.
139 Cf. Austern 1988, p. 47; Koldau 2005a, pp. 233–234; Forney 2010, pp. 84, 91, 104–109; Munro 2010, p. 67.

We have already seen, in Chapter Eleven (§ 11.4.5.), that the fictional (or perhaps autobiographical) character of the Leiden schoolmistress encouraged her pupils to play Psalms rather than dances on their keyboard instruments. Outside fiction, the actual presence of this repertoire in the musical training of Dutch and Flemish girls is witnessed by the contents of the manuscript collection (1599) of Susanne van Soldt (c.1587–1615?), a twelve-year old girl of Dutch origins who lived in London, and whose keyboard anthology included ten Psalm arrangements (whose style suggests they might have been used for accompanying singing rather than as properly instrumental works) and an arrangement of Lasso's *Susanne ung jour*, together with secular pieces.

Instrumental performance of psalmody is mentioned also by a Puritan author and diarist, Lady Grace Sherrington Mildmay (1552–1620), who used to improvise lute arrangements of the Psalms within the framework of her daily meditations. We have also seen how closely such practices resemble *lauda*-singing and their instrumental arrangements in the Italian monasteries or the plainchant *glosa* composed by Gracia Baptista and presumably performed in her convent, if not in many others.

We have observed that religious noblewomen used to organise household worships, which could be based on Calvinist Psalms (for example in the case of Louise Juliana of Orange Nassau), on Lutheran hymns or Psalm-paraphrases (as was done by Inger of Austråt) or on vernacular sung poetry (as Margaretha von Anhalt did), but these examples could be multiplied.

It is particularly remarkable, in my opinion, that, in spite of the limitations imposed on careers as church musicians for women in all Churches, several of the musical works composed and published by women in this period are on sacred texts. Even more than in the case of their male counterparts, whose sincere religious inspiration might sometimes have been replaced by the requirements of their jobs as church musicians, these works testify to a direct involvement and a personal concern for matters of faith, expressed through the medium of music and perhaps encouraged by it.

If, as we have frequently seen in this book, the success of the Reformations as "reforming" movements was closely connected to educational aspects and to the "formation" of the young, then the role of mothers and relatives, as well as of female professionals or religious teachers and educators was crucial, for transmitting beliefs, forms of prayer and values to the new and future generations.

Thus, paraphrasing Wagner Oettinger's statement, quoted in Chapter Five (§ 5.3.4.5.), that "music saved the Evangelical Church for Luther"[140], I think it safe to assert that women, and their music, "saved" several Churches by passing on faith, and by living deeply religious lives interspersed with music.

In this Chapter we have encountered several forms of music-making, numerous witnesses about musical practices, and some examples of musical creativity (or creativity with music and in music) by sixteenth-century women, in the field of spiritual and sacred music. We have discussed how the connection linking femininity, faith and music was seen by some sixteenth-century authors, but, in spite of their perplexities, how important music was in the religious experience of contemporaneous girls and women. We have observed how music was created, performed and lived in the Evangelical zones and in those which remained Catholic or reverted to Catholicism, discussing some particular figures and their works, but especially the overall framework for the experience of music and spirituality by the women of the Reformations.

---

140 Wagner Oettinger 2001, p. 209. Cf. *ibid.*, p. 45; Hsia 1992, pp. 107–108; Pettegree 2005, p. 46; Fisher 2014, p. 172.

# Conclusions

> Protestant Christianity has enriched the
> entire Christendom through its church songs, its
> great church music and its unceasing
> theological reflection[1].
>
> [Pope John Paul II]

Five hundred years have elapsed since an Augustinian Doctor of theology voiced his dissent against the sale and purchase of indulgences. Half a millennium in which culture, science, technology, economy and society have changed deeply and dramatically. And yet our present-day culture, science and society, as well as the faith of Christians worldwide, are deeply intertwined with the history of the Reformations and with their heritage.

In Chapter One, I proposed a brief historical overview of the sixteenth century: even at a first glance, it is thought-provoking to realise how deeply has the "*cuius regio eius religio*" principle influenced, at least in certain zones, the confessional proportions in the population until now.

In Chapter Two, we have surveyed the perspectives on music and on its social and spiritual role as seen in the culture of the sixteenth century. If many issues which were crucial in the sixteenth century seem less important today, and if other concerns of today's world were unthinkable five hundred years ago, still other points remain impressively relevant to the current situation. The debate on the educational role of music, for example, is alive and well, and throughout the world there is an abundance of both theory and practice showing the invaluable benefits of musical education for children and the young. Moreover, if philosophical and aesthetical discussions on the power of music to move have reached today a high level of sophistication, it is nonetheless true that no univocal response has been given as to "how" music actually moves us: many researchers are investigating this topic both from the theoretical viewpoint and from those of psychology, psychoacoustics and neurology.

More to the point, in Chapter Three we have discussed objections and criticism to sixteenth-century music, which coalesced around theoretical and practical issues. Several of these problems, though sometimes in a different form, remain at the centre of present-day debates on church music among theologians and liturgists of several Christian Churches. The Catholic Church, for example,

---

1 Pope John Paul II (Karol Wojtyła), Speech at the Cathedral of Paderborn (22.6.1996), §7, my translation; available online at http://bit.ly/2b3PaY2.

has dramatically reshaped the forms of her worship following the Second Vatican Council (1962–5), accepting several stimuli from the Protestant Churches (such as the use of the vernacular, the active role of the congregation, the necessity for songs which every parishioner could join in singing) and, at the same time, reaffirming the value of liturgical beauty as a fundamental element of worship. For many people, especially in certain contexts, church is today the only place where one is allowed or invited to sing aloud, and where live music is played and sung by non-professionals. Some of Luther's chorales or some Psalms taken from the Genevan Psalter may well be the only example of "early music" with which many Christians are familiar; their tunes did not need the Early-Music movement to be revived, since they had been in constant use for five hundred years; they are, in brief, the only example of sixteenth-century music which is known and performed by non-specialists. In a world where musical practice is more and more confined to professionalism and to digital reproduction, this live experience is also a powerful symbol of the true and real relationships one should be able to build within the context of the Church.

On the other hand, the quest for a balanced position between types of music which please but are ultimately imperfectly suited for prayer and others which are theoretically better but leave contemporary assemblies cold is still open: this closely mirrors Bernardino Cirillo's concerns as to which music can truly help believers in their spiritual life, and the Church in her pastoral role.

The concepts of sacred music discussed by the principal Reformers in Chapter Four have largely shaped the subsequent theology of music in the Churches they founded. The contribution of some Reformers, and of Luther in particular, to the very concept of a "theology of music", i.e. of a theological discourse about music and its role in Christian life, should not be underestimated. These reflections had, of course, actual embodiment in the different musical practices and cultures of the Churches, and thus shaped the thought about music and the dissemination of musical culture both inside and outside the Churches. Though history is not made by hypotheses, it seems however safe to assert that the extraordinary contribution of the German philosophy of music to this branch of thought is probably an indirect consequence of Luther's insight. Conversely, some distinctive shades of Calvin's perspective on music resonate suggestively in the fascinating writings on music of the Reformed theologian Karl Barth (1886–1968).

It is even easier to discern the continuing influence of these perspectives in the actual practices of today's Churches. In Chapter Five we examined the forms taken by Lutheran music in the first century of its life. Many hymns dating from the very first years of Luther's Reformation, and some which were included in the first published hymnals are still sung by members of the Lutheran Church, and many have been translated, adapted and disseminated within song collections officially adopted by other confessions. Moreover, very little knowledge of music history is sufficient to show how early Lutheran tunes are pervasively woven within the fabric of later masterpieces, not all of which are classifiable as "sacred" music proper. Many Chorale Preludes by Johann Sebastian Bach, which have unforgettable melodies of their own, are intrinsically shaped by the notes of the Lutheran tune constituting their backbone and their genetic code, to use biological similes. The Armed Men, in the *Zauberflöte* (1791) by Wolfgang Amadeus Mozart (1756–1791), sing on the tune of an early Lutheran Chorale, while *Ein feste Burg* is heard in the *Reformation Symphony* (1829–30) by Felix Mendelssohn Bartholdy (1809–1847), to name but three of the greatest composers.

The beauty and immediacy of the Calvinist Psalm tunes are similarly part of the shared musical heritage of Western culture, well beyond confessional boundaries. An open-air Mass in the presence of Pope Francis was opened, in June 2015, by the communal singing of an Italian Catholic hymn set to the tune of Psalm 134 [133] in the Genevan Psalter (the "Old 100th", as it is known in the English-speaking word); fascinatingly, and possibly purposefully, this happened the day before the first visit ever of a Catholic Pope to a Waldensian Temple. The same tune had greeted Pope Francis' predecessor, Pope Benedict XVI, on his arrival in Scotland (2010), while the Church of Scotland had celebrated its 450th anniversary on the notes of the same Psalm. A Lutheran hymn on that same melody had been harmonised by Bach, while its tune found its way in "art-music" through works by Mendelssohn, Ralph Vaughan Williams (1872–1958), Paul Hindemith (1895–1963) and Benjamin Britten (1913–1976), to limit myself once more to some of the most famous examples.

The splendour of English Cathedral music continues to the present-day, and while it is always a treat to listen to the best Anglican choirs, whose level is probably unsurpassed, even from a purely historical viewpoint the importance of this tradition for the research, revival, recording and performance of the polyphonic repertoire should be emphasised. Significantly, within this musical and spiritual framework, in February 2016 a Catholic Vesper service in Latin was celebrated once more, after little less than five hundred years, in the Royal Chapel of Hampton Court. Music was an integral component of this ecumenical initiative, and the repertoire selected by Harry Christophers with The Sixteen represented a consistent continuation of the cross-confessional musical tradition of English church music (works by Taverner, Tallis and William Cornysh [1465–1523]).

The Catholic Church continues to make use, albeit in a limited form, of the "Gregorian" plainchant as transmitted in the *Editio Medicæa*, while the music of Palestrina represented for centuries a model of compositional elegance and of proper church style by virtue of its musical beauty, of course, but also due to its particular role as the musical flag of the Catholic Reformation.

We have also seen how music was seen, by some religious men and women, as a means for creating unity and peace, especially where they had been broken. Today, realities such as the *West-Eastern-Divan Orchestra* (founded in 1999 by Daniel Barenboim) bear witness to this power of music to pacify conflicting and rival factions.

The contribution of today's women to the musical and spiritual life of their religious communities (as composers, theologians of music, liturgists, church musicians, hymn-writers, performers of sacred music etc.) is invaluable, and, in the contexts where religious practice is livelier, even today some religious songs are learnt by children from their mothers and female relatives.

This was just a colloquial survey, by means of conclusion, but it aimed at showing how the study of music in the context of the sixteenth-century Reformations is far from being a merely antiquarian interest. It is not the study of a dead object, which can be dissected at leisure and whose relevance for the life of contemporary people is cultural at best. It is instead a field which even today is full of resonances, some of which are among the most important and cherished in the lives of millions of believers.

It is therefore a necessary study, and one which requires enormous respect. While academic research should try and be as unbiased as possible, it should also, in my opinion, be primarily concerned with the actual lives and experiences of the actual people it discusses.

It is a field of study in which much remains to be done, and the very limits of this book reveal the scope of what can still be discovered: sources, both musical and textual, to be unearthed and analysed, especially in the less common languages; theological debates on how the distinct Christian theologies of music impacted on each other, on the overall philosophical thought on music, and on the actual practices of the Churches, within a single confession, in comparison with the others and as a net of influences; studies on the social aspects of religious singing, on the repertories whose transmission has been more difficult, or on performance practices; studies on the reception of the individual repertories of worship and devotion, of the theoretical positions on sacred music, of the official pronouncements of the Churches; studies on women's music, for example in the convents outside Italy and in some Protestant Churches etc. It is my hope, of course, that this book has provided an introduction and a starting point to those wishing to engage with these and other related topics.

I suggested that Chapter One was just a sketchy frame for the picture which was to follow, and which possibly resembles more closely a mosaic than a painting. It is however a mosaic to which I hope many of my readers will contribute with their own findings, research, insights and perspectives.

For those who believe in Christ, moreover, studying the music of the Reformations can be also a way for enhancing the reciprocal knowledge among members of different Christian confessions, for showing the beauty of the various forms of worship, and therefore for contributing to the building of unity through the respectful and amazed contemplation of the splendour of these heritages. This is, in my opinion, a cultural, historical, religious and social responsibility, as well as a fascinating endeavour for all those wishing to engage in it.

# Glossary

| | |
|---|---|
| A cappella | Vocal music without instrumental accompaniment. |
| Abgesang | Second section of the → *Barform*. |
| Accentus | In contrast with → concentus, a style of singing which prizes clear delivery (→ syllabic style, melodic sobriety) over aesthetic beauty. |
| Adiaphoron/Adiaphora | Inessential aspect of faith or liturgy, which may or may not be accepted without altering substantially the content of faith. |
| Alternatim | Sung or played in alternation: between two choirs, or between instruments and singing. |
| Ambrosian | Referring to St Ambrose (c.339–397), bishop of the Church of Milan; by extension, may refer to the diocese and rites of the Milanese Church (Ambrosian rite). |
| Anabaptist | Literally, "re-baptiser": refers to those rejecting the validity of infant baptism, and who therefore undergo a new baptism in adult age. |
| Antiphon | A short prayerful introduction recited or sung before (and after) a Psalm or canticle within the → Office (Liturgy of the Hours). "Marian" antiphons (such as the *Salve Regina* or *Regina cœli*) are recited/sung independently from psalms or canticles, and normally conclude the daily prayer after → Compline. |
| Antiphonal | In contrast to → responsorial, one of the possible forms of performance of psalmody and hymns, whereby one choir answers to another. (May also indicate a liturgical book). |
| Apocalyptical | Referring to the end of the world, particularly when the events narrated in the Book of Revelation (also indicated as *Apocalypse*) are believed to be imminent. |
| Augmentation | In contrast with → diminution, a musical process whereby the rhythmic values (durations) of notes are proportionally augmented (i.e. slowed down). |
| Augustinian | Referring to St Augustine of Hippo (354–430), one of the most important and influential figures of Western thought. May refer, thus, to his philosophy/theology, or to the members of the religious order of the Augustinians, or to their monastic rule which is adopted by other religious orders as well. |
| Barform | Poetic/musical form typical of medieval German poetry (of the *Minnesinger* and → *Meistersinger*). Stanzas in the Barform are constituted by two → *Stollen* (making together the *Aufgesang*) and one → *Abgesang*, making together an AAB structure. |
| Benedictine | Referring to St Benedict of Nursia (c.480-c.543), who is considered to be the founder of Western monasticism. His monastic rule is based on the principle of the *"ora et labora"* (i.e. pray and work) and has been adopted by numerous religious families. |
| Bicinium/Bicinia | Polyphonic form for two voices. |
| Bishop | In the Catholic Church, a presbyter (priest) designated by the Pope to be the spiritual leader of a diocese, i.e. a geographical zone surrounding a Cathedral Church. Bishops are considered to be the successors |

| | |
|---|---|
| | of the Apostles and to form the chain of tradition connecting today's Church with that founded by Christ. Bishops are also found among some Protestant Churches, though the terms of their ministry vary depending on the → confession. |
| Breviary | A book containing the prescribed Liturgy of the Hours, or Office; Catholic priests are bound to recite it daily, and many religious orders adopt it in turn; others adopt modified versions of the Hours. |
| Brief/Bull | Official Papal pronouncements, whose content may regard canonisations, matters of Church discipline, organisation etc. |
| Canon | 1. In music: a compositional process whereby the same melody is played or sung by one or more voices (*comes*), normally starting with a chronological delay after the first (*dux*). May also involve more sophisticated processes, such as (but not limited to) augmentation, diminution, inversion or retrogradation.<br>2. In the Catholic liturgy of Mass: prayer pronounced by the celebrating priest(s) and including the consecration of bread and wine. Its formulation showed remarkable continuity through the centuries.<br>3. A Church minister.<br>4. Biblical canon: the list of books held to be divinely inspired in the Bible. The list may vary depending on → confessions. |
| Canonisation | A process of the Catholic Church whereby it is affirmed that a deceased person is certainly among the saved, in heaven, and may receive the appellation of "saint". There are various degrees in this process: typically, a person is proclaimed to be a "Blessed" before canonisation (but not all "blessed" are later canonised). |
| Canticle | May indicate:<br>1. A poetic prayer similar to a Psalm and of Scriptural origin, but which is not contained within the Book of Psalms (→ Psalter). There are Old Testament canticles (e.g. in the prophetic books) and New Testament canticles, the most famous of which is the *Magnificat* (with the *Benedictus* and *Nunc Dimittis*).<br>2. By extension, a spiritual song or poetry of free composition. |
| Cantional, -style | Compositional process whereby a given melody (→ *cantus firmus*), which may also be a Lutheran chorale, is sung by the upper part of an ensemble; contrast with → *Tenorlied*, whereby the given melody is sung by the tenor. |
| Cantor | Latin for "singer"; person responsible for the musical aspect of worship. |
| Cantus firmus | Originally, a melody from the → plainchant repertoire, which was sung in long rhythmic values and upon which new voices were added. Later, it could be taken from a variety of other provenances, including the secular repertoire. |
| Cardinal | In the Catholic Church, a person entitled to electing the → Pope (and to be elected as Pope, though virtually it is not required that a Pope has been a Cardinal). Though normally Cardinals are bishops, virtually it is not required that they are ordained priests. |

| | |
|---|---|
| Catechism | 1. The content of faith, i.e. the dogmas held to be true by a Church.<br>2. The catechetic process, i.e. the religious instruction whereby the content of faith is transmitted, particularly to children.<br>3. The book/books where such contents are written, frequently in the form of questions and answers. |
| Chalcedonian | Referring to the Council of Chalcedon (451AD), which formulated the orthodox doctrine of Christ's double nature (and therefore this doctrine is called "Chalcedonian" in turn): it affirms that Jesus Christ is true God and true man, and that these two natures are united (*hypostatic union*) without confusion. This dogma therefore qualifies as heretic the competing beliefs, i.e. that Christ is a half-God, or is a God appearing in human form, or is a particularly saintly man without divine qualities. |
| Chantre | See → *cantor*; refers to the *cantors* in zones under French linguistic influence (e.g. the Church of Strasbourg). |
| Chapel | 1. A (normally) small-sized church (but, for example, the Palatine Chapel of Mantua, Santa Barbara, is very large!), frequently attached to secular institutions.<br>2. The musicians employed by an ecclesiastical establishment (such a Cathedral Church) or a private patron. |
| Chapel Master | The person responsible for coordinating and directing the → Chapel (and, particularly in the past, also for composing part of the repertoire performed by the Chapel itself). |
| Choirbook | In contrast with → partbook, a book of music which contains all parts of a polyphonic composition, albeit written separately on facing pages. |
| Choral | A musical piece sung by a choir, or anything which refers to a choir. |
| Chorale | 1. The Lutheran Church → *Lied*, with its various musical and textual origins and forms.<br>2. By extension, the four-part harmonisation of these melodies in the → *cantional* form. |
| Choraliter | Sung in unaccompanied (→ a cappella) → monody. |
| Christocentric | "Centred on Christ": for example, a form of worship which addresses first and foremost the Lord; in contrast, for example, with excessive veneration for the Virgin Mary or the Saints. An → orthodox Catholic devotion should always be Christocentric, even when it addresses Mary or the Saints, but abuses under this aspect have provoked → iconoclastic reactions. |
| Church Fathers | Theologians and religious writers of the first centuries of the Church, who are acknowledged as "Fathers of the Church" for their proximity to the Apostolic era, for their holy lives, for their → orthodox doctrine and teachings, which are held as true by most Churches. |
| Cistercian | Adjective indicating a monk or the religious family following the rule of St Bernard of Clairvaux (1090–1153). |
| Communion | 1. The act by which Christians communicate with Christ by eating and drinking the consecrated bread and wine (the different Churches maintain different concepts of how this partaking is realised). |

| | |
|---|---|
| | 2. The deep union among members of the mystical body of Christ, the Church: may be the union among individual believers, among different Churches... |
| Compline | The last of the Hours constituting the Liturgy of the Hours, or → Office. |
| Concentus | In contrast with → accentus, a style of singing which favours aesthetic beauty over clarity of delivery. |
| Concertato | In the period under discussion, a compositional style whereby instruments intermingle and/or are contrasted with voices, normally with the participation of a basso continuo; starts to be documented in sacred music during the sixteenth century. |
| Conclave | The election of Popes by the Cardinals, who are enclosed for the entire time required by the process. |
| Confession | 1. Of faith: the affirmation of one's creed. For this reason, martyrs are sometimes indicated as "confessors" (of faith). |
| | 2. Confessional belonging: since different Churches may held different doctrines as true ("confess" them), by extension a Church, in its difference from another Church, is defined as a Confession. Thus one's belonging to a Church (i.e. Catholic, Lutheran, Calvinist, Anglican etc.) is his or her confession or confessional belonging. |
| | 3. Of sins: the act whereby an individual or a group of people admit to their sinfulness and ask God for forgiveness. In the Catholic Church, it is one of the seven sacraments and involves the individual confession of one's sins to a priest and the reception of the priest's absolution in the name of Christ. |
| Congregation | A group of faithful, from the Latin *grex* (flock). |
| Consistory | 1. In the Catholic Church, a formal gathering of Cardinals, during which the Pope may "create" the new Cardinals. |
| | 2. In many Reformed Churches, a governing body of the Church, usually formed by the elders. |
| Contrafactum/ Contrafacta | Creative process whereby an existing vocal piece is given a new text. |
| Cori spezzati | Compositional technique whereby a vocal ensemble is "broken" (*spezzato*, in Italian) into multiple choirs, originating → polychorality. |
| Cornett | Wind instrument, often played in combination with → sagbuts. |
| Council | Ecclesiastical gathering; in the Catholic Church, may be an Ecumenical Council (i.e. involving the entire Church), convoked by the Pope with the aim of defining doctrinal aspects (→ dogma). May also indicate local gatherings, for which the appropriate name should rather be → synod (but the distinction is rather recent and not binding). |
| Counterpoint/ Contrapuntal | Compositional process whereby melodies are combined, in order to be sung and heard together, and following precise rules. |
| Creed | The → dogmas held as true by a Church; in most cases, are contained in the two *symbols of faith* (Apostolic and Nicene), whose Latin form takes its name, "Credo", from its first word ("I believe"). |

| | |
|---|---|
| Deacon | An ordained minister of the Catholic Church (frequently a man preparing for → priesthood); other Churches have deacons, the terms of whose ministry depend on the → confession. |
| Devotio moderna | Spiritual movement of the late Middle Ages (fourteenth- to sixteenth century) aiming at the Church's renewal through that of its individual members. Flourished especially in north-western Europe, and was influenced by the *Imitation of Christ*. |
| Diminution | For the purpose of this book, may indicate:<br>1. the process opposite of → augmentation (i.e. the proportional reduction of rhythmic values, or durations, in a melody);<br>2. the process whereby the time between two or more notes is "filled in" with shorter notes, which may be improvised. |
| Doge | From the Latin "*dux*", leader: the elected leader of the Republic of Venice. |
| Dogma | A doctrine held to be true by a Church, and whose belief constitutes an indisputable element of what it means to be a member of that Church. |
| Dominican | Refers to St Dominic of Guzman (1170–1221), founder of the Order of Preachers (OP), an order of friars whose peculiar charisma is to study and to preach. Thomas Aquinas was a Dominican. |
| Dowry | Money and/or valuables which used to be brought by brides into their new families, and also by girls entering religious life to their convent. When this habit had become a request, it might be waivered for special reasons, such as the girl's musical abilities which were deemed to be adequate replacements for the economic value of the dowry. |
| Doxology | Form of liturgical praise; the "greater doxology" is the *Gloria* in the → Mass Ordinary, the "lesser doxology" is recited at the end of psalms and canticles in the → Office. |
| Ecclesiology | The theological discipline which focuses on the Church. |
| Elevation | The act whereby a Catholic priest lifts up the host, immediately after its consecration, and offers it to the congregation's gaze. |
| Enclosure | The condition of some religious institutes (and of nearly all the female convents, at certain points of the history of the Church), whereby the nuns or monks live in spaces clearly separated from those that seculars can access. |
| Episcopal | Adjective referring to the bishop. |
| Eschatology | In theology, a discourse which refers to the end of the present world and the establishment of Christ's kingdom. |
| Eucharist | Literally, thanksgiving. May refer (but is not limited) to the celebration of the Catholic Mass, and particularly to the consecration and distribution of the bread and wine. |
| Excommunication | An act by which an individual or a group of individuals is excluded from → communion with his/her/their Church. May be used as a disciplinary measure in Church matters. |
| Exegesis | Interpretation, with particular reference to the interpretation of the Bible, both as concerns its historical/critical aspects and its theological content. |

| | |
|---|---|
| Faburden | Not to be confused with → fauxbourdon or → falsobordone. Faburden is a musical technique whereby a "treble" parallels the → *cantus firmus* singing a fourth above it, whereas the "faburden" proper sings below the *cantus firmus* at intervals of fifth and third. |
| Falsobordone | Not to be confused with → faburden and → fauxbourdon; it is a style of simple chordal harmonisation used for → psalmody. |
| Fauxbourdon | Not to be confused with → faburden or → falsobordone. Fauxbourdon is a technique of improvised polyphony, whereby the → *cantus firmus* is paralleled by a second voice, singing a fourth below, while a third part, often composed, sings above the *cantus firmus*. |
| Figural/Figuraliter | In contrast with → choraliter, sung in polyphony. |
| Free will | Doctrine according to which human beings are given the faculty of choosing between good and evil. It is affirmed by the Catholic Church, which maintains that this faculty is hindered, but not abolished, by the → original sin; it formed the object of a harsh controversy between Luther and Erasmus. |
| Geisslerlieder | Songs of the penitent (i.e. self-disciplining) German confraternities. |
| Gradual | Element of the *Proprium Missæ*, sung before the Gospel reading, accompanying the deacon's or priest's ascent to the ambo (thus *gradual* from *gradus*, Latin for step). |
| Graduale/Gradual | Liturgical book which contains, among others, the → graduals, but also the other sung elements of the Mass according to the liturgical year. It omits the spoken section which are found in the → Missal. |
| Gregorian | 1. Referring to St Gregory the Great (c.540–604), who disposed a reform of the liturgical plainchant. In consequence, that Latin-texted repertory is called – albeit improperly – "Gregorian".<br>2. Referring to Pope Gregory XIII (1502–1585), who introduced a calendar reform in 1582, aiming at correcting the errors caused by the use of the Julian calendar. |
| Harmony | In musical theory, the discipline which studies the sequences of chords. |
| Hausandacht | German for "house worship", i.e. the family prayers fostered by the Lutheran spirituality. |
| Hebdomadarius | In a religious community, the person in charge of presiding the → Office during a week. |
| Heresy | Doctrine held to be false or erroneous by a Church. |
| Heterodox | Contrary of → orthodox; something other ("etéra") than the right ("orthè") belief ("dòxa"). |
| Homiletics | Discipline studying how homilies should be created and delivered. |
| Homophony | Compositional technique whereby all parts sing or play with the same rhythm, i.e. simultaneously. |
| Huguenot | A word whose origin is still being debated, indicating the French-speaking Reformed Calvinists. |
| Humanism | Philosophical and cultural current, originating in the fifteenth century, which focused on human beings, on their abilities, on their education, and which valued the (re)discovery of ancient sources. In southern Europe, it took a more "secular" form (e.g. with the study of Greek |

| | |
|---|---|
| | and Roman culture), whereas in northern Europe it was more distinctly religious. In later centuries, the term assumed other meanings. |
| Hussite | Referring to Jan Hus (c.1349–1415), who gathered many followers which later coalesced around two competing currents: the Bohemian Brethren (or Hussites proper), who separated from the Catholic Church, and the Utraquist Church, which reunited with Catholicism. |
| Hymn | A poetic prayer, not directly taken from Scripture but of free composition; may indicate an item of the Catholic Office, but also the Lutheran → Lied. |
| Iamb/Iambic | Metrical foot of the Greek and Latin prosody, constituted by a short and a long syllable. |
| Iconoclasm | Refers to thoughts and acts aiming at the suppression or destruction of religious imagery (and sometimes of all imagery), in the belief that the veneration for sacred images is a form of idolatry. Condemned by the Church at the Council of Nicaea (787), but has periodically resurfaced in the history of the Church. |
| Idolatry | Act whereby the worship which ought to be given to God only is given instead to a creature, to an inanimate object, or to a product of imagination. |
| Idolothites | Meat that had been sacrificed to idols, and that therefore pious Jews were not allowed to eat. St Paul discusses it in 1 Corinthians 8:1 and 10:23: though Christians are freed from the requirements of Jewish Law, and therefore could eat that meat without sinning, they may choose not to eat it out of regard for those who would be scandalised or offended. This doctrine is applied to the discussion of → adiaphora. |
| Imitation | Compositional element, whereby a (in most cases melodic) fragment heard in a voice is later quoted, in an identical or modified form, in another voice. The strictest form of imitation is the → canon. |
| Imitation Mass | Or Parody Mass: compositional technique whereby the musical material for a → Mass composition is taken from an entire pre-existing polyphonic work. |
| Incarnation | In theology, the doctrine referring to the "becoming flesh" (i.e. a human being) of the divine Son of God, the eternal Logos. |
| Incipit | Latin for "beginning". |
| Indulgence | In traditional Catholic teaching, the possibility of shortening the time of a soul's purification in → Purgatory through prayers or good deeds. The scandal which arose when indulgences were sold was one of the crucial elements which propelled Luther's Reformation. |
| Introit | Element of the *Proprium Missæ*, sung as the priest(s) enter the presbytery in order to begin the Mass. |
| Jesuit | Refers to the religious family and spirituality inspired by the teachings of St Ignatius Loyola (1491–1556) [therefore also "Ignatian"], founder of the "Society of Jesus" (in Latin, "Societas Jesu", hence the abbreviation SJ), whose members are commonly known as Jesuits. |
| Justification | The process by which God makes a sinner "just", i.e. holy. For Luther, it depends on the sinner's faith (*sola fide*) and on God's Grace (*sola* |

|   |   |
|---|---|
| | *gratia*), but not on the human capability of "earning" that Grace through "merits". |
| Kanzeldienst | German for "pulpit service", i.e. a form of worship in the German vernacular which took place on Sunday morning in between the two main services. |
| Kapellmeister | → Chapel Master. |
| Kerygma | Greek for "preaching"; used to indicate the basic kernel of the Christian faith. |
| Kyrie | Greek for "Lord", in the vocative; may indicate the "Kyrie eleison" ("Lord, have mercy"), an element of the *Ordinarium Missæ* whereby God's forgiveness is invoked. |
| Lehre | German for "doctrine"; may indicate the content of faith. |
| Leise/Leisen | Originating from a contraption and deformation of "Kyrie eleison" (→ Kyrie), used as a refrain or concluding invocation in many devotional songs in the German vernacular ("Kyrioleis" and then "leis"), came to indicate such songs. |
| Lied/Lieder | German for "song". |
| Litany | A → responsorial (or, on some occasions, → antiphonal) form of prayer, whereby a soloist (or a first choir) proposes a number of different appellations (e.g. devotional titles applied to the Virgin Mary, or invocations to a series of saints etc.), and is answered by the congregation with an unvarying response (e.g. "pray for us", or "have mercy on us" when addressed to God or to the Lord). |
| Lollard/Lollardy | Religious movement inspired by the teachings of John Wycliffe (c.1331–1384), and considered to be among the forerunners of the Protestant Reformation. |
| Madrigal | Genre of vocal music, mostly in the vernacular and frequently with a secular text (but exceptions are possible in both cases), originating in Italy. Has no fixed form but depends on that of the chosen lyrics. |
| Maestro di cappella | → Chapel Master. |
| Magisterium | 1. In the Catholic Church: the pronouncements of Popes and Council which progressively define the → dogma, i.e. what Catholics hold as a fundamental truth.<br>2. The Magisterial Reformation indicates the process whereby the early Protestantism defined its relation with secular power (magistrates). |
| Mass | May indicate the act of worship which is the principal liturgical form of the Catholic Church, but also (in music) the five items of the → Mass Ordinary, whose composition and collection constitutes a "Mass". |
| Mass Ordinary | Five items with (normally) fixed text in the Catholic Mass: *Kyrie*, *Gloria*, *Credo*, *Sanctus/Benedictus* and *Agnus Dei*. Textual variants are mostly constituted by → tropes, but tended to be reduced with time (but *Kyrie* tropes are still in use). *Gloria* and *Credo* are recited/sung only on feast-days, and *Gloria* is omitted in Advent and Lent. |

| | |
|---|---|
| Matins | Morning prayer in the Office of the Hours (a term used by several Evangelical Churches as well as by Catholics, who may also speak of "Lauds"). |
| Meistersinger | German poets/musicians of the 14th-16th century, who developed and codified the earlier tradition of the Minnesinger, turning it from a courtly discipline to a bourgeois and urban form of creativity. |
| Melisma/melismatic | Compositional element whereby several notes are sung on a single syllable. |
| Mensural | System of organisation and notation of note-values (durations) in polyphonic music. |
| Metrical prosody | Form of organisation of the verbal elements in poetry, whereby the succession of long and short syllables is ruled and codified. |
| Minorite | "Friars Minor": a friar or friars who follow the rule of St Francis of Assisi (c.1881–1226); other friars who follow the same rule are the Capuchins and the Conventuals. |
| Missal | Liturgical book which contains the prayers which have to be recited or sung by the Catholic priest who intends to celebrate a valid Mass. |
| Mode/Modes | Forms of organisation of the melodic intervals (in most cases tones and semitones) within the octave. Greek modal theory associated the different *tones* with an *ethos*, a moral character. Greek names were later superimposed onto the modes of Western → plainchant, which are musically entirely different from their Greek eponyms. The modern tonal system is basically grounded on the major and minor mode. |
| Monody | Contrary of → polyphony: a single melodic line. |
| Motet | Genre comprising, in the vast majority of the cases, Latin-texted sacred polyphonic music. Lyrics may come from Scriptural fragments, from → Proper elements (of the *Proprium Missæ* or of the Office), but also be free devotional poetry; neither its text nor the collocation of its performance within the framework of liturgy are fixed. |
| Nicene | Refers to the theology and pronouncements originating in Nicaea and in the Councils which took place there. |
| Notational | Referring to how music is written (notated). |
| Office (of the Hours) | Also "Liturgy of the Hours": Mass and Office constitute the two main liturgical forms of the Catholic Church. The Office is articulated into several moments throughout the day (and part of the night), the most important of which are Lauds (or → Matins) and → Vespers. It is composed vastly (but not exclusively) by the singing or reciting of Biblical psalms and canticles. |
| Oratory | 1. The rhetorical discipline of creating and delivering a good speech. 2. A (normally) small-sized sacred building, not coincident with a church. 3. Members and sympathisers of the Congregation of the Oratory, a religious family founded by St Filippo Neri (1515–1595) and focusing on lay spirituality. |
| Ordinary | See → Mass Ordinary. |

| | |
|---|---|
| Organ – organum | The organ is a musical instrument which came to be associated with sacred music. The *organum* is a form of early polyphony. |
| Original sin | Catholic doctrine according to which the "original sin" committed by Adam and Eve in their rebellion to God is "passed on", through generation, to all human beings (with the exception of the Virgin Mary and of Jesus). Human beings are freed from it through Baptism and by virtue of Christ's passion, death and resurrection. This doctrine is held by various other confessions, though many admit variants, sometimes very substantial. |
| Orthodox | Contrary of → heterodox, indicates the "right" ("orthè") belief ("dòxa"), i.e. a doctrine which corresponds to the → dogma held as true by a Church. It is thus possible to speak of "Lutheran orthodoxy" or "Catholic orthodoxy", referring to the beliefs held, respectively, by the official Lutheran or Catholic Church.<br><br>Not to be confused with the Orthodox Church, which actually comprises various rites and confessions, originally typical of Eastern Europe (after the schism of 1054). |
| Parlatory | Zone of the convents and monasteries where the religious people can meet with the seculars or those not belonging to the religious community. |
| Parody Mass | → Imitation Mass. |
| Partbook | In contrast with → choirbook, a book of music which contains the single parts of a polyphonic composition. |
| Pastor | The spiritual guide of many Protestant Churches, as distinguished from the sacramental → priesthood of the Catholics. |
| Patristic | Refers to the era or to the teachings of the → Church Fathers. |
| Pietism/Pietist | Spiritual current of Lutheranism, focused on individual piety, devotion and the downplaying of Christ's divine nature in favour of his humanity. |
| Plainchant | From the Latin *cantus planus*, the → monodic form of sung liturgical prayer. Does not coincide with → Gregorian: Gregorian plainchant is a form, albeit one of the most important, of plainchant. |
| Polychorality | Compositional technique whereby two or more choral ensembles (choirs) are musically contrasted with each other (e.g. singing in alternation, and/or placed at different points of space). |
| Polyphony | Contrary of → monody: the compresence of two or more melodic lines. |
| Pope | The bishop of Rome; for Catholics, the successor of St Peter and the earthly vicar of Christ. Is elected by and (normally) among the → Cardinals; the institution represented by the Pope and his actions is the "papacy". The leading role of the Pope among the → bishops, who are considered to be the successors of the Apostles, is justified on the basis of the doctrine of the "primacy of Peter", i.e. the pastoral ministry conferred by Christ to Peter. During the Reformation era, this role was contested by the Evangelicals; thus, the adjective "popish" started to be derogatorily applied to Catholic (or Catholic-looking) things and habits, whereas Catholics could be indicated as "papists". |

| | |
|---|---|
| Predestination | Doctrine according to which human beings are "predestined" by God for salvation or damnation; in its most radical formulation, it implies that human acts and thoughts are a consequence of God's original choice about them, and do not influence it. |
| Prelate | An high-ranked member of the clergy. |
| Presbyterian | A type of Church which is governed by a college of "elders" (from the Greek *presbyteros*, elder). |
| Priesthood | 1. Universal: Christians maintain that Baptism bestows upon a person receiving it a "priestly" dignity; thus the Church can be defined as a "kingdom of priests". <br> 2. Ministerial/Ordained: for Catholics, some among the Baptised are called to "ministerial" or "ordained" priesthood, which is conferred through a sacrament and enables the priest to act *"in figura Christi"* (for example celebrating Mass or absolving penitents in the sacrament of penance). |
| Prior/Prioress | The leader of some religious communities (others have abbots/abbesses, "fathers" or "mothers", "superiors" in general). |
| Proper | A liturgical item whose text is not the same for all worships but varies depending on the liturgical year and feasts. It comprises, but is not limited to, the *Proprium Missæ*, consisting of *Introit, Gradual, Alleluia* or *Tract, Sequence, Offertory* and *Communion*; psalm antiphons are other examples of proper items. |
| Psalmody | The act of singing or reciting psalms and canticles. Practised by the Church following pre-Christian (Jewish) rituals, constitutes the root of the → Office. Sung in unaccompanied → monody, represented the only form of official worship envisaged by Calvin for his Church. |
| Psalter | The collection of the 150 Biblical Psalms, found in the Book of Psalms. Not to be confused with the psaltery, a musical instrument. |
| Purgatory | In traditional Catholic teaching, a state in which a soul is purified from his/her sins before entering its ultimate state of bliss ("heaven" or "paradise"). Purgatory is typical for the souls of those who are "saved" (in contrast to the "damned"). |
| Puritan | A current of the English Protestantism: the term was originally derogatory, indicating the "godly" who opposed the maintenance of "popish" practices in the Evangelical Church of England. |
| Recto tono | The singing/reciting style whereby longish portions of liturgy are read and intoned on a single pitch. |
| Recusant | Within the framework of the Anglican Reformation, indicates a person who maintained his or her Catholic beliefs and refused to pledge allegiance to the Church of England and to attend its services. |
| Regular | As opposed to secular: a person following a religious rule (*regula*), i.e. belonging in a religious order. Thus, there can be "regular" and "secular" clergy. |
| Responsorial | In contrast with → antiphonal, a form of psalmodic recitation or singing whereby a soloist is answered by a choir or congregation. |
| Sagbut/Sackbut | Wind instrument resembling the modern trombone. |

| | |
|---|---|
| Schism | The division between two branches of the Church, which are no more in → communion with each other. |
| Septuagint | A very influential translation of the Hebrew Bible into Greek, traditionally attributed to "seventy" (*septuaginta*) experts. |
| Sequence | Element of the *Proprium Missæ*, is constituted by sung poetry, normally not directly taken from Scriptural sources. In the late Middle Ages, the number of Sequences increased dramatically, until just a few of them were officially adopted in the Catholic worship. Several of them were reworked by Luther as vernacular → Lieder for his Church. |
| Serenissima | Appellation applied to the "Serenissima [i.e. "most serene"] Repubblica di Venezia", the Republic of Venice. |
| Simony | The act of exchanging spiritual values or benefits for material gain. |
| *Sola fide* | One of the pillars of Lutheran theology: God's → justification of sinners requires from humans *faith only* (*sola fide*) as the necessary and sufficient condition. |
| *Sola gratia* | Another of the pillars of Lutheran theology: God justifies human beings by his Grace alone (*sola gratia*), and salvation cannot be "earned" by good works. |
| *Sola scriptura* | Another of the pillars of Lutheran theology: against the Catholic concept of → Magisterium as the authoritative form of Biblical → exegesis, for Luther the Bible could and should be interpreted freely (i.e. under the guide of the Holy Spirit, but not of Magisterium) by all Christians. |
| Soteriology | In theology, the discipline studying how humans are saved by God in Christ. |
| Stollen | One of the two "A" elements of the "AAB" form called *Barform* in the German sung poetry. Two *Stollen* make an *Aufgesang*. |
| Syllabic style | Compositional style whereby there is one-to-one correspondence between syllables and notes; as opposed to → melismatic. |
| Synod | A gathering of members of the Church (principally bishops), normally with the aim of defining important matters of faith or discipline. Properly, it indicates gatherings of a more local character in contrast with Ecumenical → Councils. |
| Tablature | Form of musical notation indicating conventionally the finger positions to be adopted instead of the pitches as in the form of notation most common today. |
| Tenebrae | A liturgy typical for Holy Week (i.e. the days preceding Easter), during which lights were progressively extinguished, thus creating darkness (*tenebra*, in Latin) in the Church. |
| Tenorlied | As opposed to → cantional, a sung form where the → cantus firmus, or given melody, is found at the tenor. |
| Theocracy | A form of civic/national government which depends on or is strictly connected with religious authorities or institutions. |
| Transubstantiation | Catholic doctrine whereby the consecration (→ Canon) changes the *substance* of bread and wine, while maintaining their outward appearance (*form*), and makes them the Body and Blood of Christ. |

| | |
|---|---|
| Tricinium/Tricinia | Polyphonic genre for three parts. |
| Trinity | One of the basic tenets of the Christian faith: God is One in Three divine Persons (Father, Son and Holy Ghost/Spirit), equal but distinct. |
| Trochee/Trochaic | A foot of metrical prosody, constituted by a long and a short syllable. |
| Trope | Insertion of newly composed text and music within a pre-existing plainchant. |
| Trost | German for "consolation"; one of the fruits of music (and of sung prayer) actively sought by Luther. |
| Typological reading | In theology, the practice of interpreting facts or texts from an earlier time in the light of the Christian Revelation. Thus, Adam can be seen as a "type" of Christ, or statements historically referring to the King David as alluding to Jesus. |
| Unison/unisonance | The musical circumstance whereby two or more people play or sing exactly the same notes at the same time. |
| Vespers | Together with Lauds (or → Matins), one of the two most important Hours of the → Office. It is sung or prayed in the late afternoon. |
| Vulgate | The translation of the Bible into Latin realised mainly by St Jerome (347–420). For centuries, constituted the authoritative Bible translation (and was officially declared to be the official Latin Bible of the Catholic Church at the Council of Trent). |
| Waldensian | Refers to the followers of Peter Waldo (c.1140-c.1205), who separated from the Catholic Church in the thirteenth century and later adhered to the Protestant Reformation. |
| Word-painting | Compositional strategy by which individual words or short idiomatical expressions are mimicked in music: for example, quick notes on words speaking of "running", "speed" etc., or dissonant harmonies on words expressing pain etc. |

# Bibliography

## Primary

All web links were last accessed on August 25th, 2016.

**A BURCK 1568**
Joachim a Burck, *Die deutsche Passion. Das ist die Historia des Leidens unsers Hernn Jhesu Christi [...]* (Wittenberg: Johann Schwertel, 1568) [RISM A/I: B 4957]; available online at http://bit.ly/2be0Rte.

**A BURCK 1572**
Joachim a Burck, *XX. Odæ sacræ Ludovici Helmboldi Mulhusini* (Erfurt: Georg Baumann, 1572) [RISM A/I: B 4961].

**A JESU 1613**
Thomas à Jesu, *De procuranda salute omnium gentium* (Antwerp: P. Bellerus, 1613).

**AARON 1516 / AARON 1978A**
Pietro Aaron, *Libri tres de institutione harmonica* (Bologna: In ædibus Benedicti Hectoris, 1516); reprint (New York NY: Broude Brothers, 1978).

**AARON 1545 / AARON 1978B**
Pietro Aaron, *Lucidario in musica di alcune oppenioni antiche, et moderne* (Venice: Girolamo Scotto, 1545) [USTC 811115]; reprint (New York NY: Broude Brothers, 1978).

**ACTA 1595**
*Acta et Constitutiones Sinodi Dioecesanae, quae fuit celebrata Wratislaviæ in Insula S. Ioannis, Anno 1592 [...]* (Nysa: Andreas Reinheckel, 1595) [USTC 243086]; available online at http://bit.ly/2bHWbd7.

**AEM 1**
*Acta Ecclesiæ Mediolanensis [...]*, vol. 1 (Padua: Typis Seminarii, 1754); available online at http://bit.ly/2clViwu.

**AGAZZARI 1607 / AGAZZARI 1933**
Agostino Agazzari, *Del sonare sopra il basso con tutti gli strumenti* (Siena: Domenico Falcini, 1607); facsimile edition (Milan: Bollettino Bibliografico Musicale, 1933).

**AGOSTINI 1595**
Agostino Agostini, *I sette salmi penitentiali imitati in Rima [...]* (Antwerp: Girolamo Porro, 1595) [USTC 806921].

**AGRIPPA 1530**
Heinrich Cornelius Agrippa von Nettesheim, *De incertitudine et vanitate scientiarum [...]* (Antwerp: Joannes Grapheus, 1530) [USTC 403838].

**ALBER 1556**
Erasmus Alber, *Widder die verfluchte lere der Carlstadter [...]* (Neubrandenburg: Anton Brenner & Walter Brenner, 1556) [USTC 706521]; available online at http://bit.ly/2c4lzwG.

**ALEOTTI 1593A**
Raffaella Aleotti, *Sacræ cantiones quinque, septem, octo et decem vocibus decantandæ [...]* (Venice: Riccardo Amadino, 1593) [USTC 808490] [RISM A/I: A 821].

ALEOTTI 1593B / ALEOTTI 1986
Vittoria Aleotti, *Ghirlanda de madrigali a quatro voci di Vittoria Aleotti* (Venice: Appresso Giacomo Vincenzi, 1593) [USTC 808491] [RISM A/I: A 822]; modern edition by Giuliana Gialdroni as *Vittoria Aleotti: Cinque Madrigali a 4 voci miste* (Rome: Pro Musica Studium, 1986).

ALISON 1599
Richard Alison, *The Psalmes of David in meter [...]* (London: Barley, 1599) [USTC 517535].

AN EXHORTACION 1544
*An exhortacion vnto praier thought mete by the kynges maiestie [...]* (London: Richarde Grafton for Thomas Barthelet, 1544) [USTC 503511]; available online at http://bit.ly/2cE3HXV.

ANE COMPENDIOUS 1565 / ANE COMPENDIOUS 1621
*Ane Compendious Booke of Godly and Spirituall Songs [...]* (Edinburgh: J. Scot [?], 1565) [USTC 516647]; (Edinburgh: Andro Hart, 1621) [STC 2181.02].

ANIMUCCIA 1563
Giovanni Animuccia, *Il primo libro delle laudi di Giovanni Animuccia, composte per consolatione a requisitione di molte persone, spirituali et devote, tanto religiosi quanto secolari* (Rome: Valerio Dorico, 1563) [USTC 809555] [RISM A/I: A 1235].

ANIMUCCIA 1567
Giovanni Animuccia, *Missarum liber primus* (Rome: Apud Haer. Valerio & Luigi Dorico, 1567) [USTC 809550] [RISM A/I: A 1236].

ANIMUCCIA 1570
Giovanni Animuccia, *Il secondo libro delle laudi [...]* (Rome: Eredi di Antonio Blado, 1570) [RISM A 1238] [USTC 809557].

AQUINAS 1952
Thomas Aquinas, *Questiones Disputatæ de Veritate*; English translation by Robert W. Mulligan, James V. McGlynn and Robert W. Schmidt as *Truth* (Chicago: Henry Regnery Company 1952–4); text available online at http://dhspriory.org/thomas/QDdeVer.htm.

ARETINO 1864
Pietro Aretino, *Il Primo Libro delle lettere di Pietro Aretino* (Milan: G. Daelli e c. Editori, 1864); available online at http://bit.ly/2cjDzUa.

ARISTOTLE 1885
Aristotle, *The Politics of Aristotle [...]*, English translation by Benjamin Jowett (Oxford: Clarendon Press, 1885).

ARISTOTLE 1943
Aristotle, *Generation of animals*, English translation by Arthur L. Peck (Cambridge MA: Harvard University Press; London: William Heinemann, 1943); available online at http://bit.ly/2bLPUxr.

ARTUSI 1600
Giovanni Maria Artusi, *L'Artusi overo delle imperfettioni della moderna musica [...]* (Venice: Giacomo Vincenzi, 1600) [USTC 811208].

ASCHAM 1545 / ASCHAM 1571
Roger Ascham, *Toxophilus, the Schole of Shootinge [...]* (London: in aedibus Edward Whitchurch, 1545) [USTC 503581]; (London: Thomas Marshe, 1571) [USTC 507248].

**ASCHAM 1570 / ASCHAM 1863 / ASCHAM 1967**
Roger Ascham, *The Scholemaster or Plaine and Perfite Way of Teachyng Children [...]*
(London: John Daye, 1570) [USTC 507056]; edited by John E. B. Mayor (London: Bell and Daldy, 1863); reprint (New York NY: AMS Press, 1967).

**ASOLA 1571**
Giovanni Matteo Asola, *Le vergini a tre voci di Giovanni Matteo Asola veronese. Libro primo* (Venice: Haer. Antonio Gardano, 1571) [USTC 811247] [RISM A/I: A 2610].

**AUGUSTINE 1960**
St Augustine of Hippo, *St Augustine on the Psalms*, edited and translated by Scholastica Hebgin and Felicitas Corrigan (New York, NY, and Mahwah NJ: Paulist Press, 1960).

**BACCI 1622**
Pietro Giacomo Bacci, *Vita del B. Filippo Neri Fiorentino, Fondatore della Congregazione dell'Oratorio [...]* (Rome: Andrea Brugiotti, 1622).

**BALBI 1587**
Ludovico Balbi (ed.), *Graduale et Antiphonarium omnium dierum festorum Ordinis minorum [...]* (Venice: Apud Angelo Gardano, 1587) [USTC 830589].

**BANCHIERI 1628 / BANCHIERI 1968**
Adriano Banchieri, *Lettere armoniche del R. P. D. Adriano Banchieri Bolognese abbate Olivetano, et Academico Dissonante [...]* (Bologna: Per Girolamo Mascheroni, 1628); available online at http://bit.ly/2bAX9eD; facsimile edition (Sala Bolognese: Arnaldo Forni, 1968).

**BARTOLI 1567**
Cosimo Bartoli, *Ragionamenti Accademici di Cosimo Bartoli Gentil'huomo et Accademico Fiorentino, sopra alcuni luoghi difficili di Dante [...]* (Venice: Francesco de Franceschi, 1567) [USTC 812413].

**BASCAPÈ 1592**
Carlo Bascapè, *De Vita et rebus gestis Caroli S. R. E. Cardinalis [...]* (Ingolstadt: Ex Officina Typographica Davidis Sartorii, 1592) [USTC 628861]; available online at http://bit.ly/2bzXAWy.

**BATTIFERRI 1564**
Laura Battiferri degli Ammannati, *I sette salmi penitentiali del santissimo profeta Davit* (Florence: appresso haer. Bernardo Giunta, 1564) [USTC 804314].

**BDS 1**
*Martin Bucers Deutsche Schriften 1: Frühschriften 1520–1524*, edited by Robert Stuppenrich, Johannes Müller, Ortwin Rudloff and Herbert Demmer (Gütersloh: Gütersloher Verlagshaus, 1960).

**BDS 6/3**
*Martin Bucers Deutsche Schriften 6/3: Martin Bucers Katechismen aus den Jahren 1534, 1537, 1543*, edited by Marijn de Kroon and Hartmut Rudolph (Gütersloh: Gütersloher Verlagshaus, 1987).

**BDS 7**
*Martin Bucers Deutsche Schriften 7: Schriften der Jahre 1538–1539*, edited by Walter Delius, Hannelore Jahr, Ernst-Wilhelm Kohls and Herbert Demmer (Gütersloh: Gütersloher Verlagshaus, 1964).

BECCADELLI 1797 / BECCADELLI 1804
Ludovico Beccadelli, *Monumenti di varia letteratura tratti dai manoscritti di Monsignor Lodovico Beccadelli arcivescovo di Ragusa*, edited by G. Morandi, 2 vols. (Bologna: Stampe di S. Tommaso d'Aquino, 1797 and 1804).

BECKER 1602
Cornelius Becker, *Psalter Davids Gesangweis [...]* (Leipzig: [s.n.], 1602) [WB 1060].

BECON 1542
Thomas Becon, *Davids Harpe ful of moost delectable armony [...]* (London: John Mayler for John Gough, 1542) [USTC 503300].

BECON 1844
Thomas Becon,*The Catechism of Thomas Becon: With other pieces written by him in the reign of King Edward the sixth*, edited by John Ayre (Cambridge: Cambridge University Press, 1844).

BEDE 1853
Bede the Venerable, *The Historical Works of the Venerable Bede*, edited and translated by J. Stevenson (London: Seeleys 1853).

BELLARMINO 1599 / BELLARMINO 2013
Roberto Bellarmino, "De Verbo Dei Scripto et Non Scripto", in *Disputationes Roberti Bellarmini e Societate Iesu, De Controversiis Christianæ Fidei, Adversus huius temporis Hæreticos [...]* (Ingolstadt: Ex Typographia Adami Sartorii, 1599); available online at http://bit.ly/2bbM5p6; English translation by Peter L. P. Simpson as *Robert Bellarmine's Disputations about Controversies of the Christian Faith* (June 2013); available online at http://bit.ly/2bg4Epl.

BERMUDO 1555
Juan Bermudo, *Comiença el libro llamado de declaraciõ de instrumẽtos musicales [...]* (Osuna: Juan de Leon, 1555); available online at http://bit.ly/2bwYBMI.

BIANCHI 1590
Filippo Bianchi, *Trattato degli huomini illustri di Bologna* (Ferrara: Vittorio Baldini, 1590).

BODENSTEIN 1905
Andreas Bodenstein von Karlstadt, "De Cantu Gregoriano Disputatio", in Hermann Barge, *Andreas Bodenstein von Karlstadt. I. Teil: Karlstadt und die Anfänge der Reformation* (Leipzig: Friedrich Brandstetter, 1905).

BOETHIUS 1867 / BOETHIUS 1989
Anicius Manlius Severinus Boethius, *Anicii Manlii Torquati Severini Boetii De institutione arithmetica libri duo, De institutione musica libri quinque [...]*, edited by Gottfried Friedlein (Leipzig: Aedibus B. G. Teubner 1867); partial English translation by Calvin M. Bower as *Fundamentals of Music*, edited by Claude V. Palisca (New Haven CT: Yale University Press, 1989).

BOLLAND AND HENSCHEN 1658
Jean Bolland and Godefroy Henschen, *Acta Sanctorum quotquot toto orbe coluntur [...] Prodit nunc tribus Tomis Februarius [...]* (Antwerp: Apud Jacobum Meursium, 1658).

BONA 1611
Vincenzo Bona, *Li dilettevoli Introiti della messa a doi chori [...] opera XVIII* (Venice: Giacomo Vincenti, 1611) [RISM A/I: B 3432].

BONAGIUNTA 1566
Giulio Bonagiunta (ed.), *Il Desiderio. Secondo libro de madrigali a cinque voci, de diversi auttori [...]* (Venice: [Aniello Sanvito] appresso Girolamo Scotto, 1566) [USTC 816026].

BORROMEO 1628
Federico Borromeo, *De linguis, nominibus, et numero angelorum libri tres* (Milan: Giorgio Rolla, 1628).

BORSIERI 1619
Girolamo Borsieri, *Il supplimento della nobiltà di Milano* (Milan: Giovanni Battista Bidelli, 1619).

BOSKOOP 1568
Cornelis Boskoop [Boscoop], *Psalmen David Vyfftich mit vier partyen seer suet ende lustich [...]* (Düsseldorf: Albert Buyss, 1568) [USTC 552017] [RISM A/I: B 3791].

BOSSEWELL 1572
John Bossewell, *Workes of armorie deuyded into three books [...]* (London: Richard Totell, 1572) [USTC 507409].

BOTTRIGARI 1599 / BOTTRIGARI 1962
Hercole Bottrigari, *Il Desiderio, overo de' concerti di varij strumenti musicali* (Bologna: Gioambattista Bellagamba, 1599) [USTC 816617]; English translation by Carol MacClintock as *Il Desiderio. Or, Concerning the Playing Together of Various Musical Instruments* ([Dallas TX]: American Institute of Musicology, 1962).

BOUDEWIJNS 1587
Katherina Boudewijns, *Het prieelken der gheestelyker wellusten [...]* (Bruxelles: Rutgerus Velpius, 1587) [USTC 402134].

BOURGEOIS 1547
Loys Bourgeois, *Cinquante Pseaulmes de David [...] à voix de contrepoint égal consonnante au verbe* (Lyon: Beringen Fres, 1547) [RISM A/I: B 3815].

BOURGEOIS 1550 / BOURGEOIS 1954
Loys Bourgeois, *Le Droict Chemin de Musique* (Geneva: [Jean Girard], 1550) [USTC 9576]; facsimile edition by André Gaillard (Kassel: Bärenreiter, 1954).

BOWNDE 1595
Nicholas Bownde, *The doctrine of the sabbath plainely layde forth [...]* (London: Porter and Man, 1595) [USTC 512751].

BRAY 1994 / BRAY 2004
Gerald Bray (ed.), *Documents of the English Reformation 1526–1701* (Cambridge: James Clarke & Co., 1994; 2004).

BREVIARIUM 1568
*Breviarium Romanum, ex decreto Sacrosancti Concilii Tridentini restitutum, Pii V Pont. Max. jussu editum* (Rome: Stamperia del Popolo Romano apud Paolo Manuzio, 1568) [USTC 820614].

BRUTO 1555
Giovanni Michele Bruto, *La institutione di una fanciulla nata nobilmente [...]* (Antwerp: Christophe Plantin chez Jehan Bellère, 1555) [USTC 29835].

BUCER 1524
Martin Bucer, *Grund und Ursach auss gotlicher schrifft der neuwerungen [...]* (Strasbourg: Wolfgang Köpfel, 1524) [USTC 660957].

BUCER 1541 / BUCER 1953
Martin Bucer, "Vorrede", in Id. (ed.), *Gesangbuch: darinn begriffen sind, die aller fürnemisten und besten Psalmen [...]* (Strasbourg: Georg Messerschmidt, 1541) [USTC 659648]; BDS 7; facsimile edition (Stuttgart: Evangelischen Verlagswerk, 1953).

## Buchanan 1566
George Buchanan, *Psalmorum Davidis paraphrasis poetica, nunc primum edita* (Geneva, Paris: Estienne, 1566) [USTC 450546]; available online at http://bit.ly/2b58cdU.

## Bugenhagen 1526 / Bugenhagen 1586 / Bugenhagen 1985
Johannes Bugenhagen, *Die historia des leydens und der Aufferstehung unsers Herrn Jhesu Christi* (Wittenberg: Hans Weiß, 1526) [USTC 636829]; *Historia des lydendes unde upstandige unses Heren Jesu Christi uth den veer Evangelisten* (Barth: Barth Herzogliche Druckerei, 1586) [USTC 663124]; facsimile of the 1586 edition edited by Norbert Buske (Berlin and Altenburg: Evangelische Haupt-Bibelgesellschaft, 1985).

## Bullinger 1852
Heinrich Bullinger, *The Decades of Henry Bullinger: The Fifth Decade*, edited by Thomas Harding (Cambridge: Cambridge University Press, 1852).

## Butler 1636
Charles Butler, *The Principles of Musik, in Singing and Setting [...]* (London: John Haviland, 1636).

## Byrd 1588
William Byrd, *Psalmes, Sonets, & Songs of Sadnes and Pietie* (London: Thomas East, 1588) [USTC 517130] [RISM A/I: B 5209].

## Byrd 1589a
William Byrd, *Songs of Sundrie Natures [...]* (London: Thomas East, 1589) [RSTC 4256] [RISM A/I: B5212].

## Byrd 1589b
William Byrd, *Liber primus sacrarum cantionum quinque vocum. Autore Guilielmo Byrd organista regio, Anglo* (London: Thomas East, 1589) [USTC 511173] [RISM A/I: B 5211]; available online at http://bit.ly/2bl55gN.

## Byrd 1591
William Byrd, *Liber secundus sacrarum cantionum quarum aliæ ad quinque, aliæ verò ad sex voces æditæ sunt Autore Guilielmo Byrd, organista regio, Anglo* (London: Thomas East, 1591) [USTC 511772] [RISM A/I: B 5216].

## Byrd 1605
William Byrd, *Gradualia: ac Cantiones sacræ, quinis, quaternis, trinisque vocibus concinnatæ* (London: Thomas East, 1605) [RISM A/I: B 5217].

## Byrd 1607
William Byrd, *Gradualia: seu cantionum sacrarum quarum aliæ ad quatuor, aliæ vero ad quinque et sex voces editæ sunt, liber secundus* (London: Thomas East, 1607) [RISM A/I: B 5219].

## Byrd 1611
William Byrd, *Psalmes, songs and sonnets: some solemne, other joyfull, framed to the life of the words [...]* (London: Thomas Snodham, 1611) [RISM A/I: B 5221].

## Byrd and Tallis 1575
William Byrd and Thomas Tallis, *Cantiones, quæ ab argumento sacræ vocantur quinque et sex partium [...]* (London: Thomas Vautrollier, 1575) [USTC 508107] [RISM A/I: T 55].

## Cacegas and Sousa 1619
Luis Cacegas and Luis Sousa, *Vida de Dom Frei Bertolameu [...]* (Viama: Niculao Carvalho, 1619).

CÆREMONIALE 1600
Cæremoniale episcoporum iussu Clementis VIII Pont. Max. novissime reformatum [...] (Rome: Tipografia Medicea Orientale, 1600) [USTC 821165].

CALDERWOOD 1843
David Calderwood, *The History of the Kirk of Scotland* (Edinburgh: The Wodrow Society, 1843).

CALVIN 1536 / CALVIN 1975
Jean Calvin, *Christianae religionis institutio [...]* (Basel: Thomas Platter & Balthasar Lasius, 1536) [USTC 621131] [*OC* I; *OS* 1]; edited and translated by Ford L. Battles as *Institution of the Christian Religion* (Atlanta GA: John Knox, 1975).

CALVIN 1541
Jean Calvin, *Les Ordonnances ecclésiastiques de l'Eglise de Genève* (Geneva: Artus Chauvin, 1541) [*OC* X$^1$; *OS* 1]

CALVIN 1542 / CALVIN 1543
Jean Calvin, *La Forme des prieres et chantz ecclesiastiques* (Geneva: Jean Girard, 1542) [USTC 9544]; ([Geneva]: [Jean Girard], 1543) [USTC 40219]; [*OC* VI; *OS* 2].

CALVIN 1559 / CALVIN 1960
Jean Calvin, *Institutio christianæ religionis* (Geneva: Robert Estienne, 1559) [USTC 450088] [*OC* II; *OS* 4]; edited by John T. McNeill and translated by Ford L. Battles as *Calvin: Institutes of the Christian Religion* (Philadelphia PA: Westminster, 1960).

CALVIN 1999A
Jean Calvin, *Commentarius in Genesim* [*OC* XXIII]; English translation by John King as *Commentary on Genesis – Volume 1* (Grand Rapids, MI: Christian Classics Ethereal Library, 1999); available online at http://bit.ly/2bmgnGe.

CALVIN 1999B
Jean Calvin, *Commentarius in lib. Psalmorum. Pars I* (*OC* XXXI); English translation by James Anderson as *Commentary on Psalms – Volume 3* (Grand Rapids, MI: Christian Classics Ethereal Library, 1999); available online at http://bit.ly/2aYr38 g.

CALVISIUS 1594
Seth Calvisius (ed.), *Hymni sacri Latini et Germanici* (Erfurt: Georg Baumann, 1594) [USTC 664518] [RISM A/I: C 257].

CAMPO 1585
Antonio Campo, *Cremona fedelissima città et nobilissima colonia de romani [...]* (Cremona: Ippolito Tromba & Ercoliano Bartoli, 1585) [USTC 818257].

CANISIUS 1905
Petrus Canisius, *Beati Petri Canisii [...] epistulæ et acta*, edited by Otto Braunsberger, vol. IV (Freiburg im Breisgau: Sumptibus Herder, 1905).

CANONES 1564
*Canones et Decreta Sacrosancti œcumenici et generalis Concilii Tridentini* (Venice: Paolo Manuzio, 1564) [USTC 860981].

CANORO 1613
*Canoro pianto di Maria Vergine sopra la faccia di Christo estinto. Poesia del Rever.mo P. Abbate Grillo [...]* (Venice: Aere. Bartholomei Magni, 1613).

CANTIQUE 1562
*Cantique et action de Grace au Seigneur [...]* (Lyon: [Benoît Rigaud], 1562) [Lyon, Bibliothèque Municipale, Rés 373717].

CANTIQUOU 1642 / CANTIQUOU 1997
*Cantiquou spirituel da beza canet er catechismou [...]* (Quimper: Machuel, 1642); edited and translated by Gwennole Le Menn (St. Brieux: Skol, 1997).

CARLERIUS/CARLIER 2001
Egidius Carlerius (Gilles Carlier), "Tractatus de duplici ritu cantu ecclesiastici", in J. Donald Cullington (ed.), *"That liberal and virtuous art": Three Humanist Treatises on Music. Egidius Carlerius, Johannes Tinctoris, Carlo Valgulio* (Newtownabbey: University of Ulster, 2001).

CASE 1588
John Case, *Apologia Musices tam Vocalis Quam Instrumentalis et Mixtae* (Oxford: Joseph Barnes, 1588) [USTC 510927]; text available online at http://bit.ly/2b0bRbm.

CASTIGLIONE 1546 / CASTIGLIONE 1560
Sabba da Castiglione, *Ricordi. Di Sabba di Castiglione* (Bologna: Per Bartolomeo Bonardo, 1546) [USTC 819591]; (Venice: Paolo Gherardo, 1560) [USTC 819599].

CASTIGLIONE 1562 / CASTIGLIONE 1965
Baldassarre Castiglione, *Il Cortigiano del Conte Baldassar Castiglione* (Venice: Appresso Francesco Rampazetto, 1562) [USTC 819526]; modern edition by Giulio Preti as *Il libro del Cortegiano* (Turin: Einaudi, 1965).

CATECHISMUS 1544
*Catechismus Ecclesiæ et Scholæ Argentoratensis* (Argentoratum [=Strasbourg]: Ex Aedibus Vuendelini Rihelij, 1544); available online at http://bit.ly/2bmnCOe.

CAUSTUN 1565
Thomas Caustun (attr.), *Mornyng and evenyng prayer and communion, set forthe in foure partes, to be song in churches, both for men and children wyth dyvers other godly prayers & anthems* (London: John Daye, 1565) [USTC 506334].

CERTAINE NOTES 1565
*Certaine notes set forth in fowre and three [...]* (London: John Daye, 1565) [STC 6418–9].

CG 6
Johann Friedrich Schannat, Joseph Hartzheim (eds.), *Concilia Germaniæ*, volume 6 (Cologne: J. W. Krakamp, 1765); available online at http://bit.ly/2bxApJ1.

CG 7
Johann Friedrich Schannat, Joseph Hartzheim (eds.), *Concilia Germaniæ*, volume 7 (Cologne: J. W. Krakamp, 1767); available online at http://bit.ly/2c3onYS.

CG 8
Johann Friedrich Schannat, Joseph Hartzheim (eds.), *Concilia Germaniæ*, volume 8 (Cologne: J. W. Krakamp, 1769); available online at http://bit.ly/2cODKme.

CHRESTIENNE INSTRUCTION 1551
*Chrestienne Instruction touchant la pompe et excez des homes débordez et femmes dissoluës* (Lyon: [s.n.], 1551) [USTC 95426].

CHRISTELYCKE LEERINGHE 1591
*Die christelycke leeringhe in zoete ende lichte muzijcke met vier partijen* (Brussels: Rutgerus Velpius, 1591) [USTC 402213].

CHRON. 4
Juan Alfonso de Polanco, *Vita Ignatii Loiolæ et rerum Societatis Jesu historia*, tome IV (1554) (Madrid: Augustinus Avrial, 1896).

Chron. 5
Juan Alfonso de Polanco, *Vita Ignatii Loiolæ et rerum Societatis Jesu historia*, tome V (1555) (Madrid: Augustinus Avrial, 1897).
Chron. 6
Juan Alfonso de Polanco, *Vita Ignatii Loiolæ et rerum Societatis Jesu historia*, tome VI (1556) (Madrid: Augustinus Avrial, 1898).
CIC 2
*Corpus Iuris Canonici Gregorii XIII [...] in duos tomos divisum [...]*, vol. 2 (Halle an der Saale: Orphanotropheus, 1747); available online at http://bit.ly/2cGoCwL.
Clarke 1805
James S. Clarke, *Naufragia, or Historical Memoirs of Shipwrecks* (London: Mawman, 1805); available online at http://bit.ly/2b4tJkN.
Clemens 1557
Jacobus Clemens non Papa, *Souterliedenks. IIII. Het sevenste musyck boexken [...]* (Antwerp: Tielman Susato, 1557) [USTC 405999] [RISM A/I: C 2711].
Colebault 1544
Jacques Colebault (Jacquet di Mantova), *Motecta quatuor vocum, nuperime summa diligentia recognita [...] Liber primus* (Venice: Girolamo Scotto, 1544) [USTC 836794] [RISM A/I: J 10].
Colebault 1555
Jacques Colebault (Jacquet di Mantova), *Il secondo libro de le messe a cinque voci. Composte da Jachet de Mantoa [...]* (Venice: Girolamo Scotto, 1555) [USTC 836799].
Colin 1554
Pierre Colin, *Liturgicon musicarum duodecim missarum* (Lyon: Jacques Moderne, 1554) [USTC 124725] [RISM A/I: C 3310].
Collectio Bullarum 1752
*Collectio Bullarum Sacrosanctae Basilicae Vaticanae. Tomus Tertius [...]* (Rome: Giovanni Maria Salvioni, 1752); available online at http://bit.ly/2cgCJVn.
Common Prayer 1549
*The Boke of the Common Prayer and Administracion of the Sacramentes, and other Rites and Ceremonies of the Churches after the Use of the Churches of England* (London: Edward Whitchurch, 1549) [USTC 517825].
Common Prayer 1550
*The Booke of Common Praier Noted* (London: Richard Grafton, 1550) [USTC 504425].
Common Prayer 1552
*The Booke of Common Prayer, and Adminystracion of the Sacramentes, and other Rytes, and ceremonies in the Churche of England* (London: Edward Whitchurch, 1552) [USTC 504757].
Common Prayer 1559
*The Booke of Common Prayer* (London: In Officina Richard Jugge & John Cawood, 1559) [USTC 516581].
Conciliorum 1962 / Conciliorum 1991
*Conciliorum Œcumenicorum Decreta*, edited by J. Alberigo, P. P. Joannou, C. Leonardi, P. Prodi, H. Jedin (Freiburg im Breisgau: Herder, 1962); third bilingual edition (Italian) (Bologna: Edizioni Dehoniane, 1991).

**Conf.**
St Augustine of Hippo, *Confessions*; English translation by J. G. Pilkington, in *Nicene and Post-Nicene Fathers, First Series*, vol. 1. Edited by Philip Schaff (Buffalo NY: Christian Literature Publishing Co., 1887); revised by Kevin Knight, available online at http://www.newadvent.org/fathers/1101.htm; English translation by Albert C. Outler (1955), LoC CCN 55–5021, available online at http://bit.ly/2bLoMmy.

**Constitutiones 1970**
Ignatius Loyola, *The Constitutions of the Society of Jesus*, English translation by George E. Ganss SJ (St Louis MO: Institute of Jesuit Sources, 1970).

**Contzen 1621**
Adam Contzen, *Politicorum libri decem [...]* (Mainz: Johannes Kinckius, 1621).

**Coppini 1607**
Aquilino Coppini (ed.), *Musica tolta da i madrigali di Claudio Monteverde [...]* (Milan: Agostino Tradate, 1607) [RISM A/I: M 3502].

**Coppini 1608**
Aquilino Coppini (ed.), *Il secondo libro della musica di Claudio Monteverdi e d'altri autori a cinque voci fatta spirituale* (Milan: Eredi di A. Tradate, 1608).

**CoR 1**
Aimé-Louis Herminjard (ed.), *Correspondance des Reformateurs dans les pays de langue française [...] Tome Premier 1512–1526* (Geneva: H. Georg, 1866); available online at http://bit.ly/2bzkgHG; reprint (Nieuwkoop: De Graaf, 1965).

**CoR 4**
Aimé-Louis Herminjard (ed.), *Correspondance des Reformateurs dans les pays de langue française [...] Tome Quatrième 1536–1538* (Geneva: H. Georg, 1872); available online at http://bit.ly/2bK1zxe; reprint (Nieuwkoop: De Graaf, 1965).

**Cortesi 1510**
Paolo Cortesi, *De cardinalatu libri tres* (San Gimignano [Castel Cortesiano]: Simone Nardi, 1510).

**Cosyn 1585**
John Cosyn, *Musike of six, and five partes. Made upon the common tunes used in singing of the psalms* (London: John Wolfe, 1585) [USTC 510268] [RISM A/I: C 4252].

**Cotton 1650**
John Cotton, *Singing of Psalmes [:] A Gospel-Ordinance* (London: J. R. and H. A., 1650).

**Coverdale 1535a**
Myles Coverdale, *Goostly Psalmes and Spirituall Songes [...]* (London: John Rastell for John Gough, 1535) [USTC 502754]; available online at http://bit.ly/2c7hSWU.

**Coverdale 1535b**
Myles Coverdale (transl.), *Biblia The Bible, that is, the Holy Scripture of the Olde and New Testament, faithfully and truly translated out of Douche and Latyn in to Englishe* (Köln: E. Cervicornus & J. Soter, 1535) [USTC 502736].

**Coyssard 1592**
Michel Coyssard, *Paraphrase des hymnes et cantiques spirituelz pour chanter aveque la doctrine chrestienne* (Lyon: Jean Pillehotte, 1592) [USTC 74384].

**Coyssard 1608**
Michel Coyssard, *Traicté du profit que toute personne tire de chanter en la Doctrine Chrestienne [...]* (Lyon: Jean Pillehotte, 1608).

CRESOLLIO 1629
Lodovico Cresollio, *Ludovici Cresollii Armorici e Societate Iesu Mystagogus [...]* (Paris: Sumptibus Sebastiani Cramoisy, 1629).
CROWLEY 1549
Robert Crowley, *The Psalter of David newely translated into Englysh metre [...]* (London, Grafton and Mierdman, 1549) [USTC 504213].
CT
*Concilium Tridentinum: Diariorum, actorum, epistularum, tractatuum, nova collectio*, edidit Societas Goerresiana, 13 vols. (Freiburg im Breisgau: Herder, 1901–2001).
DA FANO 1532
Giovanni da Fano, *Opera utilissima vulgare contra le pernitiosissime heresie Lutherane per li simplici* (Bologna: Giovanni Battista Falli & Niccolò Zoppino, 1532) [USTC 833004].
DAMAN 1579
William Daman, *The psalms of David in English meter, with notes of foure partes set unto them, to the use of the godly Christians for recreatyng them selves, in stede of fond and unseemly ballades* (London: John Daye, 1579) [USTC 518921] [RISM A/I: D 829].
DAMAN 1591
William Daman, *The second booke of the musicke conteining all the tunes of Davids Psalmes* (London: Thomas East, 1591) [USTC 518767] [RISM A/I: D 831].
DATHEEN 1566
Petrus Datheen, *Die psalmen des konincklijkcke profeten Davids ende ander lof sangen [...]* (Emden: [s.n.], 1566) [USTC 405330].
DAVID OF AUGSBURG 1899
David of Augsburg, *De exterioris et interioris hominis compositione*, edited by PP. Collegii S. Bonaventuræ (Quaracchi [Florence]: Ex Typographia Eiusdem Collegii, 1899).
DE ÁVILA 1971
Juan de Ávila, *Obras completas*, edited by Luis Sala Balust and Francisco Martín Hernández (Madrid: Biblioteca de Autores Cristianos, 1971).
DE AZPILCUETA 1545
Martín de Azpilcueta, *Commento en romance a manera de repetición latina y scholástica [...], dist. prima* (Coimbra: [João de Barreira], 1545) [USTC 342695].
DE AZPILCUETA 1561
Martín de Azpilcueta, *Libro de la oración, horas canónicas y otros officios divinos* (Coimbra: João de Barreira, 1561) [USTC 342698].
DE AZPILCUETA 1569
Martín de Azplicueta, *Manuale de' confessori, et penitenti [...]*, Italian translation by Fra Cola di Guglinisi (Venice: Gabriele Giolito De Ferrari, 1569) [USTC 811664].
DE AZPILCUETA 1578
Martín de Azpilcueta, *Enchiridion sive manuale de oratione et horis canonicis* (Rome: Iosephus de Angelis, 1578) [USTC 811683].
DE BERTRAND 1582
Antoine de Bertrand, *Airs spirituels contenant plusieurs hymnes et cantiques, mis en musique à quatre et cinq parties* (Paris: Adrian Le Roy et Robert Ballard, 1582) [USTC 1697] [RISM A/I: B 2413].
DE CASTELNAU 1823
Michel de Castelnau, *Memoires* (Paris: Foucault, 1823).

DE FABRIS 1584
Melchior de Fabris, *Wegweyser aller Creutzferter, Kirchferter, Walfarter oder Pilgram andacht [...]* (Munich: Adam Berg, 1584) [USTC 706273]; available online at http://bit.ly/2be8qNU.

DE GRASSIS 1505
Paris de Grassis, *De tonis sive tenoribus orationum et aliorum omnium quae intra totum annum solemniter cantanda sunt*, manuscript (1505?), Vat. Lat. 12343.

DE GRASSIS 1563 / DE GRASSIS 1580 / DE GRASSIS 1582
Paris de Grassis, *De caeremoniis cardinalium et episcoporum in eorum diocesibus libri duo* (Venice: Antonio Blado, 1563) [USTC 833977]; (Rome: In Aedibus Populi Romani, 1580), available online at http://bit.ly/2bpFgw0; (Venice: Pietro Dusinelli, 1582) [USTC 833983].

DE GRASSIS 1884
Paris de Grassis, *Il Diario di Leone X di Paride de Grassi [...]*, edited by Pio Delicati and Mariano Armellini (Rome: Tipografia della Pace, 1884).

DE JUSSIE 1611
Jeanne de Jussie, *Le Levain du Calvinisme ou commencement de l'hérésie de Genève [...]* (Chambéry: Frères Du Four, 1611).

DE KERLE 1562
Jacobus de Kerle, *Preces speciales pro salubri generalis concilii successu, ac conclusione [...]* (Venice: Antonio Gardano, 1562) [USTC 837015] [RISM A/I: K 445]; available online at http://bit.ly/2bi8W04.

DE L'ESTOCART 1582A
Paschal de L'Estocart, *Premier livre des octonaires de la vanité du monde [...]* (Lyon: Barthelemi Vincent, 1582) [RISM A/I: L 2072].

DE L'ESTOCART 1582B
Paschal de L'Estocart, *Sacræ cantiones quatuor, quinque, sex et septem vocum liber primus* (Lyon [=Geneva]: [Jean I de Laon pour] Barthelemy Vincent, 1582) [USTC 451580] [RISM A/I: L 2071].

DE L'ESTOCART 1583
Paschal de L'Estocart, *Cent cinquante pseaumes mis en rime [...]* (Geneva: Eustace Vignon, 1583) [USTC 75058] [RISM A/I: L 2076].

DE MONTE 1581
Philippus de Monte, *Primo Libro de Madrigrali Spirituali a Cinque Voci* (Venice: Angelo Gardano, 1581) [USTC 843222] [RISM A/I: M 3317].

DE RAEMOND 1610
Florimond de Raemond, *L'histoire de la naissance, progres et decadence de l'herésie de ce siècle* (Paris: Veuve de Guillaume de la Nove, 1610).

DE RORE 1548
Cipriano de Rore, *Musica di Cipriano Rore sopra le stanze del Petrarcha in laude della Madonna [...]* (Venice: Antonio Gardano, 1548) [USTC 853287] [RISM B/I: 1548|10].

DE SOTO 1558
Pedro de Soto, *Preces speciales pro salute populi Christiani [...]* (Dillingen: Apud Sebald Mayer, 1558) [USTC 686372].

DE TYARD 1555
Pontus de Tyard, *Solitaire Second ou Prose de la Musique* (Lyon: Jean de Tournes, 1555) [USTC 39158].

DE VETERI 1522
*De veteri et novicio deo [...]* (Wittenberg: Melchior Lotter d. J., 1522) [USTC 630089]; available online at http://bit.ly/2cp9sfQ.

DE VICTORIA 1600
Tomás Luis de Victoria, *Missæ, Magnificat, motecta, psalmi, et alia quam plurimam [...]* (Madrid: Apud Juan Flamenco, 1600) [USTC 342351] [RISM A/I: V 1435].

DE VIO 1570 / DE VIO 1897
Tommaso de Vio, *Secunda Secundæ Summæ Theologiæ [...] Cum Commentariis [...] D. D. Thomæ de Vio, Caietani [...]* (Rome: [Giulio Accolti: Hær. Antonio Blado & Giovanni Gigliotti], 1570) [USTC 859546]; modern edition ("Editio Leonina") as *Sancti Thomæ de Aquino Opera omnia iussu Leonis XIII P.M. edita [...] Secunda secundæ Summæ Theologiæ a quæstione LVII ad quæstionem CXXII [...]* (Rome: Ex Typographia Polyglotta S. C. de Propaganda Fide, 1897); available online at http://bit.ly/2bzTyO9.

DE' RICCI 1850
Caterina de' Ricci, *Due Capitoli e una Lauda di S. Caterina de' Ricci* (Prato: Tip. Guasti, 1850).

DEL BENE 1563
Giovanni Del Bene (ed.), *Musica spirituale. Libro primo di canzon et madrigali a cinque voci [...]* (Venice: Girolamo Scotto, 1563) [USTC 804281].

DEL LAGO 1540
Giovanni del Lago, *Breve introduttione di musica misurata [...]* (Venice: Ex prælo Brandino & Ottaviano II Scotto, 1540) [USTC 826010].

DEL NENTE 1743
Ignazio del Nente, *Vita e costume ed intelligenze spirituali della venerabile madre suor Domenica del Paradiso [...]* (Florence: Francesco Moücke, 1743).

DEMANTIUS 1631
Christoph Demantius, *Deutsche Passion, nach dem Evangelisten S. Iohanne [...] mit sechs Stimmen uffs neue componiret* (Freiberg: Erben Georg Hoffmann, 1631) [RISM A/I: D 1543].

DÉSIRÉ 1560 / DÉSIRÉ 1977
Artus Désiré, *Le contrepoison des cinquante-deux chansons de Clément Marot* (Paris: Pierre Gaultier, 1560) [USTC 30772]; modern edition by Jacques Pineaux (Geneva: Librairie Droz SA, 1977).

DIVERSI AVISI 1565
*Diversi avisi particolari dall'Indie di Portogallo [...]* (Venice: Michele Tramezzino, 1565) [USTC 801179].

DKL
Konrad Ameln, Markus Jenny and Walther Lipphardt (eds.), *Das deutsche Kirchenlied: Kritische Gesamtausgabe der Melodien*; vol. I: *Verzeichnis der Drucke* [RISM B: VIII/1–2], 2 volumes (Kassel: Bärenreiter, 1975/1980).

DONI 1647
Giovanni Battista Doni, *De Praestantia Musicæ Veteris. Libri Tres [...]* (Florence: Typis Amatoris Massæ Forolivien., 1647); available online at http://bit.ly/2bbzFJi.

ECCARD 1597
Johannes Eccard, *Geistliche Lieder auf den Choral oder die gemeine Kirchenmelodey [...]* (Königsberg: Georg Osterberger, 1597).

EEN DVYTSCH 1572
*Een dvytsch musyck boeck daer inne begrepen syn vele schoone liedekens [...]* (Louvain: Pierre I Phalèse, 1572) [USTC 405434]; available online at http://bit.ly/2bKf01E.

EISENGREIN 1581
Martin Eisengrein, *Unser liebe Fraw zu Alten Oetting [...]* (Ingolstadt: Wolfgang Eder, 1581) [USTC 701865].

ELYOT 1537 / ELYOT 1962
Thomas Elyot, *The boke named the Gouernour [...]* (London: Thomas Berthelet, 1537); modern edition by S. E. Lehmberg as *The Book Named the Governor* (London: Dent, 1962).

EPISTOLÆ MIXTÆ 1900
*Epistolæ Mixtæ ex variis Europæ locis ab anno 1537 ad 1556 scriptæ [...]*, tome III (Madrid: Augustinus Avrial, 1900).

ERASMI OPERA OMNIA / COLLECTED WORKS OF ERASMUS
Jean LeClerc (ed.), *Desiderii Erasmi Opera Omnia*, 10 vols. (Leiden: Pieter van der Aa, 1703–6); English edition by C. R. Thompson et al. as *Collected Works of Erasmus* (Toronto: University of Toronto Press, 1974 ff.).

ERASMUS 1519
Desiderius Erasmus, *Farrago nova epistolarum [...]* (Basel: Johann Froben, 1519) [USTC 657310].

ERASMUS 1532
Desiderius Erasmus, *Declarationes ad censuras lutetiæ vulgatas [...]* (Basel: Hieronymus Froben & Nikolaus Episcopius, 1532) [USTC 632043].

ERASMUS ET AL. 1642
Desiderius Erasmus et al., *Epistolarum D. Erasmi Roterodami Libri XXXI Et P. Melanchthoni libri IV. quibus adjiciuntur Th. Mori & Lud. Vivis Epistolae [...]* (London: Flesher and Young, 1642).

FAIGNIENT 1568
Noé Faignient, *Chansons, madrigales, et motetz a quatre, cincq et six parties* (Antwerp: Chez Veuve Hans de Laet, 1568) [USTC 61098] [RISM A/I: F 61]; available online at http://bit.ly/2bdywo1.

FEATLEY 1609
Daniel Featley (ed.), *The workes of the very learned and reverend father in God Iohn Iewvel* (London: John Norton, 1609) [USTC 14579].

FIAMMA 1570
Gabriele Fiamma, *Rime spirituali del reverendo domino Gabriel Fiamma, canonico regolare lateranense; esposte da lui medesimo* (Venice: Francesco De Franceschi, 1570) [USTC 829390].

FICINO 1489 / FICINO 1989 / FICINO 1995
Marsilio Ficino, *De vita libri tres [...]* (Florence: Antonio di Bartolommeo Miscomini, 1489) [USTC 994998]; English translation by Carole V. Kaske and John Clark as *Marsilio Ficino: Three Books on Life*, Medieval & Renaissance Text & Studies, vol. 57 (Binghamton NY: The Renaissance Society of America, 1989); Italian translation by Alessandra Tarabochia Canavero as *Sulla vita* (Milan: Rusconi, 1995).

FICINO 1975
Marsilio Ficino, *The Philebus Commentary*, edited and translated by Michael J. B. Allen (Berkeley and Los Angeles CA: University of California Press, 1975).

FIGLIUCCI **1583**
Felice Figliucci, *De la Politica, Overo Scienza Civile secondo la Dottrina d'Aristotile [...]* (Venice: Presso Gio. Battista Somascho, 1583) [USTC 829479].

FIGULUS **1575**
Wolfgang Figulus, *Vetera nova, carmina sacra et selecta de Natali Domini nostri Jesu Christi [...] Zwantzig artige und kurtze Weynacht Liedlein [...]* (Frankfurt: Johann Eichorn, 1575) [USTC 552855] [RISM A/I: F 722].

FINCK **1556** / FINCK **1969**
Hermann Finck, *Practica Musica [...]* (Wittenberg: Hær. Georg Rhau, 1556) [USTC 685426]; facsimile edition (Sala Bolognese: Arnaldo Forni, 1969).

FIRST BOOK **1972**
*The First Book of Discipline* [of the Scottish Kirk], edited by James K. Cameron (Edinburgh: St Andrew Press, 1972).

FIRST BOOKE **1582**
*The First Booke of the Christian Exercise appertayning to resolution [...]* (Rouen: Parsons's Press, 1582) [USTC 203087].

FOIRM **1567**
*Foirm na nurrnuidheadh agas freasdal na sacramuinteadh, agas foirceadul an chreidimh Christuidhe andso sios* (Edinburgh: Robert Lekpreuik, 1567) [USTC 515610].

FONTES NARRATIVI I
MHSI vol. 66. *Fontes narrativi de S. Ignatio de Loyola et de Societatis Jesu initiis*, vol. I: *Narrationes scriptæ ante annum 1557*, edited by Dionysius Fernández Zapico and Candidus de Dalmases (Rome: apud Monumenta Historica Soc. Iesu, 1943).

FORME OF PRAYERS **1556**
*Forme of Prayers and Ministration of Sacrements, used in the Englishe Congregation at Geneva [...]* (Geneva: Jean Crespin, 1556) [USTC 450073].

FORME OF PRAYERS **1558**
*Forme of Prayers and Ministration of Sacrements. 62 psalms. Catechisme* (Geneva: Pierre-Jacques Poullain & Antoine Reboul, 1558) [USTC 450083].

FORME OF PRAYERS **1560**
*[Forme of Prayers and Ministration of the Sacrements &c. 87 psalms.] Catechisme or manner to teach children the Christian religion* ([Geneva]: Zacharie Durant, 1560) [USTC 452372].

FORME OF PRAYERS **1562**
*The Forme of Prayers and Ministration of the Sacraments &c. used in the English Churche at Geneva. Whereunto are also added the Praiers which they use there in the Frenche Church* (Edinburgh: Robert Lekpreuik, 1562) [USTC 505965].

FORME OF PRAYERS **1564**
*The Forme of Prayers and Ministration of the Sacraments &c used in the English Church at Geneva, approved & received by the Churche of Scotland whereunto are also added sondrie other prayers, with the whole psalmes of David in English meter* (Edinburgh: Robert Lekpreuik, 1564) [USTC 506228].

FRANCHI **1575**
Cirillo Franchi, *Echo, seu aemula quaedam vocum repercussio [...]* (Bologna: Società Tipografica Bolognese, 1575) [USTC 830756].

FRÓIS **1599**
Luigi Fróis, *Lettera Annua del Giappone dell'Anno MDXCVI [...]*, Italian translation by P. Francesco Mercati (Rome: Appresso Luigi Zannetti, 1599) [USTC 831063].

FUENFF SCHOENE 1592
*Fuenff schoene newe geistliche gesenge [...]* ([S.l.]: [s.n.], 1592) [USTC 656989].
FULKE 1573
William Fulke, *Praelections upon the sacred and holy Revelation of S. John*, English translation by George Gyffard (London: Thomas Purfoot, 1573) [USTC 507647].
GAFFURIUS 1492
Franchinus Gaffurius, *Theorica Musicæ* (Milan: Ioannes Petrus de Lomatio, 1492) [USTC 994866].
GAFFURIUS 1496 / GAFFURIUS 1512 / GAFFURIUS 1968
Franchinus Gaffurius, *Practica musicæ* (Milan: Ioannes Petrus de Lomatio, 1496) [USTC 994869]; (Venice: Agostino Zani, 1512) [USTC 831337]; available online at http://bit.ly/2aUrndl; English translation by Clement A. Miller, in *Musicological Studies and Documents* 20 (Dallas TX: The American Institute of Musicology, 1968).
GAFFURIUS 1518
Franchinus Gaffurius, *De harmonia musicorum instrumentorum opus* (Milan: per Gottardo Da Ponte, 1518) [USTC 831336].
GALILEI 1581
Vincenzo Galilei, *Dialogo della musica antica, et della moderna* (Florence: Giorgio Marescotti, 1581) [USTC 831522].
GARDINER 1933
Stephen Gardiner, *The Letters of Stephen Gardiner*, edited by J. A. Muller (Cambridge: Cambridge University Press, 1933).
GASTOLDI 1591
Giovanni Giacomo Gastoldi, *Balletti a cinque voci con li suoi versi per cantare, sonare et ballare [...]* (Venice: R. Amadino, 1591) [USTC 831963].
GERRITS 1592
Soetken Gerrits, *Een Nieu Gheestelijck Liedtboecxken [...]* (Haarlem: Gillis Rooman, 1592) [USTC 423077].
GESANGBUCH 1575
*Gesangbuch Der Brüder in Behemen vnd Meherrn, Die man auß haß vnd neyd, Picharden, Waldenses, &c. nennet* (Nuremberg: Dietrich Gerlach, 1575) [DKL 1575[02]].
GHERARDINI 1585
Arcangelo Gherardini, *Il primo libro de' madrigali à cinque voci [...]* (Ferrara: Vittorio Baldini, 1585) [USTC 832534] [RISM A/I: G 1762].
GIGLER 1569
Andreas Gigler, *Gesang Postill, Das ist: Evangelia [...]* (Graz: Andreas Franck, 1569).
GIUSSANO 1610 / GIUSSANO 1855
Giovanni Pietro Giussano, *Vita di S. Carlo Borromeo, Prete Cardinale del titolo di santa Prassede. Arcivescovo di Milano* (Rome: Stamperia della Camera Apostolica, 1610); available online at http://bit.ly/2bOsR8Z; (Napoli: Tipografia Arcivescovile, 1855); available online at http://bit.ly/2bIyjqN.
GLAREANUS 1547 / GLAREANUS 1967 / GLAREANUS 1965
Henricus Glareanus, *Dodecachordon* (Basel: Henricus Petri, 1547) [USTC 553084]; facsimile edition (New York: Broude Brothers, 1967); English translation by Clement A. Miller, 2 vols., in *Musicological Studies and Documents* 6 (Dallas: The American Institute of Musicology, 1965).

GODEAU 1637 / GODEAU 1676

Antoine Godeau, *Paraphrase des Pseaumes de David, mise en vers français par Mgr. Antoine Godeau, évêque de Grasse et de Vence* (Paris: Jean Camusat, 1637); (Paris: Pierre Le Petit, 1676).

GOUDIMEL 1564

Claude Goudimel, *Les cent cinquante pseaumes de David [...]* (Paris: Le Roy & Ballard, 1564) [USTC 16881] [RISM A/I: G 3202].

GOUDIMEL 1565

Claude Goudimel, *Les Pseaumes mis en rime françoise par Clément Marot et Theodore de Bèse. Mis en musique à quatre parties par Claude Goudimel* (Geneva: François Jaqui, 1565) [RISM A/I: G 3206]; facsimile reprint (Kassel: Bärenreiter, 1935).

GOUDIMEL 1568

Claude Goudimel, *Les cent cinquante pseaumes de David [...]* (Paris: Le Roy & Ballard, 1568) [USTC 30410].

GRADUALE 1580

*Graduale Sacrosanctæ Romanæ Ecclesiæ, integrum et completum iuxta ritum Missalis novi ex decreto sacrosancti Concilii Tridentini restituti* (Venice: Ex officina Peter Liechtenstein, 1580) [USTC 820804].

GRADUALE 1614

*Graduale de tempore, iuxta ritum Sacrosanctæ Romanæ Ecclesiæ. Cum Cantu Pauli V Pont. Max. Iussu Reformato* (Rome: Typographia Medicæa, 1614).

GRADUALE 1615

*Graduale de sanctis, iuxta ritum Sacrosanctæ Romanæ Ecclesiæ. Cum Cantu Pauli V Pont. Max. Iussu Reformato* (Rome: Typographia Medicæa, 1615).

GRAU 1543 / GRAU 1865

Friedrich Grau ("Nausea") von Waischenfeld ("Blancicampianus"), *Friderici Nauseæ Blancicampiani episcopi Viennensis ad Paulum III Pontificem maximum Miscellanearum pro Tridentina eademque œcumenica synodo conciliarium libri VIII [Libri octo sylvarum synodalium]*, 1543 (Bayerische Staatsbibliothek Cod. Lat. Mon. 11096); books V and VI in Theodor Wiedemann (ed.), "Ad invictissimum Cæsarem Ferdinandum de summe necessario tollendis ex catholica ecclesia abusibus, ad reformandum totum ecclesiæ corpus quod alioquin nullam sit unquam pacem habiturum. Nach Cod. 11817 der kaiserlichen Hofbibliothek Wien herausgegeben", *Österreichische Vierteljahresschrift für katholische Theologie*, 4 (1865), pp. 556–610.

GUARINI 1621

Marc'Antonio Guarini, *Compendio historico dell'origine, accrescimento, e Prerogative delle Chiese, e Luoghi Pij della Città, e Diocesi di Ferrara [...]* (Ferrara: Heredi di Vittorio Baldini, 1621).

GUERRERO 1584

Francisco Guerrero, *Liber Vesperarum [...]* (Rome: Domenico Basa, 1584) [USTC 835161] [RISM A/I: G 4873].

GUERRERO 1589

Francisco Guerrero, *Canciones y villanescas espirituales, quinta parte* (Venice: Iago Vincentio [=Giacomo Vincenzi], 1589) [USTC 343009] [RISM A/I: G 4876].

**GUERRERO 1597**
Francisco Guerrero, *Motecta quæ partim quaternis, partim quinis, alia senis, alia octonis et duodenis concinuntur vocibus* (Venice: Giacomo Vincenzi, 1597) [USTC 835165] [RISM A/I: G 4877].

**GUICCIARDINI 1567**
Lodovico Guicciardini, *Descrittione di tutti i Paesi Bassi, altrimenti detti Germania inferiore [...]* (Antwerp: appresso Willem Silvius, 1567) [USTC 405351].

**GUICCIARDINI, LOTTINI AND SANSOVINI 1588**
Francesco Guicciardini, Giovanni Francesco Lottini, Francesco Sansovini, *Propositioni Overo Considerationi in materia di cose di Stato [...]* (Venice: Presso Altobello Salicato, 1588) [USTC 835416].

**GUIDETTI 1582**
Giovanni Domenico Guidetti (ed.), *Directorium chori ad usum sacrosanctæ Basilicæ Vaticanæ [...]* (Rome: Apud Robert Granjon, 1582) [USTC 835481].

**HANDL 1959**
Jacob Handl, *Opus musicum*, edited by Emil Bezecny and Josef Mantuani [Denkmäler der Tonkunst in Österreich, vols. 12, 24, 30, 40, 48, 51, 52] (Vienna: Artaria, 1899–1919; reprint Graz: Akademische Druck, 1959).

**HARINGTON 1804**
John Harington, *Nugæ Antiquæ*, edited by Henry Harington (London: Vernon and Hood, 1804).

**HARIOT 1590**
Thomas Hariot, *A Briefe and True Report of the New Found Land of Virginia [...]* (Frankfurt: Johann Wechel, 1590) [USTC 511530].

**HARTKNOCH 1686**
Christoph Hartknoch, *Preussische Kirchen-Historia [...]* (Frankfurt am Main, Leipzig, Danzig: Beckenstein, 1686).

**HATON 1857**
Claude Haton, *Memoires*, edited by Felix Bourquelot (Paris: Imprimerie Impériale, 1857).

**HAYM 1590**
Johannes Haym von Themar, *Schoene Christenliche Catholisch Weinnaecht oder kindtleß wiegen Gesang [...]* (Augsburg: Josias Wörli, 1590) [USTC 692156] [*DKL* 1590[15]].

**HECYRUS 1561**
Kryštof Hecyrus (Christoph Schweher), *Veteres ac Piae Cantiones Praecipuorum Anni Festorum [...] Omnia quatuor vocibus composita [...]* (Nuremberg: Johan vom Berg & Ulrich Neuber, 1561) [USTC 552746] [RISM A/I: S 2474].

**HECYRUS 1581**
Kryštof Hecyrus (Christoph Schweher), *Christliche Gebet und Gesäng auff die heilige zeit und Fayertage uber das gantze Jar [...]* (Praha: Michal Peterle, 1581) [USTC 621525].

**HEMMEL 1569**
Sigmund Hemmel [Hemmeln], *Der gantz Psalter Davids, wie derselbig in teutsche Gesang verfasset [...]* (Tübingen: Ulrich Morhart, 1569) [USTC 553285] [RISM A/I: H 5020].

**HERBENUS 1496 / HERBENUS 1957**
Matthaeus Herbenus, *De natura cantus ac miraculis vocis*, 1496 (Bayerische Staatsbibliothek Cod. Lat. Mon. 10277, fols. 2$^r$-56$^v$); modern edition by Joseph Smits van Waesberghe as "Herbeni Traiectensis De natura cantus ac miraculis vocis", in *Beiträge zur rheinischen Musikgeschichte*, 22 (Cologne: Arno Volk, 1957).

**HERMAN 1560**
Nicolaus Herman, *Die Sontags Evangelia, [...] uber das gantze Jar [...]* (Wittenberg: hær. Georg Rhau, Samuel Selfisch, 1560) [USTC 637293].

**HERMAN 1562**
Nicolaus Herman, *Die Historien von der Sindfludt, Joseph, Mose, Helia, Elisa, und der Susanna [...]* (Wittenberg: hær Georg Rhau, Samuel Selfisch, 1562) [USTC 636856].

**HERPOL 1565**
Homer Herpol, *Novum et insigne opus musicum [...]* (Nuremberg: Ulrich Neuber & Johann Berg's Erben, 1565) [RISM A/I: H 5187].

**HET IERST 1551 / HET IERST 1989**
*Het ierst Musyck Boexken [...]* (Antwerp: Tielman Susato, 1551) [USTC 405102]; modern edition by Eugeen Schreurs and Martine Sanders (Peer: Alamire, 1989).

**HEYMAIR 1578**
Magdalena Heymair, *Die Sonteglichen Episteln uber das gantze Jar [...]* (Augsburg: [s.n.], 1578) [USTC 637310].

**HOOKER 1876**
Richard Hooker, "Laws of Ecclesiastical Polity", in John Keble (ed.), *The Works of That Learned and Judicious Divine, Mr. Richard Hooker: with an Account of His Life and Death* (Oxford: Clarendon Press, 1876).

**HORACE 1836**
Horace, *The Works of Horace*, edited and translated by C. Smart (Philadelphia PA: Joseph Whetham, 1836); available online at http://bit.ly/2c39Z31.

**HORN 1544**
Johann Horn (ed.), *Ein Gesangbuch der Brüder inn Behemen und Merherrn [...]* (Nuremberg: Johann Günther, 1544) [USTC 643545].

**INJUNCTIONS 1559 / INJUNCTIONS 1914**
*Injunctions geven by the Quenes Majestie [...]* (London: Richard Jugge & John Cawood, 1559) [USTC 515522]; modern edition by Henry Gee and William John Hardy, in *Documents Illustrative of English Church History* (London: Macmillan, 1914), pp. 417–442; available online at http://bit.ly/2bM6394.

**INSTITUTIO ORATORIA**
Marcus Fabius Quintilianus, *Institutio oratoria*; Latin text available online at http://bit.ly/2bCTLxS; English translation by Harold Edgeworth Butler (1920–22) available online at http://bit.ly/2c2MreV.

**INSTITUTUM 1757**
*Institutum Societatis Jesu, Auctoritate Congregationis generalis XVIII. Meliorem in ordinem digestum, auctum et recusum. Volumen Primum* (Prague: Typis Universitatis Carolo Ferdinandeæ in Collegio Societatis Jesu ad S. Clementem, 1757); available online at http://bit.ly/2buGjdo.

**JARDIN MUSICAL 1556**
*Jardin musical, contenant plusieurs belles fleurs de chansons [...]* (Antwerp: Hubert Walerant and Hans de Laet, 1556) [USTC 41342].

**JESPERSSØN 1573**
Niels Jesperssøn, *Gradual: en almindelig Sangbog* (København: Laurentz Benedicht, 1573) [USTC 303268].

### João IV 1649 / João IV 1666
João IV of Portugal, *Defensa de la musica moderna contra la errada opinion del Obispo Cyrillo Franco [...]* ([Lisbon?]: [Pedro Crasbeeck?], [1649?]); Italian translation as *Difesa della musica moderna contro la falsa opinion del vescovo Cirillo Franco, tradotta di spagnuolo in italiano* ([Perugia?]: [Angelo Laurenzi?], 1666).

### John of Salisbury 1993
John of Salisbury, *Policraticus I-IV*, edited by K. S. B. Keats-Rohan (Turnhout: Brepols, 1993).

### Joris s.d. / Joris 1972
David Joris, *Een Geestelijck Liedt-Boecxken, Inhoudende veel schoone sinrijcke Christelijcke Liedekens [...]* ([S.l.]: [s.n.], [s.d.]) [USTC 430015]; facsimile edition in *Mennonite Songbooks: Dutch series* (Amsterdam: Frits Knuf, 1972).

### Joye 1530
George Joye (ed. and transl.), *Hortulus animæ. The Garden of the Soule [...]* (Strasbourg [=Antwerp]: Francis Foxe [=Merten de Keyser], 1530) [USTC 410249].

### Klinge 1562
Konrad Klinge, *Loci Communes Theologici [...]* (Cologne: apud Hær. Arnold Birckmann, 1562) [USTC 673403].

### Klingenstein 1605
Bernard Klingenstein (ed.), *Triodia sacra. Sive modi musici ternis vocibus [...]* (Dillingen: In officina Typographica Adami Meltzer, 1605) [British Library, shelfmark C.255.a].

### Knaust 1571
Heinrich Knaust, *Gassenhawer Reuter und Bergliedlin [...]* (Frankfurt am Main: haer. Christian Egenolff, 1571) [USTC 658745].

### Lanfranco 1533
Giovanni Maria Lanfranco, *Scintille di Musica [...]* (Brescia: per Lodovico Britannico, 1533) [USTC 837338].

### Łaski 1554
Jan Łaski, *Forma ac ratio tota ecclesiastici ministerij [...]* (Emden: C. Egenolff & Egidius van der Erve, 1554) [USTC 505020].

### Lasso 1570
Orlando di Lasso, *Recueil du melange contenant plusieurs chansons a quatre et cinq parties* (London: Thomas Vautrollier, 1570) [USTC 76588] [RISM A/I: L 835].

### Lasso 1575
Orlando di Lasso, *Mellange d'Orlande de Lassus, contenant plusieurs chansons a quatre parties [...]* (La Rochelle: Pierre Haultin, 1575) [USTC 47565] [RISM A/I: L 882].

### Lasso 1576
Orlando di Lasso, *Thresor de musique, contenant chansons a quatre, cinq & six parties* ([Geneva?]: [Simon Goulart?], 1576) [USTC 61854] [RISM B/I: 1576|4].

### Lasso 1588
Orlando di Lasso, *Teutsche Psalmen: geistliche Psalmen, mit dreyen Stimmen [...]* (Munich: Johann vom Berg, 1588) [USTC 696349] [RISM B/I 340: 1588|12].

### Lasso 1597
Orlande de Lassus (Orlando di Lasso), *Cinquante Pseaumes de David, avec la musique a cinq parties d'Orlande de Lassus [...]* (Heidelberg: Jerome Commelin, 1597) [USTC 553033] [RISM B/I 375: 1597|6].

**LE CHALLEUX 1579**
Nicolas Le Challeux, "Une petite Histoire d'un Massacre commis par les Hespagnols sur quelques François en la Floride", in Girolamo Benzoni, *Histoire nouvelle du Nouveau monde* (Geneva: Eustace Vignon, 1579) sig. AA.ij [USTC 2611].

**LE FÈVRE 1578**
Guy Le Fèvre de la Boderie, *Hymnes Ecclesiastiques, Cantiques Spirituels, & autres Meslanges Poëtiques* (Paris: pour Robert Le Mangnier, 1578) [USTC 1925].

**LE JEUNE 1598**
Claude Le Jeune, *Dodecacorde contenant douze pseaumes de David* (La Rochelle: Jérôme Haultin, 1598) [USTC 6300] [RISM A/I: L 1679].

**LE JEUNE 1606**
Claude Le Jeune, *Octonaires de la vanité et inconstance du monde, mis en musique à 3 & à 4 parties* (Paris: Pierre Ballard, 1606) [RISM A/I: L 1693].

**LE MAISTRE 1559**
Mattaeus Le Maistre, *Catechesis numeris musicis inclusa [...]* (Nuremberg: Johann vom Berg, Ulrich Neuber, 1559) [USTC 554104] [RISM A/I: L 1841].

**LECHNER 1582**
Leonhard Lechner, *Newe Teutsche Lieder mit fünff und vier Stimmen* (Nuremberg: Katharina Gerlach, hær. Johann vom Berg, 1582) [USTC 552196] [RISM A/I: L 1296].

**LECHNER 1960**
Leonhard Lechner, *Historia der Passion und Leidens unser einigen Erlosers und Seligmachers Jesu Christi* (1593); modern edition by Konrad Ameln (Kassel: Bärenreiter, 1960); available online at http://bit.ly/2byvGsl.

**LEDESMA 1573**
Jaime [Diego de] Ledesma, *Modo per insegnar la dottrina christiana [...]* (Rome: per hær. Antonio Blado, 1573) [USTC 837697].

**LEDESMA 1576**
Jaime Ledesma, *Dottrina Christiana, a modo di Dialogo del Maestro, & Discepolo [...]* (Venice: appresso Cristoforo Zanetti, 1576) [USTC 837698].

**LEISENTRIT 1567**
Johann Leisentrit, *Geistliche Lieder und Psalmen der alten Apostolischer recht und warglaubiger Christlicher Kirchen [...]* (Bautzen: Johann Wolrab, 1567) [USTC 658907].

**LETTERE VOLGARI 1564**
*Lettere volgari di diversi nobilissimi huomini, et eccellentissimi ingegni, scritte in diverse materie [...]* (Venice: [Paolo Manuzio], 1564) [USTC 804348]; available online at http://bit.ly/2caoghH.

**LIVIUS 1829**
Titus Livius, *Titi Livii Patavini Historiarum Liber Primus et selecta quædam capita* (Cambridge: Sumptibus Hilliard et Brown, 1829); available online at http://bit.ly/2bQOaou.

**LM 3**
*Lainii Monumenta. Epistolae et acta Patris Jacobi Lainii [...] Tomus Tertius (1558)* (Madrid: Gabriel López del Horno, 1913), available online at http://bit.ly/2bwSSpt.

**LM 7**
*Lainii Monumenta. Epistolae et acta Patris Jacobi Lainii [...] Tomus Septimus (1563–1564)* (Madrid: Gabriel López del Horno, 1916), available online at http://bit.ly/2bitcxP.

**LM 8**
*Lainii Monumenta. Epistolae et acta Patris Jacobi Lainii [...] Tomus Octavus (1564–1565)* (Madrid: Gabriel López del Horno, 1917), available online at http://bit.ly/2be23 L5.

**LODI E CANZONI 1576**
*Lodi e Canzoni spirituali per cantar insieme con la Dottrina Christiana* (Milan: per Pacifico da Ponte, 1576) [USTC 805318].

**LOERSFELD 1524 / LOERSFELD 1983**
*Eyn enchiridion oder handbuechlein [...]* (Erfurt: Johann Loersfeld, 1524) [USTC 655582]; available online at http://bit.ly/2bOZHaO; modern reprint edited by Konrad Ameln (Kassel: Bärenreiter, 1983).

**LOPES 1590**
Lodovico Lopes [Luis López], *Dell'instruttorio della conscienza [...]*, translated into Italian by Camillo Camilli (Venice: Appresso Francesco de' Franceschi, 1590) [USTC 838618].

**LOSSIUS 1553**
Lucas Lossius, *Psalmodia, hoc est Cantica Sacra Veteris Ecclesiae selecta [...]* (Nuremberg: apud Gabriel Hain, 1553) [USTC 688163] [RISM A/I: L 2874]; available online at http://bit.ly/2bbQdEs.

**LOUIS 1555**
Jean Louis [Louys], *Pseaulmes cinquante de David composeez musicalement* (Antwerp: Hubert Waelrant & Hans de Laet, 1555) [USTC 41205] [RISM A/I: L 2888].

**LQ 3**
*Litterae Quadrimestres ex universis praeter Indiam et Brasiliam locis [...], Tomus Tertius (1554–1555)* (Madrid: Augustinus Avrial, 1896); available online at http://bit.ly/2c1USLu.

**LQ 4**
*Litterae Quadrimestres ex universis praeter Indiam et Brasiliam locis [...], Tomus Quartus (1556)* (Madrid: Augustinus Avrial, 1897); available online at http://bit.ly/2fxvsWq.

**LQ 6**
*Litterae Quadrimestres ex universis praeter Indiam et Brasiliam locis [...], Tomus Sextus (1559–1560)* (Madrid: Oficina Typographica "La Editorial Ibérica", 1925); available online at http://bit.ly/2bAqgxx.

**LQ 7**
*Litterae Quadrimestres ex universis praeter Indiam et Brasiliam locis [...], Tomus Septimus (1561–62)* (Rome: [s.n.], 1932); available online at http://bit.ly/2bdjPAG.

**LUCRETIUS 1921 / LUCRETIUS 2004**
Titus Lucretius Carus, *De Rerum Natura*; English translation by William Ellery Leonard as *On The Nature of Things* (New York NY: E. P. Dutton & Co., 1921; 2004).

**LUTHER 1524**
Martin Luther (ed.), *Etlich Cristlich lider, lobgesang und psalm, dem rainen wort Gottes gemeß auß der heyligen schrifft* (Nuremberg [=Wittenberg]: Jobst Gutknecht, 1524) [USTC 653963]; available online at http://www.dilibri.de/id/437482.

**LUTHER 1529**
Martin Luther, "Eine neue Vorrede Martini Luthers", in Martin Luther (ed.), *Geistliche Lieder* (Wittenberg: Klug, 1529).

**LUTHER 1533**
Martin Luther (ed.), *Geistliche Lieder auffs new gebessert [...]* (Wittenberg: Klug, 1533) [USTC 658881].

**LUTHER 1538A**
Martin Luther, "Encomion musices", first version (Latin) in Georg Rhau (ed.), *Symphoniæ Iucundæ [...]* (Wittenberg: apud Georg Rhau, 1538) [USTC 552490] [RISM B/I: 153818]; available in Leaver 2007, pp. 313–324, and in Loewe 2013, pp. 600–605.

**LUTHER 1538B**
Martin Luther, "Vorrede auf alle gute Gesangbücher [Frau Musika]", in Johannes Walther, *Lob und Preis der loeblichen Kunst Musica* (Wittenberg: Georg Rhau, 1538) [USTC 673095]; available online at http://bit.ly/2c4iP3F and in Leaver 2007, pp. 74–75.

**LUTHER 1545**
Martin Luther, "Vorrede d. Mart. Luth.", in *Geystliche Lieder [...]* (Leipzig: Valentin Bapst, 1545) [USTC 659758] [*DKL* I/1, 1545$^{01}$].

**LW 31**
*Luther's Works: American Edition, vol. 31: Career of the Reformer I* (St Louis: Concordia, 1957).

**LW 32**
*Luther's Works: American Edition, vol. 32: Career of the Reformer II* (Philadelphia: Fortress Press, 1958).

**LW 41**
*Luther's Works: American Edition, vol. 41: Church and Ministry III* (Philadelphia: Fortress Press, 1966).

**LW 46**
*Luther's Works: American Edition, vol. 46: The Christian in Society III* (Philadelphia: Fortress Press, 1967).

**LW 49**
*Luther's Works: American Edition, vol. 49: Letters II* (Philadelphia: Fortress Press, 1972).

**LW 53**
*Luther's Works: American Edition, vol. 53: Liturgy and Hymns* (Philadelphia: Fortress Press, 1965).

**MACHIAVELLI 1532 / MACHIAVELLI 2010**
Niccolò Machiavelli, *Il Principe de Niccolo Macchiavelli, al Magnifico Lorenzo di Piero de Medici [...]* (Florence: Bernardo Giunta, 1532) [USTC 839314]; English translation by W. K. Marriott as *The Prince* (Campbell CA: FastPencil, 2010).

**MAFFEI 1562**
Giovanni Camillo Maffei, *Delle lettere del s. r. Giovanni Camiello Maffei da Solofra [...]*, 2 vols. (Naples: appresso Raimondo Amato, 1562) [USTC 839486].

**MAGDEBURG 1565**
Johann Magdeburg, *Der Psalter Davids gesangsweiß, in teutsche Reime verfaßt durch Johann Magdeburg* (Frankfurt: [s.n.], 1565).

**MAGDEBURG 1572**
Joachim Magdeburg, *Christliche und tröstliche Tischgesenge mit vier Stimmen [...]* (Erfurt: Georg Baumann, 1572) [RISM A/I: MM 125 I,1].

**MALINGRE 1533**
[Matthieu Malingre (ed.)], *Plusieurs belles et bonnes chansons que les chrestiens peuvent chanter en grande affection de cueur* ([Neufchâtel]: [Pierre de Vingle], 1533) [USTC 9720].

**Mansi 29**
Giovanni Domenico Mansi et al. (eds.), *Sacrorum conciliorum nova, et amplissima collectio [...] Editio novissima*, vol. 29 (Venice: Antonio Zatta, 1788); available online at http://bit.ly/2c04XZm.

**Mansi 32**
Giovanni Domenico Mansi et al. (eds.), *Sacrorum conciliorum nova, et amplissima collectio [...] Editio novissima*, vol. 32 (Paris: Welter 1902); available online at http://bit.ly/2byXdeb.

**Mansi 33**
Giovanni Domenico Mansi et al. (eds.), *Sacrorum conciliorum nova, et amplissima collectio [...] Editio novissima*, vol. 33 (Paris: Welter 1902); available online at http://bit.ly/2bcfzkT.

**Mansi 34**
Giovanni Domenico Mansi et al. (eds.), *Sacrorum conciliorum nova, et amplissima collectio [...] Editio novissima*, vol. 34 (Paris: Welter 1902); available online at http://bit.ly/2bPptcW.

**Mansi 35**
Giovanni Domenico Mansi et al. (eds.), *Sacrorum conciliorum nova, et amplissima collectio [...] Editio novissima*, vol. 35 (Paris: Welter 1902); available online at http://bit.ly/2c2hwQw.

**Mansi 36bis**
Louis Petit and Jean-Baptiste Martin (eds.), *Collectio Conciliorum Recentiorum Ecclesiae Universae [...] Tomus Praeliminaris bis [...]* [=Mansi 36bis] (Paris: Hubert Welter, 1913); available online at http://bit.ly/2bxXiSl.

**Mareschall 1606**
Samuel Mareschall, *Der gantz Psalter, von Ambrosio Lobwasser D., Hiebevor auss der Frantzösischen Composition [...]* (Basel: Ludwig König, 1606) [RISM A/I: M 623].

**Martin 1581 / Martin 1969**
Gregory Martin, *Roma Sancta*, manuscript (1581) [National Library of Australia, MS 1097, Clifford Collection, no. 41]; modern edition by George Bruner Parks (Rome: Edizioni di Storia e Letteratura, 1969).

**Mathesius 1586**
Johannes Mathesius, *Sÿrach Mathesii das ist Christliche, lehrhaffte, trostreiche und lustige Erklerung [...]* (Leipzig: Johann Beyer, 1586) [USTC 695703].

**Mei 1960**
Girolamo Mei, *Letters on Ancient and Modern Music to Vincenzo Galilei and Giovanni Bardi*, edited by Claude V. Palisca (Rome: American Institute of Musicology, 1960).

**Melville 1598**
James Melville, *A Spirituall Propine of a Pastour to his People* (Edinburgh: Robert Waldegrave, 1598) [USTC 513734].

**Melville 1842**
James Melville, *The Autobiography and Diary of Mr James Melvill [...]*, edited by Robert Pitcairn (Edinburgh: The Wodrow Society, 1842).

**Merbecke 1550**
John Merbecke, *A Concordance, that is to saie, a worke wherein by the ordre of the letters of the A. B. C. ye maie redely finde any worde conteigned in the whole Bible [...]* (London: Richard Grafton, 1550) [USTC 504506].

**MES 1561**
G[h]erardus Mes, *Het achste musyck boeck mit vier partien [...]* (Antwerp: Tielman Susato, 1561) [USTC 406090] [RISM A/I: M 2384].

**MISSALE 1570**
*Missale Romanum ex decreto sacrosancti Concilii Tridentini restitutum* (Rome: Apud Haer. Bartolomeo Faletti & Giovanni Varisco, 1570) [USTC 819996].

**MOLANUS 1570**
Johannes Molanus [van der Meulen or Vermeulen], *De picturis et imaginibus sacris, liber unus* (Louvain: apud Hieronymus Welleus, 1570) [USTC 401471].

**MOLANUS 1594**
Johannes Molanus [van der Meulen or Vermeulen], *De historia sacrarum imaginum et picturarum [...]* (Louvain: apud Jean Bogard, 1594) [USTC 403611].

**MORALES 1544 / MORALES 1952 / MORALES 1984**
Cristóbal de Morales, *Missarum Liber Primus* (Rome: Valerio e Luigi Dorico, 1544) [USTC 843419] [RISM A/I: M 3580]; modern edition by Higinio Anglés (Barcelona: Consejo Superior de Investigaciones Científicas, 1952); reprint (Madrid: Consejo Superior de Investigaciones Científicas, 1984).

**MORE 1516 / MORE 1995 / MORE 1996 / MORE 2005**
Thomas More, *Libellus vere aureus [...] deque nova insula Utopia* (Louvain: Thierry Martens, 1516) [USTC 400360]; modern edition as *Utopia: Latin Text and English Translation*, edited by R. M. Adams et al. (Cambridge: Cambridge University Press, 1995); Italian translation by Ortensio Lando (1548) as *L'utopia*, edited by Massimo Baldini (Rome: Armando, 1996; reprint 2005).

**MORIGIA 1585 / MORIGIA 1595**
Paolo Morigia, *La nobilità di Milano [...]* (Milan: Pacifico Da Ponte, 1585) [USTC 843599]; (Milan: Pacifico da Ponte, 1595) [USTC 843624].

**MORLEY 1597**
Thomas Morley, *A Plaine and Easie Introduction to Practicall Musicke [...]* (London: Peter Short, 1597) [USTC 513465].

**MÜNTZER 1523**
Thomas Müntzer, *Deutzsch Kirchenampt vorordnet, auffzuheben den hinterlistigen deckel unter welchem das liecht der welt vorhalten war [...]* (Eilenburg: Nikolaus Widemar, 1523) [USTC 635752].

**MÜNTZER 1524**
[Thomas Müntzer], *Deutsch Evangelisch Messze, etwann durch die Bepstlischen pfaffen* (Allstedt: Müntzerpresse, 1524) [USTC 635723]; available online at http://bit.ly/1efojSj.

**MÜNTZER 1968**
Thomas Müntzer, *Schriften und Briefe*, edited by Günther Franz and Paul Kirn (Gütersloh: Gerd Mohn, 1968).

**NADAL 2**
*Epistolae P. Hieronymi Nadal Societatis Jesu ab anno 1546 ad 1577 [...], Tomus Secundus (1562–1565)* (Madrid: Typis Augustini Avrial, 1899) available online at http://bit.ly/2bCFfs2.

**NAVARRE 1971**
Marguerite de Navarre, *Chansons spirituelles*, critical edition by Georges Dottin (Geneva: Droz, Textes Littéraires Français, 1971).

**NEWE DEUDSCHE 1544**
*Newe deudsche geistliche Gesenge [...]* (Wittenberg: Georg Rhau, 1544) [USTC 552087] [RISM B/I: 1544|21].

**OC**
Jean Calvin, *Joannis Calvini opera quæ supersunt omnia*, edited by Edouard Cunitz, Johann-Wilhelm Baum, Eduard Wilhelm Eugen Reuss (Brunswick: C. A. Schwetschke, 1863–1900), 59 tomes in 58 volumes; available online at http://bit.ly/2b3xSrr.

**OFFICIA PASCHALIA 1539**
*Officia Paschalia de Resurrectione et Ascensione Domini* (Wittenberg: Georg Rhau, 1539) [RISM B/I: 1539|14]; available online at http://bit.ly/2aZzG2 A.

**ORDER 1548**
*The order of the communion* (London: John Daye, 1548) [USTC 503975]; available online at http://bit.ly/2c7 g4xb.

**ORNITOPARCHUS 1519**
Andreas Ornitoparchus, *Musice active micrologus [...]* (Leipzig: [Author?], 1519).

**OS 1**
Jean Calvin, *Joannis Calvini Opera Selecta*, edited by Petrus Barth, vol. I, *Scripta Calvini ab anno 1533 usque ad annum 1541 continens* (Munich: Christian Kaiser, 1926).

**OS 2**
Jean Calvin, *Joannis Calvini Opera Selecta*, edited by Petrus Barth and Dora Scheuner, vol. II, *Tractatus Theologicus minores ab anno 1542 usque ad annum 1564 editos continens* (Munich: Christian Kaiser, 1952).

**OS 4**
Jean Calvin, *Joannis Calvini Opera Selecta*, edited by Petrus Barth, vol. IV, *Institutionis Christianae religionis 1559 librum III continens* (Munich: Christian Kaiser, 1931).

**OSIANDER 1586**
Lucas Osiander, *Fünfftzig geistliche Lieder und Psalmen [...]* (Nuremberg: Katharina Gerlach, 1586) [USTC 553628] [RISM A/I: O 142].

**P-KDG**
Giovanni Pierluigi da Palestrina, *Erste kritisch durchgesehene Gesamtausgabe*, edited by Franz Xaver Haberl, 33 vols. (Leipzig: Breitkopf und Härtel, 1862–1907).

**PALEOTTI 1582 / PALEOTTI 2002**
Gabriele Paleotti, *Discorso intorno alle imagini sacre et profane [...]* (Bologna: per Alessandro Benacci, 1582) [USTC 805736]; modern edition (Rome: Libreria Editrice Vaticana, 2002).

**PALEOTTI 1842**
Gabriele Paleotti, *Acta Concilii Tridentini, Anno MDLXII et MDLXIII usque in finem Concilii [...]*, edited by Joseph Mendham (London: Jacob Duncan, 1842).

**PALESTRINA 1567**
Giovanni Pierluigi da Palestrina, *Missarum liber secundus* (Rome: hær. Valerio & Luigi Dorico, 1567) [USTC 846192] [RISM A/I: P 660].

**PALESTRINA 1570**
Giovanni Pierluigi da Palestrina, *Missarum liber tertius* (Rome: hær. Valerio & Luigi Dorico, 1570) [USTC 846195] [RISM A/I: P 664].

**PALESTRINA 1575**
Giovanni Pierluigi da Palestrina, *Motettorum quæ partim quinis, partim senis, partim octonis vocibus concinantur. Liber tertius* (Venice: Apud Haer. Girolamo Scoto, 1575) [USTC 846202] [RISM A/I: P 711].

**PALESTRINA 1581**
Giovanni Pierluigi da Palestrina, *Il primo libro de madrigali a cinque voci, di Giovanni Petr'Aloysio Prenestino* (Venice: Angelo Gardano, 1581) [USTC 856211] [RISM A/I: P 761].

**PALESTRINA 1582**
Giovanni Pierluigi da Palestrina, *Missarum cum quatuor et quinque vocibus, liber quartus* (Venice: Angelo Gardano, 1582) [USTC 846212] [RISM A/I: P 667].

**PARKER AND TALLIS 1567**
Matthew Parker and Thomas Tallis, *The Whole Psalter [...]* (London: John Daye, 1567) [USTC 506691].

**PEACHAM 1622 / PEACHAM 1634 / PEACHAM 1906**
Henry Peacham, *The Compleat Gentleman* (London: Francis Constable, 1622); (London, Francis Constable, 1634); modern reprint of the 1634 edition (Oxford: Clarendon Press, 1906).

**PEARSON 1844**
George Pearson (ed.), *Writings and Translations of Myles Coverdale [...]* (Cambridge: Cambridge University Press, 1844).

**PEVERNAGE 1578 / PEVERNAGE 1602**
Andreas Pevernage, *Cantiones aliquot sacræ, sex, septem et octo vocum* (Douai: Jean Bogard, 1578) [USTC 406390] [RISM A/I: P 1669]; (Frankfurt: Nikolaus Stein, 1602) [RISM A/I: P 1675].

**PG 29**
Jacques Paul Migne (ed.), *Patrologia cursus completus. Series græca*, vol. 29 *S. Basilius Cæsariensis Episcopus* (Paris: Imprimérie Catholique, 1857); available online at http://bit.ly/2bKinG3.

**PG 54**
Jacques Paul Migne (ed.), *Patrologia cursus completus. Series græca*, vol. 54 *S. Joannes Chrysostomus* (Paris: Imprimérie Catholique, 1862); available online at http://bit.ly/2besx1J.

**PG 55**
Jacques Paul Migne (ed.), *Patrologia cursus completus. Series græca*, vol. 55 *S. Joannes Chrysostomus* (Paris: Imprimérie Catholique, 1862); available online at http://bit.ly/2bDOR61.

**PG 56**
Jacques Paul Migne (ed.), *Patrologia cursus completus. Series græca*, vol. 56 *S. Joannes Chrysostomus* (Paris: Imprimérie Catholique, 1862); available online at http://bit.ly/2bN6IWm.

**PIDOUX 1962**
Pierre Pidoux (ed.), *Le Psautier Huguenot du XVIe siècle; mélodies et documents* (Basel: Bärenreiter, 1962), 2 vols.

**PL 15**
Jacques Paul Migne (ed.), *Patrologia cursus completus. Series latina*, vol. 15 *Sancti Ambrosii Mediolanensis Episcopi, Opera omnia [...] Tomi primi Pars posterior* (Paris: Imprimérie Catholique, 1845); available online at http://bit.ly/2bzSRp9.

**PL 22**
Jacques Paul Migne (ed.), *Patrologia cursus completus. Series latina*, vol. 22 *Sancti Eusebi Hieronymi Stridonensis Presbyteri, Opera omnia [...] Tomus primus* (Paris: Imprimérie Catholique, 1845); available online at http://bit.ly/2bzSRp9.

**PL 36**
Jacques Paul Migne (ed.), *Patrologia cursus completus. Series latina*, vol. 36 *Sancti Aurelii Augustini, Hipponensis Episcopi, Opera omnia [...] Tomus Quartus, pars prior* (Paris: Imprimérie Catholique, 1865.); available online at http://bit.ly/2bLPuI2.

**PL 37**
Jacques Paul Migne (ed.), *Patrologia cursus completus. Series latina*, vol. 37 *Sancti Aurelii Augustini, Hipponensis Episcopi, Opera omnia [...] Tomus Quartus, pars altera* (Paris: Imprimérie Catholique, 1865.); available online at http://bit.ly/2bg2ysw.

**PLATO 1967**
Plato, *Plato in Twelve Volumes*, volumes 10–11, translated by Robert Gregg Bury (Cambridge MA: Harvard University Press; London: William Heinemann, 1967–8); available online at http://bit.ly/2cr9geX.

**PLATO 1969**
Plato, *Plato in Twelve Volumes*, volumes 5–6, translated by Paul Shorey (Cambridge MA: Harvard University Press; London: William Heinemann, 1969); available online at http://bit.ly/2c3tsRe.

**PONTIFICALE ROMANUM 1572**
*Pontificale Romanum. Ad omnes pontificias ceremonias, quibus nunc utitur sacrosancta Romana Ecclesia accomodatum [...]* (Venice: Lucantonio II Giunta, 1572) [USTC 820684].

**PONTIFICALE ROMANUM 1595**
*Pontificale Romanum Clementis VIII Pont. Max. iussu restitutum atque editum* (Rome: apud Giacomo Luna, 1595) [USTC 821099].

**PONZIO 1588 / PONZIO 1959**
Pietro Ponzio, *Ragionamento di musica [...]* (Parma: apresso Erasmo Viotti, 1588) [USTC 850867]; facsimile reprint edited by Suzanne Clercx (Kassel: Bärenreiter, 1959).

**PONZIO 1595**
Pietro Ponzio, *Dialogo [...] ove si tratta della theorica e prattica musica [...]* (Parma: Erasmo Viotti, 1595).

**PORTA 1575**
Costanzo Porta, *Litaniæ Deiparæ Virginis Mariæ ex Sacra Scriptura depromptæ [...]* (Venice: Giorgio Angelieri, 1575) [USTC 850951] [RISM A/I: P 5179].

**POSSEVINO 1594**
Giovan Battista Possevino, *Hinni sacri del Breviario Rom. [...]* (Perugia: appresso hær. Andrea Bresciano, 1594) [USTC 851116].

**POSTHIUS 1608**
Johann Posthius, *Die Sontags Evangelia gesangsweise* (Amberg: Forster, 1608) [*DKL* 1608[11]].

**POWODOWSKI 1591**
Hieronim Powodowski, *Agenda seu ritus sacramentorum ecclesiasticorum [...]* (Kraków: Jan Januszowski, 1591) [USTC 242844].

**PRAETORIUS 1607**
Michael Praetorius, *Musarum Sioniarum motectæ et psalmi latini [...]* (Nuremberg: Abraham Wagenmann, [1607?]) [RISM A/I: P 5361].

**PRIMER 1545**
*The Primer set foorth by the Kinges Maiestie and his clergie [...]* (London: Edward Whitchurch, 1545) [USTC 503616].

**PRYNNE 1632**
William Prynne, *Histriomastix* (London: Michael Sparke, 1633 [=1632]).

**PSALMEN 1567**
*Psalmen Vnd Geistliche Lieder sampt dem Christlichen Catechismo/Kirchenceremonien vnd Gebeten* (Heidelberg: Harnisch, 1567) [*DKL* 1567⁰⁴].

**PSALMES OF DAVID 1594**
*The CL psalms of David in meter. For the use of the Kirk of Scotland* (Middelburg: Richard Schilders, 1594) [USTC 429535].

**PUSSOT 1858**
Jean Pussot, *Journalier ou mémoires [...]*, edited by E. Henry et Ch. Loriquet (Reims: P. Regnier, 1858).

**RATHGEB 1602**
Jacob Rathgeb, *Kurtze und warhaffte Beschreibung der Badenfahrt [...]* (Tübingen: Erhardus Cellius, 1602).

**RAUSCHER 1531**
Andreas Rauscher (ed.), *Geistliche lieder auffs new gebessert [...]* (Erfurt: Andreas Rauscher, 1531) [USTC 658874] [*DKL* 1531⁰³].

**RAZZI 1563**
Serafino Razzi (ed.), *Libro primo delle laudi spirituali [...]* (Venice: hær. Bernardo Giunta, 1563) [USTC 852086] [RISM B/I: 1563I6].

**RECUEIL 1555**
*Recueil de plusieurs chansons spirituelles tant vieilles que nouvelles [...]* ([S.l.]: [s.n.], 1555) [USTC 9387].

**REFORMATIO LEGUM ECCLESIASTICARUM 1571**
*Reformatio legum ecclesiasticarum [...]* (London: John Daye, 1571) [USTC 507300]; available online at http://bit.ly/2c3zrpr.

**RELATIONE 1570**
*Relatione de tutto il successo occorso nell'archibugiata tirata all'Illustriss. et Reverendiss. Cardinale Borromeo Arcivescovo di Milano* (Milan: G. B. Pontio, [1570]) [USTC 804784]; available online at http://bit.ly/2bzZVlP.

**RHAU 1955**
Georg Rhau, *Musikdrucke aus den Jahren 1538 bis 1545*, edited by Hans Albrecht; vol. I, *Balthasar Resinarius. Responsorium Numero Octoginta*, edited by Inge-Maria Schroeder; Preface translated by Walter E. Buszin (Kassel: Bärenreiter, 1955).

**RHODES 1637**
John Rhodes, *The countrie mans comfort. Or Religious Recreations fitte for all well disposed persons. Which was printed in the yeere of our Lord 1588. And since corrected, amended, and enlarged by the same author. I. R.* (London: M. D[awson], 1637); text available online at http://bit.ly/2bhRau8.

**RINALDI 1656**
Odorico Rinaldi (ed.), *Annali Ecclesiastici tratti da quelli del Cardinal Baronio [...] Parte II [...]* (Rome: appresso Vitale Mascardi, 1656).

**RIVOLA 1656**
Francesco Rivola, *Vita di Federico Borromeo* (Milan: Dionisio Gariboldi, 1656).

**ROBERTS 1583**
Thomas Roberts, *The Catechisme in meter for the easier learning [...]* (London: Robert Walley, 1583) [USTC 509842].

Rossetto 1529
Biagio Rossetto [Rossetti], *Libellus de rudimentis musices [...]* (Verona: per Stefano Nicolini da Sabbio, 1529) [USTC 853504].

Ruffo 1570
Vincenzo Ruffo, *Vincentii Ruffi moderatoris [...] missæ quatuor concinnatæ ad ritum Concilii Mediolani* (Milan: Giovanni Antonio degli Antoni, 1570) [USTC 853798] [RISM A/I: R 3054].

Sadoleto 1533
Jacopo Sadoleto, *De liberis recte instituendis [...]* (Lyon: apud Sébastien Gryphe, 1533) [USTC 156026].

Sahagún 1583
Bernardino de Rivera de Sahagún, *Psalmodia christiana y sermonario de los sanctos del año [...]* (Mexico: en casa de Pedro Ocharte, 1583).

Salmi 1588
*I Salmi di David tradotti dalla lingua Hebrea nella italiana. Divisi in cinque parti* (Paris: chez Jean Mettayer, 1588) [USTC 806311].

Sanudo 1969
Marino Sanudo [Sanuto], *I Diarii*, 58 vols. (Venice: F. Visentini, 1879–1903); facsimile edition (Sala Bolognese: Arnaldo Forni, 1969).

Sanudo 1980
Marino Sanudo [Sanuto], *De origine, situ et magistratibus Urbis Venetae ovvero la città di Venetia (1493–1530)*, edited by Angela Carracciolo Aricò (Milan: Cisalpino-La Goliardica, 1980).

Savonarola 1955
Girolamo Savonarola, *Prediche sopra Ezechiele*, edited by Roberto Ridolfi, 2 vols. (Rome: A. Belardetti, 1955).

Savonarola 1971
Girolamo Savonarola, *Prediche sopra Amos e Zaccaria*, edited by Paolo Ghiglieri, 3 vols. (Rome: A. Belardetti, 1971–1972).

Savonarola 1976
Girolamo Savonarola, *Operette spirituali*, edited by Mario Ferrara (Rome: A. Belardetti, 1976).

Scherer 1588
Georg Scherer, *Ein Predig vom Fronleichnamsfest und Umbgang [...]* (Ingolstadt: David Sartorius, 1588) [USTC 645509].

SCT
*Sacrosanctum Concilium Tridentinum. Cum citationibus ex utroque Testamento, Juris Pontificii Constitutionibus, aliisque S. Rom. Eccl. Conciliis* (Padua: Ex Typographia Seminarii, 1722); available online at http://bit.ly/2bD8Lff.

Seagar 1553
Francis Seagar, *Certayne Psalmes Select out of the Psalter of David [...]* (London: Nicholas Hill for William Seres, 1553) [USTC 504860].

Second livre 1555
*Le second livre des chansons spirituelles composées à l'utilité de tous vrays Chrestiens [...]* ([Geneva]: [Jean Girard], 1555) [GLN-1430].

Selnecker 1569
Nikolaus Selnecker, *Der gantze Psalter des Koeniglichen Propheten Davids [...]* (Nuremberg: Christoph Heußler, 1569) [USTC 633374] [*WB* 898].

SENECA 1604
Antonio Seneca, *Prattica del governo spirituale e temporale de monasterii delle monache* (Vatican City: Archivio segreto [A. A. Armadio I-XVIII, ms. 6492]), manuscript (1604).

SERMONS 1839
*Sermons or Homilies Appointed to be Read in Churches in the Time of Queen Elizabeth of Famous Memory. New Edition* (London: The Society for Promoting Christian Knowledge, 1839).

SERVIN 1565
Jean Servin, *Les cent cinquante Pseaumes de David, composez en trois parties [...]* (Orléans: Louis Rabier, 1565) [USTC 505].

SERVIN 1579
Jean Servin, *Psalmi Davidis a G. Buchanano versibus expressi* (Lyon [=Geneva]: Charles Pesnot, 1579) [USTC 450808]; available online at http://bit.ly/2b0gLKV.

SESSANTA SALMI 1560
*Sessanta salmi di David, tradotti in rime volgari italiane* (Geneva: Jean-Baptiste Pinereul, 1560) [USTC 450096].

SLÜTER 1525
Joachim Slüter, *Ein gantz schone unde seer nutte gesangk boek [...]* (Rostock: Ludwig Dietz, 1525) [USTC 643391].

SLÜTER 1531
Joachim Slüter (ed.), *Geystlyke leder uppt nye gebetert [...]* (Rostock: Ludwig Dietz, 1531) [USTC 659789].

SONNIUS 1571
Franciscus Sonnius, *Een bequaem maniere om jonghers soetelijck by sanck te leeren [...]* (Antwerp: Antonius Thielens, 1571) [USTC 411676].

SOTO 1588
Francisco Soto de Langa (ed.), *Il terzo libro delle Laudi spirituali a tre e quattro voci [...]* (Rome: Alessandro Gardano, 1588) [USTC 806397] [RISM B/I: 1588|11].

SOUTER LIEDEKENS 1540
*Souter Liedekens Ghemaect ter eeren Gods op alle die Psalmen van Dauid [...]* (Antwerp: Symon Cock, 1540) [USTC 403021].

SPACCINI 1911 / SPACCINI 1919
Giovanni Battista Spaccini, *Cronaca modenese (1588–1636)*, 2 vols., edited by G. Bertoni, T. Sandonnini, and P. E. Vicini, Monumenti di storia patria delle provincie modenesi, Serie delle Cronache, 16–17 (Modena: Giovanni Ferraguti e C., 1911 and 1919).

SPANGENBERG 1545
Johann Spangenberg, *Cantiones ecclesiasticæ latinæ [...] Kjrchengesenge Deudsch auff die Sontage [...]* (Magdeburg: Michael Lotther, 1545) [USTC 613392].

SPANGENBERG 1568
Cyriacus Spangenberg, *Von der ewigen vorsehung und Goetlichen gnadenwahl* (Eisleben: Andreas Petri, 1568) [USTC 631037]; available online at http://bit.ly/2bbYzYI.

SPANGENBERG 1571
Cyriacus Spangenberg, *Cithara Lutheri. Die schoenen, Christlichen trostreichen psalmen und geistlichen lieder [...]* (Mühlhausen: Georg Hantzsch, 1571) [USTC 622623].

STERNHOLD 1549
Thomas Sternhold, *Certayne Psalmes chosen out of the Psalter of David & drawen into English metre* (London: Edward Whitchurch[e], 1549) [USTC 504280].

STERNHOLD AND HOPKINS 1549

Thomas Sternhold and John Hopkins, *Al such psalmes of David as Thomas Sternehold [...] didde in his life time draw into English Metre* (London: Edward Whitchurch, 1549) [USTC 504306].

STERNHOLD AND HOPKINS 1562

Thomas Sternhold and John Hopkins, *The Whole Booke of Psalmes, collected into Englysh metre [...]* (London: John Daye, 1562) [USTC 506042].

STRIGENITZ 1610

Gregor Strigenitz, *Spiritus Effusus [...]* (Leipzig: Bartholomæi Voigt, 1610); available online at http://bit.ly/2b40Vz6.

STROZZI 1588

Lorenza Strozzi, *In singula totius anni solemnia. Hymni [...]* (Florence: Apud Filippo II Giunta, 1588) [USTC 857688].

STUBBES 1583 / STUBBES 1836

Phillip Stubbes, *The Anatomie of Abuses [...]* (London: John Kingston for Richard Jones, 1583) [USTC 509868]; reprinted from the third edition of 1585, edited by William Turnbull (London: Pickering, 1836).

SUAREZ 1655

Joseph Maria Suarez [Josephus Maria Suaresius], *Prænestes antiquæ libri duo* (Rome: Typ. Angeli Bernabò hæredis Manelfi, 1655).

SURGANT 1506

Johannes Ulrich Surgant, *Manuale curatorum predicandi prebens modu [...]* (Basel: Michael Furter, 1506) [USTC 674825].

SYLVIUS 1529

Peter Sylvius [Penick], *Summa und Schutz der waren Evangelischen lere [...]* ([Leipzig]: [Nickel Schmidt & Valentin Schumann], 1529) [USTC 694899]; available online at http://bit.ly/2bB4tWx.

TANSILLO 1585

Luigi Tansillo, *Le lagrime di san Pietro del signor Luigi Tansillo da Nola. Mandate in luce da Giovan Battista Attendolo, da Capua* (Vico Equense: Appresso Giovanni Battista Cappelli & Giuseppe Cacchi, 1585) [USTC 858051].

THE PRAISE OF MUSICKE 1586

*The Praise of Musicke [...]* (Oxford: Joseph Barnes, 1586) [USTC 510509]; facsimile edition (New York NY and Hildesheim: G. Olms, 1980); text available online at http://bit.ly/2bmMy7d.

THE SECOND TOME OF HOMILEES 1571

*The Second Tome of Homilees* (London: Richard Jugge and John Cawood, 1571) [USTC 507336].

THESAURO 1525 / THESAURO 1568

*Thesauro della sapientia evangelica* (Milan: Per Gottardo da Ponte, [1525?]) [USTC 802420]; (Milan: Valerio & Girolamo Meda, 1568) [USTC 801260].

THOMISSØN 1569

[Hans Thomissøn], *Salmebog* (Copenhagen: Lor. Benedicht, 1569) [USTC 302364]; available online at http://bit.ly/2cfabgt.

TINCTORIS 1957
Johannes Tinctoris, *Proportionale Musices*, edited and translated by Albert Seay as "The 'Proportionale Musices' of Johannes Tinctoris", *Journal of Music Theory*, vol. 1, no. 1 (March, 1957), pp. 22–75.

TINCTORIS 1963
Johannes Tinctoris, "Complexus effectuum musices", in Edmond de Coussemaker (ed.), *Scriptorum de musica medii aevi nova series a Gerbertina altera*, 4 vols. (Paris: Durand, 1864–1876); reprint (Hildesheim: Olms, 1963), vol. IV, pp. 191–195.

TINCTORIS 1976
Johannes Tinctoris, *Opera omnia*, edited by William Melin (Rome: American Institute of Musicology, 1976).

TRITONIUS 1507
Petrus Tritonius, *Melopoiæ sive harmoniæ tetracenticæ super XXII genera carminum [...]* (Augsburg: Johann Rimann [Erhard Öglin], 1507) [RISM A/I: T 1249].

TYE 1553
Christopher Tye, *The Actes of the Apostles, translated into Englyshe metre [...]* (London: Nicholas Hill for William Seres, 1553) [USTC 504886] [RISM A/I: T 1445].

ULENBERG 1582
Kaspar Ulenberg, *Die Psalmen Davids* (Köln: Haer. Johann Quentel, 1582) [USTC 637051].

UTENHOVE 1566
Jan Utenhove, *De Psalmen Davidis, in Nederlandischer sangs-ryme* (London: John Daye, 1566) [USTC 407629].

VALÉRY 1599
Magdaleine Valéry, *La Montaigne des pucelles. Den maeghdenbergh [...]* (Leiden: Jan Paets, 1599) [USTC 80745].

VAN CAMPEN 1532
Johannes van Campen, *Psalmorum omnium juxta Hebraicam veritatem paraphrastica interpretatio* (Paris: Apud Claude Chevallon, 1532) [USTC 138137].

VAN TURNHOUT 1569
Gerardus van Turnhout, *Sacrarum ac aliarum cantionum trium vocum* (Louvain: Pierre Phalèse, 1569) [USTC 83694] [RISM A/I: T 1434].

VAN VAERNEWIJCK 1873
Marcus van Vaernewijck, *Van die beroerlicke tijden in die Nederlanden en voornamelijk in Ghendt 1566–1568*, edited by F. Vanderhaeghen II, vol. II (Ghent: C. Annoot-Braeckman, 1873).

VAUX 1854
William Sandys Wright Vaux (ed.), *The World Encompassed by Sir Francis Drake* (London: The Hakluyt Society, 1854).

VEELDERHANDE LIEDEKENS 1558
*Veelderhande gheestelicke liedekens [...]* ([Emden]: Gellius Ctematius, 1558) [USTC 408040].

VEHE 1537 / VEHE 1567
Michael Vehe, *Ein new gesangbuechlin geystlicher lieder vor aller gutthe Christen nach Ordenung Christlicher Kirchen* (Leipzig: Nikolaus Wolrab, 1537) [USTC 644905]; (Mainz: Franz Behem, 1567) [USTC 644906]; available online at http://bit.ly/2b62oSC.

VENEGAS DE HENESTROSA 1557
Luis Venegas de Henestrosa (ed.), *Libro de cifra nueva para tecla, harpa y vihuela* (Alcalà de Henares: Juan de Brocar, 1557) [USTC 342303].

**VERMIGLI 1587**
Pietro Martire [Peter Martyr] Vermigli, *Loci Communes [...]* (Zürich: Froschoviana officina, 1587) [USTC 673427].

**VERMIGLI 1994**
Pietro Martire [Peter Martyr] Vermigli, *Early Writings: Creed, Scripture, Church*, translated by Mariano di Gangi, edited by Joseph C. McClelland, with a biographical introduction by Philip M. J. McNair (Kirksville: Sixteenth Century Journal Publishers, 1994).

**VESPERARUM PRECUM 1540**
*Vesperarum precum officia psalmi feriarum et dominicalium [...]* (Wittenberg: Georg Rhau, 1540) [RISM B/I: 1540|5].

**VICENTINO 1555**
Nicola Vicentino, *L'antica musica ridotta alla moderna prattica [...]* (Rome: Appresso Antonio Barrè, 1555) [USTC 863179].

**VIRET 1554 / VIRET 1556**
Pierre Viret, *Des Actes des Vrais Successeurs de Jésus Christ [...]* (Geneva: Jean Girard, 1554) [USTC 694]; Italian translation as *De' fatti de veri successori di Giesu Christo [...]* (Geneva: Gianluigi Paschale, 1556) [USTC 450394].

**VIRET 1564 / VIRET 1584**
Pierre Viret, *Les Cauteles, Canon et Ceremonies de la Messe [...]* (Lyon: [Jean Saugrain] pour Claude Ravot, 1564) [USTC 77832]; English translation as *The Cauteles, Canon, and Ceremonies [...]* (London: Thomas Vautrollier for Andrew Maunsell, 1584) [USTC 510138].

**VIVES 1524**
Juan Luis Vives, *De institutione fœminæ christianæ, libri tres* (Antwerp: apud Michael Hillenius Hoochstratanus impensis Franciscus Birckman, 1524) [USTC 403719].

**WA 10**[I/1]
*Luthers Werke: Kritische Gesamtausgabe. Weihnachtspostille 1522* (Weimar: Böhlau, 1910).

**WA 12**
*Luthers Werke: Kritische Gesamtausgabe. Reihenpredigt über 1. Petrus 1522; Predigten 1522/23; Schriften 1523* (Weimar: Böhlau, 1891).

**WA 18**
*Luthers Werke: Kritische Gesamtausgabe. Schriften 1525* (Weimar: Böhlau, 1908).

**WA 19**
*Luthers Werke: Kritische Gesamtausgabe. Schriften 1526* (Weimar: Böhlau, 1897).

**WA 26**
*Luthers Werke: Kritische Gesamtausgabe. Vorlesung über 1. Timotheus 1528; Schriften 1528* (Weimar: Böhlau, 1909).

**WA 30**[II]
*Luthers Werke: Kritische Gesamtausgabe. Schriften 1529/30. Zweite Abteilung* (Weimar: Böhlau, 1909).

**WA 35**
*Luthers Werke: Kritische Gesamtausgabe. Lieder* (Weimar: Böhlau, 1923).

**WA 44**
*Luthers Werke: Kritische Gesamtausgabe. Genesisvorlesung (Cap. 31–40) 1543/45* (Weimar: Böhlau, 1915).

**WA 50**
*Luthers Werke: Kritische Gesamtausgabe. Schriften 1536/39* (Weimar: Böhlau, 1914).

**WA 6**
*Luthers Werke: Kritische Gesamtausgabe. Schriften, Predigten, Disputationen 1519/20* (Weimar: Böhlau, 1888).
**WA BR**
*Luthers Werke: Kritische Gesamtausgabe. Briefwechsel*, 18 volumes (Weimar: Böhlau, 1930–1985).
**WA DB**
*Luthers Werke: Kritische Gesamtausgabe. Die Deutsche Bibel*, 12 volumes (Weimar: Böhlau, 1906–1961).
**WA TR**
*Luthers Werke: Kritische Gesamtausgabe. Tischreden*, 6 volumes (Weimar: Böhlau, 1912–1921).
**WALASSER 1574**
Adam Walasser, *Catholische Teutsche und lateinische Gesang [...]* (Tegernsee: Tegernsee Klosterdruckerei, 1574) [USTC 620702].
**WALDIS 1553**
Burkhard Waldis, *Der Psalter in newe gesangs weise [...]* (Frankfurt: Christian Egenolff, 1553) [USTC 634281].
**WALTHER 1524 / WALTHER 1878**
Johannes Walther, *Geystliche Gesangk buchleyn* (Wittenberg: Josef Klug, 1524) [USTC 659783] [RISM A/I: W 167]; modern edition as *Wittembergisch geistlich Gesangbuch von 1524*, edited by Otto Kade (Berlin: Trautwein, 1878); available online at http://bit.ly/2b7UQff.
**WALTHER 1970**
Johannes Walther, *Johann Walter sämtliche Werke*, edited by Otto Schroeder and Joachim Stalmann, 6 vols. (Kassel: Bärenreiter; St Louis: Concordia, 1953–1970).
**WEISSE 1531**
Michael Weisse (ed.), *Ein new Geseng Buchlen* (Jungbunzlau [Mladá Boleslav]: Jirík Štyrsa, 1531) [USTC 644927].
**WESEL 1556**
*Psalmes of David in metre* ([Wesel]: Hugh Singleton, 1556) [USTC 516558].
**WHOLE BOOKE 1592**
*The Whole Booke of Psalmes with their wonted tunes, as they are song in churches, composed into foure parts [...]* (London: Thomas East, 1592) [USTC 512271].
**WHOLE PSALMES 1563**
*The Whole Psalmes in foure partes whiche may be song to al musicall instruments, set forth for the encrease of vertue and abolishyng of other vayne and triflying ballades* (London: John Daye, 1563) [USTC 506173].
**WILLAERT 1559**
Adrian Willaert, *Musica Nova* (Venice: Antonio Gardano, 1559); available online at http://bit.ly/2bbPSBs.
**WITHER 1619**
George Wither, *A Preparation to the Psalter* (London: N. Okes, 1619).
**WITZEL 1541**
Georg Witzel, *Odæ christianæ. Etliche Christliche Gesenge, Gebete und Reymen [...]* (Mainz: Franz Behem, 1541) [USTC 679156].

**WITZEL 1550**
Georg Witzel, *Psaltes Ecclesiasticus. Chorbuch der heiligen Catholischen Kirchen Deudsch [...]* (Cologne: Johann Quentell, 1550) [USTC 688545].

**WYSS 1901**
Bernhard Wyss, *Die Chronik des Bernhards Wyss, 1519–1530*, edited by Georg Finsler (Basel: Basler Buch- und Antiquariats-Handlung, 1901).

**YNCONVENIENTES S.D.**
*Ynconvenientes, y gravísimos daños que se siguen de que las Religiones tengan Música de canto de Órgano,* manuscript, s.d. (Madrid: Biblioteca Nacional, MS 14059.11).

**Z**
Huldreich [Huldrych] Zwingli, *Huldreich Zwinglis Sämtliche Werke. Unter Mitwirkung des Zwinglivereins in Zürich*, edited by Emil Egli, Georg Finsler, Walther Köhler, Oskar Farner, Fritz Blanke, Leonhard von Muralt, Edwin Künzli, Rudolf Pfister, 13 volumes (vols. 88–101 of the *Corpus Reformatorum*, indicated here as Z I [=vol. 88]-XIII [=vol. 101]) (Berlin: Schwetschke; Leipzig: Heinsius; Zurich: Berichthaus and Theologischer Verlag, 1905–1990).

**ZACCONI 1592 / ZACCONI 1975**
Lodovico Zacconi, *Prattica di musica [...] parte prima* (Venice: appresso Girolamo Polo, 1592) [USTC 864072]; facsimile edition (Sala Bolognese: Arnaldo Forni, 1975).

**ZARLINO 1558 / ZARLINO 1999**
Gioseffo Zarlino, *Le istitutioni harmoniche [...]* (Venice: Pietro da Fino, 1558) [USTC 864226]; facsimile edition (Sala Bolognese: Arnaldo Forni, 1999).

**ZELL 1534**
Katharina Zell (ed.), *Von Christo Jesu unserem saeligmacher [...]* (Strasbourg: Jakob Frölich, 1534) [USTC 702779].

**ZWICK 1540**
Johannes Zwick (ed.), *Nüw gsangbuechle von vil schoenen psalmen und geistlichen liedern [...]* (Zürich: Christoph I Froschauer, 1540) [USTC 678764].

**ZWINGLI 1983**
Huldreich [Huldrych] Zwingli, *On Providence and Other Essays*, edited by Willian John Hinke (Durham: The Labyrinth Press, 1983).

# Secondary

All web links were last accessed on August 25th, 2016.

**ABRAHAM 1974**
Gerald Abraham, *The Tradition of Western Music* (Berkeley and Los Angeles CA: University of California Press, 1974).

**ACKERMANN 2002**
Peter Ackermann, *Studien zur Gattungsgeschichte und Typologie der römischen Motette im Zeitalter Palestrinas* (Paderborn: Ferdinand Schöningh, 2002).

**AERKE 2010**
Kristiaan Aerke, "Word as a Weapon in a Holy Mission: Anna Bijns" in Lia van Gemert et al. (eds.), *Women's Writing from the Low Countries 1200–1875. A Bilingual Anthology* (Amsterdam: Amsterdam University Press, 2010), pp. 160–175.

**AHMED 1990**
Ehsan Ahmed, "Marguerite de Navarre's *Chansons Spirituelles* and the Poet's Passion", *Bibliothèque d'Humanisme et Renaissance*, vol. 52, no. 1 (1990), pp. 37–52.

**AMELN 1955**
Konrad Ameln, "Eine ältere Auflage des Konstanzer 'Nüw gsangbüchle'", *JLH*, no. 1 (1955), pp. 97–99.

**AMELN 1956**
Konrad Ameln, "Das Achtliederbuch vom Jahre 1523/24", *JLH*, no. 2 (1956), pp. 89–91.

**AMELN 1980**
Konrad Ameln, "'Herzlich tut mich erfreuen': Wandlungen einer Melodie", in Detlef Altenburg (ed.), *Ars musica musica scientia* (Cologne: Verlag der Arbeitsgemeinschaft für rheinische Musikgeschichte, 1980), pp. 10–16.

**AMELN 1986**
Konrad Ameln, "Kirchenliedmelodien der Reformation im Gemeindegesang des 16. und 17. Jahrhunderts", in Alfred Dürr and Walther Killy (eds.), *Das protestantische Kirchenlied im 16. und 17. Jahrhundert: Text-, musik- und theologiegeschichtliche Probleme* (Wiesbaden: Otto Harrassowitz, 1986), pp. 61–71.

**AMELN 1989**
Konrad Ameln, "Luthers Kirchenlied und Gesangbuch: offene Fragen", *JLH*, no. 32 (1989), pp. 19–28.

**ANDERSON 1976**
Daniel L. Anderson, *The Theology of German Anabaptism as Seen Through the Hymnody of Its Major Forefathers* (Th. M. Thesis: Dallas Theological Seminary, 1976).

**ANFOSSO 1913**
Luigi Anfosso, *Storia dell'archibugiata tirata al Card. Carlo Borromeo (S. Carlo) in Milano la sera del 26 ottobre 1569* (Milan: Sacchetti, 1913).

**ANTTILA 2013**
Miikka E. Anttila, *Luther's Theology of Music. Spiritual Beauty and Pleasure* (Berlin and New York NY: De Gruyter, 2013).

**APLIN 1978**
John Aplin, "A Group of English Magnificats 'Upon the Faburden'", *Soundings*, no. 7 (1978), pp. 85–100.

**APLIN 1979**
John Aplin, "The Survival of Plainsong in Anglican Music: Some Early *Te Deum* Settings", *J-AMS*, vol. 82 (1979), pp. 247–275.

**APLIN 1980**
John Aplin, "'The Fourth Kind of Faburden': The Identity of an English Four-Part Style", *ML*, no. 61 (1980), pp. 245–265.

**APLIN 1981**
John Aplin, "The origins of John Day's 'Certaine Notes'", *ML*, no. 62 (1981), pp. 295–299.

**ARNOLD AND WYATT 1940**
John Henry Arnold and Edward Gerald Penfold Wyatt (eds.), *Walter Howard Frere: A Collection of His Papers on Liturgical and Historical Subjects* (London: Oxford University Press, 1940).

**ATLAS 1998**
Allan W. Atlas, *Music in Western Europe, 1400–1600* (New York NY and London: W. W. Norton and Company, 1998).

**ATLAS 2006**
Allan W. Atlas, "Music for the Mass", in James Haar (ed.), *European Music 1520–1642* (Woodbridge: The Boydell Press, 2006), pp. 91–100.

**AUKSI 1979**
Peter Auksi, "Simplicity and Silence: The Influence of Scripture on the Aesthetic Thought of the Major Reformers", *Journal of Religious History*, no. 10 (1979), pp. 343–364.

**AUKSI 1995**
Peter Auksi, *Christian Plain Style. The Evolution of a Spiritual Ideal* (Montreal and Kingston: McGill-Queen's University Press, 1995).

**AUSTERN 1988**
Linda Phyllis Austern, "Nature, Culture, Myth, and the Musician in Early Modern England", *J-AMS*, vol. 51, no. 1 (Spring 1988), pp. 1–47.

**AUSTERN 1993**
Linda Phyllis Austern, "'Alluring the Auditorie to Effeminacie': Music and the Idea of the Feminine", *ML*, no. 74 (1993), pp. 343–354.

**AUSTERN 2011**
Linda Phyllis Austern, "'For Musicke is the Handmaid of the Lord': Women, Psalms, and Domestic Music-Making in Early Modern England", in Linda Phyllis Austern, Kari Boyd McBride and David L. Orvis (eds.), *Psalms in the Early Modern World* (Aldershot: Ashgate, 2011), pp. 77–114.

**AVOLIO 2008**
Fabio Avolio, *La musica sacra nel Concilio di Trento e lo stile contrappuntistico di Giovanni Pierluigi da Palestrina; Analisi delle elaborazioni vocali, ad opera di Anerio e Suriano, della Missa Papae Marcelli* (Rome: Aracne, 2008).

**BAADE 2005**
Colleen Baade, "'Hired' Nun Musicians in Early Modern Castile", in Thomasin LaMay (ed.), *Musical Voices of Early Modern Women. Many-Headed Melodies* (Aldershot: Ashgate, 2005), pp. 287–310.

**BAADE 2010**
Colleen Baade, "Nun Musicians as Teachers and Students in Early Modern Spain", in Russell E. Murray jr, Susan Forscher Weiss, Cynthia J. Cyrus (eds.), *Music Education in the*

*Middle Ages and the Renaissance* (Bloomington IN: Indiana University Press, 2010), pp. 262–286.

**BAILEY 1987**
Adrienne Thompson Bailey, "Music in the Liturgies of the Reformers: Martin Luther and Jean Calvin", *Reformed Liturgy and Music*, vol. 21 (1987), pp. 74–79.

**BAINI 1828**
Giuseppe Baini, *Memorie storico-critiche della vita e delle opera di Giovanni Pierluigi da Palestrina*, 2 vols. (Rome: Dalla Società Tipografica, 1828); available online at http://bit.ly/2bexx9B.

**BAINTON 1971**
Roland H. Bainton, *Women of the Reformation in Germany and Italy* (Minneapolis MN: Augsburg Fortress, 1971).

**BAINTON 1973**
Roland H. Bainton, *Women of the Reformation in France and England* (Minneapolis MN: Augsburg Fortress, 1973).

**BAINTON 1977**
Roland H. Bainton, *Women of the Reformation: From Spain to Scandinavia* (Minneapolis MN: Augsburg Fortress, 1977).

**BANNARD 1919**
Yorke Bannard, "Calvin as Musical Reformer", *The Monthly Musical Record*, no. 49 (1919), pp. 151–152.

**BARDSLEY 2007**
Sandy Bardsley, *Women's Roles in the Middle Ages* (Westport CT: Greenwood Press, 2007).

**BARGE 1905**
Hermann Barge, *Andreas Bodenstein von Karlstadt* (Leipzig: Friedrich Brandstetter, 1905).

**BAROFFIO 1995**
Bonifacio G. Baroffio, "Il Concilio di Trento e la musica", in Danilo Curti and Marco Gozzi (eds.), *Musica e Liturgia nella Riforma Tridentina* (Trento: Provincia Autonoma di Trento – Servizio Beni Librari e Archivistici, 1995), pp. 9–18.

**BATAILLON 1991**
Marcel Bataillon, *Erasme et l'Espagne*, edited by Daniel Devoto and Charles Amiel, 3 vols. (Geneva: Droz, 1991).

**BATIFFOL 1912**
Pierre Batiffol, *History of the Roman Breviary*, translated by Atwell M. Y. Baylay (London: Longmans, 1912); available online at http://bit.ly/2bOokBu.

**BC**
Robert Kolb and Timothy J. Wengert (eds.), *The Book of Concord: The Confessions of the Evangelical Lutheran Church*, English translation by Charles Arand, Eric Gritsch, Robert Kolb, William Russel, James Schaaf, Jane Strohl, and Timothy J. Wengert (Minneapolis MN: Augsburg Fortress, 2000).

**BECK 1964**
Hermann Beck, "Das Konzil von Trient und die Probleme der Kirchenmusik", *Kirchemusikalisches Jahrbuch*, vol. 48 (1964), pp. 108–117.

**BEGGIAO 1978**
Diego Beggiao, *La Visita pastorale di Clemente VIII (1592–1600): aspetti di riforma post-tridentina a Roma* (Rome: Libreria Editrice della Pontificia Università Lateranense, 1978).

**BENHAM 1980**
Hugh Benham, *Latin Church Music in England, c. 1460–1575* (New York NY: Da Capo Press, 1980).

**BENTE 1989**
Martin Bente et al., *Bayerische Staatsbibliothek. Katalog der Musikhandschriften: I Chorbücher und Handschriften in chorbuchartiger Notierung*, Kataloge Bayerischer Musiksammlungen, Band 5/1 (Munich: G. Henle, 1989).

**BERDES 1993 / BERDES 1996**
Jane L. Berdes, *Women Musicians of Venice. Musical Foundations, 1525–1855* (Oxford UK and New York NY: Oxford University Press, 1993; 1996²).

**BERGER 2006**
Karol Berger, "Concepts and Developments in Music Theory", in James Haar (ed.), *European Music 1520–1642* (Woodbridge: The Boydell Press, 2006), pp. 304–328.

**BERGIN 2009**
Patrick Bergin jr, "*Preces speciales:* Prototype of Tridentine Musical Reform", *The Ohio State Online Music Journal*, vol. 2 (2009), available online at http://osomjournal.org/issues/2/bergin/.

**BERGQUIST 1999**
Peter Bergquist (ed.), *Orlando di Lasso Studies* (Cambridge: Cambridge University Press, 1999).

**BERGQUIST 2006**
Peter Bergquist, "Germany and Central Europe, I: 1520–1600", in James Haar (ed.), *European Music 1520–1642* (Woodbridge: The Boydell Press, 2006), pp. 329–352.

**BERNIER 1937**
Alfred Bernier, "Intorno alla Edizione Medicea del canto gregoriano. Un documento inedito (?)", *Note d'archivio per la storia musicale*, vol. XIV, no. 2 (1937), pp. 91–93.

**BERNSTEIN 1998**
Jane A. Bernstein, *Music Printing in Renaissance Venice: The Scotto Press (1539–1572)* (Oxford UK and New York NY: Oxford University Press, 1998).

**BERNSTEIN 2001**
Jane A. Bernstein, *Print Culture and Music in Sixteenth-Century Venice* (Oxford UK and New York NY: Oxford University Press, 2001).

**BERTOGLIO 2017**
Chiara Bertoglio, "Cats, Bulls and Donkeys: Bernardino Cirillo on Sixteenth-Century Church Music", *EM*, vol. 45 (2017), forthcoming.

**BESUTTI 1991**
Paola Besutti, "Giovanni Pierluigi da Palestrina e la liturgia mantovana", in Lino Bianchi and Giancarlo Rostirolla (eds.), *Atti del II Convegno internazionale di studi palestriniani. Palestrina e la sua presenza nella musica e nella cultura europee dal suo tempo ad oggi* (Palestrina: Fondazione G. P. da Palestrina, 1991), pp. 157–164.

**BESUTTI 1993**
Paola Besutti, "Un modello alternativo di Controriforma. Il caso mantovano", in Oscar Mischiati and Paolo Russo (eds.), *La Cappella musicale nell'Italia della Controriforma* (Florence: Olschki, 1993), pp. 111–122.

**BIRELEY 1999**
Robert Bireley, *The Refashioning of Catholicism, 1450–1700: A Reassessment of the Counter Reformation* (Washington DC: The Catholic University of America Press, 1999).

BIZZARINI 2012
Marco Bizzarini, *Federico Borromeo e la musica. Scritti e carteggi* (Milan: Biblioteca Ambrosiana; Rome: Bulzoni, 2012).
BLACK 2006
Christopher F. Black, "Society", in Euan Cameron (ed.), *The Sixteenth Century* (Oxford UK and New York NY: Oxford University Press, 2006), pp. 89–115.
BLACKBURN 1992
Bonnie J. Blackburn, "Music and Festivities at the Court of Leo X: A Venetian View", *EMH*, no. 11 (1992), pp. 1–37.
BLACKBURN 2007
Bonnie J. Blackburn, "How to Sin in Music: Doctor Navarrus on Sixteenth-Century Singers", in Melania Bucciarelli and Berta Joncus (eds.), *Music as Social and Cultural Practice. Essays in Honour of Reinhard Strohm* (Woodbridge: The Boydell Press, 2007), pp. 86–104.
BLANKENBURG 1952
Walter Blankenburg, "Calvin", in *MGG* vol. 2 (1952), cols. 653–666.
BLANKENBURG 1961
Walter Blankenburg, "Der Gottesdienstliche Liedgesang der Gemeinde", in Karl Ferdinand Müller and Walter Blankenburg (eds.), *Leiturgia: Handbuch des Evangelischen Gottesdienstes*, vol. 4 (Kassel: Johannes Stauda-Verlag, 1961), pp. 559–660.
BLANKENBURG 1975
Walter Blankenburg, "Church Music in Reformed Europe" and "The Music of the Bohemian Brethren", in Friedrich Blume (ed.), *Protestant Church Music. A History* (New York NY and London: W. W. Norton and Company, 1974; London: Victor Gollancz, 1975), pp. 507–608.
BLUME 1964 / BLUME 1974 / BLUME 1975
Friedrich Blume, *Geschichte der Evangelischen Kirchenmusik* (Kassel: Bärenreiter, 1964); English translation with additions as Friedrich Blume (ed.), *Protestant Church Music. A History* (New York NY and London: W. W. Norton and Company, 1974; London: Victor Gollancz, 1975).
BOËS 1958
Adolf Boës, "Die Reformatorischen Gottesdienste in der Wittenberger Pfarrkirche von 1523 an und die 'Ordenung der gesenge der Wittenbergischen Kirchen' von 1543–44", *JLH*, no. 4 (1958), pp. 1–40.
BORDIER 1870 / BORDIER 1969
Henri Léonard Bordier (ed.), *Le Chansonnier Huguenot dans le XVIe siècle* (Paris: Librairie Tross, 1870; reprint Geneva: Slatkine Reprints, 1969).
BORGERDING 1998
Todd M. Borgerding, "Preachers, 'Pronunciatio', and Music. Hearing Rhetoric in Renaissance Sacred Polyphony", *MQ*, vol. 82, no. 3/4 (Winter 1998), pp. 586–598.
BORGERDING AND STEIN 2006
Todd M. Borgerding and Louise K. Stein, "Spain, I: 1530–1600", in James Haar (ed.), *European Music 1520–1642* (Woodbridge: The Boydell Press, 2006), pp. 422–454.
BORROMEO 1993
Agostino Borromeo, "La storia delle cappelle musicali vista nella prospettiva della Storia della Chiesa", in Oscar Mischiati and Paolo Russo (eds.), *La Cappella musicale nell'Italia della Controriforma* (Florence: Olschki, 1993), pp. 229–238.

**BOSSY 1985**
John Bossy, *Christianity in the West* (Oxford UK and New York NY: Oxford University Press, 1985).

**BOWERS 1986**
Jane Bowers, "The Emergence of Women Composers in Italy, 1566–1700", in Jane Bowers and Judith Tick (eds.), *Women Making Music. The Western Art Tradition, 1150–1950* (Champaign IL: The Board of Trustees of the University of Illinois, 1986), pp. 116–167.

**BOWERS 1999**
Roger Bowers, *English Church Polyphony: Singers and Sources from the 14th to the 17th Century* (Aldershot: Ashgate, 1999).

**BOYCE 2006**
James J. Boyce, "Singing a New Song unto the Lord: Catholic Church Music", in Raymond F. Bulman and Frederick J. Parrella (eds.), *From Trent to Vatican II: Historical and Theological Investigations* (Oxford UK and New York NY: Oxford University Press, 2006), pp. 137–160.

**BOYD 1950**
Dorothy Boyd, "Calvin's Preface to the French Metrical Psalms", *Evangelical Quarterly*, no. 22 (1950), pp. 249–254.

**BOYDELL 2001**
Barra Boydell, "Cathedral Music, City and State: Music in Reformation and Political Change at Christ Church Cathedral, Dublin", in Fiona Kisby (ed.), *Music and Musicians in Renaissance Cities and Towns* (Cambridge: Cambridge University Press, 2001), pp. 131–142.

**BRACHIN 1975**
Pierre Brachin, "La 'Fête de rhétorique' de Gand (1539)," in Jean Jacquot (ed.), *Fêtes et cérémonies au temps de Charles Quint*, vol. 2 (Paris: Éditions du CNRS, 1975), pp. 255–279.

**BRADING 2006**
David A. Brading, "Europe and a World Expanded", in Euan Cameron (ed.), *The Sixteenth Century* (Oxford UK and New York NY: Oxford University Press, 2006), pp. 174–199.

**BRADY, OBERMAN AND TRACY 1995**
Thomas A. Brady, Heiko Augustinus Oberman, and James D. Tracy (eds.), *Handbook of European History, 1400–1600: Late Middle Ages, Renaissance, and Reformation*, 2 vols. (Leiden and New York NY: Brill, 1994–1995).

**BRAUNER 1994**
Mitchell P. Brauner, "The Repertory of the Papal Chapel and the Counter-Reformation", in Bernhard Janz (ed.), *Studien zur Geschichte der Päpstlichen Kapelle: Tagungsbericht Heidelberg 1989* (Vatican City: Biblioteca Apostolica Vaticana, 1994), pp. 333–349.

**BRAUNER 1998**
Mitchell P. Brauner, "Traditions in the Repertory of the Papal Choir in the Fifteenth and Sixteenth Centuries", in Richard Sherr (ed.), *Papal Music and Musicians in Medieval and Renaissance Rome* (Oxford UK and New York NY: Oxford University Press, 1998), pp. 167–176.

**BRAY 1995**
Roger W. Bray (ed.), *The Blackwell History of Music in Britain. The Sixteenth Century* (vol. 2 of *The Blackwell History of Music in Britain*) (Oxford: Blackwell Publishing, 1995).

**BRAY 2006**
Roger W. Bray, "England, I: 1485–1600", in James Haar (ed.), *European Music 1520–1642* (Woodbridge: The Boydell Press, 2006), pp. 487–508.
**BRAY 2011**
Roger W. Bray, "William Byrd's English Psalms", in Linda Phyllis Austern, Kari Boyd McBride and David L. Orvis (eds.), *Psalms in the Early Modern World* (Aldershot: Ashgate, 2011), pp. 61–76.
**BREDNICH 1974 / BREDNICH 1975**
Rolf Wilhelm Brednich, *Die Liedpublizistik im Flugblatt des 15. bis 17. Jahrhunderts*, 2 vols. (Baden-Baden: Bibliotheca Bibliographica Aureliana, 1974–1975).
**BRETT 1989**
Philip Brett (ed.), *The Marian Masses: The Byrd Edition V* (London: Stainer and Bell, 1989).
**BRETT 2007**
Philip Brett, *William Byrd and His Contemporaries. Essays and a Monograph* (Berkeley and Los Angeles CA: University of California Press, 2007).
**BRODERSEN 2008**
Christiane and Kai Brodersen (eds.), *The "Erfurt Enchiridion": a Hymn Book of 1524* (Speyer: Kartoffeldruck-Verlag, 2008).
**BROOKS 2000**
Jeanice Brooks, *Courtly Song in Late Sixteenth-Century France* (Chicago IL: The University of Chicago Press, 2000).
**BROOKS 2006**
Jeanice Brooks, "France, II: 1560–1600", in James Haar (ed.), *European Music 1520–1642* (Woodbridge: The Boydell Press, 2006), pp. 171–182.
**BROWN 1976 / BROWN 1999**
Howard Mayer Brown, *Music in the Renaissance* (Englewood Cliffs NJ: Prentice-Hall, 1976); second edition, revised by Louise K. Stein (Englewood Cliffs NJ: Prentice-Hall, 1999).
**BROWN 2005**
Christopher Boyd Brown, *Singing the Gospel: Lutheran Hymns and the Success of the Reformation* (Cambridge MA: Harvard University Press, 2005).
**BROWN 2008**
Christopher Boyd Brown, "Devotional Life in Hymns, Liturgy, Music and Prayer", in Robert Kolb (ed.), *Lutheran Ecclesiastical Culture 1550–1675* (Leiden and New York NY: Brill, 2008), pp. 205–258.
**BRUINSMA 1949**
Henry Allen Bruinsma, *The 'Souterliedekens' and its Relation to Psalmody in the Netherlands* (PhD Dissertation: University of Michigan, 1949).
**BRYANT 1993**
David Bryant, "Una cappella musicale di Stato: la Basilica di San Marco", in Oscar Mischiati and Paolo Russo (eds.), *La Cappella musicale nell'Italia della Controriforma* (Florence: Olschki, 1993), pp. 67–74.
**BRYANT AND QUARANTA 2007**
David Bryant and Elena Quaranta, "Traditions and Practices in Fifteenth- and Sixteenth-Century Sacred Polyphony: The Use of Solo Voices with Instrumental Accompaniment", in Melania Bucciarelli and Berta Joncus (eds.), *Music as Social and Cultural Practice. Essays in Honour of Reinhard Strohm* (Woodbridge: The Boydell Press, 2007), pp. 105–118.

**BUBENHEIMER 1989**
Ulrich Bubenheimer, *Thomas Müntzer. Herkunft und Bildung* (Leiden and New York NY: Brill, 1989).
**BÜSSER 1949**
Fritz Büsser, "Calvin und die Kirchenmusik", *Musik und Gottesdienst*, no. 3 (1949), pp. 97–106.
**BUSZIN 1958**
Walter E. Buszin, *Luther on Music* (Saint Paul MN: North Central Publishing Company, 1958).
**BUSZIN 1963**
Walter E. Buszin, "The Dynamic Power of Christian Hymnody", in Theo Hoelty-Nickel (ed.), *The Musical Heritage of the Church*, vol. VI (Valparaiso IN: Valparaiso University, 1963), pp. 38–54; text available online at http://bit.ly/2bNqPCU.
**BUTIN 1994**
Philip Butin, "John Calvin's Humanist Image of Popular Late-Medieval Piety and its Contribution to Reformed Worship", *Calvin Theological Journal*, no. 29 (1994), pp. 419–431.
**CALDECOTT 2009**
Stratford Caldecott, *Beauty for Truth's Sake: the Re-Enchantment of Education* (Grand Rapids MI: Brazos Press, 2009).
**CALDWELL 1991**
John Caldwell, *The Oxford History of English Music*, I. *From the Beginnings to c. 1715* (Oxford UK and New York NY: Oxford University Press, 1991).
**CAMERON 2004**
Averon Cameron, "The Cult of the Virgin in Late Antiquity: Religious Development and Myth-Making", *Studies in Church History*, no. 39 (2004), pp. 1–21.
**CAMERON 2006**
Euan Cameron, "The Turmoil of Faith", in Euan Cameron (ed.), *The Sixteenth Century* (Oxford UK and New York NY: Oxford University Press, 2006), pp. 145–173.
**CAMERON 2012**
Euan Cameron, *The European Reformation* (Oxford UK and New York NY: Oxford University Press, 1991; 2012²).
**CAMPIONE 2011**
Francesco Paolo Campione, *La regola del Capriccio. Alle origini di una idea estetica* (Palermo: Centro Internazionale Studi di Estetica, 2011).
**CARPENTER 1960**
Hoyle Carpenter, "Microtones in a Sixteenth Century Portuguese Manuscript", *Acta Musicologica*, vol. 32 (1960), pp. 23–28.
**CARRER 1845**
Luigi Carrer (ed.), *Lettere scelte del Cardinale Pietro Bembo; riscontrate coll'edizioni del 1548 e 1552 e corredate di note da L. Carrer* (Venice: Girolamo Tasso, 1845).
**CARRERAS AND GARCÍA 2001 / CARRERAS AND GARCÍA 2005**
Juan José Carreras and Bernardo García García (eds.), *La Capilla Real de los Austrias* (Madrid: Fundación Carlos de Amberes, 2001); English translation by Yolanda Acker and Tess Knighton as *The Royal Chapel in the Time of the Habsburgs: Music and Court Ceremony in Early Modern Europe* (Woodbridge: The Boydell Press, 2005).

**CARRUTHERS-CLEMENT 1982**
Ann Carruthers-Clement, *The Madrigals and Motets of Vittoria/Raphaela Aleotti* (PhD Dissertation: Kent State University, 1982).
**CARTER 2006**
Tim Carter, "The Concept of the Baroque", in James Haar (ed.), *European Music 1520–1642* (Woodbridge: The Boydell Press, 2006), pp. 38–57.
**CASIMIRI 1932**
Raffaele Casimiri, "Lettere di musicisti (1579–1585) al Cardinal Sirleto", *NASM*, vol. 9 (1932), pp. 97–111.
**CASIMIRI 1936 / CASIMIRI 1939**
Raffaele Casimiri, "Disciplina musicale e maestri di cappella dopo il Concilio di Trento nei maggiori istituti ecclesiastici di Roma", *NASM*, vol. 12 (1936), pp. 1–26; vol. 16 (1939), pp. 1–14.
**CASIMIRI 1940**
Raffaele Casimiri, "Annibale Zoilo (1540?-1592) e la sua famiglia: nuovi documenti biografici", *NASM*, vol. 17 (1940), pp. 1–25.
**CATTIN 1990**
Giulio Cattin, *Musica e liturgia a San Marco* (Venice: Fondazione Levi, 1990).
**CATTIN 2012**
Giulio Cattin, "La musica sacra nel Veneto dopo il Concilio di Trento", *Odeo Olimpico*, no. 27 (2007–2010) (Vicenza: Accademia Olimpica, 2012), pp. 347–354.
**CAVALLO 2006**
Paolo Cavallo, "Circolazione e produzione di musica a stampa nel Pinerolese fra Cinquecento e Ottocento", in Marco Fratini (ed.), *Libri, biblioteche e cultura nelle valli valdesi in età moderna* (Turin: Claudiana, 2006), pp. 233–270.
**CAZEAUX 1975**
Isabelle Cazeaux, *French Music in the Fifteenth and Sixteenth Centuries* (New York NY: Praeger, 1975).
**CÉARD 2008**
Jean Céard, "Un essai d'hymnaire catholique: les *Hymnes ecclésiastiques* de Guy Le Fèvre de la Boderie", in Elizabeth Vinestock and David Foster (eds.), *Writers in Conflict in Sixteenth-Century France: Essays in honour of Malcolm Quainton* (Durham: Durham University Press, 2008), pp. 283–301.
**CHARVAZ 1838**
André Charvaz, *Origine dei Valdesi e carattere delle primitive loro dottrine. Ricerche istoriche* (Turin: Bocca, 1838).
**CHOLAKIAN 2006**
Patricia F. and Rouben C. Cholakian, *Marguerite de Navarre: Mother of the Renaissance* (New York NY: Columbia University Press, 2006).
**CHRISTENSEN 1979**
Carl C. Christensen, *Art and the Reformation in Germany* (Athens OH: Ohio University Press, 1979).
**CIABATTONI 2010**
Francesco Ciabattoni, *Dante's Journey to Polyphony* (Toronto: University of Toronto Press, 2010).

**CLARK AND REHDING 2001**
Suzannah Clark and Alexander Rehding (eds.), *Music Theory and Natural Order from the Renaissance to the Early Twentieth Century* (Cambridge: Cambridge University Press, 2001).

**CLASSEN 2002**
Albrecht Classen, *'Mein Seel fang an zu singen'. Religiöse Frauenlieder der 15.–16. Jahrhunderts. Kritische Studien und Textedition* (Leuven: Peeters, 2002).

**CLIVE 1957 / CLIVE 1958**
Harry Peter Clive, "The Calvinist Attitude to Music and its Literary Aspects and Sources", *Bibliothèque d'Humanisme et Renaissance*, no. 19 (1957), pp. 80–102, 294–319; no. 20 (1958), pp. 79–107.

**COATS 1994**
Catherine Randall Coats, "Reactivating Textual Traces: Martyrs, Memory and the Self in Theodore Beza's *Icones* (1581)", in W. Fred Graham (ed.), *Later Calvinism: International Perspectives* (Kirksville MO: Sixteenth Century Publishers, 1994), pp. 19–28.

**COELHO AND POLK 2006**
Victor Coelho and Keith Polk, "Instrumental Music", in James Haar (ed.), *European Music 1520–1642* (Woodbridge: The Boydell Press, 2006), pp. 527–556.

**COLLINS JUDD 2000**
Cristle Collins Judd, *Reading Renaissance Music Theory. Hearing with the Eyes* (Cambridge: Cambridge University Press, 2000).

**COLLINSON 1988**
Patrick Collinson, *The Birthpangs of Protestant England. Religious and Cultural Change in the Sixteenth and Seventeenth Centuries* (London: Macmillan, 1988).

**CORSINI 1980**
Eugenio Corsini, *Apocalisse prima e dopo* (Turin: SEI, 1980).

**COX 1846**
John Edmund Cox (ed.), *The Works of Thomas Cranmer: Miscellaneous Writings and Letters of Thomas Cranmer* (Cambridge: Cambridge University Press, 1846); available online at http://bit.ly/2bhWRVV.

**CRAIG 2010**
John Craig, "Psalms, Groans and Dog-Whippers: The Soundscape of Sacred Space in the English Parish Church, 1547–1642", in Will Coster and Andrew Spicer (eds.), *Sacred Space in Early Modern Europe* (Cambridge: Cambridge University Press, 2010), pp. 104–123.

**CRAMER 1904**
Samuel Cramer (ed.), *Offer des Heeren*, Bibliotheca Reformatoria Neerlandica (Gravenhage: Martinus Nijhoff, 1904).

**CRESSY 1993**
David Cressy, "Literacy in Context: Meaning and Measurement in Early Modern England", in John Brewer and Roy Porter (eds.), *Consumption and the World of Goods* (Abingdon UK and New York NY: Routledge, 1993), pp. 305–319.

**CROCI 2010**
Marco Croci, "Un inaspettato tributo. Il secondo libro di madrigali di Annibale Zoilo (1563), dedicato 'al Reverendissimo Monsignor Tolomeo Gallio'", in [Editor unknown], *Il cardinal Tolomeo Gallio* (Como: NodoLibri, 2010), pp. 59–82.

CROOK 1994
David Crook, *Orlando di Lasso's Imitation Magnificats for Counter-Reformation Munich* (Princeton NJ: Princeton University Press, 1994).
CROOK 2009
David Crook, "A Sixteenth-Century Catalog of Prohibited Music", *J-AMS*, vol. 62 (2009), pp. 1–78.
CROOK 2015
David Crook, "The Exegetical Motet", *J-AMS*, vol. 68, no. 2 (Summer 2015), pp. 255–316.
CROUZET 2006
Denis Crouzet, "*Ira Dei Super Nos*", in James B. Collins and Karen L. Taylor (eds.), *Early Modern Europe. Issues and Interpretations* (Oxford: Blackwell Publishing, 2006), pp. 90–100.
CULLEY 1970
Thomas D. Culley, *Jesuits and Music*, I: *A Study of the Musicians Connected with the German College in Rome during the 17$^{th}$ Century and of their Activities in Northern Europe* (Rome and St Louis MO: Sources and Studies for the History of the Jesuits, 1970).
CULLEY AND MCNASPY 1971
Thomas D. Culley and Clement J. McNaspy, "Music and the Early Jesuits (1540–1565)", *Archivum historicum Societatis Jesu*, no. 40 (1971), pp. 213–245.
CUMMINGS 2006
Anthony Cummings, "The Motet", in James Haar (ed.), *European Music 1520–1642* (Woodbridge: The Boydell Press, 2006), pp. 130–156.
D'ACCONE 1971
Frank A. D'Accone, "The Musical Chapels at the Florentine Cathedral and Baptistery during the First Half of the 16th Century", *J-AMS*, vol. 24, no. 1 (Spring 1971), pp. 1–50.
D'ALVARENGA 2002 / D'ALVARENGA 2004 / D'ALVARENGA 2005
João Pedro d'Alvarenga, "Towards an Understanding of Post-Tridentine Portuguese Polyphony, with Special Reference to the Motets of Manuel Cardoso (with an Analysis of *Non mortuis* and *Sitivit anima mea*)"; Portuguese original first published in *Estudos de musicologia* (Lisbon: Colibri, Centro de História da Arte da Universidade de Évora, 2002), pp. 105–152; English translation by David Cranmer in *Escola de música da Sé de Évora* (Casa do Sul: 2004), pp. 143–202; revised by the author in May 2005; available online at http://bit.ly/2bffpfz.
DALGLISH 1978
William Dalglish, "The Origin of the Hocket", *J-AMS*, vol. 31 (1978), pp. 3–20.
DALLA LIBERA 1961
Sandro Dalla Libera, "Cronologia musicale della Basilica di San Marco in Venezia", *Musica Sacra*, vol. 85, nos. 2 and 6 (1961), pp. 25–27, 88–91, 135–136.
DAMILANO 1977
Piero Damilano, "Liturgia e musica nell'epoca palestriniana", in Francesco Luisi (ed.), *Atti del Convegno di Studi palestriniani, 28 settembre-2 ottobre 1975* (Palestrina: Fondazione Giovanni Pierluigi da Palestrina, 1977).
DAVIS 1973
Natalie Zemon Davis, "The Rites of Violence: Religious Riot in Sixteenth-Century France", *Past & Present*, no. 59 (May 1973), pp. 51–91.

DAVIS 1975
Natalie Zemon Davis, *Society and Culture in Early Modern France* (Stanford CA: Stanford University Press, 1975).

DAWSON 2012
Jane E. A. Dawson, "'Hamely with God': A Scottish View on Domestic Devotion", in Jessica Martin and Alec Ryrie (eds.), *Private and Domestic Devotion in Early Modern Britain* (Aldershot: Ashgate, 2012), pp. 33–52.

DE ANGELIS 1950
Pietro de Angelis, *Musica e musicisti nell'Arcispedale di Santo Spirito in Saxia dal Quattrocento all'Ottocento*, Collana di studi storici sull'Ospedale di Santo Spirito in Saxia e sugli ospedali romani, 6 (Rome: Ferri, 1950).

DEAN 1997
Jeffrey Dean, "Listening to Sacred Polyphony c. 1500", *EM*, vol. 25, no. 4 (November 1997), pp. 611–638.

DEFORD 2015
Ruth I. Deford, *Tactus, Mensuration and Rhythm in Renaissance Music* (Cambridge: Cambridge University Press, 2015).

DI FONZO 1998
Claudia Di Fonzo, *Della musica e di Dante: paralipomeni lievi*, in "Scritti offerti a Francesco Mazzoni dagli allievi fiorentini" (Florence: Pubblicazioni della SDI, 1998), pp. 47–61; available online at http://bit.ly/2bw0trf.

DIEFENDORF 1991
Barbara Diefendorf, *Beneath the Cross. Catholics and Huguenots in Sixteenth-Century Paris* (Oxford UK and New York NY: Oxford University Press, 1991).

DIEFENDORF 1993
Barbara Diefendorf, "The Huguenot Psalter and the Faith of French Protestants in the Sixteenth Century", in Barbara B. Diefendorf and Carla Alison Hesse (eds.), *Culture and Identity in Early Modern Europe (1500–1800): Essays in Honour of Natalie Zemon Davis* (Ann Arbor MI: University of Michigan Press, 1993), pp. 41–63.

DOBBINS 1992
Frank Dobbins, *Music in Renaissance Lyons* (Oxford: Clarendon Press, 1992).

DOMPNIER 2013
Bernard Dompnier, *I linguaggi della convinzione religiosa. Una storia culturale della Riforma cattolica* (Rome: Bulzoni, 2013).

DRINKER 1995
Sophie Drinker, *Music and Women: The Story of Women in their Relation to Music* (New York NY: The Feminist Press at The University of New York, 1995).

DUFFY 1992
Eamon Duffy, *The Stripping of the Altars: Traditional Religion in England c. 1400-c. 1580* (New Haven CT: Yale University Press, 1992).

DUGUID 2014
Timothy Duguid, *Metrical Psalmody in Print and Practice. English "Singing Psalms" and Scottish "Psalm Buiks"*, c. 1547–1640 (Aldershot: Ashgate, 2014).

DUHR 1907
Bernard Duhr, *Geschichte der Jesuiten in den Ländern deutscher Zunge im XVI. Jahrhundert* (Freiburg im Breisgau: Herder, 1907).

**DUMANOIR 2003**
Virginie Dumanoir (ed.), *Música y literatura en la España de la Edad Media y del Renacimiento* (Madrid: Casa de Velázquez, 2003).

**DUNNING 1970**
Albert Dunning, *Die Staatsmotette, 1480–1555* (Utrecht: Oosthoew, 1970).

**DURANT 1957**
Will Durant, *The Reformation* (New York NY: Simon & Schuster, 1957).

**ECO 1970 / ECO 1988**
Umberto Eco, *Il problema estetico in Tommaso d'Aquino* (Milan: Gruppo Editoriale Fabbri, Bompiani, Sonzogno, 1970); English translation by Hugh Bredin as *The Aesthetics of Thomas Aquinas* (Cambridge MA: Harvard University Press, 1988).

**EGAN 1961**
Patricia Egan, "'Concert' Scenes in Musical Paintings of the Italian Renaissance", *J-AMS*, vol. 14, no. 2 (Summer 1961), pp. 184–195.

**EIRE 1986 / EIRE 1989**
Carlos M. N. Eire, *War Against the Idols. The Reformation of Worship from Erasmus to Calvin* (Cambridge: Cambridge University Press, 1986; paperback 1989).

**EISENBICHLER 1998**
Konrad Eisenbichler, *The Boys of the Archangel Raphael. A Youth Confraternity in Florence, 1411–1785* (Toronto: University of Toronto Press, 1998).

**ELLINWOOD 1948**
Leonard Ellinwood, "Tallis' Tunes and Tudor Psalmody", *Musica Disciplina*, vol. 2, nos. 3–4 (1948), pp. 189–203.

**ELTON 1990**
Geoffrey Rudolph Elton (ed.), *The Reformation 1520–1559* (Cambridge: Cambridge University Press, 1990).

**ERICHSON 1886**
Alfred Erichson, *L'Eglise française de Strasbourg au seizième siècle d'après des documents inédits* (Strasbourg: Librairie C. F. Schmidt, 1886).

**FABBRI 1985**
Paolo Fabbri, *Monteverdi* (Turin: EDT, 1985).

**FABBRI 1993**
Paolo Fabbri, "La normativa istituzionale", in Oscar Mischiati and Paolo Russo (eds.), *La Cappella musicale nell'Italia della Controriforma* (Florence: Olschki, 1993), pp. 17–38.

**FARNER 1957**
Oskar Farner, "Eine neuentdeckte Äußerung Zwinglis über den Gemeindegesang", *JLH*, no. 3 (1957), p. 130.

**FELCH 2008**
Susan M. Felch (ed.), *Elizabeth Tyrwhit's Morning and Evening Prayers* (Aldershot: Ashgate 2008).

**FELLERER 1951**
Karl Gustav Fellerer, "Das Tridentinum und die Kirchenmusik", in G. Schreiber (ed.), *Das Weltkonzil von Trient, sein Werden und Wirken* (Freiburg im Breisgau: Herder, 1951), vol. I, pp. 447–462.

**FELLERER 1953**
Karl Gustav Fellerer, "Church Music and the Council of Trent", *MQ*, vol. 39, no. 4 (Oct. 1953), pp. 576–594.

**FENLON 1980**
Iain Fenlon, *Music and Patronage in Sixteenth-Century Mantua* (Cambridge: Cambridge University Press, 1980).

**FENLON 1981**
Iain Fenlon (ed.), *Music in Medieval and Early Modern Europe: Patronage, Sources, Texts* (Cambridge: Cambridge University Press, 1981).

**FENLON 1989**
Iain Fenlon, *The Renaissance. From the 1470s to the End of the Sixteenth Century* (Basingstoke and London: Macmillan, 1989).

**FENLON 1992**
Iain Fenlon, "Patronage, music, and liturgy in Renaissance Mantua", in Thomas Forrest Kelly (ed.), *Plainsong in the age of polyphony* (Cambridge: Cambridge University Press, 1992), pp. 209–235.

**FENLON 2002**
Iain Fenlon, *Music and Culture in Late Renaissance Italy* (Oxford UK and New York NY: Oxford University Press, 2002).

**FENLON 2006**
Iain Fenlon, "Music, Print, and Society in Sixteenth-Century Europe", in James Haar (ed.), *European Music 1520–1642* (Woodbridge: The Boydell Press, 2006), pp. 280–303.

**FENLON 2009**
Iain Fenlon, "Varieties of Experience: Music and Reform in Renaissance Italy", in Abigail Brundin and Matthew Treherne (eds.), *Forms of Faith in Sixteenth-Century Italy* (Aldershot: Ashgate, 2009), pp. 199–214.

**FENLON AND HAAR 1988**
Iain Fenlon and James Haar, *The Italian Madrigal in the Early Sixteenth Century* (Cambridge: Cambridge University Press, 1988).

**FERER 2012**
Mary Tiffany Ferer, *Music and Ceremony at the Court of Charles V. The* Capilla Flamenca *and the Art of Political Promotion* (Woodbridge: The Boydell Press, 2012).

**FERGUSON 1948**
Wallace K. Ferguson, *The Renaissance in Historical Thought: Five Centuries of Interpretation* (Boston: H. Mifflin, 1948).

**FERGUSON 1993**
Everett Ferguson, "Towards a Patristic Theology of Music", in Elizabeth Anne Livingston (ed.), *Studia Patristica* 24 (Leuven: Peeters Press, 1993), pp. 266–283.

**FERGUSON 2011**
Jamie H. Ferguson, "Miles Coverdale and the Claims of Paraphrase", in Linda Phyllis Austern, Kari Boyd McBride and David L. Orvis (eds.), *Psalms in the Early Modern World* (Aldershot: Ashgate, 2011), pp. 137–154.

**FERRONI 1978**
Giulio Ferroni (ed.), *Poesia Italiana. Il Cinquecento* (Milan: Garzanti, 1978).

**FILIPPI 2013**
Daniele V. Filippi, "Carlo Borromeo e la musica, 'a lui naturalmente grata'", in Antonio Addamiano and Francesco Luisi (eds.), *Atti del Congresso Internazionale di Musica Sacra (Roma, 26 maggio – 1 giugno 2011)* (Vatican City: Libreria Editrice Vaticana, 2013), vol. II, pp. 665–676.

**FILIPPI 2015A**
Daniele V. Filippi, "A Cultural History of the Motet in Milan. Preliminary Findings", Paper read at the conference "Mapping the Post-Tridentine Motet" (Nottingham: April 2015).

**FILIPPI 2015B**
Daniele V. Filippi, "A Sound Doctrine: Early Modern Jesuits and the Singing of the Catechism", *EMH*, no. 34 (2015), pp. 1–43.

**FILIPPI 2016A**
Daniele V. Filippi, "'Ask the Jesuits to Send Verses from Rome': The Society's Networks and the European Dissemination of Devotional Music", in Robert Aleksander Maryks (ed.), *Exploring Jesuit Distinctiveness. Interdisciplinary Perspectives on Ways of Proceeding within the Society of Jesus* (Leiden and New York NY: Brill, 2016), pp. 62–80.

**FILIPPI 2016B**
Daniele V. Filippi, "Introduction", *Journal of Jesuit Studies*, no. 3 (2016), pp. 357–364.

**FINCHAM AND TYACKE 2007**
Kenneth Fincham and Nicholas Tyacke, *Altars Restored: The Changing Face of English Religious Worship, 1547-c. 1700* (Oxford UK and New York NY: Oxford University Press, 2007).

**FINSCHER 1990**
Ludwig Finscher (ed.), *Die Musik des 15. und 16. Jahrhunderts* (Laaber: Laaber Verlag, 1990).

**FISHER 2001**
Alexander J. Fisher, "Song, Confession and Criminality: Trial Records as Sources for Popular Musical Culture in Early Modern Europe", *Journal of Musicology*, no. 18 (2001), pp. 616–657.

**FISHER 2004**
Alexander J. Fisher, *Music and Religious Identity in Counter-Reformation Augsburg, 1580–1630* (Aldershot: Ashgate, 2004).

**FISHER 2007**
Alexander J. Fisher, "'Per mia particolare devotione': Orlando di Lasso's *Lagrime di San Pietro* and Catholic Spirituality in Counter-Reformation Munich", *J-RMA*, vol. 132, no. 2 (2007), pp. 167–220.

**FISHER 2010**
Alexander J. Fisher, "Themes of Exile and (Re-)Enclosure in Music for the Franciscan Convents of Counter-Reformation Munich During the Thirty Years' War", in Lynne Tatlock (ed.), *Enduring Loss in Early Modern Germany: Cross-Disciplinary Perspectives* (Leiden and New York NY: Brill, 2010), pp. 281–306.

**FISHER 2014**
Alexander J. Fisher, *Music, Piety and Propaganda: the Soundscapes of Counter-Reformation Bavaria* (Oxford UK and New York NY: Oxford University Press, 2014).

**FISHER 2015**
Alexander J. Fisher, "*Thesaurus Litaniarum:* The Symbolism and Practice of Musical Litanies in Counter-Reformation Germany", *EMH*, no. 34 (2015), pp. 45–95.

**FISKEN 1985**
Beth Wynne Fisken, "Mary Sidney's *Psalmes:* Education and Wisdom", in Margaret Patterson Hannay (ed.), *Silent but for the Word* (Kent OH: Kent State University Press, 1985), pp. 166–183.

FLYNN 1995
Jane Flynn, "The Education of Choristers in England during the Sixteenth Century", in John Morehen (ed.), *English Choral Practice, 1400–1650* (Cambridge: Cambridge University Press, 1995), pp. 180–199.

FORNEY 1994
Kristine K. Forney, "The Role of Secular Guilds in the Musical Life of Antwerp", in Barbara Haggh, Frank Daelmans, and André Vanrie (eds.), *Musicology and Archival Research* (Brussels: Archives et Bibliothéques en Belgique, 1994), pp. 441–461.

FORNEY 2006
Kristine K. Forney, "The Netherlands, 1520–1640", in James Haar (ed.), *European Music 1520–1642* (Woodbridge: The Boydell Press, 2006), pp. 246–279.

FORNEY 2010
Kristine K. Forney, "A Proper Musical Education for Antwerp's Women", in Russell E. Murray jr, Susan Forscher Weiss, Cynthia J. Cyrus (eds.), *Music Education in the Middle Ages and the Renaissance* (Bloomington IN: Indiana University Press, 2010), pp. 84–125.

FOXE 1965
John Foxe, *The Acts and Monuments of John Foxe*, edited by George Townsend (New York NY: AMS Press, 1965).

FRANDSEN 2010
Mary Frandsen, "*Salve Regina / Salve Rex Christe*. Lutheran Engagement with the Marian Antiphons in the Age of Orthodoxy and Piety", *Musica Disciplina*, vol. 55 (2010), pp. 129–218.

FREEDMAN 2000
Richard Freedman, *The Chansons of Orlando di Lasso and their Protestant Listeners: Music, Piety and Print in Sixteenth-Century France* (Rochester NY: University of Rochester Press, 2000).

FREEDMAN 2003
Richard Freedman, "Le Jeune's 'Dodecacorde' as a Site for Spiritual Meanings", *Revue de Musicologie*, vol. 89, no. 2 (2003), pp. 297–309.

FREEDMAN 2006
Richard Freedman, "France, I: 1520–1560", in James Haar (ed.), *European Music 1520–1642* (Woodbridge: The Boydell Press, 2006), pp. 157–170.

FREEDMAN 2011
Richard Freedman, "Listening to the Psalms among the Huguenots: Simon Goulart as Music Editor", in Linda Phyllis Austern, Kari Boyd McBride and David L. Orvis (eds.), *Psalms in the Early Modern World* (Aldershot: Ashgate, 2011), pp. 37–60.

FREEDMAN 2013
Richard Freedman, *Music in the Renaissance* (New York NY and London: W. W. Norton and Company, 2013).

FREY 1985
Herman-Walther Frey (ed.), "Das Diarium der Sixtinischen Sängerkapelle in Rom für das Jahr 1596", *Analecta Musicologica*, no. 21 (1985), pp. 129–204.

FROMSON 1992
Michele Fromson, "A Conjunction of Rhetoric and Music: Structural Modelling in the Italian Counter-Reformation Motet", *J-RMA*, vol. 117, no. 2 (1992), pp. 208–246.

**FUGGER AND SCHEIDGEN 2008**
Dominik Fugger and Andreas Scheidgen (eds.), *Geschichte des katholischen Gesangbuchs* (Tübingen: A. Francke Verlag, 2008).

**FULLER 1996**
Sarah Fuller, "Defending the *Dodecachordon:* Ideological Currents in Glarean's Modal Theory", *J-AMS*, vol. 49 (1996), pp. 191–224.

**FUMERTON 2012**
Patricia Fumerton (ed.), *Broadside Ballads from the Pepys Collection* (Tempe AZ: Arizona Center for Medieval and Renaissance Studies, 2012).

**GALAND-HALLYN AND HALLYN 2001**
Perrine Galand-Hallyn and Fernand Hallyn (eds.), *Poétiques de la Renaissance. Le modèle italien, le monde franco-borgognon et leur héritage en France au XVIe siècle* (Geneva: Droz, 2001).

**GALLO 2011**
Franco Alberto Gallo, "L'eredità della musica medievale. Conclusioni", in Vera Minazzi (ed.), *Atlante storico della musica nel medioevo* (Milan: Jaca Book, 2011), p. 267.

**GANGWERE 2004**
Blanche Gangwere, *Music History During the Renaissance Period 1520–1550. A Documented Chronology* (Westport CT: Praeger, 2004).

**GARCÍA PÉREZ AND OTAOLA GONZÁLEZ 2014**
Amaya García Pérez and Paloma Otaola González (eds.), *Francisco de Salinas. Música, teoría y matemática en el Renacimiento* (Salamanca: Ediciones Universidad de Salamanca, 2014).

**GARSIDE 1951**
Charles Garside jr, "Calvin's Preface to the Psalter: a Re-Appraisal", *MQ*, no. 37 (1951), pp. 566–577.

**GARSIDE 1966**
Charles Garside jr, *Zwingli and the Arts* (New Haven CT: Yale University Press, 1966).

**GARSIDE 1967**
Charles Garside jr, "Some Attitudes of the Major Reformers toward the Role of Music in the Liturgy", *McCormick Quarterly*, no. 21 (1967), pp. 151–168.

**GARSIDE 1979**
Charles Garside jr, "The Origins of Calvin's Theology of Music: 1536–1543", *Transactions of the American Philosophical Society*, no. 69 (1979), pp. 5–35.

**GASPARI 1961**
Gaetano Gaspari, *Catalogo della biblioteca musicale G. B. Martini di Bologna*, edited by Napoleone Fanti et al., 4 vols. (Sala Bolognese: Forni, 1961).

**GASSNER AND QUINN 1969 / GASSNER AND QUINN 2002**
John Gassner and Edward Quinn (eds.), *The Reader's Encyclopedia of World Drama* (New York NY: Crowell, 1969; Mineola NY: Courier Dover Publications, 2002).

**GEMBERO USTÁRROZ 2007**
María Gembero Ustárroz, "Migraciones de músicos entre España y América (siglos XVI-XVIII): Estudio preliminar", in María Gembero Ustárroz and Emilio Ros-Fábregas (eds.), *La música y el Atlántico: Relaciones musicales entre España y Latinoamérica* (Granada: Universidad de Granada 2007), pp. 17–58.

**GÉROLD 1954**
Theodore Gérold, "Protestant Music on the Continent", in Gerald Abraham (ed.), *The New Oxford History of Music*, vol. 4, *The Age of Humanism*, 1540–1630 (London: Oxford University Press, 1954), pp. 419–465.

**GETZ 2001**
Christine Getz, "Simon Boyleau and the Church of the 'Madonna of Miracles': Educating and Cultivating the Aristocratic Audience in Post-Tridentine Milan", *J-RMA*, vol. 126, no. 2 (2001), pp. 145–168.

**GETZ 2005**
Christine Getz, *Music in the Collective Experience in Sixteenth-Century Milan* (Aldershot: Ashgate, 2005).

**GETZ 2015**
Christine Getz, "Canonising San Carlo: Sermonising, the Sounding Word, and Image Construction in the Music for Carlo Borromeo", *EMH*, no. 34 (October 2015), pp. 133–189.

**GHIGLIONE 1986**
Natale Ghiglione, "S. Carlo e la Musica sacra", in [Editor unknown], *San Carlo e il suo tempo. Atti del Convegno Internazionale nel IV centenario della morte* (Rome: Edizioni di Storia e Letteratura, 1986), vol. II, pp. 1013–1020.

**GIBSON 2009**
Kirsten Gibson, "Music, Melancholy and Masculinity in Early Modern England", in Ian Biddle and Kirsten Gibson (eds.), *Masculinity and Western Musical Practice* (Aldershot: Ashgate, 2009), pp. 41–67.

**GILLINGHAM 2008**
Susan Gillingham, *Psalms Through the Centuries* (Oxford: Wiley-Blackwell, 2008).

**GLIXON 2003**
Jonathan Glixon, *Honoring God and the City: Music at the Venetian Confraternities, 1260–1807* (Oxford UK and New York NY: Oxford University Press, 2003).

**GOZZI 1995**
Marco Gozzi, "Le edizioni liturgico-musicali dopo il Concilio", in Danilo Curti and Marco Gozzi (eds.), *Musica e Liturgia nella Riforma Tridentina* (Trento: Provincia Autonoma di Trento – Servizio Beni Librari e Archivistici, 1995), pp. 39–56.

**GRAY 1963 / GRAY 1968**
Hanna H. Gray, "Renaissance Humanism: The Pursuit of Eloquence", *Journal of the History of Ideas*, no. 24 (1963), pp. 497–514, reprinted in Paul Oskar Kristeller and Philip P. Wiener (eds.), *Renaissance Essays: from the Journal of the History of Ideas* (New York NY: Harper & Row, 1968), pp. 199–216.

**GRAZIOSI 1996**
Elisabetta Graziosi, "Scrivere in convento: devozione, encomio e persuasione nelle rime delle monache fra Cinque e Seicento", in Gabriella Zarri (ed.), *Donna, disciplina, creanza cristiana dal XV al XVII secolo – Studi e testi a stampa* (Rome: Edizioni di Storia e Letteratura, 1996), pp. 303–331.

**GRAZIOSI 2005**
Elisabetta Graziosi, "Arcipelago sommerso: le rime delle monache tra obbedienza e trasgressione", in Gianna Pomata and Gabriella Zarri (eds.), *I Monasteri femminili come centri di cultura fra Rinascimento e Barocco* (Rome: Edizioni di Storia e Letteratura, 2005), pp. 145–174.

**GREEN 2001**
Ian Green, "'All people that on earth do dwell. Sing to the Lord with cheerful voice': Protestantism and Music in Early Modern England", in Simon Ditchfield (ed.), *Christianity and Community in the West: Essays for John Bossy* (Aldershot: Ashgate, 2001), pp. 148–164.

**GREENGRASS 2006**
Mark Greengrass, "Politics and Warfare", in Euan Cameron (ed.), *The Sixteenth Century* (Oxford UK and New York NY: Oxford University Press, 2006), pp. 58–88.

**GRIJP 1994**
Louis Peter Grijp, "The Souterliedekens by Gherardus Mes (1561): An Enigmatic Pupil of Clemens non Papa, and Popular Song of the Mid-Sixteenth Century," in Albert Clement and Eric Jas (eds.), *From Ciconia to Sweelinck: Donum Natalicium Willem Elders* (Amsterdam and Atlanta GA: Rodopi, 1994), pp. 245–254.

**GRINDAL 2011**
Gracia Grindal, *Preaching from Home. The Stories of Seven Lutheran Women Hymn-Writers* (Grand Rapids MI: Eerdmans, 2011).

**GRITSCH 1989**
Eric W. Gritsch, *Thomas Müntzer. A Tragedy of Errors* (Minneapolis MN: Augsburg Fortress, 1989).

**GROOTE AND VENDRIX 2012**
Inga Mai Groote and Philippe Vendrix, "The Renaissance Musician and Theorist Confronted with Religious Fragmentation: Conflict, Betrayal and Dissimulation", in Isabel Karremann, Cornel Zwierlein, Inga Mai Groote (eds.), *Forgetting Faith? Negotiating Confessional Conflict in Early Modern Europe* (Berlin and New York NY: De Gruyter, 2012), pp. 163–198.

**GRUNEWALD, JÜRGENS AND LUTH 2004**
Eckhard Grunewald, Henning P. Jürgens und Jan R. Luth (eds.), *Der Genfer Psalter und seine Rezeption in Deutschland, der Schweiz und den Niederlanden. 16.–18. Jahrhundert* (Tübingen: Max Niemeyer Verlag, 2004).

**GUICHARROUSSE 1995**
Hubert Guicharrousse, *Les musiques de Luther* (Geneva: Labor et Fides, 1995).

**GUILLOT 1991**
Pierre Guillot, *Les Jésuites et la musique. Le Collège de la Trinité à Lyon 1565–1762* (Liège: Pierre Mardaga, 1991).

**HAAR 1988**
James Haar, "Cosimo Bartoli on Music", *EMH*, no. 8 (1988), pp. 37–79.

**HAAR 2006**
James Haar, "The Concept of the Renaissance", in James Haar (ed.), *European Music 1520–1642* (Woodbridge: The Boydell Press, 2006), pp. 20–37; "Madrigal", *ibid.*, pp. 225–245.

**HABERL 1892**
Franz Xaver Haberl, "Die Cardinalskommission von 1564 und Palestrinas Missa Papae Marcelli", *Kirchenmusikalisches Jahrbuch*, vol. 7 (1892), pp. 82–97.

**HABERL 1966**
Ferdinand Haberl, "Jacobus de Kerle e le sue Preci speciali per il Concilio di Trento", *Quadrivium*, vol. 7 (1966), pp. 31–37.

HAEMIG 2001
Mary Jane Haemig, "Elisabeth Cruciger (1500?-1535): The Case of the Disappearing Hymn Writer", *SCJ*, vol. 32, no. 1 (Spring 2001), pp. 21–44.

HAMLIN 2000
Hannibal Hamlin, "'Very Mete to be Used of All Sortes of People': The remarkable popularity of the 'Sternhold and Hopkins' Psalter", *The Yale University Library Gazette*, vol. 75, no. 1/2 (October 2000), pp. 37–51.

HAMLIN 2012
Hannibal Hamlin, "Sobs for Sorrowful Souls: Versions of the Penitential Psalms for Domestic Devotion", in Jessica Martin and Alec Ryrie (eds.), *Private and Domestic Devotion in Early Modern Britain* (Aldershot: Ashgate, 2012), pp. 211–236.

HANDSCHIN 1949
Jacques Handschin, "Gesungene Apologetik", *Miscellanea Liturgica in honorem L. C. Mohlberg*, no. 23 (Rome: Edizioni Liturgiche, 1949), vol. 2, pp. 76–106.

HANLON 1961
Sister Joseph Damien Hanlon, "Richard Dering, Catholic Musician of Stuart England", *The Catholic Historical Review*, vol. 46, no. 4 (Jan. 1961), pp. 428–452.

HANNAY 1985
Margaret Patterson Hannay, "'Doo what Men May Sing': Mary Sidney and the Tradition of Admonitory Dedication", in Margaret Patterson Hannay (ed.), *Silent but for the Word* (Kent OH: Kent State University Press, 1985), pp. 149–165.

HANNAY 1998
Margaret Patterson Hannay, "Literary Context", in Mary Sidney Herbert, *The Collected Works of Mary Sidney Herbert, Countess of Pembroke. Vol. II, The Psalmes of David*, edited by M. P. Hannay et al. (Oxford: Clarendon Press, 1998).

HARDIE 2002
Jane Hardie, "'Wanted, one *Maestro de Capilla*': A Sixteenth-Century Job Description", in David Crawford and G. Grayson Wagstaff (eds.), *Encomium Musicæ: Essays in Memory of Robert J. Snow* (Hillsdale NY: Pendragon Press, 2002), pp. 269–284.

HARNESS 2006
Kelley Harness, *Echoes of Women's Voices: Music, Art, and Female Patronage in Early Modern Florence* (Chicago IL: The University of Chicago Press, 2006).

HARPER 1991
John Harper, *The Forms and Orders of Western Liturgy* (Oxford UK and New York NY: Oxford University Press, 1991).

HARRÁN 1995
Don Harrán, "Investigation Through Interrogation: the Case of Female Poets and Feminist Poetry in the Sixteenth-Century Madrigal", *Recercare*, vol. 7 (1995), pp. 5–46.

HART 1898
Albert Bushnell Hart (ed.), *American History told by Contemporaries* vol. 1 (New York NY: Macmillan, 1898); available online at http://bit.ly/2bA368p.

HARTINGER 1972
Walter Hartinger, "Ain schöner Catholischer Rueff. Zur Genese eines barocken Wallfahrtsliedes", *Bayerisches Jahrbuch für Volkskunde* (1972–5), pp. 195–210.

HARTMANN 1862
Julius Hartmann, *Johannes Brenz: Leben und ausgewählte Schriften* (Elberfeld: Verlag von R. L. Friderichs, 1862).

HAUGAARD **1981**
William P. Haugaard, "The Continental Reformation of the Sixteenth Century", in John H. Westerhoff III and O. C. Edwards jr (eds.), *A Faithful Church: Issues in the History of Catechesis* (Wilton: Morehouse-Barlow Co., 1981), pp. 109–173.

HAYBURN **1979**
Robert Hayburn, *Papal Legislation on Sacred Music, 95 A.D. to 1977 A. D.* (Collegeville PA: The Liturgical Press, 1979).

HEAL **2007**
Bridget Heal, *The Cult of the Virgin Mary in Early Modern Germany: Protestant and Catholic Piety, 1500–1648* (Cambridge: Cambridge University Press, 2007).

HEIZER **1974**
Robert F. Heizer, *Elizabethan California: A Brief and Sometimes Critical Review of Opinions on the Location of Francis Drake's Five Weeks' Visit with the Indians of Ships Land in 1579* (Ramona CA: Ballena Press, 1974).

HENDRICKSON **2003** / HENDRICKSON **2005**
Marion Lars Hendrickson, *Musica Christi: a Lutheran Aesthetic* (PhD Thesis: University of Durham, 2003); available online at http://etheses.dur.ac.uk/1089/; (New York NY: Peter Lang, 2005).

HENDRIX **2004**
Scott Hendrix, *Recultivating the Vineyard. The Reformation Agendas of Christianization* (Louisville KY: Westminster John Knox, 2004).

HENNIG **1977**
Kurt Hennig, *Die geistliche Kontrafaktur im Jahrhundert der Reformation* (Hildesheim: Georg Olms Verlag, 1977).

HERL **2004**
Joseph Herl, *Worship Wars in Early Lutheranism: Choir, Congregation and Three Centuries of Conflict* (Oxford UK and New York NY: Oxford University Press, 2004).

HIGMAN **2000**
Francis Higman, "Music", in Andrew Pettegree (ed.), *The Reformation World* (Abingdon UK and New York NY: Routledge, 2000), pp. 491–505.

HIGMAN **2004**
Francis Higman, "Censorship and the Genevan Psalter", in Eckard Grunewald, Henning P. Jürgens, Jan R. Luth (eds.), *Der Genfer Psalter und seine Rezeption in Deutschland, der Schweiz und den Niederland* (Berlin and New York NY: De Gruyter, 2004), pp. 33–44.

HILL **1979**
John Walter Hill, "Oratory Music in Florence, I: 'Recitar Cantando', 1583–1655", *Acta Musicologica*, vol. 51, no. 1 (January-June 1979), pp. 108–136.

HILLERBRAND **2004**
Hans J. Hillerbrand, *Encyclopedia of Protestantism*, 4 vols. (Abingdon UK and New York NY: Routledge, 2004).

HILLERBRAND **2007**
Hans J. Hillerbrand, *The Division of Christendom. Christianity in the Sixteenth Century* (Louisville KY: Westminster John Knox, 2007).

HIS **1999**
Isabelle His, "'Sous lesquels ont esté mises des paroles morales': Un cas de contrafactum de psaumes entre 1598 et 1618", *Revue de Musicologie*, vol. 85, no. 2 (1999), pp. 189–225.

**HOEKSTRA 2013**
Gerald R. Hoekstra, "Andreas Pevernage's *Cantiones sacrae* (1578) as a Counter-Reformation Statement of Confessional Loyalty in the Low Countries", in *SCJ*, no. 44/1 (Spring 2013), pp. 3–24.

**HOELTY-NICKEL 1960**
Theodore Hoelty-Nickel, "Luther and Music", in George Wolfgang Forell (ed.), *Luther and Culture: Martin Luther Lectures*, vol. 4 (Decorah IA: Luther College Press, 1960), pp. 143–211.

**HONEGGER 1970**
Marc Honegger, *Les Chansons spirituelles de Didier Lupi et les débuts de la musique protestante en France* (Doctoral Thesis: Paris, 1970).

**HONEGGER 1982**
Marc Honegger, "La place de Strasbourg dans la musique au XVIe siècle", *International Review of the Aesthetics and Sociology of Music*, vol. 13, no. 1 (June 1982), pp. 5–19.

**HORNE 1985**
Brian L. Horne, "A Civitas of Sound: On Luther and Music", *Theology* (January 1985), pp. 21–28.

**HRUZA 2002**
Lucy Hruza, "Multiple Settings of the *Salve Regina* Antiphon: Tomás Luis de Victoria's Contribution to the Renaissance Veneration of the Virgin", in David Crawford and G. Grayson Wagstaff (eds.), *Encomium Musicæ: Essays in Memory of Robert J. Snow* (Hillsdale NY: Pendragon Press, 2002), pp. 409–434.

**HSIA 1992**
Ronnie Po-chia Hsia, *Social Discipline in the Reformation. Central Europe 1550–1750* (Abindgon UK and New York NY: Routledge, 1992).

**HSIA 2004**
Ronnie Po-chia Hsia (ed.), *A Companion to the Reformation World* (Oxford: Blackwell Publishing, 2004).

**HUCKE 1984**
Helmut Hucke, "Das Dekret 'Docta Sanctorum Patrum' Papst Johannes' XXII", *Musica Disciplina*, vol. 38 (1984), pp. 119–131.

**HUFTON 1996**
Olwen Hufton, *The Prospect before Her: A History of Women in Western Europe, 1500–1800* (New York NY: Alfred A. Knopf, 1996).

**HUGHES 1966**
Philip E. Hughes, *The Register of the Company of Pastors in the Time of Calvin* (Grand Rapids MI: Eerdmans, 1966).

**HULMES 1993 / HULMES 2004**
Edward Hulmes, "The Qur'ān and the Bible", in Bruce M. Metzger and Michael D. Coogan (eds.), *The Oxford Companion to the Bible* (Oxford UK and New York NY: Oxford University Press, 1993; online edition, 2004).

**HUNTER 1920 / HUNTER 1999**
A. Mitchell Hunter, *The Teaching of Calvin. A Modern Interpretation* (Glasgow: Maclehose, Jackson & Co., 1920); available online at http://bit.ly/2bitiaa; (Eugene OR: Wipf and Stock Publishers, 1999).

HUSTAD 1952
Donald P. Hustad, *Jubilate! Church Music in the Evangelical Tradition* (Carol Stream IL: Hope Publishing Company, 1952).

IRWIN 1983
Joyce Irwin, "Music and the Doctrine of *Adiaphora* in Orthodox Lutheran Theology", in *SCJ*, no. 14 (1983), pp. 157–172.

IRWIN 1993
Joyce Irwin, *Neither Voice Nor Heart Alone: German Lutheran Theology of Music in the Age of the Baroque* (New York NY: Peter Lang, 1993).

JACKSON 1997
Susan Jackson, "Who is Katherine? The Women of the Berg & Neuber – Gerlach – Kaufmann Printing Dynasty", in Eugeen Schreurs, Henri Vanhulst (ed.), *Music Fragments and Manuscripts in the Low Countries / Alta Capella / Music Printing in Antwerp and Europe in the 16$^{th}$ Century*, Yearbook of the Alamire Foundation 2 (Leiden: Alamire, 1997), pp. 451–463.

JACOBS 1871
Eduard Jacobs, "Ein bisher unbekanntes, während der Belagerung von Magdeburg im Jahre 1550–51 gedrucktes niederdeutsches Gesangbuch", *Geschichtsblätter für Stadt und Land Magdeburg*, no. 6 (1871), pp. 161–201.

JANSON 1995
P. J. Janson, "A Reason to Sing", *Reformation & Revival Journal*, vol. 4, no. 4 (Fall 1995), pp. 15–29.

JANSSEN 1907 / JANSSEN 1966
Johannes Janssen, *History of the German People at the Close of the Middle Ages*, vol. 11: *Art and Popular Literature to the Beginning of the Thirty Years' War*, translated by A. M. Christie, edited by Ludwig Pastor (London: Kegan Paul, Trench, Trübner & Co., 1907); available online at http://bit.ly/2bnEKQr; (New York NY: AMS Press, 1966).

JEDIN 1942
Hubert Jedin, "Il Missale Romanum usato a Trento nel 1561–63", *Il Concilio di Trento*, vol. I, no. 1 (1942), pp. 65–66.

JEDIN 1946 / JEDIN 1957
Hubert Jedin, *Katholische Reformation oder Gegenreformation? Ein Versuch zur Klärung der Begriffe nebst einer Jubiläumsbetrachtung über das Trienter Konzil* (Luzern: Stocker, 1946); Italian translation by Marola Guarducci as *Riforma cattolica o Controriforma? Tentativo di chiarimento dei concetti con riflessioni sul concilio di Trento* (Brescia: Morcelliana, 1957).

JEDIN 1973 FF.
Hubert Jedin, *Il Concilio di Trento*, 4 vols. (Brescia: Morcelliana, 1973–1984).

JENNY 1962
Markus Jenny, *Geschichte des deutschschweizerischen Evangelischen Gesangbuches im 16. Jahrhundert* (Basel: Bärenreiter, 1962).

JENNY 1983
Markus Jenny, "Kirchenlied, Gesangbuch, und Kirchenmusik", in Gerhard Bott (ed.), *Martin Luther und die Reformation in Deutschland: Ausstellung zum 500. Geburtstag Martin Luthers* (Frankfurt: Insel, 1983), pp. 293–322.

JEPPESEN 1930
Knud Jeppesen, "Wann entstand die Marcellus-Messe?", in [Editor unknown], *Festschrift für Guido Adler* (Wien: Universal, 1930), pp. 126–136; available online at http://bit.ly/2bCcmxA.

JEPPESEN 1944
Knud Jeppesen, "Marcellus-Probleme", *Acta Musicologica*, vol. 16 (1944), pp. 11–38.

JEPPESEN 1946 / JEPPESEN 1970
Knud Jeppesen, *The Style of Palestrina and the Dissonance* (Oxford: Oxford University Press, 1946; Mineola NY, Dover Publications, 1970).

JEPPESEN 1953
Knud Jeppesen, "Pierluigi da Palestrina, Herzog Guglielmo Gonzaga und die neugefundenen Mantovaner-Messen Palestrina's", *Acta Musicologica*, vol. 25 (1953), pp. 132–179.

JEPPESEN 1975
Knud Jeppesen, "Problems of the *Pope Marcellus Mass:* Some Remarks on the *Missa Papae Marcelli* by Giovanni Pierluigi da Palestrina", in Lewis Lockwood (ed.), *Palestrina. Pope Marcellus Mass* (New York NY and London: W. W. Norton and Company, 1975), pp. 99–130.

JEŻ 2007
Tomasz Jeż, "The motets of Jacob Handl in Inter-Confessional Silesian Liturgical Practice", *De Musica Disserenda*, vol. 3, no. 2 (2007), pp. 37–48.

JOBY 2005
Christopher Richard Joby, *Calvinism and the Arts: A Re-Assessment* (PhD Thesis: Durham University, 2005).

JOLDERSMA 2010
Hermina Joldersma, "Adamant Voices from Prison: Female Anabaptists", in Lia van Gemert et al. (eds.), *Women's Writing from the Low Countries 1200–1875. A Bilingual Anthology* (Amsterdam: Amsterdam University Press, 2010), pp. 176–189.

KAPLAN 2007
Benjamin J. Kaplan, *Divided by Faith: Religious Conflict and the Practice of Toleration in Early Modern Europe* (Cambridge MA: Harvard University Press, 2007).

KAUFMANN 1966
Henry W. Kaufmann, *The Life and Works of Nicola Vicentino* (Rome: American Institute of Musicology, 1966).

KELLEY 1973
Donald R. Kelley, *François Hotman. A Revolutionary's Ordeal* (Princeton NJ: Princeton University Press, 1973).

KELSEY 1990
Harry Kelsey, "Did Francis Drake Really Visit California?", *The Western Historical Quarterly*, vol. 21, no. 4 (November 1990), pp. 444–462.

KENDRICK 1994
Robert L. Kendrick, "Four Views of Milanese Nuns' Music", in E. Ann Matter and John Coakley (eds.), *Creative Women in Medieval and Early Modern Italy* (Philadelphia PA: University of Pennsylvania Press, 1994), pp. 324–342.

KENDRICK 1996
Robert L. Kendrick, *Celestial Sirens: Nuns and Their Music in Early Modern Milan* (Oxford: Clarendon Press and Oxford University Press, 1996).

**KENDRICK 2002**
Robert L. Kendrick, *The Sounds of Milan, 1585–1650* (Oxford UK and New York NY: Oxford University Press, 2002).

**KENDRICK 2006**
Robert L. Kendrick, "Federico Borromeo e l'estetica della musica sacra", *Studia Borromaica*, no. 20 (2006), pp. 339–350.

**KENDRICK 2009**
Robert L. Kendrick, "'Honore a Dio, e allegrezza alli santi e consolazione alli putti': The Musical Projection of Litanies in Sixteenth-Century Italy", in Simon Ditchfield (ed.), *Sanctorum 6: Plasmare il suono. Il culto dei santi e la musica (secc. XVI-XVIII)* (Rome: Viella, 2009), pp. 15–46.

**KENNEDY 1982**
T. Frank Kennedy, *Jesuits and Music: The European Tradition, 1547–1622* (PhD Dissertation: University of California at Santa Barbara, 1982).

**KERMAN 1994**
Joseph Kerman, *Write All These Down: Essays on Music* (Berkeley and Los Angeles CA: University of California Press, 1994).

**KIM 2005**
Hyun-Ah Kim, *Renaissance Humanism and John Merbecke's "The Booke of Common Praier Noted" (1550)* (PhD Thesis: Durham University, 2005); available online at http://etheses.dur.ac.uk/2767/.

**KIM 2008**
Hyun-Ah Kim, *Humanism and the Reform of Sacred Music in Early Modern England. John Merbecke the Orator and* The Booke of Common Praier Noted *(1550)* (Aldershot: Ashgate, 2008).

**KIM 2015**
Hyun-Ah Kim, "Death, Music and the Appropriateness of Emotions in Reformation England: Humanist Portrayals of Burial and Mourning in *Musica Rhetorica*", in Elizabeth C. Tingle and Jonathan Willis (eds.), *Dying, Death, Burial and Commemoration in Reformation Europe* (Aldershot: Ashgate, 2015), pp. 67–88.

**KIRÁLY 2014**
Péter Király, "Foreign Musicians and Their Influence in Sixteenth- and Seventeenth-Century Hungary", in Gábor Almási et al. (ed.), *A Divided Hungary in Europe. Exchanges, Networks and Representations, 1541–1699, Vol. I* (Newcastle upon Tyne: Cambridge Scholars Publishing, 2014), pp. 253–270.

**KIRBY 1961**
Franck Eugene Kirby, "Hermann Finck on Methods of Performance", *ML*, vol. 42, no. 3 (1961), pp. 212–220.

**KIRKMAN 2010**
Andrew Kirkman, *The Cultural Life of the Early Polyphonic Mass: Medieval Context to Modern Revival* (Cambridge: Cambridge University Press, 2010).

**KNIGHTON 1992**
Tess Knighton, "The *a cappella* Heresy in Spain: An Inquisition into the Performance of the *Cancionero* Repertory", *EM*, vol. 20 (1992), pp. 561–581.

**KNIGHTON 1996**
Tess Knighton, "Transmisión, difusión y recepción de la polifonía franco-neerlandesa en el reino de Aragón a principios del siglo XVI", *Artigrama*, no. 12 (1996), pp. 19–38.

**KOENIGSBERGER 1968**
Helmut Georg Koenigsberger, *Europe in the Sixteenth Century*, English translation by George L. Mosse (London: Longmans; New York NY: Holt, Rinehard and Winston, 1968).

**KOENIGSBERGER 1986**
Helmut Georg Koenigsberger, *Politicians and Virtuosi: Essays in Early Modern History* (London: Hambledon Press, 1986).

**KOLB AND NESTINGEN 2001**
Robert Kolb and James A. Nestingen (eds.), *Sources and Contexts of the Book of Concord* (Minneapolis MN: Augsburg Fortress, 2001).

**KOLDAU 2005A**
Linda Maria Koldau, "Frauen in der deutschen Musikkultur der Frühen-Neuzeit", *Archiv für Musikwissenschaft*, vol. 62, no. 3 (2005), pp. 220–248.

**KOLDAU 2005B**
Linda Maria Koldau, *Frauen-Musik-Kultur: ein Handbuch zum deutschen Sprachgebiet der Frühen-Neuzeit* (Cologne: Böhlau Verlag, 2005).

**KOLDE 1883**
Theodor Kolde (ed.), *Analecta Lutherana: Briefe und Actenstücke zur Geschichte Luthers* (Gotha: Friedrich Andreas Perthes, 1883); available online at http://bit.ly/2bAT371.

**KONNERT 2008**
Mark Konnert, *Early Modern Europe: The Age of Religious War, 1559–1715* (Toronto: University of Toronto Press, 2008).

**KÖRNDLE 1998**
Franz Körndle, "Das musikalische Ordinarium Missae nach 1400", in Horst Leuchtmann and Siegfried Mauser (eds.), *Messe und Motette* (Laaber: Laaber Verlag, 1998), pp. 154–188.

**KÖRNDLE 2006**
Franz Körndle, "Between Stage and Divine Service: Jesuits and Theatrical Music", in Gauvin Alexander Bailey, Steven J. Harris, John W. O'Malley and T. Frank Kennedy (eds.), *The Jesuits II: Cultures, Sciences and the Arts 1540–1773* (Toronto: University of Toronto Press, 2006), pp. 479–497.

**KORRICK 1990**
Leslie Korrick, "Instrumental Music in the Early 16th-Century Mass: New Evidence", *EM*, vol. 18, no. 3 (August, 1990), pp. 359–365, 367–370.

**KREMER 2001**
Joachim Kremer, "Change and Continuity in the Reformation Period: Church Music in North German Towns, 1500–1600", in Fiona Kisby (ed.), *Music and musicians in Renaissance Cities and Courts* (Cambridge: Cambridge University Press, 2001), pp. 118–130.

**KREUZER 1973**
Bernhard Kreuzer, *A Study of $16^{th}$ and $17^{th}$ century Protestant German Hymnody* (PhD Dissertation: University of Iowa, 1973).

**KRISTELLER 1961**
Paul Oskar Kristeller, *Renaissance Thought: the Classic, Scholastic, and Humanist Strains* (New York NY: Harper & Row, 1961); available online at http://bit.ly/2bwXPRQ.

**KÜMIN 2001**
Beat Kümin, "Masses, Morris and Metrical Psalms: Music in the English Parish, c. 1400–1600", in Fiona Kisby (ed.), *Music and Musicians in Renaissance Cities and Towns* (Cambridge: Cambridge University Press, 2001), pp. 70–81.

**KURTZMAN 2002**
Jeffrey G. Kurtzman, "Palestrina's *Magnificats:* A Brief Survey", in David Crawford and G. Grayson Wagstaff (eds.), *Encomium Musicæ: Essays in Memory of Robert J. Snow* (Hillsdale NY: Pendragon Press, 2002), pp. 637–662.

**LAMAY 2005**
Thomasin K. LaMay (ed.), *Musical Voices of Early Modern Women* (Aldershot: Ashgate, 2005).

**LAMBERT 1917**
James F. Lambert, *Luther's Hymns* (Philadelphia PA: General Council Publication House, 1917).

**LATOUR 2015**
Melinda Latour, "Disciplining Song in Sixteenth-Century Geneva", *The Journal of Musicology*, vol. 32, no. 1 (Winter 2015), pp. 1–39.

**LAUBE 2014**
Matthew Laube, "'Hymnis Germanicis Davidis, Lutheri & aliorum priorum virorum': Hymnbooks and confessionalisation in Heidelberg, 1546–1620", in Michael Fischer, Norbert Haag, Gabriele Haug-Moritz (eds.), *Musik in Neuzeitlichen Konfessionskulturen (16. bis 19. Jahrhundert). Räume – Medien – Funktionen* (Ostfildern: Jan Thorbecke Verlag, 2014), pp. 85–102.

**LE HURAY 1967 / LE HURAY 1978 / LE HURAY 2008**
Peter Le Huray, *Music and the Reformation in England 1549–1660* (London: Herbert Jenkins Ltd, 1967; Cambridge: Cambridge University Press, 1978; 2008).

**LEACH 2006**
Elizabeth Eva Leach, "Gendering the Semitone, Sexing the Leading Tone: Fourteenth-Century Music Theory and the Directed Progression", *Music Theory Spectrum*, vol. 28, no. 1 (Spring 2006), pp. 1–21.

**LEACH 2009**
Elizabeth Eva Leach, "Music and Masculinity in the Middle Ages", in Ian Biddle and Kirsten Gibson (eds.), *Masculinity and Western Musical Practice* (Aldershot: Ashgate, 2009), pp. 21–40.

**LEAVER 1973**
Robin A. Leaver, "Lutherans and Plainsong", *MT*, vol. 114, no. 1566 (1973), pp. 795–796.

**LEAVER 1989**
Robin A. Leaver, "The Lutheran Reformation", in Iain Fenlon, *The Renaissance. From the 1470s to the End of the Sixteenth Century* (Basingstoke and London: Macmillan, 1989), pp. 263–285.

**LEAVER 1991**
Robin A. Leaver, *'Goostly Psalmes and Spirituall Songes': English and Dutch Metrical Psalms from Coverdale to Utenhove, 1535–66* (Oxford: Clarendon Press, 1991).

**LEAVER 1995**
Robin A. Leaver, "Theological Consistency, Liturgical Integrity, and Musical Hermeneutics in Luther's Liturgical Reforms", *Lutheran Quarterly*, no. 9 (Summer 1995), pp. 117–138.

**LEAVER 1998**
Robin A. Leaver, "Liturgical Music as Corporate Song 1: Hymnody in Reformation Churches", in Robin A. Leaver and Joyce Ann Zimmerman (eds.), *Liturgy and Music. Lifetime Learning* (Collegeville PA: The Liturgical Press, 1998), pp. 281–307.

**LEAVER 2004A**
Robin A. Leaver, "Luther as Musician", *Lutheran Quarterly*, no. 18 (2004), pp. 125–183.

**LEAVER 2004B**
Robin A. Leaver, "Hymnody in English and Dutch Exile Congregations ca. 1552–1561", *JLH*, no. 43 (2004), pp. 152–179.

**LEAVER 2004C**
Robin A. Leaver, "Genevan Psalm Tunes in the Lutheran Chorale Tradition", in Eckard Grunewald, Henning P. Jürgens, Jan R. Luth (eds.), *Der Genfer Psalter und seine Rezeption in Deutschland, der Schweiz und den Niederland* (Berlin and New York NY: De Gruyter, 2004), pp. 145–166.

**LEAVER 2006**
Robin A. Leaver, "The Reformation and Music", in James Haar (ed.), *European Music 1520–1642* (Woodbridge: The Boydell Press, 2006), pp. 371–400.

**LEAVER 2007**
Robin A. Leaver, *Luther's Liturgical Music. Principles and Implications* (Grand Rapids MI: Eerdmans, 2007).

**LEGG 1891**
John Wickham Legg, "Some Imitations of the Te Deum", *Transactions of the St. Paul's Ecclesiological Society*, no. 3 (1891), pp. 34–40.

**LEICHTENTRITT 1944**
Hugo Leichtentritt, "The Reform of Trent and Its Effect on Music", *MQ*, vol. 30, no. 3 (July 1944), pp. 319–328.

**LEITE 1956**
Serafim Leite (ed.), *Monumenta Brasiliae: 1. (1538–1553)* (Rome: Monumenta Historica Societatis Jesu, 1956); available online at http://bit.ly/2bIfbKL.

**LEITMEIR 2002**
Christian Thomas Leitmeir, "Catholic Music in the Diocese of Augsburg c. 1600: A Reconstructed Tricinium Anthology and Its Confessional Implications", *EMH*, no. 21 (2002), pp. 117–173.

**LEJEUNE 2010**
Jérôme Lejeune, *Réforme & Contre-Réforme. Reformation & Counter-Reformation* (Brussels: Outhere Music – Ricercar [RIC 101], 2010).

**LESLIE 1969**
Robert Homer Leslie, *Music and the Arts in Calvin's Geneva* (PhD Dissertation: McGill University, 1969).

**LEVRI 1944**
Mario Levri, "La Cappella musicale del Madruzzo e i Cantori del Concilio", *Il Concilio di Trento*, vol. 2, no. 4 (October 1943) (Trento: Arti Grafiche Saturnia, 1944), pp. 394–405.

**LEVY 1953**
Kenneth Jay Levy, "'Susanne un jour': The History of a 16$^{th}$-Century Chanson", *Annales musicologiques*, no. 1 (1953), pp. 375–408.

**LEWIS 1954**
Clive S. Lewis, *English Literature in the Sixteenth Century* (Oxford: Oxford University Press, 1954).

**LEYERLE 2001**
Blake Leyerle, *Theatrical Shows and Ascetic Lives. John Chrysostom's Attack on Spiritual Marriage* (Berkeley and Los Angeles CA: University of California Press, 2001).

LINDBERG 1996 / LINDBERG 2010
Carter Lindberg, *The European Reformations* (Oxford: Blackwell Publishing 1996; Oxford: Wiley-Blackwell 2010²).

LINDMAYR-BRANDL 2005
Andrea Lindmayr-Brandl, "Neuer Glaube gegen Alte Macht. Spuren der Reformation im Salzburger Musikleben des 16. Jahrhunderts", in Peter Wollny (ed.), *Musikgeschichte im Zeichen der Reformation* (Beeskow: Ortus, 2005), pp. 87–95.

LOCKWOOD 1957
Lewis H. Lockwood, "Vincenzo Ruffo and Musical Reform After the Council of Trent", *MQ*, no. 43 (1957), pp. 342–371.

LOCKWOOD 1966
Lewis H. Lockwood, "Some Observations on the Commission of Cardinals and the Reform of Sacred Music (1565)", *Quadrivium*, no. 7 (1966), pp. 39–55.

LOCKWOOD 1969 / LOCKWOOD 1970
Lewis H. Lockwood, *The Counter-Reformation and the Masses of Vincenzo Ruffo* (Vienna: Universal Edition, 1969; Venice: Fondazione Giorgio Cini, 1970).

LOCKWOOD 1974
Lewis H. Lockwood, "Music and Religion in the High Renaissance and the Reformation", in Charles E. Trinkaus and Heiko A. Oberman (eds.), *The Pursuit of Holiness in Late Medieval and Renaissance Religion* (Leiden and New York NY: Brill, 1974), pp. 496–504.

LOCKWOOD 1975
Lewis H. Lockwood (ed.), *Palestrina. Pope Marcellus Mass* (New York NY and London: W. W. Norton and Company, 1975).

LOEWE 2013
J. Andreas Loewe, "'Musica est optimum': Martin Luther's Theory of Music", *ML*, vol. 94, no. 4 (2013), pp. 573–605.

LONGFELLOW 2012
Erica Longfellow, "'My now solitary prayers': *Eikon balisike* and Changing Attitudes toward Religious Solitude", in Jessica Martin and Alec Ryrie (eds.), *Private and Domestic Devotion in Early Modern Britain* (Aldershot: Ashgate, 2012), pp. 53–72.

LÓPEZ-CALO 1963
José López-Calo, *La música en la catedral de Granada en el siglo XVI* (Granada: Fundación Rodríguez Acosta, 1963).

LÓPEZ-CALO 1969
José López-Calo, "La Contre-Réforme en Italie: Palestrina et le Concile de Trente", in Jacques Porte (ed.), *Encyclopédie de musiques sacrées* (Paris: Labergerie, 1969), vol. 2, pp. 397–403.

LORENZ 1995
Ralph Lorenz, *Pedagogical Implications of* Musica Practica *in Sixteenth-Century Wittenberg* (PhD Dissertation: Indiana University, 1995).

LORENZO ARRIBAS 2011
Josemi Lorenzo Arribas, "Gracia Baptista y otras organistas del siglo XVI ibérico", *Revista de Musicología*, vol. 34, no. 2 (2011), pp. 263–284.

LOUISON LASSABLIÈRE 2003
Marie-Joëlle Louison Lassablière, "La *Chrestienne Instruction*", in Jean Pironon and Jacques Wagner (eds.), *Formes Littéraires du théologico-politique de la Renaissance au XVIIIe*

siècle: Angleterre et Europe, Actes du colloque de Clermont-Ferrand, 19–21 septembre 2002 (Clermont-Ferrand: Presses Universitaires Blaise-Pascal, 2003), pp. 101–114.

**LOVATO 1995**
Antonio Lovato, "Teoria e didattica del canto piano", in Danilo Curti and Marco Gozzi (eds.), *Musica e Liturgia nella Riforma Tridentina* (Trento: Provincia Autonoma di Trento – Servizio Beni Librari e Archivistici, 1995), pp. 57–68.

**LOWE 2003**
Kate J. P. Lowe, *Nuns' Chronicles and Convent Culture in Renaissance and Counter-Reformation Italy* (Cambridge: Cambridge University Press, 2003).

**LOWINSKY 1946 / LOWINSKY 1967**
Edward Elias Lowinsky, *Secret Chromatic Art in the Netherlands Motet* (New York NY: Russel and Russel 1946; 1967).

**LOWINSKY 1989**
Edward Elias Lowinsky, *Music in the Culture of the Renaissance and Other Essays*, edited by Bonnie J. Blackburn, 2 vols. (Chicago IL: University of Chicago Press, 1989).

**LUBECUS 1967**
Franz Lubecus, *Bericht über die Einführung der Reformation in Göttingen im Jahre 1529* (Göttingen: Heinz Reise, 1967).

**LUNELLI 1947**
Renato Lunelli, "La polifonia nel Trentino con speciale riguardo al Concilio", *Il Concilio di Trento*, vol. 3, no. 1 (June 1947), pp. 78–98.

**LÜTTEKEN 2013**
Laurenz Lütteken, "Theory of Music and Philosophy of Life: the *Dodekachordon* and the Counter-Reformation", in Iain Fenlon and Inga Mai Groote (eds.), *Heinrich Glarean's Books: the Intellectual World of a Sixteenth-Century Musical Humanist* (Cambridge: Cambridge University Press, 2013), pp. 38–46.

**MACCLINTOCK 1979 / MACCLINTOCK 1982**
Carol MacClintock (ed.), *Readings in the History of Music in Performance* (Bloomington IN: Indiana University Press, 1979; Bloomington IN: Indiana University Press, Midland Books, 1982).

**MACCULLOCH 2003**
Diarmaid MacCulloch, *Reformation. Europe's House Divided 1490–1700* (London: Penguin, 2003).

**MACDONALD 1991**
Alasdair MacDonald, "Mary Stewart's Entry to Edinburgh: an Ambiguous Triumph", *Innes Review*, vol. 42, no. 2 (1991), pp. 101–110.

**MACE 1964**
Dean T. Mace, "Musical Humanism, the Doctrine of Rhythmus, and the Saint Cecilia Odes of Dryden", *Journal of the Wardburg and Courtauld Institutes*, no. 27 (1964), pp. 251–292.

**MACEY 1983**
Patrick Paul Macey, "Savonarola and the Sixteenth-Century Motet", *J-AMS*, vol. 36, no. 3 (Autumn 1983), pp. 422–452.

**MACEY 1992**
Patrick Paul Macey, "*Infiamma il mio cor:* Savonarolan Laude by and for Dominican Nuns in Tuscany", in Craig A. Monson (ed.), *The Crannied Wall: Women, Religion, and the Arts in Early Modern Europe* (Ann Arbor MI: University of Michigan Press, 1992), pp. 161–189.

**MACEY 1998**
Patrick Paul Macey, *Bonfire Songs: Savonarola's Musical Legacy* (Oxford: Clarendon Press, 1998).
**MACEY 1999**
Patrick Paul Macey (ed.), *Savonarolan laude, motets and anthems*, volume 116 (Madison WI: A-R Editions, 1999).
**MACKERNESS 1964 / MACKERNESS 2010**
Eric David Mackerness, *A Social History of English Music* (Abindgon UK and New York NY: Routledge, 1964; 2010).
**MACY 2011**
Laura Macy, "Geronimo Cavaglieri, the *Song of Songs* and Female Spirituality in Federigo Borromeo's Milan", *EM*, vol. 39, no. 3 (2011), pp. 349–358.
**MAGER 1986**
Inge Mager, "Lied und Reformation: Beobachtungen zur reformatorischen Singbewegung in norddeutschen Städten", in Alfred Dürr and Walther Killy (eds.), *Das protestantische Kirchenlied im 16. und 17. Jahrhundert: Text-, musik- und theologiegeschichtliche Probleme* (Wiesbaden: Otto Harrassowitz, 1986), pp. 25–38.
**MANIATES 1979**
Maria Rika Maniates, *Mannerism in Italian Music and Culture, 1530–1630* (Manchester: Manchester University Press, 1979).
**MARCUS 2000**
Kenneth H. Marcus, "A Veritable Break with the Past: Sacred Music in Fifteenth-Century Basel", in Nancy van Deusen (ed.), *Medieval Germany. Associations and Delineations* (Ottawa: Institute of Mediaeval Music, 2000), pp. 163–172.
**MARCUS 2001**
Kenneth H. Marcus, "Hymnody and Hymnals in Basel, 1526–1606", *SCJ*, vol. 32, no. 3 (Autumn 2001), pp. 723–741.
**MARI 2008**
Licia Mari, "Il Diario di Santa Barbara (1572–1602): prima ricognizione di un'inaspettata fonte mantovana", in Alberto Colzani, Andrea Luppi and Maurizio Padoan (eds.), *Barocco Padano 5. Atti del XIII Convegno internazionale sulla musica italiana nei secoli XVII-XVIII* (Como: AMIS, 2008), pp. 467–503.
**MARI 2013**
Licia Mari, "Liturgia e musica tra Roma e Mantova. Ulteriori indagini relative alla Basilica Palatina di Santa Barbara", in Renata Salvarani (ed.), *I Gonzaga e i Papi. Roma e le corti padane fra Umanesimo e Rinascimento (1418–1620). Atti del convegno Mantova-Roma, 21–26 febbraio 2013* (Vatican City: Libreria Editrice Vaticana, 2013), pp. 159–178.
**MARSH 2013**
Christopher Marsh, *Music and Society in Early Modern England* (Cambridge: Cambridge University Press, 2013).
**MARSHALL 1989**
Sherrin Marshall (ed.), *Women in Reformation and Counter-Reformation Europe: Public and Private Worlds* (Bloomington IN: Indiana University Press, 1989).
**MARVIN 2002**
Clara Marvin, *Giovanni Pierluigi da Palestrina: A Guide to Research* (Abindgon UK and New York NY: Routledge, 2002).

**MASETTI ZANNINI 1985**
Gian Lodovico Masetti Zannini, "Espressioni musicali in monasteri femminili del primo Seicento a Bologna", *Strenna Storica Bolognese*, no. 35 (1985), pp. 191–205.

**MASETTI ZANNINI 1993**
Gian Lodovico Masetti Zannini, "'Suavità di canto' e 'purità di cuore'. Aspetti della musica nei monasteri femminili romani", in Oscar Mischiati and Paolo Russo (eds.), *La Cappella musicale nell'Italia della Controriforma* (Florence: Olschki, 1993), pp. 123–142.

**McCARTHY 2007**
Kerry McCarthy, *Liturgy and Contemplation in Byrd's Gradualia* (Abindgon UK and New York NY: Routledge, 2007).

**McCULLOUGH 2013**
Peter McCullough, "Music Reconciled to Preaching: A Jacobean Moment?", in Natalie Mears and Alec Ryrie (eds.), *Worship and the Parish Church in Early Modern Britain* (Aldershot: Ashgate 2013), pp. 109–130.

**McKEE 1998**
Elsie Ann McKee, *Katharina Schütz Zell*, 2 vols. (Leiden and New York NY: Brill, 1998).

**McKEE 2003**
Elsie Ann McKee, "Reformed Worship in the Sixteenth Century", in Lukas Vischer (ed.), *Christian Worship in Reformed Churches Past and Present* (Grand Rapids MI: Eerdmans, 2003), pp. 3–31.

**MEARS 2013**
Natalie Mears, "Special Nationwide Worship and the Book of Common Prayer in England, Wales and Ireland, 1533–1642", in Natalie Mears and Alec Ryrie (eds.), *Worship and the Parish Church in Early Modern Britain* (Aldershot: Ashgate 2013), pp. 31–73.

**MECONI 2003**
Honey Meconi, *Pierre de la Rue and Musical Life at the Habsburg-Burgundian Court* (Oxford UK and New York NY: Oxford University Press, 2003).

**MEIER 1990**
Bernhard Meier, "Rhetorical Aspects of the Renaissance Modes", *J-RMA*, vol. 115, no. 2 (1990), pp. 182–190.

**MILLER 1966**
Clement A. Miller, "Erasmus on Music", *MQ*, no. 52 (1966), pp. 332–349.

**MILNER 2011**
Matthew Milner, *The Senses and the English Reformation* (Aldershot: Ashgate, 2011).

**MILSOM 1982**
John Milsom, "A New Tallis Contrafactum", *MT*, no. 123 (1982), pp. 429–431.

**MILSOM 1995**
John Milsom, "Sacred Songs in the Chamber", in John Morehen (ed.), *English Choral Practice 1400–1650* (Cambridge: Cambridge University Press, 1995), pp. 161–179.

**MILSOM 2007**
John Milsom, "Caustun's Contrafacta", *J-RMA*, vol. 132, no. 1 (2007), pp. 1–31.

**MISCHIATI 1977**
Oscar Mischiati, "'Ut verba intelligerentur': circostanze e connessioni a proposito della Missa Papae Marcelli", in Francesco Luisi (ed.), *Atti del convegno di Studi palestriniani, 28 sett.–2 ott. 1975* (Palestrina: Fondazione G. P. da Palestrina, 1977), pp. 415–426.

MISCHIATI 1993
Oscar Mischiati, "Profilo storico e istituzionale della Cappella Musicale in Italia", in Oscar Mischiati and Paolo Russo (eds.), *La Cappella musicale nell'Italia della Controriforma* (Florence: Olschki, 1993), pp. vii-x.

MISCHIATI 1995
Oscar Mischiati, "Il Concilio di Trento e la polifonia. Una diversa proposta di lettura e di prospettiva storiografica", in Danilo Curti and Marco Gozzi (eds.), *Musica e Liturgia nella Riforma Tridentina* (Trento: Provincia Autonoma di Trento – Servizio Beni Librari e Archivistici, 1995), pp. 19–30.

MOLITOR 1901 / MOLITOR 1967
Raphael Molitor, *Die Nach-Tridentinische Choral-Reform zu Rom. Ein Beitrag zur Musikgeschichte des XVI. und XVII. Jahrhunderts*, 2 vols. (Leipzig: Leuckart, 1901–1902); first volume available online at http://bit.ly/2bRgZRm; (Hildesheim: Georg Olms Verlag, 1967).

MONSON 1989
Craig A. Monson, "Elena Malvezzi's Keyboard Manuscript: A New Sixteenth-Century Source", *EMH*, no. 9 (1989), pp. 73–128.

MONSON 1992
Craig A. Monson, *The Crannied Wall. Women, Religion and the Arts in Early Modern Europe* (Ann Arbor MI: University of Michigan Press, 1992).

MONSON 1993A
Craig A. Monson, "La pratica della musica nei monasteri femminili bolognesi", in Oscar Mischiati and Paolo Russo (eds.), *La Cappella musicale nell'Italia della Controriforma* (Florence: Olschki, 1993), pp. 143–160.

MONSON 1993B
Craig A. Monson, "Molti concerti, poca concordia: monache, parrocchiani, e musica nella chiesa e convento dei ss. Vitale e Agricola, 1550–1730", in Gina Fasoli (ed.), *Vitale e Agricola: Il culto dei protomartiri di Bologna attraverso i secoli* (Bologna: EDB, 1993), pp. 195–200.

MONSON 1995 / MONSON 2009
Craig A. Monson, *Disembodied Voices: Music and Culture in an Early Modern Italian Convent* (Berkeley and Los Angeles CA: University of California Press, 1995); Italian translation by Riccardo James Vargiu as *Voci incorporee. Musica e cultura in un convento italiano della prima età moderna* (Bologna: Bononia University Press, 2009).

MONSON 1997
Craig A. Monson, "Byrd, the Catholics, and the Motet: The Hearing Reopened", in Dolores Pesce (ed.), *Hearing the Motet: Essays on the Motet of the Middle Ages and Renaissance* (Oxford UK and New York NY: Oxford University Press, 1997), pp. 348–374.

MONSON 2002
Craig A. Monson, "The Council of Trent Revisited", *J-AMS*, vol. 55 (2002), pp. 1–37.

MONSON 2003
Craig A. Monson, "The Composer as 'Spy': The Ferraboscos, Gabriele Paleotti, and the Inquisition", *ML*, vol. 84, no. 1 (February 2003), pp. 1–18.

MONSON 2005
Craig A. Monson, "Ancora uno sguardo sulle suore musiciste di Bologna", in Gianna Pomata and Gabriella Zarri (eds.), *I Monasteri femminili come centri di cultura fra Rinascimento e Barocco* (Rome: Edizioni di Storia e Letteratura, 2005), pp. 3–26.

**MONSON 2006**
Craig A. Monson, "Renewal, Reform, and Reaction in Catholic Music", in James Haar (ed.), *European Music 1520–1642* (Woodbridge: The Boydell Press, 2006), pp. 401–421.

**MONSON 2010**
Craig A. Monson, *Nuns Behaving Badly. Tales of Music, Magic, Art and Arson in the Convents of Italy* (Chicago IL: The University of Chicago Press, 2010).

**MONSON 2012**
Craig A. Monson, *Divas in the Convent. Nuns, Music, and Defiance in Seventeenth-Century Italy* (Chicago IL: The University of Chicago Press, 2012).

**MONTER 1967**
E. William Monter, *Calvin's Geneva* (New York NY: Wiley and Sons, 1967).

**MONTFORD 1999**
Kimberlyn Montford, *Music in the Convents of Counter-Reformation Rome* (PhD Thesis: Rutgers University, 1999).

**MONTFORD 2006**
Kimberlyn Montford, "Holy Restraint: Religious Reform and Nuns' Music in Early Modern Rome", *SCJ*, vol. 37, no. 4 (Winter 2006), pp. 1007–1026.

**MORANDI 1804**
Giambattista Morandi (ed.), *Monumenti di varia letteratura tratti dai manoscritti di Monsignor Lodovico Beccadelli arcivescovo di Ragusa* (Bologna: Stampe di S. Tommaso d'Aquino, 1804).

**MORAWSKA 2002**
Katarzyna Morawska, *The History of Music in Poland: 1500–1600. The Renaissance* (Warsaw: Sutkowski Edition, 2002).

**MORELLI 1993**
Arnaldo Morelli, "Le cappelle musicali a Roma nel Seicento: Questioni di organizzazione e di prassi esecutiva", in Oscar Mischiati and Paolo Russo (eds.), *La Cappella musicale nell'Italia della Controriforma* (Florence: Olschki, 1993), pp. 175–204.

**MORUCCI 2012**
Valerio Morucci, "Cardinals' Patronage and the Era of Tridentine Reforms: Giulio Feltro della Rovere as Protector of Sacred Music", *The Journal of Musicology*, vol. 29, no. 3 (Summer 2012), pp. 262–291.

**MÜLLER 1911**
Nikolaus Müller, *Die Wittenberger Bewegung 1521 und 1522* (Leipzig: M. Heinsius, 1911).

**MULLINAX 1984**
Allen Bruce Mullinax, "Martin Bucer and the Strasbourg Songbook: 1541" (M. C. M. Thesis: Southern Baptist Theological Seminary, 1984).

**MUNRO 2010**
Gordon Munro, "'Sang Schwylls' and 'Music Schools': Music Education in Scotland, 1560–1650", in Russell E. Murray jr, Susan Forscher Weiss, Cynthia J. Cyrus (eds.), *Music Education in the Middle Ages and the Renaissance* (Bloomington IN: Indiana University Press, 2010), pp. 65–83.

**NALLE 1992**
Sara T. Nalle, *God in La Mancha: Religious Reform and the People of Cuenca* (Baltimore MD: Johns Hopkins University Press, 1992).

**NANNI 2012**
Stefania Nanni (ed.), *La musica dei semplici. L'altra controriforma* (Rome: Viella, 2012).

**NAUERT 2006**
Charles G. Nauert, "The Mind", in Euan Cameron (ed.), *The Sixteenth Century* (Oxford UK and New York NY: Oxford University Press, 2006), pp. 116–144.

**NAWROCKA-WYSOCKA 2009**
Arleta Nawrocka-Wysocka, "Lutheran Hymn-Singing in Masuria: Ecclesiastic Norms and the Local Tradition", in Piotr Dahlig (ed.) and John Comber (transl.), *Traditional Musical Cultures in Central-Eastern Europe. Ecclesiastical and Folk Transmission* (Warsaw: The Institute of Musicology, University of Warsaw and The Warsaw Learned Society, 2009), pp. 365–380.

**NETTL 1948 / NETTL 1967**
Paul Nettl, *Luther and Music* (Philadelphia PA: The Muhlenburg Press, 1948; New York NY, Russell and Russell, 1967).

**NEWCOMB 1980**
Anthony Newcomb, *The Madrigal at Ferrara, 1579–1597* (Princeton NJ: Princeton University Press, 1980).

**NICHOLS 1823**
John Nichols, *The Progresses and Public Processions of Queen Elizabeth*, vol. 1 (London: For John Nichols, 1823); available online at http://bit.ly/2bQwtE5.

**NISCHAN 1994**
Bodo Nischan, *Prince, People and Confession: Second Reformation in Brandenburg* (Philadelphia PA: University of Pennsylvania Press, 1994).

**NIXON 1984**
Howard M. Nixon, "Day's *Service Book*, 1560–1565", *British Library Journal*, no. 10 (1984), pp. 1–31.

**NOLL 2007**
Mark Noll, "Singing the Word of God", *Christian History and Biography*, no. 95 (2007), pp. 15–19.

**NOONE 1998**
Michael John Noone, *Music and Musicians in the Escorial Liturgy under the Habsburgs, 1563–1700* (Rochester NY: University of Rochester Press, 1998).

**NUGENT 1990**
George Nugent, "Anti-Protestant Music for Sixteenth-Century Ferrara", *J-AMS*, vol. 43, no. 2 (Summer 1990), pp. 228–291.

**NUGENT 1997**
George Nugent, "Some Reflections on Patronage: Palestrina and Mantua", in Jessie Anne Owens and Anthony M. Cummings (eds.), *Music in Renaissance Cities and Courts: Studies in Honor of Lewis Lockwood* (Michigan MI: Harmonie Park Press, 1997), pp. 241–252.

**O'MALLEY 1993**
John W. O'Malley, *The First Jesuits* (Cambridge MA: Harvard University Press, 1993).

**O'REGAN 1984**
Noel O'Regan, "The Early Polychoral Music of Orlando di Lasso: New Light from Roman Sources", *Acta Musicologica*, vol. 56 (1984), pp. 234–251.

**O'REGAN 1992**
Noel O'Regan, "Processions and their Music in Post-Tridentine Rome", *Recercare*, no. 4 (1992), pp. 45–80.

**O'REGAN 1994**
Noel O'Regan, "Palestrina, a Musician and Composer in the Market-Place", *EM*, vol. 22, no. 4 (November 1994), pp. 441, 558, 560, 562, 566, 568, 570, 572.

**O'REGAN 1995**
Noel O'Regan, *Institutional Patronage in Post-Tridentine Rome: Music at SS. Trinità dei Pellegrini 1559–1650* (London: Royal Musical Association, 1995).

**O'REGAN 1999A**
Noel O'Regan, "Orlando di Lasso and Rome: Personal Contacts and Musical Influences", in Peter Bergquist (ed.), *Orlando di Lasso Studies* (Cambridge: Cambridge University Press, 1999), pp. 132–158.

**O'REGAN 1999B**
Noel O'Regan, "Marenzio's Sacred Music: The Roman Context", *EM*, vol. 27, no. 4 (November 1999), pp. 608–620.

**O'REGAN 2000**
Noel O'Regan, "Asprilio Pacelli, Ludovico da Viadana and the Origin of the Roman *Concerto Ecclesiastico*", *Journal of Seventeenth-Century Music*, vol. 6, no. 1 (2000); available online at http://sscm-jscm.org/jscm/v6/no1/oregan.html

**O'REGAN 2006**
Noel O'Regan, "Italy, II: 1560–1600", in James Haar (ed.), *European Music 1520–1642* (Woodbridge: The Boydell Press, 2006), pp. 75–90.

**O'REGAN 2008**
Noel O'Regan, "Choirboys in Early Modern Rome", in Susan Boynton and Eric Rice (eds.), *Young Choristers 650–1700* (Woodbridge: The Boydell Press, 2008), pp. 216–240.

**O'REGAN 2009**
Noel O'Regan, "Church Reform and Devotional Music in Sixteenth-Century Rome: The Influence of Lay Confraternities", in Abigail Brundin and Matthew Treherne (eds.), *Forms of Faith in Sixteenth-Century Italy* (Aldershot: Ashgate, 2009), pp. 215–232.

**O'REGAN 2012**
Noel O'Regan, "Tomás Luis de Victoria's role in the development of a Roman polychoral idiom in the 1570s and early 1580s", *Revista de Musicología*, vol. 35, no. 1 (2012), pp. 203–218.

**O'REGAN 2013A**
Noel O'Regan, "Music and the Counter-Reformation", in Alexandra Bamji, Geert H. Janssen and Mary Laven (eds.), *The Ashgate Research Companion to the Counter-Reformation* (Aldershot: Ashgate, 2013), pp. 337–354.

**O'REGAN 2013B**
Noel O'Regan, "From Rome to Madrid: the Polychoral Music of Tomás Luis de Victoria", in Juan José Carreras and Iain Fenlon (eds.), *Polychoralities: Music Identity and Power in Italy, Spain and the New World* (Kassel: Reichenberger, 2013), pp. 35–50.

**O'REGAN 2014**
Noel O'Regan, "Music, Memory and Faith: How did singing in Latin and the vernacular influence what people knew and thought about their faith in Early Modern Rome?", *The Italianist*, vol. 34, no. 3 (2014), pp. 437–448.

**OBERMAN 1963 / OBERMAN 2000**
Heiko Augustinus Oberman, *The Harvest of Medieval Theology* (Cambridge MA: Harvard University Press, 1963; Grand Rapids MI: Baker Academic, 2000).

**OGASAPIAN 2004**
John Ogasapian, *Music of the Colonial and Revolutionary Era* (Westport CT and London: Greenwood Press, 2004).

**OLSON 1972**
Oliver K. Olson, "Theology of Revolution: Magdeburg, 1550–1551", *SCJ*, no. 3 (1972), pp. 56–79.

**ONGARO 1986**
Giulio M. Ongaro, *The Chapel of St Mark's at the Time of Adrian Willaert (1527–1562): A Documentary Study* (PhD Dissertation: University of North Carolina at Chapel Hill, 1986).

**ONGARO 2006**
Giulio M. Ongaro, "Italy, I: 1520–1560", in James Haar (ed.), *European Music 1520–1642* (Woodbridge: The Boydell Press, 2006), pp. 58–74.

**ØSTREM 2003**
Eyolf Østrem, "Luther, Josquin and *des fincken Gesang*", in Eyolf Østrem, Jens Fleischer and Nils Holger Petersen (eds.), *The Arts and the Cultural Heritage of Martin Luther* (Copenhagen: Museum Tusculanum Press, 2003), pp. 51–80.

**ØSTREM AND PETERSEN 2008**
Eyolf Østrem and Nils Holger Petersen, *Medieval Ritual and Early Modern Music: The Devotional Practice of Lauda Singing in Late-Renaissance Italy* (Turnhout: Brepols, 2008).

**OTTEN 1993**
Franz Otten, '*[M]it hilff gottes zw tichten… got zw lob vnd zw auspreittung seines heilsamen wort*': *Untersuchungen zur Reformationsdichtung des Hans Sachs* (Göppingen: Kümmerle, 1993).

**OWENS 1998**
Jessie Ann Owens, *Composers at Work: The Craft of Musical Composition 1450–1600* (Oxford UK and New York NY: Oxford University Press, 1998).

**OWENS 2006**
Jessie Ann Owens, "La musica inglese dalla Riforma alla Restaurazione", in Jean-Jacques Nattiez (ed.), *Enciclopedia della Musica*, vol. 1 (La musica europea dal gregoriano a Bach) (Turin: Giulio Einaudi; Milan, Il Sole 24 Ore, 2006), pp. 358–379.

**OZMENT 1980**
Steven Ozment, *The Age of Reform 1250–1550: An Intellectual and Religious History of Late Medieval and Reformation Europe* (New Haven CT: Yale University Press, 1980).

**PADOAN 2003**
Maurizio Padoan, "Ritualità e tensione innovativa nella musica sacra in area padana nel primo barocco", in Fabio Carboni, Valeria de Lucca and Agostino Ziino (eds.), *Tullio Cima, Domenico Massenzio e la musica del loro tempo* (Rome: IBIMUS Istituto Bibliografico Musicale, 2003), pp. 269–320.

**PAGAN 1897**
John H. Pagan, *Annals of Ayr: In the Olden Time, 1560–1692* (Ayr: Alex Fergusson, 1897).

**PAGE 1996**
Daniel Bennett Page, *Uniform and Catholic: Church Music in the Reign of Mary Tudor (1553–1558)* (PhD Thesis: Brandeis University Waltham MA, 1996).

**PALISCA 1953**
Claude Palisca, *The Beginnings of Baroque Music: Its Roots in Sixteenth-Century Theory and Polemics* (PhD Thesis: Harvard University, 1953).

PALISCA 1985
Claude Palisca, *Humanism in Italian Renaissance Musical Thought* (New Haven CT: Yale University Press, 1985).
PALISCA 1989
Claude Palisca, *The Florentine Camerata: Documentary Studies and Translations* (New Haven CT: Yale University Press, 1989).
PALISCA 1990
Claude Palisca, "Mode Ethos in the Renaissance", in Lewis Lockwood et al. (eds.), *Essays in Musicology: A Tribute to Alvin Johnson* (Philadelphia PA: American Musicological Society, 1990), pp. 126–139.
PALISCA 1997
Claude Palisca, "Bernardino Cirillo's Critique of Polyphonic Church Music of 1549: its Background and Resonance", in Jessie Anne Owens and Anthony M. Cummings (eds.), *Music in Renaissance Cities and Courts: Studies in Honor of Lewis Lockwood* (Michigan MI: Harmonie Park Press, 1997), pp. 282–292.
PALLAS 1906
Karl Pallas, *Die Registraturen der Kirchenvisitatoren im ehemals sächs. Kurkreise* vol. II, Part 1 (Halle: Hendel, 1906).
PARRISH 1958 / PARRISH 1986
Carl Parrish (ed.), *A Treasury of Early Music* (New York NY and London: W. W. Norton and Company, 1958; 1986).
PASTINA 1958
Giuseppe Pastina et al., "Gesuiti, teatro dei", in Fedele D'Amico, Luigi Squarzina and Francesco Savio (eds.), *Enciclopedia dello spettacolo*, vol. V (Florence: Le Maschere, 1958).
PASTOR 1950
Ludwig von Pastor, *Storia dei Papi nel periodo della Riforma e Restaurazione cattolica. Pio IV (1559–1565)* (Rome: Desclée, 1950).
PAYNE 1993
Ian Payne, *The Provision and Practice of Sacred Music at Cambridge Colleges and Selected Cathedrals, c. 1547-c. 1646: A Comparative Study of the Archival Evidence* (New York NY and London: Garland, 1993).
PECKLERS AND OSTDIEK 2011
Keith Pecklers and Gilbert Ostdiek, "The History of Vernaculars and the Role of Translation", in Edward Foley (ed.), *A Commentary on the Order of Mass of the Roman Missal* (Collegeville PA: The Liturgical Press, 2011), pp. 35–72.
PELIKAN 1964
Jaroslav Pelikan, *Obedient Rebels: Catholic Substance and Protestant Principle in Luther's Reformation* (New York NY: Harper, 1964).
PENDLE 1991 / PENDLE 2001
Karin Pendle, "Musical Women in Early Modern Europe", in Karin Pendle (ed.), *Women & Music: A History* (Bloomington IN: Indiana University Press, 1991; 2001$^2$), pp. 57–96.
PENDLE AND BOYD 2012
Karin Pendle and Melinda Boyd, *Women in Music: A Research and Information Guide* (Abindgon UK and New York NY: Routledge, 2012).

**PERRY 1888**
George G. Perry, "The Visitation of the Monastery of Thame, 1526", *English Historical Review*, no. 3 (1888), pp. 704–722.

**PETERSEN 2012**
Nils Holger Petersen, "The *Quarant'Ore:* Early Modern Ritual and Performativity", in Peter Gillgren and Mårten Snickare (eds.), *Performativity and Performance in Baroque Rome* (Aldershot: Ashgate 2012), pp. 115–133.

**PETRACCIA 2010**
Arianna Petraccia, *La pittura a L'Aquila 1560–1630* (PhD Thesis: Rome, Università degli Studi Roma Tre, 2010).

**PETTEGREE 1999**
Andrew Pettegree, *Huguenot Voices: The Book and the Communication Process during the Protestant Reformation* (Greenville, NC: Department of History, East Carolina University, 1999).

**PETTEGREE 2000**
Andrew Pettegree (ed.), *The Reformation World* (Abingdon UK and New York NY: Routledge, 2000).

**PETTEGREE 2002**
Andrew Pettegree, *Europe in the Sixteenth Century* (Oxford: Wiley-Blackwell, 2002).

**PETTEGREE 2003**
Andrew Pettegree, "Protestant Printing During the French Wars of Religion: The Lyon Press of Jean Saugrain", in Thomas A. Brady, Katherine G. Brady, Susan Karant-Nunn, James D. Tracy (eds.), *The Work of Heiko A. Oberman. Papers from the Symposium on His Seventieth Birthday* (Leiden and New York NY: Brill, 2003), pp. 109–129.

**PETTEGREE 2005**
Andrew Pettegree, *Reformation and the Culture of Persuasion* (Cambridge: Cambridge University Press, 2005).

**PHILLIPS 1978**
Peter Phillips, "Performance Practice in 16th-Century English Choral Music", *EM*, vol. 6, no. 2 (1978), pp. 195–199.

**PHILLIPS 1991**
Peter Phillips, *English Sacred Music, 1549–1649* (Oxford: Gimell, 1991).

**PIDOUX 1955**
Pierre Pidoux, "Über die Herkunft der Melodien des Hugenotten-Psalters", *JLH*, no. 1 (1955), pp. 113–114.

**PIETRANGELI 1994**
Carlo Pietrangeli, *Guide rionali di Roma* (Rome: Palombi, 1994).

**PINEAUX 1971**
Jacques Pineaux, *La poésie des protestants de langue française (1559–1598)* (Paris: Librairie Klincksieck, 1971).

**PIPERNO 2008**
Franco Piperno, "Istituzioni ecclesiastiche e musica nell'Italia della prima età moderna", in Erika Bellini (ed.), *Arte organaria e musica per organo nell'età moderna. L'Umbria nel quadro europeo* (Perugia: Deputazione di Storia Patria per l'Umbria, 2008), fasc. II, pp. 195–206.

PIRROTTA 1966
Nino Pirrotta, "Music and Cultural Tendencies in Fifteenth-Century Italy", *J-AMS*, vol. 19 (1966), pp. 152–155.

PIRROTTA 1984
Nino Pirrotta, *Music and Culture in Italy from the Middle Ages to the Baroque: A Collection of Essays* (Cambridge MA: Harvard University Press, 1984).

PITKIN 2015
Barbara Pitkin, "The Reformation of Preaching: Transformations of Worship Soundscapes in Early Modern Germany and Switzerland", *Yale Journal of Music & Religion*, vol. 1, no. 2 (2015), pp. 5–20.

PLASS 1959
Ewald M. Plass (ed. and transl.), *What Luther Says: An Anthology* (St Louis MO: Concordia Publishing House, 1959).

POLLMANN 2006
Judith Pollmann, "'Hey ho, let the cup go round!'. Singing for Reformation in the Sixteenth Century", in Heinz Schilling and István György Tóth (eds.), *Religion and Cultural Exchange in Europe, 1400–1700* (Cambridge: Cambridge University Press, 2006), pp. 294–316.

POPE 1952
Isabel Pope, "The Spanish Chapel of Philip II", *Renaissance News*, no. 5 (1952), pp. 1–4, 34–38.

POPE 1954
Isabel Pope, "Musical and Metrical Form of the Villancico", *Annales Musicologiques*, no. 2 (1954), pp. 189–214.

PORTER 2009
James Porter, "The Geneva Connection: Jean Servin's Settings of the Latin Psalm Paraphrases of George Buchanan (1579)", *Acta Musicologica*, vol. 81, no. 2 (2009), pp. 229–254.

PORTNOY 1949
Julius Portnoy, "Similarities of Musical Concepts in Ancient and Medieval Philosophy", *The Journal of Aesthetics and Art Criticism*, vol. 7, no. 3 (March 1949), pp. 235–243.

POWERS 1982
Harold S. Powers, "Modal Representation in Polyphonic Offertories", *EMH*, no. 2 (1982), pp. 43–86.

POWERS 1997
Katherine Powers, *The Spiritual Madrigal in Counter-Reformation Italy: Definition, Use and Style* (PhD Thesis: University of California at Santa Barbara, 1997).

PRESCOTT 1991
Anne Lake Prescott, "Musical Strains: Marot's Double Role as Psalmist and Courtier", in Marie-Rose Logan and Peter L. Rudnytsky (eds.), *Contending Kingdoms: Historical, Psychological, and Feminist Approaches to the Literature of Sixteenth-Century England and France* (Detroit MI: Wayne State University Press, 1991), pp. 42–68.

PRIZER 1998
William F. Prizer, "Music in Ferrara and Mantua at the Time of Dosso Dossi", in Luisa Ciammitti, Steven F. Ostrow and Salvatore Settis (eds.), *Dosso's Fate: Painting and Court Culture in Renaissance Italy* (Los Angeles CA: The Getty Research Institute for the History of Art and the Humanities, 1998), pp. 290–304.

PRODI 1959
Paolo Prodi, *Il Cardinale Gabriele Paleotti (1522–1597)* (Rome: Edizioni di Storia e Letteratura, 1959).

PRODI 2014
Paolo Prodi, *Arte e pietà nella Chiesa tridentina* (Bologna: Il Mulino, 2014).

PUGLIESE 1993
Annunziato Pugliese, "La cappella musicale del Cardinale Ippolito II d'Este", in Oscar Mischiati and Paolo Russo (eds.), *La Cappella musicale nell'Italia della Controriforma* (Florence: Olschki, 1993), pp. 381–394.

QUITSLUND 2008
Beth Quitslund, *The Reformation in Rhyme: Sternhold, Hopkins, and the English Metrical Psalter, 1547–1603* (Aldershot: Ashgate, 2008).

QUITSLUND 2012
Beth Quitslund, "Singing the Psalms for Fun and Profit", in Jessica Martin and Alec Ryrie (eds.), *Private and Domestic Devotion in Early Modern Britain* (Aldershot: Ashgate, 2012), pp. 237–258.

RADECKE 1996
Thomas Radecke, *450: Meister Joachim – Joachim von Burck (1546–1610)* (Burg und Mühlhausen: Stadtverwaltung, 1996).

RAINOLDI 2000
Felice Rainoldi, *Traditio canendi. Appunti per una storia dei riti cristiani cantati* (Rome: Edizioni Centro Liturgico Vincenziano, 2000).

RAMOS LÓPEZ 2005
Pilar Ramos López, "Music and Women in Early Modern Spain: Some Discrepancies between Educational Theory and Musical Practice", in Thomasin LaMay (ed.), *Musical Voices of Early Modern Women. Many-Headed Melodies* (Aldershot: Ashgate, 2005), pp. 97–118.

RAMOS LÓPEZ 2008
Pilar Ramos López, "Mysticism as a Key Concept of Spanish Early Music Historiography", in Zofia Fabiańska, Alicja Jarzębska, Wojciech Marchwica, Piotr Poźniak and Zygmunt M. Szwycykowski (eds.), *Early Music: Context and Ideas (II International Conference in Musicology, Kraków)* (Krakow: Jagiellonian University, 2008); available online at http://www.campusvirtual.unirioja.es/titulaciones/musica/fotos/13_ramos.pdf.

RAMOS-KITTRELL 2016
Jesús A. Ramos-Kittrell, *Playing in the Cathedral. Music, Race and Status in New Spain* (Oxford UK and New York NY: Oxford University Press, 2016).

RANDALL 1999
Catharine Randall, *Building Codes: the Aesthetics of Calvinism in Early Modern Europe, New Cultural Studies* (Philadelphia PA: University of Pennsylvania Press, 1999).

RASMUSSEN 1988
Niels Krogh Rasmussen OP, "Liturgy and Liturgical Arts", in John O'Malley (ed.), *Catholicism in Early Modern History: A Guide to Research* (St Louis MO: Center for Reformation Research, 1988), pp. 273–297.

RASMUSSEN 1995
Mary Rasmussen, "The Case of the Flutes in Holbein's *The Ambassadors*", *EM*, vol. 23, no. 1 (Feburary 1995), pp. 114–123.

RAYNOR 1972
Henry Raynor, *A Social History of Music* (New York NY: Schocken Books, 1972).

REARDON 2002
Colleen Reardon, *Holy Concord within Sacred Walls: Nuns and Music in Siena, 1575–1700* (Oxford UK and New York NY: Oxford University Press, 2002).

REARDON 2005
Colleen Reardon, "The Good Mother, the Reluctant Daughter, and the Convent: A Case of Musical Persuasion", in Thomasin LaMay (ed.), *Musical Voices of Early Modern Women. Many-Headed Melodies* (Aldershot: Ashgate, 2005), pp. 271–286.

REES 1991
Owen Rees, *Sixteenth- and Early Seventeenth-Century Polyphony from the Monastery of Santa Cruz, Coimbra, Portugal* (PhD Dissertation: Cambridge University, 1991).

REES 2002
Owen Rees, "'Recalling Cristóbal de Morales to Mind': Emulation in Guerrero's *Sacræ Cantiones* of 1555", in David Crawford and G. Grayson Wagstaff (eds.), *Encomium Musicæ: Essays in Memory of Robert J. Snow* (Hillsdale NY: Pendragon Press, 2002), pp. 365–394.

REES 2006
Owen Rees, "Risposte musicali alla Riforma e alla Controriforma", in Jean-Jacques Nattiez (ed.), *Enciclopedia della Musica*, vol. 1 (La musica europea dal gregoriano a Bach) (Turin: Giulio Einaudi editore; Milan: Il Sole 24 Ore, 2006), pp. 341–357.

REESE 1959
Gustave Reese, *Music in the Renaissance* (New York NY and London: W. W. Norton and Company, 1959).

REEVE AND SCREECH 1990
Anne Reeve and Michael Andrew Screech (eds.), *Erasmus' Annotations on the New Testament: Acts – Romans – I and II Corinthians*, facsimile edition of the final Latin text (Basel: Froben, 1535), with all earlier variants (Leiden and New York NY: Brill, 1990).

REID 1971
W. Stanford Reid, "The Battle Hymns of the Lord: Calvinist Psalmody of the Sixteenth Century", in Carl S. Meyer (ed.), *Sixteenth Century Essays and Studies* (St Louis MO: The Foundation for Reformation Research, 1971), vol. 2, pp. 36–54.

RESPIGHI 1900
Carlo Respighi, *Nuovo studio su Giovanni Pierluigi da Palestrina e l'emendazione del Graduale Romano* (Rome: Desclée, 1900), pp. 80–88.

REU 1918
Johann Michael Reu, *Catechetics, or Theory and Practice of Religious Instruction* (Chicago IL: Wartburg Publishing House, 1918); available online at http://bit.ly/2bl5ij9.

REYNOLDS 1989
Christopher Reynolds, "Rome: A City of Rich Contrast", in Iain Fenlon (ed.), *The Renaissance: From the 1570s to the End of the Sixteenth Century* (London: Macmillan, 1989), pp. 63–101.

RIEDEL 1967
Johannes Riedel, *The Lutheran Chorale: Its Basic Traditions* (Minneapolis MN: Augsburg Fortress, 1967).

RIOU 2000
Yves-François Riou, "Marie en Bretagne, III: l'exemple des 'Cantiquou spirituel' (Quimper 1642)", in Jean Longère (ed.), *La Vierge dans la catéchèse, hier et aujourd'hui* (Paris: Médiaspaul Éditions, 2000), pp. 107–126.

**ROBINSON 1842**
Hastings Robinson (ed.), *The Zurich Letters A. D. 1558–1579* (Cambridge: Cambridge University Press, 1842); available online at http://bit.ly/2bYyL7k.

**ROBINSON-HAMMERSTEIN 1989**
Helga Robinson-Hammerstein, *The Transmission of Ideas in the Lutheran Reformation* (Dublin: Irish Academic Press, 1989), pp. 141–171.

**ROBLEDO ESTAIRE 1984**
Luis Robledo Estaire, "La música en la corte madrileña de los Austrias", *Revista de musicología*, vol. 10, no. 3 (1984), pp. 753–796.

**RODIN 2012**
Jesse Rodin, *Josquin's Rome: Hearing and Composing in the Sistine Chapel* (Oxford UK and New York NY: Oxford University Press, 2012).

**ROMITA 1936 / ROMITA 1947**
Fiorenzo Romita, *Jus musicae liturgicae. Dissertatio historico-iuridica* (Turin: Marietti, 1936; Rome: Edizioni Liturgiche, 1947).

**ROPCHOCK 2015**
Alanna Victoria Ropchock, *The Body of Christ divided: Reception of Josquin's* Missa Pange Lingua in *Reformation Germany* (PhD Dissertation: Case Western Reserve University, 2015).

**RORKE 1984**
Margaret Ann Rorke, "Sacred Contrafacta of Monteverdi Madrigals and Cardinal Borromeo's Milan", *ML*, vol. 65, no. 2 (April 1984), pp. 168–175.

**ROSAND 1977**
Ellen Rosand, "Music in the Myth of Venice", *Renaissance Quarterly*, vol. 30, no. 4 (Winter 1977), pp. 511–537.

**ROSEN 1998**
Charles Rosen, *The Romantic Generation* (Cambridge MA: Harvard University Press, 1998).

**ROSTIROLLA 1977**
Giancarlo Rostirolla, "La Cappella Giulia in San Pietro negli anni del magistero di Giovanni Pierluigi da Palestrina", in Francesco Luisi (ed.), *Atti del Convegno di Studi Palestriniani, 28 settembre – 2 ottobre 1975* (Palestrina: Fondazione G. P. da Palestrina, 1977), pp. 174–181.

**ROSTIROLLA 1993**
Giancarlo Rostirolla, "La Bolla 'De Communi Omnium' di Gregorio XIII per la restaurazione della Cappella Giulia", in Oscar Mischiati and Paolo Russo (eds.), *La Cappella musicale nell'Italia della Controriforma* (Florence: Olschki, 1993), pp. 39–66.

**ROSTIROLLA 2001**
Giancarlo Rostirolla, "Laudi e canti religiosi per l'esercizio spirituale della Dottrina cristiana al tempo di Roberto Bellarmino", in Giancarlo Rostirolla, Denis Zardin and Oscar Mischiati, *La lauda spirituale tra Cinque e Seicento. Poesie e canti devozionali nell'Italia della Controriforma* (Rome: IBIMUS Istituto Bibliografico Musicale, 2001), pp. 275–472.

**ROTH 1998**
Adalbert Roth, "Liturgical (and Paraliturgical) Music in the Papal Chapel towards the End of the Fifteenth Century: A Repertory in Embryo", in Richard Sherr (ed.), *Papal Music and Musicians in Medieval and Renaissance Rome* (Oxford UK and New York NY: Oxford University Press, 1998), pp. 125–137.

ROWLAND-JONES 1998
Anthony Rowland-Jones, "The Minuet: Painter-Musicians in Triple Time", *EM*, vol. 26, no. 3 (August 1998), pp. 415–424, 427, 429, 431.

RUFF 2005
Anthony Ruff, "Metrical Psalmody of the Catholic Reformation", *GIA Quarterly*, vol. 16 (2005), pp. 16–19, 42–45.

RUINI 1994
Cesarino Ruini, "Liturgia e musica sacra nella cattedrale fino all'epoca del Concilio di Trento", in Rossana Dalmonte (ed.), *Musica e società nella storia trentina* (Trento: U. C. T., 1994), pp. 39–77.

RUINI 1995
Cesarino Ruini, "Antiphonaria, Gradualia et Psalteria quae at divinas laudes... Un ruolo per il manoscritto", in Danilo Curti and Marco Gozzi (eds.), *Musica e Liturgia nella Riforma Tridentina* (Trento: Provincia Autonoma di Trento – Servizio Beni Librari e Archivistici, 1995), pp. 31–38.

RUPP AND WATSON 1969 / RUPP AND WATSON 2006
Ernest Gordon Rupp and Philip Saville Watson (eds.), *Luther and Erasmus: Free Will and Salvation* (Louisville KY: Westminster John Knox, 1969; 2006).

RUPPRICH 1973
Hans Rupprich, *Geschichte der deutschen Literatur*, vol. IV/2 ("Vom späten Mittelalter bis zum Barock. Zweiter Teil. Das Zeitalter der Reformation 1520–1570") (Munich: C. H. Beck, 1973).

RUSSELL 1986 / RUSSELL 2002
Paul A. Russell, *Lay Theology in the Reformation. Popular Pamphleteers in Southwest Germany 1521–1525* (Cambridge: Cambridge University Press, 1986; paperback 2002).

RUSSELL 1996
Conrad Russell, "The Reformation and the Creation of the Church of England, 1500–1640", in John Morrill (ed.), *The Oxford Illustrated History of Tudor and Stuart Britain* (Oxford UK and New York NY: Oxford University Press, 1996), pp. 258–292.

RYDEN 1959
Ernest Edwin Ryden, *The Story of Christian Hymnody* (Rock Island IL: Augustana Press, 1959).

RYE 1865
William Brenchley Rye, *England as seen by Foreigners in the Days of Elizabeth and James the First [...]* (London: John Russell Smith, 1865); available online at http://bit.ly/2bPSNhv.

RYRIE 2006
Alec Ryrie, *The Origins of the Scottish Reformation* (Manchester: Manchester University Press, 2006).

RYRIE 2012
Alec Ryrie, "Sleeping, Waking and Dreaming in Protestant Piety", in Jessica Martin and Alec Ryrie (eds.), *Private and Domestic Devotion in Early Modern Britain* (Aldershot: Ashgate, 2012), pp. 73–92.

SALISBURY 1996
Joyce E. Salisbury, "Gendered Sexuality", in Vern L. Bullough and James A. Brundage (eds.), *Handbook of Medieval Sexuality* (New York NY and London: Garland, 1996), pp. 81–102.

**SALMEN 2001**
Walter Salmen, "Dances and Dance Music, c. 1300 – c. 1530", in Reinhard Strohm and Bonnie J. Blackburn (eds.), *Music as Concept and Practice in the Late Middle Ages* (Oxford UK and New York NY: Oxford University Press, 2001), pp. 162–190.

**SARTORI 1952**
Claudio Sartori, "Monteverdiana", *MQ*, vol. 38, no. 3 (July 1952), pp. 399–413.

**SCHAEFER 1994**
Edward Schaefer, "A Reexamination of Palestrina's Role in the Catholic Reformation", *Choral Journal*, vol. 35, no. 1 (1994), pp. 19–25.

**SCHALK 1988**
Carl F. Schalk, *Luther on Music, Paradigms of Praise* (St Louis MO: Concordia Publishing House, 1988).

**SCHEITLER 2010**
Irmgard Scheitler, "Lied und katholische Katechese im 16. und 17. Jahrhundert", *JLH*, no. 49 (2010), pp. 163–185.

**SCHENKEVELD-VAN DER DUSSEN 2010**
Riet Schenkeveld-van der Dussen, "Women's Writing from the Low Countries 1575–1875", in Lia van Gemert et al. (eds.), *Women's Writing from the Low Countries 1200–1875. A Bilingual Anthology* (Amsterdam: Amsterdam University Press, 2010), pp. 39–63; "A Blind Guide: Soetken Gerijts", *ibid.*, pp. 206–216; "A Model of Godly Reformed Womanhood: Cornelia Teellinck", *ibid.*, pp. 217–221.

**SCHERF 1998**
Gregor Scherf, *Giovanni Battista Aleotti (1546–1636). "Architetto mathematico" der Este und der Päpste in Ferrara* (Marburg: Tectum Verlag, 1998).

**SCHMIDT 1993**
Lothar Schmidt, "Le cappelle di corte nei paesi tedeschi nell'età della Controriforma. Aspetti dello stato di ricerca", in Oscar Mischiati and Paolo Russo (eds.), *La Cappella musicale nell'Italia della Controriforma* (Florence: Olschki, 1993), pp. 239–250.

**SCHNEIDER-BÖKLEN 1994**
Elisabeth Schneider-Böklen, "Elisabeth Cruciger: die erste Dichterin des Protestantismus", *Gottesdienst und Kirchenmusik*, vol. 2 (March/April 1994), pp. 32–40.

**SCHOUSBOE 1974 / SCHOUSBOE 1975**
Torben Schousboe, "Protestant Church Music in Scandinavia", in Friedrich Blume (ed.), *Protestant Church Music. A History* (New York NY and London: W. W. Norton and Company, 1974; London: Victor Gollancz, 1975), pp. 609–636.

**SCHREIBER 1951**
Georg Schreiber, "Der Barock und das Tridentinum. Geistesgeschichtliche und kultische Zusammenhängen", in Georg Schreiber (ed.), *Das Weltkonzil von Trient. Sein Werden und Wirken*, 2 vols. (Freiburg im Breisgau: Herder, 1951).

**SCHREICH-STUPPAN 2009**
Hans-Peter Schreich-Stuppan, "'Esaltar la sua gloria... per coniungersi alla compagnia degli angeli'. Die italienischen Genfer Psalter in der Geschichte des evangelischen Kirchengesangs", *JLH*, no. 48 (2009), pp. 145–178.

**SCHUETTE 1982**
Evelyn C. Schuette, "The Reformation and Musical Influences on Martin Luther's Early Protestant Hymnody", *Reformed Liturgy and Music*, no. 16 (Summer 1982), pp. 99–106.

SCOTT 2006
Tom Scott, "The Economy", in Euan Cameron (ed.), *The Sixteenth Century* (Oxford UK and New York NY: Oxford University Press, 2006), pp. 18–57.

SCRIBNER 1981 / SCRIBNER 1994
Robert W. Scribner, *For the Sake of Simple Folk: Popular Propaganda for the German Reformation* (Oxford UK and New York NY: Oxford University Press, 1981; Oxford: Clarendon Press, 1994).

SCRIBNER 1987
Robert W. Scribner, *Popular Culture and Popular Movements in Reformation Germany* (London: The Hambledon Press, 1987).

SEHLING 1902 / SEHLING 1955
Emil Sehling, *Die evangelischen Kirchenordnungen des 16. Jahrhunderts* (Leipzig: Riesland, 1902–1913); vol. 1 available online at http://bit.ly/2bPV38w; (Tübingen: Mohr, 1955).

SETTARI 1994
Olga Settari, "The Czech Sacred Song from the Period of the Reformation", *Studia Minora Facultatis Philosophicae Universitatis Brunensis*, no. 29 (1994), pp. 5–11.

SFREDDA 2010
Nicola Sfredda, *La musica nelle chiese della Riforma* (Turin: Claudiana, 2010).

SHAW 1974 / SHAW 1975
Watkins Shaw, "Church Music in England from the Reformation to the Present Day", in Friedrich Blume (ed.), *Protestant Church Music. A History* (New York NY and London: W. W. Norton and Company, 1974; London: Victor Gollancz, 1975), pp. 691–732.

SHERR 1978
Richard Sherr, "From the Diary of a Sixteenth-Century Papal Singer", *Current Musicology*, no. 25 (1978), pp. 84–98.

SHERR 1984
Richard Sherr, "A Letter from Paolo Animuccia: A Composer's Response to the Council of Trent", *EM*, vol. 12, no. 1 (February 1984), pp. 74–78.

SHERR 1992
Richard Sherr, "The 'Spanish Nation' in the Papal Chapel, 1492–1521", *EM*, vol. 20, no. 4 (1992), pp. 601–609.

SHERR 1994
Richard Sherr, "Competence and Incompetence in the Papal Choir in the Age of Palestrina", *EM*, vol. 12, no. 4 (1994), pp. 606–630.

SHERR 1997
Richard Sherr, "Ceremonies for Holy Week, Papal Commissions, and Madness (?) in Early Sixteenth-Century Rome", in Jessie Anne Owens and Anthony M. Cummings (eds.), *Music in Renaissance Cities and Courts: Studies in Honor of Lewis Lockwood* (Michigan MI: Harmonie Park Press, 1997), pp. 391–403.

SHERR 1998
Richard Sherr (ed.), *Papal Music and Musicians in Medieval and Renaissance Rome* (Oxford UK and New York NY: Oxford University Press, 1998).

SIEGELE 1962 / SIEGELE 1989
Ulrich Siegele, "Osiander, Lucas", in *MGG* vol. 10 (1962; 1989), cols. 428–429.

SLIM 1980
H. Colin Slim, "Mary Magdalene, Musician and Dancer", *EM*, vol. 8, no. 4 (October 1980), pp. 460–473.

SLIM 1992
H. Colin Slim, "Music and Dancing with Mary Magdalen in a Laura Vestalis", in Craig A. Monson (ed.), *The Crannied Wall: Women, Religion, and the Arts in Early Modern Europe* (Ann Arbor MI: University of Michigan Press, 1992), pp. 109–160.

SMIALEK 1989
William Smialek, *Polish Music: A Research and Information Guide* (New York NY and London: Garland, 1989).

SMITHER 1969
Howard E. Smither, "Narrative and Dramatic Elements in the Laude Filippine, 1563–1600", *Acta Musicologica*, vol. 41, nos. 3/4 (July/Dec. 1969), pp. 186–199.

SNYDER 2010
Timothy Snyder, *Bloodlands: Europe Between Hitler and Stalin* (New York NY: Basic Books, 2010).

SNYDER AND HUEBERT-HECHT 1996
C. Arnold Snyder and Linda Agnes Huebert-Hecht, *Profiles of Anabaptist Women: Sixteenth-Century Reforming Pioneers* (Waterloo: Canadian Corporation for Studies in Religion, 1996).

SOERGEL 1993
Philip M. Soergel, *Wondrous in His Saints: Counter-Reformation Propaganda in Bavaria* (Berkeley and Los Angeles CA: University of California Press, 1993).

SOLFAROLI CAMILLOCCI 2005
Daniela Solfaroli Camillocci, "Ginevra, la Riforma e suor Jeanne de Jussie. La petite chronique di una clarissa intorno alla metà del Cinquecento", in Gianna Pomata and Gabriella Zarri (eds.), *I Monasteri femminili come centri di cultura fra Rinascimento e Barocco* (Rome: Edizioni di Storia e Letteratura, 2005), pp. 275–296.

SOOY 2006
Mark S. Sooy, *Essays on Martin Luther's Theology of Music* (Greater Grand Rapids MI: Blue Maroon, 2006).

SPELMAN 1948
Leslie P. Spelman, "Calvin and the Arts", *The Journal of Aesthetics and Art Criticism*, vol. 6, no. 3 (March 1948), pp. 246–252.

SPITZER 1963
Leo Spitzer, *Classical and Christian Ideas of World Harmony* (Baltimore MD: The Johns Hopkins University Press, 1963).

STÄHELIN 1927 / STÄHELIN 1934
Ernst Stähelin, *Briefe und Akten zum Leben Oecolampads: zum 400jährigen Jubiläum der Basler Reformation*, 2 vols. (Quellen und Forschungen zur Reformationsgeschichte, vols. 10 and 19) (Leipzig: Heisius Nachfolger, 1927 and 1934).

STARR 2010
Pamela F. Starr, "Music Education and the Conduct of Life in Early Modern England: A Review of the Sources", in Russell E. Murray jr, Susan Forscher Weiss, Cynthia J. Cyrus (eds.), *Music Education in the Middle Ages and the Renaissance* (Bloomington IN: Indiana University Press, 2010), pp. 193–206.

STEFANI 1966
Gino Stefani, "Palestrina. La poetica del 'bene ornateque loqui'", *Musica Sacra*, vol. 90, no. 4–5 (1966), pp. 108–114.

**STEIDL 1918**
Peter D. Steidl, *Vor Frues Sange fra Danmarks Middelalder* (Copenhagen: København Katholsk Forlag, 1918); available online at http://bit.ly/2bQ0VPh.

**STERNFELD 1948**
Frederick W. Sternfeld, "Music in the Schools of the Reformation", *Musica Disciplina*, vol. 2, nos. 3–4 (1948), pp. 99–122.

**STEVENS 1961 / STEVENS 1979**
John E. Stevens, *Music and Poetry in the Early Tudor Court* (London: Methuen and Co., 1961; Cambridge: Cambridge University Press, 1979).

**STEVENSON 1961**
Robert Murrell Stevenson, *Spanish Cathedral Music in the Golden Age* (Berkeley CA: University of Califonia Press; Cambridge: Cambridge University Press, 1961).

**STEVENSON 1964**
Robert Murrell Stevenson, *Spanish Music in the Age of Columbus* (The Hague: Nijhoff, 1964).

**STEVENSON 1966**
Robert Murrell Stevenson, *Protestant Church Music in America* (New York NY and London: W. W. Norton and Company, 1966).

**STEVENSON 1973**
Robert Murrell Stevenson, *Music in Aztec and Inca Territory* (Berkeley and Los Angeles CA: University of California Press, 1973).

**STEVENSON 1974 / STEVENSON 1975**
Robert Murrell Stevenson, "Protestant Music in America", in Friedrich Blume (ed.), *Protestant Church Music. A History* (New York NY and London: W. W. Norton and Company, 1974; London, Victor Gollancz, 1975), pp. 637–690.

**STEVENSON 2002**
Jane Stevenson, "Conventual Life in Renaissance Italy: The Latin Poetry of Suor Laurentia Strozzi (1514–1591)", in Laurie J. Churchill, Phyllis R. Brown and Jane E. Jeffrey (eds.), *Women Writing Latin: from Roman Antiquity to Early Modern Europe* (Abingdon UK and New York NY: Routledge, 2002), pp. 109–132.

**STINGER 1998**
Charles L. Stinger, *The Renaissance in Rome* (Bloomington IN: Indiana University Press, 1998).

**STJERNA 2009**
Kirsi Stjerna, *Women and the Reformation* (Oxford: Blackwell Publishing, 2009).

**STRAUSS 1978**
Gerald Strauss, *Luther's House of Learning: Indoctrination of the Young in the Lutheran Reformation* (Baltimore MD: Johns Hopkins University Press, 1978).

**STRAUSS 1988**
Gerald Strauss, "The Reformation and Its Public in an Age of Orthodoxy", in Ronnie Po-Chia Hsia (ed.), *The German People and the Reformation* (Ithaca: Cornell University Press, 1988), pp. 192–214.

**STROHM 1993**
Reinhard Strohm, *The Rise of European Music, 1380–1500* (Cambridge: Cambridge University Press, 1993).

**STRUNK 1950 / STRUNK 1998**
Oliver Strunk (ed.), *Source Readings in Music History from Classical Antiquity through the Romantic Era*, revised edition by Leo Treitler (New York NY and London: W. W. Norton and Company, 1950; 1998).
**SYDNOR 1992**
James Rawlings Sydnor, "Hymnody: Sung Prayer", *Reformed Liturgy and Music* (Fall 1992), pp. 184–188.
**TANG 2016**
Kaijan Tang, *Setting off from Macau: Essays on Jesuit History during the Ming and Qing dynasties* (Leiden and New York NY: Brill, 2016).
**TARBÉ 1866**
Prosper Tarbé, *Recueil de poesies calvinistes [1550–1566]* (Reims: [s.n.], 1866).
**TARGOFF 2001**
Ramie Targoff, *Common Prayer: The Language of Public Devotion in Early Modern England* (Chicago IL: The University of Chicago Press, 2001).
**TARRY 1973**
Joe E. Tarry, "Music in the Educational Philosophy of Martin Luther", *Journal of Research in Music Education*, no. 21 (1973), pp. 355–365.
**TARUSKIN 2010**
Richard Taruskin, *Music from the Earliest Notations to the Sixteenth Century*, vol. I of Richard Taruskin, *The Oxford History of Western Music* (Oxford UK and New York NY: Oxford University Press, 2010).
**TEMPERLEY 1979**
Nicholas Temperley, *The Music of the English Parish Church*, 2 vols. (Cambridge: Cambridge University Press, 1979).
**THOMAS 2001**
Jennifer Thomas, "The Core Motet Repertory of 16th Century Europe: A View of Renaissance Musical Culture", in Barbara Haggh (ed.), *Essays on Music and Culture in Honor of Herbert Kellman* (Paris and Tours: Minerve, 2001), pp. 335–376.
**THOMPSON 1984**
Glenda Goss Thompson, "Mary of Hungary and Music Patronage", *SCJ*, no. 15 (1984), pp. 410–418.
**TODD 1995**
Margo Todd (ed.), *Reformation to Revolution: Politics and Religion in Early Modern England* (Abingdon UK and New York NY: Routledge, 1995).
**TOMLINSON 1998**
Gary Tomlinson, "The Renaissance. Introduction", in Oliver Strunk (ed.), *Source Readings in Music History from Classical Antiquity through the Romantic Era*, revised edition by Leo Treitler (New York NY and London: W. W. Norton and Company, 1998), pp. 281–289.
**TOMLINSON 2006**
Gary Tomlinson, "Renaissance Humanism and Music", in James Haar (ed.), *European Music 1520–1642* (Woodbridge: The Boydell Press, 2006), pp. 1–19.
**TROCMÉ LATTER 2015**
Daniel Trocmé Latter, *The Singing of the Strasbourg Protestants, 1524–1541* (Aldershot: Ashgate, 2015).

TUDOR-CRAIG 1989
Pamela Tudor-Craig, "Henry VIII and King David", in Daniel Williams (ed.), *Early Tudor England: Proceedings of the 1987 Harlaxton Symposium* (Woodbridge: The Boydell Press, 1989), pp. 351–369.

ULTAN 1977
Lloyd Ultan, *Music Theory: Problems and Practices in the Middle Ages and Renaissance* (Minneapolis MN: University of Minnesota Press, 1977).

URSPRUNG 1913
Otto Ursprung, *Jacobus de Kerle (1531/32–1591). Sein Leben und seine Werke* (Munich: H. Beck, 1913).

URSPRUNG 1926
Otto Ursprung (ed.), *Die "Preces Speciales" etc. für das Konzil von Trient, 1562 komponiert von Jacobus de Kerle* (Augsburg: B. Filser, 1926).

VAN AELST 2010
José van Aelst, "An Urban Anchoress: Berta Jacobs", in Lia van Gemert et al. (eds.), *Women's Writing from the Low Countries 1200–1875. A Bilingual Anthology* (Amsterdam: Amsterdam University Press, 2010), pp. 98–111.

VAN DER HEYDEN 1921
L. J. van der Heyden (ed.), "Het kerspel Groessen en zijn 'kerkenboeck'", *Archief voor de geschiedenis van het Aartsbisdom Utrecht*, no. 46 (1921), pp. 1–107.

VAN DER POEL 2010
Dieuwke van der Poel, "'Just Like a Rose in Bloom': Women and Religious Song", in Lia van Gemert et al. (eds.), *Women's Writing from the Low Countries 1200–1875. A Bilingual Anthology* (Amsterdam: Amsterdam University Press, 2010), pp. 144–159.

VAN DER POEL AND JOLDERSMA 2010
Dieuwke van der Poel and Hermina Joldersma, "Women's Writing from the Low Countries 1200–1575", in Lia van Gemert et al. (eds.), *Women's Writing from the Low Countries 1200–1875. A Bilingual Anthology* (Amsterdam: Amsterdam University Press, 2010), pp. 21–38.

VAN ELSLANDER 1975
Antonin van Elslander, "Les Chambres de rhétorique et les fêtes du règne de Charles Quint", in Jean Jacquot (ed.), *Fêtes et cérémonies au temps de Charles Quint*, vol. 2 (Paris: Éditions du CNRS, 1975), pp. 281–285.

VAN GEMERT 2010
Lia van Gemert et al. (eds.), *Women's Writing from the Low Countries 1200–1875. A Bilingual Anthology* (Amsterdam: Amsterdam University Press, 2010).

VAN ORDEN 1999
Kate van Orden, "The Reign of Music", in Francis Maes (ed.), *The Empire Resounds: Music in the Days of Charles V* (Leuven: Leuven University Press, 1999), pp. 65–81.

VAN ORDEN 2000
Kate van Orden, "Cheap Print and Street Song following the Saint Bartholomew's Massacres of 1572", in Kate van Orden (ed.), *Music and the Cultures of Print* (New York NY and London: Garland, 2000), pp. 271–324.

VAN ORDEN 2005
Kate van Orden, *Music, Discipline, and Arms in Early Modern France* (Chicago IL: The University of Chicago Press, 2005).

**VAN ORDEN 2006**
Kate van Orden, "Chanson and Air", in James Haar (ed.), *European Music 1520–1642* (Woodbridge: The Boydell Press, 2006), pp. 193–224.

**VAN ORDEN 2015**
Kate van Orden, *Materialities. Books, Readers, and the Chanson in Sixteenth-Century Europe* (Oxford UK and New York NY: Oxford University Press, 2015).

**VAN RENSBURG AND SPIES 2011**
Henriette van Rensburg and Bertha M. Spies, "Musikale ontlening en die voortbestaan van melodiese spore uit die verlede", *TD Die Joernaal vir Transdissiplinêre Navorsing in Suider-Afrika*, no. 7 (July 2011), pp. 1–24; available online at http://bit.ly/2blRvhf.

**VANDERWILT 1995**
Jeffrey T. Vanderwilt, "John Calvin's Theology of Liturgical Song", *Christian Scholar's Review*, vol. 25, no. 1 (1995), pp. 63–82.

**VANHULST 1999**
Henri Vanhulst, "The Musical World of Charles V", in Hugo Soly (ed.), *Charles V, 1500–1558, and his Time* (Antwerp: Mercatorfonds, 1999), pp. 501–511.

**VANHULST 2008**
Henri Vanhulst, "La musique et l'éducation des jeunes filles d'après *La Montaigne des pucelles / Den Maeghden-Bergh* de Magdaleine Valéry (Leyde, 1599)", in Mark Delaere and Pieter Bergé (eds.), *"Recevez ce mien petit labour". Studies in Renaissance Music in Honour of Ignace Bossuyt* (Leuven: Leuven University Press, 2008), pp. 269–278.

**VANTI 1936**
Mario Vanti, *Un umanista del Cinquecento: Mons. Bernardino Cirillo, Commendatore e Maestro Generale dell'Ordine di S. Spirito in Roma (1554–1575)* (Rome: Università Gregoriana, 1936).

**VECCHI 1965**
Giuseppe Vecchi, *Il Concilio di Trento, S. Carlo e la musica* (Bologna: Tipografia compositori, 1965).

**VEIT 1986**
Patrice Veit, *Das Kirchenlied in der Reformation Martin Luters: eine thematische und semantische Untersuchung* (Stuttgart: Steiner, 1986).

**VERSTEGEN 2007**
Ian Verstegen, "Reform and Renewed Ambition: Cardinal Giulio Feltrio della Rovere", in Ian Verstegen (ed.), *Patronage and Dynasty. The Rise of the Della Rovere in Renaissance Italy* (Kirksville MO: Truman State University Press, 2007), pp. 89–110.

**VILADESAU 2000**
Richard Viladesau, *Theology and the Arts. Encountering God through Music, Art and Rhetoric* (Mahwah NJ: Paulist Press, 2000).

**VOGEL 1887**
Emil Vogel, "Claudio Monteverdi", in Friedrich Chrysander, Philipp Spitta and Guido Adler (eds.), *Vierteljahrsschrift für Musikwissenschaft* III (Leipzig: Breitkopf & Härtel, 1887), pp. 315–450.

**WAGNER OETTINGER 2001**
Rebecca Wagner Oettinger, *Music as Propaganda in the German Reformation* (Aldershot: Ashgate, 2001).

**WAGSTAFF 2007**
G. Grayson Wagstaff, "Morales, Spanish Traditions, Liturgical Works, and the Problem of Style", in Owen Rees and Bernadette Nelson (eds.), *Cristóbal de Morales: Sources, Influences, Reception* (Woodbridge: The Boydell Press, 2007), pp. 63–83.

**WALKER 1941 / WALKER 1942**
Daniel. P. Walker, "Musical Humanism in the 16th and Early 17th Centuries", *The Music Review*, vol. 2 (1941), pp. 1–13, 111–121, 220–227, 288–308; vol. 3 (1942), pp. 55–71.

**WANGERMÉE 1968**
Robert Wangermée, *Flemish Music and Society in the Fifteenth and Sixteenth Centuries* (New York NY: Praeger, 1968).

**WARNER 1984**
Thomas E. Warner, "European Musical Activities in North America before 1620", *MQ*, vol. 70, no. 1 (Winter 1984), pp. 77–95.

**WATT 1991**
Tessa Watt, *Cheap Print and Popular Piety 1550–1640* (Cambridge: Cambridge University Press, 1991).

**WB**
Philipp Wackernagel, *Bibliographie zur Geschichte des deutsches Kirchenliedes im XVI. Jahrhundert* (Frankfurt am Main: Heyder & Zimmer, 1855); available online at http://bit.ly/2bbnOkm; (Hildesheim: Georg Olms Verlag, 1987).

**WEBB 1967**
Douglas Webb, "Les hymnes dans l'Eglise d'Angleterre", *La Maison-Dieu*, no. 92 (1967), pp. 136–144.

**WEBER 1979**
Edith Weber, *La musique protestante de langue française* (Paris: Honoré Champion, 1979).

**WEBER 1980**
Edith Weber, *La musique protestante en langue allemande* (Paris: Honoré Champion, 1980).

**WEBER 1982 / WEBER 2008**
Edith Weber, *Le Concile de Trente et la musique: De la Réforme à la Contre-Réforme* (Paris: Honoré Champion, 1982; 2008²).

**WEBER 1989**
Edith Weber, "Le style 'Nota contra notam' et ses incidences sur le Choral Luthérien et sur le Psautier Huguenot", *JLH*, no. 32 (1989), pp. 73–93.

**WEGMAN 2003**
Rob C. Wegman, "Johannes Tinctoris and the 'New Art'", *ML*, no. 84 (2003), pp. 171–188.

**WEGMAN 2005**
Rob C. Wegman, *The Crisis of Music in Early Modern Europe* (Abingdon UK and New York NY: Routledge, 2005).

**WEINMANN 1917**
Karl Weinmann, "Zur Geschichte von Palestrinas Missa Papae Marcelli", *Jahrbuch der Musikbibliothek Peters*, vol. 23 (1917), pp. 23–42.

**WEINMANN 1919 / WEINMANN 1974**
Karl Weinmann, *Das Konzil von Trient und die Kirchenmusik. Eine historisch-kritische Untersuchung* (Leipzig: Breitkopf & Härtel, 1919; Hildesheim: Georg Olms Verlag, 1974).

**WEINMANN 1920**
Karl Weinmann, "Die päpstliche Kapelle unter Paul IV", *Vierteljahrsschrift für Musikwissenschaft* (1919–1920), pp. 54–72.

**WEISS AND TARUSKIN 1984 / WEISS AND TARUSKIN 2008**
Piero Weiss and Richard Taruskin (eds.), *Music in the Western World* (Belmont CA: Thomson, 1984; 2008).

**WENDLAND 1976**
John Wendland, "'Madre non mi far monaca': The Biography of a Renaissance Folksong", *Acta Musicologica*, vol. 48, no. 2 (July/December 1976), pp. 185–204.

**WENGERT 1989**
Timothy Wengert, "Caspar Cruciger, 1504–1548: The Case of the Disappearing Reformer", *SCJ*, no. 20 (1989), pp. 417–441.

**WESSLER 2011**
Jonathan Mehrings Wessler, *An Examination of the Relationship between Johann Spangenberg's* Cantiones Ecclesiasticae/Kirchengesenge Deudsch *and Martin Luther's* Formula Missæ et Communionis *and* Deutsche Messe (DMA Thesis: University of Rochester 2011); available online at http://bit.ly/2b0f6PX.

**WETZEL AND HEITMEYER 2013**
Richard Wetzel and Erika Heitmeyer, *Johan Leisentrit's* Geistliche Lieder und Psalmen, 1567. *Hymnody of the Counter-Reformation in Germany* (Plymouth: Rownam and Littlefield, 2013).

**WHALE 1936**
John Seldon Whale, "Calvin", in Nathaniel Micklem (ed.), *Christian Worship: Studies in its History and Meaning* (London: Oxford University Press, 1936), pp. 154–171.

**WHITE 2005**
Micheline White, "Protestant Women's Writing and Congregational Psalm Singing: from the Song of the Exiled 'Handmaid' (1555) to the Countess of Pembroke's *Psalmes* (1599)", *Sidney Journal*, no. 23 (2005), pp. 61–82.

**WHITE 2011**
Micheline White, "Women's Hymns in Mid-Sixteenth-Century England: Elisabeth Cruciger, Miles Coverdale, and Lady Elizabeth Tyrwhit", *ANQ: A Quarterly Journal of Short Articles, Notes and Reviews*, vol. 24, nos. 1–2 (2011), pp. 21–32.

**WIESNER 1988**
Merry Wiesner, "Women's Response to the Reformation", in Ronnie Po-Chia Hsia (ed.), *The German People and the Reformation* (Ithaca NY: Cornell University Press, 1988), pp. 148–172.

**WILLIS 1975**
Arthur J. Willis (ed.), *Church Life in Kent: Being Church Court Records of the Canterbury Diocese, 1559–1565* (London: Phillimore, 1975).

**WILLIS 2009**
Jonathan Willis, "'By these Means the Sacred Discourses Sink More Deeply into the Minds of Men': Music and Education in Elizabethan England", *History*, vol. 94, no. 3 (2009), pp. 294–309.

**WILLIS 2010**
Jonathan Willis, *Church Music and Protestantism in Post-Reformation England. Discourses, Sites and Identities* (Aldershot: Ashgate, 2010).

**WILLIS 2013**
Jonathan Willis, "Protestant Worship and the Discourse of Music in Reformation England", in Natalie Mears and Alec Ryrie (eds.), *Worship and the Parish Church in Early Modern Britain* (Aldershot: Ashgate 2013), pp. 131–150.

**WISTREICH 2007**
Richard Wistreich, *Warrior, Courtier, Singer. Giulio Cesare Brancaccio and the Performance of Identity in the Late Renaissance* (Aldershot: Ashgate, 2007).
**WITTWER 1934**
Max Wittwer, *Die Musikpflege im Jesuitenorden unter besonderer Berücksichtigung der Länder deutscher Zunge* (Doctoral Thesis: Greifswald, 1934).
**WITVLIET 1997**
John D. Witvliet, "The Spirituality of the Psalter: Metrical Psalms in Liturgy and Life in Calvin's Geneva", *Calvin Theological Journal*, no. 32 (November 1997), pp. 280–282.
**WITVLIET 2003**
John D. Witvliet, *Worship Seeking Understanding: Windows into Christian Practice* (Grand Rapids MI: Baker Academic Press, 2003).
**WRIGHT 1993**
J. Robert Wright, *They Still Speak. Readings for the Lesser Feasts* (New York NY: Church Hymnal Corporation, 1993).
**WRIGHTSON 1989**
James Wrightson, *The "Wanley" Manuscripts: A Critical Commentary* (New York NY and London: Garland, 1989).
**WRIGHTSON 1995**
James Wrightson, *The Wanley Manuscripts* (Madison WI: A-R Editions, 1995).
**WURSTEN 2008**
Dick Wursten, "Did Clément Marot really offer his *Trente Pseaulmes* to the Emperor Charles V in January 1540?", *Renaissance Studies*, vol. 22, no. 2 (April 2008), pp. 240–250.
**WÜRZBACH 1981 / WÜRZBACH 1990**
Natasha Würzbach, *Anfänge und gattungstypische Ausformung der englischen Straßenballade* (Munich: Fink, 1981); English translation by Gayna Walls as *The Rise of the English Street Ballad, 1550–1650* (Cambridge: Cambridge University Press, 1990).
**ZAGER 1999**
Daniel Zager, "Post-Tridentine liturgical change and functional music: Lasso's cycle of polyphonic Latin hymns", in Peter Bergquist (ed.), *Orlando di Lasso Studies* (Cambridge: Cambridge University Press, 1999), pp. 41–63.
**ZANOVELLO 2009**
Giovanni Zanovello, "'In oratorio nemo aliquid agat': Savonarola, lo spazio sacro e la musica", in Mary Jennifer Bloxam, Gioia Filocamo and Leofranc Holford-Strevens (eds.), *Uno gentile et subtile ingenio. Studies in Renaissance Music in Honour of Bonnie J. Blackburn* (Turnhout: Brepols 2009), pp. 129–136.
**ZIEGLER 1995**
Walter Ziegler, "Typen des Konfessionalisierung in katholischen Territorien Deutschland", in Wolfgang Reinhard and Heinz Schilling (eds.) *Die katholische Konfessionalisierung: Wissenschaftliches Symposion der Gesellschaft zur Herausgabe des Corpus Catholicorum und des Vereins für Reformationsgeschichte 1993* (Gütersloh: Gütersloher Verlagshaus, 1995), pp. 405–418.
**ZIM 2011**
Rivkah Zim, *English Metrical Psalms. Poetry as Praise and Prayer, 1535–1601* (Cambridge: Cambridge University Press, 2011).

ZINCKGRAF 1948
June Barbara Zinckgraf, *The Music of the French Reformation in the 16<sup>th</sup> Century* (M. S. M. Thesis: Union Theological Seminary, April 1948).

ZUFFI 2011
Stefano Zuffi, *Le parole dell'arte* (Milan: Giangiacomo Feltrinelli, 2011).

ZUR MÜHLEN 2002
Karl-Heinz zur Mühlen, "On the Critical Reception of the Thought of Thomas Aquinas in the Theology of Martin Luther", in Paul van Geest, Harm Goris and Carlo Leget (eds.), *Aquinas as Authority* (Leuven: Peeters 2002), pp. 65–86.

# Index of Names

Within the book's main text, the most common spelling, version or variant of the cited names has been adopted (e.g. Henry IV, John Calvin, Palestrina, Caravaggio). In the following Index of Names, name variants are listed in italics, with references to the privileged spelling; this spelling is listed in bold type and is provided with birth and death dates.

This Index includes only historical and religious figures, and not living people or scholars cited in the text. Married women are listed first with their maiden name, and then with their husband's family name. People who are commonly known with their Graecised, Latinised or Anglicised name(s) are listed under their original name, when this could be identified. Commonly-Anglicised names of rulers are listed under the original language, but the Anglicised version follows immediately: e.g. Friedrich (Frederick). Family names including (but not limited to) particles such as "de", "von", "van" are listed, respectively, under "D", "V" and "V". Friars, monks and nuns who adopted a religious given name instead of their Christian name are listed under the name given at Baptism, but the religious name is listed as a variant of the given name: e.g. Tommaso (Paolo) Giustiniani; this does not apply when the religious name includes a dedicatory appendix (such as Thomas à Jesu), in which case the religious name is listed separately. Popes are listed under their family- and Christian name, and their pontifical name is listed separately. Minimal spelling variants, which were very common in the sixteenth century, have been omitted.

*A Burck, Joachim (see Moller, Joachim).*
*A Burgk, Joachim (see Moller, Joachim).*
*À Kempis (see Haemerkken, Thomas).*
*À Lasco, Johannes (see Łaski, Jan).*
**Aaron (Aron),** Pietro (c.1480-a.1545):   144
*Adamson, Elizabeth (see Adamsoun, Elizabeth).*
**Adamsoun (Adamson),** Elizabeth (?-1555):   584
*Adrian VI (see Florensz, Adriaan).*
**Aerontsdochter,** Hillegont (?-?):   674
**Agazzari,** Agostino (1578-1640):   422
**Agresti,** Livio ("Ritius", "Ricciutello") (1505-1579):   423
*Agricola, Martin (see Sore, Martin).*
**Agrippa von Nettesheim,** Heinrich Cornelius (1486-1535):   11 f., 122, 129, 135 f., 143, 394, 453
*Alba (see Álvarez de Toledo y Pimentel, Fernando).*
**Alber (Alberus),** Erasmus (c.1500-1553):   174, 186, 200, 287, 538
*Albert of Austria (see von Habsburg, Albrecht VII).*
*Albert of Brandenburg (see von Brandenburg, Albrecht).*
*Albert of Mainz (see von Brandenburg, Albrecht).*
*Albert V (see von Wittelsbach, Albrecht V).*
*Alberti, Gasparo (see de Albertis, Gasparo).*
*Alberus, Erasmus (see Alber, Erasmus).*
**Aldobrandini,** Ippolito (Clement VIII) (Pope) (1536-1605):   47, 445, 448, 669
**Aleotti,** Beatrice (b.1575-?):   667
**Aleotti,** Giambattista "L'Argenta" (1546-1636):   667 f.
**Aleotti,** Raffaella (Vittoria?) (c.1570-a.1646):   667 f., 672
**Aleotti,** Valeria (?-1625):   667
**Aleotti,** Vittoria (Raffaella?) (1575-a.1620):   667
**Alighieri,** Dante (c.1265-1321):   92, 545
**Alison (Allison),** Richard (c.1560-b.1610):   361, 369 f.
**Allegri,** Antonio "Correggio" (1489-1534):   457
*Allison, Richard (see Alison, Richard).*
*Almeutes (see Saunier, Antoine).*

*Alva (see Álvarez de Toledo y Pimentel, Fernando).*
**Álvarez de Toledo y Pimentel (Alva, Alba),** Fernando (Duke) (1507-1582): 44, 523
*Ambrose (see Ambrosius).*
**Ambrosius (Ambrose)** *of Milan* (St) (c.339-397): 71, 169, 261, 288, 500, 690
**Amerbach,** Bonifacius (1495-1562): 542
*Ammannati, Laura (see Battiferri Ammannati, Laura).*
**Ancina,** Giovanni Giovenale (Blessed) (1545-1604): 493
**Andreae,** Jakob (1528-1590): 173, 193, 200, 228
**Anerio,** Felice (1560-1614): 451
**Angela** *of Foligno* (Blessed) (1248-1309): 90
**Angus,** John (?-c.1595): viii, 362
**Anicius,** Gregorius (Gregory I) (Pope)/(St) (c.540-604): 145, 695
**Animuccia,** Giovanni (c.1520-1571): 449, 458, 461, 463f., 471, 493f., 504, 601
**Animuccia,** Paolo (?-c.1563): 449
**Anna** *of Cologne* (?-?): 674
**Antegnati,** Graziadio (1525-1590): 511
*Antesignanus (see Davantès, Pierre).*
**Anthony** (St) (?-1597): 489
**Antico,** Andrea *da Montona* (c.1480-1538): 11
*Aquinas (see d'Aquino, Tommaso).*
**Arascione,** Giovanni (1546-a.1589): 493
**Arcadelt,** Jacob (c.1507-1568): viii, 22, 160, 321, 396, 424, 581
**Aretino,** Pietro (1492-1556): 124f., 162, 350, 393, 628
**Ariosto,** Lodovico (1474-1533): 14, 22
**Aristophanes** (c.446BC-c.386BC): 213
**Aristotle** (c.384BC-c.322BC): 7, 10, 12, 60-62, 71f., 124, 128, 156, 168
*Aron, Pietro (see Aaron, Pietro).*
**Artusi,** Giovanni Maria (1540-1613): 669
**Ascham,** Roger (1515-1568): 129
**Asola,** Giovanni Matteo (1524-1609): 405, 471, 500
**Assandra,** Caterina (1590-a.1618): 627
**Athanasius** *of Alexandria* (St) (c.295-373): 67

*Athesinus, Petrus (see Treybenreif, Peter).*
**Attaingnant,** Pierre (c.1494-c.1552): 18
**Auger,** Edmond (1530-1591): 532, 580, 611
*Augustine (see Augustinus).*
**Augustinus (Augustine)** *of Hippo* (St) (354-430): 67–69, 71, 78, 82, 88, 90f., 116, 132, 154, 168, 170f., 176f., 181, 185, 192, 204, 221, 299, 370, 601, 656, 662, 690
**Aurelius Propertius,** Sextus (c.50BC-a.15BC): 168

**Bach,** Johann Sebastian (1685-1750): 255, 308, 624, 687
**Baerts,** Martha (?-1560): 651
**Baini,** Giuseppe (1775-1844): 422
**Balbi,** Ludovico (c.1545-1604): 445
**Baldung,** Hans "Grien" (c.1484-1545): 126
**Baldwin,** John (c.1560-1615): 380
**Ballard,** Pierre (c.1580-1639): 324
**Banchieri,** Adriano (1568-1634): 23, 503
**Baptista,** Gracia (?-?): 671f, 683
**Barbarelli da Castelfranco,** Giorgio "Giorgione" (c.1477-1510): 15f.
**Baronio (Baronius),** Cesare (Cardinal) (1538-1607): 492f.
*Baronius, Cesare (see Baronio, Cesare).*
**Barth,** Karl (1886-1968): 686
**Bartoli,** Cosimo (1503-1572): 158f.
**Bartolommea** (?-a.1585): 664
**Bascapè,** Prospera Corona (c.1550-1624): 662
*Basil (see Basilius).*
**Basile,** Adriana (c.1580-c.1640): 627
**Basilius (Basil)** *of Caesarea* (St) (c.329-379): 67–69, 157, 181, 186f., 191, 193f., 227, 591, 601
**Battiferri Ammannati,** Laura (1523-1589): 679
**Bauldeweyn (Bauldewijn),** Noel (c.1480-1529): 504
*Bauldewijn, Noel (see Bauldeweyn, Noel).*
**Beccadelli,** Ludovico (1501-1572): 88, 155, 158f., 162, 390f., 410f., 423
*Beccon, Thomas (see Becon, Thomas).*
**Becker,** Cornelius (1561-1604): 284, 544

Becon (Beccon), Thomas (c.1511-1567): 137, 148, 152, 168f., 175, 191, 350
Bede (Venerable) (c.673-735): 90, 145
Belcari, Feo (1410-1484): 662
Bellarmine, Robert (see Bellarmino, Roberto).
Bellarmino (Bellarmine), Roberto (Robert) (St) (1542-1621): 174, 233–235, 469, 486
Belle, Jan (?-1566): 314
Bembo Gradenigo, Elena (1528-a.1543): 125
Bembo, Pietro (Cardinal) (1470-1547): 14, 125, 129, 393, 628
Benedict (Benedetto) of Nursia (Norcia) (St) (c.480-c.543): 690
Benno von Meissen (of Meissen) (St) (c.1010-1106): 521, 553f.
Bermudo, Juan (c.1510-c.1565): 94
Bernard of Clairvaux (St) (1090-1153): 692
Beza (see de Bèze, Théodore).
Bezona, Laura (?-a.1575): 662
Bidembach, Balthasar (see Bidenbach, Balthasar).
Bidenbach (Bidembach), Balthasar (1533-1578): 312
Bidermann, Jakob (1578-1639): 99
Bijns, Anna (1493-1575): 679f.
Blackhall, Andro (c.1535-1609): viii, 359
Blahoslaus, Johannes (see Blahoslav, Jan).
Blahoslav (Blahoslaus), Jan (Johannes) (1523-1571): 296
Blancicampianus (see Grau von Waischenfeld, Friedrich).
Blarer (Blaurer) von Giersberg, Ambrosius (1492-1564): 329
Blaurer, Ambrosius (see Blarer, Ambrosius).
Bodenstein, Andreas von Karlstadt (1486-1541): 32f., 87f., 143, 165, 176, 179f., 186, 195, 197, 200, 204, 209, 216
Bodin, Jean (1530-1596): 13
Boethius, Severinus (c.480-524): 61, 67, 71, 126, 149
Bold, Richard (?-1602): 565
Boleyn, Anne (Queen consort) (c.1501-1536): 37
Bolsec, Jérôme-Hermès (?-c.1585): 547f., 561
Bona, Valerio (c.1560-c.1620): 630

Bonaventura (Bonaventure) da Bagnoregio (St) (c.1221-1274): 133
Bonaventure (see Bonaventura).
Boncompagni, Ugo (Gregory XIII) (Pope) (1502-1585): 46, 116, 395, 423, 449f., 504, 510, 580, 695
Boni (Bony), Guillaume (c.1530-c.1594): 327, 473
Bony, Guillaume (see Boni, Guillaume).
Borghese, Camillo (see Borghesi, Camillo).
Borghese, Camillo (Paul V) (Pope) (1550-1621): 451, 469
Borghesi (Borghese), Camillo (1552-1612): 660
Borghi, Faustina (c.1574-?): 656
Borromeo, Carlo (St) (1538-1584): 127, 383, 394, 398, 400, 405, 431, 437f., 455, 460–462, 465, 467, 471, 495, 500–502, 505, 510, 596, 657, 664f., 669, 676
Borromeo, Federigo (Cardinal) (1564-1631): 60, 68f., 76, 78, 89, 97, 99f., 103, 122, 127, 139, 147, 151, 176, 430, 494, 502f., 583, 601, 665f., 674f.
Borsieri, Girolamo (1588-1629): 670
Böschenstein, Johannes (1472-1540): 66
Boscoop, Cornelis (see Boskoop, Cornelis).
Boskoop (Boscoop), Cornelis (c.1525-1573): 331
Bossewell, John (?-1580): 333, 336, 344
Bottrigari, Ercole (1531-1612): 668f.
Boudewijns (Boudewyns), Katharina (c.1520-a.1603): 680
Boudewyns, Katharina (see Boudewijns, Katharina).
Bourgeois, Loys (c.1510-1561): 308, 322, 645
Bovia, Laura (c.1565-1629): 671, 675
Bovio, Giacomo (?-?): 671
Bownd, Nicholas (see Bownde, Nicholas).
Bownde (Bownd), Nicholas (?-1613): 369
Boyleau, Simon (?-1586): 502
Braghettone, Daniele (see Ricciarelli, Daniele).
Brahe, Tycho (1546-1601): 14
Brant, Sebastian (c.1458-1521): 112
Brenz, Johannes (1499-1570): 189

**Briant (Bryant),** Alexander (St) (1556-1581): 565
**Britten,** Benjamin (1913-1976): 687
**Bruegel,** Pieter "The Elder" (c.1525-1569): 16
**Bruno,** Giordano (1548-1600): 13
**Bruto,** Giovanni Michele (1517-1592): 628f., 633
*Bryant, Alexander (see Briant, Alexander).*
**Bucer (Butzer),** Martin (1491-1551): 38, 40, 131, 165, 168, 197, 218–221, 225, 238, 270, 290–294, 298, 305, 329, 338, 347, 533, 588–590
**Buchan,** John (?-c.1608): 362
**Buchanan,** George (1506-1582): 13, 314, 322, 359, 572, 672
**Buchstab,** Johannes (1499-1529): 214
**Bugenhagen,** Johannes (1485-1558): 33, 35, 275, 286, 289, 585, 592, 614f.
**Bullinger,** Heinrich (1504-1575): 36, 214, 227f.
**Buonarroti,** Michelangelo (1475-1564): 15f., 158f., 161–163
**Burkhardt,** Georg "Spalatin" (1484-1545): 251–253, 257
**Butler,** Charles (1560-1647): 93, 117, 152, 583
*Butzer, Martin (see Bucer, Martin).*
**Byrd,** William (c.1539-1623): 362, 371, 373, 377–381, 442, 505, 528f., 560, 562, 565, 575, 581, 620, 622

**Caccini,** Giulio (c.1550-1618): 497
*Caesar, Julius (see Julius Caesar, Gaius).*
*Cajetan, Thomas (see de Vio Caetani, Tommaso).*
**Calderwood,** David (1575-1650): 536, 547, 584
**Caliari,** Paolo "Veronese" (1528-1588): 15f., 508
**Calvi,** Ippolita (?-a.1578): 664
*Calvin, John (see Cauvin, Jehan).*
*Calvisius, Seth (see Kalwitz, Seth).*
*Campana, Paola Giustina (see Carpani, Paola Giustina).*
**Campanella,** Tommaso (1568-1639): 13

**Campbell of Kinzeancleugh,** Elizabeth (?-1574): 648
*Campensis, Johannes (see van Campen, Jan).*
**Campi,** Antonio (c.1522-1587): 677
**Campion,** Edmund (St) (1540-1581): 528, 565
**Campion,** Thomas (1567-1620): 362
*Canisius, Peter (see Kanijs, Pieter).*
**Cara,** Marchetto (c.1470-1525): 20
**Carafa,** Gian Pietro (Paul IV) (Pope) (1476-1559): 42, 394, 399, 484
*Caravaggio (see Merisi, Michelangelo).*
*Carlerius, Aegidius (see Carlier, Gilles).*
**Carlier (Carlerius),** Gilles (Aegidius) (c.1405-c.1470): 65, 93, 147, 149, 152
*Carniolus, Jacobus (see Handl, Jacob).*
**Carpani (Campana),** Paola Giustina (?-a.1575): 663
**Carpentarius,** Georgius (c.1487-1531): 542
*Carpentras (see Genet, Elzéar).*
**Case,** John (c.1539-1600): 228, 360
**Casini,** Giovanni Filippo (Gianfilippo) (1520-1584): 600
*Castiglione, Baldesar (see Castiglione, Baldassarre).*
**Castiglione,** Baldassarre (Baldesar) (1478-1529): 128–130
*Casulana, Maddalena (see Mezari, Maddalena).*
*Catherine of Aragon (see de Trastámara, Catalina).*
*Catullus (see Valerius Catullus, Gaius).* 168
**Caustun,** Thomas (c.1520-1569): 370
**Cauvin (Calvin),** Jehan (John) "Charles d'Espeville (?)" (1509-1564): 6, 37–39, 43f., 71, 131, 165, 168, 170f., 176f., 180, 182–187, 191, 197, 200f., 219–225, 238, 290f., 294, 296, 298–301, 303–311, 315f., 321–323, 325, 332, 354f., 358, 385, 387, 399, 426, 479, 538, 540, 547f., 557, 561, 583, 589f., 598, 643f., 646, 653, 686, 700
**Cavazzoni,** Girolamo (c.1525-a.1577): 511
**Cavazzoni,** Marco Antonio (c.1485-1569): 25
**Cavenaghi,** Prospera Vittoria (?-a.1575): 662

**Cecilia** (St) (?-c.230AD): 629
*Celiano, Livio (see Grillo, Angelo).*
**Certon,** Pierre (a.1510-1572): 321, 581
*Cervantes (see de Cervantes Saavedra, Miguel).*
**Cervini degli Spannocchi,** Marcello (Marcellus II) (Pope) (1501-1555): 42, 88, 118, 122, 383, 153, 178, 396, 422–425
**Cesis,** Sulpitia (1577-a.1619): 627, 656
*Chandieu, Antoine (see de la Roche Chandieu, Antoine).*
*Charles IX (see de Valois-Angoulême, Charles IX).*
*Charles V (see von Habsburg, Karl V).*
*Christ (see Jesus).*
*Christophorus of Padua (see Cristoforo).*
*Chrysostom (see Ioannes).*
**Cima,** Andrea (1580-1627): 438
**Ciocchi del Monte,** Giovanni Maria (Julius III) (Pope) (1487-1555): 396
**Cirillo,** Bernardino (1500-1575): 59, 64, 75 f., 96 f., 101 f., 108, 123, 132 f., 143, 150 f., 153–163, 177, 390, 402, 409–411, 414, 423 f., 450, 499, 686
*Claire (see Scifi, Chiara).*
**Clavijo del Castillo,** Bernardina (?-?): 673
**Clavijo del Castillo,** Bernardo (1549-1626): 673
**Clemens (Clement),** Jacobus "Non Papa" (c.1510-c.1555): viii, 19, 21, 314, 331, 622
*Clemens non Papa (see Clemens, Jacobus).*
*Clement VIII (see Aldobrandini, Ippolito).*
**Cock,** Symon (c.1505-a.1548): 330
**Colebault,** Jacques (Jacquet) de Mantua (1483-1559): 96, 396, 398, 401, 457, 509, 559
**Colin,** Pierre (?-a.1561): 99, 115, 122, 391
**Colonna d'Avalos,** Vittoria (1490-1547): 679
**Comin Robusti,** Jacopo "Tintoretto" (1518-1594): 15 f.
**Compère,** Loyset (c.1445-1518): 19
**Contarini,** Gasparo (Cardinal) (1483-1542): 38, 42
**Contzen,** Adam (1571-1635): 283, 519, 532
*Copernicus, Nicolaus (see Kopernik, Mikołaj).*

**Coppini,** Aquilino (?-1629): 99 f., 472, 503, 583
*Cordubensis, Franciscus (see de Córdoba, Francisco).*
**Cornysh,** William (1465-1523): 687
*Correggio (see Allegri, Antonio).*
**Cortellini,** Camillo (1561-1630): 671
**Cortesi,** Paolo (1465-1510): 97, 130 f., 146
**Costeley,** Guillaume (c.1530-1606): 63
**Cosyn,** John (?-1609): 361
**Cotton,** John (1585-1652): 646
*Countess of Pembroke (see Sidney Herbert, Mary).*
*Coverdale, Miles (see Coverdale, Myles).*
**Coverdale,** Myles (Miles) (1488-1569): 194, 289, 302, 333, 346–349, 613, 642, 646, 649
**Coyssard,** Michel (1547-1623): 485, 563
**Cranach,** Lucas "The Elder" (c.1472-1553): 16, 543
**Cranmer,** Thomas (1489-1556): 36, 40, 173, 226, 338 f., 341–343, 348, 350, 354, 406, 536
**Crassot,** Richard (c.1530-a.1580): 321
**Crecquillon,** Thomas (c.1505-1557): 19
*Cresollio, Lodovico (see de Cressolles, Louis).*
*Creuziger, Caspar (see Cruciger, Caspar).*
**Cristoforo (Christophorus)** da Padova (of Padua) (1500-1569): 180, 187, 413
**Croke,** John (1489-1554): 350
**Crowley,** Robert (c.1517-1588): 333, 350
*Cruciger, Elisabeth (see von Meseritz Cruciger, Elisabeth).*
**Cruciger (Creuziger),** Caspar (1504-1548): 641
**Cyriacus** (St) (?-c.303): 217

*da Fano, Giovanni (see Pili, Giovanni).*
*da Modena, Salvatore (see Essenga, Salvadore).*
**da Nola (Nolla),** Giovanni Domenico (c.1510-1592): 471
*da Palestrina, Giovanni (see Pierluigi, Giovanni).*
*da Parma, Paola (see Massarenghi, Paola).*
*da Volterra, Daniele (see Ricciarelli, Daniele).*
**Dachser,** Jakob (?-1567): 294

Dachstein, Wolfgang (c.1487-1553): 294, 306, 329, 598
dal Paradiso, Domenica (see Narducci, Domenica).
d'Albret, Jeanne (Queen) (1528-1572): 645
Daman, William (c.1540-1591): 361
d'Anjou, Francis (see de Valois-Angoulême, François).
d'Aquino ("Aquinas"), Tommaso (Thomas) (St) (1225-1274): 12f., 67-72, 76, 81, 87f., 91, 149, 196, 205, 232, 234, 394, 601, 694
Darnley, Henry (see Stuart, Henry).
Daser, Ludwig (c.1525-1589): 564
Datheen (Dathenus), Petrus (c.1531-1588): 313, 332, 528
Dathenus, Petrus (see Datheen, Petrus).
Davantès, Pierre "Antesignanus" (c.1525-1561): 308
David (King) (c.1040BC-c.970BC): 168f., 185, 193, 199f., 222, 347, 369, 545, 548, 551, 589, 610, 647, 702
David of Augsburg (c.1200-1272): 139
Day, John (c.1522-1584): 354, 360, 370
de Albertis (Alberti), Gasparo (c.1480-c.1560): 477
de Azpilcueta, Martín "Doctor Navarrus" (1491-1586): 74, 76, 87, 106f., 115, 118, 123, 134-136, 148, 150, 414
de Baïf, Jean-Antoine (1532-1589): 14f., 20f., 96, 323, 580, 672
de' Bardi, Giovanni (Count) (1534-1612): 63
de Beaulieu, Eustorg (c.1495-1552): 326, 619
de Bertrand, Antoine (c.1530-c.1581): 327, 473, 563
de Bèze (Beza), Théodore (1519-1605): 43, 173f., 187, 200, 228, 283, 307f., 312, 519, 545f., 580, 645
de' Bianchi, Tommasino (see Lancillotto, Thomasino).
de Bisschop, Ludovicus "Episcopius" (c.1520-1595): 314
de Bouchefort, Jeannet (?-a.1572): 557f.
de Bourbon, Catherine (1559-1604): 645
de Bourbon, Henri (Henry) IV de Navarre (King) (1553-1610): 45-47, 303, 323

de Braganza, João (John) IV (King) (1604-1656): 155
de Cabezón, Antonio (1510-1566): 672
de Castelnau, Michel (c.1520-1592): 317
de Cervantes Saavedra, Miguel (1547-1616): 15
de Córdoba (de Cordova, Cordubensis), Francisco (Franciscus) (?-a.1586): 232
de Cordova, Francisco (see de Córdoba, Francisco).
de Cressolles (Cresollio), Louis (Lodovico) (1568-1634): 81, 153, 463
de Dinteville, Jean (1504-1555): 569
de Fabris, Melchior (see von Fabris, Melchior).
de Févin, Antoine (c.1470-c.1511): 504
de Goisson, Ursmar (1524-1578): 484
de Grassis, Paris (c.1470-1528): 77, 146, 466f.
de Guise, Charles (Cardinal) (1524-1574): 402
de Guise, Francis (see de Guise, François).
de Guise, François (Francis) (Duke) (1519-1563): 44
de Guise, Marie (Mary) (Regent) (1515-1560): 43
de Guise, Mary (see de Guise, Marie).
de Jussie (Jussy), Jeanne (1503-1561): 653
de Jussy, Jeanne (see de Jussie, Jeanne).
de Kerle, Jacobus (c.1531-1591): 383, 401, 405-407, 425, 442, 458
de la Roche Chandieu, Antoine (1534-1591): 326
de la Rue, Pierre (c.1452-1518): 19, 107
de Laet, Hans (Jean) (c.1525-c.1567): 326
de Lassus, Roland (see di Lasso, Orlando).
de L'Estocart, Paschal (c.1538-a.1587): 299, 323, 325, 473, 618
de Ligny, Charles (?-c.1624): 379, 560
de Lorraine, Renée of Bavaria (Duchess) (1544-1602): 678
de Loyola, Ignatius (see de Loyola, Ignacio).
de Loyola (of Loyola), Ignacio (Ignatius) (St) (1491-1556): 39, 137, 430, 482-486, 586, 593f., 601f., 696
de Macque, Jean (c.1548-1614): 493
de Malherbe, François (1555-1628): 580
de Mantua, Jacquet (see Colebault, Jacques).

**de Marle,** Nicolas (?-?):   504
**de' Medici,** Alessandro di Ottaviano (Leo XI) (Pope) (1535-1605):   659, 664
**de' Medici,** Caterina (Catherine) (Queen consort) (1519-1589):   42f., 45f., 303
**de' Medici,** Giovanni Angelo (Pius IV) (Pope) (1499-1565):   459, 579
**de' Medici,** Giovanni di Lorenzo (Leo X) (Pope) (1475-1521):   32, 122, 136, 396
**de' Medici,** Giulio di Giuliano (Clement VII) (Pope) (1478-1534):   35
*de' Medici, Lucrezia (see Tornabuoni de' Medici, Lucrezia).*
**de Mendoza,** Blasina (?-?):   673
**de Montaigne,** Michel (1533-1592):   13
**de Monte,** Philippe (1521-1603):   22, 528, 679
**de Morales,** Cristóbal (1500-1553):   99, 127, 396, 431, 513
**de Poitiers,** Diane (c.1499-1566):   303
**de Polanco,** Juan Alfonso (1517-1576):   593
**de Raemond,** Florimond (1540-1601):   647
**de' Ricci,** Caterina (1522-1590):   661
**de Rivera,** Bernardino *de Sahagún* (1499-1590):   490, 599
**de Ronsard,** Pierre (1524-1585):   15, 20, 473, 532
**de Rore,** Cipriano (c.1515-1565):   22f., 286, 462, 471, 557, 619, 622
**de Rossi,** Giovanni Maria (c.1522-1590):   401
*de Sahagún, Bernardino (see de Rivera, Bernardino).*
**de Selve,** Georges (c.1508-1541):   569
**de Sermisy,** Claudin (c.1490-1562):   21, 327, 598
*de Smet, Christoffel (see de Smit, Christoffel).*
**de Smit (de Smet, Fabritius),** Christoffel (?-1564):   528
**de Soto,** Pedro (Petrus) (1493-1563):   406
*de Soto, Petrus (see de Soto, Pedro).*
**de Trastámara,** Catalina (Catherine) *de Aragón (of Aragon)* (Queen consort) (1485-1536):   36f.
**de Tyard,** Pontus (c.1521-1605):   76, 177
**de Valdés,** Juan (c.1500-1541):   37f.

**de Valois-Angoulême,** Charles IX (King) (1550-1574):   46, 63
**de Valois-Angoulême,** François (Francis) *d'Anjou* (Duke) (1555-1584):   46
**de Valois-Angoulême,** François (Francis) I (King) (1494-1547):   31, 34–36, 42, 302, 644
**de Valois-Angoulême,** François (Francis) II (King) (1544-1560):   43
**de Valois-Angoulême,** Henri (Henry) II (King) (1519-1559):   42, 303, 318, 560
**de Valois-Angoulême,** Henri (Henry) III (King) (1551-1589):   46f.
**de Valois-Angoulême,** Marguerite (Margaret) *de Navarre, de France* (Queen consort) (1553-1615):   45
**de Valois-Angoulême,** Marguerite (Margaret) *de Navarre* (Queen consort) (1492-1549):   37
**de Valois-Orléans,** Louis XII (King) (1462-1515):   557
**de Valois-Orléans,** Renée "Renée de France" (Duchess) (1510-1574):   303, 557–559
**de Vega,** Lope (1562-1635):   15
**de Victoria,** Tomás Luis (1548-1611):   431, 458, 488, 506f., 514f., 661
**de Vingle,** Pierre (1495-1536):   538
**de Vio Caetani (Cajetan),** Tommaso (Thomas) (1469-1534):   32, 91, 154, 196
**de Wert,** Giaches (1535-1596):   509
*Decius, Nikolaus (see Tech, Nikolaus).*
**del Bene,** Giovanni (1513-1559):   471
**del Lago,** Giovanni (c.1490-1544):   64
**della Rovere,** Francesco (Sixtus IV) (Pope) (1414-1484):   395
**della Rovere,** Giuliano (Julius II) (Pope) (1443-1513):   162f., 395f.
**della Rovere,** Giulio Feltrio (Cardinal) (1533-1578):   437, 439, 455, 464, 499f.
**della Valle,** Pietro (1586-1652):   443
**Demantius,** Christoph (1567-1643):   286
**des Freux (Frusius),** André (c.1515-1556):   483, 586
**des Marets,** Clément "Marot" (1496-1544):   15, 20, 298, 300, 302–307, 312, 318, 349, 352, 532, 535, 540, 545–547, 557, 560, 580, 598, 610, 619, 644

*Des Pres, Josquin (see Desprez, Josquin).*
**Descartes,** René (1596-1650): 97
**Désiré,** Artus (c.1510-1579): 302, 540f.
*d'Espeville, Charles (see Cauvin, Jehan).*
**Desportes,** Philippe (1546-1606): 580
**Desprez (Des Pres, Des Prez),** Josquin (c.1450-1521): 19, 107, 133, 158, 211, 238, 259, 396f., 400, 613
**d'Este,** Ercole II (Duke) (1508-1559): 557f.
**d'Este Gonzaga,** Isabella (Marchioness) (1474-1539): 20
**d'Euse,** Jacques-Arnaud (John XXII) (Pope) (c.1244-1334): 73f., 78, 115, 131f., 149, 153, 411f., 464
**di Lasso (de Lassus),** Orlando (Roland) (c.1532–1594): 22f., 97, 263, 286, 321, 326f., 400, 431, 458, 472f., 475, 487f., 500, 505, 515–518, 581, 619, 621f., 634, 683
**Dietrich,** Sixt (c.1494-1548): 263
**Dirks,** Elisabeth (Lijsbeth, Lijsken) (?-1549): 652
*Dirks, Lijsbeth (see Dirks, Elisabeth).*
*Dirks, Lijsken (see Dirks, Elisabeth).*
*Doctor Navarrus (see de Azpilcueta, Martín).*
*Domenica dal Paradiso (see Narducci, Domenica).*
**Domingo (Dominic)** de Guzman (of Guzman) (St) (1170-1221): 694
*Donatello (see Donato di Niccolò di Betto Bardi).*
**Donato di Niccolò di Betto Bardi** "Donatello" (c.1386-1466): 158
**Doni,** Giovanni Battista (1595-1647): 133
*dos Mártires, Bartolomeu (see Fernandes, Bartolomeo).*
**Dow,** Robert (1553-1588): 380
**Dowland,** John (1563-1626): 361f.
*Draconi (see Dragoni, Giovanni Andrea).*
**Dragoni (Draconi),** Giovanni Andrea (c.1540-1598): 445
**Drake,** Francis (Sir) (c.1540-1596): 320f.
*Dressellio, Geremia (see Drexel, Jeremias).*
**Drexel (Dressellio),** Jeremias (Geremia) (1581-1638): 485
**du Caurroy,** Eustache (1549-1609): 619

**du Faur de Pibrac,** Guy (1529-1584): 326, 473
*Duchess Elisabeth von Brandenburg (see von Hohenzollern, Elisabeth).*
**Ducis,** Benedictus (c.1492-1544): 263
*Duke Ernst I (see Guelph von Brunswick-Lüneburg, Ernst I).*
*Duke of Alva (see Álvarez de Toledo y Pimentel, Fernando).*
**Dürer,** Albrecht (1471-1528): 16
**Durie,** John (1537-1600): 547
**Duval,** Jacques (?-1549): 559

*Earl of Bothwell (see Hepburn, James).*
*Earl of Moray (see Stewart, James).*
*Earl of Surrey (see Howard, Henry).*
**East (Este),** Thomas (c.1540-1609): 361
**Eber,** Paul (1511-1569): 193, 267, 279, 287, 638f.
**Eccard,** Johannes (1553-1611): 259, 263, 516, 615
*Eck, Johann (see Maier, Johann).*
**Eeuwouts (Eeuwoutsdochter) Teellinck Hoffer,** Suzanna (1551-1625): 645
**Eeuwouts (Eeuwoutsdochter) Teellinck Limmens,** Cornelia (c.1553-1576): 645, 649
*Eeuwoutsdochter, Cornelia (see Eeuwouts Tellinck Limmens, Cornelia).*
*Eeuwoutsdochter, Suzanna (see Eeuwouts Tellinck Hoffer, Suzanna).*
*El Greco (see Theotokópoulos, Doménikos).*
**Elyot,** Thomas (c.1490-1546): 151
**Emser,** Hieronymus (c.1478-1527): 538, 554
*Episcopius (see de Bisschop, Ludovicus).*
**Erasmus,** Desiderius *of Rotterdam* (c.1469-1536): 6, 11, 30f., 49f., 54, 66, 68, 77f., 82–84, 87, 103, 107, 111, 115, 117–121, 125, 141, 152, 162, 168, 170, 209, 213, 218, 220, 227, 245, 277, 283, 329, 335f., 342, 588, 644, 695
*Ernst "The Confessor" (see Guelph, Ernst I).*
*Esaiasdochter, Anneke (see Esaiasdochter Jans, Anna).*
**Esaiasdochter Jans (Jansz),** Anna (Anneke) (c.1509-1539): 650f.

*Esch, Johannes (see van Essen, Jan).*
**Essenga,** Salvadore *da Modena* (?-1575): 678
*Este, Thomas (see East, Thomas).*

**Fabius Quintilianus (Quintilian),** Marcus (c.35AD-c.100AD): 63, 65, 70, 76, 84, 128, 149, 440
*Fabritius, Christoffel (see de Smit, Christoffel).*
*Faelli, Giovanni Battista (see Faello, Giovanni Battista).*
**Faello (Phaello, Faelli),** Giovanni Battista (?-c.1557): 558
**Faignient,** Noé (b.1540-b.1600): 314
**Farel,** Guillaume (William) (1489-1565): 37f., 304
*Farel, William (see Farel, Guillaume).*
**Farnaby,** Giles (c.1563-1640): 361
**Farnese,** Alessandro (Cardinal) (1520-1589): 156, 163
**Farnese,** Alessandro (Paul III) (Pope) (1468-1549): 37f., 163, 396, 409
**Farnese,** Ranuccio (Cardinal) (1530-1565): 156, 163, 678
**Farrant,** Richard (c.1525-1580): 378
**Fernandes,** Bartolomeo (Bartolomeu) *dos Mártires* (1514-1590): 111
**Fernandes,** Gaspar (1566-1629): 442
**Ferrabosco,** Alfonso "The Elder" (1543-1588): 378, 402
**Ferrabosco,** Domenico Maria (1513-1574): 402
**Festa,** Sebastiano (c.1490-1524): 370
**Festa,** Costanzo (c.1485-1545): 396
**Fiamma,** Gabriele (1533-1585): 472, 678
**Fiaschi,** Giulia (?-?): 669
**Ficino (Ficinus),** Marsilio (Marsilius) (1433-1499): 11f., 81, 94, 126, 160
*Ficinus, Marsilius (see Ficino, Marsilio).*
**Fiesco,** Giulio (c.1519-1586): 669
**Figliucci,** Felice (c.1525-c.1590): 88, 139
**Finck,** Hermann (1527-1558): 141, 144, 150
**Fletcher,** Francis (c.1555-c.1619): 320
**Florensz,** Adriaan (Adrian VI) (Pope) (1459-1523): 30, 560
**Fontana,** Giovanni (1537-1611): 669

**Franc,** Guillaume (c.1505-c.1571): 308
**Francesco (Francis)** *d'Assisi* (of Assisi) (St) (c.1881-1226): 698
*Franchi, Cirillo (see Franco, Cirillo).*
*Francis d'Anjou (see de Valois-Angoulême, François).*
**Franco (Franchi),** Cirillo (?-1585): 155
*Frederick I (see von Württemberg, Friedrich I).*
*Frederick III (see von Wettin, Friedrich III).*
*Frederick III (see von Wittelsbach, Friedrich III).*
*Frederick IV (see von Wittelsbach-Simmern, Friedrich IV).*
*Frederick The Wise (see von Wettin, Friedrich III).*
**Froschauer,** Christoph (c.1490-1564): 329
*Frusius, André (see des Freux, André).*
*Fugger, Sybille (see von Everstein, Sybille).*
**Fulke,** William (1538-1589): 192
**Fursa** (St) (?-650): 90

**Gabrieli,** Andrea (c.1532-1585): 86, 445, 467, 508
**Gabrieli,** Giovanni (c.1554-1612): 508
*Gaffurius, Franchinus (see Gafori, Franchino).*
**Gafori (Gaffurius),** Franchino (Franchinus) (1451-1522): 59, 63f., 128, 141, 143f., 149f.
*Galen (see Galenus Claudius, Aelius).*
**Galenus (Galen) Claudius,** Aelius (129-c.200): 14, 129
**Galilei,** Galileo (1564-1642): 14, 24, 168
**Galilei,** Vincenzo (c.1520-1591): 24, 59, 63, 65, 88f., 92
*Gallus, Jacobus (see Handl, Jacob).*
**Gardane (Gardano),** Antoine (Antonio) (1509-1569): 18, 406
*Gardano, Antonio (see Gardane, Antoine).*
**Gardiner,** Stephen (1497-1555): 120f., 141, 149
**Garnet (Garnett),** Henry (1555-1606): 565
*Garnett, Henry (see Garnet, Henry).*
*Gastoldi, Giangiacomo (see Gastoldi, Giovanni Giacomo).*
**Gastoldi,** Giovanni Giacomo (Giangiacomo) (c.1554-1609): 24, 255
**Genet,** Elzéar "Carpentras" (c.1470-1548): 396

*Gerrijts, Soetken (see Gerrits, Soetjen).*
**Gerrits (Gerrijts),** Soetjen (Soetken) (c.1540-1572): 651f., 680
**Gerrits,** Vrou (c.1580-1605): 652
**Gesualdo,** Carlo da Venosa (Prince) (1566-1613): 23
**Gherardini,** Arcangelo (?-a.1587): 678
*Ghiberti, Gian Matteo (see Giberti, Giovanni Matteo).*
**Ghislieri,** Antonio, Michele (Pius V) (Pope)/(St) (1504-1572): 45, 446, 449
**Ghoyvaers,** Lijsbet (?-?): 674
**Giberti (Ghiberti),** Giovanni Matteo (Gian Matteo) (1495-1543): 127, 176, 391
**Gigler,** Andreas (?-1570): 608
**Giles** (St) (c.650-c.710): 536
**Ginés,** Teodora (1530-1598): 627
*Giorgione (see Barbarelli da Castelfranco, Giorgio).*
*Giustinian, Paolo (see Giustinian, Tommaso).*
**Giustinian,** Tommaso (Paolo) (1476-1528): 122, 421
**Giustiniani,** Vincenzo (Marquis) (1564-1637): 95, 151
*Glarean, Heinrich (see Loris, Heinrich).*
**Godeau,** Antoine (1605-1672): 317
**Gombert,** Nicolas (c.1495-c.1560): 19, 21, 370
**Gomez Rengifo,** Francisco (?-a.1580): 321
**Gonzaga,** Ercole (Cardinal) (1505-1563): 398f., 401, 406, 410, 508, 559
**Gonzaga,** Federico (Cardinal) (1540-1565): 106
**Gonzaga,** Guglielmo (Duke) (1538-1587): 120, 455, 508-511
**Gottfried** *of Strasbourg* (c.1180-c.1215): 617
**Goudimel,** Claude (c.1514-1572): 299, 312, 317, 323, 330, 563, 589, 645
**Goulaine de Laudonnière,** René (c.1529-1574): 319
**Goulart,** Simon (1543-1628): 327, 473
*Gradenigo, Elena (see Bembo Gradenigo, Elena).*
*Grandison, John (see Grandisson, John).*
**Grandisson (Grandison),** John (1292-1369): 373

**Grau von Waischenfeld,** Friedrich "Nausea", "Blancicampianus" (1496-1552): 409-411, 420
**Greff,** Joachim (1510-1552): 239
*Gregory I (see Anicius, Gregorius).*
*Gregory XIII (see Boncompagni, Ugo).*
**Greiter (Greitter),** Matthias (c.1494-1550): 294, 306, 308, 329
*Greitter, Matthias (see Greiter, Mathias).*
**Grey,** Henry (Lord) (1517-1554): 227
**Grey,** Jane (Lady) (c.1536-1554): 41
*Grien (see Baldung, Hans).*
**Grillo,** Angelo "Livio Celiano" (c.1557-1629): 472, 670
**Groote,** Geert (1340-1384): 30
**Grossi,** Lodovico *da Viadana* (c.1560-1627): 86
**Grünewald,** Matthias (c.1470-1528): 16
**Gualteruzzi,** Carlo (1500–1577): 155
**Gualteruzzi,** Ugolino (c.1521-a.1571): 155, 390
**Guarini,** Giovanni Battista (1538-1612): 22
**Guarini,** Marco Antonio (c.1570-c.1638): 668
**Guelph,** Ernst I "The Confessor" *von Brunswick-Lüneburg* (Duke) (1497-1546): 654
**Guéroult,** Guillaume (c.1507-1569): 326, 619
**Guerrero,** Francisco (1528-1599): 64, 99, 127, 141, 151, 431, 443, 462, 473f., 513
**Guicciardini,** Lodovico (1521-1589): 682
**Guidetti,** Giovanni Domenico (c.1532-1592): 450-452
**Guidiccioni,** Lelio (1582-1643): 81, 153
*Guise, Francis (see de Guise, François).*
*Guise, Mary (see de Guise, Marie).*
*Gustav I (see Vasa, Gustav I).*

**Haemerkken,** Thomas *À Kempis* (c.1380-1471): 30
*Haendel, Georg Friedrich (see Händel, Georg Friedrich).*
*Handel, George Frederick (see Händel, Georg Friedrich).*
**Händel (Haendel, Handel),** Georg Friedrich (1685-1759): 624

**Handl (Gallus)**, Jacob (Jacobus) "Carniolus" (1550-1591):  458
**Harington**, John (1561-1612):  363
**Harriot**, Thomas (1560-1621):  320
**Harzer**, Balthasar "Resinarius" (c.1485-c.1544):  263, 266, 614
**Hassler**, Hans Leo (1564-1612):  255
**Haton**, Claude (c.1534-c.1605):  317
**Haym**, Johannes *von Themar* (?-1593):  609
*Hecyrus, Christoph (see Schweher, Kryštof).*
*Hecyrus, Christophorus (see Schweher, Kryštof).*
**Heinz (Heintz)**, Wolff (c.1490-c.1552):  199, 263
**Helgesen (Heliae)**, Poul (Paulus) (c.1485-c.1535):  551
*Heliae, Paulus (see Helgesen, Poul).*
**Hellinck**, Lupus (c.1493-1541):  266, 581, 622
**Hellriegel**, Ursula (c.1530-a.1543):  652
**Helmbold**, Ludwig *of Mühlhausen* (1532-1598):  259
**Hemmel**, Sigmund (c.1520-1565):  312
*Henry IV of Bourbon (see de Bourbon, Henri IV).*
*Henry of Navarre (see de Bourbon, Henri IV).*
**Hepburn**, James *Earl of Bothwell* (Lord) (c.1534-1578):  43
**Herben (Herbenus)**, Mathieu (Matthaeus) *of Maastricht* (1451-1538):  78, 121, 143, 152, 186, 188, 204
*Herbenus, Matthaeus (see Herben, Mathieu).*
*Herbert, Mary (see Sidney Herbert, Mary).*
**Herman**, Nikolaus (c.1500-1561):  251, 283, 539, 608, 617, 638 f.
**Hernández Palero**, Francisco (c.1533-1597):  672
**Herpol**, Homer (c.1510-c.1574):  608
**Herrgott (Herrgottin)**, Kunegunda (Kunigunde, Kunegund) (?-1547):  633
*Herrgottin, Kunegunda (see Herrgott, Kunegunda).*
*Heshusius, Tilemann (see Hesshus, Tilemann).*
**Hesshus (Heshusius)**, Tilemann (1527-1588):  283, 532
**Heugel**, Johann (c.1510-c.1585):  312
*Heussgen, Johannes (see Huschin, Johannes).*

**Heymair**, Magdalena (c.1535-a.1586):  639 f., 643
**Hieronymus (Jerome)**, Eusebius Sophronius (St) (347-420):  67 f., 70 f., 83, 91, 125, 148-151, 170, 177, 200, 300, 545, 702
**Hindemith**, Paul (1895-1963):  687
**Hoby**, Margaret (Lady) (1571-1633):  371
*Hockland, Robert (see Okeland, Robert).*
**Holbein**, Hans "The Younger" (c.1497-1543):  16, 269, 569-571, 577
**Hooker**, Richard (1554-1600):  192, 227
**Hopkins**, John (c.1520-1570):  351 f., 354
*Horace (see Horatius Flaccus, Quintus).*
**Horatius (Horace) Flaccus**, Quintus (65BC-8BC):  95, 168, 591
*Horn, Johannes (see Roh, Jan).*
*Hosius, Stanislaus (see Hozjusz, Stanisław).*
*Hospenthal, Christina (see Jacobs, Berta).*
**Hotman**, François (1524-1590):  13
**Howard**, Henry *Earl of Surrey* (Lord) (c.1515-1547):  350
**Hozjusz (Hosius)**, Stanisław (Stanislaus) (1504-1579):  391 f., 410
**Hus**, Jan (c.1369-1415):  30, 111, 253 f., 295, 297, 551, 696
**Huschin (Heussgen)**, Johannes "Oecolampadius" (1482-1531):  214, 328 f., 589 f.

*Inger of Austråt (see Ottesdotter Rømer, Inger).*
**Ioannes (John)** "Chrysostom" (St) (c.349-407):  67 f., 84, 177, 532, 611
**Isaac**, Heinrich (c.1450-1517):  19, 107
*Isidore (see Isidorus).*
**Isidorus (Isidore)** *of Seville* (St) (c.560-636):  126

**Jacobs (Hospenthal)**, Berta (Christina) "Suster Bertken" (c.1426-1514):  674
*Jacquet de Mantua (see Colebault, Jacques).*
**Jambe-de-Fer**, Philibert (c.1515-c.1566):  307, 321, 563
**Janequin**, Clément (c.1485-1558):  21, 25, 321, 507, 581, 618
*Jans, Anna (see Esaiasdochter Jans, Anna).*
*Jerome (see Hieronymus, Eusebius Sophronius).*

**Jesperssøn,** Niels (1518-1587): 289
**Jesus "Christ"** (c.4BC-c.30AD): xii, xxvii, 3–5, 7–9, 33, 90, 157, 162, 166, 179, 181, 183, 196–198, 201, 207, 209f., 211, 218, 224, 230, 244, 249, 251, 280, 283, 285f., 297, 301f., 306, 364, 369, 388, 397, 410, 414f., 423, 435, 485, 489, 495, 508, 525, 535, 538f., 541–545, 551f., 564, 566, 570, 584, 586, 630, 644, 665, 670, 673, 689, 691–694, 699, 701f.
**Jewel (Jewell),** John (1522-1571): 190, 368, 584f., 646
*Jewell, John (see Jewel, John).*
*John Chrysostom (see Ioannes).*
*John IV of Portugal (see de Braganza, João IV).*
*John of Avila (see Juan).*
**John** *of Salisbury* (c.1120-1180): 116, 126, 131, 147, 152
*John Paul II (see Wojtyła, Karol).*
*John XXII (see d'Euse, Jacques Arnaud).*
**Jonas,** Justus "The Elder" (1493-1555): 113, 252, 275
**Joye,** George (c.1495-1553): 336, 347
**Juan (John)** de Avila (of Avila) (St) (1499-1569): 593
**Judith** (Queen) (?-?): 344
**Julius Caesar,** Gaius (Caius) (100BC-44BC): 162
*Julius II (see della Rovere, Giuliano).*
*Julius III (see Ciocchi del Monte, Giovanni Maria).*
*Justinian (see Justinianus Augustus, Flavius).*
**Justinianus (Justinian) Augustus,** Flavius (c.483-565): 12

**Kalwitz (Calvisius),** Seth (1556-1615): 256
**Kanijs (Canisius),** Pieter (Peter) (St) (1521-1597): 410, 582, 585, 594
**Kantz,** Kaspar (c.1483-1544): 217, 243
*Karlstadt (see Bodenstein, Andreas).*
**Kemp,** Andro (?-a.1570): 362, 596
*Kempff, Pancratius (see Kempff, Pankraz).*
**Kempff,** Pankraz (Pancratius) (?-a.1562): 555
**Kepler,** Johannes (1571-1630): 14

*Kerle, Jacobus (see de Kerle, Jacobus).*
*King Francis I (see de Valois-Angoulême, François I).*
*King Francis II (see de Valois-Angoulême, François II).*
*King Gustav I (see Vasa, Gustav I).* 35
*King Henry II (see de Valois-Angoulême, Henri II).*
*King Henry III (see de Valois-Angoulême, Henri III).*
*King Henry IV of France (see de Bourbon, Henri IV).*
*King John IV of Portugal (see de Braganza, João IV).*
**Kirbye,** George (c.1565-1634): 361
**Klinge,** Konrad (c.1483-1556): 542
**Klingenstein,** Bernard (c.1545-1614): 443, 599, 615
**Knoepken,** Andreas (c.1468?-1539): 641
**Knox,** John (c.1513-1572): 41, 349, 358, 648
**Kopernik (Copernicus),** Mikołaj (Nicolaus) (1473-1543): 14
**Kotter,** Hans (c.1480-1541): 294

*Lady Culross (see Melville, Elizabeth).*
**Laínez,** Diego (1512-1565): 594, 600
**Lancillotto,** Thomasino (Tommasino) "de' Bianchi" (c.1503-1554): 399
**Lanfranco,** Giovanni Maria (c.1490-1545): 77
**Lardinois,** Everard "Mercurian" (1514-1580): 487
*L'Argenta (see Aleotti, Giambattista).*
**Łaski (à Lasco),** Jan (Johannes) (1499-1560): 38, 40, 353
**Lawson,** James (1538-1584): 584
**Le Challeux,** Nicolas (?-a.1565): 320
**Le Jeune,** Cécile (?-a.1613): 645
**Le Jeune,** Claude (c.1528-1600): 65, 299, 323–325, 327, 473, 563, 571, 619, 622, 645
**Le Maistre,** Mattheus (Mattaeus) (c.1505-1577): 278
**Lechner,** Leonhard (c.1553-1606): 280, 286
*Ledesma, Diego (see Ledesma, Jaime).*

*Ledesma, Giacomo (see Ledesma, Jaime).*
**Ledesma,** Jaime (Giacomo, Diego) (c.1519-1575): 592–594, 596
**Le Fèvre de la Bodérie,** Guy (1541-1598): 610
**Lefèvre d'Étaples,** Jacques (c.1455-c.1536): 11
**Leisentrit (Leisentritt),** Johannes (1527-1586): 605–607, 617
*Leisentritt, Johannes (see Leisentrit, Johannes).*
*Lekpreuik, Robert (see Lekprevik, Robert).*
**Lekprevik (Lepreuik, Leprevik, Lekpreuik),** Robert (?-1581): 358
*Leo X (see de' Medici, Giulio di Giuliano).*
*Leo XI (see de' Medici, Alessandro di Ottaviano).*
**Leonardo** da Vinci (1452-1519): 15
*Lepreuik, Robert (see Lekprevik, Robert).*
*L'Estocart, Paschal (see de L'Estocart, Paschal).*
**Leyser,** Polycarp (1552-1610): 544
*Limmens, Cornelia (see Eeuwouts Tellinck Limmens, Cornelia).*
**Livius (Livy),** Titus (c.59BC-17AD): 145
*Livy (see Livius, Titus).*
**Lobwasser,** Ambrosius (1515-1585): 261, 298, 312, 330, 536f., 543f., 589
**Loersfeld (Loersfelt),** Johannes (?-a.1528): 121, 131, 137
*Lopes, Lodovico (see Lopez, Luis).*
**Lopez (Lopes),** Luis (Lodovico) (1520-1596): 87, 128, 153
*Lord Darnley (see Stuart, Henry).*
**Loris,** Heinrich (Henricus) "Glarean" ("Glareanus") (1488-1563): 54, 59, 64, 81, 323, 330, 401f., 406, 414, 450
*Lossius, Lucas (see Lotze, Lucas).*
*Lottini, Giovanfrancesco (see Lottini, Giovanni Francesco).*
**Lottini,** Giovanni Francesco (Giovanfrancesco) (1512-1572): 130
**Lotze (Lossius),** Lucas (1508-1582): 189, 276, 287, 290, 592, 612
**Louys (Louis),** Jean (c.1530-1563): 314
*Loyola, Ignatius (see de Loyola, Ignacio).*
**Lucretius Carus,** Titus (c.99BC-c.55BC): 591

**Ludovisi,** Ludovico (Cardinal) (1595-1632): 402
**Lupi,** Didier Second (c.1520-a.1559): 326
*Luther, Katharina (see von Bora, Katharina).*
**Luther,** Martin (1483-1546): xxv, xxviii f., xxxi, 5–7, 11, 16, 19, 27, 29–36, 38f., 66, 69f., 73, 101, 106, 113, 126, 147, 164f., 169–171, 173, 176, 179–184, 186, 188–193, 195, 197, 199, 201–213, 215–218, 220–222, 225, 234, 236–259, 261f., 264–272, 274–286, 288–293, 295–297, 301f., 305, 308–311, 335, 338, 341, 346f., 384–387, 393, 398, 414, 421, 426, 432, 447, 464, 479f., 487, 501, 519, 524f., 527, 532f., 536, 538–540, 546, 549, 551–554, 556, 569f., 574, 585, 588f., 594, 597f., 604f., 609, 611, 614–617, 622, 628, 636–638, 652, 654, 656, 684, 686, 695f., 701f.
**Luzzaschi,** Luzzasco (c.1545-1607): 503

**Machiavelli,** Niccolò (1469-1527): 1, 13
*Madonna Paola da Parma (see Massarenghi, Paola).*
**Madruzzo,** Cristoforo (Cardinal) (1512-1578): 39, 559
**Maffei,** Giovanni Camillo (c.1510-a.1573): 138
*Magdalene (see Mary Magdalene).*
*Mahu, Etienne (see Mahu, Stephan).*
**Mahu,** Stephan (Etienne) (a.1480-a.1541): 266, 581, 622
**Maier,** Johann von Eck (1486-1543): 32
*Maistre Jan (see Maistre Jhan).*
**Maistre Jhan (Jean, Jan)** (c.1485-1538): 471, 557f.
**Malingre,** Matthieu (Thomas) (?-1572): 305, 541
*Malingre, Thomas (see Malingre, Matthieu).*
**Malvezzi,** Elena (1526-1563): 661
*Marbeck, John (see Merbecke, John).*
*Marcellus II (see Cervini degli Spannocchi, Marcello).*
**Marenzio,** Luca (c.1553-1599): 23, 445
**Mareschall** Samuel (1554-1640): 330, 589

*Margaret de Navarre (see de Valois-Angoulême, Marguerite).*
*Margaret of Austria (see von Habsburg, Margarethe).*
*Margaret of France (see de Valois-Angoulême, Marguerite).*
*Margaret of Parma (see Margaretha).*
**Margaretha (Margaret)** *of Parma* (Duchess) (1522-1586): 44
*Marot, Clément (see des Marets, Clément).*
**Marschalk von Pappenheim (von Calde),** Walpurga (?-a.1571): 652
**Martin,** Gregory (c.1542-1582): 78, 122, 456, 466, 657
**Martinengo,** Massimiliano Celso (1515-1557): 307
**Mary** "Magdalene" (St) (?-?): 629 f.
**Mary** *of Bethany* (St) (?-?): 630
*Mary of Hungary (see von Habsburg, Maria).*
**Mary** *of Nazareth* (St) (c.18BC-?): 3, 9, 22, 83, 110 f., 244, 249, 255, 285, 371, 379, 410, 475, 489, 539, 561, 570, 610, 668, 670, 692, 697, 699
*Mary Queen of Scots (see Stuart, Mary).*
**Massarelli,** Angelo (1510-1566): 397
**Massarenghi (Mazzarenghi, Massarengo),** Giovanni Battista (1569-c.1596): 678
**Massarenghi (Mazzarenghi, Massarengo),** Paola "Paola da Parma" (1565-?): 678
*Massarengo, Giovanni Battista (see Massarenghi, Giovanni Battista).*
*Massarengo, Paola (see Massarenghi, Paola).*
**Mathelda** *of Hackerborn* (c.1240-1298): 90
**Mathesius,** Johannes (1504-1565): 182, 192, 212, 273, 278-281
**Mauduit,** Jacques (1557-1627): 563
*Maximilian The Great (see von Wittelsbach, Maximilian I).*
**Mayer,** Sebald (?-a.1576): 406
*Mazzarenghi, Giovanni Battista (see Massarenghi, Giovanni Battista).*
*Mazzarenghi, Paola (see Massarenghi, Paola).*
**Mei,** Girolamo (1519-1594): 24, 63, 89, 92, 160

*Melanchthon, Philip (see Schwarzerdt, Philipp).*
**Melville,** Elizabeth Culross (Lady) (c.1578-c.1640): 649
**Melville,** James (1556-1614): 369, 613
**Mendelssohn Bartholdy,** Felix (1809-1847): 687
*Merbeck, John (see Merbecke, John).*
**Merbecke (Marbeck, Merbeck),** John (c.1510-c.1585): 137, 341-343
*Mercurian, Everard (see Lardinois, Everard).*
**Merisi,** Michelangelo "Caravaggio" (1571-1610): 16
**Merlotti (Merulo),** Claudio (1533-1604): 467
*Merulo, Claudio (see Merlotti, Claudio).*
**Mes,** Gerardus (?-?): 331
**Meyer,** Gregor (c.1510-1576): 330
**Mezari,** Maddalena "Casulana" (c.1544-c.1590): 678 f.
**Miki,** Paul (St) (c.1556-1597): 489
**Moderne (Moderno),** Jacques (Giacomo) (c.1500-1560): 54
*Moderno, Giacomo (see Moderne, Jacques).*
*Molanus, Jan (see van der Meulen, Jan).*
**Moller,** Joachim À Burck (Burgk) (1546-1610): 95, 259, 286, 516
**Montecalvi,** Giulia (?-a.1585): 663, 675
**Monteverdi,** Claudio (1567-1643): 25, 61, 472, 503, 583, 670
**Monteverdi,** Giulio Cesare (1573-c.1630): 61
**Morandi,** Angela (?-?): 663
*Moray, James (see Stewart, James).*
**More,** Thomas (St) (1478-1535): 36, 97
**Morigia,** Paolo (1525-1604): 677
**Morley,** Thomas (c.1557-1602): 152, 369, 373
**Morone (Moroni),** Giovanni (Cardinal) (1509-1580): 42, 127, 135, 383, 398-400, 402, 416
*Moroni, Giovanni (see Morone, Giovanni).*
**Moulu,** Pierre (c.1484-c.1550): 397
**Mouton,** Jean (c.1459-1522): 19, 133, 396 f.
**Mozart,** Wolfgang Amadeus (1756-1791): 687
**Mundy,** John (1555-1630): 362

Mundy, William (1529-1591):   337
Müntzer, Thomas (c.1489-1525):   34, 165, 216–218, 243, 248, 251, 258, 530
*Musculus, Wolfgang (see Müslin, Wolfgang).*
Müslin, Wolfgang "Musculus" (1497-1563):   264, 268

Nadal, Jerome (1507-1580):   533
Nanino, Giovanni Maria (c.1544-1607):   445
Narducci, Domenica dal Paradiso (1473-1553):   666
*Nasco, Giovanni (see Nasco, Jan).*
Nasco, Jan (Giovanni, Jhan) (c.1510-1561):   471
*Nasco, Jhan (see Nasco, Jan).*
*Nausea, Friedrich (see Grau von Waischenfeld, Friedrich).*
Navagero, Bernardo (Cardinal) (1507-1565):   127, 399, 416
Neri, Filippo (Philip) (St) (1515-1595):   31, 430, 458, 471, 490–494, 502, 584, 698
*Neri, Philip (see Neri, Filippo).*
*Nettesheim (see Agrippa von Nettesheim, Heinrich Cornelius).*
*Nolla, Giovanni Domenico (see da Nola, Giovanni Domenico).*
Norton, Thomas (1532-1584):   354
Nowell, Alexander (c.1507-1602):   344

Obrecht, Jacob (c.1457-1505):   107, 613
Ochino, Bernardino (1487-1564):   37–40
*Ockland, Robert (see Okeland, Robert).*
*Oecolampadius, Johannes (see Huschin, Johannes).*
Okeland (Hockland, Ockland), Robert (?-b.1548):   340
Olthof, Statius (1555-1629):   314, 359, 572
*Orange Nassau, Louise Juliana (see van Oranje Nassau, Louise Juliana).*
Ormaneto, Nicolò (c.1515-1577):   501
*Ornitoparchus, Andreas (see Vogelsang, Andreas).*
Osiander, Lucas "The Elder" (1534-1604):   208, 212, 248, 262, 266, 312, 610
*Otello, Gerolamo (see Ottello, Gerolamo).*
Othmayr, Caspar (1515-1553):   21, 240

Ott, Hans (?-1546):   108
Ottello (Otello), Gerolamo (1520-1581):   483
Ottesdotter Rømer, Inger *of Austråt* (c.1475-1555):   648, 683
*Ovid (see Ovidius Naso, Publius).*
Ovidius (Ovid) Naso, Publius (43BC-c.17AD):   168
Oxenbridge Tyrwhit (Tyrwhitt), Elizabeth (Lady) (c.1510-1578):   649

Paleotti, Alfonso (1531-1610):   402
Paleotti, Camillo (1520-1594):   402f.
Paleotti, Gabriele (Cardinal) (1522-1597):   66, 80, 91, 167, 180, 232, 382f., 398, 402–405, 412, 415, 450, 601, 671, 675f.
*Palestrina (see Pierluigi, Giovanni).*
Palladius, Peder (1503-1560):   289
*Paola da Parma (see Massarenghi, Paola).*
*Pappenheim, Walpurga (see Marschalk von Pappenheim, Walpurga).*
Parker, Matthew (1504-1575):   361, 368, 526
Pasquier, Jean (?-?):   327
Pathie, Rogier (c.1510-a.1564):   370
*Paul (see Paulus).*
*Paul III (see Farnese, Alessandro).*
*Paul IV (see Carafa, Gian Pietro).*
*Paul V (see Borghese, Camillo).*
Pauli, Simon "The Elder" (1534-1591):   642
Paulus (Paul) *of Tarsus* (St) (c.5AD-c.67AD):   xii, 70f., 91, 121, 168–170, 188, 195, 200f., 215, 219, 223f., 233, 247, 570, 696
Peacham, Henry "The Younger" (1578-c.1644):   202, 336
Peebles, David (?-c.1579):   viii, 359, 362, 596
Pellegrini, Vincenzo (c.1562-1631):   438
*Pendasio, Federico (see Pendaso, Federico).*
Pendaso (Pendasio), Federico (c.1525-1603):   671
Penick, Peter (Petrus) "Sylvius" (1470-1547):   552
Peretti di Montalto, Felice (Sixtus V) (Pope) (1521-1590):   47, 438
Peri, Jacopo "Zazzerino" (1561-1633):   497
Pesciolini, Biagio (c.1535-1611):   405, 500

**Petrarca (Petrarch),** Francesco (1304-1374):   14, 20, 22, 471, 648
*Petrarch (see Petrarca, Francesco).*
**Petrucci,** Alessandro (c.1560-1628):   660, 665
**Petrucci,** Ottaviano (1466-1539):   18, 95
*Pevernage, Andreas (see Pevernage, Andries).*
**Pevernage,** Andries (Andreas) (c.1542-1591):   321, 581, 620f.
**Pfitzner,** Hans (1869-1949):   422
*Phaello, Giovanni Battista (see Faello, Giovanni Battista).*
*Philip II (see von Habsburg, Philipp II).*
*Philip of Hesse (see von Hesse, Philipp).*
**Piccolomini,** Ascanio I (c.1548-1597):   665
**Piccolomini,** Enea Silvio (Pius II) (Pope) (1405-1464):   29
**Pierluigi,** Giovanni da Palestrina (c.1525-1594):   viii, 64, 120, 183, 383, 394, 396f., 400f., 422–425, 429, 431, 433, 437, 442f., 449-452, 455f., 458, 462–464, 466, 471, 504–507, 509, 515, 621, 687
**Pili,** Giovanni da Fano (1469-1539):   558
**Pipelare,** Matthaeus (c.1450-c.1515):   462
*Pius II (see Piccolomini, Enea Silvio).*
*Pius IV (see de' Medici, Giovanni Angelo).*
*Pius V (see Ghislieri, Antonio Michele).*
**Planson,** Jean (c.1545-a.1612):   473
**Plato** (c.428BC-c.348BC):   10, 14, 60-62, 65, 126, 131, 160f., 168, 218, 220, 222
**Pole,** Reginald (Cardinal) (1500-1558):   38f., 41f., 391, 565
**Ponet (Poynet),** John (c.1514-1556):   365
*Pontio, Pietro (see Ponzio, Pietro).*
**Ponzio (Pontio),** Pietro (1532-1596):   65, 90, 95, 108, 151–153
**Porta,** Costanzo (c.1528-1601):   405, 455, 464, 475, 499f., 621
**Possevino,** Giovanni Battista (c.1552-c.1622):   148, 447
**Posth (Posthius),** Johann (Johannes) (1537-1597):   608
*Posthius, Johannes (see Posth, Johann).*
**Powodowski,** Hieronim (1543-1613):   609
*Poynet, John (see Ponet, John).*

*Praetorius, Michael (see Schultheiß, Michael).*
*Propertius (see Aurelius Propertius, Sextus).*
**Prudentius Clemens,** Aurelius (348-413):   642
**Prynne,** William (1600-1669):   130
**Pussot,** Jean (1568-1626):   535
*Puteanus, Ericius (see van der Putten, Hendrik).*

*Quintilian (see Fabius Quintilianus, Marcus).*
*Quintilianus (see Fabius Quintilianus, Marcus).*
**Quirini (Querini),** Vincenzo (Pietro) (1478-1514):   122, 421

**Rabelais,** François (c.1490-1553):   15
*Ractius, Serafino (see Razzi, Serafino).*
*Ragasanus, Hieronymus (see Ragazzoni, Gerolamo).*
**Ragazzoni (Ragasanus),** Gerolamo (Hieronymus) (1537-1592):   127, 399, 419
*Raphael (see Sanzio, Raffaello).*
**Rathgeb,** Jacob (1578-1614):   375
**Rauscher,** Andreas (?-a.1535):   641
**Razzi (Ractius),** Serafino (1531-1613):   470, 661f.
**Regnart,** Jacob (c.1540-1599):   538
**Remen,** Marigen (?-?):   674
*Renée of Bavaria (see de Lorraine of Bavaria, Renée).*
*Renée of France (see de Valois-Orléans, Renée).*
*Resinarius, Balthasar (see Harzer, Balthasar).*
**Rhau (Rhaw),** Georg (1488-1548):   203, 266, 288, 585, 592, 613–615, 622
*Rhaw, Georg (see Rhau, Georg).*
**Rhodes,** John (?-a.1606):   364
*Ribault, Jean (see Ribaut, Jean).*
**Ribaut (Ribault),** Jean (1520-1565):   319f.
**Ricci,** Matteo (1552-1610):   39
**Ricciarelli,** Daniele da Volterra, "il Braghettone" (c.1509-c.1566):   158
*Ricciutello (see Agresti, Livio).*
**Richafort,** Jean (c.1480-c.1547):   21, 133, 397
*Ritius (see Agresti, Livio).*

Roberts, Thomas (?-a.1583): 364, 368, 370, 591f.
Roh (Horn), Jan (Johann) (c.1490-1547): 296
Rømer, Inger (see Ottesdotter Rømer, Inger).
Rosselli, Francesco (see Roussel, François).
Rossetto (Rossetti), Biagio (c.1470-c.1547): 77, 139, 148, 151, 176, 201, 391, 411
Roussel, Gérard (c.1500-a.1555): 304, 646f.
Roussel (Rosselli), François (Francesco) (c.1510-a.1577): 401
Rovigo, Francesco (c.1540-1597): 511
Rucellai, Annibale (?-1601): 423
Ruffo, Vincenzo (c.1508-1587): 78, 81, 99, 142, 286, 405, 424, 433, 455, 460, 464, 471, 500f., 505, 515
Rupsch, Conrad (c.1475-c.1530): 248, 259

Sachs, Hans (1494-1576): 255f.
Sadler, John (1513-1596): 380
Sadoleto, Jacopo (Cardinal) (1477-1547): 61, 99, 127, 131, 143
Saftleven, Cornelis (1607-1681): 143
Salvatore da Modena (see Essenga, Salvadore).
Sanchez de Avila, Díaz "Thomas à Jesu" (1564-1627): 274
Sanudo (Sanuto), Marino "The Younger" (1466-1536): 145, 659
Sanuto, Marino (see Sanudo, Marino).
Sanzio, Raffaello (Raphael) (1483-1520): 15
Saul (King) (c.1080BC-c.1010BC): 169, 193, 200
Saunier, Adam (see Saunier, Antoine).
Saunier, Antoine (Adam) "Almeutes" (?-a.1547): 598
Savonarola, Girolamo (1452-1498): 30f., 71, 110, 120, 136, 141, 147, 430, 470, 492f., 622, 661f.
Scandelli, Antonio (see Scandello, Antonio).
Scandello (Scandellus, Scandelli), Antonio (Antonius) (1517-1580): 286
Scandellus, Antonius (see Scandello, Antonio).
Schilders, Richard (c.1538-c.1634): 362

Schultheiß, Michael "Praetorius" (1571-1621): 621
Schütz Zell, Katharina (c.1497-1562): 625, 643f.
Schuyt, Cornelis (1557-1616): 313
Schwarzerdt, Philipp (Philip) "Melanchthon" (1497-1560): 32, 36, 39, 46, 113, 187, 189, 275f., 289, 398, 555, 587, 592, 641
Schwebel, Johann (1490-1540): 243
Schweher, Kryštof (Christoph) "Hecyrus" (c.1520-1593): 606f.
Scifi, Chiara (Claire) of Assisi (St) (c.1194-1253): 90
Seager (Segar), Francis (?-1563): 360
Second, Didier (see Lupi, Didier).
Selneccer, Nikolaus (see Selnecker, Nikolaus).
Selnecker (Selneccer), Nikolaus (1530-1592): 211, 254
Seneca, Antonio (1542-1626): 148, 657–659, 664
Senfl, Ludwig (see Sennfl, Ludwig).
Sennfl (Senfl), Ludwig (c.1486-c.1543): 21, 205, 239, 266, 577, 581, 615, 622
Servetus, Michael (c.1509-1553): 14, 41
Servin, Jean (c.1529-1609): 322f., 359, 572
Sessa, Claudia (c.1570-c.1619): 627, 670
Seymour, Jane (Queen consort) (c.1508-1537): 37
Shakespeare, William (1564-1616): 15
Shepherd, John (see Sheppard, John).
Sheppard (Shepherd), John (1515-1558): 337, 360, 370
Sherrington Mildmay, Grace (Lady) (c.1552-1620): 683
Sherwin, Raphe (see Sherwin, Ralph).
Sherwin, Ralph (Raphe) (St) (1550-1581): 565
Sidney Herbert, Mary of Pembroke (Countess) (1561-1621): 649
Singleton, Hugh (?-c.1593): 352
Sirleto, Guglielmo (Cardinal) (1514-1585): 88, 118, 153, 178
Sixtus IV (see della Rovere, Francesco).
Sixtus V (see Peretti di Montalto, Felice).

Slüter, Joachim (c.1490-1532): 289, 347
Smith, Alexander (?-a.1574): 613
Solomon (King) (c.1011BC-c.931BC): 199
Somenza, Corona (c.1530-1609): 677
Sonnius, Franciscus (see van de Velde, Franciscus).
Soranzo, Vittore (1500-1558): 178
Sore, Martin "Agricola" (1486-1556): 266
Soriano, Francesco (c.1548-1621): 451f., 462
Soto de Langa, Francisco (c.1534-1619): 493f.
Southwell, Robert (St) (c.1561-1595): 565
Spalatin, Georg (see Burkhardt, Georg).
Spangenberg, Cyriacus (1528-1604): 194, 278
Spangenberg, Johann (1484-1550): 241, 266
Spengler, Lazarus (1479-1534): 254, 278, 617
Speratus, Paul (1484-1551): 247, 254
Speth, Andreas (see Spethe, Andreas).
Spethe (Speth), Andreas (?-?): 314
St Ambrose (see Ambrosius).
St Augustine (see Augustinus).
St Basil (see Basilius).
St Benno (see Benno).
St Bonaventure (see Bonaventura).
St Claire (see Scifi, Chiara).
St Dominic (see Domingo).
St Francis (see Francesco).
St Isidore (see Isidorus).
St Jerome (see Hieronymus, Eusebius Sophronius).
St John Chrysostom (see Ioannes).
St John of Avila (see Juan).
St Paul (see Paulus).
Sternhold, Thomas (1500-1549): 349–352, 354f., 360, 589, 649
Stewart, James Earl of Moray (Lord) (c.1531-1570): 362
Stoltzer, Thomas (c.1480-1526): 262f., 266, 622
Strigenitz, Gregor (1548-1603): 641
Strozzi, Lorenza (c.1516-1591): 671f.
Stuart, Henry (Lord Darnley) (King consort) (1545-1567): 43

Stuart, James VI and I (King) (1566-1625): 43, 301, 359, 362f.
Stuart, Mary "Queen of Scots" (Queen) (1542-1587): 43, 47, 359, 362, 546
Stubbes (Stubbs), Philip (c.1555-c.1610): 129f., 393
Sturm (Sturmius), Johannes (Ioannes) (1507-1589): 588
Sturmius, Joannes (see Sturm, Johannes).
Sulpitia, Claudia (?-a.1575): 662
Sulzer, Simon (1508-1585): 330
Surgant, Johann Ulrich (c.1450-1503): 215
Susato, Tielman (c.1510-a.1570): 183, 192, 331
Suster Bertken (see Jacobs, Berta).
Sweelinck, Jan Pieterszoon (1562-1621): 313f.
Swibberts, Peter (see Swybbertszoon, Peter).
Swybbertszoon (Swibberts), Peter (c.1535-1573): 313
Sylvius, Petrus (see Penick, Peter).

Tallis, Thomas (c.1505-1585): viii, 337, 360f., 370f., 373, 377–379, 564, 687
Tansillo, Luigi (1510-1568): 472, 517
Tasso, Torquato (1544-1595): 14, 22
Taverner, John (1490-1545): 138, 336, 340, 687
Tech (Decius), Nikolaus (c.1485-a.1546): 249
Teellinck, Cornelia (see Eeuwouts Tellinck Limmens, Cornelia)
Teellinck, Suzanna (see Eeuwouts Tellinck Hoffer, Suzanna).
Teniers, David "The Younger" (1610-1690): 143
Theotokópoulos, Doménikos "El Greco" (1541-1614): 16
Thomas à Jesu (see Sanchez de Avila, Díaz).
Thomas à Kempis (see Haemerkken, Thomas).
Thomissøn, Hans (1532-1573): 289
Thorn, Lambert (Lampertus) (?-c.1528): 527
Thorn, Lampertus (see Thorn, Lambert).
Tibullus, Albius (c.55BC-19BC): 168
Tinctoris, Johannes (c.1435-1511): 63, 144f.

**Tinelli,** Ercole (?-a.1593): 150, 659
*Tintoretto (see Comin Robusti, Jacopo).*
**Tirs,** Catherina (?-1604): 673
*Titian (see Vecellio, Tiziano).*
**Tomkins,** Thomas (1572-1656): 373
**Tornabuoni de' Medici,** Lucrezia (1425-1482): 661
**Treybenreif,** Peter (Petrus) "Tritonius", "Athesinus" (1465-c.1525): 95
*Tritonius, Petrus (see Treybenreif, Peter).*
**Trombetti,** Ascanio (1544-1590): 86
**Tromboncino,** Bartolomeo (c.1470-c.1535): 20
**Truchsess von Waldburg,** Otto (Cardinal) (1514-1573): 383, 398, 400–402, 405f., 460, 515
**Tuccio,** Stefano (1540-1597): 99
**Tudor,** Edward VI (King) (1537-1553): 40f., 173, 227, 338, 343, 348–350, 589
**Tudor,** Elizabeth I (Queen) (1533-1603): 42f., 45, 47, 173, 228, 336, 344–346, 354f., 357, 363–365, 375f., 378f., 381, 574, 601, 634
**Tudor,** Henry VIII (King) (1491-1547): 33, 36, 38, 40, 335–337, 342f., 347–350, 378
**Tudor,** Mary I (Queen) (1516-1558): 36, 41f., 313, 342, 344, 351, 406
**Tye,** Christopher (c.1505-b.1573): 336f., 340, 369, 378, 564
**Tyndale,** William (c.1494-1536): 37
*Tyrwhit, Elizabeth (see Oxenbridge Tyrwhit, Elizabeth).*

*Ulenberg, Caspar (see Ulenberg, Kaspar).*
**Ulenberg,** Kaspar (Caspar) (1549-1617): 516, 581, 609f.
**Utenhove,** Jan (c.1516-1566): 313, 332, 528

**Valerius Catullus,** Gaius (c.84BC-c.54BC): 168
**Valéry,** Magdaleine (Magdeleine) (?-a.1599?): 600
*Valéry, Magdeleine (see Valéry, Magdaleine).*
**Valla,** Lorenzo (c.1405-1457): 83
**Vallick,** Jacob (c.1515-a.1571): 595, 599

*van Aken, Janneken (see van Houtte, Janneken).*
*van Campen, John (see van Campen, Jan).*
**van Campen (Campensis),** Jan (Johannes, John) (c.1491-1538): 347
**van de Velde,** Franciscus "Sonnius" (c.1506-1576): 595f.
**van der Meulen (Molanus),** Jan (1533-1585): 80
**van der Putten (Puteanus),** Hendrik (Ericius) (1574-1646): 503, 583
**van Essen (Esch),** Jan (Johannes) (?-1523): 527
*van Heemskerck, Maarten (see van Veen, Maarten).*
**van Houtte,** Janneken *van Aken* (?-1557): 652
**van Kessel,** Ferdinand (c.1648-c.1696): 143
**van Marnix,** Filips *van Sint Aldegonde* (Lord) (1540-1598): 523
**van Nassau (van Oranje, Orange Nassau),** Willem (William) I "The Silent" (Prince) (1533-1584): 44, 46, 634
*van Nijevelt, Willem (see van Nyewelt, Willem).*
**van Nyewelt (Nijevelt),** Willem (?-1543): 330
**van Oranje (Orange) Nassau,** Louise Juliana (Countess) (1576-1644): 634, 645, 648, 683
*van Sint Aldegonde, Filips (see van Marnix, Filips).*
**van Soldt,** Susanne (c.1587-c.1615): 683
**van Turnhout,** Gerardus (c.1520-1580): 314, 582
**van Vaernewijck,** Marcus (1518-1569): 318, 534
**van Veen,** Maarten *van Heemskerck* (1498-1574): 331
**van Wesel (Vesalius),** Andries (Andreas) (1514-1564): 14
**van Wilder,** Philippe (c.1500-1554): 370
**Vasa,** Gustav I (King) (1496-1560): 35
**Vaughan-Williams,** Ralph (1872-1958): 687
**Vecchi,** Orazio (1550-1605): 23, 445, 678
**Vecellio,** Tiziano (Titian) (c.1490-1576): 15f.

Vehe, Michael (1485-1539): 599, 603-606, 609-611, 617
Velpius, Rutgeert (Rutgerus, Rutger) (c.1540-c.1614): 596
*Velpius, Rutger (see Velpius, Rutgeert).*
*Venosa, Carlo (see Gesualdo, Carlo).*
Verdelot, Philippe (c.1480-c.1532): 22
Vergelius (Virgil) Maro, Publius (70BC-19BC): 168
*Vermigli, Peter Martyr (see Vermigli, Pietro Martire).*
Vermigli, Pietro Martire (Peter Martyr) (1499-1562): 38, 40, 169, 185, 187, 190, 196, 201, 295, 338, 368
*Veronese (see Caliari, Paolo).*
*Vesalius, Andreas (see van Wesel, Andries).*
*Viadana, Lodovico (see Grossi, Lodovico).*
Vicentino, Nicola (1511-c.1576): 22, 59f., 62f., 150, 177, 501, 622
Viret, Pierre (c.1511-1571): 174f., 201
*Virgil (see Vergelius Maro, Publius).*
*Virgin Mary (see Mary of Nazareth).*
Vitelli, Vitellozzo (Cardinal) (1531-1568): 383, 398, 400, 460f., 467
Vives, Juan Luis (1492-1540): 151, 664
*Voes, Heinrich (see Vos, Hendrik).*
Vogelsang, Andreas "Ornitoparchus" (c.1490-a.1520): 144
von Anhalt, Margaretha (Princess) (1473-1530): 680, 683
von Bernhausen, Anna (c.1553-?): 585
von Bora Luther, Katharina (1499-1552): 34
von Brandenburg, Albrecht (Albert) (Cardinal) (1490-1545): 31
von Braunschweig-Calenberg-Göttingen, Anna Maria (1532-1568): 642
von Bruck, Arnold (c.1500-1554): 266, 581, 615, 622
*von Calde, Walpurga (see Marschalk von Pappenheim, Walpurga).*
*von Eberstein, Sybille (see von Everstein, Sybille).*
*von Eck, Johann (see Maier, Johann).*
von Everstein (Eberstein) Fugger, Sybille (c.1531-1589): 585
von Fabris (de Fabris), Melchior (?-?): 476f.

*von Giersberg, Ambrosius (see Blarer, Ambrosius).*
von Habsburg, Albrecht (Albert) VII *of Austria* (Archduke) (1559-1621): 670
von Habsburg, Ferdinand I (Emperor) (1503-1564): 41f., 127, 383, 400, 410, 416f., 422
von Habsburg, Isabella Clara Eugenia (Archduchess) (1566-1633): 670
von Habsburg, Karl (Charles) V (Emperor) (1500-1558): 32, 35, 40-42, 303, 554, 560
von Habsburg, Margaret (Margarethe) "Margaret of Austria" (Duchess) (1480-1530): 634
von Habsburg, Margarethe (Margaret) "Margaret of Austria, Queen of Spain" (Queen) (1584-1611): 670
von Habsburg, Maria *of Hungary* (Queen consort) (1505-1558): 622, 634
von Habsburg, Philipp (Philip) II (King) (1527-1598): 41f., 44, 514
von Habsburg, Rudolf II (Emperor) (1552-1612): 529
von Hesse, Philipp (Philip) I (Landgrave) (1504-1567): 35
von Hohenzollern, Elisabeth *von Braunschweig-Lüneburg, von Brandenburg* (Duchess) (1510-1558): 634, 642
von Hohenzollern, Amalie (1557-1603): 656
*von Karlstadt (see Bodenstein, Andreas).*
von Meseritz Cruciger, Elisabeth (c.1500-1535): 266, 640-642
*von Themar, Johannes (see Haym, Johannes).*
von Wettin, Friedrich (Frederick) III *von Sachsen (of Saxony)* "The Wise" (Elector) (1463-1525): 32f., 238, 248
von Wittelsbach, Albrecht (Albert) V (Duke) (1528-1579): 524
von Wittelsbach, Friedrich (Frederick) III (Elector) (1515-1576): 317
von Wittelsbach, Maximilian I "The Great" (Elector) (1573-1651): 283
von Wittelsbach-Simmern, Friedrich (Frederick) IV (Elector) (1574-1610): 634
von Wittelsbach, Wilhelm (William) V (Duke) (1548-1626): 516, 678

**von Württemberg,** Friedrich (Frederick) I (Duke) (1557-1608): 375
**von Zütphen,** Heinrich (c.1488-1524): 258, 527
**Vos (Voes),** Hendrik (Heinrich) (?-1523): 527

**Wagner,** Richard (1813-1883): 138
**Walasser,** Adam (c.1520-1581): 609
*Waldburg, Otto (see Truchsess von Waldburg, Otto).*
**Waldis,** Burkhard (c.1490-1556): 312
**Waldo,** Peter (c.1140-c.1205): 702
**Walpole,** Henry (St) (1558-1595): 528
*Walter, Johann (see Walther, Johann).*
**Walther (Walter),** Johann (1496-1570): 173, 188, 192, 203, 212, 236, 248, 259f., 266, 269, 286, 297, 309, 570, 597, 617, 641
**Wedderburn,** James (c.1495-1553): 349
**Wedderburn,** John (c.1505-c.1553): 349, 642
**Wedderburn,** Robert (c.1510-c.1555): 349
**Weisse,** Michael (c.1488-1534): 254, 296f., 643
**Weston,** William (1550-1615): 565
**Whitbroke,** William (c.1501-1569): 340
**Whittingham,** William (c.1524-1579): 352f.
*Wicelius, Georg (see Witzel, Georg).*
**Wilde,** Mechthild (?-1535): 654
**Willaert,** Adrian (c.1490-1562): 22, 96, 115, 133, 455, 457, 471, 508, 622
**Willaert,** Caterina (?-?): 679
*William of Orange (see van Nassau, Willem).*
*William V (see von Wittelsbach, Wilhelm V).*
*Wissenburg, Wolfgang (see Wissenburger, Wolfgang).*

**Wissenburger (Wissenburg),** Wolfgang (c.1494-1575): 243
**Wither,** George (1588-1667): 546
**Wittweiler,** Johann Georg (c.1556-1633): 485
**Witzel (Wicelius),** Georg (1501-1573): 609
**Wode (Wood),** Thomas (?-1592): vii-ix, 362
**Wojtyła,** Karol (John Paul II) (Pope) (1920-2005): 685
**Wolfe,** John (c.1548-1601): 361
*Wood, Thomas (see Wode, Thomas).*
**Wyatt,** Thomas (1503-1542): 349f.
**Wycliffe,** John (c.1331-1384): 30, 697
**Wyss,** Bernhard (1463-1531): 212

**Xavier,** Francis (St) (1506-1552): 39, 595

**Zacconi,** Lodovico (1555-1627): 140
**Zarlino,** Gioseffo (1517-1590): 60f., 63, 65, 76, 115f., 140f., 143, 149f., 152f., 169, 184f., 323f., 448f., 572
*Zazzerino (see Peri, Jacopo).*
**Zell,** Mathias (Matthäus) (1477-1548): 34, 38, 643f.
**Zibramonti,** Aurelio (?-1589): 510
**Zili,** Dominik (1494-1571): 328
**Zoilo,** Annibale (c.1537-1592): 423, 429, 449–451, 509
**Zoilo,** Giovanni Domenico (c.1531-1576): 423
**Zwick,** Johannes (c.1496-1542): 328f.
**Zwingli,** Huldrych (Ulrich) (1484-1531): 33, 36, 38, 165, 169f., 175f., 178–180, 196, 200, 212–216, 222, 225, 227, 241, 291, 304, 328f., 347, 398f., 426
*Zwingli, Ulrich (see Zwingli, Huldrych).*

# Index of Subjects

Within the following Index of Subjects, there are main subjects (e.g. "Worship") and secondary subjects which depend on the former (e.g. "Anglican [worship]"). The secondary subjects are indented and follow the main subjects. In the case of synonyms, page occurrences are indicated only once, but the synonym is referenced. Thus: "Re-Baptism" is found as a secondary subject under "Baptism", but page occurrences are found under "Anabaptism". In this case, readers will find an arrow directing them to the main entry, and the entire line will be printed in italics:
*Re-Baptism → Anabaptism.*
When two or more subjects are not synonyms, but are strictly related with each other, readers will find a reference, indicated with an asterisk and in italics, after the listing of page occurrences:
Ex opere operato   9, 233, 386, 481 *Sacraments.*
In both cases, secondary subjects are listed under their main subject followed by a vertical slash (|):

→ *Jewish | Cantillation*
\**Jewish | Cantillation*


Act of Supremacy   37, 42, 336f.
Adiaphora   71, 181, 195f., 200, 384, 690, 696
Advent
– As a period of the liturgical year   249, 697
– As the Kingdom's coming   34, 197–199, 275, 280, 542, 640, 690, 694
Aesthetics   xxviii, 15–20, 50–53, 59, 61, 68, 71f., 76, 81, 84–102, 111, 117, 119, 123, 138–141, 169, 187, 196, 260f., 284, 287, 300, 307, 310, 312, 324, 327, 341f., 345, 350, 353, 363, 374, 383, 385, 388f., 402, 407, 412, 427f., 430, 443, 449–454, 457, 459, 461f., 464, 468, 481f., 498–501, 505–507, 513, 517, 569, 574, 580f., 603, 620, 623, 658, 685, 690, 693
Affaire des Placards   37, 303, 557
Affects   50, 57–59, 61–64, 75–78, 89, 94, 96–98, 109f., 123, 126, 133, 156–160, 163, 168, 187, 190, 204, 206, 211, 220, 223, 227, 260, 263, 283, 324, 388, 393, 404, 406, 423f., 427, 439, 454, 468, 472, 480–482, 512, 515, 583, 596 *Imitation | Imitation of affects, *Passion | Human passions*
Agnus Dei   157, 243, 247, 249, 339, 343, 377, 697 *Ordinarium Missæ*
Alternatim   118f., 173, 199, 249, 264, 272, 393, 448, 690
Alumbrados   30
Amboise (Conspiracy of)   43, 546
Ambrosian   *Milan*
– Church   71, 127, 139, 394, 430f., 438, 440, 497, 500–503, 583, 662–664, 670, 676f., 690
– Hymns   71, 250, 288
– Rites   690
America   28, 319f., 442, 474, 490, 526
– Latin   28, 442, 474, 490
– Northern   319f.
Anabaptism   523, 527f.
– Martyrs   33, 36, 527, 650–652 *Martyrdom, *Songs | Of martyrdom*
– Poets/Authors   650–652, 680
– Theology   9, 33, 386, 690
Anthems   viii, 334, 339, 343, 370, 372f., 377f. *Worship | Anglican*

Animal cries   130 f., 141–145, 159, 162, 411, 542 *Birdsong*
Antichrist   198, 520, 542 f., 547, 551 *Apocalyptic perspectives*
Anticlericalism   29, 523, 538, 551, 617 *Clergy*
Antiphonal style   118, 214, 250, 286, 374, 456, 639, 660, 690, 697, 700
Antiphons   110, 239 f., 249, 251, 290, 371, 378, 450, 690, 700
Apocalyptic perspectives   34, 197 f., 275, 366, 542 f., 636, 640, 642, 690 *Antichrist*
*Apologia* → Augsburg | Apology
Architecture   16, 82, 98, 159, 172, 233, 327, 430, 459, 481, 485, 657
Aristocracy   19, 23, 26, 42 f., 52 f., 136, 141, 155, 303, 326, 359, 371, 398, 430 f., 499, 508, 557–559, 582, 627 f., 633 f., 636, 640, 644, 654, 656, 664, 669 f., 672, 676–678, 680
Ars perfecta   19 f., 261, 515
Ascension   179, 250, 288, 489
Asia   28, 39, 421, 469, 489 f., 508, 525
Assumption   489, 535
Augsburg   26, 32, 36, 40 f., 44, 266, 295, 400 f., 443, 521, 530, 548, 554, 556, 560, 577, 582, 599, 609, 622
– Apology   113, 187, 189
– Confession (Confessio Augustana)   36, 38, 41, 113, 189, 208, 234, 290
– Diet (1530)   36, 577
– Interim (1548)   40, 521, 530, 554–556, 567, 577
– Peace (1555)   41, 44
Augustinian
– Monks/Nuns   31, 34, 38, 69, 106, 170, 180 f., 248, 258, 346, 413, 527, 537, 656, 660, 667, 685, 690
– Perspective   90, 171, 181, 211, 220, 690
– Rule   656, 673, 690
Authorship   58, 256, 633, 638, 640–642, 655, 674
Ave Maria   246, 266, 331, 535, 564, 595, 615

Balletti   24, 255
Baptism   4, 7, 9, 230, 565, 690, 699 f.
– Infant baptism   9, 33, 386, 690
– Re-Baptism → Anabaptism
Baroque   xxviii, 15, 25, 62, 86, 389, 404, 454, 457, 472, 481, 485, 621
Basel   37, 214, 219, 243, 299, 304, 328–330, 542, 552, 561, 589 f.
– Council → Councils and Synods | Basel (1431–49)
Battles
– Kappel (1531)   36, 213
– Lepanto (1571)   28, 45, 47
– Mohács (1526)   28, 35
– Mühlberg (1547)   40, 554
– Pavia (1525)   34, 254, 617
Bells   51, 179, 376, 534 f., 593, 653 f.
Benedictines   viii, 472, 654, 690
Bestiality   128, 130 f., 140, 142 f. *Animal cries, *Dehumanisation*
Beauty   xxix, 15, 48, 69, 71 f., 77, 79–81, 91, 116, 119, 154, 167, 177, 180, 182, 184, 204, 206–208, 210, 212, 225, 230, 233 f., 250, 261 f., 279, 292 f., 297, 300, 302, 345, 360, 378, 389, 396, 403, 412, 450 f., 462, 482, 485, 508, 510 f., 513 f., 520, 532 f., 546, 500, 565, 572 f., 583, 586, 589, 601, 614 f., 619, 622–624, 627, 641, 647 f., 655, 657, 659, 665, 670, 677, 686–689
Bible   4, 6–9, 11, 17, 31 f., 37, 50, 66, 70, 80, 84, 88, 104, 109–111, 122, 131 f., 147 f., 164, 166–169, 171 f., 174, 178, 181, 184 f., 187, 193, 195–199, 202, 204, 206, 208, 214, 220 f., 223 f., 227, 230, 234 f., 241 f., 244–247, 249–253, 278, 291–294, 300–303, 305, 307, 318, 320, 324, 326, 331, 344, 346–348, 351, 355 f., 369 f., 371, 373, 378, 386 f., 389, 392, 410, 414, 418, 426, 468, 472, 475, 492, 523, 525–527, 540, 542, 545 f., 548, 555, 565, 570 f., 592, 605, 607, 615 f., 621, 637–643, 645 f., 649–651, 668, 691, 694, 698, 700–

702 *Scripture, *Sola Scriptura, *Typological reading
– Interpretation   4, 6, 109, 117, 166 f., 169, 197 f., 202, 204, 208, 224, 233, 278, 301 f., 307, 353, 356, 359, 386, 392, 468, 492, 520, 546, 565, 570, 608, 617, 694, 701 f.
– Liturgy/worship and Bible   8, 70–72, 88, 109, 121 f., 147, 166 f., 169–171, 174 f., 185, 188, 195 f., 199–202, 204, 206, 208 f., 214 f., 219, 220 f., 223–225, 230 f., 233 f., 242, 244–247, 249–253, 270, 291–294, 299, 301, 305, 315, 344, 346–360, 363, 373, 410, 418, 435, 579–581, 608, 621, 639, 649, 651, 654, 668, 681, 683, 698, 700
– Musical instruments in the Bible   66, 71 f., 87 f., 169 f., 196, 199–202, 223, 323, 571 *Instrumental music
– Printing   53 f., 284, 308, 356
– Translations   11, 32, 37, 66, 167, 252, 284, 300–302, 305–307, 331, 346–350, 516, 520, 532, 544–547, 579, 605, 610 f., 622, 644, 701 f. *Metrics | Metrical Psalters, *Psalmody | In the vernacular, *Septuagint, *Vulgate
Birdsong   21, 129, 131 f.
Bohemian Brethren   30 f., 165, 218, 238, 253 f., 278, 295–297, 329, 465, 610, 643, 696 *Hussites, *Hymnbooks | Hussite, *Utraquists, *Worship | Bohemian Brethren
Bologna   40, 66, 155, 402, 409, 551, 655, 657, 663, 671 f., 675 f.
Book-burning   523 f.
Book of Common Prayer   40, 173, 245, 333, 339–346, 351 f.
Brethren of Common Life   30, 673 f. *Devotio Moderna
Breviary   338, 348, 410, 420, 429, 435, 446–448, 509, 516, 691 *Office of the Hours
Broadsheets   247, 258, 265, 284, 348 f., 364 f., 520, 525, 530 f.

Calendar Reform   46, 521, 556, 560, 695
Cameratas   24, 63 *Intermedi, *Opera

Canticles   viii, 70, 110, 117, 205, 234, 245, 248, 251, 303, 305–308, 322, 330, 343, 345, 350, 352, 354, 360, 362, 368, 372, 374, 377, 417, 476, 478, 600, 607, 610, 690 f., 694, 698, 700 *Magnificat, *Office of the Hours
Cantional style   261 f., 269, 272, 312, 315, 330, 332, 543, 610, 691 f., 701
Canzona   25
Capuchins   37, 558, 698
Cardinals' Commission   430, 459–461, 470, 500 f.
Carmelites   274, 547, 551, 630
Carols   111 f., 254, 368, 469, 680
Catechism   35, 39, 45, 166, 187–189, 207, 219, 246, 277 f., 291, 316, 364, 368, 420, 468, 485, 489, 532, 561, 567, 581 f., 590–598, 600, 619, 632, 638, 643, 677, 692 *Metrics | Metrical Catechisms, *Songs | Catechism songs
– Anglican   364, 368, 591, 598
– Catholic   39, 416, 420, 430, 468, 485 f., 489, 532, 592–594, 596–598, 600, 609, 619
– Lutheran   35, 206 f., 237, 246, 257, 274, 277 f., 588, 597 f.
– Reformed   316, 359, 598
– Strasbourg   219, 291, 598
Celibacy/Clerical marriage   7, 33–35, 40, 230, 394, 437, 538, 612, 653 *Clergy | Married, *Priesthood | Ordained
Chanson   21, 25, 101, 108, 133, 157, 161, 177, 303, 305, 322, 326 f., 330, 507, 540, 559, 619
– Chanson spirituelle   63, 98, 305, 326 f., 371, 473, 541, 559, 618 f., 644
Chansonnier Huguenot → Hymnbooks | Huguenot
Chapels   viii, 105, 132, 140–142, 201, 238, 285, 308, 317, 325, 341, 376, 383, 394–398, 400 f., 431, 437, 443, 449, 455, 460, 466, 498 f., 501, 504 f., 507, 509, 514, 529, 558 f., 633, 634 f., 692, 697
– English Royal   145, 202, 228, 337, 339, 371 f., 375, 378 f., 634
– Giulia   395–397, 449, 461 f., 504, 663, 675

- *Sistine* → *Sistine Chapel | Choir*
Children   xxviii, 7, 9, 124, 129f., 151, 198, 218, 267, 272, 274, 277–280, 283, 291, 306, 311, 316, 329, 345, 364, 367–369, 386, 416, 437, 470, 489f., 499, 525, 538, 561, 587–591, 593–595, 597–600, 607, 632, 636–638, 643, 647, 664, 682, 685, 688, 692 *Education, *Pedagogy, *Schoolchildren
Choirbooks   145, 481, 692
Chorales   172, 247–249, 254–265, 267, 269f., 272, 278–284, 288–290, 294, 309f., 312, 330, 444, 447, 450, 465, 543, 575, 609–611, 618, 681, 686f., 691f.
Christmas   51, 105, 112, 249–251, 253f., 282f., 442, 469, 474, 551, 617, 642, 668, 675, 680
Church Fathers   6, 11, 50, 66–68, 71, 84, 87f., 123, 125, 157, 168, 170f., 176f., 204, 228, 252, 324, 392, 398, 413, 440, 591f., 692, 699
Clergy   xxviii, 7f., 29f., 33, 53, 70, 103, 119–121, 135, 152, 154, 175, 232, 245, 274f., 279–282, 285, 344, 346, 353, 386f., 394f., 402, 410, 415, 418f., 430, 436, 441f., 476, 481, 495, 498–500, 502, 537f., 540, 551, 585, 603, 612, 700 *Anticlericalism, *Priesthood | Ordained
- Formation   30, 39, 121, 275, 386, 408, 417, 429, 436–438, 486, 499, 505 *Seminaries
- Married   7, 33f., 40, 612, 643, 667 *Celibacy/Clerical marriage
- Morality   29, 39, 55f., 130, 134f., 154, 162, 386f., 391, 393–395, 415, 436f., 441, 481, 491, 500, 502, 551
Communion   vi, xxix, 8, 30, 33, 40, 67, 148, 173, 181, 185f., 213, 231, 263, 274, 281, 290, 317, 340, 343, 364, 370, 377, 386, 476, 479, 491, 566–568, 572f., 586, 612, 616, 624, 658, 692–694, 700f. *Eucharist
- Among Churches   386, 566–568, 572f., 616, 624, 692 *Ecumenism
- As a moment of worship   263, 364, 377, 658

- Under both kinds   8, 30, 33, 40, 612 *Utraquists
- Within the Church   67, 148, 173, 181, 185, 186, 274, 281, 317, 381, 388, 476, 479, 491, 568, 586, 693 *Love | Of the faithful for one another, *Music | Creates communion
Compline   239f., 305f., 338, 690, 693 *Office of the Hours
- And death   239f., 305f. *Death
Concertato   25, 86, 260, 264, 377, 493, 508, 658, 693
Conciliarism   29
*Confessio Augustana* → *Augsburg | Confession (Confessio Augustana)*
Confessionalisation   xxx, 44, 173, 273, 519, 521–525, 543, 545f., 548–553, 562, 566f., 576, 607, 612, 619 *Music | And confessionalisation
*Confession of Magdeburg* → *Magdeburg | Confession*
Confessio Tetrapolitana   38
Confraternities   55f., 110, 253, 429, 431, 435, 470, 475, 477f., 480, 495–497, 504, 581, 598, 695
Congregational singing   51, 113, 173, 184f., 189, 199, 207, 209, 214, 217, 220, 231, 237, 241, 244, 248, 261f., 264, 268–273, 287, 291–295, 304, 315, 328f., 349, 355–357, 372, 399, 421, 470, 479, 532, 536, 560f., 603, 607, 609, 636, 638, 643, 646f., 649
Consecration   7f., 88, 118, 201, 691, 694, 701 *Elevation, *Real Presence, *Transubstantiation
Constance   93, 119, 150, 153, 328f., 439f.
- Synod → *Councils and Synods | Constance (1567)*
Continuo   25, 86, 454, 693 *Monody | Accompanied
Contrafacta   247, 309, 324f., 327, 365, 370, 472f., 476, 486f., 520, 523, 539, 542, 548–552, 555, 566, 577f., 598f., 611, 615, 624, 633, 638, 652, 693
- From Latin into vernacular   248, 340f., 577f.

Index of Subjects —— 821

- From secular into sacred    105, 112, 248, 254–256, 281, 321, 327 f., 331, 370, 470–473, 487, 492 f., 502, 517, 542, 599, 649, 665
- Polemical    252, 255 f., 285, 520, 539–541, 547–552, 558 *Polemics, *Songs | Polemical
- Satirical    256, 538, 540 f., 550 f.

Convents    93, 149, 402, 418 f., 466, 492, 503, 514, 583, 632, 634 f., 640, 644, 646, 653–677, 682 f., 688, 694, 699 *Enclosure, *Monasteries, *Nuns

Corpus Christi    379, 474, 476, 496, 535

Councils and Synods
- Avignon (1594)    469
- Basel (1431–49)    74, 119, 134, 391
- Besançon (1571)    439 f.
- Cambrai (1565)    439
- Constance (1567)    93, 119, 150, 153, 439 f.
- Chalcedon (451)    692
- Dordrecht (1574)    313
- Fifth Lateran (1512–7)    31, 122, 391, 421
- Milan (1565)    127, 139, 394, 440
- Nicaea (787)    8, 696, 698
- Prague (1565)    440
- Ravenna (1568)    141, 439 f.
- Second Vatican (1962–5)    7, 203, 229, 686
- Sens (1528)    78, 152, 157, 175
- Toledo (1565–6)    128, 439 f., 512
- Trent (1545–63)    xxvi, xxviii, xxx, 39, 45, 61, 66, 73 f., 91, 102, 105 f., 114, 119, 127, 132, 139, 154 f., 170, 176, 180, 187, 229 f., 234, 243, 382 f., 385, 404, 407–434, 436, 438–441, 444–446, 452–454, 457, 459, 467 f., 474, 481, 485, 491, 499, 502, 509 f., 512 f., 574, 595, 656, 658, 675, 702
- Trent (1593)    153, 440
- Wroclaw (1592)    469

Counter-Reformation    xxvi, xxviii, 16, 39, 42, 45, 387 f., 406, 428, 435, 442, 453, 465, 482, 505 f., 516 f., 534 f., 549, 553, 560 f., 581, 595, 605 f., 615, 621, 679

Credo (Creed)    74, 83, 90, 94 f., 118 f., 157, 179, 214, 243, 249, 271, 305, 307, 331, 339, 341, 392 f., 439, 448, 464, 564, 595, 597 f., 658, 693, 697 *Ordinarium Missæ

Cross    7, 183, 194, 207, 211, 477, 525, 543, 557, 651 *Easter, *Good Friday, *Resurrection, *Victimæ paschali

Cujus regio eius religio    35, 41, 44, 611, 685 *Speyer | Diets

Dance/Dancing    viii, 21, 24 f., 53, 72, 84, 87 f., 118, 150, 153, 158, 175, 177 f., 185 f., 222, 251, 254, 257, 316, 326, 330, 392, 440, 474, 513, 562, 600, 639, 683

Death    3, 5, 128, 239 f., 250, 306, 319, 365 f., 489, 520, 525 f., 528, 541, 617 f., 645, 650 *Compline | And death

Decalogue    305, 343, 352, 354, 538, 570, 594 f., 598

Dehumanisation    130 *Animal cries, *Bestiality

Denmark    35, 45, 289, 347

Devotio Moderna    30, 391, 673, 694 *Brethren of Common Life

Devotion    11, 30, 56, 71–73, 75 f., 91, 98, 104 f., 109–112, 118 f., 133 f., 147 f., 157 f., 160, 163 f., 176–178, 180 f., 185–187, 190, 194, 199, 214, 219, 222, 224 f., 229–232, 237, 242, 246 f., 250 f., 253, 261 f., 267, 280, 282, 286, 299, 304, 314, 321, 325, 327 f., 331, 337, 346, 349, 355, 357, 360, 362–364, 366 f., 369–371, 380, 382, 385, 387 f., 395, 407, 411, 416, 426 f., 430 f., 435 f., 468–480, 484, 486, 494–497, 500 f., 512 f., 516 f., 520 f., 524, 535, 539–542, 545, 551, 553, 557, 560 f., 563, 565, 567 f., 573 f., 576, 579, 581 f., 588, 590, 594, 599–603, 606, 608, 610 f., 618, 621–623, 626, 631, 636, 639, 647 f., 655–657, 662, 665 f., 673 f., 677, 680–682, 688, 692, 697–699 *Heartfelt devotion, *Love | Of the faithful for God, *Piety

Devotional music    109–112, 231, 237, 251, 262, 299, 321–327, 337, 346, 360, 362, 364, 371, 380, 388, 407, 430, 470–480, 486, 495–497, 500 f., 513, 516 f., 520, 539, 541 f., 551, 560 f., 563, 565, 567 f., 574, 582, 599 f., 608, 611, 618,

621f., 626, 631, 636, 648, 655f., 662, 673, 677, 681f., 697f.
Directorium chori   444, 450f.
Discant   73, 83, 143, 262, 360
Docta Sanctorum Patrum (Decretal)   73f., 78, 115, 131f., 149, 153, 411f., 464
Dogma   6f., 30, 37, 39f., 45, 48, 60, 132, 178, 181, 189f., 207, 210f., 240, 274, 278, 305, 365f., 384–387, 411, 446, 497, 519, 521f., 530f., 539, 551, 554, 572–574, 577, 582, 585, 590, 593, 597, 680, 692–694, 697, 699
Dominicans   12f., 28, 30, 71, 86, 110, 406, 470, 492, 497, 541, 603, 661f., 672f., 694
Dowry waivers   633, 663f., 694
Durch Adams Fall   254, 278, 285, 617
Dutch Revolt   44–47, 523 *Netherlands

Early modern   xxviif., 1, 49f., 54, 69, 80, 101f., 104f., 116, 236, 449, 479, 551, 573, 626, 674
Easter   51, 112, 249f., 309, 338f., 552, 675, 701 *Cross, *Resurrection, *Victimæ paschali
Ecumenism   v, vii, xif., xxvif., 8, 266, 515, 572, 607, 616, 621–624, 687 *Communion | Among Churches
Edinburgh   vii, 362, 536, 547 *Scotland
Editio Medicæa   106, 429, 451f., 462, 509, 514, 613, 687
Education   11, 14, 27, 35, 39, 56f., 61f., 68, 79, 88, 111, 121, 128–130, 160, 165–167, 181, 187–191, 198, 212, 218, 220f., 228, 231f., 237, 263, 272, 274–278, 284, 287f., 291, 298, 306, 310, 315f., 329, 335, 350, 359, 365, 367f., 371, 386, 394, 417, 429, 437f., 477f., 481, 486–488, 491, 497f., 506, 587–599, 601f., 627–629, 631, 633f., 636–638, 643, 653, 663, 683, 685, 695 *Children, *Pedagogy, *Schoolchildren
Effeminacy   61, 65, 99, 124, 126–130, 140, 146–149, 151f., 175, 626, 628f. *Music | And femininity/effeminacy
Ein feste Burg   252, 258, 278, 281, 288, 556, 687

Ein newes Lied   258, 284, 527, 554
Elevation   8, 83, 88, 118, 143, 231, 392, 658, 694 *Consecration, *Real Presence, *Transubstantiation
Elizabethan Injunctions   173, 228, 345, 355, 372, 601
Emden   38, 41, 44, 313, 351
Enclosure   154, 471, 634f., 654f., 657f., 660, 663, 669, 676, 694 *Convents, *Monasteries, *Nuns
English Civil War   43, 47, 345, 373
Erhalt uns, Herr   217, 258, 537f., 549, 617
Eucharist   9, 33, 43, 104, 118, 120, 179, 183f., 207, 209, 230–232, 235, 244f., 290, 343, 385f., 392, 410, 415, 448, 460, 468, 476, 479, 481, 497, 604, 694 *Lord's Supper, *Mass
Evensong   339–341, 343, 354, 377 *Worship | Anglican
Ex opere operato   9, 233, 386, 481 *Sacraments
Exorcism   585f.

Faburden   83, 107, 695
Faith   vii, xxvi, 2–5, 9, 16, 25, 27, 29, 31, 34, 47, 50, 52, 68, 101, 105, 136, 163, 166, 185, 187–189, 194f., 197, 206f., 210, 213, 232, 244, 276f., 282f., 292, 305, 315f., 359, 367, 379, 396, 416, 426f., 430, 434, 476f., 479, 489, 491, 507, 520–529, 535f., 544, 557, 562, 566, 568, 573, 578, 582, 584f., 587, 590, 595–602, 612, 616, 618f., 625, 630, 637f., 645, 650–652, 682–685, 690, 692f., 696f., 701f. *Sola fide
Fall (of Adam and Eve)   3, 11, 90, 206, 210, 386, 695, 699 *Free will, *Justification
Falsobordone   475, 484, 695
Fauxbourdon   107, 695 *Improvised polyphony
Ferrara   23, 132f., 303, 508, 551, 557, 559, 667, 669–671, 676
Finland   290
Florence   13, 24, 30f., 55, 60, 63, 430, 470f., 492–495, 497, 659, 662, 664f., 671f.
Flute   87, 200f., 203, 375, 569–571, 669

Formula of Concord  46, 208, 212, 262, 278
Franco-Flemish musical tradition  19, 22, 25, 53, 107, 144, 240, 260f., 323, 379, 407, 509, 515, 529, 533
Free will  6, 11, 39, 283, 386, 695 *Fall (of Adam and Eve)
Franciscans  28, 37, 110, 232, 455, 490, 536, 538, 542, 679
French Wars of Religion  44, 318, 530, 563, 579
Frottola  20, 95, 260

Geneva  viii, 41, 43, 170, 220, 352–355, 358f., 542, 547f., 653f.
– Consistory  178, 316, 542, 546, 561
– Psalter and tunes  44, 220, 224, 298f., 304–315, 319–325, 328, 330, 332, 354, 356, 362, 528, 543f., 546–548, 552, 562, 580f., 590, 609f., 613, 621, 644, 672, 686f. *Worship | Calvinist/Reformed
– Reformation  36–38, 40, 298, 304–306, 315, 326, 328, 374, 548, 561, 583, 590, 653f.
Gestures  73, 78, 94, 129, 140, 149–151, 178, 344, 512
Gloria  157, 214, 243, 249, 264, 339, 341, 343, 410, 440, 464, 694, 697 *Ordinarium Missæ
Gnesio-Lutherans  39, 555f.
Gnosticism  94, 181
Godly ballads  334, 364–366
Good Friday  397, 557f. *Cross, *Easter, *Passion | Of Christ
Grace  4–6, 9, 32, 39, 71, 92f., 125, 178, 183, 192f., 195, 199–201, 207f., 210, 233, 239, 283, 319, 386f., 412, 434f., 539, 567, 570f., 577, 586, 612, 617, 639, 641, 696f., 701 *Law, *Sola gratia
Gradual (song)  242f., 247, 249, 290, 379f., 442, 529, 560, 562, 575, 695
Gradual/Graduale (book)  77, 289, 444f., 451, 695
Gravity  65, 68, 73, 90, 151–153, 171, 176f., 221, 374, 410
Greek music  24, 49, 58f., 168
– Genera  22, 63, 159
– Modes  12, 58, 60f., 64f., 156, 698

– Philosophy  21, 60–65, 68f., 71f., 126, 131, 156, 160f., 165, 168, 191, 218, 220, 222, 561, 610
– Theory  58f., 62f. *Music | Theory
Gregorian chant  93, 106, 110, 132, 192, 217f., 245, 287, 290, 292, 308f., 389, 452, 506, 541, 549, 687, 695 *Monody | Unaccompanied, *Plainchant

Harmonisations  172, 224, 248, 260f., 267, 311–316, 322, 330f., 360–362, 369, 372f., 580, 589, 596, 613, 687, 692, 695 *Psalter | Harmonised
Harmony  xxix, 16, 49f., 57, 60–62, 65, 67, 72, 93, 99, 107, 133, 186, 189f., 192, 194, 210, 228, 317, 322, 332, 360, 382, 407, 412, 494, 561, 568–573, 575, 577, 629f., 647, 663, 666, 677, 680, 695, 702
Harpsichord  669, 675
Heartfelt devotion  31, 71, 147f., 170, 174, 176, 186, 209, 213, 215, 220f., 224f., 227, 291, 293, 304, 317, 399, 412f., 479, 496, 517, 572, 582, 647, 658 *Devotion, *Love | Of the faithful for God, *Piety
Heaven  3, 5f., 60, 80, 91, 94, 162f., 179, 182–186, 192, 212f., 226, 236, 382, 412, 415, 457, 480, 489, 567, 575, 577, 596f., 666, 691, 700
Hell  5f., 584
Hocket  73, 411
Holy Spirit  67, 185, 193f., 206, 210, 222f., 570, 591, 636, 639, 641f., 701 *Theology | Trinitarian
Homorhythmic  12, 18, 20, 22, 85, 95, 316f., 322f., 361, 377, 389, 424, 427, 454, 457, 471, 474, 477, 494, 501, 506, 510, 575, 668
Hope  16, 25f., 44, 48, 194, 207, 211, 565, 568, 577, 586, 628, 632, 642
Humanism  xxvii, 10–18, 21, 24, 27, 49–66, 68f., 72, 74–79, 82–84, 88f., 92f., 95f., 100, 102, 106, 109, 112, 115f., 119, 121, 131, 145, 155f., 160, 164–166, 168f., 173, 177, 186f., 218, 220f., 239, 247, 252, 259f., 275f., 278, 288, 293,

300, 302f., 307, 310, 312, 314, 322–324, 332, 341f., 359, 374, 392, 426, 438f., 445, 449f., 464, 515, 567, 574f., 581, 587–589, 591, 610, 620, 624, 628, 657, 664, 672, 674, 695f.
– Christian   11, 31, 50, 57, 60, 64, 66, 68, 75, 82–84, 300, 312, 323, 330, 403, 672, 696
– Esoteric   11, 54
– Exoteric   54, 82
– Ode   95f., 172, 342, 672
– Pagan   10f., 168, 581
Hungary   26, 35, 312, 512, 622, 634
Hussites   30f., 149, 253f., 295–297, 602, 696 *Bohemian Brethren, *Hymnbooks | Hussite, *Utraquists, *Worship | Bohemian Brethren
Hymnaria   264, 602
Hymnbooks/Songbooks   289, 298, 328f., 331, 562, 613, 616–619, 624, 651
– Catholic   265, 479, 553, 602–609, 617f., 673f.
– Huguenot   298, 305, 540–542, 562, 598
– Hussite   254, 296f., 643f. *Bohemian Brethren, *Hussites, *Utraquists, *Worship | Bohemian Brethren
– Lutheran   251, 254, 256, 264–269, 289, 297, 314, 336, 543, 562, 570f., 602–609, 617f., 638, 641f.
– Strasbourg   291–294, 643f.
– Use of   267–269, 291–294, 479, 531, 562

Iconoclasm   ix, 8, 33, 44, 178f., 325, 426, 536, 692, 696 *Idolatry, *Images
Idolatry   147, 178, 180, 201, 539, 696 *Iconoclasm, *Idolothites
Idolothites   71, 696 *Idolatry
Images   v, 8, 33, 80, 178f., 198, 232, 404, 426, 696 *Iconoclasm, *Idolatry
Imitation   696
– As a musical technique   12, 18f., 22, 109f., 119–122, 134, 160, 172, 260, 278, 331, 335, 340, 361, 372, 393, 424, 454, 456, 458f., 461, 464, 494, 501, 506, 510, 512f., 668

– Imitation Mass   108, 132, 134, 157, 506, 517, 696, 699 *Mass | As a musical genre
– Imitation of affects   18, 57f., 62, 64, 94, 96f., 131 *Affects
– Imitation of nature   15, 24, 126, 131, 411 *Naturalism
Improvised polyphony   83, 101, 107, 141, 145, 360, 656, 695 *Fauxbourdon, *Polyphony
Incarnation   3, 90, 178f., 181, 210f., 696
Index of the forbidden books   42, 404, 420, 436, 472
Individualism   26f., 98, 149, 172, 231, 645
Indulgences   5, 31f., 414, 685, 696 *Purgatory
Inquisition   42, 399, 403, 436, 541, 558f.
Instrumental music   viif., 25, 49, 53, 65f., 68, 71, 84–88, 97, 124f., 142, 150, 154, 169f., 173, 180, 187, 193, 196, 199–202, 212, 214, 216, 219, 223, 226, 228, 233, 237, 260f., 263f., 294, 299, 307, 311, 316f., 323, 325f., 334f., 370, 372, 375–377, 392, 411, 413, 418, 428, 443, 448, 450, 458, 466f., 478, 489f., 499f., 508, 511, 562, 569–572, 575, 600, 626, 629f., 636, 648, 655f., 659f., 663, 665, 668f., 672f., 675, 677, 681–683, 699f. *Bible | Musical instruments in the Bible
Intelligibility   12, 18, 58, 71, 74, 77, 79, 81f., 85, 93, 95f., 98, 109, 119–122, 131, 172–175, 201, 207f., 226, 234, 245, 259, 272, 307, 340, 345, 386f., 389, 393, 404f., 412, 415, 418, 422, 424, 426f., 429, 431, 439, 442, 452–457, 460–462, 464, 467, 499–502, 506, 510, 567, 575, 657 *Pronuntiatio/pronunciation
Intercession   9, 178, 287, 475, 526f., 539, 554, 605, 644, 662 *Litanies | Of the saints, *Saints
Intermedi   24 *Opera
Introit   118, 249, 290, 410, 630, 696, 700

Jesuits   28, 39, 98, 283, 410, 423, 425, 430, 453, 465, 473, 482–490, 495, 497, 504, 515, 532f., 549f., 563, 580–

## Index of Subjects

582, 585, 592f., 594f., 598–602, 609, 619, 636, 679, 696
– Colleges   86, 140, 437, 453, 486–488, 589, 599
– Missionaries   28, 469, 489f., 528f., 565, 595
– Plays   98f., 430, 485, 488f., 589
– Rule   137, 430, 482–484, 594, 601f.
Jewish   3, 66, 87, 137, 147, 169, 214, 301, 545, 696, 700
– Cantillation   66
– Worship   71, 87, 169, 200, 202, 214, 223, 251
Jubilus   69, 71, 116, 145 *Melismatic style
Justification   5–7, 38, 183f., 200f., 207f., 239, 258, 279, 386, 696f., 701 *Predestination, *Salvation, *Sola fide, *Sola gratia, *Sola scriptura, *Soteriology

Kanzeldienst   113, 697
Knights' Revolt   26, 34
Kyrie   157, 249, 264, 343, 697 *Ordinarium Missæ

Lamentations   110, 146, 397, 506, 516, 528
Lascivia/Lascivious   65, 68, 87f., 99, 103, 124–129, 132f., 136f., 139, 147, 150–152, 157, 174f., 228, 322, 383, 392–394, 404–406, 410f., 413–415, 426f., 439f., 487, 489, 499, 504, 626, 628f., 661
Lauda/laude   110f., 442, 458, 470–472, 476, 486, 490–494, 496, 502, 584, 596, 598, 659, 661f., 674, 683
Laudesi   55f., 492, 497 *Piagnoni
Law   3f., 71, 200f., 211, 223, 570f., 696
– Law of Love → Love | Law of love
– Works of the Law   4, 200f., 612 *Grace, *Sola gratia
Lent   33, 240, 249, 496, 697
Leise   112, 240, 247, 249, 309, 552, 617, 654, 697
Lieder → Chorales
Litanies   53, 105, 430, 442, 474–477, 490, 533, 535, 540, 585, 678, 697
– English   337f., 341f., 475, 536 *Worship | Anglican

– Lutheran   238, 286f., 338, 475 *Worship | Lutheran
– Of Loreto   475
– Of the saints   475, 697 *Intercession, *Saints
– Sacra Scriptura   475 *Bible, *Scripture
Literacy   26f., 53f., 66, 79, 166, 244f., 267, 276, 280, 300, 316, 329, 359, 366, 368, 398, 421, 461, 476, 567, 601f., 610, 631, 636, 645, 648, 650, 673, 682
– Musical   viii, 54, 237, 267, 316, 359f., 368, 371, 565, 582, 631, 648, 655, 682
Liturgy   vii, xxvi, 3, 8, 17, 19, 33, 42f., 45, 55–57, 69, 76, 81, 83f., 86f., 90, 93, 95f., 98, 101, 108–110, 117–119, 137, 157, 160, 165, 203, 211, 217, 220, 226, 229, 237–251, 257, 262f., 266–271, 287–294, 297, 300, 304, 306, 325, 333–346, 352–354, 358, 360, 373, 375, 377–384, 387–396, 403, 410–412, 416, 418, 420–423, 429–431, 435f., 438–452, 458, 467f., 478f., 481, 483f., 486f., 491, 495–499, 501, 505–507, 509–514, 516f., 529, 536, 551f., 558, 568, 574f., 579, 609, 613, 621, 647, 653f., 656, 664f., 668, 688, 690f., 693–695, 697–701 *Service, *Worship
– Concept of Liturgy   98, 101, 103–105, 109, 183–185, 188–190, 206–209, 214, 225, 230–235, 241–245, 292–294, 340, 342–344, 347, 353, 385, 387, 434f., 439, 444, 446, 450f., 464, 479, 481, 491, 495, 568f., 572f., 665, 685f.
– Language of Liturgy   30, 103f., 106, 112f., 119–122, 172–174, 217, 229–234, 237, 241–245, 247, 249–251, 273, 287, 289, 292f., 337–342, 346, 350, 378, 380, 383, 421, 435, 437, 444, 468f., 536, 562, 609, 618, 620, 654, 686
Lollards   30, 348, 648, 697
London   38, 190, 338f., 349, 353f., 372, 569, 683
Lord's Prayer   74, 118, 227, 244, 266, 305, 307, 331, 354, 392f., 523, 594f., 598, 600, 615, 645

Lord's Supper  33, 207, 241, 341, 352, 377
  *Eucharist, *Mass
Love
– God's for created beings  xxix, 6, 125 f., 181, 570 f., 625
– Law of love  4, 571
– Of the faithful for God  4, 67 f., 90, 92 f., 136, 496, 523, 570, 583 f., 630 *Devotion, *Heartfelt devotion, *Piety
– Of the faithful for one another  67, 570 f. *Communion | Within the Church, *Music | Creates communion
– Sexual love and marriage  14, 35, 123–130, 181, 183, 213, 218, 280, 440, 473, 512, 560, 583, 616, 625 f., 637
Lute  25, 183, 203, 317, 212, 369, 376, 403, 443, 569–571, 630, 648, 659, 669, 683
Lutheran hymns → Chorales
Lutheran Lieder → Chorales
Lyon  54, 321 f., 535, 547, 560, 563
– Publishers  54, 563

Madrid  514, 661, 673
Madrigal  20–23, 85, 101, 108, 152, 160 f., 177, 374, 401, 424, 464, 471 f., 487, 493, 503, 506, 515, 517, 583, 599, 665, 667 f., 671, 697
– Rappresentativo  23 f.
– Spiritual  98, 111, 251, 371, 430, 470–472, 478 f., 486, 501, 503, 583, 665, 678 f.
Magdeburg  248, 295, 530, 555
– Confession  40
Magisterium  6, 50, 70, 72–74, 176, 384, 412, 432, 697, 701
Magnificat  110, 120, 141, 305, 377, 397, 400, 405, 442, 447, 466, 470, 478, 506, 513, 691 *Canticles, *Office of the Hours, *Vespers
Manichaeism  94, 181
Mannerism  15, 426
Mantua  20, 38, 96, 106, 120, 396, 398, 401, 431, 449, 453, 455–457, 508–511, 559, 670 f., 692
Marburg Colloquy  36, 179
Marian Exiles  41 f., 226, 344, 351–355, 357 f., 363, 373, 526

Martyrdom  34, 258, 318 f., 351, 379, 489, 502, 525–530, 553, 562–565, 637, 650–652, 693 *Anabaptism | Martyrs, *Songs | Of martyrdom
Mass  8, 37, 74, 88, 91, 101, 104 f., 109, 118, 120, 132–135, 155–161, 214 f., 230 f., 237, 241–245, 249, 257, 276, 293, 329, 339 f., 358, 385 f., 393 f., 402, 408, 410 f., 413, 415, 418, 444, 446, 460 f., 467, 469 f., 479, 481, 484, 486, 495, 524, 532, 537 f., 542, 562, 604, 609, 617, 658, 675, 687, 691, 694–698, 700 *Eucharist, *Liturgy, *Lord's Supper, *Worship | Catholic
– As a musical genre  85, 99, 107–109, 138, 142, 155–161, 177, 372, 377, 379, 388, 400 f., 405, 422–425, 429, 439, 442, 450, 455 f., 460–465, 467 f., 470, 478, 487, 489, 496, 499 f., 501, 504–508, 532, 559, 564 f., 601, 624, 697
– As good deed  5, 183 f., 207, 211, 233, 235, 385 f., 464
– As sacrifice  7, 33, 183 f., 207, 230, 235, 385 f., 418, 463 f., 481
– Cantus firmus Mass  108, 110, 132 f., 157–161, 450, 462
– German  217, 237, 241–245, 255, 266, 293 *Liturgy | Language of Liturgy
– Ordinary → Ordinarium Missæ
– Parody/Imitation Mass → Imitation | Imitation Mass
– Paraphrase Mass  108, 132, 134, 462
– Polyphonic  91, 99, 107 f., 132 f., 138, 157–160, 334, 338, 396, 402, 411, 422–425, 429, 439, 442, 450, 455 f., 460–464, 467 f., 470, 478, 484, 486 f., 496, 499 f., 501, 504–508, 557 f., 564 f. *Polyphony
Massacre of St Bartholomew  45, 319, 330, 563 *Persecution
Matins  246, 339–341, 343, 354, 377, 474, 483, 698, 702 *Office of the Hours, *Worship | Anglican
Medicean Edition → Editio Medicæa
Melismatic style  18, 23, 70, 76, 81, 115–117, 132, 145, 172, 218, 245, 375, 393, 403, 440, 449, 510, 698 *Jubilus

Memorisation   67, 75, 189, 208, 217, 240, 245, 251f., 257, 259, 268, 276f., 284, 300f., 311, 359, 387, 477, 486, 488, 532, 548, 575, 592, 594, 596f., 640, 644
Mensural   73, 341, 444, 449f., 698 *Music | Theory, *Notation, *Rhythm
Metrics   12, 14, 17, 21, 54, 75, 78f., 94f., 97, 106, 112, 115, 166, 257, 300, 310, 323, 338, 445, 449f., 540, 558, 575, 672, 679, 696, 698, 702 *Prosody
– Metrical Catechisms   364, 368, 591–596, 598 *Catechism, *Songs | Catechism songs
– Metrical Psalters   vii, 76, 221, 226, 294, 298–304, 306f., 310–314, 318f., 333, 345–365, 367–369, 373, 376, 380, 547, 572, 580, 589, 644, 648f. *Bible | Translations, *Psalter
Middle Ages   xxix, 10, 12, 57, 60, 79, 106, 126, 157f., 205, 260, 446, 449, 492, 694, 701
Milan   71, 127, 139, 394, 430f., 438, 440, 455, 461, 497, 500–503, 511, 583, 596, 662–665, 670, 676f., 690 *Ambrosian
Missal   410, 420, 429, 435, 446–448, 509, 695, 698 *Mass
Mission/Missionary   28, 39, 45, 166, 319, 358, 421, 469, 489f., 506, 528, 565, 595 *Jesuits | Missionaries
Modes   12, 58–65, 77, 85, 94–97, 106–109, 123, 153, 157f., 160f., 244, 228, 259, 323–325, 377, 388, 406, 424, 510, 513, 572, 575, 698 *Music | Theory, *Tonality
– Church modes   12, 58, 63–65, 156, 406
– Greek → Greek music | Modes
– Ethos of the modes   12, 50, 58–65, 71, 75, 96f., 123, 157–161, 228, 323f., 406, 427, 698 *Greek music | Philosophy
– Modal theory   59, 64f., 73, 85, 96, 98, 123, 323–325, 406, 427, 572, 698 *Greek music | Theory, *Music | Theory
Monasteries   82, 105f., 113, 141, 466, 514, 552, 644, 699 *Convents, *Enclosure
– Dissolution   26, 37, 371, 636
– Female   90, 93, 149, 154, 217, 383, 402, 404, 408, 418f., 502f., 514, 583, 626f., 631f., 634–636, 640f., 646, 653–677, 682f., 688, 694 *Nuns
Monody   12, 20, 23–25, 58f., 89, 106, 116, 172, 261f., 267, 271–273, 286f., 341, 369f., 372, 399f., 412, 433, 452–454, 491–493, 595, 613, 645, 698–700
– Accompanied   12, 18, 20, 23–25, 58, 85, 106, 261, 376, 378, 389, 427, 442, 452, 454, 533, 626, 632 *Continuo
– Unaccompanied   12, 172, 217, 224, 271, 296, 299, 317, 321f., 325, 353, 568, 618, 692 *Gregorian chant, *Plainchant, *Psalmody | Huguenot, *Psalmody | Reformed, *Psalmody | Scottish
Motets   viii, 22, 25, 85, 98, 101, 103–105, 107–110, 118, 122, 133, 152, 157, 160f., 203, 239f., 249–251, 261–264, 266, 272, 286, 323, 326, 360, 377f., 380, 396, 405f., 430, 442f., 447f., 458, 468, 470, 472–474, 476, 478, 487, 493f., 496, 500f., 513, 515, 528, 534, 558f., 577, 582, 601, 608, 615, 620–622, 627, 656, 658, 668, 670, 675, 678, 698
Munich   99, 400f., 460, 465, 487, 515f., 524, 536f., 553, 564, 587
Münster   36, 560, 673
Music
– And catechism → Songs | Catechism songs
– And confessionalisation   173, 273, 519–567, 576, 607f., 612, 619 *Confessionalisation
– And femininity/effeminacy   61, 65, 92f., 99, 104, 116, 123–130, 146–149, 151–153, 175, 403, 415, 419, 583, 626–631, 647, 678, 684 *Effeminacy
– And identity   xxvif., 44, 54, 194, 197, 237, 258, 281f., 289, 297–299, 315, 317–319, 346, 355, 363, 366, 382, 522f., 525f., 531, 549, 562, 564, 566, 607, 650, 654f., 681f.
– And morality/ethics   61–65, 69, 84, 88, 92, 97, 102, 114, 116f., 119, 122–154, 160, 162f., 168, 174–178, 183, 190f., 222, 282, 292, 316, 365f., 382, 387, 389, 393–395, 403, 415, 427, 430, 487, 502, 562, 588f., 628, 637, 639, 659, 661, 676, 698
– And politics   v, 19, 53–55, 64f., 104, 238, 252, 269, 284, 305, 319, 324, 333–

335, 350, 355, 362–364, 366, 375, 378, 381, 403, 441, 498, 507–509, 512, 522f., 529, 543, 546f., 554, 557–559, 566, 572, 578 *Politics
- And propaganda   xxixf., 19, 104, 164, 181, 190, 194, 238, 256, 258, 265, 283f., 311, 368, 387f., 398, 420, 480, 482, 520f., 523f., 531, 542f., 547–549, 553f., 559f., 566, 579, 611, 619, 646 *Propaganda, *Songs | Propaganda songs
- And society   49–53, 61, 64f., 84, 93, 103, 110, 123f., 135f., 187, 215f., 218, 223, 238, 271, 274, 282, 284, 294, 298, 302, 310, 316f., 327, 332f., 355, 357, 363–367, 371–376, 381, 420, 430, 433, 441, 458, 465, 470f., 475–482, 485f., 491, 497, 499f., 502, 521, 529, 531, 534, 542, 549, 555–561, 567, 577f., 582, 587, 589, 608, 610, 624, 627, 631–636, 639, 648, 650, 652, 654f., 664, 669, 677, 682, 685, 688f. *Sixteenth-century | Society/Social issues
- And words/text → Word/Music relationship
- And worship → Worship | Theological role of music in worship
- As a gift of God   130, 171, 181–183, 196, 199, 206–208, 210f., 221f., 228, 298, 416, 574 *Theology | Of music
- As a source of comfort   ix, 67, 90, 130, 181, 192, 194, 207, 231, 237, 279–281, 300, 319, 345, 355, 368, 476, 483, 544, 584, 586f., 605, 618, 628, 632, 638f., 682
- As a waste of time/money   125, 136f., 176, 628f., 635
- Creates communion   vi, 67, 185f., 274, 281, 317, 476, 567–573, 586, 624 *Communion | Within the Church, *Love | Of the faithful for one another
- Devotional → Devotional music
- Greek → Greek music
- Internationalism   19, 23, 53–55, 95, 517, 521, 563, 567, 576, 619, 624, 634 *National features in music
- Instruments → Instrumental music (*Flute, *Harpsichord, *Lute, *Organ, *Trumpets, *Viols)
- Literacy → Literacy | Musical
- Music printing → Printing | Music printing
- National styles → National features in music
- Passion settings → Passion | Musical settings of the Passion
- Thaumaturgic   193, 200, 206, 585–587, 602
- Theory   v, xxvi, xxixf., 12, 16f., 24, 50–55, 58–60, 62–64, 73, 77, 94, 96–100, 108, 115–141, 153, 157, 168, 205, 225, 279, 323f., 401f., 406, 427, 572 *Greek music | Theory, *Mensural, *Modes, *Modes | Modal theory, *Tonality
- Theology of music → Theology | Of music
- Vocal music → Frottola, → Madrigals, → Mass | As a musical genre, → Motets, → Monody, → Polyphony, → Songs, → Word/Music relationship (etc.)
Mysticism   7, 11, 16, 30, 34, 51, 53, 62, 68f., 80, 90–93, 163f., 167, 181, 184, 193f., 204, 206, 212, 230, 343, 403, 412, 426, 430, 457, 464, 479, 503, 506, 567, 573, 575, 582–586, 602, 624, 626, 630, 665f., 673f., 681, 693

Nantes (Edict of)   47, 323
Naples   26, 37, 493
National features in music   18f., 23, 54f., 85, 96, 107, 140, 143–146, 576 *Music | Internationalism
Naturalism   12, 22, 24, 58, 80f., 94, 97, 403, 419, 450, 657 *Imitation | Imitation of nature
Neo-Platonism   11, 21, 60, 62, 64, 68f., 126, 165, 168, 191, 561, 610 *Sixteenth-century | Philosophy
Netherlands   26, 38, 41f., 44, 46f., 98, 298, 312–314, 325, 331, 553, 595, 634, 645, 649f. *Dutch Revolt
Nominalism   70
Norway   45, 289, 648
Notation   66, 86, 98, 106f., 270, 293, 311, 341, 343, 368, 444, 451, 609, 611, 698, 701 *Mensural, *Tablatures
Nun freut euch   258, 283, 285, 539
Nuns   34, 51, 55, 69, 86, 90, 93, 139, 148f., 154, 402, 418f., 471, 483, 502f., 583, 625–627, 630–636, 640–642,

644, 653–677, 680, 694 *Convents, *Enclosure, *Monasteries | Female

Office of the Hours   74, 93, 101, 105, 109–111, 118, 135 f., 153 f., 217, 237, 239, 245 f., 251, 257, 300, 340, 348, 396, 417, 430, 438, 442, 446, 448, 469, 482–484, 486, 512, 545, 551, 579, 597, 602, 609, 657 f., 665, 672, 680, 690 f., 693–696, 698, 700, 702

Opera   24 f., 85 f., 255, 497 *Cameratas, *Intermedi

Opere operato → Ex opere operato

Oratory
– As the art of speech   75, 77, 156, 166–168 *Rhetoric
– Congregation of (Oratorians)   430, 458, 471, 480, 482, 491–495, 497, 502, 504, 584, 698 *Lauda/Laude

Ordinarium Missæ   98, 104, 108–110, 119 f., 133, 158, 160, 234, 241–245, 249, 339 f., 377, 379, 393, 397, 424, 439, 448, 460 f., 464, 467, 478, 506, 564, 694, 697 f.

Organ   86–88, 91, 118–120, 128, 134, 137, 149, 153, 173, 178 f., 196, 199–201, 212, 215, 240, 260, 263 f., 269, 271 f., 294, 313, 325 f., 330, 341, 344, 359, 363, 372, 375 f., 378, 392 f., 401, 413, 418, 443, 448, 466 f., 481, 500, 511, 533, 537, 607, 639, 656, 658, 660, 663–665, 668 f., 671, 673, 675, 699

Original sin → Fall (of Adam and Eve)

Painting   vii, xxxiii, 15 f., 76, 79, 121, 158 f., 163, 179, 232 f., 269, 331, 423, 426, 457, 508, 569–572, 577, 688 f.

Pamphlets   88, 141 f., 149, 162, 398, 530–532, 549, 554, 618, 643 *Polemics

Paris   21, 45–47, 96, 304, 311, 534, 541, 559, 563

Partbooks   vii f., 340, 343, 361 f., 481, 619, 692, 699

Passion
– As a musical genre: Responsorial   285
– As a musical genre: Through-composed   286

– Human passions   62, 76, 94, 97, 124, 126, 160, 190 f., 503, 583
– Musical settings of the Passion:   95, 171, 238, 255, 260, 285 f., 297, 308, 397, 477
– Of Christ   7, 244, 397, 410, 485, 543, 699 *Cross, *Good Friday
– Passion tones   208, 244, 286

Pater Noster → Lord's Prayer

Patristic → Church Fathers

Patronage   18, 33, 49, 53, 120, 136 f., 162, 303, 396, 398, 406, 431, 433, 455 f., 462–465, 498–500, 504, 507, 509, 557, 622 f., 627, 633–636, 644 f., 692

Peasants   26 f., 34, 84, 111, 592, 632
– Peasants' War   34

Pedagogy   xxxi, 27, 51, 57, 61 f., 66, 69, 79, 85, 121, 129 f., 164 f., 188 f., 206, 233, 237, 262, 272, 278, 311, 316, 350, 367, 487, 567, 587, 589, 593, 597, 599 f., 624, 639 f., 643, 679 *Children, *Education, *Schoolchildren

Penny-ballads   18, 364 f.

Pentecost   112, 248, 250, 570 f., 675

Persecution   xxvii, 192, 194, 258, 281, 299, 302, 307, 311, 317–319, 349, 351 f., 357 f., 379, 399, 502 f., 525 f., 528, 539, 543, 546–548, 556, 559–566, 628, 637, 650–652 *Martyrdom, *Songs | Of martyrdom

Petrarchism   14, 20, 22, 648 *Sixteenth-century | Literature

Philippists   39

Piagnoni   31, 111, 492, 662 *Lauda/laude, *Laudesi

Pietism   269, 699

Piety   17, 31, 51, 55 f., 72, 76, 98, 101, 103 f., 110, 133, 157–162, 181, 186–190, 198, 222, 225 f., 230, 232, 237, 242, 246 f., 250, 252 f., 257, 264–268, 276, 280, 282, 327, 329, 334, 348, 363–366, 368, 388, 391, 395, 420, 428, 430, 434 f., 463, 469–471, 478–480, 488, 491, 496 f., 516, 539, 545 f., 567, 576, 581–583, 590, 594, 602 f., 605, 618, 624, 644 f., 648, 682, 699 *Devotion, *Heartfelt devotion, *Love | Of the faithful for God

Pilgrimages  53, 55, 104f., 112, 253, 430, 474, 476–478, 496, 534f., 539, 604, 616f.
Placards → Affaire des Placards
Plainchant  52, 59, 73, 76, 81f., 93, 101, 105–111, 115f., 120, 131f., 135, 142, 159, 163, 173, 216, 240, 245, 248, 250f., 259–261, 267, 269, 273, 287, 290, 292f., 297, 309f., 338, 341, 348, 373, 388, 397, 399, 417, 423, 429, 438, 441, 444–453, 481, 487, 505, 509f., 513f., 550–552, 558, 575, 577f., 605, 612f., 616, 654, 658, 672f., 683, 687, 691, 695, 698f., 702 *Gregorian chant, *Monody | Unaccompanied
– Revision of  287, 444–449, 505, 509
Pléiade  20f. *Sixteenth-century | Literature
Poissy (Colloquy of)  43
Poland  38, 46, 312, 512, 544, 580
Polemical songs → Songs | Polemical songs
Polemics  xxix, xxxi, 19, 104, 137, 196, 198f., 204, 240, 252, 256, 283, 285, 295, 299, 301f., 520, 523, 530f., 538–543, 547–560, 577f., 604, 611, 617, 649, 681 *Contrafacta | Polemical, *Pamphlets, *Songs | Polemical
Politics  v, viii, xxvif., 1, 11, 13, 19, 25–48, 53–57, 62, 64, 71f., 84, 104, 156, 215f., 238, 252, 269, 284, 305, 319, 324, 333–335, 350, 355, 362–364, 366, 373, 375, 378, 381, 403, 441, 498, 507–512, 521–523, 529, 543, 546f., 554, 557–559, 566, 572, 576, 578, 608, 654 *Music | And politics
Polychorality  12, 85, 96, 454–459, 474, 478, 488, 494, 508, 515, 575, 668, 693, 699
Polyphony  viii, xxix, 12, 18f., 21, 24f., 50f., 53f., 58, 63, 65, 73f., 77–83, 87, 89–95, 98, 101, 105–111, 116, 119f., 125, 127, 132–136, 139, 141–143, 145–147, 149, 156, 159, 161, 172f., 186, 200, 204, 214–216, 224, 226, 228, 233f., 239f., 246, 248, 260–262, 266, 270–274, 282, 285f., 288, 292, 294f., 299, 307f., 311–314, 316f., 321–327, 331, 334, 336f., 340f., 343f., 359–362, 368, 370–373, 376f., 379, 383, 388, 393f., 396–400, 402f., 407, 410f., 414, 416–419, 422–426, 428–430, 433, 439, 442, 448f., 452–461, 467, 475f., 478, 484, 490–492, 496, 500f., 504, 506, 510, 512, 514f., 525, 529, 533, 558, 562, 568, 585, 588, 612f., 616, 626, 630, 645, 655f., 658, 660, 662, 665, 667, 675f., 678, 681–684, 687, 690, 692, 695f., 698f., 702
Poor Clares  653, 663, 673
Preaching  28, 30, 34, 39, 71f., 78, 81, 171, 182, 184, 188f., 205, 208f., 211, 231f., 274, 278–280, 330, 359, 365, 421, 437f., 470, 480, 483–485, 490, 492, 525, 534, 559, 573, 583, 594f., 600, 610, 694, 697
Predestination  6, 46, 350, 548, 700 *Justification, *Salvation, *Sola fide, *Sola gratia, *Sola scriptura, *Soteriology
Priesthood  6–9, 51, 70, 135, 171, 206, 209, 217, 230f., 237, 257, 269, 279, 343, 384–386, 394, 415, 437, 481, 484, 539f., 637, 644, 690f., 693f., 698–700
– Of all believers  6, 51, 171, 206, 230, 237, 257, 269, 279, 384, 386, 539f., 637, 700 *Baptism
– Ordained  7, 209, 217, 230, 232, 275, 386, 540, 691, 694, 699f. *Anticlericalism, *Clergy, *Sacraments
Primers  112, 336, 338, 341
Printing  18, 20, 27, 49, 53f., 265, 284, 292, 308, 316, 348, 354, 356, 358, 362, 366, 406, 451, 530f., 580, 645
– Music printing  18–20, 49, 53f., 86, 109, 113, 116, 247, 253f., 258, 265, 268, 289, 292f., 296, 307f., 311, 319, 330, 349, 361, 364–366, 424, 444f., 447, 449, 463, 470, 515, 520, 531, 541, 548, 554f., 576, 596, 602f., 608, 617–619, 628, 667f., 672, 678f.
Processions  55, 104f., 110, 112, 253, 287, 337f., 442, 468, 470, 474–478, 496, 504, 534–536, 540, 551, 553, 617, 656, 658, 666, 677
Promiscuity  154, 660f., 676

Pronuntiatio/pronunciation   75, 77, 106, 115, 122, 132, 144, 226f., 321, 403, 439, 454 *Intelligibility
Propaganda   xxixf., 164, 181, 190, 194, 238, 256, 258, 265, 283f., 311, 368, 388, 395, 398, 420, 480, 482, 520f., 523f., 530–532, 542, 547–549, 553f., 559, 560, 566, 579, 611, 619, 646 *Music | And propaganda, *Songs | Propaganda songs
Proper   104, 109, 244, 249, 379, 447, 695f., 698, 700f.
Prosody   76, 78, 82, 96f., 116, 166, 168, 300, 310, 323, 342, 449–452, 575, 605, 696, 698, 702 *Metrics
Psalm-motets   157, 239, 262, 577, 622
Psalmody   67f., 130, 152, 181, 194, 214f., 219–221, 224, 227, 246, 252f., 294, 298–332, 344–363, 367–373, 376, 380, 386, 465, 476f., 524, 545, 560, 567, 579, 584, 589, 591, 601f., 607, 619, 622, 624, 626, 634, 645–648, 690f., 695, 700
– Anglican   333, 344–373, 579, 591, 598, 648f.
– Catholic   110f., 113, 308, 325, 362, 405, 410, 417, 457f., 476f., 489, 516, 525, 528f., 532, 535, 545f., 579–581, 601, 609f., 613, 619 *Office of the Hours
– Huguenot   44, 95, 317f., 320f., 368, 520, 524f., 526, 530–535, 540f., 562, 579, 610 *Monody | Unaccompanied
– In Latin   110, 174, 245f., 300, 314, 319f., 327, 347, 359, 417, 458, 487, 489, 525f., 528f., 545, 572, 579, 609, 672, 700
– In literature   300–304, 315, 323, 349f., 532, 580f., 610, 644, 648, 672
– In the Office of the Hours   110, 174, 245f., 251, 300, 654, 694, 698, 700 *Office of the Hours
– In the vernacular   111, 113, 170, 219–224, 245f., 251–253, 255, 261f., 289, 294, 298, 303–327, 329, 348–363, 410, 516, 520, 524, 528, 530, 534–536, 540, 542, 545–548, 556, 579–581, 589f., 607, 609, 613, 620, 626, 634, 645–648, 650, 654, 686f.
– Metrical → Metrics | Metrical Psalters

– Reformed   viii, 96, 170, 184, 191, 220–224, 231, 252, 261, 296, 298–327, 330, 351–358, 363, 368, 370, 373, 450, 479, 520, 524f., 526, 528, 530–535, 537, 540, 543–548, 560, 562, 572, 575, 579–581, 584, 589f., 598, 600, 609f., 618f., 621, 626, 634, 644–649, 681, 683, 686f., 700 *Monody | Unaccompanied
– Scottish   viii, 314, 333, 346, 353f., 358–360, 362, 369, 536, 546f., 579, 584, 596, 613, 648f., 687 *Monody | Unaccompanied
Psalter   66, 246, 251, 304, 444, 700
– Coverdale   194, 289, 302, 333, 346–349, 613, 642, 646, 649
– de Bèze   283, 307f., 312, 519, 545f., 580 *Psalmody | Reformed
– Genevan → Geneva | Genevan Psalter and tunes
– Harmonised   224, 299, 312, 314, 316, 321–327, 331, 346, 360–363, 373, 580f., 610, 613, 619, 645, 683 *Harmonisations
– Lobwasser   261, 298, 312, 330, 536f., 543f., 589
– Marot   15, 20, 298, 300, 302–307, 312, 318, 349, 352, 532, 540, 545–547, 557, 560, 580, 598, 610, 619, 644 *Psalmody | Reformed
– Martinengo   307 *Psalmody | Reformed
– Metrical → Metrics | Metrical Psalters
– Parker   361, 368, 526 *Psalmody | Anglican
– Souterliedekens → Souterliedekens
– Sternhold   349–352, 354f., 360, 589, 649 *Psalmody | Anglican
– Sternhold and Hopkins   301f., 333, 348, 351f., 354–358, 364, 368, 370, 526, 591 *Psalmody | Anglican
– Utenhove   313, 332, 528 *Psalmody | Reformed
– Wedderburn   349, 642 *Psalmody | Scottish
– Wesel   352, 649 *Psalmody | Reformed
Purgatory   5, 211, 541, 696, 700 *Indulgences

Quadrivium and Trivium   77, 205

Rationalism  51, 62, 81, 92, 204, 231, 257
Real presence  8, 33, 481, 497, 535 *Consecration, *Elevation, *Transubstantiation
Relics  8, 32, 80
Renaissance  2, 10, 15, 49, 54, 57f., 60, 62, 75, 86, 110, 131, 389, 426, 457
Responsorial style  257, 285f., 476, 598, 690, 697, 700
Resurrection  197, 209–211, 224, 244, 250, 552, 630, 699 *Easter, *Victimæ paschali
Rhetoric  12, 18, 22, 50, 56–58, 65, 75–77, 81, 83, 89, 92, 94–96, 115, 156f., 165–168, 186, 188, 205, 251, 257f., 300, 362, 412, 438, 468, 472, 480f., 485, 512, 680, 698 *Oratory | As the art of speech
Rhythm  16–18, 21, 24, 53, 58, 61, 65, 68, 72, 77f., 81, 94–96, 106, 115f., 140, 150, 153, 175, 177f., 188, 217, 240, 251, 253, 257, 260, 262, 270, 300, 309f., 321, 323f., 332, 341f., 403, 407, 444, 450, 474, 635, 690f., 694f. *Mensural
Ricercare  25
Rome  5, 11, 31–33, 35–38, 40f., 45, 58, 66, 86, 142, 145, 155, 199, 337, 395f., 400, 424, 431, 438, 445f., 458–461, 471, 488, 491–493, 497, 502f., 509–511, 516, 550, 569, 586, 598, 657f., 665, 699
– Basilica of St Peter  5, 32, 142, 395
– Sack of  35f., 396
Rosary  246

Sacraments  8f., 33, 39, 132, 233, 352, 386, 392, 434f., 481, 497, 680, 693, 699f. *Ex opere operato
Sacred Images → Images
Saints  4, 8f., 83, 90, 178, 184, 244, 249, 255, 258, 287, 339, 364, 379, 446, 474f., 503, 539, 554, 561, 605, 610, 643f., 662, 692, 697 *Intercession, *Litanies | Of the saints
Salvation  3–7, 9, 39, 178, 183, 195, 207f., 210, 239, 279, 365f., 386, 539, 612, 625, 643f., 700f. *Justification, *Predestination, *Sola fide, *Sola gratia, *Sola scriptura, *Soteriology
Salve Regina  110, 533, 539, 690
Sanctus  118, 157, 159, 243, 247, 249, 440, 565, 697 *Ordinarium Missæ
Schmalkaldic
– League  36, 38, 40, 45f.
– Wars  40, 554
Scholastic theology  12f., 57, 60, 69, 276
Schoolchildren  277f., 280, 291, 311, 589f., 607, 636 *Children, *Education, *Pedagogy
Science  1, 14f., 51, 72, 77, 85, 152, 157, 168f., 185, 205, 333, 344f., 465, 569f., 645, 685
Scotland  vii-ix, 41–43, 298, 312, 314, 346, 348f., 353f., 358–360, 362f., 369, 538, 546, 584, 596, 613, 642, 648f., 682, 687 *Edinburgh
– Gaelic  358
– Kirk  41, 43, 333, 349, 353, 358–360, 362, 369, 547, 687
– Music schools  359, 596, 613, 682
– Psalmody → Psalmody | Scottish
– Reformation  vii-ix, 41–43, 312, 314, 348f., 353f., 358–360, 362f., 369, 538, 546, 596, 648f.
– Worship → Worship | Scottish
Scribes  116, 449, 627, 640, 656, 673
Scripture  4–6, 9, 17, 70, 84, 109f., 122, 148, 166, 168, 171f., 174, 178, 187, 193, 195f., 198f., 206, 208, 214, 220f., 227, 230, 235, 241, 244, 250–252, 291f., 294, 304, 307, 318, 351, 355, 371, 378, 384, 386, 389, 392, 410, 414, 418, 426, 468, 475, 492, 525, 540, 542, 545f., 555, 565, 570, 615f., 621, 637–642, 649–651, 668, 691, 696, 698, 701 *Bible, *Sola scriptura
Sculpture  10, 158f., 178, 232f., 426
Secular influences/elements in sacred music  73f., 84, 87, 101, 103, 105, 108, 112, 118, 132–135, 137, 150f., 157, 177, 199, 201, 222, 240, 247f., 251, 253–259, 281f., 296, 305f., 313, 321, 327f., 330f., 349, 356, 362, 365, 370, 388, 393, 401, 411, 413f., 422, 441, 443,

457, 462, 465, 467, 470–474, 487, 492f., 502–504, 506–508, 513, 517, 520, 522, 541f., 548–550, 599f., 616, 618, 640, 642, 645, 649, 651f., 665, 674, 680, 691, 697
Seminaries   39, 391, 408, 417, 429, 436–438, 486, 499, 505 *Clergy | Formation, *Education
Senses   50, 98, 180, 193, 430, 485
Septuagint   302, 347, 545, 701 *Bible | Translations
Service (as an act of worship)   74, 103, 110, 113, 154, 172, 190, 215, 223, 243–245, 263, 268, 281, 294, 306, 313, 334, 339f., 343, 359, 364, 375–379, 395, 404, 417f., 460, 470, 484, 495, 502, 504, 524, 536f., 550, 567, 577, 585, 588, 598, 601f., 614, 616, 639, 657, 687, 697, 700 *Liturgy, *Worship
Sequences   83, 105, 112, 117, 242, 248–250, 253, 309, 338, 429, 443f., 446f., 541, 552, 570, 617, 695, 700f. *Proper
Settlement   40–42, 354
Sexuality → Love | Sexual love and marriage
Siena   660, 665, 678
Sistine Chapel
– Choir   78, 395–397, 456
– Frescoes   15, 158, 162
Six Articles   38, 40, 337
Sixteenth-century
– Culture   xxx, 1, 10–17, 25–28, 48f., 51–54, 56–65, 72, 74–77, 82–85, 94, 99, 101f., 115, 119, 121, 125, 129, 156, 164, 166–171, 302–304, 312, 317, 349–351, 355, 359, 363, 381, 385, 388f., 396, 398, 421, 429, 432f., 436–438, 441, 450, 454, 463, 465, 485f., 489, 497f., 500, 508, 515, 542, 549, 557, 569, 574, 577, 581f., 587f., 591, 608, 610f., 620, 623f., 631–636, 638, 640, 648, 654–656, 674, 677, 679
– Economy   xxvi, 1, 5, 25–28, 34, 45, 48, 53f., 271, 282, 334f., 372f., 375, 381, 437, 441, 465, 496f., 507, 510, 550, 554, 577, 582, 587, 658
– Explorations   1, 28, 319, 421, 490
– Literature and poetry   12, 14f., 17, 20–23, 28, 54, 56–58, 62, 66, 74–76, 79,

95f., 117, 124, 158, 166, 221, 237, 247, 249, 251, 257–259, 262, 302–305, 307, 310, 314f., 324–328, 349–352, 357, 359, 364–366, 446, 470–473, 485f., 494, 501, 515, 517, 532, 540, 560, 580f., 605, 608–610, 618f., 640, 642, 644, 648–653, 672–674, 678–680, 683
– Medicine   14
– Philosophy   1, 10–14, 29, 56–65, 68, 74–76, 82–85, 88, 126, 164–171, 220, 228, 450, 569, 574, 610, 685 *Neo-Platonism
– Physics   14, 63, 168
– Science   v, 1, 14, 51, 57, 77, 85, 168
– Society/Social issues   xxvii, 1, 13, 25–48, 50, 52–54, 84, 93, 103, 110, 135f., 264, 271, 274, 282, 284, 302, 310, 317, 327, 332f., 355, 357f., 363–367, 372f., 376, 381, 383, 385, 390, 420, 430, 433, 436, 438, 441, 447, 458, 465, 470, 475–477, 479, 481f., 485f., 489, 491, 496f., 499f., 507, 513f., 521, 529, 531, 534, 542, 549, 555–557, 560f., 577f., 582f., 587f., 595, 608, 612, 624, 627, 631–636, 639, 643, 648, 650, 652, 654–656, 664, 669, 674, 677f., 682, 685, 688 *Music | And society
– Visual arts   v, xxix, 8, 10, 15–17, 33, 39, 80f., 85, 98, 102, 126, 158, 168, 172, 178–180, 182, 197, 201, 222, 232, 313, 383, 396, 403f., 425–427, 435, 450f., 477, 514, 521, 569–573 *Architecture, *Painting, *Sculpture
Society of Jesus → Jesuits
Sola fide   5, 9, 206, 384, 386, 696, 701 *Faith, *Justification, *Salvation, *Soteriology
Sola gratia   5f., 147, 163, 171, 178, 184, 195, 206f., 384, 386, 697, 701 *Justification, *Grace, *Law, *Salvation, *Soteriology
Sola scriptura   5f., 171, 178, 187, 196, 206, 208, 244, 384, 386, 637, 701 *Bible, *Justification, *Salvation, *Scripture, *Soteriology
Songbooks → Hymnbooks

Songs   viii, 21, 24, 29, 38, 52f., 66, 69f.,
74f., 78, 83f., 89, 95, 103–105, 111–
113, 118, 120, 122, 125f., 128–131,
134f., 137, 143, 147, 150f., 153, 157, 172,
178, 180, 185, 189, 199, 201, 205f.,
208, 211, 213, 215, 217–220, 222f.,
225, 227, 231, 237–240, 243, 246–
249, 251–259, 261, 265–269, 274, 278,
280–285, 289, 291, 293–299, 303,
306f., 309–311, 313f., 314–318, 321f.,
326–330, 335, 338, 342, 345–347, 351,
354–356, 359, 365f., 368, 370f., 376,
380, 410, 416, 430, 442, 469f., 473f.,
476, 478, 485, 487, 490, 492, 495f.,
513, 515, 520–528, 530–532, 534–545,
547–556, 559–563, 567, 570, 574f.,
577–611, 613–620, 623, 625, 627, 630,
632–634, 636–640, 642–645, 649–
652, 654f., 661f., 664–666, 673f.,
680–682, 685–688, 691, 695, 697
– Catechism songs   189, 206f., 246, 277f.,
364, 368, 468, 485, 489, 581, 590–598,
600, 609, 619, 632 *Catechism, *Metrics |
Metrical Catechisms
– News songs   53, 240, 258, 284, 364f.,
520, 548
– Of martyrdom   258, 351, 525–530, 553,
565, 637, 650–652 *Martyrdom
– Polemical songs   104, 198, 252, 256,
285, 295, 523, 531, 538f., 541, 543, 549–
553, 555f., 558, 560, 577f., 604, 617, 681
*Contrafacta | Polemical, *Polemics
– Propaganda songs   xxixf., 164, 181, 190,
238, 256, 258, 283f., 388, 480, 520f., 531,
542f., 554 *Music | And propaganda,
*Propaganda
Soteriology   5, 212, 701 *Justification, *Pre-
destination, *Salvation
Souterliedekens   19, 299, 313f., 330f., 579,
613, 651
Sovereignty   13, 47
Speyer   35, 41, 553
– Diets   35 *Cujus regio eius religio
Sankt Gallen   328, 537
Stoicism   10, 13
Strasbourg   5, 34, 37–39, 165, 218–220,
238, 243, 268, 270, 290–295, 298,
303–309, 315, 328f., 333, 338, 347,
351, 532f., 539, 561, 583, 588, 590,
598, 609, 616, 643f., 647, 692 *Wor-
ship | Strasbourg
Subjectivity   18, 25, 58, 167, 227, 263, 283,
472, 479, 491, 649
Sweden   35, 45, 289f.
Syllabic style   23, 78, 95, 117, 172f., 226,
240, 245, 259f., 310, 322, 331, 339–
342, 348, 350, 353, 361, 370, 372, 374,
377, 449, 501, 575, 690, 701
Symbol   xxix, 8, 16f., 33, 50f., 75, 79–81,
89f., 100, 116, 119, 129, 149, 167, 175,
182, 186f., 198, 204, 210f., 224, 226,
233f., 237, 240, 257, 260, 264, 267,
269, 276f., 281, 287, 306, 311, 313,
336, 374, 379, 401–403, 412, 415, 426,
433, 444, 446, 450f., 453, 459, 462,
476f., 479, 481, 490f., 497, 499, 508,
510, 516, 536, 549, 555, 559, 564–573,
577, 616, 624, 629f., 635, 654f., 660,
665, 668, 686, 693

Tablatures   264, 672, 701 *Notation
Tempo   65, 140, 148, 153, 177, 356
Tenebrae   100, 701
Ten Commandments → Decalogue
Tenorlied   21, 260f., 691, 701
Theatricality   18, 65, 70, 91, 128, 149f.,
231, 374, 480, 485, 487, 508, 512, 589
Theology   xxix, 1–9, 12f., 28, 31f., 33, 35–
46, 51, 55, 60, 66, 122, 166f., 237, 239,
241, 243f., 256–258, 275–280, 283,
288, 290, 295, 302, 307, 309, 312, 316,
322, 328f., 334, 342, 344, 352–357,
366, 384–387, 433f., 446, 461f., 480,
483, 519, 521, 548, 552, 554–556, 578,
604, 607–609, 612, 614f., 639, 641–
644, 665, 673, 681, 685, 690, 694,
696, 698, 701f.
– Chalcedonian   3, 75, 166, 179–181, 692,
696, 699
– Of creation   3, 93f., 103, 133, 178–183,
204, 206, 210, 215, 228, 232, 247, 434f.,
571, 616–618, 637
– Of music   v, 17, 50, 60–74, 79–82, 88,
92–94, 100, 102, 123, 135, 147, 164–235,

237, 260, 262, 272, 279, 322, 328 f., 334 f., 384 f., 387, 389 f., 403, 412, 414, 434, 441, 444, 480–482, 567–575, 601, 604, 615, 620, 623 f., 638, 649, 656, 658, 665, 685 f., 688
– Of worship → Worship | Theological role of music in worship
– Trinitarian   3, 75, 111, 166, 179, 210, 407, 568 f., 702 *Holy Spirit
Thirty Years' War   47
Tonality   xxix, 50, 86, 106, 259, 452, 698, *Modes, *Modes | Modal theory, *Music | Theory
Tradition   v, xxvii, 6, 10 f., 19–21, 23–25, 31, 33, 39 f., 50, 53, 58 f., 66, 70–72, 89, 95, 98, 103, 105, 107, 112, 122 f., 132 f., 144 f., 147, 156, 164, 166, 168, 170 f., 176, 178, 183 f., 193, 195, 202, 213, 221, 228 f., 237 f., 240, 242–245, 248–253, 255–261, 264 f., 284–290, 292, 297–299, 302, 309 f., 313, 324, 327, 329–334, 337 f., 341, 343, 346, 348, 351, 355, 358, 361, 363, 370–374, 377, 381, 384–395, 402, 405, 407, 418, 432, 442, 444 f., 447, 449, 454, 465, 479, 490, 492 f., 500, 506, 511, 513 f., 523, 526 f., 533, 537, 541 f., 544 f., 548 f., 558, 561–563, 565 f., 571 f., 574, 579, 582, 588, 598, 602, 604–609, 613, 616, 618, 621–624, 630, 633, 648 f., 661, 673 f., 677 f., 681, 687, 691, 696, 698, 700 f.
Transubstantiation   7 f., 33, 386, 481, 497, 535, 701 *Consecration, *Elevation, *Real Presence
Trent → Councils and Synods | Trent (1545–63)
Trinity → Theology | Trinitarian
Tropes   117, 309, 343, 410, 444, 446, 697, 702
Trumpets   87 f., 200 f., 319, 535, 650
Typological reading   72, 224, 302, 520, 544, 546, 702 *Bible, *Scripture

Utraquists   30, 696 *Bohemian Brethren, *Communion | Under both kinds, *Hussites, *Hymnbooks | Hussite, *Worship | Bohemian Brethren

Vanity   71, 128, 135–137, 146–153, 175 f., 182, 223, 325, 347, 415, 419, 463, 487, 492, 591, 658 f., 665
Venice   15, 25, 38, 45, 122, 140, 158, 406, 431, 445, 458 f., 466 f., 472, 493, 507–509, 511, 515, 569, 628, 659, 661, 694, 701
– Basilica of St Marco   467, 507, 659
– Ospedali   677
Verba testamenti   244, 393
Verse composition   334, 376–378
Vespers   64, 96, 110, 246, 288, 402, 447, 457, 462, 477, 484, 490, 533, 537, 613, 675, 687, 698, 702 *Magnificat, *Office of the Hours
Victimæ paschali   112, 250, 309, 552 *Easter, *Resurrection
Villancico   23, 458, 474, 513
Viols   378, 380, 659, 675
Virtuosity   17, 23, 25, 70, 140, 146–149, 158, 160, 163, 392, 440, 647, 656
Volume (of sound)   94, 96, 140–143, 149, 458
Vulgate   169, 300, 302, 331, 347, 545, 702 *Bible | Translations

Wartburg   32 f., 216
Western Schism   29
Wittenberg   31–33, 35, 40, 141 f., 149, 162, 182, 192, 202, 216, 238, 250, 256, 264, 267 f., 287–290, 292 f., 295, 329, 347, 523, 536, 570, 592, 616, 641
Word/Music relationship   12, 17 f., 20–24, 50, 58, 61 f., 65, 67, 69, 71, 74–85, 89, 94–100, 107, 109, 115–122, 131, 133, 148, 159 f., 166–169, 172–174, 186–190, 194, 200 f., 204 f., 208, 212, 216, 218, 222–224, 226, 234, 251, 263, 293, 310 f., 322 f., 325, 337, 342, 359, 374, 381 f., 393, 404, 407, 410, 412, 419, 422, 426–428, 438–440, 449 f., 452–466, 468, 485, 494, 506, 512, 575, 585, 601, 616 f., 620 f., 641, 657

Word-painting  12, 18, 20, 22 f., 58, 94 f., 310, 323, 381, 407, 454, 457, 459, 506, 575, 702
Worms  32, 269
Worship  v, xxvi, xxviii f., 3, 9, 49 – 51, 78 – 80, 83 f., 87 f., 102 – 105, 122, 127, 135 – 138, 142, 163 – 167, 173 – 176, 179 – 181, 183 – 185, 188 f., 194 – 196, 199 – 201, 224 f., 287 – 289, 332, 357 – 363, 379, 381 f., 519 – 521, 524, 533, 537, 550, 560, 562, 577, 581 f., 598 f., 603 – 605, 607 – 609, 611 f., 619, 639, 643, 646, 649, 651, 661, 681, 683, 688 f., 691 f., 695 – 697, 700 *Liturgy, *Service
– Anglican  40, 138, 190, 194, 225 f., 334 – 338, 340, 343 – 346, 348, 351 – 354, 360, 367, 372 f., 375 f. *Evensong, *Matins
– Bohemian Brethren  295 – 297 *Bohemian Brethren, *Hussites, *Hymnbooks | Hussite, *Utraquists
– Calvinist/Reformed  viii, 41 f., 47, 66, 79, 170, 174, 176, 180, 183, 185, 190, 195 f., 200 f., 219 – 225, 231, 233, 295, 298 f., 301, 304 f., 307, 311, 313 – 316, 321, 325, 327 – 329, 344, 351, 360, 541, 608, 700 *Geneva | Psalter and tunes, *Psalmody | Reformed
– Catholic  53, 55 f., 109, 112 – 114, 117 – 120, 153 f., 173, 183 – 185, 188, 200, 217, 229 – 235, 246, 285, 287, 292, 332, 343 f., 385 – 388, 390 f., 393 f., 396 f., 399 f., 406 f., 410, 412, 416, 418, 420 – 422, 430, 434 – 436, 444, 464, 466 – 470, 474, 478 f., 481, 484, 495, 500, 612 f., 654 f., 658, 664 f., 669 – 671, 675, 677, 686, 697, 701
– Jewish → Jewish | Worship
– Lutheran  35, 179, 183 f., 186, 188 f., 195 f., 200, 204 – 209, 217, 231, 233, 235, 254, 257, 241 – 249, 266 – 274, 279 – 281, 287, 293, 314, 479, 587 f., 605, 612 f., 639, 695
– Scottish  viii, 41, 358 – 360, 362 *Scotland
– Strasbourg  38, 219 f., 291 – 295, 351 f., 353, 643 f. *Strasbourg
– Theological role of music in worship  68, 70 – 73, 80, 93, 98, 102, 147, 149, 166 f., 169 – 171, 175, 179 f., 183 – 186, 188 f., 195 f., 200, 204 – 209, 212 – 215, 219 – 224, 230 – 235, 567 f., 572 – 574

Zurich  33, 36, 165, 212, 214 f., 227, 304, 328 f., 351

www.ingramcontent.com/pod-product-compliance
Lightning Source LLC
Chambersburg PA
CBHW031932290426
44108CB00011B/524